The
Cherry Red
Non-League Newsdesk
Annual 2003

by
James Wright

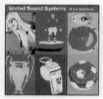

COMPILED BY
James Wright
Non-League Newsdesk
6 Harp Chase
Taunton
Somerset TA1 3RY
(Tel: 01823 324938 / 07786 636659 Fax: 01823 327720)
E-mail: james@nlnewsdesk.co.uk

DESIGNED BY
Nigel Davis
Broomhouse Farmhouse
George Nympton
South Molton
Devon EX36 4JF
(Tel: 01769 572257/ 07768 204784)
E-mail: NigelDavis@aol.com

PUBLISHED BY
James Wright

PRINTED BY
Bookcraft
First Avenue
Westfield Trading Estate
Midsomer Norton
Bath BA3 4BS
Tel: 01761 419167

ISBN 0-9539198-3-8

FRONT COVER
In his club's inaugural fixture, Drew Watkins (left) of AFC Wimbledon gets to grips with Craig Edwards at Sutton United

CONTENTS

WWW.NLNEWSDESK.CO.UK

CONTRIBUTORS

We are indebted to the following league and association officials, and individual contributors, whose help in supplying results and information during the 2002-03 campaign and close season has enabled the publication of this Annual

Chris McCullough, Graham Jones, Cyril Windiate, Geoff Jenkins, Phil Mitcham, Frank Harwood, Phil Hiscox, John Mugridge, Trevor Schorah, Ian Hallett, Peter Godfrey, Steve Adlem, Robert Errington, John Buxton, Len Llewellyn, Steve Clark, Ian Craig, Roger Allen, Brian King, Adrian Marson, Kevin Folds, Nick Robinson, Mike Wilson, Paul Rivers, Mervyn Miles, David Lumley, John Deal, Scott White, Mike Quigley, Neil Juggins, Norman Harvey, Bill Gardner, David Thompson, Alan Gorham, Robert Hurst, Dennis Strudwick, John Hansford, David Wilcox, Duncan Bayley, Wayne Williamson, Richard Rundle, Mike Sampson, Terry Knott, Alan Constable, Jane Phillips, Philip Lewis, Jeremy Biggs, Andy Awbery, Alan Wilson, Derrick Procter, Philip Rhodes, Peter Ackrill, Martin Allen, Jim Wicks, Paul Beard, Hilary Redmond, Dennis Johnson, Jim Bean, Barbara Ely, Jim Milner, Ron Bridges, R C Sutherland, Tom Clark, Del Saunders and Kieran O'Connor.

SOME CONVENTIONS USED WITHIN THIS BOOK

Results grids:- *W-L: Points awarded to home side. L-W: Points awarded to away side. n/p: Game not played. n/a: Game not scheduled, or not played due to one side having withdrawn. M: Scoreline awarded by management committee (e.g. 0м0 denotes a goalless awarded for an unplayed game). bcd: Behind closed doors.*

Some standard abbreviations:- *PF: Playing Field or Playing Fields; aet: after extra time; INT: Intermediate; INV: Invitation*

Inter-league movement:- *Promoted/relegated clubs are listed in no hierarchical or alphabetical preference*

League tables:- *All tables are final .*

Order of entries:- *The leagues in this book appear alphabetically. Entries in the index are also entirely alphabetic. Some cup competitions, though largely arranged alphabetically, may be somewhat sorted hierarchically. For example, the Sussex Senior Cup appears before the Sussex RUR Charity Cup.*

Cup competitions:- *Ties are sorted alphabetically within rounds except F A competitions which are reproduced in draw order. Penalty shoot-out scores are indicated in parenthesis, the first listed side's score preceding the second listed side. So (3-4p) means the second listed side won 4-3 on penalties.*

League sponsors: *League sponsors names have been dropped. This is for alphabetical ease of reference, and historical continuity only. Non-League football is indebted to its many sponsors, and their generosity is recognised on a separate page later in the book.*

TIME TO CONSOLIDATE

I find it hard to believe that this, already, is the fourth edition of this Annual. The publication's short life has been somewhat turbulent, so I would like to begin by putting readers in the picture as to exactly what has happened.

I launched this Annual in 2000 as an accompaniment to my weekly magazine *Non-League Newsdesk*. Within a year, *Non-League Media Plc* acquired Newsdesk and its Annual and published the second (2001) edition (I remained editor).

The demise of *Non-League Media Plc* saw both titles revert to me and, at short notice, I published last year's edition. Many readers have asked me what has become of *Non-League Newsdesk*. Well, it is lying dormant. While *The Non-League Paper* and various web resources are providing such excellent statistical coverage, I doubt sales would justify a relaunch. This position may be reassessed should the market place change again.

So, can you have an Annual to a periodical that no longer appears? I'm not sure, but here it is anyway. One thing of which I am sure is that the book desperately needs a period of stability, and this edition is the first step to providing such. So expect little change within these pages to a design and format that has proved popular over the first three editions.

I recognise that I compounded last year's confusion by moving house a few weeks after publication (at the time contracts were exchanged I had no idea that I would be publishing the book and that orders would be coming to my home). Apologies to all whose orders were delayed because they went to the incorrect address.

Through all the above commotion, the one constant has been the backing of our sponsor *Cherry Red Records*. Our sincere thanks go again to Iain McNay for not only the sponsorship, but his wise advice on the design and marketing of this book.

So, what about this edition? Well, we have retained pretty much the same format as in previous years. The major addition this time around is the inclusion of full round by round result listings for county senior cups. In previous years we listed only the results of finals. And we have extended our coverage deeper into the Welsh pyramid – most of the new senior leagues added are from Wales.

The level of information for top sides remains unchanged – the one-liners for top clubs proved popular last year, so have been freshened up. The web addresses have been updated as appropriate. Please note that the sites listed are not necessarily club official sites.

We have attempted to gather all the information regarding summer inter-league moves but, with a printer's deadline of July 8th (necessary to ensure the early publication that is the raison d'etre of this book), some matters will inevitably slip through the net. Changes will be notified on the "amendments" section of the website throughout the summer and early part of the season (have a look at the site (www.nlnewsdesk.co.uk) – Nigel has given it a major revamp). If you do not have internet access, send me an SAE whenever you would like to see a list of amendments.

Nigel and I have checked, double-checked and then re-checked the statistical content of the book. But if you do spot any faux pas please let us know and we will issue an amendment on the website. And please feel free to let me have any general comments about this book. I do not promise to act upon all suggestions, but I will of course read them in an attempt to identify any consensus. To appear so early in the season this book has to be concise. 256 pages are sufficient only to scratch the surface of a mound of information that could be published, so we have to cherry pick. Past experience tells me that for every reader who says there are, as an example, too few minor league tables, there is another who thinks there are too many. But we need to please you because we hope you will purchase the Annual for years to come, so all opinions are very welcome.

Staying on the subject of sales – book early for next year! The long awaited restructuring of our game is finally upon us, and as ever this Annual will be there to tell you exactly who has gone where. It's going to be fun!

JAMES WRIGHT

WWW.NLNEWSDESK.CO.UK

ANGLIAN COMBINATION

	Acle United	Attleborough Town	Beccles Town	Blofield United	Cromer United	Diss Town Res.	Gorleston Res.	Kirkley	Lowestoft Town Res.	Mulbarton United	North Walsham Town	Scole United	Sprowston Athletic	St Andrews	Wells Town	Wroxham Res.
Acle United	P	1-3	2-0	2-2	2-5	2-2	3-2	0-5	0-1	5-2	0-0	1-0	1-2	1-0	4-1	2-1
Attleborough Town	0-1	R	4-2	6-2	3-3	1-1	0-8	1-1	2-2	7-2	5-0	1-0	1-2	1-1	4-2	1-0
Beccles Town	4-0	2-1	E	1-1	3-0	2-0	2-0	0-2	3-1	3-0	3-1	2-0	0-0	0-4	2-2	1-4
Blofield United	1-1	3-5	0-2	M	2-1	6-0	1-2	1-2	1-2	4-2	3-1	2-3	2-1	1-2	3-1	5-5
Cromer United	1-0	1-2	4-0	3-1	I	3-1	10-0	2-2	5-2	5-1	5-2	6-2	3-4	3-3	2-1	3-1
Diss Town Res.	4-0	3-2	2-4	3-2	2-3	E	0-2	1-13	1-0	3-1	1-1	1-2	1-1	1-0	2-0	1-3
Gorleston Res.	1-4	2-3	4-1	4-2	1-3	4-0	R	0-3	1-4	7-1	1-1	2-2	0-2	0-1	2-1	1-2
Kirkley	2-1	6-0	2-2	7-1	0-1	7-1	2-1	D	4-0	7-0	2-0	8-2	2-1	2-1	1-0	5-0
Lowestoft Town Res.	0-0	4-1	1-1	3-3	3-1	1-0	3-1	0-5	I	2-1	3-1	0-1	0-2	1-3	2-1	5-0
Mulbarton United	1-5	0-5	2-4	0-4	4-2	0-2	0-1	0-4	0-5	V	0-3	0-11	0-6	1-1	4-2	5-0
North Walsham Town	0-5	1-2	0-0	1-1	1-2	2-0	2-3	2-3	2-1	0-2	I	2-0	0-3	0-3	3-1	5-3
Scole United	1-5	2-2	0-0	1-0	1-3	4-1	1-0	0-1	4-0	4-1	1-1	S	1-1	0-1	1-1	2-0
Sprowston Athletic	2-0	1-2	2-0	1-0	3-2	1-2	1-2	0-2	0-1	1-3	2-1	3-0	I	1-1	1-1	1-3
St Andrews	0-0	4-0	1-1	1-2	3-0	1-1	1-1	3-2	0-1	1-3	0-1	1-0	1-0	S	0-2	1-1
Wells Town	0-3	0-0	1-0	2-4	2-0	3-3	1-2	3-1	1-1	3-1	2-2	0-0	3-4	3-0	O	1-1
Wroxham Res.	2-2	3-2	4-3	1-3	0-2	1-2	2-2	0-5	4-0	6-0	2-1	0-0	0-1	1-2	1-4	N

Premier Division		P	W	D	L	F	A	Pts
Kirkley		30	24	4	2	110	25	76
Cromer United		30	18	3	9	84	52	57
Sprowston Athletic		30	17	4	9	59	32	55
St Andrews		30	14	9	7	52	27	51
Attleborough Town		30	14	7	9	67	60	49
Acle United		30	13	7	10	53	45	46
Beccles Town		30	12	8	10	48	45	44
Lowestoft Town Res.		30	13	5	12	49	51	44
Gorleston Res.		30	12	5	13	57	58	41
Blofield United		30	10	6	14	63	66	36
Scole United		30	9	9	12	38	47	36
Wroxham Res.		30	9	6	15	54	68	33
Wells Town		30	7	9	14	44	56	30
North Walsham Town		30	7	7	16	37	59	28
Diss Town Res.	-3	30	8	7	15	41	76	28
Mulbarton United	-3	30	4	2	24	31	120	11

SENIOR CUP
(Premier and Division One teams)

FIRST ROUND

Anglian Windows 1 **Scole United** 3
Attleborough Town 3 Great Yarmouth Town Res. 0
Blofield United 2 Dereham Town Res. 1
Cromer United 5 Brandon Town 2
Diss Town Res. 3 **Lowestoft Town Res.** 5
Halvergate United 1 Beccles Town 1 *aet* (5-4p)
Kirkley 1 Hindringham 0
Loddon United 2 **Acle United** 4
Mattishall 5 Thorpe Village 2
Mulbarton United 1 **Wroxham Res.** 2
Sprowston Athletic 1 **Norwich Union** 1 *aet* (6-7p)
Sprowston Wanderers 0 **North Walsham Town** 3
St Andrews 3 Hempnall 1
Watton United 2 **Stalham Town** 4
Wells Town 2 Gorleston Res. 1
Wymondham Town 1 **Fakenham Town Res.** 4

WWW.CHERRYRED.CO.UK

PREMIER DIVISION CONSTITUTION 2003-04

ACLE UNITED . . . . Bridewell Lane, Acle, Norfolk 01493 751372
ATTLEBOROUGH TOWN . . . . Recreation Ground, Station Road, Attleborough, Norfolk 01953 455365
BECCLES TOWN . . . . College Meadow, Beccles, Suffolk 01502 712221
BLOFIELD UNITED. . . . . Old Yarmouth Road, Blofield, Norwich, Norfolk. 01603 712576
CROMER TOWN. . . . . Cabbell Park, Mill Road, Cromer, Norfolk. 01263 512185
DISS TOWN RESERVES. . . . . Brewers Green Lane, Diss, Norfolk. 01379 651223
GORLESTON RESERVES . . . . Emerald Park, Wood Farm Lane, Gorleston, Norfolk. 01493 602802
HALVERGATE UNITED. . . . . Playing Field, Wickhampton Road, Halvergate, Norfolk. 01493 700349
LOWESTOFT TOWN RESERVES . . . . Crown Meadow, Love Road, Lowestoft, Suffolk 01502 573818
NORTH WALSHAM TOWN . . . . Sports Centre, Greens Road, North Walsham, Norfolk 01692 406888
NORWICH UNION . . . . Pinebanks, White Farm Lane, Harvey Lane, Thorpe, Norfolk 01603 434457
SCOLE UNITED. . . . . Ransome Avenue Playing Field, Scole, Diss, Norfolk 01379 741204
SPROWSTON ATHLETIC . . . Sprowston Sports & Social Club, Blue Boar Lane, Sprowston, Norwich, Norfolk 01603 427688
ST ANDREWS . . . . Thorpe Recreation Ground, Laundry Lane, Thorpe, Norfolk 01603 300316
WELLS TOWN . . . . Beach Road, Wells-next-the-Sea, Norfolk. 01328 710907
WROXHAM RESERVES . . . . Trafford Park, Skinners Lane, Wroxham, Norfolk 01603 783538

Kirkley are promoted to the Eastern Counties League. Mulbarton United drop to Division One replaced by Norwich Union and Halvergate United. Cromer United become Cromer Town.

	Anglian Windows	Brandon Town	Dereham Town Res.	Fakenham Town Res.	Great Yarmouth Res.	Halvergate United	Hempnall	Hindringham	Loddon United	Mattishall	Norwich Union	Sprowston Wanderers	Stalham Town	Thorpe Village	Watton United	Wymondham Town
Anglian Windows		1-2	1-6	4-3	4-2	2-3	0-3	1-2	0-7	1-2	4-3	5-2	0-4	3-0	2-0	1-2
Brandon Town	8-0		1-3	0-2	1-4	1-3	3-3	3-2	5-3	2-2	0-3	0-0	3-1	8-0	1-0	3-2
Dereham Town Res.	4-1	0-5	D	3-1	2-0	0-1	0-1	2-1	4-2	0-0	5-2	7-0	1-2	3-1	3-1	1-1
Fakenham Town Res.	2-0	9-1	1-1	I	4-1	2-3	1-1	2-2	1-2	1-1	1-2	2-1	3-0	4-1	0-3	2-1
Great Yarmouth Town Res.	4-1	1-1	1-2	2-5	V	0-2	2-1	2-2	1-2	0-2	3-1	0-4	4-1	0-3	2-3	
Halvergate United	4-1	2-2	4-1	3-0	2-1	I	3-1	2-1	3-0	3-0	3-1	3-1	0-1	5-3	2-2	6-0
Hempnall	3-1	4-4	4-1	3-0	1-0	1-1	S	2-0	0-0	5-1	2-2	2-2	0-1	5-0	2-3	6-0
Hindringham	4-2	4-0	1-0	2-3	4-1	2-3	0-3	I	4-1	4-0	1-1	3-1	2-1	9-1	1-0	5-1
Loddon United	4-0	3-2	2-0	2-0	1-2	3-3	1-1	4-2	O	3-2	2-3	3-1	1-1	8-5	4-1	0-0
Mattishall	6-1	0-2	0-0	0-2	2-1	0-4	4-2	1-3	6-5	N	2-2	1-2	1-1	1-0	3-4	4-1
Norwich Union	6-0	1-0	2-2	2-0	2-0	2-2	2-0	4-1	2-4	4-1		5-0	1-1	3-1	2-0	2-1
Sprowston Wanderers	3-1	1-0	0-2	1-0	4-1	0-0	2-0	2-4	1-2	2-3	0-4	O	2-3	2-2	0-2	2-0
Stalham Town	2-0	1-2	0-1	3-0	5-1	2-4	0-2	1-1	0-2	3-3	1-1	1-1	N	5-2	3-2	3-1
Thorpe Village	2-2	2-3	1-4	2-2	3-4	1-3	2-2	1-2	2-2	0-3	0-6	3-4	0-2	E	0-2	2-1
Watton United	5-0	0-1	1-2	1-0	1-0	0-2	4-1	1-2	1-2	3-0	2-3	3-1	0-3	6-3		2-1
Wymondham Town	2-3	1-0	0-4	0-5	4-3	0-2	0-2	1-3	0-2	1-1	0-1	1-3	2-3	2-4	1-3	

SECOND ROUND
Attleborough Town 3 Blofield United 2
Cromer United 10 Mattishall 3
Fakenham Town Res. 4 St Andrews 1
Halvergate United 1 **Kirkley** 4
Lowestoft Town Res. 6 **Wroxham Res.** 5
(Lowestoft expelled)
Norwich Union 4 Scole United 1
Stalham Town 4 North Walsham Town 1
Wells Town 2 Acle United 0

QUARTER-FINALS
Cromer United 3 Fakenham Town Res. 0
Kirkley 2 Wells Town 0
Norwich Union 0 **Attleborough Town** 3
Stalham Town 4 Wroxham Res. 2 *aet*

SEMI-FINALS
Cromer United 3 Attleborough Town 1
Kirkley 2 Stalham Town 0

FINAL
(10th May at Norwich United)
Kirkley 2 **Cromer United** 3 *aet*

DON FROST MEMORIAL CUP (League champions v Senior Cup holders) (24th Aug. at Norwich Utd) Kirkley 2 Cromer United 0

Division One

	P	W	D	L	F	A	Pts
Halvergate United	30	22	6	2	79	33	72
Norwich Union	30	20	7	3	78	36	67
Loddon United	30	17	6	7	77	53	57
Dereham Town Res.	30	17	5	8	64	38	56
Hindringham	30	17	4	9	74	47	55
Stalham Town	30	15	6	9	58	40	51
Hempnall	30	13	9	8	63	40	48
Watton United	30	15	1	14	55	46	46
Brandon Town	30	13	6	11	64	58	45
Fakenham Town Res.	30	12	5	13	60	47	41
Mattishall	30	11	8	11	55	61	41
Sprowston Wanderers	30	8	6	16	41	66	30
Anglian Windows	30	7	1	22	42	100	22
Great Yarmouth Res. -3	30	7	2	21	43	72	20
Wymondham Town -3	30	4	3	23	29	83	12
Thorpe Village	30	2	5	23	46	108	11

DIVISION ONE CONSTITUTION 2003-04

ANGLIAN WINDOWS . . . . Horsford Manor, Cromer Road, Norwich, Norfolk 01603 404723
BRANDON TOWN. . . . . Remembrance Playing Field, Church Road, Brandon, Suffolk 01842 813177
DEREHAM TOWN RESERVES. . . . . Aldiss Park, Norwich Road, Dereham, Norfolk 01362 690460/693677
FAKENHAM TOWN RESERVES . . . . Clipbush Lane, Fakenham, Norfolk 01328 856222/855859
GT YARMOUTH TOWN RES. . . . . Wellesley Road Rec Ground, Sandown Road, Gt Yarmouth, Norfolk 01493 843373/842936
HEMPNALL . . . . Bungay Road, Hempnall, Norfolk 01508 498086
HINDRINGHAM . . . . Wells Road, Hindringham, Norfolk 01328 878608
HOLT UNITED. . . . . Sports Centre, Kelling Road, Holt, Norfolk 01263 711217
HORSFORD UNITED. . . . . Holt Road, Horsford, Norfolk. 01603 893317
LODDON UNITED . . . . George Lane Playing Fields, Loddon, Norwich, Norfolk 01508 528497
MATTISHALL . . . . Mattishall Playing Fields, South Green, Mattishall, Norfolk 01362 850246
MULBARTON UNITED. . . . . Mulberry Park, Mulbarton, Norwich, Norfolk. 01508 570626
SPROWSTON WANDERERS . . . . . Sprowston Cricket Club, Barkers Lane, Sprowston, Norwich, Norfolk. 01603 404042
STALHAM TOWN . . . . Rivers Park, Steppingstone Lane, Stalham, Norwich, Norfolk . . . . None
WATTON UNITED . . . . Watton Playing Field, Dereham Road, Watton, Norfolk 01953 881281
WYMONDHAM TOWN . . . . Kings Head Meadow, Wymondham, Norfolk 01953 607326

Norwich Union and Halvergate United are promoted to the Premier Division replaced by Mulbarton United. Thorpe Village drop to Division Two replaced by Horsford United and Holt United.

	Aylsham Wanderers	Bradenham Wanderers	Bungay Town	Caister United	Gayton United	Holt United	Horsford United	Lakeford Rangers	Mundford	Norwich St Johns	Oulton Broad & LR.	Poringland Wanderers	Reepham Town	Swaffham Town Res.	Thorpe Rovers	Wortwell
Aylsham Wanderers		2-0	4-0	3-0	1-0	3-1	2-2	0-1	7-0	3-1	4-1	4-1	5-1	4-4	2-1	0-1
Bradenham Wanderers	0-7		0-2	0-3	1-9	0-6	0-3	1-1	1-0	2-1	0-1	2-6	0-5	0-0	0-1	0-2
Bungay Town	1-3	3-0	D	2-1	2-4	0-5	1-3	1-1	3-2	3-1	1-0	1-0	2-1	3-0	0-1	1-1
Caister United	1-2	8-0	3-3	I	2-7	0-3	1-3	5-0	3-3	3-2	2-0	0-0	1-1	0-4	0-1	1-2
Gayton United	1-3	5-0	1-4	3-1	V	0-2	3-3	3-0	1-2	9-1	4-0	5-0	0-2	2-1	1-1	3-1
Holt United	3-2	10-0	4-2	4-0	6-0	I	3-3	3-0	2-1	5-3	3-2	4-0	2-0	1-0	1-0	2-1
Horsford United	3-2	6-0	2-0	4-0	2-0	3-1	S	6-0	8-2	3-2	3-1	4-1	7-0	2-0	1-0	2-1
Lakeford Rangers	2-2	4-1	2-2	2-1	2-5	0-0	1-4	I	2-2	1-6	4-1	0-2	1-3	2-0	2-0	1-0
Mundford	1-3	4-1	6-2	1-4	1-1	2-3	2-5	1-3	O	3-1	3-2	2-2	0-1	2-5	2-1	1-1
Norwich St Johns	2-4	2-0	2-3	1-2	1-3	1-3	1-1	3-0	3-3	N	3-2	2-1	2-1	2-1	1-4	1-1
Oulton Broad & Lowestoft Railway	0-4	5-4	1-2	0-0	1-0	0-6	0-2	1-1	2-1	3-5		2-1	1-3	1-2	3-4	2-4
Poringland Wanderers	3-0	1-1	2-1	3-2	3-1	1-4	1-4	1-0	6-0	0-1	5-2	T	4-1	0-0	2-0	2-2
Reepham Town	0-2	1-0	4-1	1-3	1-3	0-0	0-0	1-3	3-0	1-1	5-1	2-1	W	1-3	2-0	0-0
Swaffham Town Res.	1-0	4-1	2-1	1-1	1-2	2-0	1-3	3-0	1-0	0-3	4-0	6-0	1-0	O	3-2	0-3
Thorpe Rovers	0-4	6-0	0-3	1-2	1-5	2-0	1-3	5-0	1-0	0-3	0-1	4-1	2-2	0-1		2-1
Wortwell	1-1	1-1	1-1	1-1	2-1	0-3	0-0	0-0	2-1	2-1	4-0	1-2	1-1	0-1	1-1	

Division Two

		P	W	D	L	F	A	Pts
Horsford United		30	25	4	1	100	28	79
Holt United		30	23	4	3	89	27	73
Aylsham Wanderers		30	20	4	6	83	33	64
Gayton United		30	16	3	11	79	46	51
Swaffham Town Res.		30	15	6	9	55	39	51
Bungay Town		30	13	6	11	50	56	45
Reepham Town		30	13	4	13	43	46	43
Wortwell		30	10	12	8	38	32	42
Poringland Wanderers		30	11	7	12	49	55	40
Thorpe Rovers		30	10	5	15	41	45	35
Norwich St Johns		30	10	5	15	58	70	35
Lakeford Rangers		30	9	7	14	36	63	34
Caister United		30	8	6	16	49	62	30
Mundford		30	6	7	17	50	80	25
Oulton Broad & Lowestoft Railway		30	6	2	22	37	82	20
Bradenham Wanderers	-3	30	2	4	24	16	109	7

JUNIOR CUP
(For Division Two, Three and Four teams)

FIRST ROUND
Corton 1 **Thetford Rovers** 2
Dersingham Rovers 3 Newton Flotman 2
Downham Town Res. 1 Beccles Caxton 0
Necton SSC 5 Swaffham Town Res. 1
Norwich United Res. 3 Long Stratton 1
Southwold Town 2 Morley Village 0
Thetford Town Res. 5 Saham Toney 1
Wortwell 5 Martham 0

SECOND ROUND
Aylsham Wanderers 2 Southwold Town 1
Bradenham Wanderers 0 **Poringland Wanderers** 3
Bungay Town 3 Zenith Windows 1
Caister United 2 **Downham Town Res.** 3
City of Norwich SOBU 2 Costessey Sports 0
Dersingham Rovers 2 **Holt United** 2 *aet*
Foster Athletic 0 Oulton Broad LR 0 *aet (3-0p)*
Gayton United 1 Thetford Town Res. 0
Great Ryburgh 2 **Wortwell** 3
Harleston Town 1 **Norwich St Johns** 4
Hellesdon 1 **Norwich CEYMS** 3
Horsford United 0 **Thetford Rovers** 4

DIVISION TWO CONSTITUTION 2003-04

AYLSHAM WANDERERS .... Sir Williams Lane, Aylsham, Norwich, Norfolk .... None
BUNGAY TOWN .... Maltings Meadow, Ditchingham, Bungay, Suffolk 01986 894028
CAISTER UNITED .... Caister Playing Fields, off Allendale Road, Caister-on-Sea, Norfolk .... None
CORTON .... Village Playing Field, Long Lane, Corton, Suffolk .... None
GAYTON UNITED .... Lime Kiln Road, Gayton, Norfolk .... None
LAKEFORD RANGERS........... Marlingford Sports Ground, Easton Road, Marlingford, Norfolk .... None
MUNDFORD.................................. The Glebe, Mundford, Thetford, Norfolk 01603 880399
NORWICH ST JOHNS .... Cringleford Recreation Ground, Oakfields Road, Cringleford, Norfolk .... None
OULTON BROAD & LOWESTOFT RAIL. . Barnard Meadow, off Peto Way, Lowestoft, Suffolk .... None
PORINGLAND WANDERERS .. Poringland Memorial Field, The Footpath, Poringland, Norwich, Norfolk ... 01508 495198
REEPHAM TOWN .... Stimpsons Piece Rec Ground, Reepham, Norwich, Norfolk .... None
SHERINGHAM......................... Weybourne Road, Sheringham, Norfolk .... None
SWAFFHAM TOWN RESERVES .... Shoemakers Lane, off Cley Road, Swaffham, Norfolk 01263 823828
THORPE ROVERS .... Dussindale Park, Pound Lane, Thorpe, Norfolk 01760 722700
THORPE VILLAGE............. Thorpe Recreation Ground, Laundry Lane, Thorpe, Norwich, Norfolk 01603 300316
WORTWELL.................... Wortwell Playing Field, opposite Bell PH, Wortwell, Norfolk................. None
Horsford United and Holt United are promoted to Division One replaced by Thorpe Village. Bradenham Wanderers drop to Division Three replaced by Sheringham and Corton.

	City of Norwich SOBU	Corton	Costessey Sports	Downham Town Res.	Foster Athletic	Great Ryburgh	Harleston Town	Hellesdon	Morley Village	Newton Flotman	Norwich CEYMS	Norwich United Res.	Sheringham	South Walsham	Thetford Town Res.	Zenith Windows
City of Norwich SOBU		2-2	1-1	1-2	0-2	6-3	2-0	0-0	1-2	2-2	1-3	2-2	0-5	3-1	2-2	0-1
Corton	3-0	D	1-2	1-1	2-9	3-1	6-0	4-1	3-1	3-1	4-1	3-2	2-2	4-1	4-2	3-1
Costessey Sports	1-1	2-0	I	2-2	3-2	1-2	5-0	10-1	1-2	4-1	2-1	6-2	1-1	1-1	3-0	2-3
Downham Town Res.	2-6	3-4	1-1	V	1-1	5-1	2-2	5-2	4-2	0-0	5-0	2-0	0-2	3-1	3-1	1-5
Foster Athletic	2-4	0-0	3-2	3-1	I	3-1	5-1	7-1	5-2	2-6	2-1	0-1	1-1	1-4	2-5	3-4
Great Ryburgh	4-3	2-3	4-5	3-3	2-2	S	4-1	3-5	2-3	3-4	2-2	2-7	0-6	0-1	1-0	5-1
Harleston Town	1-5	1-5	1-1	2-5	0-6	2-2	I	3-2	3-4	2-3	1-1	3-5	1-4	2-4	3-4	2-4
Hellesdon	4-2	2-4	0-2	2-2	1-4	0-0	1-1	O	4-5	6-2	4-0	2-0	1-7	2-6	0-1	4-2
Morley Village	1-2	4-4	3-3	2-5	1-1	2-0	8-0	5-0	N	1-0	3-3	2-3	2-6	2-1	0-1	4-2
Newton Flotman	2-2	0-5	2-3	2-1	2-1	2-2	4-1	3-0	2-3	T	1-1	1-4	1-3	2-1	3-3	1-2
Norwich CEYMS	1-3	1-4	1-3	4-2	0-6	1-0	3-0	4-1	1-1	4-0	H	1-4	1-3	2-1	3-1	2-2
Norwich United Res.	3-3	2-3	1-2	2-2	2-4	1-1	6-0	5-0	4-3	1-3	3-3	R	2-1	7-0	2-2	3-5
Sheringham	1-0	4-3	2-2	9-0	2-1	3-3	4-4	6-1	8-1	4-1	5-1	26-0	E	4-5	1-4	2-2
South Walsham	1-3	1-3	0-3	5-0	0-9	4-2	7-1	4-2	2-1	1-0	1-0	0-1	0-2	E	1-1	3-3
Thetford Town Res.	1-2	0-4	4-3	0-4	3-3	4-1	3-3	5-0	3-0	1-0	0-3	0-1	0-4	0-0	E	2-1
Zenith Windows	4-1	1-7	0-2	3-2	2-3	2-2	4-0	3-2	2-1	4-3	3-4	4-3	1-4	0-1	2-2	

Mundford 0 **Norwich United Res.** 2
Necton SSC 4 Thorpe Rovers 3
Sheringham 2 Lakeford Rangers 0
South Walsham 0 **Reepham Town** 2

THIRD ROUND
Bungay Town 0 **Norwich United Res.** 2
City of Norwich SOBU 0 **Gayton United** 5
Downham Town Res. 0 **Norwich St Johns** 3
Holt United 1 Poringland Wanderers 0
Necton SSC 3 Reepham Town 1 *aet*
Norwich CEYMS 0 **Aylsham Wanderers** 5
Sheringham 2 Foster Athletic 0
Wortwell 5 Thetford Rovers 2

QUARTER-FINALS
Aylsham Wanderers 4 Norwich St Johns 2
Gayton United 3 Norwich United Res. 2
Holt United 2 Necton SSC 1
Sheringham 2 Wortwell 0

SEMI-FINALS
Gayton United 4 Sheringham 0
Holt United 2 Aylsham Wanderers 2 *aet* (4-1p)

FINAL
(9th May at Wroxham)
Holt United 4 Gayton United 1

Division Three		P	W	D	L	F	A	Pts
Sheringham		30	22	7	1	140	37	73
Corton		30	21	5	4	97	50	68
Costessey Sports		30	16	9	5	79	43	57
Foster Athletic		30	15	6	9	93	55	51
Zenith Windows		30	15	3	12	73	73	48
Morley Village		30	13	5	12	73	76	44
Norwich United Res.	*-3*	30	13	6	11	79	86	42
Downham Town Res.		30	10	10	10	69	71	40
City of Norwich SOBU		30	10	9	11	60	59	39
Thetford Town Res.		30	10	9	11	57	63	39
South Walsham		30	11	5	14	49	64	38
Newton Flotman		30	10	6	14	58	70	36
Norwich CEYMS		30	9	7	14	52	70	34
Great Ryburgh	*-3*	30	5	9	16	58	85	21
Hellesdon		30	5	5	20	51	105	20
Harleston Town		30	1	7	22	37	118	10

DIVISION THREE CONSTITUTION 2003-04

BRADENHAM WANDERERS .... Hale Road, Bradenham, Norfolk. .... None
CITY OF NORWICH SOBU .... Britannia Barracks, Mousehold, Norwich, Norfolk .... None
COSTESSEY SPORTS .... Longwater Lane, Old Costessey, Norfolk .... None
DERSINGHAM ROVERS .... behind Feathers Hotel, Dersingham, Norfolk 01485 542707
DOWNHAM TOWN RESERVES........ Memorial Field, Lynn Road, Downham Market, Norfolk 01366 388424
FOSTER ATHLETIC........ Fosters Sports & Social Club, Ferry Road, Clenchwarton, King's Lynn, Norfolk 01553 773968
HARLESTON TOWN .... Rec & Memorial Leisure Centre, off Wilderness Lane, Harleston, Norfolk ... 01379 854519
HELLESDON .... Hellesdon Community Centre, Woodview Road, Hellesdon, Norwich, Norfolk 01603 427675
MORLEY VILLAGE.................. Golf Links Road, Morley St Peter, Wymondham, Norfolk........................ None
NEWTON FLOTMAN.......... Newton Flotman Village Centre, Grove Way, Newton Flotman, Norfolk 01508 471289
NORWICH CEYMS .... Hilltops Sports Centre, Swardeston, Norwich, Norfolk 01508 578826
NORWICH UNITED RESERVES .... Plantation Park, off Plantation Road, Blofield, Norwich, Norfolk 01603 716963
SOUTH WALSHAM .... The Playing Field, South Walsham, Norfolk. .... None
SOUTHWOLD TOWN .... Southwold Common, Southwold, Suffolk .... None
THETFORD TOWN RESERVES........ Recreation Ground, Mundford Road, Thetford, Norfolk 01842 766120
ZENITH WINDOWS.............. Rhone Poulenc Social Club, Sweet Briar Road, Norwich, Norfolk.............. 01603 787667
Sheringham and Corton are promoted to Division Two replaced by Bradenham Wanderers. Great Ryburgh have resigned. Southwold Town and Dersingham Rovers move up from Division Four.

	Beccles Caxton	Dersingham Rovers	Long Stratton	Martham	Necton SSC	Saham Toney	Southwold Town	Thetford Rovers
Beccles Caxton	D	2-4	1-1	6-6	2-1	3-5	0-4	7-4
Dersingham Rovers	6-1	I	7-1	6-1	3-0	4-0	1-1	3-2
Long Stratton	3-2	1-1	V	4-1	2-2	7-0	1-1	1-4
Martham	2-2	2-4	1-1		1-3	5-3	1-2	2-6
Necton SSC	3-6	2-4	2-3	4-2	F	8-0	0-1	6-1
Saham Toney	4-6	0-7	1-4	4-6	1-3	O	3-4	1-6
Southwold Town	1-2	0-0	6-0	3-2	3-1	8-0	U	5-2
Thetford Rovers	5-0	4-0	0-2	4-2	4-3	4-1	2-2	R

	Beccles Caxton	Dersingham Rovers	Long Stratton	Martham	Necton SSC	Saham Toney	Southwold Town	Thetford Rovers
Beccles Caxton	D	7-2	3-0	5-2	4-2	5-2	0-3	4-2
Dersingham Rovers	5-2	I	2-0	8-1	4-2	9-3	0-2	4-0
Long Stratton	2-2	1-1	V	2-0	2-3	3-1	2-4	2-5
Martham	2-2	0-2	2-0		2-2	3-0	1-3	2-5
Necton SSC	3-1	2-4	5-1	4-1	F	10-0	0-2	5-1
Saham Toney	2-2	1-4	2-4	3-5	1-4	O	0-12	1-12
Southwold Town	3-0	4-2	2-0	1-0	2-0	5-0	U	2-1
Thetford Rovers	5-0	2-0	2-1	5-2	7-5	6-2	2-2	R

Teams played each other four times

Division Four	P	W	D	L	F	A	Pts
Southwold Town	28	22	5	1	88	23	71
Dersingham Rovers	28	19	4	5	97	44	61
Thetford Rovers	28	17	2	9	103	67	53
Beccles Caxton	28	11	6	11	77	84	39
Necton SSC	28	12	2	14	85	65	38
Long Stratton	28	9	7	12	51	63	34
Martham	28	5	5	18	57	94	20
Saham Toney -1	28	1	1	26	41	159	3

WWW.CHERRYRED.CO.UK

DIVISION FOUR CONSTITUTION 2003-04

ACLE UNITED RESERVES .... Bridewell Lane, Acle, Norfolk.
ATTLEBOROUGH TOWN RESERVES . Recreation Ground, Station Road, Attleborough, Norfolk 01493 751372
BECCLES CAXTON .... Caxton Meadow, adj. Beccles Station, Beccles, Suffolk 01953 455365
BECCLES TOWN RESERVES .... College Meadow, Beccles, Suffolk 01502 712829
BLOFIELD UNITED RESERVES.......... Old Yarmouth Road, Blofield, Norwich, Norfolk........... 01502 712221
HALVERGATE UNITED RESERVES.... Playing Field, Wickhampton Road, Halvergate, Norfolk........... 01603 712576
HEMPNALL RESERVES .... Bungay Road, Hempnall, Norfolk........... 01493 700349
KIRKLEY RESERVES.............. Kirkley Recreation Ground, Walmer Road, Lowestoft, Suffolk........... 01508 498086
LONG STRATTON .... Manor Road Playing Fields, Long Stratton, Norwich, Norfolk........... 01502 513549
MARTHAM .... Coronation Recreation Ground, Rollesby Road, Martham, Norfolk .... None
NECTON SSC..... Necton Playing Field, Tuns Road, Necton, Norfolk........... 01760 723864
SPROWSTON ATH. RESERVES .. Sprowston S&S Club, Blue Boar Lane, Sprowston, Norwich, Norfolk........... 01603 427688
ST ANDREWS RESERVES.......... Thorpe Recreation Ground, Laundry Lane, Thorpe, Norfolk........... 01603 300316
STALHAM TOWN RESERVES....... Rivers Park, Steppingstone Lane, Stalham, Norwich, Norfolk........... None
THETFORD ROVERS.................. Euston Park, Euston, near Thetford, Norfolk........... None
WELLS TOWN RESERVES .... Beach Road, Wells-next-the-Sea, Norfolk.........01328 710907
Southwold Town and Dersingham Rovers are promoted to Division Three. Saham Toney leave the league. Arriving from Reserve Division One are the reserve sides of Kirkley, Attleborough Town, Hempnall, Sprowston Athletic, Beccles Town, Blofield United, St Andrews, Halvergate United, Wells Town, Stalham Town and Acle United.

Division Five (new division) constitution 2003-04: Aylsham Wanderers Reserves, Brandon Town Reserves, Bungay Town Reserves, Cromer Town Reserves, Gayton United Reserves, Loddon United Reserves, Mattishall Reserves, Mulbarton United Reserves, Mundford Reserves, North Walsham Town Reserves, Norwich Union Reserves, Poringland Wanderers Reserves, Scole United Reserves, South Walsham Reserves, Thorpe Village Reserves, Watton United Reserves

Division Six (new division) constitution 2003-04: Caister United Reserves, CNSOBU Reserves, Costessey Sports Reserves, Foster Athletic Reserves, Halvergate United Reserves, Thorpe Rovers Reserves, Harleston Town Reserves, Hindringham Reserves, Holt United Reserves, Horsford United Reserves, Norwich CEYMS Reserves, Norwich St Johns Reserves, Reepham Town Reserves, Sprowston Wanderers Reserves, Thetford Rovers Reserves, Wortwell Reserves, Wymondham Town Reserves

Reserve Div. One	P	W	D	L	F	A	Pts
Kirkley Res.	30	22	5	3	108	34	68
Attleborough Res.	30	18	6	6	68	32	60
Hempnall Res.	30	18	3	9	54	36	57
Sprowston Ath. Res.	30	16	6	8	100	59	54
Beccles Town Res.	30	16	6	8	70	47	54
Blofield Utd Res.	30	16	6	8	70	64	54
St Andrews Res.	30	16	4	10	74	42	52
Halvergate Utd Res.	30	16	3	11	70	57	51
Wells Town Res.	30	14	4	12	55	41	46
Stalham Town Res.	30	9	7	14	53	58	34
Acle United Res.	30	10	4	16	52	75	34
South Walsham Res.	30	9	4	17	36	86	31
Scole Utd Res. -3	30	8	4	18	35	54	25
North Walsham Res.	30	6	2	22	51	90	20
Bungay Town Res.	30	4	8	18	44	92	20
Mulbarton Utd Res.	30	5	2	23	39	116	17

Reserve Div. Two	P	W	D	L	F	A	Pts
Loddon United Res.	30	22	2	6	110	50	68
Norwich Union Res.	30	22	2	6	74	33	68
Watton Utd Res.	30	20	7	3	98	31	67
Cromer Utd Res. -3	30	20	4	6	94	46	61
Aylsham Wdrs Res.	30	18	3	9	85	52	57
Brandon Town Res.	30	17	3	10	77	60	54
Mattishall Res.	30	16	5	9	71	41	53
Gayton United Res.	30	16	3	11	82	59	50
Poringland W. Res.	30	14	3	13	79	68	45
Mundford Res.	30	9	6	15	55	74	33
Thorpe Village Res.	30	10	3	17	49	87	33
Foster Athletic Res.	30	9	3	18	58	77	30
Caister Utd Res. -3	30	8	1	21	38	77	22
Sprow. Wd. Res. -4	30	7	2	21	59	99	19
Wym'dham Res. -6	30	7	3	20	46	67	18
Lakeford Rgrs Res.	30	0	0	30	19	173	0

Reserve Div. Three	P	W	D	L	F	A	Pts
Costessey Spts Res.	22	16	3	3	86	28	51
Holt United Res.	22	14	5	3	71	33	47
Thetford Rov. Res.	22	14	2	6	80	36	44
Hindringham Res. -3	22	13	8	1	59	31	44
Horsford Utd Res.	22	12	5	5	49	30	41
Norw. St Johns Res.	22	10	6	6	54	40	36
Norw. CEYMS Res.	22	7	3	12	34	64	24
CNSOBU Res.	22	5	4	13	34	58	19
Harleston T. Res. -3	22	6	3	13	39	63	18
Reepham Town Res.	22	5	3	14	40	69	18
Thorpe Rovers Res.	22	5	1	16	45	103	16
Wortwell Res.	22	3	1	18	33	73	10

CAMBRIDGESHIRE LEAGUE

	Comberton United	Cottenham United	Debden	Fordham	Foxton	Great Paxton	Great Shelford	Hemingford United	Mildenhall Town Res.	Newmarket Town Res.	Over Sports	Sawston United	Tuddenham Rovers	Waterbeach	West Wratting	Wisbech Town Res.
Comberton United	P	2-1	6-1	4-1	2-2	0-1	2-5	2-3	0-1	0-1	2-1	0-2	0-2	7-2	1-2	3-1
Cottenham United	1-2	R	6-1	2-0	0-2	1-3	1-1	0-0	3-3	2-1	1-2	1-1	2-3	1-4	2-2	1-3
Debden	2-2	0-6	E	1-0	0-2	1-4	1-3	3-2	0-6	3-6	1-7	1-4	1-4	0-5	1-1	2-2
Fordham	0-2	2-2	5-1	M	4-2	1-1	4-2	1-2	6-3	2-2	2-2	1-1	3-1	3-1	4-2	2-0
Foxton	2-2	1-3	2-2	3-0	I	2-2	0-2	1-0	1-0	2-0	0-5	0-2	2-2	2-0	1-5	3-1
Great Paxton	2-1	0-3	2-0	4-3	1-2	E	1-2	2-0	4-3	1-3	2-5	2-1	2-5	1-1	2-2	1-0
Great Shelford	6-3	1-1	7-1	5-2	2-4	3-3	R	0-0	4-1	0-1	2-1	3-1	1-1	0-0	1-2	3-3
Hemingford United	1-1	3-2	2-0	1-8	2-0	1-1	3-2	D	2-0	2-2	0-0	2-4	1-5	2-5	0-4	2-2
Mildenhall Town Res.	1-1	0-2	6-0	0-1	2-0	0-2	1-1	2-1	I	1-0	3-0	1-3	6-1	2-0	0-2	3-5
Newmarket Town Res.	1-0	2-3	4-0	2-1	2-2	0-1	2-5	2-1	0-3	V	2-2	1-3	1-1	1-2	2-1	0-0
Over Sports	3-1	1-2	11-1	3-4	8-0	3-2	4-1	2-2	1-0	3-0	V	2-5	2-3	1-3	1-1	0-2
Sawston United	2-0	4-0	7-0	4-1	6-0	2-1	3-1	4-1	5-0	2-2	3-1	I	1-3	1-1	1-2	3-0
Tuddenham Rovers	1-1	3-2	4-0	2-1	2-2	3-2	3-0	0-1	1-3	2-0	3-1	1-3	S	1-3	1-3	1-2
Waterbeach	1-0	6-1	6-1	1-2	4-1	1-4	5-1	2-0	6-2	3-2	0-1	1-2	2-0	I	3-4	2-2
West Wratting	5-0	3-0	4-0	5-1	6-1	5-2	2-1	5-0	2-0	7-1	1-3	2-0	7-2	3-1	O	2-0
Wisbech Town Res.	0-0	3-0	1-2	3-1	2-4	2-4	1-1	5-0	1-0	4-2	0-0	1-2	2-2	1-2	1-3	N

Premier Division	P	W	D	L	F	A	Pts
Sawston United	30	22	6	2	85	27	72
West Wratting	30	22	5	3	96	34	71
Waterbeach	30	17	3	10	75	50	54
Over Sports	30	14	6	10	78	48	48
Great Paxton	30	14	6	10	60	56	48
Tuddenham Rovers	30	13	6	11	62	59	45
Fordham	30	12	6	12	67	64	42
Foxton	30	11	6	13	45	69	39
Great Shelford	30	9	9	12	63	62	36
Mildenhall Town Res.	30	11	3	16	53	55	36
Cottenham United	30	9	7	14	52	59	34
Newmarket Town Res.	30	9	7	14	46	59	34
Wisbech Town Res.	-3 30	9	9	12	50	51	33
Hemingford United	30	8	8	14	37	67	32
Comberton United	30	8	7	15	47	54	31
Debden	30	3	4	23	28	130	13

PREMIER DIVISION CUP

FIRST ROUND
Debden 1 Newmarket Town Res. 0
Fordham 4 West Wratting 0
Foxton 4 Waterbeach 3 *aet*
Great Paxton 3 **Comberton United** 4
Great Shelford 1 **Tuddenham Rovers** 3
Mildenhall Town Res. 1 Hemingford United 1 *aet*
Hemingford 2 **Mildenhall Town Res.** 3 *replay*
Over 0 Cottenham 0 *aet*, Cottenham 4 **Over** 4 *replay*
Sawston United 4 Wisbech Town Res. 1
QUARTER-FINALS
Comberton United 1 **Foxton** 2
Debden 1 **Tuddenham Rovers** 2
Mildenhall Town Res. 1 **Fordham** 3
Sawston United 5 Over Sports 1
SEMI-FINALS
Fordham 3 Tuddenham Rovers 2
Foxton 3 Sawston United 2
FINAL *(5th May at Cambridge City)*
Fordham 2 **Foxton** 2 *aet* (1-4p)

PREMIER DIVISION CONSTITUTION 2003-04

COTTENHAM UNITED . . . . Lambs Lane, Cottenham, Cambridge, Cambridgeshire 01954 250873
FORDHAM . . . . Recreation Ground, Carter Street, Fordham, Cambridgeshire . . . . None
FOXTON . . . . Recreation Ground, Foxton, Cambridgeshire . . . . None
FULBOURN INSTITUTE . . . . Fulbourn Recreation, Home End, Fulbourn, Cambridgeshire . . . . None
GREAT PAXTON . . . . Recreation Ground, High Street, Great Paxton, Cambridgeshire . . . . None
GREAT SHELFORD . . . . Recreation Ground, Woollards Lane, Great Shelford, Cambridgeshire 01223 842590
HEMINGFORD UNITED . . . . . . Memorial Playing Fields, Manor Road, Hemingford Grey, Cambridgeshire . . . . None
LINTON GRANTA . . . . Recreation Ground, Meadow Lane, Linton Granta, Cambridgeshire . . . . None
MILDENHALL TOWN RESERVES . . . . . Recreation Way, Mildenhall, Bury St Edmunds, Suffolk. 01638 713449
NEWMARKET TOWN RESERVES . Cricket Field Road, off New Cheveley Road, Newmarket, Suffolk 01638 663637
OVER SPORTS . . . . The Green, Over, Cambridgeshire. . . . . None
SAWSTON UNITED . . . . Spicers Sports Ground, New Road, Sawston, Cambridgeshire . . . . None
TUDDENHAM ROVERS . . . . Ramsey Field, The Green, Tuddenham, Cambridgeshire . . . . None
WATERBEACH . . . . Recreation Ground, Waterbeach, Cambridgeshire . . . . None
WEST WRATTING . . . . Recreation Ground, Bull Lane, West Wratting, Cambridgeshire . . . . None
WISBECH TOWN RESERVES . . . . Fenland Park, Lerowe Road, Wisbech, Cambridgeshire . . . . 01945 584176. Fax: 01945 584333
Comberton United and Debden drop to Senior A replaced by Fulbourn Institute and Linton Granta.

	Bassingbourn	Bluntisham Rangers	Brampton	Eaton Socon	Fulbourn Institute	Gamlingay United	Girton United	Hardwick	Huntingdon Town	Huntingdon United	Lakenheath	Linton Granta	Littleport Town	Soham Town Rangers Res.	Somersham Town Res.	Whittlesford United
Bassingbourn		2-1	2-1	0-2	0-2	0-3	1-2	0-5	2-3	3-1	2-1	0-1	2-2	0-5	2-4	1-0
Bluntisham Rangers	7-0		2-3	1-3	2-2	0-2	0-2	2-1	2-3	2-2	2-0	2-2	0-1	1-1	0-3	4-2
Brampton	1-2	1-2		1-1	2-5	0-2	1-3	2-2	1-0	2-0	1-0	2-1	3-2	7-0	0-1	6-0
Eaton Socon	3-0	1-1	2-0	*S*	1-4	3-2	2-1	3-1	2-2	1-1	0-5	0-6	2-4	1-4	3-3	2-1
Fulbourn Institute	2-0	6-0	3-3	3-0	*E*	3-0	2-2	2-0	5-1	4-0	6-1	2-1	2-2	4-0	11-2	3-2
Gamlingay United	0-1	3-1	2-1	1-1	0-3	*N*	0-1	0-3	2-3	3-6	7-0	1-1	0-3	2-1	2-0	5-0
Girton United	2-1	2-2	1-2	1-0	0-6	1-1	*I*	1-0	0-3	1-3	0-1	2-1	0-4	6-0	2-0	1-4
Hardwick	4-1	1-0	1-0	1-3	2-5	0-0	3-1	*O*	1-3	4-0	0-2	0-2	0-1	2-0	2-0	3-1
Huntingdon Town	1-1	4-1	3-1	2-4	1-2	0-0	0-1	1-2	*R*	0-1	7-2	2-1	1-3	4-1	3-1	4-0
Huntingdon United	1-1	3-2	3-0	1-2	1-3	0-0	0-2	1-1	2-3		4-0	0-1	0-5	4-2	0-2	4-2
Lakenheath	3-1	0-0	0-3	0-1	0-7	3-1	2-2	2-1	0-4	2-2		1-3	2-0	5-2	3-2	2-4
Linton Granta	3-1	2-1	1-3	3-3	2-2	5-2	0-3	2-0	3-0	2-1	4-0		7-0	4-3	6-1	5-1
Littleport Town	9-0	0-2	4-1	3-2	2-0	1-0	1-1	5-2	2-0	7-1	5-0	1-2	*A*	8-1	8-2	6-1
Soham Town Rangers Res.	2-4	0-4	1-4	0-2	1-4	0-2	1-2	4-2	2-6	3-1	4-2	0-2	0-12		6-3	6-0
Somersham Town Res.	2-0	2-4	3-5	1-4	0-2	3-5	1-5	2-1	2-3	1-2	2-0	0-3	1-12	1-2		1-5
Whittlesford United	1-0	1-2	3-1	2-1	1-6	3-2	1-2	0-1	1-2	1-2	1-2	1-6	1-1	0-0	4-2	

Senior A

		P	W	D	L	F	A	Pts
Fulbourn Institute		30	24	5	1	111	29	77
Linton Granta		30	20	5	5	78	32	65
Littleport Town		30	20	4	6	118	36	64
Huntingdon Town		30	17	3	10	70	47	54
Girton United		30	16	5	9	49	43	53
Eaton Socon		30	14	7	9	55	55	49
Gamlingay United		30	11	6	13	50	47	39
Brampton		30	12	3	15	56	54	39
Bluntisham Rangers		30	10	6	14	50	54	36
Hardwick		30	11	3	16	47	52	36
Huntingdon United	-3	30	10	5	15	47	64	32
Lakenheath		30	9	5	16	47	85	32
Soham Town Rangers Res.		30	10	1	19	53	98	31
Whittlesford United	-3	30	10	3	17	48	76	30
Bassingbourn		30	8	3	19	30	74	27
Somersham Town Res.	-3	30	5	2	23	47	110	14

WILLIAM COCKELL CUP

FIRST ROUND
Bassingbourn 0 **Huntingdon Town** 2
Brampton 1 **Littleport Town** 3
Eaton Socon 3 Huntingdon United 0
Fulbourn Institute 13 Somersham Town Res. 2
Gamlingay United 0 **Linton Granta** 1
Girton United 0 **Bluntisham Rangers** 1
Lakenheath 6 Whittlesford United 1
Soham Town Rangers Res. 2 Hardwick 1

QUARTER-FINALS
Eaton Socon 0 **Bluntisham Rangers** 5
Fulbourn Institute 2 Littleport Town 0
Lakenheath 1 Huntingdon Town 1 *aet*
Huntingdon Town 0 **Lakenheath** 1 *replay*
Linton Granta 10 Soham Town Rangers Res. 0

SEMI-FINALS
Bluntisham Rangers 1 **Fulbourn Institute** 4
Lakenheath 1 **Linton Granta** 3

FINAL
(5th May at Cambridge City)
Fulbourn Institute 4 Linton Granta 0

SENIOR A CONSTITUTION 2003-04

BASSINGBOURN .... South End, Bassingbourn, Cambridgeshire .... None
BLUNTISHAM RANGERS .... Mill Lane, Bluntisham, Huntingdon, Cambridgeshire .... None
BRAMPTON .... Thrapston Road Playing Fields, Brampton, Huntingdon, Cambridgeshire .... None
COMBERTON UNITED .... Recreation Ground, Hines Lane, Comberton, Cambridgeshire .... None
DEBDEN .... Recreation Ground, High Street, Debden, Saffron Walden, Essex .... None
EATON SOCON .... River Road, Eaton Ford, St Neots, Cambridgeshire .... None
GAMLINGAY UNITED .... Gamlingay Village College, Station Road, Gamlingay, Cambridgeshire .... None
GIRTON UNITED .... Girton Recreation, Cambridge Road, Girton, Cambridgeshire .... None
HARDWICK .... Egremont Road, Hardwick, Cambridgeshire .... None
HISTON 'A' .... Bridge Road, Impington, Cambridge, Cambridgeshire .... 01223 232301. Fax: 01223 237373
HUNDON .... North Street, Hundon, Cambridgeshire .... None
HUNTINGDON UNITED .... Storey Close, Sapley Road, Huntingdon, Cambridgeshire .... None
LAKENHEATH .... The Nest, Wings Road, Lakenheath, Cambridgeshire .... None
LITTLEPORT TOWN .... Sports Centre, Camel Road, Littleport, Cambridgeshire .... None
SOHAM TOWN RANGERS RESERVES .... Julius Martins Lane, Soham, Ely, Cambridgeshire ...... 01353 720732. Club/Fax: 01353 722139
WHITTLESFORD UNITED .... The Lawn, Whittlesford, Cambridgeshire .... None

Fulbourn Institute and Linton Granta go up to the Premier Division replaced by Debden and Comberton United. Huntingdon Town have moved up to the United Counties League. Somersham Town Reserves drop to Senior B replaced by Histon 'A' and Hundon.

	Balsham	Cambridge Univ. Press	Camden United	Cherry Hinton	Cottenham United Res.	Ely City Res.	Grampian	Great Chesterford	Great Shelford Res.	Histon 'A'	Hundon	Melbourn	Milton	Papworth	Romsey Mill	West Row Gunners
Balsham		4-3	2-4	0-6	2-2	2-6	1-7	1-4	1-5	0-5	1-10	1-0	0-3	0-5	2-2	0-1
Cambridge University Press	7-0		5-4	4-3	1-1	4-1	2-1	5-1	1-0	1-6	1-3	1-0	7-3	0-3	2-2	1-2
Camden United	4-0	1-1		0-2	8-1	7-0	0-2	1-1	5-3	0-0	2-1	5-1	3-1	2-1	3-2	2-3
Cherry Hinton	2-0	1-1	5-6	*S*	5-0	1-3	0-1	2-0	3-2	1-2	3-3	1-1	0-4	1-0	0-0	2-2
Cottenham United Res.	1-2	3-2	0-2	2-3	*E*	0-0	1-1	2-1	1-4	1-3	1-1	0-4	1-2	3-1		1-4
Ely City Res.	6-1	1-2	0-4	3-1	3-1	*N*	0-3	2-2	5-3	1-3	0-4	0-4	2-3	2-0	2-1	0-1
Grampian	9-1	2-1	3-2	1-0	8-1	3-0	*I*	1-0	3-1	2-3	2-1	1-0	3-2	4-2	3-1	1-2
Great Chesterford	2-3	5-3	4-4	0-3	2-1	0-1	1-3	*O*	1-2	1-3	2-4	1-3	0-2	1-1	1-2	1-2
Great Shelford Res.	3-1	1-4	2-0	2-4	3-0	2-2	3-1	2-0	*R*	0-0	1-1	1-1	5-2	3-1	0-5	1-0
Histon 'A'	3-2	1-3	2-0	1-1	3-0	6-1	3-1	4-0	1-2		7-1	5-1	3-2	1-0	0-4	2-1
Hundon	5-1	2-3	0-2	4-2	7-1	4-2	2-2	4-2	0-0			3-1	7-3	4-1	2-1	2-2
Melbourn	1-0	1-1	3-0	0-3	4-0	3-0	4-2	4-0	0-0	3-3	0-3	*B*	3-3	1-4	6-6	0-0
Milton	1-1	0-1	0-3	1-3	4-4	0-4	0-0	4-1	5-4	1-2	3-4	4-0	*B*	0-4	1-1	1-3
Papworth	2-2	1-3	0-0	0-3	2-1	2-1	2-1	2-2	0-4	1-3			0-4		0-1	0-4
Romsey Mill	5-0	0-3	3-1	1-2	1-1	2-2	1-4	0-3	3-1	0-2	3-5	1-6	1-4	3-0		0-1
West Row Gunners	9-0	2-1	0-0	6-3	4-2	2-0	3-1	1-1	1-2	2-3	1-2	6-1	2-0	1-0	3-4	

Senior B		P	W	D	L	F	A	Pts
Histon 'A'		30	21	5	4	82	34	68
Hundon		30	20	5	5	97	52	65
Grampian		30	20	2	8	76	39	62
West Row Gunners		30	19	5	6	71	34	62
Cambridge University Press		30	16	5	9	74	55	53
Camden United		30	15	6	9	75	48	51
Cherry Hinton		30	15	5	10	70	50	50
Great Shelford Res.		30	12	5	13	57	60	41
Melbourn	-3	30	10	8	12	57	60	35
Milton		30	10	5	15	64	73	35
Romsey Mill		30	9	7	14	57	63	34
Papworth		30	10	4	16	42	55	34
Ely City Res.	-3	30	10	4	16	50	71	31
Great Chesterford		30	4	7	19	40	71	19
Cottenham United Res.		30	3	7	20	33	88	16
Balsham	-3	30	4	4	22	31	123	13

PERCY OLDHAM CUP

FIRST ROUND
Cambridge University Press 7 Balsham 1
Cottenham United Res. 2 West Row Gunners 2 *aet*
West Row Gunners 0 Cottenham United Res. 1 *replay*
Ely City Res. 5 Papworth 0
Grampian 2 Great Chesterford 1
Great Shelford Res. 5 Histon 'A' 2
Hundon 1 **Camden United** 3
Melbourn 2 Cherry Hinton 1
Romsey Mill 3 Milton 2
QUARTER-FINALS
Cambridge University Press 2 Melbourn 0
Camden United 0 **Romsey Mill** 2
Cottenham United Res. 0 **Grampian** 2
Ely City Res. 1 **Great Shelford Res.** 3
SEMI-FINALS
Cambridge University Press 1 **Grampian** 3
Romsey Mill 6 Great Shelford Res. 1
FINAL
(7th May at Cambridge City)
Grampian 3 Romsey Mill 2

SENIOR B CONSTITUTION 2003-04

CAMBRIDGE UNIVERSITY PRESS .... CUP Sports Ground, Shaftesbury Rd, Cambridge .... None
CAMDEN UNITED .... Jesus Green, Chesterton Road, Cambridge, Cambridgeshire .... None
CASTLE CAMPS .... Recreation Ground, Bumpstead Road, Castle Camps, Cambridgeshire .... None
CHERRY HINTON............. Recreation Ground, Cherry Hinton, Cambridge, Cambridgeshire......................... None
ELY CITY RESERVES .... The Unwin Ground, Downham Road, Ely, Cambridgeshire 01353 662035
GRAMPIAN .... Sports Ground, Grampian Foods, Little Wratting, Cambridgeshire 01223 842590
GREAT SHELFORD RESERVES . Recreation Ground, Woollards Lane, Great Shelford, Cambridgeshire .... None
MELBOURN....................... The Recreation Ground, The Moor, Melbourn, Cambridgeshire .... None
MILTON....................... Milton Recreation Ground, The Sycamores, Milton, Cambridgeshire .... None
NEEDINGWORTH UNITED .... Mill Field, Holywell Road, Needingworth, Cambridgeshire .... None
PAPWORTH..................... Chequers Lane, Papworth Everard, Cambridgeshire .... None
ROMSEY MILL .... Teversham Recreation Ground, High Street, Teversham, Cambridgeshire .... None
SAWSTON UNITED RESERVES ..... Spicers Sports Ground, New Road, Sawston, Cambridgeshire .... None
SOMERSHAM TOWN RESERVES..... West End Ground, St Ives Road, Somersham, Huntingdon 01487 843384
WEST ROW GUNNERS..................... Chapel Row, West Row, Cambridgeshire .... None
WILLINGHAM .... Recreation Ground, West Fen Road, Willingham, Cambridgeshire .... None
Hundon and Histon 'A' go up to Senior A replaced by Somersham Town Reserves. Castle Camps and Sawston United Reserves arrive from Division 1A replacing Great Chesterford and Balsham. Cottenham United Reserves drop to Division 1B replaced by Needingworth United and Willingham.

WWW.CHERRYRED.CO.UK

Division 1A

	P	W	D	L	F	A	Pts
Castle Camps	22	18	1	3	92	26	55
Sawston United Res.	22	17	1	4	72	23	52
West Wratting Res.	22	16	2	4	65	32	50
Barton Mills	22	13	2	7	57	37	41
Fulbourn Institute Res.	22	10	4	8	37	39	34
JM Sports	22	9	4	9	37	36	31
Saffron Crocus	22	8	2	12	40	54	26
Sandon	22	7	2	13	46	61	23
Fowlmere	22	6	4	12	37	51	22
Sawston Rovers	22	5	4	13	43	64	19
AFC Newmarket	22	3	6	13	28	68	15
Whittlesford Utd Res.	22	3	2	17	20	83	11

Division 1B

	P	W	D	L	F	A	Pts
Needingworth United	24	18	4	2	104	24	58
Willingham	24	15	4	5	68	33	49
Haddenham Rovers	24	14	5	5	74	33	47
Waterbeach Res.	24	14	5	5	65	34	47
Swavesey Institute	24	12	5	7	57	27	41
Littleport Town Res.	24	12	1	11	73	36	37
Over Sports Res.	24	12	1	11	46	38	37
Soham United	24	10	2	12	71	65	32
St Ives Rangers	24	8	4	12	44	64	28
Buckden	24	9	1	14	58	88	28
Stretham Hotspurs	24	6	5	13	52	71	23
Little Downham	24	5	3	16	42	90	18
Earith United	24	1	0	23	13	164	3

Div 1 Play-off: Needingworth United 1 Castle Camps 3

Division 2A

	P	W	D	L	F	A	Pts
Wickhambrook	24	20	1	3	107	27	61
Harston	24	18	2	4	78	36	56
Linton Granta Res.	24	16	3	5	89	36	51
Saffron Rangers	24	16	0	8	68	40	48
Cherry Hinton Res.	24	14	2	8	97	53	44
Great Shelford 'A'	24	12	3	9	88	40	39
Comberton United Res.	24	10	6	8	63	38	36
Great Chesterford Res.	24	11	2	11	57	46	35
Litlington Athletic	24	9	1	14	49	74	28
Gransden Chequers	24	7	4	13	59	60	25
Fulbourn Hospital	24	2	2	20	27	153	8
Dullingham	24	2	1	21	19	146	7
Bassingbourn Res. -9	24	4	3	17	23	75	6

Division 2B

	P	W	D	L	F	A	Pts
Ely Crusaders	24	21	1	2	77	24	64
Great Paxton Res.	24	17	1	6	62	33	52
Bottisham Sports	24	14	9	1	60	28	51
Huntingdon Town Res.	24	14	3	7	51	27	45
Godmanchester Res.	24	11	3	10	54	46	36
Brampton Res.	24	11	2	11	49	38	35
Bluntisham Rgrs Res.	24	10	4	10	49	44	34
Isleham United	24	9	5	10	39	34	32
Sutton United	24	9	3	12	53	52	30
Wicken Amateurs	24	6	2	16	46	74	20
Lode	24	5	5	14	42	84	20
Warboys Town Res.	24	4	5	15	25	59	17
Longstanton -3	24	2	3	19	22	86	6

Div 2 Play-off: Ely Crusaders 4 Wickhambrook 0

Division 3A

	P	W	D	L	F	A	Pts
Thaxted	24	17	4	3	76	34	55
Orwell	24	12	8	4	55	34	44
Great Chishill	24	12	5	7	51	49	41
Mott McDonald	24	12	3	9	46	36	39
Ashdon Villa	24	11	5	8	61	54	38
Barrington	24	10	7	7	59	53	37
Fowlmere Res.	24	11	3	10	48	58	36
Fulbourn Institute 'A'	24	10	3	11	57	45	33
Foxton Res.	24	10	3	11	52	50	33
Steeple Morden	24	6	4	14	49	64	22
Duxford United	24	5	5	14	42	77	20
Guilden Morden -6	24	7	4	13	45	50	19
Balsham Res. -6	24	4	4	16	34	71	10

Division 3B

	P	W	D	L	F	A	Pts
Camb. Univ. Press Res.	24	21	3	0	88	17	66
Hemingford Utd Res.	24	16	3	5	70	39	51
Eaton Socon Res.	24	14	4	6	75	52	46
Tuddenham Rov. Res.	24	14	4	6	69	50	46
Fenstanton	24	12	3	9	70	48	39
Milton Res.	24	10	5	9	46	41	35
Gamlingay United Res.	24	10	1	13	46	54	31
Fordham Res.	24	9	3	12	53	72	30
Huntingdon Utd Res.	24	9	2	13	45	47	29
Hardwick Res.	24	8	4	12	51	64	28
Lakenheath Res.	24	7	1	16	49	90	22
Girton United Res.	24	4	5	15	41	72	17
Mepal Sports	24	3	0	21	32	89	9

Div 3 Play-off: Cambridge University Press 'A' 1 Thaxted 0

Division 4A

	P	W	D	L	F	A	Pts
Melbourn Res.	24	18	2	4	84	26	56
Bayer	24	16	3	5	75	33	51
Abington United	24	16	2	6	66	41	50
Sawston United 'A'	24	13	5	6	51	31	44
Grampian Res.	24	12	4	8	75	49	40
Elsworth Sports	24	11	5	8	73	52	38
Eaton Socon 'A'	24	11	4	9	76	56	37
Withersfield	24	11	3	10	67	46	36
Sawston Rovers Res.	24	10	4	10	62	61	34
Wilbraham	24	5	4	15	44	64	19
Camden United Res.	24	5	4	15	55	95	19
Papworth Res.	24	6	0	18	37	115	18
Saffron Rangers Res. -6	24	2	0	22	17	113	0

Division 4B

	P	W	D	L	F	A	Pts
Bluntisham Rgrs 'A'	26	21	3	2	110	33	66
Cottenham United 'A'	26	17	3	6	55	33	54
BRJ Huntingdon	26	16	6	4	83	44	54
Ely City 'A'	26	12	4	10	48	52	40
Soham United Res.	25	11	6	8	67	54	39
St Ives Town 'A'	26	11	5	10	48	49	38
W. Row Gunners Res.	26	11	4	11	64	56	37
Witchford	26	10	6	10	59	54	36
Isleham United Res.	26	9	6	11	42	54	33
Barton Mills Res.	25	10	3	12	67	62	33
Needingworth Res.	26	8	8	10	53	59	32
Littleport Town 'A'	26	8	5	13	71	83	29
Swavesey Institute Res.	26	5	2	19	32	67	17
Little Downham Res.	26	1	1	24	19	118	4

Div 4 Play-off: Bluntisham Rangers 'A' 4 Melbourn Res. 1

Division 5A

	P	W	D	L	F	A	Pts
Hundon Res.	24	18	3	3	88	32	57
Camb. Univ. Press 'A'	24	17	3	4	89	39	54
Linton Granta 'A'	24	17	3	4	64	24	54
Harston Res.	24	13	5	6	73	49	44
Saffron Crocus Res.	24	12	7	5	49	33	43
Hardwick 'A'	24	11	4	9	59	62	37
Girton United 'A'	24	10	4	10	51	42	34
Steeple Morden Res.	24	8	6	10	54	56	30
Comberton United 'A'	24	7	1	16	40	75	22
Barton	24	6	3	15	36	61	21
Barrington Res.	24	5	3	16	28	80	18
Newport Veterans	24	4	3	17	33	60	15
Litlington Athletic Res.	24	4	3	17	27	78	15

Division 5B

	P	W	D	L	F	A	Pts
The Vine	26	19	4	3	75	22	61
Huntingdon Town 'A'	26	16	3	7	67	28	51
Hemingford Utd 'A'	26	14	6	6	70	41	48
Sutton United Res. -6	26	17	3	6	72	29	48
Haddenham Rov. Res.	26	14	2	10	59	44	44
Pymore	26	13	5	8	53	46	44
Willingham Res.	26	12	5	9	40	39	41
Fenstanton Res.	26	13	2	11	49	65	41
Bottisham Sports Res.	26	10	4	12	55	64	34
Exning Athletic	26	10	2	14	47	58	32
Milton 'A'	26	7	4	15	60	69	25
Earith United Res. -3	26	6	3	17	35	65	18
Lode Res. -3	26	4	2	20	41	99	11
Cottenham Utd 'B' -3	26	4	1	21	38	92	10

Div 5 Play-off: The Vine 0 Hundon Res. 1

CENTRAL MIDLANDS LEAGUE

	Askern Welfare	Barton Town OB	Blackwell MW	Bottesford Town	Carlton Town	Clipstone Welfare	Dinnington Town	Dunkirk	Graham Str. Prims	Greenwood Mead.	Heanor Town	Holbrook	Nettleham	Retford United	Ripley Town	Rolls Royce Leisure	Sandiacre Town	South Normanton A.	Sutton Town	Teversal
Askern Welfare		1-0	0-0	6-2	2-3	2-3	3-1	0-2	2-0	0-2	1-1	1-1	0-2	0-0	0-3	1-2	1-2	0-2	1-4	2-1
Barton Town Old Boys	3-2		2-0	3-1	1-2	1-2	0-2	2-0	2-1	2-0	2-1	1-0	1-1	2-3	3-1	2-1	3-2	2-5	2-3	1-2
Blackwell Miners Welfare	1-5	0-4	S	10-2	3-5	1-3	3-5	1-5	2-2	3-3	0-3	3-4	0-2	2-1	1-0	3-5	0-1	1-2	1-6	0-3
Bottesford Town	1-4	3-1	4-10	U	2-2	1-1	0-5	4-4	2-1	0-3	0-1	0-3	1-4	0-4	0-3	1-2	1-3	1-4	1-0	2-2
Carlton Town	2-2	5-1	1-2	4-0	P	2-0	1-0	1-2	5-0	0-0	1-2	1-2	2-3	1-1	3-2	2-1	2-0	1-0	2-2	2-2
Clipstone Welfare	4-0	4-2	1-3	2-2	1-1	R	0-3	1-1	4-1	1-2	0-4	1-2	2-1	0-2	2-2	2-4	1-1	1-0	3-2	3-2
Dinnington Town	2-0	5-0	2-0	4-0	0-1	2-0	E	3-2	2-0	2-0	1-0	1-1	0-0	1-1	4-0	5-1	1-5	1-2	3-1	2-0
Dunkirk	1-0	3-1	1-2	6-0	1-3	2-1	3-4	M	1-1	0-1	3-1	2-1	3-1	0-0	1-1	4-0	1-4	1-3	2-3	1-3
Graham Street Prims	1-2	2-1	1-0	5-1	1-4	4-1	1-1	0-2	E	5-4	1-3	1-2	3-1	0-4	2-2	5-3	1-0	1-3	2-3	1-3
Greenwood Meadows	0-0	1-2	2-2	1-1	0-0	3-1	1-1	4-0	4-2	D	5-3	0-2	1-2	1-2	1-2	0-2	1-2	0-1	2-3	2-4
Heanor Town	1-3	0-2	4-1	6-0	0-1	3-1	3-0	4-2	5-1		I	3-0	0-0	1-1	3-1	3-2	2-2	4-0	0-2	1-0
Holbrook	4-1	3-1	3-1	6-1	1-3	2-0	2-2	0-1	3-1	4-1	0-0	V	2-1	0-1	1-3	2-2	2-2	4-0	1-3	1-0
Nettleham	0-5	2-3	3-1	2-5	2-2	1-0	2-2	0-1	1-2	1-3	0-4	1-1	I	0-3	1-2	3-2	2-0	2-1	1-3	1-5
Retford United	1-1	3-0	2-3	6-0	4-3	1-1	1-1	5-1	4-0	0-1	0-0	0-2	2-1	S	0-3	2-1	2-2	2-1	2-0	2-1
Ripley Town	3-0	1-3	3-2	7-0	0-1	5-0	0-3	2-1	2-0	0-1	1-1	4-0	2-1	0-2	I	3-1	2-4	2-2	5-3	2-0
Rolls Royce Leisure	4-1	4-1	2-0	3-0	0-1	5-0	0-3	2-1	2-0	0-1	0-1	1-1	4-0	2-1	1-2	O	1-0	2-1	1-3	1-1
Sandiacre Town	2-2	1-2	2-1	2-3	1-2	1-2	2-3	1-1	4-2	1-1	0-2	4-2	1-1	1-2	2-2	4-1	N		1-2	1-2
South Normanton Athletic	2-0	7-1	6-0	9-0	4-3	2-2	1-3	2-1	3-1	0-4	2-2	4-2	2-3	2-2	3-3	4-1	1-2		0-0	1-2
Sutton Town	2-2	1-0	3-1	2-0	0-1	0-1	3-2	3-2	3-1	7-0	0-5	1-1	1-1	0-0	1-0	1-0	3-3	1-2		2-1
Teversal	5-0	1-2	3-1	1-0	2-2	1-1	3-1	1-4	3-1	1-2										

Supreme Division

	P	W	D	L	F	A	Pts
Carlton Town	38	22	9	7	80	46	75
Sutton Town	38	23	5	10	75	47	74
South Normanton Athletic	38	22	5	11	103	67	71
Retford United	38	19	11	8	69	40	68
Teversal	38	20	6	12	90	53	66
Dinnington Town	38	19	9	10	78	50	66
Holbrook	38	17	12	9	67	49	63
Sandiacre Town	38	17	10	11	67	60	61
Ripley Town	38	17	9	12	81	57	60
Rolls Royce Leisure	38	19	3	16	72	64	60
Heanor Town	38	17	6	15	78	50	57
Dunkirk	38	17	6	15	75	64	57
Barton Town Old Boys	38	18	1	19	62	77	55
Nettleham	38	11	9	18	52	72	42
Greenwood Meadows	38	11	8	19	48	71	41
Clipstone Welfare	38	11	7	20	50	73	40
Askern Welfare	38	10	9	19	53	70	39
Graham Street Prims	38	9	4	25	55	93	31
Blackwell MW	38	8	4	26	65	106	28
Bottesford Town	38	4	5	29	40	151	17

Reserve Prem. Division

	P	W	D	L	F	A	Pts
Shirebrook Town Res.	32	25	2	5	104	29	77
Worksop Town Res.	32	21	4	7	93	38	67
Carlton Town Res.	32	20	5	7	82	49	65
Graham St. Prims Res.	32	19	6	7	67	43	63
Clipstone Welfare Res.	32	18	6	8	81	53	60
Long Eaton Utd Res.	32	18	4	10	87	45	58
Retford United Res.	32	17	7	8	72	43	58
Holbrook Res.	32	11	8	13	68	49	41
Sandiacre Town Res.	32	11	8	13	53	54	41
Teversal Res.	32	10	8	14	74	62	38
Heanor Town Res.	32	11	4	17	62	91	37
Greenwood Mdws Res.	32	10	6	16	50	56	36
Radford Res.	32	9	8	15	60	66	35
Thoresby CW Res.	32	7	11	14	39	64	32
Rolls Royce Leis.Res.	32	9	4	19	62	92	31
Ollerton Town Res.	32	5	1	26	41	152	16
Selston Res.	32	2	6	24	25	134	12

WWW.NLNEWSDESK.CO.UK

SUPREME DIVISION CONSTITUTION 2003-04

ASKERN WELFARE .... Welfare Sports Ground, Doncaster Road, Askern, Doncaster, South Yorkshire ... 01302 700957
BARTON TOWN OLD BOYS .... Marsh Lane, Barton-on-Humber, North Lincs. ... 07900 105204
BLACKWELL MINERS WELFARE . Welfare Ground, Primrose Hill, Blackwell, Alfreton, Derbyshire ... 01773 811295
CLIPSTONE WELFARE .... Lido Ground, Clipstone Road West, Mansfield, Nottinghamshire ... 01623 655674
DINNINGTON TOWN ...... Resource Centre, 131 Laughton Road (The Stute), Dinnington, South Yorkshire ... 01909 518555
DUNKIRK .... Ron Steel Sports Ground, Trentside Farm, Lenton Lane, Clifton Bridge, Nottingham, Nottinghamshire ... 0115 985 0803
GEDLING MINERS WELFARE .... Plains Road, Mapperley, Nottingham, Nottinghamshire ... 01332 668656
GRAHAM STREET PRIMS ..... Asterdale Sports Centre, Borrowash Road, Spondon, Derby, Derbyshire ... 0115 986 5913
GREENWOOD MEADOWS........ Old Lenton Lane, Clifton Bridge, Nottingham, Nottinghamshire ... 01773 713742
HEANOR TOWN .... The Town Ground, Mayfield Avenue, Heanor, Derbyshire ... 01332 880259
HOLBROOK .... Welfare Ground, Shaw Lane, Holbrook, Derbyshire ... 0797 427074
KIVETON PARK .... Hard Lane, Kiveton Park, Sheffield, South Yorkshire ... 01522 750007
NETTLEHAM .... Mulsanne Park, Field Close, Nettleham, Lincoln, Lincolnshire ... 0115 986 8255
PELICAN .... Brian Wakefield Sports Ground, Lenton Lane, Nottingham, Nottinghamshire ... 0115 942 3250
RADFORD .... Radford Road West, off Radford Road, Radford, Nottingham, Nottinghamshire ... 0794 945 4694
RETFORD UNITED .... Canon Park, Leverton Road, Retford, Nottinghamshire ... 01773 742287
RIPLEY TOWN .... Waingroves Brick Works, Peasehill Road, Ripley, Derbyshire ... 0115 963 0134
ROLLS ROYCE LEISURE .... Rolls Royce Sports & Social, Watnall Road, Hucknall, Nottinghamshire ... 0115 939 2880
SANDIACRE TOWN .... St Giles Park, Stanton Road, Sandiacre, Nottingham, Nottinghamshire ... 01623 555944
TEVERSAL........ Teversal Grange Sports & Social, Carnarvon Street, Teversal, Sutton-in-Ashfield, Nottinghamshire

Carlton Town, Sutton Town and South Normanton Athletic are promoted to the Northern Counties East League. Bottesford Town drop to the Premier Division from which Pelican, Kiveton Park, Radford and Gedling Miners Welfare are promoted.

WWW.CHERRYRED.CO.UK

	Bentley Colliery	Blidworth Welfare	Forest Town	GAD Khalsa Sports	Gedling MW	Harworth Coll. Inst.	Kimberley Town	Kiveton Park	Ollerton Town	Pelican	Radford	Selston	Sheffield City	Thoresby Coll. Welf.	Thorne Colliery	Welbeck M. Welfare	Yorkshire Main
Bentley Colliery	P	1-2	0-0	3-1	2-2	5-0	0-0	3-3	0-0	1-3	1-6	7-3	3-1	2-1	3-0	5-2	2-1
Blidworth Welfare	0-1	R	1-1	5-2	0-3	4-2	0-0	0-2	3-2	0-2	1-1	3-3	1-3	1-0	0-1	2-0	1-0
Forest Town	0-4	0-6	E	3-2	1-2	2-3	1-1	4-2	2-0	0-2	1-1	2-2	0-1	3-1	2-2	3-2	1-1
GAD Khalsa Sports	1-1	2-4	1-5	M	1-7	1-3	2-2	2-8	0-2	1-3	1-2	4-3	5-0	0-6	1-1	3-3	0-2
Gedling Miners Welfare	5-2	3-1	1-2	1-0	I	4-1	4-2	1-1	1-1	0-1	4-1	3-1	4-5	1-0	1-1	3-3	0-2
Harworth Colliery Institute	4-2	2-0	1-3	4-2	0-1	E	3-1	2-3	2-1	0-3	3-1	2-1	2-2	4-1	0-3	3-1	2-4
Kimberley Town	1-1	1-0	1-1	3-1	0-1	1-2	R	1-6	0-2	0-6	0-2	3-1	0-0	0-1	2-3	2-0	2-2
Kiveton Park	3-3	2-1	6-1	5-1	0-0	3-2	2-0		2-1	3-2	2-1	0-1	1-1	3-0	4-1	2-3	5-0
Ollerton Town	2-1	1-0	1-2	0-0	0-0	4-1	3-0	2-4		0-2	3-0	2-1	4-0	3-1	0-2	5-0	7-1
Pelican	1-3	2-1	6-0	4-2	0-0	4-1	1-0	3-3	0-2	D	2-1	5-1	4-1	0-1	2-1	8-0	6-1
Radford	4-1	4-1	2-0	1-1	4-1	2-0	3-2	2-0	1-2	2-2	I	3-0	1-0	2-0	1-0	7-1	3-0
Selston	1-5	2-1	0-0	2-2	3-2	2-3	1-0	2-7	0-2	1-5	0-6	V	1-4	0-2	3-6	2-2	1-0
Sheffield City	2-3	2-3	0-0	1-1	0-7	2-1	1-1	1-3	0-0	1-3	0-2	0-0	I	1-4	2-3	2-2	1-0
Thoresby Colliery Welfare	0-0	1-4	1-0	1-2	1-1	3-1	1-1	1-3	0-0	1-3	0-2	0-0	0-1	S	3-1	1-0	5-1
Thorne Colliery	5-2	4-0	1-2	4-1	1-2	1-0	5-1	2-2	3-3	1-1	1-1	2-1	2-2	3-1	I	6-2	4-0
Welbeck Miners Welfare	5-7	2-2	4-2	0-0	2-3	2-2	6-2	0-2	3-4	0-0	0-3	0-0	3-1	5-3	6-0	O	10-0
Yorkshire Main	3-4	0-4	0-6	0-4	0-11	2-7	0-3	0-1	0-2	0-5	1-3	0-3	1-2	5-1	2-4	1-7	N

Premier Division

	Adj	P	W	D	L	F	A	Pts
Pelican		32	22	6	4	89	28	72
Kiveton Park		32	21	6	5	95	46	69
Radford		32	21	6	5	76	28	69
Gedling Miners Welf.	-3	32	19	8	5	78	36	62
Thorne Colliery	-1	32	17	7	7	90	51	57
Ollerton Town		32	16	7	9	60	34	55
Bentley Colliery		32	15	9	8	78	62	54
Thoresby CW		32	13	7	12	50	55	46
Harworth Colliery Inst.		32	14	2	16	63	71	44
Forest Town		32	11	10	11	50	58	43
Blidworth Welfare		32	12	5	15	52	52	41
Sheffield City		32	8	8	16	44	67	32
Kimberley Town		32	6	8	18	35	64	26
Welbeck MW		32	6	8	18	60	92	26
Selston		32	6	7	19	43	87	25
GAD Khalsa Sports		32	4	9	19	47	89	21
Yorkshire Main		32	3	3	26	29	119	12

Reserve Division One

	Adj	P	W	D	L	F	A	Pts
Pelican Res.		26	20	3	3	88	25	63
Ripley Town Res.	-3	26	21	3	2	83	21	63
Carlton Town 'A'		26	19	2	5	80	32	59
Blackwell MW Res.		26	16	5	5	68	40	53
Sutton Town Res.		26	13	4	9	63	52	43
Forest Town Res.		26	10	10	6	50	30	40
Shirebrook Town 'A'		26	7	6	13	45	49	27
Radford 'A'		26	8	3	15	41	87	27
South Normanton Res.		26	8	2	16	45	69	26
Welbeck MW Res.		26	7	4	15	34	70	25
Nettleham Res.		26	7	3	16	37	59	24
Blidworth Welfare Res.		26	6	5	15	47	80	23
Thoresby Coll. W. 'A'		26	5	6	15	36	69	21
Kimberley Town Res.		26	4	6	16	26	60	18

RESERVES CUP FINAL
(8th April at South Normanton Athletic)
Holbrook Res. 1 Shirebrook Town Res. 0

PREMIER DIVISION CONSTITUTION 2003-04

APPLEBY FRODINGHAM ATH. . . Brumby Hall Sports Ground, Ashby Road, Scunthorpe, North Lincs 01724 843024
BENTLEY COLLIERY . . . . Bentley Miners Welfare, The Avenue, Bentley, Doncaster, South Yorkshire 01302 874420
BLIDWORTH WELFARE. . . Blidworth Social Centre, Mansfield Road, Blidworth, Mansfield, Nottinghamshire 01623 793361
BOTTESFORD TOWN . . . . Birch Park, Ontario Road, Bottesford, Lincolnshire 01623 793361
FOREST TOWN . . . Forest Town Welfare Sports Ground, Clipstone Road, West Forest Town, Mansfield, Nottinghamshire 01724 871883
HARWORTH COLLIERY INSTITUTE. . . Recreation Ground, Scooby Road, Bircotes, Doncaster 01302 624678
KIMBERLEY TOWN . . . . The Stag Ground, Nottingham Road, Kimberley, Nottinghamshire 01302 750614
MATLOCK UNITED . . . . Cavendish Road Playing Fields, Cavendish Park, Matlock, Derbyshire 0115 938 2788
OLLERTON TOWN . . . . Walesby Lane, New Ollerton, Nottingham, Nottinghamshire . . . . None
PUNJAB UNITED . . . . The Wharf, Shardlow, Derby, Derbyshire . . . . None
RADCLIFFE OLYMPIC . . . . Wharf Lane, Radcliffe-on-Trent, Nottingham, Nottinghamshire . . . . None
RAINWORTH MINERS WELFARE . . . . Kirklington Road, Rainworth, Nottinghamshire . . . . None
SELSTON. . . . . Parish Hall Ground, Mansfield Road, Selston, Nottinghamshire . . . . None
SHEEPBRIDGE . . . . Sheepbridge Miners Welfare, Chesterfield, Derbyshire 01773 810411
SHEFFIELD CITY . . . . Meadowhall Stadium, 101 Ferrars Road, Tinsley, Sheffield, South Yorkshire . . . . None
SOUTHWELL CITY. . . . . War Memorial Recreation Ground, Bishops Drive, Southwell, Nottinghamshire 0114 242 4244
THORESBY COLLIERY WELFARE. Welfare Ground, Fourth Avenue, Edwinstowe, Nottinghamshire 01636 814386
THORNE COLLIERY . . . . Moorends MW, Grange Road, Moorends, Thorne, Doncaster, South Yorkshire 01623 822283
WELBECK MINERS WELFARE . . . . Elkesley Road Sports Ground, Meden Vale, Mansfield . . . Colliery: 01623 842611. Welfare: 842267
YORKSHIRE MAIN . . . . Yorkshire Main Miners Welfare, Edlington Lane, Edlington, Doncaster, South Yorkshire 01709 864075
Pelican, Kiveton Park, Radford and Gedling Miners Welfare go up to the Supreme Division replaced by Bottesford Town. GAD Khalsa Sports have disbanded. Newcomers are Sheepbridge (Matlock & District League), Appleby Frodingham Athletic (Lincs League), Matlock United (Mids Regional Alliance), Radcliffe Olympic, Rainworth Miners Welfare and Southwell City (all Notts Alliance) and Punjab United (East Midlands Senior League).

LEAGUE CUP

FIRST ROUND

Bentley Colliery 2 **Rolls Royce Leisure** 4
Bottesford Town 0 **Thoresby Colliery Welfare** 2
Gedling Miners Welfare 2 Pelican 1
Nettleham 2 **Teversal** 3
Retford United 6 Yorkshire Main 0
Sutton Town 0 **Carlton Town** 2
Thorne Colliery 3 Radford 2

SECOND ROUND

Barton Town Old Boys 4 Greenwood Meadows 0
Blackwell MW 4 Thoresby CW 4
Thoresby Colliery Welfare 4 **Blackwell Miners Welfare** 4 *aet (3-4p) replay*
Dinnington Town 4 GAD Khalsa Sports 0
Dunkirk (w/o) Stanton Ilkeston (scr.)
Forest Town 3 Askern Welfare 3
Askern Welfare 3 Forest Town 2 *replay*
Gedling Miners Welfare 0 **Ollerton Town** 1
Harworth CI 0 **Welbeck Miners Welfare** 2
Heanor Town 1 Ripley Town 0
Holbrook 6 Retford United 1
Kimberley Town 1 Rolls Royce Leisure 1
Rolls Royce Leisure 5 **Kimberley Town** 2 *replay*
(ineligible player – Kimberley Town reinstated)
Nettleham **Kiveton Park**
Sandiacre Town 1 South Normanton Athletic 0
Selston 2 Blidworth Welfare 1
Sheffield City 0 **Clipstone Welfare** 2
Teversal 2 **Graham Street Prims** 3
Thorne Colliery 0 **Carlton Town** 1

THIRD ROUND

Carlton Town 4 Clipstone Welfare 1
Dinnington Town 2 Selston 1
Dunkirk 4 Sandiacre Town 1
Graham Street Prims 2 Ollerton Town 0
Heanor Town 2 Barton Town Old Boys 0
Holbrook 6 Welbeck Miners Welfare 0
Kimberley Town 1 **Blackwell Miners Welfare** 4
Kiveton Park 2 Askern Welfare 2
Askern Welfare 1 **Kiveton Park** 2
replay

QUARTER-FINALS

Blackwell Miners Welfare 3 Graham Street Prims 3
Graham Street Prims 2 **Blackwell Miners Welfare** 4 *replay aet*
Carlton Town 4 Kiveton Park 1
Heanor Town 0 **Dunkirk** 3
Holbrook 1 **Dinnington Town** 6

EMI-FINALS

Dinnington Town 2 Carlton Town 1
(at Clipstone Welfare)
Dunkirk 4 Blackwell Miners Welfare 3 *aet*
(at Heanor Town)

FINAL

(4th May at Alfreton Town)
Dinnington Town 2 Dunkirk 0

FLOODLIGHT CUP

FIRST ROUND

(Ties played over two legs)
Blackwell Miners Welfare 0 Sutton Town 1,
Sutton Town 3 Blackwell Miners Welfare 1
Blidworth Welfare 1 Harworth Colliery Institute 2,
Harworth Colliery Institute 2 Blidworth Welfare 1
Carlton Town 1 Clipstone Welfare 2,
Clipstone Welfare 4 Carlton Town 4
Heanor Town 3 Sandiacre Town 3,
Sandiacre Town 2 **Heanor Town** 3
Kimberley Town 0 Dunkirk 2,
Dunkirk 5 Kimberley Town 0
Nettleham 0 Bottesford Town 1,
Bottesford Town 0 **Nettleham** 2
Retford United (scr.) Rolls Royce Leisure (w/o),
Rolls Royce Leisure (w/o) Retford United (scr.)
South Normanton Athletic 3 Graham Street Prims 0,
Graham Street Prims 0 **South Normanton Athletic** 2

QUARTER-FINALS

(Ties played over two legs, except South Normanton v Rolls Royce Leisure)
Dunkirk 4 Clipstone Welfare 0,
Clipstone Welfare 2 **Dunkirk** 4
Harworth Colliery Institute 0 Nettleham 1,
Nettleham 1 **Harworth Colliery Institute** 4
South Normanton Athletic 1 **Rolls Royce Leisure** 2,
Sutton Town 2 Heanor Town 1,
Heanor Town 2 **Sutton Town** 2

SEMI-FINALS

(Ties played over two legs)
Dunkirk 3 Rolls Royce Leisure 0,
Rolls Royce Leisure 3 **Dunkirk** 3
Harworth Colliery Institute 0 Sutton Town 3,
Sutton Town 7 Harworth Colliery Institute 1

FINAL

(16th April at Clipstone Welfare)
Dunkirk 2 Sutton Town 2 *aet (7-8p)*

COMBINED COUNTIES LEAGUE

	Wal	Wim	Ash	Bed	ChU	ChH	Chi	Cob	Cov	Far	Fel	Fri	God	Har	Mer	NGr	RPV	Rea	San	Sou	Vik	Wlt	Wes	Wit
AFC Wallingf'd		3-0	2-0	6-2	8-0	4-1	4-2	3-0	5-0	3-0	2-0	4-0	3-0	4-1	3-0	2-2	0-1	4-0	7-1	2-0	7-0	0-3	6-0	1-0
AFC Wimbledon	3-2		5-3	5-1	4-3	2-1	1-2	4-0	3-2	0-0	0-1	1-0	2-1	3-1	1-0	4-3	5-1	2-0	2-1	2-2	5-0	3-0	5-0	0-2
Ash United	2-3	3-2		1-2	1-0	3-5	2-2	1-0	6-1	7-0	3-2	5-0	0-3	2-1	2-3	3-5	0-3	3-1	3-0	2-1	2-0	1-0	2-3	1-2
Bedfont	0-1	1-2	2-4		1-0	2-2	3-0	4-0	6-1	2-0	3-2	2-1	0-4	5-1	3-1	2-0	1-2	2-0	1-2	3-5	6-0	1-0	2-3	1-2
Chessington Utd	0-2	1-3	1-0	0-2	P	0-1	1-0	0-1	9-0	1-1	1-4	1-2	3-1	2-1	0-0	0-1	0-1	2-0	0-0	2-3	5-0	1-2	1-1	1-3
Chessington & H.	0-1	0-3	2-2	1-3	2-1	R	2-2	2-1	7-0	1-1	0-2	2-1	4-1	1-0	0-1	0-3	1-1	1-2	0-3	5-1	1-2	1-1	1-2	0-4
Chipstead	0-3	2-3	2-1	1-0	2-1	4-4	E	0-0	3-2	3-1	0-0	5-2	0-0	4-3	2-2	1-0	0-3	1-1	1-2	3-3	5-1	3-0	1-2	2-1
Cobham	1-1	0-5	1-5	1-5	0-2	0-5	3-3	M	4-0	6-1	1-1	0-0	2-3	0-4	2-4	1-2	0-5	2-4	1-2	1-3	7-1	2-2	0-1	0-6
Cove	0-1	1-4	1-4	0-12	1-2	0-4	4-2	1-1	I	1-1	0-2	4-4	1-3	2-5	0-2	1-1	0-5	2-2	1-1	0-2	0-4	1-3	1-2	0-6
Farnham Town	0-5	0-1	3-3	1-3	1-4	1-4	3-2	0-3	3-0	E	1-4	1-6	2-2	3-0	0-4	0-4	2-2	1-1	0-5	2-2	1-1	0-2	1-3	1-6
Feltham	0-1	1-2	1-2	5-0	4-0	2-2	6-1	4-1	5-1	4-1	R	3-2	5-1	0-2	1-1	1-1	4-0	0-0	0-3	2-1	5-1	4-1	2-3	1-0
Frimley Green	0-1	0-5	4-0	1-3	2-3	2-3	1-1	1-1	3-2	2-1	1-0		3-2	5-1	0-2	1-1	1-1	4-0	0-0	0-3	2-1	5-1	4-1	2-3
Godalming & G.	1-2	1-3	3-1	4-2	2-0	3-1	3-1	2-1	5-1	3-0	3-0	2-1	D	1-0	4-6	1-4	0-5	2-1	1-2	2-1	1-0	1-1	2-0	0-1
Hartley Wintney	1-1	2-0	1-8	3-1	4-1	1-0	4-0	1-1	1-3	3-0	0-2	1-0	3-5	I	1-3	2-1	3-2	1-0	1-1	1-0	1-0	3-1	0-4	0-2
Merstham	0-4	0-2	0-4	0-1	0-3	3-0	1-0	1-2	2-1	1-1	1-1	1-3	3-2	2-1	V	0-2	1-4	2-2	2-1	0-0	1-0	2-2	1-2	3-5
North Greenford	4-2	2-6	1-2	1-1	2-0	4-2	4-2	5-0	5-2	4-2	0-3	3-2	1-3	1-3	4-5	I	1-1	3-3	2-0	5-1	3-2	5-4	2-4	1-2
Raynes Pk Vale	1-3	0-5	3-4	1-1	0-1	3-2	0-3	1-4	1-2	3-0	0-3	5-2	2-2	4-5	1-1	1-3	S	2-1	3-0	4-2	3-1	3-1	5-0	2-4
Reading Town	0-0	0-2	2-0	1-2	0-5	2-1	2-0	2-0	4-0	1-2	3-1	0-3	1-1	0-3	2-0	3-0	4-1	I	0-2	1-3	5-1	2-1	1-4	0-0
Sandhurst Town	1-2	1-2	2-2	3-1	7-0	1-0	0-1	2-2	3-0	2-0	1-1	3-2	2-0	3-0	4-1	1-1	0-2	1-3	O	4-2	7-0	5-2	0-3	1-4
Southall	1-3	0-0	2-1	2-3	3-0	3-2	2-2	5-0	2-0	2-0	1-1	3-2	0-1	2-0	3-1	4-0	0-0	0-0	4-2	N	2-1	6-1	5-2	2-3
Viking Greenf'd	1-3	0-4	1-4	1-3	0-3	1-0	1-2	0-1	1-2	0-2	2-4	2-6	0-5	1-3	0-4	1-7	0-3	1-1	2-1	6-1		2-2	1-3	1-3
Walton Casuals	1-2	0-5	2-3	1-1	1-3	1-0	2-0	1-1	1-0	1-2	2-4	2-6	0-5	1-3	0-4	1-7	0-3	1-1	0-4	0-1	0-4		0-1	1-3
Westfield	0-2	0-4	1-0	0-4	1-1	3-1	4-1	1-2	6-0	2-0	0-0	2-2	1-2	1-2	2-0	1-4	5-2	2-1	1-1	1-0	1-1	2-3		1-2
Withdean	3-1	2-0	4-1	2-0	3-0	2-2	2-0	5-1	4-0	7-1	0-0	3-0	3-1	0-0	4-0	4-1	4-3	5-0	2-0	2-0	9-0	3-1	1-0	

Premier Division

		P	W	D	L	F	A	Pts
Withdean		46	40	4	2	143	32	124
AFC Wallingford		46	37	4	5	129	33	115
AFC Wimbledon		46	36	3	7	125	46	111
Feltham		46	25	10	11	101	48	85
Bedfont		46	25	5	16	106	73	80
Sandhurst Town		46	23	9	14	86	57	78
Godalming/Guildford		46	25	3	18	95	75	78
Raynes Park Vale		46	24	5	17	101	79	77
Ash United		46	23	5	18	110	83	74
North Greenford Utd		46	22	7	17	104	87	73
Hartley Wintney		46	23	4	19	88	84	73
Southall		46	19	11	16	91	77	68
Westfield		46	19	9	18	75	86	66
Chessington & Hook		46	18	9	19	96	80	63
Reading Town		46	18	6	22	67	79	60
Chipstead		46	16	10	20	92	87	58
Merstham		46	16	10	20	61	80	58
Walton Casuals		46	12	10	24	60	95	46
Chessington United		46	13	6	27	54	84	45
Frimley Green		46	13	5	28	65	98	44
Cobham	-3	46	11	10	25	61	108	40
Farnham Town		46	5	9	32	45	130	24
Cove		46	5	6	35	46	160	21
Viking Greenford	+3	46	3	2	41	35	175	14

Division One

		P	W	D	L	F	A	Pts
Raynes PV Res.	+2	28	20	3	5	73	44	65
Westfield Res.		28	18	6	4	72	31	60
Ash United Res.		28	16	6	6	78	46	54
Sandhurst Town Res.		28	15	5	8	70	42	50
North Greenford Res.		28	13	9	6	58	45	48
Farnham Town Res.		28	12	6	10	53	55	42
Feltham Res.	-1	28	12	6	10	50	46	41
Cobham Res.	-3	28	11	10	7	52	47	40
Bedfont Res.		28	10	8	10	56	48	38
Hartley Wintney Res.		28	11	3	14	53	63	36
Chess'gton/H. Res.	+3	28	6	5	17	36	63	26
Merstham Res.		28	6	5	17	46	60	23
Cove Res.		28	6	5	17	44	79	23
Chessington Utd Res.		28	5	6	17	48	73	21
Frimley Green Res.		28	5	5	18	35	82	20

DIVISION ONE CUP FINAL
(9th May at Ashford Town (Middx))
Westfield Res. 1 Raynes Park Vale Res. 0

DIVISION ONE SHIELD FINAL
(14th May at Sandhurst Town)
Westfield Res. 1 **Raynes Park Vale Res. 2**

LEAGUE CUP

FIRST ROUND
AFC Wallingford 4 Godalming & Guildford 0
Chipstead 2 **Feltham** 5
Cobham 0 **Chessington & Hook United** 2
Farnham Town 1 **Withdean** 3
Merstham 4 Viking Greenford 1
Raynes Park Vale 1 Bedfont 0 *aet*
Reading Town 0 **Southall** 2
Walton Casuals 1 **AFC Wimbledon** 1 *aet* (1-4p)

SECOND ROUND
AFC Wimbledon 1 **Southall** 5
Ash United 4 Frimley Green 0
Chessington & Hook United 3 **AFC Wallingford** 6
Merstham 1 Feltham 1 *aet* (5-4p)
North Greenford United 2 Cove 1

Raynes Park Vale 0 **Hartley Wintney** 4
Westfield 2 Chessington United 1
Withdean 1 Sandhurst Town 0

QUARTER-FINALS
Ash United 3 Southall 2
North Greenford United 1 AFC Wallingford 1 *aet* (4-3p)
Westfield 2 Merstham 1
Withdean 4 Hartley Wintney 0

SEMI-FINALS
Ash United 3 North Greenford United 0
Withdean 1 Westfield 0

FINAL
(2nd May at Woking)
Ash United 0 **Withdean** 1

PREMIER DIVISION CONSTITUTION 2003-04

AFC WALLINGFORD . . . . Wallingford Sports Park, Hithercroft, Wallingford, Oxfordshire 01491 835044
AFC WIMBLEDON . . . . Kingsmeadow Stadium, Kingston Road, Kingston-upon-Thames, Surrey 020 8547 3335/3336
ASH UNITED . . . . Youngs Drive, Ash, near Aldershot, Surrey 01252 320385
BEDFONT . . . . The Orchard, Hatton Road, Bedfont, Middlesex 020 8890 7264
CHESSINGTON UNITED . . . . River Lane, Leatherhead, Surrey 01372 363995
CHESSINGTON & HOOK UNITED . . . . Chalky Lane, Chessington, Surrey 01372 729892
CHIPSTEAD . . . . High Road, Chipstead, Surrey 01737 553250
COBHAM . . . . Leg o'Mutton Field, Anvil Lane, Downside Bridge Road, Cobham, Surrey 01932 865959
COVE . . . . Oak Farm, Romayne Close, Cove, Farnborough, Hampshire 01252 543615
FARNHAM TOWN . . . . Memorial Ground, West Street, Farnham, Surrey 01252 715305
FELTHAM . . . . The Arena, Shakespeare Avenue, Feltham, Middlesex 020 8384 0907
FRIMLEY GREEN . . . . Frimley Green Recreation Ground, Frimley Green Road, Frimley Green, Surrey . . . . None
GODALMING & GUILDFORD . . . . Wey Court, Meadrow, Godalming, Surrey 01483 417520
HARTLEY WINTNEY . . . . Memorial Playing Fields, Green Lane, Hartley Wintney, Hampshire 01252 843586
HORLEY TOWN . . . . The New Defence, Court Lodge Road, Horley, Surrey . . . . t.b.a.
MERSTHAM . . . . Merstham Recreation Ground, Weldon Way, Merstham, Surrey 01737 644046
NORTH GREENFORD UNITED . . . . Berkeley Fields, Berkeley Avenue, Greenford, Middlesex 020 8422 8923
RAYNES PARK VALE . . . . Grand Drive, Raynes Park, London . . . . 020 8540 8843. Fax: 020 8542 2193
READING TOWN . . . . Scours Lane, Tilehurst, Reading, Berkshire 0118 945 3555
SANDHURST TOWN . . . . Bottom Meadow, Memorial Park, Yorktown Road, Sandhurst, Berkshire 01252 873767
SOUTHALL . . . . t.b.a. . . . . t.b.a.
WALTON CASUALS . . . . Franklyn Road Sports Ground, Waterside Drive, Walton, Surrey 01932 787749
WESTFIELD . . . . Woking Park, Kingfield, Woking, Surrey 01483 771106
WITHDEAN . . . . Worthing FC, Woodside Road, Worthing, West Sussex 01903 239575
Viking Greenford have folded. Horley Town move up from the Surrey County Senior League.

DIVISION ONE (FORMERLY SURREY COUNTY SENIOR LEAGUE) CONSTITUTION 2003-04

AFC GUILDFORD . . . . Spectrum Leisure Centre, Parkway, Guildford, Surrey 01483 444777
BOOKHAM . . . . Chrystie Recreation Ground, Dorking Road, Bookham, Surrey 01372 459482
CHOBHAM & OTTERSHAW . . . . Chobham Recreation Ground, Station Road, Chobham, Surrey 01276 857876
COLLIERS WOOD UNITED . . . . Wibbundune Sports Ground, Robin Hood Way, London SW20 . . . . 020 8394 1946
CONEY HALL . . . . Tie Pigs Lane, Coney Hall, Hayes, Kent 020 8942 8062
CRANLEIGH . . . . Snoxhall Fields, Knowle Lane, Cranleigh, Surrey 01483 275295
CRESCENT ROVERS . . . . Wallington Sports & Social Club, Mollison Drive, Wallington, Surrey 020 8647 2558
DITTON . . . . Long Ditton Recreation Ground, Windmill Lane, Ditton, Surrey 020 8398 7428
FARLEIGH ROVERS . . . . Parsonage Field, Harrow Road, Farleigh, Warlingham, Surrey 01884 626483
HERSHAM RBL . . . . West End Recreation Ground, West End Lane, Esher, Surrey 01372 463535
MERROW . . . . The Urnfield, Downside Road, Guildford, Surrey . . . . None
MONOTYPE . . . . Perrywood Sports & Social, Honeycrock Lane, Salfords, Crawley, West Sussex 01737 557509
NETHERNE VILLAGE . . . . Woodplace Lane, Coulsdon, Surrey 01306 884112
SEELEC DELTA . . . . Dorking FC, Meadowbank, Mill Lane, Dorking, Surrey . . . . None
SHEERWATER . . . . Blackmore Crescent, Sheerwater Estate, Woking, Surrey 01428 643072
SHOTTERMILL & HASLEMERE . . . . Woolmer Hill Sports Ground, Haslemere, Surrey 01784 465204
STAINES LAMMAS . . . . Laleham Recreation Ground, The Broadway, Laleham, Staines, Middlesex 020 8337 4995
WORCESTER PARK . . . . Skinners Field, Green Lane, Worcester Park, Surrey . . . .
Horley Town move up to the Premier Division. Croydon Municipal Officers have temporarily disbanded. Newcomers are Coney Hall (Surrey South Eastern Combination), Monotype (Crawley & District League) and Merrow (Surrey Intermediate League West).

CORNWALL COMBINATION

	Falmouth Tn Res.	Goonhavern	Hayle	Helston Athletic	Illogan RBL	Ludgvan	Marazion Blues	Mousehole	Mullion	Newquay Res.	Penryn Ath. Res.	Penzance Res.	Perranwell	Porthleven Res.	RNAS Culdrose	St Agnes	St Ives Town	St Just	Truro City Res.	Wendron CC Utd
Falmouth Town Res.		5-2	2-8	1-3	0-2	3-1	0-4	4-1	6-2	1-10	4-1	1-2	5-4	2-0	2-1	0-5	1-3	1-2	0-4	0-1
Goonhavern	3-1		1-4	0-2	3-0	7-0	3-0	1-1	0-1	2-2	1-1	1-0	0-2	4-2	1-3	2-2	4-2	0-1	3-0	
Hayle	7-1	3-0		1-0	2-1	5-0	5-0	6-1	1-2	3-1	1-2	3-2	1-1	2-1	1-3	1-0	3-0	2-2	7-0	
Helston Athletic	4-1	1-3	3-0		1-1	4-3	7-2	5-0	2-0	2-2	2-2	2-1	0-0	2-1	4-0	3-1	2-0	1-0	0-1	4-1
Illogan RBL	5-2	4-4	2-0	3-3		10-0	2-1	1-0	6-0	2-1	1-1	4-0	3-2	2-1	7-1	3-2	0-1	3-0	4-0	0-1
Ludgvan	0-5	1-4	0-3	0-1	0-12		1-2	0-5	1-4	1-3	0-1	1-4	1-5	1-4	2-5	0-11	1-4	0-10	0-8	1-2
Marazion Blues	4-2	1-5	0-4	0-5	0-3	1-2		3-1	1-3	2-8	3-2	0-4	2-4	0-5	1-3	0-10	0-3	1-3	5-3	0-4
Mousehole	3-2	1-2	2-1	1-2	0-1	3-1	4-0		1-0	3-3	0-4	3-0	3-1	2-0	0-2	1-5	2-4	1-0	0-3	
Mullion	3-1	2-4	0-5	1-2	2-1	5-1	2-0	4-1		1-2	4-1	1-7	1-0	3-2	0-0	0-2	2-0	0-0	2-0	1-0
Newquay Res.	2-0	7-0	1-1	2-1	0-5	2-0	6-1	5-1	5-3		0-1	3-1	4-1	9-0	5-3	1-1	5-2	1-1	5-3	1-0
Penryn Athletic Res.	2-3	6-2	0-1	3-1	2-0	2-0	5-1	5-3	3-2	2-0		1-3	4-3	0-1	3-0	1-1	3-1	2-1	1-1	
Penzance Res.	3-1	3-0	0-1	2-2	2-2	8-0	4-0	5-2	1-1	4-1	2-1		1-2	3-3	1-2	1-2	0-4	1-1	4-1	
Perranwell	2-2	1-3	1-1	2-1	1-1	9-1	6-0	3-1	0-1	3-3	1-2		1-2	0-1	0-1	2-4	2-2	0-4	1-2	
Porthleven Res.	3-1	5-0	1-6	0-0	0-3	4-1	2-1	3-0	0-1	3-2	0-4	1-4	1-0		3-3	1-2	1-2	0-3	3-1	
RNAS Culdrose	1-2	5-0	1-3	1-0	1-0	7-1	1-1	2-0	1-4	1-1	3-1	0-0	0-3	4-1		1-1	0-2	0-3	3-1	
St Agnes	4-2	6-2	1-1	1-2	2-1	8-2	3-1	4-4	1-1	7-1	2-0	7-1	2-2	7-0	3-1		2-0	4-1	2-1	1-1
St Ives Town	6-2	0-3	2-0	5-0	0-5	5-1	2-2	1-2	0-1	0-3	3-0	2-0	0-2	0-3	1-0		1-5	1-2	2-0	
St Just	2-2	0-5	1-2	1-0	0-4	8-1	5-2	2-0	2-3	3-0	1-0	0-0	5-0	4-1	2-1	2-1		8-1	1-3	
Truro City Res.	3-2	1-0	1-3	0-9	1-3	2-2	3-1	1-1	1-3	1-3	2-0	5-1	2-0	0-0	2-0	5-0	4-1	2-1		0-1
Wendron CC United	3-1	0-3	0-4	1-3	4-4	4-0	4-0	0-2	1-3	1-3	2-0	5-1	2-1	0-0	2-0	2-0	5-2	2-4	4-2	

	P	W	D	L	F	A	Pts
St Agnes	38	28	5	5	126	39	89
Hayle	38	25	6	7	106	37	81
Illogan RBL	38	23	9	6	109	39	78
Helston Athletic	38	22	9	7	87	42	75
Newquay Res.	38	21	9	8	110	66	72
St Ives Town	38	21	4	13	83	50	67
Mullion	38	20	5	13	68	66	65
St Just	38	19	7	12	89	57	64
Goonhavern	38	19	5	14	81	74	62
Penryn Athletic Res.	38	16	8	14	67	60	56
Wendron CC United	38	17	5	16	72	72	56
Penzance Res.	38	16	6	16	80	68	54
Truro City Res.	38	14	4	20	65	84	46
Perranwell	38	11	8	19	73	70	41
RNAS Culdrose -3	38	12	8	18	57	68	41
Porthleven Res.	38	11	6	21	54	85	39
Mousehole	38	11	4	23	52	94	37
Falmouth Town Res.	38	11	2	25	72	116	35
Marazion Blues	38	6	1	31	41	142	19
Ludgvan	38	1	1	36	27	190	4

LEAGUE CUP

PRELIMINARY ROUND
Goonhavern 3 **Penryn Athletic Res.** 4
Mousehole 0 **Illogan RBL** 5
Perranwell 0 **Newquay Res.** 1
St Agnes 1 Porthleven Res. 1
Porthleven Res. 2 **St Agnes** 5 *replay*

FIRST ROUND
Falmouth Town Res. 1 **St Just** 5
Helston Athletic 2 Ludgvan 0
Marazion Blues 2 **Wendron CC Utd** 3
Newquay Res. 4 Hayle 2
Penryn Athletic Res. 2 **St Ives Town** 5
Penzance Res. 3 Illogan RBL 2

St Agnes 5 RNAS Culdrose 0
Truro City Res. 2 Mullion 1

QUARTER-FINALS
Newquay Res. 2 St Ives Town 0
St Agnes 6 Penzance Res. 2
(St Agnes expelled - ineligible player)
St Just 1 Helston Athletic 1
Helston Athletic 1 St Just 0 *replay*
Wendron CC Utd 4 Truro City Res. 2

SEMI-FINALS
Helston 1 Penzance Res. 0 *(at Hayle)*
Wendron 1 **Newquay Res.** 6 *(at Penryn)*

FINAL *(20th April at Porthleven)*
Newquay Res. 3 Helston Athletic 2

SUPPLEMENTARY CUP

PRELIMINARY ROUND
Marazion Blues 2 **Mullion** 3
Mousehole 1 **Goonhavern** 2
Penryn Athletic Res. 1 **Illogan RBL** 4
Perranwell 2 Porthleven Res. 1

QUARTER-FINALS
Goonhavern 3 Mullion 2
Hayle 6 Ludgvan 0
Perranwell 0 **Illogan RBL** 1
RNAS Culdrose 4 Falmouth Res. 0

SEMI-FINALS
Goonhavern 0 Illogan 0 *(at Wendron)*
Illogan 2 Goonhavern 0 *(replay at Truro)*
Hayle 1 RNAS Culdrose 1 *(at St Ives)*
RNAS Culdrose 2 Hayle 0 *(replay at Porthleven)*

FINAL *(18th May at Penryn Athletic)*
RNAS Culdrose 0 Illogan RBL 0 aet

FINAL REPLAY *(31st May at Penryn)*
Illogan RBL 2 RNAS Culdrose 1

CONSTITUTION 2003-04

FALMOUTH TOWN RESERVES ...... Bickland Park, Bickland Water Road, Falmouth, Cornwall ... 01326 375156
GOONHAVERN ... Reen Manor Park, Goonhavern, Newquay, Cornwall ... 01872 572493
HAYLE ... Trevassack Park, Viaduct Hill, Hayle, Cornwall ... 01736 757157
HELSTON ATHLETIC ... Kellaway Park, Helston, Cornwall ... 01326 573742
ILLOGAN RBL ... Oxland Park, Illogan, Cornwall ... 01209 216488
LUDGVAN ... Ludgvan Community Centre, Fairfield, Ludgvan, Cornwall ... 01736 740774
MARAZION BLUES ... Trevenner, Marazion, Cornwall ... 01736 711020
MOUSEHOLE ... Trungle Parc, Paul, Cornwall ... None
MULLION ... Clifden Parc, Mullion, Cornwall ... 01326 240676
NEWQUAY RESERVES ... Mount Wise, Clevedon Road, Newquay, Cornwall ... 01637 872935
PENRYN ATHLETIC RESERVES ... Kernick, Kernick Road, Penryn, Cornwall ... 01326 375182
PENZANCE RESERVES ... Penlee Park, Alexandra Place, Penzance, Cornwall ... 01736 361964
PERRANWELL ... Perran-ar-Worthal Playing Fields, Perran-ar-Worthal, Cornwall ... 01872 870202
PORTHLEVEN RESERVES ... Gala Parc, Methleigh Mill, Porthleven, Cornwall ... 01326 574181 / 574754
RNAS CULDROSE ... Sports Field, RNAS Culdrose, Helston, Cornwall ... 01326 574181 / 574754
ST AGNES ... Enys Park, West Polperro, St Agnes, Cornwall ... 01326 574121x7167
ST IVES TOWN ... The Saltings, Lelant, Cornwall ...
ST JUST ... Lafrowda Park, St Just, Cornwall ... 01736 788503
TRURO CITY RESERVES ... Treyew Road, Truro, Cornwall ... 01872 278853
WENDRON CC UNITED ... Underlane, Carnkie, Cornwall ... 01209 860946
No change.

CYMRU ALLIANCE

	Airbus UK	Amlwch Town	Buckley Town	Cemaes Bay	Flint Town United	Gresford Athletic	Guilsfield	Halkyn United	Holyhead Hotspurs	Holywell Town	Lex XI	Llandudno Town	Llanfairpwll	Llangefni Town	Mold Alexandra	Porthmadog	Ruthin Town
Airbus UK		1-2	0-4	4-2	0-2	0-2	0-0	4-3	2-1	2-0	4-3	3-3	4-0	2-1	2-1	1-0	2-0
Amlwch Town	2-1		0-2	0-0	3-0	2-0	0-0	0-0	2-2	5-1	1-0	1-1	1-1	3-4	2-1	0-1	3-1
Buckley Town	3-1	3-0		16-1	2-0	5-2	6-1	2-2	1-1	3-1	2-3	3-3	1-0	1-2	2-1	2-3	4-1
Cemaes Bay	1-9	0-2	0-4		1-0	1-1	2-3	0-4	0-3	3-0	5-3	0-8	2-0	2-1	6-0	0-9	0-3
Flint Town United	3-2	4-1	0-0	5-1		1-5	3-0	3-3	3-0	0-1	2-4	1-3	4-1	1-2	0-4	1-1	0-3
Gresford Athletic	0-4	2-3	3-2	8-0	0-1		5-1	2-2	1-0	3-1	0-2	1-3	3-0	1-2	1-2	0-6	2-3
Guilsfield	1-1	2-0	0-3	1-2	3-4	2-2		1-4	2-5	0-3	3-3	1-2	1-2	4-2	1-3	0-3	1-6
Halkyn United	0-3	2-2	1-2	3-2	1-1	2-1	2-1		1-3	3-0	2-1	1-1	2-1	0-3	0-0	1-0	0-2
Holyhead Hotspurs	1-3	4-0	2-2	4-1	0-0	3-2	2-2	4-1		2-2	1-2	0-4	2-1	1-3	3-0	1-1	1-4
Holywell Town	0-2	2-1	0-1	2-1	1-2	1-0	3-5	1-2	2-3		3-10	1-2	0-0	1-6	0-0	0-1	3-1
Lex XI	0-4	2-2	2-2	16-0	2-3	1-0	0-0	1-4	5-3	7-3		1-0	0-1	3-2	2-2	1-3	1-3
Llandudno Town	2-2	4-0	2-1	5-0	4-0	2-0	1-0	9-2	2-2	2-0	2-0		2-1	3-3	1-0	0-3	4-2
Llanfairpwll	4-4	1-0	0-3	2-1	1-1	1-1	2-3	3-0	1-0	2-3	1-2			2-1	0-1	0-3	2-0
Llangefni Town	3-0	2-1	0-1	3-2	4-1	6-0	7-0	1-2	2-1	7-0	1-0	2-1	3-1		2-1	0-1	1-0
Mold Alexandra	1-0	1-4	0-2	2-2	1-2	2-2	0-2	1-1	1-3	3-1	0-3	0-1	4-1	1-0		0-3	1-3
Porthmadog	4-1	6-0	2-0	5-2	3-1	2-1	8-0	2-0	5-1	8-1	4-1	4-0	2-1	3-0			3-2
Ruthin Town	1-2	4-1	0-0	3-1	3-1	1-1	3-0	1-2	2-1	7-1	8-1	4-1	7-1	0-1	1-1	0-2	

		P	W	D	L	F	A	Pts
Porthmadog		32	28	2	2	106	19	86
Llandudno Town		32	20	7	5	81	41	67
Buckley Town		32	19	7	6	85	34	64
Llangefni Town		32	21	1	10	78	39	64
Airbus UK		32	17	5	10	70	50	56
Ruthin Town		32	17	3	12	79	45	54
Halkyn United		32	14	9	9	56	57	51
Lex XI		32	13	5	14	83	72	44
Amlwch Town		32	11	9	12	45	55	42
Holyhead Hotspurs		32	11	8	13	60	62	41
Flint Town United		32	11	7	14	50	61	40
Mold Alexandra		32	8	7	17	35	56	31
Gresford Athletic		32	8	6	18	52	64	30
Llanfairpwll		32	8	5	19	35	66	29
Guilsfield		32	7	7	18	43	86	28
Cemaes Bay		32	7	3	22	41	129	24
Holywell Town	-9	32	4	5	23	33	96	8

LEAGUE CUP

PRELIM. ROUND
Airbus UK 2 **Porthmadog** 4
Holyhead 0 **Buckley Town** 1

FIRST ROUND
Amlwch 2 **Cemaes Bay** 3
Buckley Town (w/o)
Rhayader Town (scr.)
Flint 0 **Mold Alexandra** 2
Lex XI 1 **Porthmadog** 5
Llandudno 2 Holywell 0
Llanfairpwll 1 Halkyn Utd 1
Halkyn United 1
Llanfairpwll 2 *replay*
Llangefni Town 1 Gresford 1
Gresford 0 **Llangefni** 4 *replay*
Ruthin Town 7 Guilsfield 0

QUARTER-FINALS
Buckley Town 4 Cemaes Bay 2
Llanfairpwll 1 **Llandudno Town** 3
Llangefni 5 Ruthin Town 3
Porthmadog 3 Mold 0

SEMI-FINALS
Buckley Town 2 Llangefni Town 0
(at Llandudno Town)
Llandudno Town 1
Porthmadog 1 *aet* (2-4p)
(at Mold Alexandra)

FINAL
(17th May at Llangefni)
Buckley Town 2
Porthmadog 4 *aet*

CONSTITUTION 2003-04

AIRBUS UK . . . . Airbus UK, Broughton, Chester, Cheshire 01244 522393
AMLWCH TOWN . . . . Lon Bach, Amlwch, Anglesey . . . . None
BUCKLEY TOWN . . . . Globe Way, Liverpool Way, Buckley, Flintshire 01407 710600
CEMAES BAY . . . . School Lane Stadium, School Lane, Cemaes Bay, Anglesey 01352 730982/762804
FLINT TOWN UNITED . . . . Cae Y Castell, March Lane, Flint, Clwyd 01407 840401
GLANTRAETH . . . . Trerdraeth, Bodorgan, Anglesey . . . . None
GRESFORD ATHLETIC . . . . Clappers Lane, Gresford, Wrexham . . . . None
GUILSFIELD . . . . Community Centre, Guilsfield, Welshpool, Powys 01352 780576
HALKYN UNITED . . . . Pant Newydd, Halkyn, Clwyd 01407 764111
HOLYHEAD HOTSPURS . . . . New Oval, Leisure Centre, Kingsland, Holyhead, Anglesey 01352 711411
HOLYWELL TOWN . . . . Halkyn Road, Holywell, Flintshire 01978 261148
LEX XI . . . . Stansty Park, Summerhill, Wrexham, ... 01492 860945
LLANDUDNO TOWN . . . . Maesdu Park, Builder Street, Llandudno, Conwy . . . . None
LLANFAIRPWLL . . . . Rear of Post Office, Llanfair, Anglesey . . . . None
LLANGEFNI TOWN . . . . Cae Bob Parry, Talwrn Road, Llangefni, Anglesey . . . . None
MOLD ALEXANDRA . . . . Alyn Park, Denbigh Road, Mold, Clwyd . . . . None
RUTHIN TOWN . . . . Memorial Playing Fields, Park Road, Ruthin, Denbighshire . . . . None

Porthmadog are promoted to the Welsh Premier League. Glantraeth are promoted from the Welsh Alliance.

DEVON COUNTY LEAGUE

Key to columns: 1 Alphington, 2 Appledore, 3 Buckland Athletic, 4 Budleigh Salterton, 5 Crediton United, 6 Cullompton Rgrs, 7 Dartington Sports, 8 Dartmouth, 9 Elburton Villa, 10 Exeter Civil Serv., 11 Heavitree United, 12 Ivybridge Town, 13 Newton Abbot, 14 Newton Abb. Spurs, 15 Ottery St Mary, 16 Plymstock United, 17 Stoke Gabriel, 18 Topsham Town, 19 University of Exeter, 20 Vospers Oak Villa

	1	2	3	4	5	6	7	8	9	10	11	12	13	14	15	16	17	18	19	20
Alphington		2-0	1-2	2-4	3-0	0-2	4-0	2-3	1-1	3-0	3-1	3-3	3-2	3-0	6-2	1-1	2-1	5-0	0-2	0-2
Appledore	0-2		4-3	1-0	2-0	1-0	1-0	0-6	0-0	1-1	4-6	2-4	2-2	2-0	1-3	0-3	1-2	3-0	3-1	0-0
Buckland Athletic	2-1	2-1		5-1	3-0	2-1	4-0	1-2	5-0	1-1	5-0	1-5	0-0	4-1	5-2	1-1	3-1	2-0	0-3	0-3
Budleigh Salterton	2-0	1-0	0-3		0-0	0-3	2-0	1-2	5-0	1-1	6-2	1-4	3-3	0-2	2-3	1-1	3-1	2-0	3-1	0-3
Crediton United	2-5	1-2	1-1	0-4		0-0	3-1	0-5	0-7	0-2	1-3	0-5	0-6	2-0	1-1	0-2	0-9	0-1	0-5	
Cullompton Rangers	1-3	3-0	1-2	1-0	1-0		1-2	1-1	1-1	1-1	1-5	0-2	4-1	1-3	0-3	1-0	1-2	1-1	1-4	2-0
Dartington Sports	2-3	2-0	0-2	4-0	1-2	4-0		0-2	2-1	6-0	1-2	6-5	0-0	1-1	8-0	3-5	2-3	6-0	1-6	2-2
Dartmouth	1-0	2-0	2-0	2-0	1-0	1-0	3-3		4-0	5-2	5-2	4-0	1-0	0-1	3-0	3-0	2-1	4-1	2-1	2-1
Elburton Villa	1-1	1-3	1-3	1-1	0-1	3-3	1-0	3-1		1-1	2-2	2-2	2-0	1-2	3-1	2-1	10-0	4-0	0-4	0-2
Exeter Civil Service	0-0	2-2	0-5	2-1	5-0	0-3	1-2	1-0			0-0	2-8	3-3	1-3	0-3	1-1	4-0	1-3	0-3	
Heavitree United	0-5	3-0	2-0	3-0	4-1	2-5	1-1	0-2	6-3	3-0		2-2	3-5	2-0	2-1	0-3	3-0	4-3	1-2	7-0
Ivybridge Town	2-1	0-1	2-1	7-2	7-1	10-1	0-2	2-1	0-0	7-1	2-0		2-3	5-1	5-2	2-1	1-1	7-1	4-1	7-2
Newton Abbot	4-1	1-0	3-1	4-3	1-2	4-0	1-0	2-1	1-1	2-1	1-0	1-2		2-1	2-0	1-4	3-3	0-0	4-1	1-0
Newton Abbot Spurs	2-2	1-1	3-0	3-1	4-0	2-1	2-2	4-0	1-1	1-1	2-1	1-0	0-1		2-1	0-0	3-1	3-3	3-1	4-0
Ottery St Mary	2-3	2-2	1-0	2-2	1-1	2-2	4-0	1-1	2-0	2-1	0-2	2-2	1-1	0-1		2-1	6-3	2-0	1-3	
Plymstock United	2-2	1-1	2-2	5-2	6-1	2-2	2-2	1-2	6-0	4-2	0-0	4-3	0-3	1-1	2-1		3-0	1-0	2-2	1-3
Stoke Gabriel	1-2	4-1	0-2	2-3	1-2	0-3	1-4	0-2	4-3	2-2	1-1	1-2	1-2	2-2		3-0		1-0	2-2	1-3
Topsham Town	0-1	2-4	1-3	0-0	5-2	0-3	0-3	2-6	0-2	0-1	2-0	0-0	2-1	1-3	1-2	1-2	2-2		1-3	2-4
University of Exeter	1-2	4-2	2-2	0-5	4-1	1-1	0-4	2-5	7-5	2-1	1-0	0-3	4-1	2-1	3-1	0-2	1-0	0-1		1-5
Vospers Oak Villa	3-2	2-1	2-2	1-2	1-1	2-1	1-1	3-2	0-2	0-1	1-2	3-2	2-3	2-0	3-0	4-1	2-0	1-0	1-0	

	P	W	D	L	F	A	Pts
Dartmouth	38	29	5	4	96	32	92
Ivybridge Town	38	26	8	4	135	55	86
Buckland Athletic	38	23	6	9	88	47	75
Vospers Oak Villa	38	21	4	13	72	57	67
Alphington	38	19	7	12	80	54	64
Newton Abbot Spurs -3	38	19	6	13	62	49	60
University of Exeter	38	19	3	16	85	76	60
Newton Abbot	38	16	11	11	67	57	59
Plymstock United	38	14	13	11	72	58	55
Cullompton Rangers	38	15	8	15	56	65	53
Ottery St Mary	38	15	6	17	63	74	51
Heavitree United	38	14	6	18	71	84	48
Dartington Sports	38	13	7	18	79	70	46
Appledore	38	12	9	17	51	69	45
Elburton Villa	38	11	10	17	67	69	43
Budleigh Salterton -1	38	12	8	18	58	77	43
Exeter Civil Service	38	9	13	16	46	79	40
Stoke Gabriel	38	7	6	25	58	92	27
Crediton United	38	7	5	26	30	109	26
Topsham Town	38	7	3	28	29	92	24

LEAGUE CUP

FIRST ROUND
Budleigh Salterton 2 Plymstock 0
Dartmouth 3 Vospers OV 1 *aet*
Ottery 1 Exeter CS 1 *aet* (2-3p)
Stoke Gabriel 1 Heavitree Utd 2

SECOND ROUND
Alphington 4 Heavitree United 1
Bud. Salterton 4 Appledore 5 *aet*
Crediton United 0 Buckland 9
Cullompton Rangers 0 Exeter CS 1
Dartmouth 7 Dartington 2 *aet*
Elburton Villa 2 Newton Abbot 1
Ivybridge 3 Newton Abbot Spurs 2
Univ. of Exeter 1 Topsham 2 *aet*

QUARTER-FINALS
Appledore 3 Buckland Athletic 0
Exeter Civil Service 0 Alphington 2
Ivybridge Town 1 Dartmouth 0
Topsham Town 0 Elburton Villa 4

SEMI-FINALS
Appledore 3 Elburton Villa 2
(at Crediton United)
Ivybridge Town 1 Alphington 0
(at Newton Abbot)

FINAL
(5th May at Cullompton Rangers)
Appledore 0 Ivybridge Town 5

CHARITY SHIELD

(11th August at Dartmouth) Dartmouth 4 Topsham Town 0

CONSTITUTION FOR 2003-04

ALPHINGTON .... The Chronicles, Alphington, Exeter, Devon 01392 279556
APPLEDORE .... Marshford, Appledore, Devon 01237 477099
BUCKLAND ATHLETIC .... Homers Lane, Kingsteignton, Devon 01626 362602
BUDLEIGH SALTERTON .... Greenway Lane, Budleigh Salterton, Devon 01395 443850
CREDITON UNITED .... Lords Meadow, Commercial Road, Crediton, Devon 01363 774671
CULLOMPTON RANGERS .... Speeds Meadow, Cullompton, Devon 01884 33090
DARTINGTON SPORTS .... Foxhole Sports Ground, Dartington, Devon 01803 868032
DARTMOUTH .... Longcross, Dartmouth, Devon 01803 832902
ELBURTON VILLA .... Haye Road, Elburton, Devon 01752 480025
EXETER CIVIL SERVICE .... Foxhayes, Exwick, Exeter, Devon 01392 273976
HEAVITREE UNITED .... Wingfield Park, Wonford Hill, Exeter, Devon 01392 273020
HOLSWORTHY .... Upcott Field, North Road, Holsworthy, Devon 01409 254295
IVYBRIDGE TOWN .... Erme Valley, Ivybridge, Devon 01752 896686
NEWTON ABBOT .... Forde Park, Coach Road, Newton Abbot, Devon 01626 335011
NEWTON ABBOT SPURS .... Recreation Ground, Newton Abbot, Devon 01626 365343
OTTERY ST MARY .... Washbrook Meadows, Butts Road, Ottery St Mary, Devon 01404 813539
PLYMSTOCK UNITED .... Dean Cross, Plymstock, Devon 01752 406776
STOKE GABRIEL .... C J Churchward Mem. Ground, Broadley Lane, Stoke Gabriel, Totnes, Devon 01803 782223
TOPSHAM TOWN .... Coronation Field, Topsham, Devon 01392 873678
UNIVERSITY OF EXETER .... University Sports Ground, Topsham, Devon 01392 264452
VOSPERS OAK VILLA .... The Mill, Plymouth, Devon 01752 363352

Holsworthy have switched from the South Western League.

WWW.CHERRYRED.CO.UK

DEVON & EXETER LEAGUE

	Bud. Salterton Res.	Cullompton Rgrs Res.	Elmore Res.	Exeter CS Res.	Exeter St Thomas	Hatherleigh Town	Okehampton Argyle	Pinhoe	Seaton Town	Sidmouth Town	St Martins	Tap & Barrel	Topsham Town Res.	Univ. of Exeter Res.	Willand Rovers Res.	Witheridge
Budleigh Salterton Res.	P	3-3	2-3	1-2	1-3	6-0	1-2	2-0	1-4	2-3	2-1	0-2	8-0	2-1	0-2	0-1
Cullompton Rangers Res.	7-4	R	6-1	4-1	3-2	1-2	4-0	0-3	3-1	2-1	2-1	0-1	5-0	2-1	3-1	1-2
Elmore Res.	2-0	1-3	E	0-5	3-1	2-2	0-5	2-3	0-1	4-2	2-0	0-4	2-0	1-5	1-3	3-2
Exeter Civil Service Res.	1-2	3-2	0-0	M	1-0	1-1	3-2	1-1	1-2	1-2	2-1	1-5	4-1	2-0	2-2	3-1
Exeter St Thomas	0-0	0-4	3-2	0-1	I	0-2	1-2	1-3	1-2	1-2	0-3	0-5	0-2	1-1	2-3	3-1
Hatherleigh Town	4-0	1-4	4-0	1-2	5-0	E	3-0	4-0	0-1	2-3	0-2	2-2	4-0	2-2	3-2	3-1
Okehampton Argyle	3-0	3-2	7-2	3-0	0-2	5-0	R	3-3	2-2	3-0	3-1	2-1	4-1	0-0	5-0	1-3
Pinhoe	0-2	2-3	2-2	1-1	3-2	1-2	2-1		3-2	1-0	4-1	5-3	2-1	2-0	2-4	4-1
Seaton Town	5-0	1-4	3-0	2-1	6-0	3-0	0-1	2-1	D	2-0	5-0	0-1	4-1	1-1	1-3	0-0
Sidmouth Town	0-2	0-2	2-1	4-2	6-1	3-3	0-4	3-5	0-5	I	0-4	0-3	1-2	4-0	1-1	2-3
St Martins	2-0	0-0	3-1	2-1	0-0	3-6	2-4	4-4	0-2	3-4	V	1-5	3-1	2-2	4-1	1-3
Tap & Barrel	3-0	1-1	4-3	4-1	4-0	8-0	1-1	6-2	1-0	3-1	1-0	I	5-2	1-0	5-0	
Topsham Town Res.	0-1	2-3	0-2	0-5	2-1	0-4	1-3	4-3	1-4	3-2	0-1	0-3	S	0-6	0-2	2-1
University of Exeter Res.	1-3	3-0	5-0	0-1	3-0	1-3	0-3	3-2	2-2	3-0	0-1	1-0	7-0	I	0-1	3-2
Willand Rovers Res.	2-2	0-1	5-0	1-1	5-2	3-1	3-2	3-1	2-1	0-3	1-5	1-0	5-0	1-0	O	1-3
Witheridge	W-L	1-1	5-1	2-2	2-0	5-1	2-1	0-0	0-0	7-1	1-2	1-1	5-0	2-1	1-0	N

Premier Division		P	W	D	L	F	A	Pts
Tap & Barrel		30	22	4	4	89	28	70
Cullompton Rangers Res.		30	19	4	7	76	42	61
Seaton Town		30	18	4	8	66	29	58
Okehampton Argyle		30	18	4	8	75	40	58
Witheridge		30	15	5	10	58	46	50
Willand Rovers Res.		30	14	6	10	56	52	48
Hatherleigh Town		30	14	5	11	65	61	47
Pinhoe	-1	30	13	6	11	65	63	44
Exeter Civil Service Res.	-4	30	13	7	10	52	47	42
St Martins		30	12	4	14	53	57	40
University of Exeter Res.		30	11	5	14	55	41	38
Budleigh Salterton Res.	-1	30	10	3	17	47	57	32
Sidmouth Town		30	10	2	18	50	75	32
Elmore Res.	-4	30	8	4	18	41	85	24
Topsham Town Res.		30	6	0	24	25	100	18
Exeter St Thomas	-2	30	4	3	23	27	77	13

EAST DEVON SENIOR CUP

FINAL

(25th May at Crediton United)

Tap & Barrel 2 Willand Rovers Res. 1

PREMIER DIVISION CONSTITUTION 2003-04

BUCKLAND ATHLETIC RESERVES . . . . Homers Lane, Kingsteignton, Devon 01626 362602
BUDLEIGH SALTERTON RESERVES . . . . Greenway Lane, Budleigh Salterton, Devon 01395 443850
CULLOMPTON RANGERS RESERVES . . . . Speeds Meadow, Cullompton, Devon 01884 33090
EXETER CIVIL SERVICE RESERVES . . . . Foxhayes, Exwick, Exeter, Devon 01392 273976
FENITON . . . . Station Road, Feniton, Devon 01404 850836
HATHERLEIGH TOWN . . . . The Playing Field, Hatherleigh, Okehampton, Devon . . . . None
OKEHAMPTON ARGYLE . . . . Simmons Park, Okehampton, Devon 01837 53997
PINHOE . . . . Station Road, Pinhoe, Exeter, Devon . . . . None
SEATON TOWN . . . . Hillymead, Colyford Road, Seaton, Devon 01395 577087
SIDMOUTH TOWN . . . . Manstone Recreation Ground, Manstone Lane, Sidmouth, Devon . . . . None
ST LOYE'S . . . . St Loye's College, Topsham Road, Exeter, Devon . . . . None
ST MARTINS . . . . Minster Park, Exminster Hospital, Exminster, Devon 01392 823909
THORVERTON . . . . Simmons Park, Thorverton, Devon 01392 264452
UNIVERSITY OF EXETER RESERVES . . . . . . University Sports Ground, Topsham, Devon 01884 33885
WILLAND ROVERS RESERVES . . . . Silver Street, Willand, Devon . . . . None
WITHERIDGE . . . . Recreation Field, Witheridge, Devon . . . . None
Elmore Reserves, Topsham Town Reserves and Exeter St Thomas drop to Senior One replaced by Thorverton, Feniton and Buckland Athletic Reserves. Tap & Barrel become St Loye's.

Senior One

	P	W	D	L	F	A	Pts
Thorverton		28	19	5	4	70	27	62
Feniton		28	18	7	3	90	33	61
Buckland Athletic Res.		28	19	3	6	79	33	60
Alphington Res.		28	15	5	8	60	31	50
North Tawton		28	15	3	10	55	50	48
University of Exeter 'A'		28	12	6	10	61	55	42
Wellington Res.		28	12	6	10	63	65	42
Exmouth Amateurs		28	12	5	11	55	48	41
Westexe Rovers	-2	28	11	8	9	41	40	39
Dawlish Town Res.		28	11	2	15	53	68	35
Beer Albion		28	9	5	14	45	62	32
Newtown		28	8	4	16	44	73	28
Barnstaple T. Res.	-4	28	9	3	16	49	60	26
Tedburn St Mary		28	4	4	20	32	90	16
Newton St Cyres	-1	28	3	0	25	33	95	8

Senior Two

	P	W	D	L	F	A	Pts
Axminster Town		28	24	2	2	119	20	74
Exmouth Town Res.		28	20	3	5	72	32	63
Halwill		28	18	5	5	87	32	59
Lympstone		28	16	6	6	70	61	54
Bideford Res.		28	15	3	10	59	57	48
Sidmouth Town Res.		28	14	2	12	59	61	44
Exmouth Amateurs Res.		28	13	3	14	47	72	36
Lifton	-1	28	11	3	14	56	63	35
Lapford		28	10	4	14	42	51	34
Bickleigh		28	8	4	16	57	72	28
Bampton		28	7	7	14	45	70	28
Dunkeswell Rovers		28	8	4	16	49	77	28
Winkleigh		28	7	6	15	56	69	27
East Budleigh		28	5	6	17	33	72	21
Pinhoe Res.	-3	28	5	4	19	37	79	16

Senior Three

	P	W	D	L	F	A	Pts
Sandford		28	21	3	4	118	47	66
Broadclyst		28	17	6	5	90	49	57
Motel Rgrs & Offwell		28	17	6	5	80	62	57
Culm United		28	18	1	9	90	62	55
Kentisbeare		28	15	5	8	69	41	50
Witheridge Res.		28	13	8	7	67	55	47
Woodbury	-4	28	14	4	10	63	61	42
Oakwood		28	10	4	14	71	73	34
Clyst Valley		28	10	3	15	52	70	33
Tipton St John		28	7	11	10	62	65	32
Sidbury United		28	7	7	14	59	74	28
Colyton		28	7	5	16	40	67	26
St Martins Res.		28	6	5	17	48	97	23
Westexe Rovers Res.		28	6	2	20	32	73	20
Extr St Thom. Res.	-1	28	5	4	19	41	86	16

Senior Four

	P	W	D	L	F	A	Pts
Heavitree/Wonford SC	-2	26	22	3	1	122	39	67
Honiton Town		26	20	2	4	86	30	62
South Zeal United		26	17	3	6	90	56	54
Bow AAC		26	14	5	7	87	62	47
Seaton Town Res.		26	13	4	9	58	46	43
Univ. of Exeter 'B'		26	12	5	9	70	49	41
Okehampton Res.		26	12	4	10	78	67	40
Newtown Res.		26	11	3	12	67	63	36
Crediton United Res.	-1	26	8	7	11	54	74	30
Crescent		26	7	3	16	52	70	24
Chulmleigh	-1	26	7	3	16	54	88	23
Silverton	-1	26	6	2	18	60	100	19
Bickleigh Res.		26	5	1	20	52	131	16
Northlew	-1	26	3	5	18	35	90	13

Intermediate One

		P	W	D	L	F	A	Pts
Heavitree Harriers	-1	24	19	3	2	106	39	59
Tap & Barrel Res.	-1	24	16	2	6	85	38	49
Cullompton Rgrs 'A'		24	16	1	7	76	52	49
Alphington 'A'		24	15	3	6	69	48	48
Broadclyst Res.	-1	24	11	6	7	54	37	38
Thorverton Res.		24	11	4	9	68	63	37
Exmouth Amateurs 'A'		24	11	2	11	58	61	35
Lympstone Res.		24	10	1	13	50	54	31
Feniton Res.		24	9	3	12	54	66	30
Uplowman Athletic		24	8	3	13	56	73	27
Axmouth United		24	7	2	15	60	72	23
Tedburn St M. Res.	-1	24	5	1	18	49	108	15
Exeter Bohemians		24	2	1	21	34	108	7

Intermediate Two

		P	W	D	L	F	A	Pts
Axminster Town Res.		26	23	2	1	101	23	71
Otterton		26	22	2	2	108	31	68
Beacon Knights		26	21	2	3	85	26	65
Amory Rovers		26	19	1	6	86	40	58
Hatherleigh Town Res.		26	13	2	11	72	51	41
Elmore 'A'	-1	26	14	0	12	74	60	41
Morchard Bishop		26	11	3	12	57	56	36
Upottery		26	11	3	12	53	59	36
Priory		26	9	4	13	47	67	31
Cheriton Fitzpaine		26	8	3	15	55	81	27
Follygate/Inwardleigh		26	7	2	17	65	86	23
Beer Albion Res.		26	4	4	18	31	95	16
Oakwood Res.	-1	26	3	2	21	35	102	10
Awliscombe United	-1	26	1	2	23	19	111	4

Intermediate Three

		P	W	D	L	F	A	Pts
The Vic	-1	26	19	4	3	112	42	60
Crescent Res.		26	17	5	4	71	45	56
Sampford Peverell		26	17	4	5	80	38	55
Kentisbeare Res.		26	15	6	5	81	48	51
Mitre United		26	15	3	8	81	56	48
Culm United Res.		26	11	6	9	61	47	39
Lords XI		26	11	4	11	89	79	37
Sidbury United Res.		26	10	2	14	56	63	32
Up & Under		26	9	4	13	91	81	31
Honiton Town Res.	-1	26	9	2	15	57	78	28
Clyst Valley Res.	-1	26	9	0	17	50	82	26
Heavitree/Won Res.	-5	26	6	7	13	60	79	20
Motel & Offwell Res.		26	5	2	19	40	111	17
Culmstock	-1	26	4	1	21	53	133	12

Intermediate Four

		P	W	D	L	F	A	Pts
North Tawton Res.		24	17	2	5	89	33	53
Budley Bulldogs		24	15	7	2	50	25	52
Sandford Res.		24	15	3	6	66	42	48
Bradninch		24	15	3	6	54	31	48
Axminster Town 'A'		24	15	2	7	74	37	47
Winkleigh Res.		24	12	2	10	58	40	38
Bow AAC Res.		24	8	6	10	56	52	30
Crediton United 'A'	-1	24	7	3	14	48	78	23
Colyton Res.		24	5	7	12	24	48	22
Seaton Town 'A'	-1	24	6	4	14	37	60	21
Bampton Res.		24	6	3	15	42	71	21
Tedburn St Mary 'A'	-1	24	4	7	13	22	66	18
Lapford Res.		24	3	7	14	31	68	16

DORSET COUNTY LEAGUE

	Allendale	Blandford Res.	Chickerell Utd	Cobham Sp. Res.	Dorchester Spts	Dorchester Utd	Gill'ham T. Res.	Hamwthy U. Res.	Portland U. Res.	Shaftesbury Res.	Sturm. Marshall	Witchampton U.
Allendale		6-0	5-3	6-0	n/a	2-3	5-1	2-0	2-0	6-0	6-0	2-0
Blandford Utd Res.	0-6	S	0-3	1-3	0-2	1-6	1-5	0-1	1-3	1-1	4-3	0-1
Chickerell United	4-0	10-0	E	4-1	7-2	2-4	1-0	3-0	0-1	2-1	4-0	2-2
Cobham Spts Res.	0-4	0-3	0-7	N	3-1	0-5	1-3	1-4	0-1	0-3	4-4	0-2
Dorchester Sports	1-5	1-2	0-1	1-2	I	0-7	1-4	5-0	0-7	2-2	1-1	1-3
Dorchester United	2-0	4-1	4-4	1-2	6-0	O	3-1	6-0	3-4	7-0	7-0	2-0
Gillingham T. Res.	0-2	8-0	1-3	5-1	5-1	0-5	R	2-1	1-0	3-1	5-4	3-2
Hamworthy U. Res.	1-2	2-2	2-1	0-1	n/a	1-2	2-5		2-0	3-1	5-0	2-2
Portland Utd Res.	2-1	2-0	0-3	3-0	n/a	1-4	2-0	2-1	D	8-1	4-1	2-0
Shaftesbury Res.	2-7	0-1	2-7	3-0	2-1	4-7	1-1	1-3	2-2	I	0-6	2-1
Sturm. Marshall	3-5	1-1	0-7	10-0	1-4	4-4	1-2	3-1	2-0	1-3	V	2-5
Witchampton Utd	2-4	3-1	2-0	3-0	4-1	3-3	0-1	3-2	4-1	4-1	3-3	

Senior Division	P	W	D	L	F	A	Pts
Dorchester United	20	15	3	2	82	30	48
Allendale	20	16	0	4	73	23	48
Chickerell United	20	13	2	5	70	25	41
Gillingham Town Res.	20	12	1	7	47	36	37
Portland United Res.	20	12	1	7	38	28	37
Witchampton United	20	9	4	7	42	33	31
Hamworthy Utd Res.	20	7	2	11	33	39	23
Sturminster Marshall	20	4	4	12	48	70	16
Shaftesbury Res.	20	4	3	13	29	70	15
Blandford United Res.	20	3	3	14	18	68	12
Cobham Sports Res.	20	3	1	16	14	72	10

Note – Dorchester Sports withdrew during the course of the season. Their results are shown opposite but are expunged from the league table.

SENIOR DIVISION CUP
SEMI-FINALS
Allendale 5 Gillingham Town Res. 0
Witchampton United 2 Dorchester United 3
FINAL (7th May at Sherborne Town)
Allendale 3 Dorchester United 1

SENIOR DIVISION CONSTITUTION 2003-04
ALLENDALE .... Redcotts Recreation Ground, School Lane, Wimborne, Dorset .... None
BLANDFORD UNITED RESERVES .... Recreation Ground, Park Road, Blandford Forum, Dorset .... None
CHICKERELL UNITED .... Redlands Sports Ground, Weymouth, Dorset .... None
COBHAM SPORTS RESERVES .... Merley Park, Merley Lane, Wimborne, Dorset 01202 885773
CRANBORNE .... Recreation Ground, Penny's Lane, Cranborne, Dorset 01747 823673
GILLINGHAM TOWN RESERVES .... Hardings Lane, Gillingham, Dorset 01202 674974
HAMWORTHY UNITED RESERVES ... The County Ground, Blandford Close, Hamworthy, Poole 01305 861489
PORTLAND UNITED RESERVES .... New Grove Corner, Grove Road, Portland, Dorset 01747 853990
SHAFTESBURY RESERVES .... Cockrams, Coppice Street, Shaftesbury, Dorset .... None
STURMINSTER MARSHALL .... Churchill Close, Sturminster Marshall, Dorset 01929 424673
SWANAGE TOWN & HERSTON .... Day's Park, off De Moulham Road, Swanage, Dorset .... None
WEYMOUTH UNITED ..... Redlands Sports Ground, Dorchester Road, Weymouth, Dorset .... 01202 889310 / 884821
WIMBORNE TOWN RESERVES .... The Cuthbury, Cowgrove Road, Wimborne, Dorset .... None
WITCHAMPTON UNITED .... Crichel Park, Witchampton, Dorset 01258 840986

Dorchester United are promoted to the Dorset Premier League replaced by Swanage Town & Herston. Dorchester Sports withdrew during the course of the season. Cranborne and Weymouth United move up from Division One. Wimborne Town Reserves join from the Wessex Combination.

	Allendale Res.	Barwick/Stoford	Cranborne	Crossways	Marina Sports	Moreton	Okeford United	Piddletrenthide	Ryl O. Cougars	Wareham Res.	Weymouth PO	Weymouth Utd
Allendale Res.	D	0-3	1-6	1-2	1-0	0-5	1-1	0-2	0-3	1-0	2-5	1-6
Barwick & Stoford	4-2	I	2-3	2-1	2-0	2-3	4-2	4-0	2-3	2-1	2-4	2-2
Cranborne	0-1	7-0	V	3-2	4-1	1-0	3-1	4-0	1-0	2-0	6-2	2-2
Crossways	4-4	1-2	1-1	I	2-2	1-1	3-1	1-1	1-1	5-1	3-2	0-1
Marina Sports	3-3	1-0	1-6	2-1	S	3-2	3-2	2-3	3-0	3-1	3-0	3-0
Moreton	5-3	0-1	0-4	0-0	3-3	I	3-1	3-1	2-3	0-2	3-3	3-0
Okeford United	2-3	1-3	0-3	2-1	0-3	0-6	O	5-1	0-11	1-0	2-4	1-2
Piddletrenthide U.	0-5	4-3	0-7	0-1	1-3	3-1	5-0	N	0-3	2-2	5-4	3-4
Royal Oak Cougars	2-2	5-1	2-7	3-0	3-0	0-0	6-0	3-2		2-0	3-1	0-1
Wareham R. Res.	3-2	1-1	1-8	1-1	2-3	3-2	1-1	4-4	1-4	O	7-2	2-3
Weymouth PO	4-2	1-2	1-2	2-4	1-0	2-0	8-2	6-3	2-0	2-1	N	2-4
Weymouth United	5-1	6-3	4-4	3-1	3-1	4-0	7-2	9-0	0-4	4-5	5-3	E

Division One		P	W	D	L	F	A	Pts
Cranborne		22	18	3	1	84	21	57
Weymouth United		22	15	3	4	75	43	48
Royal Oak Cougars		22	14	3	5	61	28	45
Barwick & Stoford		22	11	2	9	47	48	35
Marina Sports	-3	22	10	4	8	42	41	31
Weymouth Post Off.		22	10	1	11	61	61	31
Crossways		22	7	8	7	39	33	29
Moreton	-6	22	7	6	9	43	40	21
Wareham Rgrs Res.		22	5	5	12	38	55	20
Allendale Res.		22	5	4	13	36	65	19
Piddletrenthide United		22	5	3	14	39	75	18
Okeford United		22	3	2	17	25	80	11

DIVISION ONE CUP
SEMI-FINALS
Allendale Res. 1 Royal Oak Cougars 5
Barwick & Stoford 0 Cranborne 5
FINAL (17th May at Hamworthy United)
Royal Oak Cougars 1 Cranborne 4

DIVISION ONE CONSTITUTION 2003-04
ALLENDALE RESERVES .... Redcotts Recreation Ground, School Lane, Wimborne, Dorset .... None
BARWICK & STOFORD .... Barwick Recreation Ground, Barwick, Yeovil, Somerset .... None
BISHOP'S CAUNDLE .... Bishop's Caundle Recreation Ground, Bishop's Caundle, Dorset .... None
CORFE MULLEN UNITED .... The Old Waterworks, Corfe Mullen, Wimborne, Dorset .... None
CROSSWAYS .... The Playing Field, Crossways, Dorset .... None
EASTON UNITED .... Grove Road Playing Field, Easton, Portland, Dorset .... None
MARINA SPORTS .... Turlin Moor, Poole, Dorset .... None
MORETON............ Recreation Field, Dick o'the Banks Road, Crossways, Dorset .... None
OKEFORD UNITED............ Recreation Ground, Okeford Fitzpaine, Dorset .... None
PIDDLETRENTHIDE UNITED .... Playing Field, Piddletrenthide, Dorset .... None
ROYAL OAK COUGARS .... The Marsh, Weymouth, Dorset .... None
STALBRIDGE .... The Park, Park Grove, Stalbridge, Dorset .... None
WAREHAM RANGERS RESERVES .... Purbeck Sports Centre, Worgret Road, Wareham, Dorset 01929 556454
WEYMOUTH POST OFFICE .... Redlands Sports Ground, Dorchester Road, Weymouth, Dorset .... None

Cranborne and Weymouth United move up to the Senior Division One. Stalbridge, Corfe Mullen United and Easton United are promoted from Division Two. Bishop's Caundle join from the Yeovil & District League.

WWW.NLNEWSDESK.CO.UK

WWW.CHERRYRED.CO.UK

Division Two (results grid)

	Chickerell Res.	Child Okeford	Corfe Mullen	Dorch. YMCA	Easton United	Kingston	Piddlehinton	Sherborne Res.	Stalbridge	Stourpaine Res.	Stur. Newt. Res.	Wool RBL
Chickerell Utd Res.	D	4-1	2-2	6-1	1-2	1-1	3-2	3-1	1-2	1-1	6-0	0-0
Child Okeford	2-3	I	4-1	0-3	1-0	0-10	1-6	1-1	1-2	2-4	4-2	3-2
Corfe Mullen Utd	4-3	5-2	V	5-1	1-4	0-2	6-2	3-2	1-0	4-1	4-5	3-5
Dorchester YMCA	2-5	6-0	1-1	I	0-3	2-1	1-4	4-0	1-2	2-5	1-3	4-1
Easton United	2-2	8-0	1-2	4-1	S	1-3	3-0	1-1	3-0	4-1	3-1	0-1
Kingston	3-2	5-2	4-1	5-2	6-2	I	7-1	1-1	2-0	5-3	6-0	2-0
Piddlehinton Utd	4-5	1-0	0-8	2-2	2-2	2-3	O	3-2	1-3	2-1	0-3	2-0
Sherborne T. Res.	0-0	3-5	4-3	1-2	0-0	1-2	3-2	N	4-1	3-1	2-0	0-1
Stalbridge	1-0	5-0	3-0	0-1	1-4	2-1	3-1	2-2		2-1	0-1	2-1
Stourpaine Res.	1-6	5-3	4-4	1-6	3-0	4-2	1-2	2-3	1-1	T	1-3	3-2
Stur. Newton Res.	2-0	1-1	1-2	2-0	1-1	3-3	0-3	1-1	0-0	0-0	W	2-1
Wool RBL	1-1	2-2	4-3	2-2	0-5	2-3	0-2	3-3	1-1	4-1	4-1	O

Division Two	P	W	D	L	F	A	Pts
Kingston	22	16	3	3	77	32	51
Stalbridge	22	12	3	7	34	28	39
Easton United	22	11	5	6	53	28	38
Chickerell United Res.	22	9	7	6	55	35	34
Corfe Mullen United	22	10	3	9	63	55	33
Sturminster Newt. Res.	22	8	5	9	32	44	29
Piddlehinton United	22	9	2	11	44	57	29
Dorchester YMCA	22	8	3	11	45	53	27
Sherborne Town Res.	22	6	8	8	38	41	26
Wool RBL	22	6	6	10	37	45	24
Stourpaine Res.	22	6	4	12	45	61	22
Child Okeford	22	5	3	14	35	79	18

DIVISION TWO CUP

SEMI-FINALS
Easton United 1 **Kingston** 1 *aet* (3-4p)
Stur. Newton Res. 0 Dorchester YMCA 0 *aet* (3-2p)
FINAL *(17th May at Corfe Mullen United)*
Sturminster Newton United Res. 0 **Kingston** 3

DIVISION TWO CONSTITUTION 2003-04

CHICKERELL UNITED RESERVES........ Redlands Sports Ground, Weymouth, Dorset .... None
DORCHESTER UNITED RESERVES. Sandringham Sports Centre, Armada Way, Dorchester, Dorset........................... None
DORCHESTER YMCA............. Recreation Ground, Weymouth Avenue, Dorchester, Dorset............................. None
HOLT UNITED RESERVES.................. Gaunts Common, Holt, Wimborne, Dorset 01258 840379
KINGSTON .... King George V Playing Field, Swanage, Dorset.
PIDDLEHINTON UNITED........ Thomas Hardye Leisure Centre, Coburg Road, Dorchester, Dorset 01305 266772
POOLE BOROUGH RESERVES .... Turlin Moor Rec, Blandford Moor, Hamworthy, Poole, Dorset ...... None. Club Office: 01202 674973
POOLE ROYAL MAIL .... Municipal pitches (t.b.a.), Poole, Dorset. None
SHERBORNE TOWN RESERVES.... Raleigh Grove, The Terrace Playing Fields, Sherborne, Dorset.................... 01935 816110
STOURPAINE RESERVES .... Dick Draper Memorial Fields, Stourpaine, Blandford Forum, Dorset.................. None
STURMINSTER NEWTON UTD RES. Barnetts Field, Honeymead Lane, Sturminster Newton, Dorset............... 01258 471406
WEYMOUTH SPARTANS .... The Marsh, Weymouth, Dorset. None
WOOL RBL.................... Wool Recreation Ground, Colliers Lane, Wool, Dorset............................. None

Stalbridge, Corfe Mullen United and Easton United move up to Division One. Child Okeford drop to Division Three North & East replaced by Holt United Reserves, Poole Borough Reserves and Poole Royal Mail (formerly Poole & Parkstone Royal Mail). Spa Hotel (who become Weymouth Spartans) are promoted from Division Three South & West. Dorchester United Reserves move up from Division Four South & West.

Division Three North & East (results grid)

	Allendale 'A'	Bere Regis	Forest Inn	Handley Sp.	Holt U. Res.	King. Lacy	Linthorpe	Milbne St A.	Poole B. Res.	Poole/Park.	Shaft'by 'A'	Stickland	Stur. M. Res.
Allendale 'A'	D	3-2	3-2	1-3	3-4	0-10	2-2	2-0	0-8	2-2	3-5	3-3	3-4
Bere Regis	6-1	I	2-0	6-0	0-4	4-6	4-3	8-0	1-1	5-6	1-3	3-4	4-2
Forest Inn	0-0	2-1	V	3-2	0-9	1-2	0-1	2-0	0-12	2-6	0-7	1-4	1-3
Handley Sports	1-6	2-0	2-2	I	1-9	2-8	3-3	2-0	2-4	5-6	0-5	3-0	3-0
Holt United Res.	4-0	4-1	8-2	8-0	S	4-1	4-3	7-0	6-2	0-1	4-0	2-1	3-1
Kingston Lacy	5-6	2-3	6-0	5-5	0-3	I	6-1	8-0	1-1	1-2	5-1	1-4	3-1
Linthorpe	0-3	2-2	7-0	2-0	1-2	0-5	O	2-1	1-3	1-1	1-0	3-0	3-1
Milborne St And.	2-2	2-3	2-0	3-2	1-7	7-3	0-2	N	2-5	1-6	1-3	2-4	4-2
Poole Borough Res.	2-2	4-1	4-0	4-1	0-0	2-3	2-2	8-1	T	3-1	3-2	3-2	9-0
Poole & Parkstone	6-1	2-4	7-2	6-5	2-4	0-9	1-3	9-0	2-3	H	0-2	3-3	5-0
Shaftesbury 'A'	8-0	0-2	2-1	0-4	4-2	1-2	6-1	1-2	6-2		R	1-1	1-2
Stickland United	2-1	3-3	3-1	3-0	1-7	0-6	4-3	2-1	3-4	1-4	1-0	E	0-2
Stur. Marsh. Res.	2-7	3-3	2-1	3-1	0-6	3-2	3-0	5-5	2-0	1-1	1-2	1-4	E

Div Three North & East	P	W	D	L	F	A	Pts
Holt United Res.	24	22	1	1	113	21	67
Poole Borough Res.	24	16	5	3	88	35	53
Shaftesbury 'A'	24	13	1	10	66	39	40
Poole/Parkstone RM	24	12	4	8	81	64	40
Kingston Lacy	24	12	2	10	98	55	38
Stickland United	24	11	4	9	52	58	37
Linthorpe	24	10	5	9	48	48	35
Bere Regis	24	10	4	10	69	64	34
Sturm. Marshall Res.	24	10	4	10	67	34	34
Allendale 'A'	24	7	6	11	54	83	27
Handley Sports	24	5	3	16	46	89	18
Milborne St Andrew	24	3	3	18	35	99	12
Forest Inn	24	3	2	19	22	95	11

DIVISION THREE NORTH AND EAST CUP

Not contested in 2002-03

DIVISION THREE NORTH & EAST CONSTITUTION 2003-04

ALLENDALE 'A'.................... Redcotts Recreation Ground, School Lane, Wimborne, Dorset............................ None
BERE REGIS .... Bere Regis Recreation Ground, Bere Regis, Dorset.................................... None
CHILD OKEFORD .... Recreation Grounds, Child Okeford, Dorset...................................... None
CRANBORNE RESERVES............... Recreation Ground, Penny's Lane, Cranborne, Dorset .... None
HANDLEY SPORTS............. Handley Recreation Ground, Sixpenny, Handley, Salisbury, Wiltshire................... None
KINGSTON LACY .... Corfe Mullen Recreation Ground, Corfe Mullen, Wimborne, Dorset................... None
LINTHORPE .... Municipal pitches (t.b.a.), Poole, Dorset....................................... None
MILBORNE ST ANDREW .... St Marys School, Puddletown, Dorset.. None
SHAFTESBURY 'A'...................... Cockrams, Coppice Street, Shaftesbury, Dorset............................... 01747 853990
STICKLAND UNITED .... Stickland Sports Ground, Hedge End, Winterborne Stickland, Dorset.................. None
STURMINSTER MARSHALL RESERVES ... Churchill Close, Sturminster Marshall, Dorset............................ None
WALLISDOWN SPORTS......................... Oakmead School, Bournemouth, Dorset .... None

Holt United Reserves, Poole Borough Reserves and Poole Royal Mail (formerly Poole & Parkstone Royal Mail) move up to Division Two replaced by Child Okeford. Forest Inn (now Ferndown Sports) drop to Division Four North & East replaced by Wallisdown Sports and Cranborne Reserves.

	Delta	Maiden NC	Martinstown	Puddletown	Southill SC	Spa Hotel	Swanage Rs.	Weym'th 'A'	Wyke Rov.	Wyke Smug.
Delta	D	3-1	4-3	3-0	7-2	0-2	0-0	1-6	0-2	4-1
Maiden Newton/Cattistock	0-2	I	2-8	1-8	3-1	1-2	2-3	4-1	1-8	n/a
Martinstown	2-5	6-2	V	1-3	4-5	2-4	2-5	3-6	5-6	2-1
Puddletown	2-1	3-1	3-3		6-1	1-2	1-3	2-0	6-1	6-1
Southill SC	4-1	0-2	4-0	2-3	3	0-5	2-1	2-2	2-2	1-0
Spa Hotel	3-0	7-0	10-0	1-1	4-0		6-3	3-0	1-1	12-1
Swanage Town & H. Res.	2-4	2-1	3-0	1-1	6-3	2-2	S	2-3	4-2	n/a
Weymouth 'A'	1-1	2-0	0-2	1-0	5-3	2-3	2-0	&	3-3	8-0
Wyke Rovers	1-0	4-0	6-4	2-3	6-0	1-2	2-0	6-3	W	4-0
Wyke Smugglers	3-7	n/a	1-2	1-6	n/a	n/a	1-2	1-4	1-3	

Div Three South & West	P	W	D	L	F	A	Pts
Spa Hotel	16	13	3	0	57	14	42
Wyke Rovers	16	9	3	4	53	34	30
Puddletown	16	9	3	4	43	24	30
Swanage T & H Res.	16	7	3	6	37	33	24
Weymouth 'A'	16	7	3	6	37	35	24
Delta	16	7	2	7	32	31	23
Southill SC	16	4	2	10	31	57	14
Martinstown	16	3	1	12	45	68	10
Maiden Nwtn/Catt.	16	3	0	13	21	60	9

DIV THREE S & W CUP

SEMI-FINALS
Martinstown 3 Wyke Rovers 2
Puddletown 2 Spa Hotel 1
FINAL (*10th May at Dorchester Town*)
Martinstown 2 Puddletown 1

Note – Wyke Smugglers withdrew during the course of the season. Their results are shown above but are expunged from the league table

DIVISION THREE SOUTH & WEST CONSTITUTION 2003-04

ABRO BOVINGTON...........................Bovington Camp, Bovington, Dorset...None
AFC HURST...Moreton Recreation Field, Moreton, Dorset...................................None
BARWICK & STOFORD RESERVES....Barwick Recreation Ground, Barwick, Yeovil, Somerset....................None
DORCHESTER UNITED 'A'.........Sandringham Sports Centre, Armada Way, Dorchester, Dorset...................None
MAIDEN NEWTON & CATTISTOCK.........Cattistock Playing Fields, Cattistock, Dorset...................None
MARTINSTOWN.................Thomas Hardye Leisure Centre, Coburg Road, Dorchester, Dorset.........01305 266772
PUDDLETOWN..............................Recreation Ground, Puddletown, Dorset..None
SOUTHILL SC....................................The Marsh, Weymouth, Dorset..None
SWANAGE TOWN & HERSTON RES.....Day's Park, off De Moulham Road, Swanage, Dorset.........01929 424673
WYKE REGIS SOCIAL CLUB.................Portland YOI, Portland, Dorset...None
WYKE ROVERS..................Redlands Sports Ground, Dorchester Road, Weymouth, Dorset.................None

Spa Hotel (who become Weymouth Spartans) are promoted to Division Two. Wyke Smugglers withdrew during the course of the season. Delta and Weymouth 'A' have resigned. ABRO Bovington, Barwick & Stoford Reserves, Mowers (who become AFC Hurst), and Wyke Regis Social Club are promoted from Division Four South & West. Newcomers are Dorchester United 'A'.

	Colehill Sports	Cranborne Res.	Donhead United	Gillingham Town 'A'	Milton Abbas Sports	Okeford United Res.	Sandford	Stalbridge Res.	Sturminster Newton Utd 'A'	Wallisdown Sports	Witchampton United Res.
Colehill Sports		1-3	3-5	2-5	2-2	1-4	2-2	4-4	0-20	0-4	5-3
Cranborne Res.	4-1	D	3-1	6-0	2-0	5-0	2-0	0-1	1-1	1-1	2-1
Donhead United	6-2	0-3	I	4-0	1-1	7-0	3-1	5-2	3-2	2-4	2-5
Gillingham Town 'A'	5-3	3-5	2-6	V	1-5	1-3	8-5	4-3	0-8	3-3	0-8
Milton Abbas Sports	4-6	0-3	0-4	0-3		4-3	1-0	3-2	1-7	0-9	3-6
Okeford United Res.	4-5	1-7	2-0	1-5	1-8	4	1-6	3-4	1-4	0-8	1-1
Sandford	6-4	1-2	1-2	2-3	3-1	8-2		3-4	7-7	4-2	3-4
Stalbridge Res.	1-6	2-10	3-1	0-4	3-2	11-1	3-4	N	2-1	2-6	3-4
Sturminster Newton Utd 'A'	7-2	0-0	2-5	2-2	6-3	5-0	2-0	1-5	&	2-6	1-0
Wallisdown Sports	5-2	3-0	7-1	4-0	3-2	6-2	4-2	11-1	7-2	E	2-0
Witchampton United Res.	8-3	1-6	1-2	0-0	5-1	4-0	0-2	3-1	6-3	1-3	

Div Four North & East	P	W	D	L	F	A	Pts
Wallisdown Sports	20	18	1	1	103	24	55
Cranborne Res.	20	15	3	2	65	18	48
Donhead United	20	12	1	7	60	44	37
Gillingham T. 'A'	20	9	3	8	52	62	30
Witchampton Res.	20	9	2	9	53	46	29
Stur. Newton 'A' -3	20	8	4	8	78	55	25
Stalbridge Res.	20	8	1	11	59	80	25
Sandford	20	7	3	10	58	52	24
Milton Abbas Sports	20	5	2	13	41	70	17
Colehill Sports	20	4	3	13	54	102	15
Okeford United Res.	20	3	1	16	30	100	10

DIVISION FOUR NORTH AND EAST CUP

Not contested in 2002-03

DIVISION FOUR NORTH AND EAST CONSTITUTION 2003-04

AC MATRAVERS ....Lytchett Matravers Recreation Ground, Lytchett Matravers, Dorset.........................None
BISHOP'S CAUNDLE RESERVES ..Bishop's Caundle Recreation Ground, Bishop's Caundle, Dorset.........None
DONHEAD UNITED..............Charlton Rembrance Field, Donhead St Mary, Shaftesbury, Dorset.............None
FERNDOWN SPORTS......................King George V Rec Ground, Ferndown, Dorset ....None
FOUNTAIN.......................Stour Provost Recreation Ground, Stour Provost, Dorset..........................None
GILLINGHAM TOWN 'A'....................Hardings Lane, Gillingham, Dorset 01747 823673
LYTCHETT RED TRIANGLE ....Sports Field, High Street, Lytchett Matravers, Dorset...........01202 624298
MILTON ABBAS SPORTS......................Hoggan Down, Milton Abbas, Dorset.................................None
OKEFORD UNITED RESERVES ....Recreation Ground, Okeford Fitzpaine, Dorset.........................None
SANDFORD ....Bovington Camp, Bovington, Dorset...................................None
STALBRIDGE RESERVES ....The Park, Park Grove, Stalbridge, Dorset...............................None
STURMINSTER NEWTON UTD 'A' ..Barnetts Field, Honeymead Lane, Sturminster Newton, Dorset....01258 471406
WITCHAMPTON UNITED RESERVES ....Crichel Park, Witchampton, Dorset.....................01258 840986

Forest Inn (now Ferndown Sports) drop from Division Three North & East to replace Wallisdown Sports and Cranborne Reserves. Colehill Sports have resigned. Newcomers are AC Matravers, Bishop's Caundle Reserves, Fountain, and Lytchett Red Triangle.

WWW.NLNEWSDESK.CO.UK

	ABRO Bov.	Barwick R.	B'dere Inn	Dorch. Boro.	Dorch. U Rs.	Easton Res.	Mowers	P'etrenthide	Thornford	Wyke Regis
ABRO Bovington	D	2-2	12-0	2-1	1-5	2-2	2-6	10-1	6-1	5-3
Barwick & Stoford Res.	2-3	I	5-1	6-2	1-3	0-2	1-3	9-2	2-1	4-5
Belvedere Inn	1-4	1-6	V	2-1	1-8	2-1	0-6	3-2	3-7	2-9
Dorchester Borough	1-9	1-5	3-1		2-5	5-1	1-8	3-6	0-5	7-1
Dorchester United Res.	3-1	5-1	7-0	6-0	4	2-0	3-2	7-0	7-1	5-1
Easton United Res.	3-0	0-6	7-0	2-1	1-3		3-4	2-0	3-0	5-4
Mowers	2-1	5-1	12-0	5-1	2-4	2-2	S	9-0	5-0	3-2
Piddletrenthide United Res.	0-7	3-1	10-3	3-6	1-9	2-9	0-9	&	1-1	2-6
Thornford	2-2	2-2	6-2	2-2	1-2	2-1	1-7	6-1	W	3-7
Wyke Regis Social Club	1-2	2-1	7-1	12-2	4-3	1-2	3-9	8-1	4-5	

Div Four South & West	P	W	D	L	F	A	Pts
Dorchester Utd Res.	18	17	0	1	87	20	51
Mowers	18	15	1	2	99	25	46
ABRO Bovington	18	10	3	5	71	36	33
Easton United Res.	18	9	2	7	46	36	29
Wyke Regis Soc. Club	18	9	0	9	80	62	27
Barwick/Stoford Res.	18	7	2	9	55	43	23
Thornford	18	6	4	8	46	57	22
Dorchester Borough	18	4	1	13	39	81	13
Piddletrenthide Res.	18	3	1	14	35	108	10
Belvedere Inn	18	3	0	15	23	113	9

DIV FOUR S & W CUP

SEMI-FINALS
Barwick & Stoford Res. 0 **Mowers** 4
Dorchester United Res. 3 Wyke Regis Social Club 0
FINAL *(17th May at Chickerell United)*
Dorchester United Res. 0 **Mowers** 1

DIVISION FOUR SOUTH & WEST CONSTITUTION 2003-04

BELVEDERE INN .... The Marsh, Weymouth, Dorset .... None
CORFE CASTLE .... Corfe Castle, Wareham, Dorset .... None
DORCHESTER BOROUGH .... Thomas Hardye Leisure Centre, Coburg Road, Dorchester, Dorset 01305 266772
EASTON UNITED .... Grove Road Playing Field, Easton, Portland, Dorset .... None
KANGAROOS .... Thomas Hardye Leisure Centre, Coburg Road, Dorchester, Dorset 01305 266772
PIDDLETRENTHIDE UNITED RESERVES ...... Playing Field, Piddletrenthide, Dorset .... None
POUNDBURY .... Thomas Hardye Leisure Centre, Coburg Road, Dorchester, Dorset 01305 266772
TERRORFINNS .... Redlands Sports Ground, Weymouth, Dorset .... None
THORNFORD .... Recreation Ground, Pound Lane, Thornford, Dorset .... None
WINFRITH .... Red Lion Ground, Winfrith, Dorset .... None

Dorchester United Reserves jump straight to Division Two while ABRO Bovington, Barwick & Stoford Reserves, Mowers (now AFC Hurst) and Wyke Regis Social Club are promoted to Division Three South & West. Newcomers are Corfe Castle, Terrorfinns, Kangaroos, Poundbury and Winfrith.

DORSET PREMIER LEAGUE

	Blandford United	Bournemouth Sports	Bridport Res.	Cobham Sports	Dorchester Town Res.	Gillingham Town	Hamworthy Recreation	Hamworthy United	Holt United	Poole Borough	Shaftesbury	Sherborne Town	Stourpaine	Sturminster Newton	Swanage T. & Herston	Wareham Rangers	Westland Sports	Weymouth Sports
Blandford United		1-2	1-2	0-1	1-2	1-4	0-3	1-5	1-1	4-2	2-1	1-1	1-2	3-2	3-0	2-1	1-3	0-2
Bournemouth Sports	1-1		0-3	1-2	1-1	0-2	0-1	0-3	3-3	4-7	2-1	2-2	4-2	5-1	6-0	1-2	1-3	7-2
Bridport Res.	3-0	2-3		2-1	3-2	0-2	2-2	0-2	1-1	3-0	1-1	1-0	4-0	0-1	2-3	1-1	1-3	3-0
Cobham Sports	3-2	0-5	2-2		1-2	0-2	0-2	0-4	2-3	1-3	3-3	0-3	2-6	3-0	2-2	1-3	0-1	3-1
Dorchester Town Res.	2-1	0-4	1-1	5-0			0-0	3-1	1-2	1-4	5-2	4-0	3-0	0-0	4-0	4-3	0-0	6-0
Gillingham Town	3-2	4-3	2-0	2-0	1-0		4-2	3-1	1-1	4-1	1-1	4-3	3-0	1-0	4-0	5-0	0-0	12-0
Hamworthy Recreation	4-0	4-2	1-0	3-0	2-1	3-0		3-0	2-0	3-3	0-2	3-1	2-0	5-1	5-1	1-2		9-1
Hamworthy United	7-1	4-1	2-0	5-2	1-0	1-2	3-1		2-1	1-0	4-0	1-0	4-2	4-0	5-2	3-1	5-1	2-4
Holt United	1-1	2-2	4-1	2-1	2-0	2-4	1-5	2-3		2-0	1-0	2-2	3-1	4-1	1-6	4-1	2-0	
Poole Borough	1-0	4-3	2-0	0-1	1-6	0-1	2-1	2-3	1-1		3-1	1-0	2-3	2-2	3-0	4-2	1-0	6-0
Shaftesbury	1-1	3-7	1-3	2-0	2-4	0-1	1-2	0-1	1-1	3-0		0-2	2-1	2-1	1-0	3-0	2-1	1-1
Sherborne Town	0-0	4-3	3-0	1-0	0-0	1-2	1-3	3-1	4-1	1-0			2-1	3-1	3-0	0-0	2-2	5-1
Stourpaine	2-1	2-2	0-1	1-2	1-0	0-2	3-1	0-3	0-1	1-7	1-2			4-2	2-1	0-4	1-3	8-0
Sturminster Newton Utd	0-1	2-2	1-1	0-1	1-1	3-3	2-1	0-1	2-2	1-2	0-1	2-0	3-4		3-1	1-0	0-4	3-0
Swanage Town & Herston	2-1	2-4	0-1	6-1	0-4	0-1	1-0	0-6	1-0	1-6	1-1	1-1	1-3	2-4		1-2	0-6	1-1
Wareham Rangers	4-1	1-0	3-6	3-1	1-2	0-0	2-3	3-3	1-6	2-0	3-0	4-2	1-1	0-0	6-1		1-3	3-2
Westland Sports	3-2	0-6	2-1	5-1	3-2	1-3	2-4	0-1	1-0	2-3	3-1	1-1	1-4	4-1	5-2	4-0		2-0
Weymouth Sports	0-3	4-4	0-3	1-2	0-6	0-5	0-5	0-8	2-4	2-5	1-1	1-5	1-6	3-1	1-0	1-2	0-1	

	P	W	D	L	F	A	Pts
Hamworthy United	34	29	1	4	103	34	88
Gillingham Town	34	27	6	1	89	25	87
Hamworthy Recreation	34	23	3	8	92	42	72
Westland Sports	34	20	5	9	73	49	65
Dorchester Town Res.	34	17	7	10	76	39	58
Sherborne Town	34	15	9	10	59	42	54
Poole Borough	34	17	3	14	73	66	54
Holt United	34	12	13	9	68	56	49
Bridport Res.	34	14	7	13	59	47	49
Wareham Rangers	34	13	7	14	64	71	46
Bournemouth Sports	34	12	8	14	91	75	44
Stourpaine	34	13	3	18	62	72	42
Shaftesbury	34	11	8	15	48	57	41
Cobham Sports	34	9	4	21	39	78	31
Sturminster Newton Utd	34	7	8	19	40	70	29
Blandford United	34	7	6	21	41	71	27
Weymouth Sports	34	4	4	26	36	138	16
Swanage Town & Herston	34	3	4	27	29	110	13

COMBINATION CUP

FIRST ROUND
Blandford 0 **Westland Sports** 1
Cobham Sports 1 **Hamworthy Recreation** 3

SECOND ROUND
Dorchester Res. 7 Swanage 0
Gillingham Town 0 **Holt** 1 *aet*
Hamworthy United 2 Bournemouth Sports 0
Poole Borough 0 **Hamworthy Recreation** 4
Shaftesbury 0 **Sherborne** 1
Sturminster Newton United 2 Wareham Rangers 1
Westland 2 Stourpaine 2 *aet*
Stourpaine 1 Westland 0 *replay*
Weymouth Sports 2 **Bridport Res.** 3

QUARTER-FINALS
Bridport Res. 1 Stourpaine 1 *aet*
Stourpaine 1 **Bridport Res.** 2
Hamworthy Recreation 3 Dorchester Town Res. 3 *aet*
Dorchester Town Res. 0 **Hamworthy Rec** 1 *replay*
Hamworthy United 3 Sturminster Newton Utd 1
Sherborne 1 **Holt United** 2

SEMI-FINALS
Hamworthy Recreation 2 Bridport Res. 1
Hamworthy United 2 **Holt United** 3

FINAL
(10th May at Hamworthy Utd)
Hamworthy Rec 0 **Holt Utd** 4

CONSTITUTION FOR 2003-04

BLANDFORD UNITED .... Recreation Ground, Park Road, Blandford Forum, Dorset .... None
BOURNEMOUTH SPORTS .... Bournemouth Sports Club, Chapel Gate, East Parley, Dorset 01202 581933
BRIDPORT RESERVES .... St Marys Field, Bridport, Dorset 01308 423834
COBHAM SPORTS .... Merley Park, Merley Lane, Wimborne, Dorset 01202 885773
DORCHESTER TOWN RESERVES .... The Avenue Stadium, Dorchester, Dorset .... 01305 262451. Fax: 01305 267623
DORCHESTER UNITED .... Sandringham Sports Centre, Armada Way, Dorchester, Dorset .... None
GILLINGHAM TOWN .... Hardings Lane, Gillingham, Dorset 01747 823673
HAMWORTHY RECREATION .. Hamworthy Rec. Club, Magna Rd, Canford Magna, Wimborne, Dorset 01202 881922
HAMWORTHY UNITED .... The County Ground, Blandford Close, Hamworthy, Poole, Dorset 01202 674974
HOLT UNITED .... Gaunts Common, Holt, Wimborne, Dorset 01258 840379
POOLE BOROUGH .... Turlin Moor Fields, Blandford Moor, Hamworthy, Poole, Dorset ...... None. Club Office: 01202 674973
SHAFTESBURY .... Cockrams, Coppice Street, Shaftesbury, Dorset 01747 853990
SHERBORNE TOWN .... Raleigh Grove, The Terrace Playing Fields, Sherborne, Dorset 01935 816110
STOURPAINE .... Dick Draper Memorial Fields, Stourpaine, Blandford Forum, Dorset .... None
STURMINSTER NEWTON UNITED .. Barnetts Field, Honeymead Lane, Sturminster Newton, Dorset 01258 471406
WAREHAM RANGERS .... Purbeck Sports Centre, Worgret Road, Wareham, Dorset 01929 556454
WESTLAND SPORTS .... Bunford Lane, Yeovil, Somerset .... 01935 703810 / 703620
WEYMOUTH SPORTS .... Weymouth College, Cranford Avenue, Weymouth, Dorset .... None

Swanage Town & Herston are relegated to the Dorset League from which Dorchester United are promoted.

EAST CORNWALL PREMIER LEAGUE

	Bodmin Town Res.	Bude	Callington T. Res.	Camelford	Dobwalls	Foxhole Stars	Launceston Res.	Liskeard Ath. Res.	Millbrook Res.	Nanpean Rovers	Padstow United	Probus	Roche	Saltash United Res.	St Blazey Res.	St Cleer	St Dennis	Sticker	Torpoint Ath. Res.	Wadebridge Res.
Bodmin Town Res.		3-2	0-0	3-0	0-5	1-2	0-0	1-4	1-4	5-0	1-1	1-1	2-0	0-2	0-2	3-1	0-0	3-0	2-0	0-3
Bude	0-3		1-2	1-2	2-0	1-5	2-2	1-3	3-2	4-1	6-1	1-0	2-0	0-2	3-1	1-1	3-2	3-1	1-2	2-0
Callington Town Res.	2-3	0-6		2-4	1-1	2-1	1-1	1-1	1-0	3-0	5-2	4-1	1-0	6-2	1-0	2-2	4-1	0-1		0-2
Camelford	1-0	0-2	7-0		1-3	0-1	2-5	1-2	3-1	1-2	3-1	2-1	1-0	0-2	1-0	2-0	3-1	0-3	1-1	
Dobwalls	4-1	2-1	3-0	1-1		1-3	3-1	2-1	0-0	5-0	2-0	2-1	3-1	0-0	3-2	2-0	1-0	2-1	0-6	6-0
Foxhole Stars	4-0	2-1	5-1	1-1	1-0		5-0	2-1	4-1	1-0	3-1	4-1	2-1	2-0	4-0	2-1	4-1	1-0	2-0	2-1
Launceston Res.	1-0	1-5	3-3	1-1	2-5	2-10		1-5	3-3	3-2	6-3	0-2	0-1	1-0	0-2	1-3	5-4	2-3	1-5	1-2
Liskeard Athletic Res.	1-0	4-1	2-1	0-1	1-1	2-2	9-0		8-1	2-1	2-1	8-0	9-0	2-2	4-0	0-2	1-0	7-2	1-1	1-1
Millbrook Res.	2-1	1-0	1-5	0-3	1-4	0-5	2-3	1-2		0-1	4-0	1-1	1-4	1-6	0-1	2-4	0-1	3-2	0-2	1-3
Nanpean Rovers	1-0	0-0	3-0	1-1	1-3	0-3	5-2	1-2	3-4		3-1	4-1	2-4	2-1	2-2	2-3	1-0	0-1	0-1	
Padstow United	1-1	2-1	2-1	1-3	2-1	2-3	4-0	0-4	4-0	4-2		4-1	0-1	1-3	3-5	1-0	0-5	3-2	1-6	0-1
Probus	2-1	3-0	3-1	0-4	0-2	0-2	5-5	3-2	2-2	1-5	0-0		2-3	1-2	1-1	1-1	3-4	3-2	3-1	0-1
Roche	0-0	0-2	4-1	1-0	3-1	0-1	0-4	4-2	1-1	3-2	3-1	3-1		1-1	0-1	3-2	0-1	1-2	0-1	0-3
Saltash United Res.	0-2	5-1	3-0	0-4	0-5	2-0	3-1	2-1	4-3	4-1	3-1	1-2	0-4		3-2	0-1	1-2	0-1	2-2	
St Blazey Res.	5-4	7-2	2-4	3-2	0-1	0-2	1-1	2-4	1-0	1-2	4-1	3-1	1-0	1-0		0-2	0-1	3-0	1-2	1-0
St Cleer	3-2	2-1	3-0	4-1	1-1	2-4	0-8	4-2	2-3	0-1	7-0	0-1	1-1	2-6	7-0		5-1	0-4	2-1	
St Dennis	2-1	2-1	3-1	1-5	1-1	1-3	2-3	2-3	0-0	0-0	2-4	0-2	1-4	6-2	5-1	0-2		0-3	0-3	
Sticker	2-4	1-3	0-0	3-1	1-0	2-3	2-1	2-3	1-0	2-0	1-4	2-3	0-1	2-4	1-3	1-3	1-1		0-2	
Torpoint Athletic Res.	3-0	1-1	4-0	2-1	1-2	2-1	3-0	0-3	3-0	1-0	1-5	1-0	2-0	7-1	0-2	3-0	3-1	1-2		1-2
Wadebridge Town Res.	2-3	3-1	2-4	0-3	1-1	1-0	2-2	2-1	5-1	1-2	3-1	1-3	0-2	2-1	2-1	0-0	1-2			

	P	W	D	L	F	A	Pts
Foxhole Stars	38	33	2	3	105	30	101
Torpoint Athletic Res.	38	26	4	8	94	32	82
Liskeard Ath. Res.	38	23	9	6	113	59	78
Dobwalls	38	23	8	7	79	39	77
St Cleer	38	21	5	12	90	55	68
Saltash United Res.	38	20	6	12	67	51	66
Camelford	38	19	5	14	68	50	62
St Blazey Res.	38	19	3	16	70	74	60
Wadebridge T. Res. -3	38	18	6	14	61	53	57
Bude	38	16	3	19	68	65	51
Roche	38	16	3	19	52	77	51
Callington Town Res.	38	14	8	16	64	81	50
St Dennis	38	13	5	20	59	75	44
Bodmin Town Res.	38	12	7	19	52	63	43
Nanpean Rovers	38	12	3	23	52	73	39
Probus	38	10	8	20	60	95	38
Padstow United	38	9	7	22	56	92	34
Launceston Res.	38	7	8	23	62	122	29
Sticker	38	8	4	26	48	88	28
Millbrook Res.	38	6	6	26	45	97	24

LEAGUE CUP

PRELIMINARY ROUND
Bude 0 **Nanpean Rovers** 3
Launceston Res. 3 Padstow United 1
Probus 0 **Sticker** 4
St Cleer 1 St Dennis 1
St Dennis 3 St Cleer 2 *replay*

FIRST ROUND
Bodmin Res. 2 Liskeard Athletic Res. 2
Liskeard Res. 3 Bodmin Res. 2 *replay*
Callington Town Res. 2 St Dennis 2
St Dennis 3 Callington Res. 2 *replay*
Camelford 3 **Saltash United Res.** 7
Launceston Res. 3 **Dobwalls** 5
Nanpean Rovers 2 **Foxhole Stars** 3
St Blazey Res. 3 **Torpoint Athletic Res.** 5

Sticker 0 **Roche** 6
Wadebridge Res. 3 Millbrook Res. 0

QUARTER-FINALS
Dobwalls 0 **Liskeard Athletic Res.** 1
Foxhole Stars 5 Wadebridge Res. 1
Saltash United Res. 2 St Dennis 2
St Dennis 1 **Saltash Utd Res.** 3 *replay*
Torpoint Athletic Res. 2 Roche 2
Roche 0 **Torpoint Athletic Res.** 1 *replay*

SEMI-FINALS
Liskeard Res. 2 Foxhole 1 *(at Saltash)*
Torpoint Athletic Res. 2 Saltash United Res. 1 *(at Liskeard Athletic)*

FINAL *(20th at St Blazey)*
Torpoint Res. 1 **Liskeard Res.** 3 *aet*

FRED BINKS MEMORIAL CUP

PRELIMINARY ROUND
Bodmin Town Res. 0 **Probus** 2
Camelford 4 Millbrook Res. 2
St Cleer 2 Callington Town Res. 1
Sticker 2 Padstow United 1

QUARTER-FINALS
Bude 3 Nanpean Rovers 0
Camelford 3 Sticker 0

Launceston Res. 0 **St Blazey Res.** 3
St Cleer 1 **Probus** 2

SEMI-FINALS
Bude 2 Camelford 0
Probus 4 St Blazey Res. 0

FINAL *(15th May at Wadebridge Town)*
Probus 1 Camelford 0

CONSTITUTION 2003-04

BODMIN TOWN RESERVES . . . . Priory Park, Bodmin, Cornwall 01208 78165
BUDE . . . . Broadclose, Bude, Cornwall . . . . None
CALLINGTON TOWN RESERVES. The Marsh, Callington Comm. College, Launceston Rd, Callington 01579 382647
CAMELFORD . . . . Tregoodwell, Camelford, Cornwall . . . . None
DOBWALLS . . . . Lantoom Park, Duloe Road, Dobwalls, Cornwall . . . . None
FOXHOLE STARS . . . . Goverseth Playing Fields, Goverseth Terrace, Foxhole, Cornwall 01726 824615
LAUNCESTON RESERVES . . . . . . Pennygillam, Pennygillam Industrial Estate, Launceston, Cornwall 01566 773279
LISKEARD ATHLETIC RESERVES . . . . . . Lux Park, Liskeard, Cornwall 01579 342665
NANPEAN ROVERS . . . . Victoria Park, Victoria Bottoms, Nanpean, Cornwall 01726 823435
PADSTOW UNITED . . . . Wadebridge Road, Padstow, Cornwall . . . . None
PROBUS . . . . Recreation Ground, Probus, Cornwall . . . . None
ROCHE . . . . Trezaise Road, Roche, St Austell, Cornwall 01726 890718
SALTASH UNITED RESERVES . . . . Kimberley Stadium, Callington Road, Saltash, Cornwall 01752 845746
ST BLAZEY RESERVES . . . . Blaise Park, Station Road, St Blazey, Cornwall 01726 814110
ST CLEER . . . . Recreation Field, St Cleer, Liskeard, Cornwall . . . . None
ST DENNIS . . . . Boscawen Park, St Dennis, Cornwall 01726 822635
ST STEPHEN . . . . Trethosa Road, St Stephen, St Austell, Cornwall . . . . None
STICKER . . . . Ennis Farm, St Stephen Road, Sticker, Cornwall 01726 71003
TORPOINT ATHLETIC RESERVES . . . . The Mill, Mill Lane, Torpoint, Cornwall 01752 812889
WADEBRIDGE TOWN RESERVES . . . . . . Bodieve Park, Bodieve Road, Wadebridge, Cornwall 01208 812537

Millbrook Reserves are relegated to the Duchy League (but have subsequently disbanded) from which St Stephen are promoted.

EASTERN COUNTIES LEAGUE

	AFC Sudbury	Bury Town	Clacton Town	Dereham	Diss Town	Ely City	Fakenham	Gorleston	Gt Yarmouth	Harwich & P.	Histon Res.	Ipswich Wd.	Lowestoft	Maldon T.	Mildenhall	Newmarket	Norwich Utd	Soham TR	Stowmarket	Tiptree Utd	Wisbech	Woodbridge	Wroxham
AFC Sudbury		1-1	3-0	4-0	0-2	6-0	2-0	4-2	2-1	2-1	1-1	4-0	1-1	2-1	5-0	2-0	2-1	4-0	4-0	2-0	4-1	2-2	1-2
Bury Town	0-2		1-0	2-2	4-1	1-1	1-1	3-3	1-1	2-2	0-2	3-1	1-0	1-2	0-2	2-2	1-0	1-2	0-0	4-0	2-1	2-1	4-1
Clacton Town	1-2	1-0		1-2	2-0	2-2	0-0	2-1	0-3	1-2	2-0	1-0	1-2	0-3	1-1	4-1	0-0	1-3	2-1	2-1	2-3	2-0	0-1
Dereham Town	0-0	1-2	1-2	P	2-0	6-1	0-2	1-1	0-2	1-1	0-2	1-3	4-0	1-5	4-0	2-2	1-4	2-3	1-3	0-3	2-3	3-5	0-5
Diss Town	5-3	1-1	3-1	0-1	R	0-1	3-2	2-0	0-1	3-1	0-3	1-2	2-1	3-1	3-1	0-1	1-1	0-1	1-1	6-1	3-1	3-1	2-3
Ely City	0-3	0-3	1-4	1-2	0-1	E	1-5	0-0	0-4	3-2	3-1	0-2	2-6	1-0	1-5	0-2	0-1	1-2	1-3	2-1	2-3	2-0	1-2
Fakenham Town	1-4	0-2	0-1	0-0	1-4	2-2	M	4-0	2-2	0-0	2-2	2-2	2-1	0-3	2-2	2-0	4-0	1-1	1-2	1-3	1-2	1-1	1-3
Gorleston	0-4	4-2	1-2	1-2	4-1	3-0	0-0	I	1-1	6-3	3-6	7-1	0-6	0-0	3-1	1-1	1-1	1-2	1-3	1-2	6-3	1-1	1-5
Great Yarmouth	1-3	1-0	0-2	2-0	1-3	4-0	0-3	0-2	E	4-1	3-2	1-4	1-1	1-2	2-0	1-0	2-1	1-1	3-3	0-0	1-3	3-0	2-1
Harwich & Parkeston	0-10	0-1	3-1	0-1	0-8	1-0	2-2	4-2	1-1	R	1-5	0-2	2-4	2-1	0-3	1-1	2-0	1-3	0-1	5-1	0-3	3-2	0-6
Histon Res.	2-3	3-1	1-4	0-0	0-4	1-1	0-1	1-1	1-1	2-3		4-3	3-2	2-1	1-2	2-0	4-1	1-3	1-2	1-4	3-1	2-2	2-3
Ipswich Wanderers	2-3	0-1	2-1	1-0	1-2	0-0	1-1	0-1	3-2	2-3	0-1	D	1-0	5-0	3-3	3-0	2-1	1-2	2-1	1-1	4-5	2-3	2-0
Lowestoft Town	0-0	2-0	1-2	8-0	3-2	5-1	2-1	4-3	0-1	4-2	3-1	1-0	I	1-0	5-0	3-3	3-0	0-1	0-4	0-0	3-1	0-0	3-2
Maldon Town	3-3	1-2	1-3	1-4	0-2	5-0	0-2	1-2	0-1	5-0	3-2	2-2	0-1	V	1-1	3-0	0-1	0-0	1-0	3-1	0-2	0-2	0-2
Mildenhall Town	1-4	2-1	1-1	1-2	0-0	2-0	2-0	1-2	1-2	2-4	2-3	2-0	2-2	1-0	I	1-1	1-2	1-3	2-2	1-3	0-2	2-0	0-2
Newmarket Town	2-2	4-1	2-1	1-1	4-3	0-0	1-2	0-0	0-1	2-2	0-1	1-1	1-3	1-0	0-1	S	0-2	0-1	0-0	1-1	1-0	0-1	0-1
Norwich United	0-3	1-0	1-1	1-0	1-1	3-1	0-1	1-1	2-1	2-0	0-0	2-0	0-1	1-0	1-1	2-1	I	2-1	1-1	1-2	3-1	1-0	1-0
Soham Town Rangers	1-1	7-2	4-4	1-2	1-2	2-2	2-0	3-0	3-1	1-0	0-0	2-1	0-1	2-1	1-1	2-1	4-3	O	3-0	1-1	1-2	3-1	1-0
Stowmarket Town	0-1	3-2	0-0	1-0	1-4	2-0	1-0	2-0	0-0	3-1	3-0	1-0	1-2	1-0	0-0	2-2	1-3	0-2	N	2-4	2-0	0-3	
Tiptree United	1-8	2-5	3-1	2-0	5-0	2-1	2-1	3-1	1-1	3-4	1-5	1-1	3-2	1-3	2-1	1-0	1-3	2-1	2-4		4-0	1-2	
Wisbech Town	0-1	3-3	1-1	2-0	1-4	2-2	4-0	3-2	2-0	4-1	5-2	2-0	3-1	3-2	1-3	3-1	3-3	4-4	4-0	1-2		2-2	1-8
Woodbridge Town	0-3	0-5	1-0	2-4	1-6	2-0	0-6	2-1	0-0	2-2	2-0	2-1	1-0	0-1	2-1	2-1	3-1	1-7	2-1	0-1	2-2		1-1
Wroxham	1-1	2-4	2-2	3-0	2-1	6-0	1-1	2-1	4-3	6-0	5-2	9-0	3-2	3-1	0-2	2-6	6-1	2-1	2-2	1-2	1-1	1-2	

Premier Division

	P	W	D	L	F	A	Pts
AFC Sudbury	44	31	10	3	122	37	103
Wroxham	44	29	6	9	121	53	93
Soham Town Rangers	44	25	11	8	91	61	86
Lowestoft Town	44	25	7	12	108	65	82
Diss Town	44	26	3	15	98	62	81
Wisbech Town	44	23	9	12	101	73	78
Stowmarket Town	44	22	9	13	65	56	75
Great Yarmouth Town	44	19	11	14	66	57	68
Bury Town	44	18	11	15	75	66	65
Mildenhall Town -1	44	18	11	15	68	65	64
Clacton Town	44	17	10	17	62	61	61
Tiptree United	44	17	7	20	73	90	58
Histon Res.	44	15	11	18	80	84	56
Fakenham Town	44	13	16	15	61	61	55
Gorleston	44	13	10	21	79	90	49
Norwich United	44	13	10	21	44	63	49
Maldon Town	44	13	8	23	57	63	47
Newmarket Town	44	11	13	20	58	76	46
Dereham Town	44	12	9	23	55	86	45
Woodbridge Town	44	11	12	21	55	96	45
Ipswich Wanderers	44	11	8	25	59	92	41
Harwich & Parkeston	44	10	6	28	58	126	36
Ely City -4	44	5	10	29	38	111	21

WWW.NLNEWSDESK.CO.UK

PREMIER DIVISION CONSTITUTION 2003-04

AFC SUDBURY .... Kingsmarsh Stadium, Brundon Lane, Sudbury, Suffolk 01787 376213
BURY TOWN .... Ram Meadow, Cotton Lane, Bury St Edmonds, Suffolk 01284 754721
CLACTON TOWN .... Rush Green Bowl, Rush Green Road, Clacton-on-Sea, Essex 01255 432590
DEREHAM TOWN .... Aldiss Park, Norwich Road, Dereham, Norfolk .... 01362 690460 / 693677
DISS TOWN .... Brewers Green Lane, Diss, Norfolk 01379 651223
FAKENHAM TOWN .... Clipbush Lane, Fakenham, Norfolk .... 01328 856222 / 855859
GORLESTON .... Emerald Park, Wood Farm Lane, Gorleston, Norfolk 01493 602802
GREAT YARMOUTH TOWN .... Wellesley Road Rec Ground, Sandown Road, Great Yarmouth, Norfolk .... 01493 843373 / 842936
HALSTEAD TOWN .... Rosemary Lane, Halstead, Essex 01787 472082
HISTON RESERVES .... Bridge Road, Impington, Cambridge, Cambridgeshire .... 01223 232301. Fax: 01223 237373
KING'S LYNN RESERVES .... The Walks Stadium, Tennyson Road, King's Lynn, Norfolk 01553 760060
LOWESTOFT TOWN .... Crown Meadow, Love Road, Lowestoft, Suffolk 01502 573818
MALDON TOWN .... Wallace Binder Ground, Park Drive, Maldon, Essex 01621 853762
MILDENHALL TOWN .... Recreation Way, Mildenhall, Bury St Edmonds, Suffolk 01638 713449
NEWMARKET TOWN .... Cricket Field Road, off New Cheveley Road, Newmarket, Suffolk 01638 663637
NORWICH UNITED .... Plantation Park, off Plantation Road, Blofield, Norwich, Norfolk 01603 716963
SOHAM TOWN RANGERS .... Julius Martins Lane, Soham, Ely, Cambridgeshire .... 01353 720732 / 722139
STOWMARKET TOWN .... Greens Meadow, Bury Road, Stowmarket, Suffolk 01449 612533
TIPTREE UNITED .... Chapel Road, Tiptree, near Colchester, Essex 01621 815213
WISBECH TOWN .... Fenland Park, Lerowe Road, Wisbech, Cambridgeshire .... 01945 584176. Fax: 01945 584333
WOODBRIDGE TOWN .... Notcutts Park, Fynn Road, off Seckford Hall Lane, Woodbridge, Suffolk 01394 385308
WROXHAM .... Trafford Park, Skinners Lane, Wroxham, Norfolk 01603 783538

Ipswich Wanderers, Harwich & Parkeston and Ely City drop to Division One replaced by Halstead Town and King's Lynn Reserves.

The Cherry Red Non-League Newsdesk Annual 2003

	CCR	COR	DOW	FEL	GOD	HAD	HAL	HAV	KLR	LEI	LME	MAR	NEE	SOM	STA	SWA	THE	WAR	WHI
Cambridge City Res.		5-0	4-2	0-1	1-0	2-0	4-2	2-0	2-3	3-3	0-2	6-0	5-1	6-1	2-3	3-1	2-0	1-0	1-6
Cornard United	2-2		1-2	2-1	1-2	0-2	1-2	1-3	1-1	4-1	0-2	1-2	2-0	2-1	1-7	0-3	3-1	0-0	2-1
Downham Town	0-1	0-3		0-0	1-2	0-1	1-2	2-1	2-5	1-1	0-1	2-2	1-4	1-2	1-1	1-1	1-0	2-3	0-1
Felixstowe & Walton Utd	2-3	1-2	5-2	D	1-1	1-5	0-1	1-2	2-3	1-3	6-0	1-1	1-2	2-1	0-2	4-1	2-1		0-3
Godmanchester Rovers	0-0	2-0	3-1	3-0	I	1-1	5-0	0-4	0-1	1-2	0-2	1-1	1-1	1-2	0-0	0-3	2-4	3-0	0-0
Hadleigh United	1-0	2-1	3-2	2-2	3-0	V	1-1	5-1	0-2	0-0	0-3	4-3	2-1	3-1	0-0	2-0	2-1	6-0	1-4
Halstead Town	1-0	1-0	8-2	3-0	0-0	0-0	I	0-1	1-2	1-0	1-1	3-1	4-3	1-0	2-0	3-0	7-1	2-1	
Haverhill Rovers	2-1	3-1	3-1	4-0	2-2	0-1	1-2	S	1-1	0-1	1-4	1-1	4-1	1-1	1-0	5-3	1-1	9-0	0-2
King's Lynn Res.	3-1	5-1	8-0	2-1	4-4	2-0	1-0	4-1	I	3-2	6-4	5-1	4-1	6-2	1-3	3-1	4-1	9-1	1-2
Leiston	1-2	1-0	2-0	2-0	3-2	0-1	1-0	1-2	4-2	O	1-2	1-0	1-3	5-1	2-2	6-2	4-1	10-1	1-0
Long Melford	0-0	2-1	0-1	1-2	3-1	0-0	0-0	2-1	2-1	1-1	N	2-2	3-1	2-2	6-2	4-1	0-1	2-0	2-3
March Town United	2-2	1-3	3-0	4-1	1-1	1-5	2-8	0-2	0-4	0-0	0-2		2-2	3-1	2-2	1-3	1-0	2-3	2-3
Needham Market	1-1	1-2	5-2	3-2	1-1	1-0	1-2	2-3	1-0	5-0	3-0	0-1		2-4	3-4	1-4	4-0	1-1	5-1
Somersham Town	1-0	3-0	5-1	0-1	2-1	1-3	2-3	5-2	2-3	1-4	1-6	3-2	1-2		0-6	0-2	0-3	3-1	1-4
Stanway Rovers	3-2	4-0	2-0	6-2	3-3	2-0	0-4	0-0	1-2	3-1	1-0	1-1	3-1	1-1	O	3-1	3-0	6-0	1-4
Swaffham Town	0-0	3-2	2-1	2-2	0-2	2-1	0-1	2-1	2-1	4-2	1-3	3-0	0-2	3-1	1-0	N	4-1	5-1	1-4
Thetford Town	1-0	1-2	1-0	2-1	0-1	2-3	1-2	2-1	0-1	0-3	1-1	1-3	1-3	0-4	0-1	1-0	E	4-0	1-4
Warboys Town	0-1	0-0	0-1	0-1	0-5	1-3	0-1	1-2	1-7	0-2	0-2	0-3	0-3	0-0	0-1	0-4	2-3		0-4
Whitton United	4-1	2-2	2-0	2-2	2-1	3-3	2-2	3-4	4-1	5-2	2-2	4-2	2-2	1-0	4-1	6-0	5-1	4-0	

Division One

	P	W	D	L	F	A	Pts
Halstead Town	36	24	7	5	76	37	79
King's Lynn Res.	36	24	4	8	108	56	76
Whitton United	36	21	8	7	93	44	71
Hadleigh United	36	20	9	7	65	40	69
Stanway Rovers	36	19	10	7	78	39	67
Long Melford	36	18	10	8	69	38	64
Leiston	36	18	9	9	76	51	63
Swaffham Town	36	18	3	15	62	62	57
Cambridge City Res.	36	16	7	13	66	49	55
Haverhill Rovers	36	16	6	14	67	55	54
Needham Market	36	15	8	13	71	59	53
Godmanchester Rovers	36	10	13	13	53	53	43
Cornard United	36	11	5	20	44	70	38
Somersham Town	36	11	5	20	59	87	38
March Town United	36	9	10	17	54	85	37
Felixstowe & Walton Utd	36	10	6	20	51	71	36
Thetford Town	36	9	5	22	38	74	32
Downham Town	36	4	6	26	33	88	18
Warboys Town	36	2	3	31	18	123	9

DIVISION ONE CONSTITUTION 2003-04

CAMBRIDGE CITY RESERVES........City Ground, Milton Road, Cambridge, Cambridgeshire........01223 357973. Fax: 01223 351582
CORNARD UNITED.............Blackhouse Lane Sports Ground, Great Cornard, Sudbury, Suffolk.....................01787 376719
DOWNHAM TOWN....................Memorial Field, Lynn Road, Downham Market, Norfolk.....................01366 388424
ELY CITY...........The Unwin Ground, Downham Road, Ely, Cambridgeshire........01353 662035
FELIXSTOWE & WALTON UNITED.....Town Ground, Dellwood Avenue, Felixstowe, Suffolk........01394 282917
GODMANCHESTER ROVERS.....Judiths Field, London Road, Godmanchester, Cambridgeshire.........01473 822165
HADLEIGH UNITED........Millfield, Tinkers Lane, off Duke Street, Hadleigh, Suffolk.....................None
HARWICH & PARKESTON.........Royal Oak, Main Road, Dovercourt, Harwich, Essex.....................01255 503649
HAVERHILL ROVERS........Hamlet Croft, Haverhill, Suffolk.....................01440 702137
IPSWICH WANDERERS.........Humberdoucy Sports Centre, Humberdoucy Lane, Ipswich, Suffolk....01473 728581. Fax: 01473 414390
KIRKLEY....................Kirkley Recreation Ground, Walmer Road, Lowestoft, Suffolk....01502 513549
LEISTON...................LTAA, Victory Road, Leiston, Suffolk.....................01728 830308
LONG MELFORD.........Stoneylands, New Road, Long Melford, Suffolk.....................01787 312187
MARCH TOWN UNITED.......GER Sports Ground, Robin Goodfellows Lane, March, Cambridgeshire.....................01354 653073
NEEDHAM MARKET........Bloomfields, Quinton Road, Needham Market, Suffolk.....................01449 721000
SOMERSHAM TOWN.....West End Ground, St Ives Road, Somersham, Huntingdon, Cambridgeshire.....................01487 843384
STANWAY ROVERS.....Hawthorns, New Farm Road, Stanway, Colchester, Essex.....................01206 578187
SWAFFHAM TOWN.....Shoemakers Lane, off Cley Road, Swaffham, Norfolk.....................01760 722700
THETFORD TOWN.....Recreation Ground, Mundford Road, Thetford, Norfolk.....................01842 766120
WARBOYS TOWN.....Sports Field, Forge Way off High Street, Warboys, Huntingdon.....................01487 823483
WHITTON UNITED.....King George V Playing Fields, Old Norwich Road, Ipswich, Suffolk.....................01473 464030

Halstead Town and King's Lynn Reserves are promoted to the Premier Division replaced by Ipswich Wanderers, Harwich & Parkeston and Ely City. Brightlingsea United withdrew without kicking a ball. Kirkley are promoted from the Anglian Combination.

LEAGUE CUP

PRELIMINARY ROUND
AFC Sudbury 4 Needham Market 1
Brightlingsea United (scr.) **Mildenhall Town** (w/o)
Cornard United 2 Harwich & Parkeston 1
Fakenham Town 4 Wisbech Town 2
Histon Res. 4 Cambridge City Res. 0
Ipswich Wanderers 0 **Soham Town Rangers** 2
Lowestoft Town 5 Godmanchester Rovers 1
Swaffham Town 3 Downham Town 2
Thetford Town 0 **Diss Town** 2
Whitton United 1 Tiptree United 0
Wroxham 5 Gorleston 0
FIRST ROUND
AFC Sudbury 4 Woodbridge Town 2
Clacton Town 5 Stanway Rovers 1
Diss Town 3 Mildenhall Town 3 *aet*
Mildenhall Town 0 **Diss Town** 5 *replay*
Fakenham Town 1 **Norwich United** 2
Felixstowe & Walton United 0 **Wroxham** 3
Halstead Town 2 **Cornard United** 4 *aet*
Histon Res. 7 Warboys Town 0
Lowestoft Town 4 Bury Town 1
Maldon Town 6 King's Lynn Res. 2
March Town United 2 Haverhill Rovers 1
Newmarket Town 1 Great Yarmouth Town 0
Soham Town Rangers 5 Dereham Town 3
Somersham Town 8 Leiston 3
Stowmarket 3 **Ely City** 1 *(Stowmarket expelled)*
Swaffham Town 1 **Hadleigh United** 3
Whitton United 4 Long Melford 0

SECOND ROUND
AFC Sudbury 0 **Clacton Town** 1
Hadleigh United 2 **Somersham Town** 3
Lowestoft Town 3 Diss Town 2
Maldon Town 3 Histon Res. 2
Newmarket Town 5 Cornard United 0
Norwich United 2 March Town United 0
Whitton United 2 Soham Town Rangers 1
Wroxham (w/o) Ely City (scr.)

QUARTER-FINALS
Clacton Town 2 Maldon Town 0
Norwich United 2 Lowestoft Town 1
Somersham Town 0 **Wroxham** 2
Whitton United 0 **Newmarket Town** 3

SEMI-FINALS
Norwich United 0 **Clacton Town** 1
Wroxham 3 Newmarket Town 1

FINAL
(16th March at Diss Town)
Clacton Town 1 **Wroxham** 2

DIVISION ONE TROPHY
(All ties prior to the Final played over two legs)

PRELIMINARY ROUND
Hadleigh United 4 Needham Market 0,
Needham Market 2 **Hadleigh United** 1
Long Melford 5 Cornard United 3,
Cornard United 2 **Long Melford** 2
March Town United 1 Downham Town 1,
Downham Town 2 **March Town United** 4
Thetford Town 2 Godmanchester Rovers 1,
Godmanchester Rovers 6 Thetford Town 1
FIRST ROUND
Cambridge City Res. 0 King's Lynn Res. 3,
King's Lynn Res. 1 Cambridge City Res. 2
Felixstowe & Walton United 2 Whitton United 5,
Whitton United 1 Felixstowe & Walton Utd 0
Hadleigh United 0 Stanway Rovers 5,
Stanway Rovers 0 Hadleigh United 2
Halstead Town (w/o) Brightlingsea United (scr.)
Leiston 0 Long Melford 0,
Long Melford 6 Leiston 1
March Town United 5 Warboys Town 1,
Warboys Town 1 **March Town United** 4
Somersham Town 0 Haverhill Rovers 0,

Haverhill Rovers 2 **Somersham Town** 3
Swaffham Town 0 Godmanchester Rovers 2,
Godmanchester Rovers 0 Swaffham Town 1
QUARTER-FINALS
Godmanchester Rovers 0 Stanway Rovers 0,
Stanway Rovers 3 Godmanchester Rovers 2
Halstead Town 1 King's Lynn Res. 2,
King's Lynn Res. 0 **Halstead Town** 2
Long Melford 1 Somersham Town 1,
Somersham Town 3 **Long Melford** 3
(Long Melford won on away goals)
Whitton United 5 March Town United 0,
March Town United (scr.) **Whitton United** (w/o)
SEMI-FINALS
Halstead Town 1 Long Melford 0,
Long Melford 0 **Halstead Town** 2
Whitton United 2 Stanway Rovers 2,
Stanway Rovers 2 **Whitton United** 3
FINAL
(5th May at Hadleigh United)
Whitton United 1 **Halstead Town** 2 *aet*

MILLENNIUM CUP
(Teams eliminated in Preliminary and First Round of League Cup)

PRELIMINARY ROUND
Downham Town 3 Dereham Town 3 *aet*
Dereham Town 4 Downham 0 *replay*
Godmanchester 2 King's Lynn Res. 0
Gorleston 3 **Fakenham Town** 5 *aet*
Halstead Town 0 **Tiptree United** 4
Ipswich Wdrs 0 **Woodbridge Town** 1
Long Melford 2 **Leiston** 4 *aet*
Mildenhall 3 Cambridge City Res. 0
Needham Market 1 **Harwich & Park.** 3
Warboys Town 0 **Swaffham Town** 1

FIRST ROUND
Bury Town 3 Felixstowe & Walton 1
Fakenham Town 6 Dereham Town 2
Godmanchester 1 Swaffham 1 *aet*
Swaffham 3 Godmanchester 0 *replay*
Great Yarmouth Town 3 Wisbech 1
Harwich & Parkeston 3 Tiptree Utd 3 *aet*
Tiptree 3 **Harwich & P.** 4 *replay aet*
Mildenhall Town 3 Leiston 0
Thetford Town 0 **Haverhill Rovers** 4
Woodbridge Town 0 **Stanway Rovers** 2

QUARTER-FINALS
Bury Town 0 **Haverhill Rovers** 1
Great Yarmouth 3 Swaffham 1 *aet*
Harwich & Parkeston 8 Fakenham 2
Mildenhall Town 2 Stanway Rovers 0
SEMI-FINALS
Harwich & Parkeston 8 Haverhill 2
Mildenhall 1 **Great Yarmouth Town** 2
FINAL
(8th May at Woodbridge Town)
Gt Yarmouth 4 Harwich & Parkeston 2

ESSEX & SUFFOLK BORDER LEAGUE

	AFC Sudbury Res.	Clacton Town Res.	Earls Colne	Felixstowe & Walton Res.	Gas Recreation	Harwich & Parkeston Res.	Kelvedon Social	Little Oakley	Mistley United	Rowhedge	St Johns (Clacton)	St Osyth	Stanway Rovers Res.	Stowmarket Town Res.	Weeley Athletic	West Bergholt
AFC Sudbury Res.	P	1-0	3-1	2-0	2-1	3-0	0-1	3-1	1-2	4-3	3-1	0-0	1-0	1-0	3-2	1-1
Clacton Town Res.	1-7	R	2-2	4-1	1-3	1-2	2-1	2-0	3-2	2-5	5-3	1-1	0-2	3-4	3-3	0-2
Earls Colne	2-4	2-3	E	6-0	0-2	4-3	3-1	4-3	2-3	2-2	6-0	9-0	1-2	1-3	2-2	0-3
Felixstowe & Walton Res.	2-0	1-0	0-3	M	1-3	1-6	1-2	0-4	0-1	1-2	1-4	1-2	0-3	1-1	2-2	0-3
Gas Recreation	2-2	3-0	3-2	3-1	I	8-5	4-2	5-0	3-1	1-1	1-2	2-1	2-3	2-0	2-3	1-2
Harwich & Parkeston Res.	3-6	3-2	3-1	5-1	3-2	E	1-1	2-2	0-6	3-1	11-0	3-2	1-2	0-3	2-0	2-5
Kelvedon Social	4-4	1-1	3-0	0-2	0-2	3-1	R	2-0	1-1	1-2	1-1	4-1	1-2	0-3	2-0	2-5
Little Oakley	2-6	0-1	2-1	3-0	0-3	1-2	3-0		2-1	0-3	1-1	0-1	1-1	4-1	1-2	1-3
Mistley United	1-4	3-2	0-1	3-0	0-3	1-2	0-6	2-0	D	2-2	2-0	2-0	1-1	0-4	1-4	0-5
Rowhedge	3-0	3-1	3-1	4-1	4-0	4-0	4-3	1-3	2-1	I	5-1	4-1	1-1	1-0	2-1	3-2
St Johns (Clacton)	1-1	2-3	2-4	2-1	2-9	1-3	L-W	1-0	3-6	3-2	V	1-4	3-3	2-4	1-5	0-3
St Osyth	0-7	4-2	0-1	3-2	1-0	1-1	1-2	1-0	1-3	1-1	5-1	I	2-3	0-0	2-1	0-11
Stanway Rovers Res.	2-0	6-1	2-0	5-0	0-3	3-1	0-3	3-1	1-0	4-1	2-1	7-0	S	1-4	1-0	4-1
Stowmarket Town Res.	1-1	3-2	3-2	5-1	3-0	4-1	2-0	4-0	4-0	2-3	6-0	2-0	2-2	I	3-1	1-3
Weeley Athletic	2-3	4-0	2-1	4-2	1-0	2-2	2-3	1-2	3-1	1-2	2-2	2-1	3-2	2-2	O	2-3
West Bergholt	3-1	2-1	1-2	7-1	2-2	3-4	2-0	4-2	2-1	0-2	7-0	5-1	6-0	2-2	2-3	N

Premier Division

	P	W	D	L	F	A	Pts
Rowhedge	30	22	4	4	81	43	70
West Bergholt	30	22	3	5	101	34	69
Stowmarket Town Res.	30	19	5	6	74	32	62
Stanway Rovers Res.	30	19	5	6	67	38	62
AFC Sudbury Res.	30	18	6	6	74	42	60
Gas Recreation	30	17	3	10	74	46	54
Harwich & Park. Res.	30	14	5	11	82	69	47
Weeley Athletic	30	11	7	12	61	57	40
Earls Colne	30	11	3	16	66	60	36
Mistley United	30	10	5	15	40	60	35
Kelvedon Social	30	9	6	15	38	53	33
St Osyth	30	8	5	17	32	78	29
Little Oakley	30	8	4	18	35	57	28
Clacton Town Res.	30	8	4	18	49	76	28
St Johns (Clacton)	30	5	6	19	41	102	21
Felixstowe & WU Res.	30	3	1	26	24	92	10

LEAGUE CUP

PRELIMINARY ROUND

Brightlingsea United 0 **Lawford Lads** 4
Clacton Town Res. 3 **Cornard United Res.** 4
Foxash Social 3 **Woodbridge Town Res.** 4
Glemsford & Cavendish United 0 **Mersea Island** 3
Great Bentley 2 Coggeshall Town 0
Halstead Town Res. 3 Felixstowe & Walton Utd Res. 1
Harwich & Parkeston Res. 0 **Weeley Athletic** 5
Hedlinghams United 1 **Boxted Lodgers** 3
Ipswich Wanderers Res. 1 **Gas Recreation** 2
Little Oakley 4 Long Melford Res. 1
Mistley United 3 Bury Town Res. 1
Needham Market Res. 2 **Hadleigh United Res.** 3
Stowmarket Town Res. 1 **Stanway Rovers Res.** 3
Sudbury Athletic 2 St Johns (Clacton) 0
West Bergholt 1 **Alresford Colne Rangers** 3

FIRST ROUND

AFC Sudbury Res. 3 Boxted Lodgers 1
Alresford Colne Rangers 3 Lawford Lads 3 *aet* (4-1p)
Cornard United Res. 2 **Stanway Rovers Res.** 4
Dedham Old Boys 2 Tiptree Heath 0
Earls Colne 5 Birch United 0
Gas Recreation 4 Halstead Town Res. 0
Hadleigh United Res. 4 Woodbridge Town Res. 2
Haverhill Rovers Res. 8 Bures United 1
Kelvedon Social 4 Whitton United Res. 3

PREMIER DIVISION CONSTITUTION 2003-04

AFC SUDBURY RESERVES . . . . Kingsmarsh Stadium, Brundon Lane, Sudbury, Suffolk 01787 376213
ALRESFORD COLNE RANGERS . . . . Ford Lane, Alresford, Essex 07796 036467
CLACTON TOWN RESERVES . . . . Rush Green Bowl, Rush Green Road, Clacton-on-Sea, Essex 01255 432590
EARLS COLNE . . . . Green Farm Meadow, Halstead Road, Earls Colne, Essex 01787 223584
GAS RECREATION . . . . Bromley Road, Colchester, Essex 01206 860383
HARWICH & PARKESTON RESERVES . . Royal Oak, Main Road, Dovercourt, Harwich, Essex 01206 503649
KELVEDON SOCIAL . . . . The Chase, High Street, Kelvedon, Essex 01255 503649
LITTLE OAKLEY . . . . War Memorial Club Ground, Little Oakley, Essex 01255 880370
MISTLEY UNITED . . . . Parish Recreation Ground, Shrubland Road, Mistley, Essex 01206 393350
ROWHEDGE . . . . Rectory Road, Rowhedge, Essex 01206 728022
ST OSYTH . . . . Cowley Park, Mill Street, St Osyth, Clacton-on-Sea, Essex . . . . None
STANWAY ROVERS RESERVES . . . . . . Hawthorns, New Farm Road, Stanway, Colchester, Essex . . . . None
STOWMARKET TOWN RESERVES . . . . Greens Meadow, Bury Road, Stowmarket, Suffolk 01206 578187
SUDBURY ATHLETIC . . . . Lucas Social Club, Alexandra Road, Sudbury, Suffolk 01449 612533
WEELEY ATHLETIC . . . . Weeley Playing Fields, Clacton Road, Weeley, Clacton-on-Sea, Essex 01787 881143
WEST BERGHOLT . . . . Lorkin Daniel Field, Lexden Road, West Bergholt, Colchester, Essex 01206 241525

St Johns (Clacton) and Felixstowe & Walton United Reserves drop to Division One replaced by Alresford Colne Rangers and Sudbury Athletic.

	Alresford Colne Rangers	Boxted Lodgers	Coggeshall Town	Dedham Old Boys	Hadleigh United Res.	Haverhill Rovers Res.	Ipswich Wanderers Res.	Lawford Lads	Needham Market Res.	Sudbury Athletic	Tiptree Heath	Tiptree United Res.	Walton Town	Whitton United Res.	Wivenhoe & University Town	Woodbridge Town Res.
Alresford Colne Rangers		2-1	0-3	0-1	2-2	6-1	6-2	4-0	6-1	5-1	4-2	3-1	0-0	2-2	2-0	4-2
Boxted Lodgers	1-2		0-4	2-2	1-6	2-2	3-1	2-1	2-1	0-5	0-2	2-3	0-4	3-3	2-3	0-3
Coggeshall Town	1-4	4-1	D	3-2	1-0	5-2	W-L	1-2	0-0	3-1	0-2	1-1	4-2	4-3	5-1	
Dedham Old Boys	0-2	3-0	2-4	I	0-1	3-5	2-2	0-0	1-0	3-3	2-2	0-4	1-1	4-2	2-0	2-1
Hadleigh United Res.	1-2	3-0	2-1	1-0	V	5-1	4-1	2-0	2-2	3-2	3-0	1-2	2-0	0-1	1-1	2-2
Haverhill Rovers Res.	1-2	2-0	1-1	2-0	1-0	I	8-0	2-3	1-3	0-3	0-2	0-3	2-0	0-0	1-2	6-1
Ipswich Wanderers Res.	1-4	1-1	1-4	L-W	3-3	2-2	S	1-1	0-3	1-5	0-2	2-6	1-0	0-6	1-6	2-1
Lawford Lads	0-3	2-0	0-0	0-0	0-0	2-2	1-2	I	4-1	2-0	1-0	1-1	5-0	4-0	0-5	2-1
Needham Market Res.	3-2	1-1	2-0	1-0	0-5	1-1	3-0	0-0	O	4-1	1-2	3-1	1-1	2-1	2-2	2-4
Sudbury Athletic	1-3	0-1	6-1	1-0	3-1	1-0	4-1	6-1	4-2	N	3-1	3-1	2-2	W-L	5-1	5-0
Tiptree Heath	1-0	0-1	0-1	1-0	5-1	1-1	3-0	1-0	1-5	1-2		4-2	0-2	0-1	0-1	2-4
Tiptree United Res.	1-1	4-1	3-0	3-0	0-0	0-0	W-L	3-1	4-1	1-3	1-0	O	1-0	2-3	1-0	6-0
Walton Town	0-3	2-1	1-0	1-1	4-0	1-1	2-1	4-2	2-0	0-1	2-4	2-0	N	0-4	2-1	6-0
Whitton United Res.	1-1	L-W	3-1	0-1	1-0	0-4	4-3	2-1	4-2	6-0	4-0	1-0	0-4	E	1-2	9-1
Wivenhoe & University Town	1-3	3-0	0-2	0-2	3-1	1-2	4-1	3-1	6-0	0-2	0-1	0-1	3-3	6-0		2-1
Woodbridge Town Res.	0-3	1-2	0-3	1-3	1-0	2-2	1-1	2-2	1-0	0-4	1-2	1-2	2-0	3-1	3-4	

Little Oakley 0 **Mistley United** 0 *aet* (3-4p)
Mersea Island 3 Weeley Athletic 2
Rowhedge 3 Hatfield Peverel 1
St Osyth 3 Bradfield Rovers 1
Sudbury Athletic 2 Great Bentley 0
Walton Town 0 **Tiptree United Res.** 2
Wivenhoe & University Town 3 Severalls Athletic 0

SECOND ROUND
AFC Sudbury Res. 3 **Sudbury Athletic** 5
Alresford Colne Rangers 3 Hadleigh United Res. 0
Dedham Old Boys 0 **Kelvedon Social** 1
Earls Colne 2 St Osyth 1
Gas Recreation 8 Mersea Island 2
Rowhedge 2 Haverhill Rovers Res. 1
Stanway Rovers Res. 2 **Mistley United** 0
Tiptree United Res. 2 **Wivenhoe & University Town** 3

QUARTER-FINALS
Gas Recreation 3 Stanway Rovers Res. 1
Rowhedge 5 Earls Colne 1
Sudbury Athletic 1 **Alresford Colne Rangers** 2
Wivenhoe & University Town 3 Kelvedon Social 1

SEMI-FINALS
Gas Recreation 0 **Rowhedge** 1
Wivenhoe & University Town 1 **Alresford Colne Rgrs** 2

FINAL *(30th April at AFC Sudbury)*
Alresford Colne Rangers 2 Rowhedge 0

Division One

		P	W	D	L	F	A	Pts
Alresford Colne Rangers		30	21	5	4	81	32	68
Sudbury Athletic		30	20	2	8	76	45	62
Tiptree United Res.		30	19	4	7	58	31	61
Walton Town	+3	30	14	9	7	53	32	54
Coggeshall Town		30	17	3	10	59	45	54
Hadleigh United Res.	+2	30	12	8	10	53	42	46
Dedham Old Boys	+2	30	11	8	11	39	41	43
Wivenhoe & Univ. Town	-4	30	14	3	13	63	47	41
Haverhill Rovers Res.		30	10	10	10	58	51	40
Whitton United Res.	-3	30	12	5	13	58	53	38
Tiptree Heath	-3	30	12	2	16	37	46	35
Lawford Lads	+3	30	7	10	13	34	48	34
Needham Market Res.		30	9	6	15	46	63	33
Woodbridge Town Res.	+5	30	7	4	19	41	82	30
Boxted Lodgers		30	7	5	18	58	70	26
Ipswich Wdrs Res.	+1 -3	30	3	6	21	31	89	13

WWW.NLNEWSDESK.CO.UK

DIVISION ONE CONSTITUTION 2003-04

BURY TOWN RESERVES .... Ram Meadow, Cotton Lane, Bury St Edmonds, Suffolk 01284 754721
COGGESHALL TOWN .... The Crops, West Street, Coggeshall, Essex 01376 562843
DEDHAM OLD BOYS .... The Old Grammar School, Dedham, Essex 01206 322302
FELIXSTOWE & WALTON UTD RESERVES . Town Ground, Dellwood Avenue, Felixstowe 01394 282917
HADLEIGH UNITED RESERVES ...... Millfield, Tinkers Lane, off Duke Street, Hadleigh, Suffolk 01473 822165
HAVERHILL ROVERS RESERVES .... Hamlet Croft, Haverhill, Suffolk 01440 702137
LAWFORD LADS .... School Lane, Lawford, Manningtree, Essex 01787 312187
LONG MELFORD RESERVES .... Stoneylands, New Road, Long Melford, Suffolk 01449 721000
NEEDHAM MARKET RESERVES .... Bloomfields, Quinton Road, Needham Market, Suffolk 01255 814874
ST JOHNS (CLACTON) .... Eastcliff Sports Ground, Dulwich Road, Holland-on-Sea, Clacton, Essex . 07889 463004
TIPTREE HEATH .... Colchester Road, Tiptree, Essex 01621 815213
TIPTREE UNITED RESERVES .... Chapel Road, Tiptree, near Colchester, Essex .... None
WALTON TOWN .... Frinton Playing Fields, Jubilee Road, Frinton-on-Sea, Essex 01473 464030
WHITTON UNITED RESERVES ... King George V Playing Fields, Old Norwich Road, Ipswich, Suffolk 01206 825380
WIVENHOE & UNIVERSITY TOWN .... Broad Lane Ground, Elmstead Road, Wivenhoe, Essex 01394 385308
WOODBRIDGE TOWN RESERVES .. Notcutts Park, Fynn Road, off Seckford Hall Lane, Woodbridge, Suffolk ....

St Johns (Clacton) and Felixstowe & Walton United Reserves drop from the Premier Division to replace promoted Alresford Colne Rangers and Sudbury Athletic. Boxted Lodgers and Ipswich Wanderers Reserves slip to Division Two replaced by Bury Town Reserves and Long Melford Reserves.

	Alresford Colne Rg. Res.	Birch United	Brightlingsea United	Bures United	Bury Town Res.	Gas Recreation Res.	Great Bentley	Halstead Town Res.	Hatfield Peverel	Long Melford Res.	Mersea Island	Mistley United Res.	Rowhedge Res.	Severalls Athletic	Weeley Athletic Res.	West Bergholt Res.
Alresford Colne Rgrs Res.		3-1	2-2	2-0	0-4	1-2	0-3	0-2	1-3	1-2	1-3	2-1	1-3	5-1	3-1	0-2
Birch United	1-1		0-2	2-3	1-9	2-1	0-1	3-3	1-5	1-3	1-4	4-1	3-2	1-4	1-2	1-3
Brightlingsea United	1-2	1-1	D	1-2	0-3	4-4	2-2	1-4	0-2	0-3	2-3	1-4	2-1	0-1	0-1	2-1
Bures United	5-2	3-0	3-1	I	0-7	3-0	2-2	1-4	0-0	0-3	1-2	1-0	1-1	1-2	2-1	7-0
Bury Town Res.	9-2	6-2	4-4	1-2	V	4-0	4-0	4-3	4-0	6-0	6-0	4-1	W-L	3-4	W-L	2-2
Gas Recreation Res.	2-3	4-0	3-3	2-1	1-5	I	1-3	1-4	2-2	1-3	2-3	3-1	2-0	1-1	1-4	1-6
Great Bentley	4-1	4-1	1-0	1-1	2-4	3-2	S	3-1	1-0	0-1	1-1	7-1	5-1	1-1	3-0	2-0
Halstead Town Res.	5-1	1-1	5-3	1-4	1-1	5-1	1-0	I	2-2	1-2	0-0	5-1	2-0	3-1	1-1	8-2
Hatfield Peverel	4-2	4-0	3-2	1-3	1-0	4-0	1-0	3-0	O	2-2	1-2	0-0	5-1	2-0	3-1	1-4
Long Melford Res.	3-3	6-3	3-2	1-0	1-1	0-1	1-1	1-2	5-1	N	1-1	2-1	1-3	2-1	3-1	1-4
Mersea Island	4-1	9-2	3-0	3-0	0-1	4-0	1-0	1-0	2-2	1-1		5-3	1-0	2-0	8-3	3-3
Mistley United Res.	1-0	5-1	2-2	2-4	3-6	1-1	0-2	3-2	2-0	0-4	0-0	T	2-1	1-1	3-0	2-3
Rowhedge Res.	1-2	2-0	0-6	0-5	1-5	2-1	1-1	1-3	2-3	1-2	0-0	4-0	W	4-0	1-4	2-1
Severalls Athletic	1-0	1-1	3-3	1-1	0-0	3-4	2-0	3-1	1-0	1-1	3-2	4-1	1-3	O	1-1	2-0
Weeley Athletic Res.	3-5	3-0	4-3	2-5	1-4	2-2	1-3	W-L	0-1	0-3	1-3	2-1	2-3	1-4		0-1
West Bergholt Res.	2-2	1-2	2-3	1-1	0-2	1-1	1-2	3-2	1-5	0-2	0-2	6-2	3-0	1-5	2-2	

Division Two

Team	Adj	P	W	D	L	F	A	Pts
Bury Town Res.	-3	30	22	5	3	109	32	68
Long Melford Res.	+3	30	19	6	5	62	37	66
Mersea Island	+3	30	18	8	4	72	38	65
Hatfield Peverel		30	16	7	7	59	38	55
Severalls Athletic		30	15	10	5	60	40	55
Great Bentley	-3	30	17	6	7	59	33	54
Bures United	+3	30	15	6	9	62	46	54
Halstead Town Res.	+3 -3	30	14	6	10	72	48	48
West Bergholt Res.		30	9	6	15	54	69	33
Alresford Colne R. Res.		30	9	4	17	49	76	31
Weeley Athletic Res.		30	8	4	18	43	70	28
Gas Recreation Res.	-3	30	7	7	16	46	76	25
Rowhedge Res.		30	7	4	19	36	66	25
Mistley United Res.		30	7	4	19	45	80	25
Brightlingsea United		30	5	8	17	53	72	23
Birch United		30	4	5	21	37	97	17

TOMMY THOMPSON CUP

FIRST ROUND
Birch United 5 Dedham Old Boys Res. 1
Bradfield Rovers 3 Hedinghams United 1
Coggeshall Town Res. 3 **Boxted Lodgers Res.** 4
Cornard Utd Res. 1 **Alresford Colne Rgrs Res.** 4
Foxash Social 2 Sudbury Athletic Res. 1
Glemsford & Cavendish Utd 2 **Earls Colne Res.** 4
Hatfield Peverel 2 Severalls Athletic 0
Kelvedon Social Res. 1 St Osyth Res. 0
Long Melford Res. 4 Bures United 1
Mersea Island 4 Great Bentley 1
Mistley United Res. 2 **Little Oakley Res.** 3
Rowhedge Res. 1 Brightlingsea United 0
St Johns (Clacton) Res. 6 Lawford Lads Res. 5
Weeley Athletic Res. 2 Halstead Town Res. 0
West Bergholt Res. 2 **Bury Town Res.** 6

SECOND ROUND
Alresford Colne Rgrs Res. 1 Bury Town Res. 0
Birch United 2 **Bradfield Rovers** 3
Boxted Lodgers Res. 3 **Kelvedon Social Res.** 4
Earls Colne Res. 2 **Gas Recreation Res.** 3

DIVISION TWO CONSTITUTION 2003-04

ALRESFORD COLNE RANGERS RESERVES........ Ford Lane, Alresford, Essex 07796 036467
BOXTED LODGERS .... The Playing Field, Cage Lane, Boxted, Colchester, Essex 01206 271969
BRADFIELD ROVERS .... The Playing Field, The Street, Bradfield, Essex.................................. None
BURES UNITED .... Recreation Ground, Nayland Road, Bures, Suffolk .... None
GAS RECREATION RESERVES.................... Bromley Road, Colchester, Essex 01206 860383
GREAT BENTLEY........................... The Green, Great Bentley, Essex 01206 251532
HALSTEAD TOWN RESERVES .... Rosemary Lane, Halstead, Essex.................................. 01787 472082
HATFIELD PEVEREL .... Strutt Memorial Field, Maldon Road, Hatfield Peverel, Essex .... None
IPSWICH WANDERERS RESERVES . Humberdoucy Sports Centre, Humberdoucy Lane, Ipswich, Suffolk 01473 728581. Fax: 01473 414390
KELVEDON SOCIAL RESERVES .... The Chase, High Street, Kelvedon, Essex................................ 01376 572240
MERSEA ISLAND .... The Glebe, Colchester Road, West Mersea, Essex 01206 385216
MISTLEY UNITED RESERVES .... Parish Recreation Ground, Shrubland Road, Mistley, Essex 01206 393350
ROWHEDGE RESERVES................... Rectory Road, Rowhedge, Essex.................................. 01206 728022
SEVERALLS ATHLETIC................ Mile End Rec Ground, Ford Lane, Colchester, Essex 01206 854712
WEELEY ATHLETIC RESERVES. Weeley Playing Fields, Clacton Road, Weeley, Clacton-on-Sea, Essex .... None
WEST BERGHOLT RESERVES ...... Lorkin Daniel Field, Lexden Road, West Bergholt, Colchester, Essex 01206 241525

Bury Town Reserves and Long Melford Reserves are promoted to Division One replaced by Boxted Lodgers and Ipswich Wanderers Reserves.
Brightlingsea United and Birch United drop to Division Three replaced by Bradfield Rovers and Kelvedon Social Reserves.

	Boxted Lodgers Res.	Bradfield Rovers	Coggeshall Town Res.	Cornard United Res.	Dedham Old Boys Res.	Earls Colne Res.	Foxash Social	Glemsford & Cav. Utd	Hedinghams United	Kelvedon Social Res.	Lawford Lads Res.	Little Oakley Res.	Mersea Island Res.	St Johns (Clacton) Res.	St Osyth Res.	Sudbury Athletic Res.
Boxted Lodgers Res.		0-2	3-1	6-0	1-1	2-4	1-3	2-0	1-2	1-3	0-6	3-0	1-4	1-8	3-1	2-1
Bradfield Rovers	3-1	D	3-1	3-3	3-0	2-0	2-0	2-2	4-0	0-5	5-1	5-0	5-1	5-2	1-0	3-3
Coggeshall Town Res.	2-1	1-1	I	5-1	2-2	0-0	5-0	2-2	0-1	4-1	1-4	0-4	1-5	2-2	2-1	2-1
Cornard United Res.	1-0	3-2	1-0	V	6-1	3-3	3-2	2-5	2-2	6-2	6-0	1-3	2-3	2-2	0-1	3-1
Dedham Old Boys Res.	2-1	3-3	6-0	7-3	I	1-2	5-0	1-8	4-2	2-6	2-1	2-2	7-1	2-1	2-4	2-7
Earls Colne Res.	4-1	1-5	0-0	2-1	4-1	S	3-0	2-2	6-1	1-3	2-0	5-0	1-3	3-3	2-1	3-1
Foxash Social	0-0	3-3	2-4	1-4	2-2	2-4	I	5-1	0-0	1-1	3-2	2-3	3-1	2-2	0-1	2-0
Glemsford/Cavendish Utd	2-0	2-4	4-1	3-1	7-0	0-0	6-1	O	4-4	1-3	5-2	4-0	6-0	5-0	2-5	1-2
Hedinghams United	7-3	2-4	1-1	3-1	0-1	4-2	2-1	5-0	N	2-3	3-2	0-6	3-3	W-L	2-2	3-2
Kelvedon Social Res.	3-0	1-1	3-1	4-3	1-2	1-1	2-2	3-3	4-2		3-1	10-0	3-2	2-1	2-1	3-1
Lawford Lads Res.	0-5	3-3	2-1	4-2	2-0	0-4	2-2	2-3	4-0	3-3	T	3-1	3-1	1-2	4-1	2-3
Little Oakley Res.	1-1	0-7	3-0	1-0	2-2	2-5	4-5	2-3	3-1	1-8	3-6	H	4-2	4-1	2-4	1-4
Mersea Island Res.	3-0	1-2	2-3	4-2	0-5	3-1	2-2	2-1	1-2	2-6	2-0	6-0	R	1-3	2-5	1-3
St Johns (Clacton) Res.	5-1	1-2	3-0	10-0	3-1	8-0	1-0	2-3	4-1	1-5	3-3	6-2	5-0	E	W-L	6-1
St Osyth Res.	0-1	0-0	7-0	3-4	2-1	1-1	3-1	2-3	2-2	1-1	4-2	4-0	1-2	5-5	E	1-4
Sudbury Athletic Res.	1-1	0-4	2-1	3-3	1-1	1-3	3-2	0-3	2-2	0-0	1-3	3-1	3-3	3-2	1-0	

Foxash Social 1 **Rowhedge Res. 3**
Hatfield Peverel 3 Weeley Athletic Res. 2
Mistley United Res. 2 **Long Melford Res. 4**
St Johns (Clacton) Res. 0 **Mersea Island 1**

QUARTER-FINALS
Gas Recreation Res. 3 Alresford Colne Rangers Res. 2
Hatfield Peverel 2 **Kelvedon Social Res. 3**
Mersea Island 4 Long Melford Res. 1
Rowhedge Res. 2 **Bradfield Rovers 4**

SEMI-FINALS
Bradfield Rovers 2 **Mersea Island 4**
Gas Recreation Res. 2 Kelvedon Social Res. 1

FINAL
(5th May at Wivenhoe Town)
Gas Recreation Res. 2 Mersea Island 0

RESERVES CUP

FINAL *(8th May at Brightlingsea United)*
Alresford Colne Rgrs Res. 2 St Johns (Clacton) Res. 0

Division Three		P	W	D	L	F	A	Pts
Bradfield Rovers	+3	30	19	9	2	89	40	69
Kelvedon Social Res.	-6	30	18	9	3	95	48	57
Earls Colne Res.		30	16	8	6	72	50	56
Glemsford & Cavendish Utd		30	16	7	7	92	57	55
St Johns (Clacton) Res.	-2	30	15	6	9	94	57	49
St Osyth Res.	+2	30	12	6	12	64	51	44
Sudbury Athletic Res.	+2	30	11	7	12	58	64	42
Dedham Old Boys Res.		30	11	7	12	68	77	40
Hedinghams United	-1	30	11	8	11	59	72	40
Lawford Lads Res.		30	11	4	15	68	74	37
Cornard United Res.	+2	30	10	5	15	69	86	37
Mersea Island Res.		30	9	4	17	61	87	31
Little Oakley Res.	+3	30	8	4	18	54	103	31
Foxash Social		30	6	10	14	49	71	28
Coggeshall Town Res.		30	7	6	17	42	70	27
Boxted Lodgers Res.	-3	30	8	4	18	43	70	25

WWW.NLNEWSDESK.CO.UK

DIVISION THREE CONSTITUTION 2003-04

BIRCH UNITED .... Colchester Road, Tiptree, Essex .... None
BOXTED LODGERS RESERVES .... The Playing Field, Cage Lane, Boxted, Colchester, Essex 01206 271969
BRIGHTLINGSEA UNITED .... North Road, Brightlingsea, Essex 01206 304199
COGGESHALL TOWN RESERVES .... The Crops, West Street, Coggeshall, Essex 01376 562843
CORNARD UNITED RESERVES ... Blackhouse Lane Sport Ground, Great Cornard, Sudbury, Suffolk 01787 376719
DEDHAM OLD BOYS RESERVES .... The Old Grammar School, Dedham, Essex 01206 322302
EARLS COLNE RESERVES .... Green Farm Meadow, Halstead Road, Earls Colne, Essex 01787 223584
                                                                                                                           01206 231309
FOXASH SOCIAL .... Foxash Playing Field, Harwich Road, Lawford, Essex .... None
GLEMSFORD & CAVENDISH UNITED .... Memorial Hall, Melford Road, Cavendish, Suffolk .... None
HEDINGHAMS UNITED .... Lawn Meadow, Yeldham Road, Sible Hedingham, Essex 01206 397211
LAWFORD LADS RESERVES .... School Lane, Lawford, Manningtree, Essex 01255 880370
LITTLE OAKLEY RESERVES .... War Memorial Club Ground, Little Oakley, Essex 01206 385216
MERSEA ISLAND RESERVES .... The Glebe, Colchester Road, West Mersea, Essex 01255 814874
ST JOHNS (CLACTON) RESERVES .. Eastcliff Sports Ground, Dulwich Road, Holland-on-Sea, Clacton .... None
ST OSYTH RESERVES .... Cowley Park, Mill Street, St Osyth, Clacton-on-Sea, Essex 01787 881143
SUDBURY ATHLETIC RESERVES ...... Lucas Social Club, Alexandra Road, Sudbury, Suffolk ....

Bradfield Rovers and Kelvedon Social Reserves are promoted to Division Two replaced by Brightlingsea United and Birch United.

ESSEX INTERMEDIATE LEAGUE

	B. Stort. Swifts	Canning Town	Epping	Frenford Snr	Harold Wood	Kelvedon Hat.	Manford Way	Rayleigh Town	Shell Club	Takeley	Wanstead T.	White Notley
B. Stortford Swifts	D	2-1	4-1	3-1	2-0	2-1	0-2	1-2	2-0	3-0	5-0	4-0
Canning Town	1-1	I	1-0	1-1	2-2	1-2	2-0	4-0	0-2	0-1	2-2	3-4
Epping	0-4	0-4	V	6-1	2-0	4-3	2-2	0-7	2-1	1-1	1-0	3-1
Frenford Senior	0-5	0-3	1-0	I	2-0	2-0	4-0	1-0	2-3	3-3	1-2	
Harold Wood Ath.	2-0	4-3	2-2	3-1	S	1-2	3-3	2-2	2-2	0-3	5-1	2-1
Kelvedon Hatch	1-3	5-1	1-1	1-1	4-1	I	2-0	2-1	4-3	4-2	5-2	2-4
Manford Way	2-0	2-1	2-1	1-0	3-1	0-1	O	0-4	3-1	0-2	1-0	3-2
Rayleigh Town	1-0	3-1	2-4	1-0	3-2	2-1	0-0	N	5-1	2-2	2-0	1-0
Shell Club Corr.	0-3	2-0	2-1	2-3	4-0	0-0	1-2	0-2	O	1-2	3-2	0-6
Takeley	0-0	4-2	2-1	1-1	2-1	3-4	3-0	4-3	1-1	O	1-0	1-0
Wanstead Town	0-4	2-3	2-0	3-3	2-0	1-0	1-1	2-2	1-0	0-3	N	0-2
White Notley	1-4	4-1	4-0	5-0	5-2	4-2	1-2	3-1	4-0	2-1	2-1	E

Division One	P	W	D	L	F	A	Pts
Bish. Stortford Swifts	22	15	2	5	52	16	47
Takeley	22	13	5	4	42	28	44
White Notley	22	14	0	8	57	34	42
Rayleigh Town	22	12	4	6	46	33	40
Manford Way	22	12	4	6	32	28	40
Kelvedon Hatch	22	12	3	7	51	39	39
Epping	22	7	4	11	32	47	25
Canning Town	22	6	4	12	37	43	22
Harold Wood Athletic	22	5	5	12	35	51	20
Frenford Senior	22	5	5	12	28	50	20
Shell Club Corr'ham	22	5	3	14	26	46	18
Wanstead Town	22	4	5	13	25	48	17

DIVISION ONE CONSTITUTION 2003-04

BISHOP'S STORTFORD SWIFTS. Silver Leys, Hadham Road (A1250), Bishop's Stortford, Hertfordshire 01279 658941
CANNING TOWN .... Southern Road Playing Field, Cave Road, London E13 .... None
EPPING .... Stonards Hill Rec Ground, Tidy's Lane, Epping, Essex .... None
FRENFORD SENIOR .... Oakfields Sports Ground, Forest Road, Barkingside, Essex .... None
HAROLD WOOD ATHLETIC ...... Harold Wood Recreation Park, Harold View, Harold Wood, Essex 01708 348827
KELVEDON HATCH .... New Hall, School Road, Kelvedon Hatch, Brentwood, Essex .... None
MANFORD WAY .... London Marathon Sports Ground, Forest Road, Hainault, Essex 01277 372153
RAYLEIGH TOWN .... Rayleigh Town Sports & Social Club, London Road, Rayleigh, Essex 020 8500 3486
SHENFIELD ASSOCIATION .... The Drive, Warley, Brentwood, Essex 01268 784001
TAKELEY .... Station Road (adj. rail bridge), Takeley, near Bishop's Stortford, Hertfordshire 01279 870404
WHITE ENSIGN .... Borough Football Combination HQ, Eastwoodbury Lane, Southend-on-Sea, Essex .... None
WHITE NOTLEY .... Oak Farm, Faulkbourne, Witham, Essex 01376 519864

Shell Club Corringham and Wanstead Town (who become Ryan) are relegated to Division Two from which White Ensign and Shenfield Association are promoted.

	Benfleet	Broomfield	Herongate Ath.	Linford Wdrs	Metpol Chig.	Mountnessing	Old Chelm.	Roydon	Sandon Royals	Shenfield Ass.	Stambridge U.	White Ensign
Benfleet	D	5-3	3-1	2-1	6-2	5-1	1-2	1-0	1-0	4-2	5-1	0-2
Broomfield	1-2	I	4-2	2-0	6-2	4-1	0-3	0-1	1-0	1-4	0-0	1-6
Herongate Athletic	1-3	0-5	V	5-1	3-1	2-4	3-2	1-0	2-4	0-1	1-1	0-2
Linford Wanderers	3-1	1-1	1-2	I	1-1	3-0	0-3	2-1	3-0	2-4	4-2	1-4
Mepol Chigwell	2-3	1-3	2-1	0-1	S	4-1	2-4	0-2	1-2	1-3	2-1	0-5
Mountnessing	5-1	2-4	4-2	2-0	1-3	I	1-2	4-2	4-2	0-2	5-2	1-4
O. Chelmsfordians	1-3	1-2	7-3	6-4	2-1	3-1	O	2-3	3-4	3-5	4-0	2-3
Roydon	1-0	3-3	3-3	1-1	1-4	1-1	1-3	N	3-1	1-0	4-0	0-1
Sandon Royals	3-3	1-3	1-0	0-0	1-0	1-3	1-1	1-2		2-2	2-1	1-3
Shenfield Assoc.	3-2	1-0	2-1	4-2	3-2	7-0	5-0	2-1	1-1	T	2-2	3-3
Stambridge United	0-3	1-2	3-1	2-0	6-3	1-2	0-7	0-2	1-1	1-0	W	3-3
White Ensign	2-0	5-1	8-0	5-0	6-2	1-0	4-0	W-L	5-1	0-0	3-0	O

Division Two	P	W	D	L	F	A	Pts
White Ensign	22	20	2	0	75	13	62
Shenfield Association +2	22	15	5	2	59	28	52
Benfleet	22	14	1	7	54	37	43
Old Chelmsfordians	22	12	2	8	61	46	38
Mountnessing +3	22	9	1	12	43	56	31
Broomfield -6	22	11	3	8	47	42	30
Roydon	22	8	5	9	32	30	29
Sandon Royals -1	22	6	6	10	30	43	23
Linford Wanderers	22	6	4	12	31	48	22
Met. Police Chigwell	22	6	1	15	39	59	19
Herongate Athletic	22	5	2	15	34	62	17
Stambridge United +3	22	2	4	16	21	62	13

DIVISION TWO CONSTITUTION 2003-04

BENFLEET .... The Club House, Woodside Extension, Manor Road, Benfleet, Rayleigh, Essex 01268 743957
BROOMFIELD .... The Angel Meadow, Main Road, Broomfield, Chelmsford, Essex 01245 443819
DEBDEN SPORTS .... Chigwell Lane, Loughton, Ilford, Essex .... None
LEIGH RAMBLERS .... Belfairs Park, Eastwood Road North, Leigh-on-Sea, Essex .... None
LINFORD WANDERERS .... Lakeside Pitches, Thurrock, Essex 01702 421077
METROPOLITAN POLICE CHIGWELL .. Met Police Sports Club, High Road, Chigwell, Essex .... None
MOUNTNESSING .... Henderson Sports & Social Club, Kenilworth Avenue, Harold Park, Romford, Essex .. 020 8500 1017 / 020 8500 2735
OLD CHELMSFORDIANS .... Lawford Lane, Roxwell Road, Chelmsford, Essex 01708 342256
ROYDON .... Roydon Playing Fields, Harlow Road, Roydon, Harlow, Essex 01245 420442
RYAN .... Blake Hall Sports Ground, Blake Hall Road, Wanstead, Essex .... None
SANDON ROYALS .... Sandon Sports Club, Rectory Chase, Sandon, Chelmsford, Essex 020 8532 9354
SHELL CLUB CORRINGHAM .... Shell Club, Springhouse Road, Corringham, Essex 01375 673100

White Ensign and Shenfield Association are promoted to Division One replaced by Shell Club Corringham and Wanstead Town (who become Ryan).
Herongate Athletic and Stambridge United are relegated to Division Three replaced by Debden Sports and Leigh Ramblers.

	Barnston	Basildon T.	Debden Spts	Galleywood	Gt Baddow	Hutton	Laindon A.	Leigh Ramb.	Leytonstone	Ramsden	Springfield	Upminster	Writtle
Barnston		5-4	0-6	4-2	4-3	1-0	6-2	2-2	5-3	1-0	1-2	2-4	3-3
Basildon Town	1-2		1-2	1-3	5-0	1-2	1-2	2-2	6-0	0-1	1-2	0-2	5-4
Debden Sports	2-0	6-0	D	6-1	3-0	3-0	W-L	3-0	4-1	1-0	2-1	7-0	6-1
Galleywood	2-4	3-2	1-0	I	0-0	2-2	3-4	0-4	2-4	2-4	0-2	0-1	4-2
Great Baddow	1-2	0-0	0-4	0-0	V	2-0	1-2	2-6	0-1	0-3	1-2	3-1	1-4
Hutton	1-1	1-3	1-6	1-2	2-1		W-L	0-3	2-1	0-2	4-1	1-1	2-1
Laindon Athletic	1-4	2-5	1-6	0-3	4-0		T	4-1	1-0	0-4	4-1	7-1	0-2
Leigh Ramblers	2-1	2-3	1-1	2-1	3-1	3-1	7-1	H	2-1	3-1	2-1	1-1	2-1
Leytonstone Utd	0-3	3-0	1-3	2-0	7-2	2-2	0-2	1-2	R	1-0	2-2	5-2	
Ramsden	6-1	0-2	1-2	5-4	3-2	3-5	0-2	2-1	4-8	E	2-1	4-8	3-2
Springfield	3-4	3-0	1-1	3-2	3-3	1-1	5-0	1-2	3-1	2-3	E	3-1	2-2
Upminster	4-0	1-3	0-5	1-2	5-1	3-1	5-0	1-2	0-1	1-4	2-0		2-3
Writtle	3-0	0-4	0-4	0-0	3-1	2-1	1-0	1-1	1-0	1-1	0-3	5-0	

Division Three		P	W	D	L	F	A	Pts
Debden Sports	-1	24	21	2	1	84	11	64
Leigh Ramblers		24	16	4	4	60	34	52
Ramsden		24	16	0	8	61	43	48
Barnston		24	13	3	8	56	57	42
Springfield	+2	24	10	4	10	46	38	36
Upminster		24	9	4	11	47	57	31
Laindon Athletic		24	10	1	13	42	58	31
Basildon Town		24	9	2	13	50	48	29
Leytonstone United		24	8	4	12	38	48	28
Writtle		24	7	5	12	45	56	26
Hutton		24	7	5	12	26	48	26
Galleywood		24	6	5	13	33	51	23
Great Baddow		24	5	2	17	29	68	11

RESERVES CHALLENGE CUP
(Res. Div One champs v Res. Cup holders)

(31st August at Bishop's Stortford Swifts)
B. Stortford Swifts Res. 2 **Rayleigh Town Res. 3**

DIVISION THREE CONSTITUTION 2003-04

BARNSTON ....High Easter Road, Barnston, Dunmow, Essex 01371 876364
BASILDON TOWN........GEC Avionics Sports Ground, Gardiners Lane South, Basildon, Essex 01268 883128
FACES ....Ford Sports & Social Club, Aldbrough Road South, Newbury Park, Ilford, Essex ....None
GALLEYWOOD......................Clarkes Field, Slades Lane, Galleywood, Chelmsford, Essex 01245 352975
GREAT BADDOW...............Great Baddow Rec, Baddow Road, Great Baddow, Chelmsford, Essex 01245 475899
HERONGATE ATHLETIC...........Adjacent to 77 Billericay Road, Herongate, Brentwood, Essex 01277 811260
HUTTON ....Polo Fields, Hall Green Lane, Hutton, Brentwood, Essex 01277 262257
LEYTONSTONE UNITED..............Ilford Wanderers RFC, Forest Road, Hainault, Essex 020 8500 4622
RAMSDEN ....Nursery Sports Ground, Downham Road, Ramsden Heath, Billericay, Essex 01268 711502
SPRINGFIELD ....Springfield Hall Park, Arun Close, Springfield, Chelmsford, Essex ....None
STAMBRIDGE UNITED...Stambridge Recreation Ground, Rochford Road, Great Stambridge, Rochford, Essex ...01702 258988
UPMINSTER ....Hall Lane Playing Fields, Hall Lane, Upminster, Romford, Essex 01708 220320
WRITTLE ....Paradise Road Playing Fields, Writtle, Chelmsford, Essex 01245 420332
WHITE NOTLEY ....Oak Farm, Faulkbourne, Witham, Essex 01376 519864

Debden Sports and Leigh Ramblers are promoted to Division Two from which Herongate Athletic and Stambridge United are relegated. Laindon Athletic have withdrawn. Newcomers are Faces.

WWW.NLNEWSDESK.CO.UK

Reserve Div One	P	W	D	L	F	A	Pts
Manford Way Res.	22	18	2	2	66	18	56
Shell Club C. Res.	22	15	2	5	53	23	47
B. Stort. Swifts Res.	22	13	5	4	58	24	44
Takeley Res.	22	11	2	9	48	39	35
Rayleigh Res. +3	22	8	4	10	33	34	31
Metpol Chig.l Res.	22	8	5	9	30	31	29
Sandon Royals Res.	22	9	2	11	41	53	29
Harold W. Res. -3	22	9	3	10	25	24	27
Frenford Snr Res.	22	6	8	8	27	48	26
Herongate Ath. Res.	22	7	2	13	25	35	23
Kelvedon H. Res.	22	5	3	14	27	47	18
Upminster Res.	22	3	2	17	21	78	11

Reserve Div Two	P	W	D	L	F	A	Pts
Broomfield Res.	22	16	4	2	54	15	52
Shenfield Ass. Res.	22	15	2	5	54	28	47
White Notley Res.	22	13	7	2	66	26	46
Epping Res.	22	10	3	9	42	27	33
Canning Town Res.	22	10	2	10	50	43	32
Roydon Res.	22	10	2	10	35	44	32
Basildon Town Res.	22	8	7	7	43	47	31
Wanstead T. Res.	22	9	0	13	48	59	27
Benfleet Res.	22	8	2	12	28	38	26
Mountnessing Res.	22	6	6	10	37	49	24
Writtle Res.	22	5	4	13	33	60	19
Great Baddow Res.	22	2	1	19	17	71	7

Reserve Div Three	P	W	D	L	F	A	Pts
White Ensign Res.	24	19	3	2	81	13	61
Debden Sports Res.	24	17	3	4	79	25	54
Old Chelm. Res.	24	16	4	4	69	33	52
Linford Wdrs Res.	24	15	5	4	69	36	50
Leigh Ramb. Res.	24	15	3	6	72	24	48
Hutton Res.	24	8	6	10	56	52	30
Laindon Ath. Res.	24	9	3	12	44	53	30
Springfield Res.	24	8	5	11	54	46	29
Stambridge U. Res.	24	8	2	14	42	66	26
Leytonstone Res. -3	24	9	2	13	40	79	26
Barnston Res.	24	6	2	16	40	71	20
Ramsden Res. +3	24	2	2	18	21	69	17
Galleywood Res.	24	1	1	22	20	89	4

RESERVES CUP
FINAL *(30th April at Maldon Town)*
Manford Way Res. 3 Rayleigh Town Res. 1

LEAGUE CUP

FIRST ROUND
Basildon Town 5 Ramsden 3
Broomfield 1 **Sandon Royals** 2
Leytonstone United 5 Writtle 0
Manford Way 1 Wanstead Town 0
Stambridge United 1 **Takeley** 2

SECOND ROUND
Barnston 2 Linford Wanderers 0
Basildon Town 1 **Leigh Ramblers** 2
Bishop's Stortford Swifts 4 Upminster 1
Debden Sports 0 **White Ensign** 2 *aet*
Epping 1 **Sandon Royals** 2
Frenford Senior 2 **Old Chelmsfordians** 3
Galleywood 1 **Sandon Royals** 3
Herongate Athletic 3 Benfleet 2 *aet*
Hutton 3 Mountnessing 1
Kelvedon Hatch 1 Springfield 1 *aet* (3-2p)
Laindon Athletic 2 **Canning Town** 6 *aet*
Leytonstone United 2 **Roydon** 3 *aet*
Manford Way 4 Shell Club Corringham 1
Metpol Chigwell 4 **Harold Wood Athletic** 5 *aet*
Rayleigh Town 3 White Notley 1
Shenfield Association 2 White Ensign 1

THIRD ROUND
Bishop's Stortford Swifts 6 Sandon Royals 0
Canning Town 1 Epping 0 *aet*
Harold Wood Athletic 3 Barnston 0
Hutton 3 Shenfield Association 2
Old Chelmsfordians 0 **Manford Way** 3
Rayleigh Town 2 **Kelvedon Hatch** 4 *aet*
Roydon 2 Leigh Ramblers 1 *aet*
White Ensign (w/o) v Herongate Athletic (scr.)

QUARTER-FINALS
Canning Town 1 **White Ensign** 3
Harold Wood Athletic 0 **Kelvedon Hatch** 4
Hutton 1 **Roydon** 2
Manford Way 0 **Bishop's Stortford Swifts** 1

SEMI-FINALS
Bishop's Stortford Swifts 3 Kelvedon Hatch 2 *aet*
Roydon 0 **White Ensign** 3

FINAL
(7th May at Southend United)
Bishop's Stortford Swifts 0 **White Ensign** 1

DENNY KING MEMORIAL CUP
(Teams eliminated in first two rounds of League Cup)

FIRST ROUND
Benfleet 3 Upminster 2
Debden Sports 2 **Ramsden** 3
Metpol Chigwell 5 Great Baddow 2
Mountnessing 1 **Springfield** 4
Shell Club Corringham 2 White Notley 1

QUARTER-FINALS
Benfleet 5 Writtle 2
Linford Wanderers 2 Metpol Chigwell 1
Ramsden 2 Shell Club Corringham 0
Springfield 2 **Galleywood** 4 *aet*

SEMI-FINALS
Linford Wanderers 3 Galleywood 0
Ramsden 0 **Benfleet** 1

FINAL *(24th May at White Notley)*
Linford Wanderers 0 **Benfleet** 1

SENIOR DIVISIONS CHALLENGE CUP
(Division One champions v League Cup holders)

(31st August May at Takeley) **Takeley** 2 Rayleigh Town 0

ESSEX SENIOR LEAGUE

	Bark'side	Basildon	Bowers	Brentw'd	Burnham	Concord	Enfield T.	Eton M.	Hullbdge	Ilford	Romford	S. Walden	S'bdgewth	S'thend M.	Stansted	W. Abbey	Woodford
Barkingside		6-2	2-0	2-1	3-0	1-2	0-2	2-0	2-0	3-5	0-1	0-0	2-0	3-4	3-1	1-1	7-0
Basildon United	3-1		2-3	0-0	2-3	1-3	1-3	2-2	3-1	1-3	1-2	3-2	1-4	1-2	3-0	0-1	2-4
Bowers United	2-1	0-4		2-1	0-0	1-3	0-1	1-1	3-0	1-3	1-2	3-0	3-2	5-4	3-1	1-2	4-3
Brentwood	3-2	2-0	1-3		1-0	0-3	0-3	1-1	5-2	0-3	0-2	3-1	0-2	1-1	2-0	0-4	3-1
Burnham Ramblers	2-0	1-2	1-2	1-2		0-4	0-3	4-2	2-2	0-1	1-2	1-0	0-1	4-0	3-0	2-1	2-0
Concord Rangers	5-2	3-1	3-1	1-1	4-1		2-0	6-3	4-1	2-2	5-0	3-2	3-0	2-3	3-1	3-2	2-1
Enfield Town	4-4	0-1	2-1	7-2	1-0	1-2		3-0	2-0	2-1	1-1	4-1	1-1	2-0	1-0	1-1	3-1
Eton Manor	1-5	4-2	2-2	1-5	0-4	0-1	1-4		5-2	2-2	3-3	2-4	0-3	1-6	1-1	0-1	3-1
Hullbridge Sports	4-1	1-3	1-2	1-1	1-3	0-4	3-4	5-2		0-5	0-4	1-1	0-3	0-4	0-3	0-2	3-1
Ilford	3-2	7-1	0-1	5-1	2-0	1-3	0-7	4-0	4-0		0-1	2-1	2-2	2-2	5-1	5-1	3-0
Romford	3-0	1-0	1-1	4-0	0-1	4-0	0-2	5-2	4-1	1-2		5-1	1-3	1-2	3-2	1-0	1-0
Saffron Walden Town	1-2	2-2	0-1	3-1	2-4	4-1	2-3	3-0	0-1	1-2	1-2		0-2	1-2	2-1	1-0	1-0
Sawbridgeworth Town	0-1	2-0	1-1	3-0	1-1	2-1	0-1	7-3	3-0	1-0	1-3	3-0		1-3	1-1	2-0	0-0
Southend Manor	1-0	4-2	1-1	1-0	2-0	4-1	1-1	2-0	2-3	3-2	1-1	4-1	1-1		3-1	1-1	5-1
Stansted	2-6	2-1	2-0	1-3	1-2	3-2	1-1	3-1	1-2	0-2	1-2	3-0	2-0	0-1		0-1	1ᴹ0
Waltham Abbey	1-2	2-2	2-3	2-3	1-1	0-1	0-1	4-0	1-0	0-4	1-0	0-0	1-2	3-1	3-1		5-0
Woodford Town	1-0	0-5	0-6	0-1	0ᴹ1	3-2	1-6	1-1	1-2	0-5	0-1	0-2	0-1	0-2	2-2	1-2	

	P	W	D	L	F	A	Pts
Enfield Town	32	23	6	3	77	28	75
Concord Rangers	32	23	2	7	83	46	71
Ilford	32	21	4	7	87	40	67
Southend Manor	32	20	7	5	73	43	67
Romford	32	21	4	7	63	34	67
Sawbridgeworth Town	32	18	7	7	57	30	61
Bowers United	32	16	6	10	58	49	54
Burnham Ramblers	32	14	4	14	45	43	46
Barkingside	32	14	3	15	66	55	45
Waltham Abbey	32	12	6	14	45	41	42
Brentwood	32	12	5	15	44	62	41
Saffron Walden Town	32	10	4	18	49	57	34
Basildon United	32	9	4	19	54	71	31
Stansted	32	8	4	20	36	64	28
Hullbridge Sports	32	5	3	24	35	90	18
Eton Manor	32	3	8	21	44	98	17
Woodford Town	32	3	3	26	22	87	12

GORDON BRASTED MEMORIAL CUP

FIRST ROUND
Barkingside 0 **Waltham Abbey** 4
SECOND ROUND
Basildon United 1 **Ilford** 3
Bowers United 1
Sawbridgeworth Town 3
Brentwood 2 **Saffron Walden Town** 4
Eton Manor 1 **Enfield Town** 4
Hullbridge Sports 0 **Concord Rangers** 4
Southend Manor 3 Stansted 1
Waltham Abbey 2 **Romford** 3
Woodford Town 1 **Burnham Ramblers** 3

QUARTER-FINALS
Burnham Ramblers 3 **Saffron Walden Town** 4 *aet*
Enfield Town 2 Concord Rgrs 1
Sawbridgeworth Town 0 **Ilford** 1
Southend Manor 3 Romford 2
SEMI-FINALS
(played over two legs)
Ilford 0 Enfield Town 0,
Enfield Town 2 Ilford 1
Southend Mnr 1 Saff. Walden 4,
Saffron Walden Town 1
Southend Manor 2
FINAL *(19th April at Burnham)*
Enfield Town 1 Saff. Walden 0

LEAGUE CUP
(All ties except Final played over two legs)

FIRST ROUND
Saffron Walden Town 5 Brentwood 1,
Brentwood 0 **Saffron Walden Town** 3
SECOND ROUND
Barkingside 3 Southend Mnr 0,
Southend M. 3 **Barkingside** 3
Basildon United 0 Concord 1,
Concord Rgrs 6 Basildon 2
Enfield Town 1 Sawbridgeworth Town 1,
Sawbridgeworth Town 1 Enfield Town 0
Eton Mnr 1 Saffron Walden 1,
Saffron Walden Town 2 **Eton Manor** 3 *aet*
Ilford 0 Hullbridge Sports 0,
Hullbridge Sports 2 **Ilford** 4
Romford 3 Burnham Ramb. 1,
Burnham Ramb. 3 **Romford** 2
Stansted 4 Woodford Town 1,
Woodford Town 2 **Stansted** 5
Waltham Abbey 0 Bowers 2,
Bowers 2 Waltham Abbey 0

QUARTER-FINALS
Barkingside 5 Stansted 1,
Stansted 1 **Barkingside** 3
Concord Rangers 2 Romford 0,
Romford 1 **Concord Rangers** 1
Ilford 0 Bowers United 1,
Bowers United 1 **Ilford** 2 *aet* (2-4p)
Sawbridgeworth Town 2 Eton Manor 1,
Eton Manor 1 **Sawbridgeworth Town** 1
SEMI-FINALS
Concord Rangers 2 Ilford 2,
Ilford 4 Concord Rangers 3 *aet*
Sawbridgeworth Town 1 Barkingside 1,
Barkingside 1 **Sawbridgeworth Town** 2
FINAL
(5th May at Barkingside)
Ilford 1 Sawbridgeworth Town 0

CONSTITUTION 2003-04

BARKINGSIDE.....Oakside, Station Road, Barkingside, Ilford, Essex.....020 8550 3611
BASILDON UNITED.....Gardiners Close, Gardiners Lane, Basildon, Essex.....01268 520268
BOWERS UNITED.....Crown Avenue, off Kenneth Road, Pitsea, Basildon, Essex.....01268 452068
BRENTWOOD.....Brentwood Centre, Doddinghurst Road, Brentwood, Essex.....01277 215151 Ext.713
BURNHAM RAMBLERS.....Leslie Field, Springfield Road, Burnham-on-Crouch, Essex.....01621 784383
CONCORD RANGERS.....Thames Road, Canvey Island, Essex.....01268 691780
ENFIELD TOWN.....Brimsdown Rovers FC, Goldsdown Road, Enfield, Middlesex.....020 8804 5491
ETON MANOR.....Leyton Pennant FC, Wadham Lodge, Kitchener Road, Walthamstow, London.....020 8527 2444
HULLBRIDGE SPORTS.....Lower Road, Hullbridge, Hockley, Essex.....01702 230420
ILFORD.....Cricklefield Stadium, High Road, Seven Kings, Ilford, Essex.....020 8514 0019
LONDON APSA.....Aveley FC, Mill Field, Mill Road, Aveley, Essex.....01708 865940. Fax: 01708 680995
ROMFORD.....Rush Green Arena, Rush Green Road, Rush Green, Romford, Essex.....01708 745678
SAWBRIDGEWORTH TOWN.....Crofters End, West Road, Sawbridgeworth, Hertfordshire.....01279 722039
SOUTHEND MANOR.....Southchurch Park Arena, Lifstan Way, Southend-on-Sea, Essex.....01702 615577
STANSTED.....Hargrave Park, Cambridge Road, Stansted, Essex.....01279 812897
WALTHAM ABBEY.....Capershotts, Sewardstone Road, Waltham Abbey, Essex.....01992 711287

Saffron Walden Town have resigned and will play friendlies only in 2003-04. Woodford Town were voted out of the league. Newcomers are London APSA from the London Intermediate League.

FOOTBALL CONFERENCE

	Barnet	Burton Albion	Chester City	Dagenham & Redbridge	Doncaster Rovers	Farnborough Town	Forest Green Rovers	Gravesend & Northfleet	Halifax Town	Hereford United	Kettering Town	Leigh RMI	Margate	Morecambe	Northwich Victoria	Nuneaton Borough	Scarborough	Southport	Stevenage Borough	Telford United	Woking	Yeovil Town
Barnet		2-2	0-3	2-1	1-2	1-2	2-0	1-4	0-0	2-1	0-2	4-0	1-1	3-4	2-1	3-0	3-1	0-2	3-0	0-0	2-1	1-1
Burton Albion	0-3		2-0	0-0	1-2	2-0	2-3	1-1	2-2	2-0	0-1	0-1	1-4	1-1	1-1	1-0	1-1	1-0	1-2	4-7	0-2	1-1
Chester City	1-1	2-1		5-2	1-0	0-2	0-1	1-1	2-0	0-1	0-0	2-1	5-0	2-1	2-3	1-2	0-0	2-0	2-0	4-1	2-2	2-2
Dagenham & Redbridge	5-1	1-2	1-0		3-3	1-0	3-1	4-0	0-0	1-0	3-1	3-1	3-0	1-1	1-1	1-1	0-1	0-0	0-0	1-3	3-1	0-4
Doncaster Rovers	2-1	1-0	0-0	5-1		1-0	4-1	0-0	2-0	1-0	1-0	3-1	1-1	3-2	0-2	1-1	2-1	0-1	2-2	5-0	2-4	
Farnborough Town	2-2	5-1	1-2	1-0	0-0		0-3	1-1	3-0	2-2	0-1	1-0	4-1	2-3	3-2	0-2	1-1	2-1	0-1	1-3	1-2	2-4
Forest Green Rovers	4-4	2-0	0-2	5-2	1-2	3-1		2-1	0-2	1-3	1-0	4-1	4-1	1-0	1-0	6-1	0-0	0-2	0-3	1-1	3-2	2-1
Gravesend & Northfleet	2-2	3-2	0-1	1-2	2-2	0-0	1-1		1-0	3-0	0-2	1-3	1-2	3-2	1-1	4-1	5-2	1-3	2-1	0-2	4-2	2-4
Halifax Town	2-4	0-1	0-0	3-3	2-1	1-0	1-1	1-2		2-1	1-0	4-0	1-0	2-2	1-0	0-5	3-1	2-1	3-4	1-0	2-0	1-1
Hereford United	4-0	4-0	0-0	2-1	2-4	2-1	1-1	3-0	1-1		2-0	0-1	1-2	1-2	2-1	1-0	1-0	2-4	0-3	0-1	0-0	
Kettering Town	1-2	1-2	0-1	1-3	0-2	1-4	2-3	1-1	0-1	2-3		0-1	1-1	3-2	2-2	3-0	1-1	0-2	1-1	2-1	0-3	1-0	2-4
Leigh RMI	4-2	4-2	0-4	1-3	0-2	3-2	1-0	0-0	0-2	0-2	2-3		2-0	1-0	1-1	0-2	4-1	1-1	1-1	2-1	1-2	
Margate	2-2	0-0	0-1	1-1	2-1	0-0	3-0	4-2	2-1	0-2	2-2	2-0		1-1	4-4	1-1	3-1	1-0	1-1	1-1	2-1	1-2
Morecambe	1-1	5-0	1-1	2-1	3-0	1-1	4-0	2-0	3-1	1-0	2-1	3-0		3-1	3-2	3-1	0-2	2-1	1-1	1-3	5-0	1-2
Northwich Victoria	1-1	1-3	1-1	0-2	1-2	0-2	2-1	1-2	0-2	2-1	1-0	3-2	3-2		1-1	3-2	3-0	1-0	1-1	1-1	1-1	
Nuneaton Borough	3-2	1-2	1-0	0-3	0-2	3-2	0-1	2-0	0-3	1-0	0-2	3-2	1-1	1-4		2-2	1-2	1-4	1-1	2-1		
Scarborough	1-1	4-1	0-1	0-1	2-5	1-0	3-0	3-2	2-1	2-1	4-1	2-0	3-2	0-1	4-1	4-1		3-2	1-4	1-1	2-1	
Southport	2-1	2-2	1-3	2-3	0-4	0-0	2-2	1-1	2-0	1-2	0-0	4-2	0-2	2-3	1-1	1-0	1-1		1-3	1-1	2-2	
Stevenage Borough	1-2	0-1	0-1	1-2	0-2	3-5	0-0	1-0	0-1	0-2	2-0	3-1	1-3	1-1	2-2	3-1	1-1	3-0		1-3	1-0	0-5
Telford United	2-1	0-2	0-1	1-2	4-4	0-2	0-1	2-1	1-2	0-1	2-0	1-1	0-0	3-0	1-5	0-6	2-1	1-1	1-5		3-0	1-1
Woking	0-0	2-2	1-0	0-0	2-2	1-1	1-1	2-2	1-2	0-1	5-0	2-1	2-1	3-2	1-0	6-0	2-1	3-0	4-0			
Yeovil Town	0-0	6-1	1-1	2-2	1-2	1-0	1-0	2-3	3-0	4-0	4-0	3-1	2-1	2-1	3-2	1-0	6-0	2-1	3-0	4-0		

	P		**HOME**					**AWAY**					**TOTAL**					
		W	D	L	F	A	W	D	L	F	A	W	D	L	F	A	Pts
Yeovil Town	42	16	5	0	54	13	12	6	3	46	24	28	11	3	100	37	95
Morecambe	42	17	3	1	52	13	6	6	9	34	29	23	9	10	86	42	78
Doncaster Rovers	42	11	6	4	28	17	11	6	4	45	30	22	12	8	73	47	78
Chester City	42	10	6	5	36	21	11	6	4	23	10	21	12	9	59	31	75
Dagenham & Redbridge	42	12	5	4	38	23	9	4	8	33	36	21	9	12	71	59	72
Hereford United	42	9	5	7	36	22	10	2	9	28	29	19	7	16	64	51	64
Scarborough	42	12	3	6	41	28	6	7	8	22	26	18	10	14	63	54	64
Halifax Town	42	11	5	5	34	28	7	5	9	16	23	18	10	14	50	51	64
Forest Green Rovers	42	12	3	6	41	29	5	5	11	20	33	17	8	17	61	62	59
Margate	42	8	9	4	32	24	7	2	12	28	42	15	11	16	60	66	56
Barnet	42	9	4	8	32	28	4	10	7	33	40	13	14	15	65	68	53
Stevenage Borough	42	7	6	8	31	25	7	4	10	30	30	14	10	18	61	55	52
Farnborough Town	42	8	6	7	37	29	5	6	10	20	27	13	12	17	57	56	51
Northwich Victoria	42	6	5	10	26	34	7	7	7	40	38	13	12	17	66	72	51
Telford United	42	7	2	12	20	33	7	5	9	34	36	14	7	21	54	69	49
Burton Albion	42	6	6	9	25	31	7	4	10	27	46	13	10	19	52	77	49
Gravesend & Northfleet	42	8	5	8	37	35	4	7	10	25	38	12	12	18	62	73	48
Leigh RMI	42	8	5	8	26	34	6	1	14	18	37	14	6	22	44	71	48
Woking	42	8	7	6	30	35	3	7	11	22	46	11	14	17	52	81	47
Nuneaton Borough	42	9	4	8	27	32	4	3	14	24	46	13	7	22	51	78	46
Southport	42	6	8	7	31	32	5	4	12	23	37	11	12	19	54	69	45
Kettering Town	42	4	3	14	23	39	4	4	13	14	34	8	7	27	37	73	31

Exeter City and Shrewsbury Town are relegated from the Football League, to which Yeovil Town and Doncaster Rovers (via play-offs – see page 45) are promoted. Kettering Town are relegated to the Isthmian League, replaced by Aldershot Town. Accrington Stanley arrive from the Northern Premier League, to which Southport return. Nuneaton Borough drop to the Southern League with Tamworth coming the other way.

CONSTITUTION FOR 2003-04

ACCRINGTON STANLEY   Manager: John Coleman   Colours: Red & white
Crown Ground, Livingstone Road, Accrington, Lancashire BB5 5BX
Tel: 01254 397869   Fax/Club: 01254 383235   www.accringtonstanley.co.uk
After a cup treble in 2002, Stanley made sure of promotion with a dominant 2002-03 campaign.

ALDERSHOT TOWN   *Manager: Terry Brown*   *Colours: Red, blue & white*
Recreation Ground, High Street, Aldershot, Hampshire GU11 1TW
Tel: 01252 320211   *Fax: 01252 324347*   *www.theshots.co.uk*
After a number of near misses, finally achieved promotion from the Isthmian League in May.

BARNET   Manager: Martin Allen   Colours: Amber & black
Underhill Stadium, Barnet Lane, Barnet, Hertfordshire EN5 2BE   www.barnetfc.com
Tel: 020 8441 6932   Fax: 020 8447 0655   Ticket office: 020 8449 6325
Again start the season under new management, Martin Allen having succeeded Peter Shreeves.

BURTON ALBION   *Manager: Nigel Clough*   *Colours: Yellow & black*
Eton Park, Princess Way, Burton-on-Trent, Staffordshire DE14 2RU
Tel: 01283 565938   *Fax: 01283 564492*   *www.burtonalbionfc.co.uk*
Season's highlight was a gripping televised FA Cup replay with Oldham, unluckily lost on penalties.

CHESTER CITY   Manager: Mark Wright   Colours: Blue & white
Deva Stadium, Bumpers Lane, Chester, Cheshire CH1 4LT
Tel: 01244 371376/317809   Fax: 01244 390265   www.chester-city.co.uk
Missed out on penalties in the play-off semis after being unbeaten in four games against Doncaster.

DAGENHAM & REDBRIDGE   *Manager: Garry Hill*   *Colours: Red, white & blue*
Glyn Hopkin Stadium, Victoria Road, Dagenham, Essex RM10 7XL   *www.daggers.co.uk*
Tel: 020 8592 7194   *Fax: 020 8593 7227*   *Club: 020 8592 1549*
Have missed out on promotion on goal difference and a golden goal in successive seasons.

EXETER CITY   Manager: Eamonn Dolan   Colours: Red, white & black
St James Park, Well Street, Exeter, Devon EX4 6PX   www.exetercityfc.co.uk
Tel: 01392 254073   Fax: 01392 425885
Become first Devon side to play in Conference following relegation after a turbulent campaign.

FARNBOROUGH TOWN   *Manager: Tommy Taylor*   *Colours: Red & white*
Aimita Stadium, Cherrywood Road, Farnborough, Hants GU14 8UD Tel: 01252 541469
Fax: 01252 375613   *www.farnborough-town.demon.co.uk*
Enjoyed a spectacular FA Cup run culminating in a visit to Highbury to play holders Arsenal.

FOREST GREEN ROVERS   Manager: Colin Addison   Colours: Black & white
The Lawn, Nympsfield Road, Forest Green, Nailsworth, Gloucestershire GL6 0ET
Tel: 01453 834860   Fax: 01453 835291   www.forestgreenrovers.com
Enjoyed best-ever Conference finish of ninth in 2002-03.

GRAVESEND & NORTHFLEET   *Manager: Andy Ford*   *Colours: Red & white*
Stonebridge Road, Northfleet, Gravesend, Kent DA11 9GN   *www.gnfc.co.uk*
Tel: 01474 533796   *Fax: 01474 324754*
Ensured a second season in the top flight after a nail-biting run-in.

HALIFAX TOWN   Manager: Chris Wilder   Colours: Blue & white
The Shay Stadium, Shaw Hill, Halifax, West Yorkshire HX1 2YS   www.halifaxafc.co.uk
Tel: 01422 341222   Fax: 01422 349487   Ticket Office: 01422 353423
The Shay, now shared with local Rugby League club, is currently undergoing a major upgrade.

HEREFORD UNITED Manager: Graham Turner Colours: White & black
Edgar Street, Hereford, Herefordshire HR4 9JU www.herefordunited.co.uk
Tel: 01432 276666 Fax: 01432 341359
Captured the Conference Fair Play award for the second time in three seasons.

LEIGH RMI Manager: Mark Patterson Colours: Red, white & black
Hilton Park, Kirkhall Lane, Leigh, Lancashire WN7 1RN www.leighrmi-mad.co.uk
Tel: 01942 743743 Fax: 01942 261843
Took 25 points from final 16 games to ensure Conference survival.

MARGATE Manager: Chris Kinnear Colours: Royal blue & white
Hartsdown Park, Hartsdown Road, Margate, Kent CT9 5QZ (see note below)
Tel: 01843 221769 Fax: 01843 221769 www.margatefc.com
Continue to play home games at Dover Athletic whilst Hartsdown Park is redeveloped.

MORECAMBE Manager: Jim Harvey Colours: Red & black
Christie Park, Lancaster Road, Morecambe, Lancashire LA4 5TJ www.morecambefc.com
Tel: 01524 411797 Fax: 01524 832230
Missed out in play-off semi-finals on penalties to a side they had topped in league campaign.

NORTHWICH VICTORIA Manager: Steve Davis Colours: Green & white
Witton Albion FC, Wincham Park, Chapel Street, Wincham, Northwich, Cheshire CW9 5HN
Tel/Fax: 01606 43008 Fax: 01606 43008 www.nvfc.co.uk
Forced into a managerial change by Jimmy Quinn's switch to relegated Shrewsbury Town.

SCARBOROUGH Manager: Russell Slade Colours: Red
McCain Stadium, Seamer Road, Scarborough, North Yorkshire YO12 4HF
Tel: 01723 375094 Fax: 01723 378733 www.scarboroughfc.co.uk
The Seadogs are currently negotiating a move to a new out of town stadium.

SHREWSBURY TOWN Manager: Jimmy Quinn Colours: Royal blue & amber
Gay Meadow, Shrewsbury, Shropshire SY2 6AB www.shrewsburytown.co.uk
Tel: 01743 360111 Fax: 01743 236384
Relegated from League in the same season that brought an FA Cup victory over Everton.

STEVENAGE BOROUGH Manager: Graham Westley Colours: White & red
Broadhall Way, Stevenage, Herts SG2 8RH www.stevenageborofc.com
Tel: 01438 223223 Fax: 01438 743666
Graham Westley controversially took over from Wayne Turner midway through last season.

TAMWORTH Manager: Darron Gee Colours: Red & black
The Lamb Ground, Kettlebrook, Tamworth, Staffordshire B79 1HA www.thelambs.co.uk
Tel: 01827 65798 Fax: 01827 62236
Promoted to Conference in May, twelve months after missing out on goal difference.

TELFORD UNITED Manager: Mick Jones Colours: White & black
New Bucks Head Stadium, Watling Street, Wellington, Telford, Shropshire TF1 2NJ
Tel: 01543 278222 Fax: 01543 273529 www.telfordunitedfc.co.uk
Looking forward to first ever Shropshire league derbies following relegation of Shrewsbury Town.

WOKING Manager: Glenn Cockerill Colours: Red, white & black
Kingfield, Kingfield Road, Woking, Surrey GU22 9AA www.wokingfc.co.uk
Tel: 01483 772470 Fax: 01483 888423
Glenn Cockerill has signed a new two year contract after guiding the Cards to safety.

WWW.CHERRYRED.CO.UK

CONFERENCE – GATES 'N DATES

	BAR	BUR	CHE	DAG	DON	FAR	FGR	G&N	HAL	HER	KET	LEI	MAR	MOR	NOR	NUN	SCA	SOU	STE	TEL	WOK	YEO
Barnet		1555 25 Jan	1347 24 Aug	1727 26 Dec	1859 4 Jan	1069 17 Sept	1144 23 Nov	1360 8 Oct	1588 22 Mar	1316 31 Aug	1198 12 Apr	1021 16 Nov	1160 15 Feb	1250 28 Sept	1093 2 Nov	1421 12 Oct	1056 22 Feb	769 18 Mar	1909 8 Mar	1067 7 Sept	1617 21 Apr	1668 20 Aug
Burton Alb.	1948 26 Aug		2183 8 Mar	1447 21 Dec	2341 6 Dec	1548 22 Mar	1598 3 Sept	1412 17 Sept	1636 7 Sept	2149 11 Oct	1570 28 Dec	1604 18 Jan	1393 28 Sept	1688 2 Nov	1833 1 Jan	2523 12 Oct	1821 17 Jan	1402 25 Mar	1523 12 Apr	1516 8 Feb	1558 23 Nov	1989 8 Oct
Chester City	1944 26 Aug	2440 24 Sept		2331	2928	2245	2210	2928	2507	2367	2273	1920	2039	3151	2564	2292	2292	1745	1523	2594	2165	3821
Dagenham	1414 18 Jan	1527 24 Sept	1870 22 Feb		1739	1542	1277	1766	1444	1235	1305	1901	1219	1494	1541	1566	1341	1905	1711	1348	2165	2588
Doncaster	3023 17 Aug	3026 14 Sept	4867 22 Feb	4294 28 Sept		3436	3508	3156	3201	3486	3764	3719	2888	2783	2941	2913	4155	3975	3477	3333	3051	5344
Farnborough	886 1 Mar	934 30 Nov	1050 29 Mar	998	947 25 Feb		500	626	1030	753	794	595	741	803	641	644	629	591	799	529	1639	2114
Forest Green	871 5 Oct	986 15 Feb	812 31 Aug	1020	986	825		711	1015	1514	685	576	763	623	676	679	751	602	645	801	901	1836
Gravesend	1358 19 Apr	1140 1 Mar	1273 5 Apr	2036	1326	1070	876		1950	1130	954	1246	1041	1040	1017	1044	1259	1054	1323	1096	1163	1404
Halifax Town	2119 8 Feb	1469 14 Dec	2178 17 Sept	1630	3082	1894	1366	1529		1299	1639	2050	1519	2122	1491	1400	1557	1544	1517	1616	1558	2222
Hereford Utd	1471 30 Nov	1780 5 Apr	2389 14 Sept	1761	2449	1910	3271	1814	1699		2062	1690	1959	2106	1400	2071	2171	1646	2322	3077	1565	2282
Kettering	1704	1743	1788	1392	1633	877	422	1070	713	1434		768	1286	1353	1386	1372	1200	2068	1481	1608	1670	2282
Leigh RMI	405 14 Sept	503 24 Aug	851 14 Dec	403	684	305	445	385	817	425	402		327	506	439	401	525	565	335	406	435	415
Margate	735 3 Sept	577 15 Mar	925 5 Oct	686	1002	635	410	1415	445	509	667	535		413	758	504	525	565	520	385	527	1083
Morecambe	1667 15 Mar	2239 26 Apr	2012	2069	1971	1024	1014	1062	1524	1437	1094	1258	1179		1252	1332	1604	1957	1954	869	1007	1343
Northwich	523 26 Apr	893 20 Aug	2305 26 Dec	720	1160	760	460	1014	896	459	608	474	1375	645		582	503	700	690	530	506	691
Nuneaton B.	868	2337 30 Nov	1371 19 Oct	1105	1759	1710	1136	969	1231	1354	1187	1549	918	718	582		1237	774	1206	1241	1007	1717
Scarborough	1266	1428	1938	1192	3435	1403	1146	1205	1835	1179	1078	950	1138	1179	1451	1629		1193	1206	1241	1192	1879
Southport	906 29 Mar	1331 30 Nov	2447 26 Dec	1002	1265	1080	880	1003	1008	1103	1327	1097	768	749	726	1311	1631		966	853	1023	1602
Stevenage B.	2130	1770	1716	2408	1803	1849	1834	1685	2000	2031	1865	2130	1809	1636	1651	1629	1815	1193		1206	2801	1879
Telford Utd	779 14 Dec	1311 19 Oct	1409	877	762	834	720	1008	880	793	802	1016	1040	726	987	1192	812	721	1768		824	1509
Woking	1761 9 Nov	1426 5 Oct	2019 19 Oct	2007	1889	1717	2721	1734	2000	2031	2160	1485	1491	1649	1786	987	1815	1768	853	1192		3332
Yeovil Town	4850 28 Dec	5691 19 Apr	8111 26 Apr	4289 9 Nov	6674 19 Oct	2231 3 Sept	2948	6487 1 Mar	2126	4738	5330	4147	4353	2154	2504	7008 28 Mar	4727	4940	7558	4003	3332	

FOOTBALL CONFERENCE PROMOTION PLAY-OFFS

SEMI-FINALS
(First legs, 1st May)
Dagenham & Redbridge 2 Morecambe 1 Att: 3447
Doncaster Rovers 1 Chester City 1 Att: 6857

SEMI-FINALS
(Second legs, 5th May)
Chester City 1 **Doncaster Rovers** 1 Att: 5702 *aet* (3-4p)
Morecambe 2 **Dagenham & Red.** 1 Att: 5405 *aet* (2-3p)

FINAL *(10th May at Stoke City)*
Doncaster Rovers 3 Dagenham & Redbridge 2 Att: 13092 *aet, golden goal*

FOOTBALL LEAGUE ASSOCIATE MEMBERS CUP

(Football League Division Two and Three teams, and top twelve Conference sides with Football League ground grading. Extra-time ties decided by golden goal)

NORTHERN FIRST ROUND
Chesterfield 2 Halifax Town 0
Lincoln City 4 York City 3
Mansfield Town 0 **Crewe Alexandra** 4
Notts County 2 **Wigan Athletic** 3
Oldham Athletic 3 **Carlisle United** 4 *aet*
Port Vale 3 Hull City 1
Rochdale 0 **Bury** 1
Scarborough 1 **Doncaster Rovers** 2 *aet*
Scunthorpe United 2 **Blackpool** 3
Shrewsbury Town 3 Morecambe 0
Southport 3 **Leigh RMI** 4
Stockport County 1 Darlington 0
Tranmere Rovers 5 Hartlepool United 0
Wrexham 2 Huddersfield Town 1

NORTHERN SECOND ROUND
Bury 1 Barnsley 0
Carlisle United 1 Stockport County 0 *aet*
Crewe Alexandra 2 Blackpool 0
Leigh RMI 3 **Wrexham** 4 *aet*
Lincoln City 1 **Shrewsbury Town** 2 *aet*
Macclesfield Town 1 **Tranmere Rovers** 2 *aet*
Port Vale 1 Chesterfield 1 *aet* (4-3p)
Wigan Athletic 0 **Doncaster Rovers** 1

NORTHERN QUARTER-FINALS
Bury 2 Tranmere Rovers 0
Carlisle United 2 Wrexham 0
Crewe Alexandra 8 Doncaster Rovers 0
Shrewsbury Town 2 Port Vale 1 *aet*

NORTHERN SEMI-FINALS
Carlisle United 3 Bury 2 *aet*
Shrewsbury Town 4 Crewe Alexandra 2

NORTHERN FINAL
(played over two legs)
Carlisle United 1 Shrewsbury Town 0,
Shrewsbury Town 0 **Carlisle United** 0

SOUTHERN FIRST ROUND
Boston United 4 Yeovil Town 2
Cambridge United 4 Rushden & Diamonds 0
Cheltenham Town 4 Colchester United 1
Chester City 1 **Plymouth Argyle** 2
Dagenham & Redbridge 1 **Kidderminster Harriers** 3
Exeter City 1 Bristol Rovers 0
Hereford United 3 **Northampton Town** 4 *aet*
Leyton Orient 3 Peterborough United 2
Oxford United 2 **AFC Bournemouth** 3
Queens Park Rangers 0 **Bristol City** 0 *aet* (4-5p)
Stevenage Borough 2 Swansea City 1
Swindon Town 6 Southend United 1
Torquay United 0 **Wycombe Wanderers** 4
Woking 0 **Luton Town** 2

SOUTHERN SECOND ROUND
AFC Bournemouth 1 Leyton Orient 0
Boston United 1 **Bristol City** 2 *aet*
Cheltenham Town 1 **Wycombe Wanderers** 2 *aet*
Exeter City 0 **Cardiff City** 3
Kidderminster Harriers 3 Swindon Town 2 *aet*
Northampton Town 2 **Cambridge United** 4
Plymouth Argyle 0 **Brentford** 1
Stevenage Borough 3 **Luton Town** 4

SOUTHERN QUARTER-FINALS
AFC Bournemouth 2 Cardiff City 1 *aet*
Brentford 2 Kidderminster Harriers 1
Bristol City 3 Wycombe Wanderers 0
Luton Town 1 **Cambridge United** 2 *aet*

SOUTHERN SEMI-FINALS
AFC Bournemouth 1 **Bristol City** 3
Brentford 1 **Cambridge United** 2 *aet*

SOUTHERN FINAL
(played over two legs)
Bristol City 4 Cambridge United 2,
Cambridge United 0 **Bristol City** 3

FINAL *(6th April at Millennium Stadium, Cardiff)*
Bristol City 2 Carlisle United 0

GLOUCESTERSHIRE COUNTY LEAGUE

	AXA	Almondsbury	DRG Stapleton	Ellwood	Hardwicke	Henbury OB	Highridge Utd	Old Georgians	Patchway Town	Pucklechurch	RG St George	Taverners	Thornbury	Totterdown	Tytherington	Viney St Swith.	Whitminster	Wotton Rovers
AXA		2-6	2-1	0-1	3-1	2-2	2-1	0-2	1-2	0-2	3-0	1-1	2-4	2-1	1-5	2-2	4-2	0-4
Almondsbury	0-0		4-1	1-1	0-0	0-1	1-4	4-0	0-1	3-2	2-0	1-3	2-4	2-1	3-2	0-0	3-0	1-2
DRG Stapleton	3-4	1-2		2-1	4-1	0-2	1-3	0-2	2-3	1-1	0-0	2-2	2-1	2-4	1-0	8-1	1-0	
Ellwood	0-1	0-3	2-0		2-1	0-1	4-1	0-1	3-1	0-0	0-0	2-3	0-3	1-3	1-1	1-0	1-1	
Hardwicke	0-7	1-6	1-3	2-4		3-2	4-1	0-2	0-3	6-2	2-1	4-1	1-3	3-0	3-0	0-2	4-2	0-2
Henbury Old Boys	1-2	0-3	2-0	2-0	0-1		6-1	2-0	0-0	6-1	5-2	1-0	2-2	2-0	1-0	4-1	3-3	1-1
Highridge United	1-0	3-1	3-2	2-0	1-2	0-1		0-2	0-0	2-0	3-0	0-3	1-0	2-1	2-3	3-1	2-0	5-0
Old Georgians	1-2	2-3	1-4	1-0	4-2	2-4	1-3		1-5	1-4	0-0	2-1	1-0	1-3	2-3	1-1	2-3	4-4
Patchway Town	1-2	2-0	2-1	1-2	2-0	0-2	2-0	0-0		4-0	3-1	4-0	2-0	3-1	3-1	2-0	4-0	1-1
Pucklechurch Sports	3-2	4-0	1-2	2-2	2-3	1-5	1-1	3-5	0-7		2-4	2-0	0-2	2-2	0-2	1-2	4-2	1-0
Roman Glass St George	4-2	1-6	0-0	2-1	6-0	2-1	2-2	2-4	0-2	2-2		1-3	0-3	2-1	2-0	2-1	1-4	1-0
Taverners	2-2	2-4	1-2	0-2	1-2	0-1	0-2	1-0	3-2	2-0	0-2		2-1	1-0	1-3	4-0	1-0	2-2
Thornbury Town	1-0	3-4	0-4	3-0	4-2	0-1	1-1	1-1	0-2	4-2	2-0	1-0		0-0	0-3	5-0	3-0	5-1
Totterdown Port of Bristol	0-3	1-4	1-1	1-1	1-1	2-1	2-1	1-0	1-3	4-0	0-2	0-1	1-1		4-0	2-1	2-2	0-1
Tytherington Rocks	3-1	0-1	0-3	4-1	4-4	3-2	1-2	3-2	1-1	1-2	3-2	1-0	2-2	4-1		3-0	3-0	1-3
Viney St Swithins	1-1	1-1	3-2	1-1	1-1	2-4	0-0	1-2	0-0	0-2	0-3	1-1	1-3	2-0	3-0		2-4	1-3
Whitminster	3-2	2-4	1-1	1-0	1-1	1-4	1-2	2-7	0-0	3-2	0-6	1-1	3-4	0-0	1-4	0-2		0-3
Wotton Rovers	3-1	2-1	2-2	2-2	7-1	1-1	4-0	6-1	0-0	4-0	1-0	1-0	2-1	1-1	2-1	3-0	1-1	

	P	W	D	L	F	A	Pts
Patchway Town	34	23	7	4	69	18	76
Henbury Old Boys	34	21	6	7	73	36	69
Wotton Rovers	34	18	11	5	70	39	65
Almondsbury	34	19	5	10	76	49	62
Tytherington Rocks	34	18	3	13	72	57	57
Highridge United	34	17	5	12	54	49	56
Thornbury Town	34	16	7	11	65	48	55
DRG Stapleton	34	13	7	14	62	52	46
AXA	34	13	6	15	59	64	45
Roman Glass St George	34	12	7	15	53	60	43
Taverners	34	12	6	16	40	46	42
Old Georgians	34	12	5	17	55	70	41
Hardwicke	34	12	5	17	57	84	41
Ellwood	34	9	9	16	36	48	36
Pucklechurch Sports	34	10	4	20	55	88	34
Totterdown Port of Bristol	34	8	9	17	39	53	33
Viney St Swithins	34	7	10	17	35	62	31
Whitminster	34	6	8	20	44	91	26

LEAGUE CUP

PRELIM. ROUND
Almondsbury 2 AXA 0
Henbury Old Boys 4 Totterdown Pt of Bristol 3

FIRST ROUND
Almondsbury 0 **Roman Glass St George** 5
DRG Stapleton 4 Highridge Utd 4 aet (9-8p)
Ellwood 2 Thornbury Town 2 aet (6-5p)
Henbury Old Boys 3 Patchway Town 1
Old Georgians 1 Pucklechurch Sports 0
Taverners 0 **Tytherington Rocks** 4 aet (3-4p)
Whitminster 2 **Hardwicke** 2 aet (4-5p)
Wotton Rovers 6 Viney St Swithins 2

QUARTER-FINALS
DRG Stapleton 1 **Henbury Old Boys** 4
Hardwicke 1 **Ellwood** 4
Roman Glass St George 4 Tytherington Rocks 3
Wotton Rovers 2 Old Georgians 1

SEMI-FINALS
Ellwood 1 **Henbury Old Boys** 3
(at Yate Town)
Roman Glass St George 1 Wotton Rovers 0
(at Yate Town)

FINAL
(9th April at Yate Town)
Henbury Old Boys 5 Roman Glass St George 1

CONSTITUTION 2003-04

AXA .... Cribbs Causeway, Bristol, South Glos 0117 950 2303
ALMONDSBURY .... Almondsbury Parish Field, Almondsbury, South Glos 01454 612240
DRG STAPLETON .... Shortwood, Carsons Road, Mangotsfield, Bristol, South Glos 0117 956 0390
ELLWOOD .... Bromley Road, Ellwood, Coleford, Gloucestershire 01594 832927
HARDWICKE .... Green Lane, Hardwicke, Gloucestershire 01452 720587
HENBURY OLD BOYS .... Lorain Walk, Henbury, Bristol, South Glos 0117 959 0475
HIGHRIDGE UNITED .... Lakemead Grove, Highridge, Bristol, South Glos 0117 978 4878
KINGS STANLEY .... Marling Close, Kings Stanley, Gloucestershire 01453 828975
OLD GEORGIANS .... St George's School PF, Johnsons Lane, Whitehall, Bristol, South Glos ... 0117 951 6888
PATCHWAY TOWN .... Scott Park, Coniston Road, Patchway, Bristol, South Glos 0117 949 3952
PUCKLECHURCH SPORTS ...... Pucklechurch Recreation Ground, Pucklechurch, Bristol, South Glos. .. 0117 937 2102
ROMAN GLASS ST GEORGE .... Bell Hill, Whiteway Road, St George, Bristol, South Glos .... None
TAVERNERS .... Highwood School, Spring Hill, Nailsworth, Gloucestershire .... None
THORNBURY TOWN .... Mundy Playing Fields, Kington Lane, Thornbury, Gloucestershire .... None
TOTTERDOWN PORT OF BRISTOL . City & Port of Bristol SC, Nibley Road, Shirehampton, Bristol 0117 982 3927
TYTHERINGTON ROCKS .. Hardwicke Playing Fields, Woodlands Rd, Tytherington, Wotton-under-Edge, Gloucestershire ... None
VINEY ST SWITHINS .... Viney Sports & Social Club, Viney Hill, Lydney, Gloucestershire 01594 510658
WOTTON ROVERS .... Synwell Playing Fields, Synwell Lane, Wotton-under-Edge, Gloucestershire ... 01453 842929
Whitminster have withdrawn and will play in the Stroud & District League. Newcomers are Kings Stanley from the Gloucestershire Northern Senior League.

GWENT COUNTY LEAGUE

	Aberbargoed Buds	Abercarn United	Blaina West Side	Clydach Wasps	Croesyceiliog	Cwmbran Celtic	Fairfield United	Goytre	Lucas Cwmbran	Mardy	Newport Corinthians	Panteg	Pill	Spencer Youth & Boys	Tillery United	Trinant
Aberbargoed Buds		0-0	5-1	1-1	3-1	1-0	4-2	2-0	5-3	1-1	3-1	2-1	3-2	6-0	8-2	5-1
Abercarn United	2-3		1-1	1-3	3-6	1-1	1-0	3-0	1-4	2-1	1-3	3-3	5-2	0-2	3-1	2-3
Blaina West Side	0-4	3-2	D	1-3	1-4	0-2	1-1	4-2	1-0	0-1	5-1	1-1	3-0	2-3	4-1	5-1
Clydach Wasps	1-1	4-1	2-1	I	2-2	1-1	5-0	1-4	5-2	0-5	2-1	2-1	2-1	0-2	8-1	2-2
Croesyceiliog	2-4	2-4	5м0	3-1	V	2-0	2-1	0-1	3-0	4-0	2-0	1-0	8-0	2-4	3-2	3-0
Cwmbran Celtic	5-4	5-1	5м0	5-2	2-2	I	2-1	0-5	3-0	2-1	1-1	3-2	1-1	1-3	4-1	3-2
Fairfield United	1-8	3-2	1-1	2-4	1-4	0-1	S	2-1	3-5	4-2	2-3	0-1	4-0	0-6	2-0	2-7
Goytre	0-0	2-0	2-0	2-0	3-1	1-0	1-1	I	4-3	2-0	3-1	0-1	6-0	4-1	4-1	2-2
Lucas Cwmbran	0-3	4-4	3-2	2-5	4-4	4-0	1-2	1-2	O	2-4	0м5	4-3	1-5	2-5	5-1	4-4
Mardy	2-2	3-1	2-1	1-3	0-2	0-3	2-0	0-0	4-3	N	1-3	3-2	6-0	0-2	2-1	1-0
Newport Corinthians	1-1	0-0	1-0	2-2	1-1	1-5	3-1	2-4	3-3	0-1		2-3	1-1	1-0	3-2	3-2
Panteg	3-2	0-2	2-1	5-2	0-3	1-0	1-1	0-1	2-2	4-2	2-4	O	5-2	0-3	5-1	5-1
Pill	1-2	0-2	4-2	4-1	3-4	2-1	3-0	1-0	2-1	1-3	1-0	3-1	N	0-2	0-4	2-6
Spencer Youth & Boys	0-3	1-3	4-1	1-1	3-2	2-3	2-0	0-2	1-2	4-2	3-3	1-1	8-1	E	2-1	6-2
Tillery United	0-9	1-3	0-2	1-6	1-4	0-8	3-5	0-4	1-2	2-2	1-6	1-1	3-0	1-0		5-2
Trinant	1-1	1-1	0-3	0-0	1-4	4-0	3-4	0-1	7-3	5-1	8-3	3-3	2-1	2-7	3-3	

Division One	P	W	D	L	F	A	Pts
Aberbargoed Buds	30	20	8	2	96	35	68
Goytre	30	20	4	6	63	27	64
Croesyceiliog	30	19	4	7	86	45	61
Spencer Youth & Boys	30	18	3	9	78	48	57
Cwmbran Celtic	30	15	6	9	67	47	51
Clydach Wasps	30	14	8	8	71	56	50
Mardy	30	12	6	12	54	57	42
Newport Corinthians	30	11	8	11	59	61	41
Panteg	30	11	7	12	59	57	40
Abercarn United	30	10	7	13	55	62	37
Trinant	30	8	8	14	75	85	32
Blaina West Side	30	9	4	17	47	63	31
Lucas Cwmbran	30	8	5	17	70	94	29
Pill	30	9	2	19	43	87	29
Fairfield United	30	8	4	18	46	79	28
Tillery United	30	4	4	22	44	110	16

DIVISION ONE CONSTITUTION 2003-04

ABERBARGOED BUDS......................Recreation Ground, Aberbargoed, Gwent...None
ABERCARN UNITED.........................Welfare Ground, Abercarn, Gwent.....................................01495 244519
BLAINA WEST SIDE.........................Duffryn Park, Blaina, Gwent...None
CLYDACH WASPS............................Recreation Ground, Clydach, Monmouthshire...None
CROESYCEILIOG.............................Woodland Road, Croesyceiliog, Gwent.....................................01633 485157
CWMBRAN CELTIC.........Cwmbran Stadium (outfield), Henllys Way, Cwmbran, Gwent...............01633 866192
GARNLYDAN ATHLETIC....................Recreation Ground, Garnlydan, Gwent.....................................01495 306952
LUCAS CWMBRAN............................Girling Sports Ground, Cwmbran, Gwent...None
MARDY..Mardy Playing Field, Mardy, Monmouthshire...None
NEWPORT CORINTHIANS.......................Coronation Park, Newport, Gwent...None
PANTEG.............................Panteg House, Greenhill Road, Griffithstown, Gwent.....................................01495 763605
PILL...Pill Harriers, Pill, Gwent.....................................01633 662668
RTB EBBW VALE...............................Eugene Cross Park, Ebbw Vale, Gwent...None
SPENCER YOUTH & BOYS............BSC Sports & Social Club, Spytty Road, Newport, Gwent.....................................01633 273790
TRINANT.......................................Trinant Recreation, Trinant, Caerphilly, Gwent.....................................01633 881352
UNDY ATHLETIC...........................Undy Playing Fields, Undy, Monmouthshire...None

Goytre are promoted to the Welsh League replaced by RTB Ebbw Vale. Fairfield United and Tillery United drop to Division Two replaced by Garnlydan Athletic and Undy Athletic.

WWW.NLNEWSDESK.CO.UK

	Abergavenny Thursdays	Abertillery Bluebirds	Christchurch Hamdden	Cromwell Youth	Garnlydan Athletic	Greenmeadow	Llanhilleth Athletic	Lliswerry	Monmouth Town	Newport Civil Service	Pentwynmawr Athletic	Rogerstone Welfare	Tranch	Trethomas Bluebirds	Undy Athletic	West Pontnewydd
Abergavenny Thursdays		0-5	2-5	1-1	1-3	0-7	2-4	1-1	3-4	1-6	3-4	0-2	0-7	2-3	0-10	1-6
Abertillery Bluebirds	10-0		3-3	0-4	1-2	2-2	3-0	1-0	3-3	4-0	1-3	1-1	3-1		0-3	3-0
Christchurch Hamdden	7-0	1-1	D	1-1	2-1	2-1	2-1	2-0	1-1	0-1	3-1	3-1	4-4	4-2	0-0	1-1
Cromwell Youth	9-2	2-5	3-2	I	0-2	3-3	3-2	3-3	3-3	3-2	0-1	4-0	4-1	1-0	L-W	2-2
Garnlydan Athletic	5-0	0-2	2-1	7-0	V	1-1	3-2	3-2	2-0	3-0	4-1	2-1	1-0	4-0	4-1	1-0
Greenmeadow	8-2	5-1	4-1	2-4	0-1	I	2-2	5-0	0-5	2-2	4-2	3-2	1-5	2-2	4-2	2-2
Llanhilleth Athletic	7-1	2-2	1-2	4-1	5-0	2-1	S	3-3	3-1	3-1	1-0	8-1	4-2	3-1	4-0	1-5
Lliswerry	4-1	2-1	1-2	1-3	4-1	1-0	3-0	I	3-0	0-3	4-0	0-0	4-2	4-1	0-2	1-1
Monmouth Town	7-1	0-3	1-8	3-5	2-8	2-2	4-1	3-1	O	1-5	1-3	1-3	2-5	2-2	4-6	1-3
Newport Civil Service	4-1	1-1	1-1	4-1	1-3	4-1	2-2	1-1	4-0	N	2-2	6-1	2-0	3-1	4-2	0-3
Pentwynmawr Athletic	4-3	1-1	0-2	2-1	2-2	0-5	0-3	1-2	1-2	3-1		3-3	2-1	5-1	3-1	0-0
Rogerstone Welfare	4-1	3-5	1-3	3-2	2-3	1-2	3-0	2-3	2-2	1-3	2-2	T	3-3	5-2	2-2	2-4
Tranch	9-1	4-1	3-3	2-0	0-2	2-0	2-2	4-0	6-1	1-3	2-3	3-2	W	4-2	2-5	2-1
Trethomas Bluebirds	17-0	0-0	0-1	3-2	1-2	1-4	4-4	6-2	1-2	2-3	0-0	0-2	0-2	O	1-1	2-2
Undy Athletic	8-0	2-0	0-0	2-2	2-0	4-3	2-3	2-1	2-0	3-2	1-2	1-1	5-5	4-2		2-3
West Pontnewydd	6-2	4-0	4-0	6-3	0-1	2-1	1-8	6-1	4-0	1-2	5M0	2-3	3-4	2-0	3-4	

Division Two

		P	W	D	L	F	A	Pts
Garnlydan Athletic		30	23	2	5	73	34	71
Undy Athletic		30	18	7	5	84	48	61
Newport Civil Service		30	17	6	7	75	44	57
Christchurch Hamdden		30	15	10	5	67	42	55
West Pontnewydd		30	15	6	9	82	50	51
Llanhilleth Athletic		30	14	6	10	84	58	48
Tranch United		30	13	6	11	83	63	45
Abertillery Bluebirds		30	11	9	10	63	51	42
Pentwynmawr Athletic		30	11	8	11	48	63	41
Greenmeadow	-3	30	12	7	11	76	58	40
Lliswerry		30	11	6	13	52	61	39
Cromwell Youth	-6	30	11	7	12	70	69	34
Rogerstone Welfare		30	9	6	15	59	74	33
Monmouth Town		30	6	6	18	58	94	24
Trethomas Bluebirds		30	4	6	20	58	78	18
Abergavenny Thursdays		30	0	2	28	32	177	2

LEAGUE CUP

FIRST ROUND

AC Pontymister 1 — Newport Civil Service 1 Pentwynmawr Athletic 0

Lliswerry 5 — Pill 2 Fleur-de-Lys 1

Abercarn 0 Blaina W. Side 4 — Race 4 Trinant 3

Abertillery Bluebirds 2 — Spencer Youth 7 Undy 0

Monmouth Town 0 — Tranch 4 Rogerstone 5

Caldicot Castle 5

Cwmffrwdoer Sports 4

Christchurch Hamdden 3

Greenmeadow 1

Clydach Wasps 2

Aberbargoed Buds 5

Cromwell Youth 0

Trethomas Bluebirds 3

Fairfield United 3 Lucas

Cwmbran 1

Hafodyrynys Bluebirds 1

New Inn AFC 0

SECOND ROUND

Abergavenny Thursdays 0 — Aberbargoed Buds 11

Brynmawr 2 Garnlydan Athletic 4

Caldicot Castle 4 Blaina West Side 2

Cwmbran Celtic 2 Spencer Youth & Boys 1

Fairfield United 9

Rogerstone Welfare 10

Govilon 3 Cefn Forest 1

DIVISION TWO CONSTITUTION 2003-04

ABERTILLERY BLUEBIRDS .... Cwmnantygroes Field, Abertillery, Gwent 01495 213999
BLAENAVON BLUES .... Recreation Ground, Blaenavon, Pontypool, Gwent .... None
CHRISTCHURCH HAMDDEN .... Glebelands Sports Stadium, Newport, Gwent .... None
COED EVA .... Cwmbran Park, Wesley Street, Cwmbran, Gwent .... None
CROMWELL YOUTH .... Hartridge Comprehensive School, Ringland Way, Newport, Gwent .... None
CWMFFRWDOER SPORTS .... Cwmffrwdoer Sports Ground, Cwmffrwdoer, Gwent .... None
FAIRFIELD UNITED .... Garndiffaith Ravine, Pontypool, Gwent .... None
LLANHILLETH ATHLETIC .... Llanhilleth Park, Llanhilleth, Gwent 01495 217840
LLISWERRY .... Spytty Park, Newport, Gwent 01633 281087
MONMOUTH TOWN .... Sports Ground, Monmouth, Monmouthshire 01600 772389
NEWPORT CIVIL SERVICE .... Civil Service Sports Ground, Shannon Road, Bettws, Gwent 01633 855576
PENTWYNMAWR ATHLETIC .... Welfare Ground, Pentwynmawr, Powys 01495 243403
ROGERSTONE WELFARE .... Welfare Ground, Rogerstone, Newport, Gwent .... None
TILLERY UNITED .... Woodland Field, Cwmtillery, Gwent .... None
TRANCH .... Welfare Ground, Tranch, Gwent .... None
WEST PONTNEWYDD .... The Birches, Pontynewydd, Pontypool, Gwent .... None

Garnlydan Athletic and Undy Athletic are promoted to Division One replaced by Fairfield United and Tillery United. Abergavenny Thursdays and Trethomas Bluebirds drop to Division Three replaced by Cwmffrwdoer Sports and Blaenavon Blues. Greenmeadow become Coed Eva.

	AC Pontymister	Blaenavon Blues	Brynmawr	Caldicot Castle	Cefn Forest	Cwmffrwdoer Sports	Fleur-de-Lys	Govilon	Hafodyrynys Bluebirds	Hilltop Sports	Marshfield	New Inn AFC	Race	Thornwell Red & White
AC Pontymister		3-2	3-3	3-2	3-4	1-4	4-4	3-5	1-2	1-1	2-2	2-1	1-4	2-3
Blaenavon Blues	3-0		4-2	3-0	6-0	0-0	5-0	2-0	2-0	5-2	5-0	3-0	2-0	5-1
Brynmawr	3-2	1-1	D	2-1	5-1	0-2	4-0	4-4	6-3	6-2	1-1	2-2	2-4	5-0
Caldicot Castle	0-1	0-2	2-1	I	3-0	2-0	1-2	2-1	1-2	3-3	4-0	0-2	0-3	0-0
Cefn Forest	1-2	2-8	1-2	2-3	V	1-4	3-2	3-0	2-3	3-1	3-3	5-2	1-1	5-6
Cwmffrwdoer Sports	3-0	3-1	5-1	3-1	8-1		4-1	3-2	3-0	5-1	6-0	6-1	1-2	8-1
Fleur-de-Lys	3-3	0-4	2-1	1-2	6-2	1-6		4-10	0-1	3-3	0-0	0-0	1-3	2-1
Govilon	3-3	2-3	2-1	6-0	8-1	2-3	2-0	T	1-2	2-3	1-3	2-1	2-3	7-0
Hafodyrynys Bluebirds	2-7	0-2	1-9	4-2	1-0	1-5	1-3	5M0	H	2-6	2-4	0-2	2-6	4-3
Hilltop Sports	3-2	1-6	1-1	0-3	2-0	2-7	4-1	3-6	4-2	R	2-0	3-1	0-7	3-0
Marshfield	3-0	0-9	2-4	4-1	1-5	2-5	1-2	3-2	1-7		E	4-2	1-10	2-3
New Inn AFC	2-7	1-3	2-1	1-4	2-6	0-4	1-2	0-1	5-1	3-1	1-1	E	2-4	1-6
Race	6-1	0-3	5-2	5-0	6-3	1-1	3-1	6-4	7-0	4-0	2-4	7-1		1-1
Thornwell Red & White	3-2	4-3	3-1	2-3	2-0	1-5	1-5	4-3	1-0	1-5	5-2	7-1	0M5	

Hilltop Sports 1 Marshfield 0
Lliswerry 4 Hafodyrynys 2
Llanhilleth Athletic 0 **Race** 4
Mardy 1 **Abertillery Bluebirds** 7
Newport Civil Service 2 Goytre 0
Panteg 2 **Blaenavon Blues** 4
Pill 3 Thornwell Red & White 1
Tillery United 1 **Christchurch Hamdden** 4
Trethomas Bluebirds 1 **Newport Corinthians** 6
W. Pontnewydd 3 **Croesyceiliog** 5

THIRD ROUND
Aberbargoed Buds 4 Abertillery Bluebirds 0
Caldicot Castle 0 **Newport Civil Service** 2
Christchurch Hamdden 2 Croesyceiliog 1

Cwmbran Celtic 3 Garnlydan 1
Govilon 3 Rogerstone Welfare 0
Hilltop Sports 1 **Blaenavon Blues** 10
Lliswerry 0 **Pill** 1
Newport Corinthians 2 Race 0

QUARTER-FINALS
Blaenavon Blues 3 Govilon 1
Christchurch Hamdden 1 **Newport Civil Service** 2
Newport Corinthians 1 Cwmbran Celtic 0
Pill 1 **Aberbargoed Buds** 3

SEMI-FINALS
Blaenavon Blues 4 Newport Civil Service 1
Newport Corinthians 1 **Aberbargoed Buds** 5

FINAL
(9th May at Newport County)
Abergargoed Buds 6 Blaenavon Blues 5

Division Three		P	W	D	L	F	A	Pts
Cwmffrwdoer Sports		26	22	2	2	104	26	68
Blaenavon Blues		26	21	2	3	92	22	65
Race		26	20	3	3	105	36	63
Thornwell Red & White		26	12	2	12	59	80	38
Hilltop Sports		26	11	4	11	63	75	37
Brynmawr		26	10	6	10	70	56	36
Govilon		26	11	2	13	79	62	35
Caldicot Castle		26	10	2	14	40	53	32
AC Pontymister		26	7	6	13	59	72	27
Hafodyrynys Bluebirds		26	9	0	17	43	85	27
Fleur-de-Lys	-3	26	8	5	13	46	70	26
Marshfield		26	7	5	14	44	87	26
Cefn Forest		26	7	2	17	55	90	23
New Inn AFC		26	5	3	18	37	82	18

DIVISION THREE CONSTITUTION 2003-04

AC PONTYMISTER .... Pontymister Recreation Ground, Pontymister, Caerphilly, Gwent .... None
ABERGAVENNY THURSDAYS .... Penypound Stadium, Abergavenny, Monmouthshire 01873 853906
BRYNMAWR .... Brynmawr Recreation Ground, Brynmawr, Gwent .... None
CALDICOT CASTLE .... Caldicot Castle Grounds, Caldicot, Gwent .... None
CEFN FOREST .... Welfare Ground, Cefn Forest, Gwent .... None
CRUSADERS .... Fields Park, Newbridge, Gwent .... None
GOVILON .... Crickhowell FC, Crickhowell, Powys .... None
HAFODYRYNYS BLUEBIRDS .... Hafodyrynys Welfare, Hafodyrynys, Gwent .... None
HILLTOP SPORTS .... Hilltop Stadium, Ebbw Vale, Gwent .... None
MARSHFIELD .... Marshfield Village Hall, Marshfield, Gwent .... None
NEW INN. .... Woodfield Road, New Inn, Gwent .... None
PILCS .... PILCS Ground, Griffithstown, Pontypool, Gwent .... None
RACE .... Pontypool College, Pontypool, Gwent .... None
THORNWELL BURT BARN .... Thornwell, Chepstow, Gwent .... None
TRETHOMAS BLUEBIRDS .... Llanfabon Drive, Trethomas, Gwent .... None
WHITEHEADS .... Whiteheads Sports Ground, Bassaleg, Gwent .... None

Cwmffrwdoer Sports and Blaenavon Blues are promoted to Division Two replaced by Abergavenny Thursdays and Trethomas Bluebirds. Whiteheads are promoted from the Newport & District League and PILCS from the East Gwent League. Fleur-de-Lys become Crusaders and Thornwell Red & White are now Thornwell Burt Barn.

HAMPSHIRE LEAGUE

Team	Aldermaston	Amesbury Town	Andover New St.	Bishops Waltham	Brading Town	East Cowes Vics	Fawley	Horndean	Hythe & Dibden	Liss Athletic	Locksheath	Lymington Town	Petersfield Town	Pirelli General	Poole Town	Portsmouth RN	Ringwood Town	Stockbridge	Vosper Thorn'croft	Winchester City
Aldermaston		0-2	1-5	1-2	0-2	0-3	3-0	1-0	2-3	2-4	0-2	4-3	0-2	1-2	0-5	0-1	2-2	1-3	1-2	1-4
Amesbury Town	3-0		2-0	5-2	1-2	0-2	1-2	2-3	1-0	2-3	3-2	5-7	4-1	3-1	2-3	3-0	1-2	1-3	1-2	1-4
Andover New Street	4-1	2-1	P	0-0	4-2	2-2	7-0	2-2	3-0	4-2	2-0	2-4	1-2	3-0	2-1	1-3	0-2	1-1	3-2	1-1
Bishops Waltham Town	0-0	1-2	1-1	R	6-1	2-1	2-0	1-1	5-3	0-2	1-2	1-2	0-1	0-1	2-3	2-0	3-2	2-1	0-1	1-1
Brading Town	1-0	2-2	1-4	3-2	E	1-4	2-1	0-0	3-0	1-1	2-1	1-2	1-0	0-1	2-3	2-0	3-2	2-1	0-1	0-5
East Cowes Victoria Ath.	4-0	5-0	4-1	1-2	2-3	M	7-0	1-0	1-2	1-0	2-0	3-2	2-1	4-1	5-0	3-1	1-2	1-3	3-0	0-7
Fawley	5-2	0-0	1-5	2-5	3-2	1-5	I	1-2	3-3	0-2	2-1	1-0	0-5	2-2	4-2	0-2	0-1	0-7	1-2	0-5
Horndean	5-0	2-0	1-1	1-0	2-0	0-0	4-0	E	1-3	3-4	2-0	0-3	4-2	1-0	0-1	1-1	2-2	2-0	0-4	0-2
Hythe & Dibden	5-1	2-2	1-3	0-1	0-1	0-1	2-4	0-1	R	1-1	1-4	1-0	2-0	2-1	2-4	1-2	5-2	2-7		0-7
Liss Athletic	3-3	5-2	5-0	4-2	8-2	2-2	3-2	1-1	4-1		7-0	4-4	2-4	2-1	2-1	2-0	5-3	2-1	0-1	2-8
Locksheath	3-0	3-5	0-1	4-0	4-1	2-5	5-1	2-4	4-0	1-1	D	1-0	1-3	4-1	5-1	1-2	1-2			0-4
Lymington Town	3-0	1-1	1-2	1-0	3-2	5-0	1-3	2-2	0-1	4-4		I	1-0	1-2	2-1	4-1	2-3	1-3	0-3	1-3
Petersfield Town	3-3	2-3	2-2	2-2	2-0	0-3	2-3	2-2	1-1	3-0	1-2	1-4	V	1-0	4-1	2-2	4-1	2-3	1-0	0-6
Pirelli General	3-3	1-0	0-2	1-2	2-0	4-3	1-2	3-1	0-0	1-2	3-1	0-0	1-0	I	0-3	1-1	5-3	2-3	1-1	0-6
Poole Town	5-1	1-3	1-1	1-0	8-1	W-L	2-1	0-0	4-0	2-0	1-3	3-1	3-0	1-0	S	0-3	1-1	5-3	2-3	1-1
Portsmouth Royal Navy	2-1	2-2	4-1	2-2	2-1	2-1	4-0	2-0	2-0	1-3	3-1	3-0	1-0		2-0	I	3-1	1-1	2-2	1-10
Ringwood Town	3-0	5-2	5-1	2-3	1-3	0-3	2-0	2-1	3-1	1-4	2-2	0-4	7-0	1-2	2-1	0-2	O	3-0	1-1	1-10
Stockbridge	7-1	7-2	2-0	2-2	4-1	2-1	4-0	2-1	1-0	3-4	2-3	2-0	4-7	0-1	1-2	1-3	4-4	N	1-2	0-2
Vosper Thornycroft	6-0	3-0	2-1	3-0	4-0	3-1	12-0	7-0	2-1	7-3	3-1	7-0	4-2	6-0	1-0	4-2	4-1			2-5
Winchester City	3-0	5-1	5-0	3-1	10-0	5-0	7-1	2-1	2-0	6-0	3-1	10-0	6-0	7-0	2-0	6-0	6-0	4-1	3-0	

Premier Division

	P	W	D	L	F	A	Pts
Winchester City	38	36	1	1	181	18	109
Vosper Thornycroft	38	29	5	4	116	40	92
East Cowes Victoria Athletic	38	23	4	11	95	47	73
Poole Town	38	22	6	10	79	54	72
Horndean	38	19	11	8	66	43	68
Locksheath	38	19	5	14	84	70	62
Liss Athletic	38	18	8	12	94	86	62
Andover New Street	38	16	9	13	73	65	57
Stockbridge	38	17	4	17	86	75	55
Petersfield Town	38	15	8	15	71	70	53
Amesbury Town	38	15	5	18	76	88	50
Ringwood Town	38	13	10	15	75	79	49
Portsmouth Royal Navy	38	14	7	17	62	84	49
Bishops Waltham Town	38	13	7	18	57	67	46
Lymington Town	38	11	11	16	75	91	44
Pirelli General	38	10	7	21	45	92	37
Brading Town	38	10	7	21	58	110	37
Fawley	38	6	5	27	43	130	23
Hythe & Dibden	38	5	7	26	46	94	22
Aldermaston	38	3	5	30	36	115	14

LEAGUE CUP

FIRST ROUND

Aldermaston 2 **Andover New Street** 4
Brading Town 1 **Horndean** 4
Broughton 2 Romsey Town 1
Co-op Sports & Hilsea 1 **Winchester City** 5
East Cowes Victoria 7 Hedge End 0
Fareham Sacred Hearts 0 **Laverstock & Ford** 1
Fleet Spurs 2 **Liss Athletic** 4
Fleetlands 5 Ludgershall Sports 2
aet (3-4p)
Hayling United 3 **DCAFC** 3
aet (3-4p)
Hythe & Dibden 2 **Netley Central Sports** 3
King's Somborne (scr.) v **QK Southampton** (w/o)
Locksheath 0 **Overton United** 5
Ordnance Survey 3 **Micheldever** 3
aet (3-4p)
Paulsgrove 0 **Verwood Town** 2
Pirelli General 2 Amesbury Town 0
Portsmouth RN 5 M & T Awbridge 1
Tadley Town 0 **Poole Town** 4
Vosper Thornycroft (w/o) v Headley Athletic (scr.)

PREMIER DIVISION CONSTITUTION 2003-04

ALDERMASTON . . . . . Aldermaston Rec Society, Automic Weapons Establishment, Aldermaston, Reading, Berkshire 0118 982 4544
AMESBURY TOWN . . . . Amesbury Recreation Ground, Amesbury, Wiltshire 01980 623489
ANDOVER NEW STREET . . . . Foxcotte Park, Charlton Down, Andover, Hampshire 01264 358358
BISHOPS WALTHAM TOWN . . Priory Park, Elizabeth Way, Bishops Waltham, Southampton, Hampshire 01489 894269
BRADING TOWN . . . . Vicarage Lane, Brading, Isle of Wight 01983 407165
EAST COWES VICTORIA ATHLETIC . Beatrice Avenue, Whippingham, East Cowes, Isle of Wight 01983 297165
FAWLEY . . . . Waterside Sports & Social Club, Long Lane, Holbury, Southampton, Hampshire 023 8089 3750
HORNDEAN . . . . Five Heads Park, Five Heads Road, Horndean, Hampshire 023 9259 1363
HYTHE & DIBDEN . . . . Ewart Recreation Ground, Jones Lane, Hythe, Southampton, Hampshire 023 8084 5264
LISS ATHLETIC . . . . Newman Collard Ground, Hill Brow Road, Liss, Hampshire 01730 894022
LOCKS HEATH . . . . Lockesheath Rec, Warsash Road, Titchfield Common, Fareham, Hampshire 01489 600932
LYMINGTON TOWN . . . . Sports Ground, Southampton Road, Lymington, Hampshire 01590 671305
PETERSFIELD TOWN . . . . Love Lane, Petersfield, Hampshire 01730 233416
POOLE TOWN . . . . Tatnam Farm, School Road, off Stanley Green/Palmer Road, Poole, Dorset 07771 604289
PORTSMOUTH ROYAL NAVY . Navy Stadium, HMS Temeraire, Burnaby Road, Portsmouth, Hampshire . . . . 023 9272 4235 / 9272 5315
RINGWOOD TOWN . . . . The Clubhouse, Long Lane, Ringwood, Hampshire 01425 473448
STOCKBRIDGE . . . . Recreation Ground, High Street, Stockbridge, Hampshire . . . . None
VTFC . . . . VT Sports Ground, Portsmouth Road, Sholing, Hampshire 023 8040 3829

Winchester City are promoted to the Wessex League. Pirelli General have folded. Vosper Thornycroft become VTFC

	AFC Portchester	Alresford Town	Clanfield	Colden Common	Co-op Sports & Hilsea	Fareham Sacred Hearts	Farnborough North End	Fleet Spurs	Fleetlands	Hayling United	Micheldever	Paulsgrove	Tadley Town	Verwood Town	Yateley Green
AFC Portchester		4-1	1-2	0-1	4-2	2-1	2-0	2-0	3-3	2-2	2-1	1-4	2-2	4-1	7-0
Alresford Town	5-1	D	2-1	0-7	4-2	1-0	2-2	1-5	0-1	0-1	2-1	1-1	1-2	0-4	1-0
Clanfield	2-2	0-2	I	4-4	1-4	7-2	2-2	1-0	2-2	0-5	2-2	0-3	1-1	1-2	0-3
Colden Common	4-2	1-1	6-2	V	4-1	3-1	5-2	1-2	4-2	1-2	0-1	2-1	1-1	0-1	3-0
Co-op Sports & Hilsea	1-1	1-2	0-3	2-3	I	1-0	1-7	2-2	1-3	0-4	2-4	1-2	2-4	0-5	0-1
Fareham Sacred Hearts	0-4	0-4	4-0	2-4	1-1	S	1-2	1-2	2-3	0-2	0-0	1-6	5-2	0-2	1-1
Farnborough North End	4-1	3-2	8-1	2-3	3-2	1-3	I	2-3	5-1	0-4	3-2	3-1	3-2	2-3	3-0
Fleet Spurs	1-1	3-1	3-2	1-1	1-1	5-1	1-1	O	0-0	3-2	1-2	2-3	2-3	2-0	0-0
Fleetlands	7-0	0-1	2-3	2-2	3-3	7-3	2-1	1-5	N	2-1	2-5	4-3	2-1	3-0	W-L
Hayling United	3-3	3-0	5-1	2-1	8-0	3-0	0-0	4-1	1-2		4-0	1-3	1-0	5-0	8-1
Micheldever	2-2	1-0	1-1	1-1	4-0	3-1	1-4	0-1	4-2	0-1		1-2	1-2	0-0	4-0
Paulsgrove	4-1	0-0	3-0	0-2	4-1	2-3	0-1	1-0	6-1	3-1	3-1	O	1-4	3-2	4-0
Tadley Town	2-0	0-0	2-2	2-0	2-1	0-3	0-0	1-2	3-1	1-3	1-2	0-1	N	1-2	5-0
Verwood Town	3-2	4-0	1-0	0-1	1-0	2-1	1-0	2-1	1-3	2-4	5-3	2-0	1-0	E	2-1
Yateley Green	1-2	2-5	3-2	1-6	0-2	1-4	1-5	2-7	2-2	3-6	0-4	1-4	1-2	1-2	

SECOND ROUND
AFC Portchester 4 Clanfield 1
Andover New Street 3 Otterbourne 2
Broughton 1 **Micheldever 2**
Colden Common 4 Laverstock & Ford 1
Fawley 0 **Poole Town 3**
Fleetlands 1 **Portsmouth Royal Navy 2**
Horndean 3 Liss Athletic 0
Lymington Town 3 Farnborough North End 0
Netley Central Sports 0 **Alresford Town 1**
Petersfield Town 2 **Overton United 3**
Pirelli General 1 East Cowes Victoria Athletic 0
QK Southampton 1 **Hamble Club 3**
Ringwood Town 2 **Bishops Waltham Town 3**
Stockbridge 4 DCAFC 2
Vosper Thornycroft 7 Verwood Town 1
Winchester City 2 Yateley Green 1

THIRD ROUND
AFC Portchester 6 Pirelli General 2
Bishops Waltham 0 **Micheldever 1**
Colden Common 7 Portsmouth RN 1
Hamble Club 4 Overton United 2
Horndean 0 **Andover New Street 1**
Lymington Town 3 Vosper Thornycroft 1
Stockbridge 3 **Poole Town 4**
Winchester City 6 Alresford Town 1

QUARTER-FINALS
AFC Portchester 3 Hamble Club 1
Andover NS 1 Lymington Town 0
Colden Common 1 **Winchester City 6**
Micheldever 0 **Poole Town 3**

SEMI-FINALS
Poole Town 2 **Andover New St 3** *aet*
(at Winchester City)
Winchester City 2 AFC Portchester 0
(at Locksheath)

FINAL
(3rd May at Andover New Street)
Andover New Street 1 **Winchester City 4**

Division One

	P	W	D	L	F	A	Pts
Hayling United	28	20	3	5	86	29	63
Verwood Town	28	19	1	8	51	38	58
Colden Common	28	16	5	7	70	39	53
Paulsgrove	28	17	2	9	66	37	53
Fleet Spurs	28	15	6	7	57	36	51
Farnborough Nth End	28	14	5	9	69	47	47
Fleetlands	28	13	6	9	63	62	45
Micheldever	28	11	6	11	51	44	39
Tadley Town	28	11	6	11	46	41	39
AFC Portchester	28	10	8	10	58	59	38
Alresford Town	28	11	5	12	39	50	38
Clanfield	28	5	8	15	43	75	23
Fareham Sac. Hearts	28	6	3	19	41	71	21
Co-op Sports & Hilsea	28	3	5	20	34	81	14
Yateley Green -1	28	3	3	22	26	91	11

DIVISION ONE CONSTITUTION 2003-04

AFC PORTCHESTER .... Portchester Community School, White Hart Lane, Portchester, Hampshire 023 9236 4399
ALRESFORD TOWN .... Alrebury Park, The Avenue, Alresford, Hampshire. 01962 735100
CLANFIELD .... Peel Park, Charlton Lane, Clanfield, Waterlooville, Hampshire. .... None
COLDEN COMMON .... Colden Common Rec, Main Road, Colden Common, Winchester, Hampshire. 01962 712365
FAREHAM SACRED HEARTS.......... Warsash Rec, Osbourne Road, Warsash, Southampton .... None
FARNBOROUGH NORTH END ..... Farnborough Gate, Ringwood Road, Farnborough, Hampshire. .... None
FLEET SPURS .... Kennels Lane, Southwood, Farnborough, Hampshire. .... None
FLEETLANDS.............................. Lederle Lane, Gosport, Hampshire 01329 239723
HAYLING UNITED .... Hayling Sports Centre, Mengham Park, Hayling Island, Hampshire 023 9263 7758
HEDGE END.......... Norman Rodaway Sports Ground, Heathhouse Lane, Hedge End, Southampton, Hampshire .... None
LAVERSTOCK & FORD... The Dell, Laverstock & Ford SC, 23 Church Road, Laverstock, Salisbury, Wiltshire. 01722 327401
MICHELDEVER............. Lord Rank Playing Field, Duke Street, Micheldever, Winchester, Hampshire. 01256 770561
OVERTON UNITED .... Recreation Centre, Bridge Street, Overton, Hampshire 023 9232 4102
PAULSGROVE .... The Grove Club, Marsden Road, off Allaway Avenue, Paulsgrove, Portsmouth, Hampshire ...... None
TADLEY TOWN .... The Green, Tadley, Hampshire .... None
VERWOOD TOWN .... Pottern Park, Pottern Way, Verwood, Dorset .... None

Headley Athletic withdrew without kicking a ball. Co-op Sports & Hilsea (who become East Lodge) and Yateley Green are relegated to Division Two
replaced by Laverstock & Ford, Overton United and Hedge End.

	Broughton	DCAFC	Hamble Club	Hedge End	Laverstock & Ford	Ludgershall Sports	M & T Awbridge	Netley Central Sports	Ordnance Survey	Otterbourne	Overton United	QK Southampton	Romsey Town
Broughton	D	1-1	3-1	1-3	0-11	2-1	3-1	0-2	1-3	3-2	1-0	4-5	4-0
DCAFC	0-0	I	3-2	1-2	1-2	4-1	3-0	4-1	0-3	0-0	0-2	0-1	2-0
Hamble Club	4-2	1-2	V	1-6	1-4	1-3	2-0	2-2	2-0	1-0	0-4	3-1	2-2
Hedge End	4-1	4-1	1-2	I	3-1	2-2	6-0	3-1	0-4	2-2	3-1	2-0	5-2
Laverstock & Ford	9-0	3-4	1-0	1-2	S	1-0	3-1	4-0	1-0	2-0	1-1	3-0	2-1
Ludgershall Sports	2-0	0-0	2-3	2-5	0-3	I	1-1	4-2	2-3	1-1	0-4	1-0	7-0
M & T Awbridge	3-2	1-2	1-1	4-2	0-2	0-4	O	0-1	0-0	0-1	1-0	3-1	3-0
Netley Central Sports	2-1	4-0	1-2	1-1	2-2	1-0	1-0	N	1-3	5-1	1-3	2-1	2-0
Ordnance Survey	4-1	0-3	2-2	1-1	0-4	4-0	2-2	2-0		3-1	4-0	0-2	1-0
Otterbourne	1-0	3-1	1-2	1-3	2-0	1-0	2-0	0-2	4-3		1-4	1-0	3-0
Overton United	4-3	5-0	0-0	0-2	1-1	4-1	4-2	3-2	1-0	2-1	T	5-1	4-0
QK Southampton	2-3	1-4	3-1	2-1	1-2	2-2	0-0	0-6	0-0	2-0	1-4	W	2-3
Romsey Town	1-4	2-2	0-2	1-1	0-3	0-3	1-2	0-7	1-2	1-2	0-5	1-2	O

Combination One	P	W	D	L	F	A	Pts
Paulsgrove Res.	22	16	4	2	57	35	52
Colden Cmn Res.	22	15	3	4	64	31	48
Liss Athletic Res.	22	15	2	5	70	36	47
Hythe/Dibden Res.	22	11	2	9	46	44	35
Fleetlands Res.	22	9	3	10	47	44	30
Hayling Utd Res.	22	8	5	9	41	39	29
Lymington T. Res.	22	7	4	11	36	51	25
Vosper T'croft Res.	22	7	4	11	30	45	25
AFC P'chester Res.	22	5	8	9	34	53	23
Laverstock/F. Res.	22	5	6	11	42	53	21
Fleet Spurs Res.	22	6	2	14	27	46	20
Clanfield Res.	22	5	3	14	38	55	18

Combination Two	P	W	D	L	F	A	Pts
Fareham T. Res.	22	20	2	0	105	9	62
Locksheath Res.	22	15	3	4	72	33	48
Pirelli General Res.	22	12	5	5	60	32	41
Overton Utd Res.	22	13	2	7	58	46	41
Bish. Waltham Res.	22	12	5	5	57	50	41
Netley CS Res.	22	11	0	11	49	47	33
Petersfield Res.	22	8	5	9	50	44	29
M&T Awb'dge Res.	22	7	2	13	37	72	23
QK South'pton Res.	22	5	7	10	37	51	22
Romsey Town Res.	22	4	6	12	28	55	18
Hamble Club Res.	22	5	3	14	39	74	18
Fawley Res.	22	0	0	22	21	100	0

COMBINATION CUP

FINAL *(23rd April at Portsmouth RN)*
Fareham T. Res. 4 Locksheath Res. 2

DIVISION TWO

Division Two	P	W	D	L	F	A	Pts
Laverstock & Ford	24	17	3	4	66	20	54
Overton United	24	16	3	5	61	26	51
Hedge End	24	15	5	4	64	33	50
Ordnance Survey	24	12	5	7	44	29	41
Netley Central Sports	24	12	3	9	49	36	39
DCAFC	24	10	5	9	38	39	35
Hamble Club	24	10	5	9	38	44	35
Otterbourne	24	10	3	11	31	37	33
Ludgershall Sports	24	7	5	12	39	44	26
Broughton	24	8	2	14	40	66	26
QK Southampton	24	7	3	14	30	51	24
M & T Awbridge	24	6	5	13	25	44	23
Romsey Town	24	1	3	20	16	72	6

DIVISION TWO CONSTITUTION 2003-04

BROUGHTON .... The Sportsfield, Buckholt Road, Broughton, Stockbridge, Hampshire 01794 301150
DCAFC .... Victoria Park, Castle Road, Salisbury, Wiltshire 01722 415089
DURLEY .... Kytes Lane, Durley, Southampton .... None
EAST LODGE .... Langstone Harbour Sports Ground, Eastern Road, Portsmouth, Hampshire .... None
HAMBLE CLUB .... Shell Mex Ground, Hamble Lane, Hamble-le-Rice, Southampton, Hampshire 07881 766085
LUDGERSHALL SPORTS .... Astor Crescent, Ludgershall, Hampshire 01264 398200
M & T AWBRIDGE .... Michelmersh & Timsbury Sports Pavilion, Mannyngham Way, Timsbury, Romsey 01794 368955
MOTTISFONT .... Bengers Lane, Mottisfont, Hampshire .... None
NETLEY CENTRAL SPORTS .... Netley Rec, Station Road, Netley Abbey, Southampton, Hampshire 023 8045 2267
ORDNANCE SURVEY .... Lordshill Recreation Ground, Southampton, Hampshire 023 8061 8812
OTTERBOURNE .... Oakwood Park, off Oakwood Avenue, Otterbourne, Hampshire 01962 714681
QK SOUTHAMPTON .... Lordshill Recreation Centre, Southampton, Hampshire 023 8073 2531
RS BASINGSTOKE .... Whiteditch Playing Field, Sherborne Road, Basingstoke, Hampshire 01256 814618
ROMSEY TOWN .... The By-Pass Ground, South Front, Romsey, Hampshire 01794 512003
YATELEY GREEN .... Sean Deveraux Park, Chandlers Lane Playing Fields, Chandlers Lane, Yateley, Hampshire .... None
Laverstock & Ford, Hedge End and Overton United are promoted to Division One replaced by Co-op Sports & Hilsea (now East Lodge) and Yateley Green. Newcomers are Durley and Mottisfont (both Southampton Senior League) and RS Basingstoke (Hellenic League).

HELLENIC LEAGUE

	Abingdon United	Almondsbury Town	Bicester Town	Bishops Cleeve	Brackley Town	Carterton Town	Didcot Town	Fairford Town	Gloucester United	Henley Town	Highworth Town	Hook Norton	North Leigh	Pegasus Juniors	Pewsey Vale	Shortwood United	Southall Town	Tuffley Rovers	Wantage Town	Wootton Bassett Town	Yate Town
Abingdon United		1-1	7-0	1-0	2-1	1-3	1-4	1-0	3-1	1-3	2-5	2-2	2-3	1-1	4-0	0-3	3-1	1-0	3-0	0-0	0-2
Almondsbury Town	0-2		1-0	1-2	0-1	0-2	1-4	1-2	1-3	3-7	0-4	1-5	0-1	4-0	2-2	0-2	4-1	1-2	0-3	1-2	0-3
Bicester Town	0-0	3-1	P	1-0	2-2	1-3	0-4	0-1	3-3	2-5	0-1	1-2	0-6	1-3	2-3	1-1	2-5	3-5	4-0	1-3	0-3
Bishops Cleeve	3-0	1-2	2-0	R	2-1	1-1	1-0	2-4	2-2	0-0	3-0	2-0	2-3	1-2	1-3	1-0	1-0	2-1	2-1	8-0	0-1
Brackley Town	2-0	0-0	4-0	1-1	E	2-2	1-0	1-3	4-0	0-1	1-2	2-2	0-2	7-0	3-0	3-1	2-2	6-1	0-3	1-0	3-3
Carterton Town	2-1	1-0	1-1	1-1	2-2	M	0-0	2-0	2-1	5-1	2-0	0-3	0-0	2-1	3-0	2-1	3-0	1-7	2-1	0-0	1-1
Didcot Town	1-2	5-1	6-0	1-0	1-0	2-2	I	0-3	2-0	1-0	0-2	5-2	0-2	2-0	2-0	3-1	1-3	1-0	7-1	2-1	0-0
Fairford Town	2-0	1-0	5-0	2-4	0-0	0-1	0-1	E	2-0	1-2	1-1	3-0	0-0	2-1	1-0	1-0	0-2	0-1	7-1	2-0	0-1
Gloucester United	0-2	0-0	2-0	1-5	0-5	0-0	0-4	0-1	R	3-0	1-3	0-0	1-4	3-2	4-3	1-3	0-2	2-4	1-1	1-3	0-2
Henley Town	2-0	4-0	1-0	4-0	2-1	0-1	3-1	0-0	2-2	D	3-0	3-1	1-2	5-0	4-1	0-0	0-2	1-3	2-1	0-0	0-1
Highworth Town	0-2	3-0	1-0	0-1	1-4	0-0	3-0	2-1	2-2	1-1	I	1-1	1-2	3-2	3-0	1-1	3-2	8-1	1-1	1-0	1-2
Hook Norton	0-2	2-1	1-1	3-0	3-4	0-2	1-0	0-4	0-2	2-0	3-0	V	2-0	3-0	2-0	3-1	1-1	4-0	1-0	0-3	1-3
North Leigh	1-1	1-1	3-2	1-0	4-0	0-2	2-0	3-2	2-0	1-1	2-5	2-0	I	2-0	3-0	2-0	3-1	0-3	0-4	1-0	2-8
Pegasus Juniors	0-3	1-2	1-2	1-4	0-5	1-1	0-2	1-2	1-4	2-0	0-6	0-3	0-2	S	4-1	5-3	2-1	1-1	1-1	1-2	2-8
Pewsey Vale	1-5	0-3	2-3	0-2	1-1	0-0	2-2	0-4	0-2	3-1	0-1	1-3	1-3	2-2	I	1-3	3-0	4-2	1-0	1-5	1-5
Shortwood United	3-2	1-3	3-0	3-1	0-0	1-1	0-3	1-1	1-2	2-2	0-0	2-1	4-2	5-3	1-0	O	1-3	3-0	4-2	1-0	1-5
Southall Town	1-2	1-0	2-3	1-3	1-2	0-1	2-2	0-1	4-3	3-2	0-1	1-1	2-3	6-1	1-0	4-2	N	2-1	4-3	5-1	3-2
Tuffley Rovers	3-2	1-1	1-1	0-0	0-4	0-2	1-0	1-4	1-3	0-0	0-3	1-2	1-0	3-0	2-3	0-1	1-3		0-4	0-1	1-2
Wantage Town	0-1	1-1	1-1	2-3	0-4	0-1	1-6	0-0	2-0	0-1	1-3	1-1	1-6	3-0	2-3	0-1	1-3	0-4		0-1	1-2
Wootton Bassett Town	0-4	1-1	2-0	2-1	2-0	1-3	0-2	0-1	2-1	1-0	0-2	2-4	1-0	2-2	1-2	1-0	0-0	1-3	0-1		0-0
Yate Town	2-1	3-2	2-1	1-3	0-0	2-3	0-2	1-1	5-0	3-2	1-3	3-1	0-3	0-2	4-0	1-0	5-0	3-2	4-0	0-0	

Premier Division	P	W	D	L	F	A	Pts
North Leigh	40	29	6	5	84	36	93
Yate Town	40	25	8	7	87	42	83
Carterton Town	40	22	17	1	61	29	83
Highworth Town	40	23	10	7	79	41	79
Didcot Town	40	22	6	12	77	39	72
Fairford Town	40	21	8	11	65	30	71
Brackley Town	40	18	12	10	84	42	66
Abingdon United	40	20	6	14	70	52	66
Bishops Cleeve	40	19	7	14	68	50	64
Henley Town	40	17	10	13	69	48	61
Southall Town	40	18	7	15	75	65	61
Hook Norton	40	15	13	12	67	55	58
Shortwood United	40	15	10	15	64	60	55
Tuffley Rovers	40	12	9	19	56	76	45
Wootton Bassett Town	40	10	10	20	36	70	40
Gloucester United -3	40	9	8	23	48	89	32
Almondsbury Town	40	8	7	25	43	77	31
Pegasus Juniors	40	8	7	25	45	108	31
Pewsey Vale	40	7	8	25	45	93	29
Bicester Town	40	5	8	27	40	99	23
Wantage Town	40	5	7	28	36	98	22

Reserve Div. One	P	W	D	L	F	A	Pts
Didcot Town Res.	26	18	4	4	60	27	58
Highworth T. Res.	26	16	7	3	55	21	55
Finchampstead Res.	26	16	4	6	69	40	52
Carterton Town Res.	26	15	5	6	50	34	50
Banbury United Res.	26	13	3	10	54	41	42
Henley Town Res.	26	12	6	8	48	47	42
Chelt. Saracens Res.	26	10	4	12	37	41	34
Kidlington Res.	26	10	4	12	31	40	34
Wootton Bassett Res.	26	8	8	10	52	45	32
Brackley Town Res.	26	9	5	12	50	43	32
Fairford Town Res.	26	8	5	13	34	49	29
North Leigh Res.	26	5	6	15	41	60	21
Bicester Town Res.	26	5	2	19	27	71	17
Headington Am. Res.	26	3	5	18	28	77	14

Reserve Div. Two West	P	W	D	L	F	A	Pts
Cirencester Utd Res.	24	17	3	4	56	30	54
Milton United Res. -3	24	16	5	3	63	17	50
Easington Spts Res.	24	14	6	4	51	22	48
Ardley United Res.	24	14	4	6	57	41	46
Hook Norton Res.	24	14	3	7	47	32	45
Wantage Town Res.	24	11	7	6	44	29	40
Almondsbury T. Res.	24	11	4	9	42	31	37
Old Woodstock Res.	24	9	4	11	45	52	31
Letcombe Res.	24	8	4	12	40	36	28
Adderbury Pk Res.	24	5	3	16	36	58	18
Clanfield Res.	24	3	6	15	32	73	15
Middle Barton Res.	24	4	3	17	22	69	15
Chipping Norton Res.	24	3	2	19	26	71	11

WWW.NLNEWSDESK.CO.UK

HELLENIC GROUND HOP 2003

Sunday	24th Aug	*Slimbridge*	v	*Shortwood United*	2.30pm
Sunday	24th Aug	*Cheltenham Saracens*	v	*Harrow Hill*	6.00pm
Monday	25th Aug	*Shrivenham*	v	*Purton*	11.00am
Monday	25th Aug	*Quarry Nomads*	v	*Headington Amateurs*	2.30pm
Monday	25th Aug	*Brackley Town*	v	*Hook Norton*	6.30pm

PREMIER DIVISION CONSTITUTION 2003-04

ABINGDON UNITED...................Northcourt Road, Abingdon, Oxfordshire...................01235 203203
ALMONDSBURY TOWN.........Oakland Park, Gloucester Road, Almondsbury, Bristol, South Glos...................01454 612220
BICESTER TOWN...................Sports Ground, Oxford Road, Bicester, Oxfordshire...................01869 241036
BISHOPS CLEEVE...................Kayte Lane, Bishops Cleeve, Cheltenham, Gloucestershire...................None
BRACKLEY TOWN...................St James's Park, Churchill Way, Brackley, Northants...................01280 704077
CARTERTON TOWN...................Kilkenny Lane, Carterton, Oxfordshire...................01993 842410
CHIPPING NORTON TOWN.........Hailey Road, Chipping Norton, Oxfordshire...................01608 642562 / 645311
DIDCOT TOWN.............Loop Meadow Stadium, Bowmont Water, off Avon Way, Didcot, Oxfordshire...................01235 813138
FAIRFORD TOWN...................Cinder Lane, London Road, Fairford, Gloucestershire...................01285 712071
GLOUCESTER UNITED.............Meadow Park, Sudmeadow Road, Hempsted, Gloucester. 01452 421400 / 311060. Fax: 01452 301330
HENLEY TOWN...................Triangle Ground, Mill Lane, Henley-on-Thames, Oxfordshire...................01491 411083
HIGHWORTH TOWN...................Elm Recreation Ground, Highworth, Swindon, Wiltshire...................01793 861109
HOOK NORTON...........Banbury United FC, The Stadium, Stadium Approach, Banbury, Oxfordshire...................01295 263354
HUNGERFORD TOWN...................Bulpit Lane, Hungerford, Berkshire.........01488 682939. Boardroom: 01488 684597
NORTH LEIGH...............Eynsham Park Hall Sports Ground, North Leigh, Witney, Oxfordshire...................01993 881427
PEGASUS JUNIORS...............Hereford Leisure Centre, Holmer Road, Hereford, Herefordshire...................01432 278178
PEWSEY VALE...................Recreation Ground, Ball Road, Pewsey, Wiltshire...................01672 562990
SHORTWOOD UNITED...........Meadowbank, Shortwood, Nailsworth, Stroud, Gloucestershire...................01453 833936
SLIMBRIDGE...................Wislow Road, Cambridge, Gloucestershire...................07831 546500
SOUTHALL TOWN...............Yeading FC, The Warren, Beaconsfield Road, Hayes, Middlesex...................020 8848 7362 / 7369
TUFFLEY ROVERS...............Glevum Park, Lower Tuffley Lane, Gloucester, Gloucestershire...................01452 423402
WOOTTON BASSETT TOWN..Gerard Buxton Sports Ground, Rylands Way, Wootton Bassett, Wiltshire...................01793 853880

Cirencester Academy withdrew before start of season. Yate Town are promoted to the Southern League. Wantage Town are relegated to Division One East. Slimbridge and Chipping Norton Town are promoted from Division One West. Hungerford Town arrive having switched from the Isthmian League.

Reserve Div. Two East		P	W	D	L	F	A	Pts
Eton Wick Res.		22	17	2	3	61	26	53
Martin Baker Spts Res.		22	14	3	5	53	32	45
Binfield Res.		22	14	1	7	45	30	43
Penn/Tylers Green Res.		22	11	4	7	54	29	37
RS Basingstoke Res.		22	10	5	7	47	40	35
Rayners Lane Res.		22	9	5	8	53	44	32
Chalfont Wasps Res.	-1	22	8	6	8	46	36	29
Bisley Sports Res.		22	8	2	12	40	53	26
Englefield Green Res.		22	8	1	13	34	49	25
Hounslow Borough Res.		22	6	6	10	34	48	24
Prestwood Res.		22	6	3	13	42	67	21
Drayton Wdrs Res.		22	1	2	19	13	68	5

LEAGUE CUP

PRELIMINARY ROUND

Ardley United 2 Shrivenham 1
Bicester Town 3 Southall Town 2
Binfield 2 RS Basingstoke 1
Bishops Cleeve 5 New College Acad. 0
Bisley Sports 1 Letcombe 0
Carterton Town 2 Martin Baker Sports 3
Cheltenham Saracens 0 Winterbourne 1
Clanfield 0 Shrivenham 4
Didcot Town 1 Finchampstead 3
Easington Sports 1 Cirencester United 2
Englefield Green 1 Rayners Lane 0
Eton Wick 3 Drayton Wanderers 1 aet
Fairford Town 2 Malmesbury Victoria 0
Headington Amateurs 5 Holyport 3
Henley Town 2 Hounslow Borough 1
Hook Norton 2 Milton United 0
Old Woodstock Town 2 Adderbury Park 1
Pegasus Juniors 2 Harrow Hill 1
Penn & Tylers Green 2 Aston Clinton 0
Pewsey Vale 3 Wootton Bassett Town 0
Prestwood 1 Chalfont Wasps 4
Purton 3 Chipping Norton Town 0
Quarry Nomads 1 Brackley Town 2
Ross Town 1 Almondsbury Town 4
Shortwood United 3 Kidlington 1
Tuffley Rovers 3 Middle Barton 0
Wantage Town 1 Highworth Town 2

FIRST ROUND

Abingdon United 3 Headington Amateurs 0
Ardley United 4 Pegasus Juniors 1
Bicester Town 0 North Leigh 1
Binfield 1 Finchampstead 3
Chalfont Wasps 1 Martin Baker Sports 0
Cirencester United 1 Pewsey Vale 2
Englefield Green Rovers 2 Brackley Town 3
Eton Wick 2 Highworth Town 4
Fairford Town 2 Winterbourne United 1 aet
Gloucester United 0 Shortwood United 4
Henley Town 5 Bisley Sports 0
Old Woodstock Town 2 Bishops Cleeve 3
Penn & Tylers Green 0 Hook Norton 1
Purton 1 Tuffley Rovers 3 aet
Shrivenham 3 Almondsbury Town 2 aet
Witney United 1 Yate Town 5

SECOND ROUND

Abingdon United 1 Finchampstead 0 aet
Bishops Cleeve 1 Chalfont Wasps 0
Highworth Town 4 Brackley Town 3
Hook Norton 0 North Leigh 4
Pewsey Vale 4 Ardley United 0
Shortwood Utd 3 Fairford Town 2 aet
Shrivenham 2 Yate Town 5
Tuffley Rovers 2 Henley Town 1

QUARTER-FINALS

Abingdon United 1 Highworth Town 0
North Leigh 1 Shortwood United 4
Pewsey Vale 1 Yate Town 2
Tuffley Rovers 0 Bishops Cleeve 1

SEMI-FINALS

(played over two legs)
Abingdon United 0 Yate Town 2,
Yate Town 2 Abingdon United 0
Shortwood United 1 Bishops Cleeve 0,
Bishops Cleeve 0 Shortwood United 0

FINAL

(10th May at Almondsbury Town)
Yate Town 3 Shortwood United 1

	Aston Clinton	Binfield	Bisley Sports	Chalfont Wasps	Drayton Wdrs	Englefield GR	Eton Wick	Finchampstead	Holyport	Hounslow Boro.	Letcombe	Martin Baker S.	Milton United	Penn & TG	Prestwood	Quarry Nomads	RS Basingstoke	Rayners Lane
Aston Clinton		n/a	n/a	0-1	n/a	n/a	n/a	n/a	1-2	n/a	n/a	n/a	n/a	n/a	1-2	n/a	1-6	n/a
Binfield	n/a		8-1	0-2	4-0	3-0	1-1	1-0	5-0	3-2	3-0	5-0	0-3	2-1	2-2	1-2	4-1	1-2
Bisley Sports	n/a	0-3		2-0	4-0	0-1	0-0	1-0	1-3	2-5	1-0	2-2	0-0	2-1	2-1	1-2	1-2	2-0
Chalfont Wasps	2-1	7-2	1-0	D	2-2	2-1	4-1	0-2	0-4	3-0	2-3	4-2	2-0	1-2	1-1	0-1	2-1	0-3
Drayton Wanderers	n/a	1-3	4-3	1-5	I	2-1	1-4	0-2	2-3	1-1	1-5	2-4	0-3	0-1	1-0	0-2	0-4	1-1
Englefield Green Rovers	n/a	3-1	2-1	0-3	2-1	V	1-1	0-3	3-0	3-1	3-1	1-1	0-4	2-3	1-2	1-5	5-2	0-3
Eton Wick	n/a	1-1	2-1	1-1	5-2	2-1		3-0	4-0	3-3	3-4	9-2	2-0	0-0	2-1	1-2	1-3	3-1
Finchampstead	n/a	2-1	2-1	1-2	2-0	2-0	0-2	O	0-2	2-0	1-1	1-1	1-3	3-4	1-0	2-0	1-0	2-2
Holyport	n/a	2-2	2-1	1-2	1-2	2-3	4-3	0-3	N	2-1	0-4	0-2	1-0	0-3	0-5	2-5	4-2	0-3
Hounslow Borough	n/a	0-8	2-4	2-1	0-0	4-2	3-4	2-2	6-1	E	1-0	5-0	2-2	1-4	4-0	4-2	2-3	1-3
Letcombe	n/a	1-3	1-0	1-3	3-0	1-4	1-2	1-6	2-0	1-0		0-0	1-1	2-0	1-0	0-1	2-2	0-2
Martin Baker Sports	n/a	0-0	1-5	2-2	0-1	2-3	1-1	0-5	2-1	1-2	0-0	E	1-2	1-2	2-0	1-4	2-6	0-2
Milton United	n/a	4-2	6-0	0-1	1-1	0-0	3-1	2-4	0-2	0-0	4-2	1-0	A	2-1	0-1	2-4	2-1	1-2
Penn & Tylers Green	n/a	2-1	2-3	0-1	3-2	2-1	1-0	1-1	0-1	4-0	2-0	5-3	1-1	S	3-0	4-1	3-2	1-0
Prestwood	n/a	2-1	1-0	0-4	1-3	3-2	1-4	0-4	0-1	2-2	0-0	0-2	1-2	2-2	T	1-2	1-3	3-1
Quarry Nomads	n/a	0-2	4-0	3-0	4-1	2-1	3-0	0-0	2-0	3-3	2-0	2-2	1-3	2-1	6-0		3-1	4-1
RS Basingstoke	5-0	1-0	1-1	3-7	7-3	1-3	0-1	2-2	2-0	0-0	1-0	0-1	0-1	0-3	3-4	1-1		0-2
Rayners Lane	n/a	3-2	3-1	0-2	3-2	4-0	2-2	0-2	3-0	1-2	3-1	2-1	5-0	1-1	1-3	2-0	5-0	

SUPPLEMENTARY CUP

PRELIMINARY ROUND
Bicester Town 2 **Didcot Town** 3 *aet*
Drayton W. (w/o) v Aston Clinton (scr.)
Easington Sports 2 Pegasus Juniors 1
Eton Wick 1 **Holyport** 3
Kidlington 3 Almondsbury 3 *aet* (5-3p)
Old Woodstock Town 0 **Ross Town** 2
Penn/Tylers G. 4 Martin Baker 3 *aet*
Rayners Lane 0 **RS Basingstoke** 1
Southall Town 1 Carterton Town 0
Witney Utd 1 **Gloucester United** 3 *aet*
Wootton Bassett 1 Adderbury Park 0
FIRST ROUND
Binfield 3 Penn & Tylers Green 1
Bisley Sports 6 Holyport 4
Cheltenham Saracens 5 Easington 1
Chipping Norton 2 Malmesbury 1
Cirencester United 0 **Slimbridge** 4
Headington 6 Englefield Green 1
Kidlington 1 **New College Academy** 2
Letcombe 0 **Wantage Town** 2
Middle Barton 3 Ross 3 *aet* (5-4p)
Milton United 1 **Didcot Town** 2
Purton 3 Gloucester United 2
Quarry Nomads 1 **Hounslow Boro.** 2
RS Basingstoke 1 Drayton Wanderers 0
Southall Town 2 Prestwood 0
Winterbourne United 4 Harrow Hill 1
Wootton Bassett Town 2 Clanfield 0

SECOND ROUND
Cheltenham Saracens 0 **Wootton Bassett Town** 1
Chipping Norton Town 1 RS Basingstoke 0
Didcot Town 3 Binfield 0
Headington Amateurs 3 Middle Barton 0
Purton 1 New College 1 *aet* (4-2p)
Slimbridge 2 Bisley Sports 1
Southall Town 7 Hounslow Borough 2
Winterbourne United 3 Wantage 1
QUARTER-FINALS
Didcot Town 5 Wootton Bassett 0
Headington Amateurs 1 **Purton** 4
Slimbridge 0 **Southall Town** 1
Winterbourne 5 Chipping Norton 1
SEMI-FINALS
(played over two legs)
Didcot Town 6 Winterbourne United 1
Winterbourne United 0 Didcot Town 0,
Purton 1 **Southall Town** 3
Southall Town 2 Purton 2
FINAL
(5th May at Abingdon United)
Didcot Town 2 Southall Town 1

Note – Aston Clinton withdrew during the course of the season. The matches they played are shown above, but the results are expunged from the league table

		P	W	D	L	F	A	Pts
Quarry Nomads		32	21	4	7	76	41	67
Penn/Tylers G.	-3	32	19	6	7	63	33	60
Finchampstead		32	17	9	6	61	32	60
Rayners Lane		32	18	5	9	66	40	59
Chalfont Wasps		32	18	4	10	67	44	58
Eton Wick		32	16	9	7	72	49	57
Milton United		32	14	9	9	53	39	51
Binfield		32	14	6	12	73	46	48
Letcombe		32	11	6	15	45	53	39
Englefield Green R.		32	12	3	17	47	62	39
RS Basingstoke		32	10	7	15	55	64	37
Bisley Sports		32	10	7	15	43	64	37
Hounslow Borough		32	9	8	15	61	73	35
Prestwood		32	8	10	14	43	63	34
Holyport		32	10	2	20	37	78	32
Martin Baker Sports		32	4	11	17	41	74	23
Drayton Wanderers		32	5	6	21	38	86	21

WWW.NLNEWSDESK.CO.UK

DIVISION ONE EAST CONSTITUTION 2003-04

BADSHOT LEA . . . . Recreation Ground, Badshot Lea, Farnham, Surrey 01252 316076
BINFIELD . . . . Stubbs Lane, Binfield, Berkshire 01344 860822
BISLEY SPORTS . . . . James Walker Sports Centre, Church Lane, Bisley, Surrey . . . . None
CHALFONT WASPS . . . . Playing Fields, Bowstridge Lane, Chalfont St Giles, Buckinghamshire 01494 875050
CHINNOR . . . . Station Road, Chinnor, Oxfordshire . . . . None
DRAYTON WANDERERS . . . . Cowley Hall, Cowley High Road, Cowley, Uxbridge, Middlesex 01895 258269
ENGLEFIELD GREEN ROVERS . . Coopers Hill Sports Ground, Coopers Hill Lane, Englefield Green, Berkshire 01784 435666
ETON WICK . . . . Haywards Meadow, Eton Wick, Slough, Berkshire 01753 852749
FINCHAMPSTEAD . . . . Memorial Ground, Finchampstead Park, Finchampstead, Berkshire 0118 973 2890
HOLYPORT . . . . Braywick Sports Centre, Braywick Road, Maidenhead, Berkshire . . . . None
HOUNSLOW BOROUGH . . . . The White Lodge, Syon Lane, Isleworth, Middlesex 020 8560 2892
LETCOMBE . . . . Bassett Road, Letcombe Regis, Berkshire 01235 768685
MARTIN BAKER SPORTS . . . . Martins Field, Tilehouse Lane, Denham, Buckinghamshire 01895 833077
MILTON UNITED . . . . Milton Hill (Potash Lane), Milton Heights, Abingdon, Oxfordshire 01235 832999
PENN & TYLERS GREEN . . . . French School Meadows, Elm Road, Penn, Buckinghamshire 01494 815346
PRESTWOOD . . . . Prestwood Sports Centre, Honor End Lane, Prestwood, Buckinghamshire 01494 865946
RAYNERS LANE . . . . Tithe Farm Social Club, 151 Rayners Lane, South Harrow, Middlesex 020 8866 9659
WANTAGE TOWN . . . . Alfredian Park, Manor Road, Wantage, Oxfordshire 01235 764781
Aston Clinton withdrew during the season. RS Basingstoke have switched to the Hampshire League. Quarry Nomads have swapped to Division One West. Wantage Town are relegated from the Premier Division. Chinnor are promoted from the Oxfordshire Senior League and Badshot Lea from the Surrey Intermediate League (West).

	Adderbury Park	Ardley United	Cheltenham Saras	Chipping Norton	Cirencester United	Clanfield	Easington Sports	Harrow Hill	Headington Amat.	Kidlington	Malmesbury Vics	Middle Barton	New College Acad.	Old Woodstock	Purton	Ross Town	Shrivenham	Slimbridge	Winterbourne Utd	Witney United
Adderbury Park		2-3	4-2	0-3	2-4	6-0	1-1	5-4	0-3	0-4	1-1	0-2	0-2	1-2	6-4	4-1	2-2	1-3	2-1	0-0
Ardley United	2-2		1-1	3-0	3-1	5-1	0-2	6-1	0-1	2-2	4-1	4-5	4-0	3-3	1-2	4-2	4-0	1-2	2-1	4-1
Cheltenham Saracens	3-0	2-5	D	0-2	4-0	1-0	1-1	1-0	3-2	1-1	2-0	4-0	3-1	1-2	0-3	3-3	0-0	1-3	1-1	2-0
Chipping Norton Town	1-0	2-1	3-1	I	1-1	3-1	1-1	2-1	4-0	1-1	2-1	2-1	3-1	1-0	2-1	5-0	4-0	1-1	1-2	2-1
Cirencester United	1-4	0-3	0-1	1-4	V	1-1	1-2	1-3	1-1	4-0	0-0	0-2	2-1	0-1	4-1	1-1	1-7	0-2	2-0	
Clanfield	0-0	0-4	1-4	0-0	2-5	I	2-1	1-0	0-3	2-2	1-2	1-0	0-1	4-3	2-1	3-5	1-1	1-1	1-1	1-1
Easington Sports	0-0	0-2	2-1	0-4	2-0	0-1	S	3-0	2-0	2-1	1-0	2-1	1-3	3-1	0-2	1-3	1-3	0-3	1-0	2-4
Harrow Hill	0-3	0-2	0-5	0-3	0-0	1-1	1-2	I	1-1	1-0	2-0	2-0	0-1	1-3	4-2	2-1	3-0	1-0	1-3	3-2
Headington Amateurs	2-3	3-2	2-2	3-3	4-1	4-0	5-4	3-1	O	2-5	2-2	3-0	2-0	0-2	1-2	2-2	1-0	0-2	0-4	1-3
Kidlington	5-2	1-0	0-2	1-2	2-3	3-2	4-2	1-1	2-2	N	1-0	1-1	2-1	1-4	2-0	2-1	1-0	1-3	2-5	2-3
Malmesbury Victoria	3-1	1-0	0-2	1-2	3-3	1-0	0-2	5-2	2-0	0-2		1-1	1-0	1-2	2-0	5-0	1-1	0-3	4-0	
Middle Barton	1-6	1-1	1-1	1-2	1-3	2-1	2-2	2-2	1-2	3-2	0-2	O	3-5	0-1	1-7	1-0	1-1	2-0		
New College Academy	1-2	1-1	4-3	2-1	3-2	0-1	0-1	0-4	2-2	1-2	2-3	4-2	N	1-2	3-0	5-0	0-2	0-4	0-3	0-0
Old Woodstock Town	1-5	1-0	2-2	0-1	0-0	5-1	1-0	7-1	3-0	5-0	2-1	2-4		E	1-2	1-0	2-3	0-6	1-3	1-0
Purton	9-1	0-1	2-0	0-3	5-0	1-0	3-1	2-0	4-5	0-4	2-1	4-0	2-1	4-0		4-1	1-2	2-0	3-1	
Ross Town	1-2	1-4	1-1	0-2	2-3	1-4	3-2	1-0	2-2	1-3	1-0	2-3	3-2	0-3	1-7	W	2-0	0-8	0-6	1-6
Shrivenham	6-0	0-3	1-0	0-0	4-0	1-4	1-2	4-1	1-1	3-0	2-1	2-0	3-2	1-2	0-1	2-2	E	2-1	1-5	2-2
Slimbridge	6-0	2-0	1-1	0-0	3-2	3-1	4-1	3-2	1-1	3-2	7-1	0-1	4-0	1-0	3-1	2-0	3-1	S	6-1	6-0
Winterbourne United	0-1	1-0	3-0	4-1	1-0	3-0	7-1	1-0	1-1	2-2	0-0	1-0	0-2	5-2	3-1	1-3	0-2	1-0	T	2-2
Witney United	1-1	1-4	1-0	0-0	1-1	4-1	1-4	1-0	3-3	3-3	0-2	2-2	1-5	1-0	2-2	2-3	1-1	0-2	2-0	

WWW.CHERRYRED.CO.UK

Division One West	P	W	D	L	F	A	Pts
Slimbridge	38	29	6	3	114	26	93
Chipping Norton Town	38	24	10	4	76	33	82
Purton	38	25	1	12	99	49	76
Winterbourne United	38	22	6	10	80	41	72
Ardley United	38	21	6	11	93	47	69
Old Woodstock Town	38	19	6	13	65	54	63
Kidlington	38	15	9	14	67	76	54
Headington Amateurs	38	13	13	12	71	70	52
Cheltenham Saracens	38	13	12	13	61	54	51
Easington Sports	38	15	6	17	54	67	51
Adderbury Park	38	14	8	16	70	85	50
Shrivenham	38	13	10	15	55	65	49
New College Academy	38	14	4	20	57	67	46
Malmesbury Victoria	38	12	8	18	54	63	44
Witney United	38	9	13	16	54	74	40
Middle Barton	38	10	9	19	49	83	39
Cirencester United	38	9	10	19	49	77	37
Harrow Hill	38	10	5	23	45	78	35
Clanfield	38	9	7	22	43	82	34
Ross Town	38	7	5	26	45	110	26

BRIAN WELLS MEMORIAL TROPHY
(Division One Play-offs)

SEMI-FINALS
Quarry Nomads v Chipping Norton Town
Slimbridge v Penn & Tylers Green
(to be played on 2nd August)

FINAL
(9th August at winners of first semi-final)
PLAY-OFF
(9th August at losers of first semi-final)

RESERVE DIVISIONS CUP FINAL
(8th May at Wantage Town)
Cirencester United Res. 0 Eton Wick Res. 0 *aet* (5-3p)

DIVISION ONE WEST CONSTITUTION 2003-04

ADDERBURY PARK.......... Adderbury Park Playing Fields, Round Close Road, Oxford, Oxfordshire .... None
ARDLEY UNITED .... Ardley Sports Ground, Oxford Road, Ardley, Bicester, Oxfordshire.................... 01869 346429
CHELTENHAM SARACENS .... Petersfield Park, Tewkesbury Road, Gloucester, Gloucestershire..................... 01242 584134
CIRENCESTER UNITED .... Cirencester Town FC, Corinium Stadium, Kingshill Lane, Cirencester... 01285 654543. Fax: 01285 654474
CLANFIELD .... Radcot Road, Clanfield, Oxfordshire.................................. 01367 810314
EASINGTON SPORTS................. Addison Road, Easington Estate, Banbury, Oxfordshire............ 01295 257006
HARROW HILL....................... Larksfield Road, Harrow Hill, Gloucestershire 01594 543873
HEADINGTON AMATEURS .... Recreation Ground, Barton, Oxford, Oxfordshire 01865 760489
KIDLINGTON....................... Yarnton Road, Kidlington, Oxfordshire 01865 841526
MALMESBURY VICTORIA .... Flying Monk Ground, Gloucester Road, Malmesbury, Wiltshire 01666 822141
MIDDLE BARTON .... Worton Road, Middle Barton, Oxfordshire 01869 347597
NEW COLLEGE ACADEMY..... Swindon Supermarine FC, Highworth Road, South Marston, Wiltshire 01793 729176
OLD WOODSTOCK TOWN .... New Road, Woodstock, Oxfordshire .... None
PURTON......................... The Red House, Purton, Wiltshire 01793 770262
QUARRY NOMADS .... Quarry Recreation Ground, St Margarets Road, Headington, Oxford 01802 865367
ROSS TOWN.............. Ross Sports Centre, The Riverside, Wilton, Ross-on-Wye, Herefordshire.......... 07787 573080
SHRIVENHAM .... Recreation Ground, Highworth Road, Shrivenham, Swindon, Wiltshire 01793 784453
WINTERBOURNE UNITED .... The Rec, Parkside Avenue, Winterbourne, Bristol, South Glos 01454 850059
WITNEY UNITED .... Marriotts Stadium, Downs Road, Culbridge, Witney, Oxfordshire .... 01993 705930 / 702549

Slimbridge and Chipping Norton Town are promoted to the Premier Division. Quarry Nomads have switched from Division One East.

HERTS SENIOR COUNTY LEAGUE

	Bedmond S&S	Bovingdon	Bushey Rangers	Chipperfield Corries	Croxley Guild	Cuffley	Elliott Star	Hadley	London Lions	Met Police Bushey	Old Parmiterians	Oxhey Jets	Sandridge Rovers	St Peters	Sun Postal Sports	Wormley Rovers
Bedmond Sports & Social	P	0-2	2-2	0-2	4-0	1-2	0-4	2-1	0-1	2-0	0-2	0-0	3-1	0-1	1-3	1-1
Bovingdon	0-2	R	0-0	0-1	7-0	0-0	2-2	4-1	2-0	0-1	2-1	3-0	4-2	2-1	3-3	2-3
Bushey Rangers	0-0	0-2	E	1-0	1-3	2-1	2-3	2-3	2-1	3-0	2-2	3-2	3-2	2-3	0-1	3-0
Chipperfield Corinthians	1-2	1-1	2-5	M	1-0	3-1	1-1	3-2	0-0	2-0	3-2	1-3	0-1	2-1	2-5	3-2
Croxley Guild	0-1	0-1	0-4	0-1	I	1-1	1-4	2-2	3-4	2-1	0-0	3-2	0-7	0-3	0-4	1-5
Cuffley	1-1	0-1	1-0	2-1	3-2	E	1-3	2-3	2-2	2-0	3-0	3-1	3-0	1-3	2-2	0-0
Elliott Star	2-4	0-0	3-0	1-2	3-0	6-0	R	1-2	2-1	5-0	2-0	0-3	1-1	2-1	3-3	
Hadley	1-2	1-0	2-3	4-2	3-0	5-0	0-2		3-1	2-0	0-3	1-2	3-2	2-4	1-3	
London Lions	2-1	4-2	1-0	0-0	5-2	4-0	2-3	3-0	D	2-2	1-0	0-5	1-2	2-0	1-2	1-1
Metropolitan Police Bushey	7-3	1-3	3-2	5-0	4-1	6-0	2-3	1-2	0-3	I	1-2	0-6	4-3	2-0	1-4	2-1
Old Parmiterians	5-2	3-2	2-1	2-1	2-0	2-5	0-4	1-1	1-5	1-1	V	1-5	1-4	1-1	1-1	0-2
Oxhey Jets	2-0	5-1	3-0	3-0	5-0	7-0	4-2	5-0	3-1	3-1	1-0	I	2-0	4-2	2-0	3-1
Sandridge Rovers	1-1	1-3	1-1	2-1	4-1	3-0	4-1	1-1	0-2	2-2	4-1	0-4	S	3-1	0-1	1-4
St Peters	0-2	2-2	1-1	1-1	3-0	1-2	3-3	4-0	2-1	3-3	0-0	1-3	1-2	I	1-4	1-1
Sun Postal Sports	2-0	2-1	4-2	0-1	7-1	3-0	7-2	3-0	3-1	3-0	1-1	2-0	2-3	2-1	O	0-0
Wormley Rovers	6-1	0-1	2-0	2-1	4-1	1-4	3-3	2-2	1-2	1-2	0-1	1-2	0-5	1-0	2-3	N

Premier Division	P	W	D	L	F	A	Pts
Oxhey Jets	30	24	1	5	91	26	73
Sun Postal Sports	30	21	5	4	79	33	68
Elliott Star	30	16	7	7	73	50	55
Bovingdon	30	14	7	9	53	37	49
Sandridge Rovers	30	14	5	11	62	50	47
London Lions	30	14	5	11	54	44	47
Chipperfield Corinth.	30	12	5	13	39	49	41
Hadley	30	12	4	14	50	60	40
Cuffley	30	11	6	13	42	64	39
Wormley Rovers	30	10	8	12	53	50	38
Bushey Rangers	30	10	6	14	47	50	36
Bedmond Spts & Soc.	30	10	6	14	38	52	36
Met. Police Bushey	30	10	4	16	52	66	34
Old Parmiterians	30	8	8	14	35	57	32
St Peters	30	7	8	15	44	52	29
Croxley Guild	30	3	3	24	24	96	12

AUBREY CUP

FIRST ROUND

Bovingdon 0 **Bedmond Sports & Social** 0 *aet* (5-6p)
Bushey Rangers 3 Codicote 3 *aet* (4-3p)
Chipperfield Corinthians 5 North Mymms 3
Croxley Guild 2 **Hatfield Town** 5 *aet*
Elliott Star 2 London Lions 1 *aet*
Hadley 1 Buntingford Town 0
Kimpton Rovers 1 **Sandridge Rovers** 3
Lemsford 3 Wormley Rovers 1
Mill End Sports & Social Ath. 2 Metropolitan Police Bushey 0
Sarratt 0 **Allenburys Sports** 3
St Peters 3 Cuffley 1
Standon & Puckeridge 4 Old Parmiterians 0
The Cheshunt Club 2 **Hinton** 6
Whitewebbs 0 **Evergreen** 3

SECOND ROUND

Bedmond Sports & Social 0 Elliott Star 0 *aet* (4-3p)
Evergreen 2 Lemsford 1
Hinton 1 **Oxhey Jets** 3
Hadley 4 **Bushey Rangers** 6
Mill End Sports & Social Ath. 3 Chipperfield Corinthians 1
Sandridge 3 Allenburys 0
Standon & Puckeridge 1 **Hatfield Town** 3
Sun Postal Sports 2 St Peters 0

QUARTER-FINALS

Bushey 2 **Sandridge Rovers** 3
Evergreen 1 Bedmond 0
Mill End 1 **Oxhey Jets** 2
Sun Postal 1 **Hatfield Town** 3

SEMI-FINALS

Evergreen 0 **Sandridge Rovers** 1 *aet*
Oxhey Jets 1 Hatfield Town 0

FINAL
(5th May at Ware)
Oxhey Jets 1 Sandridge 0

WWW.NLNEWSDESK.CO.UK

PREMIER DIVISION CONSTITUTION 2003-04

BEDMOND SPORTS & SOCIAL .. Toms Lane Recreation Ground, Toms Lane, Bedmond, Hertfordshire.................... 01923 267991
BOVINGDON .... Green Lane, Bovingdon, Hemel Hempstead, Hertfordshire 01442 832628
BUSHEY RANGERS .... Moatfield, Bournehall Lane, Bushey, Hertfordshire 020 8386 1875
CHIPPERFIELD CORINTHIANS............ Queens Street, Chipperfield, Hertfordshire 01923 269554
CUFFLEY .... King George's Playing Fields, Northaw Road East, Cuffley, Hertfordshire 07815 174434
ELLIOTT STAR................... Pursley Football Ground, London Road, Shenley, Hertfordshire .... None
HADLEY .... Hadley Sports Ground, Brickfield Lane, Arkley, Barnet, Hertfordshire 020 8449 1144
HATFIELD TOWN............ Birchwood Leisure Centre, Longmead, Birchwood, Hatfield, Hertfordshire 01707 270772
HINTON .... Holtwhites Sports & Social, Kirkland Drive, Enfield, Middlesex...................... 020 8363 4449
LONDON LIONS .... Laing Sports, Rowley Lane, Barnet, Hertfordshire 020 8441 6051
METROPOLITAN POLICE BUSHEY .. Met. Police Sports Club, Aldenham Road, Bushey, Watford .... 01923 243947. Fax: 01923 245963
MILL END SPORTS & SOCIAL.... King George V Playing Fields, Penn Road, Mill End, Hertfordshire................... 01923 776892
OLD PARMITERIANS .... Parmiters School, High Elms Lane, Garston, Watford, Hertfordshire 01923 682805
OXHEY JETS .... The Boundary Stadium, Little Oxhey Lane, South Oxhey, Hertfordshire 020 8421 6277
SANDRIDGE ROVERS .... Spencer Recreation Ground, Sandridge, St Albans, Hertfordshire 01727 835506
WORMLEY ROVERS. .... Wormley Sports Club, Church Lane, Wormley, Hertfordshire.................... 01992 460650

Sun Sports are promoted to the Spartan South Midlands League. Croxley Guild and St Peters (who become London Road) are relegated to Division One replaced by Hatfield Town, Hinton and Mill End Sports & Social.

	Allenburys Sports	Buntingford Town	Codicote	Evergreen	Hatfield Town	Hinton	Kimpton Rovers	Lemsford	Mill End S & S Ath.	North Mymms	Sarratt	Standon/Puckeridge	The Cheshunt Club	Whitewebbs
Allenburys Sports		2-1	1-3	1-1	2-4	1-2	3-2	3-1	0-5	5-0	3-1	1-0	4-4	1-3
Buntingford Town	2-1	D	0-3	1-3	0-2	0-4	1-1	1-2	1-4	3-1	1-1	0-2	0-2	1-4
Codicote	5-0	7-0	I	3-1	1-4	1-1	1-0	0-1	0-1	0-0	W-L	7-0	5-0	2-2
Evergreen	0-1	1-1	0-0	V	4-0	1-1	3-1	4-0	1-0	7-0	4-0	1-0	4-1	0-3
Hatfield Town	4-0	3-2	1-2	0-0	I	1-1	1-4	1-4	1-0	2-0	W-L	3-1	5-1	1-0
Hinton	4-0	6-0	2-2	1-1	3-1	S	11-0	1-1	1-1	1-1	8-1	5-1	5-0	1-0
Kimpton Rovers	1-4	2-0	0-9	2-2	3-6	0-3	I	2-3	1-4	5-2	4-0	1-3	3-3	5-1
Lemsford	2-0	2-1	2-1	1-1	3-1	0-2	1-1	O	2-2	5-0	8-0	2-2	0-4	7-2
Mill End S & S Ath.	3-0	4-0	1-2	0-3	1-5	0-0	6-1	1-2	N	4-2	4-0	1-0	3-0	3-0
North Mymms	3-4	1-1	1-1	0-3	2-6	1-7	5-0	0-4	1-1		4-1	0-3	2-5	2-4
Sarratt	3-7	2-6	1-3	0-6	2-5	3-5	3-2	0-3	0-3	1-2	O	1-5	1-3	1-6
Standon/Puckeridge	3-1	0-1	1-1	1-2	2-4	1-1	3-2	4-2	0-3	2-0	W-L	N	6-1	0-0
The Cheshunt Club	2-3	4-2	4-2	1-1	0-3	3-2	5-2	2-0	4-6	4-2	1-2	3-3	E	0-3
Whitewebbs	0-2	4-2	1-2	4-1	2-2	1-0	6-2	2-1	1-0	6-0	5-0	1-3	4-1	

Division One	P	W	D	L	F	A	Pts
Hatfield Town	26	17	3	6	66	40	54
Hinton	26	14	10	2	78	22	52
Mill End S&S Ath.	26	15	5	6	61	27	50
Codicote	26	14	7	5	63	25	49
Evergreen	26	13	9	4	55	23	48
Lemsford	26	14	5	7	59	38	47
Whitewebbs	26	14	4	8	64	40	46
Standon/P'ridge	26	11	5	10	46	44	38
Allenburys Sports	26	12	2	12	50	59	38
Cheshunt Club	26	10	4	12	58	73	34
Kimpton Rovers	26	5	4	17	47	89	19
Buntingford Town	26	4	4	18	28	68	16
North Mymms	26	3	5	18	32	85	14
Sarratt	26	2	1	23	24	98	7

RESERVES CUP

FINAL *(26th April at Sandridge Rovers)*
Oxhey Jets Res. 6 St Peter Res. 0

DIVISION ONE CONSTITUTION 2003-04

ALLENBURYS SPORTS .... Glaxo Smith Kline, Westfield, Park Road, Ware, Hertfordshire .... None
BENINGTON .... Benington Recreation Ground, Town Lane, Benington, Hertfordshire .... None
BUNTINGFORD TOWN .... Buntingford Community Centre, Luynes Rise, Buntingford, Hertfordshire .... None
CODICOTE .... John Clements Memorial Ground, Bury Lane, Codicote, Hertfordshire 01438 821072
CROXLEY GUILD .... Croxley Guild of Sport, The Green, Croxley Green, Hertfordshire 01923 770534
EVERGREEN .... Southway, Abbots Langley, Hertfordshire 01923 267812
KIMPTON ROVERS ... Kimpton Recreation Ground, High Street, Kimpton, Hitchin, Hertfordshire .... None
KNEBWORTH .... Old Knebworth Lane, Knebworth, Stevenage, Hertfordshire .... None
LEMSFORD .... Lemsford Village Hall, Brocket Road, Lemsford, Hertfordshire 01707 333548
LITTLE MUNDEN .... Trinity, Fahams Hall Road, Ware, Hertfordshire .... None
LONDON ROAD .... William Bird Playing Fields, Toulmin Drive, St Albans, Hertfordshire 01727 852401
LOUGHTON .... Avondale Close, Loughton, Essex .... None
NORTH MYMMS .... Welham Green Recreation, Dellsome Lane, Welham Green, Hertfordshire .... 01707 266972 / 260338
SARRATT .... King George V Playing Fields, King Georges Avenue, Sarratt, Hertfordshire .... None
STANDON & PUCKERIDGE .... Station Road, Standon, near Ware, Hertfordshire 01920 823460
WHITEWEBBS .... The Whitewebbs Centre, Whitewebbs Lane, Enfield, Middlesex 01992 760716

The Cheshunt Club have withdrawn. Hatfield Town, Hinton and Mill End Sports & Social are promoted to the Premier Division replaced by Croxley Guild and St Peters (who become London Road). Newcomers are Knebworth, Little Munden (both Hertford & District League), Benington (after a year of inactivity) and Loughton (Ilford & District League).

CHAIRMAN'S CUP

Group A	P	W	D	L	F	A	Pts
The Cheshunt Club	3	2	1	0	5	2	7
Whitewebbs	3	2	0	1	7	5	6
Buntingford Town	3	1	0	2	2	4	3
Standon & Puckeridge	3	0	1	2	2	5	1

Whitewebbs 1 The Cheshunt Club 3, The Cheshunt Club 1 Standon & Puckeridge 1, Standon & Puckeridge 0 Buntingford Town 1, Whitewebbs 3 Buntingford Town 1, Buntingford Town 0 The Cheshunt Club 1, Standon & Puckeridge 1 Whitewebbs 3

Group B	P	W	D	L	F	A	Pts
Hinton	3	2	1	0	3	2	7
Allenburys Sports	3	1	2	0	10	5	5
Lemsford	3	1	1	1	8	4	4
Kimpton Rovers	3	0	0	3	4	14	0

Lemsford 1 Hinton 2, Allenburys Sports 8 Kimpton Rovers 3, Allenburys 1 Lemsford 1, Hinton 1 Allenburys Sports 1, Kimpton Rovers 1 Lemsford 6, Hinton v Kimpton *(points awarded to Hinton)*

SEMI-FINALS

Allenburys Sports 2 The Cheshunt Club 1

Whitewebbs 3 Hinton 1

FINAL

(30th April at Oxhey Jets)

Whitewebbs 2 Allenburys Sports 2 aet (5-3p)

Reserve Division One	P	W	D	L	F	A	Pts
Oxhey Jets Res.	26	19	5	2	96	27	62
Bovingdon Res.	26	18	6	2	63	29	60
Elliott Star Res.	26	18	5	3	81	38	59
Sun Postal Sports Res.	26	14	4	8	61	51	46
London Lions Res.	26	12	7	7	56	40	43
Hadley Res.	26	12	6	8	60	42	42
Hatfield Town Res.	26	12	4	10	65	68	40
Old Parmiterians Res.	26	10	5	11	57	61	35
Met. Police Bushey Res.	26	7	3	16	49	75	24
North Mymms Res.	26	7	2	17	36	73	23
Bedmond Sports & Social Res.	26	5	7	14	42	65	22
Croxley Guild Res.	26	6	3	17	37	75	21
Sandridge Rovers Res.	26	4	6	16	39	62	18
Chipperfield Corinthians Res.	26	3	7	16	46	82	16

Reserve Division Two	P	W	D	L	F	A	Pts
Hinton Res.	24	15	6	3	55	35	51
Standon & Puckeridge Res.	24	16	1	7	61	37	49
Codicote Res.	24	13	6	5	56	42	45
Lemsford Res.	24	12	2	10	45	34	38
Cuffley Res.	24	11	3	10	47	49	36
Evergreen Res.	24	9	8	7	48	31	35
St Peters Res.	24	11	2	11	38	46	35
Bushey Rangers Res.	24	10	4	10	41	40	34
Wormley Rovers Res.	24	8	7	9	46	37	31
Buntingford Town Res.	24	7	6	11	35	47	27
Allenburys Sports Res.	24	6	5	13	39	59	23
Kimpton Rovers Res.	24	6	2	16	33	63	20
Mill End Sports & Social Res.	24	6	0	18	40	64	18

HUMBER PREMIER LEAGUE

	Beverley Town	Bridlington Spts Club	Bridlington Town Res.	Driffield	Easington United	Hedon United	Hider Foods	Hutton Cranswick Utd	Keyingham	North Ferriby Res.	Pocklington Town	Reckitts	Sculcoates Amateurs	St Andrews Sutton	Westella & Willerby	Withernsea
Beverley Town		2-0	1-0	4-4	0-1	2-0	0-2	1-2	3-4	0-1	3-1	2-3	2-1	2-1	1-0	1-0
Bridlington Sports Club	3-6		1-4	0-3	1-3	2-2	1-2	2-6	2-3	1-2	4-2	2-4	1-5	3-2	3-3	4-0
Bridlington Town Res.	0-2	0-0		0-3	3-4	5-4	1-2	0-3	0-1	0-2	0-0	1-3	3-5	2-2	5-2	2-3
Driffield	1-1	3-1	2-4		4-1	3-0	0-1	0-1	4-1	3-4	1-0	3-6	2-0	4-0	0-2	2-2
Easington United	0-0	2-0	3-3	2-0		3-1	3-1	3-3	2-2	4-2	4-3	1-1	2-3	5-3	2-3	1-0
Hedon United	3-1	1-1	2-3	0-1	2-1		0-0	2-2	0-3	0-4	1-2	0-2	0-5	0-1	2-4	1-0
Hider Foods	0-0	7-0	1-1	5-0	3-1	5-2		5-4	6-1	2-1	4-0	2-3	2-1	4-2	1-2	2-1
Hutton Cranswick United	1-1	6-3	1-0	0-0	1-2	5-0	0-0		1-0	3-2	4-1	1-0	3-5	2-1	3-1	4-1
Keyingham	2-4	2-1	2-3	1-7	0-5	0-0	3-5	1-7		0-9	2-4	1-3	1-2	3-2	1-2	6-1
North Ferriby United Res.	3-2	6-3	3-0	3-0	2-2	1-1	3-0	1-2	6-2		4-1	0-2	3-0	0-5	2-2	4-0
Pocklington Town	0-5	3-2	1-1	1-1	0-1	3-1	2-1	1-1	3-1	1-2		0-1	1-1	2-3	1-3	2-3
Reckitts	3-3	2-0	4-0	5-2	1-0	5-0	3-0	2-1	6-0	7-5	6-0		4-0	2-0	4-3	7-0
Sculcoates Amateurs	4-3	3-4	2-0	1-0	3-1	3-4	2-0	0-4	2-3	0-0	4-0	2-2		1-3	0-0	2-2
St Andrews Sutton	0-2	1-5	1-0	5-2	1-1	2-0	2-1	0-4	2-1	2-6	4-0	0-3	1-3		3-2	1-0
Westella & Willerby	3-2	0-1	1-1	2-2	6-1	7-1	1-1	0-1	2-1	2-3	5-3	0-1	1-3	3-2		1-1
Withernsea	1-1	3-5	1-5	0-3	1-4	3-1	1-1	1-0	1-0	2-5	2-0	0-1	2-1	3-1	1-5	

		P	W	D	L	F	A	Pts
Reckitts		30	26	3	1	96	29	81
Hutton Cranswick Utd		30	19	6	5	76	36	63
North Ferriby Utd Res.		30	18	5	7	89	52	59
Hider Foods		30	16	6	8	66	41	54
Easington United		30	15	7	8	65	53	52
Sculcoates Amateurs		30	15	6	9	68	52	51
Westella & Willerby		30	14	7	9	71	50	49
Beverley Town		30	13	7	10	57	44	46
Driffield	-3	30	12	6	12	60	53	39
St Andrews Sutton		30	12	2	16	53	66	38
Withernsea		30	8	5	17	36	73	29
Keyingham		30	8	2	20	48	95	26
Bridlington Town Res.		30	6	7	17	44	65	25
Bridlington Sports Club		30	7	4	19	56	88	25
Pocklington Town		30	6	5	19	38	75	23
Hedon United		30	3	6	21	29	80	15

LEAGUE CUP

FIRST ROUND
Bridlington Sports Club 2 **Reckitts** 7
Bridlington Town Res. 2 **Pocklington Town** 3
Driffield 1 **Sculcoates Amateurs** 7
Hedon United 1 **Westella & Willerby** 2
Hutton Cranswick United 0 **Easington United** 3
Keyingham 2 **Beverley Town** 6
St Andrews Sutton 0 **Hider Foods** 2
Withernsea 1 **North Ferriby United Res.** 3

QUARTER-FINALS
Beverley Town 1 **Reckitts** 2
Easington United 3 Sculcoates Amateurs 2
Hider Foods 0 **Pocklington Town** 2
North Ferriby Utd Res. 3 Westella & Willerby 2

SEMI-FINALS
Pocklington Town 3 Easington United 1
(at Hall Road Rangers)
Reckitts 3 North Ferriby United Res. 0
(at Hall Road Rangers)

FINAL
(9th May at Hall Road Rangers)
Reckitts 2 Pocklington Town 0

WWW.NLNEWSDESK.CO.UK

CONSTITUTION 2003-04

BEVERLEY TOWN . . . . Recreation Ground, Norwood, Beverley, East Yorkshire. . . . . None
BRIDLINGTON SPORTS CLUB . . . . Dukes Park, Moorfield Road, Bridlington, East Yorkshire. 01262 606016
BRIDLINGTON TOWN RESERVES . . Queensgate Stadium, Queensgate, Bridlington, East Yorkshire 01262 606879
DRIFFIELD . . . . Allotment Lane, Driffield, East Yorkshire. . . . . None
EASINGTON UNITED. . . . . Low Farm, Beck Street, Easington, Hull, East Yorkshire . . . . None
EAST HULL AMATEURS . . . . Brooklands Park, Chamberlain Road, Hull, East Yorkshire 01482 794193
HEDON UNITED. . . . . Drapers Lane, Hedon, Hull, East Yorkshire . . . . None
HIDER FOODS . . . . Blackburn Sports Club, Prescott Avenue, Brough, East Yorkshire . . . . None
HUTTON CRANSWICK UNITED . . . . Rotsea Lane, Hutton Cranswick, East Yorkshire . . . . None
KEYINGHAM . . . . BP Sports Field, Hedon Road, Hull, East Yorkshire 01482 896113
POCKLINGTON TOWN . . . . The Balk, Pocklington, York, North Yorkshire. . . . . None
RECKITTS. . . . . Humberside Police Sports Club, Inglemire Lane, Hull, East Yorkshire. 01482 856954
SCULCOATES AMATEURS . Hull & East Riding Sports Ground, Chanterlands Avenue, Hull, East Yorkshire 01482 446701
ST ANDREWS SUTTON . . . . Hall Road Rangers FC, Dene Park, Dunswell, East Yorkshire 01482 850101
WESTELLA & WILLERBY . . . . Hull YPI, Chanterlands Avenue, Hull, East Yorkshire . . . . None
WITHERNSEA . . . . Hull Road, Withernsea, East Yorkshire. . . . . None

North Ferriby United Reserves have withdrawn. East Hull Amateurs move up from the East Riding County Amateur League.

ISTHMIAN LEAGUE

	ALD	AYL	BAS	BED	BIL	STO	BOR	BRA	CAN	CHE	ENF	FOR	GRA	HAM	HAR	HAY	HEN	HEY	HIT	KIN	MAI	PUR	STA	SUT
Aldershot Town		1-0	0-3	2-1	0-0	0-0	1-0	3-0	1-0	1-2	2-0	2-1	2-1	4-0	0-1	1-0	6-2	2-0	1-0	2-1	1-1	1-0	5-1	3-2
Aylesbury Utd	3-2		1-1	0-1	1-2	3-3	1-1	1-6	2-1	4-1	2-0	3-2	3-0	0-0	3-0	0-1	2-1	2-2	1-0	0-0	1-1	1-0	1-0	0-4
Basingstoke T.	0-1	2-2		2-1	2-0	3-1	1-1	2-1	2-1	1-2	2-3	3-0	3-1	3-1	1-2	3-1	0-2	2-1	3-0	0-1	3-2	2-1	3-1	1-0
Bedford Town	1-2	4-0	0-0		2-0	3-1	0-4	1-0	2-1	0-4	8-2	0-2	1-0	1-0	1-1	2-1	2-3	1-2	2-1	5-2	0-0	2-0	2-0	2-1
Billericay Town	0-1	1-1	1-0	4-0	*P*	1-1	0-0	1-2	1-1	0-0	0-1	1-3	4-1	0-2	1-0	1-0	0-0	1-0	2-0	1-2	0-2	1-3	1-0	2-0
Bishop's Stortf'd	1-1	2-2	3-1	1-1	1-0	*R*	1-4	1-1	1-1	2-1	1-0	0-1	1-3	4-1	0-2	2-3	1-2	2-1	0-0	1-2	0-2	3-4	2-2	1-0
Boreham Wood	0-1	1-2	1-5	0-1	1-3	1-1	*E*	1-2	1-3	0-0	2-1	3-2	0-2	0-0	2-2	2-0	1-1	0-0	2-2	2-1	0-3	0-0	1-1	3-0
Braintree Town	2-1	2-2	0-3	2-0	1-0	1-3	0-1	*M*	2-4	1-2	1-3	1-0	1-1	3-1	2-4	2-0	1-3	1-3	1-2	1-2	0-0	2-2	2-2	0-1
Canvey Island	0-1	2-1	4-0	1-1	3-0	0-4	1-0	1-1	*I*	4-1	10-1	3-1	2-0	4-0	2-1	2-2	4-4	4-1	3-1	1-1	3-2	2-2	6-1	2-0
Chesham United	1-3	1-3	3-2	1-3	0-2	3-1	3-1	1-1	2-4	*E*	2-2	2-2	2-1	1-0	1-1	2-3	1-1	3-0	2-1	0-4	0-0	1-1	1-3	2-0
Enfield	1-2	0-0	3-1	1-2	1-1	0-2	1-1	1-2	1-0	1-0	*R*	1-1	1-2	0-0	1-0	0-0	2-3	0-5	2-2	1-1	1-0	0-1	1-4	
Ford United	2-3	1-2	2-3	2-0	0-2	3-2	1-1	3-0	1-3	2-0	3-1	*D*	1-0	3-0	3-3	1-3	3-3	2-2	2-2	2-0	1-1	1-1	1-1	3-4
Grays Athletic	0-0	3-1	1-2	0-0	1-0	1-0	2-1	1-2	1-2	1-0	3-0	1-2		1-1	4-1	1-0	0-2	0-2	1-1	1-1	1-4	2-1	0-1	0-0
Hampton & RB	1-3	5-1	0-2	0-2	1-1	1-0	0-4	0-1	0-2	1-3	0-1	2-3	1-1	*I*	0-2	1-1	1-1	1-1	1-0	0-2	1-1	1-1	2-3	1-3
Harrow Borough	0-2	2-2	1-2	0-2	1-2	2-2	2-0	2-2	1-2	3-0	4-0	0-4	1-0		*V*	1-3	1-3	2-1	2-0	2-1	1-1	1-2	0-4	0-1
Hayes	1-0	1-1	1-0	2-0	0-2	2-0	0-0	1-3	2-1	1-0	4-0	2-0	1-1	6-0		*I*	0-0	2-2	2-1	2-2	0-2	1-2	3-0	2-2
Hendon	1-3	3-1	2-1	2-0	0-3	0-2	2-0	1-0	1-3	3-0	3-1	1-0	3-3	1-1	2-0	1-1		0-0	2-2	1-1	1-1	1-2	0-2	0-2
Heybridge Swifts	0-4	1-0	2-4	1-0	1-1	3-3	1-0	2-0	0-2	0-0	2-1	4-4	1-1	1-0	0-1	0-4		*S*	1-2	2-4	0-0	3-3	1-3	1-2
Hitchin Town	1-3	2-3	1-0	2-1	1-0	0-1	2-1	0-0	2-3	1-1	7-1	2-2	3-1	1-0	2-3	2-0	1-1	2-4	*I*	0-0	2-3	1-1	1-2	2-0
Kingstonian	0-2	1-0	1-0	2-1	2-2	2-0	3-1	0-0	1-4	0-4	5-1	4-2	0-2	1-1	1-3	1-1	0-1	4-0	0-0	*O*	2-0	0-1	0-2	2-1
Maidenhead Utd	1-2	2-1	2-2	3-2	1-0	2-3	2-1	2-3	1-1	5-0	3-3	0-4	2-1	1-0	1-1	0-1	2-1	1-2	1-2	4-4	*N*	1-0	0-1	4-1
Purfleet	1-2	1-0	1-0	3-0	0-0	2-1	0-0	1-1	3-2	6-0	5-2	2-2	3-1	5-2	4-2	1-2	1-0	1-2	1-2	1-0	1-0		1-0	0-2
St Albans City	2-0	3-1	1-2	1-2	1-1	3-2	2-4	2-1	1-0	0-3	1-2	2-0	1-0	1-4	2-0	0-1	2-2	1-3	2-2					2-1
Sutton United	1-1	3-2	1-1	0-0	1-2	2-1	3-2	3-1	0-2	3-2	2-1	4-1	2-0	1-0	3-0	2-1	2-3	2-0	3-1	1-1	2-2	1-1	2-4	

Premier Division		HOME					AWAY					TOTAL					
	P	W	D	L	F	A	W	D	L	F	A	W	D	L	F	A	Pts
Aldershot Town	46	17	3	3	41	16	16	3	4	40	20	33	6	7	81	36	105
Canvey Island	46	14	7	2	63	27	14	1	8	49	29	28	8	10	112	56	92
Hendon	46	10	5	8	29	28	12	8	3	41	28	22	13	11	70	56	79
St Albans City	46	11	5	7	36	31	12	3	8	37	34	23	8	15	73	65	77
Basingstoke Town	46	14	3	6	44	27	9	4	10	36	33	23	7	16	80	60	76
Sutton United	46	13	6	4	44	29	9	3	11	33	33	22	9	15	77	62	75
Hayes	46	13	6	4	38	19	7	7	9	29	35	20	13	13	67	54	73
Purfleet	46	13	4	6	42	23	6	11	6	26	25	19	15	12	68	48	72
Bedford Town	46	14	3	6	42	27	7	6	10	24	31	21	9	16	66	58	72
Maidenhead Utd	46	8	7	8	40	37	8	10	5	35	26	16	17	13	75	63	65
Kingstonian	46	10	5	8	32	29	6	12	5	39	35	16	17	13	71	64	65
Billericay Town	46	10	5	8	27	21	7	6	10	19	23	17	11	18	46	44	62
Bishop's Stortford	46	9	8	8	39	35	7	5	11	35	37	16	11	19	74	72	59
Hitchin Town	46	7	8	8	36	32	8	5	10	33	35	15	13	18	69	67	58
Ford United	46	8	7	8	42	39	7	5	11	36	45	15	12	19	78	84	57
Braintree Town	46	6	4	13	28	38	8	8	7	31	33	14	12	20	59	71	54
Aylesbury United	46	9	8	6	34	33	4	7	12	28	42	13	15	18	62	75	54
Harrow Borough	46	8	4	11	31	36	7	5	11	23	39	15	9	22	54	75	54
Grays Athletic	46	9	6	8	26	24	5	5	13	27	35	14	11	21	53	59	53
Heybridge Swifts	46	8	7	8	29	38	5	7	11	23	42	13	14	19	52	80	53
Chesham United	46	8	7	8	35	39	6	3	14	21	42	14	10	22	56	81	52
Boreham Wood	46	6	8	9	24	32	5	7	11	26	26	11	15	20	50	58	48
Enfield	46	5	8	10	21	31	4	3	16	26	70	9	11	26	47	101	38
Hampton & Rich.	46	2	8	13	20	41	1	6	16	15	45	3	14	29	35	86	23

Aldershot Town are promoted to the Football Conference replaced by Kettering Town. Chesham United, Boreham Wood and Enfield slip to Division One North replaced by Northwood and Hornchurch. Hampton & Richmond Borough drop to Division One South replaced by Bognor Regis Town and Carshalton Athletic. Purfleet become Thurrock.

WWW.CHERRYRED.CO.UK

	ALD	AYL	BAS	BED	BIL	BIS	BOR	BRA	CAN	CHE	ENF	FOR	GRA	HAM	HAR	HAY	HEN	HEY	HIT	KIN	MAI	PUR	StA	SUT
Ald.	—	1835 / 1 Apr	2289 / 20 Aug	2078 / 8 Feb	2288 / 9 Nov	1964 / 4 Jan	1748 / 1 Feb	1694 / 24 Aug	2058 / 17 Sep	1770 / 19 Oct	2049 / 5 Apr	1848 / 24 Jan	1875 / 7 Sep	2012 / 8 Mar	1704 / 1 Oct	1774 / 12 Nov	3419 / 26 Apr	1813 / 21 Sep	1989 / 14 Dec	1956 / 26 Nov	2018 / 4 Mar	2018 / 7 Dec	2883 / 19 Apr	2564 / 26 Dec
Ayl.	905 / 5 Oct	—	433 / 14 Dec	726 / 9 Nov	446 / 24 Aug	405 / 1 May	356 / 17 Sep	402 / 8 Mar	716 / 7 Sep	802 / 26 Dec	521 / 31 Aug	336 / 14 Apr	504 / 25 Jan	352 / 8 Mar	503 / 19 Oct	512 / 1 Oct	642 / 26 Apr	632 / 21 Sep	332 / 18 Mar	968 / 26 Apr	518 / 12 Oct	402 / 7 Dec	664 / 20 Aug	421 / 15 Feb
Bas.	1617 / 8 Apr	386 / 17 Aug	—	389 / 10 Sep	368 / 22 Mar	391 / 9 Nov	252 / 1 Oct	338 / 19 Oct	575 / 26 Aug	407 / 8 Feb	429 / 14 Sep	293 / 12 Apr	354 / 28 Dec	517 / 3 Sep	423 / 21 Sep	411 / 21 Dec	355 / 16 Nov	375 / 26 Apr	319 / 18 Jan	484 / 1 Feb	308 / 21 Apr	311 / 22 Feb	387 / 7 Dec	367 / 26 Oct
Bed.	693 / 24 Sep	422 / 25 Mar	352 / 25 Feb	—	502 / 5 Apr	469 / 9 Nov	404 / 1 Oct	535 / 20 Aug	510 / 29 Oct	547 / 31 Aug	493 / 29 Mar	431 / 15 Feb	526 / 1 Mar	330 / 17 Sep	415 / 7 Dec	574 / 26 Apr	547 / 16 Nov	446 / 22 Oct	326 / 26 Dec	605 / 19 Apr	559 / 25 Jan	573 / 4 Jan	763 / 5 Oct	559 / 24 Aug
Bill.	1089 / 15 Mar	582 / 28 Dec	242 / 4 Mar	503 / 3 Sep	—	467 / 14 Dec	170 / 7 Sep	238 / 20 Aug	540 / 31 Oct	507 / 21 Sep	348 / 22 Oct	420 / 21 Dec	609 / 23 Nov	313 / 3 May	406 / 17 Aug	438 / 25 Jan	547 / 15 Oct	344 / 15 Oct	326 / 29 Mar	508 / 19 Apr	238 / 25 Jan	439 / 4 Jan	287 / 1 Nov	559
Bish.	894 / 26 Aug	439 / 3 Sep	378 / 15 Mar	501 / 17 Aug	265 / 25 Feb	—	318 / 21 Dec	409 / 24 Sep	379 / 28 Jan	356 / 14 Sep	355 / 10 Sep	359 / 21 Apr	291 / 15 Feb	336 / 12 Apr	343 / 17 Aug	304 / 7 Dec	341 / 15 Apr	471 / 29 Apr	421 / 5 Oct	392 / 16 Nov	327 / 26 Apr	310 / 18 Jan	388 / 28 Jan	365 / 1 Mar
Bore.	439 / 4 Nov	292 / 28 Apr	152 / 1 Mar	304 / 18 Jan	222 / 19 Apr	318 / 17 Sep	—	—	164 / 24 Sep	290 / 14 Dec	178 / 14 Dec	121 / 5 Apr	157 / 21 Apr	208 / 12 Nov	159 / 28 Dec	214	238 / 29 Mar	143	219 / 9 Sep	168 / 2 Dec	155 / 7 Dec	138 / 31 Aug	268 / 18 Apr	190 / 26 Apr
Bra.	757 / 28 Dec	260 / 22 Oct	304 / 1 Mar	270 / 11 Feb	320 / 22 Mar	431 / 20 Aug	754 / 5 Apr	—	575 / 22 Feb	331 / 18 Jan	243 / 30 Nov	294 / 1 Mar	352 / 24 Sep	193 / 19 Apr	419 / 12 Apr	407 / 31 Aug	611 / 15 Mar	619	401 / 4 Apr	483 / 7 Oct	509 / 9 Nov	766 / 31 Aug	703 / 2 Nov	779 / 31 Aug
Can.	3553 / 15 Apr	612 / 18 Jan	407 / 22 Mar	613 / 4 Feb	242 / 8 Apr	316 / 25 Jan	238 / 8 Mar	575 / 22 Feb	—	—	354 / 26 Oct	163 / 19 Apr	106 / 1 Mar	405 / 21 Sep	332 / 12 Dec	307 / 17 Sep	293 / 7 Dec	278 / 18 Dec	272 / 24 Aug	284 / 1 Oct	151 / 19 Oct	223 / 19 Oct	324 / 31 Aug	252 / 14 Dec
Ches.	671 / 2 Nov	589 / 21 Apr	220 / 18 Jan	333 / 22 Apr	242 / 12 Apr	—	283 / 17 Aug	304 / 8 Mar	305 / 21 Dec	—	5 Oct	66 / 22 Oct	135 / 8 Apr	220 / 26 Oct	61 / 8 Apr	96 / 2 Oct	159 / 7 Dec	78 / 21 Dec	121 / 3 May	158 / 29 Mar	94 / 7 Sep	87 / 21 Sep	320 / 15 Mar	212 / 29 Apr
Enf.	395 / 4 Sep	105 / 16 Apr	101 / 25 Jan	131 / 18 Dec	107 / 15 Feb	144 / 26 Mar	117 / 21 Mar	243 / 30 Nov	354 / 26 Oct	68 / 22 Feb	—	28 Dec	209 / 26 Aug	64 / 26 Aug	12 Mar	2 Oct	96 / 17 Aug	159	150 / 21 Oct	169 / 21 Sep	86 / 21 Sep	106 / 21 Sep	208 / 15 Mar	101 / 9 Nov
Ford	426 / 14 Sep	152 / 10 Sep	142 / 31 Aug	194 / 21 Aug	112 / 11 Apr	135 / 11 Mar	102 / 8 Feb	131 / 22 Mar	265 / 1 Oct	66 / 22 Oct	66 / 28 Dec	—	78 / 19 Oct	144 / 12 Nov	131 / 8 Mar	131 / 9 Nov	131 / 2 Oct	121 / 1 Mar	233 / 19 Apr	275 / 18 Mar	208 / 19 Oct	183 / 24 Aug	340 / 26 Apr	140 / 5 Apr
Gra.	675 / 18 Jan	261 / 14 Sep	279 / 24 Aug	197 / 14 Sep	303 / 11 Mar	295 / 22 Mar	255 / 9 Nov	352 / 24 Sep	586 / 8 Feb	135 / 8 Apr	135 / 26 Aug	156 / 7 Dec	—	78 / 17 Sep	237 / 8 Mar	265 / 19 Oct	156 / 3 Sep	115 / 21 Dec	190 / 15 Mar	208 / 19 Oct	222 / 22 Feb	149 / 26 Dec	269 / 7 Sep	329 / 20 Aug
Ham.	705 / 22 Oct	302 / 8 Feb	210 / 17 Sep	170 / 1 Oct	202 / 7 Dec	298 / 21 Sep	204 / 22 Feb	193 / 19 Apr	405 / 21 Sep	220 / 26 Oct	64 / 19 Oct	144 / 12 Nov	155 / 22 Oct	—	259 / 10 Sep	440 / 20 Aug	206 / 18 Jan	195 / 15 Mar	195 / 23 Nov	183 / 26 Dec	185 / 1 Oct	148 / 24 Aug	276 / 10 Sep	292 / 14 Dec
Harr.	731 / 1 Mar	285 / 16 Nov	173 / 5 Apr	252 / 4 Mar	252 / 14 Dec	250 / 18 Mar	226 / 3 May	419 / 12 Apr	316 / 17 Aug	160 / 5 Apr	61 / 12 Mar	173 / 8 Mar	175 / 17 Sep	192 / 25 Jan	—	305 / 20 Aug	377 / 24 Aug	206 / 27 Mar	323 / 26 Oct	301 / 18 Jan	483 / 3 Sep	174 / 19 Apr	144 / 24 Sep	279 / 4 Jan
Hay.	1305 / 29 Mar	294 / 21 Dec	226 / 26 Nov	286 / 23 Nov	268 / 24 Sep	380 / 3 May	306 / 26 Aug	407 / 31 Aug	226 / 1 Apr	173 / 3 May	96 / 2 Oct	247 / 19 Oct	249 / 21 Apr	173 / 7 Sep	305 / 20 Aug	—	231 / 12 Apr	231	280 / 31 Aug	410 / 15 Oct	292 / 22 Aug	235 / 10 Sep	229 / 11 Mar	394 / 19 Apr
Hen.	511 / 1 May	259 / 1 Oct	201 / 22 Oct	416 / 19 Oct	203 / 3 Apr	307 / 22 Mar	194 / 13 Nov	611 / 15 Mar	595 / 16 Nov	362 / 24 Aug	243 / 1 Mar	180 / 5 Oct	240 / 25 Jan	240 / 7 Sep	240 / 24 Aug	231 / 12 Apr	—	257 / 12 Apr	252 / 5 Apr	287 / 18 Jan	173 / 3 Sep	170 / 5 Apr	255 / 25 Jan	273 / 5 Oct
Hey.	503 / 15 Feb	400 / 3 May	215 / 23 Nov	310 / 29 Apr	292 / 1 Mar	249 / 12 Nov	217 / 19 Oct	619	406 / 3 Sep	591 / 1 Oct	215 / 15 Feb	180 / 3 May	326 / 21 Apr	173 / 9 Nov	201 / 8 Feb	170 / 31 Aug	257 / 12 Apr	—	327 / 15 Feb	323 / 12 Apr	292 / 5 Apr	170	588 / 8 Mar	208 / 8 Mar
Hit.	974 / 17 Aug	474 / 26 Aug	322 / 26 Aug	765 / 3 May	208 / 11 Mar	432 / 22 Feb	202 / 25 Mar	401 / 4 Apr	251 / 25 Jan	277 / 22 Mar	261 / 4 Feb	247 / 28 Apr	303 / 21 Dec	345 / 7 Dec	218 / 9 Nov	252 / 5 Apr	280 / 15 Oct	252 / 31 Aug	—	230 / 14 Dec	323 / 8 Feb	144 / 24 Aug	334 / 22 Mar	208 / 24 Dec
King.	1220 / 12 Apr	324 / 24 Apr	400 / 17 Sep	562 / 21 Dec	543 / 5 Oct	624 / 1 Oct	407 / 28 Dec	483 / 7 Oct	488 / 28 Dec	291 / 20 Aug	351 / 19 Apr	267 / 1 Apr	466 / 21 Dec	232 / 1 Mar	327 / 26 Apr	463 / 22 Apr	387 / 14 Dec	449 / 18 Sep	217 / 24 Sep	—	323 / 17 Aug	191 / 9 Nov	229 / 8 Feb	902 / 25 Jan
Mai.	847 / 10 Sep	334 / 29 Mar	303 / 26 Dec	270 / 14 Sep	317 / 31 Aug	232 / 19 Oct	252 / 3 May	509 / 9 Nov	421 / 15 Mar	301 / 15 Mar	358 / 24 Sep	237 / 16 Nov	301 / 1 Mar	256 / 28 Dec	235 / 29 Apr	345 / 21 Apr	297 / 22 Mar	178 / 29 Apr	221 / 3 Sep	301 / 22 Oct	—	606 / 28 Dec	295 / 25 Jan	299 / 19 Apr
Pur.	728 / 3 May	372 / 26 Oct	302 / 26 Oct	317 / 14 Dec	362 / 24 Sep	232 / 7 Sep	178 / 25 Jan	766 / 31 Aug	608 / 16 Nov	241 / 23 Nov	241 / 18 Jan	326 / 29 Mar	256 / 28 Dec	458 / 23 Nov	452 / 21 Dec	139 / 18 Feb	235 / 10 Sep	156	751 / 22 Oct	301 / 17 Aug	606 / 28 Dec	—	271 / 1 Mar	466 / 17 Sep
St A.	1538 / 21 Dec	249 / 5 Mar	442 / 3 May	613 / 22 Feb	718 / 19 Oct	428 / 8 Mar	703 / 21 Sep	703 / 2 Nov	707 / 9 Nov	591 / 9 Nov	215 / 4 Feb	452 / 17 Aug	452 / 12 Apr	543 / 17 Aug	452 / 18 Jan	457 / 8 Feb	310 / 22 Mar	401 / 26 Aug	751 / 14 Sep	611 / 10 Sep	446 / 15 Apr	410 / 1 Oct	—	412 / 5 Nov
Sutt.	2002 / 21 Apr	588 / 21 Sep	567 / 29 Mar	719 / 28 Dec	537 / 18 Jan	419 / 26 Nov	506 / 23 Nov	779 / 31 Aug	643 / 12 Apr	484 / 10 Sep	533 / 15 Mar	463 / 3 Sep	422 / 11 Mar	292 / 14 Dec	491 / 26 Aug	393 / 8 Apr	437 / 22 Oct	514 / 8 Feb	487 / 16 Nov	821 / 18 Sep	401	401 / 18 Apr	446 / 17 Sep	—

WWW.NLNEWSDESK.CO.UK

CONSTITUTION FOR 2003-04

AYLESBURY UNITED   Manager: Chris Boothe   Colours: Green & white
The Stadium, Buckingham Road, Aylesbury, Buckinghamshire HP20 2AQ
Tel: 01296 436350   Fax: 01296 395667   www.aylesburyunited.co.uk
   Fantastic run to FA Trophy semi-finals ended only by eventual winners Burscough.

BASINGSTOKE TOWN   *Manager: Ernie Howe*   *Colours: Blue & yellow*
The Camrose Ground, Western Way, Basingstoke, Hants RG22 6EZ *www.btfc.co.uk*
Tel: 01256 464353/327575   Fax: 01256 473299   Boardroom: 01256 325063
   Will miss Hampshire derbies following promotion of local rivals Aldershot Town.

BEDFORD TOWN   Manager: Kevin Wilson   Colours: Blue & white
The New Eyrie, Meadow Lane, Cardington, Bedford, Bedforshire MK44 3SB
Tel: 01234 838448   Fax: 01234 831990   www.bedfordeagles.net
   Ended 2002-03 with a shock defeat at the hands of Dunstable in Beds Senior Cup final.

BILLERICAY TOWN   *Manager: Justin Edinburgh*   *Colours: Blue & white*
New Lodge, Blunts Wall Road, Billericay, Essex CM12 9SA
Tel: 01277 655177   Club: 01277 652188   www.billericaytownfc.co.uk
   Under a new manager following arrival of former Spurs defender Justin Edinburgh.

BISHOP'S STORTFORD   Manager: Martin Hayes   Colours: Blue & white
Woodside Park, Dunmow Road, Bishop's Stortford, Hertfordshire CM23 5GZ
Tel: 01279 306456   Fax: 01279 306457   www.stortfordfc.co.uk
   Ended the season with cup success in the Herts Charity Cup.

BOGNOR REGIS TOWN   *Manager: Jack Pearce*   *Colours: White & green*
Nyewood Lane, Bognor Regis, West Sussex PO21 2TY   *www.therocks.co.uk*
Tel: 01243 822325   Fax: 01243 866151
   Jack Pearce has been at the helm of Bognor Regis for over thirty years.

BRAINTREE TOWN   Manager: Gary Bellamy   Colours: Yellow & navy blue
Cressing Road, Braintree, Essex CM7 6RD   www.braintreetownfc.co.uk
Tel: 01376 345617   Fax: 01376 323369
   Played a memorial match in the summer in memory of a Braintree fan lost in action in Iraq.

CANVEY ISLAND   *Manager: Jeff King*   *Colours: Yellow, blue & white*
Park Lane, Canvey Island, Essex SS8 7PX   *www.canveyfc.com*
Tel: 01268 682991   Fax: 01268 698586
   Endured disappointment of finishing runners-up for second successive season.

CARSHALTON ATHLETIC   Manager: Billy Smith   Colours: White & maroon
War Memorial Sports Ground, Colston Avenue, Carshalton, Surrey SM5 2PW
Tel: 020 8642 8658   Fax: 020 8643 0999   www.carshaltonathletic.com
   Surprisingly parted company with manager Graham Roberts despite gaining promotion.

FORD UNITED   *Manager: Craig Edwards*   *Colours: Blue*
Carlton Drive, Ilford, Essex IG6 1NA
Tel: 020 8550 3611   www.fordunited.com
   Recently vacated long-term ground at Rush Green to move in with Barkingside FC.

GRAYS ATHLETIC   Manager: Mark Stimson   Colours: Royal blue
Recreation Ground, Bridge Road, Grays, Essex RM17 6BZ   www.graysathletic.co.uk
Tel: 01375 377753/391649   Fax: 01708 851473
   Have made the brave decision to go full-time, with a young squad, for 2003-04.

HAYES   *Manager: Willy Wordsworth*   *Colours: Red, white & black*
Townfield House, Church Road, Hayes, Middlesex UB3 2LE
Tel: 020 8573 4598   Fax: 020 8573 2075   www.hayesfc.co.uk
   Formed in 1909 as Botwell Mission, hence club nickname The Missioners.

HENDON Manager: Dave Anderson Colours: White & green
LOOT Stadium, Claremont Road, Cricklewood, London NW2 1AE
Tel: 020 8201 9494 Fax: 020 8905 5966 Club: 020 8455 9185
Retained Middlesex Senior Cup – club's 14th success in the competition.

HEYBRIDGE SWIFTS Manager: Mark Hawkes Colours: Black & white
Scraley Road, Heybridge, Maldon, Essex CM9 7BL
Tel: 01621 852978 www.heybridgeswifts.com
Begin the season under new management following the arrival of Mark Hawkes in the hot seat.

HITCHIN TOWN Manager: Robbie O'Keefe Colours: Yellow & green
Top Field, Fishponds Road, Hitchin, Hertfordshire SG5 1NU www.hitchintownfc.co.uk
Tel: 01462 434483/459028 Fax: 01462 482463
Ex-Chelsea and England star Kerry Dixon has joined as number two to Robbie O'Keefe.

HORNCHURCH Manager: Mick Marsden Colours: Red & white
The Stadium, Bridge Avenue, Upminster, Essex RM14 2LX www.urchins.org
Tel: 01708 222307/220080
Pulled off coup by signing Russian international keeper Dmitri Kharine last season.

KETTERING TOWN Manager: Dominic Genovese Colours: Red
Rockingham Road, Kettering, Northants NN16 9AW www.ketteringtownfc.co.uk
Tel: 01536 483028/410815 Fax: 01536 412273 Clubhouse: 01536 410962
Face new experience of Isthmian League football following second relegation in three seasons.

KINGSTONIAN Manager: Kim Harris Colours: Red, white & black
Kingsmeadow Stadium, 422a Kingston Road, Kingston-upon-Thames, Surrey KT1 3PB
Tel: 020 8547 3335/3336 Fax: 020 8974 5713 www.kingstonian.net
The last team to successfully defend the F A Trophy, winning the last two Wembley finals.

MAIDENHEAD UNITED Manager: John Dreyer Colours: Black & white
York Road, Maidenhead, Berkshire SL6 1SQ Tel: 01628 636314
Club: 01628 624739 www.maidenheadunitedfc.co.uk
John Dreyer has taken over from long-serving Maidenhead manager Alan Devonshire.

NORTHWOOD Manager: Tony Choules Colours: Red
Chestnut Avenue, Northwood, Middlesex HA6 1HR www.northwoodfc.com
Tel: 01923 827148 Fax: 020 8428 1533
Followed up 2002 League Cup win with Division One North championship a year later.

ST ALBANS CITY Manager: Steve Cook Colours: Yellow, blue & white
Clarence Park, Clarence Road, St Albans, Hertfordshire AL1 4PL www.sacfc.co.uk
Tel: 01727 864296 Fax:01727 866235 Club:01727 866819
Picked up prolific goalscorer Nic McDonnell from Crawley Town during summer.

SUTTON UNITED Manager: John Rains Colours: Chocolate & amber
Borough Sports Ground, Gander Green Lane, Sutton, Surrey SM1 2EY Tel: 020 8644 4440
Fax: 020 8644 5120 www.btinternet.com/~suttonunited
Ended season on high note with victory over Kingstonian in Surrey Senior Cup final.

THURROCK Manager: Colin McBride Colours: Green & yellow
Thurrock Hotel, Ship Lane, Grays, Essex RM15 4HB www.thurrockfc.com
Tel: 01708 868901 Fax: 01708 866703 Club: 01708 865492
Club has changed its name from Purfleet this summer.

	Arlesey Town	Aveley	Barking	Barton Rov.	Berkhamsted	E. Thurrock	Gt Wakering	Harlow Town	Hemel Hemp.	Hertford T.	Hornchurch	Leyton Penn.	Marlow	Northwood	Oxford City	Slough Town	Thame Utd	Tilbury	Uxbridge	Wealdstone	Wembley	Wingate & F.	Wivenhoe	Yeading
Arlesey Town		0-0	0-0	1-0	2-2	2-0	0-4	1-2	0-0	6-0	2-2	3-1	0-0	2-3	1-0	1-0	3-3	0-2	0-1	3-3	3-2	0-0	1-1	2-1
Aveley	3-3		1-2	2-1	0-3	1-0	1-1	1-0	1-1	1-0	0-2	0-1	1-0	1-2	0-0	1-1	1-2	2-0	2-1	1-2	2-0	1-0	3-1	1-1
Barking & EH	3-1	1-3		0-3	3-5	4-0	0-4	3-1	0-1	1-0	1-1	2-0	1-2	0-0	0-0	2-1	2-1	1-0	0-1	2-0	1-5	0-2	3-4	2-3
Barton Rovers	1-0	1-1	1-2	D	0-0	0-4	0-0	1-0	2-0	2-1	0-1	1-2	2-0	1-2	0-0	0-0	2-1	2-1	1-0	0-1	2-0	1-5	0-2	2-3
Berkhamsted	1-2	1-2	2-2	3-1	I	3-0	4-2	2-2	1-0	4-0	1-1	2-0	1-4	3-4	4-2	3-1	2-3	3-0	0-1	1-5	3-1	1-0	6-2	3-2
East Thurrock	2-1	0-1	0-4	2-5	1-1	V	5-0	0-0	2-0	5-1	4-3	0-1	3-3	2-3	2-1	0-2	1-1	3-1	1-0	2-2	5-0	2-0	3-3	3-2
Great Wakering	2-3	1-1	4-3	2-1	1-1	0-4	I	1-1	0-2	3-3	2-0	0-0	2-0	0-1	2-2	0-0	0-1	0-3	2-1	5-0	1-1	3-2	3-2	3-2
Harlow Town	3-1	2-1	3-2	0-0	1-1	1-0	2-0	S	0-2	0-2	0-0	0-0	2-1	1-3	0-0	2-2	0-0	0-1	0-3	2-1	5-0	1-1	3-2	2-0
Hemel Hempst'd	1-1	0-1	2-1	2-1	2-3	4-1	2-3	0-2	I	3-1	1-3	2-1	1-0	3-2	1-0	2-2	3-1	3-2	1-3	1-2	2-1	1-0	1-0	2-0
Hertford Town	2-4	0-3	1-3	0-4	2-2	1-1	1-1	1-2	0-2	O	1-2	2-2	2-6	0-5	0-1	1-3	1-3	0-1	1-3	3-2	2-0	3-3	0-1	2-0
Hornchurch	4-3	0-1	5-1	1-1	5-3	1-1	2-1	1-1	2-2	2-2	N	2-1	0-3	1-0	3-0	1-1	1-3	1-3	0-1	1-3	3-2	2-0	3-3	0-1
Leyton Pennant	0-1	0-2	1-2	1-0	1-1	0-2	1-2	0-1	0-2	2-3	0-0		2-1	0-3	1-0	0-1	0-2	0-1	2-3	2-4	1-2	2-1	1-0	2-1
Marlow	1-0	4-3	1-3	2-1	3-1	0-0	1-4	0-0	4-1	0-2	4-1	2-3	O	1-0	1-2	2-3	2-1	2-0	0-0	2-0	0-1	2-2	2-1	1-4
Northwood	6-0	1-1	1-2	2-1	2-0	4-2	4-0	1-4	2-1	5-1	2-0	5-0	1-1	N	1-0	1-2	2-3	2-1	2-0	0-0	2-0	0-1	2-2	1-4
Oxford City	0-1	0-0	4-1	2-1	0-2	2-0	1-2	3-2	1-1	3-0	1-2	2-1	2-0	0-3	E	1-1	1-1	5-0	1-0	0-3	1-1	2-1	5-0	2-2
Slough Town	3-0	1-1	3-1	1-0	3-2	2-0	4-0	1-1	0-1	2-2	1-1	5-1	2-0	2-1	3-0	N	2-0	5-1	1-1	0-1	2-1	0-3	4-0	0-2
Thame United	2-1	1-1	2-1	1-0	1-1	1-3	2-0	0-0	8-2	0-0	0-1	3-1	4-0	0-1	1-0	1-1	O	2-0	5-1	1-1	0-1	2-1	0-3	0-2
Tilbury	1-4	1-1	0-1	3-1	2-1	1-1	1-1	3-2	1-1	1-2	1-1	0-2	0-3	3-0	1-6	0-0	3-0		1-4	2-0	4-2	5-0	0-1	7-0
Uxbridge	2-0	2-0	1-1	5-0	1-2	1-1	0-0	3-1	1-0	4-1	3-2	0-0	0-0	1-0	0-1	2-1	1-4	1-0		2-1	1-1	0-3	3-1	1-0
Wealdstone	1-3	0-2	2-2	2-3	3-0	3-0	4-2	1-1	0-2	4-1	0-0	0-0	1-0	0-1	2-1	1-2	4-1	2-1	1-0	R	1-0	2-1	1-1	3-1
Wembley	0-3	2-6	2-2	2-3	0-2	1-1	2-3	1-5	1-1	3-1	0-4	1-1	2-2	0-2	2-2	2-1	2-1	0-0	4-1	2-1	T	3-2	3-2	2-0
Wingate & Fin.	1-2	1-2	0-3	1-0	0-4	3-0	3-0	1-4	1-4	2-3	4-1	4-3	1-2	1-1	2-3	1-0	2-1	0-0	0-0	4-1	4-1	H	1-1	0-3
Wivenhoe Town	3-1	2-1	1-2	1-2	1-1	4-1	0-1	1-3	0-2	3-1	1-5	1-2	1-3	0-0	0-1	1-2	2-2	1-2	2-0	1-4	5-2	1-1		2-2
Yeading	2-1	3-5	1-1	1-1	0-1	5-1	0-1	2-1	1-2	5-1	1-2	2-1	1-0	1-2	0-1	1-1	1-1	1-0	1-1	2-1	3-2	1-1	2-1	

Division One North

	P	HOME					AWAY					TOTAL					
		W	D	L	F	A	W	D	L	F	A	W	D	L	F	A	Pts
Northwood	46	17	2	4	66	26	11	5	7	43	30	28	7	11	109	56	91
Hornchurch	46	13	7	3	46	25	12	8	3	39	23	25	15	6	85	48	90
Hemel Hempstead	46	15	2	6	41	31	11	5	7	29	24	26	7	13	70	55	85
Slough Town	46	14	5	4	47	20	8	3	12	38	39	22	13	11	85	59	79
Uxbridge	46	13	6	4	35	18	10	4	9	27	23	23	10	13	62	41	79
Aveley	46	10	6	7	27	24	11	8	4	39	24	21	14	11	66	48	77
Berkhamsted Town	46	13	3	7	54	37	8	10	5	38	31	21	13	12	92	68	76
Wealdstone	46	14	4	5	51	30	8	4	11	34	38	22	8	16	85	68	74
Thame United	46	13	5	5	50	17	7	7	9	34	34	20	12	14	84	51	72
Harlow Town	46	11	6	6	28	21	9	6	8	38	32	20	12	14	66	53	72
Marlow	46	11	4	8	39	31	8	6	9	35	32	19	10	17	74	63	67
Barking & E. Ham	46	9	3	11	32	38	10	6	7	41	38	19	9	18	73	76	66
Yeading	46	11	6	6	37	28	7	5	11	40	41	18	11	17	77	69	65
Great Wakering R.	46	9	8	6	36	31	8	6	9	28	39	17	14	15	64	70	65
Oxford City	46	10	8	5	39	25	7	5	11	16	26	17	13	16	55	51	64
Arlesey Town	46	8	10	5	33	27	9	2	12	36	44	17	12	17	69	71	63
East Thurrock Utd	46	11	6	6	48	35	6	4	13	27	44	17	10	19	75	79	61
Wingate & Finchley	46	8	5	10	38	41	7	6	10	32	33	15	11	20	70	74	56
Barton Rovers	46	9	4	10	23	27	6	3	14	30	38	15	7	24	53	65	52
Tilbury	46	8	5	10	30	43	6	2	15	25	53	14	7	25	55	96	49
Wivenhoe Town	46	5	5	13	30	43	4	6	13	26	51	9	11	26	56	94	38
Leyton Pennant	46	4	4	15	18	35	5	3	15	20	46	9	7	30	38	81	34
Wembley	46	4	7	12	33	53	3	4	16	24	58	7	11	28	57	111	32
Hertford Town	46	3	4	16	25	54	3	2	18	21	65	6	6	34	46	119	24

Northwood and Hornchurch are promoted to the Premier Division with Enfield, Boreham Wood and Chesham United moving in the opposite direction. Hertford Town and Wembley (after losing a play-off against Metropolitan Police – see page 74) are relegated to Division Two replaced by Cheshunt and Leyton. Marlow and Slough Town switch to Division One South. Dunstable Town are promoted from the Spartan South Midlands League. Leyton Pennant become Waltham Forest.

	ARL	AVE	B/EH	BAR	BER	EAS	GtW	HAR	HEM	HER	HOR	LEY	MAR	NOR	OXF	SLO	THA	TIL	UXB	WEA	WEM	WIN	WIV	YEA
Arl.		142 11 Feb	110 25 Feb	356 26 Dec	136 1 Mar	125 15 Feb	165 5 Apr	124 25 Mar	209 20 Aug	142 14 Jan	226 16 Nov	173 15 Mar	152 3 May	242 30 Nov	158 3 Dec	181 24 Sep	132 19 Apr	215 18 Jan	167 29 Mar	233 28 Jan	185 7 Sep	152 14 Dec	184 24 Aug	180 19 Oct
Ave.	82 18 Mar		145 26 Dec	67 19 Apr	88 11 Mar	150 25 Jan	118 4 Jan	101 1 Mar	71 14 Dec	86 7 Sep	151 24 Sep	82 26 Oct	79 25 Feb	133 15 Mar	63 5 Apr	135 1 Apr	91 24 Aug	90 30 Nov	62 15 Feb	138 22 Oct	101 20 Aug	113 3 May	95 26 Nov	63 29 Mar
Bark.	142 26 Aug	111 21 Apr		97 25 Jan	81 1 Apr	148 28 Dec	105 24 Sep	107 16 Nov	102 26 Apr	74 29 Mar	182 10 Sep	76 12 Apr	152 17 Aug	109 21 Dec	71 1 May	194 8 Oct	103 22 Oct	77 18 Feb	82 15 Mar	153 1 Mar	77 15 Feb	113 12 Oct	117 26 Oct	100 7 Dec
Bart.	147 21 Apr	80 21 Dec	91 19 Oct		86 12 Apr	104 3 May	50 28 Jan	136 29 Mar	131 18 Jan	106 15 Mar	82 26 Oct	50 4 Feb	71 10 Sep	82 2 Nov	116 1 Mar	155 15 Feb	63 17 Sep	106 26 Aug	88 17 Aug	213 16 Nov	54 25 Feb	80 30 Nov	78 28 Sep	36 14 Jan
Berk.	128 1 Oct	102 22 Feb	119 22 Mar	111 7 Sep		101 28 Sep	106 19 Apr	141 18 Jan	368 26 Dec	116 20 Aug	80 30 Nov	134 19 Oct	151 8 Feb	145 21 Sep	98 8 Mar	240 3 May	135 4 Jan	116 23 Nov	90 17 Dec	252 24 Aug	111 14 Dec	87 12 Nov	106 5 Apr	89 4 Mar
East	128 21 Sep	129 19 Oct	101 24 Aug	62 7 Dec	80 9 Nov		110 21 Jan	125 26 Oct	92 22 Feb	155 26 Apr	140 18 Feb	65 15 Oct	81 1 Oct	121 8 Feb	85 7 Sep	140 20 Aug	91 5 Apr	120 4 Mar	67 28 Jan	104 18 Mar	101 29 Mar	83 19 Apr	77 14 Dec	90 18 Jan
Gt W.	137 10 Sep	165 26 Aug	121 8 Feb	140 11 Jan	125 21 Dec	185 21 Apr		161 17 Aug	132 21 Sep	104 22 Feb	295 3 May	102 1 Oct	140 12 Apr	122 17 Dec	122 12 Oct	155 14 Jan	135 25 Jan	147 28 Dec	119 30 Nov	178 15 Mar	135 16 Nov	112 22 Oct	125 29 Mar	78 1 Apr
Harl.	169 23 Oct	114 2 Oct	123 8 Mar	118 13 Nov	125 12 Oct	113 23 Nov	124 14 Dec		160 4 Jan	138 26 Dec	120 15 Jan	163 21 Sep	78 29 Jan	145 25 Jan	129 9 Nov	186 5 Apr	108 7 Sep	114 22 Feb	95 3 May	139 19 Apr	104 24 Aug	120 22 Mar	136 21 Aug	99 8 Feb
Hem.	99 11 Mar	175 17 Aug	76 30 Nov	65 17 Dec	320 21 Apr	80 3 Dec	95 15 Feb	110 26 Aug		78 16 Nov	170 29 Mar	67 10 Sep	83 21 Dec	229 3 May	62 22 Oct	300 15 Mar	94 1 Apr	104 12 Apr	101 26 Oct	225 26 Nov	98 1 Mar	101 25 Jan	84 24 Sep	89 8 Apr
Hert.	147 22 Mar	70 12 Apr	85 4 Mar	75 9 Nov	85 4 Feb	103 30 Nov	105 28 Sep	170 21 Apr	151 8 Mar		139 26 Aug	120 3 May	75 22 Oct	108 11 Feb	64 24 Apr	230 1 Mar	112 12 Oct	84 5 Nov	75 21 Dec	187 1 Apr	65 25 Sep	67 25 Mar	81 18 Mar	120 17 Aug
Horn.	219 2 Nov	417 8 Feb	388 5 Apr	204 23 Nov	583 26 Apr	269 22 Mar	253 7 Dec	197 15 Oct	194 28 Jan	182 25 Feb		245 18 Mar	288 22 Feb	190 1 Oct	210 24 Aug	236 14 Dec	230 9 Nov	247 19 Oct	306 18 Jan	340 20 Aug	319 19 Apr	177 4 Feb	542 26 Dec	310 21 Sep
Leyt.	61 9 Nov	50 4 Mar	83 7 Sep	40 24 Aug	61 25 Jan	109 1 Apr	54 1 Mar	78 15 Apr	72 5 Apr	45 7 Dec	103 8 Apr		66 24 Apr	52 12 Oct	53 22 Mar	115 19 Apr	41 28 Sep	32 3 Dec	43 24 Sep	75 14 Dec	23 14 Jan	61 20 Aug	52 11 Mar	55 26 Apr
Mar.	104 7 Dec	103 18 Jan	102 14 Dec	160 5 Apr	130 24 Sep	132 1 Mar	140 7 Sep	104 26 Apr	167 19 Apr	74 11 Mar	181 29 Apr	119 16 Nov		177 29 Mar	177 20 Aug	273 24 Aug	110 18 Mar	78 17 Dec	154 15 Apr	264 15 Feb	152 19 Oct	114 4 Jan	94 15 Mar	110 26 Oct
Nor.	104 26 Apr	153 9 Nov	283 19 Apr	178 20 Aug	178 15 Feb	113 24 Sep	189 22 Mar	216 19 Oct	265 7 Dec	159 24 Aug	305 1 Mar	203 18 Jan	142 12 Nov		155 14 Dec	418 4 Jan	174 23 Nov	184 8 Mar	240 11 Mar	567 26 Dec	196 28 Sep	214 5 Apr	128 7 Sep	182 15 Oct
Oxf.	140 22 Feb	124 10 Sep	87 10 Dec	98 1 Oct	91 18 Mar	119 12 Apr	114 18 Jan	157 15 Mar	172 1 Feb	108 21 Sep	174 28 Dec	99 25 Feb	107 1 Apr	151 17 Aug		232 19 Oct	202 7 Dec	114 21 Dec	153 21 Apr	192 29 Mar	107 26 Oct	112 8 Feb	117 26 Apr	147 26 Aug
Slou.	384 8 Feb	397 8 Mar	377 22 Feb	410 21 Sep	330 7 Dec	307 15 Apr	346 23 Nov	385 10 Sep	425 9 Nov	295 28 Jan	361 17 Aug	304 21 Dec	517 28 Dec	448 26 Aug	393 25 Jan		249 4 Feb	325 22 Mar	505 12 Apr	394 17 Dec	338 26 Apr	290 18 Mar	311 22 Oct	338 21 Apr
Tha.	151 21 Dec	91 28 Dec	91 25 Mar	121 8 Feb	154 26 Aug	124 10 Sep	122 19 Oct	110 12 Apr	89 15 Oct	138 18 Jan	412 15 Mar	110 22 Feb	142 21 Apr	157 26 Oct	351 3 May	275 29 Mar		132 17 Aug	97 4 Mar	189 25 Feb	83 10 Dec	167 21 Sep	110 16 Nov	82 1 Oct
Til.	47 4 Feb	86 26 Apr	84 20 Aug	65 4 Jan	46 26 Oct	71 22 Oct	91 8 Oct	114 28 Sep	70 5 Sep	58 5 Apr	131 25 Jan	61 29 Mar	55 25 Mar	131 16 Nov	n/a 19 Apr	97 26 Nov	52 14 Dec		72 1 Mar	112 24 Sep	63 7 Dec	75 26 Dec	55 15 Feb	47 15 Mar
Uxb.	71 18 Feb	74 21 Sep	87 9 Nov	85 14 Dec	80 25 Mar	96 8 Mar	84 26 Apr	100 7 Dec	120 18 Mar	88 19 Apr	76 12 Oct	102 8 Feb	123 22 Mar	110 22 Oct	65 4 Feb	366 6 Sep	90 20 Aug	70 1 Oct		220 5 Apr	110 4 Jan	117 24 Aug	105 25 Jan	156 22 Feb
Wea.	303 23 Nov	182 8 Apr	237 1 Oct	268 8 Mar	338 28 Dec	262 26 Aug	294 9 Nov	308 21 Dec	342 22 Mar	320 19 Oct	266 14 Sep	281 17 Aug	302 21 Sep	412 21 Apr	267 28 Sep	432 18 Jan	277 26 Apr	309 8 Feb	202 10 Sep		265 4 Feb	301 22 Feb	277 7 Dec	263 12 Apr
Wem.	bcd 29 Apr	62 15 Apr	82 21 Sep	46 22 Oct	58 17 Aug	48 14 Sep	59 8 Mar	70 28 Dec	76 1 Oct	62 8 Feb	69 21 Dec	78 21 Apr	63 25 Jan	130 22 Feb	50 8 Apr	158 30 Nov	68 22 Mar	50 3 May	108 26 Aug	200 4 Mar		61 9 Nov	66 12 Oct	54 10 Sep
Win.	133 17 Aug	82 7 Dec	115 18 Jan	68 26 Apr	89 29 Mar	72 21 Dec	61 25 Feb	131 26 Nov	139 19 Oct	84 26 Oct	130 12 Apr	84 2 Nov	140 26 Aug	81 17 Sep	79 24 Sep	78 15 Oct	62 15 Feb	60 15 Apr	100 28 Dec	160 11 Mar	93 15 Mar		84 1 Mar	110 16 Nov
Wiv.	172 28 Dec	71 22 Mar	112 23 Nov	81 22 Feb	75 10 Sep	114 17 Aug	80 12 Nov	52 4 Mar	108 8 Feb	85 15 Oct	174 21 Apr	93 26 Aug	85 9 Nov	129 12 Apr	87 15 Apr	75 8 Apr	65 8 Mar	81 21 Sep	145 19 Oct	216 3 May	112 18 Jan	87 1 Oct		105 2 Nov
Yead.	82 25 Jan	45 17 Dec	68 3 May	68 22 Mar	57 22 Oct	71 12 Oct	56 20 Aug	85 24 Sep	84 24 Aug	67 14 Dec	78 15 Feb	85 30 Nov	89 23 Nov	315 11 Jan	98 4 Jan	251 26 Dec	68 1 Mar	67 9 Nov	83 9 Oct	191 7 Sep	83 5 Apr	58 8 Mar	46 19 Apr	

DIVISION ONE NORTH CONSTITUTION FOR 2003-04

ARLESEY TOWN
Manager: Nicky Ironton   *Colours:* Navy & sky blue
Hitchin Road, Arlesey, Bedfordshire SG15 6RS
Tel: 01462 734504   *Boardroom:* 01462 734512

AVELEY
Manager: Ian Bodley   *Colours:* Blue & white
Mill Field, Mill Road, Aveley, Essex RM15 4TR
Tel: 01708 865940   *Fax:* 01708 680995

BARKING & EAST HAM UNITED
Manager: Richard Thomas   *Colours:* Blue & white
Mayesbrook Park, Lodge Avenue, Dagenham RM8 2JR
Tel: 020 8595 6900/6511

BARTON ROVERS
Manager: Dick Newman   *Colours:* Blue & white
Sharpenhoe Road, Barton-le-Cley, Beds MK45 4SD
Tel: 01582 707772   *Fax:* 01582 882398

BERKHAMSTED TOWN
Manager: t.b.a.   *Colours:* White & black
Broadwater, Lower Kings Rd, Berkhamsted HP4 2AA
Tel: 01442 862815   *Fax:* 01442 865054

BOREHAM WOOD
Manager: Steve Browne   *Colours:* White, black, red
Meadow Park, Broughinge Road, Boreham Wood,
Hertfordshire WD6 5AL
Tel: 020 8953 9883   Fax/Club: 020 8207 7982

CHESHAM UNITED
Manager: Steve Bateman   *Colours:* Maroon, sky blue
Meadow Park, Amy Lane, Amersham Road, Chesham,
Bucks HP5 1NE   *Tel:* 01494 783964
Fax: 01494 794244   *Club:* 01494 791057

CHESHUNT
Manager: Andy Leese   *Colours:* Amber & black
The Stadium, Theobalds Lane, Cheshunt EN8 8RU
Tel: 01992 626752   *Fax:* 01992 626752

DUNSTABLE TOWN
Manager: Paul Reeves   *Colours:* Sky, navy & white
Creasey Park, Brewers Hill Road, Dunstable,
Bedfordshire   *Tel:* 01582 667555

EAST THURROCK UNITED
Manager: Andy McDonald *Colours:* Amber & black
Rookery Hill, Corringham, Stanford-le-Hope, Essex
SS17 9LB   *Tel:* 01375 644166
Fax: 01375 641009   *Boardroom:* 01375 641009

ENFIELD
Manager: Terry Back   *Colours:* White & blue
Boreham Wood FC, Meadow Park, Broughinge Road,
Boreham Wood, Hertfordshire WD6 5AL
Tel: 020 8953 9883   *Fax:* 020 8207 7982
Boardroom: 020 8953 5097

GREAT WAKERING ROVERS
Manager: Alan Hull   *Colours:* Green & white
Burroughs Park, Little Wakering Hall Lane, Great
Wakering, Southend-on-Sea, Essex SS3 0HG
Tel: 01702 217812

HARLOW TOWN
Manager: Tommy Cunningham
Harlow Sportscentre, Hammarskjold Road, Harlow,
Essex CM20 2JF   *Colours:* Red & white
Tel: 01279 445319   *Fax:* 01279 635846

HEMEL HEMPSTEAD TOWN
Manager: Tony Kelly   *Colours:* Red & white
Vauxhall Road, Adeyfield, Hemel Hempstead,
Hertfordshire HP2 4HW   *Tel:* 01442 259777

LEYTON
Manager: Costas Sophocleus
The Hare & Hounds Ground, 282 Lea Bridge Road,
Leyton, London E10 7LD
Tel: 020 8539 5405   *Colours:* Blue & white

OXFORD CITY
Manager: Paul Lee   *Colours:* Blue & white
Court Place Farm, Marsh Lane, Marston, Oxford OX3
0NQ
Tel: 01865 744493   *Clubroom:* 01865 742492

THAME UNITED
Manager: Mark West   *Colours:* Red & black
Windmill Road, Thame, Oxfordshire OX9 2DR
Tel: 01844 213017   *Fax:* 01844 260139

TILBURY
Manager: Paul Joynes   *Colours:* Black & white
Chadfields, St Chad's Road, Tilbury, Essex RM18 8NL
Tel: 01375 843093   *Fax:* 01375 859496

UXBRIDGE
Manager: George Talbot   *Colours:* Red & white
Honeycroft, Horton Road, West Drayton UB7 8HX
Tel: 01895 443557   *Fax:* 01895 445830
Boardroom: 01895 445830

WALTHAM FOREST
Manager: Hakan Ramis Hayrettin
Wadham Lodge Sports Ground, Kitchener Road,
Walthamstow, London E17 4JP
Tel: 020 8527 2444   *Colours:* White, navy blue

WEALDSTONE
Manager: Gordon Bartlett   *Colours:* Blue & white
Edgware Town FC, White Lion Ground, High Street,
Edgware, Middlesex HA8 5AQ
Tel: 020 8952 6799   *Fax:* 020 8907 4421

WINGATE & FINCHLEY
Manager: Adam Lee   *Colours:* Blue & white
The Abrahams Stadium, Summers Lane, Finchley,
London N12 0PD   *Tel:* 020 8446 2217
Fax: 020 8343 8194

WIVENHOE TOWN
Manager: Neil Northcott   *Colours:* Blue & yellow
Broad Lane Ground, Elmstead Road, Wivenhoe, Essex
CO7 7HA   *Tel:* 01206 825380

YEADING
Manager: Johnson Hippolyte
The Warren, Beaconsfield Road, Hayes, Middlesex
UB4 0SL   *Tel:* 020 8848 7369
Clubhouse: 020 8846 7362 *Colours:* Red & black

WWW.CHERRYRED.CO.UK

	Ashford (Mx)	Banstead	Bognor Regis	Bracknell	Bromley	Carshalton	Chertsey	Cor. Casuals	Croydon	Croydon Ath.	Dulwich H.	Egham Town	Epsom & E.	Horsham	Leatherhead	Lewes	Met. Police	Molesey	Staines Town	Tooting & M.	Walton & H.	Whyteleafe	Windsor & E.	Worthing
Ashford (Middx)		0-0	0-1	0-0	1-1	0-2	2-0	1-1	1-0	0-2	0-5	1-3	1-1	0-1	0-1	0-3	2-1	1-2	1-1	1-1	2-1	1-1	0-3	4-0
Banstead Athletic	2-3		0-1	0-1	3-3	0-2	3-1	4-0	2-3	0-1	4-1	3-2	4-0	1-1	1-1	1-0	2-5	0-1	2-1	0-4	1-0	1-2		0-0
Bognor Regis	8-0	1-0		0-1	1-1	1-0	6-0	1-1	3-1	2-0	0-1	3-1	3-0	1-3	0-0	0-2	4-0	1-1	3-0	3-0	3-0	3-0	2-1	3-0
Bracknell Town	1-1	1-1	3-1	D	2-1	1-4	4-2	3-2	2-2	0-3	0-4	0-1	0-3	1-2	5-2	1-2	0-3	0-0	2-2	3-0	1-0	0-1	1-0	1-4
Bromley	2-1	2-2	2-1	2-0	I	0-3	4-1	2-0	0-1	1-1	1-2	1-0	1-0	1-0	3-2	2-3	0-2	2-2	2-3	3-0	3-1	1-1	0-0	1-3
Carshalton Ath.	1-0	1-0	1-0	2-2	1-4	V	1-0	2-2	1-0	2-1	2-0	0-1	2-0	4-1	2-1	1-1	1-1	2-3	1-2	2-1	1-1	1-0	2-1	2-1
Chertsey Town	0-5	1-0	0-2	1-1	1-4	0-2	I	0-1	4-1	1-2	1-2	1-2	0-3	1-1	2-8	1-5	1-2	2-2	0-1	0-7	1-6	1-4	1-2	0-1
Corinthian Cas.	1-2	0-1	0-3	0-0	0-0	0-0	1-2	S	1-1	1-1	1-2	0-4	1-0	1-2	3-0	1-0	3-0	1-0	0-3	1-1	1-1	1-0	1-1	1-1
Croydon	2-1	0-0	0-6	1-1	1-1	1-2	3-1	0-1	I	1-1	1-0	3-1	0-0	0-2	1-2	1-3	1-0	3-1	0-1	2-2	2-0	0-2	2-0	4-1
Croydon Athletic	0-1	1-1	1-0	0-1	1-2	0-1	2-0	0-4	3-0	O	0-2	2-1	1-1	0-5	2-2	1-1	1-3	1-1	1-5	2-0	2-3	2-3	2-3	0-0
Dulwich Hamlet	2-0	0-0	0-0	0-2	1-0	3-1	4-2	0-1	2-1	2-1	N	2-0	3-1	3-1	3-2	2-2	1-1	1-0	4-0	1-1	2-3	2-0	2-2	
Egham Town	0-3	0-1	1-6	0-3	1-0	1-1	3-3	3-1	1-0	1-1	3-0		0-3	1-0	1-1	1-5	0-0	2-1	2-1	2-0	3-3	0-1	1-1	1-3
Epsom & Ewell	3-0	1-3	1-1	3-2	1-2	1-4	3-0	0-0	4-0	1-0	3-3	1-0	O	1-1	2-1	0-7	1-0	1-0	1-0	2-2	1-0	1-3	4-0	1-5
Horsham	1-0	2-0	1-2	3-3	1-1	0-1	4-0	0-1	6-1	2-1	1-0	1-1	2-1	N	0-1	6-2	0-2	2-3	0-1	4-2	1-0			3-3
Leatherhead	2-0	2-1	0-0	1-1	1-0	0-3	3-2	5-2	4-2	3-1	0-2	1-0	0-2		E	0-1	6-2	0-1	0-1	1-1	4-0	1-0		0-2
Lewes	5-2	0-2	2-2	2-0	1-0	3-1	7-0	5-0	0-2	3-2	2-0	2-0	1-0	0-0			1-1	3-2	2-2	0-1	1-1	1-1	6-2	0-2
Met. Police	1-1	1-3	0-2	2-2	2-2	1-2	2-1	2-1	3-2	3-0	1-1	2-3	0-1	0-1	2-1	0-3	S	0-2	2-2	0-2	0-1	0-2	1-1	1-1
Molesey	0-2	0-1	1-5	1-1	2-1	1-1	1-2	1-0	0-4	0-1	0-0	0-1	0-1	4-1	0-7	3-1		O	1-2	0-2	0-7	0-0	1-0	1-1
Staines Town	0-2	1-1	0-3	1-0	1-2	2-2	2-2	2-0	2-1	1-0	5-0	2-1	1-1	1-1	1-2	4-1	1-2	4-1	U	1-2	0-7	0-0	1-0	0-0
Tooting/Mitcham	3-1	1-2	4-0	2-3	0-1	0-2	5-0	0-1	1-0	1-2	1-2	3-4	1-4	2-0	1-1	2-4	1-1	3-2		T	1-3	1-2	3-3	0-4
Walton & Her.	0-2	1-1	1-0	3-1	2-3	5-2	1-2	2-0	3-1	1-3	4-2	0-0	2-3	1-3	2-2	0-2	3-0	1-2	2-2	0-2	H	2-2	0-2	2-4
Whyteleafe	0-1	1-0	3-1	0-1	1-2	3-1	3-3	5-0	4-1	0-0	0-0	2-1	2-4	1-1	0-2	1-0	1-2	3-0	1-2	2-2			2-0	4-1
Windsor & Eton	1-1	5-0	0-2	2-0	0-1	1-1	1-0	1-1	2-3	0-1	1-0	3-2	4-3	3-1	0-2	0-0	1-1	3-1	2-1	5-2	1-4	1-2		2-0
Worthing	5-0	3-2	1-1	2-2	0-1	2-0	3-1	3-1	5-2	0-1	2-3	0-0	1-3	2-1	2-2	1-3	3-1	4-3	0-2	0-3	0-0	4-3		

WWW.NLNEWSDESK.CO.UK

Division One South	P	HOME W	D	L	F	A	AWAY W	D	L	F	A	TOTAL W	D	L	F	A	Pts
Carshalton Athletic	46	15	4	4	36	21	13	4	6	37	23	28	8	10	73	44	92
Bognor Regis Town	46	15	4	4	52	13	11	6	6	40	21	26	10	10	92	34	88
Lewes	46	13	6	4	48	23	11	10	2	58	27	24	16	6	106	50	88
Dulwich Hamlet	46	13	7	3	41	22	10	5	8	32	27	23	12	11	73	49	81
Whyteleafe	46	12	6	5	45	23	9	7	7	29	28	21	13	12	74	51	76
Bromley	46	11	5	7	36	29	10	8	5	34	24	21	13	12	70	53	76
Walton & Hersham	46	9	7	7	42	34	11	6	6	45	29	20	13	13	87	63	73
Horsham	46	10	5	8	45	31	11	4	8	35	27	21	9	16	80	58	72
Epsom & Ewell	46	12	5	6	37	34	7	7	9	30	32	19	12	15	67	66	69
Egham Town	46	9	8	6	30	34	10	2	11	32	37	19	10	17	62	71	67
Tooting & Mitcham	46	5	4	14	36	45	13	5	5	47	33	18	9	19	83	78	63
Worthing	46	10	5	8	44	38	7	7	9	34	37	17	12	17	78	75	63
Windsor & Eton	46	11	5	7	39	29	7	4	12	27	36	18	9	19	66	65	63
Leatherhead	46	9	8	6	39	28	7	5	11	32	38	16	13	17	71	66	61
Staines Town	46	8	9	6	32	30	6	7	10	25	33	14	16	16	57	63	58
Banstead Athletic	46	8	5	10	35	34	6	10	7	23	25	14	15	17	58	59	57
Ashford T. (Middx)	46	5	8	10	18	30	9	3	11	29	40	14	11	21	47	70	53
Croydon	46	9	6	8	28	31	6	2	15	28	56	15	8	23	56	87	53
Croydon Athletic	46	5	7	11	24	38	8	6	9	28	28	13	13	20	52	66	52
Bracknell Town	46	6	5	12	29	44	6	11	6	28	30	12	16	18	57	74	52
Corinthian Casuals	46	7	7	9	25	26	5	7	11	25	42	12	14	20	50	68	50
Molesey	46	5	5	13	19	39	8	4	11	33	40	13	9	24	52	79	48
Metropolitan Police	46	6	5	12	26	38	6	5	12	24	38	12	10	24	50	76	46
Chertsey Town	46	2	3	18	20	64	1	4	18	23	75	3	7	36	43	139	16

Carshalton Athletic and Bognor Regis Town are promoted to the Premier Division replaced by Hampton & Richmond Borough. Chertsey Town are relegated to Division Two (Metropolitan Police are reprieved after winning a play-off against Wembley – see page 74). Slough Town and Marlow arrive having switched from Division One North.

DIVISION ONE SOUTH CONSTITUTION FOR 2003-04

ASHFORD TOWN (MIDDX)
Manager: Nathan Wharf   *Colours:* Orange & white
Short Lane, Stanwell, Staines, Middlesex TW19 7BH
Tel: 01784 245908

BANSTEAD ATHLETIC
Manager: Bob Langford   *Colours:* Amber & black
Merland Rise, Tadworth, Surrey KT20 5JG
Tel: 01737 350982   *Fax:* 01737 831175

BRACKNELL TOWN
Manager: Alan Taylor   *Colours:* Red & white
Larges Lane, Bracknell, Berkshire RG12 3AN
Tel/Fax: 01344 300933   *Club:* 01344 412305

BROMLEY
Manager: Stuart McIntyre   *Colours:* White & black
Hayes Lane, Bromley, Kent BR2 9EF
Tel: 020 8313 3992   *Boardroom:* 020 8460 5291

CORINTHIAN CASUALS
Manager: Trevor Waller
Colours: Chocolate, pink & sky blue
Hook Rise South, Tolworth, Surrey KT6 7NA
Tel: 020 8397 3368

CROYDON
Manager: Micky Read   *Colours:* Sky & navy blue
Croydon Sports Arena, Albert Road, South Norwood,
London SE25 4QL
Tel: 020 8654 8555/3462   *Fax:* 020 8654 3373

CROYDON ATHLETIC
Manager: Hayden Bird   *Colours:* Maroon & white
Mayfield, off Mayfield Rd, Thornton Heath CR7 6DN
Tel: 020 8664 8343   *Fax:* 020 8664 8343

DULWICH HAMLET
Manager: Martin Eede   *Colours:* Navy blue & pink
Champion Hill Stadium, Edgar Kail Way, East Dulwich
SE22 8BD   *Fax:* 020 7501 9255
Tel: 020 7274 8707/7501 9323

EGHAM TOWN
Manager: Byron Walton
Colours: Blue, yellow, white
Runnymede Stadium, Tempest Rd, Egham TW20 8HX
Tel: 01784 435226   *Boardroom:* 01784 436466

EPSOM & EWELL
Manager: Adrian Hill   *Colours:* Blue & white
Banstead Athletic FC, Merland Rise, Tadworth, Surrey
KT20 5JG   *Tel:* 01737 350982

HAMPTON & RICHMOND BOROUGH
Manager: Alan Devonshire *Colours:* Red, blue & white
Beveree Stadium, Beaver Close, Station Road,
Hampton, Middlesex TW12 2BX
Tel: 020 8941 2838   *Fax/Club:* 020 8979 2456
Boardroom: 020 8941 4936

HORSHAM
Manager: John Maggs   *Colours:* Yellow & green
Queen Street, Horsham, West Sussex RH12 5AD
Tel: 01403 252310   *Boardroom:* 01403 255787

LEATHERHEAD
Manager: Alex Inglethorpe *Colours:* Green & white
Fetcham Grove, Guildford Rd, Leatherhead KT22 9AS
Tel: 01372 360151   *Fax:* 01372 362705

LEWES
Manager: Steven King   *Colours:* Red & black
The Dripping Pan, Mountfield Road, Lewes, East
Sussex BN7 2BN   *Tel:* 01273 472100

MARLOW
Manager: Derek Sweetman *Colours:* Blue & white
Alfred Davis Ground, Oak Tree Road, Marlow,
Buckinghamshire SL7 3ED
Tel: 01628 483970   *Fax:* 01628 477032

METROPOLITAN POLICE
Manager: Paul Carruth   *Colours:* Blue
Imber Court Sports Club, Ember Lane, East Molesey,
Surrey KT8 0BT
Tel: 020 8398 1267   *Boardroom:* 020 8398 7358

MOLESEY
Manager: Steve Moss   *Colours:* Black & white
412 Walton Road, West Molesey, Surrey KT8 0JG
Tel: 020 8979 4823   *Fax:* 020 8979 9103
Boardroom: 020 8941 7989

SLOUGH TOWN
Manager: t.b.a.   *Colours:* Yellow & blue
Windsor & Eton FC, Stag Meadow, St Leonards Road,
Windsor, Berks SL4 3DR *(groundshare to be confirmed)*
Tel: 01753 860656   *Fax:* 01753 860656

STAINES TOWN
Manager: Steve Cordery   *Colours:* Old gold & blue
Wheatsheaf Park, Wheatsheaf Lane, Staines, Middlesex
TW18 7AH   *Tel:* 01784 455988

TOOTING & MITCHAM UNITED
Manager: Richard Cadette *Colours:* White & black
Imperial Fields, Bishopsford Road, Morden SM4 6BF
Tel: 020 8648 3248   *Boardroom:* 020 8685 9229

WALTON & HERSHAM
Manager: Matt Alexander   *Colours:* Red & white
Stompond Lane, Walton-on-Thames, Surrey KT12 1HF
Tel: 01932 244967   *Fax:* 01932 885814
Boardroom: 01932 245363

WHYTELEAFE
Manager: Lee Richardson   *Colours:* Green & white
15 Church Road, Whyteleafe, Surrey CR3 0AR
Tel: 020 8660 5491   *Fax:* 020 8645 0422

WINDSOR & ETON
Manager: Dennis Greene   Colours: Red & green
Stag Meadow, St Leonards Road, Windsor SL4 3DR
Tel: 01753 860656   *Fax:* 01753 860656

WORTHING
Manager: Barry Lloyd   *Colours:* Red & white
Woodside Road, Worthing, West Sussex BN14 7HQ
Tel/Fax: 01903 239575

WWW.CHERRYRED.CO.UK

	ASH	BAN	BOG	BRA	BRO	CAR	CHE	COR	CRO	Cath	DUL	EGH	EPS	HOR	LEA	LEW	MET	MOL	STA	TOO	WAL	WHY	WIN	WOR
Ash.		79 / 20 Aug	85 / 22 Mar	159 / 15 Oct	126 / 15 Feb	155 / 30 Nov	86 / 28 Sep	64 / 4 Feb	61 / 2 Nov	109 / 7 Sep	148 / 24 Sep	94 / 23 Nov	117 / 12 Apr	113 / 9 Apr	124 / 15 Oct	91 / 19 Oct	110 / 19 Apr	270 / 26 Dec	1123 / 5 Apr	159 / 12 Nov	177 / 3 May	133 / 11 Mar	138 / 14 Dec	73 / 1
Ban.	30 / 4 Mar		128 / 8 Mar	45 / 9 Nov	87 / 26 Aug	160 / 10 Sep	141 / 8 Mar	35 / 24 Sep	75 / 28 Sep	81 / 15 Feb	60 / 17 Aug	106 / 21 Apr	91 / 12 Apr	126 / 29 Apr	71 / 15 Oct	51 / 30 Nov	62 / 19 Apr	79 / 19 Oct	102 / 5 Apr	42 / 31 Mar	65 / 4 Feb	62 / 21 Dec	190 / 18 Jan	496 / 5 Apr
Bog.	256 / 16 Nov	243 / 4 Jan		308 / 5 Apr	283 / 19 Oct	553 / 20 Aug	203 / 20 Aug	197 / 24 Sep	201 / 28 Sep	315 / 1 Mar	301 / 18 Jan	252 / 21 Apr	255 / 15 Oct	206 / 19 Oct	1003 / 26 Apr	220 / 24 Aug	247 / 26 Oct	240 / 19 Apr	408 / 7 Dec	193 / 29 Mar	367 / 14 Dec	190 / 16 Nov		
Brac.	96 / 15 Mar	89 / 10 Sep	115 /		163 / 8 Oct	80 / 20 Aug	120 / 21 Sep	85 / 21 Dec	125 / 18 Mar	139 / 26 Oct	158 / 21 Apr	86 / 28 Jan	206 / 29 Mar	102 / 15 Oct	152 / 7 Dec	79 / 22 Feb	87 / 15 Oct	170 / 29 Mar	115 / 7 Dec	178 / 26 Aug	153 / 17 Aug	168 / 8 Feb	312 / 16 Nov	349 /
Bro.	312 / 11 Feb	225 / 7 Sep	390 /	12 Apr /		307 /	180 / 5 Apr	272 / 12 Oct	301 / 14 Dec	311 / 25 Feb	282 / 16 Nov	242 / 3 May	280 / 29 Mar	372 / 8 Feb	348 / 4 Mar	341 / 26 Oct	165 / 19 Apr	305 / 30 Nov	276 / 26 Dec	204 / 7 Dec	317 / 26 Apr	312 / 15 Mar	379 / 24 Aug	288 /
Car.	291 / 11 Apr	333 / 21 Sep	297 /	332 / 18 Mar	469 /		298 / 19 Apr	451 / 26 Apr	345 / 9 Nov	325 / 19 Aug	341 / 25 Jan	274 / 23 Sep	336 / 7 Dec	248 / 3 Feb	370 /	26 Oct /	252 / 24 Aug	270 / 26 Oct	740 /	313 / 22 Mar	417 / 12 Oct	379 / 4 Jan	123 / 7 Sep	108 /
Cher.	112 / 5 Apr	138 / 16 Nov	125 /	143 /	124 / 22 Oct	153 /		164 /	101 /	84 /	92 /	104 / 4 Feb	112 / 26 Aug	107 / 21 Apr	109 / 25 Jan	142 / 24 Sep	164 / 15 Feb	280 / 26 Dec	101 / 15 Apr	149 / 14 Jan	84 / 11 Mar	123 / 22 Mar	80 / 29 Mar	93 /
Cor.	55 / 26 Apr	100 / 4 Mar	74 /		126 / 21 Dec	181 /	50 / 17 Aug		114 / 1 Mar	119 / 8 Apr	69 / 26 Aug	62 / 12 Apr	107 / 4 Feb	101 /	70 / 15 Mar	53 / 25 Jan	54 / 7 Sep	80 /	162 / 15 Apr	87 / 21 Sep	126 / 1 Oct	95 /	65 / 20 Aug	95 / 26 Oct
Croy.	97 / 8 Feb	72 / 12 Oct	95 /	74 / 16 Nov	242 / 17 Aug	160 / 18 Dec	81 / 2 Oct	73 /	47 / 25 Feb	185 / 15 Mar	88 /	136 / 15 Sep	112 / 28 Dec	86 / 30 Aug	117 / 29 Mar	89 /	74 / 7 Sep	75 / 15 Apr	136 / 24 Aug	117 /	140 /	77 /	253 /	267 /
CAth.	73 / 29 Mar	49 / 21 Sep	98 /	97 / 20 Aug	185 / 21 Apr	202 / 23 Nov	108 / 15 Mar	102 / 2 Dec	86 / 8 Apr	161 / 21 Apr	52 / 4 Mar	107 /	80 / 19 Oct	235 / 22 Feb	153 / 12 Apr	83 / 19 Apr	214 / 16 Nov	192 / 24 Aug	273 / 14 Dec	269 / 8 Feb	259 / 26 Oct	253 / 7 Sep	26 Oct /	5 Mar / 118
Dul.	279 / 1 Oct	216 / 21 Sep	154 / 1 Oct	126 /	109 / 21 Apr	168 / 7 Jan	52 /	296 / 9 Nov		107 /	239 / 26 Aug	265 /	235 / 17 Aug	232 /	357 /	288 /	153 / 8 Mar	187 / 18 Jan	86 / 24 Aug	131 / 28 Dec	86 / 19 Oct	104 / 18 Jan	103 /	
Egh.	217 / 12 Apr	65 / 14 Dec	85 / 17 Sep	67 /	85 / 28 Apr		52 / 4 Mar	76 /	73 /	239 / 3 May	7 Dec /	67 / 15 Apr	15 Apr /	91 /	140 / 1 Feb	88 / 7 Sep	58 / 5 Apr	153 / 30 Nov	18 Jan /	104 / 25 Feb	112 / 21 Sep	98 / 24 Aug	88 / 29 Mar	56 / 8
Eps.	94 / 7 Apr	89 / 9 Nov	136 / 12 Oct	89 / 14 Jan	136 / 24 Aug	228 / 8 Feb	85 / 5 Apr	73 / 18 Mar	227 /	113 / 25 Jan	61 /	22 Mar /		123 /	152 / 21 Sep	135 / 16 Nov	68 / 14 Dec	183 / 20 Aug	304 / 19 Apr	139 / 22 Feb	112 / 15 Mar	98 / 29 Mar	88 /	408 /
Hor.	193 / 26 Oct	136 /	549 /	199 /	234 / 29 Mar	642 / 3 May	501 / 9 Nov	305 / 9 Nov	152 / 24 Aug	313 / 14 Dec	398 / 11 Jan	328 / 1 Mar		1 Oct /	356 /	565 /	183 / 14 Dec	304 / 4 Jan	319 / 5 Apr	318 / 26 Apr	323 / 15 Mar	252 / 19 Apr	156 / 24 Sep	408 /
Lea.	158 / 17 Dec	165 / 7 Sep	232 /	219 /	124 /		167 / 23 Nov	158 / 25 Jan	108 /	224 / 14 Dec	129 / 11 Jan	140 /	261 /	123 /		135 /	104 /	139 /	68 / 8 Mar	124 /	210 / 8 Mar	565 /	252 /	161 /
Lew.	292 / 24 Aug	232 / 21 Jan	207 / 1 Mar	237 / 21 Apr	152 / 3 May	251 /	174 / 9 Nov	240 / 22 Mar	262 /	223 / 22 Oct	282 / 21 Dec	192 / 8 Mar	140 / 15 Apr	383 / 1 Oct	462 / 21 Sep	349 / 16 Nov	204 / 20 Aug	144 / 4 Jan	142 / 5 Apr	142 / 11 Mar	5 May /	3 Dec /	144 / 19 Apr	161 / 20 Aug
Met.	125 / 1 Apr	112 / 4 Feb	114 / 3 May	112 /	130 / 25 Jan	257 / 26 Oct	273 / 24 Aug	241 /	240 / 15 Feb	112 /	223 /	192 /	105 / 19 Oct	151 / 19 Oct	180 / 22 Feb	29 Mar /	147 /	271 / 14 Dec	183 / 15 Mar	304 / 11 Mar	233 / 3 Dec	169 / 15 Apr	494 /	384 /
Mol.	80 / 26 Feb	275 / 18 Apr	220 / 12 Apr	130 / 26 Oct	100 /	460 /	98 / 24 Aug	262 / 22 Mar	61 / 21 Dec	180 / 3 Dec	282 / 10 Sep	161 / 17 Aug	105 / 8 Aug	151 / 21 Apr	186 / 20 Aug	144 / 5 Apr	269 / 23 Nov		175 / 24 Sep	185 /	168 / 10 Sep	95 /	95 / 27 Aug	150 /
Stain.	601 / 10 Sep	207 / 1 Oct	177 / 28 Dec	176 / 4 Mar	208 / 1 Dec	1147 / 28 Jan	237 / 29 Mar	282 / 26 Aug	320 / 15 Feb	451 / 18 Mar	265 / 12 Oct	186 / 11 Mar	201 / 4 Mar	105 / 25 Apr	188 / 20 Aug	140 / 17 Aug	235 / 26 Apr	135 /	4 Mar /	1 Feb /	160 / 17 Aug	95 / 21 Sep	95 / 15 Oct	29 Apr /
Toot.	236 / 10 Sep	258 /	258 /	237 / 3 May	196 / 26 Apr	534 / 22 Feb	254 / 18 Jan	282 / 28 Dec	320 / 17 Aug	180 / 29 Mar	288 / 26 Oct	201 / 4 Mar	105 / 5 Nov	383 / 10 Sep	186 / 21 Apr	349 / 5 Apr	204 / 19 Nov	147 /	271 /		358 / 17 Aug	216 / 21 Apr	174 / 2 Oct	332 /
Walt.	154 / 29 Mar	109 /	492 /	88 / 18 Sep	113 / 25 Mar	155 / 26 Nov	174 / 24 Aug	106 / 15 Feb	119 / 19 Apr	180 / 24 Sep	103 / 1 Mar	105 / 5 Nov	288 / 4 Mar	151 / 19 Oct	144 / 8 Apr	138 / 5 Apr	89 / 14 Dec	188 / 20 Aug	203 / 7 Sep	215 /		251 / 12 Apr	137 /	141 / 8 Feb
Why.	116 / 7 Dec	275 / 18 Apr	114 / 28 Sep	150 /	309 / 5 Oct	460 / 18 Jan	98 / 6 Aug	172 / 15 Feb	172 / 23 Nov	238 / 24 Aug	142 / 15 Feb	161 / 9 Nov	98 / 12 Nov	149 / 21 Dec	184 / 22 Mar	100 / 25 Feb	4 Mar /	127 / 7 Sep	188 / 24 Sep	234 / 7 Sep	137 / 18 Mar		177 / 5 Apr	278 / 15 Oct
Win.	88 / 18 Apr	98 /	111 /	88 / 24 Sep	135 / 9 Nov	146 / 26 Aug	84 / 7 Jan	90 /	98 /	156 / 28 Dec	154 / 8 Mar	98 / 21 Dec	320 / 12 Nov	138 / 21 Dec	120 / 7 Dec	129 / 17 Dec	72 / 15 Feb	116 / 1 Mar	187 / 1 Feb	24 Sep /	114 / 21 Apr	88 / 10 Sep		125 / 26 Apr
Wor.	247 / 14 Sep	217 / 21 Apr	932 / 8 Mar	221 /	339 / 28 Dec	382 /	159 / 23 Nov	403 / 22 Mar	252 / 10 Sep	318 / 12 Oct	265 / 21 Dec	320 / 26 Apr	443 / 8 Feb	138 /	163 / 10 Apr	350 / 1 Apr	309 / 21 Sep	254 / 9 Nov	318 / 3 May	394 /	151 / 25 Feb	309 / 30 Nov	169 / 18 Mar	

	Abingdon Town	Camberley Town	Chalfont St Peter	Cheshunt	Clapton	Dorking	Edgware Town	Flackwell Heath	Hungerford Town	Kingsbury Town	Leighton Town	Leyton	Tring Town	Ware	Witham Town	Wokingham Town
Abingdon Town		4-0	3-1	1-2	2-2	2-1	1-1	2-3	0-0	1-1	3-1	5-1	6-1	1-0	0-0	2-0
Camberley Town	0-3		1-4	2-3	1-2	2-0	0-0	0-2	1-3	0-1	2-1	0-3	2-0	0-1	0-1	1-3
Chalfont St Peter	1-2	0-1	D	0-4	0-3	1-0	1-3	1-4	1-2	3-0	5-3	1-3	2-1	0-3	0-0	1-3
Cheshunt	4-1	2-1	3-0	I	3-0	1-0	6-1	3-1	0-0	7-0	2-1	1-1	3-2	2-1	3-1	4-1
Clapton	2-2	2-1	2-0	0-5	V	3-3	0-5	2-4	2-0	0-2	1-1	3-1	3-2	0-1	1-1	2-1
Dorking	2-2	2-0	2-2	3-6	0-1	I	1-2	2-1	1-1	1-1	0-7	0-1	1-3	3-0	1-1	2-1
Edgware Town	0-3	0-1	0-4	1-3	0-1	3-6	S	3-0	0-1	1-6	1-0	1-2	3-1	1-2	4-0	5-0
Flackwell Heath	0-4	3-2	1-0	0-2	2-1	3-0	3-1	I	1-3	2-0	1-0	0-2	3-2	2-1	1-2	9-1
Hungerford Town	1-1	1-0	5-1	1-3	3-0	2-0	3-2	1-1	O	2-2	1-0	0-2	1-1	1-1	1-1	2-2
Kingsbury Town	1-1	1-1	2-2	2-0	2-1	0-0	1-0	2-2	0-0	N	1-1	0-2	1-0	1-0	2-0	0-1
Leighton Town	3-3	2-1	2-0	0-5	0-1	3-0	8-0	3-3	2-3	5-2		0-1	0-1	2-1	2-0	2-3
Leyton	8-0	3-0	4-0	5-2	1-0	4-0	3-1	3-0	3-2	0-0	1-3	T	1-3	3-0	3-5	5-0
Tring Town	2-0	3-0	1-1	1-6	0-2	3-1	2-1	0-2	3-1	7-1	2-7	0-2	W	2-3	2-1	1-0
Ware	3-5	0-1	0-2	1-4	3-2	4-2	3-1	2-1	1-1	3-2	0-3	0-0	3-1	O	1-2	3-3
Witham Town	0-4	7-2	2-0	0-0	1-0	3-2	2-1	1-1	0-3	0-0	1-1	0-1	2-1	4-2		1-0
Wokingham Town	1-1	3-2	2-0	1-2	2-1	1-9	0-0	0-4	2-6	1-3	0-2	0-6	0-0	1-2	1-4	

Division Two

	P	W	D	L	F	A	Pts
Cheshunt	30	25	3	2	91	29	78
Leyton	30	21	5	4	77	22	68
Flackwell Heath	30	17	3	10	52	44	54
Abingdon Town	30	14	11	5	65	42	53
Hungerford Town	30	12	12	6	49	36	48
Leighton Town	30	14	3	13	61	43	45
Witham Town	30	12	8	10	40	43	44
Ware	30	12	5	13	47	53	41
Clapton	30	12	5	13	40	47	41
Tring Town	30	11	5	14	49	58	38
Kingsbury Town	30	9	11	10	38	48	38
Edgware Town	30	10	3	17	49	65	33
Wokingham Town	30	7	7	16	34	81	28
Dorking	30	6	6	18	49	63	24
Chalfont St Peter	30	6	5	19	34	63	23
Camberley Town	30	4	4	22	23	61	16

DIVISION TWO CONSTITUTION 2003-04

ABINGDON TOWN...Culham Road, Abingdon, Oxfordshire..................................01235 521684
CAMBERLEY TOWN...........Krooner Park, Krooner Road, off Frimley Road, Camberley, Surrey .... 01276 65392. Fax: 01276 516613
CHALFONT ST PETER.........Mill Meadow, Amersham Road, Chalfont St Peter, Buckinghamshire.......................01753 885797
CHERTSEY TOWN...................................Alwyns Lane, Chertsey, Surrey.
CLAPTON ....Old Spotted Dog Ground, Upton Lane, Forest Gate, London......01932 561774 / 571792
DORKING ....Meadowbank, Mill Lane, Dorking, Surrey...............................01306 884112
EDGWARE TOWN ....White Lion Ground, High Street, Edgware, Middlesex........020 8952 6799. Fax: 020 8952 6799
FLACKWELL HEATH.......Wilks Park, Magpie Lane, Flackwell Heath, High Wycombe, Buckinghamshire.............01628 523892
HERTFORD TOWN.................Hertingfordbury Park, West Street, Hertford, Hertfordshire.....................01992 583716
KINGSBURY TOWN...................Silver Jubilee Park, Townsend Lane, Kingsbury, London ....020 8205 1645 / 8205 5204
LEIGHTON TOWN................Bell Close, Lake Street, Leighton Buzzard, Bedfordshire........01525 373311. Fax: 01525 370142
TRING TOWN....................Pendley Sports Centre, Cow Lane, Tring, Hertfordshire.................01442 824018 / 823075
WARE ....Wodson Park, Wadesmill Road, Ware, Hertfordshire.......................01920 463247
WEMBLEY ....Vale Farm, Watford Road, Sudbury, Wembley, Middlesex.......020 8904 8169 / 8908 5461
WITHAM TOWN............................Spa Road, Witham, Essex....................................01376 511198 / 520996
WOKINGHAM TOWN..........Egham Town FC, Runnymede Stadium, Tempest Road, Egham, Surrey..........01784 435226 / 436466

Cheshunt and Leyton are promoted to Division One North from which Wembley and Hertford Town are relegated. Chertsey Town are relegated from Division One South following their defeat in the play-off (see page 74). Hungerford Town have switched to the Hellenic League.

ISTHMIAN LEAGUE CUP

FIRST ROUND
Aveley 4 Bracknell Town 0
Banstead Athletic 2 Tring Town 0
Barton Rovers 4 Croydon Athletic 1
Berkhamsted Town 4 Arlesey Town 4 *aet*
Arlesey Town 3 Berkhamsted Town 2 *replay*
Chertsey Town 3 Camberley Town 2 *aet*
Cheshunt 6 Hertford Town 0
Clapton 2 Whyteleafe 2 *aet*
Whyteleafe 1 Clapton 0 *replay*
Corinthian Casuals 3 Edgware Town 1
East Thurrock United 3 Wokingham Town 1
Epsom & Ewell 1 **Ashford Town (Middx)** 4
Great Wakering Rovers 0 **Bromley** 1
Hemel Hempstead Town 1 **Leyton** 3 *aet*
Horsham 1 Abingdon Town 1 *aet*
Abingdon Town 0 **Horsham** 3 *replay*
Leighton Town 0 **Chalfont St Peter** 2
Lewes 3 Wivenhoe Town 0
Leyton Pennant 0 **Flackwell Heath** 1
Metropolitan Police 2 **Hornchurch** 6
Molesey 4 Barking & East Ham United 3
Tilbury 2 **Hungerford Town** 3
Ware 0 **Marlow** 1
Wembley 6 Kingsbury Town 0
Windsor & Eton 5 Egham Town 2
Wingate & Finchley 6 Dorking 5 *aet*
Witham Town 3 Leatherhead 0

SECOND ROUND
Ashford Town (Middx) 3 Heybridge Swifts 1
Aveley 2 Marlow 0
Barton Rovers 1 **Braintree Town** 3
Billericay Town 5 Enfield 0
Bromley 0 **Bedford Town** 1
Chalfont St Peter 1 **Arlesey Town** 2
Chesham United 2 **Sutton United** 3 *aet*
Cheshunt 1 Aldershot Town 0
Corinthian Casuals 2 Carshalton Athletic 1
Croydon 2 Banstead Athletic 0
Dulwich Hamlet 2 Chertsey Town 0
Flackwell Heath 0 **Aylesbury United** 3
Ford United 3 **Purfleet** 0
Harlow Town 1 **Grays Athletic** 2
Hayes 0 **Canvey Island** 1
Hendon 4 Staines Town 2
Horsham 1 **Boreham Wood** 3
Hungerford Town 0 Bishop's Stortford 0 *aet*
Bishop's Stortford 7 Hungerford Town 1 *replay*
Lewes 3 Maidenhead United 3 *aet*
Maidenhead United 0 **Lewes** 1 *replay*
Leyton 3 Wealdstone 0
Molesey 0 **Hampton & Richmond Borough** 1
Northwood 4 Hornchurch 2

Slough Town 1 **Kingstonian** 3 *aet*
St Albans City 3 Bognor Regis Town 2
Thame United 2 **East Thurrock United** 3 *aet*
Tooting & Mitcham United 1 **Worthing** 4
Uxbridge 1 **Basingstoke Town** 2
Walton & Hersham 0 **Hitchin Town** 1
Wembley 5 Oxford City 3
Whyteleafe 0 **Yeading** 3
Windsor & Eton 0 **Harrow Borough** 4
Witham Town 1 **Wingate & Finchley** 2 *aet*

THIRD ROUND
Ashford Town (Middx) 1 **St Albans City** 2
Aveley 2 Northwood 1
Aylesbury United 3 Sutton United 2
Billericay Town 3 Ford United 1
Bishop's Stortford 3 Basingstoke Town 1
Braintree Town 1 **Harrow Borough** 3
Cheshunt 1 **Canvey Island** 5
Croydon 1 **Wingate & Finchley** 3
East Thurrock United 0 **Grays Athletic** 1
Hendon 2 Arlesey Town 1
Hitchin Town 4 Boreham Wood 0
Kingstonian 3 Worthing 0
Lewes 6 Hampton & Richmond Borough 0
Leyton 3 **Bedford Town** 4 *aet*
Wembley 0 **Dulwich Hamlet** 2
Yeading 4 Corinthian Casuals 0

FOURTH ROUND
Bedford Town 1 **Yeading** 2
Billericay Town 1 Bishop's Stortford 1 *aet*
Bishop's Stortford 3 Billericay Town 0
Grays Athletic 1 Aylesbury United 0
Harrow Borough 2 **Lewes** 3
Hendon 5 Wingate & Finchley 2 *aet*
Hitchin Town 1 **Canvey Island** 3
Kingstonian 3 Aveley 1
St Albans City 1 **Dulwich Hamlet** 2

QUARTER-FINALS
Bishop's Stortford 1 **Yeading** 4
Canvey Island 6 Grays Athletic 0
Dulwich Hamlet 4 Lewes 1
Hendon 1 Kingstonian 0 *aet*

SEMI-FINALS
(played over two legs)
Canvey Island 4 Hendon 2, Hendon 2 **Canvey Island** 2
Dulwich H. 1 Yeading 3, **Yeading** 3 Dulwich Hamlet 1

FINAL
(5th May at Hornchurch)
Canvey Island 0 **Yeading** 2

ISTHMIAN RELEGATION PLAY-OFF
(To determine third relegation place to Division Two, played over two legs)

(First leg, 6th May)
Wembley 2 Metropolitan Police 3 Att: 71

(Second leg, 10th May)
Metropolitan Police 3 Wembley 0 Att: 255

ISTHMIAN CHARITY SHIELD
(League Cup winners v League champions)

(10th September at Northwood)
Northwood 4 Gravesend & Northfleet 2

ISTHMIAN ASSOCIATE MEMBERS CUP
(Division Two clubs)

Group A	P	W	D	L	F	A	Pts	Group B	P	W	D	L	F	A	Pts
Flackwell Heath	6	4	2	0	11	4	14	Hungerford Town	6	3	2	1	16	9	11
Chalfont St Peter	6	3	2	1	17	9	11	Camberley Town	6	1	4	1	11	10	7
Leighton Town	6	1	1	4	10	10	4	Abingdon Town	6	2	1	3	9	12	7
Wokingham Town	6	1	1	4	8	23	4	Dorking	6	2	1	3	11	16	7

Chalfont St Peter 0 Flackwell Heath 2
Chalfont St Peter 2 Leighton Town 1
Chalfont St Peter 3 Wokingham Town 3
Flackwell Heath 1 Leighton Town 1
Flackwell Heath 2 Chalfont St Peter 2
Flackwell Heath 2 Wokingham Town 0
Leighton Town 0 Chalfont St Peter 2
Leighton Town 0 Flackwell Heath 2
Leighton Town 6 Wokingham Town 0
Wokingham Town 1 Chalfont St Peter 8
Wokingham Town 1 Flackwell Heath 2
Wokingham Town 3 Leighton Town 2

Abingdon Town 2 Camberley Town 2
Abingdon Town 2 Dorking 3
Abingdon Town 3 Hungerford Town 0
Camberley Town 1 Abingdon Town 2
Camberley Town 2 Hungerford Town 2
Camberley Town 3 Dorking 1
Dorking 1 Hungerford Town 4
Dorking 2 Abingdon Town 0
Dorking 2 Camberley Town 2
Hungerford Town 1 Camberley Town 1
Hungerford Town 4 Abingdon Town 0
Hungerford Town 5 Dorking 2

Group C	P	W	D	L	F	A	Pts	Group D	P	W	D	L	F	A	Pts
Cheshunt	6	6	0	0	16	1	18	Leyton	6	5	1	0	21	4	16
Kingsbury Town	6	4	0	2	10	9	12	Ware	6	4	0	2	11	14	12
Tring Town	6	1	0	5	7	14	3	Clapton	6	2	0	4	7	12	6
Edgware Town	6	1	0	5	4	13	3	Witham Town	6	0	1	5	3	12	1

Cheshunt 3 Edgware Town 0
Cheshunt 3 Tring Town 0
Cheshunt 4 Kingsbury Town 0
Edgware Town 0 Cheshunt 1
Edgware Town 0 Kingsbury Town 1
Edgware Town 1 Tring Town 3
Kingsbury Town 0 Cheshunt 2
Kingsbury Town 3 Tring Town 2
Kingsbury Town 4 Edgware Town 1
Tring Town 0 Kingsbury Town 2
Tring Town 1 Cheshunt 3
Tring Town 1 Edgware Town 2

Clapton 0 Leyton 2
Clapton 0 Ware 2
Clapton 3 Witham Town 0
Leyton 2 Witham Town 1
Leyton 4 Clapton 0
Leyton 4 Ware 0
Ware 1 Witham Town 0
Ware 2 Leyton 8
Ware 4 Clapton 1
Witham Town 0 Clapton 3
Witham Town 1 Leyton 1
Witham Town 1 Ware 2

QUARTER-FINALS
Cheshunt 1 Chalfont St Peter 0
Flackwell Heath 2 Ware 1 *aet*
Hungerford Town 3 **Kingsbury Town** 3 *aet* (5-6p)
Leyton 4 Camberley Town 0

SEMI-FINALS
Cheshunt 5 Kingsbury Town 0
Flackwell Heath 2 Leyton 2 *aet*
Leyton 2 Flackwell Heath 0 *replay*

FINAL (6th May at Leyton)
Leyton 2 Cheshunt 0

KENT COUNTY LEAGUE

	Bearsted	Beauwater	Crockenhill	Greenways	Kennington	Lydd Town	Milton Athletic	New Romney	Old Roan	Sevenoaks Town	Sheerness East	Snodland	Stansfeld O & B Club	Wickham Park
Bearsted		4-1	4-2	0-3	3-0	4-2	1-0	0-0	2-2	0-2	0-0	6-0	1-2	2-0
Beauwater	0-2	P	3-5	1-1	1-1	1-0	0-2	3-0	0-2	0-2	2-3	3-1	0-4	2-1
Crockenhill	0-1	0-2	R	2-2	2-3	1-1	1-3	5-0	1-2	1-3	1-1	2-2	2-3	3-0
Greenways	1-1	0-0	1-3	E	4-2	3-3	2-1	2-2	2-5	1-1	1-1	3-0	4-3	2-1
Kennington	1-1	0-0	1-1	3-1	M	0-1	2-1	3-1	2-1	1-0	1-4	1-2	0-3	4-1
Lydd Town	3-2	3-2	1-0	3-2	2-1	I	6-5	2-1	1-1	1-3	3-3	3-0	2-1	0-6
Milton Athletic	1-2	0-1	3-2	1-0	2-2	3-1	E	0-0	1-2	0-2	0-1	5-0	1-3	4-0
New Romney	2-2	2-1	1-0	3-1	3-2	0-2	0-6	R	1-3	0-4	3-5	2-2	1-3	
Old Roan	2-1	0-0	4-1	1-2	4-0	4-1	3-3	6-2		1-1	5-0	2-0	1-1	4-1
Sevenoaks Town	1-1	8-1	5-1	1-0	1-1	4-0	4-1	0-0	2-3		4-1	6-2	0-1	1-1
Sheerness East	1-1	0-1	1-2	5-3	4-2	2-1	3-1	3-1	2-1	1-3	D	0-0	2-2	2-0
Snodland	2-2	3-2	4-2	1-3	1-4	3-4	1-2	1-4	0-1	1-5	2-1	I	1-1	0-0
Stansfeld O & BC	0-2	7-0	3-0	2-0	2-0	0-1	3-0	3-1	3-1	1-2	4-3	5-1	V	6-1
Wickham Park	0-0	3-2	0-0	1-4	0-1	0-2	4-1	1-3	0-3	0-1	1-0	1-0	1-6	

CHAMPIONS TROPHY

(24th August at Bearsted)
Bearsted 1 **Stansfeld** 1 *aet* (4-5p)

Premier Division	P	W	D	L	F	A	Pts
Sevenoaks Town	26	17	6	3	65	22	57
Stansfeld O&BC	26	17	4	5	71	29	55
Old Roan	26	15	7	4	63	32	52
Lydd Town	26	14	4	8	49	52	46
Bearsted	26	11	10	5	45	28	43
Sheerness East	26	11	7	8	48	42	40
Greenways	26	10	7	9	50	47	37
Kennington	26	8	7	11	38	47	31
Milton Athletic	26	9	3	14	47	46	30
New Romney	26	7	6	13	36	61	27
Beauwater	26	7	4	15	29	56	25
Wickham Park	26	6	4	16	27	54	22
Crockenhill	26	5	6	15	40	54	21
Snodland	26	5	5	16	33	71	20

PREMIER DIVISION CONSTITUTION 2003-04

BEARSTED . . . . Honey Lane, Otham, Maidstone, Kent 07711 128034
BEAUWATER . . . . Beauwater Leisure Sports Club, Nelson Road, Northfleet, Kent 01474 359222
CRAY VALLEY PAPER MILLS . . . . . Badgers Sports Ground, Middle Park Avenue, Eltham, London 020 8850 4273
CROCKENHILL . . . . Wested, Eynsford Road, Crockenhill, Swanley, Kent 01322 662097
GREENWAYS . . . . Beauwater Leisure Sports Club, Nelson Road, Northfleet, Kent . . . . None
KENNINGTON . . . . Kennington Cricket Club, Ulley Road, Ulley Road, Kennington, Kent 01797 321904
LYDD TOWN . . . . The Lindsey Field, Dengemarsh Road, Lydd, Romney Marsh, Kent 01797 564213
MILTON ATHLETIC . . . . UK Paper Sports Ground, Gore Court Road, Sittingbourne, Kent 01795 564213
NEW ROMNEY . . . . The Maud Pavilion, Station Road, New Romney, Kent 01797 364858
OLD ROAN . . . . The Playing Fields, John Roan School, Kidbrooke Park Road, London 020 8856 1915
SHEERNESS EAST . . . . Sheerness East WMC, 47 Queensborough Road, Halfway, Sheerness, Kent 01795 662049
STANSFELD O & B CLUB . . . . . . Greenwich University Sports Ground, Kidbrooke Lane, Eltham, London 020 8850 0210
TENTERDEN TIGERS . . . . Recreation Ground, High Street, Tenterden, Kent 01580 762703
WICKHAM PARK . . . . Wickham Park Sports Club, 228-230 Pickhurst Rise, West Wickham, Kent 020 8777 2550

Sevenoaks Town are promoted to the Kent League. Snodland are relegated to Division One West replaced by Cray Valley Paper Mills. Tenterden Tigers are promoted from Division One East.

WWW.NLNEWSDESK.CO.UK

INTER-REGIONAL CHALLENGE CUP

FIRST ROUND EAST
Betteshanger 3 Tenterden Tigers 1, Bromley Green 0 **Bliby** 5
Lydd Town 1 Smarden 0, New Romney 1 **St Margarets** 2
Norton 1 **Kennington** 2 *aet*, Snowdown 0 **Sheerness East** 6
FIRST ROUND WEST
AFC Blackheath 1 **Bly Spartans** 2
Bearsted 2 Belvedere 0
Crockenhill 2 Eynsford 2 *aet* (4-3p)
Oakwood 4 Wickham Park 2
Phoenix Sports 1 Snodland 0
Sevenoaks Town 10 Thames Poly 2
Stansfeld O & B Club 2 Fleetdown United 0
SECOND ROUND EAST
Betteshanger Welfare 5 St Margarets 3
Kennington 0 **Bliby** 2
Milton Athletic 5 Lydd Town 2
University of Kent 1 **Sheerness East** 2

SECOND ROUND WEST
Aylesford PM 1 Bearsted 0, Beauwater 0 **Stansfeld O&BC** 2
Cray Valley 3 Pembury 0, Holmesdale 0 **Crockenhill** 2
Moonshot Athletic 2 Greenways 1, Rusthall 0 **Oakwood** 2
Sevenoaks 2 **Old Roan** 2 *aet* (5-6p), Snodland 2 **Bly Spar.**
THIRD ROUND WEST
Aylesford PM 2 Cray Valley 0, Bly Spartans 1 **Crockenhill** 2
Old Roan 1 **Oakwood** 4, **Stansfeld** 5 Moonshot Athletic 3 *aet*
QUARTER-FINALS
Bliby 3 Crockenhill 2, Milton Athletic 0 **Oakwood** 2
Sheerness East 3 Aylesford Paper Mills 0
Stansfeld O & B Club 7 Betteshanger Welfare 1
SEMI-FINALS
Sheerness East 6 Bliby 0
Stansfeld O & B Club 2 Oakwood 1
FINAL *(24th April at Ashford Town)*
Sheerness East 2 **Stansfeld O & B Club** 2 *aet* (1-3p)

LES LECKIE CUP *(For Senior Eastern Region clubs)*

FIRST ROUND
Betteshanger Welfare 1 **Smarden** 3, Bliby 3 **Kennington** 4
New Romney 1 **Lydd Town** 4 *aet*, **Norton** 3 Bromley Green 1
Snowdown 0 **Tenterden** 2, **University** 2 Sheerness East 1
QUARTER-FINALS
Lydd Town 3 Betteshanger 2, Norton Spts 0 **Milton Athletic** 2

Tenterden Tigers 3 **St Margarets** 3 *aet* (4-5p)
University of Kent 2 **Kennington** 3
SEMI-FINALS
Milton Athletic 3 Kennington 2, St Margarets 1 **Lydd** 2
FINAL *(8th May at Chatham Town)*
Milton Athletic 2 **Lydd Town** 2 *aet* (4-5p)

	Betteshanger Welf.	Bliby	Bromley Green	Norton Sports	Smarden	Snowdown CW	St Margarets	Tenterden Tigers	Univ. of Kent
Betteshanger W.	D	2-2	n/a	1-2	8-2	1-0	1-1	0-3	1-4
Bliby	2-2	I	5-2	3-1	7-0	0-4	2-2	n/a	2-3
Bromley Green	2-2	1-5	V	2-2	6-2	3-1	0-2	n/a	n/a
Norton Sports	n/a	5-1	n/a		8-0	5-1	n/a	1-2	1-4
Smarden	1-4	n/a	1-3	0-5	O	0-2	n/a	1-5	1-1
Snowdown CW	n/a	1-3	1-2	n/a	2-1	N	n/a	2-2	n/a
St Margarets	n/a	n/a	n/a	2-0	4-1	2-1	E	n/a	1-0
Tenterden Tigers	3-4	2-1	1-1	5-3	n/a	2-1			2-2
Univ. of Kent	1-1	1-4	2-1	n/a	2-0	2-1	5-3	2-0	E

	Betteshanger Welf.	Bliby	Bromley Green	Norton Sports	Smarden	Snowdown CW	St Margarets	Tenterden Tigers	Univ. of Kent
Betteshanger W.	D	2-1	1-1	1-2	n/a	3-3	0-0	n/a	n/a
Bliby	n/a	I	0-1	2-0	7-1	n/a	3-0	2-4	n/a
Bromley Green	2-5	n/a	V	1-2	n/a	n/a	2-0	3-2	2-1
Norton Sports	2-2	n/a	1-3		6-0	2-3	1-0	2-1	1-3
Smarden	1-7	0-6	0-1	n/a	O	2-1	1-4	1-1	1-8
Snowdown CW	2-2	0-1	0-1	2-2	3-4	N	4-3	0-3	3-0
St Margarets	1-3	2-2	0-0	0-3	2-0	1-3	E	2-2	6-0
Tenterden Tigers	1-2	6-1	2-1	n/a	3-1	4-2	8-1		3-0
Univ. of Kent	2-1	4-3	5-2	4-0	n/a	3-4	n/a	n/a	E

Teams played each other three times

Division One East	P	W	D	L	F	A	Pts
Tenterden Tigers	24	14	5	5	67	36	47
University of Kent	24	14	3	7	59	44	45
Bromley Green	24	11	5	8	43	43	38
Bliby	24	11	4	9	65	46	37
Betteshanger Welfare	24	9	10	5	56	41	37
Norton Sports	24	11	3	10	57	43	36
St Margarets	24	8	6	10	40	44	30
Snowdown Colliery Welfare	24	8	4	12	45	50	28
Smarden	24	1	2	21	20	105	5

DIVISION ONE EAST CONSTITUTION 2003-04

BETTESHANGER WELFARE .... Welfare Ground, Cavell Square, Mill Hill, Deal, Kent. 01304 372080
BLIBY .... Sandyacres Sports & Social, Sandyhurst Lane, Ashford, Kent. 01233 627373
BROMLEY GREEN .... The Swan Centre, Newtown Road, South Willesborough, Ashford, Kent. .... None
NORTON SPORTS. .... Norton Park, Provender Lane, Norton, Kent. .... None
SMARDEN .... The Minnis, Smarden, Ashford, Kent. 01795 520088
SNOWDOWN COLLIERY WELFARE .... Spinney Lane, Aylesham, Canterbury, Kent. .... None
ST MARGARETS. .... Alexander Field, Kingsdown Road, St Margarets-at-Cliffe, Dover, Kent. 01304 840278
TYLER HILL .... Bekesbourne Recreation Ground, Bekesbourne, Canterbury, Kent. .... None
UNIVERSITY OF KENT .... The Playing Fields, University of Kent, off Giles Lane, Canterbury, Kent. .... None
WOODSTOCK PARK .... Woodstock Park, Sittingbourne, Kent. .... None

Tenterden Tigers are promoted to the Premier Division. Tyler Hill and Woodstock Park are promoted from Division Two East.

	AFC B'hth	Aylesford	Belvedere	Bly Spart.	Cray Valley	Eynsford	Fleetdown	Holmesdale	Moonshot	Oakwood	Pembury	Phoenix	Rusthall	Thames P.
AFC Blackheath		2-0	1-0	3-0	1-1	0-2	3-1	0-1	2-1	2-1	3-0	2-3	4-2	1-2
Aylesford Paper M.	2-4	D	3-1	1-1	1-4	0-0	1-1	1-4	2-1	0-1		6-2	0-1	2-1
Belvedere	2-2	2-1	I	1-0	1-1		4-1	3-2	0-3	2-1	5-0	2-4	2-1	1-1
Bly Spartans	0-3	2-6	3-0	V	4-2	2-0	1-0	4-1	3-0	2-0	4-2	4-1	0-1	3-1
Cray Valley Ppr M.	2-1	3-1	1-2	2-1		5-0	11-1	2-1	2-1	1-7	0-3	3-1	2-2	1-3
Eynsford	1-2	1-2	3-2	2-3	3-3	O	2-0	2-1	0-2	0-0	2-2	2-1	2-1	2-0
Fleetdown United	0-3	0-4	0-1	6-3	0-1	2-0	N	1-0	1-2	2-2	4-1	1-0	3-0	5-3
Holmesdale	4-3	0-0	0-0	2-0	1-3	0-0	0-3	E	2-2	0-4	1-1	4-1	3-1	7-1
Moonshot Athletic	2-4	2-1	4-2	4-1	2-1	1-0	1-0	0-5		1-3	2-1	3-1	2-1	7-1
Oakwood	2-2	2-0	3-2	W-L	0-1	0-1	0-1	1-1	2-3	W	0-1	3-0	1-1	1-2
Pembury	W-L	6-1	3-2	0-3	1-6	0-3	3-2	2-0	2-2	1-2	E	1-0	1-2	2-0
Phoenix Sports	1-2	1-4	2-2	1-2	1-4	1-0	2-0	0-6	2-2	2-3	2-1	S	2-1	3-1
Rusthall	2-4	0-2	5-0	1-0	0-3	3-3	2-3	2-2	0-0	0-1	2-2	2-1	T	1-1
Thames Poly	3-3	6-3	0-1	3-1	2-1	5-1	3-1	1-1	1-1	3-2	3-2	2-0	1-4	

Division One West	P	W	D	L	F	A	Pts
Cray Valley PM	26	16	5	5	74	33	53
AFC Blackheath	26	15	4	7	57	35	49
Moonshot Athletic	26	12	5	9	51	45	41
Holmesdale	26	10	8	8	45	36	38
Fleetdown United	26	12	2	12	42	50	38
Thames Poly -1	26	11	5	10	50	52	37
Oakwood	26	10	6	10	37	31	36
Bly Spartans	26	12	0	14	46	45	36
Aylesford P. Mills	26	11	3	12	46	48	36
Belvedere	26	10	6	10	41	46	36
Pembury	26	10	2	14	34	55	32
Eynsford	26	8	6	12	29	42	30
Rusthall	26	7	6	13	42	46	27
Phoenix Sports	26	8	2	16	37	67	26

DIVISION ONE WEST CONSTITUTION 2003-04

AFC BLACKHEATH .... Eltham Town FC, The Oaks, Footscray Road, Eltham, Kent. 020 8850 0695
APM MEARS .... Cobdown Sports & Social Club, Ditton Corner, Station Road, Aylesford, Kent. 01622 717771
BELVEDERE. .... Belvedere Sports & Social Club, 101a Woolwich Road, Abbey Wood, London. 01322 436724
BLY SPARTANS .... Bly Spartans Sports Ground, Watling Street, Strood, Kent. 07761 224384
BROMLEIANS SPORTS .... Scrubbs Farm, Lower Gravel Road, Bromley, Kent. 020 8462 5068
EYNSFORD .... Westminster Fields, The Street, Horton Kirby, Kent. 01322 865193
FLEETDOWN UNITED. .... Heath Lane, Dartford, Kent. 01322 273848
HALLS .... Princes Golf & Leisure Club, Darenth Road, Dartford, Kent. 01322 276565
HOLMESDALE .... Holmesdale Sports & Social Club, Oakley Road, Bromley Common, Kent. 020 8462 4440
MOONSHOT ATHLETIC .... Ten Em Bee Sports Ground, Old Bromley Road, Downham, Kent. 020 8313 9510
OAKWOOD. .... Honey Lane, Otham, Maidstone, Kent. .... None
PEMBURY .... Woodside Recreation Ground, Henwoods Mount, Pembury, Kent. 07970 026628
SNODLAND. .... Potyn's Field, Paddlesworth Road, Snodland, Kent. 01634 243961
THAMES POLY .... Greenwich University Sports Ground, Kidbrooke Lane, Eltham, London. 020 8850 0210

Cray Valley Paper Mills are promoted to the Premier Division replaced by Snodland. Phoenix Sports and Rusthall drop to Division Two West replaced by Bromleians Sports and Halls. Aylesford Paper Mills become APM Mears.

WWW.CHERRYRED.CO.UK

	Betteshanger Res.	Kennington Res.	Lydd Town Res.	New Romney Res.	Sheerness E. Res.	St Margarets Res.	Tenterden Res.	Tyler Hill	University Res.	Woodstock Park
Betteshanger Welfare Res.	D	0-0	1-0	0-4	0-5	7-0	2-5	0-4	1-1	0-5
Kennington Res.	2-3	I	2-1	1-0	2-1	n/a	2-0	1-1	2-0	0-9
Lydd Town Res.	3-1	3-2	V	0-4	2-2	n/a	3-1	0-2	2-1	1-5
New Romney Res.	1-1	1-3	0-2		2-2	n/a	4-0	2-2	5-0	3-4
Sheerness East Res.	1-0	2-1	2-0	3-2	T	15-0	4-2	0-0	2-2	1-2
St Margarets Res.	n/a	n/a	n/a	n/a	n/a	W	n/a	1-6	n/a	n/a
Tenterden Tigers Res.	6-0	1-3	4-0	2-4	1-2	n/a	O	0-4	3-2	1-5
Tyler Hill	10-1	3-0	2-1	7-1	7-1	n/a	3-0		8-0	2-2
University of Kent Res.	2-2	0-3	7-0	0-10	1-1	n/a	1-2	1-7	E	1-0
Woodstock Park	7-1	1-6	12-0	2-1	3-0	n/a	5-2	2-3	9-0	

Division Two East	P	W	D	L	F	A	Pts
Tyler Hill	16	12	4	0	65	12	40
Woodstock Park	16	12	1	3	73	22	37
Kennington Res.	16	9	2	5	30	26	29
Sheerness East Res.	16	7	5	4	29	27	26
New Romney Res.	16	6	3	7	44	29	21
Tenterden Tig. Res.	16	5	0	11	30	44	15
Lydd Town Res.	-1 16	5	1	10	18	48	15
Univ. of Kent Res.	16	2	4	10	19	57	10
Betteshanger Res.	16	2	4	10	13	56	10

Note – St Margarets Reserves withdrew during the course of the season. Their results are shown opposite but have been expunged from the league table

DIVISION TWO EAST CONSTITUTION 2003-04

BETTESHANGER WELFARE RESERVES . . Welfare Ground, Cavell Square, Mill Hill, Deal 01304 372080
BORDEN VILLAGE . . . . Borden & Playstool Parish Council Ground, Borden, Kent . . . . None
KENNINGTON . . . . Kennington Cricket Club, Ulley Road, Ulley Road, Kennington, Kent . . . . None
LYDD TOWN RESERVES . . . . The Lindsey Field, Dengemarsh Road, Lydd, Romney Marsh, Kent 01797 321904
NEW ROMNEY RESERVES . . . . The Maud Pavilion, Station Road, New Romney, Kent 01797 364858
SHEERNESS EAST RESERVES . . . Sheerness East WMC, 47 Queensborough Road, Halfway, Sheerness 01795 662049
SHEPPEY UNITED . . . . Medways Ports Authority Ground, Sheerness, Kent 01795 668054
TENTERDEN TIGERS RESERVES . . . . Recreation Ground, High Street, Tenterden, Kent 01580 762703
UNIVERSITY OF KENT RESERVES . . The Playing Fields, Univ. of Kent, off Giles Lane, Canterbury . . . . None
St Margarets Reserves withdrew during the course of the season. Tyler Hill and Woodstock Park are promoted to Division One East. Newcomers are Borden Village and Sheppey United.

	Borough Utd	Bromleians Sp.	Eltham Palace	Farnboro. OBG	Halls	Larkfield/NHW	Old Bexleians	Orpington	Otford United	Platt United	Sutton Athletic	Westerham
Borough United	D	0-2	2-0	1-4	1-3	5-3	0-0	1-4	0-2	2-3	2-1	1-5
Bromleians Sports	3-0	I	3-1	2-1	2-2	2-1	3-1	2-2	2-0	2-1	5-1	1-0
Eltham Palace	1-0	1-3	V	2-1	0-3	1-2	2-0	1-0	0-1	1-0	1-2	4-4
Farnborough OBG	4-4	0-1	4-1		2-3	2-2	3-0	2-0	0-0	5-0	2-0	1-3
Halls	2-0	2-0	5-0	3-0	T	0-4	0-1	1-2	3-1	4-1	0-1	1-3
Larkfield & NHW	3-5	0-3	1-2	4-4	0-1	W	7-1	0-1	2-2	3-3	1-4	6-2
Old Bexleians	0-3	0-2	2-1	1-1	1-5	1-2	O	3-2	1-5	2-2	1-7	1-4
Orpington	1-1	1-0	3-2	0-4	0-0	5-2	6-1		1-0	5-0	4-0	3-1
Otford United	2-0	1-6	3-1	2-2	2-2	1-0	0-5	1-3	W	2-0	1-1	2-1
Platt United	3-5	3-2	2-3	2-1	0-3	4-4	1-0	0-5	3-1	E	3-5	1-3
Sutton Athletic	3-2	0-5	3-4	4-2	0-2	2-4	1-3	0-8	3-1	3-1	S	3-1
Westerham	3-2	1-2	3-3	1-3	2-3	2-1	4-1	2-3	3-1	5-1	3-1	T

Division Two West	P	W	D	L	F	A	Pts
Bromleians Sports	22	17	2	3	53	19	53
Halls	22	15	4	3	52	18	49
Orpington	22	15	3	4	59	24	48
Westerham	22	12	2	8	59	45	38
Sutton Athletic	22	10	1	11	45	56	31
Farnborough OB Guild	22	8	6	8	48	37	30
Otford United	22	8	5	9	36	38	29
Eltham Palace	22	7	3	12	31	47	24
Larkfield & N Hythe W.	22	5	6	11	48	53	21
Borough United	22	6	3	13	37	52	21
Platt United	22	5	4	13	35	65	19
Old Bexleians	22	3	3	16	21	70	12

DIVISION TWO WEST CONSTITUTION 2003-04

BOROUGH UNITED . . . . Glentworth Club, Lowfield Street, Dartford, Kent 01322 401802
BRIDON ROPES . . . . Meridian Sports Club, Charlton Park Road, Charlton, London 020 8856 1923
ELTHAM PALACE . . . . Beaverwood Lodge, Beaverwood Road, Chislehurst, Kent 01689 826949
FARNBOROUGH OLD BOYS GUILD Farnborough (Kent) Sports Club, High St, Farnborough, Kent . . . . None
LANES END . . . . Waller Park, Darenth, Dartford, Kent . . . . None
LARKFIELD & NEW HYTHE WDRS . . Larkfield Sports Ground, New Hythe Lane, Larkfield, Aylesford . . . . None
OLD BEXLEIANS . . . . Bexley Grammar School, Danson Lane, Welling, Kent 01689 834902
ORPINGTON . . . . Westcombe Park & Orpington SC, Goddington Lane, Orpington, Kent 01959 524405
OTFORD UNITED . . . . Otford Recreation Ground, High Street, Otford, Sevenoaks, Kent 01322 526159
PHOENIX SPORTS . . . . Phoenix Sports Club, Mayplace Road East, Bexleyheath, Kent 01322 556159
PLATT UNITED . . . . Stonehouse Field, Longmill Lane (off A25), Platt, Kent 01892 517224
RUSTHALL . . . . Jockey Farm, Nellington Lane, Rusthall, Tunbridge Wells, Kent 020 8856 1126
SAMUEL MONTAGU YOUTH CLUB. . Samuel Montagu Youth Club, Broadwalk, Kidbrooke, London 01322 280507
SUTTON ATHLETIC. . . . . The Roaches, Parsonage Lane, Sutton-at-Hone, near Dartford, Kent 01959 561106
WESTERHAM . . . . Westerham Sports Association, King George V PF, Costells Meadow, Westerham, Kent . . . . None
Bromleians Sports and Halls are promoted to Division One West replaced by Rusthall and Phoenix Sports. Lanes End and Samuel Montagu Old Boys are promoted from Division Three. Newcomers are Bridon Ropes.

	Chipstead	Chislehurst	Colour	Guru Nanak	Kingsdown	Lanes End	Leaves G.	NPI	O Addeyans	S Montagu	Staplehurst	Tonbdge Inv	T. Malling
Chipstead		3-3	4-0	5-3	4-4	0-2	2-5	2-2	4-2	1-2	2-2	4-2	1-3
Chislehurst	0-6		4-3	3-2	4-5	1-3	1-3	1-3	0-2	1-2	1-6	1-1	2-2
Colour Athletic	1-2	2-4	D	2-1	1-4	0-1	0-0	0-4	1-5	1-3	3-8	1-4	2-1
Guru Nanak	1-0	6-0	1-0	I	2-2	0-3	1-3	1-3	2-3	1-2	2-2	1-2	2-1
Kingsdown Racers	7-1	3-0	2-1	4-0	V	8-0	W-L	0-7	5-2	1-2	3-2	6-2	3-2
Lanes End	10-0	7-1	7-1	4-0	3-3		W-L	3-0	6-0	3-1	4-1	1-1	2-1
Leaves Green	2-5	L-W	4-1	0-5	0-3	1-2	T	3-1	3-5	1-2	2-3	1-2	1-3
NPI	2-1	4-0	5-0	1-0	0-5	3-0	4-1	H	W-L	0-1	1-1	5-0	4-3
Old Addeyans	2-0	2-0	5-3	2-0	5-1	2-3	0-2	1-10	R	2-1	3-5	4-0	3-1
Sam. Montagu YC	3-2	4-1	5-1	2-3	3-0	1-1	7-0	4-0	1-0	E	1-0	5-5	2-2
Staplehurst	6-1	2-1	1-3	1-1	0-3	1-4	8-6	1-1	3-1	2-2	E	2-2	4-2
Tonbridge Invicta	2-2	2-0	1-0	7-2	2-2	0-3	2-2	1-0	4-4	1-4	5-5		3-0
Town Malling	3-0	3-0	1-0	3-1	5-3	1-1	2-1	0-2	1-1	2-0	2-0	1-2	

Division Three		P	W	D	L	F	A	Pts
Lanes End		24	18	4	2	73	27	58
Sam. Montagu YC		24	16	4	4	61	31	52
Kingsdown Racers		24	15	4	5	77	48	49
NPI		24	15	3	6	62	29	48
Old Addeyans		24	12	2	10	57	56	38
Tonbridge Invicta		24	9	9	6	53	56	36
Staplehurst		24	9	8	7	66	56	35
Town Malling Utd		24	10	4	10	45	41	34
Chipstead		24	7	5	12	52	70	26
Guru Nanak		24	6	3	15	39	55	21
Chislehurst		24	4	3	17	29	76	15
Leaves Green	-6	24	6	2	16	41	60	14
Colour Athletic		24	3	1	20	27	77	10

DIVISION THREE CONSTITUTION 2003-04

CHIPSTEAD .... Chipstead Rec, Chevening Road, Chipstead, near Sevenoaks, Kent .... None
CHISLEHURST .... Coldharbour Leisure Centre, Chaple Farm Road, New Eltham, Kent. 020 8851 8692
COLOUR ATHLETIC .... Putlands Sports & Leisure Centre, Mascalls Court Road, Paddock Wood, Kent. 01892 838290
GURU NANAK .... Milton Barracks, off Trinity Road, Gravesend, Kent .... None
HALSTEAD .... Halstead Parish Council Recreation Ground, Halstead, Kent. .... None
KINGSDOWN RACERS. .... Gamecock Meadow, West Kingsdown, Kent. .... None
LEAVES GREEN .... Hayes Country Club, West Common Road, Hayes, Kent. 020 8462 3846
MERIDIAN SPORTS .... Seven Acres Sports & Social Club, London 020 8310 4170
NPI .... Putlands Sports Centre, Mascalls Court Road, Paddock Wood, Kent 01892 838290
OLD ADDEYANS. .... Blackheath Park, Blackheath, London .... None
STAPLEHURST. .... King George V Playing Field, Loose Road, Loose, Maidstone, Kent .... None
TONBRIDGE INVICTA. ...... Swanmead Sports Ground, Swanwead Way, off Cannon Lane, Tonbridge, Kent .... None
TOWN MALLING UNITED .... Old County Ground, Norman Road, West Malling, Kent .... 01732 350473 .... 07803 164818
Lanes End and Samuel Montagu Youth Club are promoted to Division Two West. Newcomers are Halstead (Sevenoaks League) and Meridian Sports.

WEST KENT CHALLENGE SHIELD

FIRST ROUND
Bromleians Sports 7 Borough Utd 1, **Chipstead** 5 Platt Utd 1
Chislehurst 2 Old Bexleians 0, Guru Nanak 0 **Old Addeyans** 4
NPI 5 Eltham Palace 2, Orpington 1 **Leaves Green** 2
Town Malling United 1 **Farnborough Old Boys Guild** 2

SECOND ROUND
Bly Spartans 1 **Aylesford Paper Mills** 3
Chipstead 4 Belvedere 2
Colour Athletic 4 **Larkfield & New Hythe Wanderers** 6
Cray Valley Paper Mills 2 AFC Blackheath 0
Farnborough Old Boys Guild 3 Phoenix Sports 2
Halls 0 **Fleetdown United** 2
Kingsdown Racers 2 Rusthall 1
Lanes End (w/o) v Leaves Green (scr)
NPI 2 Moonshot Athletic 1, **Oakwood** 9 Chislehurst 0
Otford United 2 **Bromleians Sports** 4
Pembury 1 Samuel Montagu Youth Club 0
Staplehurst 0 **Holmesdale** 4
Sutton Athletic 2 **Tonbridge Invicta** 4
Thames Poly 8 Old Addeyans 4, **Westerham** 2 Eynsford 1

THIRD ROUND
Cray Valley Paper Mills 4 NPI 2
Holmesdale 2 Chipstead 1
Kingsdown Racers 2 **Bromleians Sports** 3
Lanes End 3 Tonbridge Invicta 0
Larkfield & New Hythe Wdrs 2 **Fleetdown United** 2 *aet* (5-6p)
Oakwood 1 Farnborough Old Boys Guild 0
Pembury 3 Aylesford Paper Mills 3 *aet* (4-2p)
Thames Poly 8 Westerham 0

QUARTER-FINALS
Bromleians Sports 2 **Fleetdown United** 3 *aet*
Holmesdale 2 Cray Valley Paper Mills 1 *aet*
Oakwood 2 Lanes End 1
Pembury 1 Thames Poly 0

SEMI-FINALS
Fleetdown United 2 **Oakwood** 4
Pembury 2 Holmesdale 1

FINAL
(29th April at Sevenoaks Town)
Pembury 0 **Oakwood** 1

Reserve Division One West	P	W	D	L	F	A	Pts
Sevenoaks Town Res.	22	16	4	2	85	28	52
Greenways Res.	22	13	3	6	49	29	42
Holmesdale Res.	22	11	3	8	67	45	36
Bearsted Res.	22	9	8	5	41	36	35
Fleetdown United Res.	22	10	4	8	46	43	34
Stansfeld O & B Club Res.	22	9	6	7	42	38	33
Otford United Res.	22	8	7	7	39	49	31
Beauwater Res.	22	8	6	8	49	43	30
Wickham Park Res.	22	6	8	8	49	50	26
Oakwood Res.	22	6	5	11	40	50	23
Snodland Res.	22	5	1	16	28	87	16
Phoenix Sports Res.	22	1	5	16	35	72	8

Reserve Division Two West		P	W	D	L	F	A	Pts
Aylesford Paper Mills Res.		24	18	3	3	84	32	57
Halls Res.		24	14	3	7	72	39	45
Orpington Res.		24	13	5	6	67	36	44
Borough United Res.		24	13	4	7	59	36	43
Bromleians Sports Res.		24	12	5	7	68	48	41
Eynsford Res.		24	9	7	8	53	59	34
Belvedere Res.		24	9	6	9	45	47	33
Town Malling United Res.		24	8	5	11	41	46	29
Westerham Res.		24	7	7	10	49	58	28
Old Bexleians Res.		24	6	8	10	40	54	26
Chipstead Res.		24	7	3	14	49	67	24
Larkfield & New HW Res.	-1	24	4	5	15	37	72	16
Chislehurst Res.		24	4	3	17	21	76	15

KENT LEAGUE

	Beckenham Town	Cray Wanderers	Deal Town	Erith Town	Faversham Town	Greenwich Borough	Herne Bay	Hythe Town	Lordswood	Maidstone United	Ramsgate	Slade Green	Thamesmead Town	Tunbridge Wells	VCD Athletic	Whitstable Town
Beckenham Town	P	0-2	2-2	3-0	2-1	3-1	1-3	6-0	4-0	0-4	1-1	2-0	1-4	3-0	1-4	2-1
Cray Wanderers	3-0	R	1-1	5-0	8-0	0-1	5-3	2-2	2-0	2-1	4-2	2-0	1-2	5-1	3-0	7-0
Deal Town	1-1	2-1	E	5-2	n/p	2-1	2-1	2-0	7-1	2-2	4-3	3-0	1-3	7-2	1-1	2-1
Erith Town	1-1	0-0	0-1	M	n/p	2-1	2-3	1-1	1-2	2-4	1-1	0-3	2-5	1-5	1-4	2-2
Faversham Town	n/p	n/p	n/p	1-5	I	1-0	0-6	2-3	0-2	1-5	0-1	n/p	0-4	2-6	0-1	n/p
Greenwich Borough	1-0	0-2	1-1	2-1	3-1	E	4-2	3-4	0-0	0-5	2-3	0-4	0-3	3-3	0-1	2-4
Herne Bay	1-2	0-1	1-3	0-1	6-1	3-1	R	3-3	1-1	1-1	4-0	0-3	2-1	3-1	1-3	1-1
Hythe Town	2-0	0-1	1-3	1-0	3-0	3-1	2-1		3-1	0-3	0-2	3-2	2-3	3-1	1-1	0-2
Lordswood	1-1	1-3	6-3	3-4	0-1	2-2	1-0	2-1	D	1-2	0-1	0-4	1-3	1-1	1-1	2-3
Maidstone United	5-2	2-1	1-2	2-0	8-1	1-1	1-1	1-1	1-1	I	2-1	4-2	2-0	0-0	0-0	4-0
Ramsgate	2-0	1-1	0-3	1-8	1-1	4-3	4-1	3-3	2-1	0-0	V	1-0	2-3	1-2	0-2	0-2
Slade Green	3-2	0-2	1-2	2-0	4-2	3-1	1-1	1-1	2-2	2-0	0-4	I	2-3	5-1	2-2	1-2
Thamesmead Town	5-0	0-1	2-2	4-3	8-0	1-0	2-0	1-2	2-1	2-2	1-4	1-0	I	2-4	1-2	3-3
Tunbridge Wells	3-0	0-1	3-0	5-2	n/p	1-1	2-1	1-2	2-2	1-1	2-1	4-1	1-3	I	1-2	1-1
VCD Athletic	1-1	3-1	1-1	1-0	1-1	6-1	2-1	1-2	7-0	1-2	0-2	0-4	0-2	3-2	O	1-2
Whitstable Town	1-0	1-1	1-0	1-1	4-2	4-1	1-2	4-0	2-1	4-2	1-2	5-3	1-1	1-1	1-0	N

Premier Division	P	W	D	L	F	A	Pts	AvPts
Cray Wanderers#	29	19	5	5	68	23	62	2.138
Maidstone United	30	18	9	3	76	31	63	2.100
Thamesmead Town	30	19	6	5	76	39	63	2.100
Deal Town#	28	15	9	4	62	40	54	1.929
Ramsgate	30	16	7	7	59	35	55	1.833
Whitstable Town#	29	15	8	6	56	45	53	1.828
VCD Athletic	30	13	9	8	51	36	48	1.600
Hythe Town	30	13	6	11	46	54	45	1.500
Slade Green#	29	10	5	14	57	54	35	1.207
Beckenham Town#	29	9	6	14	41	53	33	1.138
Herne Bay	30	9	7	14	53	54	34	1.133
Tunbridge Wells#	29	7	8	14	53	66	29	1.000
Lordswood	30	5	9	16	37	66	24	0.800
Greenwich Borough	30	5	5	20	36	70	20	0.667
Erith Town#	29	4	6	19	36	71	18	0.621
Faversham Town	22	2	1	19	18	88	7	0.318

(# Finishing position determined by a points per game average following resignation of Faversham Town)

LEAGUE CUP

FIRST ROUND
Beckenham Town 1 **Herne Bay** 2
Cray Wanderers 2 Thamesmead Town 1
Deal Town 3 Greenwich Borough 1
Erith Town 1 Whitstable Town 0
Faversham Town 2 **Maidstone United** 5
Lordswood 0 **Slade Green** 3
Tunbridge Wells 3 Hythe Town 0
VCD Athletic 3 Ramsgate 2
QUARTER-FINALS
Deal Town 3 Slade Green 2
Maidstone United 0 **Cray Wanderers** 2
Tunbridge Wells 3 Herne Bay 2
VCD Athletic 2 Erith Town 0 *aet*
SEMI-FINALS
(played over two legs)
Deal Town 0 VCD Athletic 1,
VCD Athletic 3 Deal Town 0
Tunbridge Wells 0 **Cray Wanderers** 2,
Cray Wanderers 3 Tunbridge Wells 1
FINAL *(3rd May at Folkestone Invicta)*
VCD Athletic 0 **Cray Wanderers** 2

WWW.NLNEWSDESK.CO.UK

PREMIER DIVISION CONSTITUTION 2003-04

BECKENHAM TOWN	Eden Park Avenue, Beckenham, Kent	020 8650 1066
CRAY WANDERERS	Bromley FC, Hayes Lane, Bromley, Kent	020 8460 5291
DEAL TOWN	Charles Sports Ground, St Leonards Road, Deal, Kent	01304 375623
ERITH TOWN	Erith Sports Centre, Avenue Road, Erith, Kent	01322 350271
GREENWICH BOROUGH	Harrow Meadow, Eltham Green Road, Eltham, London	0961 851 0370
HERNE BAY	Winchs Field, Stanley Gardens, Herne Bay, Kent	01227 374156
HYTHE TOWN	Reachfields Stadium, Fort Road, Hythe, Kent	01303 264932
LORDSWOOD	Lordswood Sports & Social, North Dane Way, Walderslade, Kent	01634 669138
MAIDSTONE UNITED	Sittingbourne FC, Central Park, Eurolink, Sittingbourne, Kent	01795 435077
RAMSGATE	Southwood, Prices Avenue, Ramsgate, Kent	01843 591662
SEVENOAKS TOWN	Greatness Park, Seal Road (on main A25), Sevenoaks, Kent	01732 741987
SLADE GREEN	The Small Glenn, Moat Lane, Slade Green, Kent	01322 351077
SPORTING BENGAL UNITED	Mile End Stadium, Rhodeswell Road, Burdett Road, Poplar, London	020 8311 4211
THAMESMEAD TOWN	Bayliss Avenue, Thamesmead, London	01892 520517
TUNBRIDGE WELLS	Culverden Stadium, Culverden Down, Tunbridge Wells, Kent	01892 520517
VCD ATHLETIC	Lordswood FC, North Dane Way, Walderslade, Kent .... 01634 669138. VCD Club:	01322 524262
WHITSTABLE TOWN	Belmont Road, Whitstable, Kent	01227 266012

Faversham Town resigned during the course of the season. Newcomers are Sevenoaks Town (Kent County League) and Sporting Bengal United (London Intermediate League).

	Beckenham Res.	Chatham Res.	Corinthian	Cray W. Res.	Danson Furness	Dartford Res.	Erith T. Res.	Erith & B. Res.	Lordswood Res.	T'mead Res.	Tun. Wells Res.	VCD Res.
Beckenham T. Res.		5-3	0-1	0-3	2-6	2-2	1-2	4-2	2-1	3-5	4-1	0-4
Chatham T. Res.	3-2	D	0-1	2-2	1-1	3-0	0-0	3-3	4-0	1-2	4-0	3-1
Corinthian	0-0	0-3	I	2-5	3-2	3-3	1-3	3-1	3-2	4-2	2-5	1-0
Cray Wdrs Res.	6-0	4-1	5-3	V	0-1	1-0	3-1	3-0	1-1	1-3	5-1	1-0
Danson Furness	3-0	2-1	2-0	0-6		2-1	2-1	1-1	2-2	3-2	5-1	4-0
Dartford Res.	1-0	3-2	1-0	1-4	4-2		0-1	0-0	0-0	1-0	0-2	1-1
Erith Town Res.	3-2	2-1	1-5	2-6	2-0	1-3	O	0-2	1-0	1-2	3-0	1-5
Erith & B'dere Res.	2-3	2-4	0-5	0-3	3-5	0-3	1-2	N	2-3	0-5	0-1	1-1
Lordswood Res.	1-3	1-0	1-1	0-1	1-1	0-1	1-2	1-5	E	1-5	3-4	3-1
Thamesmead Res.	3-5	1-2	4-1	0-2	5-3	1-0	n/p	7-2	3-0		5-2	3-2
Tunbridge W. Res.	2-2	1-1	0-2	0-5	1-0	0-1	0-1	1-2	2-2	1-2	N	6-5
VCD Athletic Res.	5-0	5-4	0-3	0-1	2-5	0-2	4-5	4-3	2-4	0-4	2-3	

Division One North	P	W	D	L	F	A	Pts
Cray Wdrs Res.	22	18	2	2	68	18	56
Thamesmead Res.	21	16	0	5	65	34	48
Danson Furness	22	12	4	6	52	39	40
Corinthian	22	11	3	8	44	40	36
Erith Town Res.	21	10	8	3	33	39	33
Dartford Res.	22	10	4	8	30	26	34
Chatham T. Res.	22	8	6	8	47	38	30
Beckenham Res.	22	7	3	12	40	59	24
Tunbridge W. Res.	22	7	3	12	34	56	24
Lordswood Res.	22	4	6	12	27	44	18
VCD Athletic Res.	22	5	2	15	44	58	17
Erith & B. Res. +3	22	3	4	15	29	62	16

Thamesmead v Erith Town not played

DIVISION ONE PLAY-OFF
(13th May at Herne Bay)
Cray Wanderers Res. 2 Deal Town Res. 3 *aet*

DIVISION ONE CUP FINAL
FINAL (10th May at Ashford Town)
Cray Wanderers Res. 3 Dover Athletic Res. 2

	Ashford Res.	Deal Town Res.	Dover Ath. Res.	Folkestone Res.	Hastings Res.	Herne Bay Res.	Hythe T. Res.	Maidstone Res.	Margate Res.	Ramsgate Res.	Sitt'gbne Res.	Whitstable Res.
Ashford Town Res.		0-2	3-2	4-2	3-0	0-2	1-0	3-0	3-0	3-0	6-0	0-2
Deal Town Res.	2-2	D	1-1	5-1	1-0	0-0	10-0	1-1	2-1	0-1	5-2	5-1
Dover Athletic Res.	3-1	2-2	I	2-2	5-1	1-0	2-0	7-1	4-4	3-0	7-2	3-3
Folkestone I. Res.	3-1	2-2	1-1	V	0-5	1-4	6-0	1-3	0-0	1-2	5-2	4-0
Hastings Utd Res.	0-1	1-2	3-2	1-0		1-1	2-1	1-1	3-1	3-0	1-1	0-0
Herne Bay Res.	0-0	0-3	1-0	4-4	0-0		5-1	2-1	3-1	0-3	4-1	1-1
Hythe Town Res.	0-2	3-4	1-4	0-2	0-9	0-9	O	3-2	0-0	3-1	3-4	2-2
Maidstone U. Res.	2-0	0-2	2-2	5-1	2-1	2-2	3-1	N	1-1	2-1	1-2	2-5
Margate Res.	2-2	1-2	2-3	2-1	0-4	1-1	2-1	2-0	E	1-5	4-1	2-1
Ramsgate Res.	1-2	1-1	3-2	2-6	4-2	3-4	3-1	0-2	2-0		3-2	1-0
Sittingbourne Res.	3-2	4-1	1-7	0-3	2-1	1-2	1-5	4-3	1-1	4-3	S	4-0
Whitstable Res.	0-4	1-2	1-3	4-3	0-1	1-2	5-0	2-2	6-1	0-1	2-3	

Division One South	P	W	D	L	F	A	Pts
Deal Town Res.	22	13	7	2	55	25	46
Dover Ath. Res.	22	12	6	4	69	35	42
Herne Bay Res.	22	11	8	3	47	26	41
Ashford T. Res.	22	12	3	7	43	26	39
Ramsgate Res.	22	11	2	9	41	42	35
Hastings Utd Res.	22	9	5	8	40	27	32
Sitt'gbne Res. -3	22	9	2	11	45	69	26
Folkestone I. Res.	22	7	4	11	49	52	25
Maidstone U. Res.	22	6	7	9	38	43	25
Whitstable Res. +3	22	5	5	12	35	46	23
Margate Res.	22	5	7	10	29	46	22
Hythe Town Res.	22	3	2	17	25	79	11

DIVISION ONE CONSTITUTION 2003-04
(NEW DIVISION CREATED BY TOP SIX FROM EACH OF THE TWO REGIONAL DIVISIONS)

ASHFORD TOWN RESERVES........The Homelands, Ashford Road, Kingsnorth, Ashford, Kent.......01233 611838. Fax: 01233 662510
CORINTHIAN..............Gay Dawn, Valley Road, Fawkham, Kent..............01474 707559 / 702335
CRAY WANDERERS RESERVES..............Oxford Road, Sidcup, Kent..............020 8300 9201
DANSON FURNESS..............Green Court Road, Swanley, Kent..............01322 666442
DARTFORD RESERVES..............t.b.a...............t.b.a.
DEAL TOWN RESERVES..............Charles Sports Ground, St Leonards Road, Deal, Kent..............01304 375623
DOVER ATHLETIC RESERVES......Hoverspeed Stadium, Lewisham Road, River, Dover, Kent........01304 822373. Fax: 01304 240041
ERITH TOWN RESERVES..............Erith Sports Centre, Avenue Road, Erith, Kent..............01322 350271
HASTINGS UNITED RESERVES......The Pilot Field, Elphinstone Rd, Hastings, East Sussex..01424 444635 / 430517. Fax: 01424 729068
HERNE BAY RESERVES..............Winchs Field, Stanley Gardens, Herne Bay, Kent..............01227 374156
RAMSGATE RESERVES..............Southwood, Prices Avenue, Ramsgate, Kent..............01843 591662
THAMESMEAD TOWN RESERVES..............Bayliss Avenue, Thamesmead, London..............020 8311 4211

DIVISION TWO CONSTITUTION 2003-04
(NEW DIVISION CREATED BY BOTTOM SIX FROM EACH OF THE TWO REGIONAL DIVISIONS)

BECKENHAM TOWN RESERVES..............Eden Park Avenue, Beckenham, Kent..............020 8650 1066
CHATHAM TOWN RESERVES..............Maidstone Road, Chatham, Kent..............01634 812114
ERITH & BELVEDERE RESERVES......Welling United FC, Park View Road, Welling, Kent.........020 8301 1196. Fax: 020 8301 5676
FOLKESTONE INVICTA RESERVES. The New Pavilion, Cheriton Road Sports Ground, Folkestone......01303 257461. Fax: 01303 255541
GROUND HOPPERS..............t.b.a...............t.b.a.
HYTHE TOWN RESERVES..............Reachfields Stadium, Fort Road, Hythe, Kent..............t.b.a.
LORDSWOOD RESERVES......Lordswood Sports & Social, North Dane Way, Walderslade, Kent..............01634 264932
MAIDSTONE UNITED RESERVES..............Salters Lane, Faversham, Kent..............01634 669138
SEVENOAKS TOWN RESERVES.....Greatness Park, Seal Road (on main A25), Sevenoaks, Kent.......01795 532738
SITTINGBOURNE RESERVES..............Central Park, Eurolink, Sittingbourne, Kent..............01732 741987
TUNBRIDGE WELLS RESERVES...Culverden Stadium, Culverden Down, Tunbridge Wells, Kent..............01795 435077
VCD ATHLETIC RESERVES..............Oakwood, Old Road, Crayford, Kent..............01892 520517
WHITSTABLE TOWN RESERVES..............Belmont Road, Whitstable, Kent..............01322 524262 / 01227 266012

Margate Reserves have left the league. Newcomers are Ground Hoppers and Sevenoaks Town Reserves.

LEICESTERSHIRE SENIOR LEAGUE

	Anstey Nomads	Barrow Town	Birstall United	Blaby & Whetstone	Coalville Town	Downes Sports	Ellistown	Friar Lane OB	Highfield Rangers	Holwell Sports	Ibstock Welfare	Kirby Muxloe SC	Leicester YMCA	Loughborough Dyn.	Ratby Sports	St Andrews SC	Thurmaston Town	Thurnby Rangers
Anstey Nomads		2-2	1-1	1-1	1-3	2-2	1-1	1-1	1-2	1-5	0-2	1-5	0-2	0-3	0-3	0-2	0-1	2-5
Barrow Town	4-0	*P*	5-1	2-0	1-1	2-0	5-0	2-3	5-0	1-0	4-1	2-2	3-0	2-1	4-1	3-1	4-0	3-0
Birstall United	4-1	3-1	*R*	1-3	2-4	0-1	3-0	1-1	2-2	0-2	2-0	2-0	0-4	0-2	0-3	1-3	0-2	1-3
Blaby & Whetstone Athletic	2-0	0-1	2-1	*E*	0-7	0-0	0-0	1-3	3-1	1-2	1-2	0-1	0-5	1-3	3-0	0-2	1-1	0-5
Coalville Town	4-0	1-1	3-0	1-0	*M*	4-3	0-0	0-0	4-1	2-0	3-2	3-0	3-2	2-2	2-1	3-1	6-1	2-0
Downes Sports	1-2	1-3	0-2	3-2	1-6	*I*	0-0	3-1	1-3	0-1	1-3	1-4	0-1	2-3	1-0	2-3	0-1	2-2
Ellistown	3-1	2-7	0-1	3-0	1-3	0-3	*E*	1-1	0-3	1-0	0-0	3-6	0-4	1-8	1-2	3-5	2-0	0-2
Friar Lane Old Boys	2-0	0-4	2-7	0-3	1-6	4-3	0-0	*R*	1-2	1-2	0-2	2-4	0-4	0-2	1-4	1-4	0-2	2-8
Highfield Rangers	3-0	3-4	0-2	0-2	2-3	1-4	1-1	1-0		2-0	0-3	0-0	3-2	1-0	4-0	0-4	4-2	1-2
Holwell Sports	0-1	2-2	4-1	4-1	1-3	3-1	5-0	1-2	4-2	*D*	0-2	0-2	3-1	1-1	2-1	3-1	3-2	0-2
Ibstock Welfare	5-0	0-1	4-1	2-1	0-1	1-1	1-0	8-1	4-1	0-2	*I*	1-3	1-1	3-4	2-1	2-1	5-0	0-3
Kirby Muxloe SC	4-0	1-4	1-0	0-0	1-2	2-0	1-2	6-2	0-2	1-2	0-2	*V*	0-1	3-1	3-0	5-1	0-0	1-1
Leicester YMCA	7-0	1-2	1-3	4-3	1-4	1-2	1-1	4-2	2-4	0-2	2-2	1-1	*I*	5-1	1-1	2-1	2-1	1-7
Loughborough Dynamo	4-2	0-1	3-3	4-2	0-2	5-1	2-0	2-1	5-3	0-3	0-3	3-0	4-2	*S*	0-1	1-0	1-0	0-2
Ratby Sports	6-2	2-2	2-1	1-0	1-5	0-2	2-1	1-0	1-0	2-1	1-2	1-2	0-2	2-0	*I*	1-3	3-3	0-2
St Andrews SC	4-0	2-2	4-0	6-0	0-2	3-2	1-1	3-1	1-0	1-0	3-1	1-1	2-7	0-0		*O*	1-0	0-5
Thurmaston Town	3-1	1-5	2-1	1-2	0-4	3-0	1-2	1-3	2-1	2-1	0-0	4-1	3-1	2-2	1-2		*N*	1-3
Thurnby Rangers	4-0	1-2	1-0	1-1	1-2	1-0	5-0	5-0	2-0	4-2	2-0	4-0	0-1	4-2	2-0	1-0		

Premier Division

	P	W	D	L	F	A	Pts
Coalville Town	34	29	5	0	101	28	92
Barrow Town	34	25	7	2	96	33	82
Thurnby Rangers	34	26	3	5	92	26	81
Loughborough Dyn.	34	19	3	12	75	55	60
Holwell Sports	34	19	2	13	61	39	59
St Andrews SC	34	18	4	12	68	56	58
Kirby Muxloe SC	34	17	6	11	63	44	57
Ibstock Welfare	34	17	4	13	68	47	55
Leicester YMCA	34	14	5	15	69	65	47
Ratby Sports	34	13	5	16	50	58	44
Highfield Rangers	34	13	3	18	53	70	42
Thurmaston Town	34	12	5	17	46	63	41
Birstall United	34	10	4	20	47	67	34
Blaby & Whetstone Ath	34	8	6	20	36	68	30
Downes Sports	34	8	5	21	44	69	29
Ellistown	34	6	10	18	30	75	28
Friar Lane Old Boys	-3 34	6	5	23	39	98	23
Anstey Nomads	34	2	6	26	24	101	12

LEAGUE CUP

PREMIER DIVISION SECTION

PRELIMINARY ROUND
Barrow Town 4 Ratby Sports 1
Holwell Sports 4 Downes Sports 1
FIRST ROUND
Anstey Nomads 4 St Andrews SC 1
Barrow Town 3 Friar Lane Old Boys 0
Blaby & Whetstone Athletic 3 Holwell Sports 1
Coalville Town 0 Kirby Muxloe SC 0 (7-6p)
Highfield Rangers 2 Loughborough Dynamo 2 (3-4p)
Ibstock Welfare (w/o) Leicester YMCA (scr.)
Thurmaston Town 1 Ellistown 6
Thurnby Rangers 4 Birstall United 0
SECOND ROUND
Anstey Nomads 1 Coalville Town 1 (5-4p)
Barrow Town 3 Blaby & Whetstone Athletic 0
Ellistown 0 Ibstock Welfare 1
Thurnby Rangers 2 Loughborough Dynamo 1

PREMIER DIVISION CONSTITUTION 2003-04

ANSTEY NOMADS . . . . Llimah International Park, Cropston Road, Anstey, Leicestershire. 0116 236 4868
BARROW TOWN . . . . Riverside Park, Meynell Road, Quorn, Leicestershire. 01509 620650
BIRSTALL UNITED . . . . Meadow Lane, Birstall, Leicestershire. 0116 267 1230
BLABY & WHETSTONE ATHLETIC . . Blaby & Whetstone Boys Club, Warwick Road, Whetstone 0116 286 4852
DOWNES SPORTS . . . . The Sports Ground, Leicester Road, Hinckley, Leicestershire 01455 615062
ELLISTOWN . . . . 1 Terrace Road, Ellistown, Coalville, Leicestershire 01530 230159
FRIAR LANE OLD BOYS . . . . Knighton Lane East, Leicester, Leicestershire 0116 283 3629
HIGHFIELD RANGERS . . . . Gleneagles Avenue, Rushey Mead, Leicester, Leicestershire 0116 266 0009
HOLWELL SPORTS . . . . Welby Road, Asfordby Hill, Melton Mowbray, Leicestershire 01664 812663
IBSTOCK WELFARE . . . . The Welfare, Leicester Road, Ibstock, Leicestershire 01530 260656
KIRBY MUXLOE SC . . . . Ratby Lane, Kirby Muxloe, Leicester, Leicestershire 0116 239 3201
LEICESTER YMCA . . . . Leicester YMCA Sports Ground, Belvoir Drive, Aylestone, Leicester, Leicestershire 0116 244 0740
LOUGHBOROUGH DYNAMO . . . . Nanpantan Sports Ground, Loughborough, Leicestershire 01509 237148
RATBY SPORTS . . . . Desford Lane, Ratby, Leicester, Leicestershire 0116 239 2474
ST ANDREWS SC . . . . Canal Street, Aylestone, Leicester, Leicestershire 0116 283 9298
STAPENHILL . . . . Maple Grove, Stapenhill, Burton-on-Trent, Staffordshire 01283 562471
THURMASTON TOWN . . . . Elizabeth Park, Thurmaston, Leicestershire 0116 260 2519
THURNBY RANGERS . . . . Dakyn Road, Thurnby Lodge Estate, Leicester, Leicestershire. 0116 243 3698

Coalville Town are promoted to the Midland Alliance. Stapenhill come up from Division One.

Division One — Results Grid

	Anstey Town	Asfordby Amateurs	Aylestone Park Old Boys	Bardon Hill Sports	Cottesmore Amateurs	Earl Shilton Albion	Epworth	Huncote Sports & Social	Leics Constabulary	Lutterworth Town	Narboro. & Littlethorpe	North Kilworth	Saffron Dynamo	Sileby Town	Stapenhill	Thringstone MW
Anstey Town		1-0	3-1	2-0	1-2	2-2	1-2	3-0	2-2	1-1	5-0	0-1	3-1	1-2	3-1	8-0
Asfordby Am.	2-3		3-2	1-2	2-1	2-1	1-7	3-1	3-1	3-2	1-0	4-2	4-2	3-6	0-3	3-1
Aylestone Pk	2-0	1-1	D	1-3	4-1	3-0	3-7	3-2	2-2	1-1	4-1	2-3	3-4	1-2		4-0
Bardon Hill	1-1	4-2	1-3	I	2-2	2-0	0-5	1-5	1-1	2-2	0-3	3-4	1-1	5-1	0-1	8-1
Cottesmore	0-1	2-0	1-3	4-2	V	0-2	0-4	1-0	1-1	3-2	2-1	3-2	7-0	2-1	2-3	2-0
Earl Shilton	1-1	1-0	2-2	2-3	0-1	I	1-4	1-0	5-1	0-4	3-3	2-0	2-2	3-3	2-2	2-0
Epworth	3-1	7-0	3-0	2-2	1-0	4-1	S	6-1	7-1	4-2	3-1	4-1	2-0	3-0		12-0
Huncote S&S	3-2	0-3	1-10	0-4	2-3	4-4	2-9	I	2-0	0-6	1-0	0-3	2-1	3-5	2-2	9-1
Leics Police	3-0	1-2	0-2	0-3	2-6	0-0	0-1	2-0	O	2-0	5-1	1-1	2-0	1-2	2-2	4-0
Lutterworth	3-1	3-0	1-3	3-1	4-5	3-2	0-3	3-0	3-0	N	6-1	5-0	2-2	2-3		1-0
Narborough	0-0	3-1	1-4	2-3	1-0	1-2	1-5	4-0	0-2			2-0	3-2	1-3	3-2	2-0
Nth Kilworth	3-1	3-2	2-7	0-3	1-2	1-3	0-2	3-0	1-1	1-2		O	2-1	1-2		6-1
Saffron Dyn.	1-4	2-0	0-4	0-5	1-3	0-4	0-6	3-1	0-3	1-0	3-2	4-1	N	2-4	1-5	0-0
Sileby Town	1-0	0-3	1-3	4-1	5-0	4-2	1-1	4-0	0-0	4-3	0-0	2-2	8-0	E	3-2	0-0
Stapenhill	3-2	3-3	2-1	3-2	3-2	1-0	0-0	3-2	6-1	2-1	4-0	4-1	4-0			3-0
Thringstone	0-1	0-3	2-5	1-2	0-3	0-4	0-10	1-1	2-9	0-4	1-8	0-3	1-6	0-7	0-3	

Combination One

	P	W	D	L	F	A	Pts
St Andrews Res.	30	23	3	4	96	38	72
Barrow Town Res.	30	22	2	6	98	32	68
Blaby/Whet. Res.	30	19	5	6	62	40	62
Thurmaston T. Res.	30	17	5	8	77	37	56
Ibstock Welf. Res.	29	17	5	7	66	35	56
Friar Lane OB Res.	29	13	5	11	61	58	44
Leics YMCA Res.	30	12	5	13	61	53	41
Downes Sports Res.	30	11	8	11	43	45	41
Coalville Town Res.	30	11	6	13	45	48	39
Highfield Rgrs Res.	30	10	5	15	51	73	35
Kirby Muxloe Res.	30	9	5	16	55	71	32
Aylestone Park Res.	30	8	8	14	35	73	32
Birstall United Res.	30	8	6	16	44	67	30
Leics Police Res.	30	8	4	18	42	53	28
Anstey Nmds Res.	30	7	7	16	32	73	28
Lutterworth T. Res.	30	3	3	24	26	98	12

Combination Two

	P	W	D	L	F	A	Pts
Ratby Sports Res.	28	23	1	4	100	26	70
Loughboro. D. Res.	28	21	4	3	104	35	67
Epworth Res.	28	18	4	6	85	44	58
Thurnby Rgrs Res.	28	18	2	8	96	50	56
Saffron Dyn. Res.	28	16	4	8	78	46	52
Holwell Sports Res.	28	14	6	8	71	43	48
Sileby Town Res. -1	28	14	4	10	77	55	45
N./Littlethorpe Res.	28	13	4	11	58	40	43
Anstey Town Res.	28	11	4	13	44	63	37
Ellistown Res.	28	9	5	14	53	61	32
Cottesmore A. Res.	28	9	4	15	63	66	31
Earl Shilton A. Res.	28	6	6	16	28	59	24
Bardon Hill Res.	28	5	3	20	38	117	18
Huncote S&S Res.	28	3	3	22	27	135	12
North Kilworth Res.	28	2	2	24	32	114	8

PRESIDENT'S CUP

FINAL *(8th May at Ibstock Welfare)*

Highfield Rgrs Res. 2 St Andrews Res. 1

Division One

		P	W	D	L	F	A	Pts
Epworth		30	27	3	0	140	21	84
Stapenhill		30	21	5	4	75	40	68
Sileby Town		30	17	6	7	80	51	57
Cottesmore Amateurs		30	17	2	11	62	50	53
Aylestone Park Old Boys		30	16	3	11	83	52	51
Lutterworth Town	-3	30	16	4	10	76	47	49
Bardon Hill Sports		30	13	6	11	67	57	45
Asfordby Amateurs		30	14	2	14	54	54	44
Anstey Town		30	12	6	12	54	54	42
Earl Shilton Albion		30	10	9	11	53	53	39
Narborough & Littlethorpe		30	11	4	15	47	52	37
Leics Constabulary		30	9	6	15	46	56	33
North Kilworth		30	8	4	18	47	81	28
Saffron Dynamo		30	7	4	19	42	93	25
Huncote S & S	-3	30	7	3	20	43	89	21
Thringstone Miners W.	-3	30	0	3	27	15	136	0

DIVISION ONE SECTION

FIRST ROUND

Aylestone Park Old Boys 0 **Narborough & Littlethorpe 2**
Bardon Hill Sports 3 North Kilworth 1
Cottesmore Amateurs 1 **Asfordby Amateurs 2**
Earl Shilton Albion 1 **Anstey Town** 1 (3-5p)
Lutterworth Town 1 **Leics Constabulary 2**
Saffron Dynamo 1 **Huncote Sports & Social 3**
Stapenhill 1 Sileby Town 0
Thringstone Miners Welfare 0 **Epworth 18**

SECOND ROUND

Anstey Town 1 Bardon Hill Sports 0
Epworth 5 Narborough & Littlethorpe 1
Leics Constabulary 3 Asfordby Amateurs 3
Stapenhill 5 Huncote S&S 1

QUARTER-FINALS (COMBINED)

Anstey Nomads 1 Stapenhill 0
Anstey Town 1 **Barrow Town 5**
Epworth 1 Ibstock Welfare 0
Thurnby Rangers 6 Leics Constabulary 1

SEMI-FINALS

Barrow Town 3 Anstey Nomads 0
Epworth 3 Thurnby Rangers 1

FINAL *(12th May at Barrow Town)*

Barrow Town 4 Epworth 2

DIVISION ONE CONSTITUTION 2003-04

ANSTEY TOWN . . . . Leicester Road, Thurcaston, Leicestershire. 0116 236 8231
ASFORDBY AMATEURS . . . . Hoby Road Sports Ground, Hoby Road, Asfordby, Leicestershire. . . . 01664 434545
AYLESTONE PARK OLD BOYS . . . Dorset Avenue, Fairfield Estate, Leicester, Leicestershire. . . . 01530 815569
BARDON HILL SPORTS . . . . Bardon Close, Coalville, Leicestershire. . . . 01530 815569
COTTESMORE AMATEURS . . . Rogues Park, Main Street, Cottesmore, Rutland. . . . 01572 813486
EARL SHILTON ALBION . . . Stoneycroft Park, New Street, Earl Shilton, Leicestershire. . . . 01455 844277
EPWORTH . . . University Sports Ground, Welford Road, Leicester, Leicestershire. . . . None
HUNCOTE SPORTS & SOCIAL . . . Enderby Lane, Thurlaston, Leicestershire. . . . 01455 888430
LEICS CONSTABULARY . . . Police Headquarters, St Johns, Enderby, Leicestershire. . . 0116 248 2198 (matchdays only)
LUTTERWORTH TOWN . . . Hall Lane, Bitteswell, Lutterworth, Leicestershire. . . . 01455 554046
NARBOROUGH & LITTLETHORPE . . . Leicester Road, Narborough, Leicestershire. . . . 0116 275 1855
NORTH KILWORTH . . . Rugby Road, North Kilworth, Leicestershire. . . . 01858 880890
ROTHLEY IMPERIAL . . . Loughborough Road, Mountsorrel, Leicester, Leicestershire. . . . 0116 237 4003
SAFFRON DYNAMO . . . Cambridge Road, Whetstone, Leicestershire. . . . 0116 284 9695
SILEBY TOWN . . . Memorial Park, Seagrave Road, Sileby, Leicestershire. . . . 01509 816104

Stapenhill are promoted to the Premier Division. Thringstone Miners Welfare are relegated to the Leicester & District League from which Rothley Imperial are promoted.

LINCOLNSHIRE LEAGUE

	Alstom S.	Appleby F.	Grimsby A.	Horncastle	Hykeham	Limestone	Linc. M Res.	Linc. U. Res.	Louth Res.	Retford T.	Skegness	Sleaford	Wyberton
Alstom Sports		3-3	1-1	2-1	0-2	1-4	1-1	2-1	4-1	6-1	4-0	1-4	0-4
Appleby Frod.	0-1		1-3	2-0	0-1	2-3	0-0	2-2	W-L	1-3	2-1	0-1	3-3
Grimsby Amat.	2-1	5-1		3-0	6-0	3-3	4-1	4-3	6-0	6-0	3-2	1-0	1-1
Horncastle Town	0-1	0-3	2-4		4-3	0-0	0-1	4-1	0-0	2-1	0-1	1-0	0-1
Hykeham Town	2-2	3-0	1-3	2-2		1-2	1-0	2-2	4-3	4-2	3-3	2-1	5-1
Limestone Rgrs	2-0	0-1	2-3	6-0	4-0		0-4	2-2	4-0	4-0	2-3	1-3	1-1
Linc. Moor. Res.	2-3	1-0	3-1	1-1	1-0	2-1		0-1	5-2	5-0	3-2	1-0	0-0
Lincoln Utd Res.	4-0	4-1	0-6	0-1	5-2	2-2	0-3		0-0	7-1	2-0	0-2	1-1
Louth United Res.	1-0	0-4	3-2	4-4	1-7	3-3	4-0	0-0		0-1	2-2	0-5	0-8
Retford Town	1-2	0-4	0-6	1-1	4-4	1-4	3-4	0-0	2-4		0-1	1-2	0-5
Skegness Town	3-4	0-2	3-1	2-1	2-1	0-3	7-2	2-0	0-0	0-1		1-2	1-1
Sleaford Town	3-2	4-2	0-2	1-1	4-0	2-1	9-1	1-1	8-2	7-0	3-0		3-1
Wyberton	3-2	4-2	2-0	2-1	2-2	1-2	1-0	3-1	2-0	5-1	1-2	1-2	

	P	W	D	L	F	A	Pts
Grimsby Amat.	24	17	3	4	76	30	54
Sleaford Town	24	17	2	5	68	24	53
Wyberton	24	12	7	5	54	30	43
Limestone Rg. +1	24	11	6	7	56	35	40
Linc. Moor. Res.	24	10	5	9	41	44	35
Alstom Sports	24	10	4	10	43	46	34
Hykeham Town	24	9	6	9	52	54	33
Skegness Town	24	9	5	10	39	43	32
Appleby Frod.	24	8	4	12	36	42	28
Lincoln U. Res. -1	24	6	9	9	39	41	26
Horncastle Town	24	6	7	11	27	41	25
Louth United Res.	24	4	7	13	30	71	19
Retford Town	24	3	3	18	24	84	12

LEAGUE CUP

FIRST ROUND

Alstom 1 **Grimsby Amateurs** 2, **Limestone** 1 Skegness 0
Lincoln United Res. 6 Horncastle Town 4 *aet*
Louth United Res. 1 Lincoln Moorlands Res. 0
Wyberton 5 Retford Town 2

QUARTER-FINALS

Appleby Frodingham Athletic 1 **Lincoln United Res.** 2
Grimsby Amateurs 4 Wyberton 0

Limestone Rangers 2 **Sleaford Town** 3
Louth United Res. 0 **Hykeham Town** 2

SEMI-FINALS

Lincoln United Res. 0 **Hykeham Town** 2
Sleaford Town 2 Grimsby Amateurs 1 *aet*

FINAL
(14th May at Lincoln Moorlands)
Hykeham Town 3 Sleaford Town 2

SUPPLEMENTARY CUP

Group One	P	W	D	L	F	A	Pts
Lincoln United Res.	12	8	1	3	35	17	25
Limestone Rangers	12	8	1	3	38	22	25
Appleby Frodingham Ath.	12	7	3	2	34	26	24
Hykeham Town	12	5	2	5	30	31	17
Alstom Sports	12	4	1	7	21	39	13
Lincoln Moorlands Res.	12	3	1	8	21	24	10
Retford Town	12	2	1	9	12	32	7

Appleby F 3 Limestone 7, Linc U. Res. 4 Linc M Res. 0, Linc M Res. 5 Alstom 0, Linc U Res. 2, Appleby F 1 Retford 0 Lincoln Utd Res. 2, Appleby F 7 Alstom 4, Linc U Res. 4 Retford 0, Appleby F 3 Retford 1, Linc U Res. 5 Alstom 2, Linc U Res. 4 Limestone 1, Retford 1 Appleby F 2, Hykeham 2 Appleby F 3, Hykeham 1 Limestone 2, Alstom 3 Linc M Res. 2, Linc M Res. 5 Retford 0, Linc U Res. 5 Hykeham 3, Limestone 4 Hykeham 1, Limestone 3 Retford 1, Limestone 2 Linc U Res. 1, Alstom 1 Appleby F 1, Hykeham 2 Linc M Res. 1, Appleby F 1 Retford 1, Retford 1 Alstom 0, Hykeham 3 Linc U Res. 2, Appleby F 4 Hykeham 1, Alstom 2 Limestone 1, Appleby Frod 3 Linc U Res. 0, Retford 4 Hykeham 4, Linc M Res. 1 Limestone 3, Hykeham 3 Alstom 1, Linc M Res. 1 Appleby Frod. 3, Retford 2 Limestone 1, Alstom 2 Linc U Res. 1, Hykeham 3 Retford 1, Limestone 2 Appleby Frod 3, Linc M Res. v Limestone 3 (points awarded to Hykeham), Alstom 3 Hykeham 7, Retford 0 Linc M Res. 3, Alstom 2 Retford 1, Limestone 6 Linc M Res. 2, Limestone 5 Alstom 1

Group Two	P	W	D	L	F	A	Pts
Sleaford Town	10	6	2	2	26	10	20
Louth United Res.	10	6	2	2	17	19	20
Skegness Town	10	4	2	4	20	13	16
Grimsby Amateurs	10	4	4	2	20	16	16
Wyberton	10	2	4	4	13	13	10
Horncastle Town	10	0	0	10	8	33	0

Wyberton 0 Sleaford 1, Horncastle 1 Sleaford 3, Horncastle 2 Louth Res. 3, Horncastle 2 Skegness 6, Grim. Am 5 Louth Res. 2, Wyberton 1 Grim. Am 2, Wyberton 0 Skegness 1, Skegness 1 Louth Res. 2, Louth Res. 1 Skegness 1, Grim Am 3 Horncastle 0, Sleaford 4 Grim Am 0, Louth Res. 3 Grim Am 2, Sleaford 5 Louth Res. 0, Wyberton 2 Horncastle 0, Louth Res. 1 Grim Am 0, Sleaford 1 Wyberton 1, Horncastle 2 Wyberton 2, Skegness 2 Horncastle 1, Sleaford 1 Wyberton 1, Horncastle 1 Wyberton 3, Horncastle 1 Grim Am 3, Sleaford 3 Skegness 2, Wyberton 2 Louth Res. 2, Grimsby Am 2 Grimsby Am 1 Wyberton 1, Skegness 3 Sleaford 0, Louth Res. 1 Horncastle 0, Skegness 2 Wyberton 2, Skegness 1 Grimsby Am 1, Sleaford 7 Horncastle 0

SEMI-FINALS

Louth United Res. 0 **Lincoln United Res.** 1
Sleaford Town 4 Limestone Rangers 3

FINAL *(21st May at Wyberton)*
Sleaford Town 6 Lincoln United Res. 1

CONSTITUTION 2003-04

ALSTOM SPORTS . . . . Ruston Marconi Sports Club, Newark Road, Lincoln, Lincolnshire 01522 882111
HARROWBY UNITED RESERVES . . . . Harrowby Fields, Harrowby Lane, Grantham, Lincolnshire 01476 590822
HORNCASTLE TOWN. . . . . The Wong, Boston Road, Horncastle, Lincolnshire . . . . None
HYKEHAM TOWN . . . . Memorial Hall Ground, Newark Road, North Hykeham, Lincoln, Lincolnshire 01522 880035
LSS LUCARLYS. . . . . Wilton Road, Humberston, Grimsby, North Lincs 01472 812936
LIMESTONE RANGERS . . . . Hollowgate Hill, Willoughton, Lincolnshire . . . . None
LINCOLN MOORLANDS RESERVES . . Moorlands Sports Ground, Newark Road, Lincoln, Lincolnshire . . . . 01522 520184 / 874111
LINCOLN UNITED RESERVES . . . . . . Ashby Avenue, Hartsholme, Lincoln, Lincolnshire. . . . 01522 696400 / 690674. Fax: 01522 696400
LOUTH UNITED RESERVES. . . . . Park Avenue, Louth, Lincolnshire 01507 607351
SKEGNESS TOWN . . . . Burgh Road, Skegness, Lincolnshire 01754 764385
SLEAFORD TOWN. Boston Road, Sleaford, Lincolnshire 01529 306959
WYBERTON. . . . . Causeway, Wyberton, Boston, Lincolnshire 01205 353525

Retford Town switch to the Notts Alliance and Appleby Frodingham Athletic to the Central Midlands League. Newcomers are LSS Lucarlys and Harrowby United Reserves. Grimsby Amateurs have folded.

LIVERPOOL COUNTY COMBINATION

Note – Marconi and REMYCA United withdrew during the season. Their results are shown below but have been expunged from the league table

	Birchfield	Bootle	Cheshire Lines	Earle	Ford Motors	Formby	Halewood Town	Lucas Sports	Marconi	Mossley Hill Ath.	Prescot Leisure	REMYCA United	Royal Seaforth	South Liverpool	South Sefton Boro.	Speke	St Aloysius	St Dominics	Tuebrook	Waterloo Dock
Birchfield		3-5	7-2	3-0	2-2	4-3	2-4	1-2	13-2	2-3	2-5	4-3	3-1	3-3	2-3	0-1	0-3	3-1	5-0	0-4
Bootle	6-2		2-1	3-1	3-2	1-2	3-0	3-0	5-2	9-1	3-0	3-3	3-0	1-2	1-2	1-1	2-3	1-2	3-2	2-2
Cheshire Lines	2-1	3-2		4-1	1-1	3-2	0-1	n/a	4-0	3-1	n/a	1-0	1-2	4-5	0-3	0-2	1-2	3-6	0-2	1-6
Earle	1-0	1-3	1-2		3-6	1-2	0-5	0-3	n/a	0-3	1-2	n/a	2-4	0-1	4-1	0-3	1-5	2-3	1-2	1-6
Ford Motors	3-0	1-2	2-2	3-1		1-1	1-1	1-1	3-1	3-1	2-1	2-2	3-0	3-0	0-2	5-1	2-2	1-2	2-0	0-1
Formby	1-1	3-0	4-2	4-1	0-2		3-1	1-3	3-2	2-0	4-5	2-2	1-2	2-7	1-3	1-4	2-3	5-4	3-1	4-4
Halewood Town	2-1	2-3	1-3	4-3	1-2	3-1		0-4	n/a	2-1	0-2	n/a	2-1	1-1	2-1	3-1	2-1	2-1	1-3	2-5
Lucas Sports	0-2	0-3	1-2	3-2	3-1	3-1	0-4		4-1	2-0	4-0	5-0	1-1	0-0	4-3	0-1	1-1	1-0	8-0	0-4
Marconi	n/a	n/a	n/a	4-8	n/a	n/a	n/a	n/a		0-4	n/a	n/a	n/a	n/a	n/a	n/a	n/a	n/a	1-1	0-2
Mossley Hill Athletic	1-3	1-4	0-0	3-3	2-6	2-2	2-5	2-6	n/a		3-3	n/a	0-3	2-1	1-0	5-4	4-3	1-0	1-0	0-2
Prescot Leisure	1-0	2-3	0-1	4-2	2-0	1-2	1-5	0-5	2-0	n/a		n/a	0-3	2-2	3-1	0-3	1-1	0-1	3-1	0-5
REMYCA United	n/a	n/a	n/a	4-3	n/a	n/a	n/a	2-1	2-1	n/a	n/a		n/a	0-0	1-3	2-2	3-1	2-1	5-3	0-3
Royal Seaforth	3-0	4-2	7-0	3-0	0-2	1-3	0-2	1-3	2-2	6-1	6-0	4-1		2-2	0-1	3-0	0-2	1-1	2-1	3-2
South Liverpool	3-3	3-0	3-0	0-0	2-4	1-1	2-1	0-0	2-0	3-3	2-0	1-0	3-2		2-2	0-1	3-0	0-2	1-1	3-2
South Sefton Borough	2-4	2-0	3-1	3-0	1-1	1-5	1-1	1-3	n/a	3-1	3-1	n/a	3-1	2-2		0-1	6-0	1-1	8-0	1-4
Speke	4-2	1-2	1-2	0-7	0-3	1-3	2-4	2-2	1-0	n/a	2-0	1-0	1-0	2-2	1-0		3-5	3-1	4-1	1-3
St Aloysius	3-1	0-0	3-1	5-0	3-5	4-2	2-2	0-0	4-0	5-2	1-7	2-1	1-0	2-2	1-4	3-5		2-0	2-3	1-3
St Dominics	3-6	2-1	3-1	4-1	1-2	3-3	4-1	1-1	3-1	5-2	0-1	5-2	2-2	1-2	1-2	2-2	1-2		2-0	2-3
Tuebrook	2-2	1-3	1-3	1-1	1-2	1-0	0-3	0-2	5-1	3-0	n/a	3-1	1-3	2-0	1-1	2-2	2-3	2-3		0-1
Waterloo Dock	3-1	2-2	5-0	6-0	0-0	1-1	2-2	1-0	5-0	3-0	1-0	3-1	2-1	4-0	1-1	1-2	2-1	7-3	4-3	

	P	W	D	L	F	A	Pts
Speke	34	26	8	0	83	25	86
Waterloo Dock	34	25	6	3	105	34	81
Lucas Sports	34	17	9	8	68	43	60
St Dominics	34	18	5	11	81	61	59
Bootle	34	18	3	13	80	56	57
St Aloysius	34	16	8	10	75	68	56
Ford Motors	34	15	10	9	73	51	55
South Liverpool	34	13	12	9	53	44	51
Formby	34	14	7	13	74	72	49
Halewood Town	34	14	6	14	67	67	48
Royal Seaforth -3	34	14	6	14	74	63	45
South Sefton Borough	34	13	5	16	65	71	44
Cheshire Lines	34	13	3	18	54	76	42
Birchfield	34	10	5	19	71	82	35
Prescot Leisure	34	10	4	20	41	69	34
Tuebrook	34	8	5	21	52	90	29
Mossley Hill Athletic	34	4	7	23	45	110	19
Earle	34	2	3	29	35	114	9

PETER COYNE/GEORGE MAHON CUP

FIRST ROUND
Formby 2 Tuebrook 1
Mossley Hill Athletic 6 Marconi 1
Speke 1 South Liverpool 0
St Aloysius 0 **Prescot Leisure** 4
Royal Seaforth 3 Prescot Leisure 1
Waterloo Dock 1 **St Dominics** 2

SECOND ROUND
Bootle 1 South Sefton Borough 0
Earle 2 Cheshire Lines 2 *aet (4-2p)*
Ford Motors 3 Mossley Hill Athletic 0
Formby 3 **Speke** 3 *aet (2-3p)*
Halewood Town 1 **Birchfield** 2
REMYCA United 0 **Lucas Sports** 5

QUARTER-FINALS
Birchfield 2 Ford Motors 2 *aet (5-4p)*
Bootle 4 Earle 2
Lucas Sports 1 St Dominics 0 *aet*
Royal Seaforth 2 **Speke** 3

SEMI-FINALS
Birchfield 0 **Lucas Sports** 4
Speke 1 **Bootle** 2

FINAL *(10th May at Formby)*
Bootle 0 **Lucas Sports** 1

LORD WAVERTREE CUP

FIRST ROUND
Formby 4 Royal Seaforth 0, Halewood Town 2
Cheshire Lines 1, Marconi (scr.) v Earle (w/o),
Mossley Hill 1 **South Sefton** 4, Prescot Leisure 1
St Aloysius 3, REMYCA United (scr.) v Ford
Motors (w/o), Tuebrook 0 **South Liverpool** 1,
Waterloo Dock 4 St Dominics 2
South Sefton Borough 1 **Waterloo Dock** 4

QUARTER-FINALS
Formby 4 Ford Motors 1, Halewood Town 1 **St
Aloysius** 2, **South Liverpool** 2 Earle 1

SEMI-FINALS
Formby 2 **Waterloo Dock** 2 *aet (2-4p)*
St Aloysius 2 **South Liverpool** 4

FINAL *(7th May at Formby)*
Waterloo Dock 5 South Liverpool 0

CONSTITUTION 2003-04
AIGBURTH PEOPLE'S HALL.... Cheshire Lines FC, Southmead Road, Allerton, Liverpool, Merseyside 0151 427 7176
BIRCHFIELD......................... Edge Hill College, St Helens Road, Ormskirk, Merseyside....................... 01695 575171
BOOTLE............................. Edinburgh Park, Townsend Lane, Liverpool, Merseyside......................... 0151 263 5267
CHESHIRE LINES .... Southmead Road, Allerton, Liverpool, Merseyside............................. 0151 427 7176
FORD MOTORS .... Ford Sports & Social Club, Cronton Lane, Widnes, Merseyside................. 0151 424 7078
HALEWOOD TOWN................... Hollies, Hollies Road, Halewood, Merseyside 0151 443 2063
LUCAS SPORTS .... Heron Eccles, Abbotshey Road, Liverpool, Merseyside........................ 0151 724 4377
MOSSLEY HILL ATHLETIC .... Athletic Club, Mossley Hill Road, Liverpool, Merseyside.................... None
PRESCOT LEISURE .... Wood Lane, Prescot, Merseyside.. None
ROYAL SEAFORTH .... William Collins Ground, Commercial Road, Liverpool, Merseyside............. None
SKELMERSDALE UTD RESERVES ..... Edge Hill College, St Helens Road, Ormskirk, Merseyside................... 01695 575171
SOUTH LIVERPOOL .... The Pavilions Sports Ground, Sandy Lane, Weston Point, Runcorn, Cheshire 01928 590508
SOUTH SEFTON BOROUGH ...... Hightown Cricket Ground, Thirlmere Road, Hightown, Merseyside............. 0151 486 1588
SPEKE .... Speke Hall Avenue, Speke, Liverpool, Merseyside............................ None
ST ALOYSIUS .... King George V, Longview Lane, Huyton, Liverpool, Merseyside............... 0151 489 2798
ST DOMINICS .... St Dominics School, Lordens Road, Huyton, Merseyside..................... None
TUEBROOK PARK.................... William Collins Ground, Commercial Road, Liverpool, Merseyside........... 0151 263 5267
WATERLOO DOCK .... Edinburgh Park, Townsend Lane, Liverpool, Merseyside..................... None
REMYCA United and Marconi withdrew during the season. Formby return to the North West Counties League. Earle have withdrawn. Newcomers are Aigburth People's Hall (I-Zingari League) and Skelmersdale United Reserves (North West Counties League Reserve Division). Tuebrook become Tuebrook Park.

WWW.NLNEWSDESK.CO.UK

MANCHESTER LEAGUE

	Atherton Town	Dukinfield Town	East Manchester	Elton Vale	Irlam Mitchell Shackleton	Leigh Athletic	Monton Amateurs	New Mills	Prestwich Heys	Rochdale Sacred Heart	Royton Town	Springhead	Stockport Georgians	Willows	Wilmslow Albion	Wythenshawe Amateur
Atherton Town	P	1-2	3-1	1-2	1-1	2-1	2-0	0-2	4-2	1-1	1-1	1-0	1-0	1-0	4-2	0-1
Dukinfield Town	0-3	R	0-3	1-3	1-2	2-2	7-1	2-1	2-0	1-1	4-2	1-0	5-1	2-1	2-1	2-0
East Manchester	1-0	3-2	E	3-3	1-3	0-3	3-1	1-3	2-2	2-1	4-2	0-4	3-5	2-2	1-3	1-4
Elton Vale	1-3	1-3	3-1	M	1-2	2-2	1-2	2-1	2-0	3-2	1-0	1-3	3-1	0-2	1-0	0-2
Irlam Mitchell Shackleton	1-4	2-0	3-0	3-2	I	1-1	2-1	2-1	2-1	3-1	3-3	4-2	1-2	1-2	6-1	2-0
Leigh Athletic	1-1	0-1	5-2	3-4	2-1	E	5-2	0-2	4-0	2-0	0-1	3-1	3-3	2-0	1-1	2-5
Monton Amateurs	0-6	1-0	2-2	1-1	2-4	2-7	R	1-2	0-2	2-2	2-1	0-1	1-4	3-0	0-2	0-1
New Mills	3-4	1-2	0-3	2-1	1-1	4-3	2-4		0-2	3-2	1-4	2-0	2-2	3-3	1-2	0-0
Prestwich Heys	0-2	0-2	2-0	1-1	3-1	1-1	6-2	3-2	D	1-1	3-2	3-0	2-3	2-1	2-2	1-0
Rochdale Sacred Heart	3-6	1-1	1-3	1-1	0-2	2-2	1-2	3-3	0-2	I	0-3	1-3	1-2	4-0	3-0	1-0
Royton Town	2-0	1-1	1-2	2-1	5-4	2-1	2-2	6-4	3-2	1-1	V	1-1	1-5	4-2	2-2	2-0
Springhead	3-1	2-0	0-2	5-2	0-1	3-2	0-2	4-2	2-2	3-3	2-7	I	2-1	4-1	4-1	1-3
Stockport Georgians	3-1	4-1	4-1	5-2	2-3	1-4	3-0	2-3	1-2	2-1	2-1	2-1	S	1-2	4-4	1-2
Willows	1-6	1-2	3-4	1-3	0-4	0-5	2-1	0-4	4-1	0-2	1-7	2-2	1-4	I	2-1	1-3
Wilmslow Albion	3-3	2-0	1-1	3-1	2-2	1-3	5-3	1-1	0-1	0-1	3-3	4-0	2-2	5-1	O	0-0
Wythenshawe Amateur	1-1	2-1	1-1	2-2	1-0	1-0	3-2	0-1	1-4	4-2	3-1	1-1	5-1	2-0	2-2	N

Premier Division

	P	W	D	L	F	A	Pts
Irlam Mitchell Shackleton	30	18	5	7	67	43	59
Wythenshawe Amateur	30	16	7	7	50	33	55
Atherton Town	30	16	6	8	64	39	54
Stockport Georgians	30	15	4	11	73	61	49
Royton Town	30	13	8	9	73	58	47
Prestwich Heys	30	13	7	10	51	47	46
Dukinfield Town	-3 30	15	4	11	50	43	46
Leigh Athletic	30	12	8	10	70	48	44
Springhead	30	12	5	13	55	56	41
New Mills	30	11	6	13	57	60	39
Elton Vale	30	11	6	13	51	58	39
East Manchester	30	11	6	13	53	67	39
Wilmslow Albion	30	8	12	10	56	57	36
Monton Amateurs	30	7	5	18	42	78	26
Rochdale Sacred Heart	30	5	10	15	43	58	25
Willows	30	6	3	21	36	85	21

GILGRYST CUP

FIRST ROUND
Atherton Town 2 Willows 0
East Manchester 0 **Dukinfield Town** 4
Elton Vale 3 Wythenshawe Amateur 2 *aet*
Irlam Mitchell Shackleton 0 **Prestwich Heys** 2
Leigh Athletic 1 **Wilmslow Albion** 6 *aet*
New Mills 2 **Springhead** 3
Rochdale Sacred Heart 0 **Stockport Georgians** 7
Royton Town 5 Monton Amateurs 0

QUARTER-FINALS
Elton Vale 1 Dukinfield Town 0
Royton Town 3 **Springhead** 4 *aet*
Stockport Georgians 2 **Atherton Town** 3 *aet*
Wilmslow Albion 2 **Prestwich Heys** 3 *aet*

SEMI-FINALS
Prestwich Heys 5 Elton Vale 3
Springhead 1 Atherton Town 1 *aet (7-6p)*

FINAL
(5th May at Elton Fold)
Prestwich Heys 4 Springhead 1

PREMIER DIVISION CONSTITUTION 2003-04

ATHERTON TOWN .... Howe Bridge Sports Centre, Howe Bridge, Lancashire 01942 884882
BREIGHTMET UNITED .... Moss Park, Bury Road, Breightmet, Manchester............................ 01204 533930
DUKINFIELD TOWN.............. Blocksages Playing Fields, Birch Lane, Dukinfield, Cheshire 0161 343 4529
EAST MANCHESTER .... Droylsden FC, Butchers Arms, Droylsden, Manchester .... 0161 370 1426 / 301 1352
ELTON VALE.................................. Elton Vale Road, Bury, Lancashire 0161 762 0666
HIGHFIELD UNITED .... Seedfield Sports Club, Parkinson Street, Bury, Lancashire. .... None
IRLAM MITCHELL SHACKLETON ..... Salteye Park, Eccles, Peel Green, Eccles, Manchester .... None
LEIGH ATHLETIC.............. Leigh Harriers AC, Madley Park, Leigh, Lancashire .... None
MONTON AMATEURS .... Granary Lane, Worsley, Manchester. 01942 673500
NEW MILLS .... Church Lane, New Mills, Derbyshire 01663 747435
PRESTWICH HEYS.................... Sandgate Road, Prestwich Heys, Manchester............................. 0161 773 8888
ROYTON TOWN .... Crompton Cricket Club Complex, Glebe Street, Shaw, Oldham, Lancashire 01706 847421
SPRINGHEAD............................. St John Street, Lees, Oldham, Lancashire 0161 627 0260
STOCKPORT GEORGIANS............... Cromley Road, Woodsmoor, Stockport, Cheshire. 0161 483 6581
WILMSLOW ALBION .... Oakwood Farm, Styal Road, Wilmslow, Cheshire 0161 483 6581
WYTHENSHAWE AMATEUR .... Longley Lane, Northendon, Wythenshawe, Manchester 0161 998 7268
Rochdale Sacred Heart and Willows (who become Swinton Town) drop to Division One replaced by Breightmet United and Highfield United.

	Ashton Athletic	Avro	Belden	Breightmet United	Highfield United	Hindsford	Hollinwood	Manchester Royal	Milton	Old Altrinchamians	Tintwistle Villa	Unsworth	Warth Fold	Whalley Range	Whitworth Valley	Wythenshawe Town
Ashton Ath.		4-0	1-1	1-3	1-1	1-3	5-4	n/a	7-0	W-L	1-1	2-2	7-3	W-L	2-0	3-1
Avro	3-1	D	1-3	2-1	2-2	1-2	4-0	n/a	1-1	5-0	6-1	2-1	2-0	3-2	0-2	3-3
Belden	1-1	2-1	I	2-5	3-6	2-2	5-3	8-1	4-3	2-2	2-1	5-1	3-4	5-2	0-3	2-2
Breightmet	5-1	1-2	2-1	V	4-2	3-1	5-0	6-2	2-0	4-2	5-2	3-5	3-3	4-0	2-2	4-2
Highfield Utd	3-1	2-2	1-4	2-0	I	1-3	6-2	n/a	2-0	W-L	2-1	0-3	6-0	6-2	W-L	5-1
Hindsford	2-1	1-2	4-5	2-1	2-2	S	4-0	n/a	4-0	W-L	5-1	2-2	6-1	1-0	2-2	0-2
Hollinwood	1-0	1-2	4-6	2-6	0-3	4-0	I	n/a	1-3	3-2	4-1	1-3	2-1	3-4	1-2	2-0
Manch. Royal	1-3	0-3	2-3	n/a	n/a	0-5	n/a	O	n/a	n/a	n/a	n/a	n/a	1-8	0-4	n/a
Milton	1-3	2-1	1-3	0-2	0-1	3-3	1-1	n/a	N	2-3	1-0	0-2	4-1	2-1	2-2	1-1
Old Alts	0-7	1-5	L-W	0-3	2-4	0-2	3-0	n/a	1-2		0-2	0-6	3-0	3-1	4-1	0-1
Tintwistle	0-7	3-2	1-2	1-0	1-4	2-4	4-3	n/a	1-3	1-0		0-1	2-4	2-1	6-3	1-0
Unsworth	0-4	1-1	1-1	0-2	2-6	0-0	1-0	n/a	1-3	3-2	1-1		4-0	1-0	1-3	2-0
Warth Fold	1-2	0-7	0-2	2-2	0-0	2-0	2-4	0-4	1-1	2-1	1-3	0-4	O	4-1	3-4	0-1
Whalley Rge	1-1	3-2	5-1	1-8	1-2	3-2	5-0	n/a	2-0	8-0	2-0	3-2	3-1	N	1-1	1-3
Whitworth V.	1-2	2-3	2-6	1-2	5-4	2-2	2-3	1-0	2-3	4-1	3-2	3-1	3-1	6-4	E	0-2
Wyth. Town	2-2	2-2	2-1	1-2	4-2	2-7	3-0	n/a	1-1	2-1	3-0	1-1	1-1	8-1	2-2	

Note – Manchester Royal withdrew during the course of the season. Their results are shown above but are expunged from the league table

Division One

		P	W	D	L	F	A	Pts
Breightmet United		28	19	3	6	81	40	60
Highfield United		28	17	5	6	74	44	56
Belden		28	15	6	7	77	62	51
Hindsford	-3	28	15	7	6	71	45	49
Ashton Athletic		28	14	7	7	68	40	49
Avro		28	14	6	8	67	44	48
Wythenshawe Town		28	11	9	8	53	47	42
Unsworth	-1	28	12	7	9	52	45	42
Whitworth Valley		28	11	5	12	63	64	38
Whalley Range		28	11	1	16	60	71	34
Milton		28	9	7	12	40	54	34
Tintwistle Villa		28	9	2	17	41	70	29
Hollinwood	-3	28	8	1	19	49	83	22
Warth Fold		28	5	5	18	38	81	20
Old Altrinchamians		28	4	1	23	29	73	13

SUPPLEMENTARY CUP

FINAL *(10th May at Atherton Town)*
Ashton Athletic Res. 2 Whalley Range Res. 1

MURRAY SHIELD

FIRST ROUND
Highfield United 6 Ashton Athletic 5
Manchester Royal (scr.) v **Milton** (w/o)
Tintwistle Villa 1 **Avro** 2
Unsworth 4 **Belden** 6
Warth Fold 5 Hollinwood 3
Whalley Range 1 **Hindsford** 2
Whitworth Valley 1 Breightmet United 1
Wythenshawe Town 7 Old Altrinchamians 1

QUARTER-FINALS
Belden 2 **Avro** 3
Hindsford 4 Wythenshawe Town 1
Milton 1 **Highfield United** 2
Whitworth Valley 4 Warth Fold 0

SEMI-FINALS
Avro 2 Whitworth Valley 1
Hindsford 1 **Highfield United** 3

FINAL
(3rd May at Springhead)
Avro 1 **Highfield United** 1 *aet* (4-5p)

OPEN TROPHY

FINAL *(30th April at New Mills)*
Dukinfield Town Res. 3
Wilmslow Albion Res. 2

Division Two

	P	W	D	L	F	A	Pts
Wilmslow Albion Res.	26	24	1	1	96	42	73
Dukinfield Town Res.	26	19	2	5	73	32	59
Stockport Georgians Res.	26	15	7	4	72	29	52
New Mills Res.	26	13	2	11	60	59	41
East Manchester Res.	26	11	4	11	49	55	37
Prestwich Heys Res.	26	11	3	12	53	50	36
Atherton Town Res.	26	11	3	12	45	49	36
Springhead Res.	26	9	6	11	59	50	33
Monton Amateurs Res.	26	10	3	13	59	69	33
Leigh Athletic Res.	26	9	4	13	54	66	31
Wythenshawe Am. Res.	26	8	7	11	50	68	31
Irlam Mit. Shack. Res.	26	7	6	13	46	64	27
Elton Vale Res.	26	8	3	15	39	64	27
Breightmet United Res.	26	1	1	24	35	93	4

Division Three

	P	W	D	L	F	A	Pts
Rochdale Sac. Ht Res.	18	14	3	1	42	23	45
Ashton Athletic Res.	18	11	4	3	52	23	37
Hindsford Res.	18	10	2	6	59	29	32
Avro Res.	18	10	2	6	43	27	32
Royton Town Res.	18	8	5	5	36	29	29
Highfield United Res.	18	7	5	6	44	33	26
Whalley Range Res.	18	6	3	9	37	59	21
Whitworth Valley Res.	18	3	4	11	18	41	13
Milton Res.	18	3	3	12	20	57	12
Old Altrinchamians Res.	18	2	1	15	23	53	7

WWW.NLNEWSDESK.CO.UK

DIVISION ONE CONSTITUTION 2003-04

AFC BLACKLEY . . . . . . Blackley New Road, Blackley, Manchester 0161 740 9591
ASHTON ATHLETIC . . . . . . Brocstedes Park, Farm Road, North Ashton, Manchester 01942 716360
AVRO . . . . . . Lancaster Club, Broadway, Failsworth, Manchester 0161 681 3083
HEYWOOD ST JAMES . . . . . . t.b.a. . . . . . . t.b.a.
HINDSFORD . . . . . . Squires Lane, Tyldesley, Lancashire . . . . . . None
HOLLINWOOD . . . . . . Lime Lane, Hollinwood, Manchester 0161 681 3385
MANCHESTER TITANS . . . . . . The Elms Playing Fields, George Street, Whitefield, Bury, Manchester 0161 767 9233
MILTON . . . . . . Springfield Park Athletic Stadium, off Bolton Road, Rochdale, Lancashire 01706 53339
OLD ALTRINCHAMIANS . . . . . . Crossford Bridge PF, Meadows Road, Sale, Cheshire 0161 767 9233
OLD STANDIANS . . . . . . t.b.a. . . . . . . t.b.a.
ROCHDALE SACRED HEART . . . . . . Fox Park, Belfield Mill Lane, Rochdale, Lancashire . . . . . . None
STAND ATHLETIC . . . . . . Ewood Bridge, Manchester Road, Haslingden, Manchester 01706 217814
SWINTON TOWN . . . . . . Agecroft Sports Ground, Agecroft Road, Salford, Manchester . . . . . . None
TINTWISTLE VILLA . . . . . . West Drive, Tintwistle, near Glossop, Derbyshire . . . . . . None
UNSWORTH . . . . . . Hillock Estate, Whitefield, Bury, Lancashire . . . . . . None
WHALLEY RANGE . . . . . . Kings Road, Chorlton-cum-Hardy, Manchester 0161 881 2618
WHITWORTH VALLEY . . . . . . Rawston Street Stadium, Whitworth, Lancashire . . . . . . None
WYTHENSHAWE TOWN . . . . . . Ericstan Park, Timpson Road, Baguley, Manchester 0161 998 5076

Manchester Royal withdrew during the course of the season. Breightmet United and Highfield United move up to the Premier Division from which Rochdale Sacred Heart and Willows (who become Swinton Town) drop. Newcomers are Heywood St James, Old Standians (Lancashire & Cheshire Amateur League) and Stand Athletic (resigned from North West Counties League during the course of this season). Belden become AFC Blackley and Warth Fold become Manchester Titans.

MID-CHESHIRE LEAGUE

	Barnton	Broadheath Central	Cheadle Heath Nomads	Chorlton Town	Crewe	Crosfields	Daten	Garswood United	Knutsford	Linotype	Middlewich Town	Padgate St Oswalds	Pilkington	Poynton	Rylands	Styal
Barnton		3-1	2-0	2-0	1-1	2-0	3-1	3-0	1-0	2-2	1-1	3-1	5-0	1-1	0-1	4-0
Broadheath Central	0-3		2-2	2-0	4-2	3-4	0-3	2-2	0-3	1-1	1-0	1-0	2-0	2-1	1-2	0-3
Cheadle Heath Nomads	1-2	1-1	D	0-4	3-2	2-5	2-0	1-0	2-5	1-3	0-3	2-0	1-1	0-1	1-4	0-1
Chorlton Town	0-2	1-0	1-2	I	0-2	0-2	1-1	1-2	1-2	2-2	0-2	2-0	1-3	0-1	1-2	0-2
Crewe	2-2	3-3	2-0	7-5	V	5-2	2-1	5-2	1-2	1-3	0-2	4-1	2-0	0-2	1-1	3-2
Crosfields	0-3	1-1	1-0	4-1	3-0	I	0-0	3-3	1-1	2-2	3-4	3-0	1-0	0-2	2-2	2-0
Daten	1-0	2-2	4-1	4-0	1-2	2-0	S	4-0	2-2	2-2	3-7	1-1	1-1	2-2	2-0	3-0
Garswood United	1-1	2-4	2-3	5-1	2-2	0-0	2-3	I	1-3	3-2	0-4	1-0	1-0	0-1	0-0	1-1
Knutsford	1-2	2-1	3-0	2-0	1-1	0-1	1-1	2-0	O	0-0	2-0	4-0	1-1	1-3	2-2	1-0
Linotype	3-1	5-0	0-1	4-1	4-2	9-0	2-1	3-0	1-1	N	0-1	8-0	0-0	1-0	4-2	1-3
Middlewich Town	0-2	0-1	4-1	2-2	3-0	4-1	2-0	5-0	1-1	1-1		5-0	6-0	1-1	2-1	1-1
Padgate St Oswalds	0-3	2-1	3-3	3-1	0-3	1-0	1-1	2-1	0-4	1-2	1-4	O	1-2	1-2	1-2	1-4
Pilkington	0-2	1-0	0-0	4-1	1-0	4-1	1-2	2-3	2-3	1-0	0-3	4-2	N	2-3	1-3	3-1
Poynton	0-2	2-2	3-3	7-1	2-0	4-2	2-1	3-1	1-1	0-3	0-0	4-0	4-1	E	3-1	4-5
Rylands	0-2	3-2	2-1	1-1	3-0	1-3	4-0	4-1	0-1	1-1	1-1	1-3	3-3	2-0		1-3
Styal	0-1	3-0	2-1	2-1	3-1	3-3	3-3	2-0	1-0	2-0	1-1	7-0	2-1	1-3	2-1	

Division One	P	W	D	L	F	A	Pts
Barnton	30	21	6	3	61	18	69
Middlewich Town	30	17	8	5	66	25	59
Poynton	30	17	6	7	62	38	57
Styal	30	17	5	8	60	41	56
Knutsford	30	15	9	6	52	29	54
Linotype	30	14	10	6	69	33	52
Rylands	30	13	8	9	52	44	47
Daten	30	12	9	9	59	42	45
Crosfields	30	11	8	11	50	59	41
Crewe	30	11	6	13	56	59	39
Pilkington	30	9	6	15	39	55	33
Broadheath Central	30	8	8	14	40	57	32
Cheadle Heath Nomads	30	7	6	17	35	63	27
Garswood United	30	6	7	17	36	67	25
Padgate St Oswalds	30	5	2	23	26	89	17
Chorlton Town	30	3	4	23	30	74	13

DIVISION ONE CUP

FIRST ROUND
Cheadle Heath Nomads 5 Padgate St Oswalds 0
Crewe 1 Daten 0
Crosfields 2 Rylands 1
Garswood United 2 Chorlton Town 1
Knutsford 1 **Barnton** 2
Linotype 3 Styal 0
Middlewich Town 4 Pilkington 1
Poynton 5 Broadheath Central 1
QUARTER-FINALS
Crewe 4 Cheadle Heath Nomads 0
Garswood United 1 Crosfields 2
Middlewich Town 5 **Barnton** 7
Poynton 2 **Linotype** 4
SEMI-FINALS
Barnton 4 Linotype 1
Crewe 3 Crosfields 4
FINAL
(1st April at Trafford)
Barnton 3 Crosfields 1

DIVISION ONE CONSTITUTION 2003-04

BARNTON . . . . Townfield, Townfield Lane, Barnton, Northwich, Cheshire . . . . None
BOLLINGTON ATHLETIC . . . . . Recreation Ground, Adlington Road, Bollington, Macclesfield, Cheshire . . . . None
BROADHEATH CENTRAL . . . . Viaduct Road, Broadheath, Altrincham, Cheshire 0161 928 5849
CHEADLE HEATH NOMADS . . . . . The Heath, Norbreck Avenue, Norbreck Avenue, Cheadle, Stockport 0161 282 6574
CREWE . . . . Cumberland Sports Ground, Thomas Street, Crewe, Cheshire 01270 537913
CROSFIELDS . . . . Crosfields Recreation Ground, Hood Lane, Great Sankey, Warrington, Cheshire 01925 411730
DATEN . . . . Culcheth Sports Ground, Charnock Road, Culcheth, Warrington, Cheshire 01925 763096
GARSWOOD UNITED . . . . The Wooders, Simms Lane End, Garswood Road, Garswood, near Wigan, Lancashire 01744 892258
GOLBORNE SPORTS . . . . Stone Cross Road, Lowton, Lancashire 01942 510161
KNUTSFORD . . . . Manchester Road, Knutsford, Cheshire . . . . None
LINOTYPE . . . . British Airways Club, Clay Lane, Timperley, Altrincham, Cheshire 0161 980 7354
MIDDLEWICH TOWN . . . . Seddon Street, Middlewich, Cheshire 01606 835842
PILKINGTON . . . . Ruskin Drive, St Helens, Merseyside 01744 22893
POYNTON . . . . London Road North, Poynton, Cheshire 01625 875765
RYLANDS . . . . Gorsey Lane, Warrington, Cheshire 01925 625700
STYAL . . . . Altrincham Road, Styal, Wilmslow, Cheshire 01625 529303

Padgate St Oswalds are relegated to Division Two replaced by Bollington Athletic and Golborne Sports. Chorlton Town have withdrawn.

	Barnton Res.	Bollington Athletic	Cheadle Heath Nmds Res.	Crewe Res.	Garswood United Res.	Golborne Sports	Linotype Res.	Lostock Gralam	Malpas	Middlewich Town Res.	Pilkington Res.	Poynton Res.	Rylands Res.	Trafford Res.	Warrington Borough	Whitchurch Alport
Barnton Res.		2-2	4-1	1-1	1-3	1-4	1-4	1-1	0-1	0-3	1-0	4-1	3-0	0-1	0-5	0-0
Bollington Athletic	6-2		4-2	2-3	6-0	1-3	5-1	2-1	2-2	0-2	2-1	3-0	2-3	3-0	3-1	6-0
Cheadle Heath Nomads Res.	2-2	3-5	D	1-2	5-0	2-3	0-2	1-3	1-1	1-5	3-3	5-4	2-2	1-3	2-4	0-5
Crewe Res.	2-0	1-2	1-5	I	3-3	0-2	0-1	2-5	1-5	2-1	0-0	1-2	1-2	2-3	6-1	4-3
Garswood United Res.	3-2	0-5	1-2	0-1	V	1-4	1-0	0-4	1-2	2-0	1-6	0-1	0-4	1-3	2-1	3-2
Golborne Sports	4-0	1-1	5-5	4-0	13-1	I	8-1	2-1	2-0	0-1	3-3	4-1	1-2	7-1	4-2	
Linotype Res.	5-0	1-4	4-1	1-1	1-0	0-1	S	1-2	3-2	4-2	0-1	5-1	3-1	3-1	3-1	4-3
Lostock Gralam	1-0	1-3	2-1	4-2	2-2	0-3	1-0	I	3-0	1-3	3-3	1-2	3-2	2-0	1-1	0-0
Malpas	3-0	1-1	4-1	3-1	4-0	1-6	0-3		O	1-2	3-1	0-1	3-0	1-0	2-0	0-0
Middlewich Town Res.	4-1	0-5	2-1	2-2	1-1	1-5	1-1	2-2	0-1	N	2-0	1-0	1-2	0-0	0-1	2-1
Pilkington Res.	2-0	0-3	5-2	5-0	3-2	1-2	2-3	3-3	0-1	2-1		2-1	4-0	4-0	0-1	1-2
Poynton Res.	2-0	2-4	5-0	1-1	9-0	0-4	1-5	2-0	0-5	2-0	4-3	T	5-1	1-1	2-3	2-1
Rylands Res.	3-2	0-4	3-2	3-3	1-0	0-4	1-2	1-0	0-1	2-2	0-2		W	1-3	1-4	0-3
Trafford Res.	2-2	1-2	2-0	6-1	1-1	0-0	2-3	5-1	2-3	4-1	2-3	1-2	0-2	O	0-1	4-0
Warrington Borough	4-1	2-1	7-1	4-0	2-1	0-2	1-2	2-2	3-0	3-4	0-5	4-4	1-1	0-1		2-2
Whitchurch Alport	4-1	3-3	9-0	0-1	4-0	0-1	4-0	1-2	0-0	4-2	1-2	2-1	5-1	5-4	1-2	

Division Two	P	W	D	L	F	A	Pts
Golborne Sports	30	23	5	2	96	28	74
Bollington Athletic	30	20	5	5	92	39	65
Malpas	30	17	6	7	60	26	57
Linotype Res.	30	18	2	10	65	54	56
Trafford Res.	30	15	6	9	63	37	51
Warrington Borough	30	14	6	10	56	48	48
Middlewich Town Res.	30	14	5	11	49	48	47
Lostock Gralam	30	12	8	10	52	52	44
Whitchurch Alport	30	12	7	11	70	51	43
Poynton Res.	30	12	6	12	67	62	42
Pilkington Res.	30	11	6	13	55	51	39
Crewe Res.	30	8	7	15	45	72	31
Rylands Res.	30	7	5	18	33	73	26
Barnton Res.	30	4	6	20	32	74	18
Cheadle Heath Nomads Res.	30	4	5	21	53	102	17
Garswood United Res.	30	4	5	21	28	98	17

DIVISION TWO CUP

FIRST ROUND
Cheadle Heath Nomads Res. 2 **Crewe Res. 7**
Garswood United Res. 0 **Bollington Athletic 2**
Golborne 5 Barnton Res. 0
Lostock G. 2 **Rylands Res. 5**
Middlewich Town Res. 0 **Poynton Res. 3**
Pilkington Res. 0 **Malpas 5**
Trafford Res. 0 **Warrington Borough 1**
Whitchurch Alport 2 **Linotype Res. 5**

QUARTER-FINALS
Bollington Athletic 0 **Golborne Sports 6**
Linotype Res. 1 **Malpas 3**
Rylands Res. 3 Poynton Res. 2
Warrington Borough 2 **Crewe Res. 3**

SEMI-FINALS
Malpas 1 **Golborne Sports 2**
Crewe Res. 2 Rylands Res. 1

FINAL
(23rd March at Trafford)
Golborne Sports 5 Crewe Res. 0

FIRST ROUND
Barnton Res. 0 **Daten 4**, Broadheath Central 0 **Lostock Gralam 1**, Cheadle Heath Res. 0 **Knutsford 6**, Garswood Res. 1 **Whitchurch Alport 4**, Middlewich Res. 0 **Chorlton Town 4**, Pilkington 0 **Rylands 2**, **Styal 5** Padgate 1, Trafford Res. 2 **Pilkington Res. 4**

QUARTER-FINALS
Daten 1 **Rylands 6**, **Lostock Gralam 1** Chorlton Town 0, Pilkington Res. 0 **Knutsford 3**, **Styal 6** Whitchurch Alport 1

SEMI-FINALS
Knutsford 1 **Styal 3**, Lostock Gralam 0 **Rylands 1**
FINAL
(9th April at Trafford)
Styal 3 Rylands 1

PRESIDENT'S CUP
(Teams eliminated in First Round of divisional cups)

WWW.NLNEWSDESK.CO.UK

DIVISION TWO CONSTITUTION 2003-04

CHEADLE TOWN RESERVES ...... Park Road Stadium, Park Road, Cheadle, Stockport, Cheshire 0161 428 2510
CLUB AZ .... t.b.a. .... t.b.a.
CURZON ASHTON RESERVES .... National Park, Katherine Street, Ashton-under-Lyne, Lancashire .... 0161 330 6033 / 6445
GAMESLEY .... t.b.a. .... t.b.a.
LOSTOCK GRALAM............. Slow and Easy Hotel, Manchester Road, Lostock Gralam, Cheshire.
MALPAS .... Malpas & District Sports Club, Oxheys, Wrexham Road, Malpas, Cheshire 01948 860662
NANTWICH TOWN RESERVES ...... Jackson Avenue, Nantwich, Cheshire. 01270 621771
PADGATE ST OSWALDS ..... Bennetts Recreation Ground, Station Road, Padgate, Warrington, Cheshire 01925 812007
SIDAC SPORTS .... Wheatsheaf Avenue, St Helens, Lancashire .... None
TRAFFORD RESERVES............ Shawe View, Pennybridge Lane, Flixton, Urmston, Manchester.... 0161 747 1727. Club: 0161 749 8217
WARRINGTON BOROUGH............ Cantilever Park, Loushers Lane, Warrington, Cheshire........ 01925 653044. Club: 01925 631932
WHITCHURCH ALPORT............. Yockings Park, Blackpark Road, Whitchurch, Shropshire........ 01948 667415
WINSFORD UNITED RESERVES .... Barton Stadium, Kingsway, Winsford, Cheshire .... 01606 593021. Club: 01606 861980
WITTON ALBION RESERVES ...... Wincham Park, Chapel Street, Wincham, Northwich, Cheshire.. 01606 43008. Club: 01606 47117

Bollington Athletic and Golborne Sports are promoted to Division One replaced by Padgate St Oswalds. Linotype Reserves, Middlewich Town Reserves, Poynton Reserves, Pilkington Reserves, Crewe Reserves, Rylands Reserves, Barnton Reserves, Cheadle Heath Nomads Reserves and Garswood United Reserves switch to a newly formed reserve division. Newcomers are Cheadle Town Reserves, Curzon Ashton Reserves (both North West Counties League), Club AZ, Gamesley (Hope Valley League), Nantwich Town Reserves, Sidac Sports (Warrington & District League), Winsford United Reserves and Witton Albion Reserves.

MIDLAND ALLIANCE

	Barwell	Biddulph Vics	Boldmere SM	Bridgnorth	Causeway Utd	Chasetown	Cradley Town	Grosvenor Pk	Halesowen H.	Ludlow Town	Oadby Town	Oldbury Utd	Pelsall Villa	Quorn	Rushall Olym.	Shifnal Town	Stafford Town	Stourbridge	Stratford T.	Studley	Wednesfield	Willenhall
Barwell		4-1	3-0	0-0	0-0	1-4	3-1	1-1	2-1	1-0	0-1	2-2	1-0	0-4	2-0	1-3	0-1	1-1	1-0		2-0	4-3
Biddulph Victoria	2-2		2-0	1-0	1-3	2-1	2-1	1-1	4-2	2-1	2-2	0-0	1-2	1-3	0-2	1-4	1-0	2-1	1-2	1-0	3-1	1-0
Boldmere St Michaels	2-0	1-0		2-1	1-2	0-1	2-0	2-2	2-0	0-4	0-4	0-2	1-4	1-1	0-3	3-0	4-2	0-2	0-1	1-5	4-0	3-0
Bridgnorth Town	1-2	0-1	0-6		0-2	1-3	1-0	3-1	1-2	2-1	1-2	2-3	1-2	2-0	0-0	0-2	2-0	2-0	0-2	0-2	4-0	2-2
Causeway United	4-3	1-2	4-1			2-1	2-0	0-2	1-1	0-1	0-3	2-1	1-0	5-2	1-2	2-2	1-3	0-4	0-1	1-4	3-0	3-3
Chasetown	4-2	2-2	2-2	0-2	3-0		0-0	2-4	2-2	5-4	3-0	2-0	0-3	0-3	0-2	2-1	1-1	0-1	1-0	2-1	8-0	1-3
Cradley Town	1-3	1-0	0-5	2-2	1-0	0-2		0-0	2-1	1-3	0-3	2-2	0-2	1-3	2-1	1-3	1-1	1-2	1-0	2-3	3-0	0-2
Grosvenor Park	2-1	1-0	0-0	6-0	5-2	3-0	1-3		3-0	1-1	1-5	4-2	6-2	0-2	2-1	1-1	1-1	1-2	1-0	2-3	3-0	1-2
Halesowen Harriers	1-3	1-2	0-2	1-2	0-3	0-2	2-2	0-3		1-1	2-5	0-5	1-1	0-3	1-3	2-1	1-2	0-3	1-3	2-3	4-0	1-2
Ludlow Town	3-2	0-1	1-0	1-1	1-2	0-1	3-2	1-2	0-1		1-2	1-5	2-0	1-2	0-0	2-2	5-1	1-2	0-7	2-3	8-0	2-2
Oadby Town	3-2	4-1	2-1	1-0	2-5	3-2	3-1	1-4	3-1	3-2		2-2	1-0	2-0	2-0	3-0	1-2	0-3	0-3	2-0	4-0	2-3
Oldbury United	0-4	1-0	1-1	2-0	2-1	3-0	2-0	2-4	5-3	1-0	2-1		2-3	2-0	4-6	3-0	2-4	0-3	0-1	0-0	4-0	2-3
Pelsall Villa	2-3	1-1	1-3	2-2	1-1	0-3	1-1	0-0	4-0	0-1	0-4	0-1		2-7	0-2	4-2	1-5	2-2	2-5	1-1	1-2	1-1
Quorn	3-1	3-2	4-1	5-1	4-1	1-2	0-0	3-0	4-1	3-0	1-1	1-3	2-2		1-1	8-0	9-2	1-1	2-1	4-1	6-0	0-3
Rushall Olympic	2-1	2-1	1-0	4-1	2-1	4-2	1-0	4-0	1-1	1-2	2-0	4-1	1-1	2-1		1-0	1-0	2-1	0-3	2-1	4-0	0-4
Shifnal Town	2-0	3-0	0-3	2-2	0-1	2-2	0-2	1-4	2-2	2-4	0-1	1-5	1-3	2-2	0-2		2-1	1-3	0-2	1-2	2-0	1-2
Stafford Town	1-3	2-3	0-1	1-2	1-3	2-4	4-2	2-0	3-1	4-1	1-3	1-1	0-2	1-5	1-2	0-0		1-3	2-1	0-2	1-2	0-4
Stourbridge	0-0	4-0	1-0	3-0	2-0	3-1	2-1	3-1	5-2	4-0	1-0	5-1	1-1	2-0	1-1				0-1	0-0	2-0	1-0
Stratford Town	3-1	6-0	3-0	4-1	4-2	2-2	5-0	1-1	2-1	1-0	2-0	1-2	6-1	3-2	1-2	3-2	2-2	1-1		4-2	8-0	2-0
Studley	4-2	1-0	3-0	3-1	4-2	0-2	2-1	4-1	3-2	3-0	1-0	0-2	8-2	5-1	0-5	3-1	1-1	2-1	1-2		6-0	1-3
Wednesfield	1-4	0-3	1-3	1-3	0-4	0-3	2-3	0-7	2-0	0-3	0-6	1-6	1-7	0-3	1-0	2-3	0-10	0-4	1-7			0-4
Willenhall Town	1-2	3-0	3-1	2-0	3-1	4-1	2-0	3-0	2-0	2-2	1-1	2-2	3-1	2-3	2-2	0-1	3-0	1-1	1-2	2-0	5-0	

		P	W	D	L	F	A	Pts
Stourbridge		42	31	8	3	96	27	101
Rushall Olympic	-3	42	31	6	5	94	37	96
Stratford Town		42	29	6	7	105	38	93
Oadby Town		42	26	7	9	87	52	85
Quorn		42	25	9	8	115	55	84
Willenhall Town		42	23	10	9	91	47	79
Studley		42	24	6	12	97	58	78
Oldbury United		42	22	7	13	88	58	73
Chasetown		42	20	8	14	79	64	68
Grosvenor Park		42	19	10	13	81	58	67
Causeway United		42	18	5	19	70	73	59
Barwell		42	17	7	18	70	68	58
Biddulph Victoria		42	17	6	19	51	69	57
Boldmere St Michaels		42	16	5	21	59	63	53
Ludlow Town		42	12	8	22	63	76	44
Bridgnorth Town		42	11	9	22	48	79	42
Stafford Town		42	11	8	23	61	93	41
Pelsall Villa		42	10	11	21	64	97	41
Cradley Town		42	8	7	27	43	87	31
Shifnal Town		42	6	7	29	43	93	25
Halesowen Harriers		42	4	6	32	44	107	18
Wednesfield		42	4	0	38	19	169	12

Midland Alliance club details can be found overleaf

LEAGUE CUP

FIRST ROUND

Barwell 1 Causeway United 1

Causeway United 2 Barwell 0 *replay*

Biddulph Victoria 1 Shifnal Town 1

Shifnal Town 3 **Biddulph Victoria** 5

replay aet

Quorn 4 Halesowen Harriers 1

Rushall Olympic 0 **Stourbridge** 2

Stratford Town 4 Cradley Town 1

Wednesfield 2 **Boldmere St Michaels** 5

SECOND ROUND

Bridgnorth Town 0 **Stratford Town** 3

Causeway United 3 Boldmere St Michaels 2

Chasetown 3 Oadby Town 2

Grosvenor Park 3 Oldbury United 0

Quorn 4 Biddulph Victoria 1

Stafford Town 0 **Ludlow Town** 1

Stourbridge 3 Pelsall Villa 1

Studley 4 Willenhall Town 0

QUARTER-FINALS

Chasetown 1 **Causeway United** 3

Ludlow Town 3 **Grosvenor Park** 4

Stourbridge 1 **Stratford Town** 4

Studley 2 Quorn 1

SEMI-FINALS

(played over two legs)

Grosvenor Park 1 Causeway United 1,

Causeway United 1 Grosvenor Park 0

Stratford Town 2 Studley 0,

Studley 1 **Stratford Town** 0

FINAL

(7th May at Oldbury United)

Causeway United 0 **Stratford Town** 1 *aet*

MIDLAND ALLIANCE CONSTITUTION 2003-04

ALVECHURCH. . . . . Lye Meadow, Redditch Road, Alvechurch, Worcestershire 0121 445 2929
BARWELL. . . . . Kirkby Road, Barwell, Leicestershire 01455 843067
BIDDULPH VICTORIA . . . . Tunstall Road, Knypersley, Stoke-on-Trent, Staffordshire. 01782 522737
BOLDMERE ST MICHAELS . . . . Church Road, Boldmere, Sutton Coldfield, West Midlands . . . . 0121 384 7531 / 373 4435
BRIDGNORTH TOWN . . . . Crown Meadow, Innage Lane, Bridgnorth, Shropshire 01746 762747
CAUSEWAY UNITED . . . . Halesowen Town FC, The Grove, Old Hawne Lane, Halesowen, West Midlands 0121 550 2179
CHASETOWN. . . . . The Scholars Ground, Church Street, Chasetown, Walsall, Staffordshire 01543 682222
COALVILLE TOWN. . . . . Owen Street Sports Ground, Owen Street, Coalville, Leicestershire 01530 833365
CRADLEY TOWN . . . . Beeches View Avenue, Cradley, Halesowen, West Midlands 01384 569658
GROSVENOR PARK . . . . The Red Lion Ground, Somerfield Road, Leamore, Bloxwich, West Midlands . . . . 01922 400600 / 405835
LUDLOW TOWN . . . . Coors Stadium, Bromfield Road, Ludlow, Shropshire 01584 876000
OADBY TOWN . . . . Invicta Park, Wigston Road, Oadby, Leicestershire 0116 271 5728
OLDBURY UNITED. . . . . The Cricketts, York Road, Oldbury, Warley, West Midlands 0121 559 5564
PELSALL VILLA . . . . The Bush Ground, Walsall Road, Heath End, Pelsall, West Midlands . . . . 01922 692748 / 682018
QUORN . . . . Farley Road, Quorn, Leicestershire 01509 620232
RACING CLUB WARWICK . . . . Townsend Meadow, Hampton Road, Warwick, Warwickshire 01926 495786
ROCESTER. . . . . Riversfield, Mill Street, Rocester, Staffordshire 01889 590463
RUSHALL OLYMPIC. . . . . Dales Lane, off Daw End Lane, Rushall, Walsall, West Midlands 01922 641021
STAFFORD TOWN . . . . Stafford Rangers FC, Aston Fields Road, Stafford, Staffordshire 01785 602430
STOURBRIDGE . . . . War Memorial Athletic Ground, High Street, Amblecote, Stourbridge, West Midlands. 01384 394040
STRATFORD TOWN . . . . Masons Road, Stratford-on-Avon, Warkickshire 01789 297479
STUDLEY . . . . BKL Sports Ground, Abbeyfield Drive, off Birmingham Road, Studley, Warwickshire. 01527 853817
WESTFIELDS . . Moor House Stadium, Hereford, Herefordshire *(*Or groundshare at Stourport Swifts FC if ground not ready)*. . . . . t.b.a.
WILLENHALL TOWN . . . . Noose Lane, Willenhall, West Midlands. 01902 636586

Halesowen Harriers have withdrawn. Shifnal Town are relegated to the Midland Combination from which Alvechurch are promoted. Wednesfield are relegated to the West Midlands Regional League which promotes Westfields. Other newcomers are Rocester and Racing Club Warwick who are both relegated from the Southern League, and Coalville Town, promoted from the Leicestershire Senior League.

JOE McGORRIAN CUP
(Midland Alliance champions v Midland Alliance Cup holders)

(3rd August at Rushall Olympic)
Stourbridge 2 Rushall Olympic 0

TONY ALLDEN MEMORIAL CUP
(Midland Combination champions v Midland Combination Challenge Cup holders)

(4th March at Highgate United)
Grosvenor Park 2 Coventry Sphinx 0

MIDLAND COMBINATION PREMIER DIVISION CONSTITUTION 2003-04

ALVESTON . . . . Home Guard Club, Main Street, Tiddington, Stratford-upon-Avon, Warwickshire 01789 297718
BOLEHALL SWIFTS. . . . . Rene Road, Bolehall, Tamworth, Staffordshire. 01827 62637
BROCTON . . . . Cannock Sports Stadium, Pye Green Road, Cannock, Staffordshire. 01543 571898
CASTLE VALE KINGS HEATH . . . . . . Vale Stadium, Farnborough Road, Castle Vale, Birmingham 0121 747 6969
COLESHILL TOWN. . . . . Pack Meadow, Packington Lane, Coleshill, Warwickshire 01675 463259
CONTINENTAL STAR . . . . Red Lion Ground, Walsall Road, Walsall, West Midlands 01922 405835
COVENTRY MARCONI . . . . . . Marconi Sports Ground, Allard Way, Copsewood, Coventry, West Midlands 024 7645 1157
COVENTRY SPHINX . . . . Sphinx Drive, Siddeley Avenue, Stoke Aldermoor, Coventry, West Midlands 024 7645 1361
DUDLEY SPORTS. . . . . Dudley Employees S&S, Hillcrest Avenue, Brierley Hill, West Midlands 01384 826420
FECKENHAM . . . . Redditch United FC, Valley Stadium, Bromsgrove Rd, Redditch, Worcestershire 01527 67450
HIGHGATE UNITED . . . . The Coppice, Tythe Barn Lane, Shirley, Solihull, West Midlands 0121 744 4194
LEAMINGTON. . . . . New Windmill Ground, Harbury Lane, Whitnash, Leamington Spa, Warwickshire 07866 348712
MASSEY-FERGUSON . . . . Banner Lane, Tile Hill, Coventry, West Midlands . . . . 024 7669 4400x2084. Club: 024 7646 5838
MEIR KA . . . . Kings Park, Hilderstone Road, Meir Heath, Stoke-on-Trent, Staffordshire 01782 388465
NUNEATON GRIFF . . . . The Pingles Stadium, Avenue Road, Nuneaton, Warwickshire . . . . 024 7637 0688. Club: 024 7673 5344
PERSHORE TOWN . . . . King George V Playing Fields, King George's Way, Pershore, Worcestershire 01386 556902
ROMULUS . . . . Sutton Coldfield Town FC, Central Ground, Coles Lane, Sutton Coldfield, West Midlands 0121 3547 2997
RUGBY TOWN . . . . Rugby Lions RFC, Webb Ellis Road, Rugby, Warwickshire 01788 334466
SHIFNAL TOWN . . . . Phoenix Park, Coppice Green Lane, Shifnal, Shropshire 01952 463667
SOUTHAM UNITED. . . . . Banbury Road, Southam, Leamington Spa, Warwickshire. 01926 812091
WEST MIDLANDS POLICE . . . . Tally Ho! Sports Ground, Pershore Road, Edgbaston, Birmingham, ... 0121 626 8228

Alveston are promoted to the Midland Alliance replaced by Shifnal Town. Cheslyn Hay, Fernhill County Sports and Handrahan Timbers have resigned. Dudley Sports are promoted from Division One. Brocton arrive from the Midland League. Kings Heath changed their name to Castle Vale Kings Heath during the course of the season.

MIDLAND COMBINATION

	Alvechurch	Alveston	Bolehall Sw.	Castle Vale	Cheslyn Hay	Coleshill T.	Cont. Star	Cov. Marconi	Cov. Sphinx	Feckenham	Fernhill CS	Handrahan T.	Highgate Utd	Leamington	Massey-Ferg.	Meir KA	Nun. Griff	Pershore T.	Romulus	Rugby Town	Southam Utd	WM Police
Alvechurch		4-2	6-1	1-0	10-1	3-2	3-2	2-0	3-3	1-1	1-2	2-1	4-2	1-2	6-0	0-1	1-0	3-1	2-2	4-0	8-3	3-2
Alveston	1-5		0-2	0-2	3-1	2-0	0-5	0-3	3-2	1-1	1-4	2-3	3-2	0-0	3-1	5-1	2-4	0-3	0-1	4-0		1-1
Bolehall Swifts	2-3	3-2		2-0	3-0	2-1	4-4	0-2	6-2	2-0	0-2	2-0	2-0	1-0	2-0	1-0	3-1	2-1	2-3	3-1	5-1	3-0
Castle Vale Kings Heath	1-3	6-5	4-1	P	2-2	0-2	1-0	0-2	3-2	3-0	0-2	2-1	4-1	1-4	1-1	0-1	1-3	4-1	0-1	4-1	3-1	4-1
Cheslyn Hay	0-4	2-2	0-1	0-7	R	2-1	2-2	0-3	0-6	1-6	0-4	1-2	1-2	0-3	2-3	2-2	4-1	0-2	1-2	3-2	3-3	0-3
Coleshill Town	0-3	2-1	2-3	0-0	1-1	E	1-1	1-5	0-3	3-1	0-2	1-1	0-2	0-3	4-2	3-2	2-1	1-3	3-0	0-4	1-2	1-1
Continental Star	0-3	5-2	0-2	0-3	2-3	2-1	M	0-2	2-0	1-1	0-1	5-1	2-4	2-4	2-3	1-4	3-0	3-2	1-3	8-1	1-2	
Coventry Marconi	2-4	4-1	2-0	4-1	5-2	1-0	2-0	I	1-2	1-1	4-1	0-0	1-0	0-1	3-4	4-2	0-1	2-0	1-2	0-1	5-0	5-0
Coventry Sphinx	0-0	3-1	1-0	2-1	2-0	3-0	2-2	1-0	E	4-0	5-0	3-2	3-2	2-4	2-4	2-3	0-0	0-4	1-3	5-8	6-2	1-0
Feckenham	4-1	4-1	0-2	1-3	4-3	0-1	3-4	0-4	0-1	R	0-3	1-0	0-1	2-3	4-1	2-3	3-1	4-3	1-5	1-1	6-1	0-1
Fernhill County Sports	0-5	2-2	1-4	3-2	3-1	2-0	5-1	1-1	1-0	4-1		2-2	2-1	0-5	2-0	0-3	1-0	4-2	2-1	1-2	0-0	1-1
Handrahan Timbers	1-2	4-2	2-1	2-2	1-1	0-1	1-1	1-2	1-2	3-1	4-2	D	0-1	0-1	1-1	2-1	6-1	0-4	0-3	1-1	0-1	3-2
Highgate United	1-4	4-0	1-2	3-2	7-0	2-0	3-1	2-1	5-3	1-2	0-0	2-0	I	0-0	4-2	1-3	0-1	4-1	3-2	0-3	6-3	2-0
Leamington	3-1	2-2	1-2	0-3	5-1	1-0	3-5	0-0	1-1	1-2	1-0	2-1	1-1	V	3-2	1-2	2-0	4-3	0-0		5-0	5-1
Massey-Ferguson	2-2	1-3	0-2	3-1	3-1	1-1	4-2	3-4	1-4	2-3	1-1	1-2	0-6	2-6	I	3-4	2-1	4-0	1-3	2-0	2-0	2-1
Meir KA	1-3	2-3	1-1	1-1	6-1	1-2	2-0	3-1	2-4	0-1	2-4	3-0	0-4	1-1	5-1	S	1-4	3-2	2-1	4-0	4-3	5-0
Nuneaton Griff	0-2	0-1	1-0	2-3	7-1	1-1	3-1	1-1	2-0	2-0	1-0	4-3	1-2	4-3	1-3	1-2	I	5-2	0-2	1-1	1-0	1-0
Pershore Town	0-2	7-2	0-2	1-1	1-1	2-3	1-1	4-3	0-2	1-0	1-3	0-2	1-3	1-2	1-2	5-3	3-3	O	5-3	2-0	6-0	3-1
Romulus	1-1	4-1	6-1	2-2	6-0	2-3	0-0	0-3	5-2	2-1	1-0	0-3	2-2	5-0	2-4				N	2-0	6-0	3-1
Rugby Town	0-1	5-0	1-1	2-0	8-2	3-1	2-2	1-0	0-3	1-1	3-1	1-1	1-1	5-0	6-0	1-0	2-1	0-3			6-0	1-0
Southam United	0-8	3-1	0-1	0-3	2-0	3-2	0-8	0-3	1-6	0-1	1-0	0-4	0-9	1-1	1-7	2-1	1-2	2-3	0-3	1-3		1-4
West Midlands Police	1-1	2-0	2-1	3-2	3-1	2-4	2-2	1-1	0-1	1-0	1-1	1-0	1-7	3-2	3-3	3-0	2-3	1-1	3-4	1-1	1-3	

Premier Division	P	W	D	L	F	A	Pts
Alvechurch	42	30	7	5	126	48	97
Coventry Marconi	42	29	5	8	94	37	92
Leamington	42	27	9	6	92	48	90
Bolehall Swifts	42	27	5	10	82	53	86
Romulus	42	24	5	13	107	58	77
Rugby Town	42	22	10	10	90	52	76
Coventry Sphinx	42	23	6	13	95	72	75
Fernhill County Sports	42	21	8	13	74	59	71
Highgate United -3	42	23	3	16	95	67	69
Meir KA	42	21	6	15	94	75	69
Castle Vale Kings Heath	42	19	6	17	86	66	63
Nuneaton Griff	42	17	3	22	66	80	54
Continental Star	42	14	9	19	86	88	51
Coleshill Town	42	13	9	20	54	68	48
Pershore Town	42	13	7	22	74	86	46
Massey-Ferguson	42	13	7	22	85	112	46
Feckenham	42	12	6	24	66	85	42
West Midlands Police	42	11	9	22	56	87	42
Handrahan Timbers	42	11	8	23	57	73	41
Alveston	42	9	7	26	66	114	34
Southam United	42	7	2	33	43	162	23
Cheslyn Hay	42	4	7	31	47	145	19

Premier Division club details opposite on page 92

Reserve Division	P	W	D	L	F	A	Pts
Tamworth Res.	32	22	2	8	97	37	68
Worcester City Res.	32	20	5	7	59	41	65
Boldmere St M. Res.	32	19	7	6	68	39	64
Solihull Boro. Res.	32	18	8	6	71	34	62
Quorn Res.	32	17	7	8	67	42	58
Rushall Olym. Res.	32	16	8	8	60	33	56
Oadby Town Res. -3	32	17	8	7	57	50	56
Gresley Rovers Res.	32	14	10	8	75	56	52
Hinckley United Res.	32	12	11	9	53	40	47
Shepshed Dyn. Res.	32	10	5	17	44	57	35
Rugby United Res.	32	9	7	16	49	68	34
Atherstone U. Res. -3	32	9	8	15	43	79	32
Bedworth Utd Res.	32	7	8	17	42	62	29
Chasetown Res.	32	7	7	18	39	72	28
Redditch United Res.	32	5	8	19	39	82	23
Highgate U. Res. -3	32	5	8	19	40	60	20
Barwell	32	3	7	22	27	78	16

WILLIE KNIBBS CHALLENGE CUP
(Premier and Division One clubs)

FIRST ROUND
Burntwood Town 4 **Coleshill Town** 6 *aet*
Cadbury Athletic 2 **Alvechurch** 4 *aet*
Castle Vale Kings Heath 1 **Cheslyn Hay** 1 *aet (7-8p)*
Continental Star 6 Old Hill Town 0
Fairfield Villa 4 Feckenham 2 *aet*
Handrahan Timbers 2 Stockingford 1
Holly Lane 3 Nuneaton Griff 2
Polesworth NW 1 **Highgate United** 2
Southam United 1 **Massey-Ferguson** 4
SECOND ROUND
Blackheath 1 **Meir KA** 3
Bloxwich Town 2 **Coleshill Town** 3
Bolehall Swifts 2 Thimblemill REC 1
Continental Star 3 **Alvechurch** 4 *aet*
Cov. Marconi 1 **Pilkington XXX** 2 *aet*
Coventry Sphinx 0 **Fairfield Villa** 2

Fernhill County Sports 2 Cheslyn Hay 0
Kenilworth Town 3 Handsaker 0
Knowle 2 Brownhills Town 1
Leamington 2 Alveston 0
Northfield 0 **Handrahan Timbers** 2
Pershore Town 4 Dudley Sports 0
Romulus 2 Massey-Ferguson 1
Rugby Town 1 **Highgate United** 2
West Midlands Police 1 **Loughborough** 0
Wilmcote Sports/Social 4 Holly Lane 2
THIRD ROUND
Fairfield Villa 1 **Highgate United** 3
Fernhill County Sports 0 **Alvechurch** 4
Handrahan Timbers 4 Kenilworth 2
Knowle 2 Bolehall Swifts 0
Leamington 5 Meir KA 2
Pershore Town 1 West Mids Police 0
Pilkington XXX 3 Coleshill Town 1

Romulus 3 **Wilmcote Sports & Social** 1
(ineligible player – Romulus expelled)
QUARTER-FINALS
Alvechurch 3 Handrahan Timbers 2 *aet*
Highgate United 1 **Pilkington XXX** 3
Pershore Town 2 **Leamington** 3
Wilmcote Sports & Social 1 Knowle 0
SEMI-FINALS
(played over two legs)
Alvechurch 2 Leamington 0,
Leamington 1 Alvechurch 1
Pilkington XXX 1 Wilmcote S&S 0,
Wilmcote S&S 4 Pilkington XXX 4
FINAL
(10th May at Moor Green)
Alvechurch 1 Pilkington XXX 1 *aet (5-4p)*

	Blackheath	Bloxwich Town	Brownhills Town	Burntwood Town	Cadbury Athletic	Dudley Sports	Fairfield Villa	Handsaker	Holly Lane	Kenilworth Town	Knowle	Loughborough	Northfield Town	Old Hill Town	Pilkington XXX	Polesworth N. Warwick	Stockingford AA	Thimblemill REC	Wilmcote Sp. & Social
Blackheath		3-3	0-3	5-1	2-1	0-5	0-2	1-1	0-1	3-3	0-1	0-2	1-6	5-1	3-2	3-0	1-2	2-2	3-3
Bloxwich Town	4-0		2-0	2-1	2-4	4-1	2-2	0-1	0-1	0-1	1-6	1-1	5-2	0-4	0-2	2-3	0-3	0-3	5-0
Brownhills Town	2-2	0-2		2-2	0-0	2-5	0-3	0-2	1-2	1-3	0-4	0-0	2-1	2-5	1-3	1-5	0-3	1-0	0-0
Burntwood Town	1-0	5-1	3-0	D	4-1	2-1	1-1	1-3	1-1	1-5	1-2	0-2	1-1	2-2	0-3	0-3	0-0	0-3	1-3
Cadbury Athletic	2-2	1-2	2-0	5-2	I	1-2	0-2	1-0	4-0	0-2	5-1	1-1	2-0	3-1	0-1	2-4	3-1	4-3	1-4
Dudley Sports	1-2	4-0	0-2	2-1	2-1	V	2-0	2-1	7-1	2-1	1-0	3-2	1-2	0-2	4-1	1-2	0-1	2-0	2-1
Fairfield Villa	1-5	3-2	2-0	0-1	3-1	0-5	I	3-3	3-1	7-0	2-0	0-0	2-0	3-2	0-2	3-1	2-5	1-0	1-0
Handsaker	1-0	2-0	2-1	1-3	3-2	1-2	0-1	S	1-0	0-2	0-0	1-0	2-0	3-0	0-5	0-1	1-2	0-0	2-3
Holly Lane	2-3	4-0	5-1	0-0	2-2	0-1	1-5	0-3	I	0-4	2-4	4-3	2-1	3-2	0-2	2-1	1-4	3-2	0-2
Kenilworth Town	2-2	2-1	3-0	2-4	4-2	3-4	2-2	4-0	3-2	O	3-5	1-1	1-4	4-2	2-4	1-0	0-2	2-3	0-1
Knowle	4-4	2-1	7-1	5-0	3-0	5-1	3-0	1-0	3-2	0-0	N	2-1	3-1	1-3	1-3	2-0	2-0	2-0	0-2
Loughborough	4-1	0-1	8-0	0-1	1-1	2-0	1-2	2-0	4-3	2-3	1-3		0-2	1-0	1-0	1-0	2-1	3-4	0-2
Northfield Town	3-4	2-1	4-1	0-0	4-1	1-5	1-2	4-2	0-1	1-0	1-2	3-2		3-3	2-4	3-3	1-4	1-1	2-0
Old Hill Town	1-5	3-2	1-1	0-2	0-1	3-1	1-1	1-1	4-1	5-1	0-0	4-4	2-5	O	2-0	3-1	1-6	2-1	2-0
Pilkington XXX	1-2	3-2	1-1	5-2	3-0	0-2	0-0	6-1	7-0	2-0	2-1	2-1	4-2	1-3	N	0-3	3-0	0-1	1-0
Polesworth North Warwick	0-0	1-3	1-0	2-1	0-1	0-1	4-0	2-0	1-0	1-2	1-3	0-1	3-1	4-0	3-0	E	3-4	0-6	0-1
Stockingford AA	2-1	5-0	3-2	2-0	4-3	3-1	4-1	6-4	7-1	2-2	3-0	3-0	1-1	6-1	0-3	1-0	E	1-1	1-3
Thimblemill REC	2-1	6-3	0-1	1-2	5-0	1-1	0-0	4-2	6-1	0-8	0-4	2-4	3-4	6-1	0-3	3-3			2-2
Wilmcote Sports & Social	1-3	2-5	2-2	5-0	2-1	1-2	5-2	4-1	2-1	0-0	1-3	5-2	0-3	3-0	1-7	3-1	1-2	2-3	

Division One

	P	W	D	L	F	A	Pts
Knowle	36	27	3	6	104	40	84
Stockingford AA	36	26	4	6	100	45	82
Pilkington XXX	36	23	5	8	92	48	74
Dudley Sports	36	24	1	11	78	47	73
Polesworth North Warwick	36	20	3	13	66	46	63
Fairfield Villa	36	18	7	11	61	53	61
Wilmcote Sports & Social	36	16	5	15	65	63	53
Northfield Town	36	15	4	17	72	71	49
Kenilworth Town	36	14	6	16	69	82	48
Blackheath	36	12	10	14	69	73	46
Loughborough	36	11	11	14	59	57	44
Thimblemill REC	36	11	10	15	69	67	43
Burntwood Town	36	11	9	16	49	69	42
Cadbury Athletic	36	11	6	19	55	72	39
Handsaker	36	11	6	19	39	64	39
Old Hill Town	36	10	8	18	70	83	38
Bloxwich Town	36	11	3	22	59	82	36
Holly Lane	36	10	4	22	54	101	34
Brownhills Town	36	5	7	24	31	98	22

PRESIDENT'S CUP

FIRST ROUND
Cadbury Ath 3 Bloxwich 1, Fairfield 0 **Thimblemill** 2
Handsaker 0 **Brownhills Town** 2

SECOND ROUND
Cadbury Athletic 4 Brownhills Town 2
Dudley Sports 3 Burntwood Town 2 *aet*
Kenilworth Town 3 Holly Lane 0
Northfield Town 2 **Wilmcote Sports & Social** 3
Old Hill 2 Blackheath 1, **Pilkington** 1 Loughborough 0
Polesworth North Warwick 2 Thimblemill REC 1
Stockingford AA 3 Knowle 0

QUARTER-FINALS
Dudley Sports 1 Kenilworth Town 0
Old Hill Town 1 Stockingford AA 0
Pilkington XXX 0 **Cadbury Athletic** 1
Wilmcote Sports & Social 1 **Polesworth North Warwick** 5

SEMI-FINALS
(played over two legs)
Cadbury 0 **Dudley Sports** 6, **Dudley Sports** 2 Cadbury 1
Polesworth 4 Old Hill Town 3, Old Hill 2 **Polesworth NW** 4

FINAL
(30th April at Rushall Olympic)
Polesworth North Warwick 4 **Dudley Sports** 5

DIVISION ONE CONSTITUTION 2003-04

BARNT GREEN SPARTAK .... Alvechurch FC, Lye Meadow, Redditch Road, Alvechurch, Worcestershire 0121 445 2929
BLACKHEATH .... Invensys Brook Compton Sports, Cakemore Road, Rowley Regis, West Midlands ..... 0121 698 3253 / 698 3256
BLOXWICH TOWN .... Abbey Park, Glastonbury Crescent, Mossley Estate, Bloxwich, West Midlands 01922 477640
BURNTWOOD TOWN .... Burntwood Memorial Institute, Rugeley Road, Burntwood, Staffordshire 01543 686308
CADBURY ATHLETIC .... Cadbury Rec, Bournville Lane, Bournville, Birmingham .. 0121 458 2000x3316 Club: 0121 454 4264
FAIRFIELD VILLA .... Recreation Road, Stourbridge Road, Fairfield, Bromsgrove, Worcestershire 01527 877049
HANDSAKER .... Hollyfields Centre Club Ltd, Woodacre Road, Erdington, Birmingham, West Midlands........... 0121 373 1018
KENILWORTH TOWN .... Gypsy Lane, off Council Lane, Kenilworth, Warwickshire 01926 850851
KNOWLE............................. Hampton Road, Knowle, Solihull, West Midlands 01564 779807
LITTLETON .... Five Acres, Pebworth Road, North Littleton, Evesham, Worcestershire .... None
LOUGHBOROUGH .... The Drome, Derby Road, Loughborough, Leicestershire 01509 610022
NORTHFIELD TOWN .... Shenley Lane, Northfield, Birmingham, West Midlands .... 0121 478 3900. Club: 0121 475 3870
OLD HILL TOWN .... Hingleys, Bluebell Road, Cradley Heath, West Midlands 01384 566827
PILKINGTON XXX ...... Triplex Sports Ground, Eckersall Road, Kings Norton, Birmingham, West Midlands 0121 458 4570
POLESWORTH NORTH WARWICK .... Hermitage Hill, Tamworth Road, Polesworth 01827 892482
STOCKINGFORD AA .... The Pavilion, Ansley Road, Stockingford, Nuneaton, Warwickshire 024 7638 7743
THIMBLEMILL REC. .... Thimblemill Road, Smethwick, Warley, West Midlands 0121 429 2459
WILMCOTE SPORTS & SOCIAL .. The Patch, Wilmcote SS Club, Aston Cantlow Rd, Wilmcote, Stratford-on-Avon......... 01789 297895

Dudley Sports are promoted to the Premier Division. Holly Lane have withdrawn. Barnt Green Spartak and Littleton are promoted from Division Two in place of relegated Brownhills Town.

	Archdale	Barnt Green Spartak	Cadbury Athletic Res.	Central Ajax	Chelmsley Town	Droitwich Spa	Earlswood Town	Enville Athletic	Fernhill County Sports Res.	Halfords	Handsworth United	Kenilworth Wardens	Leamington Hibernian	Littleton	West Hagley	West Midlands Police Res.
Archdale		0-8	1-5	3-0	4-3	2-3	3-2	1-1	0-1	2-1	3-2	n/a	3-2	2-3	0-0	1-0
Barnt Green Spartak	5-0		3-2	2-1	4-0	4-0	2-2	4-0	3-0	5-2	5-0	n/a	5-1	0-3	6-2	7-2
Cadbury Athletic Res.	2-2	0-1	D	4-1	6-4	4-1	2-2	0-0	0-0	0-2	1-2	1-0	2-2	1-1	1-0	1-0
Central Ajax	3-1	0-2	10-2	I	3-0	3-4	1-2	0-2	3-3	1-3	6-1	3-2	2-0	0-3	2-3	6-1
Chelmsley Town	1-1	1-3	1-3	0-1	V	1-3	0-3	1-2	1-3	1-2	2-2	1-0	1-2	0-4	1-1	2-5
Droitwich Spa	3-1	0-3	4-3	3-0	5-2	I	1-0	1-1	2-3	2-2	5-0	3-1	3-3	1-0	6-2	2-2
Earlswood Town	3-2	0-1	1-3	0-2	1-1	1-1	S	2-2	1-0	3-2	4-1	n/a	2-2	2-1	0-1	1-1
Enville Athletic	0-4	0-2	2-3	4-3	1-1	1-1	1-0	I	1-0	1-0	1-1	7-0	2-2	1-3	1-0	0-0
Fernhill County Sports Res.	2-2	2-2	4-1	3-1	1-2	0-0	2-0	0-2	O	1-3	1-2	2-7	0-2	2-1	1-1	1-1
Halfords	4-2	0-1	0-0	1-1	6-0	1-0	0-0	1-2	1-0	N	2-0	n/a	3-1	0-8	1-1	2-0
Handsworth United	4-1	5-2	3-1	3-2	2-5	1-4	0-0	2-1	4-2	1-2		1-5	2-0	0-6	1-1	1-2
Kenilworth Wardens	1-2	0-4	n/a	3-3	3-3	n/a	1-5	n/a	n/a	n/a	1-5	T	1-7	n/a	0-2	
Leamington Hibernian	4-0	1-1	1-5	0-0	2-2	0-1	1-0	3-4	2-1	2-0	n/a		W	5-3	3-1	
Littleton	4-2	3-2	6-1	1-2	2-1	3-1	2-0	4-0	5-3	0-3	4-0	n/a	1-1	O	3-0	2-3
West Hagley	2-1	1-1	0-0	2-1	3-3	2-5	1-0	1-3	1-0	0-1	3-1	5-3	0-2	3-1		1-0
West Midlands Police Res.	2-4	3-1	1-1	3-0	4-1	1-4	3-5	2-1	1-2	1-1	4-2	3-3	4-3	2-1	2-2	

Note – Kenilworth Wardens withdrew during the course of the season. Their results are shown above but are expunged from the league table

Division Two

		P	W	D	L	F	A	Pts
Barnt Green Spartak		28	20	4	4	85	31	64
Littleton		28	20	1	7	78	32	61
Droitwich Spa		28	14	7	7	65	47	49
Halfords		28	14	6	8	47	36	48
Fernhill County Sports Res.		28	11	6	11	49	44	39
Enville Athletic	-3	28	11	9	8	34	39	39
Cadbury Athletic Res.		28	10	8	10	54	56	38
West Midlands Police Res.		28	10	7	11	51	58	37
Earlswood Town		28	9	8	11	38	39	35
West Hagley		28	9	8	11	37	50	35
Leamington Hibernian		28	8	8	12	45	57	32
Archdale		28	9	5	14	48	70	32
Central Ajax	-3	28	9	3	16	55	56	27
Handsworth United	-9	28	9	4	15	43	72	22
Chelmsley Town		28	2	6	20	38	80	12

CHALLENGE VASE

FIRST ROUND
Kenilworth Wardens 4 Enville Athletic 1

SECOND ROUND
Archdale 0 **Barnt Green Spartak** 2
Central Ajax 0 **Littleton** 1
Droitwich Spa 3 West Midlands Police Res. 0
Fernhill County Sports Res. 1 **Earlswood Town** 3
Halfords 3 Kenilworth Wdns 2 *aet*
Handsworth Utd 2 **West Hagley** 1
(ineligible player – Handsworth United expelled)
Leamington Hibernian 3 Chelmsley Town 1 *aet*
Wilnecote Sports (scr) v **Cadbury Athletic Res.** (w/o)

QUARTER-FINALS
Barnt Green Spartak 5 Halfords 1 *aet*
Cadbury Athletic Res. 0 **Littleton** 5
Earlswood 2 Droitwich Spa 1
West Hagley 1 Leamington Hibernian 1 *aet (4-3p)*

SEMI-FINALS
(played over two legs)
Littleton 2 Earlswood Town 0, **Earlswood Town** 2 Littleton 0 *aet (4-3p)*
West Hagley 1 Barnt Green Spartak 1, **Barnt Green Spartak** 5 West Hagley 1

FINAL
(5th May at Studley)
Barnt Green Spartak 1 **Earlswood Town** 3

WWW.NLNEWSDESK.CO.UK

DIVISION TWO CONSTITUTION 2003-04

ARCHDALE . . . . Windermere Drive, Warndon, Worcester, Worcestershire 01905 451410
BROWNHILLS TOWN . . . . Holland Park, The Parade, Brownhills, Walsall, West Midlands 07951 518532
CADBURY ATHLETIC RESERVES . . . . Bournville Lane, Bournville, Birmingham . . . . 0121 458 2000x3316. Club: 0121 454 4264
CENTRAL AJAX . . . . Ajax Park, Hampton Road, Warwick, Warwickshire 01926 496295
CHELMSLEY TOWN . . . . The Pavilions, Coleshill Road, Marston Green, Birmingham, West Midlands 0121 779 5400
CONTINENTAL STAR RESERVES . . . . Holly Lane S & S Club, Holly Lane, Erdington, Birmingham 0121 373 0979
DROITWICH SPA . . . . Droitwich Spa Leisure Centre, Briar Mill, Droitwich, Worcestershire . . . . None
EARLSWOOD TOWN . . . . Malthouse Lane, Earlswood, Solihull, West Midlands 01564 703989
ENVILLE ATHLETIC . . . . Enville Athletic Club, Hall Drive, Enville, Stourbridge, West Midlands 01384 872368
FERNHILL HEATH SPORTS . . . . . Droitwich Spa Leisure Centre, Briar Mill, Droitwich, Worcestershire . . . . None
HANDSWORTH UNITED . . . . M & B Sports Ground, City Road, Edgbaston, Birmingham . . . . None
HEATHER ATHLETIC . . . . St John's Park, Ravenstone Road, Heather, Leicestershire 01530 263986
LEAMINGTON HIBERNIAN . . . Racing Club Warwick FC, Townsend Meadow, Hampton Road, Warwick 01926 495786
NEWHALL UNITED . . . . Hewfields Ground, St Johns Drive, Newhall, Swadlincote, Derbyshire 01283 551029
TIPTON TOWN RESERVES . . . . . Tipton Sports Academy, Wednesbury Oak Rd, Tipton, West Midlands 0121 502 5534. Club: 0121 556 5067
WELLESBOURNE . . . . Loxley Close Fields, Loxley Close, Wellesbourne, Warwickshire 01789 842646
WEST HAGLEY . . . . The Dell Stadium, Bryce Road, Pennsnett, Brierley Hill, West Midlands 01384 812943
WEST MIDLANDS POLICE RESERVES . . . Tally Ho!, Pershore Road, Edgbaston, Birmingham 0121 626 8228

Barnt Green Spartak and Littleton are promoted to Division One replaced by Brownhills Town. Wilnecote Sports resigned before start of season while Kenilworth Wardens during its course. Halfords return to Stratford Alliance. Wellesbourne, Newhall United, Tipton Town Reserves and Continental Star Reserves are promoted from Division Three. Newcomers are Heather Athletic (formerly Heather St Johns) from the Leicester & District League). Fernhill County Sports Reserves become Fernhill Heath Sports.

	Birchfield Oaklands	Birmingham United	Chasetown 'A'	Coleshill Town Res.	Continental Star Res.	Inkberrow	Kenilworth Town Res.	Knowle Res.	Massey-Ferguson Res.	Newhall United	Northfield Town Res.	Romulus Res.	Rugby Town Res.	Tipton Town Res.	Wellesbourne	Wilmcote Sports & Social
Birchfield Oaklands		4-2	3-2	3-5	2-1	0-5	4-3	1-3	3-3	3-3	2-1	0-1	4-1	5-0	0-6	1-6
Birmingham United	2-7	D	3-3	1-2	2-5	1-2	1-4	5-6	0-4	4-5	2-0	1-4	7-4	1-1	2-8	1-1
Chasetown 'A'	3-2	4-0	I	4-0	2-1	2-0	2-1	2-4	2-1	5-2	2-0	7-1	2-2	3-5	3-6	2-1
Coleshill Town Res.	2-1	0-1	1-3	V	2-2	2-1	5-1	1-1	1-4	0-2	2-2	9-0	3-2	0-2	1-3	2-1
Continental Star Res.	5-0	6-1	4-2	5-1	I	4-0	3-3	1-2	6-1	5-5	2-0	2-0	5-2	2-3	2-3	5-0
Inkberrow	2-6	3-1	4-0	3-1	0-2	S	1-2	4-0	0-0	0-0	2-1	2-1	0-4	1-2	2-4	0-0
Kenilworth Town Res.	1-8	2-2	2-4	0-2	0-5	1-2	I	0-3	1-2	2-4	3-2	3-4	0-3	3-3	1-8	1-4
Knowle Res.	1-2	9-2	1-5	2-3	2-4	1-1	5-1	O	1-1	1-2		9-0	1-3	3-3	1-1	1-4
Massey-Ferguson Res.	4-1	5-2	2-4	5-4	1-6	2-3	10-1	2-3	N	1-3	4-0	0-2	8-1	1-3	3-5	11-0
Newhall United	6-2	2-1	2-1	3-0	4-0	4-0	7-0	5-1	2-2		2-5	2-0	3-0	10-1	1-4	5-1
Northfield Town Res.	4-3	3-0	1-3	0-4	2-1	3-1	0-2	3-1	0-2	1-5	T	3-1	2-1	1-5	0-3	2-0
Romulus Res.	3-2	1-4	4-0	2-0	3-3	1-2	0-1	1-0	1-4	4-3	6-1	H	4-2	3-1	0-7	0-2
Rugby Town Res.	3-5	1-3	0-10	5-2	2-9	0-4	4-6	1-5	5-3	0-3	0-0	1-2	R	0-2	0-5	2-4
Tipton Town Res.	3-1	2-0	0-3	2-1	2-1	1-2	6-0	3-3	1-2	6-1	6-3	2-0	6-2	E	4-5	4-1
Wellesbourne	2-1	5-4	4-2	3-1	6-1	4-1	2-0	8-2	1-2	1-3	6-0	2-1	4-1	1-3	E	3-1
Wilmcote Spts & Soc. Res.	3-1	2-0	2-1	3-6	1-4	0-6	2-6	3-2	0-6	2-7	0-0	2-5	1-2	1-2	2-9	

Division Three

		P	W	D	L	F	A	Pts
Wellesbourne		30	24	4	2	129	43	76
Newhall United		30	22	3	5	107	48	69
Tipton Town Res.		30	19	5	6	82	52	62
Continental Star Res.		30	17	5	8	102	53	56
Chasetown 'A'		30	17	3	10	88	62	54
Massey-Ferguson Res.		30	15	3	12	95	64	48
Inkberrow		30	14	4	12	54	50	48
Romulus Res.		30	14	2	14	58	73	44
Knowle Res.		30	12	5	13	82	73	41
Birchfield Oaklands	-3	30	13	1	16	81	85	37
Coleshill Town Res.	-3	30	12	3	15	63	67	36
Northfield Town Res.		30	10	3	17	41	73	33
Wilmcote S&S Res.		30	7	4	19	43	104	25
Kenilworth Town Res.		30	7	3	20	51	108	24
Birmingham United		30	5	4	21	56	105	19
Rugby Town Res.	-3	30	5	2	23	50	122	14

CHALLENGE TROPHY

(Reserve Division teams)

FINAL (24th April at Quorn)

Quorn Res. 4 Solihull Borough Res. 0

CHALLENGE URN

FIRST ROUND
Wilmcote Sports & Social Res. 0 Knowle Res. 3
SECOND ROUND
Birchfield Oaklands 2 Continental Star Res. 3 *aet*
Birmingham United (w/o) v Droitwich Sports (scr.)
Coleshill Town Res. 3 Chasetown 'A' 2
Massey-Ferguson Res. 3 Kenilworth Town Res. 0
Newhall United 5 Knowle Res. 0
Northfield Town Res. 1 Romulus Res. 2
Rugby Town Res. 3 Inkberrow 5 *aet*
Wellesbourne 2 Tipton Town Res. 1
QUARTER-FINALS
Birmingham Utd 3 Inkberrow 5, Newhall 0 Coleshill Res. 4
Romulus Res. 2 Continental Star Res. 3
Wellesbourne 4 Massey-Ferguson Res. 3
SEMI-FINALS (played over two legs)
Inkberrow 1 Cont. Star Res. 1, Cont. Star Res. 1 Inkberrow 2
Coleshill Town Res. 0 Wellesbourne 4,
Wellesbourne 5 Coleshill Town Res. 0
FINAL (15th May at Stratford Town)
Wellesbourne 4 Inkberrow 1

DIVISION THREE CONSTITUTION FOR 2003-04

ATTLEBOROUGH VILLAGE . . . Pingles Stadium, Avenue Road, Attleborough, Nuneaton, Warwickshire 02476 370688
BIRMINGHAM UNITED . . . . . . Oldbury Leisure Centre, Newbury Road, Oldbury, Warley, West Midlands 0121 552 1818
BLACKHEATH RESERVES . Invensys Brook Compton Sports, Cakemore Road, Rowley Regis, West Midlands . . . . . 0121 698 3253 / 698 3256
BOLEHALL SWIFTS RESERVES . . . . Rene Road, Bolehall, Tamworth, Staffordshire 01827 62637
CASTLE VALE KINGS HEATH RES. . Vale Stadium, Farnborough Road, Castle Vale, Birmingham 0121 747 6969
FECKENHAM RESERVES . . The Playing Fields, The Square, Mill Lane, Feckenham, Redditch, Worcestershire 01527 892611
HEATHER ATHLETIC RESERVES . . . . St John's Park, Ravenstone Road, Heather, Leicestershire 01530 263986
HIMLEY ATHLETIC . . . . Portland Club, Portland Road, Edgbaston, Birmingham . . . . None
INKBERROW . . . . Inkberrow Village Hall, Sands Lane, Inkberrow, Worcestershire 01386 795414
KENILWORTH TOWN RESERVES . Campion School, Sydenham Drive, Leamington Spa, Warwickshire 01926 743200
KNOWLE RESERVES . . . . Hampton Road, Knowle, Solihull, West Midlands 01564 779807
MASSEY-FERGUSON RESERVES . . . . Banner Lane, Tile Hill, Coventry, West Midlands . . . . 024 7669 4400x2084. Club: 024 7646 5838
MILE OAK ROVERS & YOUTH . . . . Price Avenue, Mile Oak, Tamworth, Staffordshire 01827 62637
NORTHFIELD TOWN RESERVES . . . . Shenley Lane, Northfield, Birmingham, West Midlands 01827 289614
UNIVERSITY OF BIRMINGHAM . . Munrow Sports Centre, The University of Birmingham, Edgbaston, Birmingham 0121 414 4117
WILMCOTE SPORTS/SOC. RES. . . The Patch, Wilmcote SS Club, Aston Cantlow Rd, Wilmcote, Stratford 01789 297895

Wellesbourne, Newhall United and Continental Stars are promoted to Division Two. Droitwich Sports withdrew before the start of the season. Rugby Town Reserves, Birchfield Oaklands, Coleshill Town Reserves, Chasetown 'A' and Romulus Reserves have resigned. Newcomers are Attleborough Village (Coventry Alliance), University of Birmingham, Himley Athletic, Blackheath Reserves (Kidderminster & District League), Bolehall Swifts Reserves, Castle Vale Kings Heath Reserves, Feckenham Reserves, Heather Athletic Reserves and Mile Oak Rovers & Youth.

MIDLAND LEAGUE

	Abbey Hulton United	Alsager	Audley & District	Ball Haye Green	Brocton	Cheadle Town OB	Dominoes	Eccleshall	Foley	Goldenhill Wanderers	Hanford	Hanley Town	Milton Rangers	Newcastle Town Res.	Norton AG	Redgate Clayton	Stallington	Vale Juniors	Wolstanton United
Abbey Hulton United		3-3	0-2	2-2	1-1	2-1	4-0	0-2	8-1	1-3	1-2	1-1	0-0	1-2	0-3	1-3	0-3	2-2	3-1
Alsager	1-0		1-3	4-0	3-1	4-1	1-1	2-3	0-1	0-1	0-1	0-2	2-0	1-1	0-0	3-0	1-3	3-1	1-0
Audley & District	1-0	1-1		2-1	2-1	1-0	3-0	1-1	4-2	0-1	1-1	1-1	1-1	1-1	0-1	0-3	2-2	2-2	5-1
Ball Haye Green	0-3	1-2	2-2		0-1	3-0	0-1	0-4	3-1	1-4	2-1	2-3	3-1	3-1	0-1	0-3	2-2	4-2	7-1
Brocton	2-0	2-1	3-1	5-1		4-0	0-1	3-5	4-0	2-2	1-2	2-0	1-4	1-0	1-2	1-0	3-3	4-2	7-1
Cheadle Town Old Boys	0-2	0-2	0-2	1-1	2-4		0-1	0-0	1-0	0-3	0-1	0-3	0-0	2-2	0-3	2-2	0-2	0-0	2-2
Dominoes	2-2	0-2	2-1	3-2	1-1	1-0		0-4	4-0	4-0	2-3	0-0	2-2	4-1	0-2	1-2	4-0	1-0	1-1
Eccleshall	3-0	1-1	1-2	2-0	0-0	5-1	1-0		5-0	2-2	2-0	1-1	2-0	8-0	2-0	2-1	0-1	2-2	0-0
Foley	2-2	2-2	2-5	2-0	2-1	3-1	1-4	0-3		4-0	0-3	1-0	1-1	1-1	1-5	2-6	4-1	1-1	1-6
Goldenhill Wanderers	4-0	2-1	3-1	5-1	2-1	1-0	1-2	2-1	4-0		4-0	1-1	1-3	6-3	0-0	0-2	2-2	4-3	7-1
Hanford	3-3	3-2	1-1	0-1	2-1	3-2	0-1	1-1	3-2	0-3		0-0	3-0	1-3	0-1	2-2	1-1	2-1	2-1
Hanley Town	2-1	2-0	2-2	2-2	1-2	4-0	3-1	0-3	3-0	6-3	3-1		1-1	5-1	1-2	2-0	5-1	0-0	4-0
Milton Rangers	0-0	1-0	0-0	5-0	1-2	1-0	2-1	1-1	1-3	1-7	2-1			0-0	1-4	1-1	1-0	2-1	2-2
Newcastle Town Res.	2-2	0-1	1-1	0-3	0-0	0-0	0-0	0-1	2-1	1-1	1-3	1-2	1-3		0-3	1-1	1-2	3-1	1-2
Norton AG	4-2	2-1	0-4	3-2	2-0	3-1	2-3	2-0	5-1	1-2	1-1	0-1	1-0			2-3	1-0	1-3	2-6	3-2
Redgate Clayton	1-4	0-0	0-1	1-2	3-2	3-0	1-1	1-6	0-0	2-1	3-2	1-1	1-0	4-2	0-3		1-3	0-1	4-1
Stallington	3-2	3-0	2-3	1-0	1-0	3-2	1-1	0-1	3-2	2-1	1-1	1-0	4-2	0-3	1-3			0-1	2-2
Vale Juniors	0-1	0-3	0-2	1-0	1-3	0-1	1-1	1-1	1-2	1-2	0-4	0-3	1-2	6-5	0-4	3-4	3-2		2-2
Wolstanton United	0-5	0-4	1-1	1-2	3-3	0-2	1-1	0-6	3-1	1-4	2-4	0-7	1-1	0-3	2-6	1-1	1-7	3-2	

	P	W	D	L	F	A	Pts
Eccleshall	36	22	12	2	85	24	78
Norton AG	36	23	4	9	79	40	73
Goldenhill Wanderers	36	21	7	8	83	55	70
Audley & District	36	18	13	5	67	38	67
Hanley Town	36	18	11	7	79	34	65
Redgate Clayton	36	18	10	8	64	46	64
Hanford	36	19	7	10	62	50	64
Stallington	36	18	8	10	67	53	62
Brocton	36	17	6	13	74	53	57
Milton Rangers	36	14	13	9	44	46	55
Alsager	36	14	8	14	53	42	50
Dominoes	36	13	11	12	51	47	50
Abbey Hulton United	36	9	11	16	59	62	38
Ball Haye Green	36	8	6	22	44	77	30
Foley	36	7	8	21	40	97	29
Newcastle Town Res.	36	5	11	20	42	79	26
Wolstanton United	36	4	11	21	46	110	23
Vale Juniors	36	4	9	23	43	78	21
Cheadle Town OB	36	2	10	24	18	69	16

WWW.NLNEWSDESK.CO.UK

LEAGUE CUP

FIRST ROUND
Ball Haye Green 0 **Goldenhill** 2
Eccleshall 1 **Brocton** 2 *aet*
Norton AG 2 Newcastle Town Res. 1

SECOND ROUND
Abbey Hulton United 2 **Goldenhill Wanderers** 2 *aet* (3-5p)
Audley & District 1 Milton Rangers 0
Brocton 6 Vale Juniors 0
Cheadle Town Old Boys 2 Alsager 2 *aet* (4-3p)
Dominoes 0 **Stallington** 1
Hanford 1 **Norton AG** 5 *aet*
Hanley 2 Redgate Clayton 2 *aet* (5-4p)
Wolstanton United 3 Foley 1

QUARTER-FINALS
Brocton 3 Stallington 2 *aet*
Cheadle Town OB 0 **Audley** 1
Hanley Town 1 Goldenhill Wanderers 0
Wolstanton Utd 1 **Norton AG** 3 *aet*

SEMI-FINALS
Hanley Town 2 Brocton 0
Norton AG 4 Audley & District 2

FINAL
(14th April at Newcastle Town)
Hanley Town 0 **Norton AG** 2

CONSTITUTION 2003-04

ABBEY HULTON UNITED......... Birches Head Road, Abbey Hulton, Stoke-on-Trent, Staffordshire 01782 544232
ALSAGER TOWN RESERVES............ The Town Ground, Wood Park, Alsager, Cheshire............................. 01270 882336
AUDLEY & DISTRICT .... Town Fields, Old Road, Bignall, Stoke-on-Trent, Staffordshire................. 01782 723482
BALL HAYE GREEN........... Rear of Ball Haye Green WMC, Ball Haye Green, Leek, Staffordshire.......... 01538 371926
CHEADLE TOWN OLD BOYS........... Cheadle Leisure Centre, Allen Street, Cheadle, Staffordshire........... 01538 753331
DOMINOES......... Springbank Stadium, Kings Park, Hilderstone Road, Meir Heath, Stoke-on-Trent, Staffordshire 01782 388465
FOLEY....................... Whitcombe Road, Meir, Stoke-on-Trent, Staffordshire........................ 01782 595274
GOLDENHILL WANDERERS.... Sandyford Sports Ground, Shelford Road, Sandyford, Stoke-on-Trent........... 01782 811977
HANFORD.................... Northwood Stadium, Keeling Road, Hanley, Stoke-on-Trent, Staffordshire......... 01782 234400
HANLEY TOWN..................... Abbey Lane, Abbey Hulton, Stoke-on-Trent, Staffordshire.............. 01782 267234
NEWCASTLE TOWN RESERVES Lyme Valley Parkway Stadium, Lilleshall Rd, Clayton, Newcastle-under-Lyne ..... 01782 662351 / 622350
NORTON AG......... Norton CC & MW Institute, Community Drive, Smallthorne, Stoke-on-Trent, Staffordshire........ 01782 838290
REDGATE CLAYTON............. Northwood Lane, Clayton, Newcastle-under-Lyne, Staffordshire............. 01782 717409
STALLINGTON............ Stallington Hospital, Fulford Lane, Stallington Road, Blythe Bridge, Staffordshire 07785 338804
VALE JUNIORS........ Audley & District FC, Town Fields, Old Road, Bignall End, Stoke-on-Trent, Staffordshire......... 01782 522737
WOLSTANTON UNITED .... Bradwell Community Centre, Riceyman Road, Bradwell, Stoke-on-Trent 01782 660818

Eccleshall are promoted to the North West Counties League. Brocton have switched to the Midland Combination. Milton Rangers take the place of their own reserve side in the Staffs County League.

NORTH BERKS LEAGUE

	Benson	Blewbury	Childrey Utd	Drayton	East Hendred	Kintbury Rgrs	Lambourn Spts	Lg Wittenham	Marcham	Saxton Rovers	Sut. Courtenay	Warborough
Benson	D	3-3	W-L	2-4	1-0	2-4	1-0	1-1	1-2	1-1	4-1	1-0
Blewbury	3-1	I	4-0	1-3	1-5	3-3	3-1	0-7	6-1	0-3	1-3	5-2
Childrey United	3-3	3-3	V	1-5	0-5	L-W	1-2	0-3	L-W	3-3	1-5	L-W
Drayton	2-3	3-4	3-3	I	1-1	0-3	2-5	4-1	3-3	2-2	1-1	3-2
East Hendred	7-0	1-3	W-L	2-0	S	3-1	1-1	1-1	2-2	2-1	1-1	1-3
Kintbury Rangers	W-L	6-0	3-0	5-0	6-0	I	3-0	1-0	2-1	0-1	5-0	1-1
Lambourn Sports	1-1	7-0	7-1	0-1	7-4	2-2	O	2-4	0-3	4-2	2-2	3-0
Long Wittenham	2-3	0-1	5-0	2-2	0-2	0-2	3-4	N	0-5	0-3	1-0	5-0
Marcham	3-1	7-1	W-L	2-0	0-2	0-1	1-1	3-6		1-4	2-3	4-3
Saxton Rovers	2-0	1-2	7-0	L-W	0-2	1-0	2-1	2-1	4-1	O	5-0	3-1
Sutton Courtenay	3-3	6-3	1-1	0-3	2-3	1-3	1-2	3-1	1-2	1-2	N	3-10
Warborough & S.	4-3	3-2	7-4	1-4	2-1	2-7	3-0	3-1	0-1	0-0	1-0	E

Division One	P	W	D	L	F	A	Pts
Kintbury Rangers	22	16	3	3	58	17	51
Saxton Rovers	22	13	4	5	49	22	43
East Hendred	22	12	4	6	46	32	40
Marcham	22	11	2	9	43	41	35
Drayton	22	9	6	7	46	44	33
Lambourn Sports	22	9	5	8	52	41	32
Warbor./Shillingford	22	10	2	10	48	52	32
Blewbury	22	9	3	10	49	69	30
Benson	22	7	6	9	35	46	27
Long Wittenham Ath.	22	7	3	12	44	42	24
Sutton Courtenay	22	5	5	12	38	57	20
Childrey United	22	0	5	17	21	66	5

DIVISION ONE CONSTITUTION 2003-04

ARDINGTON & LOCKINGE.............White Road, Ardington, Wantage, Oxfordshire ....None
BENSON.........................Benson Recreation Ground, Benson, Oxfordshire ....None
BLEWBURY .... Bohams Road, Blewbury, Oxfordshire ....None
DRAYTON........................Recreation Ground, Lockway, Drayton, Abingdon, Oxfordshire ....None
EAST HENDRED ....Hendred Sports & Social Club, Mill Lane, East Hendred, Oxfordshire....01235 821008
FARINGDON TOWN.....................Tucker Park, Faringdon, Oxfordshire.....................01367 241759
KINTBURY RANGERS ....Inkpen Road, Kintbury, Hungerford, Berkshire.............01488 657001
LAMBOURN SPORTS ....Bockhampton Road, Lambourn, Berkshire ....None
LONG WITTENHAM ATHLETIC .. Bodkins Sports Field, East End of Village, Long Wittenham, Oxon ......None
MARCHAM ....Moreland Road, Marcham, Abingdon, Oxfordshire.....................None
SAXTON ROVERS ....Recreation Ground, Caldecott Road, Abingdon, Oxfordshire ....None
WARBOROUGH & SHILLINGFORD.................Village Green, Warborough, Oxfordshire ....None

Sutton Courtenay and Childrey United are relegated to Division Two from which Ardington & Lockinge and Faringdon Town are promoted.

	Ardington & L.	Botley United	Coleshill United	Faringdon T.	Grove Rangers	Hanney United	Harwell Inter	Harwell Village	Saxton R. Res.	Shriv'ham Res.	Stanford-in-V.	Steventon
Ardington & Lock.	D	3-0	5-1	0-0	2-2	3-2	4-1	1-2	3-0	5-0	5-1	5-2
Botley United	0-5	I	1-0	2-1	0-2	8-0	2-1	0-1	1-2	1-4	0-2	1-3
Coleshill United	2-2	1-3	V	2-2	2-3	4-0	3-2	6-1	2-2	0-3	3-1	2-2
Faringdon Town	3-2	0-0	3-2	I	2-1	5-1	0-0	1-0	5-0	1-0	1-1	4-2
Grove Rangers	4-1	4-2	1-4	0-3	S	5-0	2-1	W-L	1-1	1-1	2-1	5-2
Hanney United	0-4	0-5	1-6	1-2	4-2	I	0-4	1-1	1-3	1-1		0-7
Harwell Inter	3-4	3-1	4-1	1-0	3-3	5-0	O	6-2	5-1	1-0	2-0	2-1
Harwell Village	2-7	0-1	1-0	0-1	0-0	8-1	0-10	N	6-2	2-0	3-2	4-1
Saxton Rovers Res.	0-7	0-4	6-3	0-7	1-2	8-0	5-3	1-1		1-1	3-1	1-1
Shrivenham Res.	1-11	2-4	1-1	0-0	0-3	1-1	1-1	6-0	3-3	T	2-5	2-1
Stanford-in-Vale	0-3	1-4	1-0	0-1	1-2	1-0	2-0	2-2	1-1	0-2	W	3-3
Steventon	1-2	1-0	4-2	5-2	2-6	8-0	2-1	7-1	1-6	4-2	1-0	O

Division Two	P	W	D	L	F	A	Pts
Ardington & Lockinge	22	16	3	3	84	27	51
Faringdon Town	22	13	6	3	44	20	45
Grove Rangers	22	13	5	4	51	33	44
Harwell International	22	11	3	8	58	34	36
Botley United	22	11	1	10	37	34	34
Steventon	22	10	3	9	61	51	33
Harwell Village	22	8	3	11	39	57	27
Saxton Rovers Res.	22	6	8	8	45	59	26
Shrivenham Res.	22	6	7	9	35	47	25
Coleshill United	22	6	5	11	47	49	23
Stanford-in-Vale	22	5	5	12	27	41	20
Hanney United	22	1	3	18	15	91	6

DIVISION TWO CONSTITUTION 2003-04

BOTLEY UNITED .... Oxford Rugby Club, Southern Bypass, North Hinksey, Oxford, Oxfordshire 01865 243984
CHILDREY UNITED .... Childrey Playing Field, Sparsholt Road, Childrey, Wantage, Oxfordshire ....None
COLESHILL UNITED .... Bottom of the Hill, Coleshill, Oxfordshire ....None
GROVE RANGERS.................Recreation Ground, Cane Lane, Grove, Wantage, Oxfordshire ....None
HARWELL INTERNATIONAL .. Main Gate, Harwell International Business Centre, Didcot, Oxfordshire ....None
HARWELL VILLAGE................Westfields Recreation Ground, Harwell, Didcot, Oxfordshire ....None
INKPEN .... Old Post Office Road, Inkpen, Newbury, Berkshire...................None
KINTBURY RANGERS RESERVES .... Inkpen Road, Kintbury, Hungerford, Berkshire 01488 657001
SAXTON ROVERS RESERVES .... Recreation Ground, Caldecott Road, Abingdon, Oxfordshire ...... 01793 ...None
SHRIVENHAM RESERVES ...... Recreation Ground, Highworth Road, Shrivenham, Swindon, Wiltshire ....None
STEVENTON .... Steventon Green, Milton Lane, Steventon, Abingdon, Oxfordshire 01793 784453
SUTTON COURTENAY .... Old Wallingford Way, High Street, Sutton Courtenay, Abingdon, Oxfordshire ....None

Ardington & Lockinge and Faringdon Town are promoted to Division One from which Sutton Courtenay and Childrey United are relegated. Stanford-in-Vale and Hanney United drop to Division Three replaced by Kintbury Rangers Reserves and Inkpen.

WWW.CHERRYRED.CO.UK

	AFC Wall. 'A'	Buckland	E. Hendred Res.	Faringdon Res.	Hagbourne U.	Harwell I. Res.	Inkpen	Kintbury Res.	Lambourn Res.	Long Witt. Res.	Northcroft	Wootton & DS
AFC Wall'ford 'A'		1-1	2-1	2-1	7-0	3-1	1-4	1-5	6-2	3-4	0-3	7-2
Buckland	0-4	D	2-1	2-1	2-1	7-2	0-4	1-4	3-1	3-3	4-1	2-2
East Hendred Res.	5-0	2-1	I	2-1	2-3	4-1	1-2	0-1	3-0	2-1	4-2	2-2
Faringdon T. Res.	1-6	1-3	1-3	V	1-0	3-0	2-2	2-5	3-2	4-1	1-4	4-2
Hagbourne United	2-4	3-3	0-1	5-2		2-0	2-5	0-3	4-2	4-3	1-5	2-4
Harwell Inter Res.	2-0	0-6	0-2	3-6	3-0		2-3	0-4	1-4	5-2	3-4	0-4
Inkpen	5-1	3-3	4-1	3-1	9-0	10-2	T	1-1	3-0	1-0	5-0	L-W
Kintbury Rgrs Res.	2-2	3-3	3-2	2-2	8-0	3-1	1-1	H	9-0	4-0	3-0	0-1
Lambourn Sp. Res.	1-3	2-2	1-3	2-0	2-0	4-2	3-2	1-5	R	2-1	2-6	1-1
L. Wittenham Res.	4-6	1-5	L-W	0-4	4-2	3-2	1-6	1-3	3-2	E	6-1	2-2
Northcroft	L-W	1-1	5-7	4-2	4-0	1-4	3-2	1-4	4-0	9-1	E	9-0
Wootton & Dry S.	2-3	0-8	2-1	4-3	2-1	8-1	2-2	2-3	1-2	2-6	0-3	

Division Three	P	W	D	L	F	A	Pts
Kintbury Rg. Res.	22	16	5	1	76	22	53
Inkpen	22	14	5	3	77	27	47
AFC Wall'ford 'A'	22	13	2	7	62	48	41
East Hendred Res.	22	13	1	8	49	34	40
Northcroft	22	12	1	9	70	50	37
Buckland	22	9	9	4	61	41	36
Wootton/Dry Sfd.	22	8	5	9	45	62	29
Faringdon T. Res.	22	7	3	12	46	56	24
Lambourn S. Res.	22	7	2	13	36	65	23
L. Wittenham Res.	22	6	2	14	47	72	20
Hagbourne United	22	5	1	16	32	76	16
Harwell Inter. Res.	22	4	0	18	35	83	12

DIVISION THREE CONSTITUTION 2003-04

AFC WALLINGFORD 'A' .... Wallingford Sports Park, Hithercroft, Wallingford, Oxfordshire 01491 835044
APPLETON ABINGDON .... Netherton Road, Appleton, Abingdon, Oxfordshire .... None
BUCKLAND .... The Croft, Buckland, Faringdon, Oxfordshire .... None
EAST HENDRED RESERVES .... Hendred Sports & Social Club, Mill Lane, East Hendred, Oxfordshire 01235 821008
FARINGDON TOWN RESERVES .... Tucker Park, Faringdon, Oxfordshire 01367 241759
HANNEY UNITED .... Hanney War Memorial Hall, West Hanney, Oxfordshire 01235 868482
LAMBOURN SPORTS RESERVES .... Bockhampton Road, Lambourn, Berkshire .... None
LONG WITTENHAM ATH. RESERVES .. Bodkins Sports Field, East End of Village, Long Wittenham .... None
NORTHCROFT .... Northcroft Park, Northcroft, Newbury, Berkshire .... None
RADLEY .... Gooseacre, Foxborough Road, Radley, Abingdon, Oxfordshire .... None
STANFORD-IN-VALE .... Cottage Road, Stanford-in-the-Vale, Faringdon, Oxfordshire .... None
WOOTTON & DRY SANDFORD . Wootton & Dry Sandford CC, Besseleigh Road, Wootton, Oxfordshire ...... None
Kintbury Rangers Reserves and Inkpen are promoted to Division Two replaced by Stanford-in-Vale and Hanney United. Hagbourne United and Harwell International Reserves drop to Division Four replaced by Appleton Abingdon and Radley.

	Appleton	Benson L.	Blewb'y Res.	Challow U.	Coleshill Res.	Grove Res.	Radley	Stanf'd Res.	S. Cour. Res.	Uffington	Warbor. Res.
Appleton Abingdon		4-2	4-0	5-2	3-0	2-2	3-3	2-3	4-0	9-1	4-0
Benson Lions	0-4	D	1-0	5-0	5-0	5-1	0-5	5-2	6-1	3-0	7-0
Blewbury Res.	2-2	2-7	I	2-1	3-3	1-2	1-2	4-0	3-0	2-2	2-4
Challow United	0-8	2-2	1-2	V	5-4	0-2	1-6	2-1	5-2	0-1	8-1
Coleshill United Res.	1-4	0-7	2-2	1-3		0-5	1-6	3-5	0-1	L-W	W-L
Grove Rangers Res.	0-4	0-1	0-2	1-6	2-1		1-0	2-0	3-1	4-2	2-1
Radley	1-5	3-1	1-2	2-0	2-1	1-2	F	5-1	5-6	4-3	1-0
Stanford-in-Vale Res.	1-2	3-1	5-2	5-3	0-3	0-3	1-4	O	4-1	2-1	0-2
Sutton Courtenay Res.	2-3	2-5	1-4	0-0	1-1	2-0	2-6	1-3	U	3-3	1-1
Uffington United	2-5	1-3	2-3	1-2	1-2	2-0	1-2	1-1	W-L	R	2-0
Warborough & S. Res.	1-4	1-1	3-1	3-0	2-1	1-1	1-2	6-1	2-7	1-0	

Division Four	P	W	D	L	F	A	Pts
Appleton Abingdon	20	16	3	1	81	23	51
Radley	20	15	1	4	65	32	46
Benson Lions	20	13	2	5	67	31	41
Grove Rangers Res.	20	11	2	7	38	31	35
Blewbury Res.	20	8	4	8	40	43	28
Stanford-in-Vale Res.	20	8	0	12	38	54	24
Warborough & S. Res.	20	7	3	10	29	45	24
Challow United	20	7	2	11	41	53	23
Uffington United	20	5	2	13	25	55	17
Sutton Courtenay Res.	20	4	4	12	34	58	16
Coleshill United Res.	20	3	3	14	24	57	12

DIVISION FOUR CONSTITUTION 2003-04

BENSON LIONS .... RAF Benson, Benson, Oxfordshire .... None
BLEWBURY .... Bohams Road, Blewbury, Oxfordshire .... None
CHALLOW UNITED.................... Reynolds Way, East Challow, Wantage, Oxfordshire .... None
DRAYTON RESERVES........... Recreation Ground, Lockway, Drayton, Abingdon, Oxfordshire .... None
GROVE RANGERS RESERVES...... Recreation Ground, Cane Lane, Grove, Wantage, Oxfordshire .... None
HAGBOURNE UNITED .... Recreation Ground, New Road, Hagbourne, Didcot, Oxfordshire .... None
HARWELL INT. RESERVES .... Main Gate, Harwell International Business Centre, Didcot, Oxfordshire .... None
MARCHAM RESERVES............... Moreland Road, Marcham, Abingdon, Oxfordshire .... None
STANFORD-IN-VALE RESERVES.... Cottage Road, Stanford-in-the-Vale, Faringdon, Oxfordshire .... None
SUTTON COURTENAY RESERVES Old Wallingford Way, High Street, Sutton Courtenay, Abingdon .... None
UFFINGTON UNITED....................... Fawler Road, Uffington, Oxfordshire .... None
WARBOROUGH & SHILLINGFORD RES....... Village Green, Warborough, Oxfordshire .... None
Appleton Abingdon and Radley are promoted to Division Three replaced by Hagbourne United and Harwell International Reserves. Coleshill United Reserves are demoted to Division Five replaced by Drayton Reserves and Marcham Reserves.

Division Five	P	W	D	L	F	A	Pts
Drayton Res.	22	16	4	2	63	17	52
Marcham Res.	22	16	3	3	66	20	51
Ardington & Lock. Res.	22	14	3	5	60	27	45
Faringdon Town 'A'	22	13	4	5	51	33	43
Buckland Res.	22	12	5	5	52	27	41
Steventon Res.	22	11	3	8	54	40	36
Benson Res.	22	10	5	7	38	35	35
Wootton & Dry S. Res.	22	6	4	12	41	61	22
Challow United Res.	22	3	8	11	19	42	17
Hanney United Res.	22	4	1	17	33	75	13
Uffington United Res.	22	2	4	16	29	88	10
Hagbourne United Res.	22	2	2	18	19	60	8

www.cherryred.co.uk

NORTH BERKS CUP

FIRST ROUND
Benson Lions 3 Blewbury 1
Buckland 0 **Lambourn Sports** 5
Challow United 0 **Wootton & Dry Sandford** 4
Childrey United 4 Northcroft 2
Coleshill United 2 **Drayton** 4
East Hendred 5 Stanford-in-Vale 1
Grove Rangers 4 Hanney United 0
Hagbourne Utd 0 **Saxton Rovers** 4
Harwell Inter 2 **Faringdon Town** 4
Inkpen 3 **Appleton Abingdon** 4
Kintbury Rangers 5 Warborough & Shillingford 0
Long Wittenham Athletic 6 Harwell Village 0
Marcham 8 Steventon 2
Radley 0 **Ardington & Lockinge** 8
Sutton Courtenay 1 **Botley Utd** 0
Uffington United 2 Benson 1

SECOND ROUND
Appleton Abingdon 0 **Marcham** 4
Ardington 8 Wootton & DS 0
Childrey United 3 **Grove Rangers** 5
Drayton 3 Saxton Rovers 1
East Hendred 2 Lambourn Sports 1
Faringdon Town 3 Benson Lions 1
Kintbury Rgrs 12 Uffington Utd 1
Long Wittenham Athletic 2 Sutton Courtenay 0

QUARTER-FINALS
Drayton 3 Marcham 0
Faringdon 2 **East Hendred** 4 *aet*
Grove Rgrs 1 **Long Wittenham** 4
Kintbury Rangers 2 Ardington 0

SEMI-FINALS
Drayton 4 Long Wittenham Athletic 0 *(at Appleton)*
Kintbury Rangers 4 East Hendred 1 *(at Saxton Rovers)*

FINAL
(10th May at Abingdon Town)
Drayton 1 **Kintbury Rangers** 2

CHARITY SHIELD

FIRST ROUND
Benson 1 **Steventon** 4
Botley United 2 Challow United 1
Buckland 0 **Drayton** 5
Childrey Utd 2 **Harwell Village** 3
East Hendred 8 Appleton 0
Faringdon Town 5 Coleshill Utd 0
Grove Rangers 3 Saxton Rovers 1
Hanney United 2 Blewbury 1
Kintbury Rgrs 10 Hagbourne 0
Long Wittenham Ath. 4 Inkpen 0
Northcroft 2 Wootton & DS 1
Radley 5 Marcham 1
Stanford-in-Vale 2 **Ardington** 4
Sutton Courtenay 1 **Lambourn** 2
Uffington United 2 **Benson Lions** 2 *aet* (1-3p)
Warborough & Shillingford 2 **Harwell International** 3

SECOND ROUND
Ardington 2 **East Hendred** 3
Benson Lions 6 Hanney United 1
Botley United 3 **Long Wittenham Athletic** 3 *aet* (1-2p)
Drayton 5 Harwell Village 0
Faringdon Town 1 **Kintbury** 2
Harwell Inter 3 Grove Rangers 2
Lambourn Sports 2 Radley 1
Steventon 4 Northcroft 2

QUARTER-FINALS
Drayton 3 Lambourn Sports 4 *aet (Lambourn Sports expelled)*
East Hendred 3 Benson Lions 1
Harwell International 1 **Steventon** 3
Kintbury 1 Long Wittenham 0

SEMI-FINALS
Kintbury Rangers 2 Drayton 0 *(at Stanford-in-Vale)*
Steventon 4 East Hendred 2 *(at Saxton Rovers)*

FINAL
(3rd May at Abingdon Town)
Kintbury Rangers 8 Steventon 0

WAR MEMORIAL CUP

PRELIMINARY ROUND
Ardington & Lock. 6 Buckland 1
Faringdon Town 4 Hagbourne 1
Northcroft 7 Inkpen 4
Wootton & DS 0 **Coleshill United** 4

FIRST ROUND
Appleton Abington 3 Ardington 2
Challow 0 **Benson Lions** 4
Faringdon Town 3 Grove Rgrs 1
Hanney United 1 **Botley United** 3
Harwell International 4 Radley 0
Harwell Village 2 Stanford-in-V. 1
Northcroft 1 **Coleshill United** 4
Uffington United 0 **Steventon** 4

QUARTER-FINALS
Appleton 6 Coleshill United 0
Benson Lions 2 **Botley United** 3
Faringdon Town 1 **Harwell International** 4
Harwell Village 0 **Steventon** 3

SEMI-FINALS
Appleton Abingdon 2 Botley 1 *(at Stanford-in-Vale)*
Harwell Inter 3 Steventon 2 *aet (at Sutton Courtenay)*

FINAL
(19th April at Wantage Town)
Appleton Abingdon 2 Harwell International 0

LEAGUE CUP

FINAL *(5th April at Didcot Town)*
Steventon Res. 1 Blewbury Res. 0

A G KINGHAM CUP

FINAL *(12th April at Abingdon United)*
Drayton Res. 3 Stanford-in-Vale Res. 2

NAIRNE PAUL CUP

FINAL *(26th April at Milton United)*
Shrivenham Res. 2 Kintbury Rangers Res. 1

NORTH WEST COUNTIES LEAGUE

	Abbey Hey	Alsager Town	Atherton C.	Atherton LR	Clitheroe	Congleton	Curzon Ash.	Fleetwood	Flixton	Glossop NE	Mossley	Nantwich	Newcastle T.	Prescot C.	Ramsbottom	Salford City	Skelmersdale	Squires Gate	St Helens T.	Warrington	Winsford Utd	Woodley Spts
Abbey Hey		2-2	3-2	2-2	1-0	1-1	1-1	1-1	2-2	1-0	0-3	1-0	1-3	0-1	0-2	3-5	0-0	2-2	0-4	1-2	3-2	1-1
Alsager Town	1-2		2-0	0-1	1-2	2-3	3-2	4-0	3-2	3-1	1-4	1-2	0-0	1-0	0-0	1-0	2-0	2-3	0-1	0-0	4-1	0-4
Atherton Collieries	1-0	1-3		3-1	1-3	0-1	0-1	2-1	3-0	1-3	0-2	2-3	2-1	1-1	1-0	0-1	0-5	2-1	1-2	0-0	1-3	3-1
Atherton LR	4-1	1-2	4-3		2-2	1-4	3-1	3-4	2-1	0-1	2-0	1-2	0-0	0-4	2-2	2-0	1-3	1-2	0-0	2-1	1-2	1-1
Clitheroe	1-0	6-1	2-0	0-0		3-0	2-1	3-2	4-0	5-0	1-2	2-1	1-2	1-1	7-1	3-0	3-2	4-2	2-1	1-0	0-0	2-1
Congleton Town	1-0	0-0	1-2	4-2	3-0	D	3-0	2-1	7-0	4-1	0-1	3-1	5-2	1-3	2-0	1-6	0-1	1-0	0-1	3-0	1-2	3-3
Curzon Ashton	2-1	1-2	0-3	3-5	0-2	1-0	I	2-3	2-7	1-2	2-1	3-2	2-0	0-0	2-2	2-1	0-0	2-2	2-1	2-1	1-0	3-3
Fleetwood Town	1-3	0-3	3-0	3-1	1-1	3-1	3-0	V	7-4	5-0	1-1	3-4	3-2	2-1	0-0	1-4	2-1	0-0	1-1	1-0		4-1
Flixton	2-1	3-2	0-2	0-0	0-3	1-1	1-2	0-1	I	3-1	0-5	0-1	0-4	0-4	0-7	0-5	3-0	1-1	4-1	1-0	1-2	0-1
Glossop North End	1-1	4-3	1-1	1-1	2-4	0-3	1-1	2-4	0-3	S	2-2	2-1	4-3	1-1	2-2	2-1	1-2	2-0	1-2	1-0	4-0	1-0
Mossley	2-1	1-2	1-1	7-2	3-1	2-3	6-0	1-0	8-0	5-0	I	0-3	1-0	3-2	3-2	1-1	1-2	1-2	2-0	1-0	4-0	1-0
Nantwich Town	3-5	1-1	1-1	0-2	0-4	2-2	1-2	3-0	3-3	1-2	5-0	O	4-4	2-2	2-2	3-2	1-1	2-1	1-3	3-2	3-1	6-1
Newcastle Town	1-3	2-0	0-3	0-0	3-1	1-3	2-0	4-0	2-2	1-3	2-1	2-1	N	1-1	3-0	0-0	2-0	4-0	4-3	3-0	5-0	2-0
Prescot Cables	6-0	4-1	4-0	4-2	4-1	3-0	2-1	9-0	2-1	0-0	6-0	1-0	2-1	O	2-1	4-3	3-1	2-2	1-1	4-0	5-2	1-4
Ramsbottom United	0-1	1-1	1-4	1-3	0-1	1-1	1-1	0-2	1-2	3-2	2-2	0-4	2-3	2-4	N	4-1	2-1	1-2	1-1	4-0	5-2	1-4
Salford City	1-1	4-0	1-2	1-1	1-4	2-1	3-1	2-0	3-0	1-1	2-2	1-2	3-1	7-0	7-0	E	0-4	1-1	2-1	1-2	0-0	0-0
Skelmersdale United	1-1	4-1	5-1	3-1	1-0	3-0	4-1	5-1	1-0	2-1	2-3	1-2	2-1	6-1				8-1	0-0	2-2	3-1	0-0
Squires Gate	4-0	0-0	3-2	2-0	0-6	3-0	3-2	1-1	2-0	4-2	1-3	0-1	1-1	0-2	2-1	2-1	1-2		2-3	2-2	0-2	2-1
St Helens Town	2-1	1-1	6-1	5-3	1-1	2-1	2-2	3-0	1-1	5-2	1-1	1-1	3-4	0-3	2-3	0-5	1-2	2-0		3-1	1-1	7-0
Warrington Town	1-1	0-2	4-0	1-1	1-2	2-2	1-0	1-4	1-4	1-0	0-3	1-1	1-2	0-0	0-1			2-3				3-2
Winsford United	0-3	2-2	2-0	2-0	1-7	2-3	0-2	2-0	0-1	1-3	0-5	0-4	1-1	1-1	1-3	2-3	1-1	2-0	1-2	1-2		3-2
Woodley Sports	2-4	1-1	2-2	2-2	1-2	1-1	3-1	3-0	4-2	2-0	0-2	5-6	1-2	2-3	1-5	2-1	1-3	0-2	0-4	1-0	4-1	

Division One	P	W	D	L	F	A	Pts
Prescot Cables	42	30	6	6	110	38	96
Clitheroe	42	28	8	6	97	38	92
Mossley	42	27	7	8	100	41	88
Newcastle Town	42	23	12	7	83	52	81
Skelmersdale United	42	22	8	12	91	51	74
Nantwich Town	42	19	11	12	90	74	68
St Helens Town	42	17	14	11	77	60	65
Congleton Town	42	19	8	15	72	62	65
Salford City	42	17	12	13	84	63	63
Fleetwood Town	42	17	9	16	73	70	60
Alsager Town	42	15	11	16	61	67	56
Squires Gate	42	13	12	17	58	71	51
Abbey Hey	42	12	13	17	56	73	49
Atherton LR	42	11	12	19	65	86	45
Ramsbottom United	42	11	11	20	73	83	44
Warrington Town	42	11	11	20	48	66	44
Woodley Sports	42	11	9	22	62	85	42
Curzon Ashton	42	11	9	22	60	87	42
Atherton Collieries	42	11	7	24	52	85	40
Glossop North End	42	10	9	23	55	104	39
Flixton	42	10	8	24	44	112	38
Winsford United	42	10	7	25	48	91	37

DIVISION ONE CONSTITUTION 2003-04

ABBEY HEY . . . . Abbey Stadium, Goredale Avenue, Gorton, Manchester 0161 231 7147
ALSAGER TOWN . . . . The Town Ground, Wood Park, Alsager, Cheshire 01270 882336
ATHERTON COLLIERIES . . . . Alder House, Alder Street, Atherton, Lancashire . . . . 01942 884649. Fax: 01942 884649
ATHERTON LR . . . . Crilly Park, Spa Road, Atherton, Greater Manchester 01942 883950
BACUP BOROUGH . . . . West View, Cowfoot Lane, Blackthorn, Bacup, Lancashire 01200 423344
CLITHEROE . . . . Shawbridge, off Pendle Road, Clitheroe, Lancashire 01200 423344
CONGLETON TOWN . . . . Booth Street Ground, off Crescent Road, Congleton, Cheshire . . . . 01260 274460. Fax: 01260 274460
CURZON ASHTON . . . . National Park, Katherine Street, Ashton-under-Lyne, Lancashire . . . . 0161 330 6033 / 0441
FLEETWOOD TOWN . . . . Highbury Stadium, Highbury Avenue, Fleetwood, Lancashire 01253 770702
GLOSSOP NORTH END . . . . Surrey Street, Glossop, Derbyshire 01457 855469
MOSSLEY . . . . Seel Park, Market Street, Mossley, Lancashire . . . . 01457 832369. Club: 01457 836104
NANTWICH TOWN . . . . Jackson Avenue, Nantwich, Cheshire 01270 621771
NEWCASTLE TOWN . . . . Lyme Valley Parkway Stadium, Lilleshall Road, Clayton, Newcastle-under-Lyne . . . . 01782 662351 / 622350
RAMSBOTTOM UNITED . . . . Riverside Ground, Acre Bottom, Ramsbottom, Lancashire 01706 822799
SALFORD CITY . . . . Moor Lane, Kersal, Salford, Manchester . . . . 0161 792 6287. Fax: 0161 792 6287
SKELMERSDALE UNITED . . . . White Moss Park, White Moss Road, Skelmersdale, Lancashire 01695 722123
SQUIRES GATE . . . . School Road, Marton, Blackpool, Lancashire 01253 798584
ST HELENS TOWN . . . . St Helens RLFC, Knowsley Road, St Helens, Lancashire 01744 23697
STONE DOMINOES . . Springbank Stadium, Kings Park, Hilderstone Road, Meir Heath, Stoke-on-Trent, Staffordshire 01782 388465
TRAFFORD . . . . Shawe View, Pennybridge Lane, Flixton, Urmston, Manchester . . . . 0161 747 1727 / 749 8217
WARRINGTON TOWN . . . . Cantilever Park, Loushers Lane, Warrington, Cheshire . . . . 01925 653044 / 631932
WOODLEY SPORTS . . . . Lambeth Grove Stadium, Lambeth Grove, Woodley, Stockport, Cheshire 0161 494 6429

Prescot Cables go up to the Northern Premier League replaced by Trafford. Flixton and Winsford United drop to Division Two replaced by Bacup Borough and Stone Dominoes.

	Ashton Town	Bacup Borough	Blackpool Mechanics	Castleton Gabriels	Chadderton	Cheadle Town	Colne	Daisy Hill	Darwen	Great Harwood Town	Holker Old Boys	Leek CSOB	Maine Road	Nelson	Norton United	Oldham Town	Padiham	Stand Athletic	Stone Dominoes
Ashton Town		1-2	3-2	2-1	3-1	1-1	2-0	0-4	1-1	0-1	1-1	0-4	0-2	0-0	3-3	6-0	5-1	n/a	1-0
Bacup Borough	1-0		1-0	4-1	6-0	0-1	4-1	4-0	0-2	2-0	3-0	4-2	4-0	1-1	4-2	1-1	0-1	n/a	2-1
Blackpool Mechanics	2-2	0-7		2-3	1-0	2-0	1-2	4-1	1-1	2-2	0-0	2-0	0-2	0-0	2-1	3-1	0-2	n/a	1-2
Castleton Gabriels	0-0	2-1	2-1	D	2-0	0-4	1-2	6-2	0-2	3-2	1-4	0-0	0-2	2-2	2-3			n/a	1-2
Chadderton	0-1	0-1	3-3	2-1	I	1-5	1-2	4-1	3-5	0-0	0-2	2-5	1-1	3-2	1-2	0-2		n/a	1-2
Cheadle Town	0-2	1-5	0-0	2-2	1-0	V	0-2	1-0	3-4	4-3	0-1	1-1	0-2	1-1	0-1	1-1	1-1	n/a	0-3
Colne	3-1	3-4	0-1	3-0	4-0	0-0	I	5-0	1-2	1-1	3-1	3-3	1-2	3-3	1-2	7-1	2-0	n/a	1-3
Daisy Hill	1-2	1-5	0-0	4-0	2-0	1-3	2-4	S	1-0	2-1	2-2	2-6	3-3	1-1	1-3	1-0	1-1	n/a	0-3
Darwen	3-1	4-2	1-2	2-1	1-0	5-0	0-3	2-0	I	0-3	2-2	5-0	4-0	0-0	0-2	1-1	1-1	n/a	3-5
Great Harwood Town	4-1	2-7	3-1	1-1	2-0	5-1	4-2	4-0	0-3	O	3-0	0-0	1-2	0-3	5-2	3-0	3-1	n/a	1-2
Holker Old Boys	3-0	1-0	3-0	2-0	5-1	0-3	3-1	3-1	2-0	5-0	N	1-1	2-4	2-0	1-2	5-2	3-1	n/a	1-2
Leek CSOB	0-0	0-4	2-0	1-2	1-3	0-1	2-1	4-0	5-1	4-0	1-3		0-1	1-1	3-0	0-2	2-2	1-1	0-3
Maine Road	1-2	2-1	1-1	1-0	3-2	3-1	3-1	4-1	3-1	2-5	3-1	0-1		1-2	2-1	5-2	2-1	n/a	1-1
Nelson	1-1	0-1	1-2	1-0	2-0	2-0	0-1	0-2	4-1	2-3	2-2	1-0	1-2	T	2-1	1-2	2-1	n/a	2-0
Norton United	2-1	1-3	1-0	1-1	0-0	1-0	3-1	0-2	4-1	2-2	1-0	2-1	4-0	0-1		2-0	1-2	n/a	3-4
Oldham Town	3-4	1-4	2-1	0-0	4-4	1-2	0-0	2-5	1-2	1-1	1-1	1-2	0-7	0-0		W	1-3	0-3	1-1
Padiham	2-0	0-2	1-1	1-2	2-0	2-1	1-2	2-2	2-0	3-1	2-0	1-1	1-2	0-7	0-0		O	3-0	1-1
Stand Athletic	n/a	1-0	1-1	n/a	n/a	3-0	n/a	7-0	n/a	n/a	n/a	n/a	2-7	n/a	3-1	2-2			n/a
Stone Dominoes	3-2	0-1	2-1	4-1	6-0	2-3	1-0	8-0	7-1	4-0	2-1	2-1	6-0	6-0	4-1	3-1	0-1	n/a	

Note – Stand Athletic withdrew during the season. Their results are shown above but are expunged from the league table

Reserve Division	P	W	D	L	F	A	Pts
Bacup Borough	34	25	2	7	91	32	77
Stone Dominoes	34	24	3	7	94	34	75
Maine Road	34	23	2	9	74	55	71
Padiham	34	20	5	9	69	42	65
Holker Old Boys	34	18	7	9	65	42	61
Great Harwood Town	34	15	7	12	64	61	52
Nelson	34	13	12	9	50	40	51
Darwen	34	14	7	13	59	64	49
Norton United	34	14	6	14	50	52	48
Colne	34	14	5	15	65	53	47
Ashton Town	34	12	9	13	49	53	45
Castleton Gabriels	34	10	8	16	43	60	38
Cheadle Town	34	10	8	16	39	56	38
Blackpool Mechanics	34	9	10	15	39	52	37
Leek CSOB	34	8	9	17	46	57	33
Daisy Hill	34	7	5	22	42	93	26
Oldham Town	34	4	12	18	40	86	24
Chadderton	34	5	5	24	33	80	20

Reserve Division	P	W	D	L	F	A	Pts
Padiham Res.	24	19	3	2	78	33	60
Skelmersdale United Res.	24	18	4	2	73	31	58
Clitheroe Res.	24	16	8	0	68	20	56
Curzon Ashton Res.	24	17	3	4	91	21	54
Ashton Town Res.	24	14	1	9	57	39	43
Maine Road Res.	24	11	3	10	60	47	36
Atherton Collieries Res.	24	9	6	9	30	34	33
Glossop North End Res.	24	6	9	9	36	36	27
Squires Gate Res.	24	5	7	12	41	60	22
Chadderton Res.	24	3	4	17	22	61	13
Daisy Hill Res.	24	3	4	17	34	80	13
Cheadle Town Res.	24	3	4	17	22	69	13
Atherton LR Res.	24	3	2	19	29	110	11

WWW.CHERRYRED.CO.UK

DIVISION TWO CONSTITUTION 2003-04

ASHTON TOWN . . . . Edge Green Street, Ashton-in-Makerfield, Wigan, Lancashire 01942 510677
BLACKPOOL MECHANICS. . . . . Jepson Way, Common Edge Road, Blackpool, Lancashire 01253 761721
CASTLETON GABRIELS . . . . . . Butterworth Park, Chadwick Lane, off Heywood Rd, Castleton, Rochdale 01706 527103
CHADDERTON . . . . Andrew Street, Chadderton, Oldham, Lancashire 0161 624 9733
CHEADLE TOWN . . . . Park Road Stadium, Park Road, Cheadle, Stockport, Cheshire 0161 428 2510
COLNE . . . . Colne Dynamoes Stadium, Holt House, Colne, Lancashire 01282 862545
DAISY HILL . . . . New Sirs, St James Street, Westhoughton, Bolton, Lancashire 01942 818544
DARWEN. . . . . Anchor Ground, Anchor Road, Darwen, Lancashire 01254 705627
ECCLESHALL . . . . Pershall Park, Chester Road, Eccleshall, Staffordshire 01785 851351
FLIXTON . . . . Valley Road, Flixton, Manchester. . . . . 0161 747 7757 / 748 2903
FORMBY. . . . . Altcar Road, Formby, Merseyside . . . . None
GREAT HARWOOD TOWN . . . . . The Showground, Wood Street, Great Harwood, Blackburn, Lancashire 01254 883913
HOLKER OLD BOYS . . . . Rakesmoor Lane, Hawcoat, Barrow-in-Furness, Cumbria 01229 828176
LEEK CSOB . . . . Leek Town FC, Harrison Park, Macclesfield Road, Leek, Staffordshire 01538 399278
MAINE ROAD . . . . Manchester County FA Ground, Branthingham Road, Chorlton-cum-Hardy, Manchester 0161 861 0344
NELSON. . . . . Victoria Park, Lomeshaye Way, Nelson, Lancashire 0161 861 0344
NORTON UNITED . . . . . Norton CC & MW Institute, Community Drive, Smallthorne, Stoke-on-Trent, Staffordshire 01782 838290
OLDHAM TOWN. . . . . Whitebank Stadium, Whitebank Road, Hollins, Oldham, Lancashire 0161 624 2689
PADIHAM . . . . Arbories Memorial Spts Ground, Well Street, Padiham, Lancashire 01282 773742
WINSFORD UNITED . . . . Barton Stadium, Kingsway, Winsford, Cheshire . . . . 01606 593021 / 861980

Bacup Borough and Stone Dominoes move up to Division One replaced by Flixton and Winsford United. Stand Athletic withdrew during the course of the season. Newcomers are Eccleshall (Midland League) and Formby (Liverpool County Combination).

LEAGUE CUP

FIRST ROUND

Cheadle Town 0 **Castleton Gabriels** 3
Colne 2 Stand Athletic 1
Great Harwood Town 3 Ashton Town 0
Holker Old Boys 2 Darwen 1
Leek CSOB 0 **Chadderton** 1
Nelson 8 Daisy Hill 1
Norton United 2 Stone Dominoes 2 *aet*
Stone Dominoes 2 Norton United 1 *replay*
Oldham Town 2 **Blackpool Mechanics** 3
Padiham 2 Bacup Borough 1

SECOND ROUND

Abbey Hey 0 **Great Harwood Town** 2
Alsager Town 1 **Castleton Gabriels** 2
Blackpool Mechanics 0 **Salford City** 3
Congleton Town 5 Atherton LR 0
Curzon Ashton 1 **Prescot Cables** 3
Fleetwood Town 0 **Skelmersdale United** 3
Flixton 3 Atherton Collieries 2
Holker Old Boys 0 **Maine Road** 5
Nelson 2 **Newcastle Town** 4
Padiham 3 Glossop North End 2
Ramsbottom United 3 Colne 1
Squires Gate 1 **Nantwich Town** 3
Stone Dominoes 0 **Mossley** 5
Warrington Town 3 Chadderton 0
Winsford United 1 **St Helens Town** 3
Woodley Sports 2 **Clitheroe** 3

THIRD ROUND

Clitheroe 4 Prescot Cables 1
Flixton 1 **Skelmersdale United** 3
Maine Road 0 **Newcastle Town** 2
Mossley 4 Nantwich Town 3
Padiham 4 Castleton Gabriels 1
Ramsbottom United 1 Great Harwood Town 0
St Helens Town 2 **Congleton Town** 4
Warrington Town 0 **Salford City** 2

QUARTER-FINALS

Clitheroe 3 Skelmersdale United 1
Padiham 2 Congleton Town 1
Ramsbottom United 2 **Newcastle Town** 4
Salford City 2 **Mossley** 4

SEMI-FINALS

(played over two legs)
Clitheroe 4 Padiham 1,
Padiham 1 **Clitheroe** 1
Mossley 4 Newcastle Town 1,
Newcastle Town 2 **Mossley** 1

FINAL

(7th May at Bury)
Clitheroe 1 **Mossley** 2

WWW.NLNEWSDESK.CO.UK

DIVISION TWO TROPHY

FIRST ROUND

Darwen 2 **Great Harwood Town** 4
Castleton Gabriels 2 Chadderton 1
Holker Old Boys 2 Norton United 1

FIRST ROUND

Ashton Town 1 Holker Old Boys 0
Castleton Gabriels 0 **Bacup Borough** 3
Cheadle Town 5 Blackpool Mechanics 2
Daisy Hill 0 **Colne** 1
Great Harwood Town 3 Nelson 1
Oldham Town 4 Leek CSOB 0
Padiham 2 **Stone Dominoes** 4
Stand Athletic (scr.) v **Maine Road** (w/o)

QUARTER-FINALS

Ashton Town 3 Colne 1
Bacup Borough 6 Cheadle Town 1
Maine Road 0 **Stone Dominoes** 1
Oldham Town 2 Great Harwood Town 2 *aet* (5-4p)

SEMI-FINALS

Oldham Town 0 **Ashton Town** 3
Stone Dominoes 6 Bacup Borough 0

FINAL

(16th April at Congleton Town)
Ashton Town 1 **Stone Dominoes** 2

NORTHANTS COMBINATION

	Brixworth All Saints	Cold Ashby Rovers	Crick Athletic	Harborough Spencer	Harpole	Heyford Athletic	Islip United	Kettering Nomads	Milton	Moulton	Potterspury	Roade	Rushden Rangers	Stanwick Rovers	Weedon	Weldon United
Brixworth All Saints	P	1-3	2-3	1-1	1-3	1-4	1-1	2-2	1-2	0-2	5-2	0-0	2-2	2-3	2-2	1-2
Cold Ashby Rovers	1-1	R	3-1	4-0	3-3	0-2	4-0	1-1	1-2	1-2	3-2	0-3	1-4	1-2	1-1	0-1
Crick Athletic	1-1	1-4	E	0-1	0-2	0-1	1-0	1-1	2-0	1-0	3-0	1-0	5-2	2-0	1-2	0-3
Harborough Spencer	0-0	2-0	1-2	M	1-6	0-8	0-2	3-1	1-3	2-2	1-2	0-4	2-3	2-0	0-1	4-2
Harpole	0-0	2-0	4-0	1-0	I	2-1	9-0	4-1	0-1	3-2	1-1	3-2	5-1	4-1	2-1	2-1
Heyford Athletic	3-3	2-1	3-2	2-2	3-2	E	2-1	3-2	4-1	2-1	2-2	1-1	1-3	4-2	6-3	1-1
Islip United	2-4	0-4	1-5	1-1	1-1	3-1	R	0-3	2-3	0-2	2-2	1-4	3-2	3-2	2-2	2-2
Kettering Nomads	2-1	3-0	4-0	0-2	1-4	3-4	1-2		1-2	1-3	4-2	0-2	4-0	0-1	4-0	1-1
Milton	5-2	2-0	2-0	4-0	3-3	2-3	3-0	3-2	D	2-1	3-0	1-3	1-0	3-2	0-0	1-0
Moulton	3-4	1-2	2-1	3-4	1-4	2-1	7-2	3-1	2-4	I	2-0	3-1	4-2	1-0	1-1	3-5
Potterspury	2-0	1-2	1-0	3-0	1-5	0-3	3-2	3-5	1-2	3-1	V	2-3	1-7	5-2	0-4	3-2
Roade	1-2	1-1	0-0	4-0	3-1	4-0	5-0	3-1	3-1	0-1	1-4	I	2-2	1-0	0-0	4-1
Rushden Rangers	1-0	0-0	3-0	5-0	3-2	2-2	1-4	5-3	1-3	2-1	6-4	1-2	S	1-3	0-0	2-2
Stanwick Rovers	7-1	1-0	0-2	0-2	1-1	1-4	4-1	2-1	1-1	3-2	3-1	0-5	1-3	I	1-1	2-1
Weedon	0-0	1-0	1-0	3-2	1-6	1-4	1-4	4-2	1-4	0-1	1-1	0-1	3-0	0-4	O	1-1
Weldon United	1-1	2-3	2-2	0-0	0-4	3-0	4-1	2-2	1-3	1-2	1-2	0-3	3-1	4-0	2-4	N

Premier Division		P	W	D	L	F	A	Pts
Milton		30	22	3	5	67	38	69
Harpole		30	20	6	4	89	35	66
Roade		30	18	6	6	66	27	60
Heyford Athletic		30	18	6	6	77	51	60
Moulton		30	16	2	12	61	51	50
Rushden Rangers		30	12	6	12	65	64	42
Crick Athletic		30	11	4	15	37	46	37
Cold Ashby Rovers		30	10	6	14	44	45	36
Weedon	-3	30	9	12	9	40	49	36
Weldon United		30	8	10	12	51	54	34
Stanwick Rovers		30	10	4	16	46	59	34
Potterspury		30	10	4	16	54	76	34
Harborough Spencer		30	8	6	16	34	67	30
Kettering Nomads		30	8	5	17	57	63	29
Brixworth All Saints		30	4	13	13	42	61	25
Islip United	-6	30	6	7	17	40	84	19

PREMIER DIV. CUP

FIRST ROUND
Cold Ashby Rovers 5 Potterspury 3
Crick Athletic 1 Brixworth All Saints 0
Harborough Spencer 4 **Weedon** 7
Harpole 1 **Moulton** 2
Islip United 1 **Weldon United** 4
Kettering Nomads 1 **Rushden Rangers** 3
Roade 2 **Milton** 3
Stanwick Rovers 1 **Heyford Athletic** 3
QUARTER-FINALS
Milton 0 **Crick Athletic** 1
Moulton 1 **Heyford Athletic** 3
Weedon 3 **Rushden Rangers** 5 *aet*
Weldon United 0 **Cold Ashby Rovers** 2
SEMI-FINALS
Cold Ashby Rovers 3 Rushden Rangers 2
Heyford Athletic 3 Crick Athletic 1
FINAL
(23rd April at Bugbrooke St Michaels)
Cold Ashby Rovers 3 Heyford Athletic 1 *aet*

PREMIER DIVISION CONSTITUTION 2003-04

CALEDONIAN STRIP MILLS...... West Glebe South Pitch One, Cottingham Road, Corby, Northants 01536 401659
COLD ASHBY ROVERS .... Stanford Road, Cold Ashby, Northants... None
CRICK ATHLETIC.................... Crick Playing Fields, Rugby Road, Crick, Northants .... None
HARBOROUGH SPENCER ..... Leisure Centre, Northampton Road, Market Harborough, Leicestershire 01858 465934
HARPOLE.......................... Playing Field, Larkhall Lane, Harpole, Northants.................................... None
HEYFORD ATHLETIC .... Nether Heyford Playing Field, Nether Heyford, Northants......................... None
KISLINGBURY .... Beech Lane, Kislingbury, Northants 01604 831225
MILTON............................ Collingtree, Milton Mansor, Northants... None
MOULTON........................... Brunting Road, Milton, Northants 01604 492675
POTTERSPURY.......................... Meadow View, Potterspury, Northants................................ 01908 542675
ROADE .... Connolly Way, Hyde Road, Roade, Northants................................ 01604 862814
RUSHDEN RANGERS........................... Hayden Road, Rushden, Northants 01933 410036
STANWICK ROVERS............. Stanwick Recreational Park, Patrick's Lane, Stanwick, Northants .... None
WEEDON .... Jubilee Field, Bridge Street, Weedon, Northants .... None
WELDON UNITED .... Oundle Road, Weldon, Northants .... None
Kettering Nomads, Brixworth All Saints and Islip United drop to Division One replaced by Caledonian Strip Mills and Kislingbury.

Division One		P	W	D	L	F	A	Pts
Caledonian Strip Mills		26	19	5	2	88	34	62
Kislingbury		26	19	3	4	65	29	60
Stanion United		26	17	3	6	59	40	54
Corby Hellenic	-3	26	12	11	3	68	35	44
Clipston		26	10	8	8	56	39	38
Corby Legion Locos	-3	26	12	4	10	62	47	37
Gretton		26	9	6	11	68	73	33
Spratton		26	7	9	10	42	45	30
Earls Barton United		26	7	5	14	50	73	26
Corby Pegasus		26	6	6	14	47	74	24
Weavers Old Boys	-3	26	7	5	14	60	71	23
Hillmorton	-3	26	7	3	16	49	82	21
Wollaston Victoria	-6	26	7	5	14	43	70	20
Geddington WMC		26	4	5	17	29	74	17

Division One Cup Final (*15th April at Raunds Town*):
Corby Hellenic 1 Caledonian Strip Mills 0

Division Two		P	W	D	L	F	A	Pts
Finedon Volta		28	16	6	6	53	32	54
Whitefield Norpol		28	16	5	7	78	51	53
Ringstead Rangers		28	15	7	6	63	47	52
Priors Marston		28	14	4	10	62	44	46
Medbourne		28	13	6	9	53	37	45
Welford Victoria		28	13	5	10	61	42	44
Kettering Park Rov.	-3	28	13	7	8	64	54	43
Burton United		28	12	4	12	54	58	40
Wilbarston		28	12	2	14	56	55	38
Ristee Towers		28	10	7	11	47	51	37
Dainite Sports		28	10	7	11	44	48	37
Wilby		28	10	4	14	55	68	34
Northants Police		28	8	3	17	40	72	27
Podington & Higham		28	6	5	17	33	69	23
West Haddon		28	4	4	20	35	70	16

Division Three		P	W	D	L	F	A	Pts
Wellingboro Darndale		28	24	1	3	116	39	73
Weedon Malt. Arms		28	20	4	4	82	37	64
Ravensthorpe Athletic		28	18	3	7	91	41	57
AFC Sovereigns	-3	28	16	3	9	79	48	48
Great Doddington		28	14	6	8	81	57	48
Brafield United	-3	28	16	3	9	84	60	48
Raunds Academy		28	15	2	11	76	65	47
North'pton Sapphires		28	14	3	11	74	65	45
Wellingborough OG		28	14	1	13	70	68	43
Rushden Arbuckle		28	9	5	14	60	70	32
W'boro. Coach & H.	-3	28	8	5	15	60	78	26
Kettering Knights		28	7	1	20	42	81	22
Irthlingborough Bulls		28	6	4	18	51	103	22
Yardley United	-3	28	4	4	20	36	104	13
Kettering Alexandra	-3	28	2	1	25	39	125	4

Division Two Cup Final (*24th April at Rushden Rangers*):
Burton United 4 Medbourne 1

Division Three Cup Final (*8th April at Rushden Rangers*):
Ravensthorpe Rangers 3 Northampton Sapphires 0

Reserve Division One		P	W	D	L	F	A	Pts
Heyford Athletic Res.		22	17	2	3	76	11	53
Kettering Nomads Res.		22	15	1	6	56	26	46
Moulton Res.		22	11	5	6	70	41	38
Milton Res.		22	12	2	8	49	45	38
Harpole Res.		22	11	1	10	43	40	34
Brixworth AS Res.	-1	22	10	3	9	47	51	32
Bugbrooke St M. 'A'		22	10	1	11	45	53	31
Clipston Res.		22	9	2	11	60	60	29
Potterspury Res.		22	8	1	13	45	74	25
Gretton Res.	-3	22	7	3	12	37	56	21
Corby Pegasus Res.		22	5	2	15	43	81	17
Harborough Res.	-3	22	3	5	14	19	52	11

Reserve Division One Cup Final (*5th April at Kislingbury*):
Heyford Athletic Res. 4 Moulton Res. 1

Reserve Division Two		P	W	D	L	F	A	Pts
Crick Athletic Res.		24	20	2	2	73	25	62
Corby Hellenic Res.	-3	24	19	3	2	105	26	57
Roade Res.		24	16	4	4	58	24	52
Earls Barton Utd Res.		24	12	2	10	45	59	38
Corby Leg. Locos Res.		24	9	5	10	80	78	32
Stanion United Res.		24	8	7	9	54	48	31
Weldon United Res.		24	8	6	10	58	60	30
Spratton Res.		24	7	9	8	51	55	30
Kislingbury Res.		24	8	5	11	47	59	29
Stanwick Rovers Res.		24	5	7	12	37	54	22
Wilby Res.		24	6	4	14	42	66	22
Bugbrooke St M. 'B'		24	3	4	17	35	97	13
Wollaston Vics Res.	-6	24	4	4	16	53	87	10

Reserve Division Three		P	W	D	L	F	A	Pts
Rushden Rangers Res.		18	15	1	2	83	14	46
Finedon Volta Res.		18	13	1	4	61	27	40
Earls Barton Utd 'A'		18	10	2	6	41	36	32
Welford Victoria Res.		18	7	2	9	39	51	23
Cold Ashby R. Res.	-3	18	7	4	7	41	44	22
Ringstead Rgrs Res.	-3	18	8	1	9	34	49	22
Kettering Pk Rov. Res.		18	6	2	10	44	44	20
Dainite Sports Res.		18	6	2	10	34	48	20
Harpole 'A'	-3	18	7	1	10	28	38	19
West Haddon Res.		18	2	2	14	27	81	8

Reserve Division Two Cup Final
(*29th April at Bugbrooke St Michaels*):
Roade Res. 3 Crick Athletic Res. 2

Reserve Division Three Cup Final
(*24th April at Rushden Rangers*):
Rushden Rangers Res. 3 Harpole 'A' 1

NORTHERN ALLIANCE

	Amble United	Bedlington Terriers 'A'	Carlisle City	Harraby Catholic Club	Newc. Benfield Saints	Newcastle University	Northbank Carlisle	Percy Main Amateurs	Ponteland United	Ryton	Seaton Delaval Amat.	Shankhouse	Spittal Rovers	Walker Central	West Allotment Celtic	Winlaton Hallgarth
Amble United	P	1-0	1-1	1-0	2-5	0-3	0-3	1-1	1-0	4-2	1-1	1-3	3-0	0-1	0-0	2-1
Bedlington Terriers 'A'	3-0	R	0-2	0-0	1-3	0-1	1-1	1-1	4-3	2-4	4-1	3-1	1-2	1-0	1-3	5-1
Carlisle City	2-0	1-0	E	1-1	2-2	0-0	2-0	3-0	2-1	5-1	4-0	3-1	3-0	0-2	3-3	5-1
Harraby Catholic Club	2-1	2-1	1-3	M	0-3	3-2	0-2	1-1	2-1	0-0	1-1	1-0	3-1	2-0	1-5	1-0
Newcastle Benfield Saints	0-2	3-0	3-0	4-0	I	1-0	3-0	1-0	4-2	2-1	6-1	2-0	3-0	1-1	0-5	2-1
Newcastle University	0-0	2-3	1-4	3-0	2-3	E	0-3	2-0	1-4	3-0	7-0	2-3	1-2	2-1	0-3	5-0
Northbank Carlisle	3-1	6-1	0-1	1-2	3-0	3-0	R	5-0	3-2	2-3	2-1	0-2	7-1	2-2	1-3	5-2
Percy Main Amateurs	1-1	0-2	3-2	1-1	0-2	1-0	1-2		2-5	1-2	2-1	1-3	1-0	0-2	1-1	1-1
Ponteland United	4-0	1-1	2-3	2-0	1-6	1-1	0-2	2-2	D	3-0	7-0	2-2	4-2	3-0	0-2	1-1
Ryton	2-3	2-0	0-1	0-3	3-3	2-1	3-0	1-0	3-4	I	8-2	2-2	5-2	3-4	1-1	0-0
Seaton Delaval Amateurs	1-0	0-0	0-1	3-3	0-7	1-1	0-2	0-2	0-2	2-4	V	1-2	1-0	1-2	0-2	0-1
Shankhouse	2-0	1-1	3-2	2-2	2-4	3-1	2-0	4-3	3-2	7-2	1-0	I	1-1	2-0	0-0	1-0
Spittal Rovers	6-0	3-2	0-1	2-4	0-2	4-4	1-1	4-2	1-3	3-0	2-0	3-4	S	3-1	0-2	2-4
Walker Central	2-2	2-1	2-4	1-1	0-2	0-1	1-2	0-0	1-1	4-0	1-2	0-3	3-0	I	0-2	1-1
West Allotment Celtic	4-1	1-1	1-1	4-0	5-1	4-1	2-3	1-1	1-2	1-0	5-1	0-0	4-1	2-3	O	0-2
Winlaton Hallgarth	1-1	3-1	0-2	1-1	1-3	3-3	2-1	7-0	3-1	2-2	2-1	2-1	2-1	1-1	0-1	N

Premier Division		P	W	D	L	F	A	Pts
Newcastle Benfield Saints		30	23	3	4	81	35	72
Carlisle City		30	20	6	4	64	29	66
West Allotment Celtic		30	19	8	3	71	25	65
Shankhouse		30	17	7	6	61	41	58
Northbank Carlisle		30	16	3	11	64	40	51
Ponteland United		30	12	6	12	65	52	42
Winlaton Hallgarth		30	10	9	11	45	50	39
Harraby Catholic Club	-6	30	11	10	9	38	47	37
Ryton		30	10	6	14	56	67	36
Walker Central	-3	30	9	8	13	38	45	32
Amble United		30	8	8	14	30	54	32
Bedlington Terriers 'A'		30	8	7	15	41	51	31
Newcastle University	-3	30	9	6	15	50	52	30
Spittal Rovers	-3	30	8	3	19	47	72	24
Percy Main Amateurs		30	4	10	16	29	61	22
Seaton Delaval Amateurs		30	3	6	21	23	82	15

CHALLENGE CUP

FIRST ROUND
Amble United 1 Walker Central 0
Bedlington Terriers 'A' 1 Harraby Catholic Club 1 *aet* (4-3p)
Carlisle City 4 Shankhouse 2
Newcastle Benfield Saints 2 Northbank Carlisle 3
Newcastle University 0 Seaton Delaval Amateurs 1
Percy Main Amateurs 2 Ryton 0
Ponteland United 2 Winlaton Hallgarth 1
Spittal Rovers 2 West Allotment Celtic 3
QUARTER-FINALS
Amble United 2 Carlisle City 3
Northbank Carlisle 2 Bedlington Terriers 'A' 4
Ponteland United 4 Percy Main Amateurs 0
West Allotment Celtic 4 Seaton Delaval Amateurs 0
SEMI-FINALS
Carlisle City 3 Bedlington Terriers 'A' 1
West Allotment Celtic 3 Ponteland United 0
FINAL
(30th April at Penrith)
Carlisle City 3 West Allotment Celtic 4 *aet*

PREMIER DIVISION CONSTITUTION 2003-04

CARLISLE CITY......................Sheepmount Sports Complex, Carlisle, Cumbria............................01228 625599
CHOPWELL TOP CLUB ....Chopwell Park, Chopwell, Newcastle-upon-Tyne, Tyne & Wear ....None
EPPLETON COLLIERY WELFARE.. Welfare Park, Welfare Road, Hetton-le-Hole, County Durham ....None
HARRABY CATHOLIC CLUB.......Harraby Community Centre, Edghill Road, Carlisle, Cumbria 0191 526 1048
NEWCASTLE UNIVERSITY....Cochrane Park, Etherstone Avenue, Newcastle-upon-Tyne, Tyne & Wear ....None
NORTHBANK CARLISLE ....Sheepmount Sports Complex, Carlisle, Cumbria.....................01228 625599
NORTHUMBRIA UNIVERSITY . Bullocksteads Sports Ground, Kenton Bank Foot, Newcastle-upon-Tyne............None
PERCY MAIN AMATEURS ..... Purvis Park, St John's Green, Percy Main, North Shields, Tyne & Wear ....None
PONTELAND UNITED ....Ponteland Leisure Centre, Ponteland, Northumberland....................0191 257 4831
RYTON.............................Kingsley Park, Crawcrook, Tyne & Wear.................................0161 825441
SEATON DELAVAL AMATEURS ....Wheatridge Park, Seaton Delaval, Northumberland...............0191 413 4448
SHANKHOUSE ....Action Park, Dudley, Cramlington, Northumberland ....None
SPITTAL ROVERS ....Newfields, Berwick-on-Tweed, Northumberland ....None
WALKER CENTRAL.........Monkchester Greene, Walker, Newcastle-upon-Tyne, Tyne & Wear ....None
WEST ALLOTMENT CELTIC ....Whitley Park, Benton, Northumberland 0191 265 7270
WINLATON HALLGARTH ....Shibdon Park, Shibdon Road, Blaydon-on-Tyne, Tyne & Wear....................None
Newcastle Benfield Saints are promoted to the Northern League replaced by Eppleton Colliery Welfare. Amble United and Bedlington Terriers 'A' have withdrawn. Chopwell Top Club and Northumbria University come up from Division One.

	Chopwell Top Club	Cowgate Sports Club	Cramlington Town	Cullercoats	Haydon Bridge United	Heaton Stannington	Hebburn Reyrolle	Newbiggin Central Welfare	Northumbria University	Procter & Gamble Heddon	Rutherford Newcastle	Walker Fosse	Wallington	Wark
Chopwell Top Club		5-2	2-1	4-1	3-2	3-2	2-1	3-0	0-1	3-0	5-1	3-1	3-1	2-1
Cowgate Sports Club	1-3	D	2-1	1-2	2-5	1-0	2-2	3-1	1-1	3-1	3-1	1-5	5-1	1-3
Cramlington Town	3-2	4-1	I	1-1	0-1	3-2	3-0	3-2	1-4	1-0	4-3	1-5	5-1	9-2
Cullercoats	0-4	2-1	1-3	V	0-6	3-1	5-1	0-1	0-4	1-2	3-2	0-5	3-1	1-0
Haydon Bridge United	1-5	5-1	2-1	4-2	I	2-1	3-0	2-2	1-4	4-4	8-2	0-2	1-2	6-2
Heaton Stannington	4-0	3-3	2-2	3-0	3-2	S	5-0	1-1	2-1	2-2	4-2	1-3	1-0	2-5
Hebburn Reyrolle	3-4	0-4	1-0	0-0	1-1	1-2	I	1-1	0-9	0-1	3-2	1-2	0-1	0-2
Newbiggin Central Welfare	0-0	3-2	4-1	1-3	1-7	1-12	2-1	O	0-7	1-4	1-4	3-3	6-1	3-3
Northumbria University	4-1	1-1	3-1	1-2	1-1	4-2	1-0	3-0	N	0-1	5-0	5-3	1-2	2-3
Procter & Gamble Heddon	3-1	0-0	3-1	2-4	1-0	3-1	3-0	1-1	0-5		5-0	2-2	1-2	7-2
Rutherford Newcastle	1-2	0-6	0-1	1-2	4-2	1-4	0-2	3-3	0-8	1-1	O	1-1	3-0	6-2
Walker Fosse	1-1	6-2	2-1	1-2	5-1	1-3	3-2	3-3	3-2	1-3	3-1	N	2-0	4-1
Wallington	1-3	1-0	0-1	3-3	2-1	3-3	2-1	1-3	0-6	0-1	1-1	2-2	E	1-1
Wark	5-7	4-2	1-3	4-1	1-1	1-9	2-4	7-5	0-3	3-4	6-2	3-6	2-1	

Division One

		P	W	D	L	F	A	Pts
Chopwell Top Club		26	19	2	5	71	41	59
Northumbria University		26	17	3	6	86	25	54
Walker Fosse		26	15	6	5	75	45	51
Procter & G. Heddon		26	14	6	6	55	39	48
Heaton Stannington		26	12	5	9	75	48	41
Cramlington Town		26	13	2	11	55	47	41
Haydon Bridge United		26	11	5	10	69	52	38
Cullercoats	-3	26	12	3	11	42	57	36
Wark		26	9	3	14	66	92	30
Newbiggin Cent. Welf.		26	6	9	11	49	79	27
Wallington		26	7	5	14	30	59	26
Cowgate Sports Club	-6	26	8	5	13	51	60	23
Rutherford Newcastle		26	4	4	18	42	85	16
Hebburn Reyrolle	-3	26	4	4	18	25	62	13

COMBINATION CUP

WWW.NLNEWSDESK.CO.UK

FIRST ROUND
Cramlington Town 3 Wallington 0
Heaton Stannington 1 **Northumbria University** 3
Hebburn Reyrolle 1 **Chopwell Top Club** 5
Procter & Gamble Heddon 3 Newbiggin Central Welfare 2
Rutherford Newcastle 1 **Haydon Bridge United** 3
Walker Fosse 0 **Cowgate Sports Club** 1

QUARTER-FINALS
Cramlington Town 5 Cowgate Sports Club 1
Haydon Bridge United 2 Cullercoats 0
Procter & Gamble Heddon 0 **Chopwell Top Club** 2
Wark 3 **Northumbria University** 4

SEMI-FINALS
Chopwell Top Club 0 **Cramlington Town** 1
Northumbria University 6 Haydon Bridge United 1

FINAL
(28th April at Percy Main Amateurs)
Cramlington Town 0 **Northumbria University** 0 *aet* (3-4p)

DIVISION ONE CONSTITUTION 2003-04

BLYTH TOWN . . . . South Newsham Sports Ground, Blyth, Northumberland . . . . None
CRAMLINGTON TOWN . . . . Sporting Club of Cramlington, Cramlington, Northumberland . . . . None
CULLERCOATS . . . . Links Avenue Ground, Broadley, Cullercoats, Northumberland . . . . None
HAYDON BRIDGE UNITED . . . . Low Hall Park, Haydon Bridge, Northumberland . . . . None
HEATON STANNINGTON . . . . Grounsell Park, Heaton, Newcastle-upon-Tyne, Tyne & Wear . . . . None
HEBBURN REYROLLE . . . . Hebburn Sports Ground, Victoria Road West, Hebburn, Tyne & Wear . . . . None
NEWBIGGIN CENTRAL WELFARE . . . Newbiggin Sports Centre Ground, Newbiggin-by-the-Sea . . . . None
NEWCASTLE EAST END RAIL CLUB . . . . . . Stotts Road, Walkergate, Newcastle-upon-Tyne . . . . None
HEDDON . . . . Grange Park, Newburn Leisure Centre, Newcastle-upon-Tyne & Wear . . . . None
RUTHERFORD NEWCASTLE . . . . Farnacres, Coach Road, Lobley Hill, Gateshead, Tyne & Wear . . . . None
WALKER FOSSE . . . . Miller's Dene, Walkergate, Newcastle-upon-Tyne, Tyne & Wear . . . . None
WALLINGTON . . . . Oakford Park, Scots Gap, Morpeth, Northumberland . . . . None
WARK . . . . Wark Sports Club, Wark, Hexham, Northumberland 01434 230259

Chopwell Top Club and Northumbria University go up to the Premier Division. Cowgate Sports Club have resigned. Blyth Town and Newcastle East End Rail Club are promoted from Division Two. Procter & Gamble Heddon become Heddon.

	Ashington Coll.	Birtley	Blyth Town	Forest Hall	Highfields Utd	Newcastle BT	Newc. EE Rail	Otterburn	Stobhill Rges	Walker SFOS	Walker Winc.	Wallsend Town
Ashington Colliers	D	3-1	0-0	8-0	1-2	3-1	1-1	6-0	1-0	4-3	3-0	2-3
Birtley	0-2	I	2-4	3-3	2-2	1-2	1-2	1-2	0-1	3-0	2-1	0-0
Blyth Town	5-0	6-2	V	3-5	6-1	6-3	1-0	3-0	4-1	7-3	1-0	2-1
Forest Hall	0-0	1-6	0-2	I	1-1	0-1	0-2	2-2	4-3	5-3	5-2	2-2
Highfields United	0-0	6-5	0-2	1-1	S	0-3	0-4	0-5	2-0	0-5	4-3	3-2
Newcastle BT	3-1	4-1	2-2	2-3	2-4	I	5-2	6-1	1-1	3-1	5-4	3-5
Newcastle EE Rail	3-1	3-4	0-2	6-3	6-3	3-2	O	3-0	2-0	3-0	2-2	5-1
Otterburn	3-2	3-3	0-1	1-2	1-1	1-3	0-1	N	4-3	1-3	8-3	0-1
Stobhill Rangers	1-0	4-2	1-4	0-2	3-1	1-1	1-5	3-0		0-0	4-2	1-1
Walker Stack FOS	0-7	0-3	1-3	0-2	4-0	2-10	0-4	6-0	0-3	T	2-2	2-6
Walker W'comblee	1-2	1-5	1-4	3-7	2-4	2-1	1-3	3-3	1-1	3-3	W	3-6
Wallsend Town	1-1	3-1	3-1	1-2	0-3	2-1	3-0	3-1	2-1	5-2	3-2	O

Division Two

		P	W	D	L	F	A	Pts
Blyth Town		22	18	2	2	69	26	56
Newc. EE Rail Club		22	15	2	5	60	31	47
Wallsend Town		22	13	4	5	54	38	43
Newcastle BT		22	11	3	8	64	46	36
Forest Hall		22	10	6	6	50	52	36
Ashington Colliers		22	10	5	7	48	28	35
Stobhill Rangers		22	7	5	10	33	39	26
Highfields United	-3	22	8	5	9	38	58	26
Birtley	-3	22	6	4	12	48	53	19
Walker Stack FOS		22	3	3	16	38	76	12
Otterburn	-13	22	6	4	12	38	57	9
Walker Wincomblee		22	1	5	16	42	78	8

AMATEUR CUP

FIRST ROUND

Birtley 2 **Forest Hall** 0

Stobhill Rangers 1 **Newcastle East End Rail Club** 2

Walker Wincomblee 2 Otterburn 2 *aet* (4-3p)

Wallsend Town 1 **Walker Stack FOS** 3

Highfields United 0 **Newcastle British Telecom** 3

Walker Wincomblee 3 Walker Stack FOS 1

SEMI-FINALS

Newcastle British Telecom 1 Blyth Town 0

Newcastle East End Rail Club 4 **Walker Wincomblee** 2

(ineligible player – Newcastle East End Rail Club expelled)

QUARTER-FINALS

Ashington Colliers 1 **Blyth Town** 1 *aet* (1-3p)

Birtley 2 **Newcastle East End Rail Club** 3

FINAL

(2nd May at Percy Main Amateurs)

Newcastle British Telecom 4 Walker Wincomblee 0

DIVISION TWO CONSTITUTION 2003-04

ALNMOUTH . . . . Amble Welfare Recreation Ground, Amble, Northumberland . . . . None
ASHINGTON COLLIERS . . . . Portland Park, North View, Ashington, Northumberland . . . . None
FOREST HALL . . . . Palmersville Community Centre, Forest Hall, Newcastle-upon-Tyne, Tyne & Wear 01670 811991
GOSFORTH BOHEMIAN GARNETT . Benson Park, Gosforth, Newcastle-upon-Tyne, Tyne & Wear . . . . None
HIGHFIELDS UNITED . . . . Swan Leisure Centre, Berwick-on-Tweed, Northumberland . . . . None
MORPETH TOWN 'A' . . . . Storey Park, Morpeth, Northumberland . . . . None
NEWCASTLE BRITISH TELECOM . . . . . Burradon Welfare Ground, Burradon, North Tyneside . . . . None
OTTERBURN . . . . RTC Sports Centre, Otterburn, Northumberland . . . . None
PRUDHOE RTH. . . . . Eastwood Park, Prudhoe, Northumberland . . . . None
SWARLAND . . . . Swarland Leisure Centre, Swarland, Northumberland . . . . None
THE WILLOWS LEAM LANE . . . . Northumbria Centre, Washington, Tyne & Wear . . . . None
WALKER BIRDS NEST FOS . . . . . Lightfoot Sports Centre, Walker, Newcastle-upon-Tyne, Tyne & Wear . . . . None
WALKER WINCOMBLEE . . . . . . Swan Hunters Ground, Wallsend, Newcastle-upon-Tyne, Tyne & Wear . . . . None
WALLSEND TOWN . . . . Langdale School Ground, Wallsend, Newcastle-upon-Tyne, Tyne & Wear . . . . None
Newcastle East End Rail Club and Blyth Town are promoted to Division One. Birtley have resigned. Newcomers are The Willows Leam Lane (Tyneside Amateur League), Alnmouth (North Northumerland League), Gosforth Bohemian Garnett (Corinthians League), Prudhoe RTH and Swarland. Stobhill Rangers become Morpeth Town 'A', Walker Stack FOS become Walker Birds Nest FOS.

STAN SEYMOUR LEAGUE CUP

FIRST ROUND

Amble United 0 **Carlisle City** 3

Cramlington Town 5 Harraby Catholic Club 2

Cullercoats 4 Newbiggin Central Welfare 0

Haydon Bridge United 2 Rutherford Newcastle 1

Heaton Stannington 1 **Seaton Delaval Amateurs** 2

Hebburn Reyrolle 3 **Winlaton Hallgarth** 4

Percy Main Amateurs 3 **Shankhouse** 4

Ponteland United 3 Northumbria University 2

Spittal Rovers 1 **West Allotment Celtic** 2

Walker Fosse 1 **Newcastle Benfield Saints** 7

SECOND ROUND

Ashington Colliers 4 Newcastle East End Rail Club 1

Bedlington Terriers 'A' 0 **Northbank Carlisle** 2

Carlisle City 3 Blyth Town 3 *aet* (5-4p)

Cowgate Sports Club 3 Walker Stack FOS 1

Cramlington Town 2 Otterburn 1

Haydon Bridge United 15 Forest Hall 1

Newcastle Benfield Saints 3 Chopwell Top Club 1

Newcastle British Telecom 1 **West Allotment Celtic** 7

Newcastle University 4 Wallsend Town 3

Ponteland United 0 **Shankhouse** 5

Procter & Gamble Heddon 3 Highfields United 0

Seaton Delaval Amateurs 2 **Birtley** 4

Walker Central 4 Cullercoats 1

Wallington 3 Stobhill Rangers 1 *aet*

Wark 5 Walker Wincomblee 2

Winlaton Hallgarth 1 **Ryton** 2

THIRD ROUND

Ashington Colliers 1 Shankhouse 0

Carlisle City 4 Wark 0

Cowgate Sports Club 2 **Newcastle Benfield Saints** 3

Cramlington Town 3 Wallington 2

Haydon Bridge United 1 **Ryton** 2

Procter & Gamble Heddon 0 **Northbank Carlisle** 5

Walker Central 0 **Newcastle University** 1

West Allotment Celtic 8 Birtley 0

QUARTER-FINALS

Ashington Colliers 0 **West Allotment Celtic** 1

Newcastle Benfield Saints 6 Ryton 3

Newcastle University 0 Cramlington Town 0 *aet* (3-0p)

Northbank Carlisle 3 Carlisle City 3 *aet* (2-4p)

SEMI-FINALS

Newcastle Benfield Saints 3 Newcastle University 0

West Allotment Celtic 5 Carlisle City 1

FINAL

(5th May at Heaton Stannington)

West Allotment Celtic 3 Newcastle Benfield Saints 2 *aet*

NORTHERN COUNTIES EAST LEAGUE

	Armthorpe Welfare	Arnold Town	Borrowash Victoria	Bridlington Town	Brigg Town	Brodsworth MW	Buxton	Eccleshill United	Garforth Town	Glapwell	Glasshoughton W.	Goole	Hallam	Harrogate Railway	Liversedge	Ossett Albion	Pickering Town	Selby Town	Sheffield	Thackley
Armthorpe Welfare		2-2	0-2	0-3	2-1	3-5	2-4	2-0	1-2	4-1	1-5	1-4	1-1	1-4	3-0	0-0	2-2	1-4	2-1	0-0
Arnold Town	3-1		1-2	1-3	2-3	3-1	0-1	2-2	4-0	3-0	3-0	0-3	1-0	3-0	6-0	1-2	2-1	1-1	0-0	1-2
Borrowash Victoria	2-4	2-1	P	1-4	0-2	2-1	0-2	0-1	2-0	3-2	1-1	0-5	1-1	3-6	2-2	0-3	2-0	4-2	2-3	2-1
Bridlington Town	2-1	3-0	7-0	R	4-0	4-0	2-1	4-0	5-1	2-0	1-1	1-0	5-1	2-1	1-0	4-0	2-1	3-1	1-0	3-1
Brigg Town	2-0	1-0	4-0	0-0	E	5-0	1-3	0-2	2-0	3-1	2-3	1-1	5-0	2-2	4-1	1-0	2-1	0-1	4-2	0-0
Brodsworth Miners Welfare	2-1	1-0	6-2	4-2	1-4	M	0-4	1-4	5-4	1-1	3-3	0-4	0-2	2-6	1-4	6-0	3-0	0-1	2-1	0-1
Buxton	3-0	0-3	3-1	4-3	2-4	5-1	I	2-0	3-0	3-2	2-3	0-2	2-1	2-1	1-2	2-2	5-0	2-1	1-1	0-0
Eccleshill United	0-2	2-1	3-0	0-2	0-0	3-0	2-0	E	3-1	2-2	4-1	1-2	2-1	0-2	0-1	1-2	1-1	1-1	4-2	0-1
Garforth Town	1-2	2-5	0-0	1-1	1-1	1-0	0-6	1-3	R	1-2	2-4	0-2	1-4	1-4	1-0	0-2	2-3	2-0	1-2	2-0
Glapwell	0-2	1-0	1-1	0-1	1-4	2-0	2-3	0-2	4-1		1-2	1-3	1-1	3-2	4-1	0-1	2-1	1-0	0-1	0-2
Glasshoughton Welfare	0-1	2-0	4-1	2-4	1-6	0-0	7-2	2-4	2-1	0-1	D	1-1	1-1	2-2	2-1	0-2	2-0	2-3	1-4	2-2
Goole	3-1	1-1	1-0	2-2	2-1	0-1	0-0	4-3	3-0	1-1	0-1	I	1-2	2-1	2-1	0-4	0-0	0-0	2-0	2-2
Hallam	1-0	1-1	6-0	2-0	1-3	1-2	1-1	4-2	0-3	1-0	3-6	1-2	V	0-6	0-3	0-2	1-1	0-4	4-0	0-5
Harrogate Railway Athletic	7-1	2-0	3-1	1-1	0-2	1-3	0-2	4-3	2-1	2-2	2-0	3-3	2-0	I	3-4	1-4	1-3	3-0	2-3	2-2
Liversedge	1-0	3-2	2-0	1-2	1-2	3-3	2-2	0-2	4-2	0-2	3-1	1-0	3-2	1-3	S	0-2	2-0	4-0	1-0	0-3
Ossett Albion	2-2	2-2	4-0	0-1	1-2	1-1	3-2	1-1	5-3	1-1	2-0	1-4	4-1	2-0	1-3	I	1-3	2-0	0-2	1-1
Pickering Town	4-1	0-1	1-2	0-1	1-0	1-4	3-3	0-0	0-1	0-1	3-0	0-2	0-2	1-0	2-1	0-3	O	4-1	0-1	1-1
Selby Town	3-1	2-2	3-1	0-2	2-2	0-3	0-1	2-2	0-3	2-0	2-1	1-1	1-5	0-3	1-2	1-0		N	3-1	0-1
Sheffield	5-3	2-0	5-0	5-1	3-0	2-2	3-1	1-1	1-1	2-3	1-1	0-2	1-1	4-1	6-0	1-2	0-3	7-1		2-0
Thackley	1-0	2-0	1-0	0-1	0-1	1-0	2-4	3-0	0-3	2-3	2-0	1-1	0-0	0-3	1-1	2-0	4-0			

Premier Division	P	W	D	L	F	A	Pts
Bridlington Town	38	29	5	4	92	33	92
Brigg Town	38	22	6	10	75	42	72
Goole	38	20	11	7	68	36	71
Buxton	38	21	7	10	84	56	70
Ossett Albion	38	21	7	10	70	52	70
Thackley	38	17	11	10	53	39	62
Sheffield	38	17	8	13	74	55	59
Eccleshill United	38	16	7	15	61	57	55
Liversedge	38	16	6	16	59	65	54
Harrogate Railway Athletic	38	15	7	16	87	71	52
Glapwell	38	14	7	17	52	59	49
Glasshoughton Welfare	38	13	9	16	65	74	48
Pickering Town	38	14	5	19	49	51	47
Brodsworth Miners Welfare	38	13	7	18	64	84	46
Arnold Town	38	12	8	18	58	53	44
Selby Town	38	11	7	20	44	73	40
Hallam	38	10	9	19	50	75	39
Armthorpe Welfare	38	10	6	22	53	85	36
Borrowash Victoria	38	9	5	24	41	97	32
Garforth Town	38	9	4	25	47	89	31

WWW.NLNEWSDESK.CO.UK

PREMIER DIVISION CONSTITUTION 2003-04

ARMTHORPE WELFARE .... Church Street, Armthorpe, Doncaster, South Yorkshire 01302 831255
ARNOLD TOWN .... King George V Playing Field, Gedling Road, Arnold, Nottinghamshire. . 0115 926 3660. Fax: 0115 975 6441
BORROWASH VICTORIA .... Robinson Construction Bowl, Borrowash Road, Spondon, Derby, Derbyshire .... 01332 669688 / 668656
BRIG TOWN .... The Hawthorns, Hawthorn Avenue, Brigg, North Lincs .... 01652 652767 / 651605
BRODSWORTH MINERS WELFARE .. Welfare Ground, Woodlands, Doncaster, South Yorkshire 01302 728380
BUXTON .... The Silverlands, Buxton, Derbyshire .... 01298 24733 / 23197
EASTWOOD TOWN .... Coronation Park, Eastwood, Nottinghamshire .... 01773 712301 / 715823
ECCLESHILL UNITED .... Plumpton Park, Kingsway, Wrose, Bradford, West Yorkshire 01274 615739
GLAPWELL .... Hall Corner, Park Avenue, Glapwell, Chesterfield, Derbyshire 01623 812213
GLASSHOUGHTON WELFARE .... Leeds Road, Glasshoughton, Castleford, West Yorkshire 01977 518981
GOOLE .... Victoria Pleasure Grounds, Marcus Street, Goole, East Yorkshire 01405 762794
HALLAM .... Sandygate Road, Crosspool, Sheffield, South Yorkshire 0114 230 9484
HARROGATE RAILWAY ATHLETIC ... Station View, Starbeck, Harrogate, North Yorkshire .... 01423 885539 / 883104
LIVERSEDGE .... Clayborn Ground, Quaker Lane, Hightown Road, Cleckheaton, West Yorkshire 01274 862108
MICKLEOVER SPORTS .... Mickleover Sports Club, Station Road, Mickleover, Derby, Derbyshire 01332 521167
OSSETT ALBION .... Dimple Wells, Ossett, Wakefield, West Yorkshire .... 01924 280450 / 273618
PICKERING TOWN .... Recreation Ground, off Mill Lane, Malton Road, Pickering, North Yorkshire 01751 473317
SELBY TOWN .... Flaxley Road Ground, Richard Street, Scott Road, Selby, North Yorkshire 01757 210900
SHEFFIELD .... Coach & Horses Ground, Stubley Hollow, Sheffield Road, Dronfield, South Yorkshire 01246 413269
THACKLEY .... Dennyfield, Ainsbury Avenue, Thackley, West Yorkshire 01274 615571

Bridlington Town are promoted to the Northern Premier League replaced by Eastwood Town. Garforth Town drop to Division One from which Mickleover Sports are promoted.

	Gedling Town	Hall Road Rangers	Hatfield Main	Lincoln Moorlands	Long Eaton United	Louth United	Maltby Main	Mickleover Sports	Parkgate	Pontefract Collieries	Rossington Main	Shirebrook Town	Staveley MW	Tadcaster Albion	Winterton Rangers	Worsbrough Bridge	Yorkshire Amateur
Gedling Town		4-1	2-0	1-1	0-1	2-1	0-2	2-2	2-2	2-3	1-1	4-5	4-0	2-1	3-1	4-0	5-1
Hall Road Rangers	2-4		0-5	4-2	1-1	3-3	2-2	1-3	2-2	2-4	3-1	1-4	4-3	1-0	0-0	0-1	0-0
Hatfield Main	2-1	1-2	D	1-3	0-1	3-1	3-0	0-2	1-0	1-2	0-1	2-2	3-2	2-0	0-0	3-0	1-1
Lincoln Moorlands	1-0	3-1	1-2	I	2-3	0-2	3-1	1-2	2-1	2-2	2-1	0-1	2-0	2-0	1-2	3-0	2-0
Long Eaton United	1-3	1-2	5-1	1-1	V	0-0	4-3	1-1	3-2	2-3	4-1	0-2	3-1	5-1	2-2	2-1	3-2
Louth United	3-4	2-1	2-0	1-4	0-2	I	3-4	1-4	0-0	3-5	2-1	1-1	0-2	3-1	1-2	1-3	2-1
Maltby Main	0-4	2-3	1-2	3-1	1-1	0-3	S	0-1	2-6	1-4	3-4	1-6	0-2	1-6	3-2	1-0	1-1
Mickleover Sports	0-1	4-1	2-0	3-1	1-3	1-0	2-1	I	2-1	0-1	3-0	1-3	4-0	1-2	1-0	1-1	1-0
Parkgate	1-1	0-3	3-4	0-3	5-1	2-0	2-1	2-4	O	4-1	1-1	0-1	3-0	4-0	3-2	0-0	1-1
Pontefract Collieries	3-3	4-2	0-1	0-0	5-4	3-0	3-0	0-3	3-3	N	4-2	1-3	3-0	2-0	3-0	3-0	0-0
Rossington Main	1-0	2-2	0-1	3-2	2-0	2-2	1-2	1-2	2-1	1-1		2-1	1-6	1-1	2-1	2-1	3-1
Shirebrook Town	6-1	6-2	5-0	1-5	2-1	1-2	3-0	0-2	1-1	7-2	1-0		2-1	1-0	0-1	4-1	3-0
Staveley Miners Welfare	1-4	1-1	0-2	1-1	2-3	2-1	1-4	0-1	1-6	1-1	1-1	1-5	O	1-2	0-2	1-1	0-1
Tadcaster Albion	0-2	0-2	1-2	1-0	0-1	1-1	1-3	1-4	2-4	2-0	1-1	1-1	1-0		0-1	0-1	0-1
Winterton Rangers	3-3	1-3	1-3	1-1	2-2	0-1	3-2	1-2	3-4	3-0	3-1	0-0	1-0	2-3	E	2-2	1-3
Worsbrough Bridge MW	1-0	1-2	0-2	1-0	1-2	2-3	2-4	0-1	3-0	3-2	3-1	3-0	1-1	4-1	3-4		0-3
Yorkshire Amateur	1-1	0-1	1-1	2-4	2-3	5-3	1-2	0-1	0-1	1-0	2-2	2-0	2-1	1-0	0-1	3-1	

Division One	P	W	D	L	F	A	Pts
Mickleover Sports	32	24	3	5	62	26	75
Shirebrook Town	32	21	5	6	79	38	68
Long Eaton United	32	17	7	8	66	52	58
Pontefract Collieries	32	16	7	9	68	56	55
Hatfield Main	32	17	4	11	49	42	55
Gedling Town	32	15	8	9	70	48	53
Lincoln Moorlands	32	14	6	12	56	62	48
Parkgate	32	12	10	10	66	52	46
Hall Road Rangers	32	12	8	12	55	67	44
Winterton Rangers	32	10	8	14	48	54	38
Yorkshire Amateur	32	10	8	14	39	45	38
Rossington Main	32	9	10	13	45	59	37
Louth United	32	10	6	16	48	62	36
Worsbrough Bridge MW	32	10	5	17	41	56	35
Maltby Main	32	10	3	19	51	80	33
Tadcaster Albion	32	6	4	22	30	59	22
Staveley Miners Welfare	32	5	6	21	34	69	21

Reserve Division		P	W	D	L	F	A	Pts
Wakefield & Emley Res.		24	17	5	2	67	21	56
Liversedge Res.		24	17	3	4	72	26	54
Thackley Res.		24	14	4	6	59	28	46
Harrogate RA Res		24	13	1	10	62	50	40
Pickering Town Res.		24	11	5	8	52	47	38
Tadcaster Albion Res.		24	11	4	9	49	51	37
Eccleshill United Res.		24	9	7	8	49	42	34
Garforth Town Res.		24	9	4	11	38	53	31
Ossett Albion Res.		24	7	5	12	38	52	26
Rossington Main Res.		24	8	0	16	40	73	24
Yorks. Amateur Res.	-3	24	5	5	14	35	57	17
Pontefract Collieries Res.		24	4	4	16	18	43	16
Selby Town Res.	-6	24	6	3	15	29	65	15

DIVISION ONE CONSTITUTION 2003-04

CARLTON TOWN . . . . Stoke Lane, Gedling, Nottingham, Nottinghamshire 0115 987 3583
GARFORTH TOWN . . . . Wheatley Park Stadium, Cedar Ridge, Garforth, Leeds, West Yorkshire 0113 286 5739
GEDLING TOWN . . . . . . Riverside Ground, rear of Ferryboat Inn, Stoke Lane, Stoke Bardolph, Nottingham 0115 940 2145
HALL ROAD RANGERS . . . . . . Dene Park, Dene Close, Beverley Road, Dunswell, near Hull, East Yorkshire 01482 850101
LINCOLN MOORLANDS . . . . Moorlands Sports Ground, Newark Road, Lincoln, Lincolnshire . . . . 01522 520184 / 874111
LONG EATON UNITED . . . . Grange Park, Station Road, Long Eaton, Nottingham, Nottinghamshire 0115 973 5700
LOUTH UNITED . . . . Park Avenue, Louth, Lincolnshire 01507 607351
MALTBY MAIN . . . . Maltby Miners Welfare, Muglet Lane, Maltby, Rotherham, South Yorkshire 0794 105 7883
PARKGATE . . . . Roundwood Sports Ground, Green Lane, Rawmarsh, South Yorkshire 01709 826600
PONTEFRACT COLLIERIES . . . . Skinner Lane, Pontefract, West Yorkshire 01977 600818
ROSSINGTON MAIN . . . . Welfare Ground, Oxford Street, Rossington, South Yorkshire 01302 865524
SHIREBROOK TOWN . . . . BRSA Sports Ground, Langwith Road, Shirebrook, Derbyshire 01623 742535
SOUTH NORMANTON ATHLETIC . ExChem Sports Ground, Lees Lane, South Normanton, Alfreton 01773 581491
STAVELEY MINERS WELFARE. . . . . Inkersall Road, Staveley, Chesterfield, Derbyshire 01246 471441
SUTTON TOWN. . . The Hoisery Mills Ground, Kingsmill Island, Mansfield Road, Sutton-in-Ashfield, Nottinghamshire 01623 552376
TADCASTER ALBION . . . . The Park, Ings Lane, Tadcaster, North Yorkshire 01937 834119
WINTERTON RANGERS . . . . West Street, Winterton, Scunthorpe, North Lincs 01724 732628
WORSBROUGH BRIDGE MW. . . . . Park Road, Worsbrough Bridge, Barnsley, South Yorkshire 01226 284452
YORKSHIRE AMATEUR . . . . Bracken Edge, Ruxholme Road, Leeds, West Yorkshire 0113 262 4093
*Mickleover Sports are promoted to the Premier Division replaced by Garforth Town. Hatfield Main have dropped to the Doncaster Senior League.
Carlton Town, Sutton Town and South Normanton Athletic arrive from the Central Midlands League.*

LEAGUE CUP

FIRST ROUND
Pontefract Collieries 1 **Rossington Main** 2
Shirebrook Town 1 Maltby Main 0
Winterton 3 **Mickleover Sports** 4 *aet*
Yorks Amateur 3 Worsbrough Bridge 1

SECOND ROUND
Arnold Town 3 **Harrogate Railway Athletic** 6
Borrowash Victoria 1 Staveley Miners Welfare 0
Brigg Town 0 **Goole** 2
Buxton 2 Gedling Town 0
Eccleshill United 0 **Hallam** 1
Glapwell 1 Rossington Main 0
Glasshoughton 1 **Bridlington Town** 4
Lincoln Moorlands 1 **Louth United** 2
Liversedge 2 **Hatfield Main** 3
Mickleover Sports 2 Brodsworth Miners Welfare 1
Ossett Albion 3 Hall Road Rangers 1
Pickering Town 4 Tadcaster Albion 0
Selby Town 2 Armthorpe Welfare 2 *aet*
Armthorpe Welfare 3 Selby 2 *replay*
Sheffield 3 Garforth Town 0
Shirebrook Town 4 Parkgate 3
Thackley 1 Yorkshire Amateur 0

THIRD ROUND
Borrowash Victoria 0 **Bridlington Town** 4
Glapwell 1 **Sheffield** 2
Goole 0 **Buxton** 2
Hallam 1 **Harrogate Railway Athletic** 2
Hatfield Main 1 **Louth United** 2
Mickleover Sports 3 Thackley 2 *aet*
Pickering Town 0 **Ossett Albion** 1
Shirebrook Town 5 Armthorpe Welfare 2

QUARTER-FINALS
Buxton 1 **Shirebrook Town** 2
Harrogate Railway Athletic 0 Sheffield 0 *aet*
Sheffield 3 Harrogate Railway Athletic 1 *replay*
Louth United 1 **Bridlington Town** 4
Mickleover Sports 2 **Ossett Albion** 3

SEMI-FINALS
Ossett Albion 3 Bridlington Town 1
Shirebrook Town 0 **Sheffield** 1

FINAL
(6th May at Brigg Town)
Ossett Albion 3 Sheffield 0

WILKINSON SWORD SHIELD
(Contested by the Division One clubs)

PRELIMINARY ROUND
Staveley Miners Welfare 1 **Maltby Main** 2

FIRST ROUND
Gedling Town 5 Louth United 0
Hatfield Main 2 Long Eaton United 0
Mickleover Sports 3 Parkgate 0
Pontefract Collieries 4 Winterton Rangers 1
Shirebrook Town 2 Hall Road Rangers 0
Tadcaster Albion 4 Lincoln Moorlands 2
Worsbrough Bridge MW 3 Rossington Main 0
Yorkshire Amateur 1 Maltby Main 0

QUARTER-FINALS
Mickleover Sports 3 Gedling Town 2
Pontefract Collieries 2 Worsbrough Bridge MW 1
Shirebrook Town 2 Tadcaster Albion 1
Yorkshire Amateur 1 **Hatfield Main** 2

SEMI-FINALS
Mickleover Sports 2 Hatfield Main 1
Pontefract Collieries 5 Shirebrook Town 2

FINAL
(First leg 8th April)
Pontefract Collieries 0 **Mickleover Sports** 2
(Second leg 21st April)
Mickleover Sports 1 Pontefract Collieries 1

PRESIDENT'S CUP
(Contested by the previous season's top eight from each division)

FIRST ROUND
Bridlington Town 5 Armthorpe Welfare 0
Gedling Town 4 Brigg Town 3
Hallam 2 Winterton Rangers 0
Harrogate Railway Athletic 3 Pickering Town 2
Lincoln Moorlands 0 **Sheffield** 3
Maltby Main 2 **Thackley** 4
Mickleover Sports 5 Worsbrough Bridge MW 1
Rossington Main 2 **Selby Town** 4

QUARTER-FINALS
Bridlington Town 4 Thackley 0
Harrogate Railway Athletic 1 Selby Town 0
Mickleover Sports 1 **Gedling Town** 2
Sheffield 5 Hallam 1

SEMI-FINALS
Harrogate Railway Athletic 3 Sheffield 1
Bridlington Town 2 Gedling Town 0

FINAL
(First leg 27th March)
Bridlington Town 2 Harrogate Railway Athetic 3
(Second leg 31st March)
Harrogate Railway Athletic 4 Bridlington Town 0

NORTHERN LEAGUE

	Bedlington	Billingham S.	Billingham T.	Brandon Utd	Chester-le-St	Consett	Dunston FB	Durham City	Esh Winning	Guisborough	Jarrow Rfg	Marske Utd	Morpeth Town	Newcastle BS	Peterlee	Prudhoe	Shildon	Tow Law	Washington	W. Auckland	Whitley Bay
Bedlington Terriers		0-2	4-5	0-1	2-2	1-1	4-1	3-2	3-0	6-0	0-1	5-1	6-0	3-0	3-1	1-1	2-2	3-1	2-1	2-2	2-1
Billingham Synthonia	0-2		0-0	2-3	4-2	3-2	0-2	0-1	4-0	3-0	3-1	3-1	3-3	2-0	3-1	2-1	4-1	2-0	2-0	2-2	4-1
Billingham Town	2-3	0-3		0-1	1-4	5-1	1-2	2-0	0-0	2-0	5-1	6-1	1-0	1-1	2-1	2-0	5-1	6-2	1-2	1-2	4-2
Brandon United	1-1	0-1	1-2		1-1	2-0	0-1	1-0	4-0	1-0	2-1	3-2	1-1	3-0	5-0	3-0	1-1	2-0	3-0	5-0	3-0
Chester-le-Street Town	0-2	4-1	1-1	0-2	D	2-1	1-0	1-2	1-1	1-0	1-2	1-1	1-2	6-3	0-1	2-1	0-0	3-1	0-5	1-1	0-3
Consett	1-1	0-2	3-3	2-2	0-1	I	1-1	1-4	2-0	5-1	0-3	0-2	1-2	2-1	2-1	3-1	0-3	1-1	0-1	3-1	1-0
Dunston Federation Brewery	3-2	2-2	1-0	0-0	0-1	1-1	V	2-1	1-0	0-1	4-2	0-1	2-1	4-2	3-1	0-1	3-1	1-1	0-1	1-2	1-2
Durham City	1-2	1-1	0-3	1-0	5-3	4-2	0-3	I	2-0	1-0	1-1	1-1	3-2	5-0	1-1	3-2	3-1	0-2	3-0	3-2	0-1
Esh Winning	0-1	3-0	0-7	0-3	4-2	1-0	1-1	2-4	S	0-0	2-6	2-1	0-4	2-1	4-1	2-0	2-0	0-1	2-1	4-1	2-1
Guisborough Town	0-1	1-1	1-2	2-4	2-1	3-1	1-2	2-4	6-0	I	3-0	4-0	2-0	3-1	4-1	2-0	0-1	1-1	4-1	2-1	
Jarrow Roofing Boldon CA	1-6	3-2	1-0	1-1	1-2	2-0	0-0	0-0	1-2	1-0	O	1-0	3-0	4-1	3-2	1-1	0-2	2-2	4-1	2-4	1-4
Marske United	0-4	2-0	1-2	3-4	1-1	2-2	0-0	2-0	1-3	3-0	3-1	N	2-4	3-1	5-1	1-1	2-3	3-1	2-1	2-0	3-0
Morpeth Town	1-1	1-0	2-2	1-2	3-1	6-0	1-0	3-1	2-2	3-0	2-2			1-1	4-1	1-3	1-3	2-2	1-1	1-0	3-0
Newcastle Blue Star	1-2	0-1	0-8	0-0	0-3	2-1	0-0	0-5	2-2	1-1	0-2	2-3	1-1		0-2	1-3	2-4	2-5	1-0	1-4	1-2
Peterlee Newtown	0-4	1-1	1-4	1-2	2-1	1-0	2-0	0-3	2-2	0-1	1-2	1-5	0-0	3-1	O	1-3	2-1	2-0	0-0	0-3	3-1
Prudhoe Town	0-3	2-0	0-3	2-3	0-0	3-1	2-3	2-1	2-2	2-1	1-1	1-3	1-1	6-4		N	1-3	2-2	0-0	1-5	0-4
Shildon	0-3	0-4	2-4	0-0	1-3	2-0	0-1	1-5	2-1	0-2	3-1	1-1	4-1	4-0	6-0	2-1	E	3-1	7-3	5-2	3-3
Tow Law Town	2-1	1-0	0-3	1-1	1-3	2-2	1-1	2-0	4-0	2-0	1-0	2-1	2-0	4-0	0-1	4-1	2-3		0-1	1-2	0-1
Washington	1-3	0-2	0-1	1-2	2-2	1-3	3-1	2-1	0-0	1-0	5-3	3-2	2-1	1-0	0-0					2-1	1-2
West Auckland Town	1-1	2-3	5-0	0-2	2-0	2-2	2-2	1-2	1-2	2-2	4-1	5-1	2-1	1-1	7-2	3-2	2-4	2-3			4-1
Whitley Bay	2-1	1-1	3-2	0-2	1-0	5-0	1-1	1-5	5-0	0-0	1-2	2-2	2-0	2-1	3-3	3-1	4-4	1-3	2-0	2-0	

Division One

	P	W	D	L	F	A	Pts
Brandon United	40	26	10	4	77	28	88
Bedlington Terriers	40	24	9	7	96	42	81
Billingham Town -3	40	23	6	11	100	53	72
Billingham Synthonia	40	21	8	11	73	47	71
Durham City	40	21	5	14	77	54	68
Shildon	40	19	7	14	83	74	64
Guisborough Town	40	19	6	15	58	43	63
Dunston Federation	40	17	11	12	52	43	62
Jarrow Roofing BCA	40	17	7	16	64	67	58
Whitley Bay -3	40	17	8	15	68	62	56
Morpeth Town	40	15	11	14	67	67	56
Washington	40	16	8	16	52	60	56
West Auckland -3	40	16	9	15	57	74	54
Chester-le-Street	40	14	11	15	60	63	53
Tow Law Town	40	14	8	18	58	63	50
Marske United	40	13	10	17	64	74	49
Esh Winning -3	40	14	8	18	51	84	47
Peterlee Newtown	40	8	9	23	44	89	33
Prudhoe Town	40	7	10	23	52	89	31
Consett	40	7	8	25	44	83	29
Newcastle Blue Star	40	3	9	28	37	105	18

LEAGUE CUP

FIRST ROUND
Billingham Synthonia 3 West Auckland Town 0
Whickham 1 Bedlington Terriers 2
Billingham Town 6 Easington Coll. 1
Eppleton CW 1 Evenwood Town 5
Murton 2 Northallerton Town 1
Newcastle BS 2 Guisborough Town 1
Prudhoe Town 4 Chester-le-Street 1
Washington 3 Kennek Ryhope CA 2
Washington Nissan 1 Consett 5
Willington 0 Horden CW 4

SECOND ROUND
Billingham Synthonia 5 Norton & Stockton Ancients 1
Billingham Town 1 Whitley Bay 2
Brandon United 5 Crook Town 1
Dunston Federation 3 Esh Winning 2
Durham City 1 Marske United 2 aet
Evenwood Town 1 Ashington 2 aet
Hebburn Town 1 Horden CW 2
Morpeth Town 6 Shotton Comrades 1
Murton 2 Newcastle Blue Star 3 aet
Penrith 3 Jarrow Roofing BCA 1
Peterlee Newtown 2 Prudhoe Town 1
Seaham Red Star 2 Alnwick Town 1
Shildon 3 Thornaby 0

Tow Law Town 2 South Shields 0
Washington 0 Consett 1

THIRD ROUND
Billingham Synthonia 2 Consett 0
Brandon United 4 Horden Colliery Welfare 0
Dunston Federation Brewery 0 Bedlington Terriers 2
Marske United 1 Newcastle BS 0
Morpeth Town 3 Ashington 1
Peterlee Newtown 2 Seaham RS 3
Shildon 2 Whitley Bay 1
Tow Law Town 1 Penrith 0

QUARTER-FINALS
Billingham Synthonia 2 Bedlington Terriers 1
Marske United 1 Tow Law Town 2
Seaham Red Star 1 Brandon United 5
Shildon 1 Morpeth Town 0

SEMI-FINALS
Shildon 0 Tow Law Town 0 aet (3-1p)
Brandon 1 Billingham Synthonia 2

FINAL
(5th May at Darlington)
Shildon 3 Billingham Synthonia 2 aet

DIVISION ONE CONSTITUTION 2003-04

BEDLINGTON TERRIERS .... Dr Pitt Welfare Ground, Park Road, Bedlington, Northumberland 01670 825485
BILLINGHAM SYNTHONIA ...... The Stadium, Central Avenue, Billingham, Cleveland 01642 532348
BILLINGHAM TOWN ...... Bedford Terrace, Billingham, Northumberland 01642 560043
BRANDON UNITED ...... Welfare Ground, rear of Commercial Street, Brandon, County Durham .... 0191 378 2957 / 378 1730
CHESTER-LE-STREET TOWN ... Moor Park, Points North, Chester Moor, Chester-le-Street, County Durham 0191 388 3363
DUNSTON FEDERATION BREWERY ... Federation Park, Wellington Road, Dunston, Gateshead 0191 493 2935
DURHAM CITY ...... Archibald Stadium, Belmont, Durham, County Durham 0191 386 9616
ESH WINNING ...... West Terrace, Waterhouses, County Durham 0191 373 3872
GUISBOROUGH TOWN ...... King George V Playing Fields, Howlbeck Road, Guisborough, Cleveland 01287 636925
HORDEN COLLIERY WELFARE. Welfare Park Ground, Park Road, Horden, Peterlee, County Durham 0191 518 2692
JARROW ROOFING BOLDON CA .. Boldon Sports Club, New Road, Boldon Colliery, Tyne & Wear 0191 519 1391
MARSKE UNITED ...... Mount Pleasant, Mount Pleasant Avenue, Marske-by-Sea, Cleveland 01642 471091
MORPETH TOWN ...... Craik Park, Morpeth Common, Morpeth, Northumberland 01670 518375
PENRITH ...... Southend Road Ground, Penrith, Cumbria .... 01768 863212 / 859990
PETERLEE NEWTOWN ...... Eden Lane, Peterlee, County Durham 0191 586 3004
SHILDON ...... Dean Street, Shildon, County Durham 01388 773877
THORNABY ...... Teesdale Park, Acklam Road, Thornaby, Stockton-on-Tees, Cleveland .... 01642 606803 / 613402
TOW LAW TOWN ...... Ironworks Road, Tow Law, Bishop Auckland, County Durham 01388 731443
WASHINGTON ...... Albany Park, Spout Lane, Concord, District 11, Washington, County Durham 0191 417 7779
WEST AUCKLAND TOWN ...... Darlington Road, West Auckland, County Durham 01388 834403
WHITLEY BAY ...... Hillheads Park, Rink Way, Whitley Bay .... 0191 291 3637 / 251 3680. Fax: 0191 291 3636

Consett, Newcastle Blue Star and Prudhoe Town drop to Division Two. Horden Colliery Welfare, Penrith and Thornaby move up.

	Alnwick Town	Ashington	Crook Town	Easington Colliery	Eppleton CW	Evenwood Town	Hebburn Town	Horden CW	Kennek Ryhope	Murton	Northallerton	Norton & Stockton	Penrith	Seaham Red Star	Shotton Comrades	South Shields	Thornaby	Washington Nissan	Whickham	Willington
Alnwick Town		0-5	5-2	3-1	3-3	2-2	0-1	3-4	0-2	0-1	3-2	0-1	0-0	0-2	1-1	2-3	1-0	3-2	1-1	2-4
Ashington	0-0		4-0	1-3	6-0	3-1	3-1	2-3	1-1	0-0	1-0	2-1	1-1	1-1	4-0	3-1	2-2	5-1	1-1	3-2
Crook Town	3-2	1-1		1-3	0-0	3-1	1-0	1-6	3-0	2-4	0-2	1-1	1-4	2-1	4-3	2-3	2-2	0-4	4-0	
Easington Colliery	3-1	1-2	4-3		1-3	1-2	1-1	1-3	2-1	3-7	4-1	1-1	2-1	4-1	3-1	1-6	4-0	0-0	2-2	
Eppleton Colliery Welfare	2-0	0-2	1-2	1-5	D	1-0	0-2	0-2	0-2	3-1	3-1	1-2	3-6	0-1	0-1	1-1	0-3	0-4	1-3	2-1
Evenwood Town	1-0	1-4	2-2	3-3	4-2	I	3-1	2-2	2-2	2-1	0-3	2-2	0-3	1-4	1-4	1-3	1-4	0-4	2-1	3-0
Hebburn Town	2-1	2-3	0-2	1-2	0-3	1-2	V	0-1	4-3	1-1	1-2	1-1	3-2	2-2	3-2	2-2	3-2	0-2	2-2	2-1
Horden Colliery Welfare	1-1	1-1	2-1	2-0	3-2	4-0	2-0	I	1-1	2-0	3-0	2-1	0-0	0-2	3-0	3-1	1-0	2-2	2-1	5-2
Kennek Ryhope CA	1-4	0-3	5-1	1-4	2-2	3-4	2-0	1-1	S	3-0	2-1	1-1	0-1	3-4	0-0	1-0	1-1	1-4	2-0	5-0
Murton	1-2	1-1	3-2	3-0	5-1	3-0	0-2	0-3	3-1	I	2-3	1-7	1-8	2-0	0-0	1-2	3-2	4-5	2-2	
Northallerton Town	3-0	1-2	5-2	1-3	3-1	5-2	3-1	2-3	3-4	1-0	O	0-0	2-3	1-2	0-1	1-2	0-4	1-2	1-1	4-1
Norton & Stockton Ancients	0-1	0-4	1-4	1-2	1-1	0-1	4-3	0-2	0-5	4-2	1-2	N	2-2	1-4	1-2	2-2	0-4	0-3	1-1	1-3
Penrith	0-0	2-2	3-0	2-0	3-1	6-1	3-0	1-0	1-0	9-0	0-0	2-0	T	1-0	4-1	2-0	0-0	2-0	2-1	8-0
Seaham Red Star	5-0	1-1	2-1	2-0	3-1	2-1	2-1	2-1	0-1	3-2	1-3	0-0	3-1	W	4-0	3-2	1-2	1-2	2-1	4-1
Shotton Comrades	1-2	0-7	4-4	1-6	3-2	1-5	0-3	0-1	2-1	2-2	1-4	1-0	1-4	1-3	O	1-3	0-2	3-3	1-2	2-4
South Shields	3-1	0-4	3-3	3-0	2-2	4-0	3-2	4-2	1-1	7-1	2-3	2-2	2-6	3-1	3-1	Q	1-2	3-1	3-3	5-2
Thornaby	2-1	2-1	5-1	1-3	1-0	5-3	4-1	0-1	3-0	0-0	4-0	1-0	3-0	1-0	2-0			2-2	4-1	4-1
Washington Nissan	2-0	1-3	3-1	6-2	4-0	3-0	1-0	1-3	5-0	5-1	3-2	2-0	0-2	0-2	5-0	3-3	0-0		5-2	13-0
Whickham	1-0	3-3	1-2	0-4	4-0	2-7	2-1	4-2	5-1	1-0	2-1	0-3	3-7	3-0	0-2	2-2	0-3			0-3
Willington	1-5	1-9	0-0	2-1	0-2	1-2	0-3	1-5	1-3	0-2	1-4	1-5	2-6	1-3	2-2	0-1	4-3	2-4		

Division Two		P	W	D	L	F	A	Pts
Penrith		38	26	10	2	102	28	88
Horden Colliery Welfare		38	26	7	5	83	38	85
Thornaby		38	25	8	5	84	32	83
Seaham Red Star		38	26	4	8	91	45	82
Ashington		38	22	13	3	101	37	79
Washington Nissan		38	21	5	12	102	57	68
Easington Colliery		38	19	5	14	83	72	62
South Shields		38	16	11	11	86	70	59
Northallerton Town		38	17	5	16	72	58	56
Whickham		38	14	9	15	68	72	51
Kennek Ryhope Comm. Assoc.		38	12	9	17	63	67	45
Hebburn Town		38	13	5	20	55	66	44
Evenwood Town		38	12	6	20	58	95	42
Murton		38	10	8	20	55	95	38
Alnwick Town	-3	38	10	8	20	50	69	35
Crook Town	-6	38	11	8	19	64	92	35
Shotton Comrades		38	8	5	26	46	103	29
Norton & Stockton Ancients		38	5	9	24	38	81	24
Willington		38	6	5	27	50	132	23
Eppleton Colliery Welfare	-15	38	6	8	24	45	87	15

CRAVEN CUP

FIRST ROUND
Easington Colliery 0 **Kennek Ryhope CA** 3
Evenwood Town 4 Murton 0
South Shields 3 Northallerton Town 2 *aet*
Thornaby 1 Eppleton Colliery Welfare 1 *aet* (5-3p)
SECOND ROUND
Alnwick Town 3 Norton & Stockton Ancients 2
Ashington 5 Whickham 0
Evenwood Town 3 Kennek Ryhope CA 1
Hebburn Town 1 **Penrith** 3
Horden Colliery Welfare 1 **South Shields** 4
Seaham Red Star 5 Shotton Comrades 1
Thornaby 6 Washington Nissan 1
Willington 4 Crook Town 1
QUARTER-FINALS
Alnwick 1 **Seaham Red Star** 2, **Ashington** 1 Penrith 0
Evenwood Town 1 Willington 0
South Shields 4 Thornaby 3 *aet*
SEMI-FINALS
Ashington 3 Seaham Red Star 1
Evenwood Town 2 South Shields 0
FINAL *(6th May at Horden CW)*
Evenwood Town 0 **Ashington** 2

WWW.NLNEWSDESK.CO.UK

J R CLEATOR CUP
(Div One champions v League Cup holders)
(10th August at Bedlington Terriers) Bedlington 0 **Durham City** 3

DIVISION TWO CONSTITUTION 2003-04
ALNWICK TOWN . . . . St James Park, Alnwick, Northumberland 01665 603162
ASHINGTON . . . . Portland Park, North View, Ashington, Northumberland 01670 811991
CONSETT . . . . Belle Vue Park, Ashdale Road, Consett, County Durham 01207 503788
CROOK TOWN . . . . Millfield Ground, West Road, Crook, County Durham 01388 762959
EASINGTON COLLIERY . . . . Welfare Park Ground, Easington Colliery, Peterlee, County Durham. 0191 527 3047
EVENWOOD TOWN . . . . Welfare Ground, Stones End, Evenwood, Bishop Auckland, County Durham. 01388 832281
HEBBURN TOWN . . . . Hebburn Sports & Social Club, Victoria Road West, Hebburn, Tyne & Wear 0191 483 5101
KENNEK RYHOPE CA . . . . Meadow Park, off Stockton Road, Ryhope, Tyne & Wear. 0191 523 6555
MURTON . . . . Recreation Park, Church Lane, Murton, Seaham, County Durham 07711 272474
NEWCASTLE BENFIELD SAINTS . Benfield Park, Benfield Road, Newcastle-upon-Tyne, Tyne & Wear 0191 265 9357
NEWCASTLE BLUE STAR. . . . . . . Wheatsheaf Sports Ground, Woolsington, Newcastle-upon-Tyne, Tyne & Wear 0191 286 0425
NORTHALLERTON TOWN. . . Calvert Stadium, Ainderby Road, Romanby, Northallerton, North Yorkshire. 01609 772418
NORTON & STOCKTON ANCIENTS . . . . . Station Road, Norton, Stockton-on-Tees, Cleveland . . . . 01642 530203 / 554031
PRUDHOE TOWN . . . . Kimberley Park, Broomhouse Road, Prudhoe, Northumberland 01661 835900
SEAHAM RED STAR . . . . Seaham Town Park, Stockton Road, Seaham, County Durham 0191 581 1347
SHOTTON COMRADES . . . . Welfare Park, Station Road, Shotton Colliery, County Durham. 0191 526 2202
SOUTH SHIELDS. . . . . Filtrona Park, Shaftsbury Avenue, Simonside Industrial Estate, South Shields. 0191 427 9839
WASHINGTON NISSAN . . . . Nissan Sports Complex, Washington Road, Sunderland, Tyne & Wear 0191 418 7493
WHICKHAM . . . . Glebe Ground, Rectory Lane, Whickham, Newcastle-upon-Tyne, Tyne & Wear 0191 420 0186
WILLINGTON . . . . Hall Lane, Hall Lane Estate, Willington, County Durham 01388 746221
Horden Colliery Welfare, Penrith and Thornaby move up to Division One replaced by Consett, Newcastle Blue Star and Prudhoe. Eppleton Colliery Welfare drop to the Northern Alliance from which Newcastle Benfield Saints arrive.

NORTHERN PREMIER LEAGUE

	Accrington	Altrincham	Ashton Utd	Barrow	Blyth Spar.	Bradford PA	Burscough	Colwyn Bay	Droylsden	Frickley	Gainsboro.	Gateshead	Harrogate T.	Hucknall	Hyde Utd	Lancaster	Marine	Runcorn FCH	Stalybridge	Vauxhall	Wake./Emley	Whitby T.	Worksop T.
Accrington Stanley		3-1	2-1	3-2	3-1	4-2	2-0	2-1	2-1	2-1	3-0	2-1	3-2	2-0	1-0	1-1	5-0	2-1	4-1	2-1	1-1	1-1	1-1
Altrincham	1-1		1-0	1-2	3-2	0-0	0-0	4-2	3-1	1-0	1-1	4-0	0-4	0-0	4-1	3-0	0-1	1-1	3-3	0-2	0-1	2-1	2-4
Ashton United	2-2	1-0		2-2	2-1	1-4	0-0	2-2	2-1	3-2	1-3	3-1	5-0	2-3	2-1	2-2	2-3	3-3	1-1	2-1	2-1	1-1	1-4
Barrow	1-0	4-0	0-3	P	2-1	3-2	3-0	2-1	0-0	2-1	3-2	2-0	1-2	1-1	3-0	2-2	1-0	3-0	1-0	1-2	1-1	2-2	3-1
Blyth Spartans	0-3	0-2	4-0	1-1	R	1-2	2-1	1-1	0-1	4-2	2-1	3-2	0-3	1-2	1-3	1-0	1-1	3-1	1-4	2-5	2-1	2-3	2-1
Bradford Park Ave.	1-1	1-1	1-1	2-2	5-1	E	3-2	4-2	3-1	2-2	1-0	2-0	1-0	0-3	5-1	0-1	2-1	3-2	2-1	1-0	1-1	2-3	0-1
Burscough	0-1	0-3	3-2	2-0	1-3	0-1	M	3-0	0-0	1-0	4-4	1-0	0-1	2-0	0-0	0-0	2-1	3-3	0-1	0-0	1-0	0-2	3-2
Colwyn Bay	1-2	2-3	1-1	3-4	1-2	2-0	1-3	I	0-3	2-3	0-3	2-3	0-1	3-6	2-0	1-1	0-2	1-3	1-1	1-1	3-2	1-1	0-2
Droylsden	2-2	1-0	0-1	0-2	7-0	2-0	1-0	2-1	E	3-1	3-0	0-2	2-1	0-0	1-5	0-1	2-0	1-1	1-1	1-1	1-0	2-1	0-1
Frickley Athletic	2-1	0-3	1-0	1-2	1-0	0-3	0-0	3-0	0-2	R	2-2	1-0	0-1	0-0	0-0	0-1	1-3	2-2	1-0	1-0	0-3	1-7	1-3
Gainsborough Trinity	1-5	2-1	1-2	0-2	3-2	2-2	0-1	2-1	1-4	2-0		0-1	1-2	2-2	4-2	2-1	0-0	1-1	1-1	2-1	4-1	0-1	4-2
Gateshead	5-1	0-0	0-1	2-2	3-0	1-1	1-0	2-2	0-2	2-2	1-1		2-3	1-5	2-1	3-3	1-2	2-3	0-1	3-2	0-1	1-3	2-3
Harrogate Town	0-2	3-0	0-1	3-2	3-1	5-2	2-1	4-1	0-0	1-2	0-2	1-3	D	2-0	3-1	1-3	1-1	3-1	1-0	2-2	1-2	0-2	2-2
Hucknall Town	2-1	4-1	2-3	0-3	0-2	1-2	3-1	2-1	2-0	1-0	0-0	1-1	1-1	I	2-0	1-1	2-1	3-3	2-2	1-2	1-1	1-2	0-0
Hyde United	3-3	0-2	1-1	1-3	1-1	3-1	1-0	0-2	1-3	2-3	1-5	0-1	1-5	0-1	V	2-3	0-2	0-2	0-1	1-0	0-1	3-3	1-4
Lancaster City	1-2	3-0	1-3	1-5	1-4	2-3	2-1	1-0	0-3	4-0	0-1	2-1	1-2	1-2	4-1	I	1-0	1-1	0-1	1-2	5-2	0-1	1-4
Marine	0-3	0-1	1-0	3-1	2-1	4-2	1-0	0-0	2-2	0-1	0-0	4-2	2-2	2-1	4-1	4-0	S	0-2	1-2	1-2	2-1	5-5	1-2
Runcorn FC Halton	0-2	3-2	3-2	1-1	2-2	2-0	0-2	6-2	0-0	0-1	0-5	1-1	2-1	0-3	1-1	1-4	2-1	I	1-0	0-5	4-1	1-1	3-0
Stalybridge Celtic	1-4	2-0	4-1	4-3	1-1	2-2	1-0	3-1	2-1	3-1	3-0	4-4	4-1	1-2	6-0	1-0	2-1	0-1	O	2-2	0-0	2-0	4-1
Vauxhall Motors	0-1	4-0	5-1	1-1	0-1	0-1	1-0	2-3	2-1	5-0	1-0	3-0	1-1	5-1	1-0	6-2	1-1	2-1	2-1	N	1-0	3-2	0-1
Wakefield & Emley	0-0	2-1	1-1	0-1	1-1	2-0	1-0	2-1	2-2	0-0	2-1	2-1	0-0	1-1	1-1	1-4	1-1	0-0	0-0	1-1		1-0	1-0
Whitby Town	0-3	0-1	3-2	1-1	4-4	0-1	0-2	1-0	5-2	3-1	3-0	2-2	4-2	3-3	3-2	2-3	2-0	0-3	1-2	2-0	1-2		0-1
Worksop Town	1-4	1-2	3-2	0-2	1-1	7-1	0-2	4-1	4-1	2-4	0-1	2-0	1-2	5-4	2-1	1-1	2-1	2-2	1-1	1-1	1-2	0-0	

Premier Division	P	HOME					AWAY					TOTAL					
		W	D	L	F	A	W	D	L	F	A	W	D	L	F	A	Pts
Accrington Stanley	44	18	4	0	53	20	12	6	4	44	24	30	10	4	97	44	100
Barrow	44	14	5	3	41	21	10	7	5	43	31	24	12	8	84	52	84
Vauxhall Motors	44	14	3	5	46	19	8	7	7	35	27	22	10	12	81	46	76
Stalybridge Celtic	44	14	5	3	52	26	7	8	7	25	25	21	13	10	77	51	76
Worksop Town	44	9	6	7	42	35	12	3	7	40	32	21	9	14	82	67	72
Harrogate Town	44	10	4	8	38	31	11	4	7	37	32	21	8	15	75	63	71
Bradford Park Ave.	44	12	6	4	42	27	8	4	10	31	43	20	10	14	73	70	70
Hucknall Town	44	8	6	8	32	28	9	7	6	40	34	17	15	12	72	62	66
Droylsden	44	11	4	7	31	21	7	6	9	31	31	18	10	16	62	52	64
Whitby Town	44	8	4	10	38	38	9	8	5	42	31	17	12	15	80	69	63
Marine	44	10	5	7	39	31	7	5	10	24	29	17	10	17	63	60	61
Wakefield & Emley	44	8	12	2	22	17	6	6	10	24	32	14	18	12	46	49	60
Runcorn FC Halton	44	9	6	7	33	37	6	9	7	36	37	15	15	14	69	74	60
Altrincham	44	9	7	6	34	27	8	2	12	24	36	17	9	18	58	63	60
Gainsborough Trin.	44	9	5	8	35	35	7	6	9	32	31	16	11	17	67	66	59
Ashton United	44	8	9	5	42	39	7	4	11	29	40	15	13	16	71	79	58
Lancaster City	44	8	1	13	33	39	8	8	6	38	36	16	9	19	71	75	57
Burscough	44	9	6	7	26	24	5	3	14	18	27	14	9	21	44	51	51
Blyth Spartans	44	9	3	10	34	40	5	6	11	33	47	14	9	21	67	87	51
Frickley Athletic	44	7	5	10	18	33	6	3	13	27	45	13	8	23	45	78	47
Gateshead	44	5	7	10	34	39	5	4	13	26	42	10	11	23	60	81	41
Colwyn Bay	44	3	5	14	28	47	2	4	16	24	52	5	9	30	52	99	24
Hyde United	44	3	4	15	22	47	2	4	16	18	51	5	8	31	40	98	23

Accrington Stanley are promoted to the Football Conference, replaced by Southport. Gateshead (via play-offs – see P118), Colwyn Bay and Hyde United drop to Division One. They are replaced by Alfreton Town, Spennymoor United and play-off winners Radcliffe Borough.

PETER SWALES CHALLENGE SHIELD

(League champions v League Cup winners)

(3rd May at Accrington Stanley)
Accrington Stanley 2 Marine 0

N.P.L. PREMIER DIVISION – GATES 'N DATES

	ACC	ALT	ASH	BAR	BLY	BPA	BUR	COL	DRO	FRI	GAI	GAT	HAR	HUC	HYD	LAN	MAR	RUN	STA	VAU	WAK	WHI	WOR
	2263 12 Apr	665 4 Dec		1334 11 Apr	1116 1 Mar	873 14 Dec	1488 2 Oct	1367 9 Oct	1195 14 Sep	936 28 Dec	1068 28 Dec	1074 6 Nov	942 8 Feb	1290 26 Apr	1318 21 Apr	925 18 Jan	602 17 Aug	892 13 Nov	1032 4 Sep	1455 21 Sep	1355 22 Mar	1134 19 Oct
Acc'gton		600 11 Mar	595 5 Apr	574 5 Nov	548 8 Feb	494 3 Sep	560 19 Apr	715 14 Sep		582 26 Aug	576 23 Nov	540 6 Nov	552 8 Feb	557 16 Nov	604 21 Apr			628 17 Aug	897 13 Nov	455 4 Sep	602 21 Sep	620 22 Mar	738 19 Oct
Alt'cham	409 24 Sep		443 14 Sep	337 12 Apr	253 8 Feb	280 12 Nov	315 19 Apr	186 26 Dec	208 11 Mar	225 21 Dec	242 15 Feb	205 26 Oct	234 17 Aug	213 22 Feb	195 26 Apr	213 30 Nov	190 19 Apr	180 28 Jan	185 15 Oct	275 20 Aug	255 10 Sep
Ashton U.	1442 2 Nov	881		841 5 Oct	1501 26 Aug	1022 31 Aug	854 26 Dec	911 11 Mar	942 1 Mar	1038 8 Feb	1004 15 Feb	877 26 Oct	1013 25 Mar	1302 16 Oct	1520 16 Apr	1218 30 Nov	757 19 Apr	870 24 Aug	977 28 Jan	1211 15 Oct	1012 20 Aug	788 10 Sep
Barrow	418	528 4 Mar	349 17 Sep		255 26 Aug	436 5 Apr	353 22 Mar	339 19 Apr	371 1 Mar	326 8 Feb	676 21 Dec	426 15 Mar	309 15 Mar	376 17 Aug	347 26 Dec	366 4 Jan	344 8 Oct	317 24 Sep	318 5 Oct	291 9 Nov	328 7 Sep	324 15 Apr
Blyth S.	760	440 31 Aug	271 14 Dec	345 25 Feb		286 5 Apr	234 22 Feb	314 15 Mar	339	426	261 24 Aug	323 21 Apr	437 4 Mar	341 15 Apr	257 1 Feb	332 5 Apr	345 21 Sep	329 23 Nov	253 9 Nov	288 4 Dec	340 11 Feb	402 25 Mar
Brad. PA	576 5 Oct	294 29 Mar	125 8 Feb	368 14 Sep	188 19 Mar		167 30 Oct	176 23 Nov	357 4 Jan		165 11 Sep	186 29 Jan	207	301 28 Dec	237 1 Feb	250 5 Apr	187 2 Nov	164 19 Apr	234 9 Apr	701 23 Nov	132 9 Apr	204 18 Mar
B'scough	450 20 Aug	447	148	346 14 Sep	193	145 23 Apr	167 24 Sep	304	132 5 Oct	171 17 Sep	165 19 Oct	237 25 Mar	188 7 Sep	207	149 20 Aug	256 17 Sep	223 26 Apr	234 26 Dec	202 24 Aug	185 21 Apr	247
Col. Bay	539	316 12 Nov	503	269 24 Aug	195 16 Nov	118 25 Feb	315 24 Sep	306 31 Aug		140	237	171	246 21 Dec	312 5 Apr	347 1 Oct	223 7 Sep	257 17 Sep	250 26 Oct	202 25 Mar	311 26 14 Dec	175 29 Mar	184 15 Mar
Droylsden	290 5 Apr	215 31 Mar	158	208 28 Dec	185 11 Nov	176 27 Mar	195	211	201 31 Aug	201	171 30 Sep	121 21 Dec	234 18 Jan	138 16 Sep	178 22 Mar	136 7 Oct	182 2 Sep	183 21 Apr	184	261 23 Nov	168 1 Mar	184
Frickley	420 26 Oct	467 1 Apr	212	286 1 Oct	212	286	147 9 Nov	147 1 Feb	137 1 Feb	121 15 Oct	121 12 Apr	234 4 Mar	138 16 Sep	119	178 24 Jun	136 16 Nov	257 2 Sep	326 15 Mar	326 7 Sep	227 21 Apr	157 12 Oct	394 7 Apr
G'boro.	273 19 Apr	264 9 Nov	187 26 Aug	254 25 Jan	495 18 Jan	266 26 Oct	176 23 Nov	173 4 Jan	357	182	353	353 8 Feb	329 29 Oct	386 8 Oct	381 17 Aug	358 7 Dec	288 15 Mar	317 4 Mar	326 7 Sep	274 17 Sep	414 5 Apr	1240 20 Aug
Gatesh'd	706 11 Jan	368 15 Feb	187 7 Sep	254 23 Nov	495 26 Dec	266 1 Feb	167 12 Oct	176 7 Dec	461 25 Sep	407 31 Aug	317 1 Oct	343 9 Nov	343	163 30 Nov	146 17 Aug	208 15 Mar	210 5 Apr	224 22 Feb	204 18 Jan	204 21 Apr	176 5 Apr	278 26 Dec
H'gate T.	332 31 Aug	302 1 Feb	227	343 21 Apr	280 7 Dec	607 19 Apr	315 8 Mar	315 24 Aug	138 9 Apr	319 1 Mar	317	317 1 Oct	259	470 11 Jan	408 19 Oct	425 22 Mar	321 14 Dec	575 20 Aug	355 21 Apr	427 7 Sep	488 15 Feb	517 19 Apr
Hucknall	652 21 Dec	485 24 Aug	325 5 Nov	199 12 Nov	142 8 Apr	150 21 Apr	195 28 Dec	195 14 Sep	138 9 Apr	251	243 1 Mar	186 14 Dec	259		262 21 Sep	192 22 Mar	166 14 Dec	225 23 Nov	219 21 Apr	233 15 Feb	196 12 Nov	485 23 Nov
Hyde Utd	677 24 Nov	325 21 Apr	363	363 14 Oct	255 12 Mar	436 15 Oct	353 4 Jan	353 9 Sep	371 9 Apr	281 5 Oct	251 22 Feb	186 12 Apr	268 7 Dec	267 9 Nov	301 31 Aug	307 19 Apr	334 23 Nov	909 10 Sep	237 21 Apr	237 31 Aug	284 24 Aug	319 4 Oct
Lancaster	677 15 Mar	325 23 Nov	279	888 1 Jan	282 18 Apr	352 19 Aug	232 4 Jan	232 9 Nov	264 9 Sep	206 22 Feb	277	253 3 Sep	294 22 Feb	289 8 Feb	301 23 Sep		364 1 Feb	364 28 Oct	316 2 Nov	333 31 Aug	295 28 Dec	398 31 Mar
Marine	361 24 Aug	231 2 Dec	254 1 Mar	252 21 Apr	265 26 Dec	288 21 Sep	233 17 Mar	113 29 Mar	263 25 Mar	241 17 Apr	291 21 Sep	252 29 Mar	224 10 Sep	239 28 Dec	224	9 Nov		364 26 Dec	268 14 Oct	324 2 Nov	230 28 Dec	339 14 Sep
Runcorn	421 1 Feb	334 5 Nov	202	343 3 Dec	202 7 Dec	265 24 Jun	502 26 Aug	690 16 Nov	138 15 Feb	429 21 Sep	338 5 Nov	227 14 Sep	311 10 Sep	169 19 Oct	164 18 Sep	208	26 Dec		397 31 Aug	401 12 Nov	222 10 Mar	102 14 Dec	242 29 Mar
S'bridge	790 7 Sep	857 5 Nov	826 18 Jan	511 3 Dec	525 26 Apr	847 28 Dec	247 10 Sep	262 5 Oct	176 26 Apr	175 5 Apr	222 5 Nov	265 19 Oct	448 8 Oct	593 23 Apr	433 12 Oct	205 3 Sep	254 1 Mar	254 14 Dec		486 17 Aug	563 2 Nov	196 21 Sep	512 8 Mar
Vauxhall	396 15 Apr	315 14 Dec	207 1 Oct	250 19 Oct	153 12 Apr	251 22 Mar	218 18 Feb	176 10 Sep	262 15 Feb	183 1 Mar	183 29 Mar	147 14 Dec	204 15 Mar	204 15 Mar	214 8 Oct	204 21 Jan	214	167 21 Jan	237 1 Apr		280	220 21 Sep	281 24 Aug
Wake.&E	452 10 Dec	318 7 Dec	308 3 Sep	243 29 Mar	211 10 Sep	449 12 Apr	218 18 Jan	265 26 Apr	176	360 26 Dec	183 12 Apr	271 8 Oct	147 2 Apr	298 26 Apr	293 12 Nov	302 17 Apr	167 15 Apr	167 9 Nov	372 14 Sep	161 19 Apr		277 5 Nov	442 24 Aug
Whitby	566 6 Apr	402 22 Feb	274 8 Oct	357 8 Mar	326 10 Sep	332 26 Apr	317 17 Aug	317 31 Aug	265 11 Jan	275 24 Sep	308 14 Sep	275 16 Nov	3 Sep	301 18 Jan	293 26 Oct	299 5 Oct	294 9 Nov	687 9 Nov	317 7 Dec	317 8 Feb	322 15 Mar		326 3 Jan
Worksop	1063 22 Feb	754 2 Nov	478 22 Mar	739 21 Sep	738 3 Sep	571 3 Dec	611 18 Jan	639 11 Jan	639 26 Oct	483 11 Mar	523 26 Apr	636 26 Apr	517 13 Dec	592 13 Dec	444 26 Aug	607 5 Apr	687 7 Feb	687 7 Sep	557 25 Feb	557 1 Oct	606 1 Oct	672 17 Sep	

WWW.NLNEWSDESK.CO.UK

CONSTITUTION FOR 2003-04

ALFRETON TOWN   Manager: David Lloyd   Colours: Red & white
Nottingham Road, Alfreton, Derbyshire DE55 7GL   www.alfretontownfc.com
Tel: 01773 830277   Fax: 01773 830277   Club: 01773 832819
        Won promotion to Premier Division at first attempt a year after elevation from NCEL.

ALTRINCHAM   *Manager: Graham Heathcote*   *Colours: Red, white & black*
Moss Lane, Altrincham, Cheshire WA15 8AP   *www.altrinchamfc.com*
Tel: 0161 928 1045   *Fax: 0161 926 9934*
        One of England's most famous non-League clubs, and celebrating its centenary in 2003.

ASHTON UNITED   Manager: Gerry Quinn   Colours: Red, white & black
Surrey Street, Hurst Cross, Ashton-under-Lyne, Lancs OL6 8DY   www.ashtonunited.co.uk
Tel: 0161 339 4158   Fax: 0161 339 4158   Club: 0161 330 1511
        Contested two finals, losing the President's Cup but triumphing in the Manchester Premier.

BARROW   *Manager: Lee Turnbull*   *Colours: Blue & white*
Holker Street Ground, Wilkie Road, Barrow-in-Furness, Cumbria LA14 5UW
Tel: 01229 820346   *Fax: 01229 820346*   *www.barrowfc.com*
        Assistant manager Lee Turnbull steps up to take over from his boss Kenny Lowe.

BLYTH SPARTANS   Manager: Paul Baker   Colours: Green & white
Croft Park, Blyth, Northumberland NE24 3JE   www.spartans.freeserve.co.uk
Tel: 01670 352373   Fax: 01670 545592   Club: 01670 354818
        Experienced a management change during last season when John Charlton was sacked.

BRADFORD PARK AVENUE   *Manager: Trevor Storton*   *Colours: Green & white*
Horsfall Stadium, Cemetary Road, Bradford, West Yorkshire BD6 2NG
Tel: 01274 604578   *Fax: 01274 604578*   *www.bpafc.com*
        Three wins from last four games gave Avenue highest-ever finish of seventh.

BURSCOUGH   Manager: Mike Marsh   Colours: Green & white
Victoria Park, Mart Lane, Burscough, Ormskirk, Lancashire L40 0SD   www.burscoughfc.co.uk
Tel: 01704 893237   Fax: 01704 893237
        Lifted FA Trophy in May, knocking out holders and Conference toppers Yeovil en route.

DROYLSDEN   *Manager: David Pace*   *Colours: Red & white*
Butchers Arms, Market Street, Droylsden, Manchester M43 7AY   *www.droylsdenfc.co.uk*
Tel: 0161 370 1426   *Fax: 0161 370 8341*   *Club: 0161 301 1352*
        David Pace doubles up as both Chairman and Team Manager at Droylsden.

FRICKLEY ATHLETIC   Manager: Phil Sharpe   Colours: Blue & white
Westfield Lane, South Elmsall, Pontefract, West Yorkshire WF9 2EQ
Tel: 01977 642460   Fax: 01977 642460   www.frickleyafc.co.uk
        Club's pinnacle was 1985-86 – runners-up in the Conference and reached FA Cup Third Round.

GAINSBOROUGH TRINITY   *Manager: Paul Mitchell*   *Colours: Blue*
The Northolme, North Street, Gainsborough, Lincs DN21 2QN   *www.gainsboroughtrinity.com*
Tel: 01427 613295   *Fax: 01427 615239*   *Club: 01427 615625*
        Have appointed former Worksop boss Paul Mitchell to succeed Phil Stant.

HARROGATE TOWN   Manager: John Reed   Colours: Yellow & black
Wetherby Road, Harrogate, North Yorkshire HG2 7SA   www.harrogatetownafc.co.uk
Tel: 01423 880675   Fax: 01423 880675   Club: 01423 883671
        Achieved excellent sixth placed finish in first season in Premier Division.

HUCKNALL TOWN   *Manager: Steve Burr*   *Colours: Yellow & black*
Watnall Road, Hucknall, Nottinghamshire NG15 6AL   *www.devoted.to/hucknalltownfc*
Tel: 0115 956 1264   *Fax: 0115 955 5808*   *Club: 0115 956 1253*
        Sacked manager Phil Starbuck despite achieving a cup double in 2003.

LANCASTER CITY   Manager: Phil Wilson   Colours: Blue & white
Giant Axe, West Road, Lancaster, Lancashire LA1 5PE   www.lancastercityfc.com
Tel: 01524 382238/841950   Fax: 01524 382238   Club: 01524 843500
 Forced into a managerial change by Tony Hesketh's move to become number two at Southport.

MARINE   *Manager: Roly Howard*   *Colours: White & black*
Rossett Park, College Road, Crosby, Liverpool, Merseyside L23 3AS   *www.marinefc.com*
Tel: 0151 924 1743   *Fax: 0151 924 1743*   *Club: 0151 924 4046*
 Could complete a 2002-03 cup double if successful in Liverpool Senior Cup this August.

RADCLIFFE BOROUGH   Manager: Kevin Glendon   Colours: Blue & white
Stainton Park, Pilkington Road, Radcliffe, Manchester M26 3PE   www.radcliffeborough.com
Tel: 0161 724 8346   Fax: 0161 723 3178   Club: 0161 724 5937
 Promoted to Premier after dramatic play-off final penalty shoot-out win over Chorley.

RUNCORN FC HALTON   *Manager: Liam Watson*   *Colours: Yellow, green & black*
Widnes RLFC, AutoQuest Stadium, Lowerhouse Lane, Widnes, Cheshire WA8 7DZ
Tel: 0151 495 2250   *Fax: 0151 423 2720*   *www.runcornfchalton.co.uk*
 Conference (then APL) champions back in 1982 – in first year after promotion from NPL.

SOUTHPORT   Manager: Mike Walsh   Colours: Old gold & black
Haig Avenue, Southport, Merseyside PR8 6JZ   www.southportfc.net
Tel: 01704 533422   Fax: 01704 533422   Club: 01704 530182
 Mike Walsh takes over as manager following relegation back to NPL.

SPENNYMOOR UNITED   *Manager: Alex Mathie*   *Colours: Black & white*
Brewery Field, Durham Road, Spennymoor, Durham DL16 6UU   *Tel/Fax: 01388 811934*
Club: 01388 814100   *www.spennymoorunited.fsnet.co.uk*
 Promoted despite having two managers during 2002-03 – Tony Lee and Jamie Pollock.

STALYBRIDGE CELTIC   Manager: David Miller   Colours: Blue
Bower Fold, Mottram Road, Stalybridge, Cheshire SK15 2RT   www.stalybridgeceltic.co.uk
Tel: 0161 338 2828   Fax: 0161 338 8256   Club: 0161 338 8443
 Enjoyed a two-legged victory over local rivals Ashton United in final of President's Cup.

VAUXHALL MOTORS   *Manager: Alvin McDonald*   *Colours: White & blue*
Vauxhall Sports Ground, Rivacre Road, Hooton, Ellesmere Port, South Wirral CH66 1NJ
Tel: 0151 328 1114   *Clubhouse: 0151 327 2294*   *www.vauxhallfc.co.uk*
 Pulled off perhaps biggest shock of 2002-03 FA Cup defeating QPR at Loftus Road.

WAKEFIELD & EMLEY   Manager: Ronnie Glavin   Colours: Maroon & sky blue
Wakefield Wildcats RLFC, Belle Vue, Doncaster Road, Wakefield, West Yorkshire WF1 5HT
www.emleyafc.free-online.co.uk   Tel: 01924 211611   Emley Fax: 01924 860323
Emley Welfare: 01924 848398/840087
 Share the Belle Vue ground with Wakefield RLFC and Leeds United Reserves.

WHITBY TOWN   *Manager: Harry Dunn*   *Colours: Royal blue*
Turnbull Ground, Upgang Lane, Whitby, North Yorks YO21 3HZ   *www.wtfc.freeserve.co.uk*
Tel: 01947 604847   *Fax: 01947 603779*   *Club: 01947 603193*
 Installation of new seats and turnstiles, and pitch work, has been accomplished this summer.

WORKSOP TOWN   Manager: Steve Ludlam   Colours: Amber, black & white
Babbage Way, off Sandy Lane, Worksop, Nottinghamshire S80 1TN   www.worksop-town.co.uk
Tel: 01909 532282   Fax: 01909 487934   Club: 01909 501911
 Ended 2002-03 season with Sheffield & Hallamshire Senior Cup success.

	Alfreton Town	Bamber Bridge	Belper Town	Bishop Auckland	Chorley	Eastwood Town	Farsley Celtic	Guiseley	Kendal Town	Kidsgrove Athletic	Leek Town	Lincoln United	Matlock Town	North Ferriby Utd	Ossett Town	Radcliffe Borough	Rossendale United	Spennymoor United	Stocksbridge PS	Trafford	Witton Albion	Workington
Alfreton Town		1-1	1-2	4-1	1-3	4-1	2-0	1-3	4-3	2-0	1-2	2-2	2-0	3-4	5-1	3-2	3-0	1-1	1-1	6-1	1-1	3-0
Bamber Bridge	0-2		0-0	1-2	2-0	2-2	4-2	1-0	1-0	2-0	0-4	2-0	0-1	0-1	2-1	0-1	0-1	1-2	3-0	5-1	1-2	1-0
Belper Town	2-5	2-1		3-1	4-2	2-1	1-2	2-1	0-3	0-0	0-1	1-0	2-1	0-0	1-0	0-0	1-0	0-1	1-3	0-1	1-2	1-0
Bishop Auckland	0-0	2-2	2-2		2-1	3-0	1-1	1-1	2-3	0-0	0-1	1-0	1-1	1-5	3-1	1-3	5-3	3-2	2-1	2-0	0-0	2-3
Chorley	2-4	3-1	1-2	4-1		3-1	1-1	2-3	5-0	3-0	3-1	2-1	4-0	2-1	1-2	2-2	1-0	2-0	0-0	4-0	1-0	1-1
Eastwood Town	0-4	0-1	0-3	1-2	0-1	D	1-4	1-3	4-4	0-0	2-3	2-1	1-0	1-1	1-0	0-3	1-0	1-0		0-3	0-3	
Farsley Celtic	0-3	2-1	0-1	3-0	3-3	2-1	I	2-2	0-1	5-4	4-3	4-1	1-5	0-1	1-1	1-0	1-1	0-1	3-0	4-3	0-1	0-3
Guiseley	2-2	3-3	0-0	7-0	2-1	4-0	0-1	V	1-2	0-0	2-2	4-0	0-3	1-2	2-6	0-0	3-1	0-2	1-2	2-0	0-1	2-2
Kendal Town	4-1	0-1	2-1	3-0	4-1	1-0	0-1	2-1	I	1-1	1-0	0-0	3-3	2-0	0-3	1-2	1-0	1-1	4-1	1-2	3-2	1-1
Kidsgrove Athletic	0-1	0-1	0-0	3-1	1-0	0-1	1-3	1-1	3-1	S	0-4	2-4	2-3	2-0	1-3	0-0	1-2	1-0	2-1	2-2	2-1	1-1
Leek Town	3-2	0-1	4-0	3-1	2-1	2-0	1-1	1-0	1-0	1-0	I	2-3	1-0	2-2	1-0	1-2	2-2	1-3	3-2	1-1	1-2	0-1
Lincoln United	1-3	1-1	0-1	3-3	1-2	6-0	4-1	2-3	3-1	0-2	0-0	O	1-5	4-2	0-0	0-1	2-2	1-0	3-1	0-0	5-0	1-2
Matlock Town	2-4	1-0	0-0	4-2	2-1	2-0	2-2	1-2	1-5	2-0	1-1		N	1-0	2-1	3-3	0-1	2-0	3-1	2-0	3-2	
North Ferriby United	2-2	2-0	0-0	1-0	1-3	5-0	2-0	3-1	1-0	1-0	4-1	2-1	0-0		7-1	4-2	1-0	2-2	0-1	3-1	2-0	3-2
Ossett Town	1-2	4-0	1-2	2-1	1-2	1-0	1-1	0-0	2-2	2-2	0-5	1-1	0-0	0-4	O	0-4	2-1	1-3	0-0	1-1	0-2	
Radcliffe Borough	2-4	2-1	1-1	1-1	1-1	3-0	2-1	2-4	5-1	0-1	4-1	0-1	2-1	7-1	4-4					4-2	4-2	1-1
Rossendale United	3-4	1-3	0-4	3-1	0-1	2-3	4-3	1-4	1-4	1-0	1-0	3-3	1-0	2-1	0-1	1-3	E	1-2	6-3	3-1	1-3	1-2
Spennymoor United	1-2	3-0	1-2	0-0	3-0	2-0	2-1	1-2	1-1	1-1	0-3	1-0	0-3	2-1	0-1	1-3		E	6-0	3-0	2-1	
Stocksbridge Pk S.	2-3	1-1	0-0	3-1	1-4	2-1	1-3	2-3	1-1	3-4	0-1	1-1	2-0	0-1	5-1	0-3	2-0			1-1	1-2	
Trafford	2-2	1-3	0-2	0-1	0-3	0-0	1-1	0-2	1-2	0-1	3-1	3-2	1-2	0-4	2-0	0-1	5-1	0-3		2-0	1-1	1-2
Witton Albion	1-2	1-2	1-1	1-0	1-1	1-1	1-2	5-0	3-1	1-0	0-0	0-4	1-1	2-0	2-2	2-0	5-3	1-1	4-1			3-2
Workington	0-3	3-3	2-1	2-2	1-1	7-2	0-1	1-0	2-1	2-1	1-5	2-1	2-1	1-3	2-1	1-2	1-2	1-2	3-0	3-3		

Division One

	P	HOME					AWAY					TOTAL					
		W	D	L	F	A	W	D	L	F	A	W	D	L	F	A	Pts
Alfreton Town	42	11	5	5	51	29	15	4	2	55	30	26	9	7	106	59	87
Spennymoor Utd	42	15	2	4	44	15	12	4	5	37	27	27	6	9	81	42	87
Radcliffe Borough	42	13	4	4	55	28	12	6	3	35	18	25	10	7	90	46	85
North Ferriby Utd	42	13	5	3	40	16	10	4	7	38	29	23	9	10	78	45	78
Chorley	42	13	4	4	47	21	8	6	7	33	30	21	10	11	80	51	73
Belper Town	42	11	5	5	28	24	9	8	4	25	18	20	13	9	53	42	73
Witton Albion	42	9	8	4	37	25	10	7	4	30	25	19	15	8	67	50	72
Matlock Town	42	11	4	6	34	28	9	6	6	33	20	20	10	12	67	48	70
Leek Town	42	11	4	6	33	24	9	5	7	30	22	20	9	13	63	46	69
Workington	42	11	4	6	42	31	8	6	7	31	29	19	10	13	73	60	67
Farsley Celtic	42	10	4	7	36	33	7	7	7	30	34	17	11	14	66	67	62
Kendal Town	42	10	5	6	34	22	8	2	11	34	36	18	7	17	68	58	61
Bamber Bridge	42	9	3	9	28	24	6	6	9	27	35	15	9	18	55	59	54
Guiseley	42	6	7	8	36	30	8	4	9	32	33	14	11	17	68	63	53
Bishop Auckland	42	9	8	4	36	30	4	2	15	22	53	13	10	19	58	83	49
Lincoln United	42	6	4	11	35	32	6	5	10	32	45	12	9	21	67	77	45
Stocksbridge Pk S.	42	5	6	10	30	34	6	3	12	24	47	11	9	22	54	81	42
Rossendale United	42	8	1	12	36	46	4	4	13	22	42	12	5	25	58	88	41
Kidsgrove Athletic	42	7	4	10	27	33	2	7	12	22	38	9	11	22	49	71	38
Ossett Town	42	4	8	9	20	34	4	1	16	19	46	8	9	25	39	80	33
Eastwood Town	42	3	4	14	18	40	2	4	15	15	52	5	8	29	33	92	23
Trafford	42	5	4	12	22	39	0	2	19	12	60	5	6	31	34	99	21

Alfreton Town, Spennymoor United and Radcliffe Borough (via play-offs) are promoted to the Premier Division from which Gateshead (via play-offs), Colwyn Bay and Hyde United are relegated. Eastwood Town drop to the Northern Counties East League, swapping places with Bridlington Town. From the North West Counties League arrive Prescot Cables in place of relegated Trafford.

PROMOTION / RELEGATION PLAY-OFFS

SEMI-FINALS *(29th April)*
Gateshead 2 **Chorley** 5 *(at Chorley)* Att: 557
Radcliffe Borough 1 North Ferriby United 0 Att: 463

FINAL
(3rd May at Radcliffe Borough)
Radcliffe Borough 2 Chorley 2 *aet* (4-2p) Att: 956

N.P.L. DIVISION ONE – GATES 'N' DATES

	ALF	BAM	BEL	BIS	CHO	EAS	FAR	GUI	KEN	KID	LEE	LIN	MAT	NFU	OSS	RAD	ROS	SPE	SPS	TRA	WIT	WOR
Alfreton T.	—	500 26 Apr	715 25 Jan	260 28 Sep	478 9 Mar	505 4 Jan	257 17 Aug	393 8 Feb	347 9 Nov	285 3 Sep	565 5 Apr	421 1 Mar	563 26 Apr	382 19 Apr	268 29 Oct	329 18 Mar	195 15 Oct	360 8 Apr	372 26 Dec	271 12 Nov	325 21 Sep	364 23 Nov
Bamber B.	271 28 Dec	—	123 21 Sep	105 26 Nov	605 21 Apr	110 7 Dec	226 24 Sep	193 1 Mar	149 21 Sep	251 16 Nov	206 29 Mar	156 14 Dec	228 5 Apr	168 15 Mar	140 22 Feb	243 9 Nov	156 24 Aug	106 5 Nov	90 13 Mar	123 30 Nov	242 18 Jan	151 19 Oct
Belper Town	608 28 Dec	204 28 Sep	—	228 26 Oct	236 28 Dec	229 22 Feb	128 26 Nov	177 7 Sep	149 14 Dec	251 18 Jan	383 26 Aug	139 14 Dec	742 21 Apr	209 5 Nov	209 17 Aug	341 12 Apr	178 10 Sep	243 15 Mar	216 23 Nov	152 24 Sep	287 19 Oct	207 8 Mar
Bishop Auck.	185 8 Oct	161 1 Feb	149 8 Feb	—	178 1 Mar	188 15 Mar	151 23 Apr	208 22 Mar	144 16 Oct	164 24 Aug	169 25 Jan	153 17 Aug	142 30 Nov	193 21 Apr	176 5 Nov	187 2 Oct	183 9 Apr	494 21 Apr	170 19 Oct	186 26 Mar	203 19 Oct	187 11 Sep
Chorley	299 7 Sep	513 26 Dec	217 30 Nov	229 26 Aug	—	272 19 Apr	151 1 Feb	331 23 Nov	216 1 Oct	267 26 Oct	254 8 Mar	206 28 Sep	223 15 Oct	272 10 Sep	223 29 Mar	290 17 Aug	276 22 Feb	249 25 Mar	308 25 Jan	209 1 Mar	129 17 Dec	240 5 Nov
Eastwood T.	360 22 Mar	155 26 Aug	149 4 Mar	123 21 Dec	135 14 Dec	—	111 18 Jan	136 9 Nov	115 24 Dec	140 24 Dec	192 28 Sep	103 29 Oct	162 17 Aug	104 10 Apr	116 28 Sep	140 23 Nov	162 12 Apr	117 19 Oct	108 20 Aug	131 25 Jan	129 16 Nov	116 8 Feb
Farsley C.	136 12 Oct	70 15 Oct	72 29 Mar	130 9 Nov	105 14 Dec	70 1 Oct	—	213 26 Dec	106 1 Feb	140 20 Aug	56 1 Apr	64 8 Mar	84 14 Dec	129 7 Sep	122 26 Apr	146 7 Sep	79 16 Nov	112 15 Mar	86 8 Apr	141 15 Feb	75 19 Apr	180 11 Nov
Guiseley	362 18 Jan	201 21 Dec	144 31 Mar	162 2 Sep	276 2 Nov	182 29 Mar	178 21 Apr	—	285 5 Apr		259 28 Dec	182 12 Apr	217 21 Sep	193 19 Oct	152 10 Feb	183 22 Feb	179 25 Nov	146 10 Sep	210 26 Aug	196 23 Nov	145 17 Mar	321 11 Nov
Kendal T.	272 15 Mar	192 12 Apr	181 19 Apr	261 24 Sep	262 18 Jan	178 26 Oct	216 8 Oct	247 10 Sep	—	172 22 Feb	263 8 Feb	197 19 Oct	160 12 Apr	208 20 Apr	205 26 Aug	192 17 Apr	169 17 Dec	162	196	167 7 Sep	191 30 Nov	215 26 Dec
Kidsgrove A.	194 8 Mar	197 17 Aug	152 2 Oct	211 23 Nov	103 12 Oct	127 16 Oct	136 13 Nov	136 19 Apr	114 26 Apr	—	376 9 Nov	170 26 Aug	143 30 Oct	94 9 Apr	191 1 Feb	187 15 Mar	137 29 Mar	207 5 Oct	114 19 Mar	167 11 Sep	265 26 Dec	231 7 Sep
Leek Town	304 10 Sep	248 12 Oct	249 19 Apr	206 23 Nov	242 16 Oct	241 11 Feb	234 26 Oct	222 26 Apr	233 22 Mar	321 12 Apr	—	244 7 Sep	302 15 Feb	252 22 Feb	181 26 Nov	171 15 Oct	176 11 Mar	285 16 Nov	210 8 Apr	209 1 Mar	307 24 Aug	135 4 Jan
Lincoln Utd	156 5 Nov	95 19 Apr	145 20 Aug	148 21 Sep	143 16 Nov	74 17 Sep	123 22 Feb	130 4 Jan	112 15 Feb	117 7 Dec	110 4 Mar	—	131 1 Oct	145 22 Feb	68 30 Nov	148 1 Oct	102 25 Mar	101 25 Mar	118 9 Nov	113 26 Oct	137 5 Apr	225 26 Apr
Matlock T.	908 1 Apr	191 10 Sep	631 26 Apr	277 4 Jan	246 24 Sep	275 5 Nov	252 8 Feb	249 7 Dec	246 24 Aug	247 8 Oct	310 19 Oct	314 18 Jan	—	290 22 Mar	245 15 Mar	251 8 Mar	192 7 Sep	274 19 Apr	241 22 Feb	307 28 Sep	307 20 Aug	225 26 Apr
Nth Ferriby	210 14 Dec	139 10 Apr	147 19 Apr	152 12 Nov	130 5 Feb	131 16 Oct	195 26 Apr	139 11 Mar	165 1 Mar	178 8 Feb	114 19 Oct	198 18 Jan	187 22 Mar	—	122 15 Oct	199 11 Jan	133	204 7 Sep	204 19 Apr	123 28 Sep	250 29 Mar	101 17 Aug
Ossett Town	281 21 Apr	161 11 Jan	208 15 Feb	173 23 Nov	204	173 12 Oct	234 19 Oct	65 24 Aug	92	134 21 Dec	138 18 Mar	173 8 Oct	273 28 Dec	169 24 Sep	—	236 1 Mar	199 1 Apr	133 11 Jan	185 21 Sep	120 18 Jan	211 26 Oct	121
Radcliffe B.	355 4 Mar	158 2 Nov	171 21 Sep	165 18 Jan	243 19 Oct	160 24 Aug	150 25 Mar	158 30 Nov	148 20 Aug	185 21 Dec	138 24 Sep	210 8 Feb	142 17 Sep	390 24 Sep	210 19 Apr	—	292 20 Aug	203 1 Apr	320 21 Sep	121 18 Jan	284 22 Feb	143 29 Oct
Rossendale	136 24 Sep	149 23 Nov	105 5 Apr	125 2 Nov	248 21 Sep	72 26 Apr	151 28 Dec	119 15 Feb	119 29 Oct	125 19 Oct	136 3 Sep	106 22 Apr	124 12 Apr	136 30 Nov	139 14 Sep	214 21 Apr	—	135 14 Dec	81 1 Mar	219 5 Nov	157 22 Feb	143 18 Jan
Spennymoor	262 19 Oct	178 8 Mar	167 1 Mar	231 11 Mar	199 22 Apr	180 26 Apr	203 28 Dec	156 15 Feb	181 3 Sep	170 8 Feb	227 21 Dec	139 18 Mar	174 18 Jan	290 22 Mar	194 9 Nov	199 21 Apr	226 24 Apr	—	113 28 Jan	123 8 Oct	250 29 Mar	161 17 Aug
Stocksbridge	215 7 Dec	132 7 Sep	181 18 Sep	117 25 Feb	215 26 Apr	162 30 Nov	155 12 Apr	182 17 Apr	145 29 Mar	197 28 Dec	204 18 Jan	138 24 Sep	234 12 Oct	165 18 Mar	179 8 Feb	172 10 Sep	123	190	—	293	172 25 Jan	111 17 Mar
Trafford	143 20 Aug	108 22 Mar	82 1 Oct	122 26 Apr	256 8 Feb	75 12 Oct	97 17 Sep	135 4 Dec	70 18 Mar	229 5 Apr	251 12 Oct	142 12 Oct	125 1 Feb	98 24 Aug	93 26 Dec	128 16 Nov	86 4 Mar	95	221 1 Oct	—	156 19 Apr	310 29 Mar
Witton Alb.	330 20 Aug	192 22 Mar	266 1 Oct	259 12 Oct	338 15 Mar	260 1 Feb	235 1 Mar	190 15 Oct	205 21 Apr	352 21 Apr	229 18 Feb	227 10 Sep	204 12 Nov	310 7 Sep	264 23 Nov	240 21 Jan	291 28 Dec	86 4 Mar	221 1 Apr	312 17 Aug	—	310 26 Aug
Workington	332 24 Aug	256 9 Nov	244 5 Apr	237 17 Sep	385 1 Mar	222 21 Sep	339 20 Aug	238 24 Apr	251 30 Nov	359 18 Feb	361 28 Dec	468 25 Jan	281 16 Nov	206 2 Nov	240 21 Jan	582 1 Feb	232 15 Apr	299 22 Mar	317 7 Dec	259 14 Dec	111 19 Apr	—

WWW.NLNEWSDESK.CO.UK

DIVISION ONE CONSTITUTION FOR 2003-04

BAMBER BRIDGE
Manager: Paul Byron   *Colours:* White & black
Irongate, Brownedge Road, Bamber Bridge, Preston,
Lancashire PR5 6UX   *Tel:* 01772 909690
Fax: 01772 909691   *Club:* 01772 909695

BELPER TOWN
Manager: Gary Marrow   *Colours:* Gold & black
Christ Church Meadow, Bridge Street, Belper,
Derbyshire DE56 1BA   *Tel:* 01773 825549

BISHOP AUCKLAND
Manager: Brian Honour   *Colours:* Sky & navy blue
Shildon FC, Dean Street, Shildon, County Durham
DL14 9SZ   *Tel:* 01388 773877

BRIDLINGTON TOWN
Manager: Billy Heath   *Colours:* Red
Queensgate Stadium, Queensgate, Bridlington, East
Yorkshire YO16 5LN   *Tel:* 01262 606879

CHORLEY
Manager: Mark Molyneaux
Victory Park, Duke Street, Chorley, Lancs PR7 3DU
Colours: White, black, red   *Tel:* 01257 263406
Fax: 01257 241625   *Club:* 01257 275662

COLWYN BAY
Manager: Jimmy Mullen   *Colours:* Sky blue, maroon
Llanelian Rd, Old Colwyn, Colwyn, Clwyd LL29 8UN
Tel/Fax: 01492 514581   *Club:* 01492 513944

FARSLEY CELTIC
Manager: Lee Sinnott   *Colours:* Blue
Throstle Nest, Newlands, Farsley, Pudsey, Leeds, West
Yorkshire LS28 5BE   *Fax:* 0113 257 1058
Tel: 0113 256 1517/255 7292

GATESHEAD
Manager: Derek Bell   *Colours:* Black & white
The International Stadium, Neilson Road, Gateshead,
Tyne & Wear NE10 0EF
Tel: 0191 478 3883   *Fax:* 0191 477 1315

GUISELEY
Manager: Neil Parsley   *Colours:* White, navy blue
Nethermoor, Otley Road, Guiseley, Leeds LS20 8BT
Tel: 01943 873223   *Club:* 01943 872872

HYDE UNITED
Manager: Steve Waywell   *Colours:* Red
Tameside Stadium, Ewens Fields, Walker Lane, Hyde,
Cheshire SK14 5PL   *Tel:* 0161 368 1031
Fax: 0161 367 7273   *Club:* 0161 368 1621

KENDAL TOWN
Manager: Mick Hoyle   *Colours:* Black & white
Parkside Road, Kendal, Cumbria LA9 7BL
Tel: 01539 727472   *Fax:* 01539 727472
Club: 01539 722469

KIDSGROVE ATHLETIC
Manager: Kevin Langley   *Colours:* Blue & white
Hollinwood Road, Kidsgrove, Stoke-on-Trent,
Staffordshire ST7 1BQ   *Tel:* 01782 782412

LEEK TOWN
Manager: John Ramshaw   *Colours:* Royal blue
Harrison Park, Macclesfield Road, Leek, Staffordshire
ST13 8LD   *Tel:* 01538 399278
Fax: 01538 399826   *Club:* 01538 383734

LINCOLN UNITED
Manager: John Wilkinson   *Colours:* White
Ashby Avenue, Hartsholme, Lincoln, Lincs LN6 0DY
Tel/Fax: 01522 696400   *Club:* 01522 690674

MATLOCK TOWN
Manager: Ernie Moss   *Colours:* Royal blue, white
Causeway Lane, Matlock, Derbyshire DE4 3AR
TelFax: 01629 583866   *Club:* 01629 553362

NORTH FERRIBY UNITED
Manager: Brian France   *Colours:* Green
Grange Lane, Church Road, North Ferriby, East
Yorkshire HU14 3AA   *Tel/Fax:* 01482 634601

OSSETT TOWN
Manager: Gary Brook   *Colours:* Red
Ingfield, Prospect Road, Ossett, Wakefield, West
Yorkshire WF5 9HA   *Tel:* 01924 272960

PRESCOT CABLES
Manager: Tommy Lawson *Colours:* Gold & black
Valerie Park, Hope Street, Prescot, Merseyside L34
6HD   *Tel:* 0151 430 0507

ROSSENDALE UNITED
Manager: Jim McBride   *Colours:* Blue & white
Dark Lane, Staghills Road, Newchurch, Rossendale,
Lancashire BB4 7UA   *Tel:* 01706 215119
Fax: 01706 230970   *Club:* 01706 213296

STOCKSBRIDGE PARK STEELS
Manager: Mick Horne   *Colours:* Yellow, royal blue
Bracken Moor Lane, Stocksbridge, Sheffield, South
Yorkshire S36 2AN
Tel/Fax: 0114 288 8305   *Club:* 0114 288 2045

WITTON ALBION
Manager: Benny Phillips   *Colours:* Red, white, black
Wincham Park, Chapel Street, Wincham, Northwich,
Cheshire CW9 6DA
Tel: 01606 43008   *Fax:* 01606 43008
Club: 01606 47117

WORKINGTON
Manager: Tommy Cassidy *Colours:* Red
Borough Park, Workington, Cumbria CA14 2DT
Tel: 01900 602871   *Fax:* 01900 602871

WWW.CHERRYRED.CO.UK

LEAGUE CUP

FIRST ROUND
Belper Town 1 **Matlock Town** 4
Blyth Spartans 2 **Bishop Auckland** 3
Burscough 1 **Colwyn Bay** 3
Chorley 1 Bamber Bridge 0
Gateshead 6 Whitby Town 3 *aet*
Guiseley 3 **Farsley Celtic** 4
Hucknall Town 0 **Gainsborough Trinity** 3
Hyde United 2 Trafford 1
Lincoln United 1 **North Ferriby United** 2
Rossendale United 2 Droylsden 1
Stocksbridge Park Steels 2 Frickley
Athletic 0
Witton Albion 3 **Marine** 5 *aet*
Workington 6 Kendal Town 0
SECOND ROUND
Altrincham 1 **Hyde United** 2
Ashton United 1 **Vauxhall Motors** 2
Barrow 3 Accrington Stanley 2
Bradford Park Avenue 2 Spennymoor
United 2 *aet* (5-4p)
Eastwood Town 3 Kidsgrove Ath. 2 *aet*
Harrogate Town 4 Bishop Auckland 0
Lancaster City 2 Leek Town 0
Marine 3 Stalybridge Celtic 0
Matlock Town 2 **Worksop Town** 3 *aet*
North Ferriby 2 **Gainsborough Trinity** 3
Ossett Town 3 Farsley Celtic 0
Radcliffe Borough 3 Colwyn Bay 2 *aet*
Runcorn FC Halton 1 **Chorley** 3
Stocksbridge PS 1 **Alfreton Town** 4
Wakefield & Emley 1 **Gateshead** 3
Workington 2 **Rossendale United** 4

THIRD ROUND
Alfreton Town 4 Eastwood Town 1
Bradford Park Avenue 4 **Ossett Town** 5 *aet*
Gateshead 1 Harrogate Town 0
Marine 1 Hyde United 0
Radcliffe Borough 2 Barrow 1
Rossendale United 4 Lancaster City 1
Vauxhall Motors 2 Chorley 1
Worksop Town 3 Gainsborough Trinity 1
QUARTER-FINALS
Gateshead 5 Alfreton Town 4 *aet*
Marine 1 Worksop Town 0
Radcliffe Borough 3 **Ossett Town** 4
Vauxhall Motors 0 **Rossendale United** 1
SEMI-FINALS
Gateshead 4 Rossendale United 0
Ossett Town 0 **Marine** 1
FINAL
(1st leg 9th April)
Gateshead 0 Marine 1
(2nd leg 24th April)
Marine 2 Gateshead 0

PRESIDENT'S CUP
(Contested by the teams eliminated in Second Round of League Cup)

FIRST ROUND
Ashton United 4 Accrington Stanley 2
Colwyn Bay 2 Altrincham 1
North Ferriby United 2 Matlock Town 1
Runcorn FC Halton 2 Leek Town 1
Spennymoor United 5 Bishop Auckland 0
Stalybridge Celtic 4 Workington 1
Stocksbridge Park Steels 0 **Kidsgrove Athletic** 3
Wakefield & Emley 2 Farsley Celtic 1
QUARTER-FINALS
Ashton United 1 North Ferriby United 0

Runcorn FC Halton 3 Spennymoor United 1
Stalybridge Celtic 3 Colwyn Bay 0
Wakefield & Emley 5 Kidsgrove Athletic 1 *aet*
SEMI-FINALS
Ashton United 1 Wakefield & Emley 0
Runcorn FC Halton 2 **Stalybridge Celtic** 4
FINAL
(First leg 29th March)
Stalybridge Celtic 4 Ashton United 2
(Second leg 24th April)
Ashton United 1 **Stalybridge Celtic** 2

CHAIRMAN'S CUP
(Contested by the teams eliminated in First Round of League Cup)

FIRST ROUND
Bamber Bridge 4 Burscough 2
Belper Town 0 **Lincoln United** 1 *aet*
Frickley Athletic 2 Whitby Town 1
Guiseley 1 **Droylsden** 3
Witton Albion 4 Trafford 2
QUARTER-FINALS
Bamber Bridge 8 Kendal Town 2

Blyth Spartans 3 Frickley Athletic 0
Droylsden 4 Witton Albion 2 *aet*
Lincoln United 0 **Hucknall Town** 2
SEMI-FINALS
Droylsden 1 Bamber Bridge 1 *aet* (7-6p)
Hucknall Town 4 Blyth Spartans 1
FINAL
(28th April at Droylesden)
Droylsden 0 **Hucknall Town** 1 *aet*

NOTTS ALLIANCE

	Attenborough	Awsworth Villa	Boots Athletic	Clifton	Cotgrave Coll. Welf.	Keyworth United	Kimberley MW	Kingswell	Linby Coll. Welfare	Newark Flowserve	Notts Police	Radcliffe Olympic	Rainworth MW	Ruddington United	Southwell City	Wollaton
Attenborough	S	0-4	1-1	0-0	0-1	1-2	0-0	2-1	3-1	1-0	1-2	0-3	0-2	1-0	2-9	2-5
Awsworth Villa	2-3	E	0-4	2-2	3-3	1-1	2-2	7-1	0-4	2-2	1-3	2-2	3-2	1-3	0-0	1-0
Boots Athletic	5-0	3-0	N	5-1	5-2	2-0	4-1	0-3	2-1	1-1	1-2	0-1	3-1	6-3	0-5	1-0
Clifton	3-0	2-1	3-1	I	2-1	4-2	3-1	5-0	2-0	3-2	3-2	2-2	1-0	1-2	1-4	1-1
Cotgrave Colliery Welfare	2-0	1-3	2-2	3-2	O	1-3	3-3	3-0	1-2	4-3	0-0	0-4	0-4	5-3	5-1	3-2
Keyworth United	1-0	1-4	1-2	2-2	2-7	R	1-1	3-4	6-3	1-2	6-3	1-4	2-2	1-1	2-2	2-1
Kimberley Miners Welfare	0-3	1-3	2-2	4-3	1-5	2-7		1-3	6-2	4-0	2-2	1-5	0-1	3-2	1-7	2-1
Kingswell	0-4	2-1	1-2	3-1	5-3	1-1	1-3		1-2	1-4	4-3	0-3	1-6	1-1	1-4	1-1
Linby Colliery Welfare	5-1	5-0	2-4	4-3	3-1	0-4	4-1	0-2	D	1-2	4-0	0-0	3-2	2-3	2-3	0-2
Newark Flowserve	2-2	1-0	0-3	2-0	0-6	1-1	0-1	3-0	1-3	I	3-1	1-1	0-3	3-2	2-0	2-1
Notts Police	0-1	2-0	1-4	2-2	0-1	2-2	2-2	1-1	3-5	3-4	V	1-4	2-3	1-0	1-2	0-4
Radcliffe Olympic	4-0	2-0	4-1	4-0	6-2	4-2	1-0	4-1	2-4	1-0	3-0	I	5-1	5-2	2-3	2-3
Rainworth Miners Welfare	1-2	4-3	1-3	0-2	1-1	2-2	1-2	3-0	1-1	3-3	2-0	0-1	S	0-1	3-1	1-0
Ruddington United	3-2	1-1	1-4	3-2	2-5	2-2	3-6	1-2	0-5	0-1	2-4	1-2	3-5	I	4-3	1-4
Southwell City	1-0	4-1	0-1	2-0	4-2	1-2	3-2	4-2	3-0	1-0	8-0	0-2	3-4	1-1	O	5-2
Wollaton	1-2	5-1	1-1	2-0	3-4	5-4	5-0	5-1	3-1	2-1	1-3	0-4	2-2	2-4	6-3	N

SENIOR CUP
(For Senior Division sides and Division One first teams)

FIRST ROUND
AC Bulwell 0 **Boots Athletic** 6
Attenborough 0 **Awsworth Villa** 1
Bilborough 6 Matrixgrade 2
Calverton MW 3 Bilsthorpe 1
Chaffoteaux 1 **Radcliffe Olympic** 5
Cotgrave CW 1 **Ruddington United** 2
Keyworth Utd 6 Stapleford Borough 2
Kingswell 3 Bestwood MW 1 *aet*
Magdala Amateurs 0 **Wollaton** 3
Newark Flowserve 6 Basford United 1
Southbank 3 Kimberley MW 1
Southwell City 3 **ASC Dayncourt** 4
SECOND ROUND
Awsworth Villa 1 **Keyworth United** 2
Bilborough 1 **ASC Dayncourt** 3
Boots Athletic 0 **Wollaton** 2
Calverton MW 0 **Rainworth MW** 3
Clifton 0 Kingswell 0 *aet*
Kingswell 2 Clifton 0 *replay*

Notts Police 1 **Ruddington United** 3
Radcliffe Olym. 5 Newark Flowserve 1
Southbank 1 **Linby Colliery Welfare** 2
QUARTER-FINALS
Keyworth United 3 Kingswell 0
Radcliffe Olympic 5 ASC Dayncourt 2
Rainworth MW 2 Linby CW 1
Wollaton 1 **Ruddington United** 2
SEMI-FINALS
Keyworth United 6 Ruddington
United 0 *(at Cotgrave)*
Radcliffe Olympic 5 Rainworth Miners
Welfare 2 *aet (at Southwell)*
FINAL *(29th April at Southwell)*
Keyworth 1 Radcliffe Olympic 1 *aet*
REPLAY *(8th May at Southwell)*
Radcliffe Olympic 4 Keyworth Utd 0

Senior Division	P	W	D	L	F	A	Pts
Radcliffe Olympic	30	23	4	3	87	28	73
Boots Athletic	30	19	5	6	73	41	62
Southwell City	30	18	3	9	87	51	57
Cotgrave Colliery W.	30	14	5	11	77	68	47
Rainworth Miners W.	30	13	6	11	61	50	45
Linby Colliery Welf.	30	14	2	14	69	62	44
Newark Flowserve	30	12	7	11	47	52	43
Clifton	30	12	6	12	56	57	42
Wollaton	30	12	5	13	70	56	41
Keyworth United	30	9	11	10	66	67	38
Kimberley Miners W.	30	9	7	14	55	79	34
Attenborough	30	10	4	16	34	61	34
Kingswell	30	9	4	17	44	81	31
Awsworth Villa	30	7	8	15	49	66	29
Ruddington United	30	8	5	17	55	81	29
Notts Police	30	7	6	17	46	76	27

SENIOR DIVISION CONSTITUTION 2003-04

ATTENBOROUGH . . . . Village Green, The Strand, Attenborough, Nottinghamshire 0115 925 7439
AWSWORTH VILLA . . . . Shilo Park, Attewell Road, Awsworth, Nottinghamshire . . . . None
BESTWOOD MINERS WELFARE . . Bestwood Workshops, Park Road, Bestwood Village, Nottingham, Nottinghamshire . . . . None
BILBOROUGH . . . . The Pavilion, Birchover Park, Birchover Road, Bilborough, Nottinghamshire 0115 928 7662
BOOTS ATHLETIC . . . . Lady Bay, West Bridgford, Nottingham, Nottinghamshire 0115 981 3112
CLIFTON . . . . Green Lane, Clifton Estate, Nottingham, Nottinghamshire 0115 984 4903
COTGRAVE COLLIERY WELFARE . . Cotgrave Welfare Scheme Sports Ground, Cotgrave, Nottinghamshire 0115 989 4414
KEYWORTH UNITED . . . . Platt Lane, Keyworth, Nottingham, Nottinghamshire 0115 937 5998
KIMBERLEY MINERS WELFARE. . . . . . Digby Street, Kimberley, Nottingham, Nottinghamshire . . . . 0115 938 2124 (Welfare)
KINGSWELL . . . . William Lee Memorial Ground, Park Road, Calverton, Nottinghamshire 0115 965 3097
LINBY COLLIERY WELFARE . . . . Church Lane, Linby Village, Linby, Nottinghamshire . . . . None
MAGDALA AMATEURS. . . . . Civil Service Sports, Wilford Lane, West Bridgford, Nottinghamshire 0115 981 1418
NEWARK FLOWSERVE . . . . Lowfields Works, off Hawton Lane, Balderton, Newark, Nottinghamshire 01636 702672
NOTTS POLICE . . . . Police Training Centre, Epperstone, Nottingham, Nottinghamshire . . . . None
RUDDINGTON UNITED. . . . . The Elms Park, Loughborough Road, Ruddington, Nottinghamshire 0115 984 4976
WOLLATON . . . . Wollaton Cricket & Sports Club, Wollaton Road, Wollaton, Nottingham, Notts 0115 913 3134
Radcliffe Borough, Rainworth Miners Welfare and Southwell City move to the Central Midlands League. Bestwood Miners Welfare, Bilborough and Magdala Amateurs are promoted from Division One.

	AC Bulwell	ASC Dayncourt	Basford United	Bestwood Miners Welfare	Bilborough	Bilsthorpe	Boots Athletic Res.	Calverton Miners Welfare	Chaffoteaux	Magdala Amateurs	Matrixgrade	Newark Flowserve Res.	Southbank	Southwell City Res.	Stapleford Borough	Wollaton Res.
AC Bulwell		2-0	4-1	5-4	2-1	0-1	6-1	4-1	2-0	3-2	3-0	5-0	0-3	4-1	2-0	2-2
ASC Dayncourt	3-1		3-2	0-2	1-1	3-0	3-1	1-2	2-4	4-1	2-0	2-1	3-3	2-0	n/a	2-0
Basford United	1-1	1-1	D	0-4	3-5	4-3	0-4	1-3	5-3	1-3	0-1	2-2	0-0	4-1	4-2	0-0
Bestwood Miners Welfare	0-1	2-2	4-1	I	0-3	3-1	1-1	1-0	4-2	6-0	3-0	0-0	3-0	0-3	0-0	3-0
Bilborough	2-6	2-3	3-1	0-3	V	1-4	2-0	3-5	1-0	5-0	2-0	1-0	5-3	3-3	n/a	3-2
Bilsthorpe	1-2	2-7	3-1	0-1	1-1	I	1-1	1-0	2-5	0-3	2-2	4-1	0-6	0-3	n/a	1-1
Boots Athletic Res.	1-0	2-5	3-0	2-1	6-3	1-1	S	0-2	4-0	1-2	W-L	0-2	0-1	2-3	n/a	5-2
Calverton Miners Welfare	1-2	1-6	3-0	1-1	1-3	2-2	4-1	I	0-0	0-2	2-1	0-3	0-4	4-5	n/a	4-2
Chaffoteaux	1-7	0-5	2-1	0-1	1-3	4-0	2-2	0-0	O	1-5	5-0	2-2	1-0	3-3	n/a	0-1
Magdala Amateurs	2-3	1-0	W-L	5-3	2-0	1-1	2-3	0-0	2-1	N	1-0	1-2	3-2	1-5	0-2	2-1
Matrixgrade	0-5	2-3	4-1	0-4	1-3	2-2	1-4	0-4	3-1	1-3		4-2	2-2	2-1	n/a	1-3
Newark Flowserve Res.	1-3	2-1	5-1	0-4	2-3	4-3	2-1	2-3	6-0	2-0	6-0	O	2-1	2-2	2-1	3-1
Southbank	1-2	4-1	2-3	1-4	0-4	2-1	0-0	0-0	0-1	1-1	3-1	3-0	N	1-1	2-1	0-1
Southwell City Res.	1-5	0-3	4-5	0-2	2-2	1-2	5-4	1-1	2-2	1-3	0-2	1-2	1-1	E	2-3	5-1
Stapleford Borough	1-4	n/a	n/a	2-2	n/a	n/a	4-1	2-4	n/a	n/a	n/a	n/a	1-7	6-1		0-3
Wollaton Res.	1-3	1-4	4-0	0-2	1-2	1-3	3-2	1-2	0-0	1-0	1-1	1-2	1-1	2-1	2-2	

Note – Stapleford Borough withdrew during the course of the season. Their results are shown in the grid but are expunged from the league table

Division One	P	W	D	L	F	A	Pts
AC Bulwell	28	22	2	4	83	33	68
Bestwood Miners W.	28	18	4	6	66	28	58
ASC Dayncourt	28	17	4	7	74	40	55
Bilborough	28	16	4	8	67	53	52
Magdala Amateurs	28	15	3	10	48	48	48
Newark Flowserve Res.	28	14	4	10	58	48	46
Calverton Miners W.	28	11	7	10	46	47	40
Boots Athletic Res.	28	10	5	13	52	54	35
Southbank	28	8	9	11	45	41	33
Southwell City Res.	28	8	8	12	58	64	32
Bilsthorpe	28	7	8	13	42	63	29
Chaffoteaux	28	7	7	14	41	63	28
Wollaton Res.	28	7	6	15	35	54	27
Basford United	28	5	5	18	39	75	20
Matrixgrade	28	5	4	19	30	73	19

INTERMEDIATE CUP
(For teams not entered in the Senior Cup)

PRELIMINARY ROUND
Bestwood Miners Welfare Res. 6 East Leake Athletic 2

FIRST ROUND
ASC Dayncourt Res. 1 **Boots Res.** 2
Attenborough Res. 0 **Santos** 6
Awsworth Res. 0 **Notts Police Res.** 6
Basford United 2 **BTSC** 10
Bestwood Miners Welfare Res. 4 Ruddington Village 1
Bottesford St Mary's 2 **Burton Joyce** 3
Chaffoteaux Res. 2 Southbank Res. 1
Clifton Res. 4 Calverton MW Res. 0
Cotgrave Colliery Welfare Res. 3 **Rainworth Miners Welfare Res.** 5
Durham Ox 2 Kimberley Miners Welfare Res. 1
Keyworth United Res. 4 Bilborough Res. 3
Kirton Brickworks 1 **Wollaton Res.** 4
Newark Town 0 **Newark Flow. Res.** 2
Pinxton NE 0 **Southwell City Res.** 9
Radcliffe Olympic Res. 3 Linby Colliery Welfare Res. 1
Ruddington United Res. 2 **Sandhurst** 1
(Ruddington United Res. expelled)

SECOND ROUND
Boots Athletic Res. 1 Santos 1 *aet*
Santos 2 Boots Athletic Res. 0
BTSC 2 **Southwell City Res.** 4
Burton Joyce 1 **Durham Ox** 4
Chaffoteaux Res. 2 **Wollaton Res.** 3
Keyworth United Res. 5 Sandhurst 0
Newark F. Res. 7 Notts Police Res. 1
Radcliffe Olympic Res. 2 **Bestwood Res.** 3

QUARTER-FINALS
Bestwood MW Res. 7 Durham Ox 1
Clifton Res. 2 Newark Flow. Res. 2 *aet*
Newark F. Res. 3 Clifton Res. 1 *replay*
Southwell Res. 2 **Keyworth Utd Res.** 4

SEMI-FINALS
Bestwood MW Res. 3 Keyworth United Res. 3 *aet (at Bilborough)*
Bestwood MW Res. 1 **Keyworth United Res.** 4 *(replay at Southwell)*
Santos 0 **Newark Flowserve Res.** 1 *(at Rainworth)*

FINAL *(6th May at Southwell City)*
Newark F. Res. 1 **Keyworth Res.** 2

DIVISION ONE CONSTITUTION 2003-04

AC BULWELL . . . . Riverleen School, Squires Avenue, Bulwell, Nottingham, Nottinghamshire . . . . None
ARNOLD SOUTHBANK . . . . Carlton Recreation Ground, Carlton Hill, Nottingham, Nottinghamshire . . . . None
BASFORD UNITED . . . . Greenwich Avenue, Bagnall Road, Basford, Nottinghamshire 0115 942 3918
BESTWOOD MW RESERVES . . Bestwood Workshops, Park Road, Bestwood Village, Nottingham, Nottinghamshire . . . . None
BOOTS ATHLETIC RESERVES . . . . Lady Bay, West Bridgford, Nottingham, Nottinghamshire 0115 981 3112
BOTTESFORD ST MARY'S . . . . Village Hall Playing Fields, Belvoir Road, Bottesford, Leicestershire . . . . None
BURTON JOYCE. . . . . Station Road, Burton Joyce, Nottinghamshire . . . . None
CALVERTON MINERS WELFARE . . Calverton Recreation Centre, Hollingwood Lane, Calverton, Nottinghamshire 0115 965 4390
DALE HOTEL . . . . Standhill Road, Carlton, Nottingham . . . . None
EAST LEAKE ATHLETIC. . . . . Costock Road, East Leake, Loughborough, Leicestershire . . . . None
KEYWORTH UNITED RESERVES . . . . Platt Lane, Keyworth, Nottingham, Nottinghamshire 0115 937 5998
NEWARK FLOWSERVE RESERVES. . . . Lowfields Works, off Hawton Lane, Balderton, Newark. 01636 702672
NUTHALL CHAFFOTEAUX . . . . . . Basil Russell Playing Fields, Maple Drive, Nuthall, Nottinghamshire 0115 938 4765
RETFORD TOWN . . . . Badworth Road, Retford, Nottinghamshire 01777 703163
SANTOS . . . . William Lee Memorial Ground, Park Road, Calverton, Nottinghamshire 0115 965 3097
WOLLATON RESERVES . . Wollaton Cricket & Sports Club, Wollaton Road, Wollaton, Nottingham, Nottinghamshire 0115 913 3134
Bestwood Miners Welfare, Bilborough and Magdala Amateurs are promoted to the Senior Division One. Bilsthorpe and Matrixgrade drop to Division Two replaced by Bestwood Miners Welfare Reserves, Bottesford St Mary's, Burton Joyce, BTSC (who become Dale Hotel), East Leake Athletic, Keyworth United Reserves and Santos. Stapleford Borough (during the season), ASC Dayncourt and Southwell City Reserves have dropped out. Retford Town arrive from the Lincs League. Southbank become Arnold Southbank and Chaffoteaux are now Nuthall Chaffoteaux.

	BTSC	Bestwood Miners W. Res.	Bottesford St Mary's	Burton Joyce	Chaffoteaux Res.	Durham Ox	East Leake Athletic	Keyworth United Res.	Kimberley Miners W. Res.	Kirton Brickworks	Newark Town	Pinxton North End	Radcliffe Olympic Res.	Ruddington United Res.	Sandhurst	Santos
BTSC		0-3	4-3	1-1	1-0	4-1	4-3	1-1	2-0	0-1	5-3	5-2	2-3	1-0	2-1	2-0
Bestwood Miners W. Res.	1-2		2-1	9-0	0-0	3-0	1-0	3-0	2-1	4-1	3-2	5-0	2-1	2-0	5-1	0-5
Bottesford St Mary's	2-2	1-1	D	5-3	2-2	2-1	6-1	2-2	3-1	0-1	2-4	7-1	1-5	5-0	5-0	2-1
Burton Joyce	3-3	4-2	5-3	I	4-0	2-1	4-4	1-4	0-1	3-2	8-2	9-1	1-3	1-3	2-0	3-5
Chaffoteaux Res.	2-1	0-2	7-2	3-2	V	4-1	0-3	2-3	5-1	2-1	3-0	2-0	3-0	2-1	6-0	0-1
Durham Ox	2-3	0-2	0-2	2-6	1-4	I	2-3	2-4	5-0	2-5	5-2	4-0	0-3	3-1	2-3	1-3
East Leake Athletic	3-2	1-3	3-5	3-3	0-0	4-2	S	2-3	3-2	3-3	2-1	3-3	4-0	4-0	2-2	
Keyworth United Res.	1-5	2-1	4-1	3-3	3-1	0-1	5-0	I	3-6	4-0	4-0	7-0	0-1	2-0	2-0	3-4
Kimberley Miners W. Res.	1-4	1-0	2-1	2-1	0-1	0-2	0-3	0-4	O	3-2	2-1	5-0	2-2	11-1	5-1	0-2
Kirton Brickworks	0-0	2-5	1-3	0-2	0-4	2-3	2-0	0-0	2-1	N	2-2	7-0	1-0	5-2	0-3	1-2
Newark Town	0-3	1-1	3-4	0-1	1-4	1-4	1-3	1-2	5-4	2-4		6-0	1-4	3-1	2-2	1-4
Pinxton North End	3-13	1-5	2-3	0-7	2-4	2-1	1-4	1-5	0-3	1-2	2-1	T	1-3	3-7	0-3	0-5
Radcliffe Olympic Res.	2-4	2-5	3-1	2-2	1-1	4-0	3-2	1-4	1-0	4-1	5-1	11-1	W	2-4	1-0	1-0
Ruddington United Res.	1-1	0-4	3-2	1-4	2-1	2-1	2-2	2-3	0-1	1-2	1-1	1-2	1-1	O	6-1	1-0
Sandhurst	0-2	1-3	0-4	2-0	1-1	0-4	1-3	0-4	0-0	4-2	1-3	2-0	1-3	4-1		1-3
Santos	3-0	4-1	4-4	4-1	2-0	2-0	3-1	1-0	4-1	2-0	6-2	15-0	2-2	2-1	3-0	

WWW.CHERRYRED.CO.UK

Division Two	P	W	D	L	F	A	Pts
Santos	30	23	3	4	94	31	72
Bestwood Miners Welfare Res.	30	21	3	6	80	34	66
Keyworth United Res.	30	19	4	7	82	42	61
BTSC	30	18	6	6	79	46	60
Radcliffe Olympic Res.	30	17	6	7	77	47	57
Chaffoteaux Res.	30	16	5	9	64	38	53
East Leake Athletic	30	14	6	10	70	63	48
Bottesford St Mary's	30	14	5	11	84	68	47
Burton Joyce	30	13	6	11	86	71	45
Kimberley Miners Welfare Res.	30	12	2	16	56	60	38
Kirton Brickworks	30	11	3	16	48	59	36
Durham Ox	30	9	0	21	53	73	27
Ruddington United Res.	30	8	3	19	44	75	27
Sandhurst	30	7	3	20	33	78	24
Newark Town	30	6	3	21	54	92	21
Pinxton North End	30	3	0	27	27	154	9

Division Three	P	W	D	L	F	A	Pts
Southbank Res.	26	20	1	5	79	43	61
Cotgrave Coll. Welfare Res.	26	17	5	4	85	48	56
Rainworth Miners W. Res.	26	16	5	5	84	34	53
Awsworth Villa Res.	26	14	7	5	60	40	49
ASC Dayncourt Res.	26	15	3	8	74	40	48
Linby Colliery Welfare Res.	26	15	2	9	86	51	47
Clifton Res.	26	11	4	11	52	47	37
Basford United Res.	26	11	3	12	67	88	36
Calverton Miners Welf. Res.	26	9	7	10	54	38	34
Bilborough Res.	26	9	3	14	63	58	30
Ruddington Village	26	7	6	13	59	73	27
Attenborough Res.	26	5	3	18	44	95	18
Notts Police Res.	26	3	4	19	46	105	13
Newark Town Res.	26	2	3	21	31	124	9

DIVISION TWO CONSTITUTION 2003-04
(DIVISION MAY BE SPLIT INTO TWO SECTIONS)

ARNOLD SOUTHBANK RESERVES Carlton Recreation Ground, Carlton Hill, Nottingham, Nottinghamshire .... None
ATTENBOROUGH RESERVES .... Village Green, The Strand, Attenborough, Nottinghamshire 0115 925 7439
AWSWORTH VILLA RESERVES .... Shilo Park, Attewell Road, Awsworth, Nottinghamshire .... None
BILBOROUGH RESERVES ... The Pavilion, Birchover Park, Birchover Road, Bilborough, Nottinghamshire 0115 928 7662
BILSTHORPE .... Bilsthorpe Colliery Welfare, Eakring Road, Bilsthorpe, Nottinghamshire .... None
CALVERTON MW RESERVES ...... Calverton Rec, Hollingwood Lane, Calverton, Nottinghamshire 0115 965 4390
CLIFTON RESERVES .... Green Lane, Clifton Estate, Nottingham, Nottinghamshire 0115 984 4903
COTGRAVE CW RESERVES .. Cotgrave Welfare, Scheme Sports Ground, Cotgrave, Nottingham, Nottinghamshire 0115 989 4414
DURHAM OX .... Ollerton Road, Wellow, Nottingham, Nottinghamshire .... None
KIMBERLEY MW RESERVES .... Digby Street, Kimberley, Nottingham, Nottinghamshire .... 0115 938 2124 (Welfare)
KIRTON BRICKWORKS.............. Kirton Brickworks, Kirton, near Ollerton, Nottinghamshire .... None
LINBY COLLIERY WELFARE RESERVES .. Church Lane, Linby Village, Linby, Nottinghamshire .... None
MAGDALA AMATEURS RESERVES .. Civil Service Sports, Wilford Lane, West Bridgford, Nottinghamshire 0115 981 1418
MATRIXGRADE .... Aspley Boys Club, Melbourne Road, Aspley, Nottinghamshire .... None
NEWARK TOWN................. The Stadium, Elm Avenue, London Road, Newark, Nottinghamshire .... None
NOTTINGHAMSHIRE .... Bluecote School, Aspley Lane, Nottingham, Nottinghamshire. .... None
NOTTS POLICE RESERVES .... Police Training Centre, Epperstone, Nottingham, Nottinghamshire .... None
NUTHALL CHAFFOTEAUX RESERVES . Basil Russell PF, Maple Drive, Nuthall, Nottinghamshire.................. 0115 938 4765
RUDDINGTON UNITED RESERVES .. The Elms Park, Loughborough Road, Ruddington, Nottinghamshire 0115 984 4976
SANDHURST .... Walesby Sports & Social Club, Retford Road, Walesby, Nottinghamshire .... None

Bilsthorpe and Matrixgrade come down from Division One replaced by Bestwood Miners Welfare Reserves, Bottesford St Mary's, Burton Joyce, BTSC (who become Dale Hotel), East Leake Athletic, Keyworth United Reserves and Santos. Radcliffe Olympic Reserves and Pinxton North End depart. Attenborough Reserves, Bilborough Reserves, Cotgrave Colliery Welfare Reserves, Linby Colliery Welfare Reserves, Arnold Southbank Reserves, Awsworth Villa Reserves, Calverton Miners Welfare Reserves, Clifton Reserves and Notts Police Reserves all come up from the now disbanded Division Three. Newcomers are Nottinghamshire and Magdala Amateurs Reserves, both Midland Amateur League.

READING LEAGUE

	Ascot Utd	Checkendon	Cookham D.	Forest OB	High./IBIS	Marlow U.	Midgham	Mortimer	Royal Mail	Unity	W. Reading	Westwood	Woodley T.
Ascot United		W-L	0-2	3-4	0-4	2-0	7-0	4-1	2-4	5-0	4-3	0-3	2-2
Checkendon Spts	4-4	S	0-1	3-1	1-5	0-6	3-0	1-1	0-0	2-0	L-W	2-3	1-1
Cookham Dean	0-1	1-1	E	0-2	1-1	3-3	4-1	2-1	2-1	1-2	1-0	1-3	0-2
Forest Old Boys	4-2	5-1	4-1	N	3-1	4-2	2-1	2-0	2-1	9-0	0-0	2-2	6-1
Highmoor/IBIS	6-0	2-2	2-2	2-3	I	4-2	4-0	0-1	2-2	2-2	2-3	2-0	
Marlow United	3-1	5-2	1-4	0-2	2-0	O	5-2	5-4	2-5	4-0	5-1	0-0	3-1
Midgham	3-2	2-3	1-3	0-6	0-3	3-1	R	1-1	1-4	1-1	0-2	3-2	2-0
Mortimer	1-1	2-2	3-6	3-0	2-1	2-2	3-1		2-1	2-1	1-0	0-1	2-0
Royal Mail	0м0	1-2	3-1	2-1	2-8	6-1	0-0	2-0		3-1	3-1	0-2	1-0
Unity	1-3	L-W	1-3	0-3	0-2	1-4	2-2	3-1	1-3	D	1-2	1-1	2-2
West Reading	0-1	1-1	0-3	3-5	2-2	1-0	2-1	0-2	0-2	3-1	I	2-1	0-3
Westwood United	0-1	0-0	1-2	2-3	1-3	2-1	1-2	1-0	0-3	0м0	4-1	V	2-0
Woodley Town	2-2	0-1	0-1	0-3	4-0	1-1	0-2	0-1	0-2	3-0	0-2	1-1	

Senior Division	P	W	D	L	F	A	Pts
Forest Old Boys	24	20	2	2	80	29	62
Royal Mail	24	15	3	6	53	29	48
Cookham Dean	24	12	5	7	39	31	41
Highmoor/IBIS	24	11	5	8	58	38	38
Westwood United	24	10	6	8	36	30	36
Ascot United	24	10	5	9	47	47	35
Marlow United	24	10	4	10	58	51	34
Mortimer	24	8	6	10	31	36	30
Checkendon Spts	24	7	9	8	32	41	30
West Reading	24	8	4	12	28	43	28
Midgham	24	6	4	14	29	61	22
Woodley Town	24	4	6	14	23	39	18
Unity	24	3	5	16	21	60	14

SENIOR DIVISION CONSTITUTION 2003-04

ASCOT UNITED.....................Ascot Race Course, Winkfield Road, Ascot, Berkshire.....................None
CHECKENDON SPORTS...............The Playing Fields, Checkendon, Reading, Berkshire.....................None
COOKHAM DEAN........Alfred Major Rec Ground, Hillcrest Avenue, Cookham Rise, Maidenhead, Berkshire.....................None
FOREST OLD BOYS.................Holme Park (Adwest), Sonning Lane, Sonning, Berkshire.....................01734 690356
HIGHMOOR/IBIS ....IBIS Sports Club, Scours Lane, Reading, Berkshire.....................None
HURST ....Cantley Park, Twyford Road, Wokingham, Berkshire.....................None
MARLOW UNITED ....Gossmore Park, Gossmore Lane, Marlow, Buckinghamshire.....................None
MIDGHAM ....Henwick Worthy Playing Fields, Thatcham, Berkshire.....................None
MORTIMER ....Alfred Palmer Memorial PF, West End Road, Mortimer, Reading, Berkshire.....................None
READING YMCA ....Emmer Green Recreation Ground, Reading, Berkshire.....................None
ROYAL MAIL.........Victoria Recreation Ground, Norcot Road, Tilehurst, Reading, Berkshire.....................None
WEST READING ....Victoria Recreation Ground, Norcot Road, Tilehurst, Reading, Berkshire.....................None
WESTWOOD UNITED............Cotswold Sports Centre, Downsway, Tilehurst, Reading, Berkshire.....................None
Woodley Town and Unity drop to the Premier Division replaced by Reading YMCA and Hurst.

	Berks CS	Emmbrook	Forest OB Res.	Goring United	Hurst	New. Henley	REME Arbor.	Read. YMCA	Roundhead U.	Shinfield	Sonning Cmn	Westwood Res.
Berks Co. Sports	P	1-1	3-1	6-0	1-2	2-1	3-0	2-1	2-1	6-2	4-0	1-0
Emmbrook Sports	0-0	R	1-2	0-0	4-0	2-1	1-1	1-3	6-0	3-1	2-2	5-0
Forest OB Res.	1-3	0-3	E	0-2	2-1	1-3	5-5	0-4	2-6	1-3	3-0	3-1
Goring United	1-3	1-1	8-2	M	1-2	0-1	W-L	1-7	L-W	1-5	1-1	0-4
Hurst	4-1	2-0	1-1	3-0	I	3-0	5-0	4-1	0-0	0-2	7-4	5-1
Newtown Henley	5-2	1-2	2-0	3-5	1-4	E	2-4	2-6	1-1	2-3	1-2	5-0
REME Arborfield	0-3	2-5	3-6	1-1	0-1	0-1	R	3-4	5-4	0-3	0-2	2-1
Reading YMCA	1-0	0-2	5-3	1-1	0-3	1-1	4-1		3-1	5-2	3-0	8-4
Roundhead United	1-0	1-0	0-2	2-4	1-4	5-2	3-2	2-3		2-1	3-0	6-0
Shinfield	0-2	1-1	3-4	3-1	2-2	3-1	1-1	4-2		D	1-4	4-1
Sonning Common	2-3	0-1	1-2	2-0	1-1	1-0	2-1	1-4	4-0	0-1	I	3-1
Westwood U. Res.	1-6	3-3	2-2	5-1	1-2	5-6	1-3	1-3	4-1	1-3	3-1	V

Premier Division		P	W	D	L	F	A	Pts
Reading YMCA		22	15	3	4	68	36	48
Hurst		22	15	3	4	55	25	48
Berks County Sports		22	15	2	5	54	25	47
Emmbrook Sports		22	11	7	4	46	22	40
Shinfield		22	12	2	8	49	42	38
Roundhead United		22	9	2	11	42	49	29
Sonning Common		22	8	3	11	33	42	27
Forest Old Boys Res.		22	8	3	11	43	58	27
Newtown Henley		22	7	3	12	43	51	24
Goring United	-1	22	5	5	12	28	52	19
REME Arborfield		22	4	3	15	34	60	15
Westwood United Res.		22	4	2	16	40	73	14

PREMIER DIVISION CONSTITUTION 2003-04

BERKS COUNTY SPORTS .. Berks County Sports & Social Club, Sonning Lane, Sonning, Reading, Berkshire.....................None
EMMBROOK SPORTS......Emmbrook Sports Ground, Lowther Road, Emmbrook, Wokingham, Berkshire..............01189 780209
FOREST OLD BOYS RESERVES......Holme Park (Adwest), Sonning Lane, Sonning, Berkshire.....................01734 690356
NEWTOWN HENLEY ....Harpsden Hall, Harpsden Village, Henley-on-Thames, Oxfordshire.....................None
READING OLD BLUES .....Berks County Sports & Social Club, Sonning Lane, Sonning, Reading, Berkshire.....................None
ROUNDHEAD UNITED ....Coley Park, St Saviours Road, Reading, Berkshire.....................None
SHINFIELD ....Millworth Lane, Shinfield, Reading, Berkshire.....................None
SONNING COMMON ......Peppard Cricket Club, Peppard Common, Stoke Row Road, Peppard, Oxfordshire.....................None
SPENCERS WOOD.....................Sol Joel, Church Road, Earley, Reading, Berkshire.....................None
UNITY ....Cintra Park, Cintra Avenue, Reading, Berkshire.....................None
WOODCOTE & STOKE ROW ....Woodcote Recreation Ground, Woodcote, Reading, Berkshire.....................None
WOODLEY TOWN ....Woodford Park, Haddon Drive, Woodley, Berkshire.....................None
Reading YMCA and Hurst are promoted to the Senior Division replaced by Woodley Town and Unity. Westwood United Reserves and Goring United are relegated to Division One replaced by Reading Old Blues, Spencers Wood and Woodcote & Stoke Row. REME Arborfield have withdrawn.

SENIOR CUP
(Senior and Premier Division teams)

SEMI-FINALS	FINAL
Forest Old Boys 3 Marlow United 0	*(21st May at Reading FC)*
Royal Mail 1 Cookham Dean 0	Forest Old Boys 5 Royal Mail 2

	AFC M'hd	Ck. D. Res.	Emm. Res.	F'stead 'A'	Frilsham	H/IBIS Res.	Reading OB	Rides Utd	Spencers W.	Woodcote	Woodley Rs.
AFC Maidenhead		0-3	0-2	4-2	1-1	0-5	1-4	1-7	0-1	0-1	0-1
Cookham Dean Res.	1-10		0-3	2-3	2-3	0-1	1-7	2-0	1-2	7-2	3-1
Emmbrook Sports Res.	2-1	0-0	*D*	2-0	0-1	1-1	0-5	4-1	1-1	0-0	4-1
Finchampstead 'A'	4-2	3-4	1-4	*I*	1-0	4-0	1-2	1-7	3-5	6-3	1-1
Frilsham & Yattendon	5-0	1-4	2-2	1-0	*V*	2-1	1-4	6-3	1-2	1-3	2-3
Highmoor/IBIS Res.	0-1	3-4	1-1	2-3	0-1		2-1	5-4	0-1	5-2	4-0
Reading Old Blues	7-1	2-0	4-2	1-1	4-2	4-1	*O*	2-0	2-1	1-4	2-0
Rides United	4-1	2-1	6-1	3-3	0-2	4-1	1-0	*N*	1-1	2-2	5-1
Spencers Wood	4-1	0-0	3-0	3-1	0-4	2-1	0-1	8-0	*E*	2-4	3-2
Woodcote & Stoke Row	1-0	0-1	1-1	2-0	2-1	4-0	2-3	3-1	1-3		2-1
Woodley Town Res.	1-1	2-1	1-0	2-0	0-2	2-4	2-2	0-2	1-2	1-4	

Division One	P	W	D	L	F	A	Pts
Reading Old Blues	20	16	2	2	58	21	50
Spencers Wood	20	13	3	4	44	25	42
Woodcote/Stoke Row	20	11	3	6	43	36	36
Frilsham/Yattendon	20	10	2	8	39	32	32
Rides United	20	9	3	8	53	45	30
Emmbrook Sp. Res.	20	7	7	6	30	30	28
Cookham Dean Res.	20	8	2	10	37	45	26
Finchampstead 'A'	20	6	3	11	38	50	21
Highmoor/IBIS Res.	20	6	2	12	35	41	20
Woodley Town Res.	20	5	3	12	23	44	18
AFC Maidenhead	20	3	2	15	25	56	11

DIVISION ONE CONSTITUTION 2003-04

COOKHAM DEAN RESERVES .. Alfred Major Rec, Hillcrest Avenue, Cookham Rise, Maidenhead, Berkshire .... None

EMMBROOK SPORTS RESERVES. Emmbrook Sports Ground, Lowther Rd, Emmbrook, Wokingham 01189 780209

FINCHAMPSTEAD 'A' .... Memorial Ground, Finchampstead Park, Finchampstead, Berkshire 0118 973 2890

FRILSHAM & YATTENDON .. Frilsham Playing Field, Frilsham Common, Frilsham, near Hermitage, Berkshire............ 01635 201847

GORING UNITED........ Gardiners Recreation Ground, Upper Red Cross Road, Goring-on-Thames, Berkshire.................... None

HENLEY YMCA .... Henley YMCA (next to Tescos), Watermans Road, Henley-on-Thames, Oxfordshire .... None

HIGHMOOR/IBIS RESERVES .... IBIS Sports Club, Scours Lane, Reading, Berkshire .... None

HURST RESERVES .... Cantley Park, Twyford Road, Wokingham, Berkshire.................................... None

OLD BELL....................... Brimpton Recreation Ground, Brimpton, Berkshire .... None

RIDES UNITED................ Rides Community Centre, Gorse Ride South, Finchampstead, Berkshire.................... None

WESTWOOD UNITED RESERVES ... Cotswold Sports Centre, Downsway, Tilehurst, Reading, Berkshire................. None

WOODLEY TOWN RESERVES .... Woodford Park, Haddon Drive, Woodley, Reading, Berkshire .... None

Reading Old Blues, Spencers Wood and Woodcote & Stoke Row are promoted to the Premier Division replaced by Westwood United Reserves and Goring United. AFC Maidenhead are relegated to Division Two replaced by Old Bell, Henley YMCA and Hurst Reserves.

	Crowthorne	Gladstone	Henley YM.	Hurst Res.	Old Bell	Twyford	Wargrave	Westw'd 'A'	Wok'hm Rs.	W'cote Res.
Crowthorne Sports		2-3	0-6	0-2	2-5	3-0	3-1	3-2	1-5	0-0
Gladstone	1-0	*D*	2-4	2-7	0-6	1-1	2-2	5-3	5-2	2-5
Henley YMCA	3-0	3-0	*I*	6-1	1-3	6-0	2-3	7-0	W-L	2-2
Hurst Res.	5-2	4-0	3-2	*V*	1-1	5-0	1-2	4-1	0-2	10-1
Old Bell	W-L	6-1	0-4	5-1		4-0	5-4	6-0	10-0	4-2
Twyford & Ruscombe	4-1	6-0	0-1	1-1	0-5		1-4	5-1	2-2	6-1
Wargrave	2-4	3-1	2-1	1-3	0-6	1-2	*T*	6-0	2-2	6-1
Westwood United 'A'	1-2	W-L	0-6	1-3	0-2	3-2	L-W	*W*	L-W	2-3
Wokingham Town Res.	1-2	1-2	0-0	1-3	5-3	1-6	0-3	L-W	*O*	7-1
Woodcote & Stoke Row Res.	3-1	2-2	0-6	0-2	1-4	2-1	1-2	W-L	15-0	

Division Two	P	W	D	L	F	A	Pts
Old Bell	18	15	1	2	75	22	46
Henley YMCA	18	12	2	4	60	16	38
Hurst Res.	18	12	2	4	56	28	38
Wargrave	18	10	2	6	44	35	32
Twyford & Ruscombe	18	6	3	9	36	42	21
Woodcote & SR Res.	18	6	3	9	40	56	21
Crowthorne Sports	18	6	1	11	26	44	19
Wokingham T. Res.	18	5	3	10	29	55	18
Gladstone	18	5	3	10	29	57	18
Westwood United 'A'	18	3	0	15	14	54	9

DIVISION TWO CONSTITUTION 2003-04

AFC MAIDENHEAD .... Desborough Park, Maidenhead, Berkshire .... None

ASCOT UNITED RESERVES........... Ascot Race Course, Winkfield Road, Ascot, Berkshire............................ None

CROWTHORNE SPORTS .... Morgan Recreation Ground, Lower Broadmoor Road, Crowthorne, Berkshire .... None

GLADSTONE .... Prospect Park, Reading, Berkshire.................................... None

NEWTOWN HENLEY RESERVES . Harpsden Hall, Harpsden Village, Henley-on-Thames, Oxfordshire .... None

RABSON ROVERS..................... Lower Whitley Rec, Basingstoke Road, Reading, Berkshire .... None

RADSTOCK..................... Cantley Park, Twyford Road, Wokingham, Berkshire............................... None

SONNING SPORTS.................... Palmer Park, Wokingham Road, Reading, Berkshire.................................. None

TWYFORD & RUSCOMBE... Twyford Recreation Ground, Loddon Hall Road, Twyford, Reading, Berkshire................... None

WARGRAVE............. Wargrave Recreation Ground, Recreation Road, Wargrave, Maidenhead, Berkshire................. None

WHITLEY ROVERS................ Sol Joel, Church Road, Earley, Reading, Berkshire............................... None

WOODCOTE & STOKE ROW RESERVES .. Woodcote Rec. Ground, Woodcote, Reading, Berkshire................... None

Old Bell, Henley YMCA and Hurst Reserves are promoted to Division One replaced by AFC Maidenhead. Wokingham Town Reserves and Westwood United 'A' have resigned. Radstock, Rabson Rovers, Newtown Henley Reserves, Whitley Rovers and Sonning Sports are promoted from Division Three. Newcomers are Ascot United Reserves.

WWW.CHERRYRED.CO.UK

INTERMEDIATE CUP
(Division One and Two teams)

FINAL
(24th May at Reading Town)
Reading Old Blues 0 **Westwood United Res.** 1

	Compton	Englefield	Goring U. Res.	High./IBIS 'A'	Mortimer Res.	N. Henley Res.	REME App.	Rabson Rovers	Radstock	Sonning Sports	Whitley Rovers	Wok'ham Wdrs
Compton		4-0	2-4	1-1	6-2	0-5	1-0	1-2	3-7	0-4	1-5	3-3
Englefield	2-2	*D*	1-2	1-4	3-2	2-1	1-2	0-11	2-5	3-1	1-3	1-6
Goring United Res.	6-4	3-2	*I*	1-1	2-1	0-0	2-3	L-W	0-3	2-3	1-2	0-5
Highmoor/IBIS 'A'	4-3	0-1	5-0	*V*	6-1	2-3	3-2	0-4	1-3	1-2	1-7	6-1
Mortimer Res.	3-0	3-2	2-0	2-3		2-2	4-1	1-10	0-3	2-2	2-3	1-2
New. Henley Res.	3-0	2-0	4-2	5-1	12-0		3-2	2-3	4-1	2-1	3-2	1-5
REME Apprentices	9-4	4-2	4-0	4-0	5-0	1-4	*T*	3-7	1-1	3-2	4-2	2-5
Rabson Rovers	3-0	4-3	8-0	3-0	8-0	1-2	2-1	*H*	3-6	2-3	2-0	3-0
Radstock	9-1	7-0	4-3	3-0	W-L	4-2	3-1	2-2	*R*	2-0	6-4	3-0
Sonning Sports	9-3	2-0	2-2	5-0	W-L	1-3	1-0	3-5	2-4	*E*	4-3	4-2
Whitley Rovers	3-2	2-2	5-3	7-6	5-2	1-3	2-0	1-3	5-2	2-2	*E*	1-2
Wokingham Wdrs	2-3	2-2	6-1	6-4	W-L	4-6	2-4	0-0	2-6	5-3	1-4	

Division Three	P	W	D	L	F	A	Pts
Radstock	22	18	2	2	84	36	56
Rabson Rovers	22	17	2	3	86	28	53
New. Henley Res.	22	16	2	4	72	35	50
Whitley Rovers	22	12	2	8	69	53	38
Sonning Sports	22	11	2	9	56	47	35
Wokingham Wdrs	22	10	3	9	61	58	33
REME App'tices	22	10	1	11	56	51	31
Highmoor/IBIS 'A'	22	7	2	13	49	65	23
Goring Utd Res.	22	5	3	14	34	67	18
Mortimer Res.	22	5	1	16	31	75	16
Englefield	22	4	3	15	31	72	15
Compton	22	4	3	15	44	86	15

DIVISION THREE CONSTITUTION 2003-04

AFC CORINTHIANS . . . . Prospect Park, Reading, Berkshire . . . . None
COMPTON . . . . Recreation Ground, Burrell Road, Compton, Newbury, Berkshire . . . . None
ENGLEFIELD . . . . Englefield Street (off A340), Englefield, Reading, Berkshire . . . . None
GORING UNITED RESERVES . . . Gardiners Rec., Upper Red Cross Road, Goring-on-Thames, Berkshire . . . . None
HIGHMOOR/IBIS 'A' . . . . IBIS Sports Club, Scours Lane, Reading, Berkshire . . . . None
MARLOW UNITED RESERVES . . . . . . Gossmore Park, Gossmore Lane, Marlow, Buckinghamshire . . . . None
MORTIMER RESERVES . . . . . Alfred Palmer Memorial PF, West End Road, Mortimer, Reading, Berkshire . . . . None
OLD LONDON APPRENTICE . . . . Victoria Park, Newbury, Berkshire . . . . None
REME ARBORFIELD . . . . Sports Pavilion, Biggs Lane, Hazelbroun Barracks, Berkshire . . . . None
SRCC . . . . Lower Whitley Rec Ground, Basingstoke Road, Reading, Berkshire . . . . None
SONNING . . . . Woodford Park, Haddon Drive, Woodley, Reading, Berkshire . . . . None
WOKINGHAM WANDERERS . . . . Laurel Park, Lower Earley, Berkshire . . . . None
Radstock, Rabson Rovers, Newtown Henley Reserves, Whitley Rovers and Sonning Sports are promoted to Division Two. Marlow United Reserves, Old London Apprentice, AFC Corinthians, SRCC and Sonning gain promotion from Division Four.

	AFC Corinthians	Marlow Utd Res.	Nettlebed United	Old London Apps	SRCC	Shinfield Res.	Sonning	Unity Res.	Woodley Town 'A'
AFC Corinthians	*D*	0-2	4-3	3-3	6-1	8-1	2-1	2-0	7-4
Marlow United Res.	2-1	*I*	6-0	4-2	4-0	0-2	1-1	5-1	7-0
Nettlebed United	2-3	2-6	*V*	0-1	2-4	1-4	1-3	0-5	L-W
Old London Apprentice	4-2	4-5	5-1		5-0	7-0	4-0	0-0	5-1
SRCC	1-4	2-4	W-L	4-1		3-0	3-1	1-6	4-1
Shinfield Res.	0-5	0-4	2-2	1-3	L-W	*F*	3-4	1-0	1-7
Sonning	4-0	1-1	5-0	1-2	6-2	5-2	*O*	3-3	0-1
Unity Res.	0-2	1-3	3-4	1-2	2-1	3-2	1-1	*U*	4-5
Woodley Town 'A'	2-2	2-1	7-2	4-6	1-6	2-0	3-3	1-3	*R*

Division Four	P	W	D	L	F	A	Pts
Marlow Utd Res.	16	12	2	2	55	19	38
Old London App.	16	11	2	3	54	27	35
AFC Corinthians	16	10	2	4	51	30	32
SRCC	16	8	0	8	32	43	24
Sonning	16	6	5	5	39	29	23
Woodley Town 'A'	16	7	2	7	41	51	23
Unity Res.	16	5	3	8	33	33	18
Shinfield Res.	16	3	1	12	19	54	10
Nettlebed United	16	1	1	14	20	58	4

Marlow United Reserves, Old London Apprentice, AFC Corinthians, SRCC and Sonning go up to Division Three. Newcomers are Tilehurst Rangers, Linear United, Prospect United, Marlow United 'A', Whitley Wood, Southurst Park, Hurst 'A', Berks County Sports Reserves and Emmbrook Sports 'A'.

DIVISION FOUR CONSTITUTION 2003-04

BERKS CO. SPORTS RESERVES . Berks County Sports & Social Club, Sonning Lane, Sonning, Reading . . . . None
EMMBROOK SPORTS 'A' . . . Emmbrook Sports Ground, Lowther Road, Emmbrook, Wokingham, Berkshire 01189 780209
HURST 'A' . . . . Cantley Park, Twyford Road, Wokingham, Berkshire . . . . None
LINEAR UNITED . . . . t.b.a. . . . . t.b.a.
MARLOW UNITED 'A' . . . . Gossmore Park, Gossmore Lane, Marlow, Buckinghamshire . . . . None
NETTLEBED UNITED . . . . The Recreation Ground, Watlington Street, Nettlebed, Oxfordshire . . . . None
PROSPECT UNITED . . . . t.b.a. . . . . None
SHINFIELD RESERVES . . . . Millworth Lane, Shinfield, Reading, Berkshire . . . . None
SOUTHURST PARK . . . . t.b.a. . . . . t.b.a.
TILEHURST RANGERS . . . . t.b.a. . . . . t.b.a.
UNITY RESERVES . . . . Cintra Park, Cintra Avenue, Reading, Berkshire . . . . None
WHITLEY WOOD . . . . t.b.a. . . . . t.b.a.
WOODLEY TOWN 'A' . . . . Woodford Park, Haddon Drive, Woodley, Reading, Berkhire . . . . None

JUNIOR CUP
(Division Three and Four teams)

FINAL
(26th April at Reading Town)
Radstock 3 Old London Apprentice 2

DIVISION FOUR CUP

FINAL
(25th May at Reading Town)
Marlow United Res. 2 SRCC 0

SOMERSET COUNTY LEAGUE

	Backwell United Res.	Bridgwater Town Res.	Brislington Res.	Burnham United	Castle Cary	Clevedon United	Fry Club	Keynsham Town Res.	Mangotsfield Utd Res.	Nailsea Town	Nailsea United	Peasedown Athletic	Portishead	Radstock Town	Stockwood Green	Wells City	Welton Rovers Res.	Westland United
Backwell United Res.		2-6	1-2	3-2	5-2	1-1	0-1	5-0	1-2	5-0	0-4	2-4	1-0	3-3	1-1	7-4	1-2	1-0
Bridgwater Town Res.	2-3	*P*	0-0	2-3	0-1	3-3	2-1	0-2	3-0	5-1	1-4	3-0	1-0	1-4	2-3	5-3	3-2	1-1
Brislington Res.	5-1	0-3	*R*	2-2	5-0	2-1	1-3	0-0	6-1	0-1	1-2	2-0	2-3	2-1	4-3	1-0	5-2	0-1
Burnham United	4-1	1-2	1-0	*E*	4-2	0-2	1-2	2-1	3-1	5-0	0-2	2-2	1-0	4-0	1-1	0-3	2-1	3-6
Castle Cary	0-0	3-2	1-0	2-3	*M*	1-5	3-1	3-1	3-2	1-3	1-1	1-1	0-2	2-2	1-2	2-0	2-1	1-3
Clevedon United	7-1	2-1	2-1	2-2	2-0	*I*	0-1	2-1	3-1	7-1	1-3	3-2	0-3	2-1	3-1	3-2	5-0	2-1
Fry Club	2-1	0-0	0-0	4-1	4-1	0-2	*E*	1-3	2-1	3-0	2-0	1-1	1-3	1-1	2-0	1-0	1-1	1-0
Keynsham Town Res.	3-1	1-1	1-2	3-2	1-0	1-0	4-3	*R*	0-1	4-1	2-2	2-1	0-3	3-2	4-1	1-1	3-1	0-3
Mangotsfield United Res.	5-1	3-0	2-1	2-1	3-0	3-1	0-1	0-4		4-1	3-3	3-0	0-0	1-2	6-1	1-1	3-1	3-1
Nailsea Town	1-4	1-3	1-2	1-2	0-4	1-2	0-3	1-1	0-5	*D*	0-2	0-0	2-5	2-3	0-3	1-3	3-1	1-1
Nailsea United	4-0	3-0	2-0	1-0	1-2	3-2	0-0	4-0	0-3	3-0	*I*	5-1	1-3	1-2	1-0	1-1	1-2	0-3
Peasedown Athletic	4-0	1-1	0-4	1-1	0-4	2-3	0-3	2-0	2-0	2-3	1-0	*V*	0-2	0-2	0-9	3-4	3-0	0-3
Portishead	2-1	2-0	3-0	2-2	3-1	1-0	0-0	1-1	0-2	0-0	1-2	3-0	*I*	1-1	2-1	0-2	0-0	1-2
Radstock Town	0-4	2-3	1-1	4-2	2-0	1-1	2-1	3-3	0-3	4-0	1-4	1-1	1-2	*S*	1-3	2-2	2-3	1-0
Stockwood Green	3-2	0-2	0-1	2-2	1-4	2-0	1-1	2-2	2-3	4-1	1-1	0-3	2-2	2-1	*I*	0-1	1-1	1-1
Wells City	0-3	2-4	0-1	3-1	1-1	1-1	2-2	1-2	2-0	6-0	3-4	4-1	0-2	2-2	0-0	*O*	1-0	0-1
Welton Rovers Res.	3-5	2-3	5-1	2-1	2-4	1-4	3-0	2-1	1-0	2-2	0-4	4-1	3-2	3-3	3-4	0-0	*N*	0-3
Westland United	2-3	3-0	3-0	4-2	3-1	0-0	2-2	2-0	3-1	3-0	3-1	0-0	1-2	1-3	2-0	3-0	0-1	

Premier Division		P	W	D	L	F	A	Pts
Nailsea United		34	20	6	8	73	39	66
Portishead		34	19	7	8	58	29	64
Westland United		34	19	6	9	64	33	63
Clevedon United		34	19	6	9	74	45	63
Mangotsfield United Res.		34	19	3	12	70	48	60
Fry Club		34	16	10	8	51	36	58
Bridgwater Town Res.		34	15	6	13	65	59	51
Brislington Res.		34	15	5	14	54	47	50
Keynsham Town Res.		34	14	8	12	55	56	50
Radstock Town		34	11	12	11	63	64	45
Castle Cary		34	13	5	16	54	66	44
Burnham United		34	12	7	15	63	66	43
Backwell United Res.	-1	34	13	4	17	70	81	42
Stockwood Green		34	10	10	14	57	63	40
Wells City		34	9	10	15	53	56	37
Welton Rovers Res.		34	10	7	17	57	75	37
Peasedown Athletic		34	5	9	20	36	81	24
Nailsea Town		34	4	5	25	29	102	17

PREM/DIV ONE CUP

FIRST ROUND
Congresbury 1 **Hengrove Athletic** 5
Glastonbury 2 **Keynsham Town Res.** 5 *aet*
Peasedown Athletic 2 **Nailsea Town** 4
Westland United 4 Blackbrook 1
SECOND ROUND
Brislington Res. 3 Crewkerne 2
Burnham United 6 Stockwood Green 1
Clevedon United 4 Mangotsfield United Res. 2
Hengrove Athletic 2 Backwell United Res. 0
Nailsea Town 1 **Bridgwater Town Res.** 3
Nailsea United 1 Shirehampton 0
Oldland Abbotonians 1 Wells City 0
Paulton Res. 4 **Keynsham Town Res.** 4 *aet (3-4p)*
Portishead 2 Castle Cary 1
Robinsons 2 **Bishop Sutton Res.** 3
Sporting Club Somerton 2 Radstock 2 *aet (4-3p)*
Team Bath Res. 2 Fry Club 1
Watchet Town 0 **Weston-super-Mare Res.** 3

PREMIER DIVISION CONSTITUTION 2003-04

BACKWELL UNITED RESERVES . . Backwell Recreation Grounds, Backwell, Bristol, North Somerset 01275 462612
BRIDGWATER TOWN RESERVES . . . Fairfax Park, College Way, Bath Road, Bridgwater, Somerset 01278 446899
BRISLINGTON RESERVES . . . . Ironmould Lane, Brislington, Bristol, North Somerset 0117 977 4030
BURNHAM UNITED . . . . Burnham Road Playing Fields, Cassis Close, Burnham-on-Sea, Somerset 01278 794615
CASTLE CARY . . . . Donald Pither Memorial PF, Castle Cary, Somerset 01963 351538
CLEEVE WEST TOWN . . . . King George V Playing Fields, Meeting House Lane, Cleeve, North Somerset 01934 832173
FRY CLUB . . . . Fry Club, Somerdale, Keynsham, Bristol, North Somerset . . . . 0117 937 6500 / 937 6501
KEYNSHAM TOWN RESERVES . . . . Crown Field, Bristol Road, Keynsham, Bristol, North Somerset 0117 986 5876
MANGOTSFIELD UNITED RESERVES . . Cossham Street, Mangotsfield, Bristol, South Glos. 0117 956 0119
NAILSEA UNITED . . . . Grove Sports Ground, Old Church, Nailsea, North Somerset 01275 856892
PAULTON ROVERS RESERVES . . . . Athletic Ground, Winterfield Road, Paulton, Somerset 01761 412911
PORTISHEAD . . . . Bristol Road Playing Fields, Portishead, Bristol, North Somerset 01275 847136
RADSTOCK TOWN . . . . Southfield Recreation Ground, Frome Hill, Radstock, Somerset 01761 435004
STOCKWOOD GREEN . . . . Bath Spa University College, Newton Park, Newton-St-Loe, Bath, Somerset . . . . None
TEAM BATH RESERVES . . University of Bath, Sports Training Village, Claverton Down, Bath, North Somerset 01225 826339
WELLS CITY . . . . The Athletic Ground, Rowdens Road, Wells, Somerset 01749 679971
WELTON ROVERS RESERVES . . . . West Clewes, North Road, Midsomer Norton, Somerset 01761 412097
WESTLAND UNITED RESERVES . . . Westland Sports Club, Winterstoke Road, Weston-super-Mare 01934 632037

Clevedon United are promoted to the Western League. Peasedown Athletic and Nailsea Town are relegated to Division One. Cleeve West Town, Team Bath Reserves and Paulton Rovers Reserves move in the opposite direction.

	Bishop Sutton Res.	Blackbrook	Cheddar	Cleve West Town	Congresbury	Crewkerne	Glastonbury	Hengrove Athletic	Oldland Abbotonians	Paulton Rovers Res.	Robinsons	Shirehampton	Sporting Club Somerton	Team Bath Res.	Timsbury Athletic	Watchet Town	Weston-super-Mare Res.	Winscombe
Bishop Sutton Res.		4-0	0-3	1-1	6-0	1-1	1-1	0-4	1-0	1-3	3-1	0-0	2-0	1-4	2-0	0-1	5-2	2-2
Blackbrook	1-3		2-7	2-3	4-1	2-4	4-4	1-3	4-1	0-6	2-1	2-1	2-1	0-8	1-1	1-1	2-2	3-2
Cheddar	3-4	2-1		1-2	1-1	3-1	1-3	0-3	3-2	0-1	2-1	1-4	1-1	2-4	1-1	2-3	0-3	1-2
Cleve West Town	1-0	6-0	6-0	D	4-0	2-0	5-0	0-1	1-0	2-2	0-0	4-0	4-1	2-1	2-1	0-1	2-1	2-1
Congresbury	0-0	2-4	6-2	1-2	I	1-1	1-0	3-1	1-4	3-2	0-1	2-2	0-0	0-1	2-0	1-3	2-2	1-3
Crewkerne	3-1	1-2	2-3	4-1	2-1	V	2-0	0-3	0-2	0-2	2-3	0-0	2-1	2-4	4-3	2-5	4-1	3-3
Glastonbury	1-3	1-0	0-2	0-2	2-1	3-1	I	1-1	2-2	0-2	3-2	1-1	4-1	0-1	1-2	1-2	2-0	1-1
Hengrove Athletic	0-0	1-0	4-0	1-0	0-0	0-1	3-0	S	3-1	1-1	2-1	1-3	1-0	1-1	2-0	1-1	2-0	0-0
Oldland Abbotonians	0-3	0-0	3-1	0-2	1-0	2-0	1-1	0-0	I	1-3	3-0	2-0	1-0	2-1	1-2	2-2	4-3	0-1
Paulton Rovers Res.	4-3	3-1	2-1	0-1	7-1	2-1	2-0	1-4	2-1	O	6-3	11-2	5-1	2-0	1-1	6-1	1-1	4-0
Robinsons	3-0	3-1	3-4	0-2	2-3	1-0	0-2	1-1	2-3	1-1	N	2-1	1-2	2-1	0-0	3-0	1-2	
Shirehampton	0-1	3-1	0-7	0-2	2-0	0-0	1-0	0-1	7-0	2-1	1-0		5-2	1-1	2-2	2-2	2-0	1-3
Sporting Club Somerton	0-4	5-1	1-3	0-2	1-2	4-2	1-1	3-0	1-3	5-4	2-2	3-3	O	1-4	1-2	0-2	1-1	1-1
Team Bath Res.	3-1	0-2	2-1	2-1	4-1	4-0	4-2	1-1	1-0	2-3	3-0	5-0	8-0	N	4-2	1-1	5-1	3-0
Timsbury Athletic	3-0	0-2	2-3	0-1	1-2	0-2	2-1	1-2	0-4	1-0	1-2	2-0	4-0	0-3	E	4-1	1-2	2-2
Watchet Town	2-0	1-3	1-1	0-1	1-2	1-4	2-0	0-2	5-2	0-1	4-0	4-2	1-1	1-2	1-1		1-2	0-1
Weston-super-Mare Res.	2-0	0-3	5-3	0-2	4-2	3-2	3-2	2-2	3-1	3-1	2-1	5-1	3-2	0-1	2-2	0-1		0-0
Winscombe	2-2	1-3	0-3	0-1	5-0	3-1	1-1	0-1	1-2	1-2	2-0	1-3	3-2	4-4	2-0	1-1	2-3	

Welton Rovers Res. 1 **Cleve West Town** 4
Westland United 5 Cheddar 3
Winscombe 2 **Timsbury** 4
THIRD ROUND
Bridgwater Town Res. 4
Sporting Club Somerton 0
Cleve West Town 0
Hengrove Athletic 2
Keynsham Town Res. 2
Portishead 3 *aet*
Nailsea Utd 6 Burnham Utd 3
Oldland Abbotonians 2 Team Bath Res. 0
Timsbury 1 **Clevedon Utd** 4
Westland United 2 Bishop Sutton Res. 1
Weston-super-Mare Res. 2 **Brislington Res.** 3

QUARTER-FINALS
Nailsea United 2 Clevedon United 1
Oldland Abbotonians 1 Brislington Res. 0
Portishead 1 Hengrove Athletic 0
Westland United 0 **Bridgwater Town Res.** 5
SEMI-FINALS
Bridgwater Town Res. 0 **Portishead** 3
Nailsea United 3 Oldland Abbotonians 1
FINAL
(13th May at Clevedon Town)
Nailsea United 1 Portishead 1 *aet* (6-5p)

Division One		P	W	D	L	F	A	Pts
Cleve West Town		34	26	3	5	69	21	81
Team Bath Res.		34	25	4	5	100	35	79
Paulton Rovers Res.		34	22	5	7	94	45	71
Hengrove Athletic		34	20	10	4	55	24	70
Weston-super-Mare Res.		34	14	7	13	61	65	49
Watchet Town		34	13	9	12	53	53	48
Bishop Sutton Res.		34	13	8	13	55	51	47
Winscombe		34	11	11	12	53	54	44
Cheddar		34	13	4	17	68	76	43
Blackbrook		34	12	5	17	55	85	41
Shirehampton		34	10	9	15	50	70	39
Oldland Abbotonians	-9	34	14	5	15	51	56	38
Crewkerne		34	11	5	18	54	67	38
Timsbury Athletic		34	10	7	17	45	54	37
Robinsons		34	9	7	18	64	62	34
Congresbury		34	9	7	18	43	75	34
Glastonbury		34	8	9	17	41	58	33
Sporting Club Somerton		34	4	9	21	45	85	21

DIVISION ONE CONSTITUTION 2003-04

BISHOP SUTTON RESERVES . . . . Lake View, Bishop Sutton, Bristol, North Somerset 01275 333097
BLACKBROOK . . . . Taunton Town FC, Wordsworth Drive, Taunton, Somerset . . . . 01823 278191. Fax: 01823 322975
CHEDDAR . . . . Bowdens Park, Draycott Road, Cheddar, Somerset 01934 743736
CONGRESBURY . . . . Broadstones Playing Fields, Stonewell Lane, Congresbury, North Somerset 01934 832150
CREWKERNE . . . . Henhayes, South Street, Crewkerne, Somerset 01460 76422
HENGROVE ATHLETIC . . . . Norton Lane, Whitchurch, Bristol, North Somerset 01275 832894
ILMINSTER TOWN . . . . Recreation Ground, Ilminster, Somerset 01460 54756
NAILSEA TOWN . . . . Fryth Way, Pound Lane, Nailsea, North Somerset . . . . None
ODD DOWN RESERVES . . . . Lew Hill Memorial Ground, Combe Hay Lane, Odd Down, Bath, North Somerset 01225 832491
OLDLAND ABBOTONIANS . . . . Aitchinson Playing Field, Castle Road, Oldland Common, Bristol 0117 932 8263
PEASEDOWN ATHLETIC . . . . Miners Welfare Park, Peasedown St John, Bath, Somerset 01761 437319
ROBINSONS . . . . Hursley Lane, Woolard Lane, Whitchurch, Bristol, North Somerset 01275 891300
SHIREHAMPTON . . . . Recreation Ground, Penpole Lane, Shirehampton, Bristol, South Glos 0117 923 5461
TIMSBURY ATHLETIC . . . . Recreation Ground, North Road, Timsbury, Somerset 01761 472523
TUNLEY ATHLETIC . . . . The Recreation Centre, Bath Road, Tunley, Somerset . . . . None
WATCHET TOWN . . . . Memorial Ground, Doniford Road, Watchet, Somerset 01984 631041
WESTON-SUPER-MARE RESERVES . . Woodspring Park, Winterstoke Road, Weston-super-Mare . . . . 01934 621618 / 635665
WINSCOMBE . . . . Recreation Ground, The Lynch, Winscombe, North Somerset . . . . 01934 842720 (Cricket Club)
Cleve West Town, Team Bath Reserves and Paulton Rovers Reserves are promoted to the Premier Division replaced by Peasedown Athletic and Nailsea Town. Glastonbury and Sporting Club Somerton drop to Division Two from which Odd Down Reserves, Ilminster Town and Tunley Athletic are promoted.

	Backwell United 'A'	Banwell	Churchill Club	Clandown	Clevedon United Res.	Cutters Friday	Dundry Athletic	Frome Town Res.	Ilminster Town	Imperial	Langford Rovers	Larkhall Athletic Res.	Nailsea United Res.	Odd Down Res.	Portishead Res.	Saltford	St George Easton-in-Gord.	Tunley Athletic
Backwell United 'A'		3-3	0-8	2-3	0-9	1-4	1-4	2-5	1-2	0-5	1-1	3-5	1-4	0-8	2-7	0-4	1-9	2-6
Banwell	9-3		3-1	4-0	2-3	3-0	3-3	3-2	3-4	4-0	4-1	1-4	3-2	0-5	0-2	2-2	2-2	3-3
Churchill Club	8-1	0-3		3-0	2-1	2-4	5-1	3-5	3-1	1-3	4-3	2-2	1-0	1-4	2-4	3-2	1-1	1-5
Clandown	2-3	0-1	1-2	D	5-2	0-3	4-3	2-2	1-4	0-2	1-1	1-0	2-3	0-4	0-3	0-5	1-1	0-1
Clevedon United Res.	3-3	1-1	2-3	1-1	I	3-2	0-1	4-1	1-3	1-1	3-0	1-1	0-1	2-3	1-5	4-1	2-1	1-1
Cutters Friday	2-1	2-0	2-3	4-1	0-2	V	1-1	0-2	4-2	2-2	0-5	3-1	2-2	0-0	1-1	2-4	0-2	0-3
Dundry Athletic	3-3	6-0	5-1	2-0	0-6	2-0	I	1-0	3-2	5-2	5-2	3-2	1-1	0-3	4-3	2-0	0-5	2-1
Frome Town Res.	9-2	5-2	0-1	2-1	2-1	1-0	1-2	S	1-2	3-1	2-2	2-2	2-1	2-1	2-2	4-1	3-3	3-0
Ilminster Town	11-1	6-1	4-1	2-0	2-0	1-0	2-0	1-0	I	3-0	4-1	6-0	1-3	0-1	2-2	4-0	3-0	2-2
Imperial	2-0	2-3	2-2	0-4	2-0	2-0	1-5	2-2	0-3	O	3-3	2-0	0-0	2-1	2-3	2-0	3-2	2-4
Langford Rovers	3-1	2-2	1-0	1-1	1-0	1-4	2-5	1-2	1-4	1-3	N	1-3	2-1	0-5	2-1	1-7	3-4	2-8
Larkhall Athletic Res.	9-0	4-1	2-1	2-2	1-1	1-0	5-2	2-3	2-2	3-0	3-1		1-1	0-6	2-3	2-2	2-2	1-6
Nailsea United Res.	5-1	1-2	3-0	1-0	3-1	1-1	5-3	1-1	1-1	0-1	2-1	8-0	T	2-3	1-2	0-2	2-5	1-1
Odd Down Res.	9-1	1-0	0-0	2-0	0-0	4-2	4-1	5-0	2-0	2-0	4-0	1-0	2-0	W	3-0	0-1	2-3	2-0
Portishead Res.	4-0	3-2	1-3	4-1	2-3	3-1	1-2	1-1	2-3	4-0	4-1	2-3	4-1	0-1	O	5-3	2-0	2-2
Saltford	3-2	4-1	2-0	1-0	3-3	3-1	3-1	2-0	1-2	3-3	2-0	1-0	2-1	0-0	3-3		2-2	1-3
St George Easton-in-Gordano	1-1	1-2	2-0	3-3	0-3	1-1	2-2	2-0	3-3	2-3	4-2	2-3	1-1	2-3	2-2	2-1		1-0
Tunley Athletic	3-0	6-2	1-2	5-1	3-1	5-0	1-1	1-2	2-2	4-0	5-2	1-2	4-1	1-1	0-0	3-2	2-1	

Division Two		P	W	D	L	F	A	Pts
Odd Down Res.	-1	34	24	5	5	92	22	76
Ilminster Town		34	22	5	7	92	43	71
Tunley Athletic		34	20	8	6	94	43	68
Dundry Athletic		34	18	6	10	81	72	60
Portishead Res.		34	16	10	8	87	58	58
Saltford		34	16	7	11	75	59	55
St George Easton-in-Gordano		34	13	14	7	74	56	53
Frome Town Res.	-6	34	16	8	10	72	57	50
Larkhall Athletic Res.		34	13	9	12	70	73	48
Churchill Club		34	14	4	16	69	72	46
Clevedon United Res.		34	11	10	13	68	56	43
Nailsea United Res.		34	11	10	13	62	53	43
Banwell		34	12	7	15	73	84	43
Imperial		34	11	8	15	51	72	41
Cutters Friday		34	9	7	18	48	66	34
Langford Rovers		34	6	6	22	51	102	24
Clandown		34	5	7	22	38	79	22
Backwell United 'A'	-2	34	1	5	28	43	173	6

DIV TWO/THREE CUP

FIRST ROUND
Churchill Club 3 Fry
Club Res. 2
Langford Rovers 4 Bristol Spartak 1
Shepton Mallet Town Res. 4 Banwell 3
Yatton Athletic 3 Dundry Athletic 0
SECOND ROUND
Cheddar Res. 3 St George Easton-in-Gordano 1
Churchill Club 0 **Clevedon United Res.** 4
Clandown 2 **Nailsea United Res.** 3
Clutton 3 **Portishead Res.** 4
Frome Collegians 2 Hengrove Athletic Res. 1
Frome Town Res. 2 **Langford Rovers** 3
Ilminster Town 3 Cutters Friday 2
Larkhall Athletic Res. 1 **Wrington-Redhill** 3
Long Ashton 4 Robinsons Res. 2 *aet*
Odd Down Res. 2 Imperial 0
Saltford 1 **Street Res.** 2
Timsbury Athletic Res. 1 **Weston St Johns Res.** 4
Tunley Athletic 9 Backwell United 'A' 0

DIVISION TWO CONSTITUTION 2003-04

BANWELL . . . . Riverside Ground, Riverside, Banwell, North Somerset 01934 820773
CHURCHILL CLUB . . . . Ladymead Lane, Churchill, North Somerset 01934 852739
CLEVEDON UNITED RESERVES . . . . Coleridge Vale, Clevedon, North Somerset 01275 871878
COMBE ST NICHOLAS . . . . Slades Cross, Combe St Nicholas, Somerset 01460 234743
CUTTERS FRIDAY . . . . The Cutters Club, Stockwood Lane, Stockwood, Bristol, North Somerset 01275 839830
DUNDRY ATHLETIC . . . . Dundry Playing Field, Crabtree Lane, Dundry, Bristol, North Somerset 0117 964 5536
FROME TOWN RESERVES . . . . Badgers Hill, Berkley Road, Frome, North Somerset . . . . 01373 453643 / 464087
GLASTONBURY . . . . Abbeymoor Stadium, Godney Road, Glastonbury, Somerset 01458 831460
IMPERIAL . . . . Bristol Imperial Sports Club, West Town Lane, Whitchurch, Brislington, North Somerset 01275 546000
LANGFORD ROVERS . . . . Westland United FC, Winterstoke Road, Weston-super-Mare, North Somerset 01934 632037
LARKHALL ATHLETIC RESERVES . Plain Ham, Charcombe Lane, Larkhall, Bath, North Somerset 01225 334952
NAILSEA UNITED RESERVES . . . . Grove Sports Ground, Old Church, Nailsea, North Somerset 01275 856892
PORTISHEAD RESERVES . . . . Bristol Road Playing Fields, Portishead, Bristol, North Somerset 01275 847136
SALTFORD . . . . Playing Fields, Norman Road, Saltford, North Somerset 01225 873725
SHEPTON MALLET RESERVES . . Old Wells Road Playing Fields, West Shepton, Shepton Mallet, Somerset 01749 344609
SPORTING CLUB SOMERTON . . . . Somerton Sports & Social Club, Gasson Lane, Somerton, Somerset 01458 273808
ST GEORGE EASTON-IN-GORDANO . . Court Hay, Easton-in-Gordano, Bristol, North Somerset 01275 374235
WORLE . . . . Worle Recreation Ground, Station Road, Worle, Weston-super-Mare, North Somerset . . . . None

Odd Down Reserves, Ilminster Town and Tunley Athletic move up to Division One replacing Glastonbury and Sporting Club Somerton. Backwell United 'A' have resigned. Clandown are relegated to Division Three replaced by Worle, Combe St Nicholas and Shepton Mallet Town Reserves.

	Bristol Spartak	Burnham United Res.	Cheddar Res.	Clutton	Combe St Nicholas	Frome Collegians	Fry Club Res.	Hengrove Athletic Res.	Long Ashton	Robinsons Res.	Shepton Mallet Town Res.	Street Res.	Timsbury Athletic Res.	Wells City Res.	Weston St Johns Res.	Worle	Wrington-Redhill	Yatton Athletic
Bristol Spartak		1-3	1-0	2-4	0-5	1-6	0-1	3-1	0-3	1-3	0-4	0-3	0-1	1-2	1-6	0-2	4-2	5-5
Burnham United Res.	1-1		3-2	3-2	2-1	4-1	0-0	6-2	2-1	0-2	1-7	1-5	4-2	0-2	2-2	3-3	1-6	4-0
Cheddar Res.	3-3	3-3	*D*	6-3	1-2	4-6	1-2	2-2	3-3	4-2	0-3	2-2	4-1	3-0	4-3	3-4	1-4	2-1
Clutton	4-0	1-4	1-4	*I*	3-5	1-3	1-2	0-6	1-4	2-3	1-5	0-4	2-4	1-3	1-7		1-3	2-3
Combe St Nicholas	1-0	5-0	4-3	8-0	*V*	2-2	1-1	4-0	5-0	4-2	0-0	3-1	3-2	3-0	0-2	2-2	4-0	6-2
Frome Collegians	3-1	7-3	5-1	4-2	2-1	*I*	3-3	4-1	0-1	1-1	1-2	2-1	2-0	1-4	0-0	1-3	4-2	1-5
Fry Club Res.	3-4	1-1	3-0	3-1	2-2	0-2	*S*	1-1	1-0	1-2	2-3	1-1	1-2	2-1	2-1	4-0	0-3	
Hengrove Athletic Res.	4-0	2-2	2-2	1-0	0-1	0-1	2-3	*I*	1-0	3-5	0-3	5-5	0-0	0-6	1-1	0-3	4-1	2-1
Long Ashton	3-5	0-7	2-2	4-1	0-4	1-2	2-2	4-1	*O*	1-4	1-5	2-0	0-4	6-2	1-1	1-2	2-2	3-3
Robinsons Res.	0-1	2-3	5-2	0-2	1-3	1-1	4-2	5-3	3-3	*N*	1-0	2-1	5-2	3-3	0-2	1-3	3-2	4-0
Shepton Mallet Town Res.	2-2	9-3	1-1	1-2	2-1	4-2	2-2	5-3	2-1	3-2		1-0	2-1	4-0	0-1	1-3	2-1	2-2
Street Res.	4-0	1-1	2-2	4-1	1-1	1-1	2-1	1-1	3-2	3-1	1-0	*T*	3-2	0-2	1-1	0-4	2-1	1-0
Timsbury Athletic Res.	3-5	1-0	1-1	1-1	1-2	1-1	2-1	2-0	1-3	0-4	2-1	1-0	*H*	0-2	2-3	0-2	6-1	2-2
Wells City Res.	5-1	2-1	2-2	6-0	0-1	3-4	2-2	5-4	2-0	3-0	0-1	1-2	7-1	*R*	3-1	1-0	3-2	0-0
Weston St Johns Res.	2-2	5-0	1-0	6-2	3-0	0-2	2-1	3-1	0-0	5-4	2-4	0-1	4-1	3-2	*E*	1-4	1-2	1-1
Worle	9-0	3-0	4-1	3-1	0-2	1-1	5-0	2-2	3-0	4-0	2-0	5-2	4-1	3-2	2-1	*E*	1-0	5-1
Wrington-Redhill	2-5	1-0	0-0	1-4	0-2	4-1	1-2	6-1	1-3	2-0	3-0	3-1	0-4	4-4	2-3		*E*	
Yatton Athletic	1-0	4-4	0-1	2-1	3-0	1-4	1-2	2-3	1-2	1-1	2-2	0-2	2-2	2-1	1-7	0-5	0-3	

Wells City Res. 6 Burnham United Res. 2

Worle 2 Shepton Mallet Town Res. 1 *aet*

Yatton Athletic 1 **Combe St Nicholas** 2 *aet*

THIRD ROUND

Clevedon United Res. 4 Street Res. 1

Combe St Nicholas 3 Wells City Res. 1

Frome Collegians 1 Long Ashton 0

Langford Rovers 1 Worle 0

Portishead Res. 1 **Ilminster** 2

Tunley Athletic 3 Nailsea United Res. 1

Weston St Johns Res. 1 **Odd Down Res.** 1 *aet* (2-4p)

Wrington-Redhill 2 **Cheddar Res.** 3

QUARTER-FINALS

Cheddar Res. 0 **Tunley Athletic** 0 *aet* (3-4p)

Frome Collegians 0 **Combe St Nicholas** 1

Langford Rovers 5 Clevedon United Res. 1

Odd Down Res. 3 **Ilminster Town** 3 *aet* (5-6p)

SEMI-FINALS

Combe St Nicholas 1 **Ilminster Town** 4

Tunley Athletic 0 **Langford Rovers** 3

FINAL

(24th April at Bridgwater Town)

Ilminster Town 3 Langford Rovers 3 *aet* (5-3p)

Division Three

		P	W	D	L	F	A	Pts
Worle		34	27	4	3	106	33	85
Combe St Nicholas		34	22	6	6	88	38	72
Shepton Mallet Town Res.		34	19	7	8	81	44	64
Frome Collegians		34	18	8	8	81	60	62
Wells City Res.		34	19	4	11	83	54	61
Weston St Johns Res.		34	16	9	9	78	52	57
Street Res.	-1	34	15	9	10	63	53	53
Robinsons Res.		34	15	5	14	79	71	50
Fry Club Res.		34	12	12	10	57	57	48
Burnham United Res.		34	12	9	13	72	87	45
Wrington-Redhill		34	13	4	17	67	74	43
Cheddar Res.		34	8	12	14	70	81	36
Long Ashton		34	9	9	16	59	75	36
Timsbury Athletic Res.		34	9	7	18	52	73	34
Yatton Athletic		34	7	10	17	52	83	31
Hengrove Athletic Res.		34	7	9	18	55	90	30
Bristol Spartak		34	8	5	21	50	101	29
Clutton		34	5	1	28	50	117	16

DIVISION THREE CONSTITUTION 2003-04

BISHOPS LYDEARD............................Darby Way, Bishops Lydeard, Somerset............................None
BRISTOL SPARTAK............................Hursley Lane, off Hursley Hill, Whitchurch, Bristol, North Somerset............................None
BURNHAM UNITED RESERVES..Burnham Road Playing Fields, Cassis Close, Burnham-on-Sea, Somerset................01278 794615
CHEDDAR RESERVES................Bowdens Park, Draycott Road, Cheddar, Somerset................01934 743736
CLANDOWN......................Greyfield Sports & Social Club, Bath Road, Paulton, Somerset................01761 412809
CLUTTON................Warwick Fields, Upper Bristol Road (A37), Clutton, near Bristol, North Somerset................None
FROME COLLEGIANS................Selwood School, Berkley Road, Frome, Somerset................None
FRY CLUB RESERVES................Fry Club, Somerdale, Keynsham, Bristol, North Somerset................0117 937 6500 / 937 6501
HENGROVE ATHLETIC RESERVES................Norton Lane, Whitchurch, Bristol, North Somerset................01275 832894
LONG ASHTON................Long Ashton Rec., Keedwell Hill, Long Ashton, North Somerset................None
ROBINSONS RESERVES................Hursley Lane, Woolard Lane, Whitchurch, Bristol, North Somerset................01275 891300
STREET RESERVES................The Tannery Ground, Middlebrooks, Street, Somerset................01458 444987
TIMSBURY ATHLETIC RESERVES................Recreation Ground, North Road, Timsbury, Somerset................01761 472523
WELLS CITY RESERVES................The Athletic Ground, Rowdens Road, Wells, Somerset................01749 679971
WESTON ST JOHNS RESERVES................Coleridge Road, Bournville Estate, Weston-super-Mare................01934 612862
WINCANTON TOWN................Wincanton Sports Ground, Moor Lane, Wincanton, Somerset................01963 31815
WRINGTON-REDHILL................Recreation Ground, Silver Street, Wrington, North Somerset................None
YATTON ATHLETIC................Hangstones Playing Fields, Stowey Road, Yatton, North Somerset................None

Worle, Combe St Nicholas and Shepton Mallet Town Reserves are promoted to Division Two replaced by Clandown. Bishops Lydeard are promoted from the Taunton League and Wincanton Town from the Yeovil & District League.

SOUTH WALES AMATEUR LEAGUE

	Barry Athletic	British Steel	Cambrian & Clydach VBC	Cardiff Corinthians Res.	Cardiff Draconians	Cwmaman Institute	Llanbradach	Llangeinor	Llantwit Fardre	Llantwit Major	Pencoed Athletic	Rhydyfelin Zenith	Taffs Well Res.	Ton & Gelli Boys Club	Ynysddu Welfare
Barry Athletic		2-1	1-3	2-1	0-1	0-2	0-3	1-1	1-2	1-2	6-0	7-1	1-1	3-1	1-2
British Steel	0-4	D	1-5	1-3	2-0	1-2	0-2	1-1	1-2	1-1	1-0	1-0	4-0	2-1	0-2
Cambrian & Clydach VBC	2-0	1-0	I	2-1	2-2	2-1	1-2	5-0	1-2	4-0	4-0	5-1	6-1	1-0	3-1
Cardiff Corinthians Res.	0-0	2-2	0-4	V	4-3	0-0	1-2	1-2	2-3	1-1	1-2	3-1	1-2	0-1	2-3
Cardiff Draconians	0-0	3-2	1-4	3-1	I	5-1	0-5	1-1	1-4	6-3	1-0	1-1	2-0	0-3	3-0
Cwmaman Institute	0-0	2-0	1-0	2-2	5-2	S	0-1	2-2	1-2	1-0	3-1	2-2	1-0	2-2	2-1
Llanbradach	1-1	2-2	0-3	4-3	4-0	3-3	I	6-1	0-2	6-3	6-1	1-1	1-1	2-0	7-1
Llangeinor	2-2	1-0	0-1	1-3	3-2	2-0	0-8	O	0-2	3-3	0-4	2-1	1-0	1-5	4-2
Llantwit Fardre	4-1	3-0	2-1	3-0	1-0	1-3	1-2	3-0	N	3-1	3-1	3-1	4-0	4-0	2-2
Llantwit Major	0-2	3-2	0-4	4-1	1-7	0-1	3-0	4-3	0-3		4-1	2-2	0-2	1-3	0-2
Pencoed Athletic	1-2	0-0	1-7	1-2	0-3	3-2	1-4	0-1	2-4	6-4		1-4	2-1	2-3	1-1
Rhydyfelin Zenith	2-1	0-5	1-3	1-4	1-4	0-4	1-3	2-2	1-1	2-4	1-5	O	1-3	0-3	2-5
Taffs Well Res.	1-2	1-4	0-2	1-0	1-1	2-2	2-4	2-0	1-1	3-1	2-0	1-1	N	0-1	4-4
Ton & Gelli Boys Club	0-2	2-1	1-1	2-2	3-3	4-2	3-3	2-0	0-1	1-2	3-1	0-3	1-0	E	3-2
Ynysddu Welfare	2-0	3-0	2-5	1-4	2-0	1-1	0-1	0-3	0-2	2-2	6-0	0-2	4-3	3-2	

Division One	P	W	D	L	F	A	Pts
Llantwit Fardre	28	23	3	2	68	23	72
Cambrian & Clydach	28	22	2	4	82	22	68
Llanbradach	28	19	5	4	83	37	62
Cwmaman Institute	28	12	9	7	48	39	45
Ton & Gelli Boys Club	28	13	5	10	50	44	44
Cardiff Draconians	28	11	6	11	55	54	39
Ynysddu Welfare	28	11	5	12	54	59	38
Barry Athletic	28	10	7	11	43	36	37
Llangeinor	28	9	7	12	37	63	34
Taffs Well Res.	28	8	6	14	37	52	30
Llantwit Major	28	8	5	15	49	73	29
Cardiff Corinthians Res.	28	7	6	15	45	54	27
British Steel	28	7	5	16	35	48	26
Pencoed Athletic	28	6	2	20	37	79	20
Rhydyfelin Zenith	28	4	7	17	36	76	19

CORONATION CUP

FIRST ROUND

Barry Athletic 3 Trelewis Welfare 1

Cardiff Cosmos Portos 3 Tondu Robins 2

Carnetown 1 Cardiff Corinthians 1 *aet* (3-1p)

Cwmaman Institute 4 Llanharry 0

Graig Metals 0 **Treforest** 3

Hirwaun Welfare 3 **Kenfig Hill** 3 *aet* (2-4p)

Llanbradach 0 **Cambrian & Clydach Vale BC** 1

Llangeinor 5 AFC Bargoed 3

Llantwit Fardre 3 Llantwit Major 3 *aet* (6-5p)

N & M Construction 3 Osborne Athletic 1

Pencoed Athletic 6 Tonyrefail Welfare 3

Red Dragon Baglan 2 **FC Abercwmboi** 2
aet (11-12p)

Rhydyfelin Zenith 2 **British Steel** 3

Taffs Well Res. 5 Cardiff Draconians 1

Trefelin BGC 3 Ynysddu Welfare 1

DIVISION ONE CONSTITUTION 2003-04

BARRY ATHLETIC . . . . Barry Athletic Ground, Paget Road, Barry Island, South Glamorgan 01446 733726
BRITISH STEEL . . . . Corus Playing Fields, Groes Margam, Port Talbot, West Glamorgan 01639 882066
CAERAU UNITED . . . . Caerau Football Ground, Humphries Terrace, Caerau, Bridgend, Mid-Glamorgan 01656 732471
CAMBRIAN & CLYDACH VALE BC . . . . Highfield, Clydach Vale, Mid-Glamorgan 01443 442649
CARDIFF CORINTHIANS . . . . . Riverside Ground, through Station Road, Radyr, Cardiff, South Glamorgan 02920 843407
CARDIFF DRACONIANS . . . . Llanidloes Road, Gabalfa, Cardiff, South Glamorgan . . . . None
CWMAMAN INSTITUTE . . . . Canolfan, Cwmaman, Rhondda, Mid-Glamorgan 01685 887100
LLANBRADACH . . . . Llanbradach Park, Llanbradach, Caerphilly, South Glamorgan . . . . None
LLANGEINOR . . . . Llangeinor Park, Llangeinor, Bridgend, Mid-Glamorgan 01656 871676
LLANTWIT MAJOR . . . . Windmill Lane, Llantwit Major, South Glamorgan . . . . None
PENCOED ATHLETIC . . . . Recreation Ground, Felindre Road, Pencoed, Bridgend, Mid-Glamorgan . . . . None
RED DRAGON BAGLAN . . . . Evans Bevans, Port Talbot, West Glamorgan 01639 820482
TAFFS WELL . . . . Rhiwddar, Parish Road, Taffs Well, Mid-Glamorgan 02920 811080
TON & GELLI BOYS CLUB . . . . Ton Pentre FC, Ynys Park, Sawmill Villas, Ton Pentre, Rhondda 01443 432813
TONDU ROBINS . . . . Pandy Park, Ynyawdre, Bridgend, Mid-Glamorgan . . . . None
YNYSDDU WELFARE . . . . Ynysddu Welfare Park, Ynysddu, South Glamorgan . . . . None
Llantwit Fardre are promoted to the Welsh League replaced by Caerau United. Pencoed Athletic and Rhydyfelin Zenith drop to Division Two replaced by Red Dragon Baglan and Tondu Robins.

	AFC Bargoed	Cardiff Cosmos Portos	Carnetown	FC Abercwmboi	Graig Metals	Hirwaun Welfare	Kenfig Hill	Llanharry	N & M Construction	Osborne Athletic	Red Dragon Baglan	Tondu Robins	Tonyrefail Welfare	Trefelin BGC	Treforest	Trelewis Welfare
AFC Bargoed		0-1	4-1	4-2	2-1	4-2	5-5	3-0	3-2	2-4	3-4	1-2	4-2	8-3	3-3	1-1
Cardiff Cosmos Portos	0-2		3-2	3-2	3-1	0-0	2-8	7-1	4-2	2-5	2-2	4-2	5-3	2-0	4-1	6-4
Carnetown	3-2	0-0	D	1-0	0-0	1-4	3-1	6-3	0-2	2-0	1-0	2-3	4-3	4-0	2-2	2-1
FC Abercwmboi	1-1	3-3	3-1	I	9-3	2-1	1-2	6-2	3-2	1-0	0-0	1-1	1-2	1-2	4-3	2-1
Graig Metals	1-0	2-1	1-2	5-0	V	2-3	2-5	4-1	2-2	4-3	1-8	2-0	3-2	0-1	1-5	1-5
Hirwaun Welfare	4-1	4-4	2-1	2-0	1-2	I	2-2	0-4	2-3	4-2	1-1	1-1	5-2	2-1	4-2	5-0
Kenfig Hill	6-3	1-2	3-1	2-0	2-2	1-1	S	3-4	2-1	2-5	2-3	3-1	3-6	3-0	2-1	5-4
Llanharry	1-1	3-2	2-3	5-3	0-2	3-4	0-2	I	2-0	1-2	1-6	2-5	1-1	2-1	0-4	4-0
N & M Construction	7-4	2-2	1-2	3-2	2-2	5-0	0-1	2-2	O	5-1	1-3	1-4	4-1	2-2	4-1	2-1
Osborne Athletic	4-1	2-0	2-3	3-1	2-1	1-2	4-4	1-2	0-1	N	1-5	1-1	7-3	0-3	1-0	2-2
Red Dragon Baglan	5-2	4-2	8-2	3-1	5-1	3-1	0-0	4-1	1-1	3-1		1-4	3-1	6-6	2-0	13-1
Tondu Robins	2-1	2-3	2-4	4-0	2-3	8-0	1-0	0-0	3-1	8-3	2-3	T	3-0	2-0	5-1	4-0
Tonyrefail Welfare	0-4	3-2	0-7	1-2	0-2	2-2	3-5	3-0	1-3	2-4	2-4	3-3	W	3-3	2-3	1-2
Trefelin BGC	4-1	1-2	3-1	2-0	1-3	1-2	1-1	2-3	2-1	4-1	1-1	4-0	1-1	O	2-2	1-2
Treforest	3-4	4-4	4-2	5-3	2-1	1-5	2-3	1-3	1-0	3-1	0-2	1-6	5-0	0-2		6-1
Trelewis Welfare	1-5	6-1	5-1	1-2	2-2	4-5	0-4	2-1	1-1	0-2	0-5	2-4	2-4	2-2	3-1	

SECOND ROUND

British Steel 1 Pencoed Athletic 2
(ineligible player – Pencoed Athletic expelled)
Carnetown 4 Kenfig Hill 3
Cwmman Inst. 1 Cambrian & CVBC 2
FC Ambercwmboi 3 Ton & Gelli Boys 2
Llangeinor 3 N & M Construction 4
Llantwit Fardre 3 Taffs Well Res. 0
Trefelin BGC 1 Cardiff Cosmos Portos 3
(ineligible player – Cardiff Cosmos Portos expelled)
Treforest 0 Barry Athletic 2

QUARTER-FINALS

Barry Athletic 3 FC Ambercwmboi 1
Cambrian & Clydach Vale BC 4 Trefelin BGC 0
Carnetown 0 British Steel 6
N & M Construction 1 Llantwit Fardre 3

SEMI-FINALS

British Steel 1 Cambrian & Clydach Vale BC 3
Llantwit Fardre 2 Barry Athletic 2 *aet* (4-2p)

FINAL

(9th May at Ton Pentre)
Cambrian & Clydach Vale BC 4 Llantwit Fardre 1

Division Two	P	W	D	L	F	A	Pts
Red Dragon Baglan	30	21	7	2	108	42	70
Tondu Robins	30	17	5	8	85	48	56
Kenfig Hill	30	16	7	7	83	60	55
Hirwaun Welfare	30	15	7	8	71	64	52
Cardiff Cosmos Portos	30	14	7	9	76	72	49
Carnetown	30	15	3	12	64	64	48
Graig Metals	30	12	6	12	58	71	42
AFC Bargoed	30	12	5	13	79	75	41
Osborne Athletic	30	12	3	15	65	72	39
Trefelin BGC	30	10	8	12	56	58	38
N & M Construction -3	30	11	7	12	63	55	37
FC Abercwmboi	30	10	4	16	56	68	34
Llanharry	30	10	4	16	54	80	34
Treforest	30	9	5	16	67	77	32
Trelewis Welfare	30	7	5	18	56	95	26
Tonyrefail Welfare	30	5	5	20	57	97	20

DIVISION TWO CONSTITUTION 2003-04

AFC BARGOED............................Bargoed Park, Bargoed, Mid-Glamorgan............................None
CARDIFF COSMOS PORTOS.......University Field, Mendip Road, Llanrumney, South Glamorgan......................02920 777377
CARNETOWN..............................Grovers Lane, Carnetown, Mid-Glamorgan............................None
FC ABERCWMBOI.................Recreation Ground, Abercwmboi, Rhondda, Mid-Glamorgan............................None
GRAIG METALS..............Pontypridd Town FC, Ynysangharad Park, Pontypridd, Mid-Glamorgan............01443 486571
HIRWAUN WELFARE.................Manchester Place, Hirwaun, Rhondda, Mid-Glamorgan.................01685 811900
KENFIG HILL..............Central Athletic Ground, Croft Goch, Kenfig Hill, Bridgend, Mid-Glamorgan.........................None
LLANHARRY................................Recreation Ground, Llanharry, Mid-Glamorgan...........................None
N & M CONSTRUCTION..................Recreation Ground, Rhoose, South Glamorgan..........................None
OSBORNE ATHLETIC....................Pentwyn Fields, Penrhiwceiber, Mid-Glamorgan............................01443 473737
RHYDYFELIN ZENITH...........Upper Boat Playing Field, Hawthorn, Rhondda, Mid-Glamorgan...........................None
TONYREFAIL WELFARE.................The Welfare Park, Tonyrefail, Mid-Glamorgan............................None
TREFELIN BGC.....................Ynys Park, Cwmavon Road, Port Talbot, West Glamorgan.................01639 882609
TREFOREST........................White Tips Stadium, Treforest, Mid-Glamorgan..................01443 485532
TRELEWIS WELFARE.................Welfare Ground, Brondeg, Trelewis, Mid-Glamorgan..................................None
Pencoed Athletic and Rhydyfelin Zenith come down from Division One to replace promoted Red Dragon Baglan and Tondu Robins.

SOUTH WALES SENIOR LEAGUE

	AFC Whitchurch	Brecon Corinthians	Bridgend Street	Butetown	Cogan Coronation	Cwmbach Royal Stars	Fairwater	Fochriw Rising Sun	Grange Albion	Hopkinstown	Pant Yr Awel	Penydarren Boys Club	Sully Sports	Ynyshir Albions
AFC Whitchurch		1-2	3-1	3-0	2-1	4-2	1-4	6-2	1-1	1-4	4-3	1-2	2-6	2-4
Brecon Corinthians	4-3	*D*	1-0	6-0	1-0	1-1	2-3	3-0	4-0	6-1	0-1	0-2	5-3	1-2
Bridgend Street	2-4	1-3	*I*	6-0	1-3	1-2	1-3	2-0	1-2	3-0	3-1	3-2	2-2	1-3
Butetown	1-4	1-2	2-0	*V*	2-1	2-2	0-0	1-1	0-1	2-3	2-0	3-0	0-1	0-4
Cogan Coronation	1-1	2-2	3-3	2-3	*I*	5-2	2-5	1-2	0-0	3-1	3-0	1-1	1-1	0-3
Cwmbach Royal Stars	3-4	0-0	2-1	7-3	2-1	*S*	1-3	0-1	3-4	2-4	1-3	2-3	0-3	1-0
Fairwater	3-3	2-1	4-0	6-1	2-1	5-2	*I*	4-1	2-2	5-0	1-3	5-1	2-2	1-1
Fochriw Rising Sun	4-5	1-2	0-3	2-4	1-1	3-3	3-2	*O*	1-1	2-2	5-3	3-3	5-6	0-6
Grange Albion	2-1	0-2	1-2	1-1	3-0	0-1	2-2	2-1	*N*	0-0	1-2	2-0	2-3	0-6
Hopkinstown	1-3	2-4	3-4	1-1	2-2	2-5	3-4	2-7	2-4		1-5	3-5	0-4	0-1
Pant Yr Awel	8-3	1-0	3-1	9-4	1-1	2-1	0-5	3-1	2-1	7-0	*O*	6-1	6-3	0-0
Penydarren Boys Club	1-6	2-2	1-0	1-4	4-1	3-3	2-4	1-4	3-1	7-1	2-2	*N*	1-1	3-2
Sully Sports	3-3	0-0	6-3	6-1	3-2	2-2	0-3	5-7	5-2	3-1	2-4	7-1	*E*	4-0
Ynyshir Albions	6-1	1-0	5-1	3-0	3-1	3-1	4-6	7-1	2-1	11-0	1-0	2-0	3-2	

Division One		P	W	D	L	F	A	Pts
Ynyshir Albions		26	20	2	4	83	27	62
Fairwater		26	18	6	2	86	39	60
Pant Yr Awel		26	16	3	7	75	47	51
Brecon Corinthians		26	14	5	7	54	30	47
Sully Sports		26	13	7	6	83	58	46
AFC Whitchurch		26	12	4	10	72	71	40
Penydarren Boys Club		26	9	6	11	52	69	33
Grange Albion		26	8	7	11	36	47	31
Cwmbach Royal Stars		26	7	6	13	51	63	27
Fochriw Rising Sun		26	7	6	13	58	78	27
Bridgend Street		26	8	2	16	46	59	26
Cogan Coronation	+3	26	4	9	13	39	51	24
Butetown *-3pts, -2gls F*		26	7	5	14	36	72	23
Hopkinstown		26	3	4	19	39	101	13

INTER-LEAGUE PLAY-OFF

(Between champions of South Wales Amateur and Senior Leagues to determine candidate for promotion to Welsh League)

(23rd May at Maesteg Park Athletic)

Llantwit Fardre 1 Ynyshir Albions 0

FIRST ROUND

AFC Llwynypia 1 **Lisvane/Llanishen** 2
AFC Whitchurch 0 **Stanleytown** 2
Butetown 1 Cwmafan Phoenix 0
Cogan Coronation 1 Tonyrefail BGC 0
Cwm Welfare 5 Llanrumney 2
Cwmbach Royal Stars 3 Cascade 1
Fairwater 7 Ystrad Mynach Sports 1
Margam Youth Centre 1 Brecon Corinthians 0
Pant Yr Awel 5 Nelson Cavaliers 1
Penrhiwfer 2 **Grange Albion** 4 *aet*
St Josephs 0 **Penydarren Boys Club** 2
Sully Sports 5 Fochriw Rising Sun 0
Tongwynlais 2 **Bridgend Street** 5
Trelai Wenvoe 0 **Hopkinstown** 2

C W BRUTY CUP

WWW.CHERRYRED.CO.UK

DIVISION ONE CONSTITUTION 2003-04

AFC WHITCHURCH . . . . Whitchurch Hospital, Park Road, Whirchurch, Cardiff, South Glamorgan . . . . None
BRECON CORINTHIANS . . . . The Rich Field, The Watton, Brecon, Powys 01874 624033
BRIDGEND STREET . . . . Willows High School, Willows Avenue, Splott, Cardiff, South Glamorgan . . . . None
CWMBACH ROYAL STARS . . . . Blaennant-Y-Groes Rec Ground, Cwmbach, Aberdare, Mid-Glamorgan . . . . None
FAIRWATER . . . . Poplar Park, Poplar Road, Fairwater, Cardiff, South Glamorgan . . . . None
FOCHRIW RISING SUN . . . . Fochriw Recreation Ground, Fochriw, Bargoed, Merthyr Tydfil, Mid-Glamorgan . . . . None
GRANGE ALBIONS . . . . Coronation Park, Sloper Road, Cardiff, South Glamorgan . . . . None
PANT YR AWEL . . . . Lewistown, Bridgend, Mid-Glamorgan . . . . None
PENRHIWFER . . . . Penrhiwfer Park, Ashdale Road, Penrhiwfer, Mid-Glamorgan . . . . None
PENYDARREN BOYS CLUB . . . . The Bont, Rockery Road, Penydarren, Merthyr Tydfil, Mid-Glamorgan . . . . None
ST JOSEPHS . . . . Maes-Y-Coed Road, Cardiff, South Glamorgan . . . . None
SULLY SPORTS . . . . Sully Sports & Social Club, South Road, Sully, South Glamorgan . . . . None
TRELAI WENVOE . . . . Station Road, Wenvoe, Cardiff, South Glamorgan . . . . None
YNYSHIR ALBIONS . . . . Ynyshir Oval, Ynyshir, Rhondda, Mid-Glamorgan . . . . None

Cogan Coronation, Butetown and Hopkinstown drop to Division Two replaced by Penrhiwfer, St Josephs and Trelai Wenvoe.

	AFC Llwynpia	Cadoxton Cons	Cascade	Cwm Welfare	Cwmafan Phoenix	Lisvane/Llanishen	Llanrumney United	Margam Youth Centre	Nelson Cavaliers	Penrhiwfer	St Josephs	Stanleytown	Tongwynlais	Tonyrefail HGC	Trelai Wenvoe	Ystrad Mynach Sports
AFC Llwynpia		0-2	0-0	3-3	3-4	1-2	1-5	2-4	0-3	1-4	1-1	2-1	2-6	1-8	3-6	1-1
Cadoxton Cons	4-1		3-0	2-0	3-1	1-2	2-1	0-1	4-5	3-5	6-4	0-2	3-5	3-2	2-2	4-5
Cascade	6-0	2-3	*D*	4-1	4-2	1-0	2-1	1-0	1-3	4-1	3-4	1-0	0-3	6-1		
Cwm Welfare	6-3	4-5	3-5	*I*	0-2	0-1	1-1	1-1	4-5	0-0	1-1	2-1	3-1	2-1	3-0	6-2
Cwmafan Phoenix	1-1	5-4	1-2	2-1	*V*	2-3	1-2	3-2	4-0	0-4	0-1	7-4	5-0	2-3	2-4	2-4
Lisvane/Llanishen	7-1	5-0	0-3	2-0	4-5	*I*	3-3	1-1	2-0	3-0	1-3	3-2	4-2	0-0	6-2	0-0
Llanrumney United	2-0	2-2	1-3	2-0	1-3	1-1	*S*	3-3	3-2	2-3	1-1	2-2	1-2	3-1	0-1	3-2
Margam Youth Centre	2-1	4-2	4-5	0-0	2-0	0-3	2-1	*I*	2-1	4-3	3-2	1-2	2-1	1-1	2-1	5-4
Nelson Cavaliers	6-0	2-4	1-0	5-6	4-2	2-1	0-0	2-3	*O*	1-4	1-0	0-2	1-1	1-1	1-1	4-3
Penrhiwfer	3-3	5-0	4-3	2-2	5-1	4-2	2-1	2-0	6-4	*N*	3-4	4-3	3-1	1-1	4-1	8-3
St Josephs	4-2	1-1	3-1	1-1	5-3	1-2	4-2	4-0	2-1	3-0		2-0	1-1	5-1	4-0	5-1
Stanleytown	2-0	2-3	1-1	3-4	4-0	3-2	4-3	2-1	3-1	2-2	1-2	*T*	6-1	4-3	1-3	1-4
Tongwynlais	3-1	2-0	1-1	1-2	5-3	3-1	1-2	5-1	4-3	2-3	1-1	4-2	*W*	3-1	0-3	2-2
Tonyrefail HGC	1-4	1-3	1-1	3-0	5-0	0-3	1-2	2-1	4-1	1-2	5-3	5-1	1-1	*O*	2-5	0-2
Trelai Wenvoe	4-2	4-4	6-0	4-2	0-1	6-2	1-0	3-0	7-0	1-1	1-2	4-0	4-1	1-0		4-2
Ystrad Mynach Sports	2-0	0-8	1-0	2-3	1-3	0-4	0-3	1-4	5-4	5-0	1-2	0-1	3-1	3-4	0-1	

SECOND ROUND

Cadoxton Cons 3 Butetown 3 *aet* (4-1p)

Cogan Coronation 3 Fairwater 1

Cwmbach Royal Stars 0 **Bridgend Street** 6

Margam Youth Centre 9 Cwm Welfare 0

Pant Yr Awel 2 Penydarren Boys Club 1

Stanleytown 0 **Grange Albion** 2 *aet*

Sully Sports 1 **Lisvane/Llanishen** 3

Ynyshir Albions 3 Hopkinstown 2

QUARTER-FINALS

Grange Albion 2 **Margam Youth Centre** 2 *aet* (2-4p)

Lisvane/Llanishen 1 Bridgend Street 1 *aet* (4-2p)

Pant Yr Awel 5 Cogan Coronation 1

Ynyshir Albions 6 Cadoxton Cons 2

SEMI-FINALS

Margam Youth Centre 2 **Lisvane/Llanishen** 3

Ynyshir Albions 1 Pant Yr Awel 0

FINAL

(14th May at Grange Albion)

Ynyshir Albions 2 **Lisvane/Llanishen** 3

Division Two	P	W	D	L	F	A	Pts
Penrhiwfer	30	20	5	5	92	57	65
Trelai Wenvoe	30	19	4	7	83	47	61
St Josephs	30	17	7	6	74	44	58
Lisvane/Llanishen	30	16	5	9	70	47	53
Margam Youth Centre	30	14	5	11	58	65	47
Cascade	30	14	4	12	70	56	46
Cadoxton Cons	30	14	4	12	81	75	46
Tongwynlais	30	12	6	12	65	68	42
Llanrumney United	30	11	8	11	56	51	41
Stanleytown	30	13	2	15	64	72	41
Cwm Welfare	30	10	8	12	61	65	38
Cwmafan Phoenix	30	12	1	17	67	81	37
Tonyrefail HGC	30	8	7	15	58	60	31
Nelson Cavaliers	30	9	4	17	62	82	31
Ystrad Mynach Spts *-3*	30	9	4	17	60	88	28
AFC Llwynpia	30	2	6	22	40	103	12

DIVISION TWO CONSTITUTION 2003-04

AFC LLWYNPIA . . . . Ynyscynon Park, Llwynypia, Rhondda, Mid-Glamorgan . . . . None
BUTETOWN . . . . Bute Park, Butetown, Cardiff, South Glamorgan. . . . . None
CADOXTON CONS. . . . . Parc Bryn-Y-Don, Dinas Powys, South Glamorgan . . . . Blue & white
CASCADE . . . . Trosnant Crescent, Penybryn, Mid-Glamorgan . . . . None
COGAN CORONATION . . . . Cogan Recreation Field, Leisure Centre, Penarth, South Glamorgan . . . . None
CWM WELFARE . . . . Mount Pleasant Park, Beddau, Pontypridd, Mid-Glamorgan . . . . None
CWMAFAN PHOENIX . . . . Parc-Y-Llyn, Cwmafan, Port Talbot, West Glamorgan . . . . None
HOPKINSTOWN . . . . Western Field, Hopkinstown, Pontypridd, West Glamorgan . . . . None
LISVANE/LLANISHEN . . . . The Village Field, Heol Y Delyn, Lisvane, Cardiff, South Glamorgan . . . . None
LLANRUMNEY UNITED . . . . Riverside Park, Llanrumney, Cardiff, South Glamorgan . . . . None
MARGAM YOUTH CENTRE . . . . Groeswen Playing Field, Margam, Port Talbot, West Glamorgan . . . . None
NELSON CAVALIERS . . . . Wern Field, Nelson, Treharris, Mid-Glamorgan. . . . . Red & black
STANLEYTOWN . . . . Tylorstown Rec, Tylorstown, Rhondda, Mid-Glamorgan . . . . None
TONGWYNLAIS. . . . . Ironbridge Road, Tongwynlais, Cardiff, South Glamorgan. . . . . None
TONYREFAIL BGC . . . . Tynybryn Park, Tonyrefail, Porth, Rhondda, Mid-Glamorgan . . . . None
YSTRAD MYNACH SPORTS . . . Tir Y Berth Welfare Ground, Ystrad Mynach, Hengoed, Mid-Glamorgan . . . . None
Cogan Coronation, Butetown and Hopkinstown come down from Division One to replace promoted by Penrhiwfer, St Josephs and Trelai Wenvoe.

SOUTH WESTERN LEAGUE

	Bodmin Town	Callington Town	Falmouth Town	Holsworthy	Launceston	Liskeard Athletic	Millbrook	Newquay	Penryn Athletic	Penzance	Plymouth Parkway	Porthleven	Saltash United	St Austell	St Blazey	Tavistock	Torpoint Athletic	Truro City	Wadebridge Town
Bodmin Town		4-3	0-4	2-2	0-1	1-5	2-3	1-0	1-1	1-4	3-6	0-3	1-5	2-3	0-4	1-2	1-2	1-2	0-4
Callington Town	4-0		1-1	2-1	2-3	2-5	2-1	2-4	2-0	1-4	1-1	1-4	4-6	1-1	0-9	4-2	3-0	2-2	0-2
Falmouth Town	2-1	2-1		1-2	1-3	0-5	3-1	2-1	3-1	1-1	1-2	1-2	2-4	3-0	0-0	2-3	2-2	5-1	0-1
Holsworthy	2-1	0-2	0-0		2-0	1-2	3-0	3-2	6-1	2-0	4-4	1-2	1-3	2-1	1-2	1-1	1-0	0-2	2-2
Launceston	3-0	3-1	6-0	1-3		0-4	5-1	1-1	5-2	0-4	0-2	1-6	2-3	2-1	0-4	3-3	4-2	2-2	
Liskeard Athletic	6-1	2-1	1-2	1-0	7-0		1-2	2-4	1-3	0-1	2-3	1-1	4-3	3-2	2-1	4-5	2-5	5-0	2-0
Millbrook	2-0	2-2	2-3	1-0	4-5	2-2		1-2	0-0	2-0	2-2	3-2	2-1	3-0	0-2	0-3	0-1	2-0	1-2
Newquay	2-3	0-5	1-0	0-2	4-1	1-2	5-3		3-1	4-1	0-2	0-3	4-1	2-1	1-3	0-2	5-0	3-2	1-3
Penryn Athletic	4-0	3-1	0-3	0-2	1-1	1-2	1-2	1-2		0-2	1-5	1-2	4-4	3-1	2-3	1-5	1-2	1-1	1-3
Penzance	1-1	1-2	1-2	0-1	1-2	0-2	4-0	2-2	0-0		0-2	3-4	2-1	4-0	0-2	2-1	3-0	0-2	0-2
Plymouth Parkway	5-0	3-2	2-1	1-2	2-2	3-1	5-3	3-1	1-2	3-1		2-1	0-3	4-1	1-3	0-3	2-1	4-1	4-1
Porthleven	10-1	3-1	3-0	2-1	0-3	3-0	3-0	3-3	1-3	1-0	2-1		2-1	3-0	0-0	1-2	1-1	1-0	3-2
Saltash United	4-0	3-2	3-2	2-2	1-4	1-2	3-1	4-1	3-0	0-2	0-1	3-2		7-2	0-3	3-1	3-3	2-1	0-2
St Austell	4-0	0-1	0-3	1-1	3-1	2-6	0-4	4-1	1-7	4-1	2-5	1-9	0-3		0-3	0-4	1-0	2-2	0-0
St Blazey	4-0	2-1	5-0	7-1	7-1	1-2	5-1	3-0	4-0	4-1	2-0	4-1	3-0	10-1		3-0	5-1	2-1	4-1
Tavistock	6-1	1-0	4-1	0-3	0-2	3-3	3-1	4-0	4-0	3-1	3-0	3-2	1-0	5-1	2-2		3-0	2-0	3-0
Torpoint Athletic	2-0	0-2	1-4	1-2	0-4	2-2	4-1	2-0	4-1	0-0	0-3	1-3	0-0	2-2	3-3	2-0		1-2	2-1
Truro City	4-0	2-2	0-1	0-2	0-3	3-5	1-2	2-2	1-0	2-1	1-2	0-3	3-1	1-1	1-3	0-4	0-1		1-1
Wadebridge Town	6-0	3-1	0-2	1-0	2-2	2-1	3-1	3-2	3-3	0-2	2-0	0-1	3-1	0-0	1-1	0-0	0-3	3-0	

	P	W	D	L	F	A	Pts
St Blazey	36	30	5	1	126	23	95
Tavistock	36	24	5	7	87	41	77
Porthleven	36	23	5	8	95	48	74
Plymouth Parkway	36	23	4	9	83	55	73
Liskeard Athletic	36	21	4	11	95	59	67
Wadebridge Town	36	17	9	10	61	46	60
Launceston	36	18	6	12	79	78	60
Holsworthy	36	17	7	12	59	48	58
Saltash United	36	17	3	16	79	68	54
Falmouth Town	36	16	5	15	60	61	53
Newquay	36	13	4	19	64	77	43
Penzance	36	12	5	19	53	55	41
Torpoint Athletic	36	11	8	17	48	69	41
Millbrook	36	12	4	20	56	80	40
Callington Town	36	11	6	19	64	80	39
Truro City	36	9	6	21	44	74	33
Penryn Athletic	36	7	7	22	51	84	28
St Austell	36	7	6	23	45	108	27
Bodmin Town	36	3	3	30	30	125	12

LEAGUE CUP

PRELIMINARY ROUND
Millbrook 1 **Porthleven** 3
Saltash United 0 **Wadebridge Town** 2
Truro City 1 **Penzance** 3

FIRST ROUND
Bodmin 1 Penzance 1 *aet*
Penzance 4 Bodmin Town 0 *replay*
Callington 3 Tavistock 0
Liskeard Athletic 2 Plymouth Parkway 1
Newquay 0 **St Austell** 1
Porthleven 7 Launceston 1
St Blazey 3 Penryn Athletic 0
Torpoint Athletic 2 Holsworthy 2 *aet*
Holsworthy 1 Torpoint Athletic 0 *replay*
Wadebridge Town 1 **Falmouth Town** 2

QUARTER-FINALS
Falmouth Town 1 **Liskeard Athletic** 3
Penzance 3 Holsworthy 1
Porthleven 4 Callington Town 1
St Austell 0 **St Blazey** 7

SEMI-FINALS
Liskeard Athletic 2 Penzance 0
(at Newquay)
St Blazey 2 Porthleven 0
(at Falmouth Town)

FINAL
(5th May at Penryn)
Liskeard Athletic 2
St Blazey 1 *aet*

CONSTITUTION 2003-04

BODMIN TOWN . . . . Priory Park, Bodmin, Cornwall 01208 78165
CALLINGTON TOWN . . . . The Marsh, Callington Community College, Launceston Road, Callington, Cornwall 01579 382647
FALMOUTH TOWN . . . . Bickland Park, Bickland Water Road, Falmouth, Cornwall 01326 375156
LAUNCESTON . . . . Pennygillam, Pennygillam Industrial Estate, Launceston, Cornwall 01566 773279
LISKEARD ATHLETIC . . . . Lux Park, Liskeard, Cornwall 01579 342665
MILLBROOK . . . . Mill Park, off Southdown Road, Millbrook, Torpoint, Cornwall 01752 822113
NEWQUAY . . . . Mount Wise, Clevedon Road, Newquay, Cornwall 01637 872935
PENRYN ATHLETIC . . . . Kernick, Kernick Road, Penryn, Cornwall 01326 375182
PENZANCE . . . . Penlee Park, Alexandra Place, Penzance, Cornwall 01736 361964
PLYMOUTH PARKWAY . . . . Manadon Arena, St Peters Road, Mandon, Plymouth, Devon. . . . . None
PORTHLEVEN . . . . Gala Parc, Methleigh Mill, Porthleven, Cornwall. . . . . 01326 574181. Club: 01326 574754
SALTASH UNITED . . . . Kimberley Stadium, Callington Road, Saltash, Cornwall 01752 845746
ST AUSTELL . . . . Poltair Park, Poltair Road, St Austell, Cornwall 01726 66099
ST BLAZEY . . . . Blaise Park, Station Road, St Blazey, Cornwall 01726 814110
TAVISTOCK . . . . Langsford Park, Crowndale Road, Tavistock, Devon 01822 614447
TORPOINT ATHLETIC . . . . The Mill, Mill Lane, Torpoint, Cornwall 01752 812889
TRURO CITY . . . . Treyew Road, Truro, Cornwall 01872 278853
WADEBRIDGE TOWN. . . . . Bodieve Park, Bodieve Road, Wadebridge, Cornwall 01208 812537
Holsworthy have switched to the Devon County League.

SOUTHERN LEAGUE

	Bath City	Cambridge City	Chelmsford City	Chippenham Town	Crawley Town	Dover Athletic	Folkestone Invicta	Grantham Town	Halesowen Town	Hastings United	Havant/Waterlooville	Hednesford Town	Hinckley United	Ilkeston Town	Moor Green	Newport County	Stafford Rangers	Tamworth	Tiverton Town	Welling United	Weymouth	Worcester City
Bath City		1-1	0-1	1-1	0-1	1-0	2-0	3-2	3-0	1-0	1-1	4-1	2-2	1-1	4-3	0-1	0-2	0-1	0-2	1-1	1-0	
Cambridge City	0-1		2-3	0-1	3-0	1-1	2-1	1-1	0-1	1-2	4-5	2-2	1-1	2-2	1-2	1-3	1-0	0-1	3-0	2-1	0-1	1-0
Chelmsford City	2-0	1-2		2-3	1-2	0-1	3-2	1-2	1-0	1-0	1-2	2-2	1-1	2-1	4-0	1-1	0-2	0-4	3-0	1-1	3-1	1-1
Chippenham Town	1-2	2-0	3-1	P	1-0	0-0	1-0	0-0	1-2	0-0	3-1	1-3	3-1	3-0	1-1	0-0	1-0	3-0	1-1	4-0	1-1	0-0
Crawley Town	1-2	4-2	0-0	1-1	R	0-3	2-2	2-0	4-0	1-1	2-1	2-2	0-2	2-1	2-2	2-0	2-4	1-0	1-1	1-0	5-0	0-0
Dover Athletic	2-0	2-1	1-0	0-1	2-1	E	2-1	2-1	0-3	1-0	0-0	1-0	2-0	1-1	1-2	0-0	0-2	0-3	0-0	2-1	0-2	2-1
Folkestone Invicta	2-4	0-3	3-2	1-2	1-3	1-2	M	0-2	2-2	1-0	3-3	2-1	1-3	3-0	1-2	1-2	2-3	1-1	2-2	3-1	1-2	2-0
Grantham Town	0-0	1-0	2-3	1-0	0-3	3-1	4-1	I	3-3	2-1	1-1	3-0	2-1	2-4	1-2	1-2	2-1	2-0	3-1	2-0	2-3	
Halesowen Town	1-1	1-1	0-2	3-2	0-2	0-0	5-0	1-0	E	2-1	1-0	0-1	2-1	2-1	0-1	1-2	1-1	0-0	0-0	0-0	0-1	0-0
Hastings United	1-1	1-1	1-2	1-0	0-1	1-1	3-2	1-2	3-2	R	1-1	2-0	1-0	3-0	3-1	1-3	0-2	2-3	0-3	1-4	1-1	1-4
Havant & W'looville	3-1	0-2	1-0	1-0	2-4	1-1	6-2	3-3	3-0	0-0		2-1	2-2	1-3	3-3	1-0	1-2	3-1	1-0	2-1	2-1	
Hednesford Town	2-2	3-2	2-2	1-3	0-0	2-2	3-1	1-0	3-2	1-0	3-0	D	0-0	6-2	0-0	1-0	2-2	0-1	2-3	4-1	0-1	2-0
Hinckley United	3-1	3-2	2-1	1-2	3-1	1-1	3-3	0-0	1-1	3-2	1-0		I	5-2	1-2	0-2	2-0	1-1	1-1	1-3	2-1	2-0
Ilkeston Town	1-1	0-2	2-2	2-6	2-1	0-1	2-1	1-2	3-1	1-5	3-1	1-1	V	2-0	1-0	2-5	0-1	1-3	1-6	3-1	3-2	
Moor Green	1-0	1-1	1-1	1-0	0-2	0-2	3-0	3-0	4-0	0-0	0-1	0-1	2-2	5-0	I	1-2	1-1	0-2	2-1	1-0	2-2	1-1
Newport County	1-1	1-1	2-5	3-1	3-3	0-1	1-2	3-2	1-1	1-1	0-0	3-2	3-0	1-1		S	1-0	0-1	0-2	3-0	2-1	
Stafford Rangers	5-0	0-1	1-1	0-0	2-1	3-1	6-0	4-0	4-2	1-1	1-3	1-2	2-2	4-0	1-0		I	1-2	2-1	1-1	0-0	2-1
Tamworth	6-1	3-1	3-1	0-1	1-1	1-2	2-0	3-1	3-1	2-0	0-3	1-0	2-0	1-1	2-2	0-0	2-1	O	1-1	2-0	3-0	1-2
Tiverton Town	2-1	0-2	3-3	1-1	0-0	4-0	0-2	4-2	0-1	3-1	0-2	3-1	1-0	3-1	2-1	0-1		N	3-1	3-0	0-0	
Welling United	1-3	1-0	0-2	1-1	2-2	0-0	2-1	2-0	0-3	1-1	2-2	1-2	2-0	1-0	1-1	1-1	1-1			4-2	0-1	
Weymouth	2-0	0-1	1-3	1-2	2-0	0-0	3-3	3-1	1-4	1-1	1-1	0-2	1-1	3-1	2-0	1-0	0-2	2-1	0-0			0-0
Worcester City	2-1	2-0	5-0	0-0	2-1	0-1	6-0	2-0	1-1	2-1	2-1	3-1	2-2	0-0	4-0	2-1	0-3	0-0	0-2	1-1	3-1	

Premier Division

	P	HOME					AWAY					TOTAL					Pts
		W	D	L	F	A	W	D	L	F	A	W	D	L	F	A	
Tamworth	42	12	6	3	42	19	14	4	3	31	13	26	10	6	73	32	88
Stafford Rangers	42	11	7	3	43	18	10	5	6	33	22	21	12	9	76	40	75
Dover Athletic	42	11	4	6	21	20	8	10	3	21	15	19	14	9	42	35	71
Tiverton Town	42	11	4	6	34	22	8	8	5	26	21	19	12	11	60	43	69
Chippenham Town	42	9	9	3	30	14	8	8	5	29	23	17	17	8	59	37	68
Worcester City	42	12	6	3	39	17	6	7	8	21	22	18	13	11	60	39	67
Crawley Town	42	9	8	4	35	24	8	5	8	29	27	17	13	12	64	51	64
Havant/Waterlooville	42	10	6	5	35	30	5	9	7	32	34	15	15	12	67	64	60
Chelmsford City	42	8	5	8	31	28	7	7	7	34	35	15	12	15	65	63	57
Newport County	42	8	7	6	30	26	7	4	10	23	26	15	11	16	53	52	56
Hednesford Town	42	10	7	4	38	24	4	6	11	21	36	14	13	15	59	60	55
Moor Green	42	8	7	6	29	19	5	7	9	20	39	13	14	15	49	58	53
Hinckley United	42	9	6	6	35	29	3	10	8	26	35	12	16	14	61	64	52
Bath City	42	8	7	6	27	22	5	6	10	23	39	13	13	16	50	61	52
Welling United	42	8	7	6	27	25	5	5	11	28	33	13	12	17	55	58	51
Grantham Town	42	10	5	6	39	28	4	4	13	20	37	14	9	19	59	65	51
Weymouth	42	7	10	4	26	22	5	5	11	18	40	12	15	15	44	62	51
Cambridge City	42	6	5	10	28	29	7	5	9	26	27	13	10	19	54	56	49
Halesowen Town	42	7	8	6	20	17	5	5	11	32	46	12	13	17	52	63	49
Hastings United	42	7	6	8	28	33	3	7	11	16	24	10	13	19	44	57	43
Ilkeston Town	42	8	3	10	32	45	2	7	12	22	47	10	10	22	54	92	40
Folkestone Invicta	42	5	4	12	35	42	2	3	16	22	63	7	7	28	57	105	28

Tamworth are promoted to the Football Conference, replaced by Nuneaton Borough. Hastings United and Folkestone Invicta are relegated to the Eastern Division, replaced by Dorchester Town and Eastbourne Borough. Halesowen Town and Ilkeston Town drop to the Western Division from which Merthyr Tydfil and Weston-super-Mare are promoted.

CHARITY SHIELD
(League champions v League cup holders)

(27th July at Kettering Town)
Kettering Town 0 **Dorchester Town** 2

CONSTITUTION FOR 2003-04

BATH CITY   Manager: Alan Pridham   Colours: Black & white
Twerton Park, Twerton, Bath, North Somerset BA2 1DB   www.bathcityfc.com
Tel: 01225 423087/313247   Fax: 01225 481391
    City have appointed former Newport boss Tim Harris to work as Head Coach for the new season.

CAMBRIDGE CITY   *Manager: Gary Roberts*   *Colours: White & black*
City Ground, Milton Road, Cambridge, Cambridgeshire CB4 1UY   *www.cambridgecityfc.com*
Tel: 01223 357973   *Fax: 01223 351582*
        Start the season with a new manager, Gary Roberts replacing David Batch.

CHELMSFORD CITY   Manager: Steve Mosely   Colours: Red
Billericay Town FC, New Lodge, Blunts Wall Road, Billericay, Essrx CM12 9SA
Tel: 01277 655177/652188   Club office: 01245 353052   www.chelmsfordcityfc.com
    Hope this will be last season in exile – new Melbourne Park could be ready during 2004-05.

CHIPPENHAM TOWN   *Manager: Tommy Saunders*   *Colours: Blue & burgundy*
Hardenhuish Park, Bristol Road, Chippenham, Wiltshire SN15 3PL   *www.chippenhamtownfc.co.uk*
Tel: 01249 650400   *Fax: 01249 650400*
    Tommy Saunders loses long-term assistant Colin Bush who has taken over at Corsham Town.

CRAWLEY TOWN   Manager: Francis Vines   Colours: Red
Broadfield Stadium, Brighton Road, Broadfield, Crawley, West Sussex RH11 9RX
Tel: 01293 410000/410001   Fax: 01293 410002   www.crawley-town-fc.co.uk
    Major summer signing is experienced ex-Sutton, Dover and Farnborough striker Joff Vansittart.

DORCHESTER TOWN   *Manager: Mark Morris*   *Colours: Black & white*
The Avenue Stadium, Dorchester, Dorset DT1 2RY   *www.the-magpies.net*
Tel: 01305 262451   *Fax: 01305 267623*
        Celebrating spectacular double of Eastern Division championship and Dorset Senior Cup.

DOVER ATHLETIC   Manager: Clive Walker   Colours: White & Black
Hoverspeed Stadium, Lewisham Road, River, Dover, Kent CT17 0PB
Tel: 01304 822373   Fax: 01304 240041   www.dover-athletic.co.uk
            Played French "neighbours" Calais this summer for Hoverspeed Trophy.

EASTBOURNE BOROUGH   *Manager: Garry Wilson*   *Colours: Red & black*
Langney Sports Club, Priory Lane, Eastbourne, East Sussex BN23 9QJ
Tel: 01323 766050   *www.eastbourneboroughfc.co.uk*
        Achieved promotion this Spring just three years after joining from Sussex County League.

GRANTHAM TOWN   Manager: Roger Ashby   Colours: Black & white
South Kesteven Sports Stadium, Trent Road, Grantham, Lincolnshire NG31 7XQ
Tel: 01476 402224   Club: 01476 402225   www.granthamtownfc.co.uk
    Begin season with new boss, John Wilkinson having quit after leading Grantham to safety.

HAVANT & WATERLOOVILLE   *Manager: Liam Daish/Mick Jenkins*
Colours: White & blue   *www.havantandwaterlooville.net*
Westleigh Park, Martin Road, Havant, Hampshire PO9 5TH
Tel: 023 9278 7822   *Fax: 023 9242 2520*   *Club: 023 9278 7855*
        Highlight of the season was a stunning run to the semi-finals of the FA Trophy.

HEDNESFORD TOWN   Manager: Ian Painter   Colours: White, red & black
Keys Park, Hill Street, Hednesford, Staffs WS12 5DW   www.hednesfordtownfc.co.uk
Tel: 01543 422870   Fax: 01543 428180
            Keys Park is often used as a reserve team venue by First Division Walsall.

WWW.CHERRYRED.CO.UK

HINCKLEY UNITED   *Manager: Dean Thomas*   Colours: Red & blue
Middlefield Lane, Hinckley, Leicestershire LE10 0RA   www.hinckleyunitedfc.co.uk
Tel: 01455 613553   Club: 01455 615012
   Significant summer signing is ex-Portsmouth and Notts County midfielder Shaun Murray.

MERTHYR TYDFIL   Manager: Andy Beattie   Colours: White & black
Pennydarren Park, Merthyr Tydfil, Mid-Glamorgan CF47 8RF   www.themartyrs.com
Tel: 01685 384102   Fax: 01685 382882
   Clinched promotion back to Premier Division on the back of devastating post-Christmas run.

MOOR GREEN   *Manager: Bob Faulkner*   *Colours: Sky & navy blue*
The Moorlands, Sherwood Road, Hall Green, Birmingham, West Midlands B28 0EX
Tel: 0121 624 2727   *www.moorgreenfc.co.uk*
   Reached second Birmingham Senior Cup final in three years, but missed out to Birmngham City.

NEWPORT COUNTY   Manager: Peter Nicholas   Colours: Amber & black
Newport Stadium, Spytty Park, Newport, Gwent NP19 4PT   www.newport-county.co.uk
Tel: 01633 662262   Fax: 01633 666107   Stadium: 01633 671815
   Appointed Peter Nicholas as manager early last season following departure of Tim Harris.

NUNEATON BOROUGH   *Manager: Alan Lewer*   *Colours: White & blue*
Manor Park, Beaumont Road, Nuneaton, Warwickshire CV11 5HD   www.nbafc.net
Tel: 024 7638 5738   *Fax: 024 7634 2690*
   Former Chester City assistant boss Alan Lewer is hoping to take Borough back to the Conference.

STAFFORD RANGERS   Manager: Phil Robinson   Colours: Black & white
Marston Road, Stafford, Staffordshire ST16 3BX   www.staffordrangers.co.uk
Tel: 01785 602430   Fax: 01785 602431
   Ensured a Staffs one-two in Premier Division by finishing runners-up to Tamworth.

TIVERTON TOWN   *Manager: Martyn Rogers*   *Colours: Yellow & black*
Ladysmead, Bolham Road, Tiverton, Devon   *www.tiverton-town-fc.co.uk*
Tel: 01884 252397   *Fax: 01884 258840*
   An era ends with retirement of record scorer and ex-Non-League Player of the Year Phil Everett.

WELLING UNITED   Manager: Paul Parker   Colours: Red & white
Park View Road, Welling, Kent DA16 ISY   www.wellingunited.co.uk
Tel: 020 8301 1196   Fax: 020 8301 5676
   Have appointed ex-England star Paul Parker in succession to the experienced Bill Williams.

WESTON-SUPER-MARE   *Manager: Frank Gregan*   *Colours: White & blue*
Woodspring Park, Winterstoke Road, Weston-super-Mare BS23 2YG   Fax: 01934 622704
Tel: 01934 621618/635665   *web.ukonline.co.uk/westonsupermareafc*
   Now at highest level in club's history following promotion from Western Division.

WEYMOUTH   Manager: Steve Claridge   Colours: Claret
Wessex Stadium, Radipole Lane, Weymouth, Dorset DT4 9JF   www.theterras.co.uk
Tel: 01305 785558   Fax: 01305 766658
   Steve Claridge replaces Geoff Butler as manager following arrival of new chairman Ian Ridley.

WORCESTER CITY   *Manager: John Barton*   *Colours: Blue & white*
St George's Lane, Worcester, Worcestershire WR1 1QT   *www.worcestercityfc.co.uk*
Tel: 01905 23003   *Fax: 01905 26668*
   Faded in latter stages of season having looked title contenders in first half of campaign.

WWW.NLNEWSDESK.CO.UK

WWW.CHERRYRED.CO.UK

	BAT	CAM	CHE	CHI	CRA	DOV	FOL	GRA	HAL	HAS	HAV	HED	HIN	ILK	MG	NEW	STA	TAM	TIV	WEL	WEY	WOR
Bath City		734 / 7 Sep	663 / 21 Sep	1972 / 26 Dec	651 / 15 Mar	818 / 24 Aug	639 / 12 Apr	610 / 10 Sep	588 / 4 Mar	536 / 20 Aug	768 / 1 Feb	702 / 16 Nov	595 / 29 Mar	628 / 4 Jan	678 / 21 Dec	898 / 11 Mar	558 / 3 May	1116 / 12 Nov	513 / 7 Dec	589 / 21 Apr	788 / 22 Mar	635 / 8 Oct
Camb'dge C.	317 / 8 Feb		407 / 21 Sep	555 / 16 Nov	536 / 5 Oct	370 / 18 Jan	416 / 24 Aug	536 / 18 Jan	343 / 14 Sep	419 / 8 Oct	648 / 26 Apr	584 / 26 Oct	444 / 16 Nov	383 / 14 Dec	285 / 21 Dec	426 / 21 Dec	522 / 11 Mar	1209 / 14 Dec	608 / 28 Apr	273 / 28 Aug	278 / 7 Dec	316 / 14 Dec
Chelmsford	535 / 1 Mar	480 / 10 Mar		429 / 7 Dec	470 / 3 Sep	486 / 21 Sep	434 / 10 Sep	481 / 15 Feb	605 / 31 Aug	504 / 14 Apr	450 / 8 Mar	618 / 26 Apr	443 / 19 Apr	455 / 4 Jan	501 / 19 Oct	496 / 14 Sep	560 / 9 Nov	627 / 14 Dec	579 / 22 Mar	535 / 5 Oct	579 / 14 Dec	421 / 24 Aug
Chippenham	1906 / 26 Aug	445 / 29 Mar	702 / 17 Aug		796 / 9 Sep	531 / 26 Apr	525 / 23 Nov	252 / 7 Jan	669 / 15 Mar	592 / 9 Nov	661 / 11 Sep	491 / 5 Apr	541 / 19 Oct	645 / 14 Sep	577 / 5 Oct	761 / 14 Dec	761 / 18 Jan	1209 / 28 Dec	608 / 12 Feb	817 / 28 Apr	273 / 4 Sep	1014 / 14 Dec
Crawley T.	886 / 28 Dec	734 / 17 Aug	880 / 19 Apr	956 /		956 / 17 Sep	970 /	389 / 1 Mar	679 / 15 Mar	783 / 25 Feb	824 / 29 Mar	863 / 17 Aug	1217 / 9 Nov	874 / 25 Jan	813 / 15 Mar	1041 / 7 Sep	848 / 14 Dec	411 / 1 May	365 / 23 Apr	872 / 26 Aug	643 / 3 May	1738 / 14 Sep
Dover Ath.	781 / 14 Dec	752 / 22 Feb	1038 / 3 Dec	1009 / 25 Jan	1038 /		1609 / 26 Dec	803 / 29 Mar	604 / 10 Mar	1004 /	744 /	662 /	810 /	756 /	703 /	1006 /	901 / 14 Sep	1127 /	715 / 24 Mar	859 / 15 Feb	851 /	1013 / 3 May
Folkestone I.	316 / 18 Jan	412 / 11 Jan	381 / 25 Jan	339 / 8 Feb	407 / 3 Sep	1446 / 26 Aug		378 / 17 Aug	351 /	401 / 19 Apr	320 / 21 Dec	325 / 15 Mar	338 / 22 Mar	339 / 5 Apr	302 / 9 Nov	456 / 28 Dec	301 / 1 Mar	413 / 19 Oct	334 / 7 Dec	338 / 17 Sep	305 / 22 Feb	344 / 7 Sep
Grantham T.	368 / 8 Mar	611 / 20 Aug	381 /	466 / 25 Jan	375 / 21 Sep	581 / 21 Sep	317 / 14 Dec		518 /	330 /	488 /	362 / 26 Dec	470 / 21 Apr	563 /	640 / 3 May	458 / 9 Nov	424 / 26 Dec	534 /	356 / 5 Apr	385 / 15 Apr	538 / 31 Aug	372 / 22 Feb
Halesowen T.	507 / 22 Mar	506 / 8 Mar	730 / 22 Feb	547 / 21 Sep	463 /	476 / 16 Nov		501 / 19 Apr		517 / 28 Dec	429 / 8 Feb	512 / 14 Dec	535 / 5 Apr	477 / 8 Oct	598 / 18 Jan	555 / 18 Mar	736 / 26 Aug	656 / 3 Sep	430 / 17 Sep	566 / 17 Aug	294 / 25 Feb	803 / 26 Oct
Hastings Utd	452 / 22 Feb	468 / 8 Mar	397 / 3 May	433 / 3 May	491 / 21 Sep	630 / 7 Sep	525 /	252 / 7 Jan	487 /		318 / 8 Feb	506 / 14 Dec	431 / 24 Aug	433 / 7 Sep	407 /	430 / 18 Mar	410 / 3 May	521 / 21 Sep	417 / 8 Mar	511 / 25 Jan	330 / 21 Jan	560 / 23 Nov
Havant & W.	357 / 1 May	411 / 24 Aug	333 / 29 Mar	286 / 24 Feb	282 / 8 Apr	274 / 20 Aug	274 / 29 Apr	389 / 1 Mar	436 / 9 Nov	294 / 21 Dec		510 /	395 /	484 / 7 Sep	409 / 5 Apr	349 / 22 Mar	490 / 11 Mar	582 / 17 Aug	401 / 19 Apr	399 / 8 Mar	346 / 17 Sep	502 / 22 Mar
Hednesford	624 / 9 Nov	516 / 24 Aug	378 / 3 Mar	291 / 22 Feb	542 / 7 Apr	525 / 3 May	525 / 3 May	644 / 2 Sep	802 / 19 Aug	471 / 21 Dec	555 /	540 /	540 / 21 Sep	545 / 3 May	647 / 14 Dec	454 / 8 Mar	23 Nov	791 / 26 Aug	452 / 15 Feb	542 / 8 Oct	480 / 17 Sep	497 / 22 Mar
Hinckley Utd	314 / 14 Sep	411 / 29 Mar	286 / 15 Feb	333 / 29 Mar	291 / 21 Apr	241 / 30 Nov	241 / 30 Nov	332 / 18 Mar	346 / 21 Dec	294 / 21 Jan	317 / 15 Apr	372 / 19 Apr		391 / 1 Feb	290 / 23 Nov	344 / 5 Oct	346 / 8 Oct	287 / 7 Sep	393 / 17 Aug	287 / 25 Jan	272 / 12 Apr	354 / 17 Sep
Ilkeston T.	575 / 17 Aug	523 / 3 May	275 / 8 Apr	395 / 21 Dec	254 / 9 Nov	475 / 5 Oct	475 / 5 Oct	703 / 26 Apr	452 / 1 Mar	402 / 15 Feb	469 / 7 Dec	523 / 18 Jan	543 / 3 Sep		494 / 1 Apr	312 / 19 Apr	495 / 25 Feb	691 / 28 Dec	440 / 17 Aug	432 / 8 Feb	363 / 22 Mar	435 / 12 Apr
Moor Green	243 / 17 Sep	230 / 21 Dec	334 / 28 Dec	335 / 22 Mar	303 / 26 Apr	297 / 29 Mar	297 / 29 Mar	295 / 8 Oct	421 / 7 Dec	256 / 14 Sep	241 / 31 Aug	486 / 26 Aug	334 / 8 Feb	326 / 22 Feb	254 / 1 Apr	254 / 19 Apr	443 / 11 Jan	1007 /	268 / 7 Sep	236 / 26 Apr	249 / 8 Mar	675 / 25 Jan
Newport Co.	856 / 25 Jan	548 / 21 Dec	890 / 3 May	741 / 16 Sep	583 / 12 Apr	884 / 31 Aug	884 / 31 Aug	571 / 7 Dec	604 / 21 Apr	667 / 8 Feb	571 / 2 Nov	628 / 16 Nov	658 / 4 Jan	887 / 24 Aug	789 / 19 Apr		548 / 5 Apr	804 / 1 Mar	674 / 9 Sep	602 / 14 Dec	906 / 19 Aug	927 / 26 Dec
Stafford Rgrs	982 / 26 Apr	785 / 31 Aug	805 / 24 Aug	758 / 24 Aug	303 /	737 / 4 Jan	737 / 4 Jan	617 / 10 Sep	1187 / 26 Dec	964 / 29 Mar	672 / 14 Jan	1675 / 17 Sep	862 / 25 Jan	808 / 20 Aug	757 / 21 Apr	631 / 3 Sep		1884 / 15 Apr	847 / 2 Nov	811 / 5 Oct	811 / 21 Dec	1301 / 8 Feb
Tamworth	831 / 5 Oct	649 / 9 Nov	805 / 31 Aug	805 /	465 / 22 Mar	650 / 8 Mar	650 / 8 Mar	868 / 21 Dec	1150 / 25 Jan	744 / 7 Dec	408 / 23 Apr	1078 / 8 Oct	1208 / 26 Dec	1583 / 21 Apr	1012 / 20 Aug	1396 / 26 Apr	844 / 10 Dec		799 / 14 Jan	740 / 14 Sep	895 / 18 Feb	1610 / 4 Jan
Tiverton T.	903 / 4 Sep	737 / 7 Sep	832 / 21 Apr	832 / 12 Mar	537 / 19 Mar	771 / 25 Jan	771 / 25 Jan	823 / 21 Dec	731 / 29 Mar	761 / 19 Oct	603 / 21 Sep	742 / 21 Sep	660 / 26 Apr	704 / 31 Aug	638 / 12 Apr	697 / 8 Oct	661 / 22 Mar	981 / 8 Feb		701 / 9 Nov	566 / 1 Apr	714 / 21 Aug
Welling Utd	635 / 19 Oct	540 / 23 Nov	669 / 26 Oct	800 / 21 Mar	303 /	443 / 25 Jan	443 / 25 Jan	583 / 16 Nov	548 / 12 Apr	540 / 3 Sep	501 / 4 Jan	518 / 22 Feb	530 / 15 Mar	520 / 21 Sep	510 / 24 Aug	559 / 30 Mar	569 / 18 Jan	651 / 23 Nov	578 / 3 May		457 / 10 Sep	558 / 31 Aug
Weymouth	551 / 25 Mar	561 / 21 Apr	679 / 20 Aug	653 / 20 Aug	654 /	668 / 21 Dec	531 / 28 Dec	723 /	602 / 19 Oct	690 / 26 Apr	655 / 25 Jan	654 / 7 Sep	604 / 14 Dec	502 / 21 Sep	604 / 15 Feb	823 / 1 Mar	702 / 17 Aug	753 / 18 Jan	808 / 26 Aug	604 / 5 Apr		583 / 31 Aug
Worcester C.	753 / 19 Apr	974 / 19 Oct	911 / 21 Dec	877 / 8 Feb	877 / 9 Dec	1258 / 19 Apr	751 / 4 Jan	1003 / 26 Apr	817 / 24 Mar	872 / 17 Aug	1003 / 5 Oct	1251 / 1 Jan	828 / 1 Dec	1008 / 2 Nov	1202 / 2 Sep	1549 / 26 Aug	2711 / 20 Sep	1530 / 9 Sep	1000 / 15 Mar	1176 / 28 Dec	826 / 29 Mar	

	Ashford Town	Banbury United	Bashley	Burnham	Chatham Town	Corby Town	Dartford	Dorchester Town	Eastbourne Boro.	Erith & Belvedere	Fisher Athletic	Fleet Town	Histon	King's Lynn	Newport IOW	Rothwell Town	Salisbury City	Sittingbourne	Spalding United	St Leonards	Stamford	Tonbridge Ang.
Ashford Town		1-2	1-0	2-1	2-0	1-0	3-0	1-5	1-0	3-1	1-4	3-1	1-1	0-0	3-2	1-0	0-1	0-1	1-0	8-1	1-1	1-1
Banbury United	3-0		2-2	1-0	4-0	3-1	1-0	2-1	0-3	3-0	1-2	4-1	1-2	2-2	2-0	2-2	0-1	4-1	4-2	2-1	1-1	2-2
Bashley	4-1	0-0		4-2	4-0	2-0	4-0	0-0	1-6	0-0	4-1	4-0	5-1	1-2	5-1	1-1	3-1	4-0	1-1	6-0	2-1	1-1
Burnham	3-4	1-0	1-2	E	1-0	4-3	3-0	1-2	0-0	2-2	3-4	2-1	1-4	0-3	2-0	1-1	1-1	3-2	1-0	1-2	0-1	4-3
Chatham Town	1-1	3-4	1-0	2-0	A	3-2	0-1	0-4	0-3	1-2	0-1	3-1	1-1	1-3	2-1	2-1	0-2	2-0	3-1	2-1	1-2	1-2
Corby Town	2-5	2-1	2-2	0-1	2-2	S	1-1	2-5	2-2	1-4	0-2	1-1	1-0	1-1	2-0	1-3	0-4	1-3	2-0	2-0	0-1	1-4
Dartford	1-1	1-2	1-3	3-6	4-0	1-1	T	1-1	1-0	0-0	2-0	3-0	4-0	2-0	1-4	1-0	2-1	4-2	2-3	0-1	4-2	2-3
Dorchester Town	3-1	3-1	0-2	3-4	4-0	3-1	3-0	E	2-1	6-2	2-0	5-1	2-1	1-0	1-1	0-2	5-1	3-0	9-0	8-1	5-1	1-1
Eastbourne Borough	2-0	1-2	2-2	3-1	3-0	2-2	4-0	1-3	R	3-0	2-0	2-1	4-1	4-1	7-0	3-1	0-0	3-0	4-0	4-0	2-1	3-2
Erith & Belvedere	1-2	4-4	1-4	4-0	3-1	1-0	4-1	0-1	0-1	N	1-2	2-1	3-4	2-4	5-3	0-2	3-2	1-4	7-0	2-3	1-2	2-2
Fisher Athletic	0-2	0-1	1-2	0-1	3-0	0-1	1-1	1-5	2-4	1-1		0-1	3-2	0-5	1-3	0-3	1-3	0-1	3-0	1-0	3-0	0-1
Fleet Town	0-0	0-1	0-1	0-1	0-2	0-0	0-0	0-0	1-2	2-1	1-3	D	3-2	1-5	0-2	0-2	0-2	1-2	0-4	1-0	0-0	1-1
Histon	3-2	0-3	6-0	2-0	3-1	1-1	5-0	0-2	0-2	6-0	2-0	4-0	I	4-2	1-1	2-1	1-1	3-0	5-1	8-1	2-3	1-1
King's Lynn	1-0	2-1	2-1	5-1	7-2	4-1	2-0	2-2	2-0	3-0	1-1	5-0	2-8	V	1-3	3-4	3-1	1-1	4-0	1-1	1-3	3-0
Newport IOW	1-1	0-3	0-4	0-1	3-1	1-2	2-0	3-0	1-0	3-0	2-3	1-0	2-1	3-0	I	0-2	0-4	1-1	1-3	2-0	1-6	2-3
Rothwell Town	1-0	0-0	0-0	2-1	2-2	3-0	0-1	2-2	2-0	5-1	3-2	3-1	3-2	2-5	2-4	S	0-1	2-0	2-1	2-1	4-2	2-1
Salisbury City	3-1	0-0	2-5	2-0	3-1	3-0	0-0	0-0	1-2	2-1	3-1	2-1	3-2	2-1	3-2	0-0	I	3-0	1-0	3-2	2-1	2-0
Sittingbourne	2-1	0-0	1-0	2-2	0-1	2-2	1-2	0-3	0-2	4-1	1-1	3-0	0-1	1-2	0-0	0-0	3-2	O	5-2	2-1	1-4	2-1
Spalding United	0-2	4-1	0-2	1-5	0-2	1-2	1-1	2-2	0-1	1-0	2-2	0-1	1-2	1-2	0-3	2-4	1-4	1-2	N	1-0	0-0	1-3
St Leonards	2-3	0-3	1-2	0-0	0-4	1-3	3-1	0-2	1-1	0-1	2-3	3-5	0-2	0-4	3-1	0-2	0-2	1-3	1-1		0-1	1-2
Stamford	1-0	2-0	1-3	2-1	2-0	3-1	2-1	0-3	1-1	3-0	0-0	2-1	2-0	3-0	2-1	0-0	2-1	1-2	4-2	6-0		0-2
Tonbridge Angels	1-1	2-2	0-0	1-2	0-0	0-1	1-0	2-2	0-1	4-0	2-0	1-4	1-0	4-1	1-0	3-2	2-1	2-1	6-1	2-1	2-0	

Eastern Division

	P	HOME					AWAY					TOTAL					
		W	D	L	F	A	W	D	L	F	A	W	D	L	F	A	Pts
Dorchester Town	42	17	1	3	70	21	11	8	2	44	19	28	9	5	114	40	93
Eastbourne Boro.	42	16	3	2	59	17	13	3	5	33	16	29	6	7	92	33	93
Salisbury City	42	16	4	1	45	19	11	4	6	36	23	27	8	7	81	42	89
Stamford	42	17	2	2	46	14	10	4	7	34	25	27	6	9	80	39	87
Bashley	42	13	6	2	56	19	10	6	5	34	25	23	12	7	90	44	81
King's Lynn	42	14	4	3	55	27	10	3	8	43	35	24	7	11	98	62	79
Rothwell Town	42	13	4	4	42	27	9	6	6	35	25	22	10	10	77	52	76
Banbury United	42	12	5	4	44	24	9	6	6	31	26	21	11	10	75	50	74
Tonbridge Angels	42	12	5	4	37	20	8	6	7	34	35	20	11	11	71	55	71
Histon	42	12	5	4	59	23	8	2	11	40	39	20	7	15	99	62	67
Ashford Town	42	12	4	5	35	22	6	5	10	28	35	18	9	15	63	57	63
Sittingbourne	42	8	6	7	30	28	7	2	12	27	41	15	8	19	57	69	53
Burnham	42	9	4	8	35	35	6	3	12	27	44	15	7	20	62	79	52
Fisher Athletic	42	5	2	14	22	43	10	3	8	35	37	15	5	22	57	80	50
Chatham Town	42	9	2	10	29	33	5	3	13	25	51	14	5	23	54	84	47
Newport IOW	42	7	3	11	26	39	5	3	13	27	48	12	6	24	53	87	42
Dartford	42	7	4	10	35	35	4	4	13	13	43	11	8	23	48	78	41
Erith & Belvedere	42	8	2	11	47	43	3	4	14	18	53	11	6	25	65	96	39
Corby Town	42	5	6	10	26	42	4	5	12	23	42	9	11	22	49	84	38
Fleet Town	42	3	6	12	11	31	5	2	14	23	49	8	8	26	34	80	32
Spalding United	42	3	4	14	20	41	1	2	18	20	67	4	6	32	40	108	18
St Leonards	42	2	3	16	19	46	2	1	18	19	70	4	4	34	38	116	16

Dorchester Town and Eastbourne Borough are promoted to the Premier Division replaced by Hastings United and Folkestone Invicta. St Leonards have resigned and join the Sussex County League from which Burgess Hill Town are promoted. Spalding United return to the United Counties League. Eastleigh arrive from the Wessex League.

WWW.CHERRYRED.CO.UK

Team	ASH	BAN	BAS	BUR	CHA	COR	DAR	DOR	EAS	E&B	FIS	FLE	HIS	KIN	NEW	ROT	SAL	SIT	SPA	SiL	STA	TON
Ashford T.	—	283 12 Apr	203 22 Mar	269 8 Feb	320 25 Jan	292 9 Nov	285 19 Apr	260 1 Mar	320 17 Aug	239 18 Jan	171 3 Dec	3249 24 Aug	228 14 Dec	209 7 Sep	2329 19 Oct	218 15 Feb	267 15 Mar	386 20 Aug	265 3 May	203 4 Jan	311 5 Oct	389 11 Jan
Banbury Utd	402 26 Oct	—	334 5 Apr	194 26 Aug	387 8 Feb	580 1 Jan	468 7 Dec	743 28 Dec	263 17 Aug	373 29 Mar	491 18 Jan	203 10 Sep	391 25 Feb	319 19 Apr	427 23 Nov	466 1 Feb	1042 21 Jan	339 19 Oct	263 28 Sep	350 14 Dec	219 24 Sep	361 26 Apr
Bashley	102 9 Apr	156 11 Feb	—	127 17 Aug	170 11 Jan	103	201 25 Jan	304 26 Aug	272	101 28 Sep	158 1 Mar	130 24 Sep	149 8 Mar	201 29 Mar	120 10 Sep	140 19 Oct	520 25 Feb	119 12 Apr	94 26 Oct	135 22 Feb	105 26 Apr	185 8 Feb
Burnham	105 7 Dec	164 8 Mar	124 20 Aug	—	118	103	124	129	122	101	83	115	115	137	119	117	158	102	102	108	101	104 22 Mar
Chatham T.	178 21 Apr	191 21 Sep	102 25 Mar		—	184 7 Sep	252 5 Apr	178 21 Dec	235 26 Oct	102 12 Apr	168 17 Dec	128 4 Jan	174 8 Mar	194 25 Jan	182 21 Apr	142 1 Mar	209 24 Sep	276 14 Jan	154 21 Sep	122 12 Oct	185 15 Feb	282 8 Mar
Corby Town	79 14 Sep	117 21 Apr	75	55	55	—	153 24 Aug	60 19 Oct	66 23 Nov	66 4 Mar	60 21 Sep	95 29 Mar	94 11 Sep	140 21 Dec	66 3 May	210 26 Dec	70 7 Dec	83 4 Jan	143 21 Aug	51 8 Feb	98 13 Nov	95 28 Sep
Dartford	228 11 Feb	337 3 May	227 28 Dec	251 10 Sep	232		—	266 29 Mar	247 4 Mar	240 23 Nov	121 18 Feb	241 12 Apr	247 28 Sep	289 17 Aug	218 8 Mar	189 14 Dec	182 18 Mar	284 18 Jan	245 8 Feb	197 21 Apr	165 17 Dec	403 26 Aug
Dorchester T.	455 28 Sep	459 24 Aug	453	459	469 30 Nov		469 9 Nov	—	776 1 Apr	423 15 Mar	370 22 Feb	602 21 Apr	536 12 Apr	1259 3 May	427 20 Aug	433 4 Jan	469 10 Sep	472 12 Oct	416 8 Mar	447 26 Oct	444 14 Dec	359 15 Feb
Eastb'rne B.	524 21 Dec	551	689	415	488	416		519 24 Sep	—	783 21 Apr	937 3 May	472 19 Oct	426 24 Aug	541 1 Mar	456 4 Jan	402 7 Dec	357 10 Dec	517 9 Nov	615 12 Apr	345 18 Feb	669 15 Mar	526 10 Sep
Erith & Bel.	161 26 Aug	117 16 Nov	85	105	96	93	282 20 Aug	137 11 Mar	140 18 Mar	—	187 4 Mar	101 19 Oct	144 7 Dec	92 1 Mar	108 4 Jan	121 25 Jan	153 22 Mar	127 3 May	129 12 Apr	115 18 Feb	97 15 Mar	184 14 Sep
Fisher Ath.	185 23 Sep	100 4 Jan	88	115	75	75	155 19 Oct	141 26 Apr	134 4 Nov	117	—	85 26 Dec	78 21 Apr	120 15 Feb	78 29 Mar	85 11 Jan	103 14 Dec	132 8 Feb	80 24 Aug	94 25 Jan	90 5 Apr	165 23 Nov
Fleet Town	114 8 Mar	207 15 Feb	82 12 Nov	169	169	115	169 8 Mar	101 26 Apr	202 19 Aug	107	175	—	151 1 Feb	221 30 Nov	121 21 Dec	133 26 Oct	287 19 Apr	136 2 Nov	203 12 Oct	173 3 May	134 22 Mar	253 17 Aug
Histon	231 17 Aug	121	148	107	127	148	148 21 Dec	217 11 Mar	227 18 Mar	241	136 14 Jan	124	—	391 26 Aug	125 25 Jan	203 25 Jan	241 22 Mar	291 3 May	103 11 Feb	81 5 Apr	217 19 Apr	214 9 Nov
King's Lynn	757 22 Feb	620 12 Oct	439	542	469	585	585 21 Dec	747 11 Mar	661 18 Mar	536	578 4 Mar	667 7 Dec	748 26 Dec	—	670 7 Dec	583 25 Jan	691 3 May	628 8 Mar	533 21 Apr	569 5 Apr	494 19 Apr	557 9 Nov
Newport IW	204	314 4 Jan	216	318	241	242	242 16 Nov	152 24 Sep	294 26 Apr	236 24 Aug	264 26 Oct	314	220	236	—	247 20 Aug	258 5 Apr	166 8 Mar	237 21 Apr	315 22 Mar	270 10 Sep	285 14 Dec
Rothwell T.	210 5 Apr	253 7 Sep	117	166	405	185	185 19 Oct	133 25 Mar	215 25 Jan	148 22 Feb	153 12 Oct	131	195	223 21 Sep	181 9 Nov	—	261 27 Aug	175 11 Mar	135 1 Mar	173 30 Nov	283 17 Aug	163 19 Apr
Salisbury C.	555 25 Mar	663 15 Mar	470	446	433	469	433 22 Mar	553 7 Sep	561 22 Mar	374 17 Aug	462 4 Mar	435 4 Mar	488 8 Feb	475 12 Nov	613 21 Dec	393 26 Oct	—	363 11 Feb	507 22 Oct	359 21 Sep	468 25 Feb	469 18 Jan
Sittingbourne	179 26 Apr	225 1 Mar	216	295	206	256	256 24 Sep	160 22 Oct	236 8 Feb	153 22 Feb	156 12 Oct	141	226	236 9 Nov	188 28 Sep	209 5 Apr	210	—	162	120 24 Aug	189 1 Apr	211 19 Oct
Spalding Utd	82 4 Mar	164	100	129	102	75	75 17 Aug	121	93 14 Dec	122	119	115	77	226	121	115	106 25 Jan	101	—	100 23 Nov	226 11 Jan	102 5 Apr
St Leonards	168 9 Sep	153	89	102	170	150	150 15 Mar	115	459 14 Dec	52	116	115	164	95	124	81 28 Apr	81	145	140	—	78 26 Aug	153 24 Mar
Stamford	241 29 Mar	189	145	201	252	220	220	242	225	208	153	171	180	236	227	320	302	177	216	210	—	166 7 Dec
Tonbridge A.	333 12 Nov	193	257	405	303	235	235	318	394	217	339	332	385	412	355	327	543	533	221	369	363	—

EASTERN DIVISION CONSTITUTION FOR 2003-04

ASHFORD TOWN
Manager: Tim Thorogood *Colours:* Green & white
The Homelands, Ashford Road, Kingsnorth, Ashford, Kent TN26 1NJ
Tel: 01233 611838   *Fax:* 01233 662510

BANBURY UNITED
Manager: Kevin Brock   *Colours:* Red & gold
The Stadium, off Station Approach, Banbury, Oxfordshire OX16 5TA
Tel: 01295 263354   *Club:* 01295 261899

BASHLEY
Manager: Barry Blankley   *Colours:* Gold & black
Bashley Recreation Ground, Bashley Road, New Milton, Hants BH25 5RY   *Tel:* 01425 620280

BURGESS HILL TOWN
Manager: Danny Bloor   *Colours:* Yellow & white
Leylands Park, Burgess Hill, West Sussex RH15 8AW
Tel: 01444 242429

BURNHAM
Manager: Jim Greenwood *Colours:* Blue & white
The Gore, Wymers Wood Road, Burnham, Slough, Berkshire SL1 8JG
Tel: 01628 602697   *Club:* 01628 602467

CHATHAM TOWN
Manager: Steve Hearn   *Colours:* Red & black
Maidstone Road, Chatham, Kent ME4 6EJ
Tel: 01634 812194   *Fax:* 01634 812194

CORBY TOWN
Manager: Rob Dunnion   *Colours:* White & black
Rockingham Triangle Stadium, Rockingham Road, Corby, Northants NN17 2AE
Tel: 01536 401007   *Club/Fax:* 01536 406640

DARTFORD
Manager: Tommy Sampson *Colours:* White & black
Gravesend & Northfleet FC, Stonebridge Road, Northfleet, Gravesend, Kent DA11 9GN
Tel: 01474 533796
Dartford Fax: 01322 400665

EASTLEIGH
Manager: Paul Doswell   *Colours:* Blue
Ten Acres, Stoneham Lane, North Stoneham, Hampshire SO50 9HT   *Tel:* 023 8061 3361

ERITH & BELVEDERE
Manager: Mike Acland   *Colours:* Blue & white
Welling Utd FC, Park View Road, Welling DA16 1SY
Tel: 020 8301 1196   *Fax:* 020 8301 5676

FISHER ATHLETIC
Manager: Bob Davies   *Colours:* Black & white
Surrey Docks Stadium, Salter Road, Rotherhithe, London SE16 2LQ
Tel: 020 7231 5144   *Fax:* 020 7252 0060

FLEET TOWN
Manager: Mick Catlin *Colours:* Navy & sky blue
Calthorpe Park, Crookham Road, Fleet, Hampshire GU13 8DP   *Tel:* 01252 623804

FOLKESTONE INVICTA
Manager: Neil Cugley   *Colours:* Black & amber
The New Pavilion, Cheriton Road Sports Ground, Folkestone, Kent CT19 5JU
Tel: 01303 257461   *Fax:* 01303 255541

HASTINGS UNITED
Manager: Steve Lovell   *Colours:* White
The Pilot Field, Elphinstone Road, Hastings, East Sussex TN34 2AX   *Tel:* 01424 444635
Fax: 01424 729068   *Club:* 01424 430517

HISTON
Manager: Steve Fallon   *Colours:* Red & black
Bridge Road, Impington, Cambridge CB4 9PH
Tel: 01223 232301   *Fax:* 01223 237373

KING'S LYNN
Manager: Peter Morris   *Colours:* Blue & gold
The Walks Stadium, Tennyson Road, King's Lynn, Norfolk PE30 5PB   *Tel:* 01553 760060

NEWPORT IOW
Manager: Steve Tate   *Colours:* Yellow
St George's Park, St George's Way, Newport, Isle of Wight PO30 2QH
Tel: 01983 525027   *Fax:* 01983 826077

ROTHWELL TOWN
Manager: Nicky Platnauer *Colours:* Blue & white
Home Close, Cecil Street, Rothwell, Northants NN14 2EZ   *Tel:* 01536 710694

SALISBURY CITY
Manager: Nicky Holmes   *Colours:* White & black
The Raymond McEnhill Stadium, Patridge Way, Old Sarum, Salisbury, Wiltshire SP4 6PU
Tel: 01722 326454   *Fax:* 01722 323100

SITTINGBOURNE
Manager: Mark Beeney   *Colours:* Red & black
Bourne Park, Eurolink, Sittingbourne, Kent ME10 3SB
Tel: 01795 435077

STAMFORD
Manager: Billy Jeffrey   *Colours:* Red & white
Newflame Stadium, Kettering Road, Stamford, Lincolnshire   *Tel:* 01780 763079

TONBRIDGE ANGELS
Manager: Alan Walker   *Colours:* Black & azure
Longmead Stadium, Darenth Avenue, Tonbridge, Kent TN10 3JW
Tel: 01732 352477   *Club:* 01732 352417

WWW.NLNEWSDESK.CO.UK

WWW.CHERRYRED.CO.UK

	Atherstone United	Bedworth United	Bromsgrove Rovers	Cinderford Town	Cirencester Town	Clevedon Town	Evesham United	Gloucester City	Gresley Rovers	Mangotsfield United	Merthyr Tydfil	Racing Club Warwick	Redditch United	Rocester	Rugby United	Shepshed Dynamo	Solihull Borough	Stourport Swifts	Sutton Coldfield Town	Swindon Supermarine	Taunton Town	Weston-super-Mare
Atherstone United		1-1	1-2	2-2	0-0	0-3	1-2	1-1	1-2	0-4	0-1	3-1	0-0	2-1	2-0	0-0	3-4	1-1	4-1	3-2	1-4	0-2
Bedworth United	2-1		2-1	2-1	0-1	0-2	2-1	2-2	1-2	0-1	2-1	2-1	1-0	1-2	1-3	1-4	0-1	3-2	0-2	0-1	0-1	0-2
Bromsgrove Rovers	3-0	1-0		5-2	5-1	5-1	0-1	2-4	4-1	2-1	1-2	1-0	0-0	4-1	3-2	1-0	1-1	3-0	2-0	1-3	3-0	0-0
Cinderford Town	2-2	1-1	1-0	W	2-1	1-1	1-3	4-0	2-2	2-1	1-1	0-0	1-0	0-0	1-2	2-3	1-2	1-0	0-1	1-0	4-0	0-2
Cirencester Town	3-1	3-1	2-0	1-1	E	0-1	1-2	0-3	1-3	2-5	2-0	1-0	2-0	1-0	2-0	2-4	0-1	0-4	3-1	3-3	5-5	0-4
Clevedon Town	1-2	1-2	1-1	2-3	2-4	S	3-1	1-1	0-0	0-2	0-1	2-1	1-0	1-0	1-0	2-1	1-1	1-1	1-2	2-1	4-0	0-1
Evesham United	3-0	4-3	3-1	4-1	2-4	1-0	T	1-0	1-0	1-0	0-2	4-0	1-2	3-0	0-0	5-1	2-1	1-3	0-0	3-2	1-2	3-5
Gloucester City	1-2	4-1	1-0	4-0	5-4	1-1	6-1	E	4-3	2-2	3-1	2-5	2-0	0-0	0-0	3-1	4-2	1-2	3-1	2-1	4-2	0-2
Gresley Rovers	4-1	1-0	2-0	3-0	3-1	2-3	3-0	1-1	R	2-1	0-1	2-0	0-0	0-0	1-1	3-3	1-1	1-2	0-1	2-1	2-3	2-1
Mangotsfield United	4-1	1-1	2-2	3-0	3-0	4-0	5-0	1-4	7-0	N	2-3	3-0	1-1	1-1	4-2	1-0	3-3	4-0	3-1	5-1	0-1	3-0
Merthyr Tydfil	5-0	1-0	2-0	0-0	2-0	1-0	2-0	3-1	2-1	1-1		3-0	2-2	4-1	3-0	3-0	2-3	1-3	2-2	4-0	1-0	1-2
Racing Club Warwick	0-4	2-3	1-1	0-2	1-2	2-2	0-6	1-6	1-5	2-2	1-2	D	0-3	1-1	1-4	2-0	1-1	1-0	0-0	2-2	1-7	0-2
Redditch United	2-0	2-1	2-1	3-0	4-0	0-1	2-1	1-0	1-2	3-3	0-1	4-1	I	0-1	3-1	4-0	2-0	5-0	4-1	2-1	1-2	3-0
Rocester	1-0	1-2	0-1	2-1	1-1	0-0	2-2	2-2	0-1	0-6	0-2	2-1	0-1	V	0-2	0-2	1-2	1-0	1-0	0-2	0-2	0-2
Rugby United	0-0	3-1	0-2	5-1	0-3	2-2	3-0	1-0	0-1	2-1	2-1	4-0	1-2	4-2	I	2-0	2-0	3-1	1-1	1-0	1-0	1-0
Shepshed Dynamo	1-2	4-1	0-5	4-0	1-2	2-1	0-1	1-0	0-0	2-1	0-2	4-3	0-4	2-0	1-0	S	1-3	1-1	0-2	0-2	0-2	0-1
Solihull Borough	1-0	1-1	2-2	1-0	2-0	2-2	2-1	4-0	4-2	0-0	4-0	2-1	5-0	0-1	1-1	1-1	I	2-0	0-0	2-0	7-2	0-3
Stourport Swifts	1-1	1-0	1-2	1-2	1-1	0-0	1-1	0-1	1-0	0-2	3-2	5-0	0-1	3-0	1-1	0-2	1-3	O	1-2	1-2	0-3	0-3
Sutton Coldfield Town	2-0	1-1	0-1	0-0	3-1	6-0	3-2	0-1	0-2	2-3	0-2	1-1	3-2	1-1	0-1	2-1	2-1	2-0	N	9-0	1-1	0-3
Swindon Supermarine	2-1	1-0	0-1	2-0	0-3	1-3	3-3	1-2	2-4	2-4	0-2	2-0	1-2	1-2	1-1	2-0	2-3	2-2	0-2		1-2	0-2
Taunton Town	2-0	5-1	0-3	0-2	1-1	1-1	3-2	0-2	3-0	1-5	1-4	2-1	3-1	1-1	1-1	1-4	1-1	3-1	2-1	1-2		2-2
Weston-super-Mare	4-1	3-3	0-1	3-3	3-1	1-1	1-3	3-2	1-0	1-1	0-2	0-1	1-0	3-2	1-0	1-1	1-2	1-0	3-1	2-1	5-1	

Western Division

	P	HOME					AWAY					TOTAL					
		W	D	L	F	A	W	D	L	F	A	W	D	L	F	A	Pts
Merthyr Tydfil	42	13	5	3	43	16	15	3	3	35	16	28	8	6	78	32	92
Weston-super-Mare	42	11	5	5	38	27	15	2	4	39	15	26	7	9	77	42	85
Bromsgrove Rovers	42	14	3	4	47	20	9	4	8	26	21	23	7	12	73	41	76
Solihull Borough	42	12	6	3	43	17	9	7	5	34	31	21	13	8	77	48	76
Gloucester City	42	13	4	4	51	31	9	5	7	36	27	22	9	11	87	58	75
Mangotsfield United	42	13	5	3	60	21	8	5	8	46	32	21	10	11	106	53	73
Redditch United	42	15	1	5	48	17	7	5	9	28	25	22	6	14	76	42	72
Rugby United	42	15	3	3	39	16	5	6	10	19	27	20	9	13	58	43	69
Gresley Rovers	42	11	5	5	37	21	8	5	8	26	33	19	10	13	63	54	67
Taunton Town	42	9	5	7	36	36	11	2	8	40	42	20	7	15	76	78	67
Sutton Coldfield Town	42	10	5	6	39	23	8	5	8	24	30	18	10	14	63	53	64
Evesham United	42	12	2	7	42	28	7	4	10	34	44	19	6	17	76	72	63
Clevedon Town	42	7	5	9	27	27	7	8	6	27	33	14	13	15	54	60	55
Cirencester Town	42	9	3	9	34	39	6	4	11	28	43	15	7	20	62	82	52
Cinderford Town	42	8	7	6	28	22	5	5	11	22	45	13	12	17	50	67	51
Shepshed Dynamo	42	8	2	11	24	33	4	4	13	24	43	12	6	24	48	76	42
Stourport Swifts	42	4	7	10	24	28	6	4	11	24	38	10	11	21	48	66	41
Bedworth United	42	8	1	12	22	32	3	6	12	24	42	11	7	24	46	74	40
Swindon Supermarine	42	5	3	13	26	39	6	2	13	26	46	11	5	26	52	85	38
Atherstone United	42	5	7	9	26	34	4	3	14	19	44	9	10	23	45	78	37
Rocester	42	5	5	11	16	30	4	5	12	18	44	9	10	23	34	74	37
Racing Club Warwick	42	2	7	12	20	55	1	2	18	13	49	3	9	30	33	104	18

Merthyr Tydfil and Weston-super-Mare are promoted to the Premier Division. Ilkeston Town and Halesowen Town are relegated in return. Rocester and Racing Club Warwick are relegated to the Midland Alliance. Yate Town are promoted from the Hellenic League. Team Bath are promoted from the Western League.

WESTERN DIVISION – GATES 'N DATES

	ATH	BED	BRO	CIN	CIR	CLE	EVE	GLO	GRE	MAN	MER	RCW	RED	ROC	RUG	SHE	SOL	STO	SUT	SWI	TAU	WSM
Atherstone		229 29 Mar	318 18 Jan	123 21 Dec	151 26 Oct	141	168	164	265	134	203	289	247	180	318	188	167 15 Feb	140	172 24 Aug	145	156 19 Oct	265 7 Sep
Bedworth U.	511 19 Apr		241 8 Mar	102 7 Dec	123 12 Oct	120 12 Apr	175 10 Sep	143 4 Mar	286 1 Mar	121 24 Mar	251 17 Aug	131 26 Apr	170 26 Oct	153 28 Dec	210 12 Nov	128 22 Oct	86 25 Feb	85 28 Jan	142 8 Feb	118 21 Dec	169 22 Mar	121 18 Jan
Bromsgrove	511 12 Oct	242 7 Sep		512 18 Mar	466 12 Apr	120	637 10 Sep	713	358 12 Nov	350 5 Apr	557 26 Oct	740 21 Apr	506 23 Nov	605 26 Dec		483 25 Feb	432 28 Jan		473 4 Jan	474 3 May	537 22 Feb	511 1 Feb
Cinderford	137 25 Jan	161 21 Sep	114		163 1 Feb	135 7 Sep	247 15 Mar	125 12 Nov	125	115 5 Apr	272	150 21 Apr	100 23 Nov	100 3 May	100 29 Apr	105 15 Feb	110 22 Mar	136 24 Sep	100 5 Apr	130 4 Jan	164 26 Oct	146 24 Sep
Cirencester	127 26 Apr	82 18 Mar	194 9 Nov			163 26 Aug	135 24 Aug	247 22 Feb	109 25 Feb	155	240 12 Oct	126 20 Aug	154 3 May	154	145 29 Apr	122 15 Feb	112 22 Mar	97	142 5 Apr	185 4 Jan	118 1 Feb	135
Clevedon T.	119 14 Dec	193 24 Aug	172 12 Apr	133 14 Dec		169 26 Aug	169 22 Feb	109 15 Mar	155 14 Sep	82 1 Jan	109 21 Dec	251 23 Nov	144 5 Apr	145 17 Aug	197 28 Sep	178 25 Jan	182 29 Mar	154 7 Dec	204 16 Nov	204 1 Feb	256 19 Apr	438 19 Oct
Evesham U.	179 1 Mar	436 25 Jan	251 14 Dec	127 10 Sep	202	26 Aug		170 22 Oct	304	154 26 Oct	1 Jan	251 5 Apr	144 1 Mar	197 22 Feb	223 9 Nov	178	182 12 Oct	169 20 Aug	154 18 Jan	204 10 Sep	256 21 Apr	438 21 Apr
Gloucester C.	324 17 Aug	345 15 Feb	234 26 Nov	134 26 Aug	92 26 Dec	92 3 May	8 Feb		209 26 Oct	144 26 Apr	325 7 Dec	253 23 Nov	110 5 Apr	223 9 Nov	223 22 Mar	129 4 Feb	114 22 Feb	202 9 Nov	92 12 Oct	127 1 Jan	236 28 Dec	137 23 Nov
Gresley Rov.	385 10 Sep	372 4 Jan	311 8 Apr	215 8 Apr	388 19 Apr	163 3 May	257	302 18 Jan		283 18 Jan	422 21 Sep	260 7 Sep	378 15 Feb	329 7 Dec	376 26 Oct	288 14 Dec	250 12 Oct	309 22 Mar	204 12 Nov	203 24 Sep	165 26 Nov	583 1 Mar
Mangotsfield	243 16 Nov	209 15 Feb	464 29 Mar	360 18 Mar	305 3 May	355 19 Apr	310 18 Mar	362	341 1 Jan		404 26 Aug	325 21 Sep	378 15 Feb	376 26 Oct	376 14 Dec	385 26 Dec	291 12 Oct	267 14 Dec	358 21 Dec	349 5 Oct	371 26 Nov	348 3 May
Merthyr T.	575 12 Apr	571 15 Mar	653 11 Jan	188 19 Oct	177 16 Nov	311 21 Apr	173 12 Apr	271 9 Nov	341 22 Mar	325 5 Apr		325 12 Apr	309 25 Jan	237 1 Mar	376 22 Oct	291 26 Dec	234 4 Mar	238 14 Dec	175 21 Apr	285 5 Oct	293 8 Feb	425 3 May
RC Warwick	119 8 Feb	101 1 Apr	1105 22 Jan	506 22 Jan	679 20 Aug	439 24 Sep	521 21 Apr	502 21 Sep	236	659	5 Nov	485	422 8 Feb	456 19 Oct	524 24 Aug	495 15 Mar	557 3 May	479 25 Jan	780 21 Dec	586 26 Dec	533 12 Nov	465 4 Jan
Redditch U.	201 22 Mar	169 9 Nov	251 17 Aug	177 11 Apr	105 21 Apr	105 28 Dec	138 2 Nov	110 21 Dec	110 15 Feb	15 Feb	422 24 Aug	7 Sep		158 21 Sep	150 4 Jan	150 16 Nov	150 27 Aug	72 19 Apr	110 1 Mar	98 19 Oct	102 26 Apr	88 29 Mar
Rocester	88 12 Nov	102	667 14 Jan	154 18 Jan	186 28 Dec	144	174 2 Nov	175 28 Jan	178 23 Nov	161 28 Sep	306 14 Dec	116 15 Mar	158 22 Oct		150 5 Apr	150 10 Sep	284 27 Aug	215 19 Apr	184 1 Mar	173 19 Oct	233 26 Apr	140 29 Mar
Rugby Utd	275 28 Dec	260	285 14 Jan	96 9 Nov	134 17 Aug	95 19 Oct	139 22 Oct	141 11 Mar	212 19 Apr	161 18 Jan	306 28 Dec	139 22 Oct	139	204	148	205 10 Sep	284 27 Aug	215 21 Sep	184 26 Oct	173 8 Mar	233 17 Aug	140 14 Dec
Shepshed D.	216 26 Aug	142 22 Feb	442 28 Dec	146 30 Nov	156 7 Sep	95 18 Mar	139 29 Mar	191 12 Apr	234 11 Mar	189 14 Dec	282 26 Apr	256 25 Mar	265 15 Feb	232	226 21 Dec	186 19 Apr	76 3 May	101 26 Oct	111 19 Apr	126 1 Mar	164 21 Sep	212 8 Feb
Solihull Bor.	141 9 Dec	152 24 Aug	19 Oct	8 Feb	23 Nov	21 Sep	19 Aug	31 Mar	7 Sep	14 Dec	26 Apr	26 Oct	11 Nov	18 Jan	25 Jan	8 Mar	186	8 Mar	214 23 Sep	152 24 Apr	164 5 Apr	212 9 Nov
Stourport S.	101 2 Nov	125 19 Oct	326 30 Nov	73 16 Nov	124 21 Apr	97 15 Feb	186 21 Apr	132 21 Dec	127 29 Mar	125 25 Jan	102 12 Nov	112 4 Jan	162 26 Dec	114 15 Mar	178 8 Feb	148 18 Jan	109 20 Aug	129 9 Nov	20 Aug	143 12 Apr	97 5 Nov	80 24 Aug
Sutton C'fld	124 25 Feb	109 14 Dec	181 19 Apr	132 17 Aug	101 15 Feb	117 30 Nov	183 26 Apr	124 19 Oct	231 28 Dec	117 1 Feb	203 8 Mar	203 22 Mar	209 12 Apr	110 26 Aug	127 10 Sep	110 2 Nov	131 22 Oct	129 9 Nov	110	112 23 Nov	139 29 Mar	161 21 Sep
Swin. Super.	105 15 Jan	116 5 Apr	221 23 Oct	125 19 Apr	147 22 Mar	135 22 Jan	137 18 Jan	226 8 Feb	139 7 Dec	222 26 Aug	189 11 Sep	137 22 Feb	127 26 Oct	101 14 Dec	124 1 Apr	155 26 Apr	157 28 Dec	165 17 Aug	139 12 Oct	112 23 Nov	135 30 Nov	121 15 Mar
Taunton T.	322 15 Jan	344 3 May	449 16 Nov	315 12 Apr	353 26 Feb	306 4 Mar	358 24 Aug	478 21 Aug	337 8 Mar	414 25 Sep	441 13 Apr	215 29 Apr	208 30 Apr	323 9 Nov	396 12 Oct	306 7 Oct	368 21 Dec	385 1 Feb	392 7 Sep	301 21 Apr	139	460 26 Dec
Weston-s-M.	197 11 Mar	208 16 Nov	345 26 Apr	155 12 Nov	253 5 Apr	325 4 Mar	217 21 Dec	242 10 Sep	302 26 Oct	431 19 Apr	273 22 Oct	211 29 Apr	196 30 Nov	231 22 Feb	200 7 Dec	214 22 Mar	270 17 Aug	226 28 Dec	207 25 Jan	248 15 Feb	370 2 6 Aug	

WESTERN DIVISION CONSTITUTION FOR 2002-03

ATHERSTONE UNITED
Manager: Jim Ginnelly/Lee Sullivan
Sheepy Road, Atherstone, Warwickshire CV9 3AD
Tel: 01827 717829   *Colours:* Red & white

BEDWORTH UNITED
Manager: Ian Drewitt   *Colours:* Green & white
The Oval, Welfare Park, Coventry Road, Bedworth, Warwickshire CV12 8NN
Tel: 024 7649 1404   *Club:* 024 7631 4302

BROMSGROVE ROVERS
Manager: George Rooney
Colours: Green, white & black
Victoria Ground, Birmingham Road, Bromsgrove, Worcestershire B61 8DS
Tel: 01527 876949   *Fax:* 01527 876265

CINDERFORD TOWN
Manager: Tommy Callinan *Colours:* White & black
Causeway Ground, Hilldene, Cinderford, Glos GL14 2QH   *Tel:* 01594 827147

CIRENCESTER TOWN
Manager: Brian Hughes   *Colours:* Red & black
Corinium Stadium, Kingshill Lane, Cirencester, Gloucestershire GL7 1DE
Tel: 01285 654543   *Fax:* 01285 654474

CLEVEDON TOWN
Manager: Steve Fey   *Colours:* Blue & white
The Hand Stadium, Davis Lane, Clevedon BS21 6TG
Tel: 01275 341913   *Club:* 01275 871600

EVESHAM UNITED
Manager: Phil Mullen   *Colours:* Red & white
Common Road, Evesham, Worcestershire WR11 4PU
Tel: 01386 442303

GLOUCESTER CITY
Manager: Chris Burns   *Colours:* Yellow & black
Meadow Park, Sudmeadow Road, Hempsted, Gloucester, Glos GL2 5HS *Tel:* 01452 421400
Fax: 01452 301330   *Club:* 01452 311060

GRESLEY ROVERS
Manager: t.b.a.   *Colours:* Red & white
Moat Ground, Moat Street, Church Gresley, Swadlincote, Derbyshire DE11 9RE
Tel: 01283 216315   *Fax:* 01283 221881

HALESOWEN TOWN
Manager: Brendan Phillips *Colours:* White
The Grove, Old Hawne Lane, Halesowen, West Midlands B63 3TB   *Tel:* 0121 550 2179

ILKESTON TOWN
Manager: Charlie Bishop   *Colours:* Red & black
The New Manor Ground, Awsworth Road, Ilkeston, Derbyshire DE7 8JF
Tel: 0115 932 4094   *Club:* 0115 930 5622

MANGOTSFIELD UNITED
Manager: Andy Black   *Colours:* Maroon & white
Cossham Street, Mangotsfield, Bristol, South Glos BS17 3EN   *Tel:* 0117 956 0119

REDDITCH UNITED
Manager: Rod Brown   *Colours:* Red & black
Valley Stadium, Bromsgrove Road, Redditch, Worcestershire B97 4RN
Tel: 01527 67450   *Fax:* 01527 67450

RUGBY UNITED
Manager: Tony Dobson   *Colours:* Sky & navy blue
Butlin Road, Rugby, Warwickshire CV21 3ST
Tel: 01788 844806   *Fax:* 01788 540202

SHEPSHED DYNAMO
Manager: Dave Williams   *Colours:* Black & white
The Dovecote, Butt Hole Lane, Shepshed, Leicestershire LE12 9BN   *Tel:* 01509 650992

SOLIHULL BOROUGH
Manager: David Busst   *Colours:* Red & white
Damson Park, Damson Parkway, Solihull, West Midlands B91 2PP   *Tel:* 0121 705 6770

STOURPORT SWIFTS
Manager: Dave Titterton   *Colours:* Black & gold
Walshes Meadow, Harold Davies Drive, Stourport-on-Severn, Worcestershire   *Tel/Fax:* 01299 825188

SUTTON COLDFIELD TOWN
Manager: Chris Keogh   *Colours:* Blue & white
Central Ground, Coles Lane, Sutton Coldfield, West Midlands B72 1NL   *Tel:* 0121 354 2997

SWINDON SUPERMARINE
Manager: Alan Dyton/Clive McGuire
Colours: Blue & white
Supermarine Sports & Social, Highworth Road, South Marston, Swindon, Wiltshire SN3 4SF
Tel: 01793 828778

TAUNTON TOWN
Manager: Russell Musker   *Colours:* Burgundy & blue
Wordsworth Drive, Taunton, Somerset TA1 2HG
Tel: 01823 278191   *Fax:* 01823 322975

TEAM BATH
Manager: Ged Roddy   *Colours:* Yellow & blue
University of Bath, Sports Training Village, Claverton Down, Bath, North Somerset
Tel: 01225 826339

YATE TOWN
Manager: Richard Thompson
Colours: White & navy blue
Lodge Road, Yate, Bristol, South Glos BS17 5LE
Tel: 01454 228103 / 228103

WWW.CHERRYRED.CO.UK

LEAGUE CHALLENGE CUP

PRELIMINARY ROUND
Crawley Town 2 Sittingbourne 0
Mangotsfield Utd 3 Gloucester City 0

FIRST ROUND
Bashley 3 Havant & Waterlooville 2
Bath City 2 **Tiverton Town** 2 *aet* (1-3p)
Bedworth United 1 Atherstone
United 0
Burnham 4 Erith & Belvedere 2
Chatham Town 0 **Chelmsford City** 3
Cirencester Town 3 Cinderford Town 1
Crawley Town 1 Hastings United 0
Dartford 2 St Leonards 0
Dover Athletic 2 Folkestone Invicta 1
Fisher Athletic 1 **Ashford Town** 3
Fleet Town 0 **Eastbourne Borough** 1
Grantham Town 3 Histon 1
Gresley Rovers 1 **Hinckley United** 2
Ilkeston Town 2 Banbury United 1 *aet*
Mangotsfield United 2
Weston-super-Mare 0
Merthyr Tydfil 0 **Chippenham Town** 1
Moor Green 2 Stafford Rangers 1
Newport County 2 Clevedon Town 0 *aet*
Newport IOW 3 Weymouth 1
Redditch Utd 4 **Evesham United** 5 *aet*
Rocester 1 **Hednesford Town** 2
Rugby United 0 Cambridge City 3
(Cambridge City expelled)
Salisbury City 3 Dorchester Town 2
Shepshed Dynamo 3 Corby Town 2
Solihull Borough 6 Racing Club
Warwick 2
Spalding United 1 **King's Lynn** 3
Stamford 3 Rothwell Town 2 *aet*
Stourport Swifts 1 **Bromsgrove
Rovers** 4
Tamworth 1 **Sutton Coldfield Town** 3
Taunton Town 3 Swindon
Supermarine 1
Tonbridge Angels 1 **Welling
United** 2 *aet*
Worcester City 0 **Halesowen Town** 1

SECOND ROUND
Ashford Town 1 **Crawley Town** 2
Bedworth United 3 Hednesford 1
Chippenham Town 2 Bashley 1
Dartford 1 **Dover Athletic** 6
Eastbourne Borough 2 **Burnham** 3 *aet*
Halesowen Town 4 Evesham United 3
Hinckley United 2 Moor Green 1
King's Lynn 2 Stamford 1
Newport IOW 3 Salisbury City 2
Rugby United 1 **Grantham Town** 2
Shepshed Dynamo 3 Ilkeston
Town 3 *aet* (4-2p)
Solihull Borough 3 Bromsgrove 0
Sutton Coldfield 2 Newport County 1
Taunton Town 1 **Mangotsfield Utd** 7
Tiverton Town 4 Cirencester Town 2
Welling United 2 **Chelmsford City** 3

THIRD ROUND
Burnham 1 **Crawley Town** 4
Dover Athletic 0 **Chelmsford City** 1
Halesowen Town 4 Sutton Coldfield 1
King's Lynn 3 Hinckley United 0
Mangotsfield United 0 **Chippenham** 1
Newport IOW 1 **Tiverton Town** 7
Shepshed Dynamo 2 **Grantham** 5
Solihull Borough 2 **Bedworth United** 3

QUARTER-FINALS
Bedworth United 0 **Halesowen Town** 2
Crawley Town 1 Chelmsford City 2
*(ineligible player – Chelmsford
expelled)*
King's Lynn 2 Grantham Town 0
Tiverton Town 2 **Chippenham Town** 3

SEMI-FINALS
Crawley Town 1 King's Lynn 0
Halesowen Town 2 Chippenham 1

FINAL 1st LEG
(15th April)
Halesowen Town 2 Crawley Town 1

FINAL 2nd LEG
(29th April)
Crawley Town 2 Halesowen Town 0

SPARTAN SOUTH MIDLANDS LEAGUE

	Beaconsfield	Bedford U&V	Biggleswade Town	Brook House	Broxbourne BV&E	Dunstable Town	Greenacres (Hemel)	Hanwell Town	Harefield United	Haringey Borough	Hillingdon Borough	Hoddesdon Town	Holmer Green	Letchworth	London Colney	Milton Keynes City	Potters Bar Town	Royston Town	Ruislip Manor	St Margaretsbury
Beaconsfield SYCOB		2-1	1-1	1-1	2-0	2-5	3-1	5-1	0-0	5-0	2-1	2-1	2-1	n/a	1-0	2-0	2-1	2-0	4-1	0-0
Bedford United & Valerio	0-2		1-4	0-2	0-1	2-2	4-1	0-2	2-2	0-4	1-1	1-2	3-1	3-2	0-2	1-3	1-1	0-3	1-2	3-2
Biggleswade Town	1-2	1-2	P	3-0	0-1	4-5	1-0	1-4	3-4	3-3	1-0	1-2	3-0	n/a	0-1	3-1	2-1	3-1	1-1	3-1
Brook House	0-2	2-0	2-1	R	1-1	1-3	1-4	1-6	0-1	1-2	1-0	1-1	1-1	1-3	2-2	2-1	1-2	2-2	1-0	1-0
Broxbourne Borough V&E	0-3	0-3	0-1	2-0	E	0-4	2-6	3-2	1-1	4-1	0-1	2-1	4-0	3-3	1-1	0-3	0-1	0-1	3-0	0-0
Dunstable Town	0-1	2-1	11-0	4-0	3-2	M	0-0	3-4	2-0	2-0	1-1	2-0	3-1	n/a	2-0	8-2	2-0	2-2	6-0	1-2
Greenacres (Hemel)	1-1	3-0	3-3	5-0	1-3	0-4	I	6-2	0-3	3-1	3-0	0-2	4-1	n/a	3-4	1-3	0-0	4-1	1-2	3-2
Hanwell Town	1-5	6-1	4-1	3-1	2-4	0-2	4-0	E	2-2	4-2	3-2	1-2	6-3	n/a	1-4	1-0	3-0	4-1	0-2	4-0
Harefield United	1-0	2-2	2-1	5-2	6-0	0-1	4-1	3-2	R	3-1	2-0	3-2	3-0	n/a	6-1	3-0	5-1	2-3	2-0	2-1
Haringey Borough	2-0	1-0	1-2	1-1	2-3	0-6	2-1	3-3	0-1		0-1	3-0	2-1	n/a	3-2	3-1	0-2	4-0	2-4	1-1
Hillingdon Borough	1-1	1-1	1-0	1-2	3-1	3-1	3-1	4-1	1-0		D	4-1	4-1	n/a	0-3	2-3	2-3	2-4	0-1	0-4
Hoddesdon Town	0-1	4-1	2-0	4-0	1-0	0-0	1-2	2-3	0-1	1-1	1-2	I	1-1	n/a	1-1	0-0	0-2	3-0	0-2	3-1
Holmer Green	1-3	0-1	0-4	1-2	2-3	0-6	1-2	4-2	1-4	3-2	2-1	1-1	V	n/a	0-6	0-1	0-6	2-1	1-2	2-6
Letchworth	3-3	n/a	3-4	n/a	n/a	n/a	n/a	n/a	n/a	2-2	n/a	n/a	n/a	I	n/a	3-2	n/a	n/a	n/a	n/a
London Colney	0-1	3-3	0-0	2-0	2-2	2-2	3-0	0-7	1-1	3-1	2-0	2-1	2-1	n/a	S	3-2	1-2	1-1		1-3
Milton Keynes City	2-0	4-1	1-1	0-2	4-4	4-2	2-0	2-2	0-1	1-2	4-1	1-2	4-1	n/a	3-2	I	1-1	1-0	1-1	2-2
Potters Bar Town	1-1	3-0	2-2	2-1	4-3	0-1	4-0	5-2	2-0	2-0	2-1	3-1		n/a	3-1	1-3	O	2-0	4-0	4-3
Royston Town	0-1	1-1	3-2	2-0	0-3	0-1	1-1	3-1	1-3	0-0	1-2	4-1	2-3	n/a	0-0	2-1	1-1	N	1-2	1-2
Ruislip Manor	2-1	0-3	1-1	0-0	5-0	1-2	2-1	1-1	0-0	0-2	2-2	4-2	1-3	n/a	0-1	1-6	2-1	1-3		
St Margaretsbury	2-3	2-1	3-1	1-2	2-1	4-2	5-2	3-1	2-2	4-0	1-1	3-2	4-0	n/a	2-5	3-1	1-2	2-1	2-1	

Note – Letchworth withdrew. Their results are shown above but have been expunged from the league table

Premier Division	P	W	D	L	F	A	Pts
Dunstable Town	36	26	6	4	104	32	84
Beaconsfield SYCOB	36	24	7	5	66	30	79
Potters Bar Town	36	23	6	7	80	42	75
Harefield United	36	21	7	8	79	45	70
St Margaretsbury	36	18	6	12	79	60	60
London Colney	36	15	10	11	65	57	55
Ruislip Manor	36	15	8	13	47	56	53
Hanwell Town	36	16	4	16	94	82	52
Milton Keynes City	36	15	7	14	58	57	52
Hoddesdon Town	36	14	9	13	54	48	51
Biggleswade Town	36	13	6	17	59	67	45
Hillingdon Borough	36	12	6	18	44	57	42
Broxbourne BV&E -3	36	13	5	18	49	64	41
Greenacres (Hemel)	36	11	6	19	66	77	39
Haringey Borough	36	10	8	18	50	70	38
Royston Town	36	10	7	19	46	63	37
Brook House -3	36	10	9	17	36	67	36
Bedford Utd & Valerio	36	7	8	21	40	74	29
Holmer Green	36	5	3	28	40	108	18

PREMIER DIV. CUP

FIRST ROUND
Haringey Borough 2 Holmer Green 0
Hillingdon Borough 4 Royston Town 2
Hoddesdon Town 0 **Potters Bar Town 3**
St Margaretsbury 0 **Brook House 2**
Milton Keynes City 1 **Ruislip Manor 2**
Potters Bar Town 0 **Beaconsfield SYCOB 1**

SECOND ROUND
Biggleswade Town (w/o) Letchworth (scr.)
Dunstable Town 2 **Bedford United & Valerio 3**
Greenacres (Hemel) 2 Hillingdon Borough 0
Hanwell Town 3 Broxbourne Borough V & E 2
Harefield 3 London Colney 2
Haringey Boro. 1 **Brook House 3**

QUARTER-FINALS
Beaconsfield SYCOB 1 **Hanwell Town 3**
Bedford United & Valerio 1 **Biggleswade Town 3**
Brook House 0 **Harefield Utd 2**
Ruislip Manor 2 Greenacres (Hemel) 0

SEMI-FINALS
Biggleswade Town 2 **Hanwell Town 4**
Ruislip Manor 0 **Harefield Utd 1**

FINAL
(30th April at Brook House)
Harefield United 0 **Hanwell Town 2**

PREMIER DIVISION CONSTITUTION 2003-04

BEACONSFIELD SYCOB . . . . Holloway Park, Slough Road, Beaconsfield, Buckinghamshire 01494 676868
BEDFORD UNITED & VALERIO . . . . Meadow Lane, Cardington, Bedford, Bedfordshire 01234 831024
BIGGLESWADE TOWN . . . . Fairfield, Fairfield Road, Biggleswade, Bedfordshire 01767 312374
BROOK HOUSE . . . . Farm Park, Kingshill Avenue, Hayes, Middlesex . . . . 020 8845 0110. Boardroom: 020 8842 1448
BROXBOURNE BOROUGH V & E . . . . The V & E Club, Goffs Lane, Cheshunt, Hertfordshire 01992 624281
GREENACRES (HEMEL) . . . . . . Hemel Hempstead Town FC, Vauxhall Road, Adeyfield, Hemel Hempstead 01442 259777
HANWELL TOWN . . . . Reynolds Field, Perivale Lane, Greenford, Middlesex 020 8998 1707
HAREFIELD UNITED . . . . Preston Park, Breakspeare Road, Harefield, Middlesex . . 01895 823474. Boardroom: 01895 822275
HARINGEY BOROUGH . . . . Coles Park, White Hart Lane, Wood Green, London 020 8889 1415
HARPENDEN TOWN . . . . Rothamsted Park, Amenbury Lane, Harpenden, Hertfordshire 01582 715724
HILLINGDON BOROUGH . . . . Middlesex Stadium, Breakspear Road, Ruislip, Middlesex 01895 639544
HODDESDON TOWN . . . . Lowfield, Park View, Hoddesdon, Hertfordshire 01992 463133
HOLMER GREEN . . . . Watchet Lane, Holmer Green, High Wycombe, Buckinghamshire 01494 711485
LEVERSTOCK GREEN . . . . Pancake Lane, Leverstock Green, Hemel Hempstead, Hertfordshire 01442 246280
LONDON COLNEY . . . . Cotlandswick Playing Fields, London Colney, Hertfordshire 01727 822132
MILTON KEYNES CITY . . Wolverton Park, Old Wolverton Road, Wolverton, Milton Keynes, Buckinghamshire 01908 318317
POTTERS BAR TOWN . . . . Parkfield, The Walk, Potters Bar, Hertfordshire 01707 654833
ROYSTON TOWN . . . . Garden Walk, Royston, Hertfordshire 01763 241204
RUISLIP MANOR . . . . Grosvenor Vale, off West End Road, Ruislip, Middlesex . . . 01895 676168. Clubhouse: 01895 637487
ST MARGARETSBURY . . . . Station Road, Stanstead St Margarets, near Ware, Hertfordshire 01920 870473

Letchworth withdrew during the course of the season. Dunstable are promoted to the Isthmian League. Harpenden Town and Leverstock Green are promoted from Division One.

	Ampthill Town	Biggleswade United	Brache Sparta	Brimsdown Rovers	Cockfosters	Colney Heath	Harpenden Town	Haywood United	Kings Langley	Langford	Leverstock Green	New Bradwell St Peter	Pitstone & Ivinghoe	Risborough Rangers	Shillington	Stony Stratford Town	The 61 FC	Tring Athletic	Welwyn Garden City
Ampthill Town		0-3	2-0	2-1	2-3	1-3	1-4	0-4	2-1	3-2	1-3	0-3	0-1	2-1	0-3	2-2	2-0	0-3	0-3
Biggleswade United	5-1		0-2	0-0	0-3	0-4	1-3	2-0	4-0	2-1	1-2	4-1	2-1	10-2	2-0	1-3	1-2	1-1	1-1
Brache Sparta	2-0	6-1		1-1	3-2	3-1	1-1	2-1	3-1	1-4	3-2	1-3	1-3	6-0	4-2	1-2	4-2	2-3	2-0
Brimsdown Rovers	1-0	1-2	2-0	D	0-1	1-4	2-1	1-1	1-1	3-0	0-4	3-1	0-5	3-1	1-2	1-1	2-0	0-1	3-1
Cockfosters	2-0	6-1	4-1	5-2	I	0-2	8-2	5-1	0-1	7-0	0-4	4-2	0-2	1-4	3-0	2-1	4-0	1-1	0-1
Colney Heath	3-0	0-2	1-0	1-0	4-0	V	3-1	0-2	6-0	5-2	2-0	7-1	0-4	4-7	1-0	1-1	1-2	1-1	1-0
Harpenden Town	7-0	2-2	2-1	2-3	6-0	4-0	I	1-1	3-0	5-0	2-1	3-0	4-2	4-0	4-0	7-0	7-0	1-1	1-0
Haywood United	5-0	1-0	2-0	2-1	4-2	3-5	1-3	S	0-3	1-2	2-2	2-1	4-5	5-1	9-0	1-1	4-2	0-1	0-4
Kings Langley	5-3	0-1	4-2	0-0	1-7	0-3	0-3	2-3	I	3-3	0-0	0-0	0-5	4-2	2-2	2-0	1-1	1-2	0-6
Langford	1-2	1-1	2-3	4-0	2-5	0-3	2-5	1-3	2-2	O	2-3	3-3	0-1	5-0	1-1	0-0	2-0	1-2	2-3
Leverstock Green	6-2	1-1	2-1	3-0	3-2	0-1	0-3	4-0	4-2	6-1	N	2-0	0-3	3-0	1-1	2-1	1-0	0-0	0-0
New Bradwell St Peter	4-2	1-3	1-2	1-4	1-3	3-0	1-8	1-1	2-2	1-0	1-5		1-4	1-1	0-2	0-3	3-3	2-2	1-3
Pitstone & Ivinghoe	4-2	1-2	3-0	3-3	4-0	3-1	0-3	4-0	5-1	2-1	4-0	1-0		5-1	2-0	1-0	5-0	2-0	3-2
Risborough Rangers	1-0	1-6	1-2	1-0	0-1	1-4	0-6	0-5	1-3	0-3	0-7	0-2	0-5	O	1-1	1-5	1-4	2-2	3-2
Shillington	3-1	2-4	0-2	0-1	3-6	0-3	0-3	3-4	2-4	2-3	0-4	4-1	1-2	3-2	N	3-0	1-0	1-0	0-1
Stony Stratford Town	1-3	2-0	1-1	1-3	0-1	3-2	0-4	4-3	3-1	1-1	0-4	3-3	1-2	2-2	6-1	E	1-1	0-5	1-0
The 61 FC	4-1	0-2	1-3	0-1	1-1	0-2	0-5	0-0	2-0	2-4	0-2	1-0	1-4	3-2	3-0	1-0		0-2	0-2
Tring Athletic	6-0	2-0	1-0	4-2	3-1	2-1	2-1	3-0	2-0	3-1	0-0	7-1	0-4	8-1	4-0	4-2	6-1		1-1
Welwyn Garden City	2-1	0-0	3-1	2-4	4-1	1-0	2-1	2-3	4-3	6-2	1-1	0-0	2-2	12-1	3-1	2-0	0-4	0-4	

Division One	P	W	D	L	F	A	Pts
Pitstone & Ivinghoe	36	30	2	4	107	33	92
Harpenden Town	36	26	4	6	122	35	82
Tring Athletic	36	24	9	3	89	31	81
Leverstock Green	36	21	8	7	82	37	71
Colney Heath	36	23	1	12	85	42	70
Welwyn Garden City	36	18	7	11	76	46	61
Cockfosters	36	19	3	14	89	66	60
Biggleswade United	36	17	6	13	68	55	57
Haywood United	36	16	6	14	78	68	54
Brache Sparta	36	17	3	16	67	61	54
Brimsdown Rovers	36	14	7	15	51	58	49
Stony Stratford Town	36	11	10	15	51	66	43
Langford	36	9	6	21	62	90	33
Kings Langley	36	8	9	19	50	89	33
The 61 FC	36	9	5	22	37	79	32
Shillington	36	9	4	23	45	94	31
New Bradwell St Peter	36	6	11	19	47	88	29
Ampthill Town	36	8	1	27	38	102	25
Risborough Rangers	36	4	4	28	35	139	16

DIVISION ONE CUP

FIRST ROUND
Biggleswade United 2 Kings Langley 1
Harpenden 9 Ampthill Town 0
Langford 0 **The 61 FC** 1
Letchworth Bridger (scr.)
Risborough Rangers (w/o)
SECOND ROUND
Biggleswade United 2 **Stony Stratford Town** 3
Brimsdown 2 Colney Heath 0
Cockfosters 2 **Tring Athletic** 3 *aet*
Leverstock Green 0 **Pitstone & Ivinghoe** 2
New Bradwell 2 **Haywood Utd** 3
Risborough Rangers 0 **Harpenden Town** 6
Shillington 2 Welwyn Gdn City 0
The 61 FC 4 Brache Sparta 3 *aet*

QUARTER-FINALS
Brimsdown Rovers 1 **Stony Stratford Town** 2
Harpenden Town 6 Shillington 2
Haywood United 3 **Pitstone & Ivinghoe** 3 *aet (1-4p)*
The 61 FC 0 **Tring Athletic** 2
SEMI-FINALS
Stony Stratford Town 2 Harpenden Town 1
Tring Athletic 6 Pitstone & Ivinghoe 3
FINAL
(5th May at Haywood United)
Stony Stratford Town 1 **Tring Athletic** 2

WWW.NLNEWSDESK.CO.UK

DIVISION ONE CONSTITUTION 2003-04

AMPTHILL TOWN . . . . Ampthill Park, Woburn Road, Ampthill, Bedfordshire 01525 404440
BIGGLESWADE UNITED . . . . Second Meadow, Fairfield Road, Biggleswade, Bedfordshire 01767 600408
BRACHE SPARTA . . . . Foxdell Recreation Ground, Dallow Road, Luton, Bedfordshire 01582 720751
BRIMSDOWN ROVERS . . . . Brimsdown Sports & Social, Goldsdown Road, Enfield, Middlesex 020 8804 5491
BUCKINGHAM ATHLETIC . . . . Stratfields Fields, Stratford Road, Buckingham, Buckinghamshire 01280 816945
COCKFOSTERS . . . . Chalk Lane, Cockfosters, Barnet, Hertfordshire 020 8449 5833
COLNEY HEATH . . . . The Pavilion Recreation Ground, High Street, Colney Heath, St Albans, Hertfordshire 01727 826188
HAYWOOD UNITED . . . . Haywood Way, Aylesbury, Buckinghamshire 01296 423324
KINGS LANGLEY . . . . Hempstead Road, Kings Langley, Hertfordshire . . . . None
LANGFORD . . . . Forde Park, Langford Road, Henlow, Bedfordshire 01462 816106
NEW BRADWELL ST PETER . . . . Bradwell Road Rec., New Bradwell, Milton Keynes, Buckinghamshire 01908 313835
PITSTONE & IVINGHOE . . . . Tring Town FC, Pendley Sport Centre, Cow Lane, Tring, Hertfordshire . . . . 01442 824018 / 823075
SHILLINGTON . . . . Playing Fields, Greenfields, Shillington, Hitchin, Hertfordshire 01462 711757
STONY STRATFORD TOWN . . . . Ostlers Lane, Stony Stratford, Buckinghamshire 01908 562267
SUN SPORTS . . . . Bellmount Wood Avenue, Watford, Hertfordshire 01923 227453
THE 61 FC . . . . Kingsway Ground, Beverley Road, Luton, Bedfordshire 01582 495417
TRING ATHLETIC . . . . Miswell Lane, Tring, Hertfordshire 01442 828331
WELWYN GARDEN CITY . . . . Herns Lane, Welwyn Garden City, Hertfordshire . . . . 01707 328470. Fax: 01707 329358
Letchworth Bridger witdrew before start of season. Harpenden Town and Leverstock Green are promoted to the Premier Division. Risborough Rangers are relegated to Division Two replaced by Buckingham Athletic. Newcomers are Sun Sports (formerly Sun Postal Sports) from the Herts Senior County League.

	Abbey National (Loughton)	Amersham Town	Buckingham Athletic	Caddington	Cranfield United	Crawley Green	Flamstead	Kent Athletic	Mursley United	Old Bradwell United	Old Dunstablians	Padbury United	Scot	Totternhoe	Winslow United
Abbey National (Loughton)		1-3	2-1	1-1	1-2	3-3	10-0	1-2	1-4	3-0	1-4	3-1	3-2	3-2	2-4
Amersham Town	3-2	D	0-1	1-1	4-3	1-1	5-1	1-0	3-2	3-4	2-3	4-0	4-1	4-1	1-1
Buckingham Athletic	4-0	9-2	I	7-1	3-0	2-0	6-1	2-0	2-0	5-2	1-0	8-2	4-1	8-0	1-1
Caddington	1-4	1-2	1-8	V	0-2	2-5	4-2	0-2	6-0	4-0	0-7	4-2	1-0	2-4	2-3
Cranfield United	2-1	1-1	0-6	3-1	I	1-0	5-1	1-5	0-3	1-1	1-2	3-1	4-1	2-0	0-1
Crawley Green	4-5	3-1	2-4	4-0	4-0	S	6-2	1-0	1-3	4-1	1-3	5-0	3-1	5-1	2-0
Flamstead	4-1	2-6	0-2	1-0	1-4	0-1	I	0-4	1-7	3-2	0-8	3-2	4-3	2-2	1-4
Kent Athletic	0-1	1-0	3-2	5-0	3-1	3-3	6-0	O	1-3	3-2	1-0	5-0	5-0	7-0	3-2
Mursley United	4-5	2-3	0-5	6-0	3-1	0-3	3-0	1-3	N	2-2	0-1	3-1	2-4	0-0	0-6
Old Bradwell United	2-1	1-7	0-3	0-0	2-2	1-2	0-0	2-2	1-3		0-7	1-0	6-1	3-3	3-6
Old Dunstablians	0-0	2-5	3-1	3-0	4-0	4-4	5-0	3-2	6-0	5-2		3-2	11-2	9-1	3-0
Padbury United	3-5	1-3	0-3	2-3	0-1	1-2	0-4	2-2	2-1	2-3	1-7	T	1-2	4-3	1-4
Scot	2-3	2-4	0-9	2-1	3-1	1-3	2-4	0-2	1-3	2-6	2-5	6-4	W	3-4	1-3
Totternhoe	0-1	3-3	0-4	2-1	1-3	1-4	1-0	0-8	1-4	3-1	0-2	1-1	4-0	O	1-2
Winslow United	0-3	4-4	0-2	2-1	2-2	4-3	0-1	2-1	2-2	6-2	0-3	4-2	3-1	2-1	

www.CHERRYRED.CO.UK

Division Two	P	W	D	L	F	A	Pts
Buckingham Athletic	28	24	1	3	113	21	73
Old Dunstablians	28	23	2	3	113	29	71
Kent Athletic	28	18	3	7	79	30	57
Crawley Green	28	17	4	7	79	45	55
Amersham Town	28	16	6	6	80	54	54
Winslow United	28	15	6	7	62	49	51
Abbey National	28	14	3	11	67	58	45
Mursley United	28	12	4	12	61	56	40
Cranfield United	28	12	4	12	46	55	40
Flamstead	28	8	2	18	38	99	26
Old Bradwell United	28	6	7	15	50	83	25
Totternhoe	28	6	5	17	40	88	23
Caddington	28	6	3	19	38	80	21
Scot	28	5	0	23	46	107	15
Padbury United	-3	28	2	2	24	38	96	5

DIVISION TWO CUP

FIRST ROUND

Amersham Town 2 Abbey National (Loughton) 1
Buckingham Athletic 5 Totternhoe 1
Cranfield United 1 Flamstead 4
Mursley United 0 Crawley Green 4
Old Bradwell United 2 Kent Athletic 3
Scot 0 Padbury United 3
Winslow United 2 Old Dunstablians 1

QUARTER-FINALS

Caddington 3 Crawley Green 7
Flamstead 1 Kent Athletic 2
Padbury 0 Amersham 1
Winslow United 0 Buckingham Athletic 2

SEMI-FINALS

Crawley Green 2 Amersham Town 1
Kent 1 Buckingham Ath 2

FINAL

(7th May at Dunstable Town)
Buckingham Athletic 0 Crawley Green 2

DIVISION TWO CONSTITUTION 2003-04

ABBEY NATIONAL (MK) . Loughton Sports & Social Club, Linceslade Grove, Milton Keynes, Buckinghamshire 01908 690668
AMERSHAM TOWN .... Spratleys Meadow, School Lane, Amersham, Buckinghamshire 01494 727428
ARLESEY ATHLETIC .... t.b.a. .... t.b.a.
CADDINGTON .... Caddington Recreation Club, Manor Road, Caddington, Bedfordshire 01582 450151
CRANFIELD UNITED .... Crawley Road, Cranfield, Bedford, Bedfordshire..................... 01234 751444
CRAWLEY GREEN .... Crawley Green Rec Ground, Crawley Green Road, Luton, Bedfordshire.................. 01582 700883
FLAMSTEAD ....Flamstead Sports Association, Friendless Lane, Flamstead, St Albans, Hertfordshire 01582 841307
KENT ATHLETIC .... Kent Social Club, Tenby Drive, Leagrave, Luton, Bedfordshire...................... 01582 582723
KENTISH TOWN... t.b.a. .... t.b.a.
MARKYATE............................... Cavendish Road, Markyate, Hertfordshire 01582 841731
MURSLEY UNITED .... Station Road, Mursley, Milton Keynes, Buckinghamshire .... None
OLD BRADWELL UNITED .... Abbey Road, Bradwell Village, Milton Keynes, Buckinghamshire..................... 01908 312355
OLD DUNSTABLIANS .... Lancot Park, Dunstable Road, Totternhoe, Bedfordshire................ 01582 663735
PADBURY UNITED.................. Playing Fields, Springfields, Padbury, Buckinghamshire .... None
RISBOROUGH RANGERS....... Windsor, Horsenden Lane, Princes Risborough, Buckinghamshire 01844 274176
SCOT .... Selbourne Avenue, Bletchley, Milton Keynes, Buckinghamshire 01908 368881
TOTTERNHOE .... Totternhoe Recreation Ground, Totternhoe, Dunstable, Bedfordshire 01582 606738
WINSLOW UNITED........... Rec. Ground, Elmfields Gate, Winslow, Buckingham, Buckinghamshire................... 01296 713057
Buckingham Athletc are promoted to Division One replaced by Risborough Rangers. Newcomers are Arlesey Athletic, Kentish Town and Markyate.

CHALLENGE TROPHY

FIRST ROUND

Abbey National (Loughton) 1 **The 61 FC** 2

Amersham Town 5 Totternhoe 2

Ampthill Town 4 Buckingham Athletic 1

Bedford United & Valerio 3 Kings Langley 1

Brimsdown Rovers 4 Shillington 1 *aet*

Colney Heath 1 **Harpenden Town** 2

Cranfield United 2 Flamstead 1

Crawley Green 2 Royston Town 2 *aet* (4-3p)

Greenacres (Hemel) 4 Scot 1

Hanwell Town 5 Stony Stratford Town 0

Haywood United 3 Caddington 1

Hillingdon Borough 0 **Beaconsfield SYCOB** 1

Hoddesdon Town 2 **Letchworth** 6

Holmer Green 1 Leverstock Green 0

Kent Athletic (w/o) Letchworth Bridger (scr.)

Langford 1 **Ruislip Manor** 3 *aet*

Milton Keynes City 3 Haringey Borough 1

Mursley United 2 **Brache Sparta** 3

Old Bradwell United 0 **Harefield United** 6

Pitstone & Ivinghoe 3 Old Dunstablians 2

Risborough Rangers 3 Biggleswade United 0

Welwyn Garden City 1 **Biggleswade Town** 3

Winslow United 0 **Dunstable Town** 5

SECOND ROUND

Ampthill Town 3 **Cockfosters** 4 *aet*

Brimsdown Rovers 0 **Harpenden Town** 2

Brook House 0 **Harefield United** 2

Broxbourne Borough V & E 3 Brache Sparta 2 *aet*

Greenacres (Hemel) 4 Biggleswade Town 0

Hanwell Town 7 Holmer Green 0

Haywood United 3 New Bradwell St Peter 0

Kent Athletic 2 **Dunstable Town** 4 *aet*

Letchworth (sc.) **Beaconsfield SYCOB** (w/o)

London Colney 3 Amersham Town 3 *aet* (5-4p)

Padbury United 1 **Cranfield United** 2

Pitstone & Ivinghoe 3 Crawley Green 2

Potters Bar Town 4 Bedford United & Valerio 2 *aet*

St Margaretsbury 1 Ruislip Manor 0

The 61 FC 0 **Milton Keynes City** 4

Tring Athletic 5 Risborough Rangers 0

THIRD ROUND

Cockfosters 2 Hanwell Town 0

Cranfield United 1 **Beaconsfield SYCOB** 2 *aet*

Dunstable Town 7 St Margaretsbury 2

Greenacres (Hemel) 2 Harpenden Town 1

Harefield United 2 Potters Bar Town 1

Haywood United 2 **Milton Keynes City** 5 *aet*

London Colney 2 Broxbourne Borough V & E 1

Pitstone & Ivinghoe 3 **Tring Athletic** 3 *aet* (4-5p)

QUARTER-FINALS

Beaconsfield SYCOB 3 Cockfosters 2

Dunstable Town 3 Tring Athletic 1

Greenacres (Hemel) 0 **Milton Keynes City** 2

Harefield United 2 London Colney 1 *aet*

SEMI-FINALS

Harefield United 3 Beaconsfield SYCOB 1

Milton Keynes City 1 **Dunstable Town** 3

FINAL 1st LEG

(18th April)

Dunstable Town 1 Harefield United 2

FINAL 2nd LEG

(21st April)

Harefield United 2 Dunstable Town 0

RESERVES CHALLENGE TROPHY

FINAL *(over two legs 8th May and 14th May)*
London Colney Res. 2 Buckingham Athletic Res 0,
Buckingham Athletic Res. 4 London Colney Res. 1

Res. Div. One	P	W	D	L	F	A	Pts
Lon. Colney Res. -3	34	21	6	7	113	47	66
Dunstable T. Res.	34	20	6	8	100	51	66
Cockfosters Res.	34	16	9	9	82	57	57
M. Keynes C. Res.	34	17	6	11	82	57	57
Harpenden T. Res.	34	17	5	12	74	71	56
Royston Town Res.	34	15	8	11	72	55	53
Langford Res.	34	15	6	13	56	55	51
Holmer Green Res.	34	14	9	11	76	73	51
Leverstock G. Res.	34	13	10	11	60	53	49
Haywood Utd Res.	34	14	4	16	71	96	46
Tring Athletic Res.	34	12	8	14	50	50	44
Potters Bar T. Res.	34	12	6	16	74	86	42
Arlesey T. Res. -6	34	13	8	13	62	58	41
Kings Langley Res.	34	11	8	15	55	69	41
Colney Heath Res.	34	11	7	16	53	64	40
Stony Stratford Res.	34	9	7	18	52	69	34
Kent Athletic Res.	34	6	10	18	43	93	28
Biggleswade U. Res.	34	7	3	24	42	113	24

Res. Div. Two East	P	W	D	L	F	A	Pts
Harefield Utd Res.	27	23	0	4	113	25	69
Welwyn GC Res.	27	21	2	4	76	32	65
Bedford U&V Res.	27	17	2	8	68	34	53
Biggleswade T. Res.	27	13	4	10	51	48	43
The 61 FC Res.	27	13	2	12	46	52	41
Crawley Green Res.	27	11	3	13	59	71	36
Cranfield Utd Res.	27	10	4	13	50	59	34
Ampthill Town Res.	27	9	4	14	43	48	31
Shillington Res.	27	4	2	21	18	72	14
Flamstead Res.	27	1	3	23	36	119	6

Res. Div. Two West	P	W	D	L	F	A	Pts
O Dunstablians Res.	27	18	5	4	68	24	59
Abbey National Res.	27	15	5	7	60	42	50
Buckingham A. Res.	27	11	14	2	63	46	47
Pitstone & Iv. Res.	27	13	6	8	45	34	45
Risborough R. Res.	27	11	6	10	50	35	39
New Bradwell Res.	27	8	7	12	45	49	31
Winslow Utd Res.	27	9	4	14	47	73	31
Old Bradwell Res.	27	8	5	14	37	42	29
Mursley United Res.	27	7	6	14	40	57	27
Totternhoe Res.	27	5	2	20	27	80	17

STAFFS COUNTY LEAGUE

	Abbey Hulton Res.	Alsagers Bank	Ball Haye G. Res.	Bradeley	Brocton Res.	Congleton Vale	Eccleshall Res.	Florence	Foley Res.	Gnosall Horns	Hanley Town Res.	Holt JCB	Milton Rgrs Res.	Penkhull	Penkridge Town	Redgate Clay. Res.	Stallington Res.	Stone Old Alleyn.	Ward Wanderers	Wedgwood S&S
Abbey Hulton United Res.		0-0	3-6	0-1	1-4	1-2	1-1	0-2	0-2	n/a	1-5	0-0	2-1	n/a	2-1	0-2	3-3	0-3	n/a	0-4
Alsagers Bank	3-1		0-2	0-0	2-0	2-6	1-5	1-3	4-0	3-2	1-2	1-3	1-3	n/a	5-2	2-0	1-5	4-4	3-1	2-4
Ball Haye Green Res.	3-0	4-1		n/a	2-0	3-0	1-2	2-0	0-1	n/a	3-2	2-0	1-1	n/a	3-0	1-3	0-0	2-0	5-0	0-2
Bradeley	n/a	n/a	n/a		n/a	2-1	0-5	0-3	4-1	n/a	n/a	1-3	n/a	5-2	n/a	1-1	2-4	n/a	n/a	n/a
Brocton Res.	0-1	1-2	1-2	n/a		1-0	0-5	1-0	2-1	3-4	0-2	0-1	0-0	n/a	1-1	2-4	0-0	0-0	n/a	1-1
Congleton Vale	1-0	0-1	1-2	n/a	1-2		2-1	2-4	3-3	3-1	3-3	1-4	2-1	1-5	1-2	0-0	3-1	2-5		1-1
Eccleshall Res.	1-2	2-2	3-1	4-1	2-1	6-2		1-2	10-0	n/a	4-1	1-0	3-0	3-0	1-1	3-2	2-2	0-1	n/a	2-2
Florence	6-1	2-1	n/a	4-0	4-0	1-2	5-2		n/a	1-0	0-1	0-0	2-1	4-1	6-0	4-4	2-0	3-1	2-1	
Foley Res.	3-3	7-0	0-2	n/a	1-0	0-1	1-7	0-0		n/a	2-2	0-2	2-1	4-1	1-5	1-6	1-0	n/a	1-2	
Gnosall Horns	n/a	n/a	n/a	n/a	2-5	n/a	1-3	1-7	1-2		n/a	n/a	n/a	2-1	1-5	0-4	n/a	n/a	n/a	0-8
Hanley Town Res.	1-0	2-2	3-0	4-1	0-0	6-4	2-2	0-0	1-2	8-0		2-2	2-1	1-2	4-1	2-4	3-1	3-0	5-0	7-1
Holt JCB	3-0	0-1	3-3	n/a	3-1	3-1	1-1	1-0	3-0	6-0	4-0		1-0	3-3	5-0	1-5	0-2	1-1	4-0	n/a
Milton Rangers Res.	0-4	0-3	1-1	3-1	3-3	1-0	0-3	2-4	0-2	n/a	1-1	3-1		1-0	1-2	2-2	3-4	3-1	1-2	2-0
Penkhull	n/a	1-0	n/a	n/a	n/a	n/a	1-3	n/a	n/a	0-4	n/a	n/a	1-0		n/a	n/a	n/a	n/a	3-0	n/a
Penkridge Town	1-0	0-1	0-5	0-0	4-1	0-0	1-6	0-3	4-4	n/a	2-2	2-1	4-1	n/a		2-2	4-1	1-3	n/a	0-2
Redgate Clayton Res.	1-1	8-1	3-2	n/a	1-0	4-1	2-3	1-1	4-2	n/a	0-2	0-2	0-2	n/a	3-3		1-0	2-0	5-2	3-0
Stallington Res.	4-1	0-2	2-0	n/a	2-3	8-1	2-3	3-3	4-1	n/a	3-0	3-1	1-0	n/a	6-2	3-2		0-1	4-0	1-1
Stone Old Alleynians	0-0	3-0	3-2	5-0	0-0	2-1	1-5	3-5	3-0	4-3	0-1	0-0	1-1	2-0	1-3	1-1			2-1	1-1
Ward Wanderers	2-2	0-1	0-3	1-2	1-0	2-3	0-1	0-3	3-0	4-1	2-2	0-3	2-5	n/a	n/a	2-3	0-1	n/a		n/a
Wedgwood Sports & Social	3-0	3-2	1-0	n/a	0-2	0-0	0-3	0-2	2-1	n/a	0-1	4-0	2-1	4-1	2-0	0-1	3-1	1-2		

Note – Bradeley, Gnosall Horns, Penkhull and Ward Wanderers withdrew during the course of the season. Their results are shown above but have been expunged from the league table

	P	W	D	L	F	A	Pts
Eccleshall Res.	30	19	7	4	90	35	64
Florence	30	19	6	5	72	31	63
Stallington Res.	30	15	8	7	74	45	53
Redgate Clayton Res.	30	16	5	9	72	49	53
Holt JCB	30	15	7	8	49	31	52
Ball Haye Green Res.	30	15	4	11	56	38	49
Hanley Town Res.	30	13	10	7	61	45	49
Wedgwood Spts/Soc.	30	12	9	9	45	39	45
Stone Old Alleynians	30	11	9	10	39	38	42
Alsagers Bank	30	11	4	15	49	72	37
Foley Res.	30	9	6	15	46	77	33
Brocton Res.	30	7	8	15	27	46	29
Milton Rangers Res.	30	6	7	17	33	55	25
Penkridge Town	30	6	7	17	42	79	25
Congleton Vale	30	7	4	19	39	76	25
Abbey Hulton Res.	30	5	7	18	28	66	22

LEAGUE CUP

FIRST ROUND
Alsagers Bank 3 Congleton Vale 2
Hanley Town Res. 3 Milton Rangers Res. 0
Penkhull 9 Gnosall Horns 0
Wedgwood Sports & Social 5 Brocton Res. 0
Wedgwood Sports & Social 3 Stone Old Alleynians 0

SECOND ROUND
Abbey Hulton United Res. 3 Penkhull 0
Ball Haye Green Res. 3 Hanley Town Res. 2
Bradeley 0 Stallington Res. 5
Foley Res. 5 Ward Wanderers 1
Holt JCB 0 Florence 1
Penkridge Town 2 Eccleshall Res. 7
Redgate Clayton Res. 5 Alsagers Bank 4

QUARTER-FINALS
Ball Haye Green Res. 7 Abbey Hulton United Res. 3 *aet*
Eccleshall Res. 2 Florence 1
Stallington Res. 5 Foley Res. 1
Wedgwood Sports & Social 3 Redgate Clayton Res. 0
Wedgwood Sports & Social 4 Redgate Clayton Res. 1 *rematch*

SEMI-FINALS
Stallington Res. 1 Eccleshall Res. 0
Wedgwood Sports & Social 0 Ball Haye Green Res. 1

FINAL
(17th March at Newcastle Town)
Stallington Res. 0 Ball Haye Green Res. 1

DIVISION ONE CONSTITUTION 2003-04

ABBEY HULTON UNITED RESERVES .. Birches Head Road, Abbey Hulton, Stoke-on-Trent, Staffordshire 01782 544232
ALSAGERS BANK .... The Drive, Alsagers Bank, Cheshire .... None
BALL HAYE GREEN RESERVES .... rear of Ball Haye Green WMC, Ball Haye Green, Leek, Staffordshire 01538 371926
BROCTON RESERVES .... Rowley Park Stadium, Averill Road, off West Road, Stafford, Staffordshire 01785 251060
CONGLETON VALE .... Back Lane, Congleton, Cheshire 01260 276975
ECCLESHALL RESERVES .... Pershall Park, Chester Road, Eccleshall, Staffordshire 01785 851351
FEATHERSTONE PRISON .... t.b.a. .... t.b.a.
FLORENCE .... Florence Colliery Sports Ground, Lightwood Road, Stoke-on-Trent, Staffordshire 01782 312881
FOLEY RESERVES .... Whitcombe Road, Meir, Stoke-on-Trent, Staffordshire 01782 595274
HANLEY TOWN RESERVES .... Abbey Lane, Abbey Hulton, Stoke-on-Trent, Staffordshire 01782 267234
HOLDITCH MINERS .... t.b.a. .... t.b.a.
HOLT JCB .... JCB Lakeside Club, Rocester, Staffordshire 01889 591057
MANOR INNE .... t.b.a. .... t.b.a.
MILTON RANGERS .... Leek Road, Milton, Stoke-on-Trent, Staffordshire .... None
PENKRIDGE TOWN .... Rodbaston Agricultural College, Penkridge, Staffordshire 01785 712209
REDGATE CLAYTON RESERVES .. Northwood Lane, Clayton, Newcastle-under-Lyme, Staffordshire 01782 717409
STALLINGTON RESERVES .. Stallington Hospital, Fulford Lane, Stallington Road, Blythe Bridge, Staffordshire 07785 338804
STONE OLD ALLEYNIANS .... Outlands Ground, Outland Road, Stone, Staffordshire .... None
WEDGWOOD SPORTS & SOCIAL .. Wedgwood Sports & Social, Barlaston, Stoke-on-Trent, Staffordshire 01782 373442

Gnosall Horns, Ward Wanderers, Penkhull and Bradeley withdrew during the course of the season. Milton Rangers come down from the Midland League so replace their reserve side. Newcomers are Featherstone Prison who have only previously played friendlies, Holditch Miners who are a merger of two Sunday sides, and Manor Inne from Newcastle, Burslem & Tunstall League. This league has now disbanded and its remaining clubs will form the rump of a new Staffs County Division Two for 2003-04.

SURREY COUNTY SENIOR LEAGUE

	AFC Guildford	Bookham	Chobham & Ottershaw	Colliers Wood United	Cranleigh	Crescent Rovers	Croydon Mu. Officers	Ditton	Farleigh Rovers	Hersham RBL	Horley Town	Netherne Village	Seelec Delta	Sheerwater	Shottermill & Haslemere	Staines Lammas	Worcester Park
AFC Guildford	P	1-1	4-0	0-3	0-2	2-0	3-0	2-1	4-0	0-4	2-2	3-1	0-1	1-2	2-1	2-1	1-1
Bookham	2-1	R	3-1	1-1	2-1	4-1	8-2	1-2	0-1	1-2	0-1	0-0	2-1	2-1	4-2	3-0	1-1
Chobham & Ottershaw	1-3	4-0	E	2-2	4-1	1-6	0-0	3-1	0-2	0-2	0-4	2-5	1-4	2-2	0-0	3-3	3-1
Colliers Wood United	1-0	3-0	6-2	M	12-0	2-4	6-1	2-2	4-2	1-1	3-2	1-0	4-0	3-2	5-0	3-2	0-1
Cranleigh	2-3	2-2	2-3	1-1	I	2-3	4-1	1-2	1-4	1-1	0-5	1-1	1-1	0-2	1-1	0-4	2-2
Crescent Rovers	1-1	1-1	5-1	1-0	8-1	E	6-1	3-5	1-4	1-2	2-0	0-0	1-1	0-5	2-0	2-4	6-1
Croydon Municipal Officers	1-1	0-1	0-5	2-4	2-4	0-0	R	1-5	0-1	1-3	0-4	1-2	2-1	2-2	2-1	3-4	2-1
Ditton	3-1	2-2	1-1	1-1	6-3	1-0	4-1		0-1	1-2	0-0	2-1	0-0	3-1	2-1	1-2	0-1
Farleigh Rovers	2-1	1-2	2-2	1-1	1-0	0-0	4-3	4-0		2-5	0-1	1-1	3-0	2-3	4-0	3-0	0-1
Hersham RBL	1-0	1-2	1-5	4-1	1-0	2-0	4-1	1-3	5-2	D	2-1	1-1	2-0	2-2	3-0	6-0	1-1
Horley Town	2-0	0-0	4-2	3-0	2-3	1-3	0-0	4-0	5-1	1-0	I	0-0	1-0	3-3	2-0	0-1	0-1
Netherne Village	0-1	1-2	0-0	1-2	W-L	1-6	5-0	2-1	2-1	4-0	1-3	V	1-2	1-0	4-0	1-2	5-1
Seelec Delta	5-0	3-1	2-3	0-0	1-3	2-4	0-0	2-3	2-1	1-2	2-2	2-2	I	0-0	7-1	3-0	1-1
Sheerwater	0-5	1-4	4-3	0-3	6-2	2-3	1-1	3-1	3-3	0-0	1-0	2-3	2-2	S	2-1	3-2	0-4
Shottermill & Haslemere	1-4	1-4	7-2	1-3	1-0	1-2	4-4	0-3	0-5	1-4	0-2	0-2	2-0	1-3	I	0-2	0-4
Staines Lammas	0-1	0-0	5-1	2-4	19-1	2-2	7-2	0-2	6-1	1-3	4-0	1-1	2-3	2-1	6-0	O	0-3
Worcester Park	1-1	1-0	1-3	0-2	5-0	4-1	4-2	4-2	2-2	1-3	0-1	L-W	2-1	4-1	2-1	1-1	N

Premier Division		P	W	D	L	F	A	Pts
Hersham RBL		32	21	6	5	71	36	69
Colliers Wood United		32	19	8	5	84	39	65
Horley Town		32	16	7	9	56	31	55
Bookham		32	15	9	8	56	40	54
Worcester Park		32	15	8	9	57	43	53
Crescent Rovers		32	15	7	10	75	54	52
Ditton		32	14	7	11	60	53	49
Netherne Village		32	13	9	10	49	38	48
AFC Guildford		32	14	6	12	50	43	48
Farleigh Rovers		32	14	6	12	61	55	48
Staines Lammas		32	14	5	13	85	59	47
Sheerwater		32	11	10	11	62	65	43
Seelec Delta		32	9	10	13	50	49	37
Chobham/Ottershaw		32	9	8	15	60	83	35
Croydon Mun. Off.		32	3	8	21	38	99	17
Cranleigh	-6	32	5	7	20	42	106	16
Shottermill/Haslemere		32	3	3	26	29	92	12

Division One		P	W	D	L	F	A	Pts
Netherne Village Res.		32	23	7	2	78	24	76
Staines Lammas Res.		32	23	1	8	92	38	70
Horley Town Res.		32	19	6	7	84	50	63
Colliers Wood U. Res.		32	18	8	6	80	35	62
Worcester Park Res.		32	17	7	8	80	53	58
Ditton Res.	-3	32	18	5	9	78	54	56
Croydon MO Res.		32	16	5	11	85	64	53
Crescent Rovers Res.		32	14	6	12	67	41	48
Sheerwater Res.		32	12	9	11	67	55	45
AFC Guildford Res.		32	13	4	15	75	73	43
Farleigh Rovers Res.		32	11	6	15	59	61	39
Bookham Res.		32	10	6	16	52	63	36
Seelec Delta Res.		32	10	6	16	51	80	36
Chobham/Ott. Res.	-3	32	11	4	17	59	74	34
Hersham RBL Res.		32	8	2	22	41	95	26
Cranleigh Res.		32	4	0	28	26	118	12
Shottermill/Has. Res.		32	3	2	27	35	131	11

LEAGUE CUP

FIRST ROUND

Seelec Delta 2 Sheerwater 2 *aet*

Sheerwater 3 Seelec Delta 2 *replay*

SECOND ROUND

Chobham & Ottershaw 0 Bookham 0 *aet*

Bookham 3 Chobham 1 *replay aet*

Colliers Wood United 1 **Sheerwater 4**

Cranleigh 1 **AFC Guildford 4**

Crescent Rovers 8 Shottermill & H. 1

Ditton 0 **Staines Lammas 1**

Farleigh Rovers 5 Worcester Park 2

Hersham RBL 5 Croydon MO 1

Netherne Village 1 Horley Town 2

(ineligible player – Horley Town expelled)

QUARTER-FINALS

AFC Guildford 3 Crescent Rovers 1 *aet*

Netherne Village 2 Hersham RBL 1

Sheerwater 2 **Farleigh Rovers 3**

Staines Lammas 6 Bookham 4

SEMI-FINALS

Farleigh Rovers 0 AFC Guildford 0 *aet*

AFC Guildford 3 **Farleigh Rovers 3**

replay aet (4-5p)

Netherne Village 3 Staines Lammas 1

FINAL

(13th May at Chipstead)

Netherne Village 2 **Farleigh Rovers 3**

DIVISION ONE CUP

FINAL

(15th May at Colliers Wood United)

Netherne Village Res. 2 Colliers Wood United Res. 1

CONSTITUTION 2003-04

(LEAGUE NOW AMALGAMATED WITH COMBINED COUNTIES LEAGUE – see P21)

SUSSEX COUNTY LEAGUE

	Arundel	Burgess Hill Town	Chichester City Utd	East Preston	Hailsham Town	Hassocks	Horsham YMCA	Littlehampton Tn	Pagham	Peacehaven & Tel.	Redhill	Ringmer	Selsey	Shoreham	Sidlesham	Sidley United	Southwick	Three Bridges	Whitehawk	Wick
Arundel		1-3	4-3	2-2	1-1	1-1	1-4	0-0	2-4	3-0	1-0	0-3	0-0	3-1	2-0	2-3	0-4	0-0	1-0	3-0
Burgess Hill Town	5-1		4-0	2-0	4-1	1-1	1-1	3-2	2-1	7-0	4-0	3-0	1-0	0-1	4-0	2-1	2-0	3-0	1-0	6-1
Chichester City United	3-1	1-0		1-3	5-2	1-1	1-4	5-1	3-1	2-0	0-0	1-2	2-0	1-0	4-1	2-1	3-1	2-4	1-1	0-1
East Preston	0-4	1-2	1-2		4-0	2-3	2-0	3-1	1-0	2-1	0-0	0-3	1-2	0-3	1-2	2-2	3-2	2-1	5-1	
Hailsham Town	1-1	0-2	2-4	3-3	D	2-0	1-0	1-1	0-1	2-3	3-0	4-0	0-1	1-3	0-1	1-2	0-3	0-0	0-1	2-1
Hassocks	3-0	1-2	1-1	2-3	2-0	I	2-2	3-0	2-1	6-2	1-2	0-3	1-4	2-1	2-1	1-0	2-4	3-1	0-2	5-0
Horsham YMCA	4-0	0-0	3-3	0-2	1-4	2-1	V	2-1	5-2	2-0	2-0	1-4	0-0	6-0	4-1	0-1	0-1	5-3	1-1	3-0
Littlehampton Town	0-0	0-3	1-5	2-1	1-2	3-0	0-2	I	0-2	3-1	2-2	1-0	0-3	1-2	1-2	1-2	0-5	0-4	2-2	
Pagham	2-1	0-1	1-1	1-0	0-0	4-0	4-0	5-2	S	1-1	0-2	1-1	1-1	2-0	1-0	0-1	0-1	4-2	1-2	7-2
Peacehaven & Telscombe	2-1	0-3	0-5	2-1	1-4	2-1	0-1	1-1	1-3	I	4-1	2-2	0-1	1-2	1-3	2-0	0-7	0-2	7-3	
Redhill	2-1	4-1	0-1	2-0	1-2	3-5	1-3	1-0	2-0	4-1	O	4-2	0-2	1-2	0-2	1-0	0-3	1-1	2-1	
Ringmer	1-0	1-2	1-1	3-0	1-0	1-3	2-1	1-0	0-0			N	1-4	3-0	3-3	0-5	0-0	4-2	0-5	2-1
Selsey	0-1	1-1	0-2	1-2	2-2	4-2	0-0	2-2	1-1	1-1	0-1	1-1		5-0	2-3	1-2	0-3	1-0	2-1	
Shoreham	1-3	1-0	0-0	4-1	5-0	2-2	1-1	1-0	1-4	0-2	3-0	0-0	1-1	O	4-0	1-1	3-2	2-4	0-1	3-3
Sidlesham	1-1	0-4	1-0	0-2	1-3	5-3	3-2	2-2	2-2	5-1	2-0	1-1	1-0	1-0	N	1-0	2-1	4-1	2-1	1-2
Sidley United	2-0	0-2	2-5	1-1	1-0	1-1	1-2	6-0	0-5	1-2	0-1	0-0	1-0	2-1	4-0	E	3-1	2-2	0-1	3-1
Southwick	2-2	1-2	0-0	0-4	1-2	3-0	1-4	0-3	4-2	1-0	0-1	5-1	1-1	3-0	0-3	2-0		1-3	4-1	6-2
Three Bridges	4-4	1-4	2-2	2-1	0-2	1-1	1-3	2-5	0-0	1-1	3-1	1-3	3-2	1-4	5-2	1-3			4-1	6-2
Whitehawk	0-1	3-2	1-2	3-2	3-1	0-1	1-4	3-1	1-2	2-3	7-1	2-1	3-0	7-0	1-1	1-0	0-2	2-1		6-0
Wick	3-1	2-4	1-4	3-1	1-0	0-1	2-4	1-1	1-5	1-2	4-4	0-1	2-1	1-4	2-3	1-2	3-2	2-5	0-5	

Division One

	P	W	D	L	F	A	Pts
Burgess Hill Town	38	29	4	5	97	27	91
Whitehawk	38	22	4	12	79	41	70
Horsham YMCA	38	21	6	11	101	51	69
Chichester City U.	38	20	9	9	79	51	69
Sidlesham	38	20	6	12	65	62	66
Southwick	38	18	6	14	67	50	60
Ringmer	38	17	9	12	55	56	60
Hassocks	38	16	8	14	67	65	56
Pagham	38	16	7	15	69	52	55
East Preston	38	16	6	16	66	54	54
Selsey	38	14	11	13	59	44	53
Redhill	38	16	5	17	53	62	53
Sidley United	38	15	6	17	55	51	51
Three Bridges	38	14	7	17	88	83	49
Hailsham Town	38	13	8	17	54	60	47
Shoreham	38	13	6	19	54	69	45
Arundel	38	11	11	16	50	65	44
Peacehaven & Tel.	38	9	5	24	43	95	32
Wick	38	7	5	26	51	123	26
Littlehampton T.	38	4	9	25	34	110	21

JOHN O'HARA LEAGUE CUP (Division One and Two clubs)

FIRST ROUND
Chichester 3 Seaford Town 2
East Grinstead Town 3 Redhill 0
Littlehampton 1 Rye & Iden 4
Steyning Town 3 Arundel 1
Whitehawk 3 Oving 2 *aet*
Wick 2 Saltdean United 5

SECOND ROUND
East Preston 3 Worthing United 0
Eastbourne Town 2 Shoreham 4
Horsham YMCA 2 Broadbridge H. 0
Mile Oak 1 Hailsham Town 0
Oakwood 1 Southwick 2 *aet*
Peacehaven 2 Crawley Down 0
Pease Pottage Village 1 Sidlesham 4
Ringmer 2 Westfield 2 *aet*
Westfield 4 Ringmer 0 *replay*
Rye & Iden 6 Whitehawk 4 *aet*
Saltdean United 3 Chichester 5
Selsey 5 Eastbourne United 0
Shinewater Association 2 Pagham 5
Sidley United 1 Lancing 2
Steyning Town 2 East Grinstead 0
Three Bridges 0 Burgess Hill 2
Wealden 1 Hassocks 2

THIRD ROUND
Burgess Hill Town 3 Horsham YMCA 2
East Preston 1 Lancing 0
Mile Oak 2 Peacehaven & Telscombe 4
Selsey 2 Hassocks 1
Shoreham 3 Chichester City Utd 0
Southwick 1 Rye & Iden United 2
Steyning Town 0 Pagham 2
Westfield 0 Sidlesham 3

QUARTER-FINALS
Burgess Hill Town 1 Sidlesham 2
Rye & Iden Utd 3 Peacehaven & Telscombe 0
Selsey 3 East Preston 0
Shoreham 3 Pagham 2

SEMI-FINALS
Rye & Iden United 1 Sidlesham 4
(at Hassocks)
Shoreham 0 Selsey 1 *(at Wick)*

FINAL
(18th April at Pagham)
Selsey 2 Sidlesham 0

DIVISION ONE CONSTITUTION 2003-04

ARUNDEL .... Mill Road, Arundel, West Sussex 01903 882548
CHICHESTER CITY UNITED .... Oaklands Park, Chichester, West Sussex 01243 785978
EAST GRINSTEAD TOWN .... East Court, East Grinstead, West Sussex 01342 325885
EAST PRESTON .... Roundstone Recreation Ground, East Preston, West Sussex 01903 776026
EASTBOURNE TOWN .... The Saffrons, Compton Place Road, Eastbourne, East Sussex 01323 723734
HAILSHAM TOWN .... The Beaconsfield, Western Road, Hailsham, East Sussex 01323 840446
HASSOCKS .... The Beacon, Brighton Road, Hassocks, West Sussex 01273 846040
HORSHAM YMCA .... Gorings Mead, off Queen Street, Horsham, West Sussex 01403 252689
PAGHAM .... Nyetimber Lane, Pagham, West Sussex 01243 266112
REDHILL .... Kiln Brow, Three Arch Road, Redhill, West Sussex 01737 762129
RINGMER .... Caburn Ground, Anchor Field, Ringmer, East Sussex 01273 812738
RYE & IDEN UNITED .... Sydney Allnut Pavillion, Rye Cricket & Football Salts, Rye, East Sussex 01797 223855
SELSEY .... High Street Ground, Selsey, Chichester, West Sussex 01243 603420
SHOREHAM .... Middle Road, Shoreham, West Sussex 01273 454261
SIDLESHAM .... Recreation Ground, Sidlesham, Chichester, West Sussex 01243 641538
SIDLEY UNITED .... Gullivers, Glovers Lane, Sidley, East Sussex 01424 217078
SOUTHWICK .... Old Barn Way, off Manor Hall Road, Southwick, Brighton, East Sussex 01273 701010
ST LEONARDS .... The Firs, Elphinstone Road, Hastings, East Sussex .... 01424 434755. Fax: 01424 716362
THREE BRIDGES .... Jubilee Field, Bridges, Crawley, West Sussex 01293 442000
WHITEHAWK .... Enclosed Ground, East Brighton Park, Brighton, East Sussex 01273 609736

Burgess Hill Town are promoted to the Southern League replaced by St Leonards. Peacehaven & Telscombe, Wick and Littlehampton Town drop to Division Two replaced by Rye & Iden United, Eastbourne Town and East Grinstead Town.

	Broadbridge H.	Crawley Down	East Grinstead	Eastbourne T.	Eastbourne U.	Lancing	Mile Oak	Oakwood	Oving	Pease Pottage	Rye & Iden Utd	Saltdean United	Seaford Town	Shinewater Ass.	Steyning Town	Wealden	Westfield	Worthing Utd
Broadbridge Heath		1-1	0-1	0-5	3-4	2-1	1-5	1-1	4-1	1-2	1-2	2-5	2-2	2-1	2-1	5-4	4-3	4-0
Crawley Down Village	0-2		1-1	1-4	1-1	1-2	1-1	2-1	2-1	6-1	0-0	3-1	3-0	5-1	0-4	0-2	0-1	1-0
East Grinstead Town	3-0	2-2		0-0	0-3	0-0	4-3	1-1	2-0	3-0	1-1	6-0	2-1	5-0	3-1	3-0	0-0	0-1
Eastbourne Town	4-2	2-0	1-1	D	5-1	2-0	4-1	3-1	3-1	2-0	1-1	3-0	2-0	2-1	4-0	0-0	4-1	3-1
Eastbourne United	3-0	2-1	2-3	0-3	I	0-2	5-1	1-2	3-2	2-0	0-3	0-4	2-1	4-3	0-1	3-3	2-2	1-1
Lancing	2-1	1-1	2-4	2-1	0-0	V	1-0	4-4	3-1	2-0	0-1	1-1	0-2	1-1	1-1	3-1	2-2	0-1
Mile Oak	4-0	0-0	0-5	0-7	2-1	2-5	I	0-3	1-1	4-1	0-1	1-2	2-4	4-1	3-2	0-0	0-1	4-3
Oakwood	2-0	2-0	3-0	1-3	2-6	3-2	2-0	S	3-1	3-0	0-2	4-1	3-1	2-1	2-4	3-4	1-3	4-0
Oving	3-1	1-2	2-2	0-2	1-3	1-3	3-0	3-1	I	2-4	0-1	0-6	2-0	3-1	1-4	0-5	0-1	2-5
Pease Pottage Village	1-2	3-0	2-1	1-7	1-4	5-1	0-0	2-1	5-1	O	1-1	0-3	0-4	1-2	0-0	1-3	0-2	1-3
Rye & Iden United	2-0	2-1	1-2	3-6	3-2	2-0	1-0	3-2	1-0	4-0	N	2-5	3-2	1-3	3-0	7-2	3-0	3-0
Saltdean United	2-5	1-1	1-1	1-1	1-3	3-0	4-1	1-2	5-0	0-1	2-3		0-1	6-2	0-2	2-1	0-0	0-2
Seaford Town	1-1	2-1	2-2	1-5	2-0	0-2	1-1	1-3	1-0	3-0	1-2	1-2	T	0-1	0-0	0-1	3-3	5-1
Shinewater Association	2-1	3-1	2-2	1-2	0-0	0-0	1-0	1-0	3-0	1-1	0-3	2-5	1-1	W	1-0	3-1	0-2	1-0
Steyning Town	1-2	1-0	5-0	0-2	2-1	1-1	2-0	3-3	0-0	1-2	0-1	0-2	0-4	1-1	O	2-1	1-0	3-0
Wealden	1-0	3-1	1-2	2-0	1-3	4-1	3-4	1-1	3-2	4-0	2-4	2-0	3-2	1-2	1-1		1-1	0-1
Westfield	2-2	1-1	0-3	3-3	1-0	1-2	3-1	0-3	3-1	4-1	0-1	2-0	1-0	0-2	1-4	3-3		6-1
Worthing United	2-0	1-3	1-2	1-1	3-1	0-0	1-2	0-1	1-1	2-1	2-1	3-4	2-2	0-2	0-3	1-0	1-0	2-3

Division Two	P	W	D	L	F	A	Pts
Rye & Iden United	34	27	4	3	77	35	85
Eastbourne Town	34	25	7	2	97	28	82
East Grinstead Town	34	17	12	5	67	39	63
Oakwood	34	17	5	12	70	55	56
Saltdean United	34	15	6	13	70	55	51
Westfield	34	13	10	11	54	53	49
Wealden	34	14	6	14	64	60	48
Eastbourne United	34	14	6	14	63	60	48
Lancing	34	12	11	11	47	49	47
Steyning Town	34	13	7	14	47	43	46
Shinewater Association	34	13	7	14	46	59	46
Seaford Town	34	11	7	16	51	51	40
Broadbridge Heath	34	11	5	18	54	74	38
Worthing United	34	11	5	18	41	64	38
Crawley Down Village	34	9	10	15	43	51	37
Mile Oak	34	9	6	19	47	74	33
Pease Pottage Village	34	9	4	21	38	79	31
Oving	34	5	4	25	37	84	19

DIVISION TWO CUP

FIRST ROUND
Crawley Down Village 0 Oakwood 6
Shinewater Association 4 Mile Oak 0
Wealden 1 Broadbridge Heath 0
SECOND ROUND
East Grinstead Town 1 Steyning Town 6
Eastbourne Town 1 Westfield 2
Eastbourne United 2 Wealden 1
Mile Oak 2 Oving 1
Oakwood 4 Saltdean United 0
Pease Pottage Village 0 Shinewater Association 1
Rye & Iden United 2 Lancing 1
Seaford Town 1 Worthing United 2 *aet*

QUARTER-FINALS
Oakwood 6 Mile Oak 0
Rye & Iden United 1 Eastbourne United 0
Shinewater Association 1 Worthing United 3
Steyning Town 1 Westfield 2
SEMI-FINALS
Rye & Iden United 2 Worthing United 1
(at Eastbourne Town)
Westfield 1 Oakwood 0
(at Eastbourne Town)
FINAL
(18th April)
at Eastbourne Town)
Westfield 0 Rye & Iden United 1

WWW.NLNEWSDESK.CO.UK

DIVISION TWO CONSTITUTION 2003-04

BROADBRIDGE HEATH . . . . The Sports Centre, Broadbridge Heath, Horsham, West Sussex 01403 265871
CRAWLEY DOWN VILLAGE . . . . . . Haven Sportsfield, Hophurst Lane, Crawley Down, West Sussex 01342 717140
EASTBOURNE UNITED ASSOCIATION . . . . . . The Oval, Channel View Road, Eastbourne 01323 726989
HAYWARDS HEATH TOWN . . . . Hanbury Park Stadium, Haywards Heath, West Sussex 01444 412837
LANCING . . . . Culver Road, Lancing, West Sussex 01903 764398
LITTLEHAMPTON TOWN . . . . The Sportsfield, St Flora's Road, Littlehampton, West Sussex 01903 713944
MIDHURST & EASEBOURNE UNITED . . . . . . Rotherfield, Dodsley Lane, Easebourne, West Sussex 01730 816557
MILE OAK . . . . Mile Oak Recreation Ground, Graham Avenue, Mile Oak, Sussex 01273 423854
OAKWOOD . . . . Oakwood Sports & Social Club, Tinsley Lane, Three Bridges, West Sussex 01293 515742
PEACEHAVEN & TELSCOMBE . . . . Piddinghoe Avenue, Peacehaven, East Sussex 01273 582471
PEASE POTTAGE VILLAGE . . . . Finches Field, Pease Pottage, Mid-Sussex 01293 538651
SALTDEAN UNITED . . . . Hill Park, Coombe Vale, Saltdean, East Sussex 01273 309898
SEAFORD TOWN . . . . The Crouch, Seaford, East Sussex 01323 892221
STEYNING TOWN . . . . The Shooting Field, Steyning, West Sussex 01903 812228
WEALDEN . . . . Wealden Sports Club, Eastbourne Road, Uckfield, East Sussex 01825 890905
WESTFIELD . . . . The Parish Field, Westfield, Hastings, East Sussex 01424 751011
WICK . . . . Crabtree Park, Coomes Way, Wick, Littlehampton, West Sussex 01903 713535
WORTHING UNITED . . . . Robert Albon Memorial Ground, Lyons Way, Worthing, West Sussex 01903 234466

Rye & Iden United, Eastbourne Town and East Grinstead Town are promoted to Division One replacing Wick, Peacehaven & Telscombe and Littlehampton Town. Oving drop to Division Three from which Haywards Heath Town and Midhurst & Easebourne United move up. Eastbourne United and Shinewater Association amalgamate to create Eastbourne United Association.

NORMAN WINGATE TROPHY *(Div One champions v John O'Hara Cup holders)*	**ROY HAYDEN TROPHY** *(Div One champions v Sussex Senior Cup holders)*
(10th August at Horsham YMCA)	*(27th July at Eastbourne Borough)*
Burgess Hill Town 3 Horsham YMCA 2	Burgess Hill Town 0 **Eastbourne Borough** 1

	Bexhill United	Bosham	Crowborough Athletic	Forest	Franklands Village	Haywards Heath Town	Hurstpierpoint	Ifield	Lingfield	Midhurst & Easebourne	Newhaven	St Francis Rangers	Storrington	Uckfield Town	Upper Beeding
Bexhill United	D	13-0	2-5	5-0	1-2	0-1	0-4	1-5	3-2	0-2	1-0	1-1	3-3	3-0	1-0
Bosham	0-5	I	0-10	1-4	1-4	0-5	0-4	1-2	0-3	0-3	1-4	1-3	2-1	3-1	1-1
Crowborough A.	7-0	4-0	V	3-1	0-0	1-2	3-0	5-1	8-0	2-1	6-0	0-1	1-0	3-0	1-2
Forest	7-0	2-3	0-1	I	0-0	1-4	1-1	0-1	1-4	2-7	5-3	1-1	1-0	4-2	4-0
Franklands Vill.	4-1	7-0	2-0	2-0	S	0-2	0-0	2-0	2-0	3-1	2-1	2-4	2-2	2-0	2-1
Haywards Heath	2-2	0-2	3-3	3-3	3-1	I	0-0	3-4	6-2	2-2	5-2	1-1	4-1	0-0	2-0
Hurstpierpoint	1-0	2-0	2-4	2-4	1-1	1-1	O	0-2	5-1	0-3	0-3	1-1	0-2	3-2	2-0
Ifield	1-1	1-1	5-4	1-0	2-1	0-2	0-4	N	0-2	0-1	3-1	0-2	2-1	7-1	0-0
Lingfield	2-0	1-2	1-1	3-2	0-0	0-4	3-2	0-1		0-4	1-0	1-5	2-1	3-1	1-3
Midhurst & E.	2-2	4-0	1-3	2-1	1-0	1-1	1-0	4-0	4-0		1-2	3-0	2-1	4-0	1-1
Newhaven	1-0	5-3	2-1	1-1	1-1	1-3	2-2	2-2	4-0	1-5	T	4-2	1-3	7-0	1-2
St Francis Rgrs	2-0	2-2	1-2	2-2	5-0	1-8	2-0	2-2	2-3	2-3	1-3	H	3-5	3-2	4-2
Storrington	1-2	5-1	1-3	1-2	0-2	0-4	0-3	6-0	2-2	0-6	1-3	2-1	R	4-1	3-1
Uckfield Town	1-2	5-1	1-3	1-3	1-2	2-3	4-1	2-0	0-1	3-4	3-0	0-3	2-4	E	3-1
Upper Beeding	0-4	1-4	3-3	1-4	2-2	0-2	0-0	1-3	2-0	0-5	1-1	1-3	3-2	2-1	E

DIV. THREE CUP

FIRST ROUND
Bosham 0 **Storrington** 7
Haywards Heath Town 1 Ifield 0
Hurstpierpoint 2 Newhaven 2 *aet*
Newhaven 3 Hurstpierpoint 2 *replay*
Midhurst & Easebourne Utd 5 Forest 1
St Francis Rangers 4 Lingfield 2
Uckfield Town 1 **Crowborough Athletic** 2
Upper Beeding 6 Bexhill United 0

QUARTER-FINALS
Franklands Village 2 Crowborough 2 *aet*
Crowborough 3 Franklands Vill. 1 *replay*
Newhaven 0 **Midhurst & Easebourne** 4
St Francis Rangers 0 **Storrington** 1
Upper Beeding 0 **Haywards Heath Town** 3

SEMI-FINALS
Haywards Heath Town 2 **Midhurst & Easebourne Utd** 3 *aet (at Horsham YMCA)*
Storrington 2 **Crowborough Athletic** 6 *aet (at Burgess Hill Town)*

FINAL
(18th April at Horsham YMCA)
Midhurst & Easebourne Utd 1
Crowborough Athletic 0

Division Three	P	W	D	L	F	A	Pts
Midhurst & Ease.	28	20	4	4	80	26	64
Haywards Heath	28	17	9	2	76	31	60
Crowborough Ath.	28	18	4	6	87	32	58
Franklands Village	28	14	8	6	48	30	50
Ifield	28	13	5	10	47	50	44
St Francis Rangers	28	12	7	9	60	52	43
Newhaven	28	12	5	11	58	54	41
Forest	28	10	6	12	56	55	36
Lingfield	28	11	3	14	38	65	36
Bexhill United	28	10	5	13	53	56	35
Hurstpierpoint	28	8	8	12	37	44	32
Storrington	28	9	4	15	53	59	31
Upper Beeding	28	5	8	15	31	61	23
Bosham	28	6	3	19	30	102	21
Uckfield Town	28	5	1	22	39	76	16

RESERVE DIVISIONS CHALLENGE CUP

FINAL *(24th April at Arundel)*
Burgess Hill Town Res. 3 Selsey Res. 2

DIVISION THREE CONSTITUTION 2003-04

BEXHILL UNITED .... The Polegrove, Bexhill-on-Sea, East Sussex 01424 220732
BOSHAM .... Recreation Ground, Walton Lane, Bosham, West Sussex 01243 574011
CROWBOROUGH ATHLETIC . Alderbrook Recreation Ground, Fermor Road, Crowborough, East Sussex 01892 661893
FOREST .... Roffey Sports & Social Club, Spooners Road, Roffey, West Sussex 01403 210221
FRANKLANDS VILLAGE .. Hardy Memorial Playing Field, Franklands Village, Haywards Heath, West Sussex 01444 440138
HURSTPIERPOINT .... Fairfield Recreation Ground, Cuckfield Road, Hurstpierpoint, West Sussex 01273 834783
IFIELD EDWARDS .... Edwards Sports & Social Club, Ifield Green, Rusper Road, Crawley, West Sussex .... None
LINGFIELD .... Godstone Road, Lingfield, Surrey 01342 834269
NEWHAVEN .... Recreation Ground, Fort Road, Newhaven, East Sussex 01273 513940
OVING .... Village Playing Field, Highfield Lane, Oving, Chichester, West Sussex 01243 778900
ST FRANCIS RANGERS .... Deaks Lane, Ansty, West Sussex 01444 454010
STORRINGTON .... Recreation Ground, Storrington, West Sussex 01903 745860
UCKFIELD TOWN .... Victoria Pleasure Grounds, Uckfield, East Sussex 01825 769400
UPPER BEEDING .... Memorial Playing Field, High Street, Upper Beeding, West Sussex .... None
WADHURST UNITED .... Sparrow Green Rec., South View Road, Wadhurst, East Sussex 01892 783527

Haywards Heath Town and Midhurst & Easebourne United are promoted to Division Two. Wadhurst United arrive from the East Sussex League. Ifield merge with Crawley & District League side Edwards Sports to create Ifield Edwards.

Reserve Premier	P	W	D	L	F	A	Pts
Eastbourne B. Res.	32	25	4	3	107	28	79
Burgess Hill Res.	32	22	4	6	83	36	70
Sidley United Res.	32	19	1	12	72	54	58
Lewes Res.	32	17	5	10	81	56	56
Hassocks Res.	32	16	7	9	61	50	55
Hailsham Res.	32	16	6	10	60	51	54
Three Bridges Res.	32	15	6	11	72	53	51
East Preston Res.	32	15	6	11	72	61	51
Horsham YM. Res.	32	15	4	13	66	60	49
Chichester CU Res.	32	14	4	14	58	61	46
Eastbourne T. Res.	32	13	6	13	62	59	45
Pagham Res.	32	13	6	13	50	61	45
Shoreham Res.	32	12	3	17	48	61	39
Selsey Res.	32	7	4	21	37	80	25
Littlehampton Res.	32	8	1	23	46	103	25
Lancing Res.	32	6	2	24	44	109	20
Peacehaven Res.	32	3	3	26	35	71	12

Reserve Div. West	P	W	D	L	F	A	Pts
Whitehawk Res.	28	21	3	4	93	30	66
Mile Oak Res.	28	20	4	4	77	25	64
Broadbridge H. Res.	28	18	4	6	83	45	58
Arundel Res.	28	15	6	7	75	44	51
Steyning Town Res.	28	15	4	9	56	48	49
Franklands V. Res.	28	14	7	7	50	47	49
Southwick Res.	28	14	1	13	52	43	43
Sidlesham Res.	28	11	6	11	54	39	39
Worthing Utd Res.	28	11	6	11	50	47	39
Forest Res.	28	10	5	13	43	63	35
Wick Res.	28	8	2	18	50	81	26
St Francis Rgrs Res.	28	7	3	18	47	77	24
Storrington Res.	28	6	3	19	25	66	21
Oving Res.	28	6	2	20	30	86	20
Haywards Heath Res.	28	5	2	21	40	84	17

Reserve Div. East	P	W	D	L	F	A	Pts
East Grinstead Res.	28	18	3	7	84	41	57
Rye & Iden Utd Res.	28	18	3	7	60	39	57
Ringmer Res.	28	16	5	7	56	44	53
Oakwood Res.	28	16	3	9	73	42	51
Westfield Res.	28	15	3	10	72	43	48
Lingfield Res.	28	13	5	10	60	46	44
Seaford Town Res.	28	10	8	10	40	43	38
Redhill Res.	28	11	4	13	65	65	37
Saltdean Utd Res.	28	11	4	13	51	62	37
Eastbourne U. Res.	28	10	6	12	44	57	36
Shinewater Res.	28	10	5	13	62	64	35
Wealden Res.	28	9	8	11	57	67	35
Crawley Down Res.	28	10	2	16	47	69	32
Crowborough Res.	28	7	4	17	51	74	25
Newhaven Res.	28	3	3	22	29	95	12

UNITED COUNTIES LEAGUE

	Blackstones	Boston Town	Bourne Town	Buckingham	Cogenhoe Utd	Daventry T.	Deeping Rgrs	Desborough	Ford Sports	Holbeach Utd	Kempston R.	Long Buckby	Newport Pag.	N'pton Spen.	Raunds Town	St Neots Town	Stewarts & L.	Stotfold	Woodford Utd	Wootton BC	Yaxley
Blackstones		3-3	1-3	0-2	1-1	2-3	2-2	4-0	2-2	0-2	2-0	4-1	2-3	3-1	6-1	1-2	1-1	1-0	0-0	2-3	0-3
Boston Town	1-1		3-2	3-1	1-0	8-0	2-1	1-1	0-2	1-4	3-2	0-0	1-2	2-0	2-0	3-0	0-1	0-0	3-0	0-1	3-2
Bourne Town	0-1	0-2	*P*	2-6	3-0	0-4	2-2	1-0	3-3	1-3	1-2	4-0	1-4	1-4	1-3	1-2	1-1	1-2	0-4	0-3	0-3
Buckingham Town	2-0	4-0	2-0	*R*	2-1	4-1	6-1	0-0	3-0	0-0	3-0	2-2	1-1	1-6	1-2	6-0	1-4	0-5	4-0	3-0	7-2
Cogenhoe United	3-0	1-0	3-3	0-5	*E*	1-1	1-2	7-3	4-0	0-2	2-2	2-0	3-2	2-3	0-2	6-1	3-1	0-0	2-1	2-1	2-0
Daventry Town	3-0	0-1	1-2	3-0	3-2	*M*	0-1	0-0	4-1	2-1	3-2	0-0	0-3	0-1	3-1	2-0	1-1	0-3	0-2	0-2	2-0
Deeping Rangers	3-2	3-0	2-0	3-0	2-1	1-0	*I*	2-2	2-2	0-0	0-3	3-2	1-1	2-0	2-1	4-2	4-0	3-3	1-1	1-2	0-0
Desborough Town	1-3	0-2	1-2	2-2	2-0	1-1	2-0	*E*	3-3	0-2	2-2	2-1	0-3	1-2	3-2	0-5	1-2	1-1	2-1	1-3	0-1
Ford Sports Daventry	3-3	4-1	1-0	0-2	0-3	1-1	0-4	1-1	*R*	0-1	1-1	1-1	1-1	1-1	1-1	1-1	1-1	1-1	2-1	2-1	0-1
Holbeach United	3-1	5-0	2-2	2-1	3-1	5-1	2-1	0-0	0-0		2-1	6-0	1-0	1-0	1-0	2-0	1-0	0-0	1-0	2-0	2-0
Kempston Rovers	2-5	0-1	1-2	0-6	0-3	2-3	0-3	0-2	0-4	0-5		5-0	1-7	0-2	3-0	2-0	1-5	3-0	0-0	3-0	0-2
Long Buckby	0-2	1-0	0-3	2-1	1-4	2-2	0-4	0-3	1-1	0-1	1-2	*D*	1-1	0-5	0-5	1-0	0-5	2-8	0-2	0-5	0-4
Newport Pagnell Town	4-0	2-1	8-1	2-1	3-1	6-1	6-1	2-0	2-1	2-2	5-0	4-0	*I*	3-2	4-0	7-1	1-2	4-1	4-0	1-1	1-3
Northampton Spencer	1-4	3-2	0-4	1-1	0-2	1-1	2-0	4-1	1-4	2-1	2-0	1-1	0-1	*V*	1-1	0-1	2-0	2-5	1-3	0-0	1-0
Raunds Town	3-1	0-1	3-0	2-2	0-2	1-1	1-2	1-2	3-4	2-2	1-0	5-0	0-3	1-0	*I*	2-1	0-0	0-2	2-1	2-0	2-1
St Neots Town	2-0	2-1	6-0	1-0	1-1	1-1	0-1	2-0	2-0	0-1	4-0	1-0	0-1	0-1	4-0	*S*	1-3	2-1	0-1	0-4	1-3
Stewarts & Lloyds Corby	2-1	1-0	6-1	0-1	0-3	1-2	3-2	2-4	2-5	2-0	3-1	0-0	2-1	2-0	3-2	2-1	*I*	2-3	3-0	0-2	4-1
Stotfold	1-4	0-3	2-2	0-1	2-3	2-3	3-1	1-1	3-1	1-2	3-0	3-5	2-0	0-3	0-2	0-4	0-4	*O*	1-1	0-2	
Woodford United	2-3	0-2	1-0	0-3	2-0	3-0	4-1	0-0	2-1	0-3	6-0	0-0	4-1	3-1	2-1	0-1	0-3	2-2	*N*	0-3	1-4
Wootton Blue Cross	2-1	2-0	1-1	1-2	1-1	1-1	0-1	2-1	2-0	4-0	2-0	1-1	1-0	0-0	2-2	4-1	3-1	3-1			1-2
Yaxley	2-1	2-0	1-1	1-2	1-1	1-1	0-1	8-1	5-0	2-1	2-0	4-0	2-1	1-1	1-0	0-0	2-2	4-1	3-1	1-2	

Premier Division

	P	W	D	L	F	A	Pts
Holbeach United	40	28	8	4	80	25	92
Newport Pagnell T.	40	27	5	8	118	43	86
Wootton Blue Cross	40	22	10	8	72	32	76
Buckingham Town	40	21	8	11	90	50	71
Deeping Rangers	40	20	9	11	68	58	69
Stewarts & Lloyds	40	21	5	14	72	56	68
Yaxley	40	20	7	13	72	52	67
Boston Town	40	20	5	15	62	55	65
Cogenhoe United	40	18	7	15	75	59	61
Daventry Town	40	15	11	14	55	66	56
Ford Sports Daventry	40	13	14	13	62	67	53
Northampton Spencer	40	14	10	16	52	60	52
St Neots Town	40	16	4	20	59	69	52
Woodford United	40	15	7	18	50	60	52
Raunds Town	40	15	6	19	52	58	51
Blackstones	40	13	9	18	72	74	48
Stotfold	40	11	13	16	67	69	46
Desborough Town	40	10	13	17	48	75	43
Bourne Town	40	8	8	24	50	94	32
Long Buckby	40	3	10	27	21	107	19
Kempston Rovers	40	4	4	32	34	102	16

LEAGUE CUP

PRELIMINARY ROUND
Boston Town 4 Cogenhoe United 1
Buckingham Town 3 Olney 1
Harrowby Utd 3 Woodford Utd 0
Kempston 2 Stew. & Lloyds 1 *aet*
Northampton Spencer 0 Wootton Blue Cross 1
Raunds Town 3 Sileby Rangers 2

FIRST ROUND
Blisworth 0 St Neots Town 1
Boston Town 6 Whitworths 1
Bourne Town 1 Deeping Rangers 0
Buckingham Town 3 Holbeach 2
Bugbrooke 1 Harrowby United 3
Desborough 1 Daventry Town 4
Eynesbury 5 Burton Park Wdrs 0
Irchester 3 Raunds Town 5 *aet*
Long Buckby 0 Rothwell Corinthians 1
Newport Pagnell (w/o) v Wellingborough Town (scr.)
ON Chenecks 1 Blackstones 6
St Ives Town 2 Cottingham 3
Stotfold 0 Kempston Rovers 4
Thrapston Town 1 Potton United 0
Wootton BC 2 Ford Sports 3
Yaxley 4 Higham Town 1

SECOND ROUND
Blackstones 2 Daventry Town 0
Boston Town 4 Rothwell Corinthians 0
Buckingham Town 3 Harrowby United 1
Cottingham 2 Newport Pagnell 4
Eynesbury Rovers 4 Kempston Rovers 2
Raunds Town 1 Bourne Town 0
St Neots Town 2 Yaxley 2 *aet* (3-2p)
Thrapston Town 4 Ford Sports Daventry 6

QUARTER-FINALS
Blackstones 1 Eynesbury Rovers 0
Boston 1 Buckingham Town 3
Newport Pagnell Town 2 Ford Sports Daventry 3
St Neots Town 1 Raunds Town 0

SEMI-FINALS
Buckingham Town 5 St Neots 1
Ford Spts Daventry 1 Blackstones 2

FINAL
(30th April at Northampton Spencer)
Buckingham Town 0 Blackstones 4

PREMIER DIVISION CONSTITUTION 2003-04

BLACKSTONES .... Lincoln Road, Stamford, Lincolnshire 01780 57835
BOSTON TOWN .... The Stadium, Tattershall Road, Boston, Lincolnshire 01205 365470
BOURNE TOWN .... Abbey Lawn, Abbey Road, Bourne, Lincolnshire 01778 422292
BUCKINGHAM TOWN .... Ford Meadow, Ford Street, Buckingham, Buckinghamshire 01280 816257
COGENHOE UNITED .... Compton Park, Brafield Road, Cogenhoe, Northants 01604 890521
DAVENTRY TOWN .... Elderstubbs, Staverton Road, Daventry, Northants 01327 706286
DEEPING RANGERS .... Outgang Road, Market Deeping, Lincolnshire 01778 344701
DESBOROUGH TOWN .... Waterworks Field, Braybrooke Road, Desborough, Northants 01536 761350
FORD SPORTS DAVENTRY .... Royal Oak Way, Daventry, Northants 01327 704914
HARROWBY UNITED .... Harrowby Fields, Harrowby Lane, Grantham, Lincolnshire 01476 590822
HOLBEACH UNITED .... Carters Park, Park Road, Holbeach, Lincolnshire 01406 424761
LONG BUCKBY .... Station Road, Long Buckby, Northants 01327 842682
NEWPORT PAGNELL TOWN .... Willen Road, Newport Pagnell, Buckinghamshire 01908 611993
NORTHAMPTON SPENCER .... Kingsthorpe Mill, Studland Road, Kingsthorpe, Northampton, Northants 01604 718898
RAUNDS TOWN .... Kiln Park, London Road, Raunds, Wellingborough, Northants .... 01933 623351 / 460941
SPALDING UNITED .... Halley Stewart Field, Winfrey Avenue, Spalding, Lincolnshire 01775 713328
ST NEOTS TOWN .... Rowley Park, Cambridge Road, St Neots, Cambridgeshire 01480 470012
STEWARTS & LLOYDS CORBY .... Recreation Ground, Occupation Road, Corby, Northants 01536 401497
STOTFOLD .... Roker Park, The Green, Stotfold, Hitchin, Hertfordshire 01462 730765
WOODFORD UNITED .... Byfield Road, Woodford Halse, Northants 01327 263734
WOOTTON BLUE CROSS .... Weston Park, Bedford Road, Wootton, Bedfordshire 01234 767662
YAXLEY .... Leading Drove, off Holme Road, Yaxley, Peterborough, Cambridgeshire 01733 244928

Spalding United are relegated from the Southern League. Kempton Rovers drop to Division One replaced by Harrowby United.

	Blisworth	Bugbrooke St Michaels	Burton Park Wanderers	Cottingham	Eynesbury Rovers	Harrowby United	Higham Town	Irchester United	N'pton ON Cheneks	Olney Town	Potton United	Rothwell Corinthians	Sileby Rangers	St Ives Town	Thrapston Town	Wellingboro. Whitworths
Blisworth		3-1	2-2	0-3	1-8	2-2	0-1	0-3	1-3	1-6	1-3	1-1	0-5	2-3	2-4	2-0
Bugbrooke	1-2		4-2	2-3	2-5	1-5	4-0	0-3	3-3	1-0	2-3	1-1	1-4	0-4	1-2	2-2
Burton Park	2-2	2-0	D	1-1	1-3	1-6	3-0	2-3	2-4	1-3	0-2	1-1	0-1	0-4	2-4	
Cottingham	2-0	5-0	2-0	I	3-1	1-4	1-1	1-1	1-2	0-1	2-4	0-0	0-1	2-1	0-0	0-1
Eynesbury	7-0	1-0	4-1	4-1	V	0-1	2-1	0-3	3-1	3-1	0-1	3-1	1-2	1-0	1-1	4-0
Harrowby U.	8-0	3-1	8-0	3-1	1-0	I	2-1	3-0	0-2	4-0	2-1	2-2	1-1	2-0	5-0	
Higham Town	0-2	2-4	2-2	0-7	0-5	1-3	S	0-2	2-4	0-0	3-1	0-3	2-2	1-2	5-1	
Irchester Utd	2-1	0-0	4-0	3-1	1-3	1-0	3-2	I	4-2	2-2	2-1	3-0	2-0	3-2	1-0	3-0
ON Cheneks	0-0	3-2	3-0	0-2	1-3	0-1	4-3	3-4	O	0-2	2-2	1-6	0-2	4-4	3-3	4-2
Olney Town	5-1	1-3	7-0	2-3	3-3	3-1	0-3	1-1	N	3-0	2-1	0-3	1-1	1-1	1-0	0-2
Potton United	5-1	2-1	4-0	0-0	3-2	2-3	1-1	1-1	3-0	5-0		2-1	3-2	2-0	0-1	4-1
Rothwell Cor.	2-0	2-0	2-0	2-0	1-3	0-4	3-2	3-1	5-1	1-4	2-2	O	1-2	2-2	2-0	2-2
Sileby Rgrs	8-0	11-1	4-0	4-1	1-1	2-0	9-2	4-1	1-2	2-1	1-3	1-4	N	9-0	2-0	3-0
St Ives Town	1-1	2-1	4-1	2-1	0-3	0-2	1-0	1-1	0-2	1-2	1-2	4-0	0-1	E	0-2	1-0
Thrapston	3-1	5-0	2-1	3-1	1-2	3-3	1-3	4-0	5-1	3-3	2-1	1-0	2-1	2-2		3-2
Whitworths	3-1	0-1	4-0	3-4	3-1	2-1	0-3	0-3	0-2	0-2	1-3	0-1	1-3	0-1		

Reserve Div One

	P	W	D	L	F	A	Pts
Bugbrooke Res.	36	22	8	6	83	39	74
Rothwell Town Res.	36	22	5	9	70	39	71
Raunds Town Res.	36	21	7	8	97	49	70
Holbeach Utd Res.	36	21	4	11	85	57	67
Sileby Rangers Res.	36	20	6	10	69	44	66
Stotfold Res.	36	19	6	11	67	50	63
Newp't Pagnell Res.	36	18	5	13	74	48	59
Yaxley Res.	36	17	6	13	84	55	57
S&L Corby Res.	36	17	4	15	71	63	55
N'pton Spencer Res.	36	15	4	17	56	70	49
Blackstones Res.	36	12	11	13	64	61	47
St Neots Town Res.	36	12	10	14	47	57	46
Desborough Res.	36	10	12	14	76	72	42
Deeping Rgrs Res.	36	11	9	16	59	73	42
Whitworths Res.	36	11	8	17	50	89	41
Cogenhoe Utd Res.	36	10	9	17	47	80	39
Thrapston T. Res.	36	10	7	19	48	82	37
ON Cheneks Res.	36	6	7	23	53	80	25
Corby Town Res.	36	2	4	30	37	129	10

Reserve Div Two

	P	W	D	L	F	A	Pts
Olney Town Res.	30	22	2	6	81	32	68
Potton United Res.	30	21	3	6	76	40	66
Bourne Town Res.	30	19	4	7	75	37	61
Cottingham Res.	30	17	5	8	100	50	56
Eynesbury Rv. Res.	30	17	5	8	78	47	56
Buckingham T. Res.	30	15	9	6	66	41	54
Daventry Town Res.	30	14	7	9	75	52	49
Blisworth Res.	30	14	4	12	60	57	46
Woodford Utd Res.	30	11	7	12	57	58	40
Rothwell Cor. Res.	30	11	5	14	52	60	38
Ford Spts Dav. Res.	30	10	6	14	53	67	36
Higham Town Res.	30	8	5	17	56	90	29
Burton Pk Wdrs Res.	30	7	6	17	44	70	27
Irchester United Res.	30	7	4	19	59	84	25
St Ives Town Res.	30	6	3	21	48	98	21
Long Buckby Res.	30	3	1	26	52	149	10

Division One

	P	W	D	L	F	A	Pts
Sileby Rangers	30	23	3	4	96	26	72
Harrowby United	30	21	4	5	81	29	67
Irchester United	30	20	4	6	63	36	64
Eynesbury Rovers	30	19	3	8	77	36	60
Thrapston Town	30	17	7	6	61	37	58
Potton United	30	16	6	8	63	40	54
Olney Town	30	14	7	9	65	43	49
Rothwell Corinthians	30	12	6	12	49	44	42
St Ives Town	30	11	9	10	47	50	42
Cottingham	30	11	6	13	49	46	39
N'pton ON Cheneks	30	9	7	14	54	74	34
Well'gboro. Whitworths	30	8	2	20	39	72	26
Bugbrooke St Mich.	30	6	4	20	40	81	22
Higham Town	30	5	5	20	35	76	20
Blisworth	30	4	6	20	30	94	18
Burton Pk Wanderers	30	2	5	23	27	92	11

WWW.CHERRYRED.CO.UK

RESERVE DIVISIONS CUP

FINAL

(23rd April at Rothwell Corinthians)

Stewarts & Lloyds Corby Res. 3 Blackstones Res. 2

DIVISION ONE CONSTITUTION 2003-04

BLISWORTH . . . . Courteenhall Road, Blisworth, Northants 01604 858024
BUGBROOKE ST MICHAELS . . . . . Birds Close, Gayton Road, Bugbrooke, Northampton, Northants 01604 830707
BURTON PARK WANDERERS . . . . Latimer Park, Polwell Lane, Burton Latimer, Northants 01536 725841
COTTINGHAM . . . . Berryfield Road, Cottingham, Northants 01536 770051
EYE UNITED . . . . Chestnut Avenue, Dogsthorpe, Eye, Peterborough, Cambridgeshire . . . . . . None
EYNESBURY ROVERS . . . . . Alfred Hall Memorial Ground, Hall Road, Eynesbury, St Neots, Cambridgeshire . . . 01480 477449
HIGHAM TOWN . . . . Vine Hall Drive, Higham Ferrers, Northants 01933 353751
HUNTINGDON TOWN . . . . Hartford Road, Huntingdon, Cambridgeshire . . . . None
IRCHESTER UNITED . . . . Alfred Street, Irchester, Northants 01933 312877
KEMPSTON ROVERS . . . . Hillgrounds Leisure, Hillgrounds, Kempston, Bedfordshire . . . 01234 852346
NORTHAMPTON ON CHENEKS . . . Old Northamptonians, Billing Road, Northampton, Northants 01604 634045
OLNEY TOWN . . . . Recreation Ground, East Street, Olney, Buckinghamshire 01234 712227
POTTON UNITED . . . . The Hollow, Biggleswade Road, Potton, Bedfordshire 01767 261100
ROTHWELL CORINTHIANS . . . . Seargents Lawn, Desborough Road, Rothwell, Northants . . . 01536 418688
SILEBY RANGERS . . . . Fernie Fields Sports Ground, Moulton, Northampton, Northants . . . 01604 670566
ST IVES TOWN . . . . Westwood Road, St Ives, Huntingdon, Cambridgeshire 01480 463207
THRAPSTON TOWN . . . . Chancery Lane, Thrapston, Kettering, Northants 01832 732470
WELLINGBOROUGH WHITWORTHS . . Whitworths, London Road, Wellingborough, Northants 01933 227324

Harrowby United are promoted to the Premier Division replaced by Kempston Rovers. Eye United are promoted from the Peterborough & District League. Huntingdon Town step up from the Cambridgeshire League.

WEARSIDE LEAGUE

	Annfield Plain	Barnard Castle Glaxo	Birtley Town	Boldon Comm. Association	Darlington Rail. Athletic	Ferryhill Athletic	Jarrow	New Marske Sports Club	North Shields	Redcar Town	Ryhope Colliery Welfare	South Shields Cleadon SC	S. Shields Harton/Westoe	Stanley United	Stokesley SC	Whitehaven Amateurs	Windscale	Wolviston
Annfield Plain		1-4	3-0	2-2	0-5	3-0	3-0	1-1	0-0	1-2	4-1	2-1	2-1	6-3	1-3	1-0	2-1	0-5
Barnard Castle Glaxo	4-1		1-6	1-3	0-5	5-2	2-2	2-5	0-2	1-1	3-4	0-1	3-3	2-1	3-4	2-2	1-5	0-3
Birtley Town	4-0	3-2		4-3	6-2	15-0	2-0	2-1	4-2	3-1	2-1	12-1	6-1	1-1	2-1	3-0	0-2	0-1
Boldon Community Assoc.	0-1	2-1	1-4		2-1	9-3	3-0	1-1	1-3	3-0	6-0	1-1	3-0	1-3	1-0	1-2	0-4	2-2
Darlington Railway Athletic	3-2	1-0	1-1	2-2		7-1	3-3	0-1	2-1	2-0	3-0	3-0	5-1	1-2	1-2	0-0	0-0	5-0
Ferryhill Athletic	2-2	0-7	3-4	1-3	0-3		5-2	1-4	0-1	1-6	1-3	5-1	0-1	2-2	1-3	6-0	0-2	1-5
Jarrow	3-0	4-1	0-5	1-2	1-3	3-2		3-2	2-7	5-0	0-4	2-2	4-1	4-2	2-2	3-0	0-3	0-1
New Marske Sports Club	6-0	5-2	1-3	0-3	2-1	7-2	7-0		0-2	4-0	1-0	5-1	3-0	5-1	2-5	2-1	2-1	1-4
North Shields	9-0	1-5	0-2	3-3	0-0	3-0	4-1	2-0		1-2	2-0	5-0	0-0	1-3	4-1	1-2	0-2	0-2
Redcar Town	2-2	2-1	0-7	1-4	2-1	5-0	7-3	1-1	1-1		0-2	1-2	0-3	3-3	0-3	0-5	0-6	0-3
Ryhope Colliery Welfare	6-2	4-2	2-2	1-4	1-1	1-3	3-0	0-0	0-2	9-1		1-0	3-2	1-3	1-5	3-1	0-1	2-5
South Shields Cleadon SC	1-1	2-0	1-3	0-2	1-1	3-0	1-2	3-2	0-5	2-1	1-1		2-4	2-1	1-3	1-2	0-1	1-4
South Shields Harton & W.	2-4	7-4	3-1	1-3	0-2	7-1	1-0	4-3	2-4	3-2	1-1	0-1		1-5	4-1	1-1	2-1	3-3
Stanley United	1-4	5-3	1-3	3-1	3-3	6-0	1-2	1-2	4-3	4-4	6-3	4-0	0-2		2-6	1-2	2-2	0-2
Stokesley SC	5-1	2-1	1-3	5-0	4-3	4-0	3-2	4-2	3-2	3-2	4-0	9-0	4-1	8-1		3-0	1-1	1-2
Whitehaven Amateurs	3-1	1-4	0-4	2-0	0-4	5-1	2-1	0-1	1-0	1-3	2-1	1-2	1-4	3-1	2-1		0-3	1-2
Windscale	1-0	1-3	2-2	1-2	1-1	3-0	5-0	1-2	1-1	3-1	3-1	0-1	1-0	2-0	0-4	2-2		2-3
Wolviston	2-0	7-1	0-1	3-1	1-0	3-0	3-1	1-4	3-2	3-3	5-0	1-2	4-4	7-1	1-0	5-2	0-2	

		P	W	D	L	F	A	Pts
Birtley Town		34	26	4	4	120	39	82
Wolviston		34	25	4	5	96	43	79
Stokesley SC		34	25	2	7	110	49	77
New Marske Spts Club		34	19	4	11	85	53	61
Boldon Comm. Assoc.		34	18	6	10	80	55	60
Windscale		34	17	7	10	63	37	58
Darlington Railway Ath.		34	15	10	9	75	40	55
North Shields		34	15	6	13	74	47	51
Whitehaven Amateurs		34	13	4	17	49	67	43
Annfield Plain		34	12	6	16	53	83	42
Ryhope CW		34	11	5	18	60	75	38
Harton & Westoe	-9	34	13	7	14	71	76	37
Cleadon SC		34	11	4	19	37	90	37
Stanley United		34	10	6	18	74	94	36
Jarrow		34	10	4	20	56	92	34
Redcar Town		34	8	7	19	54	96	31
Barnard Castle Glaxo		34	8	4	22	71	98	28
Ferryhill Athletic		34	4	2	28	44	138	14

CONSTITUTION 2003-04

ANNFIELD PLAIN . . . . Derwent Park, West Road, Annfield Plain, County Durham . . . . None
BARNARD CASTLE GLAXO . Glaxo Sports & Social Club, Harmire Road, Barnard Castle, County Durham 01833 638926
BIRTLEY TOWN. . . . . Birtley Sports Complex, near AEI Cables, Birtley, Chester-le-Street, County Durham . . . . None
BOLDON COMMUNITY ASSOCIATION . . . . . Boldon Welfare, New Road, Boldon Colliery . . . . 0191 536 4180 (Cricket Club)
DARLINGTON RAILWAY ATHLETIC . . Darlington Rail Athletic Club, Brinkburn Road, Darlington 01325 468125
FERRYHILL ATHLETIC. . . Mainsforth Sports Complex, Morrison Terrace, Ferryhill Station, County Durham 01740 657345
GATESHEAD . . . . The International Stadium, Neilson Road, Gateshead, Tyne & Wear. . . 0191 478 3883. Fax: 0191 477 1315
JARROW. . . . . Perth Green Community Association, off Inverness Road, Jarrow, Tyne & Wear. 0191 489 3743
NEW MARSKE SPORTS CLUB . . New Marske Sports Club, Pontiac Rd, New Marske, Redcar, Cleveland 01642 479808
NORTH SHIELDS . . . . Ralph Gardner Park, West Percy Road, Chirton, North Shields, Tyne & Wear . . . . None
RYHOPE COLLIERY WELFARE . . . . . Ryhope Recreation Park, Ryhope Street, Ryhope, Sunderland. 0191 521 2843
SOUTH SHIELDS CLEADON SC . . . Jack Clark Park, Horsley Hill Road, South Shields, Tyne & Wear 0191 454 2023
SOUTH SHIELDS HARTON & WESTOE . Harton Colliery Welfare, Boldon Lane, South Shields 0191 456 6166
STOKESLEY SC. . . . . Stokesley Sports Club, Broughton Road, Stokesley, North Yorkshire 01642 710051
WASHINGTON NISSAN . . . . Nissan Sports Complex, Washington Road, Sunderland, Tyne & Wear 0191 418 7493
WHITEHAVEN AMATEURS . . . . County Sports Field, Coach Road, Whitehaven, Cumbria . . . . None
WINDSCALE . . . . Falcon Field, Smithfield, Egremont, Cumbria 01946 820421
WOLVISTON. . . . . Metcalfe Park, Wynyard Road, Wolviston, Cleveland. 01740 644761
Stanley United and Redcar Town have resigned. Newcomers are Gateshead Reserves (newly formed) and Nissan UK (formerly Washington Nissan Reserves in Wearside Combination).

WEARSIDE LEAGUE CUP

FIRST ROUND
Barnard Castle Glaxo 3 **Windscale** 5
Ferryhill Athletic 1 **North Shields** 3

SECOND ROUND
Birtley Town 4 Annfield Plain 1
Darlington Railway Athletic 4 Stanley
United 2
Jarrow 1 **New Marske
Sports Club** 1 *aet* (3-4p)
Redcar Town 0 **North
Shields** 1
South Shields Harton & Westoe 3 Whitehaven
Amateurs 0
Stokesley SC 2 Ryhope Colliery
Welfare 1
Windscale 1 Boldon Community
Association 0
Wolviston 2 **South Shields Cleadon SC** 4 *aet*

QUARTER-FINALS
New Marske Sports Club 0 **Darlington Railway
Athletic** 4
North Shields 4
Stokesley SC 3
South Shields Harton & Westoe 1 **Birtley
Town** 2
Windscale 2 South Shields
Cleadon SC 1

SEMI-FINALS
Birtley Town 4
Windscale 1
North Shields 2 **Darlington Railway
Athletic** 3 *aet*

FINAL *(16th May at Birtley Town)*
Birtley Town 1 **Darlington Railway
Athletic** 3 *aet*

MONKWEARMOUTH CHARITY CUP

FIRST ROUND
Stanley United 3 Annfield
Plain 1
Windscale 4 Whitehaven
Amateurs 1

SECOND ROUND
Boldon Community Association 0 **Darlington Railway
Athletic** 2
Ferryhill Athletic 3 Wolviston 2
Jarrow 1 **North Shields** 3
New Marske Sports Club 0 **Birtley Town** 1
South Shields Cleadon SC 4 Ryhope
Colliery Welfare 2
Stanley United (w/o) Redcar Town (scr.)
Stokesley SC 2 **South Shields Harton &
Westoe** 5
Windscale 1 **Barnard Castle
Glaxo** 2

QUARTER-FINALS
Ferryhill Athletic 1 South Shields Cleadon SC 0
North Shields 2 Birtley Town 0
South Shields Harton & Westoe 4 Barnard Castle Glaxo 0
Stanley United 0 **Darlington Railway Athletic** 5

SEMI-FINALS
Darlington Railway Athletic 3 South Shields
Harton & Westoe 1 *aet*
North Shields 6 Ferryhill
Athletic 0

FINAL *(21st April at Darlingon Railway Athletic)*
Darlington Railway Athletic 0 **North Shields** 3

SUNDERLAND SHIPOWNERS CUP

FIRST ROUND
New Marske Sports Club 3 North
Shields 0
Redcar Town 5 Windscale 0

SECOND ROUND
Barnard Castle Glaxo 3 Jarrow 2
Darlington Railway Athletic 3 Boldon
Community Association 1
Redcar Town 1 **Birtley Town** 5
Ryhope Colliery Welfare 1 **Stokesley SC** 7
South Shields Cleadon SC 2 Whitehaven
Amateurs 0
South Shields Harton & Westoe 2 Annfield
Plain 0
Stanley United 8 Ferryhill
Athletic 0
Wolviston 1 New Marske
Sports Club 0

QUARTER-FINALS
Darlington Railway Athletic 1 Birtley Town 0
South Shields Cleadon SC 1 Barnard Castle Glaxo 0
Stokesley SC 3 South Shields Harton & Westoe 1
Wolviston 3 Stanley United 2

SEMI-FINALS
South Shields Cleadon SC 2 **Darlington Railway
Athletic** 2 *aet* (4-5p)
Wolviston 3 Stokesley SC 1

FINAL *(5th May at Wolviston)*
Wolviston 1 Darlington Railway Athletic 0

WELSH ALLIANCE

	Bethesda Athletic	Bodedern	Caerwys	Conwy United	Denbigh Town	Glan Conwy	Glantraeth	Llandudno Junction	Locomotive Llanberis	Penmaenmawr Phoenix	Prestatyn Town	Rhydymwyn	Rhyl Res.	Sealand Leisure	Y Felinheli
Bethesda Athletic		0-0	3-2	4-2	1-3	7-1	2-1	3-0	1-0	2-0	2-0	1-2	3-1	2-0	1-2
Bodedern	3-1		6-0	8-0	2-1	1-1	1-1	0-1	3-0	6-0	3-0	2-0	1-1	3-1	2-3
Caerwys	3-3	0-2		3-2	2-0	3-1	1-3	1-7	0-1	5-2	3-4	5-6	4-0	0-5	2-0
Conwy United	0-4	0-2	4-1		0-3	4-0	1-6	1-1	1-2	1-1	3-0	1-1	0-1	0-3	1-6
Denbigh Town	2-1	0-2	4-2	3-2		2-1	1-2	3-3	2-2	4-0	5-0	2-1	2-1	1-1	4-0
Glan Conwy	5-0	0-3	1-2	3-0	1-0		1-6	1-1	2-2	1-3	2-2	1-1	1-6	1-1	1-3
Glantraeth	5-3	2-2	8-1	9-0	1-1	19-0		4-1	3-2	3-2	6-1	7-0	1-6	6-0	2-0
Llandudno Junction	0-5	3-3	3-3	4-2	0-2	1-3	0-2		3-1	2-2	6-2	3-2	1-0	3-2	3-1
Locomotive Llanberis	4-2	1-1	2-0	4-0	2-2	2-1	2-0	1-4		2-1	0-2	1-1	1-3	5-1	0-0
Penmaenmawr Phoenix	0-7	0-3	0-3	4-2	0-8	6-2	0-3	2-2	2-3		1-1	0-2	0-1	0-3	3-3
Prestatyn Town	2-4	0-1	2-0	0-1	0-1	1-1	2-2	1-4	2-0	3-0		3-2	1-5	0-0	1-1
Rhydymwyn	2-7	0-2	5-3	2-0	0-1	3-2	1-1	2-0	1-2	2-1	0-0		1-1	5-0	2-0
Rhyl Res.	2-3	2-0	1-1	2-0	0-1	2-1	2-1	0-1	7-1	4-0	5-2			2-0	0-0
Sealand Leisure	0-1	0-1	2-2	3-2	3-1	2-2	0-9	0-1	3-1	4-2	1-0	1-6	3-3		5-3
Y Felinheli	2-1	1-2	1-5	6-1	1-5	5-4	0-5	2-0	0-3	0-2	0-2	2-1	1-0	1-2	

		P	W	D	L	F	A	Pts
Glantraeth		28	19	5	4	118	33	62
Bodedern		28	18	7	3	65	19	61
Denbigh Town		28	17	5	6	64	31	56
Bethesda Athletic		28	17	2	9	74	44	53
Rhyl Res.		28	15	6	7	62	31	51
Locomotive Llanberis		28	12	7	9	47	42	43
Llandudno Junction		28	12	7	9	57	53	43
Rhydymwyn		28	11	6	11	52	54	39
Sealand Leisure		28	10	6	12	44	63	36
Y Felinheli	-3	28	10	4	14	44	60	31
Caerwys		28	9	4	15	57	78	31
Prestatyn Town		28	7	7	14	32	58	28
Glan Conwy		28	4	8	16	41	88	20
Penmaenmawr Phoenix		28	4	5	19	35	83	17
Conwy United		28	4	3	21	31	86	15

COOKSON CUP

SEMI-FINALS
Llandudno Junction 0 **Glantraeth** 2
Rhyl Res. 4 Sealand Leisure 1
FINAL
(8th May at Bethesda Athletic)
Rhyl Res. 2 Glantraeth 0

ALVES CUP

SEMI-FINALS
Denbigh Town 2 Caerwys 0
Y Felinheli 2 Locomotive Llanberis 1
FINAL
(15th May at Bethesda Athletic)
Denbigh Town 2 Y Felinheli 0

WWW.NLNEWSDESK.CO.UK

CONSTITUTION 2003-04

BETHESDA ATHLETIC .... Parc Meurig Park, Bethesda, Gwynedd........................... None
BODEDERN............................ Secondary School, Holyhead Road, Bodedern, Anglesey............................ None
CAERWYS .... Lon Yr Ysgol, Caerwys, Flintshire.. None
CONWY UNITED .... Penmaen Road, Morfa, Gwynedd 01492 573080
DENBIGH TOWN............................... Central Park, Denbigh, Denbighshire .... None
GLAN CONWY .... Cae Ffwt, Llanrwst Road, Glan Conwy, Gwynedd .... None
LLANDUDNO JUNCTION................. Victoria Gardens, Llandudno Junction, Gwynedd .... None
LLANDYRNOG UNITED .... t.b.a. .... t.b.a.
LLANRUG UNITED......................... Eithon Duon, Llanrug, Gwynedd 01286 677543
LOCOMOTIVE LLANBERIS .... Ffordd Padarn, Llanberis, Gwynedd............................ None
PENMAENMAWR PHOENIX............. Cae Sling, Conwy Road, Penmaenmawr, Gwynedd........................... None
PRESTATYN TOWN .... Bastion Road, Prestatyn, Clwyd... None
RHYDYMWYN .... Vicarage Road, Rhydymwyn, Denbighshire .... None
RHYL RESERVES .... Belle Vue, Grange Road, Rhyl, Clwyd .... 01745 338327. Fax: 01745 338327
SEALAND LEISURE .... Welsh Road Playing Fields, Sealand, Clwyd........................... None
Y FELINHELI .... Cae Seilo, Y Felinheli, Gwynedd.. None
Glantraeth are promoted to the Cymru Alliance. Llandyrnog United arrive from the Clwyd League and Llanrug United from the Gwynedd League.

WELSH LEAGUE

	Bettws	Briton Ferry Athletic	Caerleon	Cardiff Civil Service	Cardiff Corinthians	Ely Rangers	Garden Village	Garw Athletic	Goytre United	Gwynfi United	Llanwern	Maesteg Park Athletic	Milford United	Neath	Penrhiwceiber Rangers	Pontardawe Town	Ton Pentre	UWIC Inter Cardiff
Bettws		1-0	3-3	4-1	3-0	3-3	3-0	3-1	0-1	3-1	6-2	8-0	7-0	0-1	7-1	4-2	1-3	1-1
Briton Ferry Athletic	1-4		2-0	2-0	3-0	1-0	1-2	2-6	2-3	2-1	0-2	2-4	6-1	0-1	2-1	3-1	0-2	3-0
Caerleon	1-2	0-0		2-2	3-0	2-0	2-2	2-2	2-1	3-1	3-0	1-2	1-0	0-2	0-1	0-0	1-1	0-1
Cardiff Civil Service	0-1	1-2	1-0	D	2-2	0-2	2-1	3-2	1-0	5-3	2-0	1-0	1-1	1-0	0-2	1-1	1-2	1-2
Cardiff Corinthians	0-1	0-0	0-6	1-0	I	0-4	2-1	2-0	2-0	2-2	1-0	3-0	5-0	0-2	3-1	1-4	2-1	1-1
Ely Rangers	0-1	1-1	4-0	1-2	1-1	V	2-0	2-0	0-0	0-1	2-2	0-1	1-1	4-2	3-1	0-3	0-1	0-3
Garden Village	1-1	1-0	3-1	1-1	2-1	3-2	I	1-4	1-2	1-0	1-6	0-2	3-0	0-2	2-4	1-3	2-0	1-1
Garw Athletic	2-1	1-0	0-1	0-1	2-1	0-3	6-0	S	1-0	2-0	4-1	1-2	2-0	1-1	4-1	5-4	3-2	1-1
Goytre United	1-3	3-2	2-0	3-0	3-0	2-1	2-0	3-0	I	0-0	0-1	1-2	5-1	1-2	2-1	2-1	1-4	1-2
Gwynfi United	0-1	3-0	1-1	4-1	4-1	2-0	0-0	0-1	1-2	O	3-1	2-2	5-3	2-3	5-2	2-1	1-6	0-1
Llanwern	0-4	0-2	2-2	3-1	1-2	2-1	2-1	1-2	0-5	2-1	N	3-1	4-0	1-2	3-0	0-0	1-4	0-4
Maesteg Park Athletic	1-2	0-2	1-1	2-3	1-0	3-0	1-4	2-0	0-3	1-1	3-0		3-0	1-1	1-1	2-3	0-1	0-3
Milford United	0-2	1-2	1-3	2-5	0-1	0-1	2-0	1-5	0-2	1-1	2-2	1-1	O	0-3	1-1	1-1	0-5	1-6
Neath	0-2	5-0	1-0	1-1	1-1	4-0	1-1	5-1	5-1	2-0	1-0	4-2		N	3-2	1-0	2-1	1-2
Penrhiwceiber Rangers	0-4	2-2	4-2	2-1	1-4	3-2	0-0	2-0	0-1	0-8	1-1	1-3	1-1	1-4	E	2-1	1-3	0-1
Pontardawe Town	0-1	1-3	0-2	0-0	5-0	2-1	2-0	0-0	1-1	2-0	1-0	3-0	5-1	0-1	1-3		0-5	2-1
Ton Pentre	2-1	2-1	3-1	1-1	1-0	2-4	3-1	7-1	3-0	2-0	1-0	3-0	9-1	0-1	3-1	3-0		1-2
UWIC Inter Cardiff	1-1	3-0	3-2	2-2	2-1	2-1	4-2	1-1	0-2	3-1	2-0	1-0	5-0	1-4	2-1	2-1	1-0	

Division One	P	W	D	L	F	A	Pts
Bettws	34	24	5	5	89	30	77
Neath	34	24	5	5	70	29	77
UWIC Inter Cardiff	34	23	7	4	67	33	76
Ton Pentre	34	22	3	9	86	35	69
Goytre United	34	19	3	12	56	39	60
Garw Athletic	34	16	5	13	61	56	53
Briton Ferry Athletic	34	14	4	16	49	53	46
Cardiff Civil Service	34	12	9	13	45	52	45
Maesteg Park Athletic	34	13	6	15	44	57	45
Pontardawe Town	34	12	7	15	51	49	43
Cardiff Corinthians	34	12	6	16	40	58	42
Caerleon	34	10	10	14	48	48	40
Llanwern	34	11	5	18	44	64	38
Gwynfi United	34	10	7	17	56	57	37
Ely Rangers	34	10	6	18	46	51	36
Garden Village	34	9	7	18	39	65	34
Penrhiwceiber Rangers	34	9	7	18	47	80	34
Milford United	34	1	8	25	26	108	11

LEAGUE CUP

FIRST ROUND

Albion Rovers 3 **Aberaman** 4
Bridgend 2 Cardiff CS 0
Caerau United 0 **Briton Ferry Athletic** 10
Caerleon 3 Fields Park Pontllanfraith 0
Caldicot Town 1 Chepstow Town 0
Dinas Powys 1 Maesteg Park Athletic 1 *aet* (4-3p)
Garden Village 5 Penrhiwceiber Rangers 2
Garw Ath 5 Ammanford 1
Goytre United 2 AFC Llwydcoed 1
Merthyr Saints 0 **UWIC Inter Cardiff** 5

Milford Utd 1 **Morriston** 2
Newport YMCA 3 Treharris Athletic 1
Pontardawe Town 5 AFC Rhondda 1
Pontlottyn Blast Furnace 4 Cwmamman United 1 *aet*
Pontypridd Town 2 **Cardiff Corinthians** 4
Porth Tywyn Suburbs 2 Newcastle Emlyn 0
Porthcawl 2 **Ton Pentre** 7
Risca & Gelli 1 Treowen 0
RTB Ebbw Vale 4 Troedyrhiw 2 *aet*
Skewen 2 Seven Sisters 0
Taffs Well 1 **Ely Rgrs** 2 *aet*
Tillery 0 **Bryntirion Ath** 1

DIVISION ONE CONSTITUTION 2003-04

BETTWS .... North Site, Bettws, Mid-Glamorgan 01656 725618
BRITON FERRY ATHLETIC .... Old Road, Briton Ferry, Neath, West Glamorgan 01639 812458
CAERLEON .... Cold Bath Road, Caerleon, Gwent 01633 420074
CARDIFF CIVIL SERVICE .... Sanatorium Road, Leckwith, Cardiff, South Glamorgan 01222 341181
CARDIFF CORINTHIANS ..... Riverside Ground, through Station Road, Radyr, Cardiff, South Glamorgan .. 02920 843407
DINAS POWYS .... Murchfield, Sunnycroft Lane, Dinas Powys, South Glamorgan .... None
ELY RANGERS .... Station Road, Wenvoe, South Glamorgan 02920 598725
GARDEN VILLAGE ...... Stafford Common, Victoria Road, Kingsbridge, Gorseinon, Swansea, West Glamorgan ... 01792 894933
GARW ATHLETIC .... Blandy Park, Pontycymmer, Mid-Glamorgan 01656 870438
GOYTRE UNITED .... Glenhafod Park, Goytre, Port Talbot, West Glamorgan 01639 898983
GRANGE HARLEQUINS .... Cardiff Athletic Stadium, Leckwith, Cardiff, South Glamorgan 02920 225345
GWYNFI UNITED .... Gwynfi Welfare, Blaengwnfi, West Glamorgan 01639 850313
LLANELLI .... Stebonheath Park, Stebonheath, Llanelli, Carmarthenshire .... 01554 772973 / 773847
LLANWERN .... BSC Sports Ground, Spytty Road, Newport, Gwent 01633 273790
MAESTEG PARK ATHLETIC .... Tudor Park, Maesteg, Mid-Glamorgan 01656 732029
NEATH .... Llandarcy Park Sports Ground, Llandarcy, West Glamorgan 01792 812036
PONTARDAWE TOWN .... Recreation Ground, Trading Estate, Pontardawe, West Glamorgan 01792 642228
TON PENTRE .... Ynys Park, Sawmill Villas, Ton Pentre, Mid-Glamorgan 01443 432813
UWIC INTER CARDIFF .... Cyncoed Road, Cardiff, South Glamorgan 02920 416155

Llanelli are relegated from the Welsh Premier League. Penrhiwceiber Rangers and Milford United drop to Division Two replaced by Dinas Powys and Grange Harlequins.

	AFC Llwydcoed	AFC Rhondda	Aberaman Athletic	Ammanford	Blaenrhondda	Bridgend Town	Dinas Powys	Fields Park Pontllanfraith	Grange Harlequins	Merthyr Saints	Morriston Town	Newport YMCA	Pontypridd Town	Porth Tywyn Suburbs	Porthcawl Town	Taffs Well	Tredegar Town	Treharris Athletic
AFC Llwydcoed		3-0	4-0	1-3	2-0	4-1	1-1	2-1	1-1	0-1	0-0	4-5	2-2	5-0	4-0	2-1	0-0	2-1
AFC Rhondda	2-0		2-2	0-1	0-3	0-4	3-3	2-1	1-2	1-2	2-4	2-2	1-1	1-2	0-0	2-3	0-0	2-1
Aberaman Athletic	1-1	3-3	*D*	1-6	3-0	3-2	0-3	5-0	3-0	1-2	3-2	0-1	1-3	2-2	2-3	1-1	4-1	2-0
Ammanford	0-1	1-4	0-1	*I*	2-0	0-2	0-4	5-0	3-2	3-1	4-3	0-1	1-0	5-0	3-3	3-0	1-3	1-1
Blaenrhondda	0-0	2-1	4-3	1-4	*V*	0-2	1-4	2-1	1-5	1-4	3-3	0-3	3-1	2-0	3-1	0-4	4-2	4-3
Bridgend Town	1-1	2-1	5-1	2-1	3-1	*I*	0-3	4-2	2-1	1-0	4-0	2-0	1-1	2-0	7-0	3-2	0-3	3-1
Dinas Powys	1-2	3-1	1-0	5-2	4-0	0-0	*S*	5-0	3-0	0-0	6-1	2-2	4-3	1-2	9-1	5-1	3-1	1-1
Fields Park Pontllanfraith	1-3	3-5	0-3	0-5	0-2	1-1	1-3	*I*	1-4	3-5	2-0	1-2	0-0	2-6	6-3	2-4	3-1	1-5
Grange Harlequins	2-2	2-1	4-2	9-0	6-2	1-1	2-3	5-0	*O*	4-1	3-0	2-1	3-1	3-3	2-5	3-1	8-0	4-1
Merthyr Saints	0-1	1-2	3-4	3-2	1-2	1-3	0-2	2-1	0-3	*N*	0-1	0-3	2-4	2-2	5-2	2-2	1-0	3-0
Morriston Town	2-5	3-2	1-3	1-1	2-0	0-1	1-4	4-0	2-2	2-1		1-5	1-4	4-0	2-0	1-4	0-4	3-0
Newport YMCA	0-3	0-1	2-2	3-1	1-0	0-0	0-0	3-1	0-1	3-1	3-2		0-4	1-1	2-1	0-1	1-0	2-0
Pontypridd Town	1-1	4-0	1-1	0-0	2-0	1-2	2-4	4-0	1-1	0-0	2-2	2-0		3-1	3-1	0-3	5-0	0-0
Porth Tywyn Suburbs	1-3	5-1	0-2	1-3	0-1	0-0	1-4	5-0	1-3	5-0	1-2	2-1	1-2	*T*	1-2	1-5	2-0	0-4
Porthcawl Town	0-1	3-5	2-4	4-2	1-2	0-3	0-3	3-2	0-1	3-2	2-2	3-0	2-2	0-1	*W*	1-0	3-1	1-3
Taffs Well	1-1	2-0	3-2	1-0	0-0	0-3	0-1	1-2	0-1	6-1	2-1	1-1	2-3	2-3	0-1	*O*	1-1	3-1
Tredegar Town	2-1	1-0	2-3	3-0	2-1	4-4	2-0	5-0	2-3	1-2	2-0	2-2	1-1	8-2	8-1	4-2		0-3
Treharris Athletic	1-4	4-0	1-1	2-2	0-0	2-2	0-0	4-1	1-2	1-1	1-2	1-0	0-0	2-1	5-1	3-2	2-4	

SECOND ROUND

Bettws 4 Tredegar Town 2
Blaenrhondda 1 **Briton Ferry** 2
Bryntirion Ath 2 Gwynfi United 1
Caerau Ely 0 **Ely Rangers** 2
Caerleon 0 **UWIC Inter Cardiff** 2
Caldicot Town 1 Skewen Ath 0
Cardiff Corries 0 **Pontardawe** 1
Dinas Powys 3 Pontlottyn BF 2
Garden Village 1 **Aberaman Ath** 4
Goytre United 1 **Bridgend Town** 2
Llanwern 1 **Pontyclun** 3
Morriston 3 RTB Ebbw Vale 2
Neath 5 Newport YMCA 2
Pentwyn Dynamo 0 **Grange Harlequins** 3
Porth Tywyn Subs 0 **Ton Pentre** 2
Risca & Gelli Utd 1 **Garw Ath** 3

THIRD ROUND

Bettws 2 Grange Quins 2 *aet* (9-8p)
Bridgend Town 0 **Aberaman Ath** 2
Briton Ferry Athletic 2 **Neath** 4
Bryntirion Athletic 0 **Pontardawe** 3
Caldicot Town 0 **Pontyclun** 1
Dinas Powys 4 Morriston Town 0
Ely Rgrs 1 **UWIC Inter Cardiff** 2
Garw 0 **Ton Pentre** 2

QUARTER-FINALS

Aberaman Ath 1 **Dinas Powys** 2
Bettws 2 Pontardawe 2 *aet* (4-3p)
Ton Pentre 2 **Neath** 4
UWIC Int. 0 **Pontyclun** 0 *aet* (4-5p)

SEMI-FINALS

Bettws 4 Pontyclun 1 *(at Maesteg)*
Dinas Powys 0 **Neath** 5 *(at Maesteg)*

FINAL

(19th May at Ton Pentre)
Bettws 0 **Neath** 3

Division Two	P	W	D	L	F	A	Pts
Dinas Powys	34	24	7	3	97	31	79
Grange Harlequins	34	22	6	6	95	46	72
Bridgend Town	34	21	9	4	73	33	72
AFC Llwydcoed	34	18	11	5	67	33	65
Taffs Well	34	15	7	12	65	54	52
Newport YMCA	34	15	7	12	50	46	52
Pontypridd Town	34	12	15	7	62	41	51
Aberaman Athletic	34	14	8	12	69	65	50
Tredegar Town	34	14	6	14	70	63	48
Ammanford	34	14	5	15	65	63	47
Blaenrhondda	34	13	4	17	45	70	43
Treharris Athletic	34	10	10	14	55	55	40
Morriston Town	34	11	6	17	55	76	39
Merthyr Saints	34	11	5	18	50	69	38
Porthcawl Town	34	10	4	20	55	98	34
Porth Tywyn Suburbs	34	9	5	20	52	79	32
AFC Rhondda	34	8	7	19	48	73	31
Fields Park Pontllanfraith	34	3	2	29	36	114	11

DIVISION TWO CONSTITUTION 2003-04

AFC LLWYDCOED . . . . Welfare Ground, Llwydcoed, Rhondda, Mid-Glamorgan . . . . None
ABERAMAN ATHLETIC . . . . Aberaman Park, Aberaman, Mid-Glamorgan 07811 065025
AMMANFORD . . . . Rice Road, Betws, Ammanford, Dyfed 01269 592407
BLAENRHONDDA . . . . Blaenrhondda Park, Blaenrhondda, Rhondda 01443 774772
BRIDGEND TOWN . . . . Coychurch Road, Bridgend, Mid-Glamorgan . . . . 01656 662974. Club: 01656 655097
MERTHYR SAINTS . . . . ICI Pavilion, Pant, Merthyr Tydfil, Mid-Glamorgan . . . . None
MILFORD UNITED . . . . Marble Hall Road, Milford Haven, Pembrokeshire 01646 693691
MORRISTON TOWN . . . . The Dingle Field, Morriston, Swansea, West Glamorgan 01792 702033
NEWPORT YMCA . . . . YMCA Grounds, Mendalgief Road, Newport, Gwent 01633 263387
PENRHIWCEIBER RANGERS . . . . . . Glasbrook, Glasbrook Terrace, Penrhiwceiber, Mid-Glamorgan 01443 473368
PONTYCLUN . . . . Ivor Park, Cowbridge Road, Pontyclun, Mid-Glamorgan 01443 222182
PONTYPRIDD TOWN . . . . Ynysangharad Park, Pontypridd, Mid-Glamorgan 01443 486571
PORTH TYWYN SUBURBS . . . . Parc Tywyn, Woodbrook Terrace, Burry Port, Dyfed . . . . 01554 833991. Club: 01554 833471
PORTHCAWL TOWN . . . . Locks Lane, Porthcawl, Mid-Glamorgan 01656 784804
SKEWEN ATHLETIC . . . . Tennant Park, Skewen, Neath, West Glamorgan 01792 813757
TAFFS WELL . . . . Rhiwddar, Parish Road, Taffs Well, Mid-Glamorgan 02920 811080
TREDEGAR TOWN . . . . Recreation Ground, Tredegar, Gwent 01495 711791
TREHARRIS ATHLETIC . . . . Athletic Ground, Commercial Terrace, Treharris, Mid-Glamorgan . . . . None
Dinas Powys and Grange Harlequins are promted to Division One, replaced by Penrhiwceiber Rangers and Milford United. AFC Rhondda and Fields Park Pontllafraith drop to Division Three replaced by Pontyclun and Skewen Athletic.

	Albion Rovers	Bryntirion Athletic	Caerau Ely	Caerau United	Caldicot Town	Chepstow Town	Cwmamman United	Newcastle Emlyn	Pentwyn Dynamo	Pontlottyn Blast Furnace	Pontyclun	RTB Ebbw Vale	Risca & Gelli United	Seven Sisters	Skewen Athletic	Tillery	Treowen Stars	Troedyrhiw
Albion Rovers		2-4	4-0	3-3	1-1	4-2	0-2	1-1	1-3	5-0	1-1	1-2	3-1	0-6	1-2	1-4	3-2	1-2
Bryntirion Athletic	3-2		1-2	2-3	1-0	7-1	3-2	5-2	0-0	4-0	0-2	4-0	5-1	4-1	0-2	4-2	1-0	2-2
Caerau Ely	1-0	1-0	D	7-0	6-2	3-1	2-0	1-0	1-1	2-2	2-0	4-2	3-1	2-2	4-1	3-3	6-1	2-1
Caerau United	1-1	1-3	1-4	I	1-3	2-2	0-1	2-3	1-0	1-4	2-4	4-3	5-1	2-3	1-4	1-1	0-2	2-3
Caldicot Town	0-2	1-0	2-0	4-1	V	2-2	3-1	6-1	3-4	3-1	1-1	2-1	4-0	2-2	5-1	2-1	2-1	1-1
Chepstow Town	2-1	2-3	1-4	2-1	0-2	I	3-3	2-3	5-1	6-2	1-4	3-1	3-3	1-2	2-3	3-1	0-0	1-3
Cwmamman United	2-5	1-0	1-3	4-2	1-2	2-3	S	1-2	1-1	2-2	7-1	0-3	1-2	2-3	2-2	2-1	1-2	
Newcastle Emlyn	3-1	0-0	1-2	3-4	0-0	0-1	5-1	I	4-3	0-1	2-2	4-2	2-2	3-1	0-3	3-1	0-1	0-1
Pentwyn Dynamo	2-3	2-2	0-3	2-3	2-0	5-3	3-2	2-3	O	5-2	1-1	3-2	1-4	1-2	0-2	1-1	3-1	2-2
Pontlottyn Blast Furnace	1-0	2-1	2-1	2-2	3-2	1-1	1-2	7-1	2-0	N	0-2	3-2	4-3	4-2	1-1	5-0	1-2	1-3
Pontyclun	2-0	0-1	1-1	2-1	1-0	5-2	2-1	2-1	1-2	4-3		7-0	1-1	2-3	0-1	5-1	2-2	3-1
RTB Ebbw Vale	2-0	0-2	3-1	5-1	2-4	0-4	2-3	2-1	3-2	0-0	1-2	T	4-0	0-1	0-3	1-4	1-0	1-2
Risca & Gelli United	1-2	1-3	2-1	5-1	0-1	5-1	1-1	2-0	2-1	1-1	0-2	1-2	H	1-0	1-1	1-1	0-1	1-1
Seven Sisters	0-1	1-0	1-0	4-1	1-1	2-2	0-1	1-0	1-1	1-2	1-3	3-0	1-2	R	1-0	2-2	2-2	2-0
Skewen Athletic	6-1	1-3	4-2	2-2	1-2	0-0	1-0	8-0	3-2	6-2	1-2	1-0	3-1	3-1	E	1-0	4-3	4-0
Tillery	1-1	1-0	1-1	3-2	2-2	2-3	1-3	3-2	1-0	5-4	3-1	1-3	3-3	5-3	1-2	E	2-3	2-0
Treowen Stars	1-1	0-1	2-2	0-1	1-2	2-1	6-1	2-0	2-1	1-1	1-1	1-2	2-1	3-0	1-2			2-1
Troedyrhiw	0-1	1-2	2-0	1-3	0-2	5-1	0-1	2-1	3-2	1-3	0-1	3-3	2-0	2-3	2-0	3-1	1-0	

Division Three

	P	W	D	L	F	A	Pts
Pontyclun	34	21	7	6	73	39	70
Skewen Athletic	34	22	4	8	78	45	70
Caldicot Town	34	19	8	7	69	43	65
Caerau Ely	34	19	7	8	77	46	64
Bryntirion Athletic	34	19	4	11	70	41	61
Seven Sisters	34	15	7	12	59	53	52
Troedyrhiw	34	15	5	14	53	52	50
Pontlottyn Blast Furnace	34	14	8	12	70	72	50
Treowen Stars	34	13	7	14	50	48	46
Tillery	34	11	10	13	64	72	43
Albion Rovers	34	11	6	17	54	64	40
Risca & Gelli United	34	10	9	15	53	65	39
Cwmamman United	34	11	5	18	57	70	38
Chepstow Town	34	10	8	16	67	84	38
Pentwyn Dynamo	34	9	8	17	59	70	35
Newcastle Emlyn	34	10	5	19	51	75	35
RTB Ebbw Vale	34	10	3	21	52	82	33
Caerau United	34	8	6	20	58	93	30

DIVISION THREE CONSTITUTION 2003-04

AFC RHONDDA .... Dinas Park, Dinas, Rhondda, Mid-Glamorgan 07890 294842
ALBION ROVERS. .... Kimberley Park, Malpas Road, Newport, Gwent .... None
BRYNTIRION ATHLETIC .... Bryntirion Park, Bryntirion, Mid-Glamorgan 01656 652702
CAERAU ELY .... Cwrt-y-Ala, Caerau, Cardiff, South Glamorgan 07790 084636
CALDICOT TOWN. .... Jubilee Way, Caldicot, Gwent 01291 423519
CHEPSTOW TOWN .... Larkfield Park, Newport Road, Chepstow, Gwent 01291 629220
CWMAMMAN UNITED .... Grenig Park, Glanamman, Ammanford, Dyfed .... None
FIELDS PARK PONTLLANFRAITH .... Istwyn Park, Pontllanffraith, Blackwood, Gwent 01495 224512
GOYTRE .... Plough Road, Penperlleni, Monmouthshire .... None
LLANTWIT FARDRE .... Tonteg Park, Tonteg, Pontypridd, Mid-Glamorgan .... None
NEWCASTLE EMLYN .... Parc Emlyn, Newcastle Emlyn, Ceredigion 01239 710007
PENTWYN DYNAMO .... Cardiff Athletic Stadium, Leckwith, Cardiff, South Glamorgan 02920 225345
PONTLOTTYN BLAST FURNACE ..... Welfare Ground, Hill Road, Pontlottyn, Mid-Glamorgan 01685 841305
RISCA & GELLI UNITED. .... Ty-Isaf Park, Pontymister Road, Risca, Gwent .... 01633 615081. Club: 01633 615689
SEVEN SISTERS .... Welfare Ground, Seven Sisters, Neath, West Glamorgan 01639 700354
TILLERY .... Woodland Field, Cwmtillery, Gwent 01495 212732
TREOWEN STARS .... Bush Park, Treowen, Gwent 01495 248249
TROEDYRHIW. .... The Willows, Troedrhiw, Mid-Glamorgan 01443 692198

Pontyclun and Skewen Athletic are promoted to Division Two replaced by AFC Rhondda and Fields Park Pontllainfraith. Caerau United are relegated to the South Wales Amateur League replaced by Llantwit Fardre. RTB Ebbw Vale drop to the Gwent County League from which Goytre are promoted.

WELSH LEAGUE (WREXHAM AREA)

	Bala Town	Borras Park Albion	Brickfield Rangers	Brymbo Broughton	Castell Alun Colts	Cefn United	Chirk AAA	Corwen Amateurs	Llangollen Town	Llanuwchllyn	Llay Welfare	Mynydd Isa	Penley	Penycae	Rhos Aelwyd	Ruthin Town Res.
Bala Town	P	3-3	5-3	0-3	2-0	0-4	1-0	0-2	0-2	2-3	1-3	0-2	3-0	1-1	0-3	1-1
Borras Park Albion	2-2	R	0-2	2-2	4-10	0-3	4-2	2-3	3-5	1-3	4-2	1-6	5-1	1-3	2-3	1-8
Brickfield Rangers	8-0	3-2	E	1-4	0-3	0-3	4-2	3-1	0-1	3-2	1-2	1-3	1-0	4-1	0-3	2-3
Brymbo Broughton	7-0	5-3	1-2	M	2-2	1-0	2-0	2-1	4-2	6-1	5-2	1-1	5-0	1-2	2-1	6-0
Castell Alun Colts	4-0	5-0	8-2	3-1	I	1-3	2-0	2-0	4-0	12-1	2-0	1-2	5-1	6-5	2-0	3-2
Cefn United	1-2	1-0	6-1	2-4	3-0	E	4-2	2-2	2-1	5-0	0-0	0-2	1-1	1-2	3-0	2-2
Chirk AAA	1-5	3-3	3-1	2-2	2-3	1-1	R	2-2	2-2	1-0	3-2	1-1	0-4	3-2	0-3	
Corwen Amateurs	0-3	0-1	1-3	1-0	2-3	2-8	2-4		0-6	1-1	1-1	2-1	2-4	0-2	1-0	0-1
Llangollen Town	0-1	8-1	1-0	1-1	1-1	2-0	4-2	3-2	D	5-1	3-3	2-2	3-0	2-3	3-2	2-1
Llanuwchllyn	2-0	2-1	2-5	3-3	1-4	1-5	1-1	2-2	0-2	I	0-2	1-4	0-0	0-1	0-3	2-5
Llay Welfare	3-2	3-4	0-4	2-1	0-3	2-3	2-0	2-4	2-3	V	1-0	2-3	1-3	2-6	1-5	
Mynydd Isa	3-1	3-1	1-1	0-0	3-2	5-0	3-1	2-0	2-1	4-2	5-2	I	4-0	3-3	2-0	1-2
Penley	0-4	0-1	2-2	1-2	0-4	0-4	0-2	4-2	2-1	5-2	2-5	2-4	S	0-3	1-2	0-3
Penycae	2-1	3-4	1-4	1-0	2-0	3-2	1-2	6-1	1-1	1-0	3-1	3-0	1-1	I	1-1	4-1
Rhos Aelwyd	3-1	1-0	2-1	2-3	2-1	3-2	3-0	3-0	3-2	5-3	2-1	6-0	1-3	3-6	O	2-5
Ruthin Town Res.	0-2	2-1	1-1	3-2	0-1	1-4	5-0	3-1	1-0	1-1	3-1	3-1	2-1	5-2	2-3	N

Premier Division		P	W	D	L	F	A	Pts
Castell Alun Colts		30	21	2	7	97	41	65
Penycae		30	19	5	6	74	47	62
Mynydd Isa		30	18	5	7	71	43	59
Ruthin Town Res.		30	18	4	8	74	48	58
Brymbo Broughton		30	16	7	7	78	44	55
Rhos Aelwyd		30	18	1	11	70	52	55
Cefn United		30	16	5	9	75	41	53
Llangollen Town		30	15	6	9	70	46	51
Brickfield Rangers		30	13	3	14	63	64	42
Bala Town	-3	30	10	4	16	43	66	31
Chirk AAA		30	8	7	15	45	71	31
Llay Welfare		30	9	3	18	50	74	30
Borras Park Albion		30	7	4	19	57	97	25
Penley		30	6	5	19	35	77	23
Llanuwchllyn		30	5	6	19	42	94	21
Corwen Amateurs		30	5	5	20	34	76	20

PREMIER DIV. CUP

FIRST ROUND
Bala Town 0 **Rhos Aelwyd** 5
Chirk AAA 1 **Mynydd Isa** 5
Corwen Amateurs 1 **Brickfield Rangers** 4
Llangollen Town 2 **Ruthin Town Res.** 4
Llanuwchllyn 5 Borras Park Albion 2
Llay Welfare 0 **Castell Alun Colts** 5
Penley 0 **Cefn United** 5
Penycae 3 Brymbo Broughton 2

QUARTER-FINALS
Castell Alun Colts 3 Penycae 2
Cefn United 3 Llanuwchllyn 0
Mynydd Isa 2 Rhos Aelwyd 1
Ruthin Town Res. 0 **Brickfield Rangers** 3

SEMI-FINALS
(played over two legs)
Brickfield Rangers 0 **Mynydd Isa** 2
Mynydd Isa 3 Brickfield Rangers 3,
Castell Alun Colts 5 Cefn United 1,
Cefn United 5 **Castell Alun Colts** 2

FINAL
(13th May at Cefn Druids)
Mynydd Isa 2 Castell Alun Colts 2 *aet* (4-2p)

WWW.NLNEWSDESK.CO.UK

PREMIER DIVISION CONSTITUTION 2003-04

BALA TOWN . . . . Castle Park, Bala, Gwynedd . . . . None
BORRAS PARK ALBION . . . . Dean Road, Wrexham, Denbighshire . . . . None
BRICKFIELD RANGERS . . . . Court Road, Wrexham, Denbighshire . . . . None
BRYMBO BROUGHTON . . . . Brymbo Sports Complex, Tanyfron, Wrexham, Denbighshire . . . . None
CASTELL ALUN COLTS . . . . Castell Alun Sports & Leisure, Hope, Wrexham, Denbighshire . . . . None
CEFN UNITED . . . . Ty Mawr, Cae-Gwilym Lane, Cefn Mawr, Wrexham, Denbighshire . . . . None
CHIRK AAA . . . . Holyhead Road, Chirk, Denbighshire . . . . None
LLANGOLLEN TOWN . . . . Tower Field, Dinbren Road, Llangollen, Denbighshire . . . . None
LLAY WELFARE . . . . The Ring, Llay, Wrexham, Denbighshire . . . . None
MYNYDD ISA BT . . . . Argoed Sports Field, Snowden Avenue, Bryn-y-Baal, Flintshire. . . . . None
PENLEY . . . . Maelor School, Penley, Wrexham, Denbighshire . . . . None
PENYCAE. . . . . Afoneitha Road, Penycae, Wrexham, Denbighshire. . . . . None
QUEENS PARK . . . . Queensway Athletics Stadium, Montgomery Road, Wrexham, Denbighshire . . . . None
RHOS AELWYD. . . . . Ponciau Park, Clarke Street, Ponciau, Denbighshire . . . . None
RHOSTYLLEN UNITED . . . . Vicarage Hill Road, Rhostyllen, Wrexham, Denbighshire . . . . None
RUTHIN TOWN RESERVES. . . . . Memorial Playing Fields, Park Road, Ruthin, Denbighshire . . . . None

Corwen Amateurs and Llanuwchllyn drop to Division One replaced by Queens Park and Rhostyllen United. Mynydd Isa become Mynydd Isa BT.

	Acrefair Yth	Airbus Res.	Bradley V.	Brymbo Res.	Corwen Res.	Glyn Ceir.	Gresford R.	Penycae Res.	Queens Pk	Rhos A. Res.	Rhostyllen	Ruthin C.	Summerhill
Acrefair Youth	D	2-0	2-3	1-0	2-1	5-1	1-0	1-1	4-1	4-1	5-3	4-0	3-0
Airbus UK Res.	2-1	I	5-1	1-2	7-0	1-2	2-1	8-0	0-1	7-0	2-4	3-0	1-0
Bradley Villa	2-1	2-2	V	2-2	6-2	3-1	2-4	4-1	1-3	5-2	2-4	2-3	4-2
Brymbo B'ton Res.	3-0	0-3	1-2	I	2-1	3-0	1-2	2-2	1-4	1-1	1-2	7-0	1-2
Corwen Ams Res.	1-8	0-2	0-7	1-4	S	1-1	2-9	0-1	1-3	0-1	2-8	2-2	3-1
Glyn Ceiriog	2-4	2-5	2-1	4-6	5-1	I	0-4	2-1	4-3	6-2	2-4	4-1	7-2
Gresford Ath. Res.	0-3	3-4	4-3	3-6	4-0	4-1	O	0-1	0-2	0-0	1-7	2-4	1-3
Penycae Res.	1-2	1-7	2-2	0-2	5-1	0-1	2-4	N	1-3	2-1	4-0	3-0	4-1
Queens Park	0-0	3-1	3-0	4-0	7-1	2-1	10-5	3-1		2-0	2-1	2-1	3-1
Rhos Aelwyd Res.	2-5	1-4	1-2	2-2	6-0	4-0	1-4	1-3	2-5		1-3	2-0	1-5
Rhostyllen United	2-1	2-0	3-4	1-0	18-0	5-1	3-1	1-3	0-4	4-0	O	3-1	3-1
Ruthin T. Colts	0-7	0-6	1-2	3-2	2-0	2-0	3-2	3-2	1-5	4-1	2-3	N	2-2
Summerhill Utd	3-3	4-2	8-2	3-1	3-2	0-3	1-2	4-1	0-4	4-2	3-2	4-0	E

Division One		P	W	D	L	F	A	Pts
Queens Park	-3	24	21	1	2	79	27	61
Rhostyllen United		24	18	0	6	90	40	54
Acrefair Youth		24	16	3	5	69	29	51
Airbus UK Res.		24	15	1	8	75	32	46
Bradley Villa		24	12	3	9	64	59	39
Summerhill Utd		24	11	2	11	57	57	35
Gresford Ath. Res.		24	10	2	12	63	59	32
Glyn Ceiriog		24	10	1	13	52	64	31
Brymbo Bro. Res.		24	8	5	11	47	44	29
Penycae Res.		24	8	3	13	38	57	27
Ruthin T. Colts		24	8	2	14	35	70	26
Rhos Aelwyd Res.		24	4	3	17	35	72	15
Corwen Ams Res.		24	1	2	21	22	116	5

DIVISION ONE CONSTITUTION 2003-04

ACREFAIR YOUTH .... The Bont Playing Field, Froncysyllte, Wrexham, Denbighshire .... None
AIRBUS UK RESERVES .... Airbus UK, Broughton, Chester, Cheshire 01244 522393
BRADLEY VILLA .... The Wauns, Bradley, Wrexham, Denbighshire .... None
BRYMBO BROUGHTON RESERVES . Brymbo Sports Complex, Tanyfron, Wrexham, Denbighshire .... None
BRYNTEG VILLAGE .... Solway Banks, Southsea, Wrexham, Denbighshire .... None
CEFN UNITED RESERVES .... Ty Mawr, Cae-Gwilym Lane, Cefn Mawr, Wrexham, Denbighshire .... None
CORWEN AMATEURS .... War Memorial Park, Corwen, Denbighshire. .... None
GLYN CEIRIOG .... The Cross, Glyn Ceiriog, Wrexham, Denbighshire .... None
GRESFORD ATHLETIC RESERVES .... Clappers Lane, Gresford, Wrexham .... None
LLANUWCHLLYN .... Village Hall, Llanuwchllyn, Gwynedd .... None
PENYCAE RESERVES .... Afoneitha Road, Penycae, Wrexham, Denbighshire .... None
RHOS AELWYD .... Ponciau Park, Clarke Street, Ponciau, Denbighshire .... None
RUTHIN TOWN COLTS .... Memorial Playing Fields, Park Road, Ruthin, Denbighshire .... None
SUMMERHILL UNITED .... Bryn Alyn School, Gwersyllt, Wrexham, Denbighshire .... None

Queens Park and Rhostyllen United are promoted to the Premier Division replaced by Llanuwchllyn and Corwen Amateurs. Corwen Amateurs Reserves drop to Division Two replaced by Cefn United Reserves and Brynteg Village.

	Bala T. Res.	Borr. P. Res.	Brynteg V.	Cast. A. Res.	Cefn U. Res.	Chirk Res.	Coedpoeth	Johnstown	L'gollen Res.	Llay Res.	Mold Res.	New Brigh.	Overton Rec
Bala Town Res.	D	1-3	3-5	2-1	0-4	1-2	0-6	2-1	2-2	1-1	2-3	1-1	3-1
Borras Park Res.	0-1	I	5-5	1-4	0-10	1-3	3-4	7-2	3-3	4-1	2-5	3-3	4-4
Brynteg Village	4-1	6-3	V	10-2	2-2	2-1	2-1	3-1	7-1	8-2	4-2	6-2	4-3
Castell AC Res.	0-3	4-3	4-5	I	3-1	2-5	2-9	4-4	2-2	5-2	5-0	1-1	1-0
Cefn United Res.	4-0	0-0	6-6	4-2	S	1-0	2-2	2-0	3-1	7-0	3-0	1-1	6-3
Chirk AAA Res.	3-4	3-1	2-2	1-1	0-2	I	1-4	3-1	2-2	4-4	2-2	2-2	3-2
Coedpoeth United	5-1	1-1	2-3	3-0	0-1	5-0	O	6-2	4-4	2-1	3-1	5-5	5-1
Johnstown	1-0	2-2	0-4	0-2	1-3	1-0	2-0	N	3-0	0-1	1-3	4-2	1-1
Llangollen Res.	1-0	3-0	3-4	0-4	1-3	1-2	3-1	1-2		4-0	2-3	3-4	2-2
Llay Welfare Res.	3-2	3-2	0-8	1-0	0-1	0-3	3-4	3-4	2-2		1-2	3-2	1-3
Mold Alex. Res.	4-0	4-0	6-5	4-1	1-2	1-2	2-2	11-0	3-1	5-0	T	2-2	2-1
New Brighton V.	4-1	2-1	4-4	5-2	0-3	0-0	2-3	1-0	1-4	5-4	0-2	W	4-3
Overton Rec.	1-2	1-2	0-10	0-0	0-5	1-2	1-2	5-2	3-2	1-4	4-1	1-1	O

Division Two		P	W	D	L	F	A	Pts
Brynteg Village		24	18	5	1	119	56	59
Cefn United Res.		24	18	5	1	76	23	59
Mold Alex. Res.		24	15	3	6	72	43	48
Coedpoeth United		24	14	5	5	79	43	47
Chirk AAA Res.		24	10	7	7	46	43	37
New Brighton V.		24	7	10	7	54	59	31
Castell AC Res.	-3	24	8	5	11	52	66	29
Bala Town Res.	-3	24	7	3	14	33	60	24
Johnstown		24	7	3	14	35	66	24
Llangollen T. Res.		24	5	7	12	48	60	22
Llay Welfare Res.		24	6	3	15	40	79	21
Borras Park Res.		24	4	7	13	51	75	19
Overton Rec.		24	3	5	16	40	72	14

DIVISION TWO CONSTITUTION 2003-04

BALA TOWN RESERVES .... Castle Park, Bala, Gwynedd .... None
BORRAS PARK ALBION RESERVES .... Dean Road, Wrexham, Denbighshire. .... None
CASTELL ALUN COLTS RESERVES....... Castell Alun Sports & Leisure, Hope, Wrexham .... None
CHIRK AAA RESERVES .... Holyhead Road, Chirk, Denbighshire. .... None
COEDPOETH UNITED .... Pengelli Playing Fields, Coedpoeth, Wrexham, Denbighshire .... None
CORWEN AMATEURS RESERVES .... War Memorial Park, Corwen, Denbighshire. .... None
JOHNSTOWN .... Moreton Playing Fields, Johnstown, Wrexham, Denbighshire .... None
LLANGOLLEN TOWN RESERVES ...... Tower Field, Dinbren Road, Llangollen, Denbighshire .... None
LLAY WELFARE RESERVES .... The Ring, Llay, Wrexham, Denbighshire .... None
MOLD ALEXANDRA RESERVES .... Alyn Park, Denbigh Road, Mold, Clwyd .... None
MYNYDD ISA BT RESERVES....... Argoed Sports Field, Snowden Avenue, Bryn-y-Baal, Flintshire .... None
NEW BRIGHTON VILLA .... New Brighton Community Centre, New Brighton, Mold, Flintshire .... None
OVERTON RECREATION .... Recreation Ground, Overton-on-Dee, Wrexham, Denbighshire .... None
RHOS AELWYD YOUTH .... Johnstown Circle, Johnstown, Wrexham, Denbighshire .... None
RUABON VILLA .... Ruabon Recreation Ground, Maes-y-Laen Lane, Ruabon, Wrexham, Denbighshire ...... None

Brynteg Village and Cefn United Reserves are promoted to Division One replaced by Corwen Amateurs Reserves. Ruabon Villa, Rhos Aelwyd Youth come up from Division Three. Newcomers are Mynydd Isa BT Reserves.

	Acrefair C.	Bor. P. Colts	B'field Res.	Broncoed	C'poeth Res.	Hawarden	J'town Colts	Penyffordd	Qu. Pk Res.	Rhos Youth	R'tyllen Res.	Ruabon V.	S'hill Res.
Acrefair Colts		2-2	5-2	3-4	0-5	2-7	3-1	2-3	n/a	4-0	3-1	1-4	10-0
Borras Park Colts	3-4		1-5	2-4	8-0	4-1	4-3	3-4	3-6	2-3	5-7	1-9	6-4
Brickfield R. Res.	2-3	7-0	D	2-2	6-0	3-2	0-3	3-2	n/a	3-5	2-2	1-10	4-3
Broncoed Tigers	8-2	1-1	1-3	I	10-1	7-1	4-2	2-3	n/a	1-4	4-4	2-1	2-0
Coedpoeth Res.	4-2	2-2	4-3	1-3	V	0-5	3-1	1-5	n/a	1-3	1-9	0-2	n/a
Hawarden Rgrs	1-4	5-0	2-2	1-2	6-2		2-1	4-4	n/a	1-11	3-3	4-6	n/a
Johnstown Colts	2-3	3-5	2-1	4-2	6-3	2-1	T	7-3	4-2	1-2	8-4	1-5	1-2
Penyffordd	8-1	2-0	2-6	1-2	12-0	3-2	5-4	H	n/a	0-6	0-5	0-3	8-2
Queens Park Res.	n/a	n/a	1-1	n/a	5-0	n/a	n/a	n/a	R	4-4	n/a	1-2	n/a
Rhos Aelwyd Youth	4-2	0-1	3-1	1-5	2-2	1-1	3-3	3-1	E	2-2	0-1	3-1	
Rhostyllen Res.	3-4	7-3	1-3	2-3	7-0	2-1	7-4	5-1	7-5	0-5	E	1-6	3-1
Ruabon Villa	6-3	4-2	7-0	0-1	5-1	5-1	2-2	2-3	n/a	1-0	6-0		9-0
Summerhill Res.	1-3	1-3	2-10	1-4	5-1	2-2	3-2	1-7	n/a	n/a	2-4	n/a	

Division Three	P	W	D	L	F	A	Pts
Ruabon Villa	20	16	1	3	85	24	49
Broncoed Tigers	20	13	3	4	68	39	42
Rhos Ael. Youth -3	20	11	4	5	58	33	34
Penyffordd	20	10	1	9	62	61	31
Rhostyllen U. Res.	20	8	4	8	72	64	28
Acrefair Colts	20	9	1	10	53	70	28
Brickfield R. Res.	20	8	3	9	55	57	27
Johnstown Colts	20	7	2	11	60	62	23
Hawarden Rgrs	20	5	4	11	51	64	19
Borras Park Colts	20	5	3	12	49	73	18
Coedpoeth U. Res.	20	4	2	14	31	97	14

Note – Queens Park Reserves and
Summerhill United Reserves withdrew
during the course of the season.
Their results are shown to the left but have
been expunged from the league table

DIVISION THREE CONSTITUTION 2003-04

BORRAS PARK ALBION COLTS	Dean Road, Wrexham, Denbighshire	None
BRADLEY VILLA RESERVES	The Wauns, Bradley, Wrexham, Denbighshire	None
BRICKFIELD RANGERS RESERVES	Court Road, Wrexham, Denbighshire	None
BRONCOED TIGERS	Mold Sports Centre, Wrexham Street, Mold, Clwyd	01352 756116
BUCKLEY TOWN RESERVES	Globe Way, Liverpool Way, Buckley, Flintshire	None
CEFN UNITED COLTS	Ty Mawr, Cae-Gwilym Lane, Cefn Mawr, Wrexham, Denbighshire	None
COEDPOETH UNITED RESERVES	Pengelli Playing Fields, Coedpoeth, Wrexham, Denbighshire	None
HAWARDEN RANGERS	Gladstone Playing Fields, Hawarden, Flintshire	None
JOHNSTOWN COLTS	Moreton Playing Fields, Johnstown, Wrexham, Denbighshire	None
MOLD JUNIORS	Alyn Park, Denbigh Road, Mold, Clwyd	None
NEW BRIGHTON VILLA RESERVES	New Brighton Community Centre, New Brighton, Mold, Clwyd	None
PENLEY RESERVES	Maelor School, Penley, Wrexham, Denbighshire	None
PENYFFORDD	Abbotts Lane Infant School, Penyffordd, Flintshire	None
RHOS AELWYD YOUTH RESERVES	Johnstown Circle, Johnstown, Wrexham, Denbighshire	None
RHOSTYLLEN UNITED RERVES	Vicarage Hill Road, Rhostyllen, Wrexham, Denbighshire	None

Queens Park Reserves and Summerhill United Reserves withdrew during the course of the season. Ruabon Villa and Rhos Aelwyd Youth go up to Division Two. Newcomers are Penley Reserves, Bradley Villa Reserves, New Brighton Villa Reserves, Buckley Town Reserves, Cefn United Colts, Mold Juniors and Rhos Aelwyd Youth Reserves.

DIVISION ONE CUP

FIRST ROUND
Airbus UK Res. 4 Gresford Athletic Res. 2
Bradley Villa 2 Acrefair Youth 1
Queens Park 7 Ruthin Colts 1
Rhos Aelwyd Res. 6 Summerhill United 0
Rhostyllen Utd 6 Glyn Ceiriog 4
QUARTER-FINALS
Bradley Villa 2 **Brymbo Broughton Res.** 5
Corwen Amateurs Res. 3 **Penycae Res.** 5
Rhos Aelwyd Res. 0 **Queens Park** 1
Rhostyllen United 4 Airbus UK Res. 2
SEMI-FINALS
(played over two legs)
Brymbo Res. 3 Penycae Res. 1,
Penycae Res. 1 **Brymbo** Res. 1
Rhostyllen United 2 Queens Park 2,
Queens Park 2 **Rhostyllen United** 3
FINAL
(6th May at Chirk AAA)
Brymbo Broughton Res. 1
Rhostyllen United 3

DIVISION TWO CUP

FIRST ROUND
Bala Town Res. 3 **Llangollen Town Res.** 4 *aet*
Castell Alun Colts Res. 1 **Borras Park Albion Res.** 5
Chirk AAA Res. 4 Mold Alexandra Res. 1
Johnstown 1 **Brynteg Village** 3
New Brighton Villa 1 **Coedpoeth United** 4
QUARTER-FINALS
Borras Park Albion Res. 2 **Overton Recreation** 5
Brynteg Village 2 Cefn United Res. 1
Llangollen Town Res. 1 **Coedpoeth United** 2
Llay Welfare Res. 2 Chirk AAA Res. 1
SEMI-FINALS
(played over two legs)
Brynteg Village 2 Coedpoeth 1,
Coedpoeth United 0 **Brynteg Village** 3
Overton Recreation 1 **Llay Res.** 7,
Llay Welfare Res. 3 Overton Recreation 0
FINAL
(7th May at Brymbo Broughton)
Brynteg Village 4
Llay Welfare Res. 1

DIVISION THREE CUP

FIRST ROUND
Brickfield Rangers Res. 2 Rhos Aelwyd Colts 1
Rhostyllen Utd Res. 1 **Penyfford** 5
Ruabon Villa 1 Acrefair Colts 0
Summerhill United Res. 2 **Borras Park Albion Colts** 4
QUARTER-FINALS
Brickfield Rangers Res. 3 Penyffordd 2
Broncoed Tigers 7 Coedpoeth United Res. 1
Hawarden Rangers 1 Borras Park Albion Colts 0
Ruabon Villa 6 Johnstown Colts 1
SEMI-FINALS
(played over two legs)
Broncoed Tigers 3 Ruabon Villa 5,
Ruabon Villa 1 Broncoed Tigers 1
Hawarden Rangers 1 Brickfield Rangers Res. 1,
Brickfield Rangers Res. 2 **Hawarden Rangers** 4
FINAL
(8th May at Llay Welfare)
Ruabon Villa 3
Hawarden Rangers 1

HORACE WYNNE CUP
(Division One, Two and Three clubs)

FINAL
(14th May at Chirk AAA)
Rhostyllen United 2 Queens Park 0

WELSH PREMIER LEAGUE

(Formerly League of Wales)

	Aberystwyth Town	Afan Lido	Bangor City	Barry Town	Caernarfon Town	Caersws	Carmarthen Town	Connah's Quay Nomads	Cwmbran Town	Flexsys Cefn Druids	Haverfordwest County	Llanelli	Newtown	Oswestry Town	Port Talbot Town	Rhyl	Total Network Solutions	Welshpool Town
Aberystwyth Town		0-0	0-1	3-1	1-1	1-3	2-0	3-1	1-1	3-0	2-1	2-0	3-1	5-1	1-0	1-1	2-2	0-0
Afan Lido	1-1		1-2	0-1	0-1	1-0	2-0	3-0	1-2	0-3	0-0	2-2	1-2	0-0	2-0	1-1	0-6	2-0
Bangor City	0-1	2-1		1-1	3-1	5-0	3-2	2-1	2-1	2-0	2-1	8-0	0-1	2-2	3-0	1-0	0-2	3-1
Barry Town	5-1	1-0	3-0		3-2	3-2	3-0	3-1	2-1	6-0	3-0	1-0	2-2	4-0	0-1	4-1	0-0	2-1
Caernarfon Town	0-3	1-1	2-2	1-4		1-2	2-1	2-0	3-1	3-3	0-1	1-1	1-2	1-1	2-1	0-2	1-1	0-0
Caersws	2-2	1-2	1-1	0-1	2-1		4-1	1-0	1-1	2-1	1-1	4-0	2-3	3-1	2-2	0-4	3-1	
Carmarthen Town	0-2	0-2	0-6	2-2	0-3	3-1		1-1	0-4	0-1	0-2	2-1	1-4	2-1	0-2	0-3	1-1	5-1
Connah's Quay Nomads	2-1	2-1	2-1	0-2	1-1	1-3	1-0		1-1	4-1	3-1	3-0	1-0	2-4	2-2	2-1	0-1	4-0
Cwmbran Town	2-1	0-2	0-0	2-3	1-0	3-2	4-0	0-2		0-0	3-1	3-2	2-1	0-0	1-1	2-0	0-0	4-0
Flexsys Cefn Druids	3-0	0-1	0-2	0-3	2-1	0-1	0-1	0-0	1-0		0-1	4-0	3-0	0-0	3-2	0-2	0-1	0-2
Haverfordwest County	0-3	1-4	0-4	2-4	3-1	3-2	0-2	1-3	4-0	2-4		2-3	2-2	0-2	2-1	1-5	0-3	0-0
Llanelli	2-3	1-3	2-5	2-3	3-3	1-2	1-2	3-5	0-3	3-1	1-3		2-3	3-1	0-2	0-3	2-3	0-1
Newtown	3-1	1-2	2-1	0-0	0-3	0-2	2-2	1-2	4-1	1-2	4-0	2-1		1-3	2-4	0-2	2-4	0-2
Oswestry Town	0-1	0-3	1-2	0-4	3-0	0-2	1-2	2-3	0-5	0-1	1-1	3-1	0-0		0-0	2-3	0-3	1-1
Port Talbot Town	0-1	0-2	0-2	0-5	3-2	0-0	0-2	0-1	1-0	2-1	1-0	4-1			0-3	1-1	1-0	
Rhyl	0-0	2-2	0-1	0-1	1-0	4-0	1-0	1-2	2-1	1-0	1-0	1-1	1-2	1-1	3-0		0-1	2-0
Total Network Solutions	3-0	1-1	4-2	1-0	0-2	2-1	2-0	2-0	1-0	2-0	1-2	3-1	1-1	2-1	1-0	5-0		2-0
Welshpool Town	1-3	0-0	1-4	0-4	1-0	0-4	1-1	1-2	1-2	3-3	0-2	1-0	1-0	6-1	2-3	0-2	1-2	

	P	HOME					AWAY					TOTAL					
		W	D	L	F	A	W	D	L	F	A	W	D	L	F	A	Pts
Barry Town	34	14	2	1	45	12	12	3	2	39	14	26	5	3	84	26	83
Total Net. Solutions	34	13	2	2	33	11	11	6	0	35	10	24	8	2	68	21	80
Bangor City	34	12	2	3	39	15	10	3	4	36	19	22	5	7	75	34	71
Aberystwyth Town	34	9	6	2	30	14	8	3	6	24	24	17	9	8	54	38	60
Connah's Quay N.	34	10	3	4	31	20	8	2	7	24	26	18	5	11	55	46	59
Rhyl	34	8	4	5	21	12	9	3	5	31	21	17	7	10	52	33	58
Afan Lido	34	5	5	7	17	21	9	5	3	27	13	14	10	10	44	34	52
Caersws	34	8	5	4	30	22	7	1	9	27	30	15	6	13	57	52	51
Cwmbran Town	34	9	5	3	27	15	5	3	9	24	25	14	8	12	51	40	50
Newtown	34	5	2	10	25	32	7	4	6	23	22	12	6	16	48	54	42
Port Talbot Town	34	6	3	8	16	24	5	3	9	20	27	11	6	17	36	51	39
Flexsys Cefn Druids	34	6	2	9	16	17	5	3	9	21	34	11	5	18	37	51	38
Haverfordwest Co.	34	4	2	11	23	43	6	3	8	17	25	10	5	19	40	68	35
Caernarfon Town	34	4	7	6	21	26	4	3	10	22	27	8	10	16	43	53	34
Carmarthen Town	34	4	3	10	17	37	5	2	10	16	29	9	5	20	33	66	32
Oswestry Town	34	2	4	11	14	32	4	6	7	22	35	6	10	18	36	67	28
Welshpool Town	34	4	3	10	20	33	3	4	10	10	29	7	7	20	30	62	28
Llanelli	34	3	1	13	28	46	1	4	12	14	43	4	5	25	42	89	17

Llanelli are relegated to the Welsh League replaced by Cymru Alliance champions Porthmadog. Oswestry Town and Total Network Solutions have amalgamated under the latter's banner. Flexsys Cefn Druids become NEWI Cefn Druids

	ABE	AFA	BAN	BAR	CFN	CAE	CAR	CQN	CWM	FLE	HAV	LLA	NEW	OSW	POR	RHY	TNS	WEL
Aberystwyth Town		357 *28 Mar*	650 *4 Jan*	1023 *6 Dec*	413 *24 Aug*	613 *24 Jan*	487 *14 Feb*	423 *4 Feb*	557 *13 Dec*	473 *19 Oct*	501 *29 Nov*	324 *21 Apr*	470 *14 Sep*	385 *12 Apr*	482 *30 Dec*	397 *25 Mar*	473 *15 Apr*	278 *8 Apr*
Afan Lido	161 *1 Apr*		288 *28 Sep*	376 *22 Nov*	140 *19 Apr*	189 *19 Oct*	266 *14 Mar*	208 *7 Dec*	247 *24 Jan*	238 *4 Jan*	259 *13 Sep*	284 *23 Aug*	125 *14 Dec*	150 *22 Mar*	438 *21 Apr*	117 *15 Feb*	182 *8 Feb*	211 *29 Oct*
Bangor City	508 *17 Sep*	424 *1 Feb*		1012 *22 Feb*	839 *26 Dec*	458 *7 Sep*	492 *18 Jan*	392 *11 Mar*	635 *24 Aug*	516 *22 Nov*	308 *14 Dec*	407 *22 Mar*	655 *2 Nov*	568 *5 Oct*	395 *19 Apr*	420 *1 Apr*	463 *7 Dec*	565 *21 Sep*
Barry Town	586 *26 Apr*	381 *11 Apr*	587 *19 Oct*		261 *14 Dec*	274 *7 Sep*	437 *17 Dec*	373 *24 Aug*	561 *21 Apr*	322 *30 Mar*	373 *27 Sep*	456 *4 Feb*	353 *4 Jan*	358 *30 Nov*	651 *13 Sep*	367 *1 Mar*	1147 *25 Jan*	326 *9 Nov*
Caernarfon Town	174 *21 Dec*	159 *30 Nov*	694 *21 Apr*	295 *17 Aug*		134 *15 Mar*	129 *9 Nov*	212 *4 Jan*	147 *19 Oct*	143 *13 Sep*	197 *15 Feb*	166 *7 Sep*	137 *6 Nov*	159 *26 Apr*	174 *25 Jan*	229 *30 Oct*	153 *28 Sep*	239 *12 Apr*
Caersws	280 *21 Sep*	201 *22 Feb*	423 *28 Mar*	380 *1 Apr*	258 *2 Nov*		230 *1 Feb*	246 *22 Mar*	208 *5 Nov*	195 *7 Dec*	240 *4 Jan*	208 *19 Apr*	605 *21 Apr*	275 *26 Oct*	205 *14 Dec*	172 *14 Sep*	303 *24 Aug*	385 *5 Oct*
Carmarthen Town	592 *4 Oct*	387 *26 Oct*	360 *14 Sep*	447 *2 Nov*	272 *22 Mar*	403 *28 Sep*		289 *12 Apr*	277 *28 Mar*	277 *14 Dec*	407 *21 Apr*	527 *6 Dec*	295 *19 Apr*	288 *11 Mar*	402 *23 Aug*	438 *25 Jan*	482 *4 Jan*	293 *22 Feb*
Connah's Quay Nomads	116 *1 Oct*	113 *26 Apr*	201 *15 Apr*	153 *20 Dec*	256 *30 Aug*	142 *9 Nov*	105 *23 Nov*		139 *1 Mar*	201 *25 Jan*	127 *19 Oct*	143 *14 Sep*	153 *28 Mar*	131 *14 Dec*	167 *28 Sep*	210 *15 Mar*	167 *1 Apr*	166 *29 Nov*
Cwmbran Town	380 *16 Aug*	240 *20 Sep*	184 *21 Dec*	375 *28 Dec*	156 *22 Feb*	131 *19 Mar*	231 *6 Sep*	126 *26 Oct*		123 *22 Mar*	144 *6 Dec*	187 *1 Nov*	112 *23 Apr*	138 *1 Feb*	175 *22 Nov*	195 *31 Aug*	185 *19 Apr*	157 *18 Jan*
Flexsys Cefn Druids	239 *22 Feb*	141 *31 Aug*	452 *11 Apr*	281 *7 Sep*	214 *17 Jan*	127 *26 Apr*	129 *17 Aug*	385 *20 Sep*	183 *8 Nov*		136 *15 Mar*	131 *5 Oct*	203 *1 Feb*	317 *26 Dec*	194 *1 Mar*	268 *29 Nov*	203 *29 Oct*	135 *21 Dec*
Haverfordwest County	512 *18 Apr*	239 *17 Jan*	272 *18 Aug*	435 *31 Jan*	257 *5 Oct*	212 *31 Aug*	424 *26 Dec*	198 *22 Feb*	212 *26 Apr*	145 *2 Nov*		312 *11 Mar*	198 *26 Oct*	184 *21 Sep*	301 *21 Mar*	148 *21 Dec*	151 *23 Nov*	189 *7 Sep*
Llanelli	225 *1 Feb*	210 *20 Dec*	181 *9 Nov*	286 *2 Oct*	163 *8 Feb*	230 *30 Nov*	142 *18 Jan*	208 *18 Jan*	156 *8 Apr*	160 *15 Feb*	127 *29 Oct*		161 *21 Sep*	167 *31 Aug*	240 *18 Oct*	104 *12 Apr*	252 *1 Mar*	202 *17 Aug*
Newtown	505 *18 Jan*	220 *17 Aug*	250 *31 Aug*	290	235 *18 Mar*	675 *26 Dec*	295 *30 Nov*	170 *7 Sep*	260 *29 Oct*	265 *28 Sep*	201 *8 Apr*	285 *25 Jan*		296 *21 Dec*	280 *15 Feb*	295 *9 Nov*	355 *3 Dec*	525 *26 Apr*
Oswestry Town	178 *23 Nov*	102 *9 Nov*	328 *14 Feb*	217 *19 Apr*	201 *6 Dec*	168 *4 Mar*	118 *29 Oct*	137 *17 Aug*	117 *28 Sep*	231 *4 Apr*	155 *25 Jan*	155 *4 Jan*	160 *24 Aug*		225 *11 Jan*	168 *19 Oct*	410 *13 Sep*	292 *28 Mar*
Port Talbot Town	155 *11 Mar*	655 *26 Dec*	193 *30 Nov*	177 *17 Jan*	177	190 *17 Aug*	236 *18 Dec*	169 *1 Feb*	231 *2 May*	172 *26 Oct*	276 *8 Nov*	287 *21 Feb*	186 *5 Oct*	173 *7 Sep*		142 *26 Apr*	117 *15 Mar*	173 *31 Aug*
Rhl	243 *7 Sep*	301 *5 Oct*	428 *18 Mar*	439 *26 Oct*	228 *11 Mar*	283	251 *21 Sep*	290 *21 Apr*	341 *4 Jan*	344 *18 Apr*	236 *24 Aug*	229 *23 Nov*	341 *22 Mar*	377 *22 Feb*	244 *30 Mar*		242 *13 Dec*	320 *1 Feb*
Total Network Solutions	336 *21 Mar*	165 *7 Sep*	282 *26 Apr*	322 *21 Sep*	235 *1 Feb*	264 *21 Dec*	158 *5 Apr*	167 *5 Oct*	197 *30 Nov*	176 *11 Mar*	192 *12 Apr*	138 *26 Oct*	236 *22 Feb*	706 *17 Jan*	195 *2 Nov*	213 *20 Aug*		628 *26 Dec*
Welshpool Town	229 *25 Oct*	98 *11 Mar*	234 *25 Jan*	244 *22 Mar*	127 *23 Nov*	238 *15 Feb*	162 *19 Oct*	249 *18 Apr*	171 *14 Sep*	181 *23 Aug*	152 *5 Apr*	127 *14 Dec*	239 *7 Dec*	223 *1 Nov*	136 *4 Jan*	194 *28 Sep*	308 *21 Apr*	

WELSH PREMIER LEAGUE GATES 'N DATES

CONSTITUTION FOR 2003-04

ABERYSTWYTH TOWN   Manager: Gary Finley   Colours: Green, black & white
Park Avenue, Aberystwyth, Ceredigion SY23 1PG   www.atfcnews.co.uk
Tel: 01970 612122   Fax: 01970 617939
    Staged a testimonial this summer against Cardiff for long-serving player Kevin Morrison.

AFAN LIDO   *Manager: Mark Robinson*   *Colours: Red*
Runtech Stadium, Princess Margaret Way, Aberavon Beach, Port Talbot, W. Glamorgan SA12 6QW
Tel/Fax: 01639 881432   *Club: 01639 892960*   *www.afanlidofc.co.uk*
    Appeared in UEFA Cup once, borrowing Port Talbot rugby ground to stage home leg in 1995-96.

BANGOR CITY   Manager: Peter Davenport   Colours: Blue
The Stadium, Farrar Road, Bangor, Gwynedd LL57 3HU   www.bangorcityfc.com
Tel: 01248 718253   Fax: 01248 716873
    As the Welsh Premier InterToto Cup representatives, Bangor began their season in June.

BARRY TOWN   *Manager: Kenny Brown*   *Colours: Blue & yellow*
Jenner Park, Barry Road, Barry, South Glamorgan CF62 9BG   *www.barrytownfc.co.uk*
Tel: 01446 735858   *Fax: 01446 701884*
    Began another Champions League qualifying campaign in July with a tie against Vardar Skopje.

CAERNARFON TOWN   Manager: Adie Jones   Colours: Yellow & green
The Oval, Marcus Street, Caernarfon, Gwynedd
Tel: 01286 675002   Fax: 01286 675002   Club: 01286 674620
    Remained in NPL following L of W inauguration in 1992, playing home games at Curzon Ashton.

CAERSWS   *Manager: Micky Evans*   *Colours: Blue & white*
Recreation Ground, Bridge Street, Caersws, Powys SY17 5DT   *www.caersws-fc.com*
Tel: 01686 688753
    Founder members of the League of Wales, joining in 1992 as Cymru Alliance champions.

CARMARTHEN TOWN   Manager: Tomi Morgan   Colours: Old gold & black
Richmond Park, Priory Street, Carmarthen, Carmarthenshire SA31 1LR
Tel: 01267 232101   Fax: 01267 222851   www.carmarthentownafc.net
    Have enjoyed one European adventure, losing to AIK Stockholm in 2001-02 InterToto Cup.

CONNAH'S QUAY NOMADS   *Manager: Neville Powell*   *Colours: White & black*
Deeside College, Kelsterton Road, Connah's Quay, Deeside, Flintshire CH5 4BR
Tel: 01244 816418   *Fax: 01244 816418*   *www.nomadsfc.co.uk*
    Manager Neville Powell signed a new two-year contract with Nomads this summer.

CWMBRAN TOWN   Manager: Brian Coyne   Colours: Blue & white
Cwmbran Stadium, Henllys Way, Cwmbran, Gwent NP44 3XL   www.cwmbranafc.co.uk
Tel: 01633 628969   Fax: 01633 863324
    Rocked by the death of popular long-serving manager Tony Willcox during course of last season.

HAVERFORDWEST COUNTY   *Manager: Deryn Brace*   *Colours: Blue*
Bridge Meadow Stadium, Bridge Meadow Lane, Haverfordwest, Pembrokeshire SA61 2EX
Tel: 01437 769048   *Fax: 01437 769048*
    Bridge Meadow Stadium hosted international football in May in the Four Nations Tournament.

NEWI CEFN DRUIDS   Manager: Steve O'Shaughnessy
Plas Kynaston Lane, Plas Kynaston, Cefn Mawr, Wrexham, LL14 3PY
Tel/Fax: 01978 824332   Club: 01978 824279   Colours: Black & white
    Change name from Flexsys Cefn Druids following a change of sponsor.

NEWTOWN   *Manager: Roger Preece*   *Colours: Red*
Latham Park, Park Lane, Newtown, Powys SY1 6XX   *www.newtown-fc.co.uk*
Tel: 01686 623120/622666   *Fax: 01686 623813*   *Club: 01686 626159*
    New era begins following departure of long serving manager Brian Coyne.

PORT TALBOT TOWN   Manager: Mark Jones   Colours: Blue & white

Victoria Park, Victoria Road, Aberavon, Port Talbot, West Glamorgan SA12 6AD

Tel: 01639 882465   Fax: 01639 886991   www.porttalbotafc.co.uk

Feature in Welsh Premier's most local derby – against Afan Lido, barely a mile away.

PORTHMADOG   *Manager: Viv Williams*   *Colours: Red & white*

Y Traeth, Porthmadog, Gwynedd   *Tel: 01766 514687*

Promoted back to the Welsh Premier after achieving a treble in 2002-03.

RHYL   Manager: John Hulse   Colours: White

Belle Vue, Grange Road, Rhyl, Clwyd LL18 4BT   www.rhylfc.com

Tel: 01745 338327   Fax: 01745 338327

Triumphed in League Cup final against former Northern Premier League rivals Bangor City.

TOTAL NETWORK SOLUTIONS   *Manager: Ken McKenna*   *Colours: Green & white*

Recreation Park, Treflan, Llansantffraid, Powys SY22 6AE   *www.saints-alive.co.uk*

Tel: 01691 828112   *Fax: 01691 828862*

Subject of a summer merger with league neighbours Oswestry Town.

WELSHPOOL TOWN   Manager: Russ Cadwallader   Colours: White & black

Maesydre Recreation Grounds, Welshpool, Powys   Tel: None

Reprieved from relegation by the merger of Oswestry Town and Total Network Solutions.

LEAGUE CUP
(All ties prior to Final over two legs)

PRELIMINARY ROUND
Haverfordwest County 1 Llanelli 1,
Llanelli 1 **Haverfordwest County** 2
Welshpool Town 1 Oswestry Town 3,
Oswestry Town 0 Welshpool Town 1
FIRST ROUND
Afan Lido 0 Port Talbot Town 2,
Port Talbot Town 1 Afan Lido 2
Bangor City 3 Newtown 1,
Newtown 2 **Bangor City** 4
Barry Town 2 Aberystwyth Town 3,
Aberystwyth Town 1 Barry Town 2 *aet*
(Aberystwyth Town on on away goals)
Caernarfon Town 3 Flexsys Cefn Druids 0,
Flexsys Cefn Druids 3 **Caernarfon Town** 2
Caersws 6 Connah's Quay Nomads 0,
Connah's Quay Nomads 0 **Caersws** 0
Carmarthen Town 3 Haverfordwest County 3,
Haverfordwest County 0
Carmarthen Town 1
Cwmbran Town 2 Oswestry Town 0,
Oswestry Town 4 Cwmbran Town 1
Rhyl 1 Total Network Solutions 1,
Total Network Solutions 0 **Rhyl** 1

QUARTER-FINALS
Aberystwyth Town 0 Carmarthen Town 1,
Carmarthen Town 1 **Aberystwyth Town** 2 *aet*
(Aberystwyth Town on on away goals)
Caernarfon Town 2 Bangor City 2,
Bangor City 4 Caernarfon Town 3 *aet*
Oswestry Town 1 Rhyl 2,
Rhyl 1 Oswestry Town 0
Port Talbot Town 0 Caersws 0,
Caersws 0 **Port Talbot Town** 2
SEMI-FINALS
Aberystwyth Town 2 Rhyl 2,
Rhyl 2 Aberystwyth Town 1,
Bangor City 2 Port Talbot Town 0
Port Talbot Town 0 **Bangor City** 5
FINAL
(3rd May at Rhyl)
Rhyl 2 Bangor City 2 *aet* (4-3p)

LEAGUE OF WALES TEAMS IN EUROPE

CHAMPIONS LEAGUE
FIRST ROUND
Skonto Riga 5 BARRY TOWN 0,
BARRY TOWN 0 Skonto Riga 1

INTERTOTO CUP
FIRST ROUND
Marek Dupnitsa 2 CAERSWS 0,
CAERSWS 1 Marek Dupnitsa 1 *(at Aberystwyth)*

U E F A CUP
QUALIFYING ROUND
Amica Wronki 5 TOTAL NETWORK
SOLUTIONS 0,
TOTAL NETWORK SOLUTIONS 2
Amica Wronki 7
BANGOR CITY 1 FK Sartid Smederevo 0,
FK Sartid Smederevo 2 BANGOR CITY 0

WESSEX LEAGUE

	AFC Newbury	AFC Totton	Alton Town	Andover	BAT Sports	Bemerton Heath H.	Blackfield & Lang.	Bournemouth	Brockenhurst	Christchurch	Cowes Sports	Downton	Eastleigh	Fareham Town	Gosport Borough	Hamble ASSC	Lymington & NM	Moneyfields	Portland United	Thatcham Town	Whitchurch United	Wimborne Town
AFC Newbury		0-4	1-2	0-3	4-0	2-0	6-1	4-0	3-1	4-0	1-4	0-3	1-1	3-0	2-0	3-2	0-2	3-3	5-0	0-1	5-1	0-0
AFC Totton	4-0		1-0	1-1	2-3	5-1	1-0	2-0	4-0	5-1	2-0	2-1	2-0	2-4	1-1	1-1	5-2	4-3	4-2	0-1	3-0	1-1
Alton Town	1-0	1-4		1-2	3-2	0-2	1-1	6-1	3-0	2-2	3-0	3-2	1-3	1-4	3-4	0-3	1-2	3-1	2-2	4-6	2-4	1-3
Andover	0-2	3-2	2-2		3-1	2-1	4-2	0-0	0-1	0-0	1-2	8-0	6-1	2-4	5-0	1-1	3-2	1-1	1-1	4-1	3-1	3-1
BAT Sports	2-1	3-2	2-3	2-1		2-0	1-1	0-0	5-0	1-0	4-1	2-1	0-1	2-0	0-0	0-1	0-3	0-2	1-0	1-1	1-0	0-1
Bemerton Heath H.	3-2	1-2	0-2	2-1	0-0	D	3-2	5-1	1-3	5-2	0-1	0-0	1-0	0-7	0-1	0-2	1-1	1-2	2-2	2-0	0-2	6-0
Blackfield & Langley	1-3	0-3	2-1	1-2	0-2	0-1	I	1-3	1-4	0-5	0-0	2-2	0-1	0-5	1-6	2-1	0-6	1-4	2-4	2-4	2-3	1-6
Bournemouth	2-3	2-3	1-1	1-1	4-2	2-1	2-1	V	1-0	2-1	1-1	2-0	0-1	3-2	0-2	0-1	2-2	0-1	1-3	0-0	6-0	1-2
Brockenhurst	4-2	0-4	0-3	4-2	1-3	1-2	2-2	1-2	I	0-2	0-3	6-2	1-2	0-1	1-3	1-2	1-1	2-3	1-1	1-3	0-2	0-7
Christchurch	3-1	0-1	1-1	3-5	2-1	4-3	0-0	1-0	1-0	S	1-2	4-1	0-6	0-1	0-1	1-2	2-1	0-2	0-2	5-2	1-0	1-4
Cowes Sports	0-0	2-0	1-2	1-4	2-0	2-3	7-0	1-0	1-1	0-0	I	8-0	1-3	0-0	1-1	2-2	1-0	0-0	1-1	1-3	3-0	0-2
Downton	2-3	2-1	1-0	0-3	1-1	2-2	1-0	1-1	3-0	0-5	1-0	O	0-4	0-3	0-2	0-3	2-1	3-7	1-1	1-0	0-6	
Eastleigh	2-1	4-0	5-1	1-3	3-2	1-1	5-0	3-2	7-1	4-0	1-0	2-0	N	1-1	2-0	5-0	0-3	0-5	1-1	4-0	2-1	
Fareham Town	1-1	1-1	2-2	2-4	1-0	3-0	5-0	2-1	4-1	0-1	2-1	1-1	0-1		3-0	2-1	1-3	2-1	1-1	3-0	5-0	1-3
Gosport Borough	3-1	1-2	0-0	3-0	4-1	1-0	4-1	8-0	4-0	1-2	4-0	1-6	1-0	0-1	O	2-1	3-1	4-0	3-0	1-0	5-1	1-1
Hamble ASSC	0-1	3-3	0-2	1-2	6-1	2-3	5-1	0-1	3-2	1-1	2-3	2-0	0-1	0-3	1-1	N	1-0	1-1	0-0	1-1	2-0	2-2
Lymington & NM	5-2	0-2	0-0	3-2	6-0	1-0	2-1	3-1	4-2	2-2	3-0	3-0	1-1	1-2	0-5	1-1	E	2-1	0-2	0-1	10-0	0-4
Moneyfields	3-1	0-3	4-3	2-1	1-2	6-0	1-2	2-1	6-0	0-1	1-1	1-2	2-2	1-3	3-2	3-0			0-2	1-1	0-3	
Portland United	3-2	0-2	3-0	3-1	0-2	1-1	3-1	6-0	1-1	6-3	0-1	3-0	4-1	0-4	2-3	0-1	4-0	0-3		2-1	5-0	0-0
Thatcham Town	1-1	1-0	3-0	3-1	0-2	1-1	6-0	2-3	2-1	1-1	2-0	1-0	0-2	2-1	0-1	0-0	1-3	2-0	0-4		2-1	3-3
Whitchurch United	1-2	0-3	1-4	1-3	0-2	2-1	0-2	1-2	1-2	0-3	0-0	2-3	0-3	0-3	2-2	0-0	0-3	1-2	0-1	0-4		0-2
Wimborne Town	3-1	1-2	2-0	2-0	1-2	4-2	6-1	3-0	1-3	1-3	5-1	1-4	3-0	2-3	1-1	3-1	1-3	4-0	5-0	8-1		

Division One

Division One	P	W	D	L	F	A	Pts
Eastleigh	42	32	7	3	115	32	103
Gosport Borough	42	27	7	8	94	43	88
AFC Totton	42	27	6	9	96	47	87
Wimborne Town	42	26	7	9	113	44	85
Fareham Town	42	22	10	10	78	47	76
Lymington & New Milton	42	22	8	12	89	56	74
Andover	42	22	7	13	95	63	73
Portland United	42	20	8	14	81	62	68
Thatcham Town	42	18	13	11	68	58	67
Moneyfields	42	18	6	18	73	68	60
BAT Sports	42	18	6	18	57	65	60
AFC Newbury	42	17	6	19	77	72	57
Christchurch	42	15	10	17	58	68	55
Bournemouth	42	15	9	18	57	67	54
Cowes Sports	42	13	13	16	57	55	52
Hamble ASSC	42	13	12	17	58	60	51
Alton Town	42	14	9	19	71	80	51
Bemerton Heath Harlequins	42	13	5	24	59	83	44
Downton	42	10	7	25	41	105	37
Brockenhurst	42	7	5	30	50	118	26
Blackfield & Langley	42	4	6	32	37	134	18
Whitchurch United	42	4	3	35	27	124	15

Combination

Combination	P	W	D	L	F	A	Pts
Eastleigh Res.	40	29	7	4	120	41	94
Weymouth Res.	40	30	4	6	99	38	94
Gosport Borough Res.	40	25	7	8	92	37	82
Winchester City Res.	40	25	1	14	114	69	76
Bashley Res.	39	23	5	11	115	55	74
Newport IOW Res.	40	20	9	11	71	64	69
Bemerton Heath Harl. Res.	40	20	7	13	100	68	67
AFC Totton Res.	40	19	8	13	92	63	65
Horndean Res.	40	18	8	14	92	88	62
Wimborne Town Res.	39	17	6	16	91	83	57
Christchurch Res.	40	15	8	17	79	80	53
Hamble ASSC Res.	40	17	2	21	68	79	53
AFC Newbury Res.	40	14	7	19	62	67	49
Brockenhurst Res.	40	12	7	21	63	117	43
Moneyfields Res.	40	11	7	22	62	89	40
BAT Sports Res.	40	12	3	25	74	98	39
Alton Town Res.	40	11	6	23	71	114	39
Lymington & NM Res.	40	10	6	24	62	85	36
Downton Res.	40	10	6	24	47	95	36
Portsmouth Royal Navy Res.	40	11	2	27	57	119	35
Andover New Street Res.	40	10	4	26	64	146	34

Wimborne Town Reserves v Bashley Reserves not played

COMBINATION CUP	**FINAL**
	(2nd May at Blackfield & Langley)
	AFC Newbury Res. 1 Wimborne Town Res. 0

DIVISION ONE CONSTITUTION 2003-04

AFC NEWBURY..............................Faraday Road, Newbury, Berkshire 01635 523222

AFC TOTTON ....Testwood Park, Testwood Place, Totton, Southampton, Hampshire 023 8086 8981

ALTON TOWN ....Bass Sports Ground, Anstey Road, Alton, Hampshire...........................01420 82465

ANDOVER ....The Portway Stadium, West Portway Industrial Estate, Andover, Hampshire................01264 391341

BAT SPORTS ....BAT Sports Ground, Southern Gardens, Ringwood Road, Totton, Hampshire..............023 8086 2143

BEMERTON HEATH HARLEQUINS .. Westwood Rec, Western Way, Bemerton Heath, Salisbury, Wiltshire........ 01722 331218 / 331925

BLACKFIELD & LANGLEY.... Gang Warily Community Centre, Newlands Road, Blackfield, Hampshire 023 8089 3603

BOURNEMOUTH....................Victoria Park, Namu Road, Winton, Bournemouth, Dorset 01202 515123

BROCKENHURST ....Grigg Lane, Brockenhurst, Hampshire.................................01590 623544

CHRISTCHURCH ....Christchurch Sporting Club, Hurn Bridge, Avon Causeway, Christchurch, Hampshire...........01202 473792

COWES SPORTS...............Westwood Park, Reynolds Close, off Park Road, Cowes, Isle of Wight................01983 293793

DOWNTON..............Brian Whitehead Sports & Social Club, Wick Lane, Downton, Salisbury, Wiltshire.............01725 512162

FAREHAM TOWN......................Cams Alders, Palmerston Drive, Fareham, Hampshire 01329 231151

GOSPORT BOROUGH....................Privett Park, Privett Road, Gosport, Hampshire 023 9250 1042

HAMBLE ASSC...............Folland Park, Kings Avenue, Hamble-le-Rice, Southampton, Hampshire.................023 8045 2173

LYMINGTON & NEW MILTON ......Fawcetts Field, Christchurch Road, New Milton, Hampshire.....................01425 628191

MONEYFIELDS ....Moneyfields Sports & Social Club, Moneyfields Avenue, Copnor, Portsmouth......023 9266 5260 / 9265 2424

PORTLAND UNITED....................New Grove Corner, Grove Road, Portland, Dorset..........................01305 861489

THATCHAM TOWN...................Waterside Park, Crookham Road, Thatcham, Berks.. 01635 862016 / 873934. Fax: 01635 873834

WHITCHURCH UNITED ....Longmeadow, Winchester Road, Whitchurch, Hampshire........................01256 892493

WIMBORNE TOWN ....The Cuthbury, Cowgrove Road, Wimborne, Dorset.........01202 889310. Club: 01202 884821

WINCHESTER CITY..........The City Ground, Hillier Way, Abbotts Barton, Winchester, Hampshire..................01962 863553

Eastleigh are promoted to the Southern League. Newcomers are Winchester City, promoted from the Hampshire League.

LEAGUE CUP
(All ties prior to Final over two legs)

FIRST ROUND	SECOND ROUND	QUARTER-FINALS
BAT Sports 1 Brockenhurst 1,	Alton Town 2 Moneyfields 2,	AFC Totton 1 Bournemouth 0,
Brockenhurst 4 BAT Sports 2	**Moneyfields** 3 Alton Town 0	Bournemouth 0 **AFC Totton** 4
Blackfield & Langley 4 Portland	Brockenhurst 2 Downton 2,	Bemerton Heath Harlequins 5
United 3,	Downton 0 **Brockenhurst** 1	Brockenhurst 2,
Portland United 3 Blackfield &	Christchurch 0 AFC Totton 2,	Brockenhurst 0 **Bemerton Heath**
Langley 0	**AFC Totton** 4 Christchurch 2	**Harlequins** 5
Cowes Sports 1 Fareham Town 1,	Cowes Sports 0 Bournemouth 2,	Lymington & New Milton 0 Eastleigh 3,
Fareham Town (scr.) **Cowes Sports** (w/o)	**Bournemouth** 3 Cowes Sports 4	**Eastleigh** 2 Lymington & New Milton 3
(ineligible player in first leg – Fareham	Lymington & New Milton 3 AFC	Moneyfields 2 Andover 1,
Town expelled)	Newbury 0,	Andover 1 **Moneyfields** 3
Gosport Borough 2 Moneyfields 1,	AFC Newbury 1 **Lymington & New**	SEMI-FINALS
Moneyfields (w/o) Gosport Borough (scr.)	**Milton** 4	Bemerton Heath Harlequins 1 AFC
(ineligible player in first leg – Gosport	Portland United 1 Bemerton Heath	Totton 1,
expelled)	Harlequins 1,	**AFC Totton** 0 Bemerton Heath
Whitchurch United 0 Thatcham Town 2,	**Bemerton Heath Harlequins** 4 Portland	Harlequins 0
Thatcham Town 1 Whitchurch United 0	United 0	*(AFC Totton won on away goals)*
Wimborne Town 3 Hamble	Thatcham Town 2 Andover 3,	Eastleigh 3 Moneyfields 0,
ASSC 1,	**Andover** 0 Thatcham Town 0	Moneyfields 0 **Eastleigh** 1
Hamble ASSC 3 **Wimborne**	Wimborne Town 1 Eastleigh 1,	FINAL *(5th May at AFC Totton)*
Town 5	**Eastleigh** 4 Wimborne Town 2	**AFC Totton** 2 Eastleigh 1

WEST CHESHIRE LEAGUE

	Aintree Villa	Ashville	Cammell Laird	Castrol Social	Christleton	Ellesmere Port	General Chemicals	Helsby	Heswall	MANWEB	Maghull	Mallaby	Newton	Poulton Victoria	Stork	Vauxhall M. Res.
Aintree Villa		2-2	0-2	2-1	1-1	3-0	1-1	4-1	1-6	2-4	1-0	2-3	1-0	1-1	n/a	2-4
Ashville	5-2		1-3	6-1	3-1	1-1	1-2	2-1	0-2	2-1	1-1	0-1	3-2	0-4	n/a	1-2
Cammell Laird	7-0	0-0	D	3-0	2-1	3-1	2-0	4-0	2-2	2-2	1-1	3-1	4-1	0-2	n/a	1-4
Castrol Social	3-0	3-2	2-4	I	2-2	0-1	1-1	4-0	2-0	3-0	2-1	1-1	3-2	0-1	n/a	0-2
Christleton	2-0	5-1	1-1	3-1	V	0-0	2-0	5-0	0-0	2-0	2-0	1-2	0-3	2-3	n/a	0-1
Ellesmere Port	0-0	0-5	0-1	1-0	3-0	I	5-0	5-0	2-2	1-3	1-5	4-2	2-5	1-3	n/a	0-3
General Chemicals	3-1	5-1	0-0	0-1	2-2	0-1	S	3-0	1-0	1-0	1-1	2-1	1-0	4-1	n/a	0-0
Helsby	0-8	2-3	0-4	0-7	0-1	0-3	1-4	I	1-3	1-6	0-1	0-4	1-2	0-7	n/a	0-7
Heswall	5-2	5-2	0-1	1-2	3-0	4-1	1-3	5-0	O	0-2	1-2	3-0	3-7	2-2	n/a	0-2
MANWEB	2-1	1-0	0-1	4-1	2-1	5-0	2-1	6-1	3-0	N	2-0	4-3	2-2	0-1	n/a	2-2
Maghull	2-3	0-4	2-3	1-1	2-2	3-1	3-1	8-0	2-2	0-3		0-0	0-1	1-1	n/a	0-2
Mallaby	1-1	5-2	1-0	0-1	4-2	0-0	1-3	8-2	1-2	1-2	0-1	O	4-2	2-3	n/a	2-5
Newton	2-0	0-1	2-1	3-1	2-1	3-1	3-0	8-0	1-3	3-2	1-1	2-0	N	2-1	n/a	1-1
Poulton Victoria	3-1	3-0	0-2	1-0	5-1	3-1	4-0	7-1	1-0	2-1	4-3	1-3	5-1	E	n/a	5-2
Stork	n/a	2-11	n/a	n/a	n/a	n/a	n/a	n/a	n/a	n/a	0-10	n/a	n/a	n/a		n/a
Vauxhall Motors Res.	3-2	3-2	1-2	1-1	4-0	3-1	2-1	11-0	3-1	4-0	2-0	0-1	2-0	1-0	n/a	

Note – Stork withdrew during the course of the season.
Their results are shown above but have been expunged from the league table

Division One

	P	W	D	L	F	A	Pts
Vauxhall Motors Res.	28	21	4	3	77	25	67
Poulton Victoria	28	20	3	5	74	32	63
Cammell Laird	28	18	6	4	59	25	60
MANWEB	28	16	3	9	61	38	51
Newton	28	15	3	10	60	44	48
General Chemicals	28	12	6	10	40	38	42
Heswall	28	11	5	12	56	46	38
Castrol Social	28	11	5	12	44	43	38
Mallaby	28	11	4	13	52	49	37
Ashville	28	10	4	14	51	58	34
Christleton	28	8	7	13	40	47	31
Maghull	28	7	9	12	41	43	30
Ellesmere Port	28	8	5	15	37	56	29
Aintree Villa	28	7	6	15	44	64	27
Helsby	28	0	0	28	12	140	0

WWW.CHERRYRED.CO.UK

PYKE CUP

FIRST ROUND
Cammell Laird 2 General Chemicals 0
Castrol Social 2 **Poulton Victoria** 3 *aet*
Ellesmere Port 1 **Vauxhall Motors Res.** 2
Helsby 0 **Ashville** 1
Maghull 1 **Heswall** 2
MANWEB 2 **Mallaby** 3
Newton 3 Aintree Villa 0
Stork (scr.) v **Christleton** (w/o)
QUARTER-FINALS
Christleton 2 **Cammell Laird** 3 *aet*
Heswall 2 Poulton Victoria 2 *aet*
Poulton Victoria 0 **Heswall** 2 *replay*
Newton 2 **Ashville** 4 *aet*
Vauxhall Motors Res. 2 **Mallaby** 3
SEMI-FINALS
Cammell Laird 2 Mallaby 0 *aet*
(at Poulton Victoria)
Heswall 0 **Ashville** 2
(at Cammell Laird)
FINAL
(5th May at Vauxhall Motors)
Cammell Laird 0 **Ashville** 1

BILL WEIGHT CUP

SEMI-FINALS
Christleton 1 **Mallaby** 2
Cammell Laird 4 Maghull 1

FINAL
(11th September at Cammell Laird)
Cammell Laird 3 Mallaby 1

DIVISION ONE CONSTITUTION 2003-04

AINTREE VILLA...................................Aintree Racecourse, Aintree, Merseyside .... None
ASHVILLE.. Villa Park, Cross Lane, Wallesey Village, Wallesey, Merseyside 0151 638 2127
CAMMELL LAIRD .... Kirklands, St Peters Road, Rock Ferry, Merseyside 0151 645 5991
CASTROL SOCIAL .... Castrol Sports & Social Club, Chester Road, Whitby, Ellesmere Port, South Wirral 0151 355 1730
CHRISTLETON..................................... Little Heath, Christleton, Chester, Cheshire.................................. 01244 332153
ELLESMERE PORT.................... Chester Road, Whitby, Ellesmere Port, South Wirral...................... 0151 200 7080/7050
GENERAL CHEMICALS........................... Picow Farm Road, Runcorn, Cheshire .... None
HELSBY... Helsby Sports & Social Club, Helsby, Cheshire 01928 722267
HESWALL.. Gayton Park, Brimstage Road, Heswall, Wirral................................ 0151 342 8172
MANWEB .... MANWEB Sports & Social Club, Thingwall Lane, Liverpool, Merseyside................. 0151 281 5364
MAGHULL .... Old Hall Field, Hall Lane, Maghull, Merseyside................................ 0151 526 7320
MALLABY.................... Balaclava, Birkenhead Park, Ashville, Ashville Road, Wirral................................... None
NEWTON... Millcroft, Frankby Road, Greasby, Wirral..................................... 0151 677 8282
POULTON VICTORIA .... Victoria Park, Rankin Street, Wallasey, Wirral............................. 0151 638 3559
VAUXHALL MOTORS RESERVES.. Vauxhall Sports Ground, Rivacre Road, Hooton, Ellesmere Port .... 0151 328 1114 / 327 2294
WEST KIRBY........................... Marine Park, Greenbank Road, West Kirby, Wirral............................... 0151 625 7734
Shell changed their name to Ellesmere Port during the course of the season. Stork resigned during the season. West Kirby come up from Division Two.

	Aintree Villa Res.	Blacon Youth Club	Cammell Laird Res.	Capenhurst Villa	Christleton Res.	Heswall Res.	Maghull Res.	Manor Athletic	Mersey Royal	Merseyside Police	Mond Rangers	New Brighton	Pavilions	Poulton Victoria Res.	Upton AA	West Kirby
Aintree Villa Res.		0-2	1-4	0-2	2-1	2-3	1-1	4-4	2-2	1-2	1-0	2-4	1-3	2-3	3-6	0-3
Blacon Youth Club	4-2		6-2	3-1	2-0	5-2	0-0	4-2	11-2	3-1	0-0	3-2	1-3	2-2	0-2	3-2
Cammell Laird Res.	3-1	3-0	D	2-1	1-0	1-0	3-0	4-1	3-0	1-1	4-2	1-2	1-1	2-2	1-0	1-2
Capenhurst Villa	3-2	3-0	0-1	I	3-0	0-2	5-3	1-4	2-1	0-1	3-1	1-3	1-4	1-2	3-3	0-3
Christleton Res.	2-1	1-7	0-1	4-0	V	0-1	2-3	7-3	4-1	1-1	1-0	3-0	0-2	1-2	0-0	2-3
Heswall Res.	2-1	2-1	1-2	2-1	1-2	I	2-0	5-1	6-0	0-0	2-1	0-2	2-2	0-3	1-2	2-2
Maghull Res.	0-3	1-1	2-1	1-3	5-2	3-1	S	2-2	3-1	2-5	2-1	3-1	1-2	0-1	3-2	2-2
Manor Athletic	1-3	1-5	2-0	1-2	1-3	3-2	0-3	I	1-2	2-6	0-2	2-2	2-1	0-1	2-4	0-1
Mersey Royal	1-2	1-5	1-6	1-4	2-5	2-4	1-1	2-3	O	0-7	3-0	3-4	1-4	1-1	0-3	1-2
Merseyside Police	0-1	4-1	2-2	0-3	1-2	1-5	0-0	2-3	3-2	N	4-1	1-2	1-0	4-3	1-0	0-4
Mond Rangers	1-2	0-0	0-1	4-3	2-2	3-2	0-8	0-2	4-1	3-4		1-4	0-2	2-1	1-1	0-2
New Brighton	0-1	2-2	2-2	2-2	1-3	3-3	3-0	3-0	3-2	2-1	5-0	T	2-0	2-3	1-3	1-1
Pavilions	1-1	1-1	1-1	2-5	0-0	4-1	1-1	6-3	3-2	3-2	2-3	2-1	W	2-0	0-3	2-1
Poulton Victoria Res.	2-1	2-1	4-2	2-1	4-0	2-3	2-1	0-0	1-1	1-0	3-2	2-1	1-0	O	4-0	4-1
Upton AA	2-1	2-0	0-0	3-1	1-1	1-2	2-0	2-1	4-1	1-3	1-2	3-5	1-3	5-2		3-5
West Kirby	4-1	0-1	2-2	0-0	1-3	6-0	1-0	3-1	3-2	2-1	4-2	2-1	3-1	4-7	3-0	

Division Two	P	W	D	L	F	A	Pts
Poulton Victoria Res.	30	21	5	4	68	38	68
West Kirby	30	19	5	6	72	43	62
Cammell Laird Res.	30	16	8	6	58	37	56
Pavilions	30	16	6	8	60	44	54
Blacon Youth Club	30	15	6	9	74	47	51
New Brighton	30	15	6	9	68	50	51
Heswall Res.	30	15	4	11	59	55	49
Upton AA	30	13	5	12	60	54	44
Merseyside Police	30	12	5	13	58	52	41
Christleton Res.	30	12	5	13	52	52	41
Capenhurst Villa	30	12	3	15	55	57	39
Maghull Res.	30	8	9	13	49	54	33
Aintree Villa Res.	30	8	4	18	45	66	28
Mond Rangers	30	7	5	18	39	70	26
Manor Athletic	30	7	4	19	48	82	25
Mersey Royal	30	2	4	24	40	104	10

WEST CHESHIRE BOWL

FIRST ROUND
Christleton Res. 0 **Upton AA** 2
Heswall Res. 2 Merseyside Police 0
Maghull Res. 2 **Capenhurst Villa** 3 *aet*
Manor Athletic 1 **Pavilions** 4
Mersey Royal 0 **Aintree Villa Res.** 3
Mond Rangers 0 **Cammell Laird Res.** 6
Poulton Victoria Res. 2 New Brighton 1 *aet*
West Kirby 3 **Blacon Youth Club** 4
QUARTER-FINALS
Blacon Youth Club 3 Upton AA 0
Cammell Laird Res. 4 Aintree Villa Res. 2
Capenhurst Villa 5 Heswall Res. 5 *aet*
Heswall Res. 2 Capenhurst Villa 0 *replay*
Poulton Victoria Res. 2 **Pavilions** 4
SEMI-FINALS
Blacon Youth Club 0 **Cammell Laird Res.** 2
(at Vauxhall Motors)
Heswall Res. 3 Pavilions 1 *(at Ashville)*
FINAL *(30th April at Vauxhall Motors)*
Cammell Laird Res. 2 Heswall Res. 1

DIVISION TWO CONSTITUTION 2003-04

AINTREE VILLA RESERVES .... Aintree Racecourse, Aintree, Merseyside .... None
ASHVILLE RESERVES .... Villa Park, Cross Lane, Wallasey Village, Wallasey, Merseyside 0151 638 2127
BLACON YOUTH CLUB.............. Cairns Crescent Playing Fields, Blacon, Chester, Cheshire............................ None
CAMMELL LAIRD RESERVES .... Kirklands, St Peters Road, Rock Ferry, Merseyside 0151 645 5991
CAPENHURST VILLA .... Capenhurst Sports Ground, Capenhurst Lane, Capenhurst ...... 0151 339 9837. Fax: 0151 355 1730
CHRISTLETON RESERVES .... Little Heath, Christleton, Chester, Cheshire............................. 01244 332153
FC PENSBY............................ Ridgewood Park, Pensby, Wirral .... None
HESWALL RESERVES .... Gayton Park, Brimstage Road, Heswall, Wirral.......................... 0151 342 8172
MAGHULL RESERVES .... Old Hall Field, Hall Lane, Maghull, Merseyside............................ 0151 526 7320
MANOR ATHLETIC..................... Unilever Sports Ground, Bromborough, Wirral .... None
MERSEYSIDE POLICE .... Police Club, Fairfield, Prescot Road, Liverpool, Merseyside ...... 0151 228 2352. Fax: 0151 259 6997
MOND RANGERS.................. Pavilions Club, Sandy Lane, Weston Point, Runcorn, Cheshire......................... 01928 590508
NEW BRIGHTON....................... Harrison Drive, Wallasey Village, Wallasey, Wirral .... None
PAVILIONS .... Pavilions Complex, Sandy Lane, Weston Point, Runcorn, Cheshire 01928 590508
POULTON VICTORIA RESERVES .... Victoria Park, Rankin Street, Wallasey, Wirral.............................. 0151 638 3559
UPTON AA.................. Cheshire County Sports & Social Club, Plas Newton Lane, Chester, Cheshire. 01244 318167
West Kirby are promoted to Division One. Mersey Royal drop to Division Three replaced by Ashville Reserves and FC Pensby.

	Ashville Res.	Capenhurst Villa Res.	Chester Nomads	Ellesmere Port Res.	FC Pensby	Grange Athletic	Manor Athletic Res.	Mond Rangers Res.	New Brighton Res.	Newton Res.	Shaftesbury	St Werburghs	Upton AA Res.	West Kirby Res.	Willaston
Ashville Res.	D	5-3	0-0	4-1	0-0	3-1	5-0	2-1	4-2	3-1	2-1	3-1	7-0	2-1	0-0
Capenhurst Villa Res.	0-3	I	0-2	2-3	0-0	0-7	0-3	1-4	1-1	2-0	2-1	2-1	0-1	1-1	0-3
Chester Nomads	0-3	4-1	V	6-3	2-1	5-1	0-2	0-1	3-1	5-0	3-2	6-1	0-1	2-1	1-0
Ellesmere Port Res.	1-1	3-1	3-2	I	0-5	0-1	0-3	2-3	1-4	3-1	3-3	4-1	2-1	1-2	0-1
FC Pensby	0-0	5-1	2-2	1-0	S	5-3	3-4	4-0	2-0	5-2	1-2	4-0	2-1	4-0	3-1
Grange Athletic	3-0	2-2	2-1	5-0	2-4	I	4-1	5-2	0-1	1-1	1-4	2-2	3-1	3-4	0-2
Manor Athletic Res.	0-1	2-0	4-1	5-2	0-4	3-3	O	2-4	1-1	2-3	1-0	2-2	3-5	3-1	0-5
Mond Rangers Res.	0-1	4-3	1-8	7-1	1-3	3-1	3-4	N	4-1	2-7	2-4	2-3	1-2	1-2	2-5
New Brighton Res.	0-2	6-0	2-2	2-0	0-2	2-2	4-0	1-0		2-3	2-2	2-2	0-2	1-0	1-1
Newton Res.	1-3	2-3	2-1	3-2	0-2	2-5	3-0	4-0	0-2		2-2	16-0	2-1	1-2	0-1
Shaftesbury	1-3	1-0	0-4	3-0	1-3	3-0	4-1	3-5	5-1	4-2	T	2-2	5-1	1-1	2-3
St Werburghs	2-5	1-2	2-4	4-0	1-2	1-2	4-3	8-1	0-4	5-2	1-3	H	1-7	1-5	0-1
Upton AA Res.	2-4	2-2	5-0	1-3	0-0	0-4	3-3	5-0	3-3	2-1	4-1	2-3	R	6-2	2-7
West Kirby Res.	1-2	3-2	0-2	4-2	0-1	0-1	3-2	3-0	3-2	0-1	0-0	4-0	4-2	E	0-3
Willaston	1-1	3-1	2-2	2-1	3-5	0-2	1-2	3-0	6-2	5-4	3-1	2-1	4-2	1-2	E

Division Three	P	W	D	L	F	A	Pts
Ashville Res.	28	21	6	1	69	24	69
FC Pensby	28	20	5	3	72	26	65
Willaston	28	18	4	6	69	37	58
Chester Nomads	28	15	4	9	68	43	49
Grange Athletic	28	13	5	10	66	52	44
West Kirby Res.	28	13	3	12	49	48	42
Upton AA Res.	28	11	4	13	64	67	37
Manor Athletic Res.	28	11	4	13	56	69	37
Shaftesbury	28	10	6	12	58	55	36
Newton Res.	28	11	2	15	68	62	35
New Brighton Res.	28	9	8	11	50	51	35
Mond Rangers Res.	28	9	0	19	54	87	27
Ellesmere Port Res.	28	7	2	19	41	78	23
St Werburghs	28	6	4	18	50	94	22
Capenhurst Villa Res.	28	5	5	18	32	73	20

WEST CHESHIRE SHIELD

FIRST ROUND
Chester Nomads 0 **Grange Athletic** 2
Ellesmere Port Res. 0 **Upton AA Res.** 3
FC Pensby 3 St Werberghs 0
Manor Athletic Res. 1 **West Kirby Res.** 4
Mersey Royal Res. (scr.) v
Capenhurst Villa Res. (w/o)
New Brighton Res. 4 Mond Rangers Res. 2 *aet*
Newton Res. 1 **Willaston** 11
Shaftesbury 1 Ashville Res. 0
QUARTER-FINALS
FC Pensby 6 Shaftesbury 2
New Brighton Res. 2 Upton AA Res. 0
West Kirby Res. 2 Capenhurst Villa Res. 1 *aet*
Willaston 2 **Grange Athletic** 4 *aet*
SEMI-FINALS
FC Pensby 0 **Grange Athletic** 5
(at Cammell Laird)
New Brighton Res. 3 West Kirby Res. 0 *(at Poulton)*
FINAL *(3rd May at Heswall)*
Grange Athletic 1 **New Brighton Res.** 1 *aet* (2-3p)

DIVISION THREE CONSTITUTION 2003-04
BRONZE SOCIAL . . . . t.b.a. . . . . t.b.a.
CAPENHURST VILLA RESERVES . . . . Capenhurst Sports Ground, Capenhurst Lane, Capenhurst . . . . . . 0151 339 9837. Fax: 0151 355 1730
CHESTER NOMADS . . . . Garrison Ground, Eaton Road, Handbridge, Chester, Cheshire. . . . . None
ELLESMERE PORT RESERVES. . . . . Chester Road, Whitby, Ellesmere Port, South Wirral. . . . . 0151 200 7080 / 7050
GRANGE ATHLETIC . . . . Stanney Grange, Ellesmere Port, South Wirral. . . . . None
MBNA . . . . t.b.a. . . . . t.b.a.
MANOR ATHLETIC RESERVES. . . . . Unilever Sports Ground, Bromborough, Wirral . . . . None
MERSEY ROYAL . . . . Unilever Sports Ground, Bromborough, Wirral. . . . . None
MOND RANGERS RESERVES. . . . . . . Pavilions Club, Sandy Lane, Weston Point, Runcorn, Cheshire. 01928 590508
NEW BRIGHTON RESERVES. . . . . Harrison Drive, Wallasey Village, Wallasey, Wirral . . . . None
NEWTON RESERVES. . . . . Millcroft, Frankby Road, Greasby, Wirral 0151 677 8282
SHAFTESBURY. . . . . Memorial Ground, Borough Road, Birkenhead, Wirral 0151 608 7165
ST WERBURGHS . . . . West Cheshire College, Old Wrexham Road, Handbridge, Chester, Cheshire. . . . . None
UPTON AA RESERVES. . . . . . . Cheshire County Sports & Social Club, Plas Newton Lane, Chester, Cheshire. 01244 318167
WEST KIRBY RESERVES. . . . . Marine Park, Greenbank Road, West Kirby, Wirral. 0151 625 7734
WILLASTON . . . . Johnston Recreation Ground, Neston Road, Willaston, South Wirral . . . . None
Ashville Reserves and FC Pensby are promoted to Division Two replaced by Mersey Royal. Mersey Royal Reserves drop out of the league replaced by newcomers Bronze Social (South Wirral League) and MBNA.

WEST LANCS LEAGUE

	BAE Barrow SC	Barnoldswick United	Blackpool Wren Rovers	Blackrod Town	Burnley United	Charnock Richard	Dalton United	Eagley	Freckleton	Fulwood Amateurs	Kirkham & Wesham	Milnthorpe Corinthians	Norcross & Warbreck	Springfields	Turton	Wyre Villa
BAE Barrow Sports Club	P	2-0	1-1	2-1	2-1	1-1	2-1	1-2	4-0	0-1	4-2	2-3	3-2	1-2	2-1	4-0
Barnoldswick United	3-2	R	4-3	3-3	3-0	1-2	2-2	2-2	2-4	1-0	0-3	1-0	3-1	5-0	0-2	0-1
Blackpool Wren Rovers	2-3	1-5	E	0-2	3-4	5-3	0-1	3-1	2-1	0-1	0-2	0-3	3-1	5-2	1-4	1-2
Blackrod Town	5-1	3-3	7-0	M	2-1	0-1	1-2	1-1	3-2	1-0	3-4	5-0	4-1	0-1	5-1	3-4
Burnley United	1-0	1-0	7-1	4-1	I	0-2	2-5	2-3	1-0	1-4	4-2	1-1	4-0	4-1	4-1	7-1
Charnock Richard	3-2	3-1	1-0	3-0	0-3	E	3-1	3-0	4-0	2-1	3-1	1-1	2-0	2-1	4-1	5-0
Dalton United	2-0	3-2	3-3	6-2	2-3	2-2	R	5-2	2-0	2-2	3-3	7-2	1-2	5-0	1-1	2-1
Eagley	3-2	1-0	0-1	0-2	3-1	1-1	3-2		1-2	3-2	0-4	4-1	2-2	5-0	0-1	2-2
Freckleton	1-0	3-2	2-0	3-1	0-1	3-2	1-2	1-0	D	0-0	3-2	1-2	4-1	3-0	1-2	2-2
Fulwood Amateurs	0-1	0-1	4-1	1-1	4-0	2-2	4-2	3-0	0-1	I	0-2	1-1	1-4	6-0	0-2	2-3
Kirkham & Wesham	1-1	2-1	1-2	1-2	4-0	2-0	0-2	3-2	5-1	4-1	V	4-0	3-0	3-2	1-1	1-3
Milnthorpe Corinthians	2-2	1-2	1-3	2-3	1-1	1-2	2-3	2-2	0-1	1-1	2-1	I	1-1	5-1	1-7	2-3
Norcross & Warbreck	0-1	2-3	2-3	1-4	0-4	0-2	3-2	1-1	2-2	2-1	0-3	0-2	S	2-2	1-1	2-2
Springfields	1-2	1-3	3-2	0-4	0-4	0-3	2-0	2-2	0-2	2-2	0-5	1-1	1-2	I	0-3	2-1
Turton	0-0	1-2	2-3	2-3	2-3	0-0	0-0	2-2	0-3	2-3	0-10	0-1	5-1	12-1	O	1-2
Wyre Villa	1-2	3-1	1-3	2-0	1-0	1-2	0-1	1-3	1-0	4-1	4-5	3-2	1-1	6-2	5-3	N

Premier Division		P	W	D	L	F	A	Pts
Charnock Richard		30	20	6	4	64	31	66
Kirkham & Wesham		30	20	2	8	87	43	62
Burnley United		30	17	2	11	69	49	53
Dalton United		30	15	7	8	72	50	52
Blackrod Town		30	15	4	11	72	52	49
Wyre Villa		30	15	4	11	61	62	49
Freckleton		30	15	3	12	47	44	48
BAE Sports Barrow	-3	30	14	5	11	50	43	44
Barnoldswick United		30	13	4	13	56	52	43
Eagley		30	10	9	11	51	55	39
Fulwood Amateurs		30	9	7	14	48	46	34
Turton		30	9	6	15	60	62	33
Blackpool Wren Rovers		30	10	2	18	51	75	32
Milnthorpe Corinthians		30	7	9	14	44	64	30
Norcross & Warbreck		30	5	8	17	37	71	23
Springfields		30	5	4	21	30	100	19

RICHARDSON CUP

FIRST ROUND
BAE Barrow Sports Club 1 **Blackpool Wren Rovers** 2
Blackrod Town 1 **Kirkham & Wesham** 2
Burnley United 3 Springfields 2
Dalton United 0 **Freckleton** 3
Eagley 2 Milnthorpe Corinthians 0
Norcross & Warbreck 1 **Charnock Richard** 4
Turton 1 **Fulwood Amateurs** 3
Wyre Villa 2 Barnoldswick United 1

QUARTER-FINALS
Blackpool Wren Rovers 3 Burnley United 3 *aet*
Burnley United 2 Blackpool Wren Rovers 1 *replay*
Eagley 5 Wyre Villa 0
Freckleton 1 **Charnock Richard** 2
Fulwood Amateurs 1 **Kirkham & Wesham** 4

SEMI-FINALS
Eagley 2 Burnley United 0
Kirkham & Wesham 5 **Charnock Richard** 6

FINAL
(23rd April at LCFA, Leyland)
Eagley 2 Charnock Richard 1

WWW.NLNEWSDESK.CO.UK

PREMIER DIVISION CONSTITUTION 2003-04

BAE BARROW SPORTS CLUB .... Vickers Sports Club, Hawcoat Lane, Barrow-in-Furness, Cumbria 01229 825296
BARNOLDSWICK UNITED .... Victory Park, West Close, Barnoldswick, Colne, Lancashire 01282 815817
BLACKPOOL WREN ROV. RESERVES .. Bruce Park, School Road, Marton, Blackpool, Lancashire 01253 760570
BLACKROD TOWN .... Blackrod Community Centre, Vicarage Road, Blackrod, Lancashire 01204 692614
BURNLEY UNITED................. Barden Sports Ground, Barden Lane, Burnley, Lancashire .... None
CHARNOCK RICHARD .... Charter Lane, Charnock Richard, Lancashire 01257 794288
COPPULL UNITED......................... Springfield Road, Coppull, Lancashire 01257 795190
DALTON UNITED .... Railway Meadow, Beckside Road, Dalton-in-Furness, Cumbria.................. 01229 462799
EAGLEY......................... Eagley Sports Complex, Dunscar Bridge, Bolton, Lancashire................. 01204 306830
FLEETWOOD HESKETH .... Fylde Road, Southport, Merseyside 01704 227968
FRECKLETON..................... Hodgson Memorial Ground, Bush Lane, Freckleton, Lancashire 01772 679139
FULWOOD AMATEURS................... Lightfoot Lane, Fulwood, Preston, Lancashire......................... 01772 861827
KIRKHAM & WESHAM.......... Recreation Ground, Coronation Road, Kirkham, Lancashire................... None
MILNTHORPE CORINTHIANS................ Strands Lane, Milnthorpe, Cumbria 01539 562135
TURTON........................... Moorfield, Edgworth, Bolton, Lancashire................................ 07929 965160
WYRE VILLA .... Hallgate Park, Stalmine Village, near Knott End, Lancashire 01253 701468

Norcross & Warbreck and Springfields are relegated to Division One replaced by Coppull United and Fleetwood Hesketh.

	Bootle	Burnley Belvedere	Carnforth Rangers	Coppull United	Crooklands Casuals	Feniscowles	Fleetwood Hesketh	Garstang	Haslingden St Mary's	Hesketh Bank	Lancashire Constabulary	Millom	Poulton Town	Tempest United	Whinney Hill
Bootle		4-1	4-1	4-3	0-0	2-2	2-1	4-3	3-0	4-1	2-6	0-3	0-0	1-1	4-1
Burnley Belvedere	0-4	D	1-5	1-6	0-2	1-4	0-4	1-3	4-3	1-0	1-0	4-1	0-0	2-1	0-0
Carnforth Rangers	2-1	3-0	I	0-3	0-0	4-2	0-3	1-1	4-3	3-2	6-0	2-2	2-0	2-2	0-1
Coppull United	1-2	4-0	2-2	V	0-0	3-2	2-1	5-0	3-0	4-0	4-0	6-0	4-0	3-3	2-0
Crooklands Casuals	0-2	2-1	3-0	0-4	I	1-0	2-2	3-0	2-4	2-1	5-4	3-1	2-2	3-3	3-1
Feniscowles	1-4	5-0	1-1	1-8	1-1	S	1-2	3-0	0-1	0-2	2-1	4-3	2-4	1-0	0-1
Fleetwood Hesketh	1-2	8-0	2-1	1-7	4-1	3-3	I	3-1	3-0	3-1	4-0	7-1	1-3	3-1	4-2
Garstang	2-1	2-0	0-1	2-2	4-1	1-3	0-1	O	3-4	1-4	5-2	2-4	3-3	1-0	4-1
Haslingden St Mary's	0-3	0-4	2-3	0-4	5-0	0-7	1-3	0-1	N	0-3	2-4	1-3	0-1	1-2	2-8
Hesketh Bank	4-1	3-1	2-3	0-2	2-2	2-2	2-4	1-1	3-1		2-0	1-0	1-4	2-1	3-2
Lancashire Constabulary	4-0	1-4	3-5	2-3	4-1	2-5	1-4	1-2	2-1	0-1		1-3	1-2	2-2	1-2
Millom	0-3	4-0	0-4	2-3	2-0	3-2	4-1	5-1	5-1	5-1	6-4	O	5-0	1-2	2-3
Poulton Town	1-3	4-0	1-1	1-2	1-1	2-2	2-2	1-1	1-0	2-1	5-0	5-4	N	0-2	2-0
Tempest United	1-4	4-0	2-0	0-2	5-1	1-1	2-4	5-0	4-2	2-3	2-2	0-4	2-2	E	6-2
Whinney Hill	1-2	1-3	1-5	0-0	0-1	3-3	2-2	3-3	0-4	1-0	4-1	3-2	1-0	1-5	

Division One

	P	W	D	L	F	A	Pts
Coppull United	28	20	6	2	90	24	66
Fleetwood Hesketh	28	18	4	6	81	44	58
Bootle	28	18	4	6	66	41	58
Carnforth Rangers	28	14	7	7	61	44	49
Millom	28	14	1	13	75	64	43
Poulton Town	28	11	10	7	49	43	43
Hesketh Bank	28	12	4	12	48	50	40
Crooklands Casuals	28	10	9	9	42	53	39
Tempest United	28	10	8	10	61	50	38
Feniscowles	28	9	8	11	60	56	35
Garstang	28	9	6	13	47	63	33
Whinney Hill	28	9	5	14	45	64	32
Burnley Belvedere	28	8	2	18	30	78	26
Haslingden St Mary's	28	5	0	23	38	83	15
Lancs Constabulary -3	28	5	2	21	49	85	14

WWW.CHERRYRED.CO.UK

PRESIDENT'S CUP

FIRST ROUND
Bootle 2 **Whinney Hill** 3
Carnforth Rangers 4 Feniscowles 2
Garstang 1 **Hesketh Bank** 3
Lancashire Constabulary 1 **Crooklands Casuals** 4
Millom 4 Coppull United 1
Poulton Town 1 **Fleetwood Hesketh** 5
Tempest United 2 Haslingden St Mary's 1
QUARTER-FINALS
Burnley Belvedere 4 Whinney Hill 1
Carnforth Rangers 2 Tempest United 2 *aet*
Tempest United 0 Carnforth Rangers 1 *replay*
(ineligible player – Carnforth Rangers expelled)
Hesketh Bank 2 Fleetwood Hesketh 1
Millom 4 Crooklands Casuals 1
SEMI-FINALS
Burnley Belvedere 1 **Hesketh Bank** 2
Millom 2 Tempest United 1
FINAL
(29th April at Lancaster City)
Millom 1 Hesketh Bank 0

DIVISION ONE CONSTITUTION 2003-04

BOOTLE..Whitehaven/Workington Road, Bootle, Cumbria............................01229 718096
BURNLEY BELVEDERE........................Holden Road, Burnley, Lancashire..........................01282 433171
CARNFORTH RANGERS........................Quarry Bank, Carnforth, Lancashire..........................None
CROOKLANDS CASUALS.........Longlands Park, Greystone Lane, Dalton-in-Furness, Cumbria..................01229 465010
EUXTON VILLA.......................Runshaw Hall Lane, Euxton, Chorley, Lancashire..........................None
FENISCOWLES....................Livesey Branch Road, Feniscowles, Lancashire..........................None
GARSTANG................Riverside Community Centre, off High Street, Garstang, Lancashire.................01995 601586
HASLINGDEN ST MARY'S............Townsend Street, Haslingden, Rossendale, Lancashire.................01706 221814
HESKETH BANK.................Hesketh Sports Field, Station Road, Hesketh Bank, Lancashire..........................None
LYTHAM ST ANNES.............Lytham Cricket Club, Church Road, Lytham St Annes, Lancashire.................01253 734137
MILLOM..................................Millom RL Club, Millom, Cumbria.................01229 772030
NORCROSS & WARBRECK.....Anchorsholme Lane, Thornton Cleveleys, near Blackpool, Lancashire.................01253 859836
POULTON TOWN...........Cottam Hall Playing Fields, Blackpool Old Road, Poulton-le-Fylde, Lancashire.................01253 896150
SPRINGFIELDS.........Preston Sports Arena, Tom Benson Way, Cottam, Preston, Lancashire.................01772 761000
TEMPEST UNITED ....Tempest Road, Chew Moor Village, Lostock, near Bolton, Lancashire.................01942 811938
WHINNEY HILL.......................Clayton-le-Moors, Accrington, Lancashire..........................None

Coppull United and Fleetwood Hesketh are promoted to the Premier Division replaced by Norcross & Warbreck and Springfields. Lancashire Constabulary drop to Division Two from which Lytham St Annes and Euxton Villa arise.

	Askam United	BAC/EE Preston	BAE Canberra	Barrow Rangers	Crosshills	Euxton Villa	Furness Cavaliers	Glaxo Ulverston R.	Lytham St Annes	Mill Hill St Peters	Pennington	Stoneclough	Thornton Cleveleys	Todmorden Boro.
Askam United		1-1	2-2	1-2	3-1	1-1	3-2	3-1	1-9	0-1	3-0	4-4	0-2	4-0
BAC/EE Preston	4-0	*D*	1-3	4-0	3-1	0-3	1-0	3-0	2-2	0-0	4-3	5-0	1-0	3-0
BAE Canberra	3-2	1-2	*I*	7-1	3-2	3-1	4-0	7-1	1-3	1-0	3-0	1-2	2-4	6-1
Barrow Rangers	3-0	2-0	0-4	*V*	2-1	5-4	1-0	4-2	3-3	0-2	2-2	4-1	0-0	3-0
Crosshills	4-3	1-4	2-3	4-2	*I*	2-2	2-1	2-1	1-3	2-1	7-2	1-1	6-3	4-0
Euxton Villa	3-2	0-3	3-2	4-0		*S*	8-0	5-0	0-0	1-0	4-3	9-0	4-2	3-1
Furness Cavaliers	0-2	1-1	1-1	2-1	2-1	1-4	*I*	2-2	1-2	1-3	1-6	1-5	0-2	4-2
Glaxo Ulverston	1-3	1-2	1-1	4-0	1-2	2-2	0-1	*O*	0-3	1-2	3-0	3-2	1-2	1-1
Lytham St Annes	1-0	2-0	3-2	6-0	3-1	2-1	5-1	2-0	*N*	1-1	2-1	1-2	2-0	4-1
Mill Hill St Peters	2-3	4-1	3-3	5-1	7-2	0-0	4-0	2-0	0-1		1-0	3-1	1-2	2-1
Pennington	1-2	2-1	3-2	1-0	0-1	1-1	3-1	4-0	2-1	1-2	*T*	1-3	1-0	1-2
Stoneclough	2-3	2-2	1-4	3-2	1-1	0-2	4-1	3-0	2-4	0-0	3-1	*W*	1-3	5-2
Thornton Cleveleys	3-0	2-0	2-1	2-4	3-0	1-0	2-2	0-2	1-2	3-0	5-1	1-2	*O*	3-5
Todmorden Boro.	2-3	1-2	1-0	2-1	3-1	1-5	3-3	1-3	1-2	0-1	2-2	4-2	2-5	

Division Two	P	W	D	L	F	A	Pts
Lytham St Annes	26	20	4	2	69	25	64
Euxton Villa	26	15	6	5	75	32	51
Mill Hill St Peters	26	14	5	7	47	26	47
BAC/EE Preston	26	14	5	7	50	32	47
Thornton Clev.	26	14	2	10	53	40	44
BAE Canberra	26	13	4	9	70	42	43
Askam United	26	11	4	11	49	55	37
Stoneclough	26	10	5	11	52	63	35
Crosshills	26	10	3	13	52	61	33
Barrow Rangers	26	10	3	13	43	65	33
Pennington	26	8	3	15	42	56	27
Todmorden Boro.	26	6	3	17	39	73	21
Glaxo Ulverston	26	5	4	17	31	59	19
Furness Cavaliers	26	4	5	17	29	72	17

Reserve Div. One		P	W	D	L	F	A	Pts
Fulwood Res.	-3	30	24	4	2	108	35	73
Freckleton Res.		30	19	5	6	61	31	62
Eagley Res.		30	16	7	7	98	62	55
Charnock Rich. Res.		30	15	7	8	65	48	52
Blackrod Town Res.		30	14	8	8	60	48	50
Turton Res.		30	14	6	10	54	45	48
Kirkham & W. Res.		30	14	4	12	69	56	46
Whinney Hill Res.		30	12	4	14	54	72	40
Norcross & W. Res.		30	10	9	11	51	63	39
Poulton Town Res.		30	10	4	16	61	71	34
Barnoldswick R.	-3	30	9	6	15	57	67	30
Tempest Res.	-3	30	10	3	17	43	69	30
Garstang Res.		30	8	5	17	43	55	29
Springfields Res.	-3	30	9	5	16	58	82	29
Milnthorpe Cor.		30	8	5	17	50	86	29
Fleetwood H Res.	-3	30	5	4	21	34	76	16

Reserve Div. Two		P	W	D	L	F	A	Pts
Coppull Utd Res.		28	22	2	4	91	34	68
Hesketh Bank Res.		28	19	6	3	74	30	63
Thornton Clev. Res.		28	17	5	6	80	37	56
Euxton Villa Res.		28	16	8	4	67	37	56
Wyre Villa Res.		28	16	5	7	77	42	53
Todmorden B. Res.		28	13	3	12	52	51	42
Carnforth Res.	-3	28	14	1	13	52	64	40
Lytham St A. Res.		28	12	3	13	55	57	39
BAC/EE Preston Res.		28	10	5	13	50	57	35
Stoneclough Res.		28	10	2	16	47	50	32
Burnley Bel. Res.		28	7	4	17	48	78	25
Burnley Utd Res.		28	7	4	17	42	77	25
Mill Hill SP Res.		28	7	3	18	52	89	24
Has'den SM. Res.	-3	28	8	2	18	55	70	23
Pennington Res.		28	4	3	21	35	104	15

TAVERN CUP

FIRST ROUND
BAC/EE Preston 1 Euxton Villa 0
BAE Canberra 3 Stoneclough 1
Glaxo Ulverston Rangers 2 Todmorden Borough 0
Lytham St Annes 4 Pennington 1
Mill Hill St Peters 3 **Crosshills** 4
Thornton Cleveleys 0 **Askam United** 1
QUARTER-FINALS
Askam United 3 **BAC/EE Preston** 0
(Askam United expelled)
Barrow Rangers 2 Crosshills 1
Furness Cavaliers 1 **BAE Canberra** 2
Lytham St Annes 2 Glaxo Ulverston Rangers 2
SEMI-FINALS
BAC/EE Preston 2 Barrow Rangers 0
Lytham St Annes 0 **BAE Canberra** 1
FINAL
(23rd April at Bamber Bridge)
BAE Canberra 1 BAC/EE Preston 0

WWW.NLNEWSDESK.CO.UK

HOUSTON CUP

FINAL *(8th April at Blackpool Wren Rovers)*
Garstang Res. 2 Charnock Richard Res. 0

DIVISION TWO CONSTITUTION 2003-04

ASKAM UNITED .... Duddon Road, Askam, Westmorland .... None
ASPULL........................... Aspull Civic Hall, Woods Road, Aspull, Wigan, Lancashire 01942 833328
BAC/EE PRESTON .... BAC Sports Ground, South Meadow Lane, Preston, Lancashire 01772 464351
BAE CANBERRA .... Samlesbury Works, Whalley Road, Samlesbury, Lancashire 01254 768888
BARROW RANGERS .... Wilkie Road, Barrow-in-Furness, Cumbria .... None
CROSSHILLS........................ Holme Lane, Crosshills, Keighley, West Yorkshire .... None
FURNESS CAVALIERS.................... Rampside Road, Barrow-in-Furness, Cumbria.......................... None
GLAXO ULVERSTON RANGERS.......... off North Lonsdale Road, Ulverston, Cumbria........................ 01229 582261
LANCASHIRE CONSTABULARY .... Police HQ, Saunders Lane, Hutton, Preston, Lancashire.................... 01772 410591
MILL HILL ST PETERS ..... opposite Mill Hill Hotel, Bridge Street, off Buncer Lane, Blackburn, Lancashire 01254 675557
PENNINGTON....................... Jubilee Park, Leigh Road, Atherton, Lancashire........................... None
RIVINGTON .... Lostock Lane (near Reebok Stadium), Bolton, Lancashire........................ None
STONECLOUGH .... Brook Street, opposite Europa Business Park, Stoneclough, Kearsley, Bolton, Lancashire .... None
THORNTON CLEVELEYS .... Bourne Way, Thornton Cleveleys, Lancashire.......................... 01253 869666
TODMORDEN BOROUGH......... Bellholme, Walsden Road (off A6033), Todmorden, Lancashire.......................... None

Lytham St Annes and Euxton Villa move up to Division One with Lancashire Constabulary making the reverse trip. Glaxo Ulverston Rangers become GSK Ulverston Rangers. Newcomers are Aspull (Wigan Youth League) and Rivington (Lancs Amateur League).

WEST MIDLANDS (REGIONAL) LEAGUE

	Brierley & Hagley	Bromyard Town	Bustleholme	Dudley Town	Ettingshall HT	Gornal Athletic	Heath Hayes	Kington Town	Ledbury Town	Little Drayton Rgrs	Lye Town	Malvern Town	Sedgley White Lions	Shawbury United	Smethwick Sikh T.	Tipton Town	Tividale	Walsall Wood	Wellington	Westfields	Wolverhampton C.	Wolverhampton U.
Brierley & Hagley A.		1-3	4-1	3-0	5-1	1-1	1-3	3-2	0-0	1-2	2-1	0-5	3-1	0-0	2-2	1-3	1-1	3-0	3-2	0-3	0-2	2-2
Bromyard Town	3-4		1-0	6-1	5-2	3-1	1-5	1-4	1-7	1-4	3-1	2-3	2-4	1-0	2-0	0-4	1-4	1-2	0-0	0-9	2-0	2-3
Bustleholme	3-5	2-1		0-2	0-2	2-0	1-2	1-2	3-1	2-4	5-2	2-2	4-0	4-0	3-3	1-2	1-2	2-1	2-3	1-4	1-2	1-1
Dudley Town	1-6	4-0	1-2	P	0-2	0-2	1-1	0-2	2-1	0-2	1-2	2-1	2-2	0-9	1-1	0-1	1-0	2-2	1-2	0-3	1-4	2-3
Ettingshall Holy Trin.	0-1	2-3	0-3	3-3	R	5-0	1-3	3-6	4-1	3-4	0-0	0-1	3-2	3-1	1-2	1-2	0-2	2-1	4-0	0-2	1-2	1-1
Gornal Athletic	0-2	2-0	2-2	1-0	5-1	E	0-2	1-6	2-4	0-5	0-4	1-0	1-3	1-2	0-0	1-1	1-1	1-3	1-1	1-5	2-1	0-4
Heath Hayes	1-1	4-3	3-2	3-3	0-4	2-2	M	0-1	3-4	1-2	0-2	0-1	0-0	4-1	2-2	1-4	1-3	9-1	1-1	1-2	2-2	0-3
Kington Town	3-1	5-0	4-1	6-2	5-1	4-1	0-0	I	0-1	2-2	1-2	4-2	1-0	1-2	3-1	1-2	2-1	4-2	8-0	2-1	4-1	3-1
Ledbury Town	2-0	2-2	6-1	4-2	5-1	5-2	0-1	1-2	E	3-1	4-1	3-2	1-1	3-3	1-1	0-4	1-1	3-3	3-0	0-1	3-3	1-1
Little Drayton Rgrs	3-0	3-0	3-0	8-0	5-1	3-1	2-1	2-1	4-2	R	1-2	0-2	3-0	2-3	3-1	1-1	2-2	4-0	1-0	3-1	5-1	1-3
Lye Town	2-3	1-0	2-1	1-2	4-2	1-1	2-2	1-1	4-0	5-1		2-1	1-1	2-0	0-2	1-2	5-1	2-0	0-1	2-1	2-0	
Malvern Town	7-1	3-2	2-2	2-1	0-0	6-0	0-2	1-1	5-2	3-4	6-0	D	2-0	1-2	6-0	0-0	3-1	4-1	1-2	0-1	1-2	2-0
Sedgley White Lions	0-0	1-3	1-1	2-0	2-4	1-0	1-1	1-2	0-1	1-1	0-1	0-2	I	0-3	1-1	0-1	1-0	1-3	1-1	0-3	2-0	3-2
Shawbury United	2-1	3-0	4-2	4-2	1-2	1-1	2-1	3-4	1-0	2-1	3-3	0-3	3-2	V	1-2	1-3	2-1	2-1	1-1	1-1	4-0	2-1
Smethwick Sikh Tem.	2-2	3-0	2-1	0-1	2-3	3-1	0-1	1-3	0-5	5-2	1-3	0-2	3-0	0-5	I	1-2	0-5	1-1	1-0	3-4	4-1	3-0
Tipton Town	2-2	4-2	3-0	5-2	0-0	4-1	7-0	0-1	3-0	0-2	3-2	1-2	0-1	3-2	0-0	S	3-3	4-0	3-0	0-1	4-2	5-2
Tividale	3-1	9-1	6-1	4-0	1-0	4-1	1-2	1-2	1-2	1-2	1-1	2-4	1-1	3-2	2-1	2-2	I	5-4	7-1	1-1	0-1	5-1
Walsall Wood	1-4	3-0	0-3	1-1	1-0	0-2	1-1	1-5	0-2	2-7	0-1	1-1	1-2	1-1	1-1	1-3	0-3	O	1-1	1-1	2-1	1-1
Wellington	1-1	4-0	1-1	3-1	2-1	3-1	0-1	3-1	2-0	3-2	1-2	1-1	3-1	2-0	1-1	0-1	4-0	1-1	N	0-1	2-1	2-1
Westfields	2-0	6-0	4-0	7-0	4-1	2-1	6-1	1-3	1-0	3-2	3-0	0-0	2-0	4-1	1-2	0-3	6-0	2-0			3-0	7-1
Wolverhampton Cas.	0-2	2-1	2-1	1-1	2-0	3-0	0-2	4-5	3-5	2-2	2-0	4-6	5-3	0-2	4-1	3-1	0-5	0-3	3-2	1-4		1-0
Wolverhampton Utd	0-1	0-2	1-3	0-0	3-0	2-0	2-1	1-4	3-1	3-0	2-0	0-2	1-1	2-2	1-1	2-0	0-1	3-3	4-0	4-2	0-3	1-1

Premier Division	P	W	D	L	F	A	Pts
Westfields	42	32	6	4	119	30	102
Kington Town	42	31	6	5	121	51	99
Tipton Town	42	27	8	7	95	40	89
Little Drayton Rangers	42	26	5	11	113	66	83
Tividale	42	22	10	10	104	53	76
Malvern Town	42	22	9	11	96	49	75
Shawbury United	42	21	9	12	86	68	72
Lye Town	42	19	7	16	69	64	64
Ledbury Town	42	18	9	15	90	75	63
Brierley & Hagley Alliance	42	17	11	14	74	73	62
Wellington	42	16	10	16	59	69	58
Heath Hayes	42	15	12	15	72	75	57
Wolverhampton Casuals	42	17	5	20	71	91	56
Wolverhampton United	42	15	8	19	66	73	53
Smethwick Sikh Temple	42	11	11	20	58	83	44
Sedgley White Lions	42	11	9	22	48	74	42
Ettingshall Holy Trinity	42	12	5	25	65	92	41
Bustleholme	42	11	7	24	69	93	40
Bromyard Town	42	11	2	29	61	125	35
Dudley Town	42	7	9	26	46	112	30
Walsall Wood	42	6	11	25	48	109	29
Gornal Athletic	42	7	7	28	41	106	28

PREMIER DIVISION CUP

FIRST ROUND
Bustleholme 4 Wellington 1
Heath Hayes 1 **Brierley & Hagley Alliance** 4
Kington Town 3 Little Drayton Rangers 2 *aet*
Ledbury Town 9 Gornal Athletic 1
Shawbury United 6 Bromyard Town 2
Wolverhampton Casuals 0 **Tividale** 6

SECOND ROUND
Bustleholme 3 Westfields 1
Dudley Town 0 **Brierley & Hagley Alliance** 3
Ettingshall HT 1 Tividale 1 *aet (4-3p)*
Ledbury Town 2 Malvern Town 0
Sedgley White Lions 0 **Kington Town** 1
Shawbury United 1 **Lye Town** 3
Tipton Town 6 Smethwick Sikh Temple 0
Wolverhampton Utd 3 Walsall Wood 2

QUARTER-FINALS
Ettingshall Holy Trinity 2 Tipton Town 1
Ledbury Town 1 **Kington Town** 2
Lye Town 2 **Bustleholme** 2 *aet (2-4p)*
Wolverhampton Utd 2 Brierley & HA 1

SEMI-FINALS
(played over two legs)
Bustleholme 2 Ettingshall Holy Trinity 3,
Ettingshall Holy Trinity 1 **Bustleholme** 3
Wolverhampton United 0 Kington Town 1
Kington Town 1 Wolverhampton Utd 0

FINAL
(15th May at Malvern Town)
Kington Town 2 Bustleholme 0

PREMIER DIVISION CONSTITUTION 2003-04

BRIERLEY & HAGLEY ALLIANCE Lye Town FC, Sports Ground, Stourbridge Rd, Lye, Stourbridge. 01384 422672
BROMYARD TOWN . . . . Delahay Meadow, Bromyard, Herefordshire. 01885 483974
BUSTLEHOLME . . . . Tipton Sports Academy, Wednesbury Oak Road, Tipton, West Midlands. . . . . 0121 502 5534 / 556 5067
DUDLEY TOWN . . . . Tividale FC, The Beeches, Packwood Road, Tividale, West Midlands 01384 211743
ETTINGSHALL HOLY TRINITY. . . . Aldersley Stadium, Aldersley Road, Tettenhall, Wolverhampton . . . . 01902 751171 / 754975
HEATH HAYES. . . . . Coppice Colliery Ground, Newlands Lane, Heath Hayes, Cannock, Staffordshire . . . . None
KINGTON TOWN. . . . . Park Road Ground, Kington, Herefordshire. 01544 231007
LEDBURY TOWN. . . . . New Street, Ledbury, Herefordshire 01531 631463
LITTLE DRAYTON RANGERS . . Greenfield Sports Club, Greenfield Lane, Market Drayton, Shropshire 01630 655088
LYE TOWN. Sports Ground, Stourbridge Road, Lye, Stourbridge, West Midlands 01384 422672
MALVERN TOWN . . . . Langland Stadium, Langland Avenue, Malvern, Worcestershire 01684 574068
NEWPORT TOWN . . . . Wolverhampton Casuals FC, Brinsford Lane, Coven Heath, Wolverhampton, West Midlands. 01902 783214
SEDGLEY WHITE LIONS. . Gornal Athletic FC, Garden Walk Stadium, Lower Gornal, Dudley, West Midlands. 01384 252285
SHAWBURY UNITED . . . . Butlers Sports Centre, Bowens Field, Wem, Shropshire 01939 233287
SMETHWICK SIKH TEMPLE. . . . . Hadley Stadium, Wilson Road, Smethwick, Warley, West Midlands 0121 434 4848
TIPTON TOWN . . . . Tipton Sports Academy, Wednesbury Oak Road, Tipton, West Midlands . . . . 0121 502 5534 / 556 5067
TIVIDALE . . . . The Beeches, Packwood Road, Tividale, West Midlands. 01384 211743
WEDNESFIELD . . . . Cottage Ground, Amos Lane, Wednesfield, West Midlands 01902 735506
WELLINGTON . . . . Wellington Playing Fields, Wellington, Herefordshire. . . . . None
WOLVERHAMPTON CASUALS . . . . Brinsford Lane, Coven Heath, Wolverhampton 01902 783214
WOLVERHAMPTON UTD. . . . . Wednesfield FC, Cottage Ground, Amos Lane, Wednesfield, Wolverhampton 01902 735506

Westfields are promoted to the Midland Alliance replaced by Wednesfield. Walsall Wood are relegated to Division One North replaced by Newport Town. Gornal Athletic are relegated to Division One South.

	Bewdley Town	Blackheath Town	Bridgnorth T. Res.	Bustleholme Res.	Chaddesley Corbett	Hinton	Ledbury Town Res.	Leominster Town	Ludlow Town Res.	Lye Town Res.	Mahal	Malvern Rangers	Malvern Town Res.	Wyre Forest Brintons
Bewdley Town	D	4-1	2-3	6-0	2-0	2-3	7-1	2-0	4-0	2-1	2-1	6-1	6-3	0-0
Blackheath Town	1-1	I	2-2	5-0	2-2	1-2	5-0	6-0	3-1	1-0	3-3	3-1	4-3	5-2
Bridgnorth T. Res.	2-3	1-1	V	6-2	1-1	2-0	6-0	0-4	2-2	1-1	4-0	4-0	2-1	0-1
Bustleholme Res.	0-1	0-3	1-2	I	0-2	0-2	3-3	1-4	1-1	1-1	1-2	3-2	3-1	4-5
Chaddesley Corbett	1-1	0-1	0-2	1-1	S	3-2	1-5	7-1	1-1	1-0	0-1	5-0	0-3	2-0
Hinton	2-3	1-2	1-3	4-0	2-1	I	1-0	7-1	2-4	4-1	1-1	8-0	3-1	3-1
Ledbury Town Res.	1-1	3-0	1-2	2-3	1-4	2-4	O	2-2	1-0	1-2	1-3	1-5	2-1	
Leominster Town	0-6	1-2	0-3	2-0	2-4	1-3	1-3	N	1-1	0-1	1-1	4-3	1-2	3-4
Ludlow Town Res.	4-4	1-4	2-0	3-2	2-4	2-3	6-1	2-2		1-0	6-1	4-2	2-0	7-1
Lye Town Res.	1-4	0-3	2-2	1-3	2-1	4-3	2-1	1-1		O	1-1	5-0	2-0	2-3
Mahal	1-2	1-1	4-3	5-1	3-5	1-3	6-0	4-0	1-0	1-0	N	1-3	3-0	4-3
Malvern Rangers	1-5	2-2	0-3	2-2	0-2	2-5	1-0	2-0	1-1	0-1	2-4	E	3-3	0-1
Malvern Town Res.	2-5	2-1	3-1	1-5	0-0	4-3	2-2	1-1	5-1	3-4	3-2	1-1		1-4
Wyre Forest Brin.	1-2	3-3	0-1	3-4	1-2	2-4	3-1	5-3	2-3	2-0	0-1	6-1	2-2	S

Division One South	P	W	D	L	F	A	Pts
Bewdley Town	26	19	5	2	83	31	62
Hinton	26	17	1	8	74	42	52
Blackheath Town	26	14	8	4	65	36	50
Bridgnorth Res.	26	14	6	6	58	34	48
Mahal	26	13	5	8	55	46	44
Chaddesley Corb.	26	12	6	8	50	37	42
Ludlow Town Res.	26	10	8	8	61	51	38
Wyre Forest Brin.	26	11	3	12	58	60	36
Lye Town Res.	26	10	5	11	36	38	35
Malvern T. Res.	26	8	6	12	52	62	30
Bustleholme Res.	26	5	5	16	38	70	20
Ledbury T. Res.	26	5	4	17	38	76	19
Leominster Town	26	4	5	17	36	74	17
Malvern Rangers	26	4	5	17	33	80	17

DIVISION ONE SOUTH CONSTITUTION 2003-04

BEWDLEY TOWN . . . . Ribbesford Meadows, Ribbesford, Bewdley, Worcestershire. 01299 405837
BLACKHEATH TOWN. . . . . . . Oldbury United FC, Cricketts, York Road, Oldbury, Warley, West Midlands 0121 559 5564
BRIDGNORTH TOWN RESERVES . . . . . Crown Meadow, Innage Lane, Bridgnorth, Shropshire 01746 762747
BUSTLEHOLME RESERVES . . Great Barr Club, Ray Hall Lane (off Newton Rd), Gt Barr, West Midlands. . . . . None
CHADDESLEY CORBETT . . . . . Chaddesley Sports Club, Longmore, Chaddesley Corbett, Worcestershire 01562 777691
CRADLEY TOWN RESERVES . . . . Beeches View Avenue, Cradley, Halesowen, West Midlands 01384 569658
GORNAL ATHLETIC . . . . Garden Walk Stadium, Lower Gornal, Dudley, West Midlands. 01384 252285
HINTON . . . . Broomy Hill, Hereford, Herefordshire . . . . None
LEDBURY TOWN RESERVES . . . . New Street, Ledbury, Herefordshire 01531 631463
LEOMINSTER TOWN . . . . Bridge Street Park, Bridge Street, Leominster, Herefordshire 01568 611172
LUDLOW TOWN RESERVES . . . . Coors Stadium, Bromfield Road, Ludlow, Shropshire. 01584 876000
MAHAL . . . . Hadley Stadium, Wilson Road, Smethwick, West Midlands 0121 434 4848
MALVERN RANGERS. . . . . Victoria Playing Fields, Pickersleigh Road, Malvern Link, Worcestershire . . . . None
MALVERN TOWN RESERVES . . . . . Langland Stadium, Langland Avenue, Malvern, Worcestershire 01684 574068
REALITY SPORTS. Kays Sports Ground, Worcester, Worcestershire. . . . . None
TENBURY UNITED . . . . Palmers Meadow, Burford, Tenbury Wells . . . . None
WYRE FOREST BRINTONS . . . . Brintons Sports Ground, Oldington Lane, Kidderminster, Worcestershire 01562 824900

Lye Town Reserves have withdrawn. Gornal Athletic are relegated from the Premier Division. Newcomers are Reality Sports (Sunday football), Tenbury United (Kidderminster & District League) and Cradley Town Reserves.

DIVISION ONE SUPPLEMENTARY CUP

FIRST ROUND
Bridgnorth Town Res. 3 Mahal 1,
Hinton 4 Malvern Rangers 0
Leominster Town **Chaddesley Corbett**
Ludlow Town Res. 5 Bustleholme Res. 2
QUARTER-FINALS
Chaddesley Corbett 1 **Lye Town Res.** 3

Ludlow Town Res. 3 Ledbury Town Res. 1
Malvern Town Res. 1 Bridgnorth Town Res. 1
aet (3-1p)
Wyre Forest Brintons 3 Hinton 1
SEMI-FINALS
(played over two legs)
Ludlow Town Res. 1 Lye Town Res. 1,

Lye Town Res. 1 **Ludlow Town Res.** 4
Wyre Forest Brintons 11 Malvern Town Res. 0,
Malvern Town Res. 2 **Wyre Forest Brintons** 2
FINAL *(14th May at Bridgnorth Town)*
Wyre Forest Brintons 1 Ludlow Town Res. 0

	Ashbourne	Bilston	Brereton	Darlaston	Gt Wyrley	Hth H. Res.	Lucas Spts	Marston W.	Morda Utd	Newport T.	Riverway	Shelfield	Shenstone	Sikh Hunt.	Wal. W. Res.	Wednesbury	W'pton Spts	Wrock. Wd	Wyrley Rgrs
Ashbourne United		1-4	2-3	0-3	3-2	6-4	1-1	4-1	3-2	3-1	3-0	n/a	7-3	7-0	7-0	4-1	3-1	4-1	2-1
Bilston Town	2-2	D	4-1	2-1	6-1	3-0	2-1	2-0	5-1	1-2	5-3	5-2	3-0	3-2	11-0	5-0	7-0	3-0	3-1
Brereton Social	2-1	2-1	I	6-1	7-1	1-0	3-3	3-2	2-1	1-3	1-1	2-3	4-1	0-6	2-4	1-1	6-1	4-1	4-1
Darlaston Town	2-7	3-3	2-4	V	4-3	2-2	4-1	2-0	1-0	1-4	0-0	n/a	2-0	3-4	5-0	5-3	4-6	2-2	1-0
Great Wyrley	2-2	0-1	2-0	2-4	I	1-2	4-2	0-0	5-4	0-3	1-2	3-2	7-0	1-1	9-0	0-1	3-1	5-0	0-1
Heath Hayes Res.	4-1	1-2	1-1	2-2	0-4	S	1-6	0-2	0-0	1-2	4-1	1-3	0-6	2-0	3-1	3-2	0-1	3-2	
Lucas Sports	5-1	0-4	4-2	4-0	1-0	4-1	I	3-0	6-3	0-4	12-0	4-1	5-0	4-3	1-0	4-1	4-2	7-1	
Marston Wolves	5-5	1-2	2-2	0-1	1-5	2-0	3-0	O	2-2	1-3	6-1	n/a	3-1	2-2	3-0	1-2	5-2	1-0	3-0
Morda United	3-0	3-3	2-1	2-1	1-1	4-1	2-3	1-0	N	0-2	2-1	n/a	0-2	2-4	2-0	2-0	3-0	4-1	3-0
Newport Town	1-0	1-1	2-0	2-0	5-0	2-1	3-3	1-2	3-0		5-1	n/a	3-4	3-0	8-0	2-0	5-2	2-0	4-1
Riverway Stafford	1-0	0-3	2-6	2-2	1-3	1-4	2-1	2-1	1-1		O	n/a	4-2	1-3	5-4	4-0	2-3	2-3	0-1
Shelfield Sports	0-3	0-1	n/a	n/a	3-2	1-2	n/a	1-1	n/a	2-4	n/a	N	1-2	n/a	9-0	3-2	n/a	2-3	n/a
Shenstone Pathfinder	2-2	1-4	2-1	3-1	2-2	1-1	1-4	1-3	1-0	0-2	2-2	n/a	E	3-1	4-4	2-1	2-1	1-2	
Sikh Hunters	1-5	0-4	L-W	1-2	3-4	2-2	2-6	2-2	0-3	2-3	2-2	7-2	2-2		6-1	5-1	1-1	2-0	4-1
Walsall Wood Res.	1-3	0-10	2-2	2-6	1-7	0-2	0-8	2-4	0-2	0-4	0-1	0-8	1-1	0-5	N	1-3	1-2	0-1	1-2
Wednesbury Town	5-3	0-4	2-5	5-1	3-3	2-4	1-2	3-1	2-3	2-5	2-2	1-1	1-1	6-0		O	7-2	1-1	2-3
Wolverhampton Sports	4-3	0-4	4-2	1-6	4-2	1-2	0-6	0-2	1-2	0-6	3-1	n/a	1-0	1-1	2-1	0-4	R	2-3	2-3
Wrockwardine Wood	1-7	1-4	1-1	2-2	2-2	2-3	0-3	2-1	1-1	0-2	4-1	n/a	0-1	0-5	4-0	0-2	2-0	T	1-0
Wyrley Rangers	0-4	0-4	1-3	0-0	1-2	2-1	1-3	2-3	3-4	1-5	1-0	n/a	1-3	6-2	2-2	2-0	0-0	2-4	H

Note – Shelfield Sports withdrew during the season. Their results are shown above but are expunged from the league table

Division One North	P	W	D	L	F	A	Pts
Newport Town	34	29	3	2	105	28	90
Bilston Town	34	28	4	2	125	29	88
Lucas Sports	34	25	3	6	124	51	78
Brereton Social	34	18	7	9	87	58	61
Ashbourne United	34	18	5	11	106	69	59
Morda United	34	16	5	13	65	57	53
Darlaston Town	34	14	8	12	76	75	50
Marston Wolves	34	14	6	14	65	58	48
Great Wyrley	34	13	7	14	84	69	46
Sikh Hunters	34	12	9	13	81	73	45
Heath Hayes Res.	34	12	6	16	55	72	42
Wrockwardine Wood	34	10	7	17	45	77	37
Wednesbury Town	34	10	5	19	68	85	35
Shenstone Pathfinder	34	9	8	17	50	81	35
Riverway Stafford	34	9	7	18	52	91	34
Wyrley Rangers	34	10	3	21	42	82	33
Wolverhampton Sports	34	9	4	21	51	101	31
Walsall Wood Res.	34	0	3	31	23	148	3

DIVISION ONE NORTH CONSTITUTION 2003-04

ASHBOURNE UNITED . . . . Rocester FC, Riversfield, Mill Street, Rocester, Staffordshire 01889 590463
BILBROOK . . . . t.b.a. . . . . t.b.a.
BILSTON TOWN . . . . Queen Street, Bilston, West Midlands 01902 491498
BRERETON SOCIAL . . . . Red Lion Ground, Armitage Lane, Brereton, Staffordshire 01889 585526
DARLASTON TOWN . . . . City Ground, Waverley Road, Darlaston, West Midlands 0121 526 4423
ECCLESHALL AFC . . . . Pershall Park, Chester Road, Eccleshall, Staffordshire 01785 851351
GREAT WYRLEY . . . . Hazelbrook, Hazel Lane, Great Wyrley, Walsall, West Midlands 01922 410366
HEATH HAYES RESERVES . Coppice Colliery Ground, Newlands Lane, Heath Hayes, Cannock, Staffordshire . . . . None
LUCAS SPORTS . . . . Lucas Sports Ground, Stafford Road, Fordhouses, Wolverhampton, West Midlands 01902 644644x4448
MARSTON WOLVES . . . . . . Goodyear Sports Ground, Stafford Road, Oxley, Wolverhampton, West Midlands 01902 327260
MORDA UNITED . . . . Weston Road, Morda, Oswestry, Shropshire 01691 659621
RIVERWAY STAFFORD . . . . Riverway, Stafford, Staffordshire . . . .
SHENSTONE PATHFINDER . . Shenstone PF (Pavilion Club), Birmingham Road, Shenstone, Lichfield, Staffordshire 01543 481658
SIKH HUNTERS . . . . Great Wyrley FC, Hazelbrook, Hazel Lane, Great Wyrley, Walsall, West Midlands 01922 410366
WALSALL WOOD . . . . Oak Park, Lichfield Road, Walsall Wood, West Midlands 01543 361084
WEDNESBURY TOWN . . . . Wolverhampton United FC, Prestwood Road West, Wednesfield, West Midlands 01902 730881
WOLVERHAMPTON SPORTS GNST . . Wolverhampton Utd FC, Prestwood Rd West, Wednesfield 01902 730881
WROCKWARDINE WOOD. . . . . New Road, Wrockwardine Wood, Shropshire 01952 613086
WYRLEY RANGERS . . . . Long Lane Park, Long Lane, Essington, Staffordshire 01922 406604

Shelfield Sports withdrew during the course of the season. Newport Town are promoted to the Premier Division replaced by Walsall Wood. Walsall Wood Reserves have withdrawn. Newcomers are Eccleshall AFC and Bilbrook (from youth football).

WEST RIDING COUNTY AMATEUR LEAGUE

	Bay Athletic	Brighouse Town	Campion	Golcar United	Hemsworth Miners Welfare	Keighley Phoenix	Littletown	Lower Hopton	Otley Town	Ovenden West Riding	Silsden	Storthes Hall	Tyersal	Wibsey
Bay Athletic		2-2	3-4	2-7	3-1	n/a	4-2	3-3	5-1	1-3	1-1	1-0	1-2	3-1
Brighouse Town	4-2		P	4-0	1-0	0-1	n/a	2-0	2-1	3-1	1-1	0-1	1-1	3-2
Campion	3-1	0-0	R	2-2	0-3	4-0	2-1	0-0	1-1	0-1	1-6	1-0	3-0	1-2
Golcar United	1-5	0-3	1-0	E	3-0	n/a	2-2	3-4	5-1	1-4	2-3	3-2	2-0	0-2
Hemsworth Miners Welfare	1-3	1-3	3-2	1-1	M	n/a	1-0	2-0	0-0	4-1	0-0	1-0	4-0	0-3
Keighley Phoenix	n/a	0-9	n/a	1-2	2-4	I	1-7	n/a	2-8	1-3	n/a	n/a	n/a	n/a
Littletown	2-2	0-1	1-3	2-3	2-0	8-0	E	0-4	5-0	1-4	1-2	2-2	5-3	1-5
Lower Hopton	7-1	0-2	1-1	2-3	1-3	8-1	1-3	R	4-2	1-2	1-2	1-2	1-1	3-1
Otley Town	1-2	0-3	3-5	3-1	2-1	n/a	2-1	3-3		2-3	0-3	3-2	4-4	2-2
Ovenden West Riding	6-1	0-2	0-0	1-1	1-4	n/a	2-1	5-2	4-1		2-4	0-3	2-2	3-2
Silsden	2-2	1-1	6-1	3-1	2-0	6-1	6-2	2-0	0-0	4-1	D	1-1	5-1	3-0
Storthes Hall	5-1	1-5	2-1	1-2	3-1	7-2	1-2	0-0	2-2	3-3	1-5	I	1-1	1-0
Tyersal	2-1	0-6	1-4	4-3	1-0	n/a	0-2	7-4	0-1	3-4	0-0	2-0	V	0-1
Wibsey	3-1	0-0	3-2	3-1	2-3	n/a	1-1	2-1	5-0	0-2	0-1	4-1	1-3	

Note – Keighley Phoenix withdrew during the season. Their results are shown above but are expunged from the league table

Premier Division	P	W	D	L	F	A	Pts
Silsden	24	17	7	0	63	19	58
Brighouse Town	24	16	6	2	54	16	54
Ovenden West Riding	24	13	5	6	55	44	44
Wibsey	24	11	3	10	45	36	36
Hemsworth Miners W.	24	11	3	10	35	33	36
Golcar United	24	9	4	11	48	51	31
Campion	24	8	6	10	37	45	30
Bay Athletic	24	8	5	11	51	64	29
Tyersal	24	7	6	11	38	56	27
Storthes Hall	24	6	6	12	35	47	24
Littletown	24	6	4	14	39	53	22
Otley Town	24	5	7	12	35	64	22
Lower Hopton	24	5	6	13	45	52	21

PREM. DIV. CUP

FIRST ROUND
Bay Athletic 1 Otley Town 0
Brighouse Town 0 **Silsden** 3
Golcar United 2 **Campion** 3
Keighley Phoenix 1 **Ovenden West Riding** 2
Tyersal 2 **Storthes Hall** 2 *aet* (2-3p)
Wibsey 2 Hemsworth Miners Welfare 0

QUARTER-FINALS
Campion 1 **Silsden** 4, Littletown 4 **Storthes Hall** 5 *aet*
Lower Hopton 4 Ovenden West Riding 1
Wibsey 6 Bay Athletic 4

SEMI-FINALS
Silsden 3 Lower Hopton 0 *(at Altofts)*
Storthes Hall 1 **Wibsey** 2 *aet (at Otley Town)*

FINAL
(16th May at Brighouse Town)
Silsden 2 Wibsey 0

BOB WEDGEWORTH MEMORIAL TROPHY
(League champions v Premier Division Cup holders)
(13th August at Hemsworth Miners Welfare)
Brighouse Town 0 **Hemsworth Miners Welfare** 1

PREMIER DIVISION CONSTITUTION 2003-04
BAY ATHLETIC.............. University of Huddersfield, Salendine Nook, Huddersfield, West Yorkshire 07796 511243
BRIGHOUSE TOWN .... St Giles Road, Hove Edge, Brighouse, West Yorkshire 07775 693647
CAMPION .... Manningham Mills Sports Ground, Scothman Road, Manningham, Bradford, West Yorkshire 01274 546726
GOLCAR UNITED .... Longfield Recreation Ground, Golcar, Huddersfield, West Yorkshire 07779 700098
HALL GREEN UNITED ... Crigglestone Sports Club, Painthorpe Lane, Crigglestone, Wakefield, West Yorkshire 01924 254544
HEMSWORTH MINERS WELF.. Fitzwilliam Sports Complex, Wakefield Road, Fitzwilliam, West Yorkshire 01977 610444
LITTLETOWN .... Beck Lane, Heckmondwike, West Yorkshire 07930 852796
OTLEY TOWN .... Old Show Ground, Pool Road, Otley, West Yorkshire........................... 01943 451025
OVENDEN WEST RIDING................ Natty Lane, Illingworth, Halifax, West Yorkshire 01422 244350
SILSDEN .... Cougar Park, Keighley, West Yorkshire 01535 235111
STEETON .... Summer Hill Lane, Steeton, West Yorkshire............................... None
STORTHES HALL .... Woodfield Park, Police Sports Ground, Lockwood, Huddersfield, West Yorkshire. .... None
TYERSAL........................... Awkwright Street, off Dick Lane, Bradford, West Yorkshire...................... 07741 007070
WIBSEY............................. Harold Park, Low Moor, Bradford, West Yorkshire 01274 690692
Keighley Phoenix withdrew during the season. Hall Green United and Steeton are promoted from Division One to which Lower Hopton descend.

	Altofts	Ardsley Celtic	Dudley Hill Athletic	Dudley Hill Rangers	Eastmoor	Halifax Irish Club	Hall Green United	Heckmondwike Town	Hunsworth	Keighley Shamrocks	Marsden	Rawdon Old Boys	Salt Old Boys	Steeton	Stump Cross	Wakefield City
Altofts		1-1	7-2	4-0	1-0	4-1	2-1	4-2	1-2	2-1	7-2	4-0	1-0	1-4	4-2	0-0
Ardsley Celtic	1-4		3-1	4-3	1-1	2-2	1-3	0-1	3-1	1-1	5-0	4-1	3-2	2-1	2-1	1-2
Dudley Hill Athletic	0-9	1-4	D	3-5	0-3	1-2	0-3	1-3	2-2	1-7	2-3	0-2	1-4	0-7	4-2	2-3
Dudley Hill Rangers	1-0	0-4	5-1	I	2-0	0-3	1-4	1-3	5-1	2-0	1-1	1-1	2-1	0-0	1-2	0-2
Eastmoor	1-3	2-5	3-1	1-4	V	2-2	4-2	4-2	3-3	1-0	1-2	7-2	1-1	0-2	3-1	1-0
Halifax Irish Club	1-4	0-3	4-1	7-1	4-1	I	0-5	2-3	1-2	0-4	3-3	4-1	0-1	1-9	3-0	2-1
Hall Green United	3-2	2-2	8-2	2-0	4-2	5-1	S	3-2	7-3	1-1	9-0	8-2	1-0	0-2	1-0	1-0
Heckmondwike Town	1-3	3-6	2-2	2-2	2-1	2-3	0-4	I	3-3	2-3	2-2	7-2	2-0	1-3	1-4	2-2
Hunsworth	1-4	2-1	4-2	2-3	1-2	4-5	2-1	3-2	O	1-4	4-3	3-3	2-2	2-6	3-7	1-1
Keighley Shamrocks	1-0	3-0	2-0	2-3	4-1	3-3	0-2	3-1	5-2	N	1-2	3-1	3-0	0-1	2-3	2-1
Marsden	4-1	5-3	3-2	1-3	0-2	3-0	0-3	5-1	0-5	1-2		2-2	2-2	2-4	0-0	2-1
Rawdon Old Boys	1-4	0-4	4-1	1-0	1-4	5-3	1-3	3-4	0-2	2-2	1-2	O	1-1	1-3	2-0	1-4
Salt Old Boys	1-0	1-3	6-2	5-1	2-3	3-0	0-2	4-0	3-0	1-1	4-1	1-0	N	1-3	2-2	5-4
Steeton	3-4	3-2	7-2	3-3	3-0	6-0	1-2	0-0	2-3	4-1	1-3	6-0	3-1	E	4-1	3-2
Stump Cross	1-3	5-2	4-1	0-1	3-1	1-1	1-3	0-3	3-2	4-3	4-3	4-1	4-0	2-7		3-6
Wakefield City	1-4	1-3	3-3	2-1	1-0	3-0	3-1	1-3	0-3	5-2	3-3	4-2	1-2	2-1		

Division One	P	W	D	L	F	A	Pts
Hall Green United	30	23	2	5	94	35	71
Steeton	30	22	3	5	103	38	69
Altofts	30	21	2	7	88	39	65
Ardsley Celtic	30	16	5	9	76	53	53
Keighley Shamrocks	30	15	5	10	67	43	50
Wakefield City	30	13	5	12	62	55	44
Dudley Hill Rangers	30	12	5	13	52	62	41
Eastmoor	30	12	4	14	55	59	40
Salt Old Boys	30	11	6	13	56	52	39
Stump Cross	30	12	3	15	65	71	39
Marsden	30	11	6	13	59	81	39
Heckmondwike Town	30	10	6	14	62	74	36
Hunsworth	30	10	6	14	67	87	36
Halifax Irish Club	30	10	5	15	58	83	35
Rawdon Old Boys	30	5	6	19	45	94	21
Dudley Hill Athletic	30	1	3	26	41	124	6

DIVISION ONE CUP

FIRST ROUND
Dudley Hill Rangers 1 **Ardsley Celtic** 5
Halifax Irish Club 2 **Eastmoor** 3
Hall Green United 4 Marsden 1
Heckmondwike Town 2 Altofts 1
Hunsworth 3 Dudley Hill Athletic 2
Keighley Shamrocks 2 Salts Old Boys 1
Steeton 7 Rawdon Old Boys 3
Wakefield City 3 **Stump Cross** 3 *aet* (9-10p)

QUARTER-FINALS
Eastmoor 1 **Keighley Shamrocks** 2 *aet*
Hall Green United 1 **Steeton** 3
Heckmondwike Town 5 Hunsworth 2
Stump Cross 3 **Ardsley Celtic** 4

SEMI-FINALS
Heckmondwike Town 2 **Ardsley Celtic** 5 *(at Littletown)*
Steeton 1 Keighley Shamrocks 0
(at Silsden)

FINAL
(13th May at Littlen)
Ardsley Celtic 1 **Steeton** 2

DIVISION ONE CONSTITUTION 2003-04

ALTOFTS .... Altofts Sports Club, Lock Lane, Altofts, Normanton, West Yorkshire 01924 892708
ARDSLEY CELTIC .... Cave Lane, Main Street, East Ardsley, Wakefield, West Yorkshire 07950 131889
DUDLEY HILL RANGERS .... Newall Park School, Bierley, West Yorkshire 07967 359883
EASTMOOR .... King George V Playing Fields, Woodhouse Road, Eastmoor, Wakefield, West Yorkshire 01924 375367
HECKMONDWIKE TOWN .... Cemetary Road, Heckmondwike, West Yorkshire 01924 442907
HUNSWORTH .... Birkenshaw Middle School, Bradford Road, Birkenshaw, West Yorkshire 07711 197741
KEIGHLEY SHAMROCKS .... Marley Stadium, Keighley, West Yorkshire 01535 609910
LOWER HOPTON .... Woodend Road, Lower Hopton, Mirfield, West Yorkshire................. 01924 492048
MARSDEN .... Fell Lane, Marsden, Huddersfield, West Yorkshire.................... 01484 844191
SALT OLD BOYS .... Esholt Cricket Club, Esholt Lane, Baildon, Bradford, West Yorkshire.................. 01274 587792
SALTS .... Salts Playing Fields, Hirst Lane, Saltaire, Shipley, West Yorkshire 01274 583427
STUMP CROSS .... Shroggs Park, Lee Mount, Halifax, West Yorkshire..................... 01422 345845
WAKEFIELD CITY .... West Yorks Sports & Social, Walton Lane, Sandal, Wakefield, West Yorkshire............... 01924 258760
WESTWOOD .... Westwood Park, Cooper Lane, Bradford, West Yorkshire............................. None

Hall Green United and Steeton are promoted to the Premier Division replaced by Lower Hopton. Dudley Hill Athletic, Rawdon Old Boys and Halifax Irish Club are relegated to Division Two from which Salts and Westwood are promoted.

WWW.NLNEWSDESK.CO.UK

Reserve Div. One	P	W	D	L	F	A	Pts
Brighouse T. Res.	24	19	3	2	97	34	60
Hemsw'th MW Res.	24	19	2	3	71	23	59
Lower Hopton Res.	24	11	6	7	53	42	39
Campion Res.	24	11	3	10	54	56	36
Keighley Sham. Res.	24	10	4	10	57	58	34
Wibsey Res.	24	9	6	9	60	67	33
Keigh. Phoenix Res.	24	9	5	10	49	59	32
Rawdon OB Res.	24	9	4	11	50	54	31
Ardsley Celtic Res.	24	9	2	13	62	58	29
Ovenden WR Res.	24	8	5	11	45	68	29
Salts Res.	24	6	8	10	53	66	26
Westbrook W. Res.	24	5	3	16	29	62	18
Littletown Res.	24	4	3	17	36	69	15

	Barclays	Bowling	Crag Road United	Dynamoes	Farnley	Green Lane	Morley Town	Roberttown	Salts	Ventus & Yeadon Celtic	Westbrook Wanderers	Westwood
Barclays	D	1-0	7-2	2-3	2-3	2-0	0-2	0-2	1-3	2-2	1-4	0-3
Bowling	1-5	I	6-2	2-0	4-2	2-0	2-4	2-2	3-3	2-3	2-4	3-5
Crag Road United	2-1	1-2	V	5-3	1-4	4-4	1-6	3-7	3-3	2-5	0-3	1-9
Dynamoes	0-6	1-3	7-2	I	1-3	4-5	2-1	1-6	2-9	2-1	1-3	2-6
Farnley	3-4	2-2	12-0	0-0	S	6-0	3-1	2-7	1-2	2-1	0-4	0-3
Green Lane	0-7	0-8	8-0	1-1	3-1	I	1-1	2-3	2-2	8-2	0-4	1-3
Morley Town	3-4	0-3	4-2	1-2	5-2	2-2	O	0-0	1-2	2-2	2-8	1-4
Roberttown	2-1	4-1	2-0	3-1	1-3	3-4	6-1	N	1-0	4-2	0-4	2-3
Salts	2-1	2-2	4-0	2-0	0-1	3-1	6-0	4-2		7-4	3-1	2-1
Ventus & Yeadon Celtic	3-2	1-1	6-2	3-0	3-2	7-2	3-1	1-5	1-5	T	2-3	0-5
Westbrook Wanderers	2-4	2-4	8-2	5-0	1-2	4-0	4-5	3-5	0-2	2-2	W	0-1
Westwood	4-2	0-3	4-1	0-0	1-1	5-1	8-0	3-1	2-4	6-2	2-2	O

Reserve Div. Two	P	W	D	L	F	A	Pts
Silsden Res.	20	14	4	2	70	27	46
Dudley Hill R. Res.	20	11	4	5	53	42	37
Steeton Res.	20	9	6	5	57	45	33
Salts Old Boys Res.	20	9	2	9	38	33	29
Wakefield City Res.	20	9	2	9	38	50	29
Hunsworth Res.	20	9	1	10	45	50	28
Crag Road Utd Res.	20	8	3	9	44	51	27
Hall Green U. Res.	20	8	2	10	47	56	26
Heckmondwike Res.	20	7	1	12	43	56	22
Tyersal Res.	20	6	3	11	34	45	21
Eastmoor Res.	20	4	4	12	36	50	16

Division Two	P	W	D	L	F	A	Pts
Salts	22	16	4	2	70	30	52
Westwood	22	16	3	3	78	29	51
Roberttown	22	14	2	6	68	41	44
Westbrook Wanderers	22	12	2	8	71	40	38
Bowling	22	10	5	7	58	44	35
Farnley	22	10	3	9	55	46	33
Barclays	22	9	1	12	55	46	28
Ventus/Yeadon Celtic	22	8	4	10	56	67	28
Morley Town	22	6	4	12	43	67	22
Green Lane	22	5	5	12	45	74	20
Dynamoes	22	5	3	14	33	69	18
Crag Road United	22	2	2	18	36	115	8

DIVISION TWO CUP

FIRST ROUND
Bowling 6 Crag Road United 1
Morley Town 3 **Westbrook Wanderers** 4
Roberttown (w/o) v Green Lane (scr.)
Salts 2 **Westwood** 3 *aet*
QUARTER-FINALS
Bowling 3 **Roberttown** 4
Dynamoes 1 **Ventus & Yeadon Celtic** 2
Farnley 5 **Westbrook Wanderers** 6 *aet*
Westwood 2 Barclays 0
SEMI-FINALS
Roberttown 1 **Westwood** 3
Westbrook Wanderers 1 **Ventus & Yeadon Celtic** 4
FINAL
(29th April at Crag Road United)
Westwood 2 **Ventus & Yeadon Celtic** 4 *aet*

RESERVES CUP

FINAL
(at Ovenden West Riding)
Brighouse Town Res. 3 Silsden Res. 2

DIVISION TWO CONSTITUTION 2003-04

BARCLAYS . . . . Crawshaw Street, Ravensthorpe, Dewsbury, West Yorkshire. 01924 497020
BOWLING . . . . Bowling Community College, Lister Avenue, Bowling, Bradfield, West Yorkshire 01274 734913
CRAG ROAD UNITED . . . . Apperley Road, Greengates, Bradford, West Yorkshire 07781 808212
DUDLEY HILL ATHLETIC . . . . Hunsworth Lane, East Bierley, West Yorkshire . . . . None
DYNAMOES . . . . Dudley Hill Athletic FC, Hunsworth Lane, East Bierley, West Yorkshire . . . . None
FARNLEY . . . . Farnley Cricket Club, Church Lane, Farnley, West Yorkshire 0113 253 5950
GREEN LANE . . . . Avenue Road Playing Fields, Bradford, West Yorkshire. 01274 733508
HALIFAX IRISH CLUB . . . . Natty Lane, Illingworth, Halifax, West Yorkshire 01422 861084
MORLEY TOWN. . . . . Glen Road, Morley, Leeds, West Yorkshire . . . . None
RAWDON OLD BOYS . . . . Hansons Field, Rawdon, Leeds, West Yorkshire 07788 554733
ROBERTTOWN. . . . . Mill Street, Birstall, West Yorkshire . . . . None
SOUTH BRADFORD . . . . Avenue Road Playing Fields, Bradford, West Yorkshire . . . . None
VENTUS & YEADON CELTIC. . . . . Dam Lane, Yeadon, Leeds, West Yorkshire 07721 468967
WESTBROOK YMCA . . . . Lawnswood YMCA, Westbrook, Leeds, West Yorkshire 0113 267 8158

Salts and Westwood are promoted to Division One. Dudley Hill Athletic, Rawdon Old Boys and Halifax Irish Club are relegated from Division One.
Newcomers are South Bradford (formerly TFD Centre). Westbrook Wanderers become Westbrook YMCA.

WEST YORKSHIRE LEAGUE

	Aberford Albion	Baildon Trinity Athletic	Bardsey	Beeston	Carlton Athletic	Horsforth St Margaret's	Knaresborough Town	Nostell Miners Welfare	Pontefract Sports & Social	Pudsey	Ripon City Magnets	Tadcaster Magnet Sports	Wakefield	Wetherby Athletic	Whitkirk Wanderers
Aberford Albion		0-2	3-2	1-1	1-3	0-1	3-1	2-2	0-1	1-0	4-0	5-0	1-3	3-1	2-1
Baildon Trinity Athletic	2-0		1-0	0-1	1-2	1-2	1-2	0-6	0-3	3-3	5-0	1-0	2-1	1-3	4-0
Bardsey	4-2	3-3	P	5-2	0-5	1-7	4-1	6-7	1-2	1-2	2-2	1-4	2-2	2-0	2-1
Beeston	1-2	2-0	1-2	R	0-5	6-1	5-1	3-2	5-2	4-1	5-5	4-3	1-0	4-4	5-2
Carlton Athletic	4-4	5-2	6-2	4-3	E	2-2	2-0	3-5	2-1	0-1	4-1	5-1	3-4	3-1	3-3
Horsforth St Margaret's	3-0	3-1	1-2	0-1	1-1	M	6-0	2-0	3-1	4-3	5-2	1-0	1-0	2-0	2-1
Knaresborough Town	1-3	4-3	0-3	2-1	0-1	1-1	I	2-3	4-0	0-1	4-1	0-0	3-2	1-1	0-0
Nostell Miners Welfare	2-3	4-1	5-2	3-1	2-4	2-2	4-4	E	2-3	5-2	7-5	3-0	6-0	3-3	1-3
Pontefract Sports & Social	3-1	2-0	2-1	6-1	0-4	1-1	4-0	0-1	R	1-3	6-0	3-0	4-4	2-1	2-2
Pudsey	4-1	1-0	6-2	1-2	1-5	0-1	2-2	0-0	2-2		4-0	1-0	1-0	1-0	1-2
Ripon City Magnets	1-3	1-2	2-0	2-2	0-9	1-1	0-1	0-1	0-0	1-3	D	2-1	3-0	2-3	0-6
Tadcaster Magnet Sports	3-4	0-0	1-1	1-3	0-1	1-1	2-2	3-6	1-1	1-1	0-0	I	4-3	3-1	2-0
Wakefield	0-0	2-2	0-2	1-4	0-3	1-3	3-0	0-3	0-1	2-2	2-1	6-1	V	2-0	0-3
Wetherby Athletic	1-1	2-1	2-2	2-3	1-1	5-1	3-0	0-4	2-3	1-3	4-3	3-0	2-0		1-2
Whitkirk Wanderers	0-2	3-1	1-0	4-2	0-1	0-2	1-0	3-2	5-2	3-3	2-1	1-1	3-1	1-4	

Premier Division		P	W	D	L	F	A	Pts
Carlton Athletic		28	20	5	3	91	37	65
Horsforth St Margaret's		28	17	7	4	60	34	58
Nostell Miners Welfare		28	16	5	7	91	57	53
Beeston		28	15	4	9	73	62	49
Pontefract Sports & Social		28	14	6	8	58	46	48
Pudsey		28	13	7	8	53	44	46
Whitkirk Wanderers		28	13	5	10	53	47	44
Aberford Albion	-3	28	13	5	10	52	47	41
Wetherby Athletic	+3	28	9	6	13	51	54	36
Bardsey		28	9	5	14	55	71	32
Baildon Trinity Athletic		28	8	4	16	40	55	28
Knaresborough Town		28	7	7	14	36	60	28
Wakefield		28	6	5	17	39	61	23
Tadcaster Magnet Sports		28	4	9	15	33	60	21
Ripon City Magnets		28	3	6	19	36	86	15

WWW.CHERRYRED.CO.UK

PREMIER DIVISION CUP

FIRST ROUND
Aberford Albion 2 Wakefield 1
Baildon Trinity Athletic 3 Knaresborough Town 0
Bardsey 4 Nostell Miners Welfare 3
(ineligible player – Bardsey expelled)
Pontefract Sports & Social 1 Tadcaster Magnets 2
Pudsey 3 Carlton Athletic 4
Ripon City Magnets 1 Horsforth St Margaret's 2
Wetherby Athletic 0 Beeston 5
QUARTER-FINALS
Baildon Trinity Athletic 1 Nostell Miners Welfare 3
Beeston 5 Tadcaster Magnet Sports 2
Carlton Athletic 0 Whitkirk Wanderers 2
Horsforth St Margaret's 1 Aberford Albion 0
SEMI-FINALS
Horsforth St Margaret's 3 Beeston 0
Whitkirk Wanderers 1 Nostell Miners Welfare 2
FINAL
(10th May at Whitkirk Wanderers)
Horsforth St Margaret's 1 Nostell Miners Welfare 0

PREMIER DIVISION CONSTITUTION 2003-04

ABERFORD ALBION .... Bunkers Hill, Main Street (South), Aberford, West Yorkshire .... None
BAILDON TRINITY ATHLETIC ..... The Dell, Cliffe Lane, West Baildon, Shipley, West Yorkshire .... None
BARDSEY .... The Sportsfield, Keswick Lane, Bardsey, West Yorkshire 01937 574286
BEESTON .... Beggars Hill, Sunnyview Gardens, Beeston Road, Beeston, Leeds, West Yorkshire 0113 270 7223
BOROUGHBRIDGE .... Aldborough Road, Boroughbridge, West Yorkshire 01423 324206
CARLTON ATHLETIC .... Carlton Cricket Club, Town Street, Carlton, West Yorkshire 0113 282 1114
HORSFORTH ST MARGARET'S .... Cragg Hill Recreation Ground, off Ring Road, Horsforth, Leeds .... None
KNARESBOROUGH TOWN .... Manse Lane, Knaresborough, West Yorkshire 0777 367 9971
NOSTELL MINERS WELFARE .... Miners Welfare Ground, New Crofton, Wakefield, West Yorkshire 01924 862348
OSSETT COMMON ROVERS .... Illingworth Park, Monor Road, Ossett, West Yorkshire .... None
PONTEFRACT SPORTS & SOCIAL . Willow Park School, Harewood Avenue, Pontefract, West Yorks .... None
PUDSEY .... Fulneck Sports Centre, Pudsey, Leeds, West Yorkshire .... None
TADCASTER MAGNET SPORTS........... Queens Gardens, Tadcaster, West Yorkshire 01937 833435
WAKEFIELD ...... Woolley Colliery, Colliery Road, Darton, Wakefield, West Yorkshire 01226 385095
WETHERBY ATHLETIC .... The Ings, Wetherby, West Yorkshire.............................. 01937 585699
WHITKIRK WANDERERS ... Whitkirk Sports & Social Club, Selby Road, Whitkirk, Leeds, West Yorkshire............... 0113 264 6623
Ripon City Magnets are relegated to Division One replaced by Boroughbridge and Ossett Common Rovers.

	Armley Athletic	Barwick	Boroughbridge	Churwell Lions	Featherstone Colliery	Howden Clough	Kirk Deighton Rangers	Mount St Mary's	Ossett Common Rovers	Pool	Robin Hood Athletic	Rothwell Athletic	Rothwell Town	Sandy Lane	Sherburn White Rose	Upper Armley Old Boys
Armley Athletic		0-8	0-3	3-6	4-0	1-8	5-4	1-1	1-5	1-7	4-2	2-11	2-0	2-4	0-6	2-3
Barwick	4-1		1-3	0-2	3-2	4-5	4-0	3-2	2-1	1-0	3-3	3-2	4-2	1-0	7-2	2-0
Boroughbridge	10-0	5-1	D	2-4	2-1	2-2	6-1	7-0	2-0	8-1	10-0	4-4	4-0	2-1	5-2	0-0
Churwell Lions	7-3	1-6	2-3	I	1-1	2-3	8-2	8-0	0-0	3-0	5-3	3-0	5-1	4-0	1-0	5-3
Featherstone Colliery	2-1	0-1	1-2	3-2	V	2-3	4-2	4-2	0-4	0-0	3-2	2-6	5-4	2-3	3-1	1-3
Howden Clough	3-0	2-1	2-2	1-1	4-0	I	3-2	2-2	1-1	4-4	4-0	4-3	0-1	1-3	4-2	3-0
Kirk Deighton Rangers	1-0	0-6	2-7	0-2	2-4	2-7	S	0-2	0-8	0-2	6-2	2-1	2-2	0-3	1-7	0-2
Mount St Mary's	3-0	0-1	1-3	4-1	1-4	1-2	5-0	I	1-5	0-1	2-0	0-5	0-0	3-5	0-3	1-1
Ossett Common Rovers	3-0	5-1	1-2	2-1	3-1	4-2	4-0	2-0	O	1-0	3-0	3-1	3-0	6-0	8-0	0-0
Pool	9-1	3-3	0-2	5-4	2-1	2-1	4-2	7-1	1-2	N	5-1	2-2	4-0	0-3	3-2	3-3
Robin Hood Athletic	1-0	0-6	0-6	0-6	0-1	4-6	4-1	1-0	2-6	4-2		2-5	3-2	0-2	3-0	2-4
Rothwell Athletic	3-1	3-1	1-4	1-3	2-1	1-1	1-1	4-2	0-1	1-1	2-1	O	3-3	2-3	2-0	4-1
Rothwell Town	7-2	1-2	0-3	0-1	2-1	1-5	5-2	3-0	0-2	1-3	2-0	4-5	N	0-1	1-1	1-2
Sandy Lane	3-0	3-0	0-1	1-6	0-2	1-1	3-0	0-2	0-0	2-3	1-2	4-2	5-0	E	4-2	1-5
Sherburn White Rose	0-4	5-1	1-4	2-6	3-2	1-2	4-1	1-3	0-3	2-1	6-0	1-3	5-2	0-2		3-1
Upper Armley Old Boys	9-2	2-0	1-3	4-2	3-2	0-0	6-2	1-1	1-6	1-0	4-2	9-2	1-2	0-0	2-3	

Division One

	P	W	D	L	F	A	Pts
Boroughbridge	30	25	4	1	117	30	79
Ossett Common Rovers	30	23	4	3	93	20	73
Churwell Lions	30	19	3	8	102	53	60
Howden Clough	30	17	8	5	84	51	59
Barwick	30	18	2	10	80	55	56
Sandy Lane	30	16	3	11	58	49	51
Pool	30	15	4	11	73	56	49
Upper Armley Old Boys	30	14	7	9	72	55	49
Rothwell Athletic	30	12	6	12	82	73	42
Featherstone Colliery	30	11	3	16	56	68	36
Sherburn White Rose	30	11	1	18	65	79	34
Mount St Mary's	30	7	6	17	40	73	27
Rothwell Town	30	7	4	19	47	74	25
Robin Hood Athletic	30	7	1	22	44	107	22
Armley Athletic	30	5	1	24	43	133	16
Kirk Deighton Rangers	30	4	1	25	41	121	13

DIVISION ONE CUP

FIRST ROUND
Armley Athletic 4 Rothwell Athletic 3
Barwick 2 Upper Armley Old Boys 0
Churwell Lions 5 Featherstone Colliery 4
Mount St Mary's 2 **Boroughbridge** 5
Robin Hood Athletic 1 **Ossett Common Rovers** 2
Rothwell Town 0 **Pool** 3
Sandy Lane 3 Kirk Deighton Rangers 0
Sherburn White Rose 1 **Howden Clough** 2

QUARTER-FINALS
Armley Athletic 2 **Boroughbridge** 6
Churwell Lions 3 **Sandy Lane** 5
Ossett Common Rovers 4 Howden Clough 0
Pool 0 **Barwick** 3

SEMI-FINALS
Boroughbridge 2 Ossett Common Rovers 1
Sandy Lane 0 **Barwick** 1

FINAL
(3rd May at Knaresborough Town)
Boroughbridge 3 Barwick 0

WWW.NLNEWSDESK.CO.UK

DIVISION ONE CONSTITUTION 2003-04

BARWICK . . . . back of Village Hall, Chapel Lane, Barwick, West Yorkshire . . . . None
CHURWELL LIONS . . . . Bruntcliffe High School, Bruntcliffe Lane, Morley, Leeds, West Yorshire . . . . None
FEATHERSTONE COLLIERY . Featherstones Miners Welfare, Cresseys Corner, Green Lane, Featherstone . . . . None
HOWDEN CLOUGH . . . . Batley Sports Centre, Batley, West Yorkshire . . . . None
KELLINGLEY WELFARE . . Kellingley (Knottingley) Social Club, Marine Villa Road, Knottingley, Wakefield 01977 673113
MOUNT ST MARY'S . . . . Welfare Sports Ground, Wakefield Road, Swillington, Leeds, West Yorkshire . . . . None
POOL . . . . Arthington Lane, Pool, Leeds, West Yorkshire 0113 284 3932
RIPON CITY MAGNETS . . . . Mallorie Park Drive, Ripon, West Yorkshire 01765 600542
ROBIN HOOD ATHLETIC . . . . behind Coach & Horse, Rothwell Haigh, Leeds, West Yorkshire 0113 282 1021
ROTHWELL ATHLETIC . . . . Royds Lane, Rothwell, Leeds, West Yorkshire . . . . None
ROTHWELL TOWN . . . . off Fifth Avenue, Leeds Road, Rothwell, Leeds, West Yorkshire . . . . None
RYHILL & HAVERCROFT SPORTS . . . . Mulberry Place, Ryhill, West Yorkshire . . . . None
SANDY LANE . . . . Haworth Road Rec Ground, Bradford, West Yorkshire . . . . None
SHERBURN WHITE ROSE . . . . Recreation Ground, Finkle Hill, Sherburn-in-Elmet, West Yorkshire . . . . None
UPPER ARMLEY OLD BOYS . . . . Churwell Hill, Morley, Leeds, West Yorkshire . . . . None

Boroughbridge and Ossett Common Rovers go up to the Premier Division replaced by Ripon City Magnets. Kirk Deighton Rangers and Armley Athletic drop to Division Two replaced by Kellingley Welfare and Ryhill & Havercroft Sports.

Premier Alliance	P	W	D	L	F	A	Pts
Carlton A. Res.	26	24	2	0	110	17	74
Whitkirk W. Res.	26	19	4	3	72	28	61
Pudsey Res.	26	19	2	5	84	30	59
Beeston Res.	26	16	3	7	63	28	51
Nostell MW Res.	26	11	6	9	52	37	39
Knaresboro. Res.	26	10	5	11	50	48	35
Baildon TA Res.	26	10	5	11	55	56	35
Bardsey Res.	26	8	9	9	48	49	33
Tad. Magnet Res.	26	9	4	13	50	62	31
Ripon City M. Res.	26	8	2	16	45	85	26
Wetherby A. Res.	26	6	7	13	44	66	25
P'fract S&S Res.	26	5	3	18	37	96	18
Aberford A. Res.	26	4	5	17	35	74	17
Wakefield Res.	26	3	3	20	29	98	12

	Boston Spartans	Camerons	Dewsbury Moor Ath.	Great Preston	Hartshead Senior	Hunslet	Kellingley Welfare	Kippax Athletic	Kippax Welfare	Pontefract Town	Ryhill & Havercroft	Stanley United	Swillington Saints	Woodhouse Hill
Boston Spartans		6-5	2-1	3-4	1-1	0-1	2-3	2-1	2-0	2-0	0-0	1-3	2-1	1-1
Camerons	1-3	D	1-0	6-1	2-2	2-3	1-4	0-2	4-2	4-3	3-0	1-1	10-2	2-1
Dewsbury Moor A.	3-3	2-1	I	4-5	2-4	1-6	1-5	1-2	2-5	3-0	0-4	3-3	2-5	3-3
Great Preston	2-5	1-4	3-1	V	1-4	1-2	0-7	3-1	3-3	2-1	0-4	7-3	2-0	5-1
Hartshead Senior	4-2	1-3	3-1	3-0	I	3-0	1-5	2-5	4-2	2-2	1-0	4-0	2-1	0-3
Hunslet	2-2	1-2	5-3	4-1	0-2	S	1-1	1-0	2-2	2-0	2-4	3-3	10-0	5-0
Kellingley Welfare	7-2	6-0	3-2	2-1	1-1	3-1	I	3-0	3-1	5-0	1-3	3-1	7-0	1-1
Kippax Athletic	1-2	3-2	5-1	3-1	1-2	5-4	2-4	O	1-4	3-0	3-4	0-7	7-1	1-4
Kippax Welfare	1-1	0-5	1-0	4-3	4-3	1-2	2-3	0-1	N	1-3	0-6	2-2	2-1	0-0
Pontefract Town	3-1	1-0	5-2	0-3	0-3	5-3	0-1	4-2	2-7		2-2	1-5	2-5	1-2
Ryhill/Havercroft	1-2	6-1	7-3	5-1	5-0	3-1	0-2	3-1	4-1	10-2	T	1-0	6-0	2-6
Stanley United	1-2	1-5	4-1	1-1	5-4	1-0	0-6	1-2	2-2	2-3	1-5	W	3-1	0-2
Swillington Saints	1-3	1-5	3-2	2-1	1-2	2-3	1-4	1-3	1-7	2-2	2-4	2-3	O	1-0
Woodhouse Hill	3-3	2-7	4-1	1-2	4-1	5-2	1-6	2-0	2-2	4-2	1-2	1-1	6-0	

RESERVES CUP

FINAL *(9th May at Robin Hood Athletic)*

Whitkirk Wanderers 'A' 3 Churwell Res. 0

Division Two	P	W	D	L	F	A	Pts
Kellingley Welfare	26	22	3	1	96	25	69
Ryhill & Havercroft Sports	26	19	2	5	91	36	59
Hartshead Senior	26	14	4	8	59	51	46
Camerons	26	14	2	10	77	55	44
Boston Spartans	26	12	7	7	55	51	43
Hunslet	26	12	4	10	66	52	40
Woodhouse Hill WMC	26	11	7	8	60	51	40
Kippax Athletic	26	13	0	13	58	52	39
Great Preston	26	10	2	14	54	74	32
Kippax Welfare	26	8	7	11	56	62	31
Stanley United	26	7	7	12	47	66	28
Pontefract Town	26	7	3	16	44	78	24
Swillington Saints	26	5	1	20	37	100	16
Dewsbury Moor Athletic	26	2	3	21	45	92	9

DIVISION TWO CUP

FIRST ROUND

Boston Spartans 1 **Hunslet** 1 *aet* (1-2p)

Hartshead Senior 2 Kellingley Welfare 1

Kippax Athletic 1 **Great Preston** 2

Kippax Welfare 1 **Pontefract Town** 2

Ryhill & Havercroft Sports 3 Dewsbury Moor Athletic 2

Stanley United 3 **Camerons** 4

QUARTER-FINALS

Great Preston 2 **Hartshead Senior** 4

Hunslet 1 **Woodhouse Hill WMC** 5

Ryhill & Havercroft Sports 4 Pontefract Town 2

Swillington Saints 1 **Camerons** 3

SEMI-FINALS

Camerons (scr.) **Hartshead Senior** (w/o)

Ryhill & Havercroft Sports 1 Woodhouse Hill WMC 0

FINAL

(26th April at Nostell Miners Welfare)

Ryhill & Havercroft Sports 2 Hartshead Senior 0

DIVISION TWO CONSTITUTION 2003-04

ARMLEY ATHLETIC . . . . Churwell Hill, Morley, Leeds, West Yorkshire . . . . None
BOSTON SPARTANS. . . . . Stables Lane, Boston Spa, near Wetherby, West Yorkshire . . . . None
CAMERONS . . . . John O'Gaunts, Sixth Avenue, Leeds Road, Rothwell, Leeds, West Yorkshire. None
DEWSBURY MOOR ATHLETIC . . . . Crawshaw Street Fields, Ravensthorpe, West Yorkshire. . . . . None
GREAT PRESTON . . . . Berry Lane, Great Preston, West Yorkshire. . . . . None
HARTSHEAD SENIOR . . . . Littletown Recreation Ground, Hartshead, West Yorkshire 01274 873365
HUNSLET. . . . . Community Sports Club, Hunslet Green, Leeds, West Yorkshire . . . . None
KIPPAX ATHLETIC . . . . Kippax Common, Valley Road, Kippax, Leeds, West Yorkshire . . . . None
KIPPAX WELFARE . . . . Longdike Lane, Kippax, Leeds, West Yorkshire . . . . None
KIRK DEIGHTON RANGERS . . . . Barfield, Kirk Deighton, West Yorkshire 01937 580240
PONTEFRACT TOWN. . . . . The Barracks Playing Field, Wakefield Road, Pontefract, West Yorkshire . . . . None
STANLEY UNITED . . . . John O'Gaunts, Sixth Avenue, Leeds Road, Rothwell, Leeds, West Yorkshire. None
SWILLINGTON SAINTS . . . . . Welfare Sports Ground, Wakefield Road, Swillington, Leeds, West Yorkshire . . . . None
WOODHOUSE HILL WMC. . . . . Woodlands School Playing Field, Woodhouse Hill, Leeds, West Yorkshire . . . . None
Kellingley Welfare and Ryhill & Havercroft Sports are promoted to Division One from which Kirk Deighton Rangers and Armley Athletic are both relegated.

WESTERN LEAGUE

Results grid (home team in rows, away team in columns). Column abbreviations: BAC = Backwell United, BAR = Barnstaple Town, BCR = Bath City Res., BID = Bideford, BIS = Bishop Sutton, BRG = Bridgwater Town, BRP = Bridport, BRI = Brislington, DAW = Dawlish Town, DEV = Devizes Town, ELM = Elmore, FRO = Frome Town, KEY = Keynsham Town, MEL = Melksham Town, ODD = Odd Down, PAU = Paulton Rovers, TEB = Team Bath, WEL = Welton Rovers.

	BAC	BAR	BCR	BID	BIS	BRG	BRP	BRI	DAW	DEV	ELM	FRO	KEY	MEL	ODD	PAU	TEB	WEL
Backwell United		1-0	3-1	2-1	7-0	1-0	5-1	0-0	5-0	4-0	3-2	2-1	2-2	2-2	1-3	2-0	0-1	4-0
Barnstaple Town	0-2	P	0-5	2-2	2-2	1-4	1-2	0-0	3-1	4-0	1-2	2-1	0-3	1-1	1-3	0-1	0-3	1-1
Bath City Res.	2-5	0-1	R	1-1	1-3	2-0	3-0	4-1	4-0	2-1	1-1	0-1	1-0	2-2	6-1	2-1	1-2	0-1
Bideford	1-0	4-0	5-1	E	7-0	1-2	1-0	1-1	1-0	6-1	2-0	1-1	4-2	1-0	5-0	1-1	5-2	11-2
Bishop Sutton	0-1	1-2	5-1	3-2	M	2-2	1-0	0-3	1-3	2-0	1-1	4-0	0-3	2-5	2-3	1-2	0-5	3-0
Bridgwater Town	1-2	2-1	2-1	3-1	3-1	I	0-0	2-0	6-1	0-0	3-1	3-2	4-0	2-4	2-0	1-1	1-3	6-0
Bridport	1-2	5-0	0-1	2-0	0-1	2-5	E	0-1	1-1	2-2	3-1	1-0	2-0	4-1	0-3	0-2	0-2	0-1
Brislington	1-2	2-1	2-0	3-0	2-2	1-0	3-0	R	6-0	5-0	2-0	1-2	2-1	5-1	3-2	1-0	3-1	4-0
Dawlish Town	1-0	0-3	2-1	0-3	4-1	2-2	1-4	1-0		2-8	2-0	0-5	0-1	3-3	1-2	2-1	0-4	6-2
Devizes Town	1-0	4-1	0-2	0-1	4-2	1-3	4-2	0-1	0-2		1-3	2-2	0-2	0-2	1-5	0-1	1-1	1-0
Elmore	1-0	2-2	2-7	0-3	3-0	0-5	0-1	0-3	1-1	4-1	D	1-2	3-3	3-1	2-1	2-3	0-7	1-2
Frome Town	0-1	0-3	0-3	2-4	3-4	1-2	2-0	1-3	3-3	3-0	1-1	I	1-0	3-2	3-0	0-4	1-3	0-0
Keynsham Town	2-4	0-0	0-3	0-3	3-1	1-1	0-0	3-3	3-4	1-1	3-2	0-1	V	0-3	4-2	1-0	0-2	3-2
Melksham Town	2-1	3-1	3-1	1-3	4-3	3-1	2-4	0-1	5-1	2-0	1-2	1-1	1-4	I	1-4	1-1	0-1	1-2
Odd Down	1-1	3-3	2-2	0-2	1-3	1-0	1-1	1-3	2-3	2-2	0-3	0-2	3-2	0-2	S	0-0	1-0	1-0
Paulton Rovers	1-0	4-1	2-0	1-1	1-2	2-2	0-0	3-3	8-0	1-1	2-0	4-1	4-3	3-1	4-0	I	3-0	2-1
Team Bath	2-1	3-0	4-1	2-1	3-0	4-1	4-0	1-1	6-0	2-2	8-0	6-0	4-2	3-1	2-1	4-0	O	7-0
Welton Rovers	2-4	1-3	4-4	0-8	2-1	0-0	1-0	0-3	2-0	3-1	2-1	1-4	2-3	3-3	0-1	2-1	4-1	N

Premier Division

	P	W	D	L	F	A	Pts
Team Bath	34	27	3	4	109	28	84
Brislington	34	22	7	5	71	28	73
Bideford	34	21	7	6	105	35	70
Backwell United	34	21	4	9	70	33	67
Paulton Rovers	34	18	9	7	68	35	63
Bridgwater Town	34	17	8	9	71	43	59
Bath City Res.	34	14	5	15	66	57	47
Melksham Town	34	12	7	15	65	68	43
Odd Down	34	12	6	16	49	67	42
Keynsham Town	34	11	7	16	55	65	40
Frome Town	34	11	7	16	49	62	40
Bishop Sutton	34	11	5	18	57	83	38
Dawlish Town	34	11	5	18	47	107	38
Bridport	34	9	8	17	40	54	35
Barnstaple Town	34	8	8	18	41	68	32
Welton Rovers	34	9	5	20	40	99	32
Elmore	34	8	7	19	45	81	31
Devizes Town	34	6	8	20	40	75	26

LES PHILLIPS CUP

PRELIMINARY ROUND
Barnstaple Town 2 Keynsham Town 0
Bideford 0 **Exmouth Town** 2
Clyst Rovers 5 Larkhall Athletic 0
Paulton Rovers 8 Weston St Johns 0
Welton Rovers 1 Frome Town 0

FIRST ROUND
Barnstaple Town 1 **Hallen** 2 *aet*
Bath City Res. 2 Minehead Town 0
Bitton 0 **Chard Town** 1
Bridgwater Town 3 Backwell United 1
Bristol Manor Farm 1 Welton Rovers 0
Clyst Rovers 2 **Cadbury Heath** 3 *aet*
Dawlish Town 3 Wellington 0
Exmouth Town 2 Calne Town 0
Ilfracombe Town 3 **Corsham Town** 5 *aet*
Odd Down 1 Paulton Rovers 1 *aet* (7-6p)
Shepton Mallet Town 2 **Bishop Sutton** 3 *aet*
Street 2 Elmore 1

PREMIER DIVISION CONSTITUTION 2003-04

BACKWELL UNITED . . . . Backwell Recreation Grounds, Backwell, Bristol, North Somerset. 01275 462612
BARNSTAPLE TOWN . . . . Mill Road, Barnstaple, Devon. 01271 343469
BIDEFORD. . . . . Sports Ground, Kingsley Road, Bideford, Devon. 01237 474974
BISHOP SUTTON . . . . Lake View, Bishop Sutton, Bristol, North Somerset. 01275 333097
BRIDGWATER TOWN. . . . . Fairfax Park, College Way, Bath Road, Bridgwater, Somerset. 01278 446899
BRIDPORT . . . . St Marys Field, Bridport, Dorset 01308 423834
BRISLINGTON. . . . . Ironmould Lane, Brislington, Bristol, North Somerset 0117 977 4030
DAWLISH TOWN . . . . Playing Fields, Sandy lane, Exeter Road, Dawlish, Devon 01626 863110
DEVIZES TOWN. . . . . Nursteed Road, Devizes, Wiltshire. 01380 722817
ELMORE . . . . Horsdon Park, Tiverton, Devon. 01884 252341
EXMOUTH TOWN. . . . . King George V Ground, Southern Road, Exmouth, Devon. 01395 263348
FROME TOWN . . . . Badgers Hill, Berkley Road, Frome, North Somerset. . . . . 01373 453643 / 464087
KEYNSHAM TOWN . . . . Crown Field, Bristol Road, Keynsham, Bristol, North Somerset 0117 986 5876
MELKSHAM TOWN . . . . The Conigre, Melksham, Wiltshire. 01225 702843
ODD DOWN. . . . . Lew Hill Memorial Ground, Combe Hay Lane, Odd Down, Bath, North Somerset. 01225 832491
PAULTON ROVERS . . . . Athletic Ground, Winterfield Road, Paulton, Somerset 01761 412907
TORRINGTON. . . . . Vicarage Field, School Lane, Great Torrington, Devon . . . . 01805 329527. Club: 01805 622853
WELTON ROVERS . . . . West Clewes, North Road, Midsomer Norton, Somerset 01761 412097

Team Bath are promoted to the Southern League and Bath City Reserves have transferred to the new Severnside Reserve team league. Torrington and Exmouth Town come up from Division One.

	Bitton	Bristol Manor Farm	Cadbury Heath	Calne Town	Chard Town	Clyst Rovers	Corsham Town	Exmouth Town	Hallen	Ilfracombe Town	Larkhall Athletic	Minehead Town	Shepton Mallet Town	Street	Torrington	Wellington	Westbury United	Weston St Johns	Willand Rovers
Bitton		2-0	1-0	1-1	5-1	2-0	0-0	1-1	4-3	1-2	0-2	3-1	1-0	1-5	1-2	0-1	0-0	4-2	0-2
Bristol Manor Farm	1-0		2-2	2-4	0-1	2-1	1-0	0-2	0-3	5-1	2-4	6-1	1-0	1-2	0-2	1-0	0-2	1-4	2-1
Cadbury Heath	1-0	1-1		3-2	1-2	0-0	4-4	0-1	2-0	1-1	2-4	2-0	1-1	0-0	2-3	3-1	0-3	3-3	1-2
Calne Town	2-2	2-1	1-0	*D*	3-0	1-1	1-1	0-1	1-2	1-0	3-1	4-0	0-1	2-3	1-1	1-1	0-0	5-2	0-2
Chard Town	1-1	4-1	1-1	3-2	*I*	1-4	3-1	0-2	1-2	3-4	0-2	4-1	2-3	2-1	3-4	1-1	1-2	3-2	0-2
Clyst Rovers	1-0	6-2	1-0	1-4	0-3	*V*	2-1	2-3	0-2	4-1	2-1	3-1	4-0	5-0	2-4	1-1	1-1	2-0	3-0
Corsham Town	0-2	0-1	4-0	0-1	1-1	1-2	*I*	2-1	0-1	1-1	1-0	0-1	3-1	1-2	3-0	2-2	2-3		0-1
Exmouth Town	2-0	1-3	3-1	1-2	1-1	2-0	2-0	*S*	3-2	2-1	3-0	4-0	3-3	3-0	1-1	1-0	3-2	4-0	2-0
Hallen	1-1	1-3	3-1	0-3	2-1	2-1	1-1	1-5	*I*	6-2	3-0	3-1	3-3	4-0	0-3	2-2	5-3	1-0	0-1
Ilfracombe Town	0-0	3-3	0-1	2-1	1-1	1-3	2-2	1-2	6-2	*O*	1-3	1-2	2-1	2-2	1-3	2-5	1-0		2-6
Larkhall Athletic	2-4	0-2	0-2	0-1	2-2	2-1	3-1	1-6	0-2	2-3	*N*	4-2	0-1	1-1	1-5	2-1	1-1	2-1	1-1
Minehead Town	0-1	1-0	1-2	0-1	0-3	1-0	0-2	0-3	0-2	1-1	2-0		0-0	3-1	0-2	3-1	1-6	5-2	1-1
Shepton Mallet Town	2-1	1-0	1-2	2-0	1-1	1-0	0-0	0-3	2-2	2-1	0-1	1-1		3-1	2-4	0-2	5-1	0-1	0-2
Street	1-5	2-2	3-3	2-0	0-3	2-1	1-1	2-2	0-1	1-3	3-1	3-1	0-1	*O*	2-1	3-1	2-6	0-4	3-0
Torrington	3-0	8-2	4-0	2-2	1-1	5-0	6-1	1-3	6-2	2-0	5-0	5-1	5-3	6-1	*N*	2-5	4-0	2-1	1-0
Wellington	0-0	3-3	1-0	1-1	2-0	2-5	1-3	0-2	0-1	5-1	3-1	3-1	2-0	0-2	2-0	*E*	2-2	0-0	1-3
Westbury United	6-1	3-1	2-1	4-3	3-2	1-4	1-0	2-2	0-2	3-3	5-0	4-3	6-3	1-2	5-1			2-4	1-0
Weston St Johns	0-3	1-3	1-2	1-0	4-1	1-1	0-2	1-3	0-3	2-1	4-2	0-1	5-0	2-5	5-1	1-0	1-2		1-3
Willand Rovers	2-2	3-1	4-5	0-2	0-2	5-1	1-2	0-0	3-3	1-0	1-3	5-1	1-2	0-0	3-5	3-1	3-4	1-0	

Team Bath 1 **Brislington** 2

Torrington 3 Melksham Town 2

Westbury United 1 **Devizes Town** 3

Willand Rovers 2 Bridport 1

SECOND ROUND

Bath City Res. 1 **Hallen** 1 aet (2-4p)

Bishop Sutton 0 **Brislington** 4

Chard Town 3 Corsham Town 2 aet

Dawlish Town 3 Bristol Manor Farm 1

Exmouth 5 Torrington 1

Odd Down 2 Devizes Town 1

Street 1 Cadbury Heath 0

Willand Rovers 0 **Bridgwater Town** 2

QUARTER-FINALS

Brislington 6 Dawlish 3

Chard Town 1 **Bridgwater Town** 2

Exmouth Town 3 Hallen 0

Street 0 **Odd Down** 4

SEMI-FINALS

Bridgwater 1 Odd Down 0

Exmouth 1 **Brislington** 2

FINAL

(3rd May at Melksham Town)

Brislington 0 **Bridgwater Town** 1

Division One

		P	W	D	L	F	A	Pts
Torrington		36	27	5	4	113	47	86
Exmouth Town		36	26	7	3	83	29	85
Westbury United		36	20	8	8	92	65	68
Hallen		36	19	6	11	70	56	63
Calne Town		36	16	9	11	62	43	57
Clyst Rovers		36	17	5	14	67	55	56
Willand Rovers		36	16	6	14	63	53	54
Bitton		36	13	10	13	50	48	49
Shepton Mallet Town		36	13	10	13	53	55	49
Chard Town		36	12	10	14	59	60	46
Bristol Manor Farm		36	14	4	18	56	71	46
Wellington		36	12	8	16	49	57	44
Larkhall Athletic		36	13	4	19	48	73	43
Cadbury Heath		36	10	11	15	49	61	41
Street	-6	36	13	7	16	59	81	40
Corsham Town		36	8	12	16	44	51	36
Weston St Johns		36	9	4	23	54	76	31
Ilfracombe Town		36	7	9	20	47	85	30
Minehead Town		36	7	5	24	34	86	26

DIVISION ONE CONSTITUTION 2003-04

BITTON . . . . Recreation Ground, Bath Road, Bristol, South Glos 0117 9323222
BRISTOL MANOR FARM . . . . The Creek, Portway, Sea Mills, Bristol, South Glos 0117 968 3571
CADBURY HEATH . . . . Springfield, Cadbury Heath Road, Warmley, Bristol, South Glos 0117 967 5731
CALNE TOWN . . . . Bremhill View, Calne, Wiltshire 01249 816716
CHARD TOWN . . . . Denning Sports Field, Zembard Lane, Chard, Somerset 01460 61402
CLEVEDON UNITED . . . . Clevedon Town FC, The Hand Stadium, Davis Way, Clevedon, North Somerset . . . . 01275 341913 / 871600
CLYST ROVERS . . . . Waterslade Park, Clyst Honiton, Devon 01392 366424
CORSHAM TOWN . . . . Southbank, Lacock Road, Corsham, Wiltshire 01249 715609
HALLEN . . . . Moorhouse Lane, Hallen, near Bristol, South Glos. 0117 950 5559
ILFRACOMBE TOWN . . . . Marlborough Park, Marlborough Road, Ilfracombe, Devon 01271 865939
LARKHALL ATHLETIC . . . . Plain Ham, Charcombe Lane, Larkhall, Bath, North Somerset 01225 334952
MINEHEAD TOWN . . . . Recreation Ground, Irnham Road, Minehead, Somerset. 01643 704989
SHEPTON MALLET TOWN . . . . Old Wells Road Playing Fields, West Shepton, Shepton Mallet, Somerset 01749 344609
SHREWTON UNITED . . . . Recreation Ground, Shrewton, Wiltshire . . . . None
STREET . . . . The Tannery Ground, Middlebrooks, Street, Somerset 01458 444987
WELLINGTON . . . . Wellington Playing Field, North Street, Wellington, Somerset 01823 664810
WESTBURY UNITED . . . . Meadow Lane, Westbury, Wiltshire 01373 823049
WESTON ST JOHNS . . . . Coleridge Road, Bournville Estate, Weston-super-Mare, North Somerset 01934 612862
WILLAND ROVERS . . . . Silver Street, Willand, Devon 01884 33885

Torrington and Exmouth Town are promoted to the Premier Division. Newcomers are Shrewton United, promoted from the Wiltshire League, and Clevedon United (Somerset County League).

WILTSHIRE LEAGUE

	Aldbourne	Biddestone	Bradford Town	Chiseldon Castrol	Corsham Town Res.	Cricklade Town	Devizes Town Res.	Malmesbury Vics Res.	Marlborough Town	Melksham Town Res.	Pewsey Vale Res.	Purton Res.	Shrewton United	Stratton Crosslink	Trowbridge Town	Warminster Town	Westbury United Res.	Wroughton
Aldbourne		2-1	0-1	3-0	4-1	3-2	2-2	3-5	3-0	0-3	2-0	1-2	0-5	0-1	1-0	2-1	2-0	1-4
Biddestone	4-3	P	2-2	2-0	1-1	5-0	4-2	1-0	1-1	3-1	6-0	2-1	1-3	0-5	1-3	1-1	1-0	3-0
Bradford Town	3-1	2-2	R	4-1	1-2	2-0	0-3	3-1	1-2	3-0	5-0	3-1	3-5	2-1	0-2	4-3	5-1	0-3
Chiseldon Castrol	0-3	1-2	0-2	E	2-0	2-4	0-1	1-1	0-0	1-2	2-4	1-2	0-6	1-3	1-2	2-4	1-2	0-3
Corsham Town Res.	0-0	1-2	1-2	3-2	M	0-2	1-3	3-0	4-0	5-1	4-2	1-2	0-5	2-2	2-0	0-1	2-1	1-0
Cricklade Town	0-2	3-0	0-0	0-0	4-3	I	1-3	6-4	1-0	2-1	3-0	1-1	4-4	1-1	2-1	3-1	3-1	3-3
Devizes Town Res.	0-2	1-1	1-4	7-2	0-0	2-0	E	3-0	2-1	0-2	1-3	5-1	4-2	1-5	1-1	2-0	3-4	3-4
Malmesbury Victoria Res.	1-1	1-3	0-1	2-3	0-5	1-1	3-3	R	1-2	0-4	1-0	1-2	2-6	0-5	0-0	0-6	1-1	2-9
Marlborough Town	2-3	2-2	3-5	2-1	3-1	0-6	0-3	1-3		2-5	1-1	3-1	0-10	0-9	2-3	0-3	1-1	1-5
Melksham Town Res.	4-1	3-1	3-5	5-0	1-2	2-0	1-3	3-0	5-0	D	2-1	4-0	1-7	1-4	0-2	1-2	0-3	5-2
Pewsey Vale Res.	1-2	2-1	2-2	1-2	1-2	2-3	3-2	1-2	1-0	1-1	I	1-0	0-3	1-0	1-1	0-4	1-3	
Purton Res.	2-0	0-2	1-1	0-4	0-3	2-0	5-0	0-1	2-0	0-3	2-1	V	1-2	0-1	2-3	1-2	2-2	0-2
Shrewton United	5-0	3-3	6-3	4-0	4-2	4-0	7-1	6-1	8-0	2-1	1-1	9-0	I	3-0	2-0	7-0	6-1	2-1
Stratton Crosslink	1-0	3-2	2-1	1-1	2-0	1-0	2-0	2-0	3-3	4-1	4-1	0-0	1-0	S	1-0	1-0	0-0	1-1
Trowbridge Town	2-0	2-0	1-2	3-0	4-0	1-0	3-1	3-0	0-0	0-0	4-1	4-1	1-1	1-0	I	2-0	0-0	4-1
Warminster Town	2-1	0-1	2-1	3-0	0-1	3-1	0-2	3-0	8-1	1-1	4-2	2-2	0-4	1-3	1-0	O	1-3	3-1
Westbury United Res.	0-2	0-1	0-1	4-1	5-3	2-2	1-0	0-0	2-0	0-1	1-2	1-3	0-3	0-3	1-0	1-4	N	0-3
Wroughton	7-0	1-2	0-2	3-1	1-0	2-1	3-2	7-1	4-2	3-0	1-0	5-1	2-2	4-1	0-2	2-1	3-1	

Premier Division		P	W	D	L	F	A	Pts
Shrewton United		34	27	5	2	147	34	86
Stratton Crosslink		34	23	7	4	76	27	76
Wroughton		34	23	3	8	94	48	72
Bradford Town		34	20	5	9	76	52	65
Trowbridge Town		34	19	6	9	53	23	63
Biddestone		34	16	8	10	63	51	56
Melksham Town Res.		34	17	2	15	68	59	53
Warminster Town		34	15	4	15	63	56	49
Aldbourne		34	15	3	16	50	62	48
Cricklade Town		34	13	8	13	59	59	47
Corsham Town Res.		34	14	4	16	56	58	46
Devizes Town Res.	-3	34	14	5	15	67	68	44
Purton Res.		34	11	6	17	41	69	39
Westbury United Res.		34	10	7	17	43	60	37
Pewsey Vale Res.		34	7	5	22	38	77	26
Malmesbury Vics Res.		34	5	7	22	35	98	22
Marlborough Town		34	5	7	22	36	109	22
Chiseldon Castrol		34	4	4	26	33	88	16

SENIOR CUP

FIRST ROUND
Marlborough Town 3
Chiseldon Castrol 3 *aet* (3-4p)
Purton Res. 1 **Shrewton Utd** 5

SECOND ROUND
Chiseldon Castrol 0
Warminster Town 4
Cricklade 4 Bradford Town 2
Malmesbury Victoria Res. 0
Aldbourne 4
Melksham Town 1 **Biddestone** 1 *aet* (2-4p)
Pewsey Vale 1 Wroughton 0
Stratton Cross. 1 **Shrewton** 4
Trowbridge 2 Devizes Res. 1
Westbury United Res. 1
Corsham Town Res. 2

QUARTER-FINALS
Biddestone 1 **Shrewton United** 6
Corsham Town Res. 0 **Aldbourne** 2
Cricklade Town 3 **Warminster Town** 4
Trowbridge Town 4 Pewsey Vale Res. 1

SEMI-FINALS
Shrewton Utd 5 Aldbourne 0
Trowbridge Town 0
Warminster Town 0 *aet* (9-8p)

FINAL
(26th April at Corsham Town)
Shrewton United 5
Trowbridge Town 2

PREMIER DIVISION CONSTITUTION 2003-04

AFC STRATTON . . . . The Crosslink Centre, Ermin Street Stratton, Swindon, Wiltshire. 01793 831511
ALDBOURNE . . . . Farm Lane, Aldbourne, Marlborough, Wiltshire. . . . . None
BIDDESTONE. . . . . Cuttle Lane, Biddestone, Chippenham, Wiltshire. 01249 713676
BRADFORD TOWN. . . . . Avon Sports Ground, Trowbridge Road, Bradford-on-Avon, Wiltshire 01225 866649
CHISELDON CASTROL . . . . . Chiseldon Sports & Social Club, Draycott Road, Chiseldon, Swindon, Wiltshire. 01793 740274
CORSHAM TOWN RESERVES. . . . . Southbank, Lacock Road, Corsham, Wiltshire. 01249 715609
CRICKLADE TOWN . . . . Cricklade Leisure Centre, Stones Lane, Cricklade, Wiltshire. 01793 750011
DEVIZES TOWN RESERVES. . . . . Nursteed Road, Devizes, Wiltshire. 01380 722817
MALMESBURY VIC. RESERVES . . . Flying Monk Ground, Gloucester Road, Malmesbury, Wiltshire 01666 822141
MARLBOROUGH TOWN . . . . Elcot Lane, Marlborough, Wiltshire 01672 514033
MELKSHAM TOWN RESERVES . . . . The Conigre, Melksham, Wiltshire. 01225 702843
PEWSEY VALE RESERVES . . . . Recreation Ground, Ball Road, Pewsey, Wiltshire 01672 562990
PURTON RESERVES. . . . . The Red House, Purton, Wiltshire. 01793 770262
SHREWTON UNITED RESERVES . . . . Recreation Ground, Shrewton, Wiltshire . . . . None
TROWBRIDGE TOWN. . . . . Woodmarsh, North Bradley, Trowbridge, Wiltshire . . . . None
WARMINSTER TOWN . . . . Weymouth Street, Warminster, Wiltshire 01985 217828
WESTBURY UNITED RESERVES. . . . . Meadow Lane, Westbury, Wiltshire 01373 823409
WROUGHTON . . . . Weir Farm, Wroughton, Wiltshire. 01793 812319

Shrewton United are promoted to the Western League. They are replaced by the club's reserve side, elevated from the Salisbury & District League.
Stratton Crosslink become AFC Stratton.

	Biddestone Res.	Blunsdon United	Calne Town Res.	Down Ampney	Dunbar Westside	Sherston Town	Stratton C. Res.	Trowbridge Res.	Wanborough Utd
Biddestone Res.		0-0	0-2	n/a	2-4	1-2	n/a	1-1	1-4
Blunsdon United	n/a	I	0-5	1-1	2-3	0-2	2-1	n/a	2-3
Calne Town Res.	0-4	n/a	N	n/a	n/a	5-0	7-3	1-1	2-2
Down Ampney	2-1	4-1	2-2	T	1-4	5-1	5-0	1-3	3-5
Dunbar Westside	n/a	2-1	5-0	5-1		4-1	0-1	8-2	n/a
Sherston Town	0-2	4-0	4-0	4-3	n/a	D	1-0	1-1	2-3
Stratton C. Res.	2-1	4-3	2-1	n/a	2-6	n/a	I	7-2	n/a
Trowbridge Res.	n/a	3-3	4-1	n/a	0-1	n/a	4-1	V	W-1
Wanborough Utd	8-2	7-2	5-1	2-1	2-2	n/a	4-0	n/a	

	Biddestone Res.	Blunsdon United	Calne Town Res.	Down Ampney	Dunbar Westside	Sherston Town	Stratton C. Res.	Trowbridge Res.	Wanborough Utd
Biddestone Res.		2-2	n/a	2-0	2-5	n/a	3-2	1-4	n/a
Blunsdon United	1-1	I	2-4	3-0	n/a	4-2	n/a	3-1	1-3
Calne Town Res.	1-4	2-0	N	1-1	2-2	3-0	3-0	n/a	3-1
Down Ampney	2-0	n/a	5-1	T	1-4	n/a	1-1	0-1	n/a
Dunbar Westside	0-0	6-1	4-1	n/a		3-1	3-1	n/a	3-1
Sherston Town	2-3	n/a	n/a	3-1	4-8	D	0-3	2-2	1-2
Stratton C. Res.	1-2	6-1	n/a	4-2	n/a	1-1	I	2-1	1-4
Trowbridge Res.	4-0	4-1	0-2	3-0	1-1	0-0	n/a	V	1-3
Wanborough Utd	4-1	n/a	n/a	7-3	3-3	3-2	3-2	1-2	

Teams played each other three times

Intermediate Division		P	W	D	L	F	A	Pts
Dunbar Westside		24	18	5	1	86	33	59
Wanborough United		24	17	3	4	80	41	54
Trowbridge Town Res.		24	10	7	7	45	41	37
Calne Town Res.		24	10	5	9	50	51	35
Stratton Crosslink Res.		24	9	2	13	47	60	29
Biddestone Res.		24	7	5	12	36	53	26
Sherston Town		24	7	4	13	40	57	25
Down Ampney		24	6	4	14	45	59	22
Blunsdon United	-1	24	4	5	15	36	70	16

JUNIOR DIVISION ONE (FORMERLY INTERMEDIATE DIVISION) CONSTITUTION 2003-04

AFC STRATTON RESERVES ...... The Crosslink Centre, Ermin Street, Stratton, Swindon, Wiltshire 01793 831511
ALDBOURNE RESERVES .... Farm Lane, Aldbourne, Marlborough, Wiltshire.................................... None
BIDDESTONE RESERVES .... Cuttle Lane, Biddestone, Chippenham, Wiltshire 01249 713676
BLUNSDON UNITED .... Sutton Park, Blunsdon, Wiltshire .... None
BROMHAM .... Jubilee Field, Bromham, Chippenham, Wiltshire 01380 850671
CALNE TOWN RESERVES .... Bremhill View, Calne, Wiltshire 01249 816716
CRICKLADE TOWN RESERVES ..... Cricklade Leisure Centre, Stones Lane, Cricklade, Wiltshire 01793 750011
DOWN AMPNEY .... Broadacre, Down Ampney, Wiltshire 01793 750414
DUNBAR WESTSIDE............... King Edward Place, Foxhill, Wanborough, Swindon, Wiltshire 01793 791282
FERNDALE RODBOURNE............ Pinehurst School, Whitworth Road, Swindon, Wiltshire .... None
MARLBOROUGH TOWN RESERVES .... Elcot Lane, Marlborough, Wiltshire 01672 514033
SHERSTON.............................. Knockdown Road, Sherston, Wiltshire .... None
TROWBRIDGE TOWN RESERVES....... Woodmarsh, North Bradley, Trowbridge, Wiltshire .... None
WANBOROUGH UNITED .... Hoopers Field, Rotten Road, Wanborough, Swindon, Wiltshire .... None
WOOTTON BASSETT UTD ... Ballards Ash Sports Ground, Malmesbury Road, Wootton Bassett, Wiltshire ... None
WROUGHTON RESERVES .... Weir Farm, Wroughton, Wiltshire 01793 812319

Aldbourne Reserves, Bromham, Cricklade Town Reserves, Ferndale Rodbourne, Marlborough Town Reserves, Purton 'A', Wootton Bassett United and Wroughton Reserves move up from the Junior Division (now Junior Division Two). Stratton Crosslink Reserves become AFC Stratton Reserves.

Junior Division		P	W	D	L	F	A	Pts
Cricklade Town Res.		32	22	7	3	100	46	73
Ferndale Rodbourne		32	20	6	6	90	45	66
Wroughton Res.		32	18	7	7	86	48	61
Aldbourne Res.	-1	32	18	8	6	89	60	61
Wootton Bassett United		32	18	6	8	108	61	60
Marlborough Town Res.		32	15	5	12	79	56	50
Dunbar Westside Res.		32	14	8	10	75	64	50
Purton 'A'		32	15	5	12	64	61	50
Bromham		32	15	3	14	79	52	48
West Swindon		32	11	9	12	39	47	42
Down Ampney Res.		32	11	5	16	53	88	38
Wanborough United Res.		32	11	3	18	53	72	36
Chiseldon Castrol Res.		32	7	7	18	39	78	28
Sporting HKQ		32	8	4	20	59	102	28
Blunsdon United Res.		32	8	3	21	56	96	27
Minety		32	7	4	21	57	92	25
Wootton Bassett Town 'A'		32	7	4	21	45	103	25

Junior Division Two (formerly Junior Division) constitution 2003-04: Blunsdon United Reserves, Chiseldon Castrol Reserves, Clarendon & Tidworth Garrison, Down Ampney Reserves, Dunbar Westside Reserves, Green Baize, Lower Stratton, Minety, New College Academy Reserves, Pinehurst Old Boys, SKS Blyskawica, Sporting HKQ, Swindon Asians, Trax and West Swindon

INTERMEDIATE CUP	JUNIOR CUP
(Intermediate Division teams)	*(Junior Division teams)*
FINAL *(12th April at Marlborough Town)*	FINAL *(26th April at Corsham Town)*
Wanborough United 4 Trowbridge Town Res. 2	Cricklade Town Res. 2 Marlborough Town Res. 0

F A CHALLENGE CUP

EXTRA PRELIMINARY ROUND	Att
Flixton 1 Goole 1	150
Holker Old Boys 0 **Bridlington Town** 2	86
West Auckland Town 2 Winsford United 1	66
Penrith 3 Brandon United 2	90
Marske United 1 **Salford City** 4	131
Maltby Main 0 **Billingham Synthonia** 6	63
Consett 4 Pontefract Collieries 1	76
Chester-le-Street Town 3 Northallerton Town 1	38
Morpeth Town 3 Curzon Ashton 2	98
Nelson 0 Norton & Stockton Ancients 0 *aet*	80
Ramsbottom United 1 Thackley 0	150
Horden Colliery Welfare 2 Armthorpe Welfare 1	52
Bridgnorth Town 4 Gedling Town 2	50
Stratford Town 4 Stourbridge 1	188
Mickleover Sports 3 Shirebrook Town 1	128
Leek CSOB 0 **Nantwich Town** 3	184
Grosvenor Park 2 Stafford Town 0	71
Newmarket Town 2 Ely City 3	111
(ineligible player – Ely City expelled)	
Dereham Town 1 **AFC Wallingford** 3	166
Saffron Walden Town 0 **Hullbridge Sports** 1	81
Bedford United & Valerio 0 **Brook House** 1	38
Potters Bar Town 1 **Milton Keynes City** 2	73
Sawbridgeworth Town 2 Harwich & Parkeston 0	69
Raunds Town 1 Ruislip Manor 0	88
Stotfold 0 Broxbourne Borough V & E 0	36
Tiptree United 1 Ipswich Wanderers 1	92
Ilford 3 Kempston Rovers 0	54
Walton Casuals 0 **Whitehawk** 4	82
Littlehampton Town 0 **Godalming & Guildford** 6	141
Greenwich Borough 1 **Three Bridges** 4	30
Deal Town 2 Chichester City United 2	231
Lymington & New Milton 2 East Preston 2	138
Moneyfields 1 Burgess Hill Town 0	120
Alton Town 1 Didcot Town 1	213
Horsham YMCA 1 **Eastleigh** 3	105
AFC Totton 3 Southwick 2	115
Ramsgate 1 Maidstone United 1	747
Chessington United 0 **Ringmer** 1	48
Reading Town 3 Farnham Town 1 *(at Farnham Tn)*	74
Paulton Rovers 5 Downton 1	40
Highworth Town 2 Fairford Town 2	216
Street 3 Keynsham Town 1	85
Portland United 6 Welton Rovers 2	247
Bishop Sutton 2 Melksham Town 1	48
Christchurch 3 Willand Rovers 0	96
(at Wimborne Town)	

EXTRA PRELIMINARY ROUND Replays	
Goole 0 Flixton 0 *aet* (5-4p)	202
Norton & Stockton Ancients 1 **Nelson** 2	70
Broxbourne Borough V & E 1 **Stotfold** 5	34
Ipswich Wanderers 3 Tiptree United 3 *aet* (7-6p)	142
Chichester City United 2 **Deal Town** 3	109
East Preston 1 **Lymington & New Milton** 2	131
Didcot Town 1 Alton Town 0	164
Maidstone United 1 Ramsgate 0	432
Fairford Town 1 **Highworth Town** 4	227

PRELIMINARY ROUND	
Shildon 2 **Salford City** 4	205
Morpeth Town 1 Woodley Sports 0	70
Hatfield Main 0 **Shotton Comrades** 1	68

Selby Town 0 Newcastle Blue Star 0	
Fleetwood Town 1 Workington 1	
Skelmersdale United 1 **Penrith** 3	
Brigg Town 2 **Kendal Town** 4	
Whitley Bay 2 Harrogate Railway Athletic 2	
Guisborough Town 2 Blackpool Mechanics 0	1.
Farsley Celtic 4 Seaham Red S	94
Glasshoughton Welfare 1 **Jarrow Roofing BCA** 3	85
Goole 0 **Mossley** 3	2.
Nelson 2 **Bishop Auckland** 3	14.
Ossett Town 0 **Worsbrough Bridge MW** 2	153
Great Harwood Town 0 Winterton Rangers 0	61
Horden Colliery Welfare 2 Trafford 1	60
Evenwood Town 1 **Durham City** 4	10
Prescot Cables 3 **Witton Albion** 6	
Parkgate 2 St Helens Town 2	
Squires Gate 1 **Lincoln United** 2	8.
Tow Law Town 2 Tadcaster Albion 1	167
Abbey Hey 0 Bamber Bridge 0	75
Louth United 4 Cheadle Town 1	42
Ramsbottom United 3 Chadderton 0	242
Matlock Town 2 Pickering Town 2	224
Maine Road 1 **Guiseley** 2	64
Spennymoor United 4 Consett 0	161
Chester-le-Street Town 2 Hall Road Rangers 0	52
Atherton LR 0 **Rossington Main** 2	64
Ashington 7 Colne 0	245
Willington 0 Atherton Collieries 0	57
Chorley 5 Liversedge 0	231
Warrington Town 2 Esh Winning 2	100
Bacup Borough 1 **Bridlington Town** 2	110
(at Rossendale United)	
Bedlington Terriers 2 Brodsworth Miners Welfare 0	198
Alnwick Town 1 **Crook Town** 2	112
Garforth Town 3 Yorkshire Amateur 1	168
Stocksbridge Park Steels 17 Oldham Town 1	110
Rossendale United 0 **Ossett Albion** 1	201
Thornaby 1 Dunston Federation Brewery 1	67
Clitheroe 1 **Radcliffe Borough** 3	229
Sheffield 0 **West Auckland Town** 4	302
South Shields 1 **Hallam** 2	103
Easington Colliery 1 **Hebburn Town** 3	51
Washington 0 **North Ferriby United** 2	71
Peterlee Newtown 2 Billingham Synthonia 1	67
Billingham Town (w/o) Gretna (scr)	
Darwen 1 **Eccleshill United** 3	64
Stourport Swifts 1 **Alfreton Town** 4	128
Rocester 3 Congleton Town 0	106
Kidsgrove Athletic 4 Buxton 1	192
Rushall Olympic 1 **Sutton Coldfield Town** 4	115
Staveley Miners Welfare 0 **Boston Town** 1	88
Halesowen Harriers 1 **Shepshed Dynamo** 3	113
Newcastle Town 0 **Leek Town** 1	223
Belper Town 0 **Gresley Rovers** 1	319
Mickleover Sports 2 Cradley Town 1	197
Redditch United 2 Grosvenor Park 1	184
Bourne Town 1 Eastwood Town 1	102
Bedworth United 1 Causeway United 1	159
Histon 2 **Quorn** 3	107
Oadby Town 2 Rugby United 2	249
Atherstone United 3 Studley 0	180
Stratford Town 3 Ludlow Town 1	133

WWW.CHERRYRED.CO.UK

Biddulph Victoria 2 Bridgnorth Town 0	174
Nantwich Town 4 Holbeach United 0	83
Chasetown 0 **Spalding United** 1	95
Corby Town 0 **Stamford** 6	168
Arnold Town 1 Racing Club Warwick 0	161
King's Lynn 1 Deeping Rangers 0	690
Willenhall Town 1 Glapwell 0	118
Pelsall Villa 1 Borrowash Victoria 1	52
Shifnal Town 1 **Blackstones** 4	73
Glossop North End 1 Boldmere St Michaels 0	89
Solihull Borough 2 Oldbury United 0	188
Barwell 1 Bromsgrove Rovers 1	168
Long Buckby 0 **Marlow** 2	74
Newmarket Town 1 **Ilford** 3	123
Barking & E. Ham Utd 4 Soham Town Rangers 3	159
Hullbridge Sports 2 **Edgware Town** 5	53
Great Yarmouth Town 2 Holmer Green 1	138
Desborough Town 1 **Romford** 2	91
Southall Town 1 **Wroxham** 6	68
Northampton Spencer 1 Yaxley 1	93
Banbury United 1 Berkhamsted Town 1	292
Hoddesdon Town 0 **AFC Sudbury** 2	110
(at Hertford Town)	
Cheshunt 3 Wembley 0	62
Maldon Town 1 Flackwell Heath 1	85
Leighton Town 2 Royston Town 2	120
Chalfont St Peter 0 **Hemel Hempstead Town** 3	112
Clacton Town 3 Sawbridgeworth Town 1	116
Wealdstone 1 **Leyton** 3	268
Cogenhoe United 0 **Diss Town** 2	92
Bowers United 1 **Arlesey Town** 4	88
Wivenhoe Town 0 **Yeading** 5	74
Stotfold 1 Hornchurch 1	68
St Neots Town 6 Stansted 0	106
Bury Town 2 **Barton Rovers** 3	191
Lowestoft Town 0 **Uxbridge** 2	282
Raunds Town 5 Burnham Ramblers 1	74
Wootton Blue Cross 3 Brackley Town 1	78
Stewarts & Lloyds Corby 1 Ford Sports Daventry 0	32
Harlow Town 0 **Aveley** 1	115
Stowmarket Town 1 **Southall** 6	106
Wisbech Town 3 Woodbridge Town 1	312
Brook House 2 **Burnham** 3	62
Hanwell Town 0 **Great Wakering Rovers** 3	79
Mildenhall Town 0 London Colney 0	138
Tilbury 4 Gorleston 3 *(at Aveley)*	57
Concord Rangers 2 **Hertford Town** 3	60
Ware 5 Milton Keynes City 1	132
Haringey Borough 0 **Northwood** 1	62
Ipswich Wanderers 2 **Leyton Pennant** 3	140
Letchworth 1 Staines Town 1	67
Clapton 0 **Beaconsfield SYCOB** 3	40
Witham Town 0 **Wingate & Finchley** 5	75
St Margaretsbury 2 Dunstable Town 0	68
(at Dunstable Town)	
East Thurrock United 1 **Harefield United** 2	116
Buckingham Town 3 Tring Town 0	103
Rothwell Town 3 Kingsbury Town 1	109
Brentwood 2 AFC Wallingford 2	52
Fakenham Town 1 **Southend Manor** 3	96
Wick 1 **Abingdon United** 4	66
Merstham 3 **St Leonards** 4	60
Three Bridges 3 Didcot Town 1	80
Erith Town 0 **Ringmer** 3	90
North Leigh 0 **Cowes Sports** 5	82
Bromley 3 Abingdon Town 2	255
Lymington & New Milton 1 Dulwich Hamlet 1	171
Redhill 1 **Peacehaven & Telscombe** 3	99
Gosport Borough 2 Wantage Town 1	122
Oxford City 0 **Cray Wanderers** 1	129
Deal Town 4 Hythe Town 2	248
Eastleigh 5 Erith & Belvedere 0	189
Fisher Athletic 7 Wokingham Town 0	108
Whyteleafe 1 Reading Town 0	170
Whitstable Town 1 **Chipstead** 2	137
Croydon Athleticc 0 Eastbourne Borough 0	185
AFC Totton 2 Thamesmead Town 0	139
Molesey 3 Hassocks 0	80
Bedfont 3 Whitehawk 1	79
Saltdean United 0 **VCD Athletic** 3	73
Beckenham Town 1 **Croydon** 2	97
Brockenhurst 3 Fleet Town 2	96
Newport IOW 1 Blackfield & Langley 1	181
Moneyfields 0 **BAT Sports** 2	104
Chertsey Town 4 Arundel 1	142
Tunbridge Wells 2 Ashford Town (Middx) 1	87
Fareham Town 1 Tooting & Mitcham United 1	249
Eastbourne Town 1 Windsor & Eton 1	208
Godalming & Guildford 3 Whitchurch United 0	82
Thame United 1 **Slough Town** 2	258
Pagham 3 Bracknell Town 2	180
Sandhurst Town 2 **Herne Bay** 6	82
Sittingbourne 2 Slade Green 2	162
Metropolitan Police 4 Lancing 0	78
Camberley Town 0 **Cove** 1	99
Horsham 2 Lordswood 0	234
Lewes 1 Thatcham Town 0	344
Chatham Town 0 Egham Town 0	150
Bognor Regis Town 1 Worthing 0	706
Banstead Athletic 1 **Leatherhead** 4	133
Westfield 1 **Dorking** 2	70
Tonbridge Angels 2 **Maidstone United** 3	1027
Hillingdon Borough 2 Chessington & Hook United 2	103
Corinthian Casuals 1 Epsom & Ewell 1	105
Walton & Hersham 2 Andover 1	147
Ashford Town 1 **Carshalton Athletic** 3	344
AFC Newbury 2 Hailsham Town 1	107
Selsey 3 Ash United 0	146
Eastbourne United 0 **Cobham** 3	102
Dartford 2 Carterton Town 2	279
Chard Town 2 Swindon Supermarine 0	79
Frome Town 0 **Shortwood United** 1	187
Bishop Sutton 1 **Cinderford Town** 3	72
Torrington 2 Westbury United 1	105
Odd Down 0 **Paulton Rovers** 2	91
Clevedon Town 2 Bitton 0	193
Highworth Town 3 Cirencester Town 0	228
Hungerford Town 2 Shepton Mallet Town 0	95
Bridport 2 **Taunton Town** 3	235
Elmore 1 **Backwell United** 2	44
Bashley 2 Mangotsfield United 2	216
Salisbury City 1 **Bideford** 2	482
Barnstaple Town 0 **Team Bath** 4	148
Corsham Town 3 Portland United 1	120
Devizes Town 5 Ilfracombe Town 2	61
Bournemouth 3 Bridgwater Town 0	115
Falmouth Town 2 Bristol Manor Farm 0	146
Merthyr Tydfil 5 Christchurch 0	353

Porthleven 0 **Dorchester Town** 5	284
Tuffley Rovers 0 **St Blazey** 1	92
Minehead Town 0 **Gloucester City** 2	144
Weston-super-Mare 4 Calne Town 0	160
Yate Town 4 Hallen 2	215
Dawlish Town 0 **Wimborne Town** 3	122
Brislington 2 Evesham United 2	144
Street 1 **Bemerton Heath Harlequins** 3	87

PRELIMINARY ROUND Replays

Newcastle Blue Star 2 **Selby Town** 4	100
Workington 1 Fleetwood Town 0 *aet*	325
Harrogate Railway Athletic 5 Whitley Bay 4	187
Seaham Red Star 1 **Farsley Celtic** 6	93
Winterton Rangers 0 Great Harwood Town 0 *aet* (3-5p)	96
St Helens Town 3 Parkgate 1	104
Bamber Bridge 2 **Abbey Hey** 2 *aet* (2-4p)	160
Pickering Town 0 **Matlock Town** 1	125
Atherton Collieries 5 Willington 1	56
Esh Winning 3 Warrington Town 1 *aet*	120
Dunston Federation Brewery 2 Thornaby 1	99
Eastwood Town 3 Bourne Town 1	162
Causeway United 1 **Bedworth United** 2 *aet*	165
Rugby United 2 **Oadby Town** 3	207
Borrowash Victoria 1 **Pelsall Villa** 4	59
Bromsgrove Rovers 4 Barwell 3	309
Yaxley 5 Northampton Spencer 1 *aet*	95
Berkhamsted Town 1 **Banbury United** 4	162
Flackwell Heath 1 Maldon Town 0	93
Royston Town 3 Leighton Town 0	110
Hornchurch 4 **Stotfold** 4 *aet* (4-5p)	384
London Colney 1 Mildenhall Town 0	75
Staines Town 1 Letchworth 0 *(at Egham Town)*	161
AFC Wallingford 4 Brentwood 1	114
Dulwich Hamlet 1 **Lymington & New Milton** 3	153
Eastbourne Borough 4 Croydon Athletic 1	412
Blackfield & Langley 0 **Newport IOW** 3	159
Tooting & Mitcham United 1 Fareham Town 0	319
Windsor & Eton 4 Eastbourne Town 2	92
Slade Green 3 Sittingbourne 1	156
Lordswood 1 **Horsham** 2	147
Egham Town 0 **Chatham Town** 1	122
Chessington & Hook United 1 **Hillingdon Borough** 3	192
Epsom & Ewell 1 **Corinthian Casuals** 2	118
Carterton Town 1 Dartford 0	103
Bitton 1 **Clevedon Town** 2	316
Mangotsfield United 0 **Bashley** 1	243
Evesham United 3 Brislington 2	147

FIRST ROUND QUALIFYING

Eccleshill United 3 St Helens Town 2	89
Bedlington Terriers 1 Ossett Albion 0	314
Radcliffe Borough 4 Abbey Hey 1	213
Esh Winning 1 **Harrogate Railway Athletic** 2	111
Horden Colliery Welfare 4 Shotton Comrades 1	93
Dunston Federation Brewery 2 Selby Town 0	101
Kendal Town 2 North Ferriby United 1	267
Workington 2 Mossley 1	289
Hallam 2 **Stocksbridge Park Steels** 3	388
Bishop Auckland 3 Rossington Main 3	118
Jarrow Roofing Boldon CA 2 **Billingham Town** 4	65
Morpeth Town 0 **Guisborough Town** 1	77
West Auckland Town 6 Chorley 3	104
Chester-le-Street Town 2 Penrith 0	68
Great Harwood Town 1 Crook Town 1	103
Bridlington Town 1 Garforth Town 0	213

Tow Law Town 5 Matlock Town 4	191
Witton Albion 1 Ramsbottom United 1	303
Farsley Celtic 3 Lincoln United 1	107
Durham City 5 Worsbrough Bridge MW 1	143
Guiseley 3 Hebburn Town 0	220
Peterlee Newtown 4 Louth United 0	58
Spennymoor United 1 Ashington 1	236
Atherton Collieries 1 Salford City 0	99
Alfreton Town 0 **Kidsgrove Athletic** 1	315
Nantwich Town 2 Rocester 0	174
Eastwood Town 1 **Redditch United** 2	162
Stamford 3 Oadby Town 1	236
Boston Town 1 Sutton Coldfield Town 1	94
King's Lynn 4 Quorn 1	699
Blackstones 2 Pelsall Villa 2	67
Bromsgrove Rovers 5 Gresley Rovers 0	794
Solihull Borough 9 Glossop North End 0	221
Willenhall Town 0 **Atherstone United** 2	167
Mickleover Sports 0 **Shepshed Dynamo** 1	244
Arnold Town 1 Biddulph Victoria 1	176
Leek Town 2 Spalding United 1	287
Stratford Town 1 **Bedworth United** 2	305
Stewarts & Lloyds Corby 0 **Burnham** 1	25
Rothwell Town 3 Southend Manor 2	142
Cheshunt 4 Edgware Town 0	69
Hertford Town 1 **AFC Wallingford** 4	115
Royston Town 3 London Colney 2	98
Hemel Hempstead Town 7 St Neots Town 1	165
Ilford 2 **Clacton Town** 3	138
Wootton Blue Cross 2 Wroxham 1	110
Raunds Town 1 **AFC Sudbury** 3	165
Barking & East Ham United 1 Banbury United 0	168
Leyton Pennant 3 Great Yarmouth Town 3	96
Staines Town 1 **Uxbridge** 2 *(at Egham Town)*	176
Harefield United 2 Barton Rovers 1	104
Tilbury 0 **Yeading** 2 *(at East Thurrock United)*	53
Beaconsfield SYCOB 5 Great Wakering Rovers 0	76
Northwood 1 **Wisbech Town** 2	214
Aveley 2 Stotfold 2	94
Diss Town 3 Romford 0	265
St Margaretsbury 1 **Arlesey Town** 2	136
Southall 2 **Yaxley** 3	41
Flackwell Heath 2 Buckingham Town 1	78
Leyton 0 **Marlow** 1	92
Wingate & Finchley 2 Ware 0	142
Bromley 2 BAT Sports 1	303
Herne Bay 3 Cowes Sports 2	192
Peacehaven & Telscombe 1 **Carterton Town** 2	71
Walton & Hersham 3 Cove 0	107
Horsham 3 Slade Green 0	273
Lewes 2 Brockenhurst 1	243
Eastleigh 2 Croydon 0	209
Abingdon United 2 **Leatherhead** 3	178
Chatham Town 2 **Godalming & Guildford** 3	207
Molesey 3 Fisher Athletic 0	88
Bognor Regis Town 4 Windsor & Eton 1	351
VCD Athletic 2 Bedfont 1	70
Tunbridge Wells 2 Selsey 2	134
Newport IOW 0 **Maidstone United** 4	455
Metropolitan Police 1 Corinthian Casuals 0	75
Hillingdon Borough 2 **Lymington & New Milton** 3	80
Gosport Borough 2 Deal Town 1	212
Eastbourne Borough 6 AFC Newbury 2	397
St Leonards 1 **Slough Town** 2	244

Tooting & Mitcham United 0 Cobham 0	353
AFC Totton 3 Pagham 1	162
Carshalton Athletic 4 Dorking 0	235
Cray Wanderers 1 Whyteleafe 0	265
Ringmer 1 **Chertsey Town** 2	120
Chipstead 1 **Three Bridges** 3	84
St Blazey 1 Bournemouth 0	201
Team Bath 3 Backwell United 1	62
Torrington 0 **Hungerford Town** 1	149
Yate Town 0 **Bideford** 4	260
Bemerton Heath Harlequins 2 Shortwood United 1	172
Merthyr Tydfil 2 Chard Town 0	461
Weston-super-Mare 3 Wimborne Town 1	243
Clevedon Town 2 Dorchester Town 0	195
Gloucester City 3 Bashley 0	305
Devizes Town 0 **Taunton Town** 1	160
Falmouth Town 1 **Evesham United** 2	191
Highworth Town 2 **Cinderford Town** 3	251
Paulton Rovers 2 Corsham Town 1	132

FIRST ROUND QUALIFYING Replays

Rossington Main 1 Bishop Auckland 1 *aet* (4-1p)	136
Crook Town 1 **Great Harwood Town** 1 *aet* (7-8p)	158
Ramsbottom United 2 **Witton Albion** 3	272
Ashington 1 **Spennymoor United** 2	283
Sutton Coldfield Town 2 Boston Town 0	72
Pelsall Villa 3 Blackstones 0	70
Biddulph Victoria 1 **Arnold Town** 2	131
Great Yarmouth Town 5 Leyton Pennant 1	182
Stotfold 0 **Aveley** 2	93
Selsey 2 Tunbridge Wells 1	164
Cobham 0 **Tooting & Mitcham United** 3	105

SECOND ROUND QUALIFYING

Chester-le-Street Town 5 Harrogate Railway Ath 5	109
Colwyn Bay 4 West Auckland Town 0	235
Hyde United 7 Tow Law Town 3	307
Guisborough Town 3 Guiseley 3	190
Stocksbridge Park Steels 0 **Ashton United** 2	270
Stalybridge Celtic 2 Workington 2	421
Bedlington Terriers 1 **Vauxhall Motors** 2	280
Durham City 3 Peterlee Newtown 0	217
Gainsborough Trinity 3 Frickley Athletic 2	351
Whitby Town 0 **Bradford Park Avenue** 4	517
Harrogate Town 2 Great Harwood Town 0	342
Marine 2 Eccleshill United 2	248
Runcorn FC Halton 2 Wakefield & Emley 0	245
Bridlington Town 3 Witton Albion 1	323
Droylsden 4 Farsley Celtic 3	210
Altrincham 1 Kendal Town 0	513
Accrington Stanley 2 Billingham Town 0	737
Spennymoor United 5 Atherton Collieries 0	226
Horden Colliery Welfare 0 **Worksop Town** 4	269
Rossington Main 0 **Radcliffe Borough** 7	160
Lancaster City 2 **Blyth Spartans** 4	357
Dunston Federation Brewery 2 Burscough 0	131
Gateshead 3 **Barrow** 4	295
Shepshed Dynamo 0 **Stafford Rangers** 2	315
Bedford Town 6 Pelsall Villa 1	461
King's Lynn 1 Cambridge City 0	1041
Bromsgrove Rovers 1 **Tamworth** 2	1115
Bedworth United 1 **Moor Green** 4	270
Ilkeston Town 7 Atherstone United 0	435
Sutton Coldfield Town 0 **Halesowen Town** 2	269
Hednesford Town 0 Hucknall Town 0	506
Redditch United 1 Leek Town 1	309

Nantwich Town 0 **Arnold Town** 3	243
Solihull Borough 0 **Grantham Town** 2	349
Worcester City 3 Stamford 3	810
Hinckley United 3 Kidsgrove Athletic 0	283
Walton & Hersham 1 Chesham United 0	228
Harefield United 4 AFC Sudbury 4	192
Grays Athletic 1 Marlow 0	237
Molesey 3 Hitchin Town 1	140
Hendon 3 Tooting & Mitcham United 0	249
Leatherhead 1 Bromley 1	321
Godalming/Guildford 0 **Hampton/Richmond Boro** 1	201
AFC Wallingford 0 **Eastbourne Borough** 1	238
Clacton Town 2 **Kingstonian** 3	465
Billericay Town 3 Yeading 1	448
Hayes 6 Bognor Regis Town 0	311
AFC Totton 2 Slough Town 2	342
Rothwell Town 1 Barking & East Ham United 0	221
Maidenhead United 1 **Welling United** 2	285
Lewes 0 Eastleigh 0	437
Horsham 2 Yaxley 0	320
Havant & Waterlooville 2 Harrow Borough 1	210
Diss Town 2 **Chertsey Town** 3	321
Canvey Island 2 Folkestone Invicta 1	429
Carshalton Athletic 1 Chelmsford City 1	577
Maidstone United 2 **Boreham Wood** 5	937
Heybridge Swifts 1 Sutton United 1	310
Uxbridge 1 **Braintree Town** 2	130
Hastings United 4 Selsey 1	400
Flackwell Heath 2 Royston Town 2	84
Hemel Hempstead Town 3 Cray Wanderers 1	181
Enfield 1 **Bishop's Stortford** 5	161
Beaconsfield SYCOB 1 **Gosport Borough** 2	80
Burnham 0 **Herne Bay** 1	65
Aldershot Town 3 Aylesbury United 1	1681
Dover Athletic 2 Basingstoke Town 0	824
Lymington & New Milton 3 Cheshunt 1	175
Carterton Town 0 **Arlesey Town** 6	173
Crawley Town 3 Great Yarmouth Town 0	723
Wisbech Town 6 VCD Athletic 1	426
Wootton Blue Cross 0 **Purfleet** 4	121
Three Bridges 1 **Aveley** 3	149
Ford United 4 Metropolitan Police 2	59
St Albans City 2 Wingate & Finchley 0	532
Tiverton Town 1 Taunton Town 1	1380
Bath City 5 Merthyr Tydfil 0	744
Weston-super-Mare 2 Clevedon Town 0	552
Gloucester City 1 Newport County 1	774
Team Bath 6 Bemerton Heath Harlequins 1	385
Bideford 3 St Blazey 1	715
Hungerford Town 2 Paulton Rovers 1	113
Evesham United 1 Cinderford Town 1	187
Chippenham Town 1 **Weymouth** 4	917

SECOND QUALIFYING ROUND Replays

Harrogate Rail. Ath. 7 Chester-le-Street Town 2 *aet*	278
Workington 3 Stalybridge Celtic 1	378
Guiseley 1 Guisborough Town 0	199
Eccleshill United 2 **Marine** 3 *aet*	176
Hucknall Town 3 Hednesford Town 3 *aet* (6-5p)	411
Leek Town 1 **Redditch United** 2	303
Stamford 1 **Worcester City** 2	365
AFC Sudbury 5 Harefield United 0	302
Bromley 2 **Leatherhead** 4	415
Slough Town 2 AFC Totton 0	360
Eastleigh 2 **Lewes** 4 *aet*	357

WWW.NLNEWSDESK.CO.UK

Chelmsford City 1 Carshalton Athletic 0 *aet*   537
Sutton United 1 **Heybridge Swifts** 2   385
Royston Town 0 **Flackwell Heath** 0 *aet* (3-5p)   152
Taunton Town 0 **Tiverton Town** 2   1365
Newport County 4 Gloucester City 0   619
Cinderford Town 0 **Evesham United** 5   171

THIRD ROUND QUALIFYING

Harrogate Railway Athletic 4 Workington 0   402
Droylsden 0 Spennymoor United 0   342
Accrington Stanley 0 Harrogate Town 0   1112
Bradford Park Avenue 3 **Bridlington Town** 5   425
Vauxhall Motors 6 Gainsborough Trinity 1   226
Durham City 1 Blyth Spartans 1   713
Barrow 3 Hyde United 1
                                                       1074
Ashton United 0 **Runcorn FC Halton** 3   347
Dunston Federation Brewery 0 **Marine** 1   297
Colwyn Bay 1 **Radcliffe Borough** 2   425
Guiseley 2 Altrincham 1
                                                       428
Ilkeston Town 6 King's Lynn 1   694
Redditch United 0 **Arnold Town** 1   465
Hinckley United 1 **Tamworth** 3   1139
Moor Green 3 Halesowen Town 1   649
Wisbech Town 1 Bedford Town 0   833
Hucknall Town 1 Worcester City 0   697
Grantham Town 1 Worksop Town 0   915
Stafford Rangers 3 Rothwell Town 0   849
Canvey Island 2 Aveley 0
                                                       423
Billericay Town 4 Braintree Town 0   715
Heybridge Swifts 1 Herne Bay 0   270
Hemel Hempstead Town 1 **Arlesey Town** 2   337
Dover Athletic 2 **Welling United** 2   1302
Molesey 3 Chertsey Town 1   287
Bishop's Stortford 1 Eastbourne Borough 0   452
Flackwell Heath 1 Purfleet 0   204
Grays Athletic 2 Hayes 1
                                                       315
AFC Sudbury 2 Walton & Hersham 0   374
Hastings United 2 Hendon 1   795
Slough Town 4 Hampton & Richmond Borough 2   537
St Albans City 1 Chelmsford City 0   839
Boreham Wood 2 Kingstonian 0   498
Leatherhead 1 **Ford United** 2   333
Horsham 1 Hungerford Town 0   607
Havant & Waterlooville 4 Evesham United 0   329
Weston-super-Mare 0 **Bath City** 5   1029
Bideford 3 Gosport Borough 1   916
Aldershot Town 2 Lewes 0   1870
Newport County 0 **Team Bath** 3   736
Lymington & New Milton 0 **Crawley Town** 2   480
Tiverton Town 4 Weymouth 2   1191

THIRD QUALIFYING ROUND Replays

Spennymoor United 3 Droylsden 2   342
Harrogate Town 3 Accrington Stanley 2   602
Blyth Spartans 3 Durham City 1   832
Welling United 1 **Dover Athletic** 3   735

FOURTH ROUND QUALIFYING

Wisbech Town 1 **Harrogate Town** 2   1061
Blyth Spartans 1 **Runcorn FC Halton** 3   851
Morecambe 3 Grantham Town 1   1055
Telford United 0 **Doncaster Rovers** 2   1012
Ilkeston Town 0 **Stafford Rangers** 5   903

Burton Albion 2 Halifax Town 1   1990
Moor Green 2 Leigh RMI 1   525
Harrogate Railway Athletic 4 Marine 2   703
Arnold Town 0 **Scarborough** 2   910
Northwich Victoria 3 Spennymoor United 1   731
Hucknall Town 1 Vauxhall Motors 1   593
Guiseley 3 Tamworth 3
                                                       724
Southport 4 Bridlington Town 1   1004
Radcliffe Borough 2 **Chester City** 4   1138
Nuneaton Borough 1 Barrow 1   1623
AFC Sudbury 1 **St Albans City** 2   702
Bishop's Stortford 1 Boreham Wood 1   969
Heybridge Swifts 2 Bideford 0   516
Bath City 1 Yeovil Town 1
                                                       3470
Slough Town 3 Canvey Island 2   875
Aldershot Town 0 **Dagenham & Redbridge** 4   2491
Hastings United 0 Kettering Town 0   1538
Havant & Waterlooville 3 Billericay Town 1   631
Hereford United 1 Arlesey Town 0   1718
Horsham 0 Team Bath 0
                                                       1543
Gravesend & Northfleet 1 **Margate** 2   1827
Forest Green Rovers 2 Ford United 1   601
Flackwell Heath 1 **Crawley Town** 4   567
Dover Athletic 1 Woking 1
                                                       1636
Barnet 0 **Tiverton Town** 2
                                                       1390
Grays Athletic 1 **Stevenage Borough** 2   757
Molesey 0 **Farnborough Town** 6   514

FOURTH ROUND QUALIFYING Replays

Vauxhall Motors 5 Hucknall Town 1   401
Tamworth 2 **Guiseley** 3
                                                       1124
Barrow 4 Nuneaton Borough 3   1919
Boreham Wood 4 Bishop's Stortford 1   903
Yeovil Town 3 Bath City 1
                                                       4393
Kettering Town 0 **Hastings United** 5   1144
Team Bath 1 Horsham 1 *aet* (4-2p)   1581
Woking 1 **Dover Athletic** 2
                                                       1806

FIRST ROUND PROPER

Farnborough Town 5 Harrogate Town 1   1090
Tiverton Town 1 Crawley Town 1   1840
Dover Athletic 0 **Oxford United** 1   4302
Northwich Victoria 0 **Scunthorpe United** 3   1680
Bury 0 **Plymouth Argyle** 3
                                                       2987
Wycombe Wanderers 2 **Brentford** 4   5673
Yeovil Town 0 **Cheltenham Town** 2   6455
Hull City 0 **Macclesfield Town** 3   8003
York City 2 Swansea City 1   2948
Chesterfield 1 **Morecambe** 2   3703
Kidderminster Harriers 2 Rushden & Diamonds 2   3079
AFC Bournemouth 2 Doncaster Rovers 1   5371
Dagenham/Redbridge 3 Havant /Waterlooville 2   1546
Team Bath 2 **Mansfield Town** 4   5469
Swindon Town 1 Huddersfield Town 0   4017
Bristol Rovers 0 Runcorn FC Halton 0   4135
Barnsley 1 **Blackpool** 4
                                                       6828

Leyton Orient 1 Margate 1	3605
Oldham Athletic 2 Burton Albion 2	5806
Barrow 2 Moor Green 0	2650
Shrewsbury Town 4 Stafford Rangers 0	5114
Southend United 1 Hartlepool United 1	4988
Hereford United 0 **Wigan Athletic** 1	4086
Forest Green Rovers 0 Exeter City 0	2147
Port Vale 0 **Crewe Alexandra** 1	5507
Scarborough 0 Cambridge United 0	2084
Stevenage Borough 1 Hastings United 0	1821
Colchester United 0 **Chester City** 1	2901
Torquay United 5 Boreham Wood 0	2739
Vauxhall Motors 0 Queens Park Rangers 0	3507
(at Chester City)	
Slough Town 1 **Harrogate Railway Athletic** 2	1687
Carlisle United 2 Lincoln City 1	4388
Heybridge Swifts 0 **Bristol City** 7	2046
Rochdale 3 Peterborough United 2	2560
Wrexham 0 **Darlington** 2	
	3418
Luton Town 4 Guiseley 0	
	5248
Southport 4 Notts County 2	3519
Tranmere Rovers 2 Cardiff City 2	5592
Northampton Town 3 Boston United 2	4136
Stockport County 4 St Albans City 1	3303

FIRST ROUND PROPER Replays

Crawley Town 3 Tiverton Town 2	3907
Rushden & Diamonds 2 Kidderminster Harriers 1	3391
Runcorn FC Halton 1 **Bristol Rovers** 3 *aet*	2434
Margate 1 Leyton Orient 0	2048
Burton Albion 2 **Oldham Athletic** 2 *aet* (4-5p)	3416
Hartlepool United 1 **Southend United** 2	4080
Exeter City 2 Forest Green Rovers 1	2951
Cambridge United 2 Scarborough 1 *aet*	3373
Queens Pk Rgrs 1 **Vauxhall Motors** 1 *aet* (3-4p)	5336
Cardiff City 2 Tranmere Rovers 1	6746

SECOND ROUND PROPER

Morecambe 3 Chester City 2	4293
Shrewsbury Town 3 Barrow 1	4210
Harrogate Railway Athletic 1 **Bristol City** 3	3249
Darlington 4 Stevenage Borough 1	3378
Oldham Athletic 1 **Cheltenham Town** 2	4416
Macclesfield Town 2 Vauxhall Motors 0	2972
Cambridge United 2 Northampton Town 2	5076
Exeter City 3 Rushden & Diamonds 1	2578
Southport 0 **Farnborough Town** 3	2534
Crawley Town 1 **Dagenham & Redbridge** 2	4516
Bristol Rovers 1 Rochdale 1	4369
Wigan Athletic 3 Luton Town 0	4544
Stockport County 0 **Plymouth Argyle** 3	3571
Southend United 1 AFC Bournemouth 1	5703
Oxford United 1 Swindon Town 0	11655
York City 1 **Brentford** 2	3517
Margate 0 **Cardiff City** 3	1461
Scunthorpe United 0 Carlisle United 0	3590
Blackpool 3 Torquay United 1	5014
Crewe Alexandra 3 Mansfield Town 0	4893

SECOND ROUND PROPER Replays

Northampton Town 0 **Cambridge United** 1	4591
Rochdale 3 Bristol Rovers 2	2206
AFC Bournemouth 3 Southend United 2	5456
Carlisle United 0 **Scunthorpe United** 1	6809

THIRD ROUND PROPER

Leicester City 2 Bristol City 0	25868
Scunthorpe United 0 **Leeds United** 2	8328

Gillingham 4 Sheffield Wednesday 1	6434
Chelsea 1 Middlesbrough 0	26062
Ipswich Town 4 Morecambe 0	18529
Preston North End 1 **Rochdale** 2	8762
Manchester City 0 **Liverpool** 1	28575
Shrewsbury Town 2 Everton 1	7266
AFC Bournemouth 0 Crewe Alexandra 0	7252
Plymouth Argyle 2 Dagenham & Redbridge 2	11754
Cambridge United 1 Millwall 1	6865
Bolton Wanderers 1 Sunderland 1	10123
Darlington 2 **Farnborough Town** 3	4253
Walsall 0 Reading 0	5987
Fulham 3 Birmingham City 1	9203
Stoke City 3 Wigan Athletic 0	9618
West Ham United 3 Nottingham Forest 2	30116
Charlton Athletic 3 Exeter City 1	18023
Sheffield United 4 Cheltenham Town 0	9132
Aston Villa 1 **Blackburn Rovers** 4	23884
Cardiff City 2 Coventry City 2	16013
Wolverhampton Wanderers 3 Newcastle United 2	27316
Southampton 4 Tottenham Hotspur 0	25589
Norwich City 3 Brighton & Hove Albion 1	17205
Arsenal 2 Oxford United 0	35432
Grimsby Town 2 Burnley 2	5350
West Bromwich Albion 3 Bradford City 1	19645
Rotherham United 0 **Wimbledon** 3	4909
Brentford 1 Derby County 0	8709
Blackpool 1 **Crystal Palace** 2	9044
Manchester United 4 Portsmouth 1	67222
Macclesfield Town 0 **Watford** 2	4244

THIRD ROUND PROPER Replays

Crewe Alex. 2 **AFC Bournemouth** 2 *aet* (1-3p)	4540
Dagenham & Redbridge 2 Plymouth Argyle 0	4530
Millwall 3 Cambridge United 2	7141
Sunderland 2 Bolton Wanderers 0 *aet*	14550
Reading 1 **Walsall** 1 *aet* (1-4p)	8767
Coventry City 3 Cardiff City 0	11997
Burnley 4 Grimsby Town 0	5851

FOURTH ROUND PROPER

Norwich City 1 Dagenham & Redbridge 0	21164
Southampton 1 Millwall 1	23809
Walsall 1 Wimbledon 0	6698
Blackburn Rovers 5 Sunderland 3	14315
Rochdale 2 Coventry City 0	9156
Fulham 3 Charlton Athletic 0	12203
Sheffield United 4 Ipswich Town 3	12757
Shrewsbury Town 0 **Chelsea** 4	7950
Stoke City 3 AFC Bournemouth 0	12004
Brentford 0 **Burnley** 3	9509
Farnborough Town 1 **Arsenal** 5 *(at Arsenal)*	35108
Manchester United 6 West Ham United 0	67181
Gillingham 1 Leeds United 1	11093
Wolverhampton Wanderers 4 Leicester City 1	28164
Watford 1 West Bromwich Albion 0	16975
Crystal Palace 0 **Liverpool** 0	25793

FOURTH ROUND PROPER Replays

Millwall 1 **Southampton** 2 *aet*	10197
Sunderland 2 Blackburn Rovers 2 *aet* (3-0p)	15410
Leeds United 2 Gillingham 1	29355
Liverpool 0 **Crystal Palace** 2	35109

FIFTH ROUND PROPER

Manchester United 0 **Arsenal** 2	67209
Southampton 2 Norwich City 0	31103
Crystal Palace 1 **Leeds United** 2	24512
Wolverhampton Wanderers 3 Rochdale 1	24033
Fulham 1 Burnley 1	12312
Stoke City 0 **Chelsea** 2	26615

F A TROPHY

PRELIMINARY ROUND

Chorley 1 Stocksbridge Park Steels 1	238
Alfreton Town 5 Guiseley 0	248
Rocester 2 Workington 2	92
Rossendale United 2 Witton Albion 2	232
Farsley Celtic 1 Ossett Town 0	140
Trafford 2 Belper Town 0	123
Lincoln United 4 Bishop Auckland 3	114
Bamber Bridge 2 Leek Town 2	201
North Ferriby United 3 Matlock Town 0	181
Radcliffe Borough 0 **Eastwood Town** 1	160
Shepshed Dynamo 2 Taunton Town 2	133
Atherstone United 0 **Gloucester City** 1	170
Rothwell Town 4 Cinderford Town 0	125
Racing Club Warwick 0 **Clevedon Town** 1	100
Bromsgrove Rovers 0 **Banbury United** 1	607
Solihull Borough 2 Sutton Coldfield Town 0	237
Mangotsfield United 4 Stourport Swifts 2	280
Merthyr Tydfil 2 Evesham United 0	391
Bedworth United 0 **Corby Town** 1	148
Croydon Athletic 0 **Tonbridge Angels** 3	198
Histon 2 Wingate & Finchley 0	98
Leyton Pennant 0 **Oxford City** 2	63
East Thurrock United 2 Sittingbourne 0	157
Fleet Town 1 Epsom & Ewell 1	142
Dorchester Town 4 Yeading 1	316
Aveley 2 Newport IOW 0	83
Spalding United 3 Barton Rovers 0	189
Harlow Town 2 Uxbridge 2	113
Bracknell Town 2 Fisher Athletic 2	122
Corinthian Casuals 4 Barking & East Ham United 3	82
Burnham 3 Arlesey Town 1	103
Wealdstone 0 Banstead Athletic 0	236
Erith & Belvedere 2 St Leonards 0	102
Hornchurch 2 **Walton & Hersham** 6	263
Metropolitan Police 1 Dulwich Hamlet 1	112
Hertford Town 1 Molesey 0	109
Northwood 0 **Tooting & Mitcham United** 2	172
Windsor & Eton 2 Ashford Town (Middx) 1	147
King's Lynn 4 Chertsey Town 0	601
Salisbury City 2 Dartford 0	410
Berkhamsted Town 6 Leatherhead 0	137
Slough Town 2 Wembley 0	341
Bashley 1 **Marlow** 2	187
Bognor Regis Town 5 Wivenhoe Town 2	303
Horsham 4 Tilbury 0	302

PRELIMINARY ROUND Replays

Stocksbridge Park Steels 1 Chorley 0	134
Workington 2 **Rocester** 2 *aet* (3-4p)	350
Witton Albion 2 Rossendale United 0	203
Leek Town 3 Bamber Bridge 1 *aet*	203
Taunton Town 3 Shepshed Dynamo 0	251
Epsom & Ewell 2 Fleet Town 0	83
Uxbridge 1 **Harlow Town** 2 *aet*	122
Fisher Athletic 4 **Bracknell Town** 7 *aet*	111
Banstead Athletic 0 **Wealdstone** 1 *aet*	101
Dulwich Hamlet 3 Metropolitan Police 1	119

FIRST ROUND

Spennymoor United 4 Witton Albion 3	248
Blyth Spartans 5 North Ferriby United 3	432
Burscough 0 Marine 0	242
Gresley Rovers 0 Harrogate Town 0	302
Droylsden 2 Ashton United 1	327
Lincoln United 2 **Alfreton Town** 3	168

Stocksbridge Park Steels 0 **Whitby Town** 1	182
Gateshead 0 **Hyde United** 2	122
Leek Town 4 Eastwood Town 1	226
Farsley Celtic 7 Trafford 2	113
Rocester 0 **Colwyn Bay** 2	108
Kidsgrove Athletic 1 Frickley Athletic 1	100
Gainsborough Trinity 3 Kendal Town 1	345
Mangotsfield United 3 Redditch United 1	216
Corby Town 0 **Rothwell Town** 5	184
Halesowen Town 4 Bath City 3	403
Grantham Town 3 Hinckley United 2	413
Banbury United 1 **Gloucester City** 1	478
Weston-super-Mare 2 Cirencester Town 2	125
Solihull Borough 7 Swindon Supermarine 1	148
Clevedon Town 2 **Hednesford Town** 4	172
Rugby United 2 Hucknall Town 1	218
Taunton Town 1 **Merthyr Tydfil** 2	346
Thame United 3 Bromley 2	120
Great Wakering Rovers 2 Ford United 2	145
Burnham 0 **Aylesbury United** 2	200
Oxford City 4 Egham Town 2	108
Corinthian Casuals 1 Croydon 0	53
Hastings United 1 Chelmsford City 0	599
Hitchin Town 3 Chatham Town 1	256
Lewes 6 Slough Town 4	320
East Thurrock United 1 **Kingstonian** 3	293
Tooting & Mitcham United 2 **Dulwich Hamlet** 3	421
Aveley 1 **Weymouth** 4	74
Harlow Town 2 Wealdstone 0	221
Horsham 2 Ashford Town 0	301
Whyteleafe 1 **Walton & Hersham** 5	148
Worthing 1 **Cambridge City** 4	256
Staines Town 1 **Epsom & Ewell** 2	126
Carshalton Athletic 2 Folkestone Invicta 1	347
Bracknell Town 0 **Heybridge Swifts** 2	136
Windsor & Eton 2 **Welling United** 2	174
Sutton United 2 Harrow Borough 1	332
Hemel Hempstead Town 2 **Histon** 3	109
Salisbury City 2 Erith & Belvedere 2	431
Berkhamsted Town 2 **Bishop's Stortford** 2	191
Eastbourne Borough 4 Hertford Town 1	355
Bognor Regis Town 2 Boreham Wood 0	306
Chippenham Town 4 Dorchester Town 1	534
Spalding United 2 Hampton & Richmond Boro 1	199
Marlow 1 Bedford Town 1	226
Tonbridge Angels 3 Maidenhead United 2	448
King's Lynn 1 **Stamford** 2	637
Enfield 1 **Basingstoke Town** 2	91

FIRST ROUND Replays

Marine 1 **Burscough** 3 *aet*	224
Harrogate Town 3 Gresley Rovers 0	276
Frickley Athletic 2 Kidsgrove Athletic 1 *aet*	92
Gloucester City 2 Banbury United 1	326
Ford United 6 Great Wakering Rovers 1 *aet*	88
Welling United 3 **Windsor & Eton** 5	247
Bishop's Stortford 2 Berkhamsted Town 0	221
Bedford Town 1 **Marlow** 2	368
Cirencester Town 3 Weston-super-Mare 2 *aet*	120
Erith & Belvedere 2 Salisbury City 0	93

SECOND ROUND

Droylsden 1 **Colwyn Bay** 2	221
Stafford Rangers 0 **Alfreton Town** 2	782
Moor Green 2 **Blyth Spartans** 3	323
Spennymoor United 1 Halesowen Town 1	268

Tamworth 4 Accrington Stanley 1 — 951
Worksop Town 4 Solihull Borough 2 — 555
Runcorn FC Halton 0 **Rugby United** 3 — 263
Histon 3 **Farsley Celtic** 4 — 141
Harrogate Town 2 Burscough 2 — 291
Vauxhall Motors 4 Frickley Athletic 2 — 185
Stalybridge Celtic 2 Rothwell Town 0 — 473
Wakefield & Emley 5 Spalding United 0 — 227
Leek Town 3 Hyde United 1 — 303
Ilkeston Town 3 Hednesford Town 1 — 436
Lancaster City 6 Stamford 1 — 181
Grantham Town 0 **Gainsborough Trinity** 1 — 525
Barrow 4 Whitby Town 2 — 853
Bradford Park Avenue 0 **Altrincham** 1 — 437
Chippenham Town 0 **Aylesbury United** 1 — 580
Hastings United 0 **Eastbourne Borough** 2 — 906
Heybridge Swifts 2 Weymouth 1 — 314
Dover Athletic 2 Ford United 0 — 804
Canvey Island 2 Carshalton Athletic 0 — 385
Windsor & Eton 3 Hitchin Town 1 — 195
Oxford City 1 Braintree Town 0 — 146
Gloucester City 0 Merthyr Tydfil 0 — 417
St Albans City 0 **Hayes** 1 — 468
Havant & Waterlooville 1 Billericay Town 1 — 277
Basingstoke Town 0 **Sutton United** 2 — 528
Horsham 1 **Thame United** 2 — 327
Kingstonian 5 Erith & Belvedere 1 — 372
Grays Athletic 3 Tiverton Town 1 — 334
Purfleet 3 Tonbridge Angels 2 — 244
Harlow Town 0 **Lewes** 3 — 178
Bishop's Stortford 2 Marlow 2 — 349
Newport County 2 Epsom & Ewell 1 — 489
Chesham United 0 Walton & Hersham 0 — 243
Bognor Regis Town 1 **Hendon** 4 — 266
Mangotsfield United 0 **Dulwich Hamlet** 1 — 297
Cambridge City 0 **Crawley Town** 1 — 327
Worcester City 1 Aldershot Town 0 — 1562
Corinthian Casuals 0 **Cirencester Town** 4 — 103

SECOND ROUND Replays
Halesowen Town 4 Spennymoor United 1 — 391
Burscough 3 Harrogate Town 2 — 160
Merthyr Tydfil 0 **Gloucester City** 1 — 340
Billericay Town 1 **Havant & Waterlooville** 2 *aet* — 327
Marlow 2 **Bishop's Stortford** 3 — 145
(ineligible player – Bishop's Stortford expelled)
Walton & Hersham 0 **Chesham United** 1 — 133

THIRD ROUND
Farsley Celtic 1 Gainsborough Trinity 1 — 217
Kettering Town 1 Altrincham 1 — 1072
Chester City 1 **Worksop Town** 2 — 1393
Leek Town 1 **Southport** 2 — 428
Alfreton Town 2 Halesowen Town 1 — 681
Leigh RMI 1 **Vauxhall Motors** 2 — 229
Rugby United 0 **Telford United** 2 — 404
Stalybridge Celtic 0 **Scarborough** 3 — 613
Northwich Victoria 3 Barrow 1 — 543
Wakefield & Emley 1 Burton Albion 0 — 802
Ilkeston Town 0 **Burscough** 3 — 248
Tamworth 3 Nuneaton Borough 0 — 2045
Lancaster City 0 **Morecambe** 1 — 2257
Colwyn Bay 1 Blyth Spartans 0 — 321
Halifax Town 4 Doncaster Rovers 1 — 1770
Woking 3 Chesham United 0 — 1284
Dover Athletic 1 Gravesend & Northfleet 0 — 814
Stevenage Borough 2 Oxford City 1 — 846
Forest Green Rovers 4 Barnet 2 — 552

Windsor & Eton 3 Thame United 2 — 307
Aylesbury United 1 Kingstonian 0 — 431
Eastbourne Borough 0 **Farnborough Town** 1 — 1576
Gloucester City 3 Lewes 2 — 338
Dagenham & Redbridge 5 Marlow 2 — 1055
Hayes 2 Crawley Town 1 — 296
Dulwich Hamlet 0 **Margate** 2 — 553
Canvey Island 5 Cirencester Town 1 — 349
Heybridge Swifts 0 Hendon 0 — 210
Worcester City 3 Newport County 2 — 1128
Purfleet 1 **Grays Athletic** 2 — 325
Hereford United 1 **Yeovil Town** 2 — 2425
Sutton United 1 **Havant & Waterlooville** 3 — 645

THIRD ROUND Replays
Gainsborough Trinity 2 Farsley Celtic 1 — 336
Altrincham 3 Kettering Town 3 *aet* (5-3p) — 436
Hendon 2 Heybridge Swifts 1 — 177

FOURTH ROUND
Colwyn Bay 0 **Havant & Waterlooville** 2 — 351
Scarborough 1 Dover Athletic 1 — 899
Halifax Town 3 Grays Athletic 2 — 1653
Windsor & Eton 1 Vauxhall Motors 1 — 351
Northwich Victoria 2 Canvey Island 1 — 708
Altrincham 0 **Aylesbury United** 1 — 732
Worksop Town 2 **Hayes** 3 — 1064
Yeovil Town 2 Morecambe 1 — 3984
Alfreton Town 1 Burscough 1 — 602
Gainsborough Trinity 0 **Forest Green Rovers** 2 — 710
Worcester City 0 **Margate** 2 — 1364
Dagenham & Redbridge 0 Southport 0 — 1307
Gloucester City 0 Woking 0 — 1073
Wakefield & Emley 0 Hendon 0 — 529
Tamworth 3 Stevenage Borough 0 — 1452
Telford United 2 **Farnborough Town** 3 — 928

FOURTH ROUND Replays
Burscough 2 Alfreton Town 0 — 190
Southport 2 Dagenham & Redbridge 2 *aet* (4-3p) — 569
Woking 0 **Gloucester City** 2 — 976
Hendon 0 **Wakefield & Emley** 1 *aet* — 245
Vauxhall Motors 0 **Windsor & Eton** 3 — 268
Dover Athletic 2 Scarborough 1 *aet* — 801

FIFTH ROUND
Dover Athletic 0 **Forest Green Rovers** 3 — 932
Margate 0 **Tamworth** 2 — 971
(at Hartsdown Park, Margate)
Farnborough Town 2 Halifax Town 0 — 863
Yeovil Town 2 Northwich Victoria 1 — 4469
Burscough 5 Wakefield & Emley 0 — 437
Aylesbury United 2 Windsor & Eton 2 — 847
Gloucester City 1 Southport 1 — 1237
Havant & Waterlooville 3 Hayes 0 — 456

FIFTH ROUND Replays
Windsor & Eton 1 **Aylesbury United** 1 *aet* (3-4p) — 577
Southport 1 **Gloucester City** 3 — 835

SIXTH ROUND
Farnborough Town 1 **Tamworth** 2 — 1312
Aylesbury United 2 Gloucester City 1 — 1435
Forest Green Rovers 1 **Havant & Waterlooville** 2 — 1016
Yeovil Town 0 **Burscough** 2 — 4934

SEMI-FINALS 1st Leg
Aylesbury United 1 Burscough 1 — 1523
Tamworth 1 Havant & Waterlooville 0 — 2165

SEMI-FINALS 2nd Leg
Burscough 3 Aylesbury United 0 — 1773
Havant & Waterlooville 1 Tamworth 1 *aet* — 1331

FINAL *(18th May at Aston Villa)*
Burscough 2 Tamworth 1 — 14265

F A VASE

FIRST ROUND QUALIFYING

Blackpool Mechanics 0 Sheffield 0 *aet*	37
Chester-le-Street Town 0 **Eccleshill United** 1	70
Nelson 2 Curzon Ashton 0	87
South Shields 0 **Holker Old Boys** 2	83
Thackley (w/o) Retford United (scr)	
West Allotment Celtic 2 Goole 1	101
Selby Town 0 **Louth United** 1	85
New Mills 1 **Northallerton Town** 5	215
Crook Town 1 **Guisborough Town** 3	80
Marske United 1 **Prudhoe Town** 2	119
Winsford United 3 Great Harwood Town 0	n/k
Brodsworth Miners Welf. 3 Jarrow Roofing BCA 2	59
Poulton Victoria 2 Hebburn Town 0	74
Easington Colliery 0 **Warrington Town** 1 *aet*	45
Hatfield Main 1 **Penrith** 2 *aet*	58
Chadderton 2 Glasshoughton Welfare 2 *aet*	68
Norton & Stockton Ancients 0 **Washington** 2	13
Oldham Town 0 **Parkgate** 6	39
Malvern Town 5 Rainworth Miners Welfare 0	63
Causeway United 6 Bolehall Swifts 0	131
(at Halesowen Town)	
Willenhall Town 6 Marconi 0	77
Bourne Town 3 Bromyard Town 3 *aet* (4-3p)	55
Kimberley Town 3 **Carlton Town** 4	43
Oldbury United 5 Dunkirk 2	25
Nettleham 2 **Shawbury United** 8 *(at Brigg Town)*	16
Handrahan Timbers 0 **Congleton Town** 3	56
Lye Town 5 Anstey Nomads 0	63
Heath Hayes 2 Tividale 0	50
Glapwell 3 Westfields 1	70
Quorn 4 Blackstones 2 *aet*	102
Biddulph Victoria 2 Kirby Muxloe SC 1	151
Blackwell Miners Welfare 1 Lincoln Moorlands 0	47
Staveley Miners Welfare 0 **Cradley Town** 1	45
Rolls Royce Leisure 3 Pegasus Juniors 1	30
Ledbury Town 3 Coventry Sphinx 2	86
Greenacres (Hemel) (w/o) Downham Town (scr)	
Ware 3 Hullbridge Sports 1	97
Whitton United 1 **Enfield Town** 3	198
Great Yarmouth Town 1 **Clacton Town** 3	105
Hoddesdon Town 5 Ruislip Manor 2 *aet*	33
(at Hertford Town)	
Fakenham Town 1 **Ely City** 3	91
Felixtowe & Walton United 2 Letchworth 0	56
Leyton 1 Brimsdown Rovers 0	101
Welwyn Garden City 2 Henley Town 1 *aet*	64
Holmer Green 3 Bugbrooke St Michaels 1 *aet*	54
Chalfont St Peter 0 **Norwich United** 2	35
Beaconsfield SYCOB 3 Harwich & Parkeston 2	38
Halstead Town 2 Thetford Town 0	112
Stowmarket Town 4 Harpenden Town 2	92
Brook House 0 **Leighton Town** 2	45
Brackley Town 1 **Buckingham Town** 4	125
Gorleston 4 Romford 1	120
Bury Town 2 Haringey Borough 1	94
Brightlingsea United (scr) **Clapton** (w/o)	
Lowestoft Town 4 Edgware Town 3	145
Biggleswade Town 1 **Cornard United** 2	34
Long Buckby 1 **Wootton Blue Cross** 5	39
Westfield 3 **Eastbourne Town** 4	30
Horsham YMCA 1 Chipstead 1 *aet*	66
Wantage Town 1 Carterton Town 0	56
Merstham 6 Hartley Wintney 0	41

Lordswood 1 **Redhill** 2	62
Whitstable Town 2 **Raynes Park Vale** 4 *aet*	116
Godalming & Guildford 1 Three Bridges 0	67
Abingdon United 3 Chessington United 0	65
Ringmer 2 Eastbourne United 0	80
Farnham Town 0 **Whitehawk** 4	60
Ramsgate 1 **Deal Town** 2	175
Hungerford Town 4 Petersfield Town 0	68
East Preston 0 **AFC Totton** 3	98
Gosport Borough 3 Chichester City United 0	142
Eastleigh 6 Peacehaven & Telscombe 0	119
Pagham 0 **Greenwich Borough** 3	59
Frome Town 4 Downton 2	177
Poole Town 0 Christchurch 0 *aet*	156
Elmore 4 Harrow Hill 0	45
Paulton Rovers 3 Barnstaple Town 0	58
Wellington 1 **Devizes Town** 2	48
Clevedon United 1 Almondsbury Town 1 *aet*	78
Falmouth Town 4 Bristol Manor Farm 2	120
Portland United 0 **Ilfracombe Town** 1	99

FIRST ROUND QUALIFYING Replays

Sheffield 3 Blackpool Mechanics 1	70
Glasshoughton Welfare 6 Chadderton 0	53
Chipstead 3 Horsham YMCA 2	78
Christchurch 2 Poole Town 0	140
Almondsbury Town 2 **Clevedon United** 4	95

SECOND ROUND QUALIFYING

Guisborough Town 2 Darwen 1	110
Woodley Sports 2 Horden Colliery Welfare 2 *aet*	67
Atherton Collieries 2 Cheadle Town 1	40
West Allotment Celtic 1 **Warrington Town** 1 *aet*	96
Bacup Borough 0 **Cammell Laird** 4	100
(at Rossendale United)	
Squires Gate 2 **Brandon United** 4 *aet*	81
Atherton LR 4 **Sheffield** 5 *aet*	56
Thornaby 4 Willington 0	45
Kennek Ryhope CA 1 **Northallerton Town** 3	32
Esh Winning 4 Whickham 0	58
Penrith 3 Stand Athletic 0	86
Bridlington Town 8 North Shields 0	178
Newcastle Blue Star 3 **Newcastle Benfield Saints** 5 *aet*	169
Louth United 1 **Armthorpe Welfare** 3	34
Fleetwood Town 2 Alsager Town 0	142
Harrogate Railway Athletic 2 Skelmersdale Utd 0	88
Alnwick Town 0 **Ashington** 7	70
Winsford United 1 **Thackley** 1 *aet*	110
Abbey Hey 8 Maltby Main 1	65
Nelson 2 Evenwood Town 1	113
Morpeth Town 3 Washington 1	42
Peterlee Newtown 3 Maine Road 1	50
Poulton Victoria 2 Seaham Red Star 1	90
Liversedge 4 Prudhoe Town 1	89
Washington Nissan 0 **Flixton** 1	36
Winterton Rangers 3 Parkgate 2 *aet*	65
Tadcaster Albion 0 **Eccleshill United** 7	54
Shildon 6 Glasshoughton Welfare 3	143
Murton 3 Rossington Main 0	25
Brodsworth Miners Welfare 2 Shotton Comrades 0	61
Pontefract Collieries 5 Holker Old Boys 1	32
Colne 1 **Hall Road Rangers** 3	55
Mossley 3 Ramsbottom United 1	240
Garforth Town 4 Formby 1	100
Worsbrough Bridge MW 0 **Yorkshire Amateur** 1	50

Lye Town 3 Dudley Town 1	61
West Midlands Police 1 **Holbeach United** 4	36
Boston Town 1 **Deeping Rangers** 2 *aet*	116
Oldbury United 6 Blackwell Miners Welfare 1	45
Buxton 1 Daventry Town 0	193
St Andrews SC 0 **Chasetown** 1	56
Brierley & Hagley Alliance 1 **Malvern Town** 2 *aet*	28
Stratford Town 13 Wednesfield 0	125
Holwell Sports 1 **Congleton Town** 2	110
Fernhill County Sports 2 Tipton Town 0	28
Cradley Town 0 **Stafford Town** 1	39
Coalville Town 0 **Mickleover Sports** 1	77
Meir KA 1 Ludlow Town 0	71
Shawbury United 0 **Boldmere St Michaels** 1	41
Gedling Town 5 Blaby & Whetstone Athletic 1	63
Highfield Rangers 2 **South Normanton Athletic** 5	50
Birstall United 1 **Borrowash Victoria** 2	59
Glapwell 0 **Carlton Town** 3	92
Barrow Town 0 **Leamington** 1	220
Willenhall Town 1 Friar Lane Old Boys 0	79
Leek CSOB 1 **Ledbury Town** 5	80
Norton United 3 Castle Vale Kings Heath 0	63
Biddulph Victoria 0 **Rugby Town** 1	61
Ibstock Welfare 8 Heath Hayes 0	82
Sutton Town 5 **Glossop North End** 6 *aet*	106
Wellington 2 **Alvechurch** 4	89
Stone Dominoes 1 **Causeway United** 2	130
Shifnal Town 0 **Rolls Royce Leisure** 1	56
Long Eaton United 2 Pershore Town 1	95
Quorn 1 **Shirebrook Town** 2	141
Nuneaton Griff 4 Bourne Town 1	55
Downes Sports 0 **Halesowen Harriers** 5	95
(at Halesowen Harriers)	
Little Drayton Rangers 1 **Pelsall Villa** 4	104
Grosvenor Park 4 Gornal Athletic 0	51
Stansted 2 Bedford United & Valerio 1	43
Eton Manor 0 **Buckingham Town** 3	40
St Margaretsbury 4 Beaconsfield SYCOB 3 *aet*	37
Ipswich Wanderers 1 Concord Rangers 1 *aet*	97
Harefield United 3 Northampton Spencer 1	77
Warboys Town 1 **Needham Market** 5	55
Burnham Ramblers 2 Somersham Town 1	46
Greenacres (Hemel) 3 Stowmarket Town 1	68
Potters Bar Town 6 Bicester Town 1	78
Broxbourne Borough V&E 3 Tring Town 2	39
March Town United 0 **Lowestoft Town** 5	62
Eynesbury Rovers 0 **Maldon Town** 4	86
Basildon United 0 **Enfield Town** 2 *aet*	178
Cheshunt 2 Leighton Town 0 *aet*	61
Biggleswade United 1 **London Colney** 2 *aet*	52
Leverstock Green 1 Cockfosters 0	53
Wootton Blue Cross 2 Holmer Green 0	71
Felixstowe & Walton United 3 Colney Heath 1	90
Welwyn Garden City 1 **Rothwell Corinthians** 2	52
Kempston Rovers 0 **Norwich United** 2	53
Woodbridge Town 0 **Haverhill Rovers** 5	75
Dunstable Town 2 **Halstead Town** 3 *aet*	43
Stanway Rovers 5 Royston Town 1	60
Clacton Town 3 Potton United 1	124
Hanwell Town 5 Ely City 2	56
Leyton 5 Hoddesdon Town 1	69
Gorleston 2 Saffron Walden Town 1 *aet*	143
St Ives Town 3 **Southall Town** 4	63
Newmarket Town 2 Ilford 1	120
Bury Town 4 Brentwood 0	139
Witham Town 1 **Yaxley** 3	40

Southall 0 **Flackwell Heath** 1	63
Diss Town 2 Sawbridgeworth Town 0	189
Hadleigh United 2 Southend Manor 2 *aet*	82
Cornard United 3 Desborough Town 1	40
Woodford Town 1 **Soham Town Rangers** 4	92
Ware 4 Bowers United 3 *aet*	91
Clapton 2 Langford 1	22
East Grinstead Town 4 Herne Bay 3	160
Bedfont 2 Hungerford Town 2 *aet*	37
Wantage Town 1 Saltdean United 0	64
Cray Wanderers 2 Godalming & Guildford 1	126
Alton Town 2 **Erith Town** 3 *aet*	75
Hythe Town 1 Deal Town 1 *aet*	103
Sidlesham 7 Redhill 0	45
VCD Athletic 2 Littlehampton Town 1	52
Whitehawk 2 Reading Town 0	92
Oakwood 1 **Lymington Town** 3	18
Chessington & Hook United 4 Beckenham Town 3	82
Greenwich Borough 4 Wokingham Town 0	15
Cobham 3 Hillingdon Borough 1 *aet*	43
Raynes Park Vale 1 **BAT Sports** 2	39
Camberley Town 0 **Withdean** 2	77
Arundel 3 Hassocks 1	70
Gosport Borough 3 Ringmer 0	132
Slade Green 6 Viking Greenford 1	51
Sandhurst Town 1 Southwick 0	67
Lymington & New Milton 11 Wick 1	130
Blackfield & Langley 1 **Eastleigh** 7	121
Eastbourne Town 2 **Winchester City** 5	191
Fareham Town 0 **Walton Casuals** 1	140
Lancing 0 **Hailsham Town** 1	79
Chipstead 1 **AFC Newbury** 3	74
AFC Totton 2 Sidley United 1	126
Abingdon United 2 Milton United 0	162
Cove 1 **Merstham** 5	32
Tunbridge Wells 0 **Didcot Town** 2	101
Whitchurch United 0 **Broadbridge Heath** 7	47
Corsham Town 2 Brislington 0	120
Falmouth Town 2 Gloucester United 1 *aet*	151
Westbury United 2 Elmore 1	104
Calne Town 2 Shepton Mallet Town 0	60
Bridport 0 **Fairford Town** 1	132
Ilfracombe Town 1 **Torrington** 2	102
Christchurch 2 Odd Down 0	78
Frome Town 0 **Liskeard Athletic** 1	161
Backwell United 6 Dawlish Town 1	43
Tuffley Rovers 3 Cullompton Rangers 1	55
Minehead Town 3 Chipping Norton Town 1	47
Hamworthy United 2 **Bitton** 3	175
Shortwood United 5 Wootton Bassett Town 1	55
Welton Rovers 3 Keynsham Town 2	65
Chard Town 0 **Highworth Town** 4	74
Paulton Rovers 3 Launceston 1	153
Cirencester Academy (scr) **Willand Rovers** (w/o)	
Street 1 **Yate Town** 2	74
Exmouth Town 0 **Bournemouth** 1	80
Bridgwater Town 9 Pewsey Vale 1	184
Newton Abbot 3 Amesbury Town 3 *aet*	70
Devizes Town 5 Bishop Sutton 1	60
Clevedon United 3 Hook Norton 2	77

SECOND ROUND QUALIFYING Replays

Horden Colliery Welfare 2 Woodley Sports 1	83
Warrington Town 3 West Allotment Celtic 1	68
Thackley 3 Winsford United 2	87
Concord Rangers 2 **Ipswich Wanderers** 3 *aet*	38
Southend Manor 4 Hadleigh United 0	40

Hungerford Town 2 **Bedfont** 5　　　　　　　　　61
Deal Town 6 Hythe Town 4 *aet*　　　　　　120
Amesbury Town 1 **Newton Abbot** 4　　　　　65

FIRST ROUND PROPER

Brandon United 3 Murton 0　　　　　　　　　54
Armthorpe Welfare 1 Bridlington Town 1 *aet*　70
Eccleshill United 1 **Poulton Victoria** 3　　　82
Pontefract Collieries 5 Penrith 0　　　　　60
Abbey Hey 3 Liversedge 0　　　　　　　　　65
Esh Winning 0 **Mossley** 2　　　　　　　　　152
Salford City 2 Thackley 1　　　　　　　　　73
Warrington Town 1 **Flixton** 2　　　　　　　72
Nelson 0 **Dunston Federation Brewery** 1　123
Garforth Town 0 **Northallerton Town** 1　　95
Horden Colliery Welfare 1 Ashington 0 *aet*　65
Peterlee Newtown 2 **Ossett Albion** 5　　　59
Hall Road Rangers 4 Hallam 3　　　　　　45
Newcastle Benfield Saints 1 **Morpeth Town** 2　78
Nantwich Town 0 **Fleetwood Town** 3　　　94
Brodsworth Miners Welfare 2 **Billingham Synth.** 6　60
Cammell Laird 4 Shildon 1　　　　　　　111
Sheffield 3 Winterton Rangers 2 *aet*　　122
Yorkshire Amateur 1 **Guisborough Town** 2　n/k
Atherton Collieries 4 **Harrogate Railway Ath.** 6 *aet* 52
Borrowash Victoria 2 Stafford Town 0　　57
Rolls Royce Leisure 0 **Long Eaton United** 2　79
Stratford Town 0 **Stourbridge** 1　　　　　171
Malvern Town 0 **Norton United** 2　　　　　93
Congleton Town 4 Oldbury United 1　　　143
Pelsall Villa 1 **Studley** 3　　　　　　　　　73
Glossop North End 1 **Ford Sports Daventry** 2　128
Barwell 4 Ledbury Town 1　　　　　　　　82
Nuneaton Griff 0 **Grosvenor Park** 1　　　40
Carlton Town 4 Lye Town 2 *aet*　　　　　43
Boldmere St Michaels 2 Halesowen Harriers 1　92
Newcastle Town 2 Buxton 0　　　　　　　101
Stewarts & Lloyds Corby 3 Deeping Rangers 0　51
Alvechurch 0 **Rugby Town** 3　　　　　　113
Holbeach United 5 Fernhill County Sports 0　n/k
Meir KA 2 **Causeway United** 3　　　　　　35
Gedling Town 2 Cogenhoe United 0　　　53
Wisbech Town 2 Chasetown 1　　　　　　335
Willenhall Town 2 South Normanton Athletic 0　95
Bridgnorth Town 0 **Shirebrook Town** 2　　72
Mickleover Sports 2 Leamington 0　　　275
Ibstock Welfare 0 **Raunds Town** 1　　　　92
Burnham Ramblers 1 **Bury Town** 4　　　　60
Hanwell Town 8 Greenacres (Hemel) 3　54
Kingsbury Town 4 Cornard United 2　　　43
Southend Manor 2 **Norwich United** 3　　　67
Gorleston 3 Newmarket Town 2　　　　132
Leverstock Green 1 **Potters Bar Town** 2 *aet*　n/k
Buckingham Town 4 Clapton 1　　　　　　96
Lowestoft Town 5 Ipswich Wanderers 1　140
London Colney 2 Broxbourne Borough V & E 0　40
Diss Town 3 Rothwell Corinthians 3 *aet*　186
St Margaretsbury 8 Stansted 0　　　　　58
Ware 3 Needham Market 0　　　　　　　120
Halstead Town 2 **Stanway Rovers** 3　　　210
Haverhill Rovers 0 **Soham Town Rangers** 3　131
Felixstowe & Walton United 0 **Leyton** 5　85
Enfield Town 3 North Leigh 1　　　　　　309
Clacton Town 0 **Southall Town** 1　　　　　98
Wootton Blue Cross 0 Cheshunt 0 *aet*　　85
Maldon Town 2 Harefield United 0　　　　76
Yaxley 5 Flackwell Heath 1　　　　　　　60

Lymington & New Milton 5 Walton Casuals 2　104
Cowes Sports 2 Greenwich Borough 1　　92
Whitehawk 3 Broadbridge Heath 0　　　50
Sandhurst Town 1 Gosport Borough 0　88
Lymington Town 0 **Selsey** 3　　　　　　　82
Chessington & Hook United 2 Abingdon United 1　72
Merstham 0 **Withdean** 5　　　　　　　　70
Maidstone United 2 **Sidlesham** 4　　　　327
Winchester City 5 Cray Wanderers 2　　231
Wantage Town 5 East Grinstead Town 2 *aet*　80
Cobham 5 BAT Sports 3　　　　　　　　35
Andover 3 AFC Newbury 1　　　　　　187
AFC Wallingford 0 **Arundel** 1　　　　　　108
Slade Green 0 **Erith Town** 2 *aet*　　　　64
Hailsham Town 1 **Brockenhurst** 2 *aet*　73
Eastleigh 4 Deal Town 0　　　　　　　　300
VCD Athletic 1 **AFC Totton** 5　　　　　　45
Thatcham Town 2 **Moneyfields** 3　　　　84
Bedfont 1 **Didcot Town** 3　　　　　　　82
St Blazey 3 Yate Town 2　　　　　　　193
Falmouth Town 2 **Devizes Town** 3 *aet*　199
Newton Abbot 0 **Willand Rovers** 1　　　90
Clevedon United 1 **Bournemouth** 2　　　155
Bridgwater Town 0 **Bitton** 1　　　　　　215
Shortwood United 1 Calne Town 0　　　　60
Christchurch 4 Tuffley Rovers 2　　　　95
Fairford Town 0 Team Bath 0 *aet*　　　　76
Wimborne Town 4 Minehead Town 0　　194
Welton Rovers 5 Highworth Town 0　　　105
Liskeard Athletic 0 **Bideford** 2　　　　　221
Corsham Town 1 Backwell United 0 *aet*　101
Melksham Town 1 **Paulton Rovers** 4　　　131
Torrington 3 Westbury United 2　　　　80
Thornaby (w/o) Kendal Town (scr)

FIRST ROUND PROPER Replays

Team Bath 5 Fairford Town 2 *aet*　　　　46
Bridlington Town 3 Armthorpe Welfare 3 *aet* (6-5p) 263
Rothwell Corinthians 0 **Diss Town** 5　　　79
Cheshunt 0 **Wootton Blue Cross** 2　　　68

SECOND ROUND PROPER

Sheffield 1 **Guisborough Town** 2　　　　122
Cammell Laird 3 **Harrogate Railway Athletic** 4　115
Pontefract Collieries 1 **Northallerton Town** 2　93
Billingham Synthonia 0 **Whitley Bay** 1　151
Consett 1 **Billingham Town** 4　　　　　　76
Dunston Federation Brewery 3 Tow Law Town 2 177
Ossett Albion 0 **Durham City** 4　　　　165
Brigg Town 2 Horden Colliery Welfare 1　179
Abbey Hey 2 Hall Road Rangers 0　　　53
Morpeth Town 2 Brandon United 1　　　68
Thornaby 1 Fleetwood Town 1 *aet*　　　57
Bridlington Town 2 Poulton Victoria 1　191
Salford City 1 **Mossley** 2　　　　　　　150
Clitheroe 3 Bedlington Terriers 1　　　485
Prescot Cables 2 West Auckland Town 1　199
Flixton 2 St Helens Town 1　　　　　　　74
Mickleover Sports 2 Raunds Town 1　　107
Borrowash Victoria 0 **Rugby Town** 3　　70
Carlton Town 1 **Oadby Town** 2　　　　　79
Shirebrook Town 5 Congleton Town 4　170
St Neots Town 0 **Newcastle Town** 3　　89
Boldmere St Michaels 1 **Rushall Olympic** 2 *aet*　92
Stewarts & Lloyds Corby 2 **Ford Sports Daventry** 3 43
Norton United 1 **Gedling Town** 2　　　　68
Causeway United 2 Long Eaton United 1　138

Willenhall Town 4 Arnold Town 0 *aet*	164
Wisbech Town 2 Holbeach United 2 *aet*	504
Barwell 0 Grosvenor Park 3	87
Heanor Town 0 Studley 2	110
Pickering Town 3 Stourbridge 2	139
Withdean 2 St Margaretsbury 2 *aet*	87
Cobham 0 Gorleston 1	44
Lowestoft Town 5 Sidlesham 0	174
Diss Town 3 Tiptree United 2	216
Sandhurst Town 3 Dorking 3 *aet*	74
Soham Town Rangers 2 Selsey 3	152
Potters Bar Town 0 Yaxley 1	79
Mildenhall Town 2 Maldon Town 4 *aet*	129
Didcot Town 1 Wootton Blue Cross 2	154
Thamesmead Town 3 Leyton 1	80
Wroxham 2 Enfield Town 0	287
Chessington & Hook United 2 Ware 4 *aet*	95
Norwich United 1 Stotfold 1	56
London Colney 2 Milton Keynes City 2 *aet*	39
Arundel 1 Erith Town 0	103
Burgess Hill Town 2 Stanway Rovers 1	202
AFC Sudbury 2 Southall Town 0	267
Ash United 4 Kingsbury Town 1	87
Whitehawk 2 Abingdon Town 0	75
Buckingham Town 2 Bury Town 0	145
Hanwell Town 2 Dereham Town 1	72
Bitton 2 Wimborne Town 1	152
Devizes Town 3 Wantage Town 2	71
Christchurch 3 Torrington 2	95
Brockenhurst 1 Bemerton Heath Harlequins 0	60
Winchester City 3 Shortwood United 2	211
St Blazey 1 Hallen 0	196
Welton Rovers 2 Bournemouth 1	67
Moneyfields 1 Paulton Rovers 0	102
Eastleigh 1 Porthleven 3	176
Bideford 5 Cowes Sports 0	225
AFC Totton 2 Andover 0	158
Team Bath 2 Lymington & New Milton 3 *aet*	56
Willand Rovers 1 Corsham Town 0	105

SECOND ROUND PROPER Replays

Fleetwood Town 4 Thornaby 1	91
Holbeach United 3 Wisbech Town 0	456
St Margaretsbury 0 Withdean 1	59
Dorking 4 Sandhurst Town 1	95
Stotfold 1 Norwich United 2 *aet*	88
Milton Keynes City 1 London Colney 0	38

THIRD ROUND PROPER

Prescot Cables 6 Flixton 2	177
Rugby Town 1 Bridlington Town 2 *aet*	213
Fleetwood Town 3 Abbey Hey 1	101
Grosvenor Park 0 Billingham Town 3	76
Pickering Town 2 Causeway United 2 *aet*	107
Dunston Federation Brewery 0 Whitley Bay 2	140
Oadby Town 2 Mickleover Sports 2 *aet*	149
Clitheroe 4 Studley 1	352
Morpeth Town 3 Willenhall Town 2	75
Brigg Town 2 Rushall Olympic 1	207
Guisborough Town 0 Mossley 1	173
Northallerton Town 6 Shirebrook Town 3	182
Durham City 7 Gedling Town 3 *aet*	152
Newcastle Town 3 Harrogate Railway Athletic 1	142
AFC Sudbury 6 Hanwell Town 0	301
Buckingham Town 4 Ash United 2	162
Moneyfields 0 Gorleston 4	142
Yaxley 0 Wroxham 1	120

Dorking 0 Ware 1	136
Holbeach United 1 Burgess Hill Town 4	218
Milton Keynes City 0 Diss Town 2	80
Wootton Blue Cross 2 Thamesmead Town 1	167
Ford Sports Daventry 1 Withdean 2 *aet*	60
Maldon Town 3 Selsey 0	97
Lowestoft Town 3 Norwich United 0	204
Whitehawk 2 Arundel 5 *aet*	87
St Blazey 5 AFC Totton 1	338
Welton Rovers 0 Christchurch 5	67
Devizes Town 2 Bitton 2 *aet*	75
Willand Rovers 4 Lymington & New Milton 5	152
Bideford 3 Porthleven 2	353
Brockenhurst 0 Winchester City 7	213

THIRD ROUND PROPER Replays

Causeway United 1 Pickering Town 2 *aet*	204
Mickleover Sports 2 Oadby Town 3	101
Bitton 0 Devizes Town 2	89

FOURTH ROUND PROPER

Lymington & New Milton 2 Mossley 3	291
Newcastle Town 0 Winchester City 1	231
Northallerton Town 0 Burgess Hill Town 3	255
Wroxham 0 Prescot Cables 2	307
Ware 0 Clitheroe 1	568
Oadby Town 4 Bideford 2	435
Wootton Blue Cross 1 Whitley Bay 2 *aet*	416
Maldon Town 3 Morpeth Town 0	261
Gorleston 3 Billingham Town 1	304
Durham City 0 AFC Sudbury 4	375
Devizes Town 3 Christchurch 1	162
Bridlington Town 5 Arundel 0	360
Withdean 2 Diss Town 2 *aet*	325
Lowestoft Town 2 Buckingham Town 0	421
Brigg Town 3 Fleetwood Town 1	332
Pickering Town 2 St Blazey 3	218

FOURTH ROUND Replay

Diss Town 3 Withdean 1	452

FIFTH ROUND

Brigg Town 4 Diss Town 1	476
Whitley Bay 1 Oadby Town 2 *aet*	684
Gorleston 1 Bridlington Town 2	450
Lowestoft Town 2 Maldon Town 3 *aet*	668
St Blazey 1 AFC Sudbury 1 *aet*	944
Mossley 2 Prescot Cables 1	665
Burgess Hill Town 1 Winchester City 2	731
Clitheroe 1 Devizes Town 3 *aet*	563

FIFTH ROUND PROPER Replay

AFC Sudbury 7 St Blazey 1	725

SIXTH ROUND PROPER

Brigg Town 2 Bridlington Town 1	942
Devizes Town 0 Maldon Town 3	491
Oadby Town 1 Winchester City 0	828
Mossley 0 AFC Sudbury 2	1010

SEMI-FINALS 1st Leg

Oadby Town 0 Brigg Town 2	1060
Maldon Town 0 AFC Sudbury 1	1163

SEMI-FINALS 2nd Leg

Brigg Town 1 Oadby Town 1	1179
AFC Sudbury 2 Maldon Town 0	1407

FINAL

(10th May at West Ham United)

AFC Sudbury 1 Brigg Town 2	6634

WWW.NLNEWSDESK.CO.UK

WELSH CUP

PRELIMINARY ROUND
Caerau Ely 5 RTB Ebbw Vale 2
Caerwys 2 Rhos Aelwyd 0
Cwmamman United 2 Pontlottyn Blast Furnace 1
Glantraeth 10 Bala Town 2

FIRST ROUND
AFC Llwydcoed 1 Newport YMCA 0
AFC Rhondda 4 Porthcawl Town 1
Airbus UK 2 Ruthin Town 0
Amlwch Town 0 **Buckley Town** 3
Bettws 2 **Caerau Ely** 3
Briton Ferry Athletic 2 **Blaenrhondda** 6 *aet*
Brymbo Broughton 3 Conwy United 2
Caerwys 3 **Brickfield Rangers** 3 *aet* (5-6p)
Caldicot Town 2 Morriston Town 1
Cardiff Civil Service 2 Tredegar Town 1
Cemaes Bay 2 Llandyrnog United 1
Cwmamman United 3 Newcastle Emlyn 2 *aet*
Denbigh Town 0 **Porthmadog** 3
Ely Rangers 1 **Aberaman Athletic** 2
Garden Village 5 Merthyr Saints 3
Garw Athletic 4 Seven Sisters 3
Glantraeth 7 Corwen Amateurs 0
Goytre United 7 Milford United 1
Gresford Athletic 6 Holywell Town 0
Gwynfi United (w/o) Penrhiwceiber Rangers (scr.)
Halkyn United 3 Flint Town United 0
Holyhead Hotspurs 3 Castell Alun Colts 1
Llandudno Town 4 Mold Alexandra 0
Llanfairpwll 3 Chirk AAA 0
Llanrhaeadr 4 Llanidloes Town 1
Maesteg Park Athletic 3 Risca & Gelli United 0
Meifod (scr.) **Presteigne St Andrews** (w/o)
Neath 2 Dinas Powys 1
Penrhyncoch 4 Guilsfield 0
Pontyclun 0 **Treowen Stars** 2
Pontypridd Town 3 **Grange Harlequins** 3 *aet* (3-4p)
Porth Tywyn Suburbs 3 Caerleon 0
Prestatyn Town 1 **Lex XI** 3 *aet*
Taffs Well 4 Cardiff Corinthians 0
Troedyrhiw 4 Fields Park Pontllanfraith 2

SECOND ROUND
Aberystwyth Town 3 Welshpool Town 0
AFC Rhondda 2 AFC Llwydcoed 2 *aet* (3-2p)
Airbus UK 2 Buckley Town 0
Blaenrhondda 0 **Cwmamman United** 1
Brymbo Broughton 2 Caernarfon Town 1
Caerau Ely 3 Grange Harlequins 2
Caldicot Town 1 **Garw Athletic** 3
Cardiff Civil Service 0 **UWIC Inter Cardiff** 1
Carmarthen Town 4 Gwynfi United 1
Cemaes Bay 4 **Lex XI** 6
Connah's Quay Nomads 3 Brickfield Rangers 0
Glantraeth 4 Porthmadog 3
Goytre United 0 **Haverfordwest County** 1

Llandudno Town 3 Gresford Athletic 1
Llanelli 1 **Cwmbran Town** 4
Llanfairpwll 3 **Halkyn United** 3 *aet* (5-6p)
Llangefni Town 3 **Pontardawe Town** 5
Neath 1 Afan Lido 1 *aet* (5-4p)
Newtown 6 Llanrhaeadr 1
Oswestry Town 2 Presteigne St Andrews 1
Port Talbot Town 1 Taffs Well 0
Porth Tywyn Suburbs 3 Garden Village 0
Rhayader Town 0 **Penrhyncoch** 5
Rhyl 5 Holyhead Hotspurs 0
Treowen Stars 2 Maesteg Park Athletic 0
Troedyrhiw 0 **Aberaman Athletic** 2

THIRD ROUND
Aberaman Athletic 0 **Barry Town** 4
Aberystwyth Town 6 Lex XI 0
AFC Rhondda 0 **Pontardawe Town** 5
Bangor City 6 Halkyn United 0
Brymbo Broughton 0 **Llandudno Town** 1
Caersws 1 Total Network Solutions 0
Connah's Quay Nomads 1 Newtown 0
Cwmbran Town 3 Cwmamman United 1
Flexsys Cefn Druids 4 Airbus UK 3
Garw Athletic 1 **Haverfordwest County** 3
Glantraeth 1 **Oswestry Town** 2
Port Talbot Town 2 Neath 1
Porth Tywyn Suburbs 1 **Ton Pentre** 2
Rhyl 2 Penrhyncoch 1
Treowen Stars 0 **Carmarthen Town** 4
UWIC Inter Cardiff 3 Caerau Ely 0

FOURTH ROUND
Barry Town 4 Pontardawe Town 1
Caersws 0 **Bangor City** 3
Carmarthen Town 0 **Cwmbran Town** 1
Llandudno Town 1 **Connah's Quay Nomads** 3
Oswestry Town 2 Haverfordwest County 1
Port Talbot Town 2 **Aberystwyth Town** 3
Ton Pentre 2 Flexsys Cefn Druids 1
UWIC Inter Cardiff 0 **Rhyl** 1

QUARTER-FINALS
Aberystwyth Town 2 **Barry Town** 3
Bangor City 0 **Cwmbran Town** 0 *aet* (3-5p)
Rhyl 1 Connah's Quay Nomads 0
Ton Pentre 3 Oswestry Town 0

SEMI-FINALS
Barry Town 1 Rhyl 0 *(at Aberystwyth Town)*
Cwmbran Town 2 Ton Pentre 1 *(at Barry Town)*

FINAL
(11th May at Llanelli)
Barry Town 2 Cwmbran Town 2 *aet* (4-3p)

F A W PREMIER CUP

(Contested by Wales's three Football League clubs its top Southern League side, and the League of Wales top eight. Football League sides and League of Wales champions are exempt until Quarter-Finals)

Group A	P	W	D	L	F	A	Pts
AFAN LIDO	6	4	0	2	10	9	12
RHYL	6	3	2	1	13	8	11
Cwmbran Town	6	2	0	4	9	12	6
Caersws	6	1	2	3	8	11	5

Group B	P	W	D	L	F	A	Pts
TOTAL NET. SOL.	6	4	1	1	15	2	13
NEWPORT COUNTY	6	1	4	1	5	7	7
Bangor City	6	1	3	2	6	11	6
Connah's Quay Nomads	6	1	2	3	7	13	5

Afan Lido 2 Caersws 1
Afan Lido 1 Cwmbran Town 0
Afan Lido 1 Rhyl 3
Caersws 2 Afan Lido 3
Caersws 2 Cwmbran Town 4
Caersws 1 Rhyl 1
Cwmbran Town 1 Afan Lido 2
Cwmbran Town 0 Caersws 1
Cwmbran Town 3 Rhyl 2
Rhyl 2 Afan Lido 1
Rhyl 1 Caersws 1
Rhyl 4 Cwmbran Town 1

Bangor City 1 Newport County 1
Bangor City 2 Connah's Quay Nomads 3
Bangor City 0 Total Network Solutions 0
Connah's Quay Nomads 1 Bangor City 2
Connah's Quay Nomads 1 Newport County 1
Connah's Quay Nomads 1 Total Net. Solutions 3
Newport County 1 Bangor City 1
Newport County 1 Connah's Quay Nomads 1
Newport County 1 Total Network Solutions 0
Total Network Solutions 5 Bangor City 0
Total Net. Solutions 4 Connah's Quay Nomads 0
Total Network Solutions 3 Newport County 0

QUARTER-FINALS
Afan Lido 0 **Wrexham** 4
Newport County 3 Swansea City 1
Rhyl 1 Barry Town 1 *aet* (5-4p)
Total Network Solutions 1
Cardiff City 3

SEMI-FINALS
Newport County 0 Cardiff City 0 *aet* (4-2p)
Wrexham 4 Rhyl 0
FINAL
(8th May at Wrexham)
Wrexham 6 Newport County 1

AMENDMENTS TO THE LAWS OF THE GAME

A t its annual meeting this year, the International Football Association Board made a small number of amendments to the Laws of the Game and the decisions thereon. However, all concerned with the game are urged to ensure that they do obtain a copy of the revised "Laws of Association Football and Guide for Players and Referees, 2003/2004", containing full details.

In accordance with earlier practice, the contents of the relevant FIFA Circular (No 847, issued 12 May 2003), with the amendments, are reproduced herein (and courtesy of the Football Association).

All amendments and decisions **must be enforced from 1 July 2003.**

Players are reminded again that they should ensure that they do not wear anything which is dangerous to themselves or other players (including any kind of jewellery).

Players and referees are reminded that **racist remarks** constitute **a dismissal offence** in accord with Law 12 (the use of offensive, insulting or abusive language) and **must** be punished accordingly.

Players, managers, coaches, referees and administrators **all** have a responsibility to ensure that the image of the national game is not tarnished either by the use, or the acceptance, of offensive language likely to incite, insult or provoke others.

Finally, a reminder is given that it is a decision of the Council of The Football Association that instructions regarding the Laws of the Game will be given only by The Football Association. **No other Association or League is permitted to do so.**

May 2003

Nic Coward
Joint Acting Chief Executive

To the national associations of FIFA

Circular no. 847

Zurich, 12 May 2003
GS/hus/mjo

Amendments to the 2003 Laws of the Game

The 117th Annual Meeting of the International Football Association Board took place in Belfast, Northern Ireland on 15th March 2003. The amendments to the Laws of the Game and various instructions and directives are listed below.

AMENDMENTS TO THE LAWS OF THE GAME AND DECISIONS OF THE BOARD

LAW 4 – THE PLAYERS' EQUIPMENT

Decision of the International F.A. Board

Decision 1

Players must not reveal undershirts, which contain slogans or advertising.
A player removing his jersey to reveal slogans or advertising will be sanctioned by the competition organisers.

Jerseys must have sleeves.

The Board agreed to remove the bullet point which permitted advertising only on players' jerseys.

The Fourth Official

New text

Bullet point 1

The fourth official may be appointed under the competition rules and officiates if any of the three match officials is unable to continue. **He assists the referee at all times.**

Bullet point 7

He must indicate to the referee when the wrong player is cautioned because of mistaken identity or when a player is not sent off having been seen to be given a second caution or when violent conduct occurs out of the view of the referee and assistant referees. The referee, however, retains the authority to decide on all points connected with play.

Reason:
By stating in bullet point 7 that "the fourth official assists the referee at all times", there is an inference that this could be in respect of matters of misconduct, the topic of the remainder of the paragraph. It is not expected or desired that the fourth official should be extending his role to include reporting cautionable offences and therefore for reasons of clarity and interpretation it is more appropriate to have the phrase in bullet point 1.

Procedures to determine the winner of a match – Kicks from the Penalty Mark

New text

The referee tosses a coin and the team whose captain wins the toss decides whether to take the first **or the second kick.**

Reason:
To give the team which wins the toss a fair choice and not to insist that they take the first kick, which can be perceived as an advantage to the team which loses the toss.

Additional instructions for Referees, Assistant Referees and Fourth Officials

New text

The Penalty Kick

It is an infringement to enter the penalty area before the kick has been taken. The goalkeeper also infringes the Laws if he moves from his goal-line before the ball has been kicked. Referees must ensure that when players infringe this Law appropriate action is taken.

Reason:
Law 14 was amended in 1997, taking away the necessity for referees to caution when player(s) entered the penalty area prior to a penalty kick being taken. The amendment also allowed the goalkeeper to move along his goal-line. Nowadays, infringements often occur at a penalty kick, yet the referee seldom takes action.

INFORMATION, INSTRUCTIONS AND DIRECTIVES

Rules of the International Football Association Board

The Board shall meet bi-annually. The Annual General Meeting shall take place in the month of **February or March, as agreed.** The Annual Business Meeting shall take place in the month of September or October, as agreed.

TEMPORARY EXPULSIONS

The Board re-affirmed the decision taken at its last meeting that the temporary expulsion of players is not permitted at any level of football.

ARTIFICIAL SURFACES

The Board recognised the advances in artificial surface technology and the major benefits of using artificial surfaces in areas with climactic problems. It also recognised that artificial surfaces allowed multiple and extended use of facilities in urban environments. The Board mandated FIFA to create clear procedures for the use of artificial surfaces, to unify the quality system and apply it worldwide, taking into consideration the best resources and knowledge available.

The amendments to the Laws of the Game take effect as from 1st July 2003 and instructions and directives from the Board are introduced with immediate effect.

LEAGUE SPONSORS

	2002-03	2003-04
Anglian Combination	Lovewell Blake	Lovewell Blake
Cambridgeshire League	Kershaw/Beaumont	Kershaw/Beaumont
Central Midlands League	Redferns International Removers	Samsan International
Combined County League	Seagrave Haulage	Seagrave Haulage
Cornwall Combination	Jolly's	Jolly's
Cymru Alliance	Huws Gray Fitlock	Huws Gray Fitlock
Devon County League	Firewatch	Firewatch
Devon & Exeter League	Jackson Vending	Jackson Vending
Dorset Premier League	Elite Teamwear	Elite Teamwear
East Cornwall Premier League	Cornish Guardian	Cornish Guardian
Eastern Counties League	Jewson	Ridgeons
Essex & Suffolk Border League	Kent Blaxill	Kent Blaxill
Essex Intermediate League	Carling	Greene King IPA
Essex Senior League	Foresters	Eastway Construction
Football Conference	Nationwide	Nationwide
Gwent County League	County Motors	County Motors
Hellenic League	Cherry Red Records	Cherry Red Records
Herts Senior County League	World Class Homes	World Class Homes
Humber Premier League		Carling
Isthmian League	Ryman	Ryman
Kent County League	British Energy	British Energy
Kent League	Go Travel	Go Travel
Leicestershire Senior League	Everards Brewery	Everards Brewery
Liverpool County Combination	Frank Armitt	Frank Armitt
Manchester League	Air Miles	Air Miles
Mid-Cheshire League	Coors/WPRC	Coors/WPRC
Midland Combination	ICIS	ICIS
Midland League	Springbank Vending	Springbank Vending
Northants Combination	Travis Perkins	Travis Perkins
Northern Alliance	Wade Associates	Wade Associates
Northern League	Albany	Albany
Northern Premier League	Unibond	Unibond
Reading League	A Quote Insurance	Opus
South Wales Amateur League	Regal Travel	Regal Travel
South Wales Senior League	Thomas, Carroll	Thomas, Carroll
South Western League	Carlsberg	Carlsberg
Southern League	Dr Martens	Dr Martens
Spartan South Midlands League	Minerva	Minerva
Sussex County League	Matthew Clark	Matthew Clark
United Counties League	Eagle Bitter	Eagle Bitter
Welsh Alliance	Tyn Lon Volvo	Pentraeth Honda
Welsh Premier League	J T Hughes Mitsubishi	J T Hughes Mitsubishi
Wessex League	Jewson	Jewson
West Cheshire League	Carlsberg	Carlsberg
West Lancs League	ASDA Logic	ASDA Logic
West Midlands (Regional) League	Express & Star	Essex & Star
West Riding County Amateur League	Mumtaz	Mumtaz
Western League	Screwfix Direct	Screwfix Direct
Wiltshire League	Skurrays	Skurrays

MAJOR COUNTY CUPS

BEDFORDSHIRE SENIOR CUP
FIRST ROUND
Barton Rovers 1 **Dunstable Town** 2
Biggleswade United 0 **Stotfold** 2
Kempston Rovers 0 **Wootton Blue Cross** 1
Leighton Town 1 **Biggleswade Town** 3 *aet*
QUARTER-FINALS
Bedford United & Valerio 0 **Dunstable Town** 4
Biggleswade Town 1 **Arlesey Town** 2
Stotfold 0 **Bedford Town** 3
Wootton Blue Cross 0 **Luton Town** 0 *aet* (3-4p)
SEMI-FINALS
Arlesey Town 0 **Dunstable Town** 1
Bedford Town (w/o) Luton Town (scr.)
FINAL
(6th May at Arlesey Town)
Dunstable Town 1 Bedford Town 0

BERKS & BUCKS SENIOR CUP
SECOND ROUND
Aylesbury United 4 Wokingham Town 0
Burnham 3 Hungerford Town 1
Slough Town 1 Wycombe Wanderers 0
Windsor & Eton 3 Abingdon Town 1
QUARTER-FINALS
Burnham 1 Chesham United 1
Chesham United 2 **Burnham** 2 *replay aet* (3-4p)
Flackwell Heath 2 Aylesbury United 2
Aylesbury United 4 Flackwell Heath 0 *replay*
Maidenhead United 3 Slough Town 1
Windsor & Eton 1 Marlow 0
SEMI-FINALS
Aylesbury United 5 Burnham 0
Windsor & Eton 0 **Maidenhead United** 5
FINAL
(5th May at Chesham United)
Aylesbury United 1 **Maidenhead United** 4

BIRMINGHAM SENIOR CUP
FIRST ROUND
Atherstone United 1 **Bromsgrove Rovers** 3
Racing Club Warwick 4 **Willenhall Town** 4 *aet* (3-4p)
Stratford Town 2 **Rushall Olympic** 3
SECOND ROUND
Banbury United 4 Causeway United 2
Bedworth United 4 Cradley Town 0
Boldmere St Michaels 2 Stourbridge 2 *aet*
Stourbridge 4 Boldmere St Michaels 0 *replay*
Bromsgrove Rovers 0 **Moor Green** 3
Burton Albion 2 Redditch United 1
Grosvenor Park 2 **Tamworth** 5
Halesowen Town 3 Studley 0
Hednesford Town 7 Rugby United 2
Rushall Olympic 1 **Nuneaton Borough** 5
Solihull Borough 2 Halesowen Harriers 0
Sutton Coldfield Town 1 Willenhall Town 0
Wednesfield 2 **Oldbury United** 6
THIRD ROUND
Banbury United 2 Stourbridge 1
Halesowen Town 1 **Birmingham City** 3
Hednesford Town 0 Oldbury United 3
(ineligible player – Oldbury expelled)
Moor Green 2 Sutton Coldfield Town 1
Nuneaton Borough 6 Bedworth United 0
Solihull Borough 0 **Walsall** 4
Tamworth 1 West Bromwich Albion 1 *aet* (4-3p)
Wolverhampton Wanderers 5 Burton Albion 0
QUARTER-FINALS
Banbury United 2 **Birmingham City** 4
Hednesford Town 1 **Wolverhampton Wanderers** 3
Moor Green 1 Tamworth 3
(ineligible player – Tamworth expelled)
Nuneaton Borough 0 **Walsall** 5
SEMI-FINALS
Moor Green 2 Wolverhampton Wanderers 1
Walsall 0 **Birmingham City** 2
FINAL *(28th April at Solihull Borough)*
Birmingham City 2 Moor Green 0 *aet*

CAMBRIDGESHIRE INVITATION CUP
PRELIMINARY ROUND
Histon 8 Whittlesey United 0
March Town United 0 **Sawston United** 2
Newmarket Town 3 Mildenhall Town 1
QUARTER-FINALS
Cambridge City 5 Fordham 0
Newmarket Town 7 Ely City 1
Soham Town Rangers 1 **Histon** 5 *aet*
Wisbech Town 0 **Sawston United** 1
SEMI-FINALS
Newmarket Town 0 **Histon** 1
Sawston United 0 **Cambridge City** 2
FINAL
(14th April at Cambridge United)
Cambridge City 2 Histon 2 *aet* (8-7p)

CHESHIRE SENIOR CUP
PRELIMINARY ROUND
Hyde United 1 **Northwich Victoria** 3
Witton Albion 5 Congleton Town 4 *aet*
FIRST ROUND
Cheadle Town 1 **Chester City** 4
Crewe Alexandra 3 Altrincham 2
Nantwich Town 1 Stockport County 1 *aet*
Stockport County 2 Nantwich Town 1 *replay*
Northwich Victoria 3 Stalybridge Celtic 1
Tranmere Rovers 1 Macclesfield Town 0
Vauxhall Motors 3 Witton Albion 2
Winsford United 2 Warrington Town 1
Woodley Sports 5 Alsager Town 5 *aet*
Alsager Town 2 **Woodley Sports** 3
QUARTER-FINALS
Crewe Alexandra 2 **Vauxhall Motors** 1
Stockport County 1 Chester City 3 *aet*
(ineligible player – Chester expelled)
Tranmere Rovers 7 Woodley Sports 1
Winsford United 0 **Northwich Victoria** 3
SEMI-FINALS
Crewe Alexandra 5 Tranmere Rovers 2
Stockport County 1 **Northwich Victoria** 2
FINAL
(25th March at Altrincham)
Northwich Victoria 1 **Crewe Alexandra** 2

CORNWALL SENIOR CUP
FIRST ROUND
Dobwalls 4 Bude 2
Goonhavern 3 Illogan RBL 1
Hayle 6 Camelford 3
Marazion Blues 1 **Mousehole** 2
Nanpean Rovers 2 **Padstow United** 2
Padstow United 1 **Nanpean Rovers** 4 *replay*
Perranwell 1 **St Just** 2
St Agnes 2 St Dennis 1
St Ives Town 2 RNAS Culdrose 0
Sticker 1 **St Cleer** 8
SECOND ROUND
Bodmin Town 3 Helston Athletic 1
Callington Town 3 Nanpean Rovers 1
Falmouth Town 7 Mousehole 0
Foxhole Stars 4 Saltash United 1
Goonhavern 1 **Penryn Athletic** 2
Hayle 7 Ludgvan 1
Liskeard Athletic 3 St Austell 0
Millbrook 3 Dobwalls 2
Mullion 1 **Launceston** 3
Penzance 4 Wendron CC United 0
St Agnes 2 St Cleer 2
St Cleer 2 **St Agnes** 3 *replay aet*
St Blazey 8 Roche 1
St Ives Town 2 **Newquay** 4
Torpoint Athletic 5 Probus 1
Truro City 0 **Porthleven** 7
Wadebridge Town 3 St Just 2
THIRD ROUND
Bodmin Town 1 Hayle 0
Callington Town 1 **Penzance** 2

Falmouth Town 1 Millbrook 1
Millbrook 2 Falmouth Town 1 *replay*
Launceston 2 Foxhole Stars 2
Foxhole Stars 0 **Launceston** 2 *replay*
Newquay 1 **Torpoint Athletic** 2
Penryn Athletic 1 **Wadebridge Town** 3
Porthleven 2 **St Blazey** 4
St Agnes 0 **Liskeard Athletic** 7
QUARTER-FINALS
Launceston 0 **Liskeard Athletic** 3
Millbrook 2 Penzance 1
St Blazey 3 Bodmin Town 0
Torpoint Athletic 2 Wadebridge Town 2
Wadebridge Town 1 **Torpoint Athletic** 1 *replay aet* (7-8p)
SEMI-FINALS
Millbrook 0 **St Blazey** 3 *(at Wadebridge Town)*
Torpoint Athletic 2 **Liskeard Athletic** 3 *aet (at Saltash United)*
FINAL
(21st April at Penzance)
St Blazey 1 Liskeard Athletic 1
FINAL REPLAY
(30th April at Millbrook)
St Blazey 1 **Liskeard Athletic** 1 *aet* (2-4p)

CORNWALL CHARITY CUP
FIRST ROUND
Bodmin Town 0 **Callington Town** 3
Falmouth Town 6 Liskeard Athletic 3
Launceston 2 **Wadebridge Town** 3
Penryn Athletic 1 **St Austell** 2
Penzance 2 Saltash United 0
Porthleven 0 **St Blazey** 2
Torpoint Athletic 4 Newquay 2
Truro City 2 Millbrook 0
QUARTER-FINALS
Falmouth Town 3 Callington Town 1
St Blazey 5 Penzance 1
Torpoint Athletic 4 Wadebridge Town 2 *aet*
Truro City 3 St Austell 0
SEMI-FINALS
Falmouth Town 6 Torpoint Athletic 0 *(at St Blazey)*
St Blazey 1 **Truro City** 2 *(at Falmouth Town)*
FINAL *(15th May at Porthleven)*
Truro City 0 **Falmouth Town** 1

CUMBERLAND CUP
FINAL
(5th May at Carlisle United)
Northbank Carlisle 4 Carlisle United 0

DERBYSHIRE SENIOR CUP
FIRST ROUND
South Normanton Athletic 3 Graham Street Prims 2
Stapenhill 1 **Ripley Town** 5
SECOND ROUND
Heanor Town 2 **South Normanton Athletic** 2 *aet* (5-6p)
Holbrook 1 **Blackwell Miners Welfare** 2
New Mills 3 **Ripley Town** 5
THIRD ROUND
Alfreton Town 3 Ripley Town 0
Belper Town 1 Glapwell 1 *aet* (5-4p)
Glossop North End 2 Blackwell Miners Welfare 1
Gresley Rovers 4 Buxton 0
Long Eaton United 2 **Ilkeston Town** 3
Matlock Town 5 Shirebrook Town 3
Mickleover Sports 3 Borrowash Victoria 0
Staveley Miners Welfare 1 **South Normanton Athletic** 2
QUARTER-FINALS
Alfreton Town 3 Glossop North End 0
Belper Town 4 Matlock Town 0
Ilkeston Town 0 **Mickleover Sports** 2
South Normanton Athletic 2 **Gresley Rovers** 3
SEMI-FINALS
Belper Town 0 **Alfreton Town** 1
Gresley Rovers 0 **Mickleover Sports** 4
FINAL
1st leg *(15th April):* Mickleover Sports 0 Alfreton Town 5
2nd leg *(29th April):* **Alfreton Town** 2 Mickleover Sports 1

DEVON St LUKES COLLEGE BOWL
FIRST ROUND
Barnstaple Town 2 **Plymouth Argyle** 5
Bideford (w/o) Exeter City (scr.)
Clyst Rovers 2 Torrington 1
Elmore 1 **Torquay United** 4
Exmouth Town 3 **Tiverton Town** 3 *aet* (1-2p)
QUARTER-FINALS
Clyst Rovers 1 **Bideford** 4
Ilfracombe Town 0 **Torquay United** 1
Tiverton Town 3 Plymouth Argyle 2
Willand Rovers 2 Dawlish Town 0
SEMI-FINALS
Tiverton Town 2 Bideford 0
Willand Rovers 0 **Torquay United** 2
FINAL
(30th July at Torquay United)
Torquay United v Tiverton Town

DORSET SENIOR CUP
Barwick & Stoford 0 **Allendale** 3
Chickerell United 1 **Shaftesbury** 3
Cobham Sports 2 Sherborne Town 1
Cranborne 3 Stourpaine 1
Crossways 1 Marina Sports 2
(ineligible player – Marina Sports expelled)
Dorchester Sports 1 **Trinidad New Star** 2
Dorchester United 3 Witchampton United 0
Okeford United 3 **Piddletrenthide United** 6
Royal Oak Cougars 0 **Poole Town** 1
St Marys 0 **Bournemouth Sports** 6
St Pauls (Jersey) 2 **Gillingham Town** 3
Sturminster Marshall 2 **Moreton** 3
Sturminster Newton Utd 3 Weymouth United 2 *aet*
Verwood Town 4 Weymouth Sports 0
Wareham Rangers 4 Poole Borough 3
West Moors 3 **Holt United** 6 *aet*
Weymouth Post Office 0 **Dorset Knob** 1
SECOND ROUND
Blandford United 2 **Gillingham Town** 5
Cobham Sports 2 Shaftesbury 1
Cranborne 0 Verwood Town 0 *aet*
Verwood Town 1 **Cranborne** 3 *replay*
Crossways 2 **Bournemouth Sports** 4 *aet*
Dorset Knob 3 **Dorchester United** 4 *aet*
Hamworthy United 5 Moreton 1
Holt United 3 Hamworthy Recreation 1
Piddletrenthide United 1 **Allendale** 3
Poole Town (w/o) Sturminster Newton Utd (scr.)
Wareham Rangers 3 Trinidad New Star 2
THIRD ROUND
Allendale 2 **Wimborne Town** 5
Bournemouth Sports 1 **Cranborne** 2
Cobham Sports 1 **Portland United** 5
Dorchester United 2 **Swanage Town & Herston** 4 *aet*
Gillingham Town 0 **Bridport** 1
Hamworthy United 2 Holt United 0
Poole Town 0 **Dorchester Town** 2
Weymouth 4 Wareham Rangers 2
QUARTER-FINALS
Bridport 8 Swanage Town & Herston 0
Dorchester Town 7 Hamworthy United 0
Portland United 2 Wimborne Town 1 *aet*
Weymouth 3 Cranborne 0
SEMI-FINALS
Portland United 0 **Dorchester Town** 2
Weymouth 2 Bridport 1
FINAL
(15th April at Dorchester Town)
Dorchester Town 2 Weymouth 0

DURHAM CHALLENGE CUP
PRELIMINARY ROUND
Annfield Plain 2 **Murton** 3
Barnard Castle Glaxo 0 **Birtley Town** 2
Billingham Synthonia 3 Shildon 2 *aet*
Boldon Community Association 3 Kennek Ryhope CA 1

Consett 2 South Shields Harton & Westoe 0
Esh Winning 7 Darlington Railway Athletic 0
Ryhope Colliery Welfare 3 Jarrow 1
Ryton 2 **Wolviston** 3
Seaham Red Star 0 **Durham City** 4
South Shields Cleadon SC 1 **Tow Law Town** 5
Spennymoor United 6 Norton & Stockton Ancients 4
Stanley United 1 **Eppleton Colliery Welfare** 4
Washington 4 Shotton Comrades 1
West Auckland Town 0 **Sunderland Res.** 1
Whickham 2 Washington Nissan 1
FIRST ROUND
Bishop Auckland 1 Evenwood Town 0
Dunston Federation Brewery 2 Billingham Town 1
Eppleton Colliery Welfare 0 **Boldon Community Association** 1
Esh Winning 1 **Billingham Synthonia** 1 *aet* (6-7p)
Gateshead 4 Consett 1
Hartlepool United Res. 0 **Birtley Town** 2 *(at Seaham Red Star)*
Horden Colliery Welfare 5 Crook Town 1
Jarrow Roofing Boldon CA 6 Easington Colliery 1
Murton 5 Chester-le-Street Town 4
Peterlee Newtown 2 **Tow Law Town** 4
Spennymoor United 3 Durham City 2
Sunderland Res. 5 Brandon United 2 *(at Durham City)*
Washington 3 Darlington Res. 2
Whickham 2 South Shields 1
Willington 5 Ryhope Colliery Welfare 0
Wolviston 5 Birtley 1
SECOND ROUND
Birtley Town 1 Bishop Auckland 0
Boldon Community Association 0 **Billingham Synthonia** 1
Jarrow Roofing Boldon CA 1 **Dunston Federation Brewery** 3
Murton 2 Tow Law Town 0
Sunderland Res. 1 **Spennymoor United** 2
Washington 1 **Gateshead** 3
Willington 0 **Horden Colliery Welfare** 5
Wolviston 3 Whickham 1
QUARTER-FINALS
Billingham Synthonia 4 Gateshead 4 *aet* (6-5p)
Birtley Town 4 Wolviston 1
Dunston Federation Brewery 3 Spennymoor United 0
Horden Colliery Welfare 5 Murton 0
SEMI-FINALS
Billingham Synthonia 1 Dunston Federation Brewery 0
Horden Colliery Welfare 2 Birtley Town 0
FINAL *(21st April at Durham City)*
Billingham Synthonia 0 **Horden Colliery Welfare** 1

EAST RIDING SENIOR CUP
FINAL
(24th April at Boothferry Park)
North Ferriby United 3 Bridlington Town 1

ESSEX SENIOR CUP
FIRST ROUND
Barkingside 0 Woodford Town 0 *aet* (4-3p)
Bowers United 3 Romford 2 *aet*
Concord Rangers 2 Burnham Ramblers 1
Hullbridge Sports 0 **Brentwood** 2
Southend Manor 3 Stansted 1
Waltham Abbey 4 Saffron Walden Town 1
SECOND ROUND
Concord Rangers 2 **Barkingside** 5 *aet*
Ilford 3 Brentwood 0
Southend Manor 3 Bowers United 2 *aet*
Waltham Abbey 3 Basildon United 2
THIRD ROUND
Barking & East Ham United 1 **Maldon Town** 4
Barkingside 0 **Waltham Abbey** 2
Billericay Town 5 Wivenhoe Town 0
East Thurrock United 2 Purfleet 1
Ford United 2 Tilbury 1
Grays Athletic 2 **Dagenham & Redbridge** 4 *aet*
Great Wakering Rovers 1 **Southend United** 2
Halstead Town 0 **Chelmsford City** 5
Harwich & Parkeston 1 **Harlow Town** 4
Heybridge Swifts 5 Clapton 2
Hornchurch 3 Southend Manor 1
Ilford 2 **Aveley** 3
Leyton Pennant 1 **Clacton Town** 2
Tiptree United 4 Stanway Rovers 0

Witham Town 3 Braintree Town 2
FOURTH ROUND
Billericay Town 1 Harlow Town 0
Canvey Island 1 **Chelmsford City** 4
Clacton Town 0 **East Thurrock United** 1
Ford United 1 **Aveley** 3
Heybridge Swifts 4 Witham Town 2
Hornchurch 1 **Southend United** 2
Maldon Town 1 **Dagenham & Redbridge** 2
Tiptree United 4 Waltham Abbey 1
QUARTER-FINALS
Dagenham & Redbridge 1 **Southend United** 4
East Thurrock United 0 **Billericay Town** 1
Heybridge Swifts 0 **Chelmsford City** 2
Tiptree United 1 **Aveley** 6
SEMI-FINALS
Aveley 1 Billericay Town 1 *aet* (3-1p)
Chelmsford City 2 Southend United 0
FINAL
(24th March at Southend United)
Chelmsford City 5 Aveley 0

GLOUCESTERSHIRE SENIOR CUP
2001-02 FINAL
(3rd September at Cirencester Town)
Cirencester Town 0 **Bristol City** 6
FIRST ROUND
Bristol Rovers 3 Cinderford Town 2
Forest Green Rovers 1 **Cheltenham Town** 5
Gloucester City 1 **Bristol City** 2
Mangotsfield United 2 Cirencester Town 0
SEMI-FINALS
Bristol City 6 Cheltenham Town 0
Mangotsfield United 1 Bristol Rovers 0
FINAL
(28th April at Mangotsfield United)
Mangotsfield United 1 Bristol City 0

GLOUCESTERSHIRE TROPHY
PRELIMINARY ROUND
Cadbury Heath 1 **Shortwood United** 3
DRG Stapleton 0 **Hallen** 2
Taverners 1 Whitminster 1 *aet* (6-5p)
Tuffley Rovers 1 **Wotton Rovers** 1 *aet* (9-10p)
FIRST ROUND
Almondsbury 4 Totterdown Port of Bristol 2 *aet*
Almondsbury Town 3 **Tytherington Rocks** 4
Bitton 4 AXA 0
Cheltenham Saracens 1 Old Georgians 1 *aet* (4-2p)
Ellwood 1 **Mangotsfield United Res.** 1 *aet* (2-4p)
Hallen 2 **Yate Town** 3
Harrow Hill 3 Gloucester United 2
Henbury Old Boys 4 Hardwicke 1
Highridge United 0 **Fairford Town** 1
Patchway Town (w/o) Cirencester Academy (scr.)
Pucklechurch 0 **Thornbury Town** 2
Slimbridge 3 Bristol Manor Farm 1 *aet*
Taverners 2 **Shortwood United** 3
Viney St Swithins 0 **Roman Glass St George** 1
Winterbourne United (w/o) Cirencester United (scr.)
Wotton Rovers 0 **Bishops Cleeve** 2
SECOND ROUND
Almondsbury 3 Shortwood United 1
Bitton 3 Mangotsfield United Res. 1
Cheltenham Saracens 0 **Henbury Old Boys** 6
Fairford Town 2 Bishops Cleeve 1
Roman Glass St George 4 Thornbury Town 3
Slimbridge 1 **Patchway Town** 4
Winterbourne United 1 **Harrow Hill** 2
Yate Town 1 Tytherington Rocks 0
QUARTER-FINALS
Harrow Hill 1 Almondsbury 0
Patchway Town 2 **Bitton** 3
Roman Glass St George 1 **Fairford Town** 2
Yate Town 2 Henbury Old Boys 1
SEMI-FINALS
Bitton 1 **Fairford Town** 3 *aet*
Yate Town 5 Harrow Hill 1
FINAL
(6th May at Oaklands Park)
Yate Town 0 **Fairford Town** 2

HAMPSHIRE SENIOR CUP
FIRST ROUND
Andover 8 RS Basingstoke 0
Andover New Street 4 **Christchurch** 5
BAT Sports 6 Hartley Wintney 2 *aet*
Blackfield & Langley 0 **Bournemouth** 1
Brockenhurst 1 Bishops Waltham Town 0
Cowes Sports 4 Portsmouth Royal Navy 2
Hamble ASSC 2 Fareham Town 1
Vosper Thornycroft 3 Lymington & New Milton 2
SECOND ROUND
AFC Totton 4 **Lymington Town** 5
Aldershot Town 2 Farnborough Town 1
Alton Town 16 Brading Town 2
Bashley 3 Vosper Thornycroft 2
Bournemouth 2 East Cowes Victoria Athletic 1
Brockenhurst 2 **Andover** 6
Cove 0 **Christchurch** 4
Cowes Sports 0 **Basingstoke Town** 2
Eastleigh 3 Newport IOW 0
Fleet Town (w/o) AFC Bournemouth (scr.)
Hamble ASSC 0 **Gosport Borough** 3
Havant & Waterlooville 6 Whitchurch United 0
Moneyfields 1 Hythe & Dibden 0
Pirelli General 1 **BAT Sports** 4
St Peters Jersey 0 **Winchester City** 7
Stockbridge 1 **Ringwood Town** 6
THIRD ROUND
Aldershot Town 3 Bournemouth 2
Andover 3 Alton Town 0
Basingstoke Town 7 Ringwood Town 1
Christchurch 3 BAT Sports 1
Eastleigh 5 Moneyfields 0
Fleet Town 1 **Bashley** 2
Lymington Town 1 **Havant & Waterlooville** 4
Winchester City 3 Gosport Borough 2
QUARTER-FINALS
Aldershot Town 2 Eastleigh 1
Andover 4 Basingstoke Town 2
Bashley 2 Winchester City 1 *aet*
Christchurch 0 **Havant & Waterlooville** 4
SEMI-FINALS
(played over two legs)
Aldershot Town 2 Andover 0,
Andover 2 **Aldershot Town** 2
Bashley 2 Havant & Waterlooville 0,
Havant & Waterlooville 1 **Bashley** 2
FINAL
(8th May at Southampton)
Bashley 1 **Aldershot Town** 2

HAMPSHIRE RUSSELL COTES CUP
FIRST ROUND
Blackfield Langley 0 **East Cowes Victoria Athletic** 3
Brockenhurst 3 **Bashley** 4.
Hamble ASSC 4 Ringwood Town 1
Hartley Wintney 0 **BAT Sports** 2
Havant & Waterlooville 3 Pirelli General 1
Lymington Town 1 **Winchester City** 3
Petersfield Town 3 **RS Basingstoke** 4
SECOND ROUND
Andover 2 Bashley 0
Bournemouth 0 **Fleet Town** 1
Christchurch 4 **Moneyfields** 5
East Cowes Victoria Athletic 2 **BAT Sports** 4
Eastleigh 6 RS Basingstoke 1
Hamble ASSC 1 **Gosport Borough** 3
Lymington & New Milton 0 **Winchester City** 1
Wimborne Town 5 Havant & Waterlooville 1
QUARTER-FINALS
Fleet Town 1 BAT Sports 0
Gosport Borough 3 Eastleigh 1
Moneyfields 2 **Andover** 3
Wimborne Town 1 **Winchester City** 2
SEMI-FINALS
Fleet Town 3 Andover 2
Gosport Borough 1 Winchester City 1 *aet* (4-2p)
FINAL
(29th April at Gosport Borough)
Gosport Borough 1 **Fleet Town** 4 *aet*

HEREFORDSHIRE CHALLENGE CUP
FINAL
(21st April at Hereford United)
Westfields 2 Kington Town 0

HERTFORDSHIRE SENIOR CUP
FIRST ROUND
Berkhamsted Town (w/o) Letchworth (scr.)
Greenacres (Hemel) 3 St Margaretsbury 2
Hemel Hempstead Town 2 **Sawbridgeworth Town** 2 *aet* (3-4p)
Hoddesdon Town 1 **Hertford Town** 4
Royston Town 1 **Broxbourne Borough V & E** 2
St Albans City 6 Ware 0
SECOND ROUND
Broxbourne Borough V & E 0 Boreham Wood 0 *aet* (5-3p)
Cheshunt 1 Bishop's Stortford 0
Greenacres (Hemel) 0 **St Albans City** 1
Hertford Town 1 **Berkhamsted Town** 4
London Colney 0 **Hitchin Town** 2
Potters Bar Town 2 Barnet 0
Stevenage Borough 7 Sawbridgeworth Town 0
Tring Town 0 **Watford** 1
QUARTER-FINALS
Berkhamsted Town 3 St Albans City 2
Broxbourne Borough V & E 2 **Stevenage Borough** 4
Cheshunt 2 Potters Bar Town 0
Hitchin Town 2 Watford 1 *aet*
SEMI-FINALS
Cheshunt 4 Stevenage Borough 2
Berkhamsted Town 4 Hitchin Town 2
FINAL
(15th April at Hemel Hempstead Town)
Cheshunt 0 **Berkhamsted Town** 2

HERTFORDSHIRE CHARITY CUP
FIRST ROUND
Bishop's Stortford 3 Hitchin Town 0
Cheshunt 1 **Boreham Wood** 2
QUARTER-FINALS
Berkhamsted Town 1 **Tring Town** 2
Boreham Wood 1 **Bishop's Stortford** 2
Hertford Town 2 **Hemel Hempstead Town** 4
Ware 0 **St Albans City** 4
SEMI-FINALS
Hemel Hempstead Town 3 St Albans City 0
Tring Town 1 **Bishop's Stortford** 9
FINAL
(29th April at Hemel Hempstead Town)
Hemel Hempstead Town 1 **Bishop's Stortford** 3

HERTFORDSHIRE SENIOR TROPHY
FIRST ROUND
Bovingdon 4 Bushey Rangers 1
Chipperfield Corinthians 6 Metropolitan Police Bushey 0
Hadley 0 **Kings Langley** 3
Leverstock Green 1 **Harpenden Town** 2
St Peters 2 **London Lions** 3
Tring Athletic 11 Croxley Guild 0
SECOND ROUND
Bovingdon 3 Elliott Star 1 *aet*
Colney Heath 5 Cuffley 1
Harpenden Town 1 **Chipperfield Corinthians** 3
Sandridge Rovers 1 **Oxhey Jets** 4
Sun Postal Sports 3 London Lions 0
Tring Athletic 3 Bedmond Sports & Social 0
Welwyn Garden City 2 Old Parmiterians 0
Wormley Rovers 7 Kings Langley 4 *aet*
QUARTER-FINALS
Chipperfield Corinthians 1 Welwyn Garden City 0
Colney Heath 4 Bovingdon 2 *aet*
Tring Athletic 2 Sun Postal Sports 1
Wormley Rovers 1 Oxhey Jets 0
SEMI-FINALS
Colney Heath 9 Chipperfield Corinthians 0
Tring Athletic 4 Wormley Rovers 1
FINAL
(8th April at Letchworth)
Tring Athletic 1 Colney Heath 0

HERTFORDSHIRE CHARITY SHIELD
FIRST ROUND
Broxbourne Borough V & E 6 Kings Langley 0
Greenacres (Hemel) 2 **London Colney** 3 *aet*
Leverstock Green 5 Colney Heath 0
Oxhey Jets 1 **Tring Athletic** 3
Potters Bar Town 6 Letchworth 2
Royston Town (w/o) Sun Postal Sports (scr.)
St Margaretsbury 0 **Sawbridgeworth Town** 1
Welwyn Garden City 2 Hoddesdon Town 2 *aet* (5-4p)
QUARTER-FINALS
London Colney 3 Royston Town 3 *aet* (4-1p)
Potters Bar Town 2 Tring Athletic 1
Sawbridgeworth Town 3 Leverstock Green 0
Welwyn Garden City 0 Broxbourne Borough
V & E 0 *aet* (4-2p)
SEMI-FINALS
London Colney 2 **Potters Bar Town** 3
Welwyn Garden City 2 **Sawbridgeworth Town** 2 *aet* (2-3p)
FINAL
(22nd April at Letchworth)
Potters Bar Town 1 Sawbridgeworth Town 1 *aet* (4-3p)

HUNTINGDONSHIRE SENIOR CUP
FINAL
(5th May at Warboys Town)
Hotpoint 3 St Neots Town 3 *aet* (5-4p)

KENT SENIOR CUP
FIRST ROUND
Ashford Town 0 **Erith & Belvedere** 2
Chatham Town 4 Fisher Athletic 0
Dover Athletic 2 **Sittingbourne** 3
Folkestone Invicta 1 Dartford 0 *aet*
Tonbridge Angels 0 **Bromley** 3
Welling United 1 Thamesmead Town 1 *aet* (3-1p)
QUARTER-FINALS
Chatham Town 3 **Bromley** 4
Folkestone Invicta 1 **Welling United** 6
Gravesend & Northfleet 2 **Erith & Belvedere** 3
Margate 3 Sittingbourne 1
SEMI-FINALS
Margate 3 Erith & Belvedere 0 *aet*
Welling United 2 Bromley 0
FINAL
(30th April at Welling United)
Welling United 1 **Margate** 2 *aet*

KENT SENIOR TROPHY
FIRST ROUND
Bearsted 2 **Lordswood** 4
Cray Wanderers 3 Slade Green 2 *aet*
Erith Town 2 Faversham Town 0
Greenwich Borough 1 Stansfeld O & B Club 1 *aet*
Stansfeld O & B Club 0 **Greenwich Borough** 2 *replay*
West Wickham 2 Milton Athletic 2 *aet*
Milton Athletic 1 **West Wickham** 2 *replay aet*
SECOND ROUND
Beckenham Town 2 **Ramsgate** 2 *aet* (0-2p)
(no replay due to numerous postponements)
Cray Wanderers 3 Tunbridge Wells 3 *aet*
Tunbridge Wells 0 **Cray Wanderers** 1 *replay*
Deal Town 2 Hythe Town 0
Greenwich Borough 2 Lordswood 1
Maidstone United 6 Crockenhill 0
Sevenoaks Town 3 Herne Bay 3 *aet*
Herne Bay 2 Sevenoaks Town 0 *replay*
West Wickham 1 **VCD Athletic** 2 *aet*
Whitstable Town 4 Erith Town 1 *aet*
QUARTER-FINALS
Cray Wanderers 3 Herne Bay 0 *aet*
Greenwich Borough 0 **VCD Athletic** 2
Maidstone United 3 Deal Town 0
Ramsgate 1 **Whitstable Town** 3
SEMI-FINALS
Cray Wanderers 4 Whitstable Town 1
Maidstone United 2 VCD Athletic 1
FINAL
(19th April at Chatham Town)
Maidstone United 3 Cray Wanderers 0

LANCASHIRE TROPHY
FIRST ROUND
Atherton LR 1 **Holker Old Boys** 3
Bamber Bridge 2 **Marine** 3
Burscough 0 **Blackpool Mechanics** 1
Chorley 2 Castleton Gabriels 0
Darwen 1 **Lancaster City** 4
Fleetwood Town 1 Skelmersdale United 0
Kendal Town 3 Atherton Collieries 0 *aet*
Leigh RMI 1 Radcliffe Borough 0
Morecambe 2 Ramsbottom United 1
Nelson 2 Bacup Borough 0
Rossendale United 4 Colne 1
Southport 4 Great Harwood Town 1
Squires Gate 1 **Flixton** 1 *aet* (2-4p)
SECOND ROUND
Accrington Stanley 2 Southport 0
Barrow 0 **Kendal Town** 1
Blackpool Mechanics 2 Nelson 1
Clitheroe 5 Holker Old Boys 1
Fleetwood Town 0 **Lancaster City** 1
Flixton 0 **Leigh RMI** 7
Morecambe 1 **Chorley** 3
Rossendale United 2 Marine 1 *aet*
QUARTER-FINALS
Accrington Stanley 3 Lancaster City 1
Chorley 5 Blackpool Mechanics 1
Kendal Town 1 Clitheroe 0
Rossendale United 2 **Leigh RMI** 4
SEMI-FINALS
Accrington Stanley 1 **Kendal Town** 2
Leigh RMI 1 Chorley 0
FINAL
(16th April at Accrington Stanley)
Leigh RMI 2 Kendal Town 0

LEICESTERSHIRE CHALLENGE CUP
FIRST ROUND
Barwell 3 Quorn 0
Kirby Muxloe SC 1 **Leicester City** 3
Thurnby Rangers 3 Coalville Town 1
QUARTER-FINALS
Barwell 1 **Hinckley United** 7
Downes Sports 3 **Leicester City** 6
Oadby Town 5 St Andrews SC 3 *aet*
Thurnby Rangers 0 **Shepshed Dynamo** 1
SEMI-FINALS
Hinckley United 0 **Leicester City** 7
(at LCFA, Holmes Park)
Oadby Town 1 **Shepshed Dynamo** 2
(at LCFA, Holmes Park)
FINAL
(29th April at Leicester City)
Leicester City 1 Shepshed Dynamo 0

LEICESTERSHIRE SENIOR CUP
FIRST ROUND
Friar Lane Old Boys 3 **Kirby Muxloe SC** 2
Thurmaston Town 1 **Loughborough Dynamo** 4
SECOND ROUND
Anstey Nomads 0 **Thurnby Rangers** 8
Anstey Town 1 **Barrow Town** 6
Asfordby Amateurs 1 **Saffron Dynamo** 4
Aylestone Park Park OB 2 Earl Shilton Albion 0
Birstall United 0 **Blaby & Whetstone Athletic** 4
Cottesmore Amateurs 2 **Holwell Sports** 3
Downes Sports 1 **Coalville Town** 4
Ellistown 13 Thringstone Miners Welfare 0
Epworth 4 Leicester YMCA 2
Friar Lane Old Boys 0 **Loughborough Dynamo** 4
Lutterworth Town 5 Barton Hill Sports 1
Narborough & Littlethorpe 5 Highfield Rangers 2
North Kilworth 2 **Loughborough** 4
Ratby Sports 4 Leics Constabulary 0
Sileby Town 1 **Ibstock Welfare** 2
St Andrews SC 6 Huncote Sports & Social 1
THIRD ROUND
Barrow Town 2 Thurnby Rangers 0
Coalville Town 4 Loughborough 0
Ellistown 1 Aylestone Park Old Boys 0
Holwell Sports 2 **Epworth** 5

Loughborough Dynamo 4 Lutterworth Town 1
Ratby Sports 5 Narborough & Littlethorpe 2
Saffron Dynamo 1 **Blaby & Whetstone Athletic** 4
St Andrews SC 1 **Ibstock Welfare** 3
QUARTER-FINALS
Blaby & Whetstone Athletic 1 Ibstock Welfare 0
Coalville Town 4 Ratby Sports 1
Ellistown 0 **Barrow Town** 6
Loughborough Dynamo 5 Epworth 3
SEMI-FINALS
Blaby & Whetstone Athletic 1 **Loughborough Dynamo** 2
(at Heather St Johns)
Coalville Town 0 **Barrow Town** 2
(at Loughborough Dynamo)
FINAL
(15th April at LCFA, Holmes Park)
Loughborough Dynamo 1 Barrow Town 0

LINCOLNSHIRE SENIOR CUP
2001-02 FINAL
(1st August at Grantham Town)
Grantham Town 0 **Scunthorpe United** 3
FIRST ROUND
Lincoln City 1 **Grantham Town** 3
Stamford 2 Boston United 1
SEMI-FINALS
Gainsborough Trinity 2 Lincoln United 1
Stamford 0 **Grantham Town** 1
FINAL
(29th April at Gainsborough Trinity)
Gainsborough Trinity 4 Grantham Town 0

LIVERPOOL SENIOR CUP
FIRST ROUND
Burscough 3 St Helens Town 2 *aet*
Prescot Cables 1 **Southport** 3
Skelmersdale United 0 **Warrington Town** 1
QUARTER-FINALS
Burscough 0 **Liverpool** 5
Marine 1 Warrington Town 0
Runcorn FC Halton 1 **Tranmere Rovers** 4 *aet*
Southport v Everton *(12th August)*
SEMI-FINALS
Marine v Southport/Everton *(t.b.a.)*
Tranmere Rovers 3 Liverpool 3 *aet* (7-6p)
FINAL *(t.b.a.)*
Tranmere Rovers v Marine/Southport/Everton

LONDON SENIOR CUP
PRELIMINARY ROUND
AFC Wimbledon 3 Brimsdown Rovers 3 *aet* (5-4p)
Barkingside 2 Civil Service 1
FIRST ROUND
AFC Wimbledon 4 Woodford Town 0
Barkingside 2 Erith Town 0
Clapton 3 Thames Poly 1
Cockfosters 1 **Bedfont** 2
Crown & Manor 1 **Haringey Borough** 4
Hoddesdon Town 2 **Leyton** 3 *aet*
Hornchurch 4 VCD Athletic 2
Romford 2 Thamesmead Town 1 *aet*
SECOND ROUND
AFC Wimbledon 2 Bedfont 1
Barkingside 2 Haringey Borough 1
Erith & Belvedere 2 **Bromley** 2 *aet* (3-4p)
Ilford 3 Hornchurch 2 *aet*
Leyton 2 **Barking & East Ham United** 3 *aet*
Romford 2 Clapton 1
Tooting & Mitcham United 2 Corinthian Casuals 0
Wingate & Finchley 1 **Cray Wanderers** 2
THIRD ROUND
AFC Wimbledon 0 **Barkingside** 3
Barking & East Ham United 2 Tooting & Mitcham United 1
Cray Wanderers 1 **Uxbridge** 2 *aet*
Croydon Athletic 0 **Romford** 1
Dulwich Hamlet 1 **Ford United** 2
Hanwell Town 2 Welling United 1
Ilford 1 **Bromley** 2
Metropolitan Police 4 Fisher Athletic 3 *aet*
QUARTER-FINALS
Barking & East Ham United 2 **Metropolitan Police** 2 (3-4p)

Barkingside 1 **Ford United** 2
Hanwell Town 0 **Bromley** 1
Romford 1 **Uxbridge** 2
SEMI-FINALS
Ford United 0 Metropolitan Police 0 *aet* (4-3p)
Uxbridge 0 **Bromley** 1
FINAL
(30th April at Dagenham & Redbridge)
Bromley 1 Ford United 0

MANCHESTER PREMIER CUP
FIRST ROUND
Abbey Hey 1 Mossley 0
Ashton United 3 Trafford 2 *aet*
Curzon Ashton 2 **Maine Road** 4
Stand Athletic (scr.) **Flixton** (w/o)
QUARTER-FINALS
Abbey Hey 0 **Droylsden** 1
Flixton 2 Chadderton 1
Maine Road 0 **Ashton United** 4
Oldham Town 0 **Salford City** 4
SEMI-FINALS
Ashton United 6 Flixton 1
Droylsden (w/o) Salford City (scr.)
FINAL
(16th April at Oldham Athletic)
Ashton United 2 Droylsden 0

MIDDLESEX SENIOR CUP
FIRST ROUND
Brook House 3 **Feltham** 3 *aet* (1-4p)
Harefield Town 0 **Hanwell Town** 6
North Greenford United 2 **Ashford Town (Middx)** 4
Potters Bar Town 7 Bedfont 3
Southall Town 5 Staines Town 2
Viking Greenford 0 **Hillingdon Borough** 6
Wealdstone 2 Enfield 0
Wembley 2 Kingsbury Town 1 *aet*
Yeading 0 **Ruislip Manor** 1
SECOND ROUND
Ashford Town (Middx) 3 Southall Town 1
Feltham 0 **Enfield Town** 1
Hanwell Town 1 **Harrow Borough** 5
Hayes 4 Potters Bar Town 1
Hendon 5 Hillingdon Borough 1
Ruislip Manor 2 Wembley 1 *aet*
Uxbridge 1 **Hampton & Richmond Borough** 3
Wealdstone 3 Northwood 0
QUARTER-FINALS
Ashford Town (Middx) 3 **Harrow Borough** 4
Enfield Town 0 Ruislip Manor 0 *aet* (5-3p)
Hampton & Richmond Borough 2 Hayes 2 *aet* (4-2p)
Wealdstone 2 **Hendon** 3
SEMI-FINALS
Harrow Borough 1 **Enfield Town** 2
Hendon 2 Hampton & Richmond Borough 0
FINAL
(21st April at Northwood)
Hendon 2 Enfield Town 0

MIDDLESEX CHARITY CUP
FIRST ROUND
Harefield United 2 Brook House 0
Hillingdon Borough 2 **Southall Town** 4
SECOND ROUND
Enfield Town 1 **Ashford Town (Middx)** 3
Kingsbury Town 1 **Enfield** 2
North Greenford United 0 **Hanwell Town** 1
Northwood 5 Potters Bar Town 1
Ruislip Manor 4 Harefield United 3
Southall Town 1 **Feltham** 2
Wembley 1 Bedfont 0
Yeading 1 **Wealdstone** 1 *aet* (4-5p)
QUARTER-FINALS
Feltham 1 Wembley 0
Hanwell Town 0 **Northwood** 2
Ruislip Manor 0 **Ashford Town (Middx)** 0 *aet* (5-6p)
Wealdstone 7 Enfield 3 *(at Ruislip Manor)*
SEMI-FINALS
Feltham 1 Ashford Town (Middx) 1 *aet* (4-2p)
Northwood 3 Wealdstone 2

FINAL
(23rd April at Harrow Borough)
Northwood 0 **Feltham** 2

NORFOLK SENIOR CUP
PRELIMINARY ROUND
Anglian Windows 2 **Norwich Union** 4
Hindringham 1 Hempnall 0
Stalham Town 1 **Watton United** 2
Wymondham Town 1 **Mattishall** 3
FIRST ROUND
Halvergate United 4 Thorpe Village 1
Loddon United 2 Hindringham 0
Sprowston Wanderers 1 **Norwich Union** 4 *aet*
Watton United 3 Mattishall 0
SECOND ROUND
Acle United 6 Loddon United 0
Blofield United 3 North Walsham Town 0
Downham Town 0 **Cromer United** 5
Halvergate United 1 Thetford Town 1 *aet*
Thetford Town 0 Halvergate United 0 *replay aet* (8-7p)
Norwich Union 1 Wells Town 1 *aet*
Wells Town 1 **Norwich Union** 4 *replay*
Scole United 7 Mulbarton United 1
Sprowston Athletic 4 St Andrews 1
Swaffham Town 2 **King's Lynn Res.** 3
Watton United 2 **Attleborough Town** 4
THIRD ROUND
Blofield United 3 Attleborough Town 1
Dereham Town 1 Diss Town 1 *aet*
Diss Town 5 Dereham Town 1 *replay*
Fakenham Town 6 Norwich Union 1
Gorleston 9 Thetford Town 0
King's Lynn Res. 2 Acle United 1
Scole United 0 **Norwich United** 3
Sprowston Athletic 0 **Cromer United** 2
Wroxham 0 **Great Yarmouth Town** 1
QUARTER-FINALS
Cromer United 0 **Gorleston** 1
Fakenham Town 1 **Diss Town** 2 *aet*
Great Yarmouth Town 0 Blofield United 0 *aet*
Blofield United 0 **Great Yarmouth Town** 5 *replay*
King's Lynn Res. 4 Norwich United 3 *aet*
SEMI-FINALS
Diss Town 4 Gorleston 1
King's Lynn Res. 1 **Great Yarmouth Town** 3
FINAL
(22nd April at Norwich City)
Diss Town 4 Great Yarmouth Town 1

NORTH RIDING SENIOR CUP
FINAL
(to be played in pre-season)
Scarborough v Middlesbrough

NORTHAMPTONSHIRE SENIOR CUP
FIRST ROUND
Daventry Town 1 **Corby Town** 3
Desborough Town 4 Long Buckby 1
Ford Sports Daventry 3 Stewarts & Lloyds Corby 2
Northampton Spencer 0 **Brackley Town** 1
Raunds Town 1 Woodford United 0 *aet*
Rothwell Town 3 Cogenhoe United 1
QUARTER-FINALS
Corby Town 0 **Brackley Town** 1
Desborough Town 0 **Northampton Town** 1 *aet*
Ford Sports Daventry 1 **Rothwell Town** 2
Raunds Town 0 **Peterborough United** 6
SEMI-FINALS
Peterborough United 1 Northampton Town 0
Rothwell Town 5 Brackley Town 0
FINAL *(28th April at Rothwell Town)*
Rothwell Town 2 Peterborough United 1

NORTHUMBERLAND SENIOR CUP
FIRST ROUND
Alnwick Town 0 **Ponteland United** 3
Bedlington Terriers 0 **Newcastle United Res.** 3
Morpeth Town 3 Prudhoe Town 1
Newcastle Benfield Saints 2 **Whitley Bay** 5
Newcastle Blue Star 0 **Amble United** 1

North Shields 1 **Shankhouse** 2
Walker Central 0 **Ashington** 2
West Allotment Celtic 1 **Blyth Spartans** 2
QUARTER-FINALS
Amble United 0 **Whitley Bay** 2
Blyth Spartans 2 Ashington 1
Morpeth Town 1 **Shankhouse** 2
Ponteland 1 **Newcastle Utd Res.** 4 *(at Newcastle Blue Star)*
SEMI-FINALS
Blyth Spartans 1 **Newcastle United Res.** 3
Whitley Bay 3 Shankhouse 0
FINAL
(7th May at Newcastle United)
Newcastle United Res. 2 Whitley Bay 0

NOTTINGHAMSHIRE SENIOR CUP
FIRST ROUND
Clifton 3 Cotgrave Colliery Welfare 2
Keyworth United 2 **Rainworth Miners Welfare** 3
Notts Police 1 **Radcliffe Olympic** 4
Retford United 1 **Wollaton** 5
Ruddington United 3 Kimberley Miners Welfare 0
Sutton Town 2 Newark Flowserve 0
SECOND ROUND
Clifton 1 **Clipstone Welfare** 2
Forest Town 0 **Blidworth Welfare** 5
Radcliffe Olympic 3 Ruddington United 0
Rainworth Miners Welfare 2 Ollerton Town 0
Sutton Town 3 Pelican 1 *aet*
Wollaton 2 Greenwood Meadows 2 *aet* (7-6p)
THIRD ROUND
Arnold Town 1 **Sutton Town** 2
Blidworth Welfare 2 **Carlton Town** 3
Boots Athletic 2 **Hucknall Town** 3
Eastwood Town 3 **Teversal** 4
Rainworth Miners Welfare 3 Wollaton 3 *aet* (5-3p)
Rolls Royce Leisure 0 **Radcliffe Olympic** 1
Southwell City 0 **Gedling Town** 2
Welbeck Miners Welfare 1 **Clipstone Welfare** 5
QUARTER-FINALS
Carlton Town 3 **Teversal** 3 *aet* (4-5p)
Gedling Town 2 Clipstone Welfare 1
Hucknall Town 1 Sutton Town 0
Rainworth Miners Welfare 2 **Radcliffe Olympic** 4
SEMI-FINALS
Gedling Town 0 **Teversal** 1
Radcliffe Olympic 3 **Hucknall Town** 4
FINAL
(24th April at Notts County)
Hucknall Town 2 Teversal 0

OXFORDSHIRE SENIOR CUP
FIRST ROUND
Ardley United 2 Adderbury Park 0
Bicester Town 2 Kidlington 1
Chinnor 2 Goring United 1
Clanfield 1 **Witney United** 2
Easington Sports 0 **Hook Norton** 2
Eynsham Association 2 **Chipping Norton Town** 4
Headington Amateurs 3 Quarry Nomads 1
Henley Town 4 Middle Barton 1
Sonning Common 0 **Carterton Town** 4
SECOND ROUND
Ardley United 4 Headington Amateurs 0
Carterton Town 3 Highfield Old Boys 1
Chinnor 2 **Bicester Town** 5
Chipping Norton Town 4 Watlington 0
Garsington 0 **Henley Town** 12
Hook Norton 2 Launton Sports 1
Witney United 2 Kidlington Old Boys 1
Worcester & Bletchington 1 **Old Woodstock Town** 3
THIRD ROUND
Carterton Town 3 Ardley United 1
Henley Town 3 Bicester Town 1
Hook Norton 2 Witney United 1
Old Woodstock Town 1 **Chipping Norton Town** 2
QUARTER-FINALS
Banbury United 1 **Thame United** 2
Chipping Norton Town 1 **Oxford City** 3
Henley Town 1 North Leigh 1 *aet* (6-5p)

Hook Norton 2 Carterton Town 0
SEMI-FINALS
Oxford City 4 Henley Town 3
(at Thame United)
Thame United 0 **Hook Norton** 1
(at Oxford City)
FINAL
(29th April at Oxford United)
Oxford City 3 Hook Norton 2
aet, golden goal

SHEFFIELD & HALLAMSHIRE SENIOR CUP
FIRST ROUND
Frecheville CA 1 **Penistone Church** 3
Frickley Athletic 3 Harworth Colliery Institute 1
Rossington Main 3 **Stocksbridge Park Steels** 7
Worsbridge Bridge MW 0 Hallam 0 *aet*
Hallam 4 Worsbrough Bridge MW 3 *replay*
SECOND ROUND
Brodsworth Miners Welfare 1 **Mexborough Main Street** 3
Doncaster Rovers 10 Yorkshire Main 0
Frickley Athletic 1 **Stocksbridge Park Steels** 2
Grimethorpe Miners Welfare 1 **Worksop Town** 4 *aet*
Maltby Main 3 Penistone Church 2
Parkgate 3 Hallam 1
South Kirkby Colliery 3 Sheffield 0
Wakefield & Emley 2 Swinton Athletic 1
(at Welfare Ground, Emley)
QUARTER-FINALS
Doncaster Rovers 7 Mexborough Main Street 0
Maltby Main 5 Wakefield & Emley 3 *aet*
Parkgate 2 **Stocksbridge Park Steels** 5
South Kirkby Colliery 1 **Worksop Town** 5
SEMI-FINALS
Doncaster Rovers 2 Maltby Main 1
Stocksbridge Park Steels 0 **Worksop Town** 4
FINAL
(6th May at Sheffield Wednesday)
Worksop Town 2 Doncaster Rovers 1

SHROPSHIRE SENIOR CUP
FIRST ROUND
Bridgnorth Town 3 **Ludlow Town** 3 (4-5p)
SEMI-FINALS
Shrewsbury Town 5 Shifnal Town 1
Telford United 3 Ludlow Town 0
FINAL
(30th July at Telford United)
Telford United 2 **Shrewsbury Town** 3

SOMERSET PREMIER CUP
FIRST ROUND
Backwell United 2 Minehead Town 1
Bishop Sutton 1 **Street** 1 *aet* (0-2p)
Bitton 4 Bridgwater Town 2
Brislington 1 **Weston-super-Mare** 1 *aet* (3-5p)
Clevedon Town 3 Frome Town 2
Paulton Rovers 4 Bristol Manor Farm 0
Team Bath 1 Keynsham Town 0
Wellington 0 **Taunton Town** 3
SECOND ROUND
Backwell United 2 Street 0
Bristol City 2 Team Bath 0
Odd Down 4 Bath City 3 *aet*
Shepton Mallet Town 2 **Clevedon Town** 3 *aet*
Taunton Town 4 Chard Town 4 *aet* (5-4p)
Welton Rovers 1 **Paulton Rovers** 2
Weston-super-Mare 4 Bitton 1
Yeovil Town 2 Mangotsfield United 1 *aet*
QUARTER-FINALS
Backwell United 0 **Clevedon Town** 1
Bristol City 4 Weston-super-Mare 1 *(at Weston)*
Taunton Town 5 Paulton Rovers 1
Yeovil Town 2 Odd Down 0
SEMI-FINALS
Bristol City 1 **Taunton Town** 2
Clevedon Town 0 **Yeovil Town** 4
FINAL
(29th April at Clevedon Town)
Yeovil Town 1 **Taunton Town** 2

STAFFORDSHIRE SENIOR CUP
FIRST ROUND
Biddulph Victoria 0 **Pelsall Villa** 1
SECOND ROUND
Burton Albion 5 Stafford Town 1
Hednesford Town 7 Chasetown 0
Leek Town 0 **Stoke City** 2
Newcastle Town 2 Rocester 1
Port Vale (w/o) Alsager Town (scr.)
Shifnal Town 3 Kidsgrove Athletic 2
Stafford Rangers 7 Pelsall Villa 0
Tamworth 1 Rushall Olympic 1
Rushall Olympic 3 Tamworth 1 *replay*
QUARTER-FINALS
Burton Albion 1 **Hednesford Town** 2
Rushall Olympic 2 **Stoke City** 2 (2-4p)
Shifnal Town 1 **Port Vale** 2
Stafford Rangers 4 Newcastle Town 0
SEMI-FINALS
Hednesford Town 2 **Stoke City** 6
Port Vale 1 **Stafford Rangers** 2
FINAL
(30th April at Port Vale)
Stafford Rangers 5 Stoke City 1

SUFFOLK PREMIER CUP
PRELIMINARY ROUND
Mildenhall Town 4 Woodbridge Town 0
QUARTER-FINALS
AFC Sudbury 3 Stowmarket Town 1
Bury Town 1 **Mildenhall Town** 2
Lowestoft Town 7 Ipswich Wanderers 0
Newmarket Town 4 Felixstowe & Walton United 1
SEMI-FINALS
Lowestoft Town 3 **Mildenhall Town** 3 *aet* (3-4p)
Newmarket Town 1 **AFC Sudbury** 2
FINAL
(5th May at Bury Town)
Mildenhall Town 0 **AFC Sudbury** 1

SURREY SENIOR CUP
FIRST ROUND
Ashford Town (Middx) 3 Egham Town 2
Chessington United 2 Redhill 1
Chipstead 4 Chessington & Hook United 3
Epsom & Ewell 4 Westfield 2
Molesey 3 Frimley Green 0
Raynes Park Vale 3 Cobham 0
SECOND ROUND
Ashford Town (Middx) 2 Dorking 1
Banstead Athletic 0 **Chessington United** 1
Corinthians Casuals 4 Merstham 3
Epsom & Ewell 0 **Walton Casuals** 1
Farnham Town 1 **Raynes Park Vale** 7
Godalming & Guildford 3 **Ash United** 4
Metropolitan Police 3 Chipstead 0
Molesey 2 **Camberley Town** 3
THIRD ROUND
Ashford Town (Middx) 2 **Metropolitan Police** 3
Camberley Town 2 **Ash United** 3
Chessington United 1 Walton Casuals 0
Corinthian Casuals 2 **Raynes Park Vale** 3
FOURTH ROUND
Ash United 2 Tooting & Mitcham United 1
Carshalton Athletic 3 Raynes Park Vale 0
Kingstonian 2 Chessington United 0
Leatherhead 4 Croydon 1
Metropolitan Police 1 **Crystal Palace** 4
Walton & Hersham 1 **Sutton United** 3
Whyteleafe 1 Chertsey Town 0
Woking 0 **Dulwich Hamlet** 1
QUARTER-FINALS
Kingstonian 4 Ash United 1
Leatherhead 0 Crystal Palace 0 *aet* (5-4p)
Sutton United 2 Carshalton Athletic 0
Whyteleafe 1 **Dulwich Hamlet** 2
SEMI-FINALS
Dulwich Hamlet 1 **Sutton United** 2
Leatherhead 2 **Kingstonian** 2 *aet* (6-7p)
FINAL *(6th May at Metropolitan Police)*
Kingstonian 1 **Sutton United** 2

SUSSEX SENIOR CUP
FIRST ROUND
Crawley Down Village 3 **Rye & Iden United** 4 *aet*
Eastbourne Town 2 Saltdean United 1 *aet*
Eastbourne United 1 Peacehaven & Telscombe 1 *aet*
Peacehaven & Telscombe 2 **Eastbourne United** 5 *replay*
Hassocks 6 Shinewater Association 1
Littlehampton Town 0 Steyning Town 0 *aet*
Steyning Town 2 Littlehampton Town 1 *replay*
Mile Oak 1 **Horsham YMCA** 5
Oakwood 1 **Broadbridge Heath** 2
Oving 1 Pease Pottage Village 0 *aet*
Sidlesham 3 Seaford Town 1
Southwick 0 **Shoreham** 2
Wealden 2 **East Preston** 3
Whitehawk 2 East Grinstead Town 0
Wick 3 Lancing 0
Worthing United 2 Westfield 1
SECOND ROUND
Bognor Regis Town 1 **Crawley Town** 3
Brighton & Hove Albion 1 Hastings United 0 *(at Worthing)*
Burgess Hill Town 1 Three Bridges 0
Chichester City United 5 Hailsham Town 1
East Preston 6 Broadbridge Heath 0
Eastbourne Borough 5 Shoreham 0
Eastbourne Town 4 Sidley United 1
Horsham 1 Hassocks 0
Horsham YMCA 5 Eastbourne United 1
Lewes 0 **Worthing** 2
Oving 1 **Rye & Iden United** 4
Pagham 2 Steyning Town 1 *aet*
St Leonards 5 Sidlesham 1
Whitehawk 3 Ringmer 0
Wick 2 Selsey 1
Worthing United 1 **Arundel** 2
THIRD ROUND
Burgess Hill Town 2 St Leonards 0
Chichester City United 1 **Pagham** 2
East Preston 1 **Brighton & Hove Albion** 2
Horsham 1 **Crawley Town** 3
Rye & Iden United 2 Arundel 1
Whitehawk 6 Eastbourne Town 6 *aet*
Eastbourne Town 2 Whitehawk 1 *replay*
Wick 1 **Eastbourne Borough** 3
Worthing 0 Horsham YMCA 0 *aet*
Horsham YMCA 1 **Worthing** 3 *replay*
QUARTER-FINALS
Crawley Town 1 Brighton & Hove Albion 0
Eastbourne Borough 3 Eastbourne Town 1
Pagham 1 Worthing 0 *aet*
Rye & Iden United 0 Burgess Hill Town 0 *aet*
Burgess Hill Town 1 **Rye & Iden United** 2 *replay*
SEMI-FINALS
Pagham 0 **Eastbourne Borough** 1 *(at Burgess Hill Town)*
Rye & Iden United 0 **Crawley Town** 3 *(at Lewes)*
FINAL
(5th May at Eastbourne Borough)
Eastbourne Borough 0 **Crawley Town** 0 *aet* (5-6p)

SUSSEX ROYAL ULSTER RIFLES CHARITY CUP
FIRST ROUND
Arundel 4 Ringmer 2 *aet*
Littlehampton Town 1 **Eastbourne United** 3
Oakwood 0 **Horsham YMCA** 2
Pagham 1 East Preston 0
Sidley United 2 Redhill 0
Three Bridges 0 **Southwick** 3
SECOND ROUND
Burgess Hill Town 8 Hassocks 0
Chichester City United 2 Lancing 2 *aet* (8-7p)
Crawley Down Village 0 **Horsham YMCA** 3
East Grinstead Town 3 **Sidlesham** 4
Eastbourne Town 4 Oving 1
Mile Oak 1 **Hailsham Town** 3
Saltdean United 1 **Arundel** 2
Selsey 4 Whitehawk 0
Shoreham 3 Pagham 0
Southwick 3 Shinewater Association 0
Steyning Town 0 **Sidley United** 1
Wealden 0 Peacehaven & Telscombe 1
(ineligible player – Peacehaven expelled)

Westfield 3 Rye & Iden United 2
Wick 1 Pease Pottage Village 0
Worthing United 1 **Seaford Town** 2
THIRD ROUND
Arundel 4 Westfield 3
Chichester City United 3 Sidlesham 2
Eastbourne United 1 **Shoreham** 3
Hailsham Town 0 **Wealden** 0 *aet* (13-14p)
Seaford Town 0 **Southwick** 4
Selsey 3 Horsham YMCA 0
Sidley United 2 Eastbourne Town 1
Wick 0 **Burgess Hill Town** 2
QUARTER-FINALS
Chichester City United 2 **Selsey** 3 *aet*
Sidley United 6 Arundel 3
Southwick 3 Shoreham 1
Wealden 1 **Burgess Hill Town** 3
SEMI-FINALS
Sidley United 2 Selsey 2 *aet* (10-9p) *(at Southwick)*
Southwick 2 Burgess Hill Town 1 *(at Hassocks)*
FINAL
(11th March at Lancing)
Southwick 2 Sidley United 1

WEST RIDING COUNTY CUP
FIRST ROUND
Armthorpe Welfare 1 Tadcaster Albion 0
Guiseley 2 Pontefract Collieries 1
Halifax Town 3 Ossett Albion 0
Liversedge 4 Glasshoughton Welfare 3
SECOND ROUND
Farsley Celtic 3 Guiseley 0
Garforth Town 1 **Eccleshill United** 2
Goole 1 Armthorpe Welfare 0 *aet*
Harrogate Town 3 Harrogate Railway Athletic 1
Hatfield Main 0 **Thackley** 3
Liversedge 4 Selby Town 1
Ossett Town 1 **Halifax Town** 2
Yorkshire Amateur 1 **Bradford Park Avenue** 4
QUARTER-FINALS
Bradford Park Avenue 1 Eccleshill United 0
Halifax Town 1 **Harrogate Town** 2
Liversedge 0 **Goole** 2
Thackley 0 **Farsley Celtic** 1
SEMI-FINALS
Goole 0 **Farsley Celtic** 1
Harrogate Town 2 Bradford Park Avenue 0
FINAL
(16th April at WRCFA, Fleet Lane, Woodlesford)
Harrogate Town 3 Farsley Celtic 1

WESTMORLAND SENIOR CUP
FINAL
(5th April at Kendal Town)
Kendal Town Res. 3 Appleby 3 *aet* (4-2p)

WILTSHIRE PREMIER SHIELD
FIRST ROUND
Chippenham Town 3 **Salisbury City** 3
Salisbury City 2 Chippenham Town 0 *replay*
Swindon Supermarine 0 Swindon Town 0
Swindon Town 1 **Swindon Supermarine** 2 *replay aet*
FINAL
(5th May at Salisbury City)
Salisbury City 3 Swindon Supermarine 1

WORCESTERSHIRE SENIOR CUP
FIRST ROUND
Stourport Swifts 0 **Halesowen Town** 3
Sutton Coldfield Town 3 Redditch United 1
QUARTER-FINALS
Evesham United 2 Sutton Coldfield Town 1
Halesowen Town 2 Worcester City 1
Kidderminster Harriers 1 **Bromsgrove Rovers** 2
Solihull Borough 2 **Moor Green** 3
SEMI-FINALS
Bromsgrove Rovers 1 **Halesowen Town** 3
Evesham United 1 Moor Green 0
FINAL
1st leg *(8th April)* Halesowen Town 2 Evesham United 0
2nd leg *(24th April)* Evesham United 0 **Halesowen Town** 1

OTHER COUNTY AND DISTRICT CUP FINALS

A E E U CUP *(10th May at Conwy United)*
Llandudno Cricketers 1 **Llangefi Town Res.** 5
A F A SENIOR CUP *(5th April at Old Owens)*
Bromleians Sports 0 **Winchmore Hill** 1
A F A INTERMEDIATE CUP *(22nd March at Old Actonians)*
Old Camdenians 3 UCL Academicals Res. 2
A F A JUNIOR CUP *(22nd March at HSBC)*
Old Aloysians 'A' 1 **UCL Academicals 'A'** 2 *aet*
A F A MINOR CUP *(22nd March at Bank of England)*
Old Magdalenians 1 **Nottsborough 'B'** 2
A F A ESSEX SENIOR CUP *(22nd March at Old Parmiterians)*
Hale End Athletic 2 Old Parkonians 0
A F A ESSEX INT. CUP *(29th March at Old Parmiterians)*
Mount Pleasant Post Office 1 **Old Buckwellians Res.** 2
A F A MIDDLESEX SENIOR CUP *(22nd March at Civil Service)*
Old Meadonians 2 Winchmore Hill 0
A F A MIDDLESEX INT. CUP *(29th March at Winchmore Hill)*
Civil Service Res. 1 **East Barnet OG Res.** 3 *aet*
A F A SURREY SENIOR CUP *(29th March at Carshalton)*
Nottsborough 5 Old Wokingians 3 *aet*
A F A SURREY INT. CUP *(29th March at Zurich Eagle Star)*
Old Tiffinians Res. 1 **Nottsborough Res.** 3
ALDERSHOT SENIOR CUP *(15th April at Aldershot Town)*
Ashford Town (Middx) 0 Fleet Town 0 *aet* (5-4p)
ANCASTER CUP *(10th May at Bourne Town)*
Bourne Town Res. 0 **Deeping Rangers Res.** 3
AXMINSTER HOSPITAL CUP *(11th May at Axminster Town)*
Budleigh Salterton Res. 2 Cullompton Rangers Res. 2 *aet* (5-3p)
B U S A CUP *(5th May at Wolverhampton Wanderers)*
Swansea University 1 Northumbria University 0
BARRITT CUP *(10th May at Bangor City)*
Glantraeth 1 **Bodedern** 2
BASINGSTOKE SENIOR CUP *(23rd April at Basingstoke Town)*
Hartley Wintney 4 AFC Newbury Res. 0
BEDFORD CUP *(18th May at Tavistock)*
Callington Town 5 Gunnislake 1
BEDS SENIOR TROPHY *(29th April at Stotfold)*
Brache Sparta 2 Langford 1 *aet*
BEDS INTERMEDIATE CUP *(4th April at Langford)*
St Josephs 2 McDonald Humphreys 1
BEDS JUNIOR CUP *(11th April at Kempston Rovers)*
Crawley Green Res. 1 Potton United Res. 0
BEDS JUNIOR TROPHY *(25th April at Ampthill Town)*
Admiral 5 Ujima 0
BEDWORTH NURSING CUP *(18th April at Bedworth United)*
Bedworth United Res. 2 Coventry Marconi 1
BERKS & BUCKS TROPHY *(26th April at Didcot Town)*
Milton Keynes City 0 **Didcot Town** 2
BERKS & BUCKS INT. CUP *(12th April at Abingdon United)*
Buckingham Athletic 3 Highmoor/IBIS 0
BERKS & BUCKS JUNIOR CUP *(5th April at Thatcham Town)*
Stony Stratford Town Res. 1 **Old Bell** 5
BIGGLESWADE & DISTRICT CUP *(13th May at Langford)*
Langford Res. 0 **Potton United Res.** 3
BILL SPURGEON CUP *(23rd April at Witham Town)*
Old Chelmsfordians 0 **Kelvedon Hatch** 3
BIRMINGHAM FLOODLIGHT CUP *(25th April at Tipton Town)*
Tipton Town 4 Rugby Town 1
BIRMINGHAM VASE *(26th April at BCFA, Great Barr)*
Polesworth North Warwick 1 **Folly Lane BCOB** 2
BIRMINGHAM JUNIOR CUP *(3rd May at BCFA, Great Barr)*
Triumph Athletic 1 **Whitnash** 2
BOURNEMOUTH CUP *(24th April at AFC Bournemouth)*
Bournemouth Electric 2 Verwood Town 1
BRADFORD & DISTRICT CUP *(10th May at Bradford Park Ave)*
Wibsey 1 **Thackley Res.** 2
BRAUNTON CUP *(11th May at Barnstaple Town)*
Boca Seniors 3 Hartland 1

BRIGHTON CHARITY CUP *(30th April at Horsham)*
Horsham 2 East Preston 1
BUCKINGHAM CHARITY CUP *(5th May at Buckingham Town)*
Buckingham Town 3 Leighton Town 1
CAMBRIAN CUP *(29th April at Penrhyncoch)*
Aberaeron 4 Penparcau 0
CAMBS PROFESSIONAL CUP *(10th August at Histon)*
Histon 3 Cambridge City 1
CAMBS CHALLENGE CUP *(21st April at Cambridge City)*
Waterbeach 2 West Wratting 2 *aet* (5-4p)
CAMBS JUNIOR INV. CUP *(23rd May at Cambridge City)*
Needingworth United 1 Barton Mills 0
CAPITAL COUNTIES FEEDER LEAGUES TROPHY
(12th April at Ware) Tring Athletic 0 **White Ensign** 1
CHESHIRE AMATEUR CUP *(4th April at Vauxhall Motors)*
Cammell Laird 4 Heswall 0
CHESTER SENIOR CUP *(2nd May at Christleton)*
Chester Nomads 3 Blacon Youth Club 3 *aet* (4-3p)
CHESTER CHALLENGE CUP *(25th April at Christleton)*
Christleton Res. 1 **Upton AA Res.** 1 *aet* (2-4p)
CORNWALL JUNIOR CUP *(21st April at Penzance)*
Biscovey 3 Cury 1
COVENTRY CHARITY CUP *(7th May at Coventry City)*
Coventry Marconi 2 Stockingford AA 1
COVENTRY EVENING TELEGRAPH CUP
(6th May at Coventry City) Coventry Marconi 1 **Folly Lane BCOB** 2
CREWE & DISTRICT CUP *(10th May)*
Crewe 3 Alsager 1
DAVENTRY CHARITY CUP *(14th May at Daventry Town)*
Banbury United 1 Woodford United 0 *aet*
DERBYSHIRE DIVISIONAL CUP SOUTH *(26th March at Belper)*
Ashbourne United 2 **Ilkeston Town Res.** 3
DEVON PREMIER CUP *(31st March at Torquay United)*
Plymstock United 2 Upton Athletic 0
DEVON SENIOR CUP *(8th April at Newton Abbot)*
Princess Yachts International 0 **Buckland Athletic Res.** 3
DEVON INTERMEDIATE CUP *(22nd April at Dawlish Town)*
Kevin Purdy Roofing 6 Farway United 0
DORSET INTERMEDIATE CUP *(24th April at Dorchester Town)*
Kingston 3 Corfe Mullen United 1
DORSET JUNIOR CUP *(1st May at Bridport)*
Bishop's Caundle 3 Spa Hotel 1
DORSET MINOR CUP *(10th April at Wimborne Town)*
Witchampton United Res. 2 Cranborne Res. 2 (3-1p)
EAST ANGLIAN CUP *(15th May at Long Melford)*
Long Melford 0 **East Thurrock United** 1
ERNIE BROWN CUP *(15th May at Polesworth North Warwick)*
Polesworth North Warwick 2 Knowle 1
ESSEX PREMIER CUP *(7th April at Heybridge Swifts)*
Ramsden 1 **Benfleet** 2
ESSEX THAMESSIDE TROPHY *(to be played in pre-season)*
Maldon Town v Ford United/Canvey Island
FARINGDON THURSDAY MEMORIAL CUP
(1st May at Faringdon Town) **Letcombe** 2 Lower Stratton 0
GLOS SENIOR AMATEUR CUP NORTH
(22nd April at Forest Green) **Kings Stanley** 1 Broadwell Amateurs 0
GLOS SENIOR AMATEUR CUP SOUTH
(8th May at Oaklands Park) **Hanham Athletic** 3 Sea Mills Park 2
GLOS INT. CUP NORTH *(9th April at Shortwood United)*
Patriots 5 Athletico Severn 0
GLOS INT. CUP SOUTH *(15th April at Oaklands Park)*
Sea Mills Park Res. 4 Rangeworthy Res. 2
GLOS JUNIOR CUP NORTH *(30th April)*
Barnwood 3 **Berkeley Town** 4
GLOS JUNIOR CUP SOUTH *(22nd April at Oaklands Park)*
Lawrence Rovers 4 Patchway Town Res. 1
GLOS MINOR CUP SOUTH *(1st May at Oaklands Park)*
Soundwell Victoria 1 Sukoshi Juniors 0

GLOS PRIMARY CUP NORTH *(17th April at Harrow Hill)*
Marshall Langton 3 Sedbury BL 0
GLOS PRIMARY CUP SOUTH *(25th March at Oaklands Park)*
Longshore United Res. 0 **Ridings High 'A'** 1
GOLDLINE TROPHY *(9th April at Bolton Wanderers)*
Atherton Collieries 0 **Prestwich Heys** 3
GOLESWORTHY CUP *(16th May at Ottery St Mary)*
Honiton Town 4 Kentisbeare Res. 2
GRANDISSON CUP *(14th May at Ottery St Mary)*
Broadclyst 2 Motel Rangers & Offwell 0
GRAVESEND HOSPITALS MALLINSON CUP *(9th April)*
Greenways Res. 1 Lanes End 0
GWENT SENIOR CUP *(3rd May at Newport County)*
Tillery 2 **Croesyceiliog** 3
GWENT AMATEUR CUP *(26th April at Newport County)*
Christchurch Hamdden 1 Panteg 0 *aet*
HALIFAX F A CUP *(30th April at Ovenden West Riding)*
Brighouse Town 5 Sowerby United 1
HANSEN CUP *(5th May at Bideford)*
Shamwickshire Rovers 2 Morwenstow 1 *aet*
HARWICH CHARITY CUP *(20th May at Woodbridge Town)*
Woodbridge Town 2 Long Melford 1
HASTINGS CUP *(30th April at Hastings United)*
Hastings United 1 Westfields 0
HERTS INTERMEDIATE CUP *(1st April at Letchworth)*
Bishop's Stortford Swifts 4 Leverstock Green Res. 2
HERTS JUNIOR CUP *(18th April at Letchworth)*
Bengeo Trinity 1 Hertford Heath 0
HINCHINGBROOKE CUP *(13th May at St Neots Town)*
St Neots Town 0 **Wootton Blue Cross** 2
HOLMAN CUP *(5th May at Lynton & Lynmouth)*
North Tawton 4 Shamwickshire Rovers Res. 3 *aet*
HOSPITALS CHARITY CUP *(3rd May)*
Halls 2 Fleetdown United Res. 0
HUDDERSFIELD & DISTRICT CUP
(12th May at Huddersfield Town) Bay Athletic 0 **Storthes Hall** 3
HUNTS PREMIER CUP *(14th May at St Neots Town)*
Stotfold 1 **Biggleswade Town** 2
HUNTS BENEVOLENT CUP *(17th April at Eynesbury Rovers)*
Yaxley Res. 2 St Ives Town Res. 0
HUNTS SCOTT GATTY CUP *(22nd April at Godmanchester)*
Yaxley Res. 2 St Neots Town Res. 0
ISLE OF WIGHT SENIOR CUP *(29th April at Newport IOW)*
Newport IOW 2 Cowes Sports 0 *aet*
J W HUNT CUP *(15th May at Wolverhampton Wanderers)*
Newport Town 0 **Old Wulfrunians** 2
JESS PIGGOTT CUP *(21st August at Sandy Albion)*
Stotfold Res. 2 Blunham 1
KEIGHLEY F A CUP *(28th April at Cougar Park)*
Silsden 4 Keighley Lifts 1
KENT INTERMEDIATE CUP *(26th April at Whitstable Town)*
Gravesend & Northfleet Res. 0 **Deal Town Res.** 1
KENT INT. CHALLENGE SHIELD *(12th April at Erith Town)*
Danson Furness 2 **Sheerness East** 3
KENT JUNIOR CUP GROUP A *(10th May at Corinthian)*
Lanes End 1 **180 Albion** 6
LANCS AMATEUR SHIELD *(3rd April at LCFA, Leyland)*
Charnock Richard 1 **Springfields** 2
LANCS AMATEUR CUP *(2nd April at LCFA, Leyland)*
Gregorians 1 **St Dominics** 2
LEEK CUP *(28th March at Ball Haye Green)*
Alsager 3 Eccleshall 0
LINCS SENIOR 'A' CUP *(14th May at Boston Town)*
Brigg Town 1 **Holbeach United** 3
LINCS SENIOR 'B' CUP *(30th April at Boston United)*
Harrowby United 0 **Sleaford Town** 1
LIVERPOOL CHALLENGE CUP
(16th April at Walton Hall Avenue) Speke 1 **Royal Seaforth** 2
LIVERPOOL JUNIOR CUP *(25th March at Walton Hall Avenue)*
Birchfield 2 Aigburth People's Hall Res. 0
LLANSANTFFRAID VILLAGES CUP *(21st April at Treflan)*
Berriew 2 Llangedwyn 1 *aet*
LONDON INTERMEDIATE CUP *(5th April at Thamesmead Town)*
Thamesmead Town Res. 0 **Cray Valley Paper Mills** 0 *aet* (3-4p)

MANCHESTER CHALLENGE TROPHY
(13th February at Branthingham Rd) **East Manchester** 3 Belden 0
MIDDLESEX SUPER CUP *(6th August at Hendon)*
Hendon 1 Enfield Town 0
MIDDLESEX PREMIER CUP *(26th March at Uxbridge)*
Uxbridge Res. 2 Hayes Res. 1 *aet*
MIDDLESEX INTERMEDIATE CUP *(16th April at Yeading)*
British Airways 3 Willesden Constantine 2
MID-CHESHIRE SENIOR CUP *(15th April at Witton Albion)*
Witton Albion 4 Northwich Victoria 3
MID-SUSSEX CHARITY CUP *(15th April at Haywards Heath)*
Forest 0 **Hassocks Res.** 4
MOORE CUP *(11th May at Bradworthy United)*
Halwill 2 Stratton United 1
MORRISON BELL *(15th May at Ottery St Mary)*
Cullompton Rangers Res. 1 **Exmouth Town Res.** 4
NORFOLK JUNIOR CUP *(9th May at Norwich City)*
Gayton United 1 **Dersingham Rovers** 6
NORFOLK PRIMARY CUP *(11th April at Dereham Town)*
King's Lynn Royals 3 Yaxham 1
NORTH BEDS CHARITY CUP *(9th May at Stotfold)*
Stotfold 1 Biggleswade United 1 *aet* (4-2p)
NORTH EAST WALES CUP *(15th May at Wrexham)*
Buckley Town 2 Airbus UK 2 *aet* (5-4p)
NORTH WALES COAST CUP *(13th May at Caernarfon Town)*
Porthmadog 3 Llandudno Town 1
NORTH WALES COAST JUNIOR CUP *(31st May at Conwy)*
Bethel 1 **Castell Rhuddlan** 2
NORTHERN CO'S CHAMPIONSHIP *(19th April at Penrith)*
Cumberland (Northbank FC) 3 Liverpool (St Aloysius) 0
NORTHANTS JUNIOR CUP *(24th April at Rushden & Diamonds)*
Sileby Rangers 3 Rothwell Corinthians 1
NORTHANTS LOWER JUNIOR CUP *(1st April at Desborough)*
Bugbrooke St Michaels Res. 1 **Caledonian Strip Mills** 2
NOTTS INTERMDIATE CUP *(23rd April at Gedling Town)*
Pelican Res. 4 Carlton Town Res. 0
NORTHUMBERLAND SENIOR BOWL
(7th May at NFA, Whitley Park)
Percy Main Amateurs 0 **Spittal Rovers** 1
NORTHUMBERLAND MINOR CUP
(9th May at NFA, Whitley Park)
Newcastle British Telecom 2 **Cramlington Town** 4
OKEHAMPTON CUP *(4th May at Okehampton Argyle)*
Hatherleigh Town 1 **Chagford** 1 *aet, Chagford won on pens*
POTTERS BAR CHARITY CUP *(7th May at Potters Bar Town)*
Cockfosters 0 **Colney Heath** 2
READING JUNIOR CUP *(23rd April)*
Henley Town Res. 3 Radstock 2
RICKMANSWORTH CHARITY CUP *(21st April)*
Evergreen 1 **Oxhey Jets** 2
RICKMANSWORTH CHARITY PLATE *(21st April)*
Bushey Rangers Res. 0 **Holywell** 1
ROBERTSBRIDGE INTERMEDIATE CHARITY CUP
(7th May at Hastings United) Peche Hill Select 1 **Rock-a-Nore** 2
ROLLESTON CHARITY CUP
(5th May at LCFA, Holmes Park) **Hinckley Utd** 6 Anstey Nomads 0
ROWE (NORTH DEVON) CHARITY CUP
(11th May at Ilfracombe Town) **Witheridge** 3 Braunton 1
ROY BAILEY MEMORIAL CUP *(12th May at Waltham Abbey)*
Cheshunt 1 **Hoddesdon Town** 2 *aet*
RUNCORN CHALLENGE CUP *(25th March at Mond Rangers)*
General Chemicals 3 FC Trannie 1
SALISBURY HOSPITAL CUP *(5th May at Bemerton Heath)*
Shrewton United 2 Downton 1
SEVENOAKS JUNIOR CHARITY CUP
(18th April at Sevenoaks Town) **Otford United Res.** 4 Seal 2
SHROPSHIRE CHARITY CUP *(23rd April at Shrewsbury Town)*
Shawbury United 3 Newport Town 2 *aet*
SHROPSHIRE JUNIOR CUP *(31st March at Shrewsbury Town)*
Clee Hill United 1 Shakespeare 0
SLOUGH JUNIOR CUP *(23rd April)*
Eton Wick Res. 3 ICI Slough 0
SMEDLEY CROOKE MEMORIAL CHARITY CUP
(1st May at Redditch) Northfield Town 0 **Fernhill County Sports** 4

SOMERSET SENIOR CUP *(5th May at Clevedon Town)*
Westland United 0 **Keynsham Town Res.** 4
SOMERSET JUNIOR CUP *(25th March at Frome Town)*
Meadow Rangers 1 **Westgate Bath** 1 *aet* (1-3p)
SOMERSET INTERMEDIATE CUP
(1st April at Cheddar)
Littleton Sports Res. 0 **Blackbrook Res.** 3
SOUTHAMPTON SENIOR CUP *(6th May at Southampton)*
Winchester City 5 Vosper Thornycroft 0
SOUTH CARDIGANSHIRE CUP *(5th May at Ffostrasol)*
Aberaeron 5 Penparcau 1
SOUTH MIDS FLOODLIGHT CUP
(1st May at Biggleswade Town)
Biggleswade Town 1 Wormley Rovers 0
SOUTH MIDS FLOODLIGHT RESERVE TEAMS CUP
(8th May at Dunstable Town)
Dunstable Town Res. 3 Hoddesdon Town Res. 1
SOUTH MOLTON Y M C A CUP *(17th May at South Molton)*
Witheridge 2 **Landkey** 4
SOUTH WALES SENIOR CUP *(30th April at Merthyr Tydfil)*
Stanleytown 1 Ynyshir Albions 0
SOUTHEND CHARITY CUP *(2nd May at Southend United)*
White Ensign 5 Rochford Town 1
STAFFS VASE *(7th April at Newcastle Town)*
Norton AG 0 **Eccleshall** 0 *aet* (1-3p)
STAFFS CHALLENGE CUP *(28th April at Rushall Olympic)*
Bilston Town 3 Blackheath Town 0
STAFFS PRESIDENT'S CUP *(31st March at Leek Town)*
Newcastle Town Res. 2 Grandy's 1
STOCKPORT & DISTRICT CUP *(8th May at Stockport County)*
Stockport Georgians Res. 3 Mellor 1
STROUD CHARITY CUP HAROLD GREENING TROPHY
(7th May at Frampton United) Slimbridge 0 **Wotton Rovers** 1
STROUD CHARITY CUP SECTION B
(6th May at Shortwood United) **Berkeley Town** 3 Tetbury Town 2
SUFFOLK SENIOR CUP *(1st April at Ipswich Town)*
Long Melford 5 Stanton 0
SUFFOLK PRIMARY CUP *(12th April)*
Claydon 0 **Bury Town Res.** 2
SURREY PREMIER CUP *(16th April at Woking)*
Tooting & Mitcham United Res. 1 **Sutton United Res.** 4
SURREY INTERMEDIATE CUP
(23rd April at Carshalton Athletic) **Nuwood** 4 Ashtead 0
SURREY JUNIOR CUP *(24th April at Egham Town)*
Warlingham Res. 2 Guildford Railway Old Boys 1

SURREY LOWER JUNIOR CUP *(13th May at Banstead Athletic)*
Anerley Athletic 5 Robin Hood 0
SUSSEX INTERMEDIATE CUP *(2nd May at Lancing)*
Eastbourne Borough Res. 4 Loxwood 1
TIPTREE CHARITY CUP *(7th May at Witham Town)*
Maldon Town Res. 2 White Notley Res. 0
TORRIDGE CUP *(1st May at Torrington)*
Torrington 5 Shamwickshire Rovers 2
WAKEFIELD & DISTRICT CUP *(9th May)*
Ardsley Celtic 3 The Station 0
WALSALL SENIOR CUP *(13th May at Walsall)*
Rocester 0 **Tividale** 1 *aet*
WALTHO CUP *(3rd May at Combe Martin)*
Braunton 1 Morwenstow 0
WELSH TROPHY *(19th April at Barry Town)*
Tillery 1 **Rhydyfelin Zenith** 4
WEM POWELL CHARITY CUP *(4th May at Wem Town)*
Shawbury United 0 **Newport Town** 4
WEST HERTS St MARY'S CUP *(5th May at Leverstock Green)*
Hemel Hempstead Town 2 Sun Postal Sports 1
WEST RIDING CHALLENGE CUP
(2nd May at WRCFA, Woodlesford) Barnoldswick Utd 0 **Silsden** 2
WEST RIDING CHALLENGE TROPHY
(25th April May at WRCFA, Woodlesford)
Park Hotel Pudsey 2 St Nicholas 2 *aet* (4-2p)
WESTWARD HO! CUP *(4th May at Barnstaple Town)*
Braunton 1 **Barnstaple AAC** 3
WHITSTABLE CHARITY CUP *(5th May at Whitstable Town)*
Canterbury Tally Ho! 2 Chislet 2 *aet* (5-3p)
WILTS SENIOR CUP *(23rd April at Chippenham Town)*
Melksham Town 2 Trowbridge Town 1 *aet*
WILTS JUNIOR CUP
147 FC 2 Rodbourne 1 *aet*
WIRRAL SENIOR CUP *(2nd May at Poulton Victoria)*
Mallaby 1 **West Kirby** 2 *aet*
WIRRAL AMATEUR CUP *(21st April at Heswall)*
Heswall Res. 0 **Cammell Laird Res.** 1
WORCS URN *(24th April at Kidderminster Harriers)*
Studley 3 Lye Town 0
WORCS JUNIOR CUP *(19th March at Worcester City)*
Bewdley Town 0 **Littleton** 1
WORCS NURSING CUP *(1st May at Worcester City)*
Archdale 3 Tolladine Sports 0
WYCOMBE SENIOR CUP *(30th April at Wycombe Wanderers)*
Chalfont Wasps 2 **Penn & Tylers Green** 3

OTHER LEAGUES

ABERYSTWYTH & DISTRICT LEAGUE

Division One	P	W	D	L	F	A	Pts
Bow Street	26	21	2	3	96	34	65
Tywyn & Bryncrug	26	19	3	4	106	31	60
Llanrhystud	26	18	1	7	65	39	55
Penrhyncoch Res.	26	15	5	6	76	44	50
Penparcau	25	15	3	7	74	41	48
Dolgellau	26	13	3	10	75	68	42
UWA Res.	26	12	3	11	58	54	39
Talybont	26	9	3	14	33	49	30
Bont	26	8	4	14	40	59	28
Llanilar	26	6	9	11	48	64	27
Aberdyfi	25	7	3	15	37	58	24
Machynlleth	26	6	6	14	30	54	24
Trawsgoed	26	7	1	18	23	82	22
Corris United	26	2	0	24	27	111	6

ALDERSHOT & DISTRICT LEAGUE

Senior Division	P	W	D	L	F	A	Pts
Frimley Town	20	13	4	3	61	33	43
Frimley Select	20	12	4	4	51	34	40
Yateley	20	13	0	7	48	41	39
Eversley Soc. Club	20	12	2	6	55	33	38
Sandhurst T. Devels	20	10	5	5	50	40	35
Anchor Blues	20	10	3	7	35	28	33
Four Marks	20	7	3	10	42	57	24
Farnboro. NE Res.	20	7	2	11	47	51	23
Bentley Athletic	20	5	5	10	34	45	20
Blackwater	20	3	4	13	31	54	13
Alton United	20	1	2	17	24	62	5

Division One	P	W	D	L	F	A	Pts
Crookham Krakatoa	26	19	4	3	86	33	61
Sandhurst Spts Club	26	17	1	8	86	50	52
Pyestock	26	16	3	7	82	48	51
Hartley Wintney 'A'	26	14	6	6	60	51	48
Frimley Town Res.	26	14	4	8	76	53	46
Courtmoor	26	14	4	8	64	47	46
Liss Athletic 'A'	26	13	4	9	58	52	43
Letef Select	26	7	9	10	43	53	30
Normandy	26	8	4	14	54	62	28
Hindhead Athletic	26	7	6	13	39	53	27
Yateley Res.	26	8	2	16	52	69	26
Fleet Spurs 'A'	26	8	2	16	52	75	26
College Town	26	8	2	16	41	72	26
Puttenham	26	2	3	21	43	118	9

Division Two	P	W	D	L	F	A	Pts
Clarence Rovers	20	14	3	3	64	33	45
Yateley Green Res.	20	14	2	4	65	26	44
Eversley SC Res.	20	14	2	4	60	34	44
Alton United Res.	20	11	6	3	59	40	39
Fleet Spurs 'B'	20	10	2	8	42	38	32
Normandy Res.	20	10	1	9	52	40	31
Frensham	20	8	3	9	43	50	27
College Town Res.	20	7	3	10	34	62	24
Yateley 'A'	20	6	0	14	52	63	18
Courtmoor Res.	20	4	1	15	30	35	13
Hindhead Ath. Res.	20	0	1	19	14	94	1

AMATEUR COMBINATION

Premier Division	P	W	D	L	F	A	Pts
Old Meadonians	20	16	3	1	55	20	51
Old Hamptonians	20	12	2	6	37	22	38
Hale End Athletic	20	8	6	6	45	36	30
Albanian	20	8	5	7	35	35	29
Old Aloysians	20	9	2	9	36	41	29
Old Wilsonians	20	8	4	8	39	39	28
UCL Academicals	20	7	6	7	40	36	27
Old Danes	20	5	5	10	33	49	20
Old Ignatians	20	6	2	12	27	46	20
Parkfield	20	4	7	9	34	45	19
Hon. Artillery Co.	20	4	4	12	30	42	16

Senior One	P	W	D	L	F	A	Pts
Old Salvatorians	20	16	1	3	58	24	49
Latymer Old Boys	20	15	2	3	50	19	47
Old Bealonians	20	13	1	6	61	24	40
Southgate County	20	10	3	7	49	38	33
Old Vaughanians	20	8	7	5	39	34	31
Old Tiffinians	20	8	3	9	44	41	27
Phoenix Old Boys	20	7	3	10	35	43	24
Card. Manning OB	20	7	0	13	41	61	21
Mill Hill Village	20	5	2	13	41	55	17
Shene Old Gramm.	19	3	3	13	28	61	12
Ulysses *-3*	19	3	3	13	32	78	9

Senior Two	P	W	D	L	F	A	Pts
Old Tenisonians	22	15	2	5	46	20	47
Old Wokingians	22	13	7	2	55	32	46
Glyn Old Boys	22	12	3	7	39	37	39
Old Isleworthians	22	11	2	9	49	44	35
Enfield Old Gramm.	22	9	6	7	41	37	33
Old Dorkinians	22	8	8	6	34	33	32
Old Manorians	22	8	7	7	46	46	31
Old Grammarians	22	8	2	12	34	41	26
Old Suttonians	22	8	2	12	37	45	26
St Marys College	22	5	4	13	35	50	19
Old Woodhouseians	22	4	6	12	35	48	18
Kings Old Boys	22	4	5	13	38	56	17

Senior Three	P	W	D	L	F	A	Pts
Economicals	20	15	1	4	75	29	46
Old Buckwellians	20	12	4	4	62	41	40
Qu. Mary Coll. OB	20	10	5	5	50	30	35
Wood Green OB	20	10	4	6	62	45	34
Univ. of Hertford	20	10	3	7	61	38	33
Pegasus	20	9	4	7	42	40	31
Old Reigatian	20	7	4	9	31	38	25
Old Minchendenians	20	6	4	10	39	55	22
Brent	20	5	5	10	31	43	20
The Rugby Clubs	20	2	7	11	29	56	13
BBC	20	3	1	16	28	95	10

Senior Four	P	W	D	L	F	A	Pts
O. Vaughanians Res.	18	11	5	2	40	27	38
John Fisher OB	18	11	3	4	56	33	36
Clapham Old Xav.	18	10	4	4	53	33	34
City of London	18	10	2	6	51	45	32
Latymer OB Res.	18	6	6	6	40	34	24
Old Sedcopians	18	7	3	8	46	49	24
Centymca	18	6	2	10	41	46	20
Old Aloysians Res.	18	3	7	8	38	37	16
O. W'houseians Res.	18	4	3	11	32	61	15
Old Tenison. Res. *-3*	18	3	3	12	24	56	9

Senior Five North	P	W	D	L	F	A	Pts
Parkfield Res.	22	15	5	2	68	25	50
Old Challoners	22	12	8	2	58	21	44
UCL Academ. Res.	22	13	3	6	65	26	42
Albanian Res.	22	13	3	6	57	56	42
Old Tollingtonians	22	10	7	5	49	35	37
Hale End Ath. Res.	22	9	2	11	54	53	29
O. Salvatorians Res.	22	7	8	7	36	40	29
Pegasus Res.	22	7	3	12	47	57	24
Egbertian	22	5	5	12	41	61	20
Mill Hill Vill. Res.	22	4	6	12	33	60	18
Old Manor. Res. *-3*	22	5	3	14	28	78	15
Old Edmontonians	22	3	5	14	47	71	14

Senior Five South	P	W	D	L	F	A	Pts
Chert. Old Salesians	22	16	3	3	70	35	51
Old Hampton. Res.	22	17	0	5	58	37	51
Old Wilsonians Res.	21	15	1	5	47	18	46
Sinjuns	22	12	4	6	68	42	40
London Welsh	22	12	3	7	61	60	39
Witan	22	9	3	10	48	50	30
Hon. Art. Co. Res.	22	8	3	11	48	54	27
Mickleham O. Box.	22	7	5	10	54	54	26
St Marys Coll. Res.	21	6	5	10	46	58	23
O. Meadonians Res.	22	4	3	15	35	63	15
Old St Marys	22	4	3	15	26	55	15
Old Grammar. Res.	22	2	5	15	45	80	11

ANDOVER & DISTRICT LEAGUE

Division One	P	W	D	L	F	A	Pts
Andover N. St. 'B'	14	11	2	1	61	29	35
ABC United	14	11	2	1	49	19	35
Station Hotel	14	9	0	5	47	32	27
Borough Arms	14	6	2	6	35	32	20
Picket Piece S&S	14	5	2	7	40	45	17
Inkpen Exiles	14	5	0	9	33	40	15
King's Somborne	14	3	1	10	22	54	10
Whitchurch Utd 'A'	14	1	1	12	24	60	4

Division Two	P	W	D	L	F	A	Pts
Andover Rail. Club	14	11	3	0	64	15	36
Screenbase	14	10	2	2	57	25	32
Royal Oak 2002	14	8	3	3	49	23	27
Over Wallop	14	7	1	6	26	41	22
Picket Piece SS Res.	14	5	1	8	33	38	16
Shipton Bellinger	14	4	2	8	27	47	14
Burghclere	14	3	1	10	29	47	10
Wallop Wanderers	14	1	1	12	17	66	4

ANGLESEY LEAGUE

	P	W	D	L	F	A	Pts
Llangefni Town Res.	14	11	0	3	62	24	33
Amlwch Town Res.	14	10	1	3	28	19	31
Holy. Gwelfor Ath.	14	8	1	5	40	31	25
Llanerchymedd	14	6	3	5	29	30	21
Llangoed & District	14	5	2	7	37	36	17
Llanfairpwll Res.	14	3	6	5	29	29	15
Llandegfan	14	2	3	9	17	49	9
Gwalchmai	14	2	2	10	18	42	8

(Holyhead Ex-Servicemen's – record expunged)

ARTHURIAN LEAGUE

Premier Division	P	W	D	L	F	A	Pts
Old Foresters	18	13	3	2	48	19	42
Old Brentwoods	18	9	2	7	44	36	29
Lancing Old Boys	18	9	2	7	32	35	29
Old Salopians	18	8	4	6	27	28	28
Old Carthusians	18	8	2	8	32	31	26
Old Harrovians	18	8	1	9	54	48	25
Old Westminsters	18	7	3	8	20	22	24
Old Etonians	18	7	3	8	32	43	24
Old Reptonians	18	3	8	7	30	34	17
Old Chigwellians	18	2	4	12	19	42	10

BASINGSTOKE & DISTRICT LEAGUE

Premier Division	P	W	D	L	F	A	Pts
Bramley United	18	15	2	1	78	26	47
New Inn	18	13	3	2	54	19	42
Wellington Social	18	8	5	5	48	27	29
Hook	18	9	2	7	40	25	29
Oakley Athletic	18	8	3	7	39	25	27
Aldermaston Res.	18	7	3	8	36	42	24
B'stoke Lab. Club	18	6	3	9	34	40	21
Oakridge West	18	6	3	9	25	42	21
Kingsclere	18	3	1	14	25	82	10
Water End	18	2	1	15	25	76	7

Division One	P	W	D	L	F	A	Pts
Tylney Hall	18	12	3	3	65	29	39
Wellington Soc. Res.	18	11	1	6	45	39	34
Headley Athletic	18	10	3	5	59	33	33
South Ham Rangers	18	11	0	7	49	30	33
New Inn Res.	18	9	3	6	51	43	30
Silchester United	18	7	4	7	42	28	25
Lamb Inn	18	7	2	9	37	46	23
Sainsburys Newbury	18	7	2	9	44	54	23
Sherborne St John	18	3	2	13	41	74	11
Ropley	18	3	0	15	23	80	9

Division Two	P	W	D	L	F	A	Pts
Nine Saxons	18	14	1	3	80	25	43
Herriard Sports	18	13	2	3	67	24	41
Aldermaston 'A'	18	13	2	3	52	21	41
Oakley Athletic Res.	18	9	2	7	36	31	29
Tadley Town 'A'	18	8	1	9	42	46	25
Overton United 'A'	18	8	1	9	35	51	25
Sherfield	18	6	0	12	28	48	18
Great Western	18	5	1	12	30	58	16
Chineham	18	5	0	13	30	57	15
Kingsclere Res.	18	4	0	14	28	67	12

BATH & DISTRICT LEAGUE

Division One	P	W	D	L	F	A	Pts
Westgate Bath	16	16	0	0	84	11	48
Odd Down Athletic	16	10	3	3	53	31	33
Bath Arsenal	16	9	2	5	38	23	29
Oval Sports	16	8	2	6	48	39	26
Bath University	16	7	2	7	27	32	23
Saltford Res.	16	5	3	8	22	31	18
Keynsham Town 'A'	16	4	3	9	19	35	15
Claverton Academ.	16	2	4	10	24	51	10
Larkhall Ath. 'A'	16	1	1	14	15	77	4

Division Two	P	W	D	L	F	A	Pts
CS Filos	24	19	1	4	75	24	58
Aces SSJ	24	17	3	4	97	40	54
Oval Sports Res. *-1*	24	15	3	6	72	48	47
Fry Club Old Boys	24	12	3	9	87	75	39
Batheaston Athletic	24	12	2	10	79	63	38
Cutters Friday Res.	24	11	5	8	59	50	38
Sothert & Pitt	24	10	5	9	54	55	35
Newton & Corston	24	9	5	10	60	49	32
WESA	24	9	1	14	76	72	28
Freshford Sports	24	8	3	13	51	68	27
Bath Spa University	24	7	2	15	40	71	23
Odd Down Ath. Res.	24	6	2	16	44	107	20
Red Star Bath	24	3	1	20	38	110	10

Division Three	P	W	D	L	F	A	Pts
CCB United	20	14	4	2	81	34	46
Oldfield Sports	20	14	4	2	67	25	46
Bath Arsenal Res.	20	14	3	3	61	31	45
Aces SSJ Res.	19	10	3	6	50	40	33
Westwood U. (Bath)	20	8	6	6	53	40	30
Top Wall	19	8	3	8	53	45	27
IPL	20	7	4	9	36	42	25
Bath Post Office	20	7	1	12	50	76	22
Wesco United	20	6	3	11	46	44	21
Express Dairies	20	4	2	14	45	71	14
Porter Butt	20	0	1	19	15	109	1

BOURNEMOUTH LEAGUE

Division One	P	W	D	L	F	A	Pts
Westover B'mouth	22	19	1	2	75	18	58
Bournemouth CS	22	16	2	4	56	22	50
B'mouth Electric *-3*	22	15	2	5	52	27	44
Burton	22	11	3	8	41	35	36
Hamw'thy Rec Res.	22	9	5	8	47	45	32
Redlynch & WU *+3*	22	8	5	9	40	47	32
Trinidad New Star	22	8	3	11	37	48	27
Southbourne	22	8	3	11	53	71	27
Dorset Knob	22	7	4	11	40	47	25
Pennington St Marks	22	5	3	14	24	39	18
Sway	22	4	4	14	34	72	16
Stourvale	22	2	5	15	29	57	11

Division Two	P	W	D	L	F	A	Pts
B'mth Electric Res.	22	14	2	6	69	43	44
AFC Highcliffe	22	14	2	6	66	42	44
West Moors	22	13	3	6	68	33	42
Bisterne United	22	11	6	5	43	34	39
N. Milton Eagles *+3*	22	9	6	7	45	49	36
Ringwood T. Res.	22	10	4	8	45	34	34
PS Abbey Life *-3*	22	10	3	9	51	47	30
Westover B. Res.	22	9	2	11	43	50	29
Chiropractic	22	9	2	11	42	52	29
J P Morgan	22	7	3	12	39	56	24
St Mary's	22	5	1	16	28	67	16
B'mouth Sports Res.	22	2	4	16	23	55	10

Division Three	P	W	D	L	F	A	Pts
Redhill Rangers	22	18	3	1	72	26	57
Burton Res.	22	15	4	3	66	24	49
Verwood T. Res.	22	12	4	6	40	28	40
Queens Park Ath.	22	10	4	8	35	35	34
B'mouth CS Res.	22	11	1	10	44	48	34
Mag./Woolsb'dge U.	22	9	4	9	43	47	31
Lym. & NM 'A'	22	8	5	9	28	25	29
Penn. St Marks Res.	22	7	5	10	42	50	26
Fordingbridge Turks	22	7	3	12	34	44	24
DMC *-1*	22	7	3	12	33	40	23
Red./Woodfalls Res.	22	4	4	14	33	67	16
Sway Res.	22	2	4	16	26	62	10

Division Four	P	W	D	L	F	A	Pts
Ferndown Town	20	13	6	1	62	30	45
Talbot Rise	20	14	2	4	71	35	44
Bisterne United Res.	20	14	2	4	61	26	44
Premier Trading	20	11	3	6	60	46	36
Burley	20	9	4	7	51	51	31
AFC Haymoor *-3*	20	8	3	9	42	28	24
Westover B. 'A'	20	7	3	10	46	49	24
Magpies & W. Res.	20	6	6	8	44	47	24
AFC Highcliffe Res.	20	2	6	12	25	59	12
Walkford SFC	20	3	3	14	27	77	12
Ringwood T. 'A'	20	2	4	14	33	74	10

Division Five	P	W	D	L	F	A	Pts
Harrington United	22	16	2	4	68	34	50
Talbot Rise Res.	22	15	3	4	79	34	48
Redlynch & W. 'A'	22	13	4	5	47	31	43
Griffin	22	14	0	8	69	35	42
PS Abbey Life Res.	22	11	1	10	57	53	34
South End Keys	22	10	3	9	50	59	33
Alderholt	22	10	1	11	56	52	31
Queens Pk Ath Res.	22	7	7	8	38	42	28
Southbourne Res.	22	6	5	11	49	50	23
Stourvale Res.	22	6	4	12	32	48	22
Portcastrian	22	3	3	16	44	80	12
St Mary's Res.	22	3	3	16	36	107	12

Division Six	P	W	D	L	F	A	Pts
Mag. & Wool. 'A'	20	15	3	2	67	24	48
Charminster Ath *+3*	20	13	1	6	66	40	43
Boscombe Celtic *-3*	20	14	2	4	76	27	41
NM Eagles Res.	20	11	3	6	56	40	36
Britannia *-1*	20	9	8	3	44	38	34
Fordingbridge Res.	20	9	3	8	52	41	30
Pheonix DB	20	7	3	10	42	48	24
Moordown United	20	7	2	11	51	75	23
New Lodge	20	5	4	11	41	58	19
Redhill Rgrs Res.	20	3	4	13	45	85	13
Redlynch & W. 'B'	20	0	1	19	25	89	1

BRIGHTON, HOVE & DISTRICT LEAGUE

Premier Division	P	W	D	L	F	A	Pts
Old Varndeanians	18	13	4	1	63	30	43
Harbour View	18	10	4	4	51	26	34
Montpelier Villa	18	9	6	3	41	24	33
Whitehawk Veterans	18	7	3	8	35	43	24
AFC St Georges	18	7	3	8	39	53	24
Rottingdean Village	18	7	2	9	31	31	23
Royal Sovereign	18	6	4	8	30	39	22
Midway	18	4	7	7	23	27	19
Meridian Athletic	18	5	4	9	24	34	19
Legal & General	18	2	3	13	29	59	9

Division One	P	W	D	L	F	A	Pts
Hanover	18	15	2	1	56	16	47
South Cent. Wdrs	18	12	2	4	67	34	38
American Express	18	10	3	5	51	37	33
Rottingdean United	18	10	3	5	45	37	33
Portslade Athletic	18	8	3	7	37	31	27
Old Varn. Res. *-3*	18	7	2	9	33	45	20
Southern Rgrs OB	18	5	2	11	35	63	17
Rot'dean V. Res. *+3*	18	3	3	12	19	37	15
Montpelier Villa Res.	18	3	6	9	31	50	15
Brighton BBOB	18	2	4	12	28	52	10

Division Two	P	W	D	L	F	A	Pts
Brighton Electricity	14	13	0	1	64	21	39
Brighton Rangers	14	10	2	2	39	17	32
Autopaints *+2*	14	6	3	5	36	42	23
Grenadier *-1*	14	6	5	3	35	33	22
Coversure Athletic	14	5	3	6	48	47	18
Ericsson	14	3	1	10	30	40	10
Midway Res. *-3*	14	3	3	8	24	49	9
Portslade A. Res. *+3*	14	1	1	12	28	55	7

Division Three	P	W	D	L	F	A	Pts
FC Midlothians	18	15	1	2	69	30	46
Portslade Sports	18	14	2	2	65	26	44
Real Conqueror *-3*	18	11	3	4	71	33	33
Legal/General Res.	18	10	1	7	42	45	31
CCK	18	6	4	8	40	60	22
Marquess of Exeter	18	6	2	10	35	35	20
Fairlight Garage *+3*	18	5	2	11	28	49	20
Old V'deanians 'A'	18	5	3	10	27	38	18
AFC Stanley	18	5	3	10	31	49	18
Ricardo	18	2	1	15	18	61	7

Division Four	P	W	D	L	F	A	Pts
Shoreham United	16	11	1	4	56	28	34
Brighton Sports	16	11	0	5	45	24	33
Whitehawk V. Res.	16	10	2	4	53	30	32
Brighton Rgrs Res.	16	10	0	6	55	31	30
Harbour V. Res. *-3*	16	9	1	6	37	31	25
Rottingdean V. 'A'	16	6	2	8	33	38	20
Meridian Ath. Res.	16	5	2	9	31	46	17
AFC Buckingham	16	3	3	10	33	54	12
Brighton BBOB Res.	16	1	1	14	19	80	4

Division Five	P	W	D	L	F	A	Pts
Master Tiles	16	14	0	2	56	22	42
Men In Black	16	13	1	2	80	29	40
Adur Athletic Res.	16	11	1	4	61	26	34
Ovingdean	16	8	1	7	51	35	25
Brighton 1664	16	7	0	9	33	45	21
Brighton A & E	16	5	2	9	43	52	17
AFC Manor	16	4	2	10	35	56	14
AFC Standen	16	2	3	11	38	80	9
Hove Palmeira	16	2	2	12	27	79	8

BRISTOL PREMIER COMBINATION

Premier Division	P	W	D	L	F	A	Pts
Bitton Res.	26	17	6	3	56	26	57
Rangeworthy	26	14	7	5	54	32	49
Hartcliffe	26	13	6	7	51	39	45
Sea Mills Park	26	14	2	10	71	46	44
Nicholas Wanderers	26	13	5	8	44	28	44
Longwell Green Sp.	26	12	6	8	45	33	42
Hillfields Old Boys	26	12	2	12	52	55	38
Highridge Utd Res.	26	10	6	10	34	45	36
Hallen Res.	26	9	7	10	47	47	34
RMC Wick	26	10	4	12	39	50	34
Hanham Athletic	26	9	6	11	51	52	33
Bristol Union	26	7	6	13	38	48	27
St Philips Marsh AS	26	4	3	19	43	82	15
Iron Acton	26	3	4	19	25	67	13

CARDIFF & DISTRICT LEAGUE

Premier Division	P	W	D	L	F	A	Pts
St Patricks	22	17	3	2	70	21	54
Pentwyn Dyn. Res.	22	15	3	4	57	33	48
Splott Albion	22	13	2	7	81	60	41
Grangет'n Cath. OB	22	9	8	5	57	44	35
Clwb Cymric	22	9	4	9	49	45	31
St Albans	22	7	6	9	51	48	27
AFC Rumney	22	8	2	12	40	63	26
Grange Quins Res.	22	6	7	9	43	50	25
Cardiff Rovers	22	5	9	8	38	36	24
The Villa	22	6	5	11	42	62	23
Cwrt-y-Vil	22	5	4	13	40	67	19
St Marys (Cardiff)	22	3	5	14	28	67	14

CENTRAL & SOUTH NORFOLK LEAGUE

Division One	P	W	D	L	F	A	Pts
Yaxham	22	20	2	0	96	15	62
Methwold Hythe	22	13	4	5	89	40	43
Hingham Athletic	22	10	5	7	62	41	35
Whissonsett	22	10	4	8	62	53	34
Bircham	22	9	5	8	46	43	32
Fakenham T. 'A'	22	9	5	8	58	67	32
Dereham T. 'A'	22	9	3	10	38	43	30
Swaffham T. 'A'	22	8	6	8	38	48	30
Holy Trinity	22	6	8	8	50	55	26
Hempnall 'A'	22	7	2	13	34	61	23
Attleborough 'A'	22	3	4	15	26	64	13
Hepworth	22	2	4	16	36	105	10

Division Two	P	W	D	L	F	A	Pts
Longham	26	20	2	4	101	32	62
Dickleburgh	26	20	2	4	121	55	62
Tacolneston	26	19	2	5	82	53	59
North Elmham	26	16	4	6	74	43	52
Old Buckenham	26	12	6	8	92	65	42
Morley Village Res.	26	11	6	9	61	57	39
Rockland United	26	11	3	12	63	81	36
Wendling	26	9	4	13	54	59	31
Necton SSC Res.	26	8	4	14	56	88	28
Stoke Ferry	26	8	3	15	71	84	27
Bridgham	26	7	4	15	55	83	25
Toftwood United	26	5	7	14	46	84	22
Feltwell United	26	5	5	16	51	81	20
Shropham United	26	3	4	19	44	106	13

Division Three	P	W	D	L	F	A	Pts
East Harling	22	19	2	1	110	21	59
Ditchingham Rov.	22	18	0	4	102	37	54
Beetley	22	15	2	5	64	31	47
Mulbarton Wdrs	22	12	2	8	60	40	38
Watton United 'A'	22	11	0	11	61	55	33
Bawdeswell	22	9	2	11	52	72	29
Yaxham Res.	22	8	2	12	50	68	26
Methwold H. Res.	22	6	4	12	49	89	22
Hingham Ath. Res.	22	7	0	15	57	79	21
Saham Toney Res.	22	7	2	13	45	65	23
Cockers	22	6	1	15	43	78	19
Wortham	22	4	3	15	34	92	15

Division Four	P	W	D	L	F	A	Pts
Redgrave Rangers	26	23	1	2	153	23	70
East Harling Res.	26	17	8	1	92	50	59
Long Stratton Res.	26	15	5	6	109	53	50
Whissonsett Res.	26	14	5	7	100	50	47
Scarning	26	12	5	9	61	57	41
North Elmham Res.	26	12	3	11	61	69	39
Harleston Town 'A'	26	11	3	12	72	65	36
Mattishall 'A'	26	11	2	13	58	76	35
Cherry Tree	26	8	8	10	38	56	32
Rockland Utd Res.	26	8	6	12	60	86	30
Great Cressingham	26	7	7	12	44	67	28
Longham Res.	26	5	7	14	40	74	22
Beetley Res.	26	2	8	16	23	70	14
Toftwood Utd Res.	26	1	4	21	17	132	7

COLCHESTER & EAST ESSEX LEAGUE

Premier Division	P	W	D	L	F	A	Pts
University of Essex	20	15	3	2	75	23	48
Tollesbury	20	14	3	3	76	32	45
Berechurch Rangers	20	14	3	3	61	22	45
Forty Fives	20	12	2	6	61	40	38
Norside	20	10	4	6	43	32	34
Eight Ash Green	20	10	2	8	64	41	32
Walton Town Res.	20	8	3	9	49	54	27
Foxash Social Res.	20	6	3	11	32	62	21
Colchester Hotspurs	20	3	2	15	21	83	11
Weeley Athletic 'A'	20	2	4	14	37	80	10
Feering United	20	1	1	18	21	71	4

Division One	P	W	D	L	F	A	Pts
Harwich Rangers	16	14	0	2	53	16	42
Brightlingsea Res.	16	14	0	2	60	25	42
Tolleshunt K E	16	11	1	4	87	45	34
Castle	16	9	2	5	49	40	29
Univ. of Essex Res.	16	8	0	8	36	38	24
Doverston	16	7	0	9	29	37	21
Nayland Rangers	16	4	1	11	21	56	13
Great Bentley Res.	16	2	1	13	29	58	7
Stoke-by-Nayland	16	0	1	15	16	65	1

Division Two	P	W	D	L	F	A	Pts
Harwich & P. 'A'	18	14	3	1	74	31	45
Clacton Town 'A'	18	13	3	2	49	18	42
Ardleigh United	18	12	1	5	53	37	37
Posties FC	18	9	2	7	42	32	29
Univ. of Essex 'A'	18	7	4	7	42	33	25
Frinton & Walton	18	6	6	6	52	45	24
Oyster	18	5	5	8	37	36	20
Wormingford	18	4	3	11	32	40	15
Kemp Athletic	18	4	3	11	25	40	15
Donyland Swifts	18	0	2	16	12	106	2

Division Three	P	W	D	L	F	A	Pts
AFC Axa	20	15	0	5	70	22	45
St Osyth 'A'	20	14	1	5	64	30	43
Royal London	20	13	3	4	40	25	42
Univ. Of Essex 'B'	20	13	0	7	60	31	39
Lawford Lads 'A'	20	12	3	5	50	31	39
Frinton & W. Res.	20	10	1	9	60	48	31
Tollesbury Res.	20	6	3	11	29	44	21
Abberton	20	6	3	11	39	67	21
Sudbury Ath. 'A'	20	5	0	15	23	65	15
Kemp Athletic Res.	20	4	1	15	25	59	13
Mistley United 'A'	20	4	1	15	26	64	13

Division Four	P	W	D	L	F	A	Pts
Stoke-by-Nay. Res.	14	9	3	2	39	23	30
Bradfield Rov. Res.	14	8	2	4	41	27	26
Ardleigh Utd Res.	14	6	6	2	37	24	24
Forty Fives Res.	14	6	4	4	38	21	22
Highwayman	14	6	1	7	31	27	19
MSX International	14	4	3	7	21	39	15
Wormingford Res.	14	2	7	5	28	31	13
Wimpole	14	1	2	11	24	67	5

CRAWLEY & DISTRICT LEAGUE

Premier Division	P	W	D	L	F	A	Pts
Monotype	22	17	3	2	84	29	54
Boca Seniors	22	16	3	3	84	38	51
TD Sports	22	14	1	7	45	32	43
Virgin	22	11	6	5	50	30	39
Phoenix	22	11	3	8	54	45	36
Oakwood 'A'	22	11	0	11	55	72	33
Horley Albion	22	9	5	8	39	46	32
Wooldridge Tavern	22	8	3	11	42	40	27
Holland Sports	22	8	3	11	45	60	27
Three Bridges 'A'	22	5	0	17	37	60	15
Bluebird Rangers	22	3	5	14	45	88	14
Edwards Sports	22	2	2	18	26	66	8

Division One	P	W	D	L	F	A	Pts
St Francis Flyers	18	12	4	2	62	30	40
Monotype Res.	18	12	2	4	61	32	38
Bewbush Athletic -1	18	12	2	4	52	32	37
Real Hydraquip	18	11	3	4	47	23	36
Trident	18	8	3	7	52	31	27
TD Sports Res. +2	18	6	7	5	31	27	27
Crawley Elite	18	7	5	6	36	43	26
Worth Park Rangers	18	3	3	12	21	71	12
Youngmans	18	2	3	13	24	62	9
Langshott	18	1	0	17	13	48	3

Division Two	P	W	D	L	F	A	Pts
Virgin Res.	22	19	3	0	89	27	60
St Francis Fly. Res.	22	19	1	2	90	37	58
FC Rocket	22	18	1	3	75	27	55
Ifield Res.	22	12	2	8	55	52	38
Oakwood 'B'	22	10	3	9	55	54	33
Phoenix Res.	22	9	0	13	28	65	27
Newtown Dynamo	22	8	2	12	61	58	26
Seebrook Rovers	22	8	0	14	40	55	24
Holland Sports Res.	22	7	0	15	52	93	21
Kingscote	22	6	2	14	39	58	20
Border Wanderers	22	4	2	16	23	68	14
W'dridge Tav. Res.	22	3	2	17	26	39	11

Division Three	P	W	D	L	F	A	Pts
Langley Green	20	15	2	3	91	33	47
Horley Albion Res.	20	14	0	6	53	39	42
Horley Town 'A'	20	13	1	6	76	51	40
Sporting Crawley	20	12	1	7	53	34	37
Crawley College +3	20	10	1	9	76	52	34
Stones	20	9	3	8	58	60	30
White Lady +2	20	8	3	9	40	39	29
Real Hydraquip Res.	20	6	2	12	36	53	20
Worth Park R. Res.	20	6	0	14	59	68	18
Crawley Hospital -4	20	6	4	10	37	64	18
Crawley Dynamos	20	2	1	17	27	113	7

DONCASTER SENIOR LEAGUE

Premier Division	P	W	D	L	F	A	Pts
Hemsworth St Pat.	24	20	1	3	64	27	61
S. Kirkby Coll. Res.	24	19	1	4	112	36	58
Armthorpe	24	18	3	3	97	18	57
Askern Welf. Res.	24	16	1	7	51	37	49
Carcroft V. WMC	24	11	4	9	63	55	37
Bawtry Town	24	10	4	10	52	64	34
Upton/Harew'd Soc.	24	9	3	12	44	70	30
Mexboro. Red Lion	24	9	1	14	41	51	28
Eden Grove	24	8	3	13	47	62	27
Kinsley Boys	24	6	5	13	41	58	23
Harworth CI Res.	24	5	4	15	35	68	19
Ackworth United	24	4	5	15	42	72	17
Sutton Rovers	24	2	3	19	25	96	9

DURHAM ALLIANCE

	P	W	D	L	F	A	Pts
Coxhoe Athletic	28	20	2	6	77	34	62
Whitehill	28	19	4	5	90	39	61
Shildon Railway	28	18	3	7	78	51	57
Black & Decker	28	17	5	6	79	41	56
Hartlepool Town	28	17	3	8	88	42	54
Brandon Station	28	16	6	6	74	32	54
Sptg Club Sund. -3	28	16	5	7	81	49	50
Cockfield	28	14	6	8	74	42	48
Belford House	28	14	6	8	68	51	48
Seaham Duke	28	10	2	16	59	68	32
Seaham Mallard	28	6	4	18	54	96	22
Birtley Town Res.	28	4	5	19	46	103	17
Simonside SC -3	28	5	0	23	49	109	12
Dur. Victoria Bdge	28	3	2	23	34	93	11
Ebchester -3	28	4	1	23	44	145	10

EAST MIDLANDS ALLIANCE

Division One	P	W	D	L	F	A	Pts
Corby St Brendans	10	8	0	2	45	23	24
Oakham Imperials	10	7	3	0	35	13	24
Corby Grampion	10	6	2	2	38	19	20
Langham	10	2	3	5	18	26	9
Corby Ravens	10	1	1	8	16	46	4
Kett. Orchard Park	10	0	3	7	12	37	3

Division Two	P	W	D	L	F	A	Pts
Kett. Orch. Pk Res.	12	9	2	1	42	17	29
Corby St Bren. Res.	12	7	2	3	45	23	23
Corb. CIC Flamingo	12	5	2	5	28	26	17
Oakham Imps Res.	12	3	1	8	30	50	10
Corby Ravens Res.	12	1	3	8	19	48	6

(The East Midlands Alliance has now merged with the Northants Combination)

ESSEX & HERTS BORDER COMBINATION

Premier Division	P	W	D	L	F	A	Pts
Canvey Island Res.	30	23	3	4	101	28	72
Hornchurch Res.	30	22	4	4	91	22	70
Gt Wakering Res.	30	18	7	5	81	34	61
Braintree Town Res.	30	18	4	8	65	34	58
Leyton Res.	30	17	5	8	77	32	56
E. Thurrock Res. -2	30	15	11	4	60	26	54
Ilford Res.	30	15	4	11	60	54	49
Witham Town Res.	30	15	3	12	62	61	48
Heybridge S. Res.	30	11	8	11	69	57	41
Ware Res.	30	11	8	11	47	67	41
Brentwood Res.	30	8	5	17	48	73	29
Tilbury Res.	30	8	5	17	38	64	29
Cheshunt Res.	30	6	3	21	40	80	21
Broxbourne B. Res.	30	4	5	21	39	99	17
Walth. Abbey Res.	30	4	4	22	30	97	16
Burnham Ram. Res.	30	5	1	24	34	114	16

Division One	P	W	D	L	F	A	Pts
Purfleet Res.	26	19	6	1	80	20	63
Barking & EH Res.	26	17	5	4	72	29	56
St Albans City Res.	26	17	4	5	74	31	55
Romford Res.	26	13	3	10	52	48	42
Bowers United Res.	26	8	11	7	32	41	35
Concord Rgrs Res.	26	9	7	10	42	49	34
Basildon Utd Res.	26	10	4	12	35	49	34
Sawb'dgeworth Res.	26	10	4	12	34	58	34
Maldon T. Res. -3	26	9	6	11	43	46	30
Southend Mnr Res.	26	8	6	12	37	45	30
Hertford Town Res.	26	7	8	11	37	41	29
Harlow Town Res.	26	6	9	11	35	47	27
Stansted Res.	26	4	8	14	27	55	20
Hoddesdon T. Res.	26	2	5	19	28	69	11

GREAT YARMOUTH & DISTRICT LEAGUE

Division One	P	W	D	L	F	A	Pts
MK United	18	13	1	4	62	34	40
King William	18	13	0	5	52	33	39
Freethorpe	18	10	1	7	47	31	31
Town Hall	18	8	4	6	41	36	28
Magdalen Arms	18	8	2	8	43	47	26
Hemsby	18	7	3	8	41	33	24
Sports United -3	18	7	3	8	47	59	21
Gorleston 'A' -3	18	5	3	10	43	57	15
Gt Yarmouth 'A' -3	18	5	2	11	39	58	14
Camden Tavern -3	18	3	3	12	32	59	9

Division Two	P	W	D	L	F	A	Pts
Prince FC	18	16	2	0	96	11	50
Gt Yarm. Ceilings	18	15	0	3	67	20	45
Centurion	18	12	2	4	92	24	38
Catfield	18	11	1	6	47	28	34
Ormesby -3	18	9	3	6	57	38	27
Halvergate Utd 'A'	18	7	1	10	38	50	22
Martham Res.	18	6	2	10	40	39	20
Reedham	18	2	3	13	25	71	9
Freethorpe Res. -3	18	2	2	14	18	85	5
MK United Res.	18	1	2	15	12	126	5

Division Three	P	W	D	L	F	A	Pts
Archers	18	15	2	1	86	18	47
Clipper Schooner	18	14	0	4	84	38	42
Salisbury Arms	18	13	1	4	72	32	40
Hemsby Res.	18	11	0	7	66	44	33
Caister United 'A'	18	10	2	6	48	39	32
Gorleston 'B' -6	18	9	2	7	52	44	23
JPH	18	3	3	12	22	64	12
Ormesby Res.	18	3	2	13	47	94	11
Heritage United	18	3	0	15	37	86	9
Town Hall Res.	18	3	0	15	31	86	9

GWENT CENTRAL LEAGUE

Division One	P	W	D	L	F	A	Pts
PILCS	26	23	2	1	103	25	71
Sebastopol	26	21	2	3	122	35	65
Usk Town	26	18	4	4	110	42	58
Tranch Res.	26	16	3	7	61	42	51
Gilwern & District	26	15	4	7	71	50	49
Goytre Res.	26	15	2	9	77	46	47
Llanarth	26	10	7	9	81	64	37
Mardy Res. -3 +3	26	7	5	14	50	89	26
Panteg Res.	26	7	3	16	52	84	24
Clydach Wasps Res.	26	6	5	15	54	78	23
Lower New Inn	26	6	3	17	44	75	21
Pontypool Town	26	4	4	18	63	102	16
Little Mill Utd -3	26	5	3	18	50	143	15
Fairfield Utd Res. -3	26	4	3	19	30	93	12

Division Two	P	W	D	L	F	A	Pts
Cwmffrwdoer Res.	22	18	4	0	121	33	58
Crickhowell	22	15	4	3	86	30	49
Blaenavon B. Res.	22	14	3	5	76	45	45
Govilon Res.	22	11	4	7	78	46	37
PILCS Res.	22	11	3	8	74	57	36
Race Res.	22	9	6	7	56	47	33
New Inn Res. -3	22	7	5	10	44	80	23
Llantilio -6	22	8	2	12	64	62	20
Prescoed	22	4	5	13	49	78	17
Pontypool T. Res.	22	5	2	15	38	103	17
Sebastopol Res.	22	5	1	16	48	95	16
Gilwern & D. Res.	22	5	1	16	37	95	16

GWYNEDD LEAGUE

Premier Division	P	W	D	L	F	A	Pts
Llanrug United	24	18	4	2	69	24	58
Beaumaris Town	24	18	2	4	95	38	56
Porthmadog Res.	24	15	3	6	78	44	48
Pwllheli	24	14	4	6	78	41	46
Llanrwst United	24	14	2	8	45	40	44
Nefyn United	24	13	3	8	75	57	42
Nantlle Vale	24	12	3	9	57	52	39
Blaenau Ffestiniog	24	10	3	11	61	58	33
Caernarfon T. Res.	24	8	0	16	53	69	24
Holyh'd Hot. Res.	24	6	3	15	36	77	21
Bangor University	24	5	2	17	42	72	17
Llanfairfechan T.	24	3	3	18	30	87	12
Deinolen	24	3	2	19	39	99	11

Division One	P	W	D	L	F	A	Pts
L'dudno Cricketers	10	10	0	0	50	15	30
Machno United	10	5	2	3	28	27	17
Bangor Univ. Res.	10	5	1	4	37	35	16
Llanrwst Utd Res.	10	2	3	5	16	28	9
Conwy United Res.	10	2	2	6	38	40	8
Llandudno Jun. Res.	10	1	2	7	18	42	5

WWW.NLNEWSDESK.CO.UK

HEREFORDSHIRE LEAGUE

Premier Division	P	W	D	L	F	A	Pts
Wellington Rangers	22	17	4	1	83	25	55
Ewyas Harold	22	14	4	4	63	39	46
Woofferton	22	14	4	4	47	25	46
Painters	22	11	2	9	54	49	35
Leominster T. Res.	22	11	1	10	50	56	34
Westfields Res.	22	8	7	7	41	39	31
Ross Utd Services	22	9	3	10	54	45	30
Hinton Res.	22	7	5	10	42	52	26
Sutton United	22	7	4	11	38	53	25
Fownhope	22	5	4	13	31	53	19
Weston Rhyn Utd	22	5	2	15	41	66	17
Pegasus Jun. Res.	22	3	2	17	26	68	11

Division One	P	W	D	L	F	A	Pts
Hereford Lads Club	16	12	2	2	40	14	38
Tupsley	16	11	1	4	55	19	34
Bartestree	16	10	2	4	45	26	32
Pencombe	16	8	2	6	37	24	26
Woofferton Res.	16	7	1	8	27	42	22
Holme Lacy	16	6	2	8	38	36	20
Weobley	16	6	2	8	36	34	20
Colwall Rangers	16	4	2	10	26	35	14
Fownhope Res.	16	1	0	15	13	87	3

Division Two	P	W	D	L	F	A	Pts
Ross Utd Serv. Res.	22	19	1	2	78	24	58
Shobdon	22	16	0	6	64	33	48
Kington Town Res.	22	15	0	7	60	34	45
Ewyas Harold Res.	22	10	6	6	76	47	36
Orleton	22	11	2	9	65	49	35
Skenfrith United	22	11	2	9	56	53	35
Burghill	22	10	3	9	38	38	33
Wel'ton Rgrs Colts	22	10	1	11	57	61	31
Leintwardine Colts	22	7	3	12	53	71	24
Weston Rhyn Res.	22	5	1	16	40	97	16
Hereford Civil Serv.	22	4	1	17	41	85	13
Dorstone United	22	2	4	16	33	69	10

Division Four	P	W	D	L	F	A	Pts
Widemarsh Rangers	22	18	2	2	89	28	56
Kingstone Rovers	22	17	3	2	88	42	54
Allpay	22	15	1	6	57	29	46
Tupsley Colts	22	13	4	5	63	43	43
Bulmers	22	9	3	10	61	48	30
Marriotts	22	8	4	10	53	54	28
Hereford Sports	22	8	2	12	43	70	26
Pegasus Colts	22	7	2	13	53	65	23
Hereford LC Colts	22	6	5	11	35	55	23
Orcop Juniors	22	6	1	15	35	77	19
Stoke Prior	22	5	3	14	30	59	18
Bartestree Res.	22	3	4	15	36	73	13

HOUNSLOW & DISTRICT LEAGUE

Premier Division	P	W	D	L	F	A	Pts
Locomotive	20	13	4	3	38	18	43
Northfield Sham. +3	20	11	2	7	54	35	38
East Fulham	20	11	4	5	64	40	37
TSL Feltham	20	10	4	6	52	34	34
Sligo Rovers	20	10	3	7	52	42	33
St. John's Ath. -3	20	11	2	7	52	33	32
Bison	20	9	5	6	41	32	32
CB Hounslow 'A'	20	7	3	10	33	40	24
Hanworth	20	4	4	12	27	62	16
Bedham Old Boys	20	4	3	13	31	61	15
Abbey	20	2	2	16	21	68	8

Division One	P	W	D	L	F	A	Pts
Eutectic	16	14	1	1	65	18	43
East Fulham Res.	16	12	2	2	57	23	38
Southall Rangers	16	7	3	6	27	26	24
CB Hounslow 'B'	16	7	2	7	30	35	23
Ashford Albion	16	6	2	8	30	30	20
Explorers Seniors	16	5	4	7	28	31	19
Trinity	16	5	0	11	26	56	15
Abbey Reserves	16	4	2	10	31	50	14
Ashford Warriors	16	2	4	10	23	48	10

Division Two	P	W	D	L	F	A	Pts
Bedfont Town	18	16	1	1	72	29	49
Spelthorne SC 'A'	18	14	1	3	95	27	43
AFC Hampton	18	12	3	3	70	32	39
N'field Sham. Res.	18	11	3	4	56	31	36
Eutectic Reserves	18	9	2	7	51	40	29
Walton Rangers	18	6	1	11	57	57	19
White Hart	18	4	3	11	26	53	15
Bedham OB Res.	18	4	2	12	23	68	14
Hounslow W. OB	18	4	1	13	26	74	13
Staines Massiv	18	1	1	16	29	94	4

ISLE OF WIGHT LEAGUE

Division One	P	W	D	L	F	A	Pts
WW Mayflower	22	16	5	1	61	22	53
Oakfield	22	16	2	4	84	23	50
Shanklin	22	13	5	4	56	23	44
E. Cowes Vics Res.	22	13	2	7	56	33	41
Cowes Sports Res.	22	12	5	5	48	29	41
Binstead & COB	22	11	3	8	59	46	36
Whitecroft & B. Sp.	22	9	7	6	61	40	34
Red Star Spartans	22	7	4	11	45	56	25
St Helens Blue Star	22	6	4	12	32	61	22
Carisbrooke United	22	3	3	16	40	87	12
Newport Town 'A'	22	3	2	17	28	90	11
Brading Town Res.	22	2	0	20	23	83	6

Division Two	P	W	D	L	F	A	Pts
Niton	18	13	4	1	75	25	43
Northwood IOW	18	12	3	3	59	23	39
Sandown	18	10	6	2	58	21	36
Plessey	18	11	3	4	47	31	36
GKN Westlands	18	6	5	7	30	52	23
Bembridge -2	18	6	4	8	45	48	20
Wakes	18	5	2	11	24	36	17
Kyngs Towne	18	4	4	10	26	39	16
Osborne Coburg	18	3	2	13	15	66	11
Seaview	18	2	3	13	17	55	9

KIDDERMINSTER & DISTRICT LEAGUE

Premier Division	P	W	D	L	F	A	Pts
Cookley Social	26	20	4	2	85	50	64
Tenbury United	26	17	2	7	78	38	53
Norton Celtic	26	13	11	2	53	26	50
Furnace Sports	26	13	5	8	45	38	44
Crad. H. Timbertree	26	11	4	11	65	50	37
Wollescote Sports	26	10	7	9	38	38	37
Parkdale Rovers	26	9	9	8	44	35	36
Two Gates	26	10	6	10	47	52	36
Barley Mow -1	26	10	5	11	53	60	34
Kinver	26	8	7	11	52	54	31
Springvale Rovers	26	7	7	12	35	55	28
Chadd. Corbett Res.	26	5	9	12	35	59	24
Oldington United	26	4	6	16	48	77	18
Quarry Bank Rgrs	26	2	4	20	29	75	10

Division One	P	W	D	L	F	A	Pts
Castle Inn 2000	28	20	7	1	76	24	67
Top Bell	28	17	7	4	66	34	58
Quarry Bank	28	16	5	7	54	37	53
Straits House	28	15	5	8	69	38	50
Birch Coppice	28	11	11	6	54	39	44
Blackheath Res.	28	11	10	7	51	38	43
Dudley Wd. Ath. -3	28	12	5	11	46	58	38
Clee Hill Utd Res.	28	10	7	11	50	49	37
Two Gates Res.	28	8	10	10	41	42	34
Rising Sun	28	8	7	13	41	59	31
Bewdley Rovers	28	6	10	12	43	54	28
Sun Celtic	28	7	7	14	48	74	28
Libertys Sports	28	6	8	14	30	57	26
Belbroughton WMC	28	5	5	18	52	62	20
Tenbury Utd Res.	28	4	4	20	29	85	16

LANCASHIRE LEAGUE

Premier Division	P	W	D	L	F	A	Pts
Morecambe Res.	28	21	2	5	122	45	65
Southport Res.	28	17	6	5	96	41	57
Chester City Res.	28	17	4	7	82	37	55
Chorley Res.	28	15	5	8	62	55	50
Burscough Res.	28	13	7	8	64	51	46
Marine Res.	28	14	4	10	43	37	46
Lancaster City Res.	28	14	2	12	58	57	44
Northwich Vic. Res.	28	12	7	9	65	51	43
Bradford Pk A. Res.	28	9	9	10	49	62	36
Bamber Bridge Res.	28	10	5	13	47	58	35
Barrow Res.	28	8	7	13	53	83	31
Accrington S. Res.	28	7	7	14	53	60	28
Ossett Town Res.	28	8	2	18	70	63	26
Guiseley Res.	28	3	7	18	36	139	16
Farsley Celtic Res.	28	4	2	22	33	94	14

LANCASHIRE & CHESHIRE AMATEUR LEAGUE

Division One	P	W	D	L	F	A	Pts
Heaton Mersey	26	18	7	1	86	25	61
Denton Town	26	16	4	6	62	49	52
Old Ashtonians	26	12	8	6	60	34	44
Rochdalians	26	11	9	6	56	50	42
Bedians	26	10	10	6	59	50	40
Hooley Bdge Celtic	26	10	8	8	54	55	38
Oldham Albion	26	10	5	11	56	58	35
Hazel Grove	26	10	4	12	55	64	34
Heywood Town	26	8	6	12	52	57	30
Old Stoconians	26	9	3	14	38	55	30
Cheadle Hulme	26	7	8	11	39	47	29
Wardle	26	7	7	12	66	85	28
Metro	26	5	7	14	64	89	22
Old Standians	26	4	4	18	39	68	16

LONDON COMMERCIAL LEAGUE

Division One	P	W	D	L	F	A	Pts
British Airways	18	15	3	0	83	26	48
New Hanford	18	12	2	4	58	27	38
Hillingdon Irish	18	9	5	4	33	26	32
Xerox Sports	18	8	6	4	44	25	30
Kodak Harrow	18	8	2	8	31	33	26
Travaux	18	7	4	7	34	41	25
Meadhurst	18	5	2	11	23	49	17
Sporting Hackney	18	4	3	11	19	41	15
Barnet Mun. Off.	18	2	6	10	16	41	12
Charing Cross Ass.	18	2	3	13	18	50	9

Division Two	P	W	D	L	F	A	Pts
New Islip	20	13	1	6	59	35	40
Heathrow Club	20	12	3	5	56	39	39
Old Alpertonians	20	10	6	4	35	27	36
Indian Gymkhana	20	8	8	4	35	29	32
Sandgate Old Boys	20	8	6	6	29	29	30
Northolt Saints	20	9	1	10	42	48	28
Northwood 'A'	20	8	3	9	35	33	27
Tradewise	20	6	4	10	31	29	22
Harefield Wed.	20	6	3	11	46	53	21
Newark Yth Assoc.	20	5	5	10	32	53	20
Sudbury Court	20	4	2	14	35	60	14

MATLOCK & DISTRICT LEAGUE

Division One	P	W	D	L	F	A	Pts
Kings Arms	22	20	1	1	93	15	61
Stonebroom	22	19	2	1	102	26	59
Batemans	22	17	2	3	71	32	53
Sheepbridge	22	14	0	8	81	52	42
Tupton Royal Oak	22	12	2	8	50	48	38
Ormond Blues	22	11	2	9	70	39	35
Wirksworth Athletic	22	6	3	13	50	50	21
Lea Holloway	22	6	2	14	37	85	20
Darley Dale Lions	22	5	2	15	33	76	17
Whitemeadow	22	5	2	15	36	84	17
Rose & Crown	22	4	2	16	39	92	14
Bell Inn	22	2	2	18	18	81	8

MID-HERTS LEAGUE

Premier Division	P	W	D	L	F	A	Pts
Harpenden Rovers	14	11	1	2	34	20	34
Colney Athletic	14	7	3	4	39	23	24
The Bull -1	14	7	4	3	29	13	24
Eliz. Allen OB Res.	14	5	1	8	27	37	16
The Baton	14	5	1	8	21	37	16
Potters Bar T. 'A'	14	4	3	7	21	26	15
Colney Heath OB	14	2	7	5	23	34	13
Cockfosters 'A' -3	14	4	2	8	25	29	11

Division One	P	W	D	L	F	A	Pts
Harp'den Rov. Res.	16	13	2	1	61	20	41
Kings Sports 'A'	16	9	2	5	35	30	29
St Albans Wdrs -3	16	8	1	7	42	36	22
London Colney 'A'	16	6	3	7	38	39	21
Court United -3	16	7	2	7	38	33	20
Redbourn	16	5	5	6	32	35	20
Marlbor. W. Lion -3	16	6	2	8	34	33	17
Eliz. Allen OB 'A'	16	4	2	10	29	52	14
Sandridge Rov. 'A'	16	3	3	10	29	60	12

Division Two	P	W	D	L	F	A	Pts
Park Str. Village -3	18	15	2	1	56	14	44
King Offa +3	18	10	4	4	51	36	37
IFK Buttles	18	10	3	5	36	37	33
The Oak Tree	18	8	3	7	45	36	27
The Bull Res. -3	18	8	3	7	30	32	24
Colney Ath. Res. -3	18	7	2	9	38	45	20
Harp. Rovers Ath.	18	4	3	11	26	46	15
Hinton 'A' -3	18	4	5	9	37	38	14
Harpenden Rov. 'A'	18	3	5	10	34	47	14
Six Bells -3	18	4	4	10	20	42	13

MID-SOMERSET LEAGUE

Premier Division	P	W	D	L	F	A	Pts
Coleford Athletic	20	17	2	1	78	21	53
Meadow Rangers	20	13	3	4	62	30	42
Mells/Vobster Utd	20	10	7	3	50	38	37
Stoke Rovers	20	9	4	7	49	38	31
Chew Magna	20	8	6	6	40	42	30
Evercreech Rovers	20	9	2	9	48	43	29
Littleton Sports	20	8	2	10	41	46	26
Chilcompton	20	7	4	9	37	41	25
Belrose -1	20	7	3	10	48	55	23
Pensford	20	3	2	15	22	67	11
Temple Cloud -1	20	1	1	18	26	80	3

Division One	P	W	D	L	F	A	Pts
Littleton Spts Res.	20	17	3	0	64	13	54
Farrington Gurney	20	14	3	3	48	24	45
Oakhill *-1*	20	12	4	4	46	22	39
Welton Rovers 'A'	20	12	2	6	51	34	38
Radstock T. Res.	20	10	4	6	45	31	34
Tunley Res. *-1*	20	7	2	11	26	34	22
Pilton United	20	5	5	10	30	39	20
Welton Arsenal	20	5	5	10	24	43	20
Glastonbury Res.	20	5	4	11	35	47	19
Frome Coll. Res.	20	3	2	15	16	54	11
Belrose Res.	20	2	2	16	28	72	8

Division Two	P	W	D	L	F	A	Pts
Peasedown SJ. Rov.	20	16	1	3	79	30	49
Norton Hill Rangers	20	14	4	2	63	22	46
Wookey	20	14	1	5	76	30	43
Farmborough	20	12	2	6	51	30	38
Welton Rovers 'B'	20	7	4	9	38	63	25
Clutton Res. *-3*	20	7	4	9	49	53	22
Clandown Res. *-2*	20	6	4	10	43	46	20
Chilcompton Res. *-5*	20	6	7	7	42	60	20
Stoke Rovers Res. *-3*	20	5	4	11	31	58	16
Interhound	20	4	2	14	26	66	14
Pilton United Res.	20	1	3	16	19	59	6

Division Three	P	W	D	L	F	A	Pts
Westfield	22	19	2	1	86	29	59
Wells City 'A' *-1*	22	17	1	4	84	24	51
Frome Sptsh'se Res.	22	16	2	4	101	33	50
Pensford Res. *-1*	22	12	5	5	59	40	40
Chew Magna Res.	22	11	2	9	58	51	35
Evercreech Res.	22	7	5	10	39	53	26
Wookey Res. *-4*	22	8	3	11	54	66	23
Radstock 'A'	22	5	6	11	27	52	21
Farr. Gurney Res.	22	5	4	13	39	66	19
Chilcompton U. *-1*	22	5	2	15	42	91	16
Frome Coll. 'A' *-6*	22	6	1	15	45	93	13
Coleford Res. *-3*	22	3	3	16	28	64	9

MID-SUSSEX LEAGUE

Premier Division	P	W	D	L	F	A	Pts
Lewes Bridgeview	24	19	2	3	88	18	59
Wisdom Sports	24	17	3	4	78	27	54
East Grinstead Utd	24	16	5	3	56	30	53
Maresfield Village	24	14	3	7	53	32	45
Handcross Village	24	10	3	11	38	34	33
Lindfield	24	10	3	11	37	59	33
Barcombe	24	10	1	13	44	47	31
Nutley	24	9	4	11	44	50	31
Cuckfield Town	24	8	6	10	42	46	30
Village of Ditchling	24	8	4	12	29	44	28
Ardingly	24	5	5	14	38	60	20
Buxted	24	4	8	12	41	71	20
Hassocks/Clayton V.	24	2	1	21	29	99	7

Division One	P	W	D	L	F	A	Pts
East Grin. U. Res.	20	14	2	4	54	35	44
Hassocks 'A'	20	13	1	6	74	39	40
Newick	20	12	2	6	49	36	38
Wisdom Sports Res.	20	11	3	6	59	37	36
Balcombe	20	9	6	5	44	27	33
Turners Hill	20	11	0	9	50	48	33
Lewes Rovers	20	9	5	6	52	38	32
Felbridge	20	6	7	7	52	48	25
Plumpton Athletic	20	4	4	12	35	70	16
Copthorne Rovers	20	3	2	15	28	81	11
Hurstpierpoint Res.	20	0	4	16	24	62	4

Division Two	P	W	D	L	F	A	Pts
Jarvis Brook	18	13	2	3	71	25	41
Wivelsfield Green	18	12	2	4	73	39	38
Peacehaven United	18	11	1	6	40	44	34
Heath Pilgrims	18	10	2	6	46	36	32
Sporting Lindfield	18	10	1	7	51	36	31
E. Grinstead T. 'A'	18	9	0	9	46	44	27
Uckfield Town Res.	18	7	3	8	39	45	24
East Grin. Utd 'A'	18	6	1	11	31	50	19
Ashurst Wood	18	3	2	13	34	57	11
Burgess Hill Ath.	18	1	2	15	23	78	5

Division Three	P	W	D	L	F	A	Pts
Maresfield V. Res.	20	15	2	3	59	21	47
Lindfield Res.	20	14	2	4	53	31	44
Forest Row	20	13	2	5	54	27	41
Rotherfield	20	13	1	6	55	20	40
Burgess Hill Albion	20	9	6	5	44	29	33
Cuckf'd Wheatsheaf	20	6	4	10	27	40	22
Nutley Res.	20	5	4	11	22	35	19
West Hoathly *-3*	20	5	7	8	20	39	19
East Grin. Mariners	20	5	2	13	24	44	17
Danehill	20	4	2	14	19	60	14
Handcross V. Res.	20	3	4	13	25	56	13

Division Four	P	W	D	L	F	A	Pts
Lewes Rovers Res.	20	14	1	5	53	31	43
Cuckfield T. Res.	20	13	2	5	46	27	41
Scaynes Hill	20	12	1	7	61	49	37
Horsted Keynes *-3*	20	11	2	7	42	26	32
Horley Athletico	20	10	2	8	54	41	32
Wealden 'A'	20	9	3	8	53	35	30
Hartfield	20	9	2	9	46	36	29
Buxted Res.	20	9	2	9	50	51	29
Lewes B'view Res.	20	8	1	11	41	41	25
Plumpton Ath. Res.	20	3	4	13	31	67	13
Uckfield Town 'A'	20	1	2	17	20	93	5

Division Five	P	W	D	L	F	A	Pts
Crawley Down 'A'	18	14	1	3	75	21	43
Franklands V. 'A'	18	13	4	1	43	14	43
V. of Ditchling Res.	18	12	2	4	45	19	38
Ardingly Res.	18	8	6	4	37	27	30
Barcombe Res.	18	8	1	9	30	33	25
Fairwarp	18	7	1	10	48	51	22
Fairfield	18	6	3	9	32	31	21
Crowboro. Ath. 'A'	18	3	3	12	26	50	12
Hillview	18	3	3	12	37	72	12
Ashurst Wood Res.	18	4	0	14	22	77	12

Division Six	P	W	D	L	F	A	Pts
Lingfield 'A'	20	13	5	2	49	23	44
Dormansland Rkts	20	13	4	3	78	42	43
Fletching	20	10	5	5	60	31	35
Wisdom Sports 'A'	20	9	7	4	45	39	34
Turners Hill Res.	20	10	3	7	57	38	33
Scaynes Hill Res.	20	8	4	8	46	46	28
East Grinst'd U. 'B'	20	7	2	11	35	47	23
Ansty S&S *+2*	20	5	5	10	39	52	22
Heath Pilgrims Res.	20	6	2	12	46	71	20
Hass. & CV Res. *-1*	20	4	4	12	34	64	15
Felbridge Res.	20	4	1	15	28	64	13

Division Seven	P	W	D	L	F	A	Pts
East Court	20	17	1	2	80	28	52
Jarvis Brook Res.	20	13	5	2	61	24	44
Balcombe Res.	20	12	3	5	43	30	39
Bolney Rovers	20	9	3	8	37	29	30
Lindfield 'A'	20	6	8	6	37	42	26
Cuckfield Town 'A'	20	7	2	11	45	52	23
V. of Ditchling 'A'	20	7	2	11	34	56	23
Hartfield Res.	20	7	1	12	49	58	22
Maresfield V. 'A'	20	6	4	10	31	50	22
Copthorne Res. *-1*	20	6	3	11	34	49	20
Plumpton Ath. 'A'	20	3	2	15	32	65	11

Division Eight	P	W	D	L	F	A	Pts
Chailey	20	17	3	0	88	23	54
Burg. Hill Ath. Res.	20	11	5	4	53	31	38
Dormansland Res.	20	12	2	6	62	50	38
Wivelsfield G. Res.	20	10	4	6	61	46	34
Rotherfield Res.	20	10	4	6	43	40	34
Uckfield Town 'B'	20	7	3	10	49	45	24
Scaynes Hill 'A'	20	6	4	10	44	68	22
Horsted Keynes Res.	20	5	4	11	37	51	19
Handcross Vill. 'A'	20	5	2	13	42	63	17
Forest Row Res.	20	5	2	13	34	72	17
Wealden 'B'	20	4	3	13	22	46	15

Division Nine	P	W	D	L	F	A	Pts
Burg. Hill Alb. Res.	20	15	2	3	80	30	47
Lindfield 'B'	20	15	2	3	65	18	47
Chailey Res.	20	13	3	4	70	40	42
Ardingly 'A'	20	11	0	9	61	36	33
Fletching Res.	20	9	2	9	63	61	29
Buxted 'A'	20	8	4	8	38	42	28
West Hoathly Res.	20	7	2	11	41	64	23
Maresfield V. 'B'	20	6	2	12	42	66	20
Hillview Res.	20	5	2	13	43	75	17
Scaynes Hill 'B'	20	5	2	13	27	71	17
Fairwarp Res.	20	4	3	13	32	59	15

MIDDLESEX LEAGUE

Premier Division	P	W	D	L	F	A	Pts
Hanworth Villa	20	16	2	2	61	13	50
Will. Constantine	20	15	2	3	50	18	47
CB Hounslow Utd	20	13	3	4	51	28	42
Spelthorne Sports *-4*	20	9	4	7	40	29	27
Wraysbury *-3*	20	9	2	9	51	38	26
Stonewall	20	8	2	10	36	61	26
FC Deport. Galicia	20	6	3	11	26	35	21
Brentford New Inn	20	6	1	13	34	50	19
Broadfields Utd *-4*	20	6	4	10	40	43	18
Neasden	20	6	0	14	25	45	18
Technicolor CAV	20	4	1	15	20	74	13

Division One	P	W	D	L	F	A	Pts
Southall Town Res.	18	13	3	2	47	20	42
Marsh Rangers	18	11	5	2	55	24	38
Actual Soccer	18	7	6	5	40	28	27
Spelthorne Spts Res.	18	8	3	7	25	23	27
Hounslow Wdrs	18	6	8	4	46	34	26
Signcraft	18	8	2	8	33	33	26
Ealing Assyrians *-3*	18	8	4	6	36	29	25
Neasden Res. *-3*	18	5	2	11	27	42	14
Hanworth Villa Res.	18	3	4	11	31	51	13
Southall Res.	18	2	1	15	16	72	7

Division Two	P	W	D	L	F	A	Pts
Harefield Ex-Serv.	18	12	4	2	46	17	40
CB Hounslow Res.	18	9	5	4	53	23	32
Stedfast United *+2*	18	7	5	6	42	46	28
North Hayes Acad.	18	8	1	9	42	44	25
Eastcote *+3*	18	6	3	9	34	36	24
Brunel University *-7*	18	7	8	3	45	22	22
Will. Const. Res.	18	6	4	8	37	38	22
Wilberforce Wdrs	18	6	3	9	34	36	21
Safeway *-6*	18	8	3	7	36	46	21
Edson	18	3	0	15	27	88	9

Division Three	P	W	D	L	F	A	Pts
Stonewall Res. *-6*	20	16	3	1	65	26	45
Hounslow W. Res.	20	14	2	4	46	25	44
Haze	20	13	2	5	71	37	41
Signcraft Res.	20	12	4	4	74	44	40
Wishing Well *-1*	20	10	3	7	58	34	32
Hare. Ex-Serv. Res.	20	8	3	9	55	50	27
Stedfast United Res.	20	7	3	10	56	53	24
Brunel Univ. Res. *-4*	20	7	4	9	35	34	21
Eastcote Res.	20	5	1	14	36	90	16
FC Tilburg Regents	20	1	3	16	32	85	6
NH Acad. Res. *-3*	20	2	2	16	35	85	5

NORTH DEVON LEAGUE

Premier Division	P	W	D	L	F	A	Pts
Shamwickshire Rov.	28	22	3	3	108	35	69
Morwenstow	28	18	5	5	87	34	59
Braunton	28	17	6	5	86	26	57
Barnstaple AAC	28	15	10	3	66	33	55
Georgeham/Croyde	28	16	3	9	61	40	51
Appledore Res. *-3*	28	16	5	7	68	43	50
Ilfracombe T. Res.	28	14	5	9	65	53	47
Bradworthy United	28	13	5	10	74	52	44
Combe Martin	28	13	4	11	60	60	43
Putford	28	11	2	15	66	64	35
Northam Lions	28	8	7	13	50	64	31
Holsworthy Res.	28	6	2	20	25	69	20
High Bickington	28	4	2	22	36	107	14
South Molton	28	4	1	23	36	108	13
Torr'gton Admirals	28	2	2	24	34	134	8

(Dolton Rangers – record expunged)

NORTH HAMPSHIRE LEAGUE

	P	W	D	L	F	A	Pts
Winchester City 'A'	24	19	2	3	83	19	59
Vernham Dean	24	13	2	9	51	38	41
Stockbridge Res.	24	10	7	7	51	43	37
Broughton Res.	24	10	0	14	46	68	30
Whitchurch U. Res.	24	7	5	12	36	64	26
Andover N. St. 'A'	24	7	3	14	53	61	24
Tadley Town Res.	24	7	3	14	47	74	24

PERRY STREET & DISTRICT LEAGUE

Premier Division	P	W	D	L	F	A	Pts
Ilminster Town Res.	20	13	3	4	52	23	42
Lyme Regis	20	11	3	6	44	25	36
Barrington	20	10	4	6	47	35	34
Merriott Rovers	20	9	5	6	45	31	32
Farway United	20	8	6	6	50	52	30
South Petherton	20	8	4	8	44	35	28
Crewkerne Res.	20	8	3	9	37	55	27
Forton Rangers	20	7	3	10	27	33	24
Shepton Beauchamp	20	6	3	11	26	47	21
Chard United	20	4	4	12	30	52	16
Combe St N. Res. *-3*	20	4	6	10	35	49	15

Division One	P	W	D	L	F	A	Pts
Chard Town Colts	20	15	0	5	43	22	45
Perry Street & YH	20	14	2	4	54	23	44
Charmouth	20	12	2	6	49	29	38
Haselbury *-1*	20	12	1	7	52	32	36
Netherbury	20	10	3	7	43	37	33
Lyme Regis Res.	20	8	4	8	40	37	28
Merriott R. Res. *-1*	20	6	6	8	40	57	23
Misterton *-3*	20	6	3	11	37	46	18
Crewkerne 'A'	20	5	3	12	25	48	18
Drimpton	20	4	2	14	30	50	14
Norton Athletic	20	4	2	14	36	68	14

WWW.NLNEWSDESK.CO.UK

PETERBOROUGH & DISTRICT LEAGUE

Premier Division	P	W	D	L	F	A	Pts
Eye United *-1*	30	25	4	1	119	31	78
Wimblington OB	30	18	7	5	70	40	61
AMP Pearl Ass.	30	17	6	7	78	43	57
Moulton Harrox	30	17	5	8	74	34	56
Leverington Sports	30	17	5	8	65	37	56
Ortonians	30	15	7	8	69	50	52
Oundle Town	30	14	6	10	65	46	48
Hotpoint	29	14	4	11	62	53	46
Whittlesey United	30	10	5	15	68	77	35
Stilton United	30	10	4	16	61	65	34
Alconbury	29	9	4	16	50	68	31
Peterboro. Sports *-1*	30	9	5	16	57	104	31
Pinchbeck United	30	5	9	16	32	63	24
Perkins Sports	30	5	7	18	27	80	22
Long Sutton Ath. *-1*	30	4	8	18	36	111	19
Ryhall United *-3*	30	4	6	20	45	76	15

PLYMOUTH & DISTRICT COMBINATION

Premier Division	P	W	D	L	F	A	Pts
Mount Gould BP	26	18	4	4	85	28	58
Plymouth CSS&L	26	16	7	3	66	35	55
Manstow	26	15	3	8	68	57	48
Wessex Rangers	26	14	4	8	67	51	46
Plympton United	26	14	3	9	50	32	45
Plymouth Univ.	26	13	4	9	61	42	43
Plymstock Utd Res.	26	12	7	7	60	43	43
Plym. Parkway Res.	26	10	6	10	62	62	36
Mainstone Sports	26	9	2	15	49	55	29
Prince Rock YC	26	7	4	15	42	81	25
Roborough	26	6	6	14	42	65	24
Tavistock Res. *-6*	26	8	4	14	52	73	22
Vospers OV Res.	26	3	7	16	41	77	16
Plym. Command *-3*	26	5	3	18	46	90	15

Division One	P	W	D	L	F	A	Pts
Princess Yachts Int.	22	18	3	1	105	21	57
Tamarside	22	17	3	2	99	22	54
Elburton Villa Res.	22	11	5	6	59	34	38
Manadon	22	11	3	8	67	52	36
Lopes Arms Rgrs	22	10	5	7	66	55	35
Old Suttonians	22	10	3	9	56	65	33
DML Spts & Social	22	9	3	10	51	62	30
Plym. Univ. Res. *-9*	22	10	3	9	50	53	24
SWEB	22	7	1	14	44	70	22
Ivybridge T. Res.	22	5	4	13	41	67	19
Horrabridge Rgrs	22	4	4	14	35	87	16
Plymouth Civil S.	22	1	1	20	26	111	4

Division Two	P	W	D	L	F	A	Pts
Kevin Purdy Roof'g	20	20	0	0	119	23	60
Morley Cars	20	13	4	3	58	31	43
Plymouth City	20	12	2	6	55	43	38
Clear View Cleaning	20	9	5	6	50	36	32
Stonehouse Glass	20	7	5	8	36	46	26
Woodside	20	8	1	11	44	71	25
Toshiba	20	7	2	11	48	55	23
Tamarside Res.	20	6	4	10	31	55	22
DH Construction	20	5	5	10	43	70	20
Gleasons S & S	20	4	2	14	32	57	14
Yealm G. Rangers	20	3	2	15	32	61	11

Division Three	P	W	D	L	F	A	Pts
Lee Moor	20	16	1	3	120	29	49
Old Suttonians Res.	20	15	1	4	114	35	46
Friendship Inn	20	13	2	5	98	55	41
Yelverton	20	12	1	7	79	57	37
Pot Black	20	12	1	7	61	51	37
Plymouth Rangers	20	11	1	8	80	64	34
Pilkington *-3*	20	7	3	10	62	61	21
Buckland MC	20	6	0	14	47	82	18
Modbury Rovers	20	6	0	14	57	121	18
Grenville Hotel	20	4	3	13	42	102	15
Qu. Arms Tamerton	20	1	1	18	37	140	4

SALISBURY & DISTRICT LEAGUE

Premier Division	P	W	D	L	F	A	Pts
George & Dragon	18	14	2	2	67	25	44
Harnham	18	10	5	3	53	28	35
PFC Durrington	18	10	2	6	48	28	32
Tisbury	18	9	3	6	40	23	30
Salisbury Arms	18	9	2	7	37	36	29
Shrewton Utd Res.	18	8	4	6	41	48	28
S. Newton/Wishford	18	7	3	8	37	50	24
Porton Sports	18	4	4	10	29	38	16
Friends Provident	18	3	1	14	15	65	10
Damerham	18	1	4	13	22	48	7

Division One	P	W	D	L	F	A	Pts
Meadow Park	18	13	4	1	67	26	43
Kings Arms	18	12	5	1	78	23	41
Royal George	18	10	4	4	65	44	34
Winterslow	18	9	4	5	40	31	31
Enford	18	8	4	6	60	42	28
Wyndham Park	18	8	2	8	25	49	26
Chalke Valley	18	4	4	10	40	56	16
Whiteparish	18	4	4	10	41	59	16
Rose & Crown	18	3	4	11	30	47	13
Tisbury Res.	18	1	1	16	11	80	4

Division Two	P	W	D	L	F	A	Pts
Stockton & Codford	20	18	0	2	84	21	54
Greyhound	20	14	2	4	69	35	44
Netheravon	20	12	2	6	64	39	38
Club Rouge	20	12	0	8	73	52	36
Salisbury Glass	20	9	2	9	60	47	29
Laverstock	20	8	3	9	47	44	27
VW Heritage	20	7	3	10	48	68	24
Victoria Hotel	20	7	1	12	56	84	22
Porton Sports Res.	20	7	0	13	31	42	21
Beacon Sports	20	3	4	13	25	67	13
Harnham Res.	20	3	3	14	25	83	12

Division Three	P	W	D	L	F	A	Pts
Castle Street Club	20	17	2	1	99	26	53
Alderbury	20	16	2	2	102	38	50
Digital Instinct	20	12	2	6	58	36	38
Hi-Flex Sports	20	12	2	6	53	38	38
Langford United	20	10	3	7	52	48	33
Anchor & Hope	20	8	3	9	55	44	27
Hogshead	20	5	3	12	37	64	18
Chalke Valley Res.	20	5	3	12	36	65	18
Royal George Res.	20	4	4	12	39	77	16
Winterslow Res.	20	5	0	15	40	87	15
Enford Res.	20	2	4	14	44	92	10

SHEFFIELD & HALLAMSHIRE COUNTY SENIOR LEAGUE

Premier Division	P	W	D	L	F	A	Pts
Wombwell Main	24	17	5	2	57	17	56
Penistone Church	24	15	4	5	43	22	49
Mexboro. Main Str.	24	15	2	7	70	39	47
Athersley Rec.	24	15	1	8	47	25	46
Hallam Res.	24	13	4	7	69	32	43
S. Kirkby Colliery	24	13	4	7	55	41	43
Parkgate Res.	24	11	3	10	56	55	36
Groves Social	24	9	5	10	46	46	32
Wickersley OB	24	9	5	10	46	56	32
Grapes Roy Hanc.	24	9	0	15	43	47	27
Thorpe Hesley	24	7	4	13	29	45	25
Swinton Athletic	24	3	1	20	26	71	10
Phoenix	24	0	2	22	16	107	2

Division One	P	W	D	L	F	A	Pts
Elm Tree	26	18	3	5	64	33	57
HSBC	26	15	7	4	70	35	52
Sheffield Lane Top	26	15	4	7	66	42	49
Oughtibdge WMSC	26	14	3	9	51	40	45
Hollinsend Amat.	26	13	5	8	57	40	44
Parramore Sports	26	11	4	11	55	48	37
Rising Sun	26	11	4	11	60	61	37
Stocksbridge Res.	26	11	2	13	50	37	35
The Wetherby	26	10	5	11	45	42	35
Frecheville CA	26	9	6	11	42	50	33
Georgia Pacific	26	10	3	13	46	60	33
Ecclesfield R. Rose	26	7	8	11	36	47	29
Avesta Polarit	26	6	6	14	45	74	24
Caribbean Sports	26	1	2	23	20	98	5

Division Two	P	W	D	L	F	A	Pts
Edlington WMC	26	22	3	1	66	23	69
High Green Villa	26	17	3	6	63	32	54
Renishaw Juniors	26	17	1	8	83	39	52
Treeton	26	13	7	6	65	39	46
Wath Athletic	26	12	8	6	60	38	44
Sheff'ld Centralians	26	13	5	8	50	44	44
Grimethorpe MW	26	11	8	7	56	48	41
Gate 13	26	10	7	9	49	54	37
Penistone Ch. Res.	26	8	5	13	40	60	29
Dinnington T. Res.	26	9	1	16	56	61	28
Davy	26	7	6	13	50	58	27
Manvers Park	26	6	6	14	49	56	24
Psalter Vigo	26	6	1	19	38	66	19
Harworth CI Colts	26	0	1	25	19	126	1

SOUTH LONDON ALLIANCE

Premier Division	P	W	D	L	F	A	Pts
Metrogas	22	18	1	3	55	24	55
Waterloo	22	16	1	5	48	23	49
Kingfisher	22	15	3	4	48	17	48
CWS	22	13	3	6	68	44	42
Johnson & Phillips	22	11	1	10	54	48	34
Long Lane	22	11	1	10	38	39	34
Cray Vall. PM Res.	22	9	3	10	45	50	30
Farnboro. OBG Res.	22	5	6	11	45	62	21
Old Roan Res.	22	6	2	14	34	68	20
T C Sports	22	5	3	14	30	41	18
Lewisham	22	3	6	13	36	57	15
Bickley Town	22	4	2	16	26	54	14

Division One	P	W	D	L	F	A	Pts
Drummond Athletic	22	14	5	3	53	27	47
RASRA	22	13	4	5	53	41	43
Brockley	22	13	3	6	51	35	42
Metrogas Res.	22	12	3	7	56	37	39
CUM	22	11	2	9	61	43	35
Penhill Standard	22	9	6	7	53	43	33
Blackheath Wd. *-3*	22	9	4	9	42	42	28
Croydon Strikers	22	8	4	10	46	50	28
Bexley	22	8	4	10	37	45	28
Catford Wanderers	22	7	4	11	43	55	25
Old Colfeians	22	4	3	15	33	56	15
CWS Res.	22	3	0	19	30	84	9

Division Two	P	W	D	L	F	A	Pts
AFC North Heath	20	14	4	2	67	30	46
Perana	20	12	4	4	62	40	40
Churchdown	20	10	7	3	63	34	37
Middle Park	20	10	6	4	60	36	36
Beckenham Royals	20	10	4	6	44	31	34
Well Hall	20	9	4	7	48	39	31
Eltham Royals	20	8	3	9	55	51	27
Wilmington	20	7	2	11	53	57	23
Swanley Town	20	3	3	14	36	85	12
Beaverwood	20	2	5	13	38	70	11
S Club Eleven	20	3	2	15	25	78	11

Division Three	P	W	D	L	F	A	Pts
Catford Wdrs 'B'	22	18	4	0	80	21	58
Old Roan 'A'	22	17	2	3	97	30	53
RASRA Res.	22	16	3	3	77	28	51
New Park	22	13	3	6	48	48	42
Eltham Invicta	22	10	5	7	47	37	35
Avery Hill College	22	8	5	9	45	62	29
Blackheath W. Res.	22	6	3	13	46	69	21
Wickham Park 'A'	22	5	4	13	33	58	19
Johnson & Ph. Res.	22	4	6	12	33	58	18
Farnboro. OBG 'A'	22	5	3	14	35	70	18
Eltham Palace Res.	22	2	8	12	36	56	14
North Kent	22	3	4	15	34	74	13

Division Four	P	W	D	L	F	A	Pts
Parkhurst Rangers	22	17	4	1	87	28	55
Old Roan 'B'	22	17	2	3	74	34	53
Metrogas 'A'	22	15	3	4	79	40	48
Oakdale Athletic	22	14	3	5	46	21	45
Ravens	22	10	5	7	60	49	35
Elliott Sports	22	10	0	12	43	40	30
Red Star Bromley	22	9	2	11	51	42	29
Bexleyheath	22	9	1	12	40	47	28
Brockley Res.	22	6	5	11	42	56	23
Guys Athletic	22	6	1	15	34	63	19
Greenwich Royals	22	2	3	17	29	78	9
Churchdown Res.	22	2	1	19	24	111	7

SOUTHAMPTON LEAGUE

Senior Premier	P	W	D	L	F	A	Pts
Nursling	22	18	3	1	64	17	57
Botley Village	22	14	6	2	35	13	48
Mottisfont	22	15	1	6	46	27	46
Eastleigh Comrades	22	11	4	7	50	31	37
Sporting BTC	22	11	2	9	38	33	35
AFC Target	22	9	1	12	42	37	28
BTC Southampton	22	8	4	10	42	46	28
Durley	22	7	4	11	37	50	25
Brendon	22	7	2	13	40	47	23
Fair Oak	22	7	2	13	39	53	23
North Baddesley	22	5	1	16	24	76	16
Old Tauntonians	22	4	2	16	30	57	14

Senior Division One	P	W	D	L	F	A	Pts
Lyndhurst *-1*	22	17	3	2	63	26	53
AFC Arrow	22	15	2	5	58	23	47
Black. & L. Res. *-4*	22	15	4	3	61	32	45
Priory Rovers	22	12	4	6	60	42	40
Otterbourne Res.	22	11	2	9	41	37	35
Cadnam United	22	8	7	7	49	55	31
Ord. Survey Res.	22	7	6	9	42	40	27
Porter *-1*	22	7	1	14	54	60	21
Hythe Aztecs	22	5	5	12	43	60	20
Mill Hill	22	6	2	14	38	66	20
Solent WTL	22	6	0	16	33	77	18
Braishfield	22	3	4	15	37	61	13

WWW.CHERRYRED.CO.UK

Senior Division Two	P	W	D	L	F	A	Pts
Capital -1	18	15	3	0	71	23	47
Wellow	18	11	3	4	50	18	36
Millbridge	18	11	1	6	59	31	34
Eastleigh Com. Res.	18	10	1	7	45	34	31
Progressive Club	18	9	1	8	34	28	28
AFC Hop	18	7	5	6	36	29	26
BTC S'pton Res.	18	6	3	9	26	36	21
M&T Awbridge 'A'	18	4	1	13	26	64	13
Burridge AFC -1	18	2	5	11	21	74	10
Burridge Sports	18	1	5	12	31	62	8

Junior Div. One	P	W	D	L	F	A	Pts
Locksley Sports	20	17	3	0	84	16	54
Hamble Harriers	20	17	1	2	85	26	52
Mottisfont Res.	20	11	5	4	46	29	38
Inter Norw. Union	20	10	3	7	47	32	33
Northend United	20	9	3	8	50	50	30
Bishopstoke WMC	20	9	2	9	37	33	29
Velmore	20	9	1	10	48	64	28
Testwood United	20	6	3	11	48	49	21
Otterbourne 'A' -1	20	5	6	9	26	42	20
Ordnance Surv. 'A'	20	2	1	17	29	94	7
Sptng BTC Res. -3	20	1	0	19	14	79	0

Junior Div. Two	P	W	D	L	F	A	Pts
Forest Town	18	13	4	1	70	31	43
Romsey Town Yth	18	11	1	6	67	40	34
Spartans	18	9	4	5	58	33	31
Compton	18	7	4	7	46	47	25
Bacardi	18	7	4	7	23	34	25
Manor	18	6	6	6	48	38	24
A & M Sports -1	18	7	2	9	37	54	22
Cadnam Utd Res.	18	6	3	9	52	49	21
Interbrew	18	4	5	9	23	49	17
Fair Oak Res. -1	18	1	5	12	32	81	7

Junior Div. Three	P	W	D	L	F	A	Pts
Lowford	18	14	2	2	64	22	44
Eastleigh Royals	18	13	3	2	72	19	42
Millers Pond -1	18	10	2	6	59	49	31
Langley Manor	18	7	5	6	36	38	26
Weston Shore	18	7	4	7	47	45	25
London Airways	18	5	5	8	35	50	20
M&T Awbridge 'B'	18	4	7	7	37	48	19
Brookwood	18	3	6	9	40	57	15
Hythe Aztec Res. -1	18	4	4	10	33	54	15
AFC Merryoak	18	3	2	13	21	62	11

Junior Div. Four	P	W	D	L	F	A	Pts
Malvern	20	19	1	0	90	20	58
Durley Res.	20	11	5	4	67	23	38
Capital Res. -8	20	14	2	4	71	33	36
Millbank AFC	20	9	3	8	38	38	30
Alma -1	20	9	2	9	40	39	28
Wildern OB -1	20	7	3	10	44	59	23
Priory Rov. Res. -1	20	7	2	11	48	53	22
WEBFC	20	6	2	12	42	58	20
Burridge AFC Res.	20	6	2	12	32	54	20
Inmar	20	5	2	13	40	86	17
Inter Northam	20	3	4	13	28	77	13

Junior Div. Five	P	W	D	L	F	A	Pts
Bush Hill	20	12	4	4	78	32	40
AFC Arrow Res.	20	12	4	4	57	48	40
City Sports	20	12	3	5	60	46	39
Wellow Res.	20	12	3	5	59	50	39
Inter Nor. U. Res. -1	20	11	3	6	59	44	35
Mayfield Rangers	20	10	1	9	56	46	31
Millbridge Res.	20	8	2	10	60	76	26
Slightly Athletic	20	8	1	11	44	66	25
Polygon United	20	4	3	13	38	50	15
QK S'pton 'A' -3	20	4	3	13	36	62	12
Compton Res.	20	2	3	15	32	59	9

Junior Div. Six	P	W	D	L	F	A	Pts
Calmore Rovers	20	16	1	3	108	35	49
Riverside	20	14	4	2	52	24	46
Keywords Direct	20	14	1	5	86	38	43
Spike Ajax	20	11	3	6	48	44	36
Braishfield Res. -1	20	9	3	8	57	49	29
Norleywood	20	7	3	10	41	47	24
East Boldre	20	7	2	11	47	67	23
Harrier PH -6	20	7	5	8	49	56	20
Welcome	20	4	3	13	29	83	15
Spar-Tec Wessex	20	3	3	14	43	86	12
AFC Aldermoor	20	3	2	15	34	65	11

SOUTHERN AMATEUR LEAGUE

Senior One	P	W	D	L	F	A	Pts
Old Salesians	22	14	6	2	45	15	48
Old Esthameians	22	10	7	5	38	22	37
Alleyn Old Boys	22	9	5	8	28	32	32
Norsemen	22	8	7	7	36	26	31
Old Owens	22	9	4	9	35	34	31
Broomfield	22	8	5	9	26	42	29
Polytechnic	22	7	7	8	33	35	28
Old Acton Assoc.	22	8	4	10	25	31	28
HSBC	22	7	6	9	26	27	27
Civil Service	22	5	10	7	27	31	25
East Barnet OG	22	6	5	11	29	34	23
BB Eagles	22	6	4	12	22	41	22

Senior Two	P	W	D	L	F	A	Pts
Winchmore Hill	22	17	2	3	56	18	53
West Wickham	22	16	4	2	45	14	52
Nottsborough	22	12	8	2	56	22	44
Old Finchleians	22	9	7	6	46	37	34
Old Parkonians	22	10	1	11	25	39	31
South Bank Cuaco	22	8	5	9	41	43	29
Old Stationers	22	7	5	10	34	40	26
Old Lyonians	22	7	3	12	45	44	24
Carshalton	22	7	3	12	36	47	24
Weirside Rangers	22	5	7	10	36	41	22
Lloyds TSB Bank	22	4	5	13	27	54	17
Crouch End Vamp.	22	3	4	15	30	78	13

Senior Three	P	W	D	L	F	A	Pts
Bank of England	18	14	2	2	50	12	44
Old Parmiterians	18	12	3	3	60	22	39
Old Westminster Cz	18	10	2	6	41	34	32
Kew Association	18	9	4	5	50	35	31
Alexandra Park	18	8	5	5	46	30	29
Old Latymerians	18	7	2	9	39	40	23
Merton	18	7	2	9	36	41	23
Ibis	18	4	2	12	22	47	14
Southgate Olympic	18	4	1	13	31	60	13
Brentham	18	3	1	14	23	77	10

Res. Division One	P	W	D	L	F	A	Pts
Polytechnic Res.	22	13	6	3	47	22	45
O. Esthameians Res.	22	12	5	5	71	30	41
West Wickham Res.	22	12	5	5	51	24	41
Norsemen Res.	22	13	2	7	54	29	41
Old Acton. A. Res.	22	11	6	5	47	34	39
HSBC Res.	22	10	5	7	37	28	35
East Barnet OG Res.	22	11	2	9	58	58	35
Old Owens Res.	22	8	3	11	45	53	27
BB Eagles Res.	22	8	1	13	58	70	25
Crouch End V. Res.	22	6	4	12	37	56	22
Old Stationers Res.	22	4	4	14	33	95	16
O. Parmiterians Res.	22	2	1	19	31	70	7

Res. Division Two	P	W	D	L	F	A	Pts
Nottsborough Res.	22	12	7	3	56	28	43
Old Finchleians Res.	22	13	4	5	62	39	43
Carshalton Res.	22	9	10	3	44	30	37
Winchmore H. Res.	22	10	4	8	47	38	34
Bank of Eng. Res.	22	9	5	8	41	40	32
Civil Service Res.	22	8	7	7	50	47	31
S. Bank Cuaco Res.	22	7	7	8	38	41	28
Alleyn OB Res.	22	5	8	9	36	46	23
Old Salesians Res.	22	5	7	10	38	53	22
Weirside Rgrs Res.	22	5	7	10	26	43	22
Broomfield Res.	22	5	6	11	31	45	21
Alexandra Park Res.	22	5	6	11	33	52	21

Res. Division Three	P	W	D	L	F	A	Pts
Ibis Res.	18	10	4	4	45	20	34
O. Latymerians Res.	18	9	6	3	37	28	33
Southgate O. Res.	18	10	2	6	49	38	32
Old Lyonians Res.	18	8	7	3	46	32	31
Kew Assoc. Res.	18	8	7	3	40	33	31
Old Parkonians Res.	18	7	2	9	24	34	23
Merton Res.	18	6	3	9	33	40	21
Brentham Res.	18	4	5	9	27	46	17
Lloyds TSB B. Res.	18	3	5	10	36	52	14
Old West. Cit. Res.	18	3	3	12	24	38	12

SUBURBAN LEAGUE

Premier Division	P	W	D	L	F	A	Pts
Hayes Res.	34	22	2	10	90	51	68
Maidenhead U. Res.	34	20	3	11	80	67	63
Carshalton Ath. Res.	34	18	4	12	67	49	58
Crawley Town Res.	34	17	7	10	56	44	58
Sutton United Res.	34	17	5	12	64	54	56
Marlow Res.	34	16	6	12	63	57	54
Basingstoke T. Res.	34	15	7	12	67	62	52
Northwood Res.	34	13	10	11	66	56	49
Berkhamsted Res.	34	14	7	13	64	61	49
Met. Police Res.	34	13	9	12	50	51	48
Kingstonian Res.	34	13	7	14	61	58	46
Wingate & F. Res.	34	13	6	15	49	61	45
Dulwich Ham. Res.	34	13	4	17	60	55	43
Brook House Res.	34	13	4	17	42	57	43
Thame United Res.	34	11	9	14	52	67	42
Walton & Her. Res.	34	11	5	18	49	63	38
Corinthian Cas. Res.	34	7	7	20	42	75	28
Hendon Res.	34	7	4	23	49	83	25

North Division	P	W	D	L	F	A	Pts
Oxford City Res.	34	25	3	6	92	31	78
Aylesbury Utd Res.	34	23	6	5	82	41	75
Boreham Wood Res.	34	19	8	7	77	48	65
Leighton Town Res.	34	19	7	8	74	39	64
Uxbridge Res.	34	16	10	8	69	46	58
Thatcham T. Res.	34	15	8	11	75	66	53
Chesham Utd Res.	34	15	7	12	73	49	52
Hanwell Town Res.	34	15	5	14	55	50	50
Beaconsfield S. Res.	34	15	5	14	55	59	50
Wembley Res.	34	13	8	13	59	65	47
Hillingdon B. Res.	34	11	9	14	62	80	42
Abingdon T. Res.	34	12	3	19	45	71	39
Ruislip Manor Res.	34	10	6	18	48	63	36
Abingdon Utd Res.	34	10	6	18	51	72	36
Hungerford T. Res.	34	7	10	17	56	79	31
Burnham Res.	34	9	4	21	53	80	31
Reading Town Res.	34	9	3	22	39	99	30
AFC Wall'ford Res.	34	8	2	24	52	79	26

South Division	P	W	D	L	F	A	Pts
Whyteleafe Res.	34	25	5	4	96	30	80
Ashford (Mx) Res.	34	22	5	7	83	40	71
Wealdstone Res.	34	20	8	6	91	41	68
Tooting & M. Res.	34	20	4	10	118	46	64
Fisher Athletic Res.	34	20	4	10	83	64	64
Croydon Ath. Res.	34	19	4	11	76	49	61
Epsom/Ewell Res.	34	17	8	9	73	61	59
Tonbridge A. Res.	34	16	7	11	67	54	55
Windsor/Eton Res.	34	15	7	12	75	64	52
Bracknell T. Res.	34	13	8	13	53	53	47
Croydon Res.	34	12	4	18	57	63	40
Molesey Res.	34	11	5	18	50	71	38
Camberley T. Res.	34	10	5	19	49	66	35
Chipstead Res.	34	9	5	20	45	94	32
Walton Cas. Res.	34	7	8	19	38	76	29
Godalming/G. Res.	34	7	6	21	32	69	27
Chertsey Town Res.	34	7	3	24	37	102	24
Fleet Town Res.	34	6	4	24	44	124	22

SUFFOLK & IPSWICH LEAGUE

Senior Division	P	W	D	L	F	A	Pts
Walsham-le-Will.	30	19	7	4	84	47	64
Ipswich Athletic	30	18	8	4	75	41	62
East Bergholt Utd	30	17	7	6	103	59	58
Old Newton United	30	16	8	6	72	37	56
Stanton	30	14	8	8	63	53	50
Westerfield United	30	14	8	8	54	44	50
Grundisburgh	30	13	8	9	63	47	47
Haughley United	30	13	6	11	72	56	45
Crane Sports	30	10	8	12	65	69	38
Stonham Aspal	30	11	5	14	58	67	38
Capel Plough	30	11	2	17	45	58	35
Melton St Audrys	30	8	9	13	44	56	33
Bramford United	30	8	6	16	43	65	30
Achilles	30	8	1	21	37	61	25
Leiston St Marg.	30	6	4	20	36	75	22
Woodbridge Ath.	30	6	1	23	31	110	19

Division One	P	W	D	L	F	A	Pts
Cockfield United	24	16	8	0	70	20	56
Felixstowe United	24	16	5	3	56	24	53
Framlingham Town	24	14	7	3	62	23	49
Ransomes Sports	24	13	8	3	66	30	47
Willis/Kesgrave U.	24	11	4	9	43	36	37
Stowupland	24	8	7	9	41	55	31
Thurston	24	7	9	8	50	31	30
Coplestonians	24	7	5	12	39	47	26
AFC Debenham	24	5	9	10	35	43	24
Brantham Athletic	24	6	6	12	34	54	24
Ipswich Exiles	24	5	8	11	37	54	23
Halesworth Town	24	5	3	16	37	83	18
John Bull Utd -6	24	3	1	20	22	92	4

Intermediate A	P	W	D	L	F	A	Pts
East Bergholt Res. -1	28	19	6	3	82	38	60
Haughley Utd Res.	28	17	6	5	71	30	57
Grundisburgh Res.	28	16	5	7	86	44	53
Achilles Res.	28	14	4	10	56	49	46
Walsham-le-W. Res.	28	13	6	9	50	41	45
Willis & Kes. Res.	28	14	3	11	62	59	45
Ipswich Ath. Res.	28	12	5	11	53	61	41
Crane Sports Res.	28	11	4	13	53	62	37
Leiston Res. -6	28	12	5	11	47	44	35
Capel Plough Res.	28	10	4	14	39	53	34
Old Newton Res.	28	9	7	12	53	69	34
Coplestonians Res.	28	9	2	17	45	52	29
Woodbridge A. Res.	28	8	4	16	40	63	28
Melton St A. Res.	28	7	3	18	48	77	24
Bramford Utd Res.	28	4	6	18	31	72	18

Intermediate B	P	W	D	L	F	A	Pts
Westerfield U. Res. -6	26	18	6	2	88	39	54
Stowupland Res.	26	17	2	7	86	44	53
Ransomes Spts Res.	26	17	1	8	78	33	52
Stonham Aspal Res.	26	14	3	9	67	48	45
Framlington T. Res.	26	12	5	9	62	52	41
Stanton Res.	26	13	2	11	51	56	41
Thurston Res.	26	12	4	10	65	61	40
Ipswich Exiles Res.	26	12	4	10	60	60	40
Felixstowe U. Res.	26	10	5	11	57	73	35
Cockfield Utd Res.	26	9	4	13	75	73	31
Brantham Athletic	26	9	2	15	45	68	29
Leiston St M Res. -6	26	9	3	14	52	82	24
AFC Debenham Res.	26	5	1	20	36	87	16
Halesworth T. Res.	26	3	2	21	37	88	11

Division Two	P	W	D	L	F	A	Pts
BT Trimley	26	20	4	2	72	19	64
Mendlesham KH	26	16	4	6	58	32	52
Wickham Market -6	26	17	4	5	71	38	49
Stradbroke United	26	12	5	9	65	42	41
Orwell Athletic	26	11	7	8	55	45	40
Wenhaston United	26	11	5	10	44	41	38
Murray Rangers	26	12	1	13	48	46	37
Coddenham Cnt. C.	26	9	4	13	49	55	31
Bacton United	26	8	4	14	48	51	28
Bramford Road OB	26	7	7	12	34	50	28
Elmswell	26	8	4	14	34	67	28
St Clements Hosp.	26	7	4	15	32	50	25
Saxmundham Sports	26	8	1	17	42	78	25
St Edmunds '65	26	7	4	15	38	76	25

Division Three	P	W	D	L	F	A	Pts
Dennington United	22	16	4	2	88	37	52
Salvation Army	22	15	5	2	64	29	50
Martlesham Athletic	22	13	4	5	63	31	43
Sproughton Sports	22	12	5	5	63	36	41
Tattingstone United	22	11	2	9	65	55	35
Needham Mkt 'A'	22	11	1	10	51	41	34
Albion Mills	22	10	3	9	32	37	33
Walsham-le-W. 'A'	22	5	6	11	39	56	21
Waterside CB	22	6	3	13	42	68	21
East Bergholt U. 'A'	22	6	3	13	44	73	21
Somersham	22	4	4	14	32	60	16
Stag Tavern	22	2	2	18	33	93	8

Division Four	P	W	D	L	F	A	Pts
AFC Hoxne	26	19	4	3	120	45	61
Whitton Maypole	26	19	2	5	99	34	59
Ipswich Postals Res.	26	16	5	5	91	50	53
Bildeston Rangers	26	16	3	7	73	36	51
Woodbridge A. 'A'	25	16	2	7	65	42	50
BT Trimley Res.	25	12	3	10	62	53	39
Haughley Utd 'A'	24	11	2	11	56	47	35
Coplestonians 'A'	26	11	2	13	48	54	35
Sproughton S. Res.	26	7	6	13	48	77	27
Sizewell/Aldeburgh	26	8	3	15	42	96	27
Wenhaston U. Res.	25	6	5	14	43	76	23
Bacton United Res.	26	5	5	16	35	67	20
Meadlands	25	5	3	17	48	80	18
Wickham Mkt Res.	26	3	5	18	39	112	14

Division Five	P	W	D	L	F	A	Pts
Claydon	24	20	2	2	90	20	62
Walton Rangers	24	20	1	3	98	37	61
Ufford Sports	24	15	1	8	63	26	46
Bramford ROB Res.	24	11	3	10	49	43	36
Needham Mkt 'B'	24	11	3	10	49	63	36
Stradbroke U. Res.	24	10	4	10	66	76	34
Parkside United	24	10	2	12	47	57	32
Salvation Army Res.	24	10	2	12	58	72	32
Murray Rgrs Res.	24	8	2	14	61	70	26
Stonham Aspal 'A'	24	7	5	12	34	47	26
Benhall St Mary	24	6	3	15	51	84	21
BT Trimley 'A'	24	6	2	16	37	71	20
Elmswell Res.	24	6	2	16	53	90	20

Division Six	P	W	D	L	F	A	Pts
Stowupland 'A'	18	13	4	1	48	23	43
Tacket Street BBOB	18	11	0	7	60	41	33
Martlesham Res.	18	10	2	6	58	39	32
Orwell Athletic Res.	18	9	1	8	31	37	28
AFC Hoxne Res.	18	8	3	7	49	38	27
Woolverstone Utd	18	7	3	8	40	36	24
Dennington U. Res.	18	6	4	8	42	51	22
St Clements H. Res.	18	6	3	9	34	38	21
The Chequers -3	18	7	0	11	39	59	18
Somersham Res.	18	2	2	14	22	61	8

Division Seven	P	W	D	L	F	A	Pts
Peasenhall United	20	17	1	2	75	36	52
Alstons	20	15	0	5	87	37	45
Jokers Nightclub	20	13	3	4	73	36	42
Old Newton Utd 'A'	20	11	5	4	61	41	38
Codd'ham CC Res.	20	11	1	8	52	48	34
Mendlesham Res.	20	7	5	8	47	39	26
Needham M. Youth	20	8	2	10	44	46	26
Albion Mills Res.	20	7	1	12	37	44	22
Claydon Res.	20	5	3	12	48	72	18
Tacket SBBOB Res.	20	5	1	14	34	58	16
Bacton United 'A'	20	0	0	20	10	111	0

SURREY SOUTH EASTERN COMBINATION

Int. Division One	P	W	D	L	F	A	Pts
Warlingham	20	15	2	3	74	25	47
Coney Hall	20	12	4	4	42	21	40
Greenside	20	12	2	6	58	36	38
Accra '94	19	11	2	6	46	30	35
Old Rutlishians	19	10	2	7	46	38	32
Battersea Ironsides	20	8	4	8	43	42	28
Surbiton Griffins	20	7	1	12	45	58	22
Ashtead	20	5	6	9	37	55	21
Oxted & District	20	5	3	12	30	56	18
Addington	20	5	1	14	26	51	16
Sutton High	20	3	5	12	24	59	14

Int. Division Two	P	W	D	L	F	A	Pts
St Andrews	20	13	3	4	62	30	42
Bletchingley	20	13	2	5	60	47	41
Woodmansterne Sp.	20	11	2	7	45	34	35
Cheam Vill. Warr.	20	11	2	7	44	35	35
Tadworth	20	10	4	6	43	33	34
Continental Stars	20	9	3	8	47	40	30
AFC Ewell	20	8	2	10	29	43	26
Thornton Hth Rov.	20	6	4	10	36	51	22
Charlwood +3	20	3	5	12	26	37	17
Croygas	20	4	5	11	39	58	17
Hawker -3	20	4	4	12	24	47	13

Int. Division Three	P	W	D	L	F	A	Pts
Nuwood	18	17	1	0	55	11	52
Wandgas Sports	18	11	2	5	60	35	35
Croydon Postal	18	11	1	6	35	30	34
Epsom Athletic	18	10	1	7	47	42	31
NPL -3	18	11	0	7	35	33	30
Caterham Old Boys	18	6	4	8	42	39	22
Old Plymouthians	18	6	3	9	37	46	21
Chipstead Old Boys	18	4	2	12	22	40	14
Nutfield	18	2	5	11	19	44	11
NCA Regus +3	18	1	3	14	19	51	9

Junior Div. One	P	W	D	L	F	A	Pts
Battersea	18	15	2	1	66	11	47
Westside	18	11	5	2	42	15	38
Warlingham Res.	18	11	3	4	48	28	36
S. Pk/Reigate T. -1	18	9	3	6	62	47	29
AC Mondial +3	18	7	3	8	26	25	27
Old Rutlishians Res.	18	6	4	8	33	36	22
Batt. Ironsides Res.	18	6	4	8	32	43	22
Little House -3	18	6	2	10	34	39	17
Crescent R. 'A' -1	18	2	5	11	22	48	10
Ashtead Res.	18	0	3	15	22	95	3

Junior Div. Two	P	W	D	L	F	A	Pts
NPL Res.	20	14	3	3	53	20	45
St Andrews Res.	20	14	3	3	52	30	45
Wandgas Spts Res.	20	13	3	4	67	36	42
Accra 94 Res. -3	20	12	3	5	39	24	36
Brixton Lambeth	20	10	3	7	55	46	33
Greenside Res. +3	20	8	1	11	43	71	28
Coney Hall Res.	20	8	3	9	48	44	27
Croygas Res.	20	7	1	12	48	58	22
Addington Res.	20	6	1	13	35	39	19
Tadworth Res	20	3	2	15	28	66	11
Sutton High Res.	20	3	1	16	22	56	10

Junior Div. Three	P	W	D	L	F	A	Pts
Cont. Stars Res.	22	17	2	3	69	29	53
NCA Regus Res. +2	22	15	3	4	70	29	50
Oxted & D. Res.	22	14	3	5	51	36	45
Cheam VW Res	22	13	4	5	65	48	43
Rusmill Res.	22	12	3	7	50	48	39
Worcester Pk 'A' -1	22	8	6	8	39	43	29
Mustard United -6	22	10	0	12	43	43	24
SP & Reigate Res	22	6	5	11	50	72	23
Wood'sterne Res	22	6	5	11	38	64	23
Old Rutlishians 'A'	22	5	1	16	26	53	19
Hawker Res.	22	4	1	17	30	38	16
Oakway Sports	22	4	3	15	39	67	15

Junior Div. Four	P	W	D	L	F	A	Pts
Sporting Wandgas	22	18	1	3	109	24	55
Nuwood Res.	22	15	4	3	77	29	49
Epsom Ath. Res. +2	22	13	4	5	65	36	45
Bletchingley Res.	22	14	2	6	70	38	44
Carshalton Ryls +3	21	9	2	10	46	55	32
Fetcham	22	10	2	10	72	81	32
Warlingham 'A' -1	22	10	2	10	51	47	31
Tadworth 'A' -3	21	9	2	10	40	49	26
Hurst View	22	6	3	13	43	61	21
Alexander Forbes	22	5	3	14	38	67	18
Crescent Rov. 'B'	22	4	4	14	32	79	16
Woodmansterne 'A'	22	1	5	16	27	104	8

TAUNTON & DISTRICT LEAGUE

Division One	P	W	D	L	F	A	Pts
Bishops Lydeard	20	17	1	2	62	20	52
Sydenham Rangers	20	15	0	5	78	37	45
Staplegrove	20	10	3	7	55	48	33
Alcombe Rovers	20	9	4	7	59	47	31
Galmington -3	20	9	4	7	61	46	28
Wellworthy Saints	20	9	1	10	49	44	28
Wyvern	20	9	1	10	43	43	28
Bridgwater Sports	20	6	3	11	37	53	21
Norton F'warren -3	20	7	1	12	35	55	19
Sampford Blues	20	4	2	14	26	73	14
Redgate	20	3	4	13	27	66	13

WEST HERTS LEAGUE

Premier Division	P	W	D	L	F	A	Pts
Hemel Hemp. Rov.	20	18	0	2	60	34	54
Kings Sports	20	15	2	3	103	28	47
Metpol Bushey 'A'	20	13	3	4	64	41	42
Duke of York	20	13	0	7	65	44	39
Agrevo	20	11	3	6	45	29	36
Jomarth Builders	20	11	0	9	56	47	33
Rose/Crown (Herts)	20	5	3	12	41	73	18
Glenn Sports	20	5	2	13	41	45	17
Oxhey Jets 'A'	20	3	5	12	27	58	14
Oxhey	20	3	4	13	33	72	13
Cassiobury Rangers	20	1	2	17	27	91	5

Division One	P	W	D	L	F	A	Pts
Oaklands Athletic	16	14	0	2	87	19	42
L'Artista	16	12	2	2	63	25	38
Oxhey Wanderers	16	12	1	3	57	26	37
H. Hemp. Rvrs Res.	16	8	3	5	44	38	27
Aldenham	16	7	1	8	46	46	22
Rifle Volunteer	16	4	3	9	31	51	15
Jomarth Build. Res.	16	4	2	10	39	50	14
Langleybury CC	16	3	2	11	22	64	11
Croxley Guild 'A'	16	1	0	15	19	89	3

Division Two	P	W	D	L	F	A	Pts
SOS Athletic	16	14	0	2	72	20	42
Tring Athletic 'A'	16	13	0	3	56	26	39
Potten End	16	10	1	5	35	27	31
Croxley Guild 'B'	16	9	1	6	46	33	28
L'Artista Res.	16	7	1	8	39	46	22
Kings Sports Res.	16	5	2	9	41	43	17
Evergreen Old Boys	16	5	2	9	25	51	17
Red Lion Rovers	16	4	1	11	34	40	13
Metpol Bushey 'B'	16	1	0	15	17	79	3

Division Three	P	W	D	L	F	A	Pts
Oxhey Jets 'B'	16	15	1	0	63	12	46
Badger Athletic	16	11	1	4	70	26	34
Coach & Horses	16	11	1	4	41	17	34
Tring Athletic 'B'	16	5	3	8	31	47	18
Bovingdon 'A'	16	5	2	9	30	53	17
H. Hempst'd Rv. 'A'	16	5	2	9	24	51	17
Oxhey Res.	16	4	3	9	25	53	15
Kings Langley 'A'	16	4	2	10	29	37	14
Hunton Bridge	16	2	5	9	31	48	11

WESTMORLAND LEAGUE

Division One	P	W	D	L	F	A	Pts
Wetheriggs United	26	19	2	5	84	30	59
Coniston	26	19	2	5	78	36	59
Carleton Rovers	26	16	5	5	72	37	53
Appleby	26	15	5	6	76	36	50
Staveley United	26	14	4	8	59	37	46
Lunesdale United	26	14	3	9	68	57	45
Kendal County	26	13	4	9	58	47	43
Windermere SC	26	11	7	8	62	51	40
Sedbergh Wanderers	26	10	3	13	65	53	33
Keswick	26	9	5	12	41	49	32
Victoria SC	26	6	3	17	36	67	21
Ambleside United	26	4	5	17	39	68	17
Burneside	26	4	4	18	23	63	16
Shap United -6	26	2	0	24	17	147	0

Division Two		P	W	D	L	F	A	Pts
Kendal Town Res.		24	22	2	0	121	14	68
Penrith Res.		24	16	4	4	87	18	52
Carvetii United		24	14	3	7	59	38	45
Greystoke		24	12	4	8	63	40	40
Wetheriggs U. Res.		24	13	1	10	51	45	40
Ibis		24	12	3	9	67	39	39
Endmoor KGR		24	11	2	11	40	46	35
Kirkoswald		24	11	1	12	49	58	34
Dent		24	8	4	12	59	63	28
Kendal Co. Res.	-3	24	7	5	12	50	81	23
Ullswater United		24	6	2	16	33	99	20
Appleby Res.		24	5	1	18	35	85	16
Grasmere		24	1	4	19	36	124	7

Division Three	P	W	D	L	F	A	Pts
Penrith Rangers	22	19	2	1	93	31	59
Keswick Res.	22	13	3	6	68	36	42
Wetheriggs Utd 'A'	22	11	6	5	58	42	39
Kirkby L'dale Rgrs	22	11	4	7	58	46	37
Windermere Res.	22	10	5	7	44	30	35
Carleton Rov. Res.	22	11	2	9	54	45	35
Coniston Res.	22	9	4	9	41	54	31
Braithwaite	22	8	5	9	54	46	29
Burneside Res.	22	6	6	10	28	54	24
Greystoke Res.	22	6	2	14	42	72	20
Carvetii Utd Res.	22	4	2	16	33	65	14
Ambleside Res. -3	22	2	3	17	26	78	6

Division Four	P	W	D	L	F	A	Pts
Kendal Celtic	18	13	2	3	73	35	41
Penrith Rangers Res.	18	12	2	4	79	25	38
Sedbergh W. Res.	18	11	1	6	58	30	34
Endmoor KGR Res.	18	11	1	6	54	42	34
Ibis Res.	18	10	2	6	57	41	32
Lunesdale Utd Res.	18	8	2	8	43	57	26
Windermere SC 'A'	18	5	3	10	30	49	18
Staveley Utd Res.	18	5	2	11	28	58	17
Penrith Academy -3	18	6	1	11	32	60	16
Dent Res.	18	2	1	15	19	76	5

WIMBLEDON & DISTRICT LEAGUE

Premier Division	P	W	D	L	F	A	Pts
Union	16	14	1	1	49	18	43
Independiente	16	12	0	4	44	23	36
Putney Corinthians	16	9	2	5	70	39	29
Brentside	16	9	1	6	43	28	28
Leamington	16	7	2	7	35	29	23
Agricola	16	6	3	7	46	60	21
Rivelino City	16	5	1	10	24	41	16
AFC Cubo	16	3	3	10	22	54	12
Colombia	16	0	1	15	25	66	1

Division One	P	W	D	L	F	A	Pts
London Study Cent.	14	12	2	0	49	15	38
Real Phoenix	14	12	1	1	61	15	37
Brompton Rovers	14	9	0	5	53	27	27
Partizan Wandsw'th	14	5	1	8	25	34	16
Wollaton Forest	14	5	1	8	23	42	16
AC Retros	14	4	2	8	24	35	14
All Action	14	4	2	8	19	37	14
London Lionhearts	14	0	1	13	16	65	1

Division Two	P	W	D	L	F	A	Pts
Brentside Res.	14	10	4	0	40	10	34
PWCA	14	9	3	2	24	14	30
Wandle	14	8	2	4	38	23	26
Stapleton	14	8	1	5	32	34	25
Hurlingham Hornets	14	7	1	6	41	30	22
Norfolk	14	5	2	7	26	37	17
FC Samba	14	1	1	12	11	48	4
Emperors Eleven	14	0	2	12	6	22	2

WORTHING & DISTRICT LEAGUE

Premier Division	P	W	D	L	F	A	Pts
Sompting	18	15	2	1	52	11	47
GSK Sports	18	13	4	1	52	19	43
Tabernacle	18	10	1	7	36	26	31
W. Worthing WMC	18	8	3	7	30	25	27
Maple Leaf Rangers	18	8	3	7	25	38	27
Warren Sports	18	8	1	9	33	31	25
The Brunswick	18	7	4	7	34	36	25
Northbrook	18	4	2	12	24	56	14
Worthing Utd 'B'	18	4	1	13	26	36	13
West Tarring WMC	18	2	1	15	24	55	7

YEOVIL & DISTRICT LEAGUE

Premier Division	P	W	D	L	F	A	Pts
Ilchester	18	14	2	2	68	22	44
Wincanton Town	18	11	2	5	55	30	35
Henstridge United	18	11	2	5	59	38	35
Pen Mill	18	11	1	6	51	29	34
Milborne Port	18	10	1	7	29	21	31
Normalair RSL	18	7	2	9	23	26	23
Stoke-sub-Hamdon	18	4	6	8	32	30	18
Keinton Mandeville	18	5	1	12	33	63	16
Castle Cary Res.	18	3	6	9	40	60	15
Glastonbury Sports	18	2	1	15	15	86	7

Division One	P	W	D	L	F	A	Pts
Victoria Sports	18	17	0	1	67	17	51
South Cheriton Utd	18	15	1	2	76	21	46
Bishop's Caundle	18	11	4	3	39	21	37
Odcombe	18	7	6	5	47	31	27
Langport Town	18	7	2	9	39	38	23
AFC Camel	18	7	0	11	23	57	21
Ansford Rovers	18	6	1	11	26	46	19
Martock United	18	5	2	11	29	49	17
Stoke-sub-H. Res.	18	3	2	13	26	55	11
Templecombe Rov.	18	2	2	14	31	68	8

Division Two	P	W	D	L	F	A	Pts
Yetminster Sharks	18	15	1	2	59	38	46
Westland Spts Res.	18	14	1	3	64	26	43
East Coker	18	13	1	4	65	30	40
Normalair RSL Res.	18	9	0	9	50	47	27
Milborne Port Res.	18	7	4	7	42	44	25
Blue Heron	18	7	2	9	56	55	23
Pen Mill Res.	18	7	2	9	36	38	23
Royal Oak Rangers	18	6	3	9	40	46	21
Armoury	18	4	1	13	30	56	13
Kingsbury Episcopi	18	0	1	17	17	79	1

Division Three	P	W	D	L	F	A	Pts
Ilchester Res.	20	18	0	2	113	34	54
Porter Blacks	20	17	1	2	108	36	52
AFC Wessex	20	12	3	5	76	43	39
Wincanton T. Res.	20	12	1	7	59	40	37
Milborne Port 'A'	20	8	4	8	50	62	28
Lyde United	20	7	2	11	37	62	23
Charlton United	20	7	1	12	56	66	22
Langport T. Res.	20	5	4	11	37	72	19
Ansford Rov. Res.	20	5	2	13	36	63	17
Martock Utd Res.	20	5	0	15	36	77	15
Montacute	20	4	2	14	44	97	14

Division Four	P	W	D	L	F	A	Pts
Victoria Sports Res.	20	16	1	3	118	21	49
Bradford Sports	20	16	1	3	104	27	49
Armoury Res.	20	13	0	7	71	39	39
Pitney	20	12	1	7	75	49	37
Keinton Mand. Res.	20	11	3	6	64	36	36
Odcombe Res.	20	11	2	7	68	43	35
Wincanton Town 'A'	20	10	1	9	72	51	31
Bish. Caundle Res.	20	8	1	11	50	54	25
Pen Mills Colts	20	3	1	16	19	178	10
Charlton Utd Res.	19	3	0	16	24	73	9
Mann United	19	0	1	18	18	112	1

YORK & DISTRICT LEAGUE

Premier Division	P	W	D	L	F	A	Pts
Pocklington Res.	26	23	2	1	80	18	71
Dringhouses	26	21	2	3	89	22	65
Malton Bacon Fact.	26	16	3	7	91	37	51
Osbaldwick	26	13	5	8	76	47	44
Dunnington	26	12	5	9	56	49	41
Huntington Rovers	26	12	3	11	53	58	39
Old Malton	26	11	3	12	63	51	36
Kartiers	26	9	5	12	36	44	32
Wigginton G'hopp.	26	9	4	13	41	58	31
Rufforth United	26	8	5	13	45	72	29
Nestle Rowntree	26	7	5	14	50	62	26
Bishopthorpe	26	7	3	16	45	68	24
Crayke	26	6	5	15	36	60	23
Riccall United	26	2	2	22	24	139	8

Division One	P	W	D	L	F	A	Pts
Wigginton Bk Hrse	24	17	3	4	62	35	54
T&L Selby	24	16	4	4	57	28	52
Copmanthorpe	24	15	3	6	66	33	48
Post Office -3	24	14	6	4	55	29	45
Haxby/Wigginton	24	11	4	9	59	56	37
Thorpe Utd	24	10	6	8	51	37	36
Haxby Town	24	11	3	10	41	50	36
New Earswick	24	10	4	10	41	46	34
St Johns College	24	8	4	12	44	55	28
South Bank	24	7	5	12	53	56	26
Norwich Union	24	4	6	14	33	59	18
Civil Service	24	4	3	17	31	71	15
Fulford United	24	1	5	18	24	62	8

All league tables in this section are final. It is the policy of some competitions to leave some oft postponed matches as unplayed if they do not affect end of season issues.

OTHER LEAGUES - SPONSORS

Aberystwyth & District League	-	*Cambrian Tyres*
Anglesey League	-	*Stena Line*
Bournemouth League	-	*Haywards Sports*
Colchester & East Essex League	-	*K E Connect*
East Midlands Alliance	-	*Dr Martens*
Gwent Central League	-	*Knauf Alcopor Insulation*
Herefordshire League	-	*Hereford Times*
Matlock & District League	-	*Hellison Trophies*
Middlesex League	-	*Select Appointments*
Mid-Somerset League	-	*Fast*
Mid-Sussex League	-	*Robert Gray*
Peterborough & District League	-	*AMP Pearl Assurance*
North Devon League	-	*Bideford Tool*
Southampton League	-	*Drew Smith Homes*
Suffolk & Ipswich League	-	*Metaltec*
Taunton & District League	-	*Somtech*
West Herts League	-	*Arlon Printers*
Westmorland League	-	*Talbot Insurance*
York & District	-	*Leeper Hare*

INDEX

The page numbers point to each team's 2002-03 league table. If a team's 2003-04 directory entry is on a different page, this precedes in brackets. Clubs subject to name changes are asterisked. Both new and old names are included in the index, and a full listing follows the index.

WWW.NLNEWSDESK.CO.UK

WWW.CHERRYRED.CO.UK

WWW.NLNEWSDESK.CO.UK

WWW.CHERRYRED.CO.UK

Brickfield Rangers Res.	167
Bridgend Street	134
Bridgend Town	163
Bridgham	224
Bridgnorth Town	(92) 91
Bridgnorth Town Res.	181
Bridgwater Sports	230
Bridgwater Town	190
Bridgwater Town Res.	128
Bridlington Sports Club	61
Bridlington Town	(120) 109
Bridlington Town Res.	61
Bridon Ropes	(77)
Bridport	190
Bridport Res.	31
Brierley & Hagley Alliance	(181) 180
Brigg Town	109
Brighouse Town	183
Brighouse Town Res.	185
Brightlingsea United	(39) 38
Brightlingsea United Res.	225
Brighton 1664	224
Brighton A & E	224
Brighton BBOB	224
Brighton BBOB Res.	224
Brighton Electricity	224
Brighton Rangers	224
Brighton Rangers Res.	224
Brighton Sports	224
Brimsdown Rovers	149
Brislington	190
Brislington Res.	128
Bristol Manor Farm	191
Bristol Spartak	131
Bristol Union	224
Britannia	224
British Airways	226
British Steel	132
Briton Ferry Athletic	162
Brixton Lambeth	230
Brixworth All Saints	104
Brixworth All Saints Res.	105
BRJ Huntingdon	16
Broadbridge Heath	155
Broadbridge Heath Res.	156
Broadclyst	26
Broadclyst Res.	26
Broadfields United	227
Broadheath Central	88
Brockenhurst	(173) 172
Brockenhurst Res.	172
Brockley	228
Brockley Res.	228
Brocton	(92) 97
Brocton Res.	152
Brodsworth Miners Welfare	109
Bromham	193
Bromleians Sports	(76) 77
Bromleians Sports Res.	78
Bromley	(70) 69
Bromley Green	76
Brompton Rovers	231
Bromsgrove Rovers	(146) 144
Bromyard Town	(181) 180
Broncoed Tigers	167
Bronze Social	(176)
Brook House	148
Brook House Res.	229
Brookwood	229
Broomfield (AFA)	229
Broomfield (AFA) Res.	229
Broomfield (Essex)	40
Broomfield (Essex) Res.	41
Broughton	54
Broughton Res.	227
Brownhills Town	(95) 94
Broxbourne Borough V&E Res.	225
Broxbourne Borough V&E	148
Brunel University	227
Brunel University Res.	227
Brymbo Broughton	165
Brymbo Broughton Res.	166
Brynmawr	51
Brynteg Village	166
Bryntirion Athletic	164
BT Trimley	230
BT Trimley 'A'	230
BT Trimley Res.	230
BTC Southampton	228
BTC Southampton Res.	229
BTSC*	124
Buckden	16
Buckingham Athletic	150
Buckingham Athletic Res.	151
Buckingham Town	157
Buckingham Town Res.	158
Buckland	99
Buckland Athletic	24
Buckland Athletic Res.	(25) 26
Buckland MC	228
Buckland Res.	100
Buckley Town	23
Buckley Town Res.	(167)
Bude	32
Budleigh Salterton	24
Budleigh Salterton Res.	25
Budley Bulldogs	26
Bugbrooke St Michaels	158
Bugbrooke St Michaels 'A'	105
Bugbrooke St Michaels 'B'	105
Bugbrooke St Michaels Res.	158
Bulmers	226
Bungay Town	10
Bungay Town Res.	12
Buntingford Town	60
Buntingford Town Res.	60
Bures United	38
Burgess Hill Albion	227
Burgess Hill Albion Res.	227
Burgess Hill Athletic	227
Burgess Hill Athletic Res.	227
Burgess Hill Town	(143) 154
Burgess Hill Town Res.	156
Burghclere	223
Burghill	226
Burley	224
Burneside	230
Burneside Res.	231
Burnham	(143) 141
Burnham Ramblers	42
Burnham Ramblers Res.	225
Burnham Res.	229
Burnham United	128
Burnham United Res.	131
Burnley Belvedere	178
Burnley Belvedere Res.	179
Burnley United	177
Burnley United Res.	179
Burntwood Town	94
Burridge AFC	229
Burridge AFC Res.	229
Burridge Sports	229
Burscough	(116) 114
Burscough Res.	226
Burton	224
Burton Albion	(44) 43
Burton Joyce	(123) 124
Burton Park Wanderers	158
Burton Park Wanderers Res.	158
Burton Res.	224
Burton United	105
Bury Town	33
Bury Town Res.	(37) 38
Bush Hill	229
Bushey Rangers	59
Bushey Rangers Res.	60
Bustleholme	(181) 180
Bustleholme Res.	181
Butetown	(135) 134
Buxted	227
Buxted 'A'	227
Buxted Res.	227
Buxton	109
Cadbury Athletic	94
Cadbury Athletic Res.	95
Cadbury Heath	191
Caddington	150
Cadnam United	228
Cadnam United Res.	229
Cadoxton Cons	135
Caerau Ely	164
Caerau United	(132) 164
Caerleon	162
Caernarfon Town	(170) 168
Caernarfon Town Res.	225
Caersws	(170) 168
Caerwys	161
Caister United	10
Caister United 'A'	225
Caister United Res.	12
Caldicot Castle	51
Caldicot Town	164
Caledonian Strip Mills	(104) 105
Callington Town	136
Callington Town Res.	32
Calmore Rovers	229
Calne Town	191
Calne Town Res.	193
Calverton Miners Welfare	123
Calverton Miners Welfare Res.	124
Camberley Town	72
Camberley Town Res.	229
Cambrian & Clydach Vale BC	132
Cambridge City	(138) 137
Cambridge City Res.	34
Cambridge University Press	15
Cambridge University Press 'A'	16
Cambridge University Press Res.	16
Camden Tavern	225
Camden United	15
Camden United Res.	16
Camelford	32
Camerons	188
Cammell Laird	174
Cammell Laird Res.	175
Campion	183
Campion Res.	185
Canning Town	40
Canning Town Res.	41
Canvey Island	(64) 62
Canvey Island Res.	225
Capel Plough	229
Capel Plough Res.	229
Capenhurst Villa	175
Capenhurst Villa Res.	176
Capital	229
Capital Res.	229
Carcroft Village WMC	225
Cardiff Civil Service	162
Cardiff Corinthians	162
Cardiff Corinthians Res.	132
Cardiff Cosmos Portos	133
Cardiff Draconians	132
Cardiff Rovers	224
Cardinal Manning Old Boys	223
Caribbean Sports	228
Carisbrooke United	226
Carleton Rovers	230
Carleton Rovers Res.	231
Carlisle City	106
Carlton Athletic	186
Carlton Athletic Res.	188
Carlton Town	(110) 17
Carlton Town 'A'	18
Carlton Town Res.	17
Carmarthen Town	(170) 168
Carnetown	133
Carnforth Rangers	178
Carnforth Rangers Res.	179
Carshalton	229
Carshalton Athletic	(64) 69
Carshalton Athletic Res.	229
Carshalton Res.	229
Carshalton Royals	230
Carterton Town	(56) 55

Mill Hill St Peters	179
Mill Hill St Peters Res.	179
Mill Hill Village	223
Mill Hill Village Res.	223
Millbank AFC	229
Millbridge	229
Millbridge Res.	229
Millbrook	136
Millbrook Res.	32
Millers Pond	229
Millom	178
Milnthorpe Corinthians	177
Milnthorpe Corinthians Res.	179
Milton (Cambs)	15
Milton (Cambs) 'A'	16
Milton (Cambs) Res.	16
Milton (Manchester)	87
Milton (Manchester) Res.	87
Milton (Northants)	104
Milton (Northants) Res.	105
Milton Abbas Sports	29
Milton Athletic	75
Milton Keynes City	148
Milton Keynes City Res.	151
Milton Rangers	(152) 97
Milton Rangers Res.	152
Milton United	57
Milton United Res.	55
Minehead Town	191
Minety	193
Misterton	227
Mistley United	36
Mistley United 'A'	225
Mistley United Res.	38
Mitre United	26
MK United	225
MK United Res.	225
Modbury Rovers	228
Mold Alexandra	23
Mold Alexandra Res.	166
Mold Juniors	(167)
Molesey	(70) 69
Molesey Res.	229
Mond Rangers	175
Mond Rangers Res.	176
Moneyfields	(173) 172
Moneyfields Res.	172
Monmouth Town	50
Monotype	(21) 225
Monotype Res.	225
Montacute	231
Monton Amateurs	86
Monton Amateurs Res.	87
Montpelier Villa	224
Montpelier Villa Res.	224
Moonshot Athletic	76
Moor Green	(139) 137
Moordown United	224
Morchard Bishop	26
Morda United	182
Morecambe	(45) 43
Morecambe Res.	226
Moreton	27
Morley Cars	228
Morley Town	185
Morley Village	11
Morley Village Res.	224
Morpeth Town	112
Morpeth Town 'A'*	(108)
Morriston Town	163
Mortimer	125
Mortimer Res.	127
Morwenstow	227
Mossley	101
Mossley Hill Athletic	85
Motel Rangers & Offwell	26
Motel Rangers & Offwell Res.	26
Mott McDonald	16
Mottisfont	(54) 228
Mottisfont Res.	229
Moulton	104
Moulton Harrox	228
Moulton Res.	105
Mount Gould Black Prince	228
Mount St Mary's	187
Mountnessing	40
Mountnessing Res.	41
Mousehole	22
Mowers*	30
MSX International	225
Mulbarton United	8
Mulbarton United Res.	12
Mulbarton Wanderers	224
Mullion	22
Mundford	10
Mundford Res.	12
Murray Rangers	230
Murray Rangers Res.	230
Mursley United	150
Mursley United Res.	151
Murton	113
Mustard United	230
Mynydd Isa*	165
Mynydd Isa BT*	(165)
Mynydd Isa BT Res.*	(166)
N & M Construction	133
Nailsea Town	(129) 128
Nailsea United	128
Nailsea United Res.	130
Nanpean Rovers	32
Nantlle Vale	225
Nantwich Town	101
Nantwich Town Res.	(89)
Narborough & Littlethorpe	83
Narborough & Littlethorpe Res.	83
Nayland Rangers	225
NCA Regus	230
NCA Regus Res.	230
Neasden	227
Neasden Res.	227
Neath	162
Necton SSC	12
Necton SSC Res.	224
Needham Market	34
Needham Market 'A'	230
Needham Market 'B'	230
Needham Market Res.	37
Needham Market Youth	230
Needingworth United	(15) 16
Needingworth United Res.	16
Nefyn United	225
Nelson	102
Nelson Cavaliers	135
Nestle Rowntree	231
Netheravon	228
Netherbury	227
Netherne Village	(21) 153
Netherne Village Res.	153
Netley Central Sports	54
Netley Central Sports Res.	54
Nettlebed United	127
Nettleham	17
Nettleham Res.	18
New Bradwell St Peter	149
New Bradwell St Peter Res.	151
New Brighton	175
New Brighton Res.	176
New Brighton Villa	166
New Brighton Villa Res.	(167)
New College Academy	58
New College Academy Res.	(193)
New Earswick	231
New Hanford	226
New Inn	223
New Inn AFC	51
New Inn AFC Res.	225
New Inn Res.	223
New Islip	226
New Lodge	224
New Marske Sports Club	159
New Mills	86
New Mills Res.	87
New Milton Eagles	224
New Milton Eagles Res.	224
New Park	228
New Romney	75
New Romney Res.	77
Newark Flowserve	122
Newark Flowserve Res.	123
Newark Town	124
Newark Town Res.	124
Newark Youth Association	226
Newbiggin Central Welfare	107
Newcastle Benfield Saints	(115) 106
Newcastle Blue Star	(113) 112
Newcastle British Telecom	108
Newcastle East End Rail Club	(107) 108
Newcastle Emlyn	164
Newcastle Town	101
Newcastle Town Res.	97
Newcastle University	106
Newhall United	(95) 96
Newhaven	156
Newhaven Res.	156
NEWI Cefn Druids*	(170)
Newick	227
Newmarket Town	33
Newmarket Town Res.	13
Newport Civil Service	50
Newport Corinthians	49
Newport County	(139) 137
Newport IOW	(143) 141
Newport IOW Res.	172
Newport Pagnell Town	157
Newport Pagnell Town Res.	158
Newport Town	(181) 182
Newport Town 'A'	226
Newport Veterans	16
Newport YMCA	163
Newquay	136
Newquay Res.	22
Newton	174
Newton & Corston	223
Newton Abbot	24
Newton Abbot Spurs	24
Newton Flotman	11
Newton Res.	176
Newton St Cyres	26
Newtown (Wales)	(170) 168
Newtown (Devon)	26
Newtown (Devon) Res.	26
Newtown Dynamo	225
Newtown Henley	125
Newtown Henley Res.	(126) 127
Nicholas Wanderers	224
Nine Saxons	223
Nissan UK	(159)
Niton	226
Norcross & Warbreck	(178) 177
Norcross & Warbreck Res.	179
Norfolk	231
Norleywood	229
Normalair RSL	231
Normalair RSL Res.	231
Normandy	223
Normandy Res.	223
Norsemen	229
Norsemen Res.	229
Norside	224
North Baddesley	228
North Elmham	224
North Elmham Res.	224
North Ferriby United	(120) 118
North Ferriby United Res.	61
North Greenford United	(21) 20
North Greenford United Res.	20
North Hayes Academicals	227
North Hayes Academicals Res.	227
North Kent	228
North Kilworth	83
North Kilworth Res.	83
North Leigh	(56) 55
North Leigh Res.	55
North Mymms	60
North Mymms Res.	60

Otterbourne 'A'	229
Otterbourne Res.	228
Otterburn	108
Otterton	26
Ottery St Mary	24
Oughtibridge War Memorial SC	228
Oulton Broad & Lowestoft Railway	10
Oundle Town	228
Oval Sports	223
Oval Sports Res.	223
Ovenden West Riding	183
Ovenden West Riding Res.	185
Over Sports	13
Over Sports Res.	16
Over Wallop	223
Overton Recreation	166
Overton United	(53) 54
Overton United 'A'	223
Overton United Res.	54
Oving	(156) 155
Oving Res.	156
Ovingdean	224
Oxford City	(68) 66
Oxford City Res.	229
Oxhey	230
Oxhey Jets	59
Oxhey Jets 'A'	230
Oxhey Jets 'B'	230
Oxhey Jets Res.	60
Oxhey Res.	230
Oxhey Wanderers	230
Oxted & District	230
Oxted & District Res.	230
Oyster	225
Padbury United	150
Padgate St Oswalds	(89) 88
Padiham	102
Padiham Res.	102
Padstow United	32
Pagham	154
Pagham Res.	156
Painters	226
Pant Yr Awel	134
Panteg	49
Panteg Res.	225
Papworth	15
Papworth Res.	16
Park Street Village	226
Parkdale Rovers	226
Parkfield	223
Parkfield Res.	223
Parkgate	110
Parkgate Res.	228
Parkhurst Rangers	228
Parkside United	230
Parramore Sports	228
Partizan Wandsworth	231
Patchway Town	48
Paulsgrove	53
Paulsgrove Res.	54
Paulton Rovers	190
Paulton Rovers Res.	(128) 129
Pavilions	175
Peacehaven & Telscombe	(155) 154
Peacehaven & Telscombe Res.	156
Peacehaven United	227
Pease Pottage Village	155
Peasedown Athletic	(129) 128
Peasedown St John Rovers	227
Peasenhall United	230
Pegasus	223
Pegasus Colts	226
Pegasus Juniors	(56) 55
Pegasus Juniors Res.	226
Pegasus Res.	223
Pelican	(17) 18
Pelican Res.	18
Pelsall Villa	(92) 91
Pembury	76
Pen Mill	231
Pen Mill Res.	231

Pen Mills Colts	231
Pencoed Athletic	(133) 132
Pencombe	226
Penhill Standard	228
Penistone Church	228
Penistone Church Res.	228
Penkhull	152
Penkridge Town	152
Penley	165
Penley Res.	(167)
Penmaenmawr Phoenix	161
Penn & Tylers Green	57
Penn & Tylers Green Res.	56
Pennington	179
Pennington Res.	179
Pennington St Marks	224
Pennington St Marks Res.	224
Penparcau	223
Penrhiwceiber Rangers	(163) 162
Penrhiwfer	(134) 135
Penrhyncoch Res.	223
Penrith	(112) 113
Penrith Academy	231
Penrith Rangers	231
Penrith Rangers Res.	231
Penrith Res.	231
Penryn Athletic	136
Penryn Athletic Res.	22
Pensford	226
Pensford Res.	227
Pentwyn Dynamo	164
Pentwyn Dynamo Res.	224
Pentwynmawr Athletic	50
Penycae	165
Penycae Res.	166
Penydarren Boys Club	134
Penyffordd	167
Penzance	136
Penzance Res.	22
Perana	228
Percy Main Amateurs	106
Perkins Sports	228
Perranwell	22
Perry Street	227
Pershore Town	(92) 93
Peterborough Sports	228
Peterlee Newtown	112
Petersfield Town	52
Petersfield Town Res.	54
Pewsey Vale	(56) 55
Pewsey Vale Res.	192
PFC Durrington	228
Pheonix DB	224
Phoenix (Sussex)	225
Phoenix (Sussex) Res.	225
Phoenix (Yorkshire)	228
Phoenix Old Boys	223
Phoenix Sports	(77) 76
Phoenix Sports Res.	78
Pickering Town	109
Pickering Town Res.	110
Picket Piece Sports & Social	223
Picket Piece Sports & Social Res.	223
Piddlehinton United	28
Piddletrenthide United	27
Piddletrenthide United Res.	30
PILCS	(51) 225
PILCS Res.	225
Pilkington (Cheshire)	88
Pilkington (Cheshire) Res.	89
Pilkington (Devon)	228
Pilkington XXX	94
Pill	49
Pilton United	227
Pilton United Res.	227
Pinchbeck United	228
Pinehurst Old Boys	(193)
Pinhoe	25
Pinhoe Res.	26
Pinxton North End	124
Pirelli General	52
Pirelli General Res.	54

Pitney	231
Pitstone & Ivinghoe	149
Pitstone & Ivinghoe Res.	151
Platt United	77
Plessey	226
Plumpton Athletic	227
Plumpton Athletic 'A'	227
Plumpton Athletic Res.	227
Plymouth City	228
Plymouth Civil Service	228
Plymouth Civil Service S&L	228
Plymouth Command	228
Plymouth Parkway	136
Plymouth Parkway Res.	228
Plymouth Rangers	228
Plymouth University	228
Plymouth University Res.	228
Plympton United	228
Plymstock United	24
Plymstock United Res.	228
Pocklington Town	61
Pocklington Town Res.	231
Podington & Higham	105
Polesworth North Warwick	94
Polygon United	229
Polytechnic	229
Polytechnic Res.	229
Pontardawe Town	162
Pontefract Collieries	110
Pontefract Collieries Res.	110
Pontefract Sports & Social	186
Pontefract Sports & Social Res.	188
Pontefract Town	188
Ponteland United	106
Pontlottyn Blast Furnace	164
Pontyclun	(163) 164
Pontypool Town	225
Pontypool Town Res.	225
Pontypridd Town	163
Pool	187
Poole & Parkstone Royal Mail*	28
Poole Borough	31
Poole Borough Res.	28
Poole Royal Mail*	(28)
Poole Town	52
Poringland Wanderers	10
Poringland Wanderers Res.	12
Port Talbot Town	(171) 168
Portcastrian	224
Porter	228
Porter Blacks	231
Porter Butt	224
Porth Tywyn Suburbs	163
Porthcawl Town	163
Porthleven	136
Porthleven Res.	22
Porthmadog	(171) 23
Porthmadog Res.	225
Portishead	128
Portishead Res.	130
Portland United	(173) 172
Portland United Res.	27
Porton Sports	228
Porton Sports Res.	228
Portslade Athletic	224
Portslade Athletic Res.	224
Portslade Sports	224
Portsmouth Royal Navy	52
Portsmouth Royal Navy Res.	172
Post Office	231
Posties FC	225
Pot Black	228
Potten End	230
Potters Bar Town	148
Potters Bar Town 'A'	226
Potters Bar Town Res.	151
Potterspury	104
Potterspury Res.	105
Potton United	158
Potton United Res.	158
Poulton Town	178
Poulton Town Res.	179

WWW.CHERRYRED.CO.UK

Team	Page	Team	Page	Team	Page
Royston Town Res.	151	Sandon	16	Shene Old Grammarians	223
Royton Town	86	Sandon Royals	40	Shenfield Association	(41) 40
Royton Town Res.	87	Sandon Royals Res.	41	Shenfield Association Res.	41
RS Basingstoke	(54) 57	Sandown	226	Shenstone Pathfinder	182
RS Basingstoke Res.	56	Sandridge Rovers	59	Sheppey United	(77)
RTB Ebbw Vale	(49) 164	Sandridge Rovers 'A'	226	Shepshed Dynamo	(146) 144
Ruabon Villa	(168) 167	Sandridge Rovers Res.	60	Shepshed Dynamo Res.	93
Ruddington United	122	Sandy Lane	187	Shepton Beauchamp	227
Ruddington United Res.	124	Santos	(123) 124	Shepton Mallet Town	191
Ruddington Village	124	Sarratt	60	Shepton Mallet Town Res.	(130) 131
Rufforth United	231	Sawbridgeworth Town	42	Sherborne St John	223
Rugby Town	(92) 93	Sawbridgeworth Town Res.	225	Sherborne Town	31
Rugby Town Res.	96	Sawston Rovers	16	Sherborne Town Res.	28
Rugby United	(146) 144	Sawston Rovers Res.	16	Sherburn White Rose	187
Rugby United Res.	93	Sawston United	13	Sherfield	223
Ruislip Manor	148	Sawston United 'A'	16	Sheringham	(10) 11
Ruislip Manor Res.	229	Sawston United Res.	(15) 16	Sherston Town	193
Runcorn Halton	(117) 114	Saxmundham Sports	230	Shifnal Town	(92) 91
Rushall Olympic	(92) 91	Saxton Rovers	98	Shildon	112
Rushall Olympic Res.	93	Saxton Rovers Res.	98	Shildon Railway	225
Rushden Arbuckle	105	Scarborough	(45) 43	Shillington	149
Rushden Rangers	104	Scarning	224	Shillington Res.	151
Rushden Rangers Res.	105	Scaynes Hill	227	Shinewater Association Res.	156
Rusmill Res.	230	Scaynes Hill 'A'	227	Shinewater Association*	155
Rusthall	(77) 76	Scaynes Hill 'B'	227	Shinfield	125
Rutherford Newcastle	107	Scaynes Hill Res.	227	Shinfield Res.	127
Ruthin Town	23	Scole United	8	Shipton Bellinger	223
Ruthin Town Colts	166	Scole United Res.	12	Shirebrook Town	110
Ruthin Town Res.	165	Scot	150	Shirebrook Town 'A'	18
Ryan*	(42)	Screenbase	223	Shirebrook Town Res.	17
Rye & Iden United	(154) 155	Sculcoates Amateurs	61	Shirehampton	129
Rye & Iden United Res.	156	Sea Mills Park	224	Shobdon	226
Ryhall United	228	Seaford Town	155	Shoreham	154
Ryhill & Havercroft Sports	(187) 188	Seaford Town Res.	156	Shoreham Res.	156
Ryhope Colliery Welfare	159	Seaham Duke	225	Shoreham United	224
Rylands	88	Seaham Mallard	225	Shortwood United	(56) 55
Rylands Res.	89	Seaham Red Star	113	Shottermill & Haslemere	(21) 153
Ryton	106	Sealand Leisure	161	Shottermill & Haslemere Res.	153
		Seaton Delaval Amateurs	106	Shotton Comrades	113
S Club Eleven	228	Seaton Town	25	Shrewsbury Town	(45)
Safeway	227	Seaton Town 'A'	26	Shrewton United	(191) 192
Saffron Crocus	16	Seaton Town Res.	26	Shrewton United Res.	(192) 228
Saffron Crocus Res.	16	Seaview	226	Shrivenham	58
Saffron Dynamo	83	Sebastopol	225	Shrivenham Res.	98
Saffron Dynamo Res.	83	Sebastopol Res.	225	Shropham United	224
Saffron Rangers	16	Sedbergh Wanderers	230	Sidac Sports	(89)
Saffron Rangers Res.	16	Sedbergh Wanderers Res.	231	Sidbury United	26
Saffron Walden Town	42	Sedgley White Lions	(181) 180	Sidbury United Res.	26
Saham Toney	12	Seebrook Rovers	225	Sidlesham	154
Saham Toney Res.	224	Seelec Delta	(21) 153	Sidlesham Res.	156
Sainsburys Newbury	223	Seelec Delta Res.	153	Sidley United	154
Salford City	101	Selby Town	109	Sidley United Res.	156
Salisbury Arms (Norfolk)	225	Selby Town Res.	110	Sidmouth Town	25
Salisbury Arms (Wilts)	228	Selsey	154	Sidmouth Town Res.	26
Salisbury City	(143) 141	Selsey Res.	156	Signcraft	227
Salisbury Glass	228	Selston	18	Signcraft Res.	227
Salt Old Boys	184	Selston Res.	17	Sikh Hunters	182
Saltash United	136	Seven Sisters	164	Silchester United	223
Saltash United Res.	32	Sevenoaks Town	(79) 75	Sileby Rangers	158
Saltdean United	155	Sevenoaks Town Res.	(80) 78	Sileby Rangers Res.	158
Saltdean United Res.	156	Severalls Athletic	38	Sileby Town	83
Saltford	130	Shaftesbury	31	Sileby Town Res.	83
Saltford Res.	223	Shaftesbury (Dorset)	176	Silsden	183
Salts	(184) 185	Shaftesbury (Dorset) 'A'	28	Silsden Res.	185
Salts Old Boys Res.	185	Shaftesbury (Dorset) Res.	27	Silverton	26
Salts Res.	185	Shamwickshire Rovers	227	Simonside SC	225
Salvation Army	230	Shankhouse	106	Sinjuns	223
Salvation Army Res.	230	Shanklin	226	Sittingbourne	(143) 141
Sampford Blues	230	Shap United	230	Sittingbourne Res.	80
Sampford Peverell	26	Shawbury United	(181) 180	Six Bells	226
Samuel Montagu Youth Club	(77) 78	Sheepbridge	(18) 226	Sizewell & Aldeburgh	230
Sandford (Devon)	26	Sheerness East	75	Skegness Town	84
Sandford (Devon) Res.	26	Sheerness East Res.	77	Skelmersdale United	101
Sandford (Dorset)	29	Sheerwater	(21) 153	Skelmersdale United Res.	(85) 102
Sandgate Old Boys	226	Sheerwater Res.	153	Skenfrith United	226
Sandhurst	124	Sheffield	109	Skewen Athletic	(163) 164
Sandhurst Sports Club	223	Sheffield Centralians	228	SKS Blyskawica	(193)
Sandhurst Town	(21) 20	Sheffield City	18	Slade Green	79
Sandhurst Town Devels	223	Sheffield Lane Top	228	Sleaford Town	84
Sandhurst Town Res.	20	Shelfield Sports	182	Slightly Athletic	229
Sandiacre Town	17	Shell Club Corringham	40	Sligo Rovers	226
Sandiacre Town Res.	17	Shell Club Corringham Res.	41	Slimbridge	(56) 58

WWW.CHERRYRED.CO.UK

WWW.CHERRYRED.CO.UK

WWW.NLNEWSDESK.CO.UK

*NAME CHANGES & MERGERS

AFC Blackley were known as **Belden**
AFC Hurst were known as **Mowers**
AFC Stratton were known as **Stratton Crosslink**
APM Mears were known as **Aylesford Paper Mills**
Arnold Southbank were known as **Southbank**
Coed Eva were known as **Greenmeadow**
Cromer Town were known as **Cromer United**
Crusaders were known as **Fleur-de-Lys**
Dale Hotel were known as **BTSC**
East Lodge were known as **Co-op Sports & Hilsea**
Eastbourne United Association are a merger of **Eastbourne United** and **Shinewater Association**
Ferndown Sports were known as **Forest Inn**
Fernhill Heath Sports were known as **Fernhill County Sports Reserves**
GSK Ulverston Rangers were known as **Glaxo Ulverston Rangers**
Heather Athletic were known as **Heather St Johns**
Heddon were known as **Procter & Gamble Heddon**
Ifield Edwards are a merger of **Ifield** and **Edwards Sports**
London Road were known as **St Peters**
Manchester Titans were known as **Warth Fold**

Morpeth Town 'A' were known as **Stobhill Rangers**
Mynydd Isa BT were known as **Mynydd Isa**
NEWI Cefn Druids were known as **Flexsys Cefn Druids**
Nuthall Chaffoteaux were known as **Chaffoteaux**
Oswestry Town have been absorbed by **Total Network Solutions**
Poole Royal Mail were known as **Poole & Parkstone Royal Mail**
Ryan were known as **Wanstead Town**
South Bradford were known as **TFD Centre**
St Loye's were known as **Tap & Barrel**
Swinton Town were known as **Willows**
Thornwell Burt Barn were known as **Thornwell Red & White**
Thurrock were known as **Purfleet**
Total Netwrok Solutions are a merger of **Total Network Solutions** and **Oswestry Town**
Tuebrook Park were known as **Tuebrook**
VTFC were known as **Vosper Thornycroft**
Walker Birds Nest FOS were known as **Walker Stack FOS**
Waltham Forest were known as **Leyton Pennant**
Westbrook YMCA were known as **Westbrook Wanderers**
Weymouth Spartans were known as **Spa Hotel**